How well do **you** want to do in this course?

A better grade starts here.
Register today for your S.O.S. Edition's online grade-boosting tools.

(Your registration code is included at the back of this textbook.)

Introducing the **S.O.S. Edition**
for *Psychology and Life...*

Get ready to study... Organize... and <u>Succeed</u>!

**We give you the tools
to take control and succeed
in your course!**

✓ Practice Tests
✓ TestXL – Online Test Prep
✓ Tutor Center – Live Tutor Support

Want help mastering the course?
Looking to change that B to an A?

Our S.O.S Edition for *Psychology and Life* offers a personalized study and review system that helps you master the principles of psychology, save time studying, and perform better on exams.

With the purchase of this textbook, you get a powerful combination of tools that includes Practice Tests with Answers, live tutoring assistance from our Tutor Center, and access to our TestXL online diagnostic testing and review system. With the S.O.S. Edition tools, you can test with confidence and complete your course with greater comprehension and higher grades!

Read on to find out how...

How will you **benefit** from using the S.O.S. Edition tools?

✓ **Reinforces** textbook concepts.

✓ Provides **feedback** on your learning progress.

✓ Helps you **maximize** your study time.

✓ Adds **variety** to your study routine.

✓ **Supports** you with live tutors who can answer your questions and help you master the text.

✓ Gives you more **control** over your grade!

" The students benefit from the individualized study plan that identifies their weak and strong areas. It saves them time because they are more aware of what they need to study. Taking the pre- and post-tests enhances their test-taking skills, and ultimately helps them earn better grades on their chapter exams. "

— **Professor Teresa R. Stalvey,
North Florida Community College***

A better grade is right here at your fingertips!

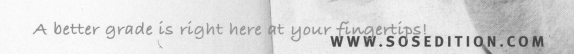

What's the best way to **review** concepts and **practice** for exams?

It's built right into your textbook!

Printed Practice Tests with Answers

Practice makes perfect when you have the right tools. What better way to review textbook concepts than with tools built in to the back of your textbook. Master the text material by utilizing the Practice Tests at the end of your S.O.S. Edition. You'll find multiple-choice and fill-in-the-blank questions for every chapter, organized by the major text sections to help you quickly connect the concepts. Answers are included for all questions to help you measure your performance. What's more, all Practice Tests are perforated so you can remove them from the text and take them with you!

> **" I recommend that students take the Practice Test after they have read each chapter. The students that use them do better on my exams. "**
>
> — *Professor Jarvis Gamble,*
> *Owens Community College*

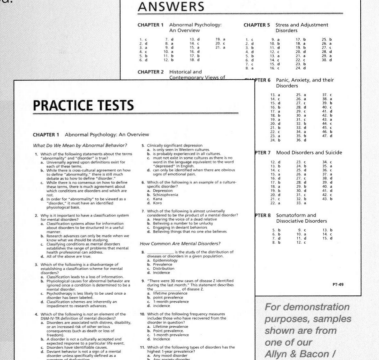

For demonstration purposes, samples shown are from one of our Allyn & Bacon / Longman S.O.S. Editions.

you go out and buy a magnet to help you with a repetitive-stress injury caused by typing too many term papers!

WHAT DO WE MEAN BY ABNORMAL BEHAVIOR?

This is an easy question to ask but a surprisingly difficult one to answer. Is talking to yourself abnormal? What about feeling depressed for weeks and weeks after a break-up? Or

drinking a bottle of vodka with friends on the weekend? Drawing the line between what is abnormal and what is just human behavior can be difficult sometimes. No two of us are alike, and although some of us can exhibit behaviors that are considered quirky, indulgent, or experimental, others with similar behavior may be considered mentally ill, afflicted, or addicted.

It may come as a surprise to you that there is still no universal agreement about what we mean by *abnormality* or *disorder*. This is not to say we do not have definitions.

The S.O.S. Edition Practice Tests (right) include questions for every major section of the textbook (above), providing you with a thorough review of the material.

PRACTICE TESTS

CHAPTER 1   Abnormal Psychology: An Overview

What Do We Mean by Abnormal Behavior?

1. Which of the following statements about the terms "abnormality" and "disorder" is true?
    a. Universally agreed upon definitions exist for each of these terms.
    b. While there is cross-cultural agreement on how to define "abnormality," there is still much debate as to how to define "disorder."
    c. While there is no consensus on how to define these terms, there is much agreement about which conditions are disorders and which are not.
    d. In order for "abnormality" to be viewed as a "disorder," it must have an identified physiological basis.

2. Why is it important to have a classification system for mental disorders?
    a. Classification systems allow for information about disorders to be structured in a useful manner.
    b. Research advances can only be made when we know what we should be studying.
    c. Classifying conditions as mental disorders establishes the range of problems that mental health professional can address.
    d. All of the above are true.

3. Which of the following is a disadvantage of establishing a classification scheme for mental disorders?
    a. Classification leads to a loss of information.
    b. Physiological causes for abnormal behavior are ignored once a condition is determined to be a mental disorder.
    c. Psychotherapy is less likely to be used once a disorder has been labeled.
    d. Classification schemes are inherently an impediment to research advances.

4. Which of the following is *not* an element of the DSM-IV-TR definition of mental disorders?
    a. Disorders are associated with distress, disability, or an increased risk of other serious consequences (such as death or loss of freedom).
    b. A disorder is not a culturally accepted and expected response to a particular life event.
    c. Disorders have identifiable causes.
    d. Deviant behavior is not a sign of a mental disorder unless specifically defined as a symptom of dysfunction.

5. Clinically significant depression
    a. is only seen in Western cultures.
    b. is probably experienced in all cultures.
    c. must not exist in some cultures as there is no word in the language equivalent to the word "depressed" in English.
    d. can only be identified when there are obvious signs of emotional pain.

6. Which of the following is an example of a culture-specific disorder?
    a. Depression
    b. Schizophrenia
    c. Kana
    d. Koro

7. Which of the following is almost universally considered to be the product of a mental disorder?
    a. Hearing the voice of a dead relative
    b. Believing a number to be unlucky
    c. Engaging in deviant behaviors
    d. Believing things that no one else believes

How Common Are Mental Disorders?

8. _____ is the study of the distribution of diseases or disorders in a given population.
    a. Epidemiology
    b. Prevalence
    c. Distribution
    d. Incidence

9. "There were 30 new cases of disease Z identified during the last month." This statement describes the _____ of disease Z.
    a. lifetime prevalence
    b. point prevalence
    c. 1-month prevalence
    d. incidence

10. Which of the following frequency measures includes those who have recovered from the disorder in question?
    a. Lifetime prevalence
    b. Point prevalence.
    c. 1-month prevalence
    d. Incidence

11. Which of the following types of disorders has the highest 1-year prevalence?
    a. Any mood disorder
    b. Any anxiety disorder
    c. Any substance-use disorder
    d. Schizophrenia

PT-1

A better grade is right here at your fingertips!

WWW.SOSEDITION.COM

Jump-start your grade with our **TestXL** online test prep system!

Who doesn't want better grades?

About **TestXL**

Designed specifically to help enhance your performance, this S.O.S. Edition's online test preparation system gauges your prior knowledge of content and creates a unique Individualized Study Plan to help you pinpoint exactly where additional study and review is needed. You can follow the plan as a guide to focus your efforts and improve upon areas of weakness with one-on-one assistance from our qualified tutors and/or by utilizing the printed Practice Tests in the back of the textbook. Additional testing features in this program help you assess your progress with the textbook material to reach your ultimate goal of success in the course.

" I like the fact that I can take a pre-test before I study the course material to test how much I know, and then I can take the post-test to see my improvement. "
— *Natalie Ricks, student**

Knowing what to study is key to your success.

TestXL Pre-Test

Why waste time studying what you already know? TestXL's Pre-Test helps you measure your level of understanding of the material in each chapter. After logging in to the S.O.S. Edition online program, you'll find the Table of Contents for your textbook, with links to Pre-Test, Post-Test, and Study Plan. Choose your chapter of interest and select Pre-Test to assess your existing knowledge about the subject matter.

You'll be prompted with multiple questions per major topic area in each chapter. Complete all of the questions, submit the test, and TestXL will produce your Individualized Study Plan (see next page) based on the results to help you focus your study efforts where they're needed most.

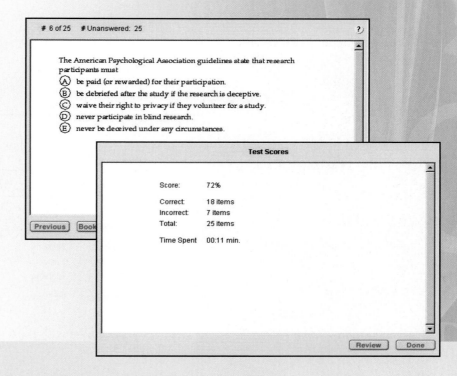

> " With the Pre-Tests, I feel like I'm learning more by being directed to specific text pages for additional study. "
>
> — *Bridget San Angelo, student**

TestXL Post-Test

Measure your progress with Post-Tests for each chapter. Organized exactly like the Pre-Tests, with multiple questions per major topic area, the Post-Tests show you how much you've improved, or where you need continued help. Continue to take the Post-Tests as often as you like, revisiting your progress in the Study Plan, which is updated every time a test is taken.

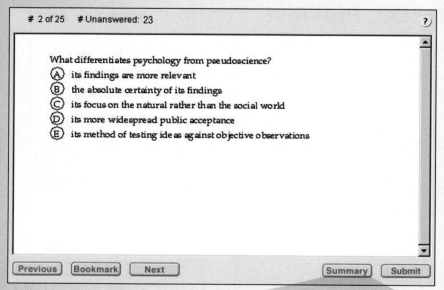

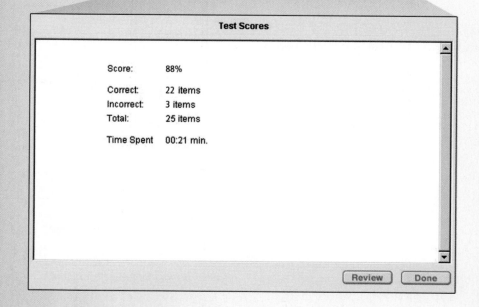

" Each time
I take a post-test,
I see an improvement
in my test score.
It challenges me
to see if I can better
my score until
it's perfect. "
— *Tammi Smith, student**

TestXL Individualized Study Plan

Maximize your study time by reviewing and following your very own Study Plan created from the results of your Pre- and Post-Tests. The Study Plan quickly identifies your areas of weakness and strength in a clear outline, directing you back to specific areas in your textbook for further study. The Study Plan helps you immediately pinpoint where additional time is needed, so you can feel confident about where you're saving time! Use this customized guide to re-study material as necessary for mastery of the material and success on your tests and in your course.

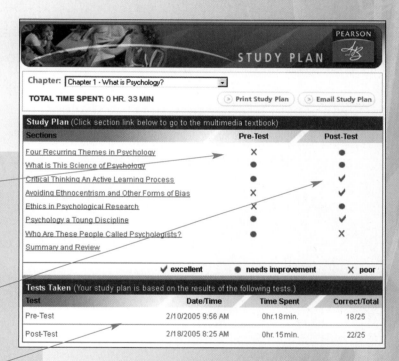

For each major topic in the chapter (shown in blue), the Study Plan "grades" your understanding based on your Pre-Test results. Ratings of "Excellent," "Needs Improvement," and "Poor" are used to identify areas of strength and weakness.

Post-Test results are included after you participate in this next stage (see opposite page). Note how most areas have improved after the Post-Test.

The Study Plan keeps a log of your Pre- and Post-Test activity, noting time spent as well as score summaries. Additional Post-Test results will appear here. You can take the Post-Tests as many times as you like, until you're comfortable with your level of mastery of the material.

> **The Individualized Study Plans help me study at a faster pace by focusing on my underscored areas.**
> — *Kim Skains, student**

A support service that's available when your instructor isn't! Our qualified tutors are on hand to assist you during key studying hours – from Sunday to Thursday, 5PM to midnight EST, during the school term.

Addison-Wesley • Allyn & Bacon • Benjamin Cummings • Longman •

The **Tutor Center**

❝ What I benefited from the most was the Tutor Center. I am a working mother, and to have the opportunity to come home late at night and still be able to have someone to help me is a true blessing. ❞

— *Jennifer Kelly, student*

Getting started on the path to success is quick and easy!

✓ **Take advantage of the Practice Tests**

At any point in your studies, you can use these tests to quiz yourself, prepare for exams, or simply gain understanding of the most important concepts in each chapter of this textbook.

✓ **Access your online resources**

The Student Starter Kit packaged with this textbook gives you a **FREE 6-month subscription** to the S.O.S. Edition's TestXL program and Tutor Center resources. You'll find your access code under the tear-off tab in the back of your book. **Follow these quick and easy steps...**

1 **GET YOUR CODE.**

Open your S.O.S. Edition to the inside back cover to find your code.

2 **LOG ON TO www.sosedition.com** and **CHOOSE YOUR TEXTBOOK.**

3 CLICK "REGISTER" AND ENTER YOUR ACCESS CODE.

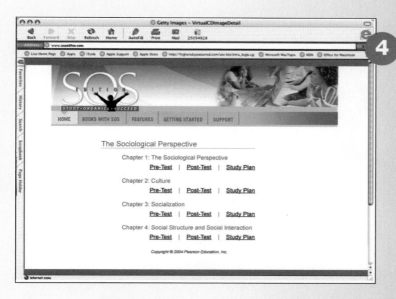

4 THAT'S IT!

You'll find the table of contents for your book with links to Pre-Test, Post-Test, and Study Plan to get started.

A better grade is right here at your fingertips!

Psychology and Life

S.O.S. Edition

Richard J. Gerrig
Stony Brook University

Philip G. Zimbardo
Stanford University

Boston   New York   San Francisco
Mexico City   Montreal   Toronto   London   Madrid   Munich   Paris
Hong Kong   Singapore   Tokyo   Cape Town   Sydney

Associate Editor, Practice Tests: Matt Latowsky
Editorial Production Service and Electronic Composition: Modern Graphics, Inc.
Composition and Prepress Buyer: Linda Cox
Manufacturing Buyer: Megan Cochran
Cover Designer, S.O.S Edition: Rubin Pfeffer

ISBN   0-205-47463-2

Printed in the United States of America
10 9 8 7 6 5 4 3 2 1   VHP   09 08 07 06 05

Psychology and Life

SEVENTEENTH EDITION

Richard J. Gerrig
Stony Brook University

Philip G. Zimbardo
Stanford University

PEARSON

Boston • New York • San Francisco

Mexico City • Montreal • Toronto • London • Madrid • Munich • Paris

Hong Kong • Singapore • Tokyo • Cape Town • Sydney

Executive Editor:	Karon Bowers
Senior Developmental Editor:	Lisa McLellan
Editorial Assistant:	Lara Torsky
Senior Marketing Manager:	Wendy Gordon
Editorial Production Administrator:	Anna Socrates
Editorial–Production Service:	Susan McNally
Composition and Prepress Buyer:	Linda Cox
Manufacturing Buyer:	Megan Cochran
Cover Administrator:	Linda Knowles
Interior Design:	Geri Davis, The Davis Group, Inc.
Photo Research:	Helane M. Prottas, Posh Pictures
Illustrations:	Monotype Composition, Inc.
Electronic Composition:	Monotype Composition, Inc.

Between the time Website information is gathered and then published, it is not
unusual for some sites to have closed. Also, the transcription of URLs can result
in unintended typographical errors. The publisher would appreciate notification
where these errors occur so that they may be corrected in subsequent editions.

Library of Congress Cataloging-in-Publication Data

Gerrig, Richard J.
    Psychology and life/Richard J. Gerrig, Philip G. Zimbardo.—17th ed.
        p. cm.
    Includes bibliographical references and index.
    ISBN: 0-205-41799-X
    1. Psychology. I. Zimbardo, Philip G. II. Title.

BF121.G47 2004
50—dc21   2004044440

Printed in the United States of America

10 9 8 7 6 5 4 3 2   VHP 09 08 07 06 05 04

To Timothy —R. J. G.

To Richard Gerrig, who has so ably taken the helm of *Psychology and Life* to sail it in challenging new directions while keeping a steady eye on all that is happening on shore. I also dedicate this book to other teachers of introductory psychology whose enthusiasm for the science, practice, and art of psychology creates a passion to learn in our next generation of students   —P. G. Z.

Brief Contents

Contents

<www.ablongman.com/gerrig17e>

<www.ablongman.com/gerrig17e>

9   Intelligence and Intelligence Assessment   284

10   Human Development Across the Life Span   314

Preface

Teaching introductory psychology is one of the greatest challenges facing any academic psychologist. Indeed, because of the range of our subject matter, it is probably the most difficult course to teach effectively in all of academia. We must cover both the micro-level analyses of nerve cell processes and the macro-level analyses of cultural systems: both the vitality of health psychology and the tragedy of lives blighted by mental illness. Our challenge in writing this text—like your challenge in teaching—is to give form and substance to all this information: to bring it to life for our students.

More often than not, students come into our course filled with misconceptions about psychology that they have picked up from the infusion of "pop psychology" into our society. They also bring with them high expectations about what they want to get out of a course in psychology—they want to learn much that will be personally valuable, that will help them improve their everyday lives. Indeed, that is a tall order for any teacher to fill. But we believe that *Psychology and Life* can help you to fill it.

Our goal has been to design a text that students will enjoy reading as they learn what is so exciting and special about the many fields of psychology. In every chapter, in every sentence, we have tried to make sure that students will want to go on reading. At the same time, we have focused on how our text will work within the syllabi of instructors who value a research-centered, applications-relevant approach to psychology.

This 17th edition of *Psychology and Life* is the fourth collaboration between Philip Zimbardo and Richard Gerrig. Our partnership was forged because we shared a commitment to teaching psychology as a science relevant to human welfare. We both could bring our teaching experience to bear on a text that balances scientific rigor with psychology's relevance to contemporary life concerns. Furthermore, Richard's expertise in cognitive psychology provided an important complement to Phil's expertise in social psychology. With Richard as lead author, *Psychology and Life* has been able to keep pace with rapid changes in psychology, particularly in areas such as cognitive neuroscience. Even

so, *Psychology and Life* remains a collaboration of like minds: Together, we celebrate both an ongoing tradition and a continued vision of bringing the most important psychological insights to bear on your students' lives. The 17th edition is a product of this fine collaboration.

Text Theme: The Science of Psychology

The aim of *Psychology and Life* is to use solid scientific research to combat psychological misconceptions. In our experience as teachers, one of the most reliable occurrences on the first day of introductory psychology is the throng of students who push forward at the end of class to ask, in essence, "Will this class teach me what I need to know?":

> *My mother is taking Prozac: Will we learn what it does?*
>
> *Are you going to teach us how to study better?*
>
> *I need to put my son in daycare to come back to school. Is that going to be all right for him?*
>
> *What should I do if I have a friend talking about suicide?*

We take comfort that each of these questions has been addressed by rigorous empirical research. *Psychology and Life* is devoted to providing students with scientific analyses of their foremost concerns. As a result, the features of *Psychology and Life* support a central theme: psychology as a science, with a focus on *applying* that science to your students' lives.

◆ PUTTING IDEAS TO THE TEST

An important goal of *Psychology and Life* is to teach the scientific basis of psychological reasoning. When our students ask us questions—what they need to know—they quite often have acquired partial answers based on the types of information that are available in the popular media. Some of that information is accurate, but often students do not know how to make sense of it. How do they learn to interpret and evaluate what they hear in the media? How can they become wiser consumers of the overabundance of research studies and surveys cited? How can they judge the credibility of these sources? To counteract this infusion of so-called reliable research, we provide students with the scientific tools to scrutinize effectively the information with which they are surrounded and to draw generalizations appropriate to the goals and methods of research.

With a feature we call **Putting Ideas to the Test,** we seek several times in each chapter to confront students

---

PUTTING IDEAS TO THE TEST

Emotional Intelligence and Everyday Well-Being

Take a moment to review the components of the definition of emotional intelligence. Can you see how people who have more of these abilities would also be better able to cope with day-to-day hassles? A pair of researchers tested the hypothesis that people high in EQ would cope better and therefore have a greater sense of psychological well-being (Slaski & Cartwright, 2002). The sample they used were middle managers working for a major retailer in England. These men and women had jobs that were reasonably demanding. Each manager completed an assessment device that measured EQ. They also reported on aspects of well-being, such as their level of psychological distress, their morale, and their quality of working life. Finally, each manager's supervisor rated his or her job performance. The researchers divided the managers into a low-EQ group and a high-EQ group. The results were quite dramatic. By comparison to the low-EQ group, the high-EQ managers reported less psychological distress, higher morale, and better quality of working life. Their bosses also rated the high-EQ group as better managers.

---

directly with the experimental basis of critical conclusions. We give each Putting Ideas to the Test study a title—"Emotional Intelligence and Everyday Well-Being," "Predicting Who Will Divorce," "Conditioning and Immune Function," "Cross-Cultural Patterns of Self-Enhancement," "Teasing, Rejection, and Violence"—so that students can access them easily. Nearly 200 Putting Ideas to the Test studies appear throughout the text. Our intention is not to maintain that each of these studies is the definitive answer to a particular research area but to open the door for further questions. Our mission is to reinvent the use of primary research in psychology and describe methodologies clearly, in language accessible to your students. In this way, your students have repeated opportunities to understand how progress is made in psychological research.

◆ PSYCHOLOGY IN THE 21ST CENTURY

At the beginning of the 21st century, our students feel as if they are living in very special times—times that are bringing with them rapid changes. Those changes provide researchers in psychology and related fields with a host of new topics to address as well as a range of new techniques to do so. To reflect these new realities, we include a special feature we call **Psychology in the 21st Century.** These sections cover a diversity of topics, all at the cutting edge: "Can Technology Restore Sight?," "Understanding Alzheimer's Disease," and "Expert Systems and Medicine." Each Psychology in the 21st Century section demonstrates the flexibility with which psychological research tackles new issues and creates new applications.

◆ PSYCHOLOGY IN YOUR LIFE

The questions we cited earlier are real questions from real students, and your students will find the answers throughout the book. These questions represent data we collected from students over the years. We asked them, "Tell us what you need to know about psychology," and we have placed those questions—your students' own voices—directly into the text in the form of **Psychology in Your Life** sections. Each chapter includes a section that addresses questions such as "Why Study Psychology?" (Chapter 1), "Why Is Eating 'Hot' Food Painful?" (Chapter 4), and "Why Are Some People Happier Than Others?" (Chapter 12). Our hope is that your students will see, in each instance, exactly why psychological knowledge is directly relevant to the decisions they make every day of their lives.

<www.ablongman.com/gerrig17e>

◆ TEXT ORGANIZATION

Psychology is a field that continues to evolve. We intend the revised organization of this edition of *Psychology and Life* to reflect the way in which psychological research is configured at the turn of the 21st century. Our text organization also incorporates feedback from the text's reviewers and users—both students and professors. They have helped us devise an organization that provides even more support to our theme of psychology as a science.

For example, we had heard from students that they sometimes found it difficult to find the continuity between Sensation and Perception when the topics were divided into separate chapters. For that reason, this edition of *Psychology and Life* features a streamlined chapter that joins the topics together (Chapter 4). The chapter provides a unified structure that allows students to understand the processes that bring sensory information to the brain and the constraints that affect the interpretation of that information once it arrives.

Because professors have responded with consistent enthusiasm, other aspects of *Psychology and Life* have remained unchanged. For example, we retained separate chapters on Social Cognition and Relationships (Chapter 16) and Social Processes, Society, and Culture (Chapter 17). Researchers in the field of social psychology have most often assumed the burden of tackling the new research issues that arise from different historical circumstances. We have divided the social psychological material into two chapters to enable us to show students how this type of research can have broad implications for their most pressing issues at both personal and societal levels.

◆ PEDAGOGICAL FEATURES

Psychology and Life has maintained a reputation for presenting the science of psychology in a way that is challenging, yet accessible, to a broad range of students, and the 17th edition is no exception. To enhance students' experience with the book, we include several pedagogical features:

➤ ***Put Yourself to the Test.*** This new feature appears at the end of every major section and provides students with thought-provoking questions to test their mastery of material before moving on.

➤ ***Recapping Main Points.*** Each chapter concludes with a chapter summary, *Recapping Main Points*, which summarizes the chapter content and is organized according to major section headings.

➤ ***Key Terms.*** Key terms are boldfaced in the text as they appear and are listed, with page references, at the end of each chapter for quick review.

Also, your students can learn how to get the most out of their text by consulting the *Student Preface: How to Use This Book,* which begins on page xxii.

PUT YOURSELF TO THE TEST

➤ What idea about emotions did Charles Darwin originate?
➤ What evidence suggests that some elements of emotional responses are innate while others are not?
➤ What roles do the autonomic and central nervous systems play in the experience of emotions?
➤ How have theories of emotion attempted to explain the relationship between physiology and feelings?
➤ In what ways do emotions serve motivational functions?
➤ What roles may emotions play in social circumstances?
➤ What impact may emotions have on cognitive functioning?

New in the 17th Edition

In addition to the new features mentioned earlier, *Psychology and Life* is fresh with the most up-to-date coverage and brimming with over 300 new references. Our goal is to be the most current, most accurate, and most accessible treatment of our discipline today. The 17th edition of *Psychology and Life* also incorporates new research on the diversity of people's life experiences. We intend our book to have meaning for the whole range of students who enroll in introductory psychology—men and women, members of diverse cultural and racial groups, traditional and nontraditional students. Wherever possible, we have brought new research to bear on cultural issues.

◆ CHAPTER-BY-CHAPTER CHANGES

CHAPTER 1

- New and improved introduction to the current psychological perspectives
- Expanded discussions of behaviorist and humanistic perspectives
- New discussion of behavioral neuroscience and cognitive neuroscience perspectives
- Expanded coverage of what psychologists do

CHAPTER 2

- Revised and expanded discussion of independent and dependent variables, including a new figure
- New Putting Ideas to the Test that examines a within-subjects study of learning emotions from TV, including a new figure
- New summary table illustrating research methods and measures
- Updated coverage of APA ethical guidelines

CHAPTER 3

- Expanded coverage of Darwin's theory of evolution
- Additional information on the Human Genome Project
- New discussion of heritability (including a Putting Ideas to the Test section and new figure)
- Expanded coverage of sociobiology and evolutionary psychology
- New Psychology in the 21st Century feature that examines techniques for unlocking the locked-in brain
- New Psychology in Your Life that uses brain research to examine the impact of music on emotions
- New section on plasticity and neurogenesis

CHAPTER 4

- Separate sensation and perception chapters now combined into one streamlined chapter
- Refined discussion of **feature detectors** (including a new figure)
- Updated discussion of pheromones
- Revised and expanded section on pain
- Revised discussion of Gestalt principles

CHAPTER 5

- New Putting Ideas to the Test that examines cross-cultural differences in reporting well-being, including new figure
- Revised and clarified discussion on the functions of consciousness

- New figure illustrating cycles of sleep
- Refined discussions of sleep disorders, including insomnia and sleep apnea, along with a new discussion on somnambulism, or sleepwalking
- Updated discussion of physiological theories of dream content
- Updated discussion of meditation, examining further the mind–body healing connection
- Updated and refined discussion of mind-altering drugs

CHAPTER 6

- New Putting Ideas to the Test examining the role of shaping to improve an athlete's performance
- New Putting Ideas to the Test discussing the link between childhood TV viewing and adult aggression, including new figure

CHAPTER 7

- New figure on proactive and retroactive interference
- New Putting Ideas to the Test examining the relationship between encoding and retrieval
- New Putting Ideas to the Test on imagination and memory construction
- New Psychology in the 21st Century feature on understanding Alzheimer's disease
- New Putting Ideas to the Test discussing amnesia and explicit and implicit memory
- New Putting Ideas to the Test examining encoding and retrieval in the hippocampus, including new images of brain scans

CHAPTER 8

- New information on comparing brain activity during automatic and controlled processing, including a new image
- New Putting Ideas to the Test examining the brain bases of deductive and inductive reasoning, including new visuals highlighting brain activity
- New Putting Ideas to the Test discussing the impact of framing on romance

CHAPTER 9

- Refined and updated discussions of the Stanford-Binet and WAIS-III tests
- New coverage on learning disorders
- New Putting Ideas to the Test examining the connections between emotional intelligence and well-being
- New Psychology in Your Life discussing the theories of intelligence and how they may generate successful approaches to classroom lessons

CHAPTER 10

- Streamlined discussion on studying development
- New Putting Ideas to the Test on voice recognition in the womb
- Expanded discussion of nature/nurture and development
- New discussion of the principle of contrast and children's hypotheses with respect to meaning acquisition
- New discussion of internal working models and attachment
- New Putting Ideas to the Test discussing research on predicting who will divorce

CHAPTER 11

- Streamlined and updated discussion of the psychology of eating, including new information on body mass index (BMI) and rising obesity rates
- New Putting Ideas to the Test on the effects of anticipated diets on restrained and unrestrained eaters, including a new figure
- New Putting Ideas to the Test on mate-choice copying in sailfin mollies, including a new figure
- New and updated discussion of early-realization rates of homosexuality and the impact of homophobia

CHAPTER 12

- New discussion of differences in the amygdala's responses to emotional stimuli
- New discussion of researcher Robert Zajonc's theory
- New Putting Ideas to the Test on the amygdala and perception of emotional events
- New research on the impact of emotions on judgments and reasoning, including a new table
- Updated coverage on traumatic events and post-traumatic stress disorder (PTSD)
- New research on the psychological impact of economic hardship
- Updated coverage and new research on stress, including using multiple strategies for coping
- New research on the impact of social support on stress
- New research on the genetic impact on smoking for men and women, including a new table
- Expanded discussion of psychoneuroimmunology
- New Putting Ideas to the Test on conditioning and immune function, including a new figure on perceived stress and immune function
- New Putting Ideas to the Test on hostility and coronary heart disease, including a new figure

CHAPTER 13

- New Putting Ideas to the Test on extraversion and the amygdala, including a new figure with new visuals from an fMRI
- New Putting Ideas to the Test on self-regulatory efficacy and adolescent behavior
- New Putting Ideas to the Test on cross-cultural patterns of self-enhancement, including a new table

CHAPTER 14

- New Putting Ideas to the Test on posttraumatic stress disorder and brain activity, including a new figure with visuals from an fMRI
- New research from the World Health Organization and the toll of depression
- Streamlined discussion of biological causes of mood disorders
- New research on bipolar disorder and brain activity, including a new figure with visuals from an fMRI
- New research and discussion of gender differences in depression
- Updated research and discussion of youth suicide
- New Putting Ideas to the Test on parents' behaviors and antisocial personality traits
- New section on psychological disorders of childhood, with coverage of attention-deficit hyperactivity disorder and autistic disorder
- New Psychology in the 21st Century feature on pinpointing interactions of nature and nurture, including a new graph

CHAPTER 15

- New research and discussion of using e-mail or the Internet for mental health care
- Clarified discussion of exposure therapy and systematic desensitization
- New Putting Ideas to the Test on treatments for acrophobia
- New Putting Ideas to the Test on an intervention for social isolation, including a new table
- New discussion of repetitive transcranial stimulation (rTMS), an alternative to ECT
- New table on drug therapies for mental illness
- Expanded discussion of antidepressant drugs, including new research
- New Psychology in the 21st Century feature on therapies and brain activity, including new visuals
- New research and discussion of the results from meta-analyses of treatments for depression, including a new figure

CHAPTER 16

- New chapter title, "Social Cognition and Relationships"

- Moved discussion of the power of the situation to Chapter 17, "Social Processes, Society, and Culture"

- New discussion and research on self-fulfilling prophecies and mothers' expectations of their children engaging in underage drinking

- New Putting Ideas to the Test on lying and attitude accessibility, including a new table on correlation between true attitude and behavioral choice

- New Psychology in Your Life on whether late night TV ads really work

- Introduced coverage of prejudice

- New research on the consequences of in-group versus out-group status

- Clarified and updated discussion of contact hypothesis

- New Putting Ideas to the Test on prejudice in East and West Germany

CHAPTER 17

- New chapter title, "Social Processes, Society, and Culture"

- New discussion (moved from previous chapter) of the power of the situation

- New Putting Ideas to the Test on the minority slowness effect

- New Putting Ideas to the Test on antisocial behavior among 5-year-old children

- New Putting Ideas to the Test on teasing, rejection, and violence

- New Putting Ideas to the Test on violent video games and hostile expectations

- New Putting Ideas to the Test on the impact of lessons from history, including a new figure with recommendations for responses to conflicts

◆ THE TOTAL PSYCHOLOGY AND LIFE TEACHING PROGRAM

A good textbook is only one part of the package of educational materials that makes an introductory psychology course valuable for students and effective for instructors. To make the difficult task of teaching introductory psychology easier for you and more interesting for your students, we have prepared a number of valuable ancillary materials in both electronic and print form.

Instructor Supplements

Instructor's Manual (0-205-42387-6). Written by Bradley N. Collins of University of Pennsylvania, this robust instructor's manual contains additional material to enrich class presentations. For each chapter of the text, the instructor's manual includes a Chapter-at-a-Glance grid, detailed lecture outlines, lecture extensions, demonstrations and activities for classroom use, updated video, media and Web resources, and other detailed pedagogical information.

Test Bank (0-205-42384-1). Written by John Caruso of the University of Massachusetts, Dartmouth, the test bank contains over 100 items per chapter, in essay, short-answer, multiple-choice, and true/false format. There are page references to in-text material, answer justification, a skill level, and a difficulty rating scale. This supplement is available for download from Supplements Central.

TestGen 5.0—Computerized Test Bank (0-205-42383-3). (Available for Windows and Macintosh) TestGen 5.0 is an integrated suite of testing and assessment tools for Windows and Macintosh. You can use TestGen to create professional-looking exams in just minutes by building tests from the existing database of questions, editing questions, or adding your own. TestGen also allows you to prepare printed network and online tests.

PowerPoint Presentation CD-ROM (0-205-42385-x). Written by Joe Davis at San Diego State University, this multimedia resource contains key points covered in the textbook; images from the textbook, with demonstrations; and a link to the companion Web site for corresponding activities.

Allyn and Bacon Transparencies for Introductory Psychology, 2004 (0-205-39862-6). Over 200 full-color transparencies, taken from the text and other sources, are designed to enhance classroom lecture and discussion.

Allyn and Bacon Digital Media Archive for Psychology, 4.0 (0-205-39537-6). This collection of media products—including charts, graphs, tables, figures, and audio and video clips—enlivens your classroom with resources that can be easily integrated into your lectures. Animation and video clips include classic psychology experiments footage.

Insights into Psychology, Volumes I and II (Part I: 0-205-39477-9; Part II: 0-205-39478-7). These interactive videos illustrate the many theories and concepts surrounding 16 areas of psychology. These videos contain two to three video clips per topic, followed by critical thinking questions that challenge students. A Video Guide provides further exploration questions and Internet resources for more information. These videos are also available on DVD from your Allyn and Bacon sales representative.

Discovering Psychology Telecourse Videos. *Psychology and Life* is the sole, premiere text accompanying the revised *Discovering Psychology* telecourse. Written, designed, and hosted by Philip Zimbardo, this set of 26 half-hour videos is available for class use from the Annenberg/CPB collection. The collection includes two completely new programs and more than 15 new sequences that bring students up-to-date on some of the latest developments in the field. A perfect complement to *Psychology and Life*, this course supplement is a landmark educational resource that reveals psychology's contribution not only to understanding the puzzles of behavior but also to identifying solutions and treatments to ease the problems of mental disorders. It has won numerous prizes and is widely used in the United States and internationally.

Discovering Psychology Telecourse Faculty Guide (0-205-42389-2). The *Telecourse Faculty Guide* provides guidelines for using *Discovering Psychology* as a resource within your course. Keyed directly to *Psychology and Life*, the faculty guide includes the complete Telecourse Study Guide plus suggested activities; suggested essays; cited studies; instructional resources including books, articles, films, and Web sites; video program test questions with answer key; textbook test questions with answer key; and a key term glossary.

Student Supplements

MyPsychLab. (0-205-43321-9). *MyPsychLab* is an exciting new learning and teaching tool designed to increase student success in the classroom and provide instructors with every resource needed to teach and administer an introductory psychology course. Designed to be used as a supplement to a traditional lecture course or for complete administration of an online course, *MyPsychLab* features a text-specific e-book—matching the exact layout of the printed textbook—with multimedia and assessment icons in the margins. These icons launch to exciting resources—stimulating animations, video clips, audio explanations, activities, controlled assessments, and profiles of prominent psychologists—to expand on the key topics students encounter as they read the text.

   MyPsychLab includes access to Research Navigator, Pearson Education's online journal database program, and the Tutor Center, which provides students with free tutoring from qualified college psychology instructors on all material in the text. Tutors are available via phone, fax, e-mail, or Internet during the Tutor Center hours of 5 P.M. to 12 A.M. EST, Sunday through Thursday. For more information, please go to www.mypsychlab.com or contact your Allyn & Bacon representative.

Discovering Psychology Telecourse Study Guide (0-205-42390-6). In consultation with Phil Zimbardo, Nancy Franklin of Stony Brook University authors the fully revised *Telecourse Study Guide* and *Telecourse Faculty Guide*. In this *Telecourse Study Guide*, each chapter corresponds to one program, expands on the material covered in the program, specifies appropriate reading assignments, and reviews material covered in the text. In addition, the study guide includes learning objectives; reading assignments; key people and terms; video program summaries and test questions with answer key; textbook test questions with answer key; essay questions; student activities; additional book, article, and film resources; and annotated Web sites. All vocabulary and review questions are keyed to *Psychology and Life*.

Grade Aid with Practice Tests (0-205-42388-4). Developed by Nancy Simpson of Trident Technical College, this is a comprehensive and interactive study guide filled with in-depth activities. Each chapter includes "Before You Read," with a brief chapter summary and chapter learning objectives; "As You Read," a collection of demonstrations, activities, and exercises; "After you Read," containing three short practice quizzes and one comprehensive practice test; "When You Have Finished," with Web links for further information; and crossword puzzles using key terms from the text. An appendix includes answers to all practice tests and crossword puzzles.

Companion Web Site. The companion Web site for *Psychology and Life*, which can be accessed at www.ablongman.com/gerrig17e, offers a wide range of resources for students. Each chapter contains learning objectives; Web links; activities; and practice tests with multiple choice, true/false, and essay questions.

Mind Matters CD-ROM (0-205-39315-2). The Allyn and Bacon Mind Matters II CD-ROM makes psychology more engaging, interactive, informative, and fun! Mind Matters II covers the "core" concepts of psychology through a combination of text, graphics, simulations, video clips of historic experiments, and activities. Assessments test comprehension at both the topic and unit levels. New to Mind Matters II are innovative modules on Personality, Developmental Psychology, and Social Psychology.

Research Navigator Guide for Psychology (0-205-37640-1). This easy-to-read guide helps point students in the right direction as they explore the tremendous array of information on psychology on the Internet. The guide also provides a wide range of additional annotated Web links for further exploration.

   This guide also contains an access code to Research Navigator, Allyn and Bacon's online collection of academic and popular journals. Research Navigator offers students three exclusive databases (Ebsco's ContentSelect, *The New York Times* on the Web, and Link Library) of credible and reliable source content to help students focus their research efforts and get the research process started.

◆ ADDITIONAL RESOURCES

For more information, please go to www.ablongman.com or contact your Allyn & Bacon representative.

How to Think Straight about Psychology, 7th Edition (0-205-36093-9). This well-known critical thinking manual by Keith Stanovich helps students become educated consumers of psychological information, particularly those topics they may encounter in the media or self-help literature.

Diversity Activities for Psychology (0-205-29638-6). This student manual, developed by Valerie Whittlesey, offers a wide variety of hands-on activities to help incorporate issues of diversity into your classroom. Activities are correlated with all major areas of psychological research, making it easy to assign this supplement with the Gerrig and Zimbardo textbook.

Ask Dr. Mike: Frequently Asked Questions about Psychology (0-205-33109-2). Developed by Mike Atkinson, author of the popular "Ask Dr. Mike" column on the Psychology PlaceTM Web site, this manual contains a collection of commonly asked student questions with in-depth answers, organized by major topics in the introductory psychology course.

Evaluating Psychological Information: Sharpening Your Critical Thinking Skills, 4th Edition (0-205-43511-4). Developed by James Bell, this workbook focuses on helping students to evaluate psychological research systematically and to improve their critical thinking skills.

APA and MLA Writing Formats (0-205-42437-6). Developed by Chalon Anderson, Amy Carrell, and Jimmy Widdifield, this workbook is a must for research writing. Starting with a quick review of grammar, the workbook proceeds into clear explanations of both APA and MLA styles with numerous examples and exercises.

Majoring in Psych?: Career Options for Psychology Undergraduates, 2nd Edition (0-205-32643-9). Focusing on the multiple ways that students can enhance their marketability while still in school, this guide from Betsy Morgan and Ann Korschgen answers the career-planning questions most psychology majors find themselves asking.

◆ PERSONAL ACKNOWLEDGMENTS

Although the Beatles may have gotten by with a little help from their friends, we have survived the revision and production of this edition of *Psychology and Life* only with a great deal of help from many colleagues and friends. We especially thank Brenda Anderson, Lisa Burckell, Turhan Canli, Joanne Davila, Tony Freitas, Sam Gaertner, Randy Grosch, Donna Hildenbrand, Daniel Klein, Hoi-Chung Leung, Sheri Levy, Jim McBurney, Anne Moyer, Donna Mumme, John Pachankis, Timothy Peterson, John Robinson, Megan Robinson, Arthur Samuel, Nancy Squires, Judy Thompson, and Pat Whitaker.

We would like to thank the following instructors of both this edition and previous ones, who read drafts of the manuscript and provided valuable feedback:

◆ REVIEWERS AND SURVEY RESPONDENTS FOR THE 17TH EDITION

Brad J. Bushman, Iowa State University
Marc Carter, Hofstra University
Sheree Dukes Conrad, University of Massachusetts, Boston
Matthew Erdelyi, Brooklyn College, CUNY
Trudi Feinstein, Boston University
Peter Gram, Pensacola Junior College
Jeremy Gray, Yale University
Rebecca Hellams, Southeast Community College
Matthew Johnson, University of Vermont
Mark Kline, Indiana University
Suzanne B. Lovett, Bowdoin College
M. Kimberly MacLin, University of Northern Iowa
Kathleen Martynowicz, Colorado Northwestern
    Community College
Lori Metcalf, Gatson College
Ann Moyer, Stony Brook University
Kelly Elizabeth Pelzel, University of Utah
Bernadette Sanchez, DePaul University
Walter Swap, Tufts University

◆ REVIEWERS FOR PREVIOUS EDITIONS

Robert M. Arkin, Ohio State University
Gordon Atlas, Alfred University
Lori L. Badura, State University of New York at Buffalo
Darryl K. Beale, Cerritos College
N. Jay Bean, Vassar College
Michael Bloch, University of San Francisco
Richard Bowen, Loyola University
Mike Boyes, University of Calgary
James Calhoun, University of Georgia
Timothy Cannon, University of Scranton
John Caruso, University of Massachusetts–Dartmouth
Dennis Cogan, Texas Tech University
Randolph R. Cornelius, Vassar College
Lawrence Dachowski, Tulane University
Mark Dombeck, Idaho State University
Victor Duarte, North Idaho College
Tami Egglesten, McKendree College
Mark B. Fineman, Southern Connecticut State University
Kathleen A. Flannery, Saint Anselm College
Rita Frank, Virginia Wesleyan College
Eugene H. Galluscio, Clemson University
Preston E. Garraghty, Indiana University
W. Lawrence Gulick, University of Delaware
Pryor Hale, Piedmont Virginia Community College
Dong Hodge, Dyersburg State Community College
Mark Hoyert, Indiana University Northwest
Richard A. Hudiburg, University of North Alabama

James D. Jackson, Lehigh University
Seth Kalichman, Georgia State University
Stephen La Berge, Stanford University
Charles F. Levinthal, Hofstra University
Leonard S. Mark, Miami University
Michael R. Markham, Florida International University
Michael McCall, Ithaca College
David McDonald, University of Missouri
Greg L. Miller, Stanford University School of Medicine
Karl Minke, University of Hawaii–Honolulu
Charles D. Miron, Catonsville Community College
J. L. Motrin, University of Guelph
William Pavot, Southwest State University
Brady J. Phelps, South Dakota State University
Gregory R. Pierce, Hamilton College
William J. Pizzi, Northeastern Illinois University
Mark Plonsky, University of Wisconsin–Stevens Point
Bret Roark, Oklahoma Baptist University
Cheryl A. Rickabaugh, University of Redlands
Rich Robbins, Washburn University
Daniel N. Robinson, Georgetown University
Mary Schild, Columbus State University

Norman R. Simonsen, University of Massachusetts–Amherst
Peggy Skinner, South Plains College
R. H. Starr, Jr., University of Maryland–Baltimore
Douglas Wardell, University of Alberta
Linda Weldon, Essex Community College
Paul Whitney, Washington State University
Allen Wolach, Illinois Institute of Technology
Jim Zacks, Michigan State University

The enormous task of writing a book of this scope was possible only with the expert assistance of all these friends and colleagues and that of the editorial staff of Allyn and Bacon. We gratefully acknowledge their invaluable contributions at every stage of this project, collectively and, now, individually. We thank the following people at Allyn and Bacon: Karon Bowers, Executive Editor; Lisa McLellan, Senior Development Editor; Julie McBurney, Development Editor; Wendy Gordon, Senior Marketing Manager; Anna Socrates, Editorial Production Administrator; Susan McNally, Project Manager; Helane Prottas, Photo Researcher.

To The Student

How to Use This Book

Y ou are about to embark with us on an intellectual journey through the many areas of modern psychology. Before we start, we want to share with you some important information that will help guide your adventures. "The journey" is a metaphor used throughout *Psychology and Life;* your teacher serves as the tour director, the text as your tour book, and we, your authors, as your personal tour guides. The goal of this journey is for you to discover what is known about the most incredible phenomena in the entire universe: the brain, the human mind, and the behavior of all living creatures. Psychology is about understanding the seemingly mysterious processes that give rise to your thoughts, feelings, and actions.

This guide offers general strategies and specific suggestions about how to use this book to get the quality grade you deserve for your performance and to get the most from your introduction to psychology.

◆ STUDY STRATEGIES

1. **Set aside sufficient time** for your reading assignments and review of class notes. This text contains much new technical information, many principles to learn, and a new glossary of terms to memorize. To master this material, you will need at least 3 hours' reading time per chapter.

2. **Keep a record of your study time** for this course. Plot the number of hours (in half-hour intervals) you study at each reading session. Chart your time investment on a cumulative graph. Add each new study ti\me to the previous total on the left-hand axis of the graph and each study session on the baseline axis. The chart will provide visual feedback of your progress and show you when you have not been hitting the books as you should.

3. **Be an active participant.** Optimal learning occurs when you are actively involved with the learning materials. That means reading attentively, listening to lectures mindfully, paraphrasing in your own words what you are reading or hearing, and taking good notes. In the text, underline key sections, write notes to yourself in the margins, and summarize points that you think might be included on class tests.

4. **Space out your studying.** Research in psychology tells us that it is more effective to do your studying regularly rather than cramming just before tests. If you let yourself fall behind, it will be difficult to catch up with all the information included in Introductory Psychology at last-minute panic time.

5. **Get study-centered.** Find a place with minimal distractions for studying. Reserve that place for studying, reading, and writing course assignments—and do nothing else there. The place will come to be associated with study activities, and you will find it easier to work whenever you are seated at your study center.

6. **Encode reading for future testing.** Unlike reading magazines and watching television (which you do usually for their immediate impact), reading textbooks demands that you process the material in a special way. You must continually put the information into a suitable form (encode it) that will enable you to retrieve it when you are asked about it later on class examinations. Encoding means that you summarize key points, rehearse sections (sometimes aloud), and ask questions you want to be able to answer about the contents of a given section of a chapter as you read.

You should also take the teacher's perspective, anticipating the kinds of questions she or he is likely to ask, and then making sure you can answer them. Find out what kinds of tests you will be given in this course—essay, fill-in, multiple choice, or true/false. That form will affect the extent to which you focus on the big ideas and/or on details. Essays and fill-ins ask for recall-type memory, while multiple-choice and true/false tests ask for recognition-type memory. (Ask the teacher for a sample test to give you a better idea of the kinds of questions for which you need to prepare.)

◆ STUDY TACTICS

1. Review the **outline of the chapter.** It shows you the main topics to be covered, their sequence, and their relationship, giving you an overview of what is to come. The outline at the start of each chapter contains first-level and second-level headings of the major topics. The section headings indicate the structure of the chapter, and they are also convenient break points, or time-outs, for each of your study periods.

2. Jump to the end of the chapter to read the **Recapping Main Points** section. There you will find the main ideas of the chapter organized under each of the first-level headings, which will give you a clear sense of what the chapter will be covering.

3. Skim through the chapter to get the gist of its contents. Don't stop, don't take notes, and read as quickly as you can (one hour maximum time allowed).

4. Finally, dig in and master the material by actively reading, underlining, taking notes, questioning, rehearsing, and paraphrasing as you go (two hours' minimum time expected). Pay particular attention to the **Put Yourself to the Test** questions at the end of each section. Use those questions to see how well you have acquired the major points of each section.

◆ SPECIAL FEATURES

1. The purpose of the **Putting Ideas to the Test** feature is to help you see the direct link between the experiments researchers conduct and the conclusions they draw. This feature allows you to see the close relationship between psychological research and application.

2. **The Psychology in Your Life** boxes also present applications of psychological research to your everyday life. Each of these boxes presents an answer to questions that we have been asked in class by our own students and that we imagine you might ask us.

3. The **Psychology in the 21st Century** boxes describe topics and techniques for research that are on the cutting edge at the beginning of the new century. Each box presents applications of psychological research relevant to your experience of these swiftly changing times.

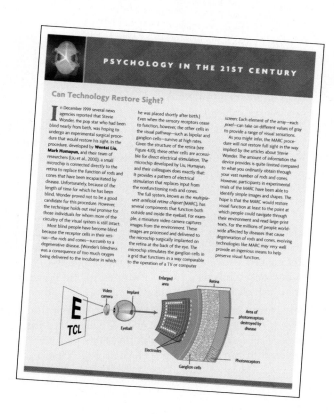

4. **Key terms and major contributors** are highlighted within the chapter in **boldface type** so they will stand out for you to notice. When you study for a test, be sure you can define each term and identify each major researcher. In addition, all key terms are listed alphabetically at the end of the chapter.

5. The key terms are also gathered together in the **glossary,** found at the end of the text. The glossary provides formal definitions of all key terms that appear in the text, and the page numbers on which they appear. Use it to refresh your memory while studying for tests.

6. Each **Put Yourself to the Test** provides questions that refer to the key points you should know before going ahead to the next section. Try to answer the questions as you finish your reading of each main section. If any of the questions stumps you, plunge back into the text and reread the appropriate material until you feel you can provide a good answer. Similarly, use these questions as a starting point for your studying before tests.

> **PUT YOURSELF TO THE TEST**
>
> ➤ What idea about emotions did Charles Darwin originate?
> ➤ What evidence suggests that some elements of emotional responses are innate while others are not?
> ➤ What roles do the autonomic and central nervous systems play in the experience of emotions?
> ➤ How have theories of emotion attempted to explain the relationship between physiology and feelings?
> ➤ In what ways do emotions serve motivational functions?
> ➤ What roles may emotions play in social circumstances?
> ➤ What impact may emotions have on cognitive functioning?

7. The **References,** also at the end of the text, present bibliographic information on every book, journal article, or media source cited in the text. It is a valuable resource in case you wish to find out more about some topic for a term paper in this or another course or just for your personal interest. A name and date set off by parentheses in the text—(Freud, 1923)—identify the source and publication date of the citation. You will then find the full source information in the References section. Citations with more than two authors list the senior author followed by the notation et al., which means "and others."

8. The **Name Index** and **Subject Index,** also at the end of the text, provide you with alphabetized listings of all terms, topics, and individuals that were covered in the text, along with their page citations.

9. Finally, your study and test performance is likely to be enhanced by using the **Grade Aid with Practice Tests** that accompanies *Psychology and Life.* It was prepared to give students a boost in studying more efficiently and taking tests more effectively. Each chapter includes "Before You Read," with a brief chapter summary and chapter learning objectives; "As You Read," a collection of demonstrations, activities, and exercises; "After You Read," containing three short practice quizzes and one comprehensive practice test; "When You Have Finished," with Web links for further information; and crossword puzzles using key terms from the text. An appendix includes answers to all practice tests and crossword puzzles.

So, there you have it—some helpful hints to increase your enjoyment of this special course and to help you get the most out of it. Our text will demand concentrated attention when you are studying to master its wealth of information. Other texts may seem to be easier because they do not give you as much depth as *Psychology and Life*, but then less in means less out.

We appreciate the opportunity your teacher has provided in selecting *Psychology and Life.* You will find it a source of valuable knowledge about a wide range of topics. Many students have reported that *Psychology and Life* has proven to be an excellent reference manual for term papers and projects in other courses as well. You might consider keeping it in your personal library of valuable resources. However, we must begin at the beginning, with the first steps in our journey.

◆ A FINAL REQUEST

Throughout this book, and through many previous editions, we have tried to make *Psychology and Life* interesting and relevant to you. We have done our best to show you the link between psychological research and your daily life—to show you that what happens in a psychologist's laboratory or clinic explains and elucidates the everyday mysteries of your mind. To do this, we have described why people react the way they do to horror movies, why some people like to eat hot peppers, and why many messages have multiple meanings. As you read, we would like you to think of relevant and interesting examples from your own life, and to send them to us (use the student feedback form on our Web site at www.ablongman.com/gerrig17e). We might even ask to publish your examples in future editions of this book!

We invite you to become part of *Psychology and Life* with us. And we can't wait to start on our journey with you.

Richard J. Gerrig
rgerrig@notes.cc.sunysb.edu

Philip G. Zimbardo
zim@psych.stanford.edu

About the Authors

Richard J. Gerrig is a professor of psychology at Stony Brook University. Before joining the Stony Brook faculty, Gerrig taught at Yale University, where he was awarded the Lex Hixon Prize for teaching excellence in the social sciences. Gerrig's research on cognitive psychological aspects of language use has been widely published. One line of work examines the mental processes that underlie efficient communication. A second research program considers the cognitive and emotional changes readers experience when they are transported to the worlds of stories. His book Experiencing Narrative Worlds was published by Yale University Press. Gerrig is a Fellow of both the American Psychological Association and the American Psychological Society.

Gerrig is the proud father of Alexandra, who at age 13 provides substantial and valuable advice about many aspects of psychology and life in the 21st Century. Life on Long Island is greatly enhanced by the guidance and support of Timothy Peterson.

Philip G. Zimbardo is a professor of psychology at Stanford University, where he has taught since 1968, after earlier teaching at Yale University, New York University, and Columbia University. His dedication to both undergraduate and graduate teaching, as well as his charismatic teaching style, has earned him many awards for distinguished teaching. Zimbardo has been a prolific, innovative researcher across a number of fields in social psychology, with more than 250 professional articles and chapters and 50 books to his credit. To recognize the breadth of his research achievements, the American Psychological Association presented Zimbardo with the Ernest Hilgard Award for lifetime contributions to general psychology. In addition, he has "crossed over" into the popular realm to introduce psychology to the general public through his best-selling trade books on shyness and his Discovering Psychology video series. Zimbardo has been President of the American Psychological Association and the Western Psychological Association.

Zimbardo is the proud father of Adam, Zara, and Tanya. His wife, Christina Maslach, is a professor of psychology at the University of California, Berkeley, and also an award-winning distinguished teacher.

1

Psychology and Life

As you begin your introductory course in psychology, what should you expect? If you are like many of the students we have taught, you will be quite pleasantly surprised by the wide-ranging terrain of contemporary psychology. We have crafted *Psychology and Life* to take you on a journey through that terrain—a journey in which rigorous research will reveal the intricacies of your human experience. Psychology and Life will lead you from the inner spaces of brain and mind to the outer dimensions of human behavior. We will investigate the processes that provide meaningful structure to your experiences, such as how you perceive the world, communicate, learn, think, and remember. We will try to understand the more dramatic expressions of human nature, such as how and why people dream, fall in love, act aggressively, and become mentally ill. Finally, we will demonstrate how psychological knowledge can be used to understand and change cultural forces at work in our lives.

As authors of *Psychology and Life,* we believe in the power of psychological expertise. The appeal of psychology has grown

3

personally for us over our careers as educators and researchers. In recent years, there has been a virtual explosion of new information about the basic mechanisms that govern mental and behavioral processes. As new ideas replace or modify old ideas, we are continually intrigued and challenged by the many fascinating pieces of the puzzle of human nature. We hope that, by the end of this journey, you too will cherish your store of psychological knowledge.

Foremost in the journey will be a scientific quest for understanding. We shall inquire about the how, what, when, and why of human behavior and about the causes and consequences of behaviors you observe in yourself, in other people, and in animals. We will explain why you think, feel, and behave as you do. What makes you uniquely different from all other people? Yet why do you often behave so much like others? Are you molded by heredity, or are you shaped more by personal experiences? How can aggression and altruism, love and hate, and madness and creativity exist side by side in this complex creature—the human animal? In this opening chapter, we consider how and why all these types of questions have become relevant to psychology's goals as a discipline.

What Makes Psychology Unique?

To appreciate the uniqueness and unity of psychology, you must consider the way psychologists define the field and the goals they bring to their research and applications. By the end of the book, we will encourage you to think like a psychologist. In this first section, we'll give you a strong idea of what that might mean.

◆ DEFINITIONS

Many psychologists seek answers to this fundamental question: What is human nature? Psychology answers this question by looking at processes that occur within individuals as well as forces that arise within the physical and social environment. In this light, we formally define **psychology** as the scientific study of the behavior of individuals and their mental processes. Let's explore the critical parts of this definition: *scientific, behavior, individual,* and *mental*.

The scientific aspect of psychology requires that psychological conclusions be based on evidence collected according to the principles of the scientific method. The **scientific method** consists of a set of orderly steps used to analyze and solve problems. This method uses objectively collected information as the factual basis for drawing conclusions. We will elaborate on the features of the scientific method more fully in Chapter 2, when we consider how psychologists conduct their research.

Behavior is the means by which organisms adjust to their environment. Behavior is action. The subject matter of psychology largely consists of the observable behavior of humans and other species of animals. Smiling, crying, running, hitting, talking, and touching are some obvious examples of behavior you can observe. Psychologists examine what the individual does and how the individual goes about doing it within a given behavioral setting and in the broader social or cultural context.

The subject of psychological analysis is most often an *individual*—a newborn infant, a teenage athlete, a college student adjusting to life in a dormitory, a man facing a midlife career change, or a woman coping with the stress of her husband's deterioration from Alzheimer's disease. However, the subject might also be a chimpanzee learning to use symbols to communicate, a white rat navigating a maze, or a sea slug responding to a danger signal. An individual might be studied in its natural habitat or in the controlled conditions of a research laboratory.

Many researchers in psychology also recognize that they cannot understand human actions without also understanding *mental processes,* the workings of the human mind. Much human activity takes place as private, internal events—thinking, planning, reasoning, creating, and dreaming. Many psychologists believe that mental processes represent the most important aspect of psychological inquiry. As you shall soon see, psychological investigators have devised ingenious techniques to study mental events and processes—to make these private experiences public.

The combination of these concerns defines psychology as a unique field. Within the *social sciences,* psychologists focus largely on behavior in individuals, whereas sociologists study the behavior of people in groups or institutions, and anthropologists focus on the broader context of behavior in different cultures. Even so, psychologists draw broadly from the insights of other scholars. Psychologists share many interests with researchers in *biological sciences,* especially with those who study brain processes and the biochemical bases of behavior. As part of the emerging area of *cognitive science,* psychologists' questions about how the human mind works are related to research and theory in computer science, artificial intelligence, and applied mathematics. As a *health science*—with links to medicine, education, law, and environmental studies—psychology

<www.ablongman.com/gerrig17e>

Most psychological study focuses on individuals—usually human ones, but sometimes those of other species. What aspects of your own life would you like psychologists to study?

seeks to improve the quality of each individual's and the collective's well-being.

Although the remarkable breadth and depth of modern psychology are a source of delight to those who become psychologists, these same attributes make the field a challenge to the student exploring it for the first time. There is so much more to the study of psychology than one expects initially—and, because of that, there will also be much of value that you can take away from this introduction to psychology. The best way to learn about the field is to learn to share psychologists' goals. Let's consider those goals.

◆ THE GOALS OF PSYCHOLOGY

The goals of the psychologist conducting basic research are to describe, explain, predict, and control behavior. These goals form the basis of the psychological enterprise. What is involved in trying to achieve each of them?

DESCRIBING WHAT HAPPENS

The first task in psychology is to make accurate observations about behavior. Psychologists typically refer to such observations as their *data* (*data* is the plural, *datum* the singular). **Behavioral data** are reports of observations about the behavior of organisms and the conditions under which the behavior occurs. When researchers undertake data collection, they must choose an appropriate *level of analysis* and devise measures of behavior that ensure *objectivity*.

In order to investigate an individual's behavior, researchers may use different *levels of analysis*—from the broadest, most global level down to the most minute, specific level. Suppose, for example, you were trying to describe a painting you saw at a museum (see **Figure 1.1**). At a global level, you might describe it by title, *Bathers,* and by artist, Georges Seurat. At a more specific level, you might recount features of the painting: Some people are sunning themselves on a riverbank, while others are enjoying the water, and so on. At a very specific level, you might describe the technique Seurat used—tiny points of paint—to create the scene. The description at each level would answer different questions about the painting.

Different levels of psychological description also address different questions. At the broadest level of psychological analysis, researchers investigate the behavior of the whole person within complex social and cultural contexts. At this level, researchers might

◆

FIGURE 1.1

Levels of Analysis

Suppose you wanted a friend to meet you in front of this painting. How would you describe it? Suppose your friend wanted to make an exact copy of the painting. How would you describe it?

study cross-cultural differences in violence, the origins of prejudice, and the consequences of mental illness. At the next level, psychologists focus on narrower, finer units of behavior, such as speed of reaction to a stop light, eye movements during reading, and grammatical errors made by children acquiring language. Researchers can study even smaller units of behavior. They might work to discover the biological bases of behavior by identifying the places in the brain where different types of memories are stored, the biochemical changes that occur during learning, and the sensory paths responsible for vision or hearing. Each level of analysis yields information essential to the final composite portrait of human nature that psychologists hope ultimately to develop.

However tight or broad the focus of the observation, psychologists strive to describe behavior *objectively*. Collecting the facts as they exist, and not as the researcher expects or hopes them to be, is of utmost importance. Because every observer brings to each observation his or her *subjective* point of view—biases, prejudices, and expectations—it is essential to prevent these personal factors from creeping in and distorting the data. As you will see in the next chapter, psychological researchers have developed a variety of techniques to maintain objectivity.

EXPLAINING WHAT HAPPENS

While *descriptions* must stick to perceivable information, *explanations* deliberately go beyond what can be observed. In many areas of psychology, the central goal is to find regular patterns in behavioral and mental processes. Psychologists want to discover *how* behavior

works. Why do you laugh at situations that differ from your expectations of what is coming next? What conditions could lead someone to attempt suicide or commit rape?

Explanations in psychology usually recognize that most behavior is influenced by a combination of factors. Some factors operate within the individual, such as genetic makeup, motivation, intelligence level, or self-esteem. These inner determinants tell something special about the organism. Other factors, however, operate externally. Suppose, for example, that a child tries to please a teacher in order to win a prize or that a motorist trapped in a traffic jam becomes frustrated and hostile. These behaviors are largely influenced by events outside the person. When psychologists seek to explain behavior, they almost always consider both types of explanations. Suppose, for example, psychologists want to explain why some people start smoking. Researchers might examine the possibility that some individuals are particularly prone to risk taking (an internal explanation) or that some individuals experience a lot of peer pressure (an external explanation)—or that both a disposition toward risk taking and situational peer pressure are necessary (a combined explanation).

Often a psychologist's goal is to explain a wide variety of behavior in terms of one underlying cause. Consider a situation in which your teacher says that to earn a good grade, each student must participate regularly in class discussions. Your roommate, who is always well prepared for class, never raises his hand to answer questions or volunteer information. The teacher chides him for being unmotivated and assumes he is not bright. That same roommate also goes to parties but never asks anyone to dance, doesn't openly defend his point of view when it is challenged by someone less informed, and rarely engages in small talk at the dinner table. What is your diagnosis? What underlying cause might account for this range of behavior? How about *shyness?* Like many other people who suffer from intense feelings of shyness, your roommate is unable to behave in desired ways (Zimbardo & Radl, 1999). We can use the concept of shyness to explain the full pattern of your roommate's behavior.

To forge such causal explanations, researchers must often engage in a creative process of examining a diverse collection of data. Master detective Sherlock Holmes drew shrewd conclusions from scraps of evidence. In a similar fashion, every researcher must use an informed imagination, which creatively *synthesizes* what is known and what is not yet known. A well-trained psychologist can explain observations by using her or his insight into the human experience along with the facts previous researchers have uncovered about the phenomenon in question. Much psychological research attempts to determine which of several explanations most accurately accounts for a given behavioral pattern.

<www.ablongman.com/gerrig17e>

PREDICTING WHAT WILL HAPPEN

Predictions in psychology are statements about the likelihood that a certain behavior will occur or that a given relationship will be found. Often an accurate explanation of the causes underlying some form of behavior will allow a researcher to make accurate predictions about future behavior. Thus, if we believe your roommate to be shy, we could confidently predict that he would be uncomfortable when asked to have a conversation with a stranger. When different explanations are put forward to account for some behavior or relationship, they are usually judged by how well they can make accurate and comprehensive predictions. If your roommate were to blossom in contact with a stranger, we would be forced to rethink our diagnosis.

Just as observations must be made objectively, scientific predictions must be worded precisely enough to enable them to be tested and then rejected if the evidence does not support them. A *scientific prediction* is based on an understanding of the ways events relate to one another, and it suggests what mechanisms link those events to certain predictors. A *causal prediction* specifies the conditions under which behaviors will change. For example, the presence of a stranger reliably causes human and monkey babies, beyond a certain age, to respond with signs of anxiety. Changes in the observed behavior, however, may depend on variations in the exact situation—such as the extent of strangeness. Would fewer signs of anxiety appear in a human or a monkey baby if the stranger were also a baby rather than an adult, or if the stranger were of the same species rather than of a different one? To improve a causal prediction, a researcher would create systematic variations in environmental conditions and observe their influence on the baby's response.

A psychological prediction

CONTROLLING WHAT HAPPENS

For many psychologists, control is the central, most powerful goal. Control means making behavior happen or not happen—starting it, maintaining it, stopping it, and influencing its form, strength, or rate of occurrence. A causal explanation of behavior is convincing if it can create conditions under which the behavior can be controlled.

The ability to control behavior is important because it gives psychologists ways of helping people improve the quality of their lives. Throughout *Psychology and Life,* you will see examples of the types of *interventions* psychologists have devised to help people gain control over problematic aspects of their lives. Chapter 15, for example, discusses treatments for mental illness. We also describe how people can harness psychological

What causes people to smoke? Can psychologists create conditions under which people will be less likely to engage in this behavior?

PSYCHOLOGY IN YOUR LIFE

A s you read this opening chapter, the question we pose as the title of this box may have come to mind once or twice: Why study psychology? Our answer to that question is quite straightforward: We believe that psychological research has immediate and crucial applications to important issues of everyday experience. One of the foremost goals of *Psychology and Life* is to highlight the personal relevance and social significance of psychological expertise.

Every semester when we begin to teach, we are faced with students who enter an introductory psychology class with some very specific questions in mind. Sometimes those questions emerge from their own experience ("What should I do if I think my mother is mentally ill?").

Why Study Psychology?
Hal Whalen
University of Vermont

"Will this course teach me how to improve my grades?"); sometimes those questions emerge from the type of psychological information that is communicated through the popular press ("Is it true that oldest children are the most conservative?" "Are women really always better parents than men?"). The challenge for us is to bring the products of scientific research to bear on questions that matter to our students.

Almost every section of *Psychology and Life* addresses concerns that our students have brought directly to us. In this edition, we have also included a special feature, boxes we call Psychology in Your Life (like this one!). Each of these boxes answers a question we have heard repeatedly both from our own students and from students who used earlier editions of this text. We hope as you read each Psychology in Your Life box that the questions your peers have posed will strike you as important and relevant to your own life. Please read these boxes carefully. Our aim has been to bring scientific evidence to bear on some of the issues that matter most to students like you. We hope that you will agree that the study of psychology will enrich your life.

forces to eliminate unhealthy behaviors like smoking and initiate healthy behaviors like regular exercise (see Chapter 12). You will learn what types of parenting practices can help parents maintain solid bonds with their children (Chapter 10); you will learn what forces make strangers reluctant to offer assistance in emergency situations and how those forces can be overcome (Chapter 17). These are just a few examples of the broad range of circumstances in which psychologists use their knowledge to control and improve people's lives. In this respect, psychologists are a rather optimistic group; many believe that virtually any undesired behavior pattern can be modified by the proper intervention. *Psychology and Life* shares that optimism.

In this introductory chapter, we will introduce some special features of *Psychology and Life*—features such as Put Yourself to the Test—that we have designed to allow you to learn more effectively from the text. The Put Yourself to the Test sections that follow the major portions of each chapter will provide a set of questions

for your careful consideration. As psychologists, we know that students acquire knowledge more thoroughly when they actively engage with the material. You should use the questions to help you solidify your understanding of the important concepts in each part of the text. Below is the first Put Yourself to the Test.

PUT YOURSELF TO THE TEST

- How does each of the four components of the definition of psychology contribute to the field's unique identity?
- With respect to the goal of describing what happens, why do different levels of analysis suit different research purposes?
- Why is there often a close relationship between explanation and prediction?
- With respect to the goal of control, why is it appropriate to characterize psychologists as "rather optimistic"?

The Evolution of Modern Psychology

I n the 21st century, it is relatively easy to define psychology and to state the goals of psychological research. As you begin to study psychology, however, it is important to understand the many forces that led to the emergence of modern psychology. At the core of this historical review is one simple principle: *Ideas matter.* Much of the history of psychology has been characterized by heated debates about what constitutes the appropriate subject matter and methodologies for a science of mind and behavior.

Our historical review will be carried out at two levels of analysis. In the first section, we will consider the period of history in which some of the critical groundwork for modern psychology was laid down. This tight focus will enable you to witness at close range the battle of ideas. In the second section, we describe in a broader fashion seven perspectives that have emerged in the modern day. For both levels of focus, you should allow yourself to imagine the intellectual passion with which the theories evolved.

◆ PSYCHOLOGY'S HISTORICAL FOUNDATIONS

"Psychology has a long past, but only a short history," wrote one of the first experimental psychologists, **Hermann Ebbinghaus** (1908/1973). Scholars had long asked important questions about human nature—about how people perceive reality, the nature of consciousness, and the origins of madness—but they did not possess the means to answer them. Consider the fundamental questions posed in the fourth and fifth centuries B.C. by the classical Greek philosophers Socrates, Plato, and Aristotle. Although forms of psychology existed in ancient Indian Yogic traditions, Western psychology traces its origin to these great thinkers' dialogues about how the mind works, the nature of free will, and the relationship of individual citizens to their community or state. Toward the end of the 19th century, psychology began to emerge as a discipline when researchers applied the laboratory techniques from other sciences—such as physiology and physics—to the study of these fundamental questions from philosophy.

A critical figure in the evolution of modern psychology was **Wilhelm Wundt,** who, in 1879 in Leipzig, Germany, founded the first formal laboratory devoted to experimental psychology. Although Wundt had been trained as a physiologist, over his research career his interest shifted from questions of body to questions of mind: He wished to understand basic processes of sensation and perception as well as the speed of simple mental processes. By the time he established his psychology laboratory, Wundt had already accomplished a range of research and published the first of several editions of *Principles of Physiological Psychology* (Kendler, 1987). Once Wundt's laboratory was established at Leipzig, he began to train the first graduate students specifically devoted to the emerging field of psychology. Those students often became founders of their own psychology laboratories around the world.

As psychology became established as a separate discipline, psychology laboratories began to appear in universities throughout North America, the first at Johns Hopkins University in 1883. These early laboratories often bore Wundt's impact. For example, after studying with Wundt, **Edward Titchener** became one of the first psychologists in the United States, founding a laboratory at Cornell University in 1892. However, at around the same time, a young Harvard philosophy professor who had studied medicine and had strong interests in literature and religion developed a uniquely American perspective. **William James,** brother of the great novelist Henry James, wrote a two-volume work, *The Principles of Psychology* (1890/1950), which many experts consider to be the most important psychology text ever written. Shortly after, in 1892, G. Stanley Hall founded the American Psychological Association. By 1900 there were more than 40 psychology laboratories in North America (Hilgard, 1986).

In 1879, Wilhelm Wundt founded the first formal laboratory devoted to experimental psychology. Suppose you decided to found your own psychology laboratory. What types of issues would you study?

In 1894, Margaret Washburn became the first woman to receive a PhD in psychology. She went on to write an influential textbook, The Animal Mind (1908). What challenges might she have faced as a pioneer woman researcher?

Almost as soon as psychology emerged, a debate arose as to the proper subject matter and methods for the new discipline. This debate isolated some of the issues that still loom large in psychology. We will describe, specifically, the tension between structuralism and functionalism.

STRUCTURALISM: THE CONTENTS OF THE MIND

Psychology's potential to make a unique contribution to knowledge became apparent when psychology became a laboratory science organized around experiments. In Wundt's laboratory, experimental participants made simple responses (saying yes or no, pressing a button) to stimuli they perceived under conditions varied by laboratory instruments. Because the data were collected through systematic, objective procedures, independent observers could replicate the results of these experiments. Emphasis on the scientific method, concern for precise measurement, and statistical analysis of data characterized Wundt's psychological tradition

When Titchener brought Wundt's psychology to the United States, he advocated that such scientific methods be used to study consciousness. His method for examining the elements of conscious mental life was *intro-*

spection, the systematic examination by individuals of their own thoughts and feelings about specific sensory experiences. Titchener emphasized the "what" of mental contents rather than the "why" or "how" of thinking. His approach came to be known as **structuralism,** the study of the structure of mind and behavior.

Structuralism was based on the presumption that all human mental experience could be understood as the combination of basic components. The goal of this approach was to reveal the underlying structure of the human mind by analyzing the component elements of sensation and other experience that form an individual's mental life. Many psychologists attacked structuralism on three fronts: (1) It was *reductionistic,* because it reduced all complex human experience to simple sensations; (2) it was *elemental,* because it sought to combine parts, or elements, into a whole rather than study complex, or whole, behaviors directly; and (3) it was *mentalistic,* because it studied only verbal reports of human conscious awareness, ignoring the study of individuals who could not describe their introspections, including animals, children, and the mentally disturbed.

One important alternative to structuralism, pioneered by the German psychologist **Max Wertheimer,** focused on the way in which the mind understands many experiences as *gestalts*—organized wholes—rather than as the sums of simple parts: Your experience of a painting, for example, is more than the sum of the individual daubs of paint. As we shall see in Chapter 4, *Gestalt psychology* continues to have an impact on the study of perception.

A second major opposition to structuralism, which we shall discuss here, came under the banner of *functionalism.*

FUNCTIONALISM: MINDS WITH A PURPOSE

William James agreed with Titchener that consciousness was central to the study of psychology; but for James, the study of consciousness was not reduced to elements, contents, and structures. Instead, consciousness was an ongoing stream, a property of mind in continual interaction with the environment. Human consciousness facilitated one's adjustment to the environment; thus, the acts and *functions* of mental processes were of significance, not the contents of the mind.

Functionalism gave primary importance to learned habits that enable organisms to adapt to their environment and to function effectively. For functionalists, the key question to be answered by research was "What is the function or purpose of any behavioral act?" The founder of the school of functionalism was the American philosopher **John Dewey.** His concern for the practical uses of mental processes led to important advances in education. Dewey's theorizing provided

<www.ablongman.com/gerrig17e>

the impetus for *progressive education* in his own laboratory school and more generally in the United States: "Rote learning was abandoned in favor of learning by doing, in expectation that intellectual curiosity would be encouraged and understanding would be enhanced" (Kendler, 1987, p. 124).

Although James believed in careful observation, he put little value on the rigorous laboratory methods of Wundt. In James's psychology, there was a place for emotions, self, will, values, and even religious and mystical experience. His "warm-blooded" psychology recognized a uniqueness in each individual that could not be reduced to formulas or numbers from test results. For James, explanation rather than experimental control was the goal of psychology (Arkin, 1990).

THE LEGACY OF THESE APPROACHES

Despite their differences, the insights of the practitioners of both structuralism and functionalism created an intellectual context in which contemporary psychology could flourish. Psychologists currently examine *both* the structure and the function of behavior. Consider the process of speech production. Suppose you want to invite a friend to the movies. To do so, the words you speak must serve the right function—*Lord of the Rings, with me, tonight*—but also have the right structure: It wouldn't do to say, "Would go *Lord of the Rings* me to with tonight you to like?" To understand how speech production works, researchers study the way that speakers fit meanings (functions) to the grammatical structures of their languages (Bock, 1990). (We will describe some of the processes of language production in Chapter 8.) Throughout *Psychology and Life,* we will emphasize both structure and function, as we review both classic and contemporary research. Psychologists continue to employ a great variety of methodologies to study the general forces that apply to all humans as well as unique aspects of each individual.

◆ CURRENT PSYCHOLOGICAL PERSPECTIVES

Suppose your friend accepts the invitation to see *Lord of the Rings.* What *perspective* does each of you bring to your viewing of the movie? Suppose one of you has read the novel on which the movie is based whereas the other has not. Or, suppose one of you likes to judge movies by the quality of the computer-generated

◆ Classroom practices in the United States were changed through the efforts of the functionalist John Dewey. What can teachers do to encourage "intellectual curiosity"?

special effects whereas the other of you is more attuned to the subtleties of the human actors' performances. You can see how these different perspectives would affect the way in which you examine the movie as it unfolds.

In a similar fashion, psychologists' perspectives determine the way in which they examine behavior and mental processes. The perspectives influence what psychologists look for, where they look, and what research methods they use. In this section, we define seven perspectives—psychodynamic, behaviorist, humanistic, cognitive, biological, evolutionary, and sociocultural. As you read the section, note how each perspective defines the causes and consequences of behavior.

A word of caution: Although each perspective represents a different approach to the central issues of psychology, you should come to appreciate why most psychologists borrow and blend concepts from more than one of these perspectives. Each perspective enhances the understanding of the entirety of human experience. In the chapters that follow, we will elaborate in some detail on the contributions of each approach, because, taken together, they represent what contemporary psychology is all about.

THE PSYCHODYNAMIC PERSPECTIVE

According to the **psychodynamic perspective,** behavior is driven, or motivated, by powerful inner forces. In this view, human actions stem from inherited instincts, biological drives, and attempts to resolve conflicts between personal needs and society's demands. Deprivation states, physiological arousal, and conflicts provide the power for behavior just as coal fuels a steam locomotive. According to this model, the organism stops reacting when its needs are satisfied and its drives reduced. The main purpose of action is to reduce tension.

Psychodynamic principles of motivation were most fully developed by the Viennese physician **Sigmund Freud** (1856–1939) in the late 19th and early 20th centuries. Freud's ideas grew out of his work with mentally disturbed patients, but he believed that the principles he observed applied to both normal and abnormal behavior. Freud's psychodynamic theory views a person as pulled and pushed by a complex network of inner and outer forces. Freud's model was the first to recognize that human nature is not always rational, that actions may be driven by motives that are not in conscious awareness.

Many psychologists since Freud have taken the psychodynamic model in new directions. Freud himself emphasized early childhood as the stage in which personality is formed. Neo-Freudian theorists have broadened psychodynamic theory to include social influences and interactions that occur over the individual's entire

Sigmund Freud, photographed with his daughter, Anna, on a trip to the Italian Alps in 1913. Freud suggested that behavior is often driven by motives outside of conscious awareness. What implications does that perspective have for the ways in which you make life choices?

lifetime. Psychodynamic ideas have had a great influence on many areas of psychology. You will encounter different aspects of Freud's contributions as you read about child development, dreaming, forgetting, unconscious motivation, personality, and psychoanalytic therapy.

THE BEHAVIORIST PERSPECTIVE

Those who take the **behaviorist perspective** seek to understand how particular environmental stimuli control particular kinds of behavior. First, behaviorists analyze the *antecedent* environmental conditions—those that precede the behavior and set the stage for an organism to make a response or withhold a response. Next, they look at the *behavioral response,* which is the main object of study—the action to be understood, predicted, and controlled. Finally, they examine the observable *consequences* that follow from the response. A behaviorist, for example, might be interested in the way in which speeding tickets of varying sizes (consequences) change the likelihood that motorists will drive with caution or abandon (behavioral responses).

The behaviorist perspective was pioneered by **John Watson** (1878–1958), who argued that psychological research should seek the laws that govern observable behavior across species. **B. F. Skinner** (1904–1990) extended the influence of behaviorism by expanding its analyses to the consequences of behaviors. Both researchers insisted on precise definitions of the phenomena studied and on rigorous standards of evidence. Both Watson and Skinner believed that the basic processes they investigated with nonhuman animals represented general principles that would hold true for humans as well.

Behaviorism has yielded a critical practical legacy. Its emphasis on the need for rigorous experimentation and carefully defined variables has influenced most areas of psychology. Although behaviorists have conducted much basic research with nonhuman animals, the principles of behaviorism have been widely applied to human problems. Behaviorist principles have yielded a more humane approach to educating children (through the use of positive reinforcement rather than punishment), new therapies for modifying behavior disorders, and guidelines for creating model utopian communities.

THE HUMANISTIC PERSPECTIVE

Humanistic psychology emerged in the 1950s as an alternative to the psychodynamic and the behaviorist models. According to the **humanistic perspective,** people are neither driven by the powerful, instinctive forces postulated by the Freudians nor manipulated by their environments, as proposed by the behaviorists. Instead, people are active creatures who are innately good and capable of choice. Humanistic psychologists study behavior, but not by reducing it to components, elements, and variables in laboratory experiments. Instead, they look for patterns in people's life histories.

According to the humanistic perspective, the main task for humans is to strive for positive development. For example, **Carl Rogers** (1902–1987) emphasized that individuals have a natural tendency toward psychological growth and health—a process that is aided by the positive regard of those who surround them. **Abraham Maslow** (1908–1970) coined the term *self-actualization* to refer to each individual's drive toward the fullest development of his or her potential. In addition, Rogers, Maslow, and their colleagues defined a perspective that strives to deal with the whole person, practicing a *holistic* approach to human psychology. They believed that true understanding requires integrating knowledge of the individual's mind, body, and behavior with an awareness of social and cultural forces.

The humanistic approach expands the realm of psychology to include valuable lessons from the study of literature, history, and the arts. In this manner, psychology becomes a more complete discipline. Humanists suggest that their view is the yeast that helps psychology rise above its focus on negative forces and on the animal-like aspects of humanity. As we shall see in Chapter 15, the humanistic perspective had a major impact on the development of new approaches to psychotherapy.

THE COGNITIVE PERSPECTIVE

The cognitive revolution in psychology emerged as another challenge to the limits of behaviorism. The centerpiece of the **cognitive perspective** is human thought and all the processes of knowing—attending, thinking, remembering, and understanding. From the cognitive perspective, people act because they think, and people think because they are human beings, exquisitely equipped to do so.

According to the cognitive model, behavior is only partly determined by preceding environmental events and past behavioral consequences, as behaviorists believe. Some of the most significant behavior emerges from totally novel ways of thinking, not from predictable ways used in the past. The ability to imagine options and alternatives that are totally different from what is or was enables people to work toward futures that transcend current circumstances. An individual responds to reality not as it is in the objective world of matter, but as it is in the *subjective reality* of the individual's inner world of thoughts and imagination. Cognitive psychologists view thoughts as both results and causes of overt actions. Feeling regret when you've hurt someone is an example of thought as a result. But apologizing for your actions after feeling regret is an example of thought as a cause of behavior.

Cognitive psychologists study higher mental processes such as perception, memory, language use, problem solving, and decision making at a variety of levels. They may examine patterns of blood flow in the brain during different types of cognitive tasks, a student's recollection of an early childhood event, or changes in memory abilities across the life span. Because of its focus on mental processes, many researchers see the cognitive perspective as the dominant one in psychology today.

THE BIOLOGICAL PERSPECTIVE

The **biological perspective** guides psychologists who search for the causes of behavior in the functioning of genes, the brain, the nervous system, and the endocrine system. An organism's functioning is explained in terms of underlying physical structures and biochemical processes. Experience and behaviors are largely understood as the result of chemical and electrical activities taking place within and between nerve cells.

Researchers who take the biological perspective generally assume that psychological and social phenomena can be ultimately understood in terms of biochemical processes: Even the most complex phenomena can be understood by analysis, or reduction, into ever smaller, more specific units. They might, for example, try to explain how you are reading the words of this sentence with respect to the exact physical processes in cells in your brain. According to this perspective, behavior is determined by physical structures and hereditary processes. Experience can modify behavior by altering these underlying biological structures and processes. Researchers might ask, "What changes in your brain occurred while you learned to read?" The task of psychobiological researchers is to understand behavior at the most precise level of analysis.

Many researchers who take the biological perspective contribute to the multidisciplinary field of **behavioral neuroscience.** Neuroscience is the study of brain function; behavioral neuroscience attempts to understand the brain processes underlying behaviors such as sensation, learning, and emotion. The advances in the brain imaging techniques that we describe in Chapter 3 have led to dramatic breakthroughs in the field of **cognitive neuroscience.** Cognitive neuroscience trains a multidisciplinary research focus on the brain bases of higher cognitive functions such as memory and language. As we shall see, brain imaging techniques allow the biological perspective to be extended into a broad range of human experience.

THE EVOLUTIONARY PERSPECTIVE

The **evolutionary perspective** seeks to connect contemporary psychology to a central idea of the life sciences, Charles Darwin's theory of evolution by natural selection. The idea of natural selection is quite simple: Those organisms that are better suited to their environments tend to produce offspring (and pass on their genes) more successfully than those organisms with poorer adaptations. Over many generations, the species changes in the direction of the privileged adaptation. The evolutionary perspective in psychology suggests that *mental abilities* evolved over millions of years to serve particular adaptive purposes, just as physical abilities did.

To practice evolutionary psychology, researchers focus on the environmental conditions in which the human brain evolved. Humans spent 99 percent of their evolutionary history as hunter–gatherers living in small groups during the Pleistocene era (the roughly 2-million-year period ending 10,000 years ago). Evolutionary psychology uses the rich theoretical framework of evolutionary biology to identify the central adaptive

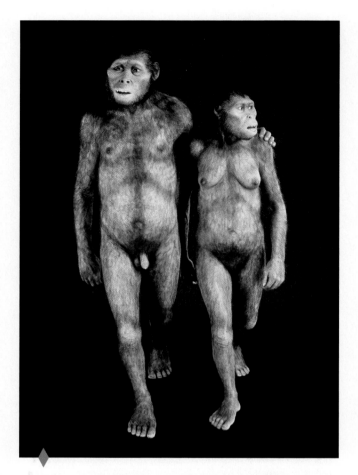

What mental abilities were needed by the Australopithecus afarensis of 4 million years ago, and how might these abilities have evolved to the present day?

problems that faced this species: avoiding predators and parasites, gathering and exchanging food, finding and retaining mates, and raising healthy children. After identifying the adaptive problems that these early humans faced, evolutionary psychologists generate inferences about the sorts of mental mechanisms, or psychological adaptations, that might have evolved to solve those problems.

Evolutionary psychology differs from other perspectives most fundamentally in its focus on the extremely long process of evolution as a central explanatory principle. Evolutionary psychologists, for example, attempt to understand the different sex roles assumed by men and women as products of evolution, rather than as products of contemporary societal pressures. Because evolutionary psychologists cannot carry out experiments that vary the course of evolution, they must be particularly inventive to provide evidence in favor of their theories.

<www.ablongman.com/gerrig17e>

THE SOCIOCULTURAL PERSPECTIVE

Psychologists who take a **sociocultural perspective** study *cross-cultural* differences in the causes and consequences of behavior. The sociocultural perspective is an important response to the criticism that psychological research has too often been based on a Western conception of human nature and had as its subject population only white, middle-class Americans (Gergen et al., 1996). A proper consideration of cultural forces may involve comparisons of groups within the same national boundaries. For example, researchers may compare the prevalence of eating disorders for white American versus African American teenagers within the United States (see Chapter 11). Cultural forces may also be assessed across nationalities, as in comparisons of moral judgments in the United States and India (see Chapter 10). Cross-cultural psychologists want to determine whether the theories researchers have developed apply to all humans, or only to more narrow, specific populations.

A cross-cultural perspective can be brought to bear on almost every topic of psychological research: Are people's perceptions of the world affected by culture? Do the languages people speak affect the way they experience the world? How does culture affect the way children develop toward adulthood? How do cultural attitudes shape the experience of old age? How does culture affect our sense of self? Does culture influence an individual's likelihood to engage in particular behaviors? Does culture affect the way individuals express emotions? Does culture affect the rates at which people suffer from psychological disorders?

By asking these types of questions, the sociocultural perspective often yields conclusions that directly challenge those generated from the other perspectives. Researchers have claimed, for example, that many aspects of Freud's psychodynamic theories cannot apply to cultures that are very different from Freud's Vienna. This concern was raised as early as 1927 by the anthropologist Bronislaw Malinowski (1927), who soundly critiqued Freud's father-centered theory by describing the family practices of the Trobriand Islanders of New Guinea, for whom family authority resided with mothers rather than with fathers. The sociocultural perspective, therefore, suggests that some universal claims of the psychodynamic perspective are incorrect. The sociocultural perspective poses a continual, important challenge to generalizations about human experience that ignore the diversity and richness of culture.

COMPARING PERSPECTIVES: FOCUS ON AGGRESSION

Each of the seven perspectives rests on a different set of assumptions and leads to a different way of looking for answers to questions about behavior. **Table 1.1**

TABLE 1.1

Comparison of Seven Perspectives in Contemporary Psychology

Perspective	Focus of Study	Primary Research Topics
Psychodynamic	Unconscious drives Conflicts	Behavior as overt expression of unconscious motives
Behaviorist	Specific overt responses	Behavior and its stimulus causes and consequences
Humanistic	Human experience and potentials	Life patterns Values Goals
Cognitive	Mental processes Language	Inferred mental processes through behavioral indicators
Biological	Brain and nervous system processes	Biochemical basis of behavior and mental processes
Evolutionary	Evolved psychological adaptations	Mental mechanisms in terms of evolved adaptive functions
Sociocultural	Cross-cultural patterns of attitudes and behaviors	Universal and culture-specific aspects of human experience

summarizes the perspectives. As an example, let's briefly compare how psychologists using these models might deal with the question of why people act aggressively. All of the approaches have been used in the effort to understand the nature of aggression and violence. For each perspective, we give examples of the types of claims researchers might make and experiments they might undertake.

- *Psychodynamic.* Analyze aggression as a reaction to frustrations caused by barriers to pleasure, such as unjust authority. View aggression as an adult's displacement of hostility originally felt as a child against his or her parents.

- *Behaviorist.* Identify reinforcements of past aggressive responses, such as extra attention given to a child who hits classmates or siblings. Assert that children learn from physically abusive parents to be abusive with their own children.

- *Humanistic.* Look for personal values and social conditions that foster self-limiting, aggressive perspectives instead of growth-enhancing, shared experiences.

- *Cognitive.* Explore the hostile thoughts and fantasies people experience while witnessing violent acts, noting both aggressive imagery and intentions to harm others. Study the impact of violence in films and videos, including pornographic violence, on attitudes toward gun control, rape, and war.

- *Biological.* Study the role of specific brain systems in aggression by stimulating different regions and then recording any destructive actions that are elicited. Also analyze the brains of mass murderers for abnormalities; examine female aggression as related to phases of the menstrual cycle.

- *Evolutionary.* Consider what conditions would have made aggression an adaptive behavior for early humans. Identify psychological mechanisms capable of selectively generating aggressive behavior under those conditions.

- *Sociocultural.* Consider how members of different cultures display and interpret aggression. Identify how cultural forces affect the likelihood of different types of aggressive behavior.

It is not only professional psychologists who have theories about why people do what they do. You probably have some convictions about whether behavior is influenced more by heredity or by environment, whether people are basically good or evil, and whether or not humans have free will. As you read about the findings based on these perspectives, keep checking psychologists' conclusions against your own views. Examine where your personal convictions come from and think about some ways you might want to broaden or modify them.

PUT YOURSELF TO THE TEST

- What are the most important contrasts between structuralism and functionalism?
- From the psychodynamic perspective, what forces drive human behavior?
- What types of relationships does the behaviorist perspective seek among observable behaviors?
- How does the humanistic perspective differ from the psychodynamic and behaviorist perspectives?
- Why does the cognitive perspective embrace behavioral processes that cannot be directly observed?
- What types of explanations for behavior does the biological perspective seek?
- Why does the evolutionary perspective put emphasis on the circumstances in which the human species evolved?
- Why is cross-cultural research critical to tests of most psychological theories?

What Psychologists Do

You now know enough about psychology to formulate questions that span the full range of psychological inquiry. If you prepared such a list of questions, you would be likely to touch on the areas of expertise of the great variety of individuals who call themselves psychologists. In **Table 1.2,** we provide our own version of such questions and indicate what sort of psychologist might address each one.

As you examine the table, you will note that there are a great many subdivisions within the profession of psychology. Some of the labels the field uses tell you about the major content of a psychologist's expertise. For example, *cognitive psychologists* focus on basic cognitive processes such as memory and language; *social psychologists* focus on the social forces that shape

TABLE 1.2

The Diversity of Psychological Inquiry

The Question	Who Addresses It?
How can people cope better with day-to-day problems?	Clinical psychologists Counseling psychologists Community psychologists Psychiatrists
How do memories get stored in the brain?	Biological psychologists Psychopharmacologists
How can you teach a dog to follow commands?	Experimental psychologists Behavior analysts
Why can't I always recall information I'm *sure* I know?	Cognitive psychologists Cognitive scientists
What makes people different from one another?	Personality psychologists Behavioral geneticists
How does peer pressure work?	Social psychologists
What do babies know about the world?	Developmental psychologists
Why does my job make me feel so depressed?	Industrial psychologists Human factors psychologists
How should teachers deal with disruptive students?	Educational psychologists School psychologists
Why do I get sick before every exam?	Health psychologists
Was the defendant insane when she committed the crime?	Forensic psychologists
Why do I always choke during important basketball games?	Sports psychologists

people's attitudes and behavior. Some of the labels identify the domains in which psychologists apply their expertise. For example, *industrial–organizational psychologists* focus their efforts on improving people's adjustment in the workplace; *school psychologists* focus on students' adjustment in educational settings.

Each type of psychologist achieves a balance between *research*—seeking new insights—and *application*—putting those insights to use in the world. There's a necessary relationship between those two types of activities. For example, we often think of *clinical psychologists* largely as individuals who apply psychological knowledge to better people's lives. However, as we shall see in Chapters 14 and 15, clinical psychologists also have important research functions. Contemporary research continues to improve our understanding of the distinctions among psychological disorders and the treatments that best ease patients' distress.

Developmental psychologists may use puppets or other toys in their study of how children behave, think, or feel. Why might it be easier for a child to express his or her thoughts to a puppet than to an adult?

PSYCHOLOGY IN THE 21ST CENTURY

The Future Is Now

Throughout *Psychology and Life,* we include brief essays that discuss transitions in the discipline of psychology as we enter the 21st century. In this chapter, we have given a brief account of how the discipline has changed, particularly with respect to theoretical perspectives, over the past 100 years. What will the next 100 years bring? It is easy to foresee changes in both the content and practice of psychology.

Although some of the topics psychologists seek to answer are timeless, such as the basic processes of language acquisition, other questions arise because of particular circumstances of human history. For example, much of the social psychological research we will review in Chapters 16 and 17 was initiated by scholars who were trying to understand the

forces that gave rise to the horrors of World War II. We cannot foretell what major social movements will grip the globe in the 21st century, but we can be reasonably certain that psychologists will respond immediately to study the origins and implications of those movements. Psychological research is also very likely to be influenced by the technologies that are shrinking the distances between individuals in diverse cultures and locations. With the World Wide Web giving people instant access to information from all over the world, questions of cultural differences and similarities are likely to loom very large in 21st-century psychology.

Even as technological innovations influence the questions psychologists wish to answer, those advances will also change the way in which researchers are able to

answer those questions. In the 20th century, the advent of computers and brain imaging devices revolutionized the study of mental processes in ways that Wundt and his colleagues in early experimental psychology could hardly have imagined. With further technological refinement, researchers may be able to pinpoint the relationship between ongoing mental processes and brain activity with amazing accuracy. Similarly, advances in the technological tools of genetics research may swiftly change the ways in which researchers tease apart the influences of nature and nurture on each individual's life course.

These are the types of issues—innovations in the content and practice of psychology—that we will address in this feature, Psychology in the 21st Century.

Take a look back at Table 1.2. We intended the list of questions to demonstrate why psychology has so many divisions. Did we manage to capture your own concerns? If you have the time, make a list of your own questions. Cross off each question as *Psychology and*

Life answers it. If, at the end of the course, you still have unanswered questions, please send them to us! (Our e-mail addresses can be found in the preface.)

Have you begun to wonder exactly how many practicing psychologists there are in the world? Surveys sug-

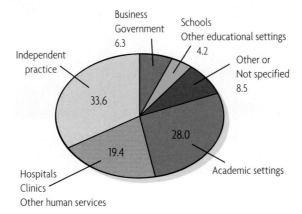

Business
Government
6.3

Schools
Other educational settings
4.2

Independent practice

Other or
Not specified
8.5

33.6

28.0

19.4

Hospitals
Clinics
Other human services

Academic settings

FIGURE 1.2

Work Settings of Psychologists

Shown are percentages of psychologists working in particular settings, according to a survey of American Psychological Association (APA) members holding doctoral degrees in psychology.

gest that the number is well over 500,000. Of that number, approximately 62,000 to 82,000 work at psychological research (see **Figure 1.2**). Although the percentage of psychologists in the population is greatest in Western industrialized nations, interest in psychology continues to increase in many countries. The International Union of Psychological Science draws together member organizations from 64 countries (Rosenzweig, 1999a). The American Psychological Association (APA), an organization that includes psychologists from all over the world, has 155,000 members (Fowler, 1999). A second international organization, the American Psychological Society, with more than 13,500 members, focuses more on scientific aspects of psychology and less on the clinical, or treatment, side. As psychology continues to contribute to the scientific and human enterprise, more people—women and men, and members of all segments of society—are being drawn to it as a career.

You're on your way. We hope *Psychology and Life* will be a worthwhile journey, full of memorable moments and unexpected pleasures. Let's go, or, as the Italians say, "Andiamo!"

PUT YOURSELF TO THE TEST

- Why does the field of psychology address such a diverse range of topics?
- Why does the field of psychology include both research and application?

Recapping Main Points

Each chapter of *Psychology and Life* ends with a section called Recapping Main Points. You should use these summaries to test your comprehension of the text. If you don't understand a summary point, plunge back into the text and reread the appropriate material until you feel confident that you understand. You can use the Put Yourself to the Test questions and these recapping sections as a starting point for your study before tests. Here's the first Recapping Main Points.

WHAT MAKES PSYCHOLOGY UNIQUE?

- Psychology is the scientific study of the behavior and the mental processes of individuals.
- The goals of psychology are to describe, explain, predict, and help control behavior.

THE EVOLUTION OF MODERN PSYCHOLOGY

- Structuralism emerged from the work of Wundt and Titchener. It emphasized the structure of the mind and behavior built from elemental sensations.
- Functionalism, developed by James and Dewey, emphasized the purpose behind behavior.
- Taken together, these theories created the agenda for modern psychology.
- Each of the seven contemporary approaches to studying psychology differs in its view of human nature, the determinants of behavior, the focus of study, and the primary research approach.

- The psychodynamic perspective looks at behavior as driven by instinctive forces, inner conflicts, and conscious and unconscious motivations.
- The behaviorist perspective views behavior as determined by external stimulus conditions.
- The humanistic perspective emphasizes an individual's inherent capacity to make rational choices.
- The cognitive perspective stresses mental processes that affect behavioral responses.
- The biological perspective studies relationships between behavior and brain mechanisms.
- The evolutionary perspective looks at behavior as having evolved as an adaptation for survival in the environment.
- The sociocultural perspective examines behavior and its interpretation in cultural context.

WHAT PSYCHOLOGISTS DO

- Psychologists work in a variety of settings and draw on expertise from a range of specialty areas. Almost any question that can be generated about real-life experiences is addressed by some member of the psychological profession.
- At the start of the 21st century, the profession of psychology has become more international in scope and more diverse in the composition of its practitioners and researchers.

 <www.ablongman.com/gerrig17e>

KEY TERMS

Key terms are highlighted within the chapter in boldface type so they will stand out. As you can see here, they are listed again at the end of the chapter with the page number on which they first appeared. When you study for a test, be sure you can define each term. In addition, all key terms are listed alphabetically and defined in the **Glossary** at the end of the book. The glossary provides definitions of the key terms and the page numbers on which they appear. You can use it to refresh your memory while studying.

behavior (p. 4)

behavioral data (p. 5)

behavioral neuroscience (p. 14)

behaviorism (p. 13)

behaviorist perspective (p. 12)

biological perspective (p. 13)

cognitive neuroscience (p. 14)

cognitive perspective (p. 13)

evolutionary perspective (p. 14)

functionalism (p. 10)

humanistic perspective (p. 13)

psychodynamic perspective (p. 12)

psychology (p. 4)

scientific method (p. 4)

sociocultural perspective (p. 14)

structuralism (p. 10)

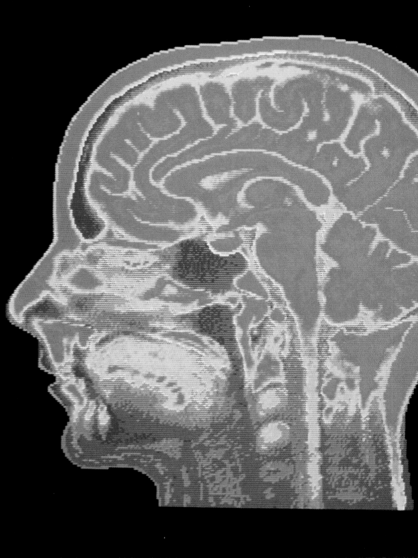

Research Methods in Psychology

You may recall that in Chapter 1 we asked you to compose a list of questions that you would like to have answered by the end of *Psychology and Life*. Students who have used the book in the past responded to this request with a range of interesting concerns. Here are some of their questions:

- Why is eating "hot" food painful?

- Is it bad to spank your children?

- Can psychology help me find a career?

- Do late night TV ads really work?

In this chapter, we describe how psychologists generate answers to questions that matter most to students. We focus on the special way in which psychology applies the scientific method to its domain of inquiry. We want you to understand how psychologists design their research: How can solid conclusions ever be drawn from the complex and often fuzzy phenomena that psychologists study—how people think, feel, and behave? Even if you never do any scientific research in your life, mastering the information in this section will be useful. The underlying purpose here is to help improve your *critical thinking skills* by teaching you how to ask the right questions and evaluate the answers about the causes, consequences, and correlates of psychological phenomena. The mass media constantly release stories that begin with, "Research shows that . . ." By sharpening your intelligent skepticism, we will help you become a more sophisticated consumer of the research-based conclusions that confront you in everyday life.

The Process of Research

Scientific theories undergo rigorous testing. Their results must be replicated by independent investigators before the theories are recognized as proven.

The research process in psychology can be divided into two major categories that usually occur in sequence: forming an idea and then testing it. The process typically begins when observations, beliefs, information, and general knowledge lead someone to come up with a new idea or a different way of thinking about a phenomenon. Where do researchers' questions originate? Some come from direct observations of events, humans, and nonhumans in the environment. Other research addresses traditional parts of the field: Some issues are considered to be "great unanswered questions" that have been passed down from earlier scholars. Often, researchers combine old ideas in unique ways that offer an original perspective. The hallmark of the truly creative thinker is the discovery of a new truth that moves science and society in a better direction.

Psychological theories, in general, are an attempt to understand how brain, mind, behavior, and environment function and how they may be related. A **theory** is an organized set of concepts that *explains* a phenomenon or set of phenomena. At the common core of most psychological theories is the assumption of **determinism,** the idea that all events—physical, mental, and behavioral—are the result of, or determined by, specific causal factors. These causal factors are limited to those in the individual's environment or within the person. Researchers also assume that behavior and mental processes follow *lawful patterns* of relationships, patterns that can be discovered and revealed through research. Psychological theories are typically claims about the causal forces that underlie such lawful patterns.

When a theory is proposed in psychology, it is generally expected both to account for known facts and to generate new ideas and hypotheses. A **hypothesis** is a tentative and testable statement about the relationship between causes and consequences. Hypotheses are often stated as if–then predictions, specifying certain outcomes from specific conditions. We might predict, for example, that *if* children view a lot of violence on television, *then* they will engage in more aggressive acts toward their peers. Research is required to verify the if–then link. Theories are of fundamental importance for generating new hypotheses. When scientific data do not bear out a hypothesis, researchers must rethink aspects of their theories. There is, therefore, continual interaction between theory and research.

When researchers are ready to put their hypotheses to the test, they rely on the **scientific method.** The scientific method is a general set of procedures for gathering and interpreting evidence in ways that limit sources of errors and yield dependable conclusions. Psychology is considered a science to the extent that it follows the rules established by the scientific method.

Because subjectivity must be minimized in the data collection and analysis phases of scientific research, procedural safeguards are used to increase objectivity. One of these safeguards needs no explanation: Researchers must keep complete records of observations and data analyses in a form that other researchers can understand and evaluate. Secrecy is banned from the research procedure because all data and methods must eventually be open for *public verifiability;* that is, other researchers must have the opportunity to inspect, criticize, replicate, or disprove the data and methods. For other aspects of the scientific method, we wish to emphasize why a particular procedure is so critical. Accordingly, each of the next two sections begins with a *challenge to objectivity* and then describes the *remedy* prescribed by the scientific method.

◆ OBSERVER BIASES AND OPERATIONAL DEFINITIONS

When different people observe the same events, they don't always "see" the same thing. In this section, we describe the problem of *observer bias* and the steps researchers take as remedies.

THE CHALLENGE TO OBJECTIVITY

An **observer bias** is an error due to the personal motives and expectations of the viewer. At times, people see and hear what they expect rather than what is. Consider a rather dramatic example of observer bias. Around the beginning of the 20th century, a leading psychologist, Hugo Munsterberg, gave a speech on peace to a large audience that included many reporters. He summarized the news accounts of what they heard and saw in this way:

> *The reporters sat immediately in front of the platform. One man wrote that the audience was so surprised by my speech that it received it in complete silence; another wrote that I was constantly interrupted by loud applause and that at the end of my address the applause continued for minutes. The one wrote that during my opponent's speech I was constantly smiling; the other noticed that my face remained grave and without a smile. The one said that I grew purple–red from excitement; and the other found that I grew chalk-white. (1908, pp. 35–36)*

It would be interesting to go back to the original newspapers, to see how the reporters' accounts were related to their political views—then we might be able to understand why the reporters "saw" what they did.

In a psychology experiment, we wouldn't expect differences between observers to be quite as radical as those reported by Munsterberg. Nonetheless, the example demonstrates how the same evidence can lead different observers to different conclusions. The biases of the observers act as *filters* through which some things are noticed as relevant and significant, and others are ignored as irrelevant and not meaningful.

We'd like you now to try the demonstration in **Figure 2.1,** to illustrate how easy it is to create an observer bias. This quick demonstration gives an idea of how the experiences you have prior to making an observation can influence how you interpret what you see.

Let's apply this lesson to what happens in psychology experiments. Researchers are often in the business of making observations. Given that every observer brings a different set of prior experiences to making those observations—and often those experiences include a commitment to a particular theory—you can see why observer biases could pose a problem. What can researchers do to ensure that their observations are minimally affected by prior expectations?

THE REMEDY

To minimize observer biases, researchers rely on standardization and operational definitions. **Standardization** means using uniform, consistent procedures in all phases of data collection. All features of the test or experimental situation should be sufficiently standardized so that all research participants experience exactly the same experimental conditions. Standardization means asking questions in the same way and scoring responses according to preestablished rules. Having results printed or recorded helps ensure their comparability across different times and places and with different participants and researchers.

Participants, as well as spectators and broadcast viewers, are subject to observer bias. How can you determine what really happened?

Look at the glass in this illustration. How would you answer the classic question: Is the glass half empty or half full?

Now suppose you watched this sequence in which water is poured into the glass. Wouldn't you be likely to describe the glass as half full?

Suppose you watched the sequence in which water is removed. Now doesn't the glass seem half empty?

FIGURE 2.1

Observer Bias

Is the glass half empty or half full?

Observations themselves must also be standardized: Scientists must solve the problem of how to translate their theories into concepts with consistent meaning. The strategy for standardizing the meaning of concepts is called *operationalization*. An **operational definition** standardizes meaning within an experiment, by defining a concept in terms of specific operations or procedures used to measure it or to determine its presence. All the variables in an experiment must be given operational definitions. A **variable** is any factor that varies in amount or kind.

In experimental settings, researchers most often wish to demonstrate a cause-and-effect relationship between two types of variables. The **independent variable** is the factor that the researcher manipulates; it functions as the causal part of the relationship. The effect part of the relationship is served by the **dependent variable,** which is what the experimenter measures. If the researcher's claims about cause and effect are correct, the value of the dependent variable will *depend* on the value of the independent variable. Imagine, for example, that you wished to test the hypothesis we mentioned earlier: that children who view a lot of violence on television will engage in more aggressive acts toward their peers. You could devise an experiment in which you manipulated the amount of violence each participant viewed (the independent variable) and then assessed how much aggression he or she displayed (the dependent variable).

Let's take a moment to put these new concepts to use in the context of a real experiment. The research project we will describe begins with the observation that the world can be sorted into people who claim to be "morning people"—they feel best performing tasks in the morning—versus others who are most definitely not morning people. Most college students fall into the *not* category! Researchers have demonstrated that people's self-judgments are correct: In laboratory tests, people most often perform best at those times of day they say they prefer (Yoon et al., 1999). But why? One theory is that performance is worse at the "wrong" time of day because the individuals suffer from a general decrease in the level of physiological arousal or alertness. This leads to a hypothesis: If you can do something to increase alertness at the wrong time of day, you should be able to lessen or eliminate performance problems.

In **Figure 2.2,** we present an experiment that tested that hypothesis (Ryan et al., 2002). The experiment focused on *older adults*, those age 65 and older. Unlike their younger selves, most older adults are morning people. In this study, the researchers wished to know that all their participants were morning people. For that reason, they had each potential participant fill out the Morningness–Eveningness Questionnaire—a measurement device that categorizes people on a scale ranging from "definitely morning" to "definitely evening" (Horne & Ostberg, 1976). The experiment used participants who were at least "moderately" morning people.

Next, the researchers needed a procedure to manipulate the independent variable—physiological arousal. As shown in Figure 2.2, the researchers used a procedure that will be quite familiar to most of you. One group consumed coffee with caffeine whereas the other group got decaf—the participants didn't know which type of coffee they had. The researchers predicted that the caffeine would produce physiological arousal that would, in turn, have an impact on the participants' ability to perform at the "wrong" time of day. To measure the dependent variable—performance—the researchers challenged the participants to memorize a 16-word list. A memory test occurred 20 minutes later. The participants received lists and memory tests once in the morning (8 A.M.) and once in the afternoon (4 P.M.) in sessions separated by 5 to 11 days.

As you can see in Figure 2.2, the independent variable had the effect on the dependent variable that the researchers expected. In circumstances of high physiological arousal—when participants consumed the coffee with caffeine—performance was more or less equal at the

The researchers manipulate the *independent variable*

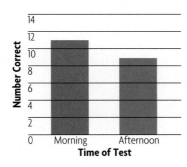

Participants consume decaffeinated coffee

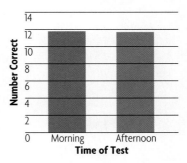

Participants consume coffee with caffeine

The researchers measure the *dependent variable*

FIGURE 2.2

Elements of an Experiment

To test their hypotheses, researchers create operational definitions for the independent and dependent variables.

two times of day. However, without the caffeine, memory performance was worse in the afternoon. As with all research results, we need to take stock of what we now know. The theory is stated in general terms—there is a relationship between physiological arousal and performance. However, the experiment uses the specific independent variable of caffeine consumption and the specific dependent variable of memory performance to stand in for "physiological arousal" and "performance." Take a moment to think about other ways in which you might operationalize these two concepts, to test the same hypothesis in different fashions. You might, for example, want to manipulate physiological arousal without using caffeine, to show that it is not the caffeine itself having magical effects. This type of concern provides a transition to our exploration of experimental methods.

◆ EXPERIMENTAL METHODS: ALTERNATIVE EXPLANATIONS AND THE NEED FOR CONTROLS

You know from day-to-day experience that people can suggest many causes for the same outcome. Psychologists face this same problem when they try to make exact claims about causality. To overcome causal ambiguity, researchers use **experimental methods:**

They manipulate an independent variable to look for an effect on a dependent variable. The goal of this method is to make strong causal claims about the impact of one variable on the other. In this section, we describe the problem of *alternative explanations* and some steps researchers take to counter the problem.

THE CHALLENGE TO OBJECTIVITY

When psychologists test a hypothesis, they most often have in mind an explanation for why change in the independent variable should affect the dependent variable in a particular way. For example, you might predict, and demonstrate experimentally, that the viewing of television violence leads to high levels of aggression. But how can you know that it was precisely the viewing of *violence* that produced aggression? To make the strongest possible case for their hypotheses, psychologists must be very sensitive to the existence of possible *alternative explanations*. The more alternative explanations there might be for a given result, the less confidence there is that the initial hypothesis is accurate. When something other than what an experimenter purposely introduces into a research setting changes a participant's behavior and adds confusion to the interpretation of the data, it is called a **confounding variable.** When the real cause of some observed behavioral effect is

Is violent behavior caused by viewing violence on television? How could you find out?

Rats Will Meet Your Expectations

Throughout *Psychology and Life,* we will be sharing with you the results from psychological research. Often, our conclusions will be based on studies conducted by several different teams of researchers, at sites all over the world. The purpose of the **Putting Ideas to the Test** feature is to give you regular opportunities to make contact with individual experiments that directly answer specific questions. Each one gives you the opportunity to see a precise relationship between experiment and insight. For this first **Putting Ideas to the Test,** we briefly describe a classic study that vividly demonstrates the way in which expectations can affect an experiment's outcome.

In this experiment, 12 students were given groups of rats that were going to be trained to run a maze. Half of the students were told that their rats were from a special *maze-bright* breed. The other students were told that their rats were bred to be *maze-dull.* As you might guess, their rats were actually all the same. Nonetheless, the students' results corresponded with their expectations for their rats. The rats labeled bright were found to be much better learners than those that had been labeled as dull (Rosenthal & Fode, 1963).

confounded, the experimenter's interpretation of the data is put at risk. Suppose, for example, that violent television scenes are louder and involve more movement than do most nonviolent scenes. In that case, the violent and the superficial aspects of the scenes are confounded. The researcher is unable to specify which factor uniquely produces aggressive behavior.

Although each different experimental method potentially gives rise to a unique set of alternative explanations, we can identify two types of confounds that apply to almost all experiments, which we will call *expectancy effects* and *placebo effects.* Unintentional **expectancy effects** occur when a researcher or observer subtly communicates to the research participants the behaviors he or she expects to find—thereby producing the desired reaction. Under these circumstances, the experimenter's expectations, rather than the independent variable, actually help trigger the observed reactions.

Robert Rosenthal has studied the phenomenon of expectancy bias and how it can distort research results (Rosenthal, 1966):

How do you suppose the students communicated their expectations to their rats? Do you see why you should worry even more about expectancy effects when an experiment is carried out within species—with a human experimenter and human participants? Expectation effects distort the content of discovery.

A **placebo effect** occurs when experimental participants change their behavior in the *absence* of any kind of experimental manipulation. This concept originated in medicine to account for cases in which a patient's health improved after he or she had received medication that was chemically inert or a treatment that was nonspecific. The placebo effect refers to an improvement in health or well-being due to the individual's *belief* that the treatment will be effective. Some treatments with no genuine medical effects have been shown, even so, to produce good or excellent outcomes for 70 percent of the patients on whom they were used (Roberts et al., 1993).

In a psychological research setting, a placebo effect has occurred whenever a behavioral response is influenced by a person's expectation of what to do or how to feel, rather than by the specific intervention or procedures employed to produce that response. Recall the 28experiment relating television viewing to later aggression. Suppose we discovered that experimental participants who hadn't watched any television at all also showed high levels of aggression. We might conclude that these individuals, by virtue of being put in a situation that allowed them to display aggression, would expect that they were *supposed* to behave aggressively and would go on to do so. Experimenters must always worry that participants change the way they behave simply because they are aware of being observed or tested. For example, participants may feel special about being chosen to take part in a study and thus act differently than they would ordinarily. Such effects can compromise an experiment's results.

THE REMEDY

Because human and animal behaviors are complex and often have multiple causes, good research design involves anticipating possible confounds and devising strategies for eliminating them. Similar to defensive strategies in sports, good research designs anticipate what the other team might do and make plans to counteract it. Researchers' strategies are called **control procedures**—methods that attempt to hold constant all variables and conditions other than those related to the hypothesis being tested. In an experiment, instructions, room temperature, tasks, the way the researcher is dressed, time allotted, the way the responses are recorded, and many other details of the situation must be similar for all participants, to ensure that their experience is the same. The only differences in participants' experiences should be those introduced by the independent variable. Let us look at remedies for the specific confounding variables, expectancy and placebo effects.

Imagine, for example, that you enriched the aggression experiment to include a treatment group that watched comedy programs. You'd want to be careful not to treat your comedy and violence participants in different ways based on your expectations. Thus, in your experiment, we would want the research assistant who greeted the participants and later assessed their aggression to be unaware of whether they had watched a violent program or a comedy. In the best circumstances, bias can be eliminated by keeping *both* experimental assistants and participants unaware of, or *blind* to, which participants get which treatment. This technique is called a **double-blind control.** Recall that in the coffee study (Figure 2.2), we specifically noted that the participants didn't know whether the beverage they were asked to consume contained caffeine or not. In fact, the design was double-blind because the experimenters administering the memory tests also did not know which participants had each kind of drink. To provide further reassurance that expectations were not responsible for the memory effects, the experimenters asked the participants to guess which type of coffee they had consumed. Participants were unable to guess correctly (Ryan et al., 2002). This result provides strong

evidence that the memory findings did not depend on the participants' expectations about the relationship between caffeine and memory performance.

To account for placebo effects, researchers generally include an experimental condition in which the treatment is not administered. We call this a **placebo control.** Placebo controls fall into the general category of controls by which experimenters assure themselves that they are making appropriate comparisons. Consider the story of a young girl who, when asked if she loved her older sister, replied, "Compared to what?" That question is one that must be asked—and satisfactorily answered—before you can really understand what a research finding means. Suppose you read that a study shows that "more than three-quarters of a group of people trying to quit smoking were able to win with the help of nicotine patches" (Andrews, 1990). Compared to what? What about the control group? In this study's placebo control group, which wore nicotine-free patches, a full 39 percent also stopped smoking! Moreover, the longer they wore those medically useless patches, the more likely they were to quit smoking (Abelin et al., 1989). So the nicotine patch was an effective treatment, but more than half of its effectiveness was due to the placebo effect of expecting that it would work. The data from control conditions provide an important baseline against which the experimental effect is evaluated.

In some research designs, which are referred to as **between-subjects designs,** different groups of participants are *randomly assigned,* by chance procedures, to an experimental condition (exposed to one or more experimental treatments) or to a control condition (not exposed to an experimental treatment). Random assignment is one of the major steps researchers take to eliminate confounding variables that relate to individual differences among potential research participants. This is the design we had in mind for the aggression experiment. The random assignment to experimental and control conditions makes it quite likely that the two groups will be similar in important ways at the start of an experiment, because each participant has the same probability of being in a treatment condition as in a control condition. We shouldn't have to worry, for example, that everyone in the experimental group loves violent television and everyone in the control group hates it. Random assignment should mix both types of people together in each group. If outcome differences are found between conditions, we can be more confident that the differences were caused by a treatment or intervention rather than by preexisting differences.

Researchers also try to approximate randomness in the way they bring participants into the laboratory. Typically, psychology experiments use from 20 to 100 participants—but experimenters would often like to generalize from this **sample** to the full **population** from which the sample is drawn. Suppose you would like to test the hypothesis that 6-year-old children are more likely to lie than 4-year-old children. You can bring only a very small subset of all of the world's 4- and 6-year-olds into your laboratory. To generalize beyond your samples, you need to have confidence that your particular 4- and 6-year-olds are comparable to any other randomly selected groups of children. A sample is a **representative sample** of a population if it closely matches the overall characteristics of the population with respect, for example, to the distribution of males and females, racial and ethnic groups, and so on. You can generalize from your sample only to the population it adequately represents. If you had only boys as participants in your lying study, you'd be incorrect to draw conclusions about girls' probable behavior.

Another type of experimental design—a **within-subjects design**—uses each participant as his or her own control. For example, the behavior of an experimental participant before getting the treatment might be compared with behavior after. Consider an experiment that assessed 12-month-old infants' ability to learn from emotional responses they witnessed on a television screen.

PUTTING IDEAS TO THE TEST

A Within-Subjects Study of Learning Emotions from TV

How do children learn which objects in their environments are *nice* and which are *nasty?* Researchers tested the idea that they acquire some of this information from passive observation of other individuals (Mumme & Fernald, 2003). In one study, 12-month-old infants had the opportunity to interact with novel objects such as a bumpy ball and a plastic valve. As shown in **Figure 2.3,** the children were seated in front of a television screen, with the objects in easy reach. The children viewed two video presentations of an actress describing one of the two objects. In the initial presentation, the actress mentioned the *target* object with a neutral tone of voice and a neutral facial expression. However, in the second presentation, the actress used a negative tone of voice and a negative expression while mentioning the same object. The actress never discussed the *distracter* object. Figure 2.3 shows the within-subjects comparison of the extent to which the infants touched each object. As you can see, when the actress's emotion became negative, the infants tended to shy away from the target object. The infants weren't just getting bored. Their behavior did not vary with respect to touching the object the actress hadn't mentioned.

Because the study was within-subjects, the experimenters could draw the strong conclusion that the infants' observation of the actress's negative emotions *changed* their willingness to interact with the object. By the way, the experimenters repeated the experiment with 10-month-old infants and discovered that those younger participants did not change their behavior based on the actress's expressed emotions (Mumme & Fernald, 2003). Thus, it's somewhere in that 2-month window between 10 and 12 months that children begin to let their behavior be guided by their observation of other people's emotional reactions.

The research methodologies we have described so far all involve the manipulation of an independent variable to look for an effect on a dependent variable. Although this experimental method often allows researchers to make the strongest claims about causal relations among variables, several conditions can make this method less desirable. First, during an experiment, behavior is frequently studied in an artificial environment, one in which situational factors are controlled so heavily that the environment may itself distort the behavior from the way it would occur naturally. Critics claim that much of the richness and complexity of natural behavior patterns is lost in controlled experiments, sacrificed to the simplicity of dealing with only one or a few variables and responses. Second, research participants typically know they are in an experiment and are being tested and measured. They may react to this awareness by trying to please the researcher, attempting to "psych out" the research purpose, or changing their behavior from what it would be if they were unaware of being monitored. Third, some important research problems are not amenable to ethical experimental treatment. We could not, for example, try to discover whether the tendency toward child abuse is transmitted from generation to generation by creating an experimental group of children who would be abused and a control group of children who would not be. In the next section, we turn to a type of research method that often addresses these concerns.

◆ CORRELATIONAL METHODS

Is intelligence associated with creativity? Are optimistic people healthier than pessimists? Is there a relationship between experiencing child abuse and later mental illness? These questions involve variables that a psychologist could not easily or ethically manipulate. To answer these questions, as we will in later chapters, requires research based on **correlational methods.** Psychologists use correlational methods when they want to determine to what extent two variables, traits, or attributes are related.

FIGURE 2.3

Infants Learn Emotional Responses

The 12-month-olds were seated so that they could interact with the same objects that appeared on the television screen. In two video presentations, an actress mentioned the target object and ignored the distracter object. The first video presentation provided a neutral baseline to measure the children's initial preference to interact with each object. In the second video presentation, the actress expressed negative emotions related to the target object. The bar graphs plot the proportion of time the infants spent touching each object—the researchers calculated this measure by dividing the amount of time the infants touched each object into the total duration of the play period. As you can see, when the actress expressed negative emotions toward an object, children touched it much less often.

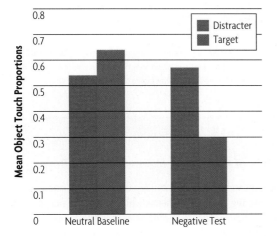

To determine the precise degree of correlation that exists between two variables, psychologists compute a statistical measure known as the **correlation coefficient (*r*).** This value can vary between +1.0 and −1.0, where +1.0 indicates a perfect positive correlation, −1.0 indicates a perfect negative correlation, and 0.0 indicates there is no correlation at all. A positive correlation coefficient means that as one set of scores increases, a second set also increases. The reverse is true with negative correlations; the second set of scores goes in the opposite direction to the values of the first scores (see **Figure 2.4**). Correlations that are closer to zero mean that there is a weak relationship or no relationship between scores on two measures. As the correlation coefficient gets stronger, closer to the ±1.0 maximum, predictions about one variable based on information about the other variable become increasingly more accurate.

Suppose, for example, researchers were interested in determining the relationship between students' sleep habits and their success in college. They might operationally define *sleep habits* as the average amount of sleep per night. *Success in college* could be defined as cumulative GPA. The researchers could assess each variable for an appropriate sample of students and compute the correlation coefficient between them. A strongly positive score would mean that the more a student sleeps, the higher his or her GPA is likely to be. Knowing a student's

"hours per night" would then allow the researchers to make a reasonable prediction about the student's GPA.

The researchers might want to take the next step and say that the way to improve students' GPAs would be to force them to sleep more. This intervention is misguided. A strong correlation indicates only that two sets of data are related in a systematic way; the correlation does not ensure that one causes the other. *Correlation does not imply causation.* The correlation could reflect any one of several cause-and-effect possibilities, or none. For example, a positive correlation between sleep and GPA might mean that (1) people who study more efficiently get to bed sooner, (2) people who experience anxiety about schoolwork cannot fall asleep, or (3) people sleep better when they are taking easy courses. You can see from this example that correlations most often require researchers to probe for deeper explanations.

Correlations may also be spurious because researchers did not make the appropriate control comparisons. Consider the supposed connection between the power blackout in New York City in 1965 and the reported jump in the birthrate nine months later. "New Yorkers are very romantic. It was the candlelight," said one new father. An official for a planned parenthood group offered the explanation that, because of the blackout, "all the substitutes for sex—meetings, lectures, card

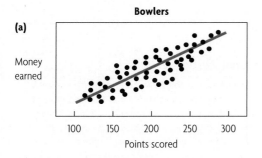

Bowlers

(a)

Money
earned

100   150   200   250   300

Points scored

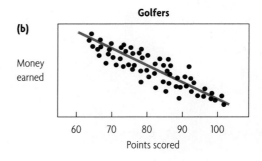

Golfers

(b)

Money
earned

60   70   80   90   100

Points scored

FIGURE 2.4

Positive and Negative Correlations

These imaginary data display the difference between positive and negative correlations. Each point represents a single bowler or golfer. (a) In general, the more points a professional bowler scores, the more money he or she will earn. Thus, there is a positive correlation between those two variables. (b) The correlation for golf is negative, because golfers earn more money when they score fewer points.

parties, theaters, saloons—were eliminated that night. What else could they do?" (*The New York Times,* 8/11/1966). The same kind of correlation is often reported after major blizzards and other disasters in many parts of the world. "Quake May Have Caused Baby Boom in Bay Area" was a more recent headline in the *San Francisco Chronicle* (Chen, 1990). However, when anyone takes the time to compare these apparently dramatic birthrate increases with the ordinary seasonal variations, the correlation turns out to be coincidence masquerading as causation. That is, there is a real correlation between *season* and birthrate—this is the control comparison for the coincidental "disaster" correlation. Clearly, we must apply the same caution to correlational results as we apply to research results that emerge from experimental methods.

We don't want to leave you with the impression that correlational methods aren't valuable research tools. Throughout *Psychology and Life,* we will see many correlational studies that have led to important insights. We'll offer just one example here to whet your appetite:

The Origins of Conduct Problems in Young Boys

What environmental factors explain why, even by age 5, some boys are displaying conduct problems while others are not? A team of researchers sought to demonstrate that this difference among boys arises, in part, from the varying amount of *destructive sibling conflict* the boys experience with their brothers and sisters (Garcia et al., 2000). The researchers reasoned that high levels of conflict with siblings might reinforce the boys' tendency toward aggressive or inappropriate responses to life situations. To measure destructive sibling conflict, the researchers videotaped hour-long play sessions between each of 180 boys and his sibling while they were playing together with different sets of toys. The videotaped play sessions were evaluated on dimensions such as the number of conflicts between the children and the intensity of those conflicts. Correlational analyses strongly supported the prediction that boys who experienced high levels of sibling conflict would also be most likely to display aggressive and delinquent behaviors.

What procedures might you follow to determine the correlation between students' sleep habits and their success in college? How would you evaluate potential causal relationships underlying any correlation?

Can you see why a correlational design is required to address this prediction? You can't randomly assign children to have a little or a lot of conflict with their siblings. You must wait to see what differences emerge after children are in one situation or the other.

◆ SUBLIMINAL INFLUENCE?

To close this section, we offer one concrete example of how psychological research has been used to assess the vigorous claims of advertisers anxious to make you believe in their products. You almost certainly have been subjected to commercials for products that promise to change your life with messages outside conscious awareness—*subliminal* messages: It's magic! One CD guarantees a better sex life; another provides a quick cure for low self-esteem; a third promises safe and effective weight loss. How? All you have to do is *listen*—in bed, while jogging, when doing your homework—to the "restful splash of ocean waves breaking on sandy shores."

"Subliminal" influence has a long history. Although it was almost certainly a hoax, a 1957 study made headlines when the "inventor" of subliminal advertising claimed that the message "Buy Popcorn" flashed on the screen during a movie yielded a 58 percent increase in popcorn sales (Rogers, 1993)! *The Wall Street Journal* once reported that a New Orleans supermarket significantly decreased stealing and cashier shortages after piping the following subliminal message into its Muzak system: "If I steal, I will go to jail." A telephone survey in Toledo, Ohio, showed that nearly 75 percent of the 400 adults surveyed were familiar with subliminal advertising (Rogers & Smith, 1993). Of that group, again, nearly 75 percent believed that subliminal advertising was used successfully by marketers. In general, the better educated the respondents were, the more likely they were to believe in the effectiveness of subliminal advertising.

You now have the knowledge to address the critical question: Do subliminal messages really influence mental states and behavior as their advocates claim? Our answer comes from an application of the experimental methods we have described (see **Figure 2.5**).

PUTTING IDEAS TO THE TEST

Evaluating Subliminal Effects

A team of experimenters set out to determine the effectiveness of listening to commercially available audiotapes designed to improve self-esteem or memory. The participants were 237 men and women volunteers, ranging from 18 to 60 years of age.

After a pretest session in which their initial self-esteem and memory were measured on standard psychological tests and questionnaires, the participants were randomly assigned to two conditions. Half of them received subliminal memory tapes, and the others received subliminal self-esteem tapes. They listened regularly to the tapes for a five-week period and then returned to the laboratory for a posttest session to evaluate their memories (using four memory tests) and self-esteem (using three self-esteem scales). The researchers were blind to which participants received which treatment (Greenwald et al., 1991).

Did the tapes boost self-esteem and enhance memory? The results from this controlled experiment indicate that there was no significant improvement shown on any of the objective measures of either self-esteem or memory. However, one very powerful effect did emerge: the placebo effect of expecting to be helped. Anticipating this placebo effect, the researchers had added another independent variable. Half the participants in each group received memory tapes that were mismarked "self-esteem" and the others received self-esteem tapes in "memory boxes." Participants *believed* their self-esteem improved if they received tapes with that label or felt that their memory improved if their tapes were labeled "memory"—even when they had been listening to the other tape!

This rigorous experiment allows for some very concrete advice: Save your money; subliminal self-help programs offer nothing more than placebo effects. An important goal of *Psychology and Life* is to provide you with such concrete conclusions based on solid experimental methods.

This experiment also gives you a specific example of the types of variables that psychologists measure—in this case, it was participants' beliefs about improvements in self-esteem and memory as well as objective measures of self-esteem and memory. In the next section, we discuss more generally the way in which psychologists measure important processes and dimensions of experience.

PUT YOURSELF TO THE TEST

- ➤ What is the relationship between a hypothesis and a theory?
- ➤ Why do standardized procedures and operational definitions help researchers overcome observer biases?
- ➤ What procedures do researchers use to combat expectancy effects and placebo effects?
- ➤ Is it always possible for an experiment with a between-subjects design to become one with a within-subjects design? Why?
- ➤ Why does correlation not imply causation?

FIGURE 2.5

Experimental Design for Testing Hypotheses About the Effectiveness of Subliminal Messages

In this simplified version of the experiment, a sample of people is drawn from a larger, general population. They are given a series of pretest measures and randomly assigned to receive subliminal tapes with either memory or self-esteem messages. They are then given posttests that objectively assess any changes in the dependent variables: memory and self-esteem. The study found no significant effects of subliminal persuasion.

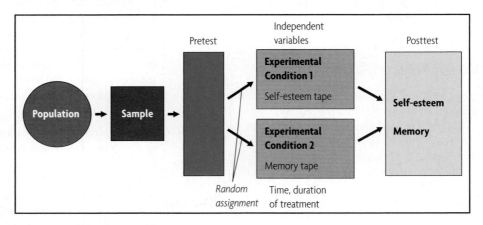

Psychological Measurement

B ecause psychological processes are so varied and complex, they pose major challenges to researchers who want to measure them. Although some actions and processes are easily seen, many, such as anxiety or dreaming, are not. Thus, one task for a psychological researcher is to make the unseen visible, to make internal events and processes external, and to make private experiences public. You have already seen how important it is for researchers to provide operational definitions of the phenomena they wish to study. Those definitions generally provide some procedure for assigning numbers to, or *quantifying,* different levels, sizes, intensities, or amounts of a variable. Many measurement methods are available, each with its particular advantages and disadvantages.

Our review of psychological measurement begins with a discussion of the distinction between two ways of gauging the accuracy of a measure: reliability and validity. We then review different measurement techniques for data collection. By whatever means psychologists collect their data, they must use appropriate statistical methods to verify their hypotheses. A description of how psychologists analyze their data is given in the Statistical Supplement, which follows this chapter. You should read it in conjunction with this chapter.

◆ ACHIEVING RELIABILITY AND VALIDITY

The goal of psychological measurement is to generate findings that are both reliable and valid. **Reliability** refers to the consistency or dependability of behavioral data resulting from psychological testing or experimental research. A reliable result is one that will be repeated under similar conditions of testing at different times. A reliable measuring instrument yields comparable scores when employed repeatedly (and when the thing being measured does not change). Consider the experiment we just described, which showed that subliminal audiotapes generate only placebo effects. That experiment used 237 participants. The experimenters' claim that the result was "reliable" means that they should be able to repeat the experiment with any new group of participants of comparable size and generate the same pattern of data.

Validity means that the information produced by research or testing accurately measures the psychological variable or quality it is intended to measure. A valid measure of *happiness,* for example, should allow us to predict how happy you are likely to be in particular situations. A valid experiment means that the researcher can generalize to broader circumstances, often from the laboratory to the real world. When we gave you advice based on the audiotapes experiment, we were accepting the researchers' claim that the results are valid. Tests and experiments can be reliable without being valid. We could, for example, use your shoe size as an index of your happiness. This would be reliable (we'd always

By watching from behind a one-way mirror, a researcher can record observations of a child without influencing or interfering with the child's behavior. Have you ever changed your behavior when you knew you were being watched?

get the same answer), but not valid (we'd learn very little about your day-to-day happiness level).

As you now read about different types of measures, try to evaluate them in terms of reliability and validity.

◆ SELF-REPORT MEASURES

Often researchers are interested in obtaining data about experiences they cannot directly observe. Sometimes these experiences are internal psychological states, such as beliefs, attitudes, and feelings. At other times, these experiences are external behaviors but—like sexual activities or criminal acts—not generally appropriate for psychologists to witness. In these cases, investigations rely on self-reports. **Self-report measures** are verbal answers, either written or spoken, to questions the researcher poses. Researchers devise reliable ways to quantify these self-reports so they can make meaningful comparisons between different individuals' responses.

Self-reports include responses made on questionnaires and during interviews. A *questionnaire* or *survey* is a written set of questions, ranging in content from questions of fact ("Are you a registered voter?"), to questions about past or present behavior ("How much do you smoke?"), to questions about attitudes and feelings ("How satisfied are you with your present job?"). *Open-ended* questions allow respondents to answer freely in their own words. Questions may also have a number of *fixed alternatives* such as *yes, no,* and *undecided.*

An *interview* is a dialogue between a researcher and an individual for the purpose of obtaining detailed information. Instead of being completely standardized, as a questionnaire is, an interview is *interactive.* An interviewer may vary the questioning to follow up on something the respondent said. Good interviewers are also sensitive to the process of the social interaction as

well as to the information revealed. They are trained to establish *rapport,* a positive social relationship with the respondent that encourages trust and the sharing of personal information.

Although researchers rely on a wide variety of self-report measures, there are limits to their usefulness. Obviously, many forms of self-report cannot be used with preverbal children, illiterate adults, speakers of other languages, some mentally disturbed people, and nonhuman animals. Even when self-reports can be used, they may not be reliable or valid. Participants may misunderstand the questions or not remember clearly what they actually experienced. Furthermore, self-reports may be influenced by social desirability—people may give false or misleading answers to create a favorable (or, sometimes, unfavorable) impression of themselves. They may be embarrassed to report their true experiences or feelings. If respondents are aware of a questionnaire's or interview's purpose, they may lie or alter the truth to get a job, to get discharged from a mental hospital, or to accomplish any other goal. An interview situation also allows personal biases and prejudices to affect how the interviewer asks questions and how the respondent answers them.

◆ BEHAVIORAL MEASURES AND OBSERVATIONS

As a group, psychological researchers are interested in a wide range of behaviors. They may study a rat running a maze, a child drawing a picture, a student memorizing a poem, or a worker repeatedly performing a task. **Behavioral measures** are ways to study overt actions and observable and recordable reactions.

One of the primary ways to study what people do is *observation.* Researchers use observation in a planned,

Jane Goodall has spent most of her adult life making naturalistic observations of chimpanzees. What has she discovered that she couldn't have discovered if the animals were not in their natural habitat?

precise, and systematic manner. Observations focus on either the *process* or the *products* of behavior. In an experiment on learning, for instance, a researcher might observe how many times a research participant rehearsed a list of words (process) and then how many words the participant remembered on a final test (product). For *direct observations,* the behavior under investigation must be clearly visible and overt and easily recorded. For example, in a laboratory experiment on emotions, a researcher could observe a participant's facial expressions as the individual looked at emotionally arousing stimuli.

A researcher's direct observations are often augmented by technology. For example, contemporary psychologists often rely on computers to provide very precise measures of the time it takes for research participants to perform various tasks, such as reading a sentence or solving a problem. Although some forms of exact measurement were available before the computer age, computers now provide extraordinary flexibility in collecting and analyzing precise information. In Chapter 3, we will describe the newest types of technologies that allow researchers to produce behavioral measures of a remarkable kind: pictures of the brain at work.

In *naturalistic observations,* some naturally occurring behavior is viewed by a researcher, who makes no attempt to change or interfere with it. For instance, a researcher behind a one-way mirror might observe the play of children who are not aware of being observed. Some kinds of human behavior can be studied only through naturalistic observation, because it would be unethical or impractical to do otherwise. For example, it would be unethical to experiment with severe deprivation in early life to see its effects on a child's later development.

When studying behavior in a laboratory setting, a researcher is unable to observe the long-term effects that one's natural habitat has in shaping complex patterns of behavior. One of the most valuable examples of naturalistic observation conducted in the field is the work of **Jane Goodall** (1986, 1990; Peterson & Goodall, 1993). Goodall has spent more than 30 years studying patterns of behavior among chimpanzees in Gombe, on Lake Tanganyika in Africa. Goodall notes that had she ended her research after 10 years—as she originally planned—she would not have drawn the correct conclusions:

> *We would have observed many similarities in their behavior and ours, but we would have been left with the impression that chimpanzees were far more peaceable than humans. Because we were able to continue beyond the first decade, we could document the division of a social group and observe the violent aggression that broke out between newly separated factions. We discovered that in certain circumstances the chimpanzees may kill and even cannibalize individuals of their own kind. On the other side of the coin, we have learned of the extraordinarily enduring affectionate bonds between family members . . . advanced cognitive abilities, [and the development of] cultural traditions. (Goodall, 1986, pp. 3–4)*

In the early stages of an investigation, naturalistic observation is especially useful. It helps researchers discover the extent of a phenomenon or to get an idea of what the important variables and relationships might be. The data from naturalistic observation often provide clues for an investigator to use in formulating a specific hypothesis or research plan.

Before we leave the topic of psychological measurement, we must emphasize that many research projects combine both self-report measures and behavioral observations. Researchers may, for example, specifically look for a relationship between how people report they will behave and how they actually behave. In addition, rather than involving large numbers of participants, some research projects will focus all their measures on a single individual or small group in a **case study.** Intensive analyses of particular individuals can sometimes yield important insights into general features of human experience. For example, in Chapter 3 you will learn that careful observations of single patients with brain damage provided the basis for important theories of the localization of language functions in the brain.

We have now described several types of procedures and measures that researchers use. Before we move on, we want to give you an opportunity to see how the same issue can be addressed in different research designs. Consider Shakespeare's question, "What's in a name?" In *Romeo and Juliet,* Juliet asserts, "That which we call a rose by any other name would smell as sweet." But is that correct? Do you think your name has an impact on the way other people treat you? Is it better to have a common, familiar name or a rare, distinctive one? Or does your name not matter at all? In **Table 2.1** we give examples of combinations of measures and methods that researchers might use to answer those questions. As you read through Table 2.1, ask yourself how willing you would be to participate in each type of study. In the next section, we consider the ethical standards that govern psychological research.

- Why can some measures be reliable but not valid?
- What factors influence the use of self-report measures?
- In what different settings do researchers use behavioral measures?

TABLE 2.1

What's in a Name?: Methods and Measures

Research Goal		Dependent Measure	
		Self-Report	**Observation**
Correlational Methods	To assess the correlation between the frequency of people's names and their experience of happiness.	Each participant's assessment of his/her own happiness.	
	To assess the correlation between the frequency of children's names and their acceptance by peers.		Children's amount of social interaction on the playground.
Experimental Methods	To determine if people judge identical photos differently when different names are assigned to them.	Participants' ratings of baby pictures to which random names have been assigned.	
	To determine if people's actual social interactions change because of name-based expectations.		The number of positive facial expressions people produce in conversation with a stranger who has introduced himself as *Mark* or *Marcus.*

Ethical Issues in Human and Animal Research

In the study that tested the effectiveness of subliminal messages, the researchers deceived the participants by mislabeling the tapes. They did so to see if the participants' expectations would lead them to believe that the messages were helpful even if objective measures of memory and self-esteem showed no improvement. Deception is always ethically suspect, but in this case, how else could researchers assess the placebo effect of false beliefs held by the participants? How should the *potential gains* of a research project be weighed against the *costs* it incurs to those who are subjected to procedures that are risky, painful, stressful, or deceptive? Psychologists ask themselves these questions on an ongoing basis (Rosenthal, 1994).

Respect for the basic rights of humans and animals is a fundamental obligation of all researchers. Beginning in 1953, the American Psychological Association has published guidelines for ethical standards for researchers. Current research practice is governed by the 2002 revision of those guidelines. Consider the issue of deception in research. The 2002 guidelines assert, "Psychologists do not deceive prospective participants about research that is reasonably expected to cause physical pain or severe emotional distress" (American Psychological Association, 2002, p. 1070). Guidelines of this sort were not always in force. For example, in Chapter 16 we describe classic experiments on *obedience to authority*. In these experiments, participants were deceived into believing that they were giving dangerous electric shocks to total strangers. Evidence from the experiments suggests that the participants were, in fact, experiencing "severe emotional distress." For that reason—although the research is quite important to an understanding of human nature—no responsible psychologist could advocate replicating the studies today. In fact, researchers no longer make decisions about issues like the use of deception in isolation. To guarantee that ethical principles are honored, special committees oversee every research proposal, imposing strict guidelines issued by the U.S. Department of Health and Human Services. Universities and colleges, hospitals, and research institutes each have *review boards* that approve and reject proposals for human and animal research. Let's review some of the factors those review boards consider.

◆ INFORMED CONSENT

At the start of nearly all laboratory research with human subjects, participants are given a description of the procedures, potential risks, and expected benefits they will experience. Participants are assured that their privacy is protected: All records of their behavior are kept strictly confidential; they must approve any public sharing of them. Participants are asked to sign statements indicating that they have been *informed* about these matters and *consent* to continue. The participants are assured in advance that they may leave an experiment any time they wish, without penalty, and are given the names and phone numbers of officials to contact if they have any grievances.

◆ RISK/GAIN ASSESSMENT

Most psychology experiments carry little risk to the participants, especially where participants are merely asked to perform routine tasks. However, some experiments that study more personal aspects of human nature—such as emotional reactions, self-images, conformity, stress, or aggression—can be upsetting or psychologically disturbing. Therefore, whenever a researcher conducts such a study, risks must be minimized, participants must be informed of the risks, and suitable precautions must be taken to deal with strong reactions. Where any risk is involved, it is carefully weighed by each institutional review board in terms of its necessity for achieving the benefits to the participants of the study, to science, and to society.

◆ INTENTIONAL DECEPTION

For some kinds of research, it is not possible to tell the participants the whole story in advance without biasing the results. If you were studying the effects of violence on television on aggression, for example, you would not want your participants to know your purpose in advance. But is your hypothesis enough to justify the deception?

We already noted that the American Psychological Association's (2002) ethical principles give explicit instructions about the use of deception. In addition to the guideline that participants not be misled about the probability of physical or emotional distress, the APA provides other restrictions: (1) the study must have sufficient scientific and educational importance to warrant deception; (2) researchers must demonstrate that no equally effective procedures excluding deception are available; (3) the deception must be explained to the participants by the conclusion of the research; and (4) participants must have the opportunity to withdraw their data once the deception is explained. In experiments involving deception, a review board may impose constraints, insist on monitoring initial demonstrations of the procedure, or deny approval.

◆ DEBRIEFING

Participation in psychological research should always be a mutual exchange of information between researcher and participant. The researcher may learn something new about a behavioral phenomenon from the participant's responses, and the participant should be informed of the purpose, hypothesis, anticipated results, and expected benefits of the study. At the end of an experiment, each participant must be given a careful **debriefing,** in which the researcher provides as much information about the study as possible and makes sure that no one leaves feeling confused, upset, or embarrassed. If it was necessary to mislead the participants during any stage of the research, the experimenter carefully explains the reasons for the deception. Finally, participants have the right to withdraw their data if they feel they have been misused or their rights abused in any way.

◆ ISSUES IN ANIMAL RESEARCH

Should animals be used in psychological and medical research? This question has often produced very polarized responses. On one side are researchers who point to the very important breakthroughs research with animals has allowed in several areas of science (Domjan & Purdy, 1995; Petrinovich, 1998). The benefits of animal research have included discovery and testing of drugs that treat anxiety and mental illnesses as well as important knowledge about drug addiction (Miller, 1985). Animal research benefits animals as well. For example, psychological researchers have shown how to alleviate the stresses of confinement experienced by zoo animals. Their studies of animal learning and social organization have led to the improved design of enclosures and animal facilities that promote good health (Nicoll et al., 1988).

To defenders of animal rights, this list of achievements does not undercut the deep error of believing that there is a "morally relevant difference separating Homo sapiens from other creatures" (Bowd & Shapiro, 1993, p. 136; see also Shapiro, 1998). To remedy this error, ethicists argue for "a shift from laboratory-based invasive research to minimally manipulative research

conducted in naturalistic and semi-naturalistic settings" (Bowd & Shapiro, 1993, p. 140). Each animal researcher must judge his or her work with heightened scrutiny.

Surveys of 1,188 psychology students and 3,982 American Psychological Association members on their attitudes toward animal research support a criterion of heightened scrutiny (Plous, 1996a, 1996b):

- Roughly 80 percent of the people surveyed believed that observational studies in naturalistic settings were appropriate. Smaller numbers (30 to 70 percent) supported studies involving caging or confinement, depending in part on the type of animal (for example, rats, pigeons, dogs, or primates). Both students and their professors disapproved of studies involving physical pain or death.

- A majority of both groups (roughly 60 percent) supported the use of animals in undergraduate psychology courses, but only about a third of each group felt that laboratory work with animals should be a required part of an undergraduate psychology major.

How do your beliefs compare to those of your peers? How would you make decisions about the costs and benefits of animal research?

PUT YOURSELF TO THE TEST

➥ What is the relationship between informed consent and intentional deception?

➥ How are risks and gains defined in the context of psychological research?

➥ What special considerations apply to research with nonhuman animals?

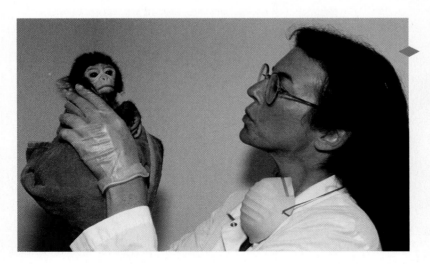

Researchers who use animal subjects are required to provide a humane environment. Do you think scientific gains justify the use of nonhuman animals in research?

Becoming a Wiser Research Consumer

In the final section of this chapter, we will focus on the kinds of critical thinking skills you need to become a wiser consumer of psychological knowledge. Honing these thinking tools is essential for any responsible person in a dynamic society such as ours—one so filled with claims of truth, with false "common sense" myths, and with biased conclusions that serve special interests. To be a *critical thinker* is to go beyond the information as given and to delve beneath slick appearances, with the goal of understanding the substance without being seduced by style and image.

Psychological claims are an ever-present aspect of the daily life of any thinking, feeling, and acting person in this psychologically sophisticated society. Unfortunately, much information on psychology does not come from the books, articles, and reports of accredited practitioners. Rather, this information comes from newspaper and magazine articles, TV and radio shows, pop psychology and self-help books. Return to the idea of subliminal mind control. Although it began as a hoax propagated by profit-minded marketing consultant James M. Vicary (Rogers, 1993)—and, as we have seen, has been rigorously discredited in the laboratory—the idea of subliminal influences on overt behavior continues to exert a pull on people's beliefs—and their wallets!

Studying psychology will help you make wiser decisions based on evidence gathered either by you or by others. You should always try to apply the insights you derive from your formal study of psychology to the informal psychology that surrounds you: Ask questions about your own behavior or that of other people, seek answers to these questions with respect to rational psychological theories, and check out the answers against the evidence available to you.

Here are some general rules to keep in mind in order to be a more sophisticated shopper as you travel through the supermarket of knowledge:

- Avoid the inference that correlation is causation.

- Ask that critical terms and key concepts be defined operationally so that there can be consensus about their meanings.

- Consider first how to disprove a theory, hypothesis, or belief before seeking confirming evidence, which is easy to find when you're looking for a justification.

- Always search for alternative explanations to the obvious ones proposed, especially when the explanations benefit the proposer.

- Recognize how personal biases can distort perceptions of reality.

- Be suspicious of simple answers to complex questions or single causes and cures for complex effects and problems.

- Question any statement about the effectiveness of some treatment, intervention, or product by finding the comparative basis for the effect: compared to what?

A news interview with an expert may include misleading sound bites taken out of context or oversimplified "nutshell" descriptions of research conclusions. How could you become a wiser consumer of media reports?

- Be open-minded yet skeptical: Recognize that most conclusions are tentative and not certain; seek new evidence that decreases your uncertainty while keeping yourself open to change and revision.

- Challenge authority that uses personal opinion in place of evidence for conclusions and is not open to constructive criticism.

We want you to apply open-minded skepticism while you read *Psychology and Life*. We don't want you to view your study of psychology as the acquisition of a list of facts. Instead, we hope you will participate in the joy of observing and discovering and putting ideas to the test.

PSYCHOLOGY IN THE 21ST CENTURY

Psychological Research and the Information Explosion

If you access the World Wide Web, you will discover an amazing range of sites devoted to topics in psychology. For example, when we first wrote these paragraphs three years ago, our preferred search engine turned up 83,760 pages mentioning schizophrenia (see Chapter 14). This morning, the search engine found "about 764,000" pages. That's some increase! No doubt the numbers will grow even higher during the short interval the publisher needs to turn our paragraphs into your textbook. These two data points make it clear why many people characterize the time in which we live as a time of *information explosion*. The challenge for all of us is to become wise consumers of all that information. How can you determine which information posted on the Web arises from legitimate sources and which does not?

In a physical library, it's much easier to determine the source of information. Most psychological research appears in *journals* that are published by organiza-

tions such as the *American Psychological Association* or the *American Psychological Society*. When research manuscripts are submitted to most journals, they undergo a process of *peer review*. Each manuscript is typically sent to two to five experts in the field. Those experts provide detailed analyses of the manuscript's rationale, methodology, and results. Only when those experts have been sufficiently satisfied do manuscripts become journal articles. This is a rigorous process. For example, in 2002, journals published by the American Psychological Association (2003) rejected, on average, 69 percent of the manuscripts submitted to them. The process of peer review isn't perfect—no doubt some worthy research projects are overlooked, and some uneven ones slip through—but, in general, this process ensures that the research you read in the vast majority of journals has met high standards.

In this context, it's easy to identify the problem with much of the information on

the Web: You often can't tell who, if anyone, has evaluated the advice a webpage offers or the claims it makes. When you accept information from a webpage, you need to assure yourself that the source is legitimate. One good approach is to look for online versions of the journals available in the library. Also, look for the webpages researchers now often maintain that summarize their projects and list relevant publications. If the information you find on those or any other webpages interests you, try to find the references and publications they list. In general, you should have the greatest confidence in the information provided on a website when the authors of the site are able to point you toward the research sources for that information. You can have confidence in the conclusions we draw throughout *Psychology and Life* because we provide research citations for each of our claims. Make sure to hold webpages to the same standard!

◆ Recapping Main Points

THE PROCESS OF RESEARCH

- In the initial phase of research, observations, beliefs, information, and general knowledge lead to a new way of thinking about a phenomenon. The researcher formulates a theory and generates hypotheses to be tested.

- To test their ideas, researchers use the scientific method, a set of procedures for gathering and interpreting evidence in ways that limit errors.

- Researchers combat observer biases by standardizing procedures and using operational definitions.

- Experimental research methods determine whether causal relationships exist between variables specified by the hypothesis being tested.

- Researchers rule out alternative explanations by using appropriate control procedures.

- Correlational research methods determine if and how much two variables are related. Correlations do not imply causation.

PSYCHOLOGICAL MEASUREMENT

- Researchers strive to produce measures that are both reliable and valid.

- Psychological measurements include self-reports and behavioral measures.

ETHICAL ISSUES IN HUMAN AND ANIMAL RESEARCH

- Respect for the basic rights of human and animal research participants is the obligation of all researchers. A variety of safeguards have been enacted to guarantee ethical and humane treatment.

BECOMING A WISER RESEARCH CONSUMER

- Becoming a wise research consumer involves learning how to think critically and knowing how to evaluate claims about what research shows.

KEY TERMS

behavioral measures (p. 35)

between-subjects designs (p. 29)

case study (p. 37)

confounding variable (p. 28)

control procedures (p. 29)

correlation coefficient (*r*) (p. 31)

correlational methods (p. 30)

debriefing (p. 39)

dependent variable (p. 26)

determinism (p. 24)

double-blind control (p. 29)

expectancy effects (p. 28)

experimental methods (p. 27)

hypothesis (p. 24)

independent variable (p. 26)

observer bias (p. 25)

operational definition (p. 26)

placebo control (p. 29)

placebo effect (p. 28)

population (p. 30)

reliability (p. 34)

representative sample (p. 30)

sample (p. 30)

scientific method (p. 24)

self-report measures (p. 35)

standardization (p. 25)

theory (p. 24)

validity (p. 34)

variable (p. 26)

within-subjects design (p. 30)

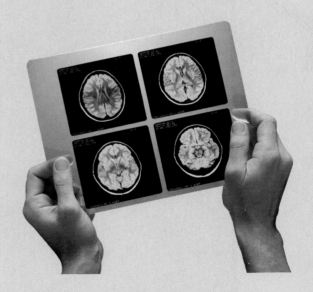

Statistical Supplement

Understanding Statistics:
Analyzing Data and Forming Conclusions

As we noted in Chapter 2, psychologists use statistics to make sense of the data they collect. They also use statistics to provide a quantitative basis for the conclusions they draw. Knowing something about statistics, therefore, can help you appreciate the process by which psychological knowledge is developed. On a more personal level, having a basic understanding of statistics will help you make better decisions when people use data to try to sway your opinions and actions.

Most students perceive statistics as a dry, uninteresting topic. However, statistics have many vital applications in your life. To demonstrate this point, we will follow a single project from its real-world inspiration to the statistical arguments that were used to bolster general conclusions. The project began in response to the types of stories that appear on newspaper front pages, about shy individuals who became *sudden murderers*. Here's an example:

> *Fred Cowan was described by relatives, co-workers, and acquaintances as a "nice, quiet man," a "gentle man who loved children," and a "real pussycat." The principal of the parochial school Cowan had attended as a child reported that his former student had received A grades in courtesy, cooperation, and religion. According to a co-worker, Cowan "never talked to anybody and*

was someone you could push around." Cowan, *however, surprised everyone who knew him when, one Valentine's Day, he strolled into work toting a semiautomatic rifle and shot and killed four co-workers, a police officer, and, finally, himself.*

This story has a common plot: A shy, quiet person suddenly becomes violent, shocking everyone who knows him. What did Fred Cowan have in common with other people who are suddenly transformed from gentle and caring into violent and ruthless? What personal attributes might distinguish them from us?

A team of researchers had a hunch that there might be a link between shyness and other personal characteristics and violent behavior (Lee et al., 1977). Therefore, they began to collect some data that might reveal such a connection. The researchers reasoned that seemingly nonviolent people who suddenly commit murders are probably typically shy, nonaggressive individuals who keep their passions in check and their impulses under tight control. For most of their lives, they suffer many silent injuries. Seldom, if ever, do they express anger, regardless of how angry they really feel. On the outside, they appear unbothered, but on the inside they may be fighting to control furious rages. They give the impression that they are quiet, passive, responsible people, both as children and as adults. Because they are shy, they probably do not let others get close to them, so no one knows how they really feel. Then, suddenly, something explodes. At the slightest provocation—one more small insult, one more little rejection, one more bit of social pressure—the fuse is lit, and they release the suppressed violence that has been building up for so long. Because they did not learn to deal with interpersonal conflicts through discussion and verbal negotiation, these sudden murderers act out their anger physically.

The researchers' reasoning led them to the hypothesis that shyness would be more characteristic of *sudden murderers*—people who had engaged in homicide without any prior history of violence or antisocial behavior—than it would of *habitual criminal murderers*—those who had committed homicide but had had a previous record of violent criminal behavior. In addition, sudden murderers should have higher levels of control over their impulses than habitually violent people. Finally, their passivity and dependence would be manifested in more feminine and androgynous (both male and female) characteristics, as measured on a standard sex-role inventory, than those of habitual criminals.

To test their ideas about sudden murderers, the researchers obtained permission to administer psychological questionnaires to a group of inmates serving time for murder in California prisons. Nineteen inmates (all male) agreed to participate in the study. Prior to committing murder, some had committed a series of crimes, whereas the other part of the sample had had no previous criminal record. The researchers collected three kinds of data from these two types of participants: shyness scores, sex-role identification scores, and impulse control scores.

Shyness scores were collected using the Stanford Shyness Survey. The most important item on this questionnaire asked if the individual was shy; the answer could be either yes or no. Other items on the scale tapped degree and kinds of shyness and a variety of dimensions related to origins and triggers of shyness.

The second questionnaire was the Bem Sex-Role Inventory (BSRI), which presented a list of adjectives, such as *aggressive* and *affectionate,* and asked how well each adjective described the individual (Bem, 1974, 1981). Some adjectives were typically associated with being "feminine," and the total score of these adjectives was an individual's femininity score. Other adjectives were considered "masculine," and the total score of those adjectives was an individual's masculinity score. The final sex-role score, which reflected the difference between an individual's femininity and masculinity, was calculated by subtracting the masculinity score from the femininity score. A combination of the masculinity and femininity scores shows up as an individual's androgyny score.

The third questionnaire was the Minnesota Multiphasic Personality Inventory (MMPI), which was designed to measure many different aspects of personality (see Chapter 14). The study used only the "ego-overcontrol" scale, which measures the degree to which a person acts out or controls impulses. The higher the individual's score on this scale, the more ego overcontrol the individual exhibits.

The researchers predicted that, compared with murderers with a prior criminal record, sudden murderers would (1) more often describe themselves as shy on the shyness survey, (2) select more feminine traits than masculine ones on the sex-role scale, and (3) score higher in ego overcontrol. What did they discover?

Before you find out, you need to understand some of the basic procedures that were used to analyze these data. The actual sets of data collected by the researchers will be used as the source material to teach you about some of the different types of statistical analyses and also about the kinds of conclusions they make possible.

Analyzing the Data

For most researchers in psychology, analyzing the data is an exciting step—statistical analysis allows researchers to discover if their predictions were correct. In this section, we will work step by step through an analysis of some of the data from the Sudden Murderers Study. If you have looked ahead, you will have seen numbers and equations. Keep in mind that mathematics is a tool; mathematical symbols are a shorthand for representing ideas and conceptual operations.

The *raw data*—the actual scores or other measures obtained—from the 19 inmates in the Sudden Murderers Study are listed in **Table S.1.** As you can see, there were

ten inmates in the sudden murderers group and nine in the habitual criminal murderers group. When first glancing at these data, any researcher would feel what you probably feel: confusion. What do all these scores mean? Do the two groups of murderers differ from one another on these various personality measures? It is difficult to know just by examining this disorganized array of numbers.

Psychologists rely on two types of statistics to help make sense of and draw meaningful conclusions from the data they collect: descriptive and inferential. **Descriptive statistics** use mathematical procedures in an objective, uniform way to describe different aspects of numerical data. If you have ever computed your grade-point average, you already have used descriptive statistics. **Inferential statistics** use probability theory to make sound decisions about which results might have occurred simply through chance variation.

◆ DESCRIPTIVE STATISTICS

Descriptive statistics provide a summary picture of patterns in the data. They are used to describe sets of scores collected from one experimental participant or, more often, from different groups of participants. They are also used to describe relationships among variables. Thus, instead of trying to keep in mind all the scores obtained by each of the participants, researchers get indexes of the scores that are most *typical* for each group. They also get measures of how *variable* the scores are with respect to the typical score—whether the scores are spread out or clustered closely together. Let's see how researchers derive these measures.

FREQUENCY DISTRIBUTIONS

How would you summarize the data in Table S.1? To present a clear picture of how the various scores are distributed, we can draw up a **frequency distribution**—a summary of how frequently each of the various scores occurs. The shyness data are easy to summarize. Of the 19 scores, there are 9 *yes* and 10 *no* responses; almost all the *yes* responses are in Group 1, and almost all the *no* responses are in Group 2. However, the ego-overcontrol and sex-role scores do not fall into easy *yes* and *no* categories. To see how frequency distributions of numerical responses can allow informative comparisons between groups, we will focus on the sex-role scores.

Consider the sex-role data in Table S.1. The highest score is +61 (most feminine) and the lowest is −33 (most masculine). Of the 19 scores, 9 are positive and 10 negative—this means that 9 of the murderers described themselves as relatively feminine and 10 as relatively masculine. But how are these scores distributed between the groups? The first step in preparing a

---

TABLE S.1

Raw Data from the Sudden Murderers Study

INMATE	SHYNESS	BSRI FEMININITY–MASCULINITY	MMPI EGO OVERCONTROL
Group 1: Sudden Murderers			
1	Yes	+5	17
2	No	−1	17
3	Yes	+4	13
4	Yes	+61	17
5	Yes	+19	13
6	Yes	+41	19
7	No	−29	14
8	Yes	+23	9
9	Yes	−13	11
10	Yes	+5	14
Group 2: Habitual Criminal Murderers			
11	No	−12	15
12	No	−14	11
13	Yes	−33	14
14	No	−8	10
15	No	−7	16
16	No	+3	11
17	No	−17	6
18	No	+6	9
19	No	−10	12

<www.ablongman.com/gerrig17e>

frequency distribution for a set of numerical data is to *rank order* the scores from highest to lowest. The rank ordering for the sex-role scores is shown in **Table S.2.** The second step is to group these rank-ordered scores into a smaller number of categories called *intervals*. In this study, 10 categories were used, with each category covering 10 possible scores. The third step is to construct a frequency distribution table, listing the intervals from highest to lowest and noting the *frequencies*—the number of scores within each interval. Our frequency distribution shows us that the sex-role scores are largely between −20 and +9 (see **Table S.3**). The majority of the inmates' scores did not deviate much from zero. That is, they were neither strongly positive nor strongly negative.

The data are now arranged in useful categories. The researchers' next step was to display the distributions in graphic form.

GRAPHS

Distributions are often easier to understand when they are displayed in graphs. The simplest type of graph is a *bar graph*. Bar graphs allow you to see patterns in the data. We can use a bar graph to illustrate how many more sudden murderers than habitual criminal murderers described themselves as shy (see **Figure S.1**).

For more complex data, such as the sex-role scores, we can use a *histogram,* which is similar to a bar graph except that the categories are intervals—number categories instead of the name categories used in the bar graph. A histogram gives a visual picture of the number of scores in a distribution that are in each interval. It is

Category	Frequency
+60 to +69	1
+50 to +59	0
+40 to +49	1
+30 to +39	0
+20 to +29	1
+10 to +19	1
0 to +9	5
−10 to −1	4
−20 to −11	4
−30 to −21	1
−40 to −31	1

easy to see from the sex-role scores shown in the histograms (in **Figure S.2**) that the distributions of scores are different for the two groups of murderers.

You can see from Figures S.1 and S.2 that the overall distributions of responses conform to two of the researchers' hypotheses. Sudden murderers were more likely to describe themselves as shy and were more likely to use feminine traits to describe themselves than were habitual criminal murderers.

TABLE S.2

Rank Ordering of Sex-Role Difference Scores

Highest	+61	−1	
	+41	−7	
	+23	−8	
	+19	−10	
	+6	−12	
	+5	−13	
	+5	−14	
	+4	−17	
	+3	−29	
		−33	Lowest

Note: + scores are more feminine; − scores are more masculine.

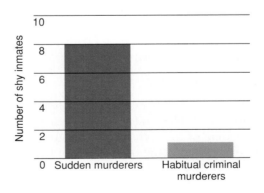

FIGURE S.1

Shyness for Two Groups of Murderers (a Bar Graph)

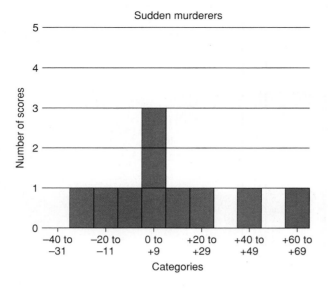

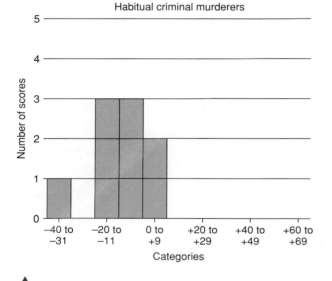

FIGURE S.2

Sex-Role Scores (Histograms)

MEASURES OF CENTRAL TENDENCY

So far, we have formed a general picture of how the scores are *distributed*. Tables and graphs increase our general understanding of research results, but we want to know more—for example, the one score that is most typical of the group as a whole. This score becomes particularly useful when we compare two or more groups; it is much easier to compare the typical scores of two groups than their entire distributions. A single, *representative* score that can be used as an index of the most typical score obtained by a group of participants is called a **measure of central tendency.** (It is located in the center of the distribution, and other scores tend

to cluster around it.) Typically, psychologists use three different measures of central tendency: the *mode,* the *median,* and the *mean.*

The **mode** is the score that occurs more often than any other. For the measure of shyness, the modal response of the sudden murderers was *yes*—eight out of ten said they were shy. Among habitual criminal murderers, the modal response was *no.* The sex-role scores for the sudden murderers had a mode of +5. Can you figure out what the mode of their ego-overcontrol scores is? The mode is the easiest index of central tendency to determine, but it is often the least useful. You will see one reason for this relative lack of usefulness if you notice that only one overcontrol score lies above the mode of 17, and six lie below it. Although 17 is the score obtained most often, it may not fit your idea of "typical" or "central."

The **median** is more clearly a central score; it separates the upper half of the scores in a distribution from the lower half. The number of scores larger than the median is the same as the number that is smaller. When there are an odd number of scores, the median is the middle score; when there are an even number of scores, researchers most often average the two scores at the middle. For example, if you rank-order the sex-role scores of only the habitual criminal murderers on a separate piece of paper, you will see that the median score is −10, with four scores higher and four scores lower. For the sudden murderers, the median is +5—the average of the fifth and sixth scores, each of which happens to be +5. The median is not affected by extreme scores. For example, even if the sudden murderers' highest sex-role score had been +129 instead of +61, the median value would still have been +5. That score would still separate the upper half of the data from the lower half. The median is quite simply the score in the middle of the distribution.

The **mean** is what most people think of when they hear the word *average.* It is also the statistic most often used to describe a set of data. To calculate the mean, you add up all the scores in a distribution and divide by the total number of scores. The operation is summarized by the following formula:

$$M = (\Sigma X)/N$$

In this formula, M is the mean, X is each individual score, Σ (the Greek letter sigma) is the summation of what immediately follows it, and N is the total number of scores. Because the summation of all the sex-role scores (ΣX) is 115, and the total number of scores (N) is 10, the mean (M) of the sex-role scores of the sudden murderers would be calculated as follows:

$$M = 115/10 = 11.5$$

Try to calculate their mean overcontrol scores yourself. You should come up with a mean of 14.4.

<www.ablongman.com/gerrig17e>

Unlike the median, the mean *is* affected by the specific values of all scores in the distribution. Changing the value of an extreme score does change the value of the mean. For example, if the sex-role score of inmate 4 were +101 instead of +61, the mean for the whole group would increase from 11.5 to 15.5.

VARIABILITY

In addition to knowing which score is most representative of the distribution as a whole, it is useful to know how representative that measure of central tendency really is. Are most of the other scores fairly close to it or widely spread out? **Measures of variability** are statistics that describe the distribution of scores around some measure of central tendency.

Can you see why measures of variability are important? An example may help. Suppose you are a grade-school teacher. It is the beginning of the school year, and you will be teaching reading to a group of 30 second graders. Knowing that the average child in the class can now read a first-grade-level book will help you to plan your lessons. You could plan better, however, if you knew how *similar* or how *divergent* the reading abilities of the 30 children were. Are they all at about the same level (low variability)? If so, then you can plan a fairly standard second-grade lesson. What if several can read advanced material and others can barely read at all (high variability)? Now the mean level is not so representative of the entire class, and you will have to plan a variety of lessons to meet the children's varied needs.

The simplest measure of variability is the **range,** the difference between the highest and the lowest values in a frequency distribution. For the sudden murderers' sex-role scores, the range is 90: $(+61) - (-29)$. The range of their overcontrol scores is 10: $(+19) - (+9)$. To compute the range, you need to know only two of the scores: the highest and the lowest.

The range is simple to compute, but psychologists often prefer measures of variability that are more sensitive and that take into account *all* the scores in a distribution, not just the extremes. One widely used measure is the **standard deviation (SD),** a measure of variability that indicates the *average* difference between the scores and their mean. To figure out the standard deviation of a distribution, you need to know the mean of the distribution and the individual scores. The general procedure involves subtracting the value of each individual score from the mean and then determining the average of those mean deviations. Here is the formula:

$$SD = \sqrt{\Sigma(X - M)^2/N}$$

You should recognize most of the symbols from the formula for the mean. The expression $(X - M)$ means "individual score minus the mean" and is commonly

called the *deviation score*. The mean is subtracted from each score, and each resulting score is squared (to eliminate negative values). Then the mean of these deviations is calculated by summing them up (Σ) and dividing by the number of observations (N). The symbol $\sqrt{}$ tells you to take the square root of the enclosed value to offset the previous squaring. The standard deviation of the overcontrol scores for the sudden murderers is calculated in **Table S.4.** Recall that the mean of these scores is 14.4. This, then, is the value that must be subtracted from each score to obtain the corresponding deviation scores.

The standard deviation tells us how variable a set of scores is. The larger the standard deviation, the more spread out the scores are. The standard deviation of the sex-role scores for the sudden murderers is 24.6, but the standard deviation for the habitual criminals is only 10.7. This shows that there was less variability in the habitual criminals group. Their scores clustered more closely about their mean than did those of the sudden murderers. When the standard deviation is small, the mean is a good representative index of the entire distribution. When the standard deviation is large, the mean is less typical of the whole group.

TABLE S.4

Calculating the Standard Deviation of Sudden Murderers' Ego-Overcontrol Scores

Score (X)	Deviation (score minus mean) (X − M)	Deviations Squared (score minus mean)² (X − M)²
17	2.6	6.76
17	2.6	6.76
13	−1.4	1.96
17	2.6	6.76
13	−1.4	1.96
19	4.6	21.16
14	−.4	.16
9	−5.4	29.16
11	−3.4	11.56
14	−.4	.16

$$\text{Standard deviation} = SD = \sqrt{\frac{\Sigma (X - M)^2}{N}} \qquad 86.40 = \Sigma (X - M)^2$$

$$\sqrt{\frac{86.40}{10}} = \sqrt{8.64} = 2.94$$

$$SD = 2.94$$

CORRELATION

Another useful tool in interpreting psychological data is the **correlation coefficient,** a measure of the nature and strength of the relationship between two variables (such as height and weight or sex-role score and ego-overcontrol score). It tells us the extent to which scores on one measure are associated with scores on the other. If people with high scores on one variable tend to have *high* scores on the other variable, then the correlation coefficient will be positive (greater than 0). If, however, most people with high scores on one variable tend to have *low* scores on the other variable, then the correlation coefficient will be negative (less than 0). If there is *no* consistent relationship between the scores, the correlation will be close to 0 (see also Chapter 2).

Correlation coefficients range from +1 (perfect positive correlation) through 0 to −1 (perfect negative correlation). The further a coefficient is from 0 in *either* direction, the more closely related the two variables are, positively or negatively. Higher coefficients permit better predictions of one variable, given knowledge of the other.

In the Sudden Murderers Study, the correlation coefficient (symbolized as *r*) between the sex-role scores and the overcontrol scores turns out to be +0.35. The sex-role scores and the overcontrol scores are, thus, positively correlated—in general, individuals seeing themselves as more feminine also tend to be higher in overcontrol. However, the correlation is modest, compared with the highest possible value, +1.00, so we know that there are many exceptions to this relationship. If we had also measured the self-esteem of these inmates and found a correlation of −0.68 between overcontrol scores and self-esteem, it would mean that there was a negative correlation. If this were the case, we could say that the individuals who had high overcontrol scores tended to be lower in self-esteem. It would be a stronger relationship than the relationship between the sex-role scores and the overcontrol scores, because −0.68 is farther from 0, the point of no relationship, than is +0.35.

◆ INFERENTIAL STATISTICS

We have used a number of descriptive statistics to characterize the data from the Sudden Murderers Study, and now we have an idea of the pattern of results. However, some basic questions remain unanswered. Recall that the research team hypothesized that sudden murderers would be shyer, more overcontrolled, and more feminine than habitual criminal murderers. After we have used descriptive statistics to compare average responses and variability in the two groups, it appears that there are some differences between the groups. But how do we know if the differences are large enough to be meaningful? If we repeated this study, with other sudden murderers and other habitual criminal murderers, would we expect to find the same pattern of results, or could these results have been an outcome of chance? If we could somehow measure the entire population of sudden murderers and habitual criminal murderers, would the means and standard deviations be the same as those we found for these small samples?

Inferential statistics are used to answer these kinds of questions. They tell us which inferences we *can* make from our samples and which conclusions we can legitimately draw from our data. Inferential statistics use probability theory to determine the likelihood that a set of data occurred simply by chance variation.

THE NORMAL CURVE

In order to understand how inferential statistics work, we must look first at the special properties of a distribution called the *normal curve.* When data on a variable (for example, height, IQ, or overcontrol) are collected from a large number of individuals, the numbers obtained often fit a curve roughly similar to that shown in **Figure S.3.** Notice that the curve is symmetrical (the left half is a mirror image of the right) and bell shaped—high in the middle, where most scores are, and lower the farther you get from the mean. This type of curve is called a **normal curve,** or *normal distribution.* (A *skewed* distribution is one in which scores cluster toward one end instead of around the middle.)

In a normal curve, the median, mode, and mean values are the same. A specific percentage of the scores can be predicted to fall under different sections of the curve. Figure S.3 shows IQ scores on the Stanford–Binet Intelligence Test. These scores have a mean of 100 and a standard deviation of 16. If you indicate standard deviations as distances from the mean along the baseline, you find that a little over 68 percent of all the scores are between the mean of 100 and 1 standard deviation above and below—between IQs of 84 and 116. Roughly another 27 percent of the scores are found between the first and second standard deviations below the mean (IQ scores between 68 and 84) and above the mean (IQ scores between 116 and 132). Less than 5 percent of the scores fall in the third standard deviation above and below the mean, and very few scores fall beyond—only about one-quarter of 1 percent.

Inferential statistics indicate the probability that the particular sample of scores obtained is actually related to whatever you are attempting to measure or whether it could have occurred by chance. For example, it is more likely that someone would have an IQ of 105 than an IQ of 140, but an IQ of 140 is more probable than one of 35.

<www.ablongman.com/gerrig17e>

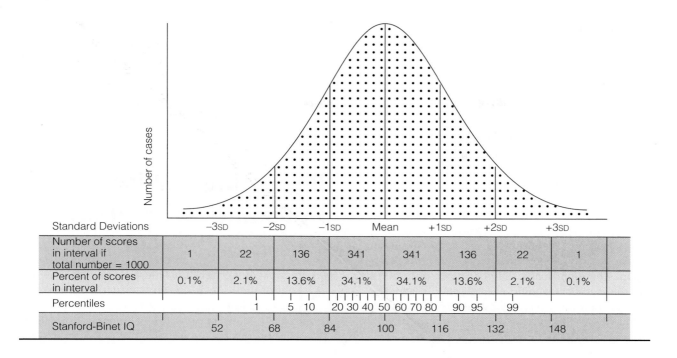

Standard Deviations		−3SD	−2SD	−1SD	Mean	+1SD	+2SD	+3SD	
Number of scores in interval if total number = 1000	1	22	136	341	341	136	22	1	
Percent of scores in interval	0.1%	2.1%	13.6%	34.1%	34.1%	13.6%	2.1%	0.1%	
Percentiles			1	5 10	20 30 40 50 60 70 80	90 95	99		
Stanford-Binet IQ		52	68	84	100	116	132	148	

FIGURE S.3

A Normal Curve

A normal curve is also obtained by collecting a series of measurements whose differences are due only to chance. If you flip a coin 10 times in a row and record the number of heads and tails, you will probably get 5 of each—most of the time. If you keep flipping the coin for 100 sets of 10 tosses, you probably will get a few sets with all heads or no heads, more sets where the number is between these extremes, and, most typically, more sets where the number is about half each way. If you made a graph of your 1,000 tosses, you would get one that closely fits a normal curve, such as the one in the figure.

STATISTICAL SIGNIFICANCE

A researcher who finds a difference between the mean scores for two samples must ask if it is a *real* difference or if it occurred simply because of chance. Because chance differences have a normal distribution, a researcher can use the normal curve to answer this question.

A simple example will help illustrate the point. Suppose your psychology professor wants to see if the gender of a person proctoring a test makes a difference in the test scores obtained from male and from female students. For this purpose, the professor randomly assigns half of the students to a male proctor and half to a female proctor. The professor then compares the mean score of each group. The two mean scores would probably be fairly similar; any slight difference would most likely be due to chance. Why? Because if only chance is operating and both groups are from the same population (no difference), then the means of male proctor and female proctor samples should be fairly close most of the time. From the percentages of scores found in different parts of the normal distribution, you know that less than a third of the scores in the male proctor condition should be greater than one standard deviation above or below the female proctor mean. The chances of getting a male proctor mean score more than three standard deviations above or below most of your female proctor means would be very small. A professor who *did* get a difference that great would feel fairly confident that the difference is a real one and is somehow related to the gender of the test proctor. The next question would be *how* that variable influences test scores.

If male and female students were randomly assigned to each type of proctor, it would be possible to analyze whether an overall difference found between the proctors was consistent across both student groups or was limited to only one sex. Imagine the data show that male proctors grade female students higher than do female proctors, but both grade male students the same. Your professor could use a statistical inference procedure to estimate the probability that an observed difference could have occurred by chance. This computation is based on the size of the difference and the spread of the scores.

By common agreement, psychologists accept a difference as "real" when the probability that it might be due to chance is less than 5 in 100 (indicated by the notation $p < .05$). A **significant difference** is one that meets this criterion. However, in some cases, even stricter probability levels are used, such as $p < .01$ (less than 1 in 100) and $p < .001$ (less than 1 in 1000).

With a statistically significant difference, a researcher can draw a conclusion about the behavior that was under investigation. There are many different types of tests for estimating the statistical significance of sets of data. The type of test chosen for a particular case depends on the design of the study, the form of the data, and the size of the groups. We will mention only one of the most common tests, the *t-test,* which may be used when an investigator wants to know if the difference between the means of two groups is statistically significant.

We can use a *t*-test to see if the mean sex-role score of the sudden murderers is significantly different from that of the habitual criminal murderers. The *t*-test uses a mathematical procedure to confirm the conclusion you may have drawn from Figure S.2: The distributions of sex-role scores for the two groups is sufficiently different to be "real." If we carry out the appropriate calculations—which evaluate the difference between the two means as a function of the variability around those two means—we find that there is a very slim chance, less than 5 in 100 ($p < .05$), of obtaining such a large *t* value if no true difference exists. The difference is, therefore, statistically significant, and we can feel more confident that there is a real difference between the two groups. The sudden murderers *did* rate themselves as more feminine than did the habitual criminal murderers. On the other hand, the difference between the two groups of murderers in overcontrol scores turns out not to be statistically significant ($p < .10$), so we must be more cautious in making claims about this difference. There is a trend in the predicted direction—the difference is one that would occur by chance only 10 times in 100. However, the difference is not within the standard 5-in-100 range. (The difference in shyness, analyzed using another statistical test for frequency of scores, is highly significant.)

So, by using inferential statistics, we are able to answer some of the basic questions with which we began, and we are closer to understanding the psychology of people who suddenly change from mild-mannered, shy individuals into murderers. Any conclusion, however, is only a statement of the *probable* relationship between the events that were investigated; it is never one of certainty. Truth in science is provisional, always open to revision by later data from better studies, developed from better hypotheses.

Becoming a Wise Consumer of Statistics

N ow that we have considered what statistics are, how they are used, and what they mean, we should briefly talk about how they can be misused. Many people accept unsupported "facts" that are bolstered by the air of authority of a statistic. Others choose to believe or disbelieve what the statistics say without having any idea of how to question the numbers that are presented in support of a product, politician, or proposal. At the end of Chapter 2, we gave you some suggestions about how you can become a wiser research consumer. Based on this brief survey of statistics, we can extend that advice to situations in which people make specific statistical claims.

There are many ways to give a misleading impression using statistics. The decisions made at all stages of research—from who the participants are to how the study is designed, what statistics are selected, and how they are used—can have a profound effect on the conclusions that can be drawn from the data.

The group of participants can make a large difference that can easily remain undetected when the results are reported. For example, a survey of views on abortion rights will yield very different results if conducted in a small conservative community in the South rather than at a university in New York City. Likewise, a pro-life group surveying the opinions of its membership will very likely arrive at conclusions that differ from those obtained by the same survey conducted by a pro-choice group.

Even if the participants are randomly selected and not biased by the methodology, the statistics can produce misleading results if the assumptions of the statistics are violated. For example, suppose 20 people take an IQ test; 19 of them receive scores between 90 and 110, and 1 receives a score of 220. The mean of the group will be strongly elevated by that one outlying high score. With this sort of a data set, it would be much more accurate to present the median or the mode, which would accurately report the group's generally average intelligence, rather than the mean, which would make it look as if the average member of this group had a high IQ. This sort of bias is especially powerful in a small sample. If, on the other hand, the number of people in this group were 2,000 instead of 20, the one extreme outlier would make virtually no difference, and the mean would be a legitimate summary of the group's intelligence.

One good way to avoid falling for this sort of deception is to check on the size of the sample—large samples are less likely to be misleading than small ones. Another check is to look at the median or the mode as well as the mean—the results can be interpreted with more confidence if they are similar than if they are different. You should always closely examine the methodology and results of the research reported. Check to see if the experimenters report their sample size, measures of variability, and significance levels. Try to find out if the methods they used measure accurately and consistently whatever they claim to be investigating.

Statistics are the backbone of psychological research. They are used to understand observations and to determine whether the findings are, in fact, correct. Through the methods we have described, psychologists can prepare a frequency distribution of data and find the central tendencies and variability of the scores. They can use the correlation coefficient to determine the strength and direction of the association between sets of scores. Finally, psychological investigators can then find out how representative the observations are and whether they are significantly different from what would be observed among the general population. Statistics can also be used poorly or deceptively, misleading those who do not understand them. But when statistics are applied correctly and ethically, they allow researchers to expand the body of psychological knowledge.

KEY TERMS

correlation coefficient *(r)* (p. 50)

descriptive statistics (p. 46)

frequency distribution (p. 46)

inferential statistics (p. 46)

mean (p. 48)

measure of central tendency (p. 48)

measures of variability (p. 49)

median (p. 48)

mode (p. 48)

normal curve (p. 50)

range (p. 49)

significant difference (p. 52)

standard deviation (SD) (p. 49)

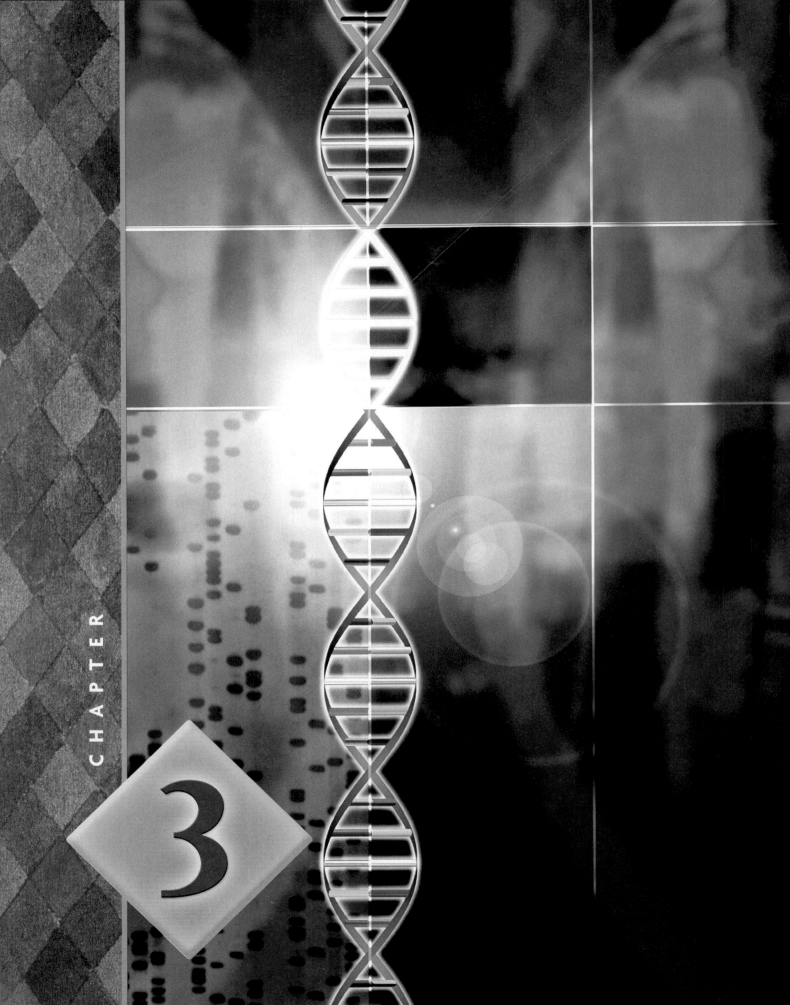

3

The Biological and Evolutionary Bases of Behavior

W hat makes you a unique individual? *Psychology and Life* provides many answers to this question, but in this chapter we will focus on the biological aspects of your individuality. To help you understand what makes you different from the people around you, we will describe the role that heredity plays in shaping your life and in forming the brain that controls your experiences. Of course, you can appreciate these differences only against the background of what you have in common with all other people. You might, therefore, think of this as a chapter about biological potential: What possibilities for behavior define the human species, and how do those possibilities emerge for particular members of that species?

In a way, this chapter stands as proof of one remarkable aspect of your biological potential: Your brain is sufficiently complex to carry out a systematic examination of its own functions. Why is this so remarkable? The human brain is sometimes likened to a spectacular computer: At only three pounds, your brain contains more cells than there are stars in our entire galaxy—over 100 billion cells that communicate and store information with astonishing efficiency. But even the world's mightiest computer is incapable of reflecting on the rules that guide its own operation. You are, thus, much more than a computer; your consciousness allows you to put your vast computational power to work, trying to determine your species' own rules for operation. The research we describe in this chapter arose from the special human desire for self-understanding.

For many students, this chapter will pose a greater challenge than the rest of *Psychology and Life*. It requires that you learn some anatomy and many new terms that seem far removed from the information you may have expected to get from an introduction to psychology. However, understanding your biological nature will enable you to appreciate more fully the complex interplay among the brain, mind, behavior, and environment that creates the unique experience of being human.

Our goal for this chapter is to allow you to understand how biology contributes to the creation of unique individuals against a shared background potential. To approach this goal, we first describe how evolution and heredity determine your biology and behavior. We then see how laboratory and clinical research provide a view into the workings of the brain, the nervous system, and the endocrine system. Finally, we describe the basic mechanisms of communication among cells in your nervous system that produce the full range of complex human behaviors.

Psychologists often wish to understand the separate impact of nature and nurture on individuals' courses through life. Why might it be easier to observe the impact of environments versus the impact of heredity?

Heredity and Behavior

In Chapter 1, we defined one of the major goals of psychology to be the discovery of the causes underlying the variety of human behavior. An important dimension of causal explanation within psychology is defined by the end points of *nature* versus *nurture,* or *heredity* versus *environment.* Consider, as we did in Chapter 1, the question of the roots of aggressive behavior. You might imagine that individuals are aggressive by virtue of some aspect of their biological makeup: They may have inherited a tendency toward violence from one of their parents. Alternatively, you might imagine that all humans are about equally predisposed to aggression and that the degree of aggression individuals display arises in response to features of the environment in which they are raised. The correct answer to this question has a profound impact on how society treats individuals who are overly aggressive—by focusing resources on changing certain environments or on changing aspects of the people themselves. You need to be able to discriminate the forces of heredity from the forces of environment.

Because the features of environments can be directly observed, it is often easier to understand how they affect people's behavior. You can, for example, actually watch a parent acting aggressively toward a child and wonder what consequences such treatment might have on the child's later tendency toward aggression; you can observe the overcrowded and impoverished settings in which some children grow up and wonder whether these features of the environment lead to aggressive behaviors. The biological forces that shape behavior, by comparison, are never plainly visible to the naked eye. To make the biology of behavior more understandable to you, we will begin by describing some of the basic principles that shape a species's potential repertoire of behaviors—elements of the theory of evolution—and then describe how behavioral variation is passed from generation to generation.

◆ EVOLUTION AND NATURAL SELECTION

In 1831, **Charles Darwin,** fresh out of college with a degree in theology, set sail from England on HMS *Beagle,* an ocean research vessel, for a five-year cruise to survey the coast of South America. During the trip, Darwin collected everything that crossed his path: marine animals, birds, insects, plants, fossils, seashells,

OUR EVOLUTIONARY FAMILY TREE

X YOU ARE HERE

and rocks. His extensive notes became the foundation for his books on topics ranging from geology to emotion to zoology. The book for which he is most remembered is *The Origin of Species*, published in 1859. In this work, Darwin set forth science's grandest theory: the evolution of life on planet Earth.

NATURAL SELECTION

Darwin developed his theory of evolution by reflecting on the species of animals he had encountered while on his voyage. One of the many places the *Beagle* visited was the Galápagos Islands, a volcanic archipelago off the west coast of South America. These islands are a haven for diverse forms of wildlife, including 13 species of finches, now known as Darwin's finches. Darwin wondered how so many different species of finches could have come to inhabit the islands. He reasoned that they couldn't have migrated from the mainland because those species didn't exist there. He suggested, therefore, that the variety of species reflected the operation of a process he came to call **natural selection.**

Darwin's theory suggests that each species of finch emerged from a common set of ancestors. Originally, a small flock of finches found their way to one of the islands; they mated among themselves and eventually their number multiplied. Over time, some finches migrated to different islands in the archipelago. What happened next was the process of natural selection. Food resources and living conditions—*habitats*—vary considerably from island to island. Some of the islands are lush with berries and seeds, others are covered with cacti, and others have plenty of insects. At first, the populations on different islands were similar—there was *variation* among the groups of finches on each island. However, because food resources on the islands were limited, birds were more likely to survive and reproduce if the shape of their beak was well suited to the

food sources available on the island. For example, birds that migrated to islands rich in berries and seeds were more likely to survive and reproduce if they had thick beaks. On those islands, birds with thinner, more pointed beaks, unsuitable for crushing or breaking open seeds, died. The environment of each island determined which among the original population of finches would live and reproduce and which would more likely perish, leaving no offspring. Over time, this led to very different populations on each island and permitted the different species of Darwin's finches to evolve from the original ancestral group.

In general, the theory of natural selection suggests that organisms well adapted to their environment, whatever it happens to be, will produce more offspring than those less well adapted. Over time, those organisms possessing traits more favorable for survival will become more numerous than those not possessing those traits. In evolutionary terms, an individual's success is measured by the number of offspring he or she produces.

Contemporary research has shown that natural selection can have dramatic effects, even in the short run. In a series of studies by **Peter** and **Rosemary Grant** (Grant & Grant, 1989, 2002; Weiner, 1994), involving several species of Darwin's finches, records were kept of rainfall, food supply, and the population size of these finches on one of the Galápagos Islands. In 1976, the population numbered well over 1,000 birds. The following year brought a murderous drought that wiped out most of the food supply. The smallest seeds were the first to be depleted, leaving only larger and tougher seeds. That year the finch population decreased by more than 80 percent. However, smaller finches with smaller beaks died at a higher frequency than larger finches with thicker beaks. Consequently, as Darwin would have predicted, the larger birds became more numerous in the following years. Why? Because only they, with their larger bodies and thicker beaks, were fit enough to respond to the environmental change caused by the drought. Interestingly, in 1983, rain was plentiful, and seeds, especially the smaller ones, became abundant. As a result, smaller birds outsurvived larger birds, probably because their beaks were better suited for pecking the smaller seeds. The Grants' study shows that natural selection can have noticeable effects even over short periods. Researchers continue to document the impact of environments on natural selection in diverse species, including the European fruit fly (Huey et al., 2000) and the stickleback fish (Rundle et al., 2000).

Although Darwin provided the foundation for evolutionary theory, researchers continue to study mechanisms of evolutionary change that fell beyond the bounds of Darwin's ideas (Gould, 2002). For example, one important question that Darwin was unable to address fully was how populations with common ancestors evolve so that one species becomes two. As you have already seen in the Grants' research with Darwin's finches, species can change rapidly in response to local environments. One explanation for the appearance of new species is that they emerge when two populations from an original species become geographically separate—and therefore evolve in response to different environmental events. However, contemporary research on evolution has uncovered many examples of new species that have emerged without that type of geographic isolation (Barton, 2000). Researchers are pursuing a variety of explanations for how species arise under those circumstances. These explanations focus, for example, on how subgroups within a species evolve different cues—such as the chemical signals fruit flies use—to recognize appropriate mates (Higgie et al., 2000). If, over time, those cues become distinct, separate species may emerge.

GENOTYPES AND PHENOTYPES

Let's return our focus to the forces that bring about change within an existing species.

The example of the ebb and flow of finch populations demonstrates why Darwin characterized the course of evolution as *survival of the fittest*. Imagine that each environment poses some range of difficulties for each species of living beings. Those members of the species who possess the range of physical and psychological attributes best adapted to the environment are most likely to survive. To the extent that the attributes that foster survival can be passed from one generation to another—and stresses in the environment endure over time—the species is likely to evolve.

To examine the process of natural selection in more detail, we must introduce some of the vocabulary of evolutionary theory. Let us focus on an individual finch. At conception, that finch inherited a **genotype,** or genetic structure, from its parents. In the context of a particular environment, this genotype determined the finch's development and behavior. The outward appearance and repertoire of behaviors of the finch are known as its **phenotype.** For our finch, its genotype may have interacted with the environment to yield the phenotype of *small beak* and *able to peck smaller seeds*.

If seeds of all types were plentiful, this phenotype would have no particular bearing on the finch's survival. Suppose, however, that the environment provided insufficient seeds to feed the whole population of finches. In that case, the individual finches would be in *competition* for resources. When species function in circumstances of competition, phenotypes help determine which individual members are better adapted to ensure survival. Recall our finch with a small beak. If only small seeds were available, our finch would be at a

selective advantage with respect to finches with large beaks. If only large seeds were available, our finch would be at a disadvantage.

Only finches that survive can reproduce. Only those animals that reproduce can pass on their genotypes. Therefore, if the environment continued to provide only small seeds, over several generations the finches would probably come to have almost exclusively small beaks—with the consequence that they would be almost exclusively capable of eating only small seeds. In this way, forces in the environment can shape a species's repertory of possible behaviors. **Figure 3.1** provides a simplified model of the process

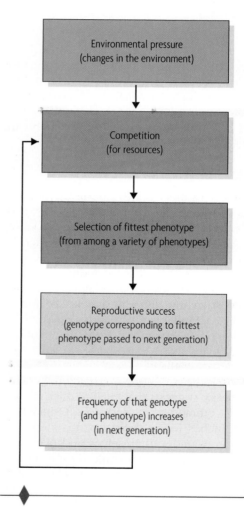

FIGURE 3.1

How Natural Selection Works

Environmental changes create competition for resources among species members. Only those individuals possessing characteristics instrumental in coping with these changes will survive and reproduce. The next generation will have a greater number of individuals possessing these genetically based traits.

of natural selection. Let us now apply these ideas to human evolution.

HUMAN EVOLUTION

By looking backward to the circumstances in which the human species evolved, you can begin to understand why certain physical and behavioral features are part of the biological endowment of the entire human species. In the evolution of our species, natural selection favored two major adaptations—bipedalism and encephalization. Together, they made possible the rise of human civilization. *Bipedalism* refers to the ability to walk upright, and *encephalization* refers to increases in brain size. These two adaptations are responsible for most, if not all, of the other major advances in human evolution, including cultural development (see **Figure 3.2**). As our ancestors evolved the ability to walk upright, they were able to explore new environments and exploit new resources. As brain size increased, our ancestors became more intelligent and developed capacities for complex thinking, reasoning, remembering, and planning. However, the evolution of a bigger brain did not guarantee that humans would become more intelligent—what was important was the kind of tissue that developed and expanded within the brain (Gibbons, 2002). The genotype coding for mobile and intelligent phenotypes slowly squeezed out other, less well-adapted genotypes from the human gene pool, affording only intelligent bipeds the opportunity to reproduce.

After bipedalism and encephalization, perhaps the most important evolutionary milestone for our species was the advent of *language* (Bickerton, 1990; Holden, 1998). Think of the tremendous adaptive advantages that language conferred on early humans. Simple instructions for making tools, finding a good hunting or fishing spot, and avoiding danger would save time, effort, and lives. Instead of learning every one of life's lessons firsthand, by trial and error, humans could benefit from experiences shared by others. Conversation, even humor, would strengthen the social bonds among members of a naturally gregarious species. Most important, the advent of language would provide for the transmission of accumulated wisdom, from one generation to future generations.

Language is the basis for *cultural evolution,* which is the tendency of cultures to respond adaptively, through learning, to environmental change. Cultural evolution has given rise to major advances in toolmaking, improved agricultural practices, and the development and refinement of industry and technology. Cultural evolution allows our species to make very rapid adjustments to changes in environmental conditions. Adaptations to the use of personal computers, for example, have arisen in only the past 20 years. Even so, cultural evolution could not occur without genotype coding for the capacities to learn and to think abstractly.

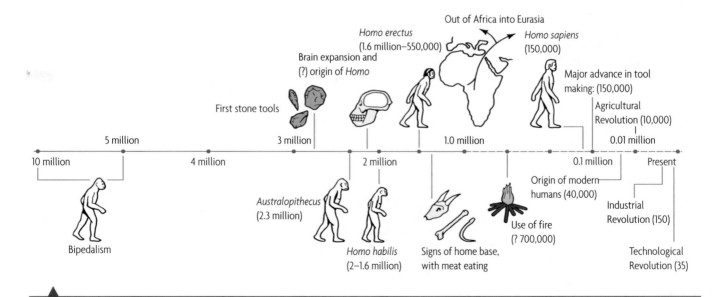

FIGURE 3.2

Approximate Time Line for the Major Events in Human Evolution

Bipedalism freed the hands for grasping and tool use. Encephalization provided the capacity for higher cognitive processes such as abstract thinking and reasoning. These two adaptations probably led to the other major advances in human evolution.

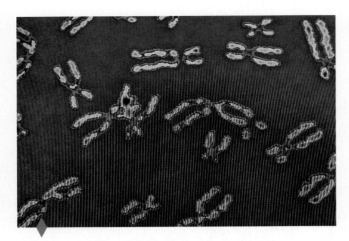

Human chromosomes—at the moment of conception, you inherited 23 from your mother and 23 from your father.

Culture—including art, literature, music, scientific knowledge, and philanthropic activities—is possible only because of the potential of the human genotype.

◆ VARIATION IN THE HUMAN GENOTYPE

You have seen that the conditions in which humans evolved favored the evolution of important shared biological potential: for example, bipedalism and the capacity for thought and language. There remains, however, considerable variation within that shared potential. Your mother and father have endowed you with a part of what their parents, grandparents, and all past generations of their family lines have given them, resulting in a unique biological blueprint and timetable for your development.

The study of the mechanisms of **heredity**—the inheritance of physical and psychological traits from ancestors—is called **genetics.**

The earliest systematic research exploring the relationship between parents and their offspring was published in 1866 by **Gregor Mendel** (1822–1884). Mendel's studies were carried out on the humble garden pea. He was able to demonstrate that the physical features of peas that emerged from different seeds—for example, whether the peas appeared *round* or *wrinkled*—could be predicted from the physical features of the plants from which the seeds had been obtained. Based on his observations, Mendel suggested that pairs of "factors"—one inherited from each parent—determined the properties of the offspring (Lander & Weinberg, 2000). Although Mendel's work originally received little attention from other scientists, modern techniques have allowed researchers to visualize and study Mendel's "factors," which we now call *genes.*

BASIC GENETICS

In the nucleus of each of your cells is genetic material called **DNA** (deoxyribonucleic acid; see **Figure 3.3)**. DNA is organized into tiny units, called **genes.** Genes contain the instructions for the production of proteins. These proteins regulate the body's physiological processes and the expression of phenotypic traits: body build, physical strength, intelligence, and many behavior patterns.

Genes are found on rodlike structures known as *chromosomes.* At the very instant you were conceived, you inherited from your parents 46 chromosomes—23 from your mother and 23 from your father. Each of these chromosomes contains thousands of genes—the union of a sperm and an egg results in only one of many billion possible gene combinations. The **sex**

FIGURE 3.3

Genetic Material

The nucleus of each cell in your body contains a copy of the chromosomes that transmit your genetic inheritance. Each chromosome contains a long strand of DNA arranged in a double helix. Genes are segments of the DNA that contain instructions for the production of the proteins that guide your individual development.

From Lester A. Lefton, Linda Brannon. *Psychology* 8e. Published by Allyn & Bacon, Boston, MA. Copyright © 2003 by Pearson Education. Reprinted by permission of the publisher.

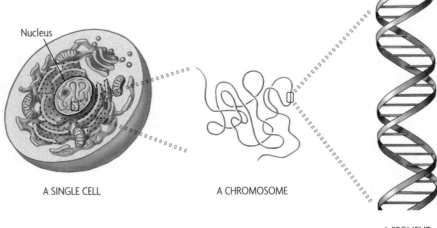

Nucleus

A SINGLE CELL   A CHROMOSOME   A SEGMENT OF DNA

chromosomes are those that contain genes coding for development of male or female physical characteristics. You inherited an X chromosome from your mother and either an X or a Y chromosome from your father. An XX combination codes for development of female characteristics; an XY combination codes for development of male characteristics.

Beginning in 1990, the U. S. government funded an effort called the *Human Genome Project*. The **genome** of an organism is the full sequence of genes found on the chromosomes with the associated DNA. An important goal of the Human Genome Project is to identify all of the 30,000 or so human genes. In 2000, a working draft of the human genome was published in parallel by researchers for the Human Genome Project and the Celera Genomics Corporation. Research is ongoing to improve on this working draft to give a full account of each human chromosome.

GENES AND BEHAVIOR

We have seen that evolutionary processes have allowed a considerable amount of variation to remain in human genotypes; the interactions of these genotypes with particular environments produce variation in human phenotypes. Researchers in the field of **human behavior genetics** unite genetics and psychology to explore the causal link between inheritance and behavior (Plomin et al., 2003).

Research in human behavior genetics often focuses on estimating the **heritability** of particular human traits and behaviors. Heritability is measured on a scale of 0 to 1. If an estimate is near 0, that suggests that the attribute is largely a product of environmental influences; if an estimate is near 1, that suggests that the attribute is largely a product of genetic influences. To tease apart environment and genes, researchers often use *adoption studies* or *twin studies*. For adoption studies, researchers obtain as much information as possible about the birth parents of children who are raised in adoptive homes. As the children develop, researchers assess the relative similarity of children to their birth families—representing genetics—and their adoptive families—representing environment.

In twin studies, researchers examine the extent to which *monozygotic (MZ)* twins and *dizygotic (DZ)* twins show similarity within pairs on particular traits or behaviors. MZ twins share 100 percent of their genetic material whereas DZ twins share roughly 50 percent. (DZ twins are no more genetically alike than any other pair of brothers and sisters.) Researchers compute heritability estimates by determining how much more alike MZ twins are than DZ twins on a particular attribute. Consider a twin study that estimated the extent to which people inherit their ability to perceive distortions in simple melodies.

The Heritability of Pitch Perception

Do your neighbors complain when you sing in the shower? To what extent is your musical ability, or lack thereof, a product of your genetic makeup? Researchers sought to answer this question for one aspect of musical expertise—the ability to perceive distortions in simple tunes (Drayna et al., 2001). Consider the example in **Figure 3.4**. Even if you can't read music, you can *see* that the notes toward the end of the musical phrase have been distorted. But would you *hear* the distortion?

In this experiment, 136 pairs of MZ twins and 148 pairs of DZ twins heard 26 brief tunes and indicated whether each melody was correct or incorrect. The scores of the MZ twins—the number correct out of 26—were more similar, with a correlation of 0.67, than the scores of the DZ twins, with a correlation of 0.44. Based on these data, the researchers obtained a heritability estimate of 0.71. This estimate suggests a large genetic component to pitch perception.

Note that this high heritability estimate does not mean that everyone in a family is going to have the same pitch perception abilities. Just as the same parents will produce some children with blue eyes and some with brown eyes, the same parents will produce some children with exceptional musical ability and some children who are more ordinary. Instead, the high heritability suggests that, with respect to pitch perception, there's relatively little room for life experiences to have an impact on how talented you may or may not become.

Even so, it's important to remember that genes are not destiny. Just because you're tall doesn't mean you will play basketball. Just because you're a woman doesn't mean you will bear children. Also keep in mind that genotypes are expressed in particular contexts. Physical size, for example, is determined jointly by genetic factors and nutritional environment. Physical strength can be developed in both males and females through special exercise programs. Intellectual growth is determined by both genetic potential and educational experiences. Neither genes nor the environment alone determines who you are or what kind of person you ultimately become.

The study of human behavior genetics most often focuses on the origins of individual differences: What factors in your individual genetic inheritance help to explain the way you think and behave? To complement human behavior genetics, two other fields have emerged that take a broader focus on how forces of natural selection affected the behavioral repertoire of humans and other species. Researchers in the field of **sociobiology** provide evolutionary explanations for the social behavior

FIGURE 3.4

Using Distorted Tunes to Study the Heritability of Pitch Perception

If you heard these two melodies played, could you tell which was correct and which was distorted?

and social systems of humans and other animal species. Researchers in **evolutionary psychology** extend those evolutionary explanations to include other aspects of human experience, such as how the mind functions.

Consider the question of happiness: How might an evolutionary perspective explain the human species's general ability to experience happiness? Buss (2000) suggested that some limits are placed on human happiness by the "discrepancies between modern and ancestral environments" (p. 15). For example, although humans evolved in the context of small groups, many people now live in large urban environments in which they are mostly surrounded by large numbers of total strangers. We might no longer have close bonds to the group of individuals that share our space—the types of bonds that could help us weather crises to experience happy lives. What can be done? Although you cannot turn back the tide of cultural evolution that has brought about these changes, you can try to counteract their negative effects by increasing your closeness to your family members and to your friends (Buss, 2000). This example reveals the contrast between the sociobiological emphasis on the human species in a particular environment versus the behavior genetic emphasis on variation within the general pattern for a species. In the remainder of *Psychology and Life*, we will present several more instances in which the evolutionary perspective sheds light on human experience. These examples range from partner choices in relationships (Chapter 11), to emotional expression (Chapter 12), to patterns of aggression (Chapter 17).

PUT YOURSELF TO THE TEST

➤ What role does competition for resources play in the process of natural selection?

➤ What are the roles of genotypes and phenotypes in evolutionary change?

➤ Why were two evolutionary advances most critical in human evolution?

➤ What important contrast exists between research in human behavior genetics and research in evolutionary psychology?

Biology and Behavior

We turn our attention now to the remarkable products of the human genotype: the biological systems that make possible the full range of thought and performance. Long before Darwin made preparations for his trip aboard the *Beagle*, scientists, philosophers, and others debated the role that biological processes play in everyday life. An important figure in the history of brain studies was the French philosopher **René Descartes** (1596–1650).

Descartes proposed what at that time was a very new and very radical idea: The human body is an "animal machine" that can be understood scientifically—by discovering natural laws through empirical observation.

Researchers who pursue these natural laws now call themselves *neuroscientists*. Today, **neuroscience** is one of the most rapidly growing areas of research. Important discoveries come with astonishing regularity. Our discussion of neuroscience begins with an overview of the techniques researchers use to hasten new discoveries. We then offer a general description of the structure of the nervous system, followed by a more detailed look at the brain itself. Finally, we discuss the activity of the endocrine system, a second biological control system that works in cooperation with your nervous system and brain.

◆ EAVESDROPPING ON THE BRAIN

Neuroscientists seek to understand how the brain works at a number of different levels—from the operation of large structures visible to the naked eye to the properties of individual nerve cells visible only under powerful microscopes. The techniques researchers use are suited to their level of analysis. Here, we discuss the techniques that have been used most often to attribute functions and behaviors to particular regions of the brain.

INTERVENTIONS IN THE BRAIN

Several research methods in neuroscience involve direct intervention with structures in the brain. These methods find their historical roots in circumstances like the story of railroad foreman Phineas Gage, who in September 1848 suffered an accident in which a 3-foot, 7-inch-long pole was blown, as the result of an unexpected explosion, clear through his head. Gage's physical impairment was remarkably slight: He lost vision in his left eye, and the left side of his face was partially paralyzed, but his posture, movement, and speech were all unimpaired. Yet, psychologically, he was a changed man, as his doctor's account made clear:

> *The equilibrium or balance, so to speak, between his intellectual faculties and animal propensities seems to have been destroyed. He is fitful, irreverent, indulging at times in the grossest profanity (which was not previously his custom), manifesting but little deference for his fellows, impatient of restraint or advice when it conflicts with his desires. . . . Previous to his injury, though untrained in schools, he possessed a well-balanced mind, and was looked upon by those who knew him as a shrewd, smart businessman, very energetic and persistent in executing all his plans of operation. In this regard his mind was radically changed, so*

> *decidedly that his friends and acquaintances said he was "no longer Gage." (Harlow, 1868, pp. 339–340)*

Gage's injury came at a time when scientists were just beginning to form hypotheses about the links between brain functions and complex behavior. The behavioral changes following the dramatic piercing of his brain prompted his doctor to hypothesize brain bases for aspects of personality and rational behavior.

At about the same time that Gage was convalescing from his injury, **Paul Broca** was studying the brain's role in language. His first research in this area involved an autopsy of a man whose name was derived from the only word he had been able to speak, "Tan." Broca found that the left front portion of Tan's brain had been severely damaged. This finding led Broca to study the brains of other persons who suffered from language impairments. In each case, Broca's work revealed similar damage to the same area of the brain, a region now known as **Broca's area.** As you shall see as *Psychology and Life* unfolds, contemporary researchers still attempt to correlate patterns of behavior change or impairment with the sites of brain damage.

The problem with studying accidentally damaged brains, of course, is that researchers have no control over the location and extent of the damage. To produce a well-founded understanding of the brain and its relationship to behavioral and cognitive functioning, scientists need methods that allow them to specify precisely the brain tissue that has been incapacitated. Researchers have developed a variety of techniques to produce **lesions,** highly localized brain injuries. They may, for example, surgically remove specific brain areas, cut the neural connections to those areas, or destroy those areas through application of intense heat, cold, or electricity. As you would guess, experimental work with permanent lesions is carried out exclusively with nonhuman animals. (Recall our discussion in Chapter 2 that the ethics of this type of animal research has now come under heightened scrutiny.) Our conception of the brain has been radically changed as researchers have repeatedly compared and coordinated the results of lesioning experiments on animals with the growing body of clinical findings on the effects of brain damage on human behavior.

In recent years, scientists have developed a procedure called **repetitive transcranial magnetic stimulation (rTMS)**, which uses pulses of magnetic stimulation to create temporary, reversible "lesions" in human participants—without any damage being done to tissue, brain regions can be briefly inactivated. This new technique enables researchers to address a range of questions that would not have been possible with nonhuman experiments. Consider an application of rTMS to study the brain bases of visual imagery.

Localizing Visual Imagery in the Brain

Take a moment to fix your eyes on an object in your environment, perhaps a tree outside the nearest window. Now close your eyes and form a mental image of that same object. What happened in your brain during these two activities? How likely do you think it is that some of the same brain regions are involved in both real acts of perception and in visual imagination? To answer this question, researchers asked participants to memorize displays with four quadrants (see **Figure 3.5**) and then visualize the displays with their eyes closed (Kosslyn et al., 1999). The participants' task was to answer questions about, for example, the relative length or width of the stripes in the different quadrants. This task was designed so that participants were obliged to form visual images. The researchers then used rTMS to "lesion" the parts of the brain participants use for ordinary vision (which we will discuss in Chapter 4). Just as in the cases in which participants made the quadrant comparisons with their eyes wide open, performance was consistently disrupted in circumstances of visual imagery. This finding strongly suggests that the same brain areas are at work when you look at a tree as when you form a visual image of a tree.

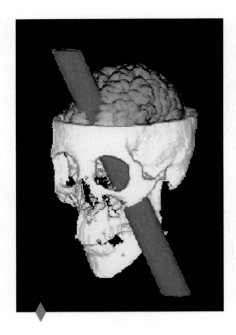

Phineas Gage's skull is preserved in the collections of the Warren Anatomical Museum, Harvard University Medical School. Why were doctors so fascinated by Gage's changes in personality?

You can see why this experiment would not be possible with nonhuman participants: How could we be certain that a rat had formed a visual image? This study illustrates why an ability to create reversible "lesions" has great potential for improving our understanding of how the brain functions.

On other occasions, neuroscientists learn about the function of brain regions by directly *stimulating* them. For example, in the mid-1950s, **Walter Hess** pioneered the use of electrical stimulation to probe structures deep in the brain. For example, Hess put electrodes into the brains of freely moving cats. By pressing a button, he could then send a small electrical current to the point of the electrode. Hess carefully recorded the behavioral consequences of stimulating each of 4,500 brain sites in nearly 500 cats. Hess discovered that, depending on the location of the electrode, sleep, sexual arousal, anxiety, or terror could be provoked by the flick of the switch—and turned off just as abruptly. For example, electrical stimulation of certain regions of the brain led the otherwise gentle cats to bristle with rage and hurl themselves upon a nearby object.

RECORDING AND IMAGING BRAIN ACTIVITY

Other neuroscientists map brain function by using electrodes to record the electrical activity of the brain in response to environmental stimulation. The brain's electrical output can be monitored at different levels of pre-

cision. At the most specific, researchers can insert ultra-sensitive microelectrodes into the brain to record the electrical activity of a single brain cell. Such recordings can illuminate changes in the activity of individual cells in response to stimuli in the environment.

For human subjects, researchers often place a number of electrodes on the surface of the scalp to record larger, integrated patterns of electrical activity. These

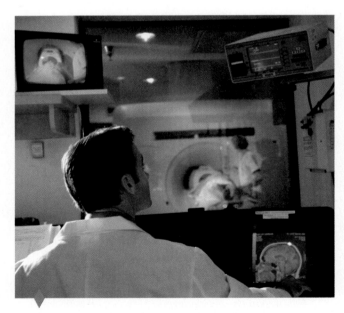

How have new imaging techniques expanded the range of questions researchers can ask?

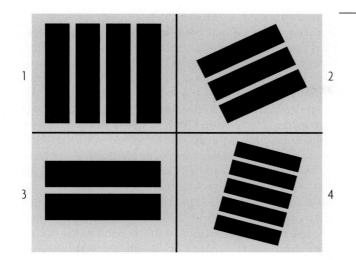

FIGURE 3.5

Test for Visual Imagery

Try to memorize this figure, quadrant by quadrant, until you can form a mental image of all four quadrants. Now cover the display with your hand. Answer this question by creating a mental visual image: Are the lines longer in quadrant 1 or quadrant 2? Confirm your answer by looking back at the figure.

electrodes provide the data for an **electroencephalogram (EEG)**, or an amplified tracing of the brain activity. EEGs can be used to study the relationship between psychological activities and brain response. For example, in one experiment, participants were asked to view a series of faces and make judgments about whether they thought they would be able to recognize each face in a later memory task. The EEGs revealed a distinctive pattern of brain activity, at the time the participants made their judgments, that predicted those instances in which the participants were, in fact, later able to recognize the faces (Sommer et al., 1995).

Some of the most exciting technological innovations for studying the brain are machines originally developed to help neurosurgeons detect brain abnormalities, such as damage caused by strokes or diseases. These devices produce images of the living brain without invasive procedures that risk damaging brain tissue.

In research with positron-emission tomography, or **PET scans,** subjects are given different kinds of radioactive (but safe) substances that eventually travel to the brain, where they are taken up by active brain cells. Recording instruments outside the skull can detect the radioactivity emitted by cells that are active during different cognitive or behavioral activities. This information is then fed into a computer that constructs a dynamic portrait of the brain, showing where different types of psychological activities are actually occurring (see **Figure 3.6**).

Magnetic resonance imaging, or **MRI,** uses magnetic fields and radio waves to generate pulses of energy within the brain. As the pulse is tuned to different frequencies, some atoms line up with the magnetic field. When the magnetic pulse is turned off, the atoms vibrate (resonate) as they return to their original positions. Special radio receivers detect this resonance and channel information to a computer, which generates images of the locations of different atoms in areas of the brain. By looking at the image, researchers can link brain structures to psychological processes.

MRI is most useful for providing clear images of anatomical details; PET scans provide better information about function. A newer technique called **functional MRI,** or **fMRI,** combines some of the benefits of both techniques by detecting magnetic changes in the flow of blood to cells in the brain; fMRI allows more precise claims about both structure and function. Researchers have begun to use fMRI to discover the distributions of brain regions responsible for many of your most important cognitive abilities, such as attention, perception, language processing, and memory (Cabeza & Nyberg, 2000).

More than 300 years have passed since Descartes sat in his candlelit study and mused about the brain; over 100 years have passed since Broca discovered that

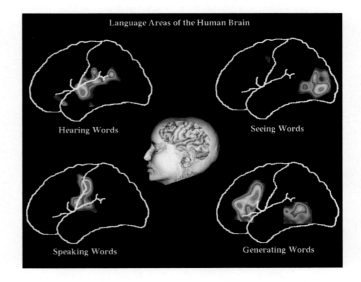

FIGURE 3.6

PET Scans of the Brain at Work

These PET scans show that different tasks stimulate neural activity in distinct regions of the brain.

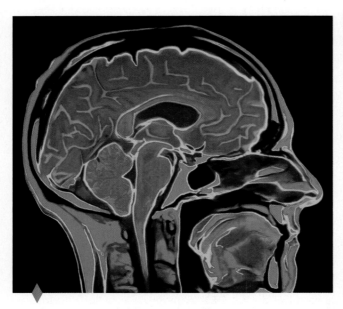
Magnetic resonance imaging (MRI) produces this color-enhanced profile of a normal brain. What is the purpose of trying to identify brain regions that underlie particular functions?

brain regions seem to be linked to specific functions. In the time since these developments, cultural evolution has provided neuroscientists with the technology necessary to reveal some of your brain's most important secrets. The remainder of this chapter describes some of those secrets.

◆ THE NERVOUS SYSTEM

The nervous system is composed of billions of highly specialized nerve cells, or *neurons,* that constitute the brain and the nerve fibers found throughout the body. The nervous system is subdivided into two major divisions: the **central nervous system (CNS)** and the **peripheral nervous system (PNS)**. The CNS is composed of all the neurons in the brain and spinal cord; the PNS is made up of all the neurons forming the nerve fibers that connect the CNS to the body. **Figures 3.7** and **3.8** show the relationship of the CNS to the PNS.

The job of the CNS is to integrate and coordinate all bodily functions, process all incoming neural messages, and send out commands to different parts of the body. The CNS sends and receives neural messages through the *spinal cord,* a trunk line of neurons that connects the brain to the PNS. The trunk line itself is housed in a hollow portion of the vertebral column, called the spinal column. Spinal nerves branch out from the spinal cord between each pair of vertebrae in the spinal column, eventually connecting with sensory receptors throughout the body and with muscles and glands. The spinal cord coordinates the activity of the left and right sides of the body and is responsible for simple, fast action

reflexes that do not involve the brain. For example, an organism whose spinal cord has been severed from its brain can still withdraw its limb from a painful stimulus. Though an intact brain would normally be notified of such action, the organism can complete the action without directions from above. Damage to the nerves of the spinal cord can result in paralysis of the legs or trunk, as seen in paraplegic individuals. The extent of paralysis depends on how high up on the spinal cord the damage occurred; higher damage produces greater paralysis.

Despite its commanding position, the CNS is isolated from any direct contact with the outside world. It is the role of the PNS to provide the CNS with information from sensory receptors, such as those found in the eyes and ears, and to relay commands from the brain to the body's organs and muscles. The PNS is actually composed of two sets of nerve fibers (see Figure 3.8). The **somatic nervous system** regulates the actions of the body's skeletal muscles. For example, imagine you are typing a letter. The movement of your fingers over the keyboard is managed by your somatic nervous system. As you decide what to say, your brain sends commands to your fingers to press certain keys. Simultaneously, the fingers send feedback about their position and movement to the brain. If you strike the wrong key (th**w**), the somatic nervous system informs the brain, which then issues the necessary correction, and, in a fraction of a second, you delete the mistake and hit the right key (th**e**).

The other branch of the PNS is the **autonomic nervous system (ANS)**, which sustains basic life processes. This system is on the job 24 hours a day, regulating bodily functions that you usually don't consciously control, such as respiration, digestion, and arousal. The ANS must work even when you are asleep, and it sustains life processes during anesthesia and prolonged coma states.

The autonomic nervous system deals with survival matters of two kinds: those involving threats to the organism and those involving bodily maintenance. To carry out these functions, the autonomic nervous system is further subdivided into the sympathetic and parasympathetic nervous systems (see Figure 3.8). These divisions work in opposition to accomplish their tasks. The **sympathetic division** governs responses to emergency situations; the **parasympathetic division** monitors the routine operation of the body's internal functions. The sympathetic division can be regarded as a troubleshooter—in an emergency or stressful situation, it arouses the brain structures for "fight or flight." Digestion stops, blood flows away from internal organs to the muscles, oxygen transfer increases, and heart rate increases. After the danger is over, the parasympathetic division takes charge, and the individual begins to calm down. Digestion resumes, heartbeat slows, and breathing is relaxed. The parasympathetic division carries out the body's nonemergency housekeeping chores, such

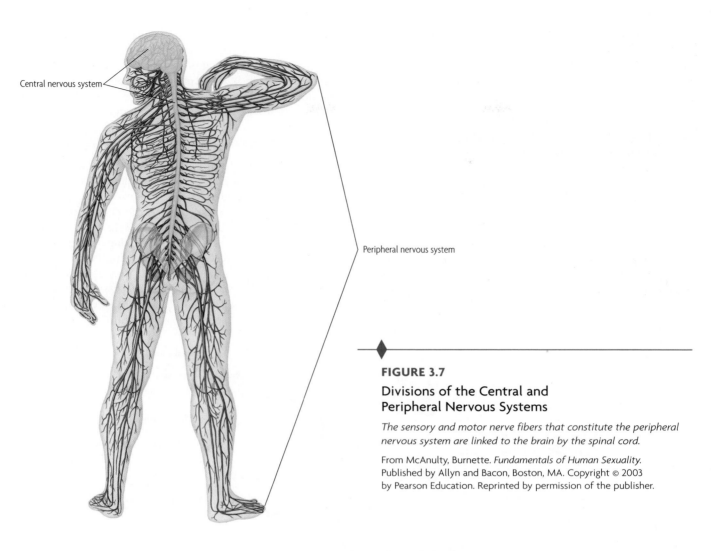

Central nervous system

Peripheral nervous system

FIGURE 3.7

Divisions of the Central and Peripheral Nervous Systems

The sensory and motor nerve fibers that constitute the peripheral nervous system are linked to the brain by the spinal cord.

From McAnulty, Burnette. *Fundamentals of Human Sexuality.* Published by Allyn and Bacon, Boston, MA. Copyright © 2003 by Pearson Education. Reprinted by permission of the publisher.

FIGURE 3.8

Hierarchical Organization of the Human Nervous System

The central nervous system is composed of the brain and the spinal cord. The peripheral nervous system is divided according to function: The somatic nervous system controls voluntary actions, and the autonomic nervous system regulates internal processes. The autonomic nervous system is subdivided into two systems: The sympathetic nervous system governs behavior in emergency situations, and the parasympathetic nervous system regulates behavior and internal processes in routine circumstances.

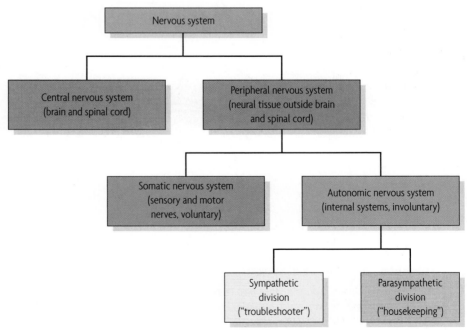

Nervous system

Central nervous system (brain and spinal cord)

Peripheral nervous system (neural tissue outside brain and spinal cord)

Somatic nervous system (sensory and motor nerves, voluntary)

Autonomic nervous system (internal systems, involuntary)

Sympathetic division ("troubleshooter")

Parasympathetic division ("housekeeping")

as elimination of bodily wastes, protection of the visual system (through tears and pupil constriction), and long-term conservation of body energy. The separate duties of the sympathetic and parasympathetic nervous systems are illustrated in **Figure 3.9.**

◆ BRAIN STRUCTURES AND THEIR FUNCTIONS

The brain is the most important component of your central nervous system. The brains of human beings have three interconnected layers. In the deepest recesses of the brain, in a region called the *brain stem,* are structures involved primarily with autonomic processes such as heart rate, breathing, swallowing, and digestion. Enveloping this central core is the *limbic system,* which is involved with motivation, emotion, and memory processes. Wrapped around these two regions is the *cerebrum.* The universe of the human mind exists in this region. The cerebrum, and its surface layer, the *cerebral cortex,* integrates sensory information, coordinates your movements, and facilitates abstract thinking and reasoning (see **Figure 3.10**). Let's look more closely at the functions of the three major brain regions, beginning with the brain stem, thalamus, and cerebellum.

THE BRAIN STEM, THALAMUS, AND CEREBELLUM

The **brain stem** is found in all vertebrate species. It contains structures that collectively regulate the internal state of the body (see **Figure 3.11**). The **medulla,** located at the very top of the spinal cord, is the center for breathing, blood pressure, and the beating of the heart. Because these processes are essential for life, damage to the medulla can be fatal. Nerve fibers ascending from the body and descending from the brain cross over at the medulla, which means that the left side of the body is linked to the right side of the brain and the right side of the body is connected to the left side of the brain.

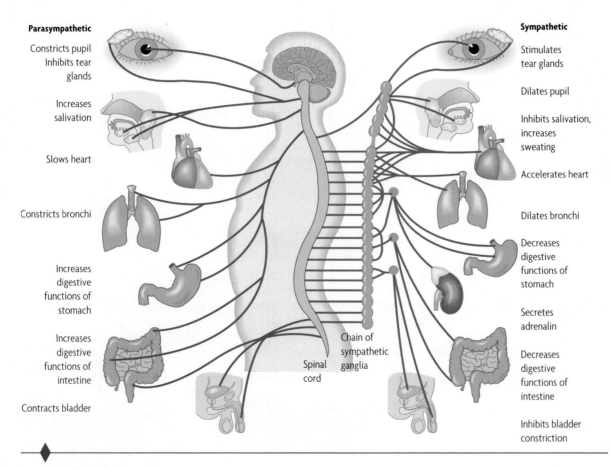

Parasympathetic

Constricts pupil
Inhibits tear glands

Increases salivation

Slows heart

Constricts bronchi

Increases digestive functions of stomach

Increases digestive functions of intestine

Contracts bladder

Sympathetic

Stimulates tear glands

Dilates pupil

Inhibits salivation, increases sweating

Accelerates heart

Dilates bronchi

Decreases digestive functions of stomach

Secretes adrenalin

Decreases digestive functions of intestine

Inhibits bladder constriction

Chain of sympathetic ganglia

Spinal cord

FIGURE 3.9

The Autonomic Nervous System

The parasympathetic nervous system, which regulates day-to-day internal processes and behavior, is shown on the left. The sympathetic nervous system, which regulates internal processes and behavior in stressful situations, is shown on the right. Note that on their way to and from the spinal cord, the nerve fibers of the sympathetic nervous system innervate, or make connections with, ganglia, which are specialized clusters of neuron chains.

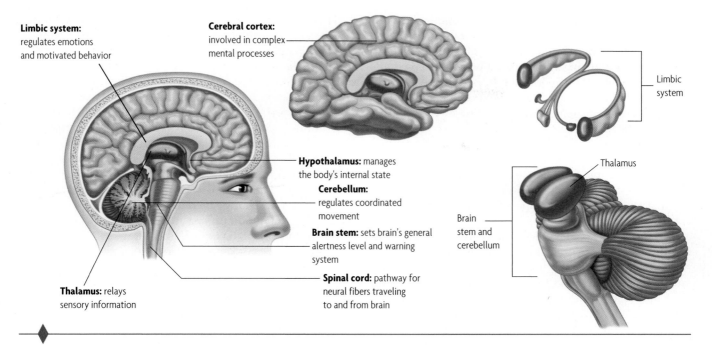

FIGURE 3.10

Brain Structures

The brain contains several major components, including the brain stem, cerebellum, limbic system, and cerebral cortex, all of which fit together in an intricate design.

Labels in figure 3.10:

Limbic system: regulates emotions and motivated behavior

Cerebral cortex: involved in complex mental processes

Limbic system

Hypothalamus: manages the body's internal state

Cerebellum: regulates coordinated movement

Brain stem: sets brain's general alertness level and warning system

Spinal cord: pathway for neural fibers traveling to and from brain

Thalamus: relays sensory information

Thalamus

Brain stem and cerebellum

FIGURE 3.11

The Brain Stem, Thalamus, and Cerebellum

These structures are primarily involved in basic life processes: breathing, pulse, arousal, movement, balance, and simple processing of sensory information.

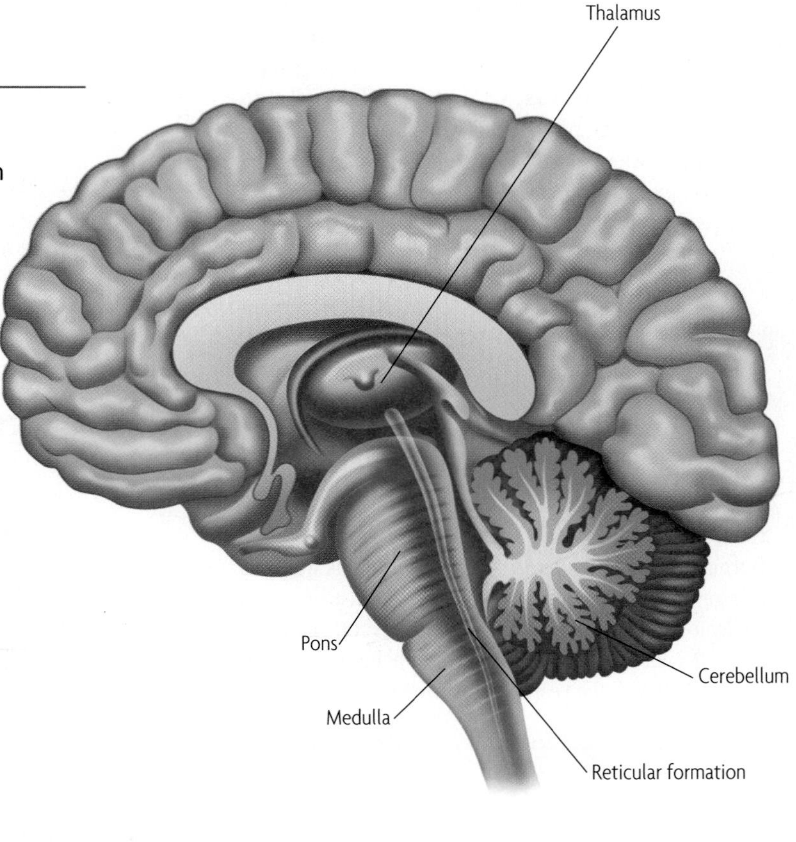

Labels in figure 3.11:

Thalamus

Pons

Medulla

Cerebellum

Reticular formation

Directly above the medulla is the **pons,** which provides inputs to other structures in the brain stem and to the cerebellum (*pons* is the Latin word for *bridge*). The **reticular formation** is a dense network of nerve cells that serves as the brain's sentinel. It arouses the cerebral cortex to attend to new stimulation and keeps the brain alert even during sleep. Massive damage to this area often results in a coma.

The reticular formation has long tracts of fibers that run to the **thalamus,** which channels incoming sensory information to the appropriate area of the cerebral cortex, where that information is processed. For example, the thalamus relays information from the eyes to cortical areas for vision.

Neuroscientists have long known that the **cerebellum,** attached to the brain stem at the base of the skull, coordinates bodily movements, controls posture, and maintains equilibrium. Damage to the cerebellum interrupts the flow of otherwise smooth movement, causing it to appear uncoordinated and jerky. More recent research suggests that the cerebellum also plays an important role in the ability to learn and perform sequences of body movements (Hazeltine & Ivry, 2002; Seidler et al., 2002).

THE LIMBIC SYSTEM

The **limbic system** mediates motivated behaviors, emotional states, and memory processes. It also regulates body temperature, blood pressure, and blood-sugar level and performs other housekeeping activities. The limbic system comprises three structures: the hippocampus, amygdala, and hypothalamus (see **Figure 3.12**).

The **hippocampus,** which is the largest of the limbic system structures, plays an important role in the acquisition of memories. Considerable clinical evidence supports this conclusion, including the notable studies of a patient, H.M., perhaps psychology's most famous subject:

CLASSIC
PUTTING IDEAS TO THE TEST

Some Consequences of Hippocampal Damage

When he was 27, H.M. underwent surgery in an attempt to reduce the frequency and severity of his epileptic seizures. During the operation, parts of his hippocampus were removed. As a result, H.M. could recall only the very distant past; his ability to put new information into long-term memory was gone. Long after his surgery, he continued to believe he was living in 1953, which was the year the operation was performed.

There are, however, some types of new memories that can still be formed after damage to the hippocampus. For example, H.M. was able to acquire new skills. This pattern suggests that if you were in an accident and sustained damage to your hippocampus, you would still be able to learn some new tasks, but you would not be able to remember having done so! As researchers have continued to focus attention on the hippocampus, they have come to a more detailed understanding of how even different regions of the structure play roles in the acquisition of different types of memories (Zeineh et al., 2003). In Chapter 7, we will return to the functions of the hippocampus for memory acquisition.

The **amygdala** plays a role in emotional control and the formation of emotional memories. Because of this control function, damage to areas of the amygdala may have a calming effect on otherwise mean-spirited individuals. (We discuss *psychosurgery* in Chapter 15.) However, damage to some areas of the amygdala also impairs the ability to recognize the emotional content of facial expressions (Adolphs et al., 1994). Those individuals who have suffered amygdala damage are most impaired with respect to negative emotional expressions, especially fear. Researchers speculate that the amygdala may play a special role in people's acquisition and use of knowledge related to threat and danger (Adolphs et al., 1999).

The **hypothalamus** is one of the smallest structures in the brain, yet it plays a vital role in many of your most important daily actions. It is actually composed of several nuclei, small bundles of neurons that regulate physiological processes involved in motivated behavior (including eating, drinking, temperature regulation, and sexual arousal). The hypothalamus maintains the body's internal equilibrium, or **homeostasis.** When the body's energy reserves are low, the hypothalamus is involved in stimulating the organism to find food and to eat. When body temperature drops, the hypothalamus causes blood-vessel constriction, or minute involuntary movements you commonly refer to as the "shivers." The hypothalamus also regulates the activities of the endocrine system.

THE CEREBRUM

In humans, the **cerebrum** dwarfs the rest of the brain, occupying two-thirds of its total mass. Its role is to regulate the brain's higher cognitive and emotional functions. The outer surface of the cerebrum, made up of billions of cells in a layer about a tenth of an inch thick, is called the **cerebral cortex.** The cerebrum is also divided into two almost symmetrical halves, the **cerebral hemispheres** (we discuss the two hemispheres at length in a later section of this chapter). The two hemispheres are connected by a thick mass of nerve fibers, collectively referred to as the **corpus callosum.** This pathway sends messages back and forth between the hemispheres.

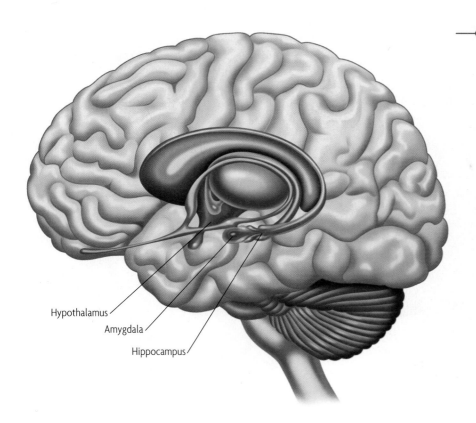

FIGURE 3.12

The Limbic System

The structures of the limbic system, which are present only in mammals, are involved in motivated behavior, emotional states, and memory processes.

Hypothalamus

Amygdala

Hippocampus

Neuroscientists have mapped each hemisphere, using two important landmarks as their guides. One groove, called the *central sulcus,* divides each hemisphere vertically, and a second similar groove, called the *lateral fissure,* divides each hemisphere horizontally (see **Figure 3.13**). These vertical and horizontal divisions help define four areas, or brain lobes, in each hemisphere. The **frontal lobe,** which is involved in motor control and cognitive activities, such as planning, making decisions, and setting goals, is located above the lateral fissure and in front of the central sulcus. Accidents that damage the frontal lobes can have devastating effects on human action and personality. This was the location of the injury that brought about such a dramatic change in Phineas Gage (Damasio et al., 1994). The **parietal lobe** is responsible for sensations of touch, pain, and temperature and is located directly behind the central sulcus. The **occipital lobe,** the final destination for visual information, is located at the back of the head. The **temporal lobe,** which is responsible for the processes of hearing, is found below the lateral fissure, on the sides of each cerebral hemisphere.

It would be misleading to say that any lobe alone controls any one specific function. The structures of the brain perform their duties in concert, working smoothly as an integrated unit, similar to a symphony orchestra. Whether you are doing the dishes, solving a calculus problem, or carrying on a conversation with a friend, your brain works as a unified whole, each lobe interacting and

cooperating with the others. Nevertheless, neuroscientists can identify areas of the four lobes of the cerebrum that are necessary for specific functions, such as vision, hearing, language, and memory. When they are damaged, their functions are disrupted or lost entirely.

The actions of the body's voluntary muscles, of which there are more than 600, are controlled by the **motor cortex,** located just in front of the central sulcus in the frontal lobes. Recall that commands from one side of the brain are directed to muscles on the opposite side of the body. Also, muscles in the lower part of the body—for example, the toes—are controlled by neurons in the top part of the motor cortex. Muscles in the upper part of the body, such as the throat, are controlled by neurons in the lower part of the motor cortex. As you can see in **Figure 3.14,** the upper parts of the body receive far more detailed motor instructions than the lower parts. In fact, the two largest areas of the motor cortex are devoted to the fingers—especially the thumb—and to the muscles involved in speech. Their greater brain area reflects the importance in human activity of manipulating objects, using tools, eating, and talking.

The **somatosensory cortex** is located just behind the central sulcus in the left and right parietal lobes. This part of the cortex processes information about temperature, touch, body position, and pain. Similar to the motor cortex, the upper part of the sensory cortex relates to the lower parts of the body, and the lower part to the upper parts of the body. Most of the area of the sensory cortex

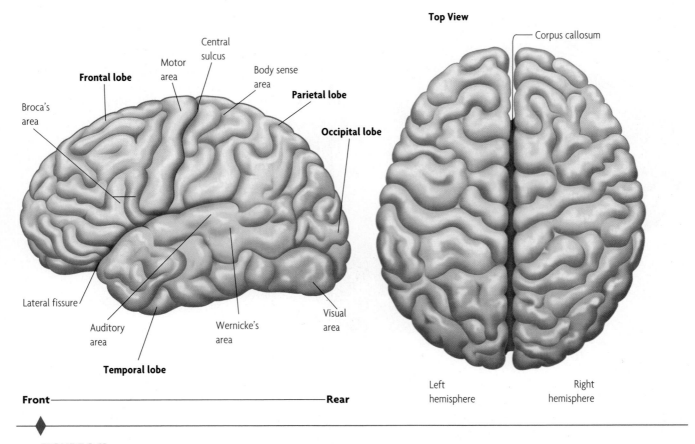

Top View

Corpus callosum

Central
sulcus

Motor
area

Body sense
area

Frontal lobe

Parietal lobe

Broca's
area

Occipital lobe

Lateral fissure

Visual
area

Auditory
area

Wernicke's
area

Temporal lobe

Front ——————————————— **Rear**

Left
hemisphere

Right
hemisphere

FIGURE 3.13

The Cerebral Cortex

Each of the two hemispheres of the cerebral cortex has four lobes.
Different sensory and motor functions are associated with specific parts of each lobe.

is devoted to the lips, tongue, thumb, and index fingers—the parts of the body that provide the most important sensory input (see Figure 3.14). And like the motor cortex, the right half of the somatosensory cortex communicates with the left side of the body, and the left half communicates with the right side of the body.

Auditory information is processed in the **auditory cortex,** which is in the two temporal lobes. The auditory cortex in each hemisphere receives information from *both* ears. One area of the auditory cortex is involved in the production of language, and a different area is involved in language comprehension. Visual input is processed at the back of the brain in the **visual cortex,** located in the occipital lobes. Here the greatest area is devoted to input from the center part of the retina, at the back of the eye, the area that transmits the most detailed visual information.

Not all of the cerebral cortex is devoted to processing sensory information and commanding the muscles to action. In fact, the majority of it is involved in

interpreting and *integrating* information. Processes such as planning and decision making are believed to occur in the **association cortex.** Association areas are distributed to several areas of the cortex—one region is labeled in Figure 3.14. The association cortex allows you to combine information from various sensory modalities to plan appropriate responses to stimuli in the environment.

How do these different areas of the brain work in unison? Consider, as an example, what happens in your brain when you speak a written word (see **Figure 3.15**). Imagine that your psychology instructor hands you a piece of paper with the word *chocolate* written on it and asks you to say the word aloud. The biological processes involved in this action are surprisingly subtle and complex. Neuroscience can break down your verbal behavior into numerous steps. First, the visual stimulus (the written word *chocolate*) is detected by the nerve cells in the retinas of your eyes, which send nerve impulses to the visual cortex (via the thalamus). The visual cortex

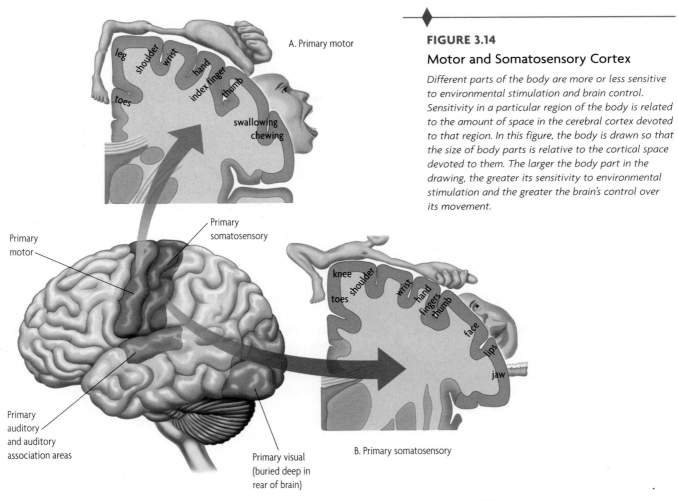

A. Primary motor

leg
shoulder
wrist
hand
index finger
thumb
toes
swallowing
chewing

Primary motor

Primary somatosensory

Primary auditory and auditory association areas

Primary visual (buried deep in rear of brain)

knee
shoulder
toes
wrist
hand
fingers
thumb
face
lips
jaw

B. Primary somatosensory

FIGURE 3.14

Motor and Somatosensory Cortex

Different parts of the body are more or less sensitive to environmental stimulation and brain control. Sensitivity in a particular region of the body is related to the amount of space in the cerebral cortex devoted to that region. In this figure, the body is drawn so that the size of body parts is relative to the cortical space devoted to them. The larger the body part in the drawing, the greater its sensitivity to environmental stimulation and the greater the brain's control over its movement.

FIGURE 3.15

How a Written Word Is Spoken

Nerve impulses, laden with information about the written word, are sent by the retinas to the visual association area of the cortex via the thalamus. The visual cortex sends the nerve impulses to an area in the rear of the temporal lobe, the angular gyrus, where visual coding for the word (the arrangement of letters and their shapes, etc.) is compared with its acoustical coding (the way it sounds). Once the proper acoustical code is found, it is relayed to an area of the auditory cortex known as Wernicke's area. Here it is encoded and interpreted. Nerve impulses are sent to Broca's area, which sends the message to the motor cortex. The motor cortex puts the word in your mouth by stimulating the lips, tongue, and larynx to act in synchrony.

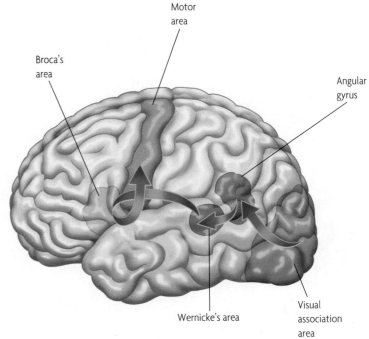

Motor area

Broca's area

Angular gyrus

Wernicke's area

Visual association area

Speaking a written word

then sends nerve impulses to an area in the rear of the temporal lobe (called the angular gyrus) where visual coding for the word is compared with its acoustical coding. Once the proper acoustical code is located, it is relayed to an area of the auditory cortex known as *Wernicke's area,* where it is decoded and interpreted: "Ah! Chocolate! I'd like some now." Nerve impulses are then sent to Broca's area, which, in turn, sends a message to the motor cortex, stimulating the lips, tongue, and larynx to produce the word *chocolate.*

That's a lot of mental effort for just one word. Now imagine what you require of your brain every time you read aloud a book or even a billboard. The truly amazing thing is that your brain responds effortlessly and intelligently, translating thousands of marks on paper into a neurological code, informing other brain areas about what's going on, and, finally, putting words in your mouth.

We have now reviewed the many important structures in your nervous system. When we began to talk about the cerebrum, we noted that each cerebral structure is represented in both hemispheres of your brain. However, the structures in those two hemispheres play somewhat different functions with respect to many types of behaviors. We turn now to those differences between your brain's two hemispheres.

◆ HEMISPHERIC LATERALIZATION

What types of information originally led researchers to suspect that there are differences in the functions of the brain's two hemispheres? Recall that when Paul Broca carried out his autopsy on Tan, he discovered damage in the left hemisphere. As he followed up this original discovery, Broca found that other patients who showed similar disruption of their language abilities—a pattern now known as *Broca's aphasia*—also had damage on the *left* side of their brains. Damage to the same areas on the *right* side of the brain did not have the same effect. What should one conclude?

The chance to investigate hemispheric differences first arose in the context of a treatment for severe epilepsy in which surgeons sever the corpus callosum—the bundle of about 200 million nerve fibers that transfers information back and forth between the two hemispheres (see **Figure 3.16**). The goal of this surgery is to prevent the violent electrical activity that accompanies epileptic seizures from crossing between the hemispheres. The operation is usually successful, and a patient's subsequent behavior in most circumstances appears normal. Patients who undergo this type of surgery are often referred to as *split-brain* patients.

To test the capabilities of the separated hemispheres of epileptic patients, **Roger Sperry** (1968) and **Michael Gazzaniga** (1970) devised situations that could allow visual information to be presented sepa-

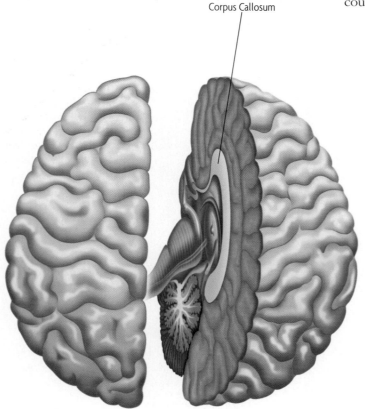

Corpus Callosum

FIGURE 3.16

The Corpus Callosum

The corpus callosum is a massive network of nerve fibers that channels information between the two hemispheres. Severing the corpus callosum impairs this communication process.

rately to each hemisphere. Sperry and Gazzaniga's methodology relies on the anatomy of the visual system (see **Figure 3.17**). For each eye, information from the *right visual field* goes to the left hemisphere, and information from the *left visual field* goes to the right hemisphere. Ordinarily, information arriving from both hemispheres is shared very quickly across the corpus callosum. But because these pathways have been severed in split-brain patients, information presented to the right or left visual field may remain only in the left or right hemisphere (see **Figure 3.18**).

Because for most people speech is controlled by the left hemisphere, the left hemisphere could "talk back" to the researchers whereas the right hemisphere could not. Communication with the right hemisphere was achieved by confronting it with manual tasks involving identification, matching, or assembly of objects—tasks that did not require the use of words. Consider the following demonstration of a split-brain subject using his left half brain to account for the activity of his left hand, which was being guided by his right half brain:

Two Hemispheres in Action

A snow scene was presented to the right hemisphere and a picture of a chicken claw was simultaneously presented to the left hemisphere. The subject selected, from an array of objects, those that "went with" each of the two scenes. With his right hand, the patient pointed to a chicken head; with his left hand, he pointed to a shovel. The patient reported that the shovel was needed to clean out the chicken shed (rather than to shovel snow). Since the left brain was not privy to what the right brain "saw" because of the severed corpus callosum, it needed to explain why the left hand was pointing at a shovel when the only picture the left hemisphere was aware of seeing was a chicken claw. The left brain's cognitive system provided a theory to make sense of the behavior of different parts of its body (Gazzaniga, 1985).

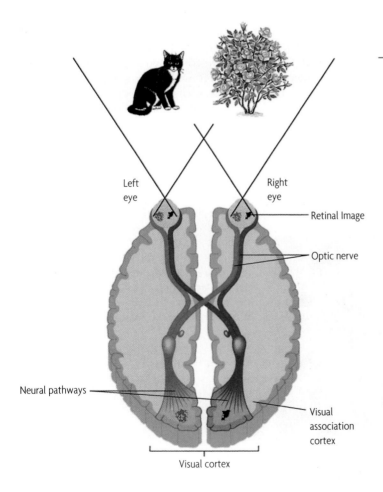

FIGURE 3.17

The Neural Pathways for Visual Information

The neural pathways for visual information coming from the inside portions of each eye cross from one side of the brain to the other at the corpus callosum. The pathways carrying information from the outside portions of each eye do not cross over. Severing the corpus callosum prevents information selectively displayed in the right visual field from entering the right hemisphere, and left visual field information cannot enter the left hemisphere.

Left eye

Right eye

Retinal Image

Optic nerve

Neural pathways

Visual association cortex

Visual cortex

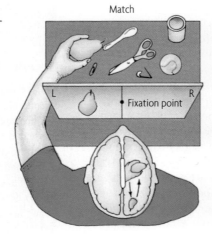
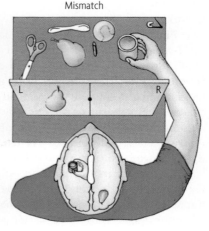

FIGURE 3.18

Coordination Between Eye and Hand

Coordination between eye and hand is normal if a split-brain patient uses the left hand to find and match an object that appears in the left visual field, because both are registered in the right hemisphere. However, when asked to use the right hand to match an object seen in the left visual field, the patient cannot do so, because sensory messages from the right hand are going to the left cerebral hemisphere, and there is no longer a connection between the two hemispheres. Here the cup is misperceived as matching the pear.

From a variety of research methods in addition to split-brain studies, we now know that, for most people, many language-related functions are *lateralized* to the left hemisphere. A function is considered lateralized when one cerebral hemisphere plays the primary role in accomplishing that function. Speech—the ability to produce coherent spoken language—is perhaps the most highly lateralized of all functions. Neuroscientists have found that only about 5 percent of right-handers and 15 percent of left-handers have speech controlled by the right hemisphere, while another 15 percent of left-handers have speech processes occurring in both sides of the brain (Rasmussen & Milner, 1977). For most people, therefore, speech is a left-hemisphere function. As a consequence, damage to the left side of most people's brains can cause speech disorders. What is interesting is that for users of languages like American Sign Language—which use systems of intricate hand positions and movements to convey meaning—left-brain damage is similarly disruptive (Corina & McBurney,

2001; Hickok et al., 2002). What is lateralized, therefore, is not speech as such, but rather, the ability to produce the sequences of gestures—either vocal or manual—that encode communicative meaning.

You should not conclude that the left hemisphere is somehow "better" than the right hemisphere. Researchers have suggested that each hemisphere has a different "style" for processing the same information. The left hemisphere tends to be more *analytical*: It processes information bit by bit. The right hemisphere tends to be more *holistic*: It processes information with respect to global patterns. It is the combined action of the right and left hemispheres—each with its particular processing style—that gives fullness to your experiences. For example, you wouldn't be surprised to learn that the left hemisphere, with its attention to fine detail, plays a key role in most forms of problem solving. However, the function of the right hemisphere becomes more apparent when problems require creative solutions or bursts of insight—the right hemisphere helps problem solvers

How have studies with individuals who use sign language influenced researchers' beliefs about the lateralization of brain function?

<www.ablongman.com/gerrig17e>

do the broader searches of memory that these types of problems require (Bowden & Beeman, 1998). (If you want to put your right hemisphere to work, you can skip ahead to try some of these types of problems on p. 266 in Chapter 8).

Although researchers can confidently make claims about the way in which functions are lateralized in the "average" brain, as with all aspects of human experience there are measurable differences among individuals. When we introduced the lateralization of speech, we also introduced a first individual difference in brain function: Left-handers are somewhat more likely to have speech dominated by their right hemisphere or equally present in both hemispheres. Another distinction that appears to matter greatly with respect to brain lateralization is male versus female: There are general differences in the way that male and female brains carry out their functions (Breedlove, 1994; Kimura, 1999). With brain imaging techniques, it has become relatively easy to look for differences in the regions of men's and women's brains that are brought into action for different tasks. For example, one team of researchers used MRI to demonstrate that the brains of men and women become activated in different ways when they make judgments based on language sounds (e.g., Does *sud*

rhyme with *wud*?). The brain activity in men was largely localized in the left hemisphere, whereas this task was more likely to engage both left- and right-brain activity for women (Shaywitz et al., 1995). Results like this one return us to the issue of *nature* versus *nurture*. Do males and females come into the world with different brains, or do life experiences modify their brains along the way? The techniques of contemporary neuroscience should allow for a rigorous answer to this question over the next several years.

We have now reviewed the many important structures of your nervous system. Let's now consider the endocrine system, a bodily system that functions in close cooperation with the nervous system to regulate bodily functions.

◆ THE ENDOCRINE SYSTEM

The human genotype specifies a second highly complex regulatory system, the **endocrine system,** to supplement the work of the nervous system. The endocrine system is a network of glands that manufacture and secrete chemical messengers called **hormones** into the bloodstream (see **Figure 3.19**). Hormones are important in everyday functioning, although they are more

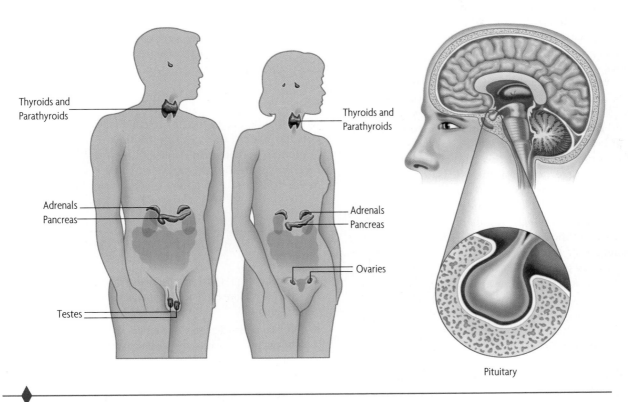

FIGURE 3.19

Endocrine Glands in Males and Females

The pituitary gland is shown at the far right; it is the master gland that regulates the glands shown at the left. The pituitary gland is under the control of the hypothalamus, an important structure in the limbic system.

vital at some stages of life and in some situations than others. Hormones influence body growth. They initiate, maintain, and stop development of primary and secondary sexual characteristics; influence levels of arousal and awareness; serve as the basis for mood changes; and regulate metabolism, the rate at which the body uses its energy stores. The endocrine system promotes the survival of an *organism* by helping fight infections and disease. It advances the survival of the *species* through regulation of sexual arousal, production of reproductive cells, and production of milk in nursing mothers. Thus, you could not survive without an effective endocrine system.

Endocrine glands respond to the levels of chemicals in the bloodstream or are stimulated by other hormones or by nerve impulses from the brain. Hormones are then secreted into the blood and travel to distant target cells that have specific receptors; hormones exert their influence on the body's program of chemical regulation only at the places that are genetically predetermined to respond to them. In influencing diverse, but specific, target organs or tissue, hormones regulate an enormous range of biochemical processes. This multiple-action communication system allows for control of slow, continuous processes such as maintenance of blood-sugar levels and calcium levels, metabolism of carbohydrates, and general body growth. But what happens during crises? The endocrine system also releases the hormone adrenaline into the bloodstream; adrenaline energizes your body so that you can respond quickly to challenges.

As we mentioned earlier, the brain structure known as the *hypothalamus* serves as a relay station between the endocrine system and the central nervous system. Specialized cells in the hypothalamus receive messages from other brain cells, commanding it to release a number of different hormones to the pituitary gland, where they either stimulate or inhibit the release of other hormones. Hormones are produced in several different regions of the body. These "factories" make a variety of hormones, each of which regulates different bodily processes, as outlined in **Table 3.1.** Let's examine the most significant of these processes.

The **pituitary gland** is often called the "master gland," because it produces about ten different kinds of hormones that influence the secretions of all the other endocrine glands, as well as a hormone that influences growth. The absence of this growth hormone results in dwarfism; its excess results in gigantic growth. In males, pituitary secretions activate the testes to secrete **testosterone,** which stimulates production of sperm. The pituitary gland is also involved in the development of male secondary sexual characteristics, such as facial hair, voice change, and physical maturation. Testosterone may even increase aggression and sexual desire. In females, a pituitary hormone stimulates production of **estrogen,**

TABLE 3.1

Major Endocrine Glands and the Functions of the Hormones They Produce

These Glands:	Produce Hormones That Regulate:
Hypothalamus	Release of pituitary hormones
Anterior pituitary	Testes and ovaries
	Breast milk production
	Metabolism
	Reactions to stress
Posterior pituitary	Water conservation
	Breast milk excretion
	Uterus contraction
Thyroid	Metabolism
	Growth and development
Parathyroid	Calcium levels
Gut	Digestion
Pancreas	Glucose metabolism
Adrenals	Fight or flight responses
	Metabolism
	Sexual desire in women
Ovaries	Development of female sexual traits
	Ova production
Testes	Development of male sexual traits
	Sperm production
	Sexual desire in men

which is essential to the hormonal chain reaction that triggers the release of ova from a woman's ovaries, making her fertile. Certain birth-control pills work by blocking the mechanism in the pituitary gland that controls this hormone flow, thus preventing the ova from being released.

PUT YOURSELF TO THE TEST

➤ What techniques have neuroscientists developed that enable them to explore the functions of different structures within the brain?

➤ Why do neuroscientists make distinctions between and within the central and peripheral nervous systems?

➤ What major functions are served by the brain stem, cerebellum, the structures of the limbic system, and the cerebrum?

➤ What processing styles are reflected by the two hemispheres of the brain?

➤ What are the major functions of the endocrine system?

The Nervous System in Action

One of the major goals of early physiologists was to better understand how the nervous system operates. Modern neuroscientists have made steady progress toward this goal, but they continue to work on solving more fine-grained pieces of the puzzle. Our objective in this section is to analyze and understand how the information available to your senses is ultimately communicated throughout your body and brain by nerve impulses. We begin by discussing the properties of the basic unit of the nervous system, the neuron.

◆ THE NEURON

A **neuron** is a cell specialized to receive, process, and/or transmit information to other cells within the body. Neurons vary in shape, size, chemical composition, and function—over 200 different types have been identified in mammal brains—but all neurons have the same basic structure (see **Figure 3.20**). There are from 100 billion to 1 trillion neurons in your brain.

Neurons typically take in information at one end and send out messages from the other. The part of the cell that receives incoming signals is a set of branched fibers called **dendrites,** which extend outward from the cell body. The basic job of the dendrites is to receive stimulation from sense receptors or other neurons. The

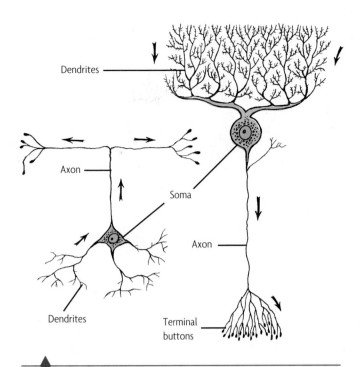

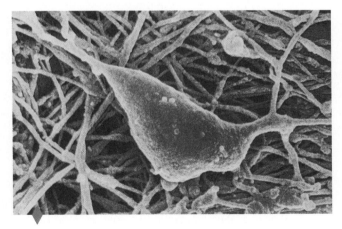

A neuron that affects contractions in the human intestine. What are the roles of the dendrites, soma, and axons in neural transmission?

cell body, or **soma,** contains the nucleus of the cell and the cytoplasm that sustains its life. The soma integrates information about the stimulation received from the dendrites (or in some cases received directly from another neuron) and passes it on to a single, extended fiber, the **axon.** In turn, the axon conducts this information along its length—which, in the spinal cord, can be several feet and, in the brain, less than a millimeter. At the other end of axons are swollen, bulblike structures called **terminal buttons,** through which the neuron is able to stimulate nearby glands, muscles, or other neurons. Neurons generally transmit information in only one direction: from the dendrites through the soma to the axon to the terminal buttons (see **Figure 3.21**).

There are three major classes of neurons. **Sensory neurons** carry messages from sense receptor cells *toward* the central nervous system. Receptor cells are highly specialized cells that are sensitive, for example, to light, sound, and body position. **Motor neurons** carry messages *away* from the central nervous system toward the muscles and glands. The bulk of the neurons in the brain are **interneurons,** which relay messages from sensory neurons to other interneurons or to motor neurons. For every motor neuron in the body

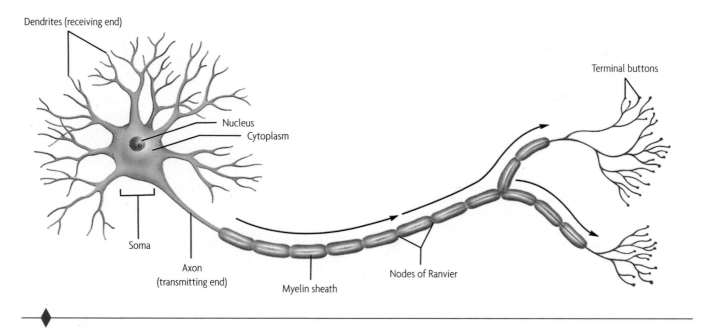

Dendrites (receiving end)

Terminal buttons

Nucleus
Cytoplasm

Soma

Axon
(transmitting end)

Myelin sheath

Nodes of Ranvier

FIGURE 3.21

The Major Structures of the Neuron

The neuron receives nerve impulses through its dendrites. It then sends the nerve impulses through its axon to the terminal buttons, where neurotransmitters are released to stimulate other neurons.

there are as many as 5,000 interneurons in the great intermediate network that forms the computational system of the brain.

As an example of how these three kinds of neurons work together, consider the pain withdrawal reflex (see **Figure 3.22**). When pain receptors near the skin's surface are stimulated by a sharp object, they send messages via sensory neurons to an interneuron in the spinal cord. The interneuron responds by stimulating motor neurons, which, in turn, excite muscles in the appropriate area of the body to pull away from the pain-producing object. It is only *after* this sequence of neuronal events has taken place, and the body has been moved away from the stimulating object, that the brain receives information about the situation. In cases such as this, where survival depends on swift action, your perception of pain often occurs after you have physically responded to the danger. Of course, then the information from the incident is stored in the brain's memory system so that the next time you will avoid the potentially dangerous object altogether, before it can hurt you.

Interspersed among the brain's vast web of neurons are about five to ten times as many glial cells (**glia**). The word *glia* is derived from the Greek word for *glue,* which gives you a hint of one of the major duties per-

formed by these cells: They hold neurons in place. In vertebrates, glial cells have several other important functions. A first function applies during development. Glial cells help guide newborn neurons to appropriate locations in the brain. A second function is housekeeping. When neurons are damaged and die, glial cells in the area multiply and clean up the cellular junk left behind; they can also take up excess neurotransmitters and other substances at the gaps between neurons. A third function is insulation. Glial cells form an insulating cover, called a *myelin sheath,* around some types of axons. This fatty insulation greatly increases the speed of nerve signal conduction. A fourth function of glial cells is to prevent toxic substances in the blood from reaching the delicate cells of the brain. Specialized glial cells, called astrocytes, make up a *blood–brain barrier,* forming a continuous envelope of fatty material around the blood vessels in the brain. Substances that are not soluble in fat do not dissolve through this barrier, and because many poisons and other harmful substances are not fat soluble, they cannot penetrate the barrier to reach the brain. Finally, neuroscientists have come to believe that glia may play an active role in neural communication by affecting the concentrations of ions that allow for the transmission of nerve impulses (Fields & Stevens-Graham, 2002).

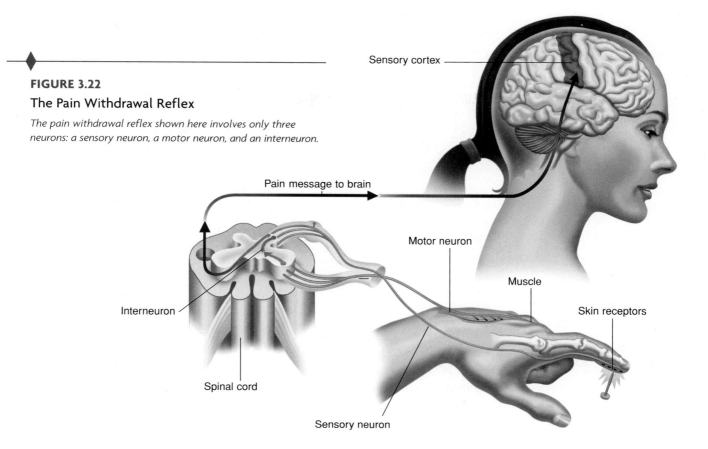

FIGURE 3.22

The Pain Withdrawal Reflex

The pain withdrawal reflex shown here involves only three neurons: a sensory neuron, a motor neuron, and an interneuron.

Sensory cortex

Pain message to brain

Motor neuron

Muscle

Skin receptors

Interneuron

Spinal cord

Sensory neuron

◆ ACTION POTENTIALS

So far, we have spoken loosely about neurons "sending messages" or "stimulating" each other. The time has come to describe more formally the kinds of electrochemical signals used by the nervous system to process and transmit information. These signals are the basis of all you know, feel, desire, and create.

The basic question asked of each neuron is: Should it or should it not *fire*—produce a response—at some given time? In loose terms, neurons make this decision by combining the information arriving at their dendrites and soma (cell body) and determining whether those inputs are predominantly saying "fire" or "don't fire." More formally, each neuron will receive a balance of **excitatory**—fire!—and **inhibitory**—don't fire!—**inputs.** In neurons, the right pattern of excitatory inputs over time or space will lead to the production of an *action potential:* The neuron fires.

THE BIOCHEMICAL BASIS OF ACTION POTENTIALS

To explain how an **action potential** works, we need to describe the biochemical environment in which neurons draw together incoming information. All neural commu-

nication is produced by the flow of electrically charged particles, called *ions,* through the neuron's membrane, a thin "skin" separating the cell's internal and external environments. Think of a nerve fiber as a piece of macaroni, filled with saltwater, floating in a salty soup. The soup and the fluid in the macaroni both contain ions—atoms of sodium (Na^+), chloride (Cl^-), calcium (Ca^+), and potassium (K^+)—that have either positive (+) or negative (–) charges (see **Figure 3.23**). The membrane, or the surface of the macaroni, plays a critical role in keeping the ingredients of the two fluids in an appropriate balance. When a cell is inactive, or in a *resting state,* there are about ten times as many potassium ions inside as there are sodium ions outside. The membrane is not a perfect barrier; it "leaks" a little, allowing some sodium ions to slip in while some potassium ions slip out. To correct for this, nature has provided transport mechanisms within the membrane that pump out sodium and pump in potassium. Successful operation of these pumps leaves the fluid inside a neuron with a slightly negative voltage (70/1,000 of a volt) relative to the fluid outside. This means that the fluid inside the cell is *polarized* with respect to the fluid outside the cell. This slight polarization is called the **resting potential.**

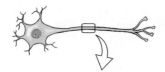

 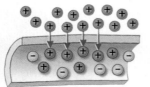 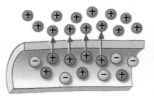 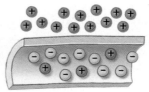

In a resting state, the fluid surrounding the axon has a high concentration of positively charged sodium ions whereas the fluid inside the axon has a high concentration of negatively charged potassium ions. This means that the fluid within the cell is *polarized* with respect to the exterior fluid, providing the neuron's resting potential.

When a nerve impulse arrives at a segment of the axon, positively charged sodium ions flow into the axon. The inflow of sodium causes the nerve cell to become *depolarized*. The nerve impulse is passed down the axon as each successive segment becomes depolarized.

Once the nerve impulse has been passed along, sodium ions flow back out of the axon to restore the resting potential.

Once the resting potential is restored, the segment of the axon is ready to transmit another impulse.

FIGURE 3.23

The Biochemical Basis of Action Potentials

Action potentials rely on an imbalance of the electrical charge of the ions present inside and outside of axons.

From Lester A. Lefton, Linda Brannon. *Psychology.* 8e. Published by Allyn and Bacon, Boston, MA. Copyright © 2003 by Pearson Education. Reprinted by permission of the publisher.

It provides the electrochemical context in which a nerve cell can produce an action potential.

The nerve cell begins the transition from a resting potential to an action potential in response to the pattern of inhibitory and excitatory inputs. Each kind of input affects the likelihood that the balance of ions from the inside to the outside of the cell will change. They cause changes in the function of **ion channels,** excitable portions of the cell membrane that selectively permit certain ions to flow in and out. Inhibitory inputs cause the ion channels to work harder to keep the inside of the cell negatively charged—this will keep the cell from firing. Excitatory inputs cause the ion channels to begin to allow sodium ions to flow in—this will allow the cell to fire. Because sodium ions have a positive charge, their influx can begin to change the relative balance of positive and negative charges across the cell membrane. An action potential begins when the excitatory inputs are sufficiently strong with respect to inhibitory inputs to *depolarize* the cell from −70 millivolts to −55 millivolts: Sufficient sodium has entered the cell to effect this change.

Once the action potential begins, sodium rushes into the neuron. As a result, the inside of the neuron becomes positive relative to the outside, meaning the neuron has become fully depolarized. A domino effect now propels the action potential down the axon. The leading edge of depolarization causes ion channels in the adjacent region of the axon to open and allow sodium to rush in. In this way—through successive depolarization—the signal passes down the axon (see Figure 3.23).

How does the neuron return to its original resting state of polarization after it fires? When the inside of the neuron becomes positive, the channels that allow sodium to flow in close and the channels that allow potassium to flow out open. The outflow of potassium ions restores the negative charge of the neuron. Thus, even while the signal is reaching the far end of the axon, the portions of the cell in which the action potential originated are being returned to their resting balance, so that they can be ready for their next stimulation.

PROPERTIES OF THE ACTION POTENTIAL

The biochemical manner in which the action potential is transmitted leads to several important properties. The action potential obeys the **all-or-none law:** The size of the action potential is unaffected by increases in the intensity of stimulation beyond the threshold level. Once excitatory inputs sum to reach the threshold level, a uniform action potential is generated. If the threshold

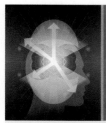
Unlocking the "Locked-in" Brain

Across the globe, tens of thousands of people have active brains trapped in inactive bodies. For example, patients with amyotrophic lateral sclerosis (ALS) experience a progressive deterioration of the nerves in the spinal cord and brain that control motor movement. Although these patients' ability to think remains unchanged, over time they lose the ability to accomplish virtually any bodily movement and, therefore, they lose the ability to communicate with the outside world. For the past several years, researchers have been exploring a variety of techniques to help people overcome what they refer to as *locked-in syndrome* (Kübler et al., 2001; Wickelgren, 2003). These techniques draw information directly from the patients' brains to help unlock the mind from the body. We will describe two approaches that show promise to restore some ability to communicate.

One technique, developed by **Emanuel Donchin** and his colleagues (Donchin et al., 2000), takes advantage of the information that is available from electroencephalograms (EEGs) (see p. 65). Research with EEGs has demonstrated that certain types of events in the external world cause distinctive brain responses. For example, when you experience a series of events from two categories, your brain emits an "oddball"

response—a pattern called the *P300*—each time you experience an event from the relatively more rare category. The *brain–computer interface* designed by Donchin and his colleagues allows patients to choose rows and columns in an array by focusing their attention

A	B	C	D	E	F
G	H	I	J	K	L
M	N	O	P	Q	R
S	T	U	V	W	X
Y	Z	1	2	3	4
5	6	7	8	9	SPACE

on oddball events. Consider the simple display in the figure. In the P300-based system, the rows and columns in the display are briefly illuminated in random order on a computer screen. People are instructed to focus their attention on a desired character, but only when the row or column in which it appears is lit up. Because those occasions are relatively rare—one out of six because there are six rows and six columns—attention to those events produces a P300. The computer finds the intersection of the appropriate row and column to identify the exact

character the individual had in mind. In that way, patients can slowly but surely spell out their messages.

Philip Kennedy and his colleagues (Kennedy et al., 2000) have explored a brain–computer interface in which electrodes are implanted directly into the patients' brains. The electrodes for the interface were specially designed so that neural tissue would grow into their hollow tips and make a strong and stable connection to the wires within them. Once the neural tissue has connected to the electrodes, the patients learn to turn the brain activity from the electrode on and off—this capability, in turn, allows them to move a cursor around a display on a computer screen. For example, one patient, JR, who had suffered a severe stroke, was able to use very limited amounts of preserved motor function—small movements of his mouth, tongue, eye, and eyebrows—to produce signals through the electrodes. Using a display similar to the one in the figure, JR was able to work his way through the messages he wished to deliver. A second computer display provided him with pre-stored messages (e.g., "I feel too cold," "I feel too warm").

Both of these pioneering techniques provide you with solid ideas about how the ordinary activities of the human brain can be harnessed to unlock the locked in.

is not reached, no action potential occurs. An added consequence of the all-or-none property is that the size of the action potential does not diminish along the length of the axon. In this sense, the action potential is said to be *self-propagating;* once started, it needs no

outside stimulation to keep itself moving. It's similar to a lit fuse on a firecracker.

Different neurons conduct action potentials along their axons at different speeds; the fastest have signals that move at the rate of 200 meters per second, the slowest plod along at 10 centimeters per second. The axons of the faster neurons are covered with a tightly wrapped myelin sheath—consisting, as we explained earlier, of glial cells—making this part of the neuron resemble short tubes on a string. The tiny breaks between the tubes are called *nodes of Ranvier* (see Figure 3.21). In neurons having myelinated axons, the action potential literally skips along from one node to the next—saving the time and energy required to open and close ion channels at every location on the axon. Damage to the myelin sheath throws off the delicate timing of the action potential and causes serious problems. Multiple sclerosis (MS) is a devastating disorder caused by deterioration of the myelin sheath. It is characterized by double vision, tremors, and eventually paralysis. In MS, specialized cells from the body's immune system actually attack myelinated neurons, exposing the axon and disrupting normal synaptic transmission (Joyce, 1990).

After an action potential has passed down a segment of the axon, that region of the neuron enters a **refractory period** (see **Figure 3.24**). During the *absolute refractory period,* further stimulation, no matter how intense, cannot cause another action potential to be generated; during the *relative refractory period,* the neuron will fire only in response to a stimulus stronger than what is ordinarily necessary. Have you

ever tried to flush the toilet while it is filling back up with water? There must be a critical level of water for the toilet to flush again. Similarly, in order for a neuron to be able to generate another action potential, it must "reset" itself and await simulation beyond its threshold. The refractory period ensures, in part, that the action potential will only travel in one direction down the axon: It cannot move backward, because "earlier" parts of the axon are in a refractory state.

◆ SYNAPTIC TRANSMISSION

When the action potential completes its leapfrog journey down the axon to a terminal button, it must pass its information along to the next neuron. But no two neurons ever touch: They are joined at a **synapse,** with a small gap between the *presynaptic membrane* (the terminal button of the sending neuron) and the *postsynaptic membrane* (the surface of a dendrite or soma of a receiving neuron). When the action potential reaches the terminal button, it sets in motion a series of events called **synaptic transmission,** which is the relaying of information from one neuron to another across the synaptic gap (see **Figure 3.25**). Synaptic transmission begins when the arrival of the action potential at the terminal button causes small round packets, called *synaptic vesicles,* to move toward and affix themselves to the interior membrane of the terminal button. Inside each vesicle are **neurotransmitters,** biochemical substances that stimulate other neurons. The action potential also causes ion channels to open that admit calcium ions into the terminal button. The influx of calcium ions causes the rupture of the synaptic vesicles and the release of whatever neurotransmitters they contain. Once the synaptic vesicles rupture, the neurotransmitters are dispersed rapidly across the *synaptic cleft* to the postsynaptic membrane. To complete synaptic transmission, the neurotransmitters attach to *receptor molecules* embedded in the postsynaptic membrane.

The neurotransmitters will bind to the receptor molecules under two conditions. First, no other neurotransmitters or other chemical substances can be attached to the receptor molecule. Second, the shape of the neurotransmitter must match the shape of the receptor molecule—as precisely as a key fits into a keyhole. If either condition is not met, the neurotransmitter will not attach to the receptor molecule. This means that it will not be able to stimulate the postsynaptic membrane. If the neurotransmitter does become attached to the receptor molecule, then it may provide "fire" or "don't fire" information to this next neuron. Once the neurotransmitter has completed its job, it detaches from the receptor molecule and drifts back into the synaptic gap. There it is either decomposed through the action of

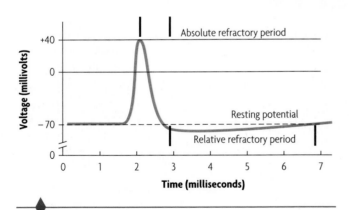

FIGURE 3.24

Timetable for Electrical Changes in the Neuron during an Action Potential

Sodium ions entering the neuron cause its electrical potential to change from slightly negative during its polarized, or resting, state to slightly positive during depolarization. Once the neuron is depolarized, it enters a brief refractory period during which further stimulation will not produce another action potential. Another action potential can occur only after the ionic balance between the inside and the outside of the cell is restored.

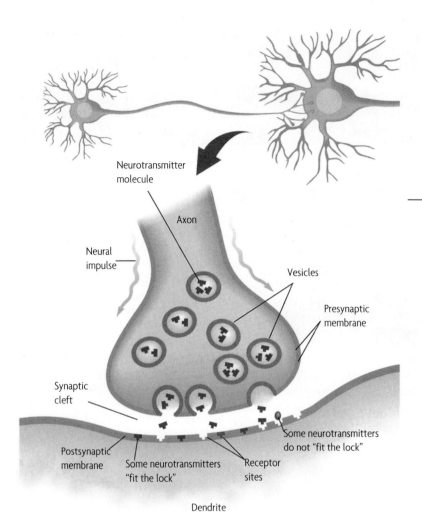

Neurotransmitter
molecule

Axon

Neural
impulse

Vesicles

Presynaptic
membrane

Synaptic
cleft

Some neurotransmitters
do not "fit the lock"

Postsynaptic
membrane

Some neurotransmitters
"fit the lock"

Receptor
sites

Dendrite

FIGURE 3.25
Synaptic Transmission

*The action potential in the presynaptic neuron causes
neurotransmitters to be released into the synaptic gap.
Once across the gap, they stimulate receptor molecules
embedded in the membrane of the postsynaptic neuron.
Multiple neurotransmitters can exist within the same cell.*

enzymes or reabsorbed into the presynaptic terminal button for quick reuse.

Depending on the receptor molecule, a neurotransmitter will have either an excitatory or an inhibitory effect. That is, the same neurotransmitter may be excitatory at one synapse but inhibitory at another. Each neuron integrates the information it obtains at synapses with between 1,000 and 10,000 other neurons to decide whether it ought to initiate another action potential. It is the integration of these thousands of inhibitory and excitatory inputs that allows all-or-none action potentials to provide the foundation for all human experience.

You may be wondering why we have taken you so deep into the nervous system. After all, this is a psychology course, and psychology is supposed to be about behavior and thinking and emotion. In fact, synapses are the biological medium in which all of these activities occur. If you change the normal activity of the synapse, you change how people behave, how they

think, and how they feel. Understanding the functioning of the synapse has led to tremendous advances in the understanding of learning and memory, emotion, psychological disorders, drug addiction, and, in general, the chemical formula for mental health. You will use the knowledge you have acquired in this chapter throughout *Psychology and Life*.

◆ NEUROTRANSMITTERS AND THEIR FUNCTIONS

Dozens of chemical substances are known or suspected to function as neurotransmitters in the brain. The neurotransmitters that have been studied most intensively meet a set of technical criteria. Each is manufactured in the presynaptic terminal button and is released when an action potential reaches that terminal. The neurotransmitter's presence in the synaptic cleft produces a

Why Does Music Have an Impact on How You Feel?

Joel Gendron
Northeastern University

Suppose you're sitting in a movie theater watching a comedy. It's likely that the soundtrack will feature music that's upbeat and lively—music you might describe as "happy." In Theater 2, a dramatic movie features "sad" music. The horror flick in Theater 3 uses music to try to build up feelings of fear. Does music really have an impact on your emotions? Researchers have turned to the brain to address this question.

As we shall see in Chapter 12, solid advances have been made in understanding the relationship between brain states and the emotions you experience. That work provides a context for examining the impact of music in the brain. We know, for example, that pleasant and unpleasant images cause different patterns of brain activity (Davidson et al., 2000). When you view pleasant stimuli, your brain produces relatively more activity in the prefrontal cortex (the forward region of your frontal lobes) of your left hemisphere; unpleasant stimuli produce relatively more activity in the same region of your right hemisphere. Does music yield the same pattern? To find out, researchers gathered EEG recordings from students while they listened to pleasant (joyful or happy) music and unpleasant (fearful and sad) music (Schmidt & Trainor, 2001). The musical passages produced the same asymmetries in brain activity found for other types of stimuli. These results suggest that, for example, happy music makes you feel happy because it involves

the same brain regions as other experiences that evoke happy feelings.

But what components of music make it seem happy or sad? One important difference is *tempo*: On the whole, faster music strikes people as happier than slower music. To determine how the brain responds to tempo differences, researchers once again recorded EEGs while students listened to music. In this case, the musical passages were relatively fast or relatively slow (Tsang et al., 2001). Once again the brain revealed an asymmetry in activation. Parallel to the earlier results, "happier" tempos produced relatively more activity in the left frontal cortex whereas "sadder" tempos produced relatively more activity on the right side of the brain.

Let's consider one more aspect of emotion and music. Have you ever had the experience of listening to music so pleasurable, it gives you "chills"? To study this phenomenon, researchers invited ten students to bring their own chill-inducing music to the laboratory (Blood & Zatorre, 2001). While the students listened to their personal favorites and neutral musical passages, the researchers monitored both physiological arousal (e.g., heart rate and respiration) as well as brain activity (using PET scans). The physiological data verified the reality of the chills. The students experienced increased heart and respiration rates when listening to their favorite music with respect to neutral music. The PET scans revealed that the chills were accompanied by increased brain activity in regions that signal pleasurable emotional arousal—the more intense the chills, the more these regions became active. The researchers explained the importance of these results: "Music recruits neural systems of reward and emotion similar to those known to respond specifically to biologically relevant stimuli, such as food and sex, and those that are artificially activated by drugs of abuse. This is quite remarkable, because music is neither strictly necessary for biological survival or reproduction, nor is it a pharmacological substance" (p. 11823).

Next time music sends shivers down your spine, you should reflect on how exactly your brain is being engaged.

biological response in the postsynaptic membrane, and if its release is prevented, no subsequent responses can occur. To give you a sense of the effects different neurotransmitters have on the regulation of behavior, we will discuss a set that has been found to play an important role in the daily functioning of the brain. This brief discussion will also enable you to understand many of the ways in which neural transmission can go awry.

ACETYLCHOLINE

Acetylcholine is found in both the central and peripheral nervous systems. Memory loss among patients suffering from Alzheimer's disease, a degenerative disease that is increasingly common among older persons, is believed to be caused by the deterioration of neurons that secrete acetylcholine. Acetylcholine is also excitatory at junctions between nerves and muscles, where it causes muscles to contract. A number of toxins affect the synaptic actions of acetylcholine. For example, botulinum toxin, often found in food that has been preserved incorrectly, poisons an individual by preventing release of acetylcholine in the respiratory system. This poisoning, known as *botulism,* can cause death by suffocation. Curare, a poison Amazon Indians use on the tips of their blowgun darts, paralyzes lung muscles by occupying critical acetylcholine receptors, preventing the normal activity of the transmitter.

GABA

GABA (gamma-aminobutyric acid) is the most common inhibitory neurotransmitter in the brain. GABA may be used as a messenger in as many as a third of all brain synapses. Neurons that are sensitive to GABA are particularly concentrated in brain regions such as the thalamus, hypothalamus, and occipital lobes. GABA appears to play a critical role in some forms of psychopathology by inhibiting neural activity; when levels of this neurotransmitter in the brain become low, people may experience the extra neural activity as feelings of anxiety. Anxiety disorders are often treated with *benzodiazepine* drugs, such as *Valium* or *Xanax,* that increase GABA activity (Ballenger, 1999). The *benzodiazepine* drugs do not attach directly to GABA receptors. Instead they allow GABA itself to bind more effectively to postsynaptic receptor molecules.

DOPAMINE, NOREPINEPHRINE, AND SEROTONIN

The *catecholamines* are a class of chemical substances that include two important neurotransmitters, *dopamine* and *norepinephrine*. Both have been shown to play prominent roles in psychological disorders, such as mood disturbances and schizophrenia. Norepinephrine appears to be involved in some forms of depression: Drugs that increase brain levels of this neurotransmitter elevate mood and relieve depression. Conversely, higher-than-normal levels of dopamine have been found in persons with schizophrenia. As you might expect, one way to treat people with this disorder is to give them a drug that decreases brain levels of dopamine. In the early days of drug therapy, an interesting but unfortunate problem arose. High doses of the drug used to treat schizophrenia produced symptoms of Parkinson's disease, a progressive and ultimately fatal disorder involving disruption of motor functioning. (Parkinson's disease is caused by deterioration of neurons that manufacture most of the brain's dopamine.) This finding led to research that improved drug therapy for schizophrenia and to research that focused on drugs that could be used in the treatment of Parkinson's disease.

All the neurons that produce *serotonin* are located in the brain stem, which is involved in arousal and many autonomic processes. The hallucinogenic drug LSD (lysergic acid diethylamide) appears to produce its effects by suppressing the effects of serotonin neurons. These serotonin neurons normally inhibit other neurons, but the lack of inhibition produced by LSD creates vivid and bizarre sensory experiences, some of which last for hours. Many antidepressant drugs, such as Prozac, enhance the action of serotonin by preventing it from being removed from the synaptic cleft (Barondes, 1994).

ENDORPHINS

The *endorphins* are a group of chemicals that are usually classified as neuromodulators. A **neuromodulator** is any substance that modifies or modulates the activities of the postsynaptic neuron. Endorphins (short for *endogenous morphines*) play an important role in the control of emotional behaviors (anxiety, fear, tension, pleasure) and pain—drugs like opium and morphine bind to the same receptor sites in the brain. Endorphins have been called the "keys to paradise" because of their pleasure–pain controlling properties. Researchers have examined the possibility that endorphins are at least partially responsible for the pain-reducing effects of acupuncture and placebos (Murray, 1995). Such tests rely on the drug *naloxone,* whose only known effect is to block morphine and endorphins from binding to receptors. Any procedure that reduces pain by stimulating release of endorphins becomes ineffective when naloxone is administered. With the injection of naloxone, acupuncture and placebos do, in fact, lose their power—suggesting that, ordinarily, endorphins help them do their work.

Researchers have also documented that gases like *carbon monoxide* and *nitric oxide* can function as neurotransmitters (Barinaga, 1993). What is most surprising about this new class of neurotransmitters is that they violate many of the normal expectations about synaptic transmission. For example, rather than binding to receptor molecules, as do the other neurotransmitters we have discussed, these gaseous transmitters appear to pass directly through the receptor cell's outer membrane. This surprising discovery should reinforce your impression that the brain possesses many secrets yet to be revealed.

Roughly 1.5 million people in the United States, including the actor Michael J. Fox, are impaired by Parkinson's disease. Research on the neurotransmitter dopamine has led to advances in understanding this disease. How does basic research in neuroscience allow for improved treatments?

◆ PLASTICITY AND NEUROGENESIS: OUR CHANGING BRAINS

You now have a good basic idea of your nervous system at work: At all times, millions of neurons are communicating to do the essential work of your body and mind. What makes the brain even more interesting, however, is one consequence of all that neural communication: The brain itself changes over time. Do you want to take a moment to change your brain? Go back a few pages and memorize the definition of *action potential.* If you are successful at learning that definition—or any other new information—you will have brought about a modification of your brain. Researchers refer to changes in the performance of the brain as **plasticity.** A good deal of research in neuroscience focuses on the physical bases for plasticity. For example, researchers examine how learning arises from the formation of new synapses or from changes in communication across existing synapses (Baudry et al., 1999).

Because brain plasticity depends on life experiences, you won't be surprised to learn that brains show the impact of different environments and activities. One classic series of studies, carried out by **Mark Rosenzweig**

and his colleagues, demonstrated the consequences for rats of being raised in impoverished or enriched environments (for reviews, see Rosenzweig, 1996, 1999b). In the impoverished environments, the rats were kept alone in their cages; in the enriched environments, the rats shared a large cage with several other rats and had playthings that were changed daily. After periods varying from a few days to several months, the experimenters examined the rats' brains. The results were dramatic. The average cortex of the rats living in the enriched environments was heavier and thicker—positive attributes—than that of their impoverished littermates. Measurable differences emerged even when the rats had been in the enriched environments for only a few days.

With brain imaging techniques, it is possible to measure very specific brain differences related to individuals' life experiences. Consider those musicians who play the violin. They are required to control the fingers of their left hands with an extremely delicate touch. If you refer back to Figure 3.14, you'll see that a good deal of sensory cortex is devoted to the fingers. Brain scans reveal that the representation of fingers of the left hand is even more enhanced for violin players, as compared to nonplayers (Elbert et al., 1995). No such increase is found for fingers of the right hand, which do not have as great a sensory role in violin playing. The extra representation of the left fingers was greatest for violinists who took up the instrument before age 12.

One important aspect of research on plasticity concerns circumstances in which humans or animals have sustained injuries to the brain or spinal cord, through strokes, degenerative diseases, or accidents. A good deal of clinical evidence confirms that the brain is sometimes able to "heal itself." For example, patients who suffer from strokes that cause disruptions in language often recover over time. In some instances, the damaged brain areas themselves have enough lingering function that recovery is possible; in other cases other brain areas take over the functions of those that were damaged (Kuest & Karbe, 2002). Researchers have also begun to develop techniques to help the brain along in the healing process. In recent years, attention has focused on *stem cells*—unspecialized cells that, under appropriate conditions, can be prompted to function as new neurons (Kintner, 2002; Wilson & Edlund, 2001). Researchers hope that stem cells may ultimately provide a means to replace damaged tissue in the nervous system with new neural growth. Because the most flexible stem cells come from embryos and aborted fetuses, stem cell research has been subject to political controversy. Still, researchers believe that stem cell research could lead to cures for paralysis and other serious malfunctions in the nervous system. For that reason, the scientific community is highly motivated to discover ways to continue research within accepted societal norms.

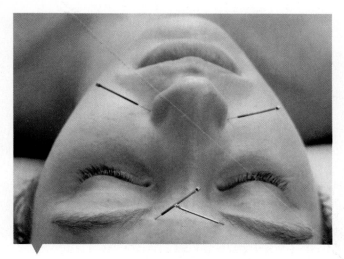

Why do patients experience pain relief from acupuncture?

Research on brain repair has accelerated in recent years in the face of important new data suggesting that **neurogenesis**—the production of new brain cells from naturally occurring stem cells—occurs in the brains of adult mammals, including humans (Gould & Gross, 2002; Gross, 2000). For nearly a hundred years, neuroscientists believed that the adult brains of mammals had their full supply of neurons—all that could happen over the adult years was that neurons could die out. However, the new data have challenged that view.

Recall, for example, that we identified the hippocampus as an important structure for the formation of certain types of memories. Now that researchers have documented neurogenesis in the adult hippocampus, they are trying to understand the role newly born neurons play in allowing memories to remain accessible over time (Kempermann, 2002).

In this chapter, we have taken a brief peek at the marvelous 3-pound universe that is your brain. It is one thing to recognize that the brain controls behavior and your mental processes but quite another to understand how the brain serves all those functions. Neuroscientists are engaged in the fascinating quest to understand the interplay among brain, behavior, and environment. You now have the type of background that will allow you to appreciate new knowledge as it unfolds.

PUT YOURSELF TO THE TEST

- ➤ What are the functions of the major types of neurons and glia?
- ➤ What are the circumstances that cause a neuron to produce an all-or-none response?
- ➤ What role do some of the most important neurotransmitters play in regulating bodily functions?
- ➤ In what ways does the brain change after birth?

Recapping Main Points

HEREDITY AND BEHAVIOR

- Species originate and change over time because of natural selection.
- In the evolution of humans, bipedalism and encephalization were responsible for subsequent advances, including language and culture.
- The basic unit of heredity is the gene. Genes determine the range of effects that environmental factors can have in influencing the expression of phenotypic traits.

BIOLOGY AND BEHAVIOR

- Neuroscientists use several methods to research the relation between brain and behavior: studying brain-damaged patients, producing lesions at specific brain sites, electrically stimulating the brain, recording brain activity, and imaging the brain with computerized devices.
- The brain and the spinal cord make up the central nervous system (CNS).
- The peripheral nervous system (PNS) is composed of all neurons connecting the CNS to the body. The PNS consists of the somatic nervous system, which regulates the body's skeletal muscles, and the autonomic nervous system (ANS), which regulates life-support processes.
- The brain consists of three integrated layers: the brain stem, limbic system, and cerebrum.
- The brain stem is responsible for breathing, digestion, and heart rate.
- The limbic system is involved in long-term memory, aggression, eating, drinking, and sexual behavior.
- The cerebrum controls higher mental functions.
- Some functions are lateralized to one hemisphere of the brain. For example, most individuals have speech localized in the left hemisphere.
- Although the two hemispheres of the brain work smoothly in concert, they typically embody different styles of processing: The left hemisphere is more analytic, while the right hemisphere is more holistic.

- The endocrine system produces and secretes hormones into the bloodstream.
- Hormones help regulate growth, primary and secondary sexual characteristics, metabolism, digestion, and arousal.

THE NERVOUS SYSTEM IN ACTION

- The neuron, the basic unit of the nervous system, receives, processes, and relays information to other cells, glands, and muscles.
- Neurons relay information from the dendrites through the cell body (soma) to the axon to the terminal buttons.
- Sensory neurons receive messages from specialized receptor cells and send them toward the CNS. Motor neurons direct messages from the CNS to muscles and glands. Interneurons relay information from sensory neurons to other interneurons or to motor neurons.
- Once the summation of inputs to a neuron exceeds a specific threshold, an action potential is sent along the axon to the terminal buttons.
- All-or-none action potentials are created when the opening of ion channels allows an exchange of ions across the cell membrane.
- Neurotransmitters are released into the synaptic gap between neurons. Once they diffuse across the gap, they lodge in the receptor molecules of the postsynaptic membrane.
- Whether these neurotransmitters excite or inhibit the membrane depends on the nature of the receptor molecule.
- New cell growth and life experiences reshape the brain after birth.

KEY TERMS

action potential (p. 82)

all-or-none law (p. 82)

amygdala (p. 70)

association cortex (p. 72)

auditory cortex (p. 72)

autonomic nervous system (ANS) (p. 66)

axon (p. 79)

brain stem (p. 68)

Broca's area (p. 63)

central nervous system (CNS) (p. 66)

cerebellum (p. 70)

cerebral cortex (p. 70)

cerebral hemispheres (p. 70)

cerebrum (p. 70)

corpus callosum (p. 70)

dendrites (p. 79)

DNA (deoxyribonucleic acid) (p. 60)

electroencephalogram (EEG) (p. 65)

endocrine system (p. 77)

estrogen (p. 78)

evolutionary psychology (p. 62)

excitatory inputs (p. 81)

frontal lobe (p. 71)

functional MRI (fMRI) (p. 65)

genes (p. 60)

genetics (p. 60)

genome (p. 61)

genotype (p. 58)

glia (p. 80)

heredity (p. 60)

heritability (p. 61)

hippocampus (p. 70)

homeostasis (p. 70)

hormones (p. 77)

human behavior genetics (p. 61)

hypothalamus (p. 70)

inhibitory inputs (p. 81)

interneurons (p. 79)

ion channels (p. 82)

lesions (p. 63)

limbic system (p. 70)

magnetic resonance imaging (MRI) (p. 65)

medulla (p. 68)

motor cortex (p. 71)

motor neurons (p. 79)

natural selection (p. 57)

neurogenesis (p. 89)

neuromodulator (p. 87)

neuron (p. 79)

neuroscience (p. 63)

neurotransmitters (p. 84)

occipital lobe (p. 71)

parasympathetic division (p. 66)

parietal lobe (p. 71)

peripheral nervous system (PNS) (p. 66)

PET scans (p. 65)

phenotype (p. 58)

pituitary gland (p. 78)

plasticity (p. 88)

pons (p. 70)

refractory period (p. 84)

repetitive transcranial magnetic stimulation (rTMS) (p. 63)

resting potential (p. 81)

reticular formation (p. 70)

sensory neurons (p. 79)

sex chromosomes (p. 60)

sociobiology (p. 61)

soma (p. 79)

somatic nervous system (p. 66)

somatosensory cortex (p. 71)

sympathetic division (p. 66)

synapse (p. 84)

synaptic transmission (p. 84)

temporal lobe (p. 71)

terminal buttons (p. 79)

testosterone (p. 78)

thalamus (p. 70)

visual cortex (p. 72)

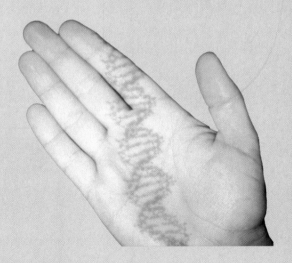

4

Sensation and Perception

Have you ever wondered how your brain—locked in the dark, silent chamber of the skull—experiences the blaze of color in a Van Gogh painting, the driving melodies and rhythms of rock 'n' roll, the refreshing taste of watermelon on a hot day, the soft touch of a child's kiss, or the fragrance of wildflowers in the springtime? Our task in this chapter is to explain how your body and brain make sense of the buzz of stimulation—sights, sounds, and so on—constantly around you. You will see how evolution has equipped you with the capability to detect many different dimensions of experience.

In this chapter, we will describe how your experience of the world relies on processes of *sensation* and *perception*. We will discover that these processes serve the dual functions of *survival* and *sensuality*. Your sensory and perceptual processes help you survive by sounding alarms of danger, priming you to take swift action to ward off hazards, and directing you toward agreeable experiences. These processes also provide you with sensuality.

Sensuality is the enjoyment of sensory experiences. What is the relationship between sensuality and survival?

Sensuality is the quality of being devoted to the gratification of the senses; it entails enjoying the experiences that appeal to your various senses of sight, sound, touch, taste, and smell.

We begin with an overview of sensory and perceptual processes—and some challenges the physical world provides to them.

Sensing, Organizing, Identifying, and Recognizing

The term **perception**, in its broad usage, refers to the overall process of apprehending objects and events in the environment—to sense them, understand them, identify and label them, and prepare to react to them. A *percept* is what is perceived—the phenomenological, or experienced, outcome of the process of perception. The process of perception is best understood when we divide it into three stages: sensation, perceptual organization, and identification/recognition of objects.

Sensation is the process by which stimulation of *sensory receptors*—the structures in our eyes, ears, and so on—produces neural impulses that represent experiences inside or outside the body. For example, sensation provides the basic facts of the visual field. Nerve cells in your eye pass information along to cells in your brain's cortex, which extract preliminary features from this input.

Perceptual organization refers to the stage in which an internal representation of an object is formed and a percept of the external stimulus is developed. The representation provides a working description of the perceiver's external environment. With respect to vision, perceptual processes provide estimates of an object's likely size, shape, movement, distance, and orientation. Those estimates are based on mental computations that integrate your past knowledge with the present evidence received from your senses and with the stimulus within its perceptual context. Perception involves *synthesis* (integration and combination) of simple sensory features, such as colors, edges, and lines, into the percept of an object that can be recognized later. These mental activities most often occur swiftly and efficiently, without conscious awareness.

Identification and recognition, the third stage in this sequence, assigns meaning to percepts. Circular objects "become" baseballs, coins, clocks, oranges, and moons; people may be identified as male or female, friend or foe, relative or rock star. At this stage, the perceptual question "What does the object look like?" changes to a question of identification—"What is this object?"—and to a question of recognition—"What is the object's function?" To identify and recognize what something is, what it is called, and how best to respond to it involves higher-level cognitive processes, which include your theories, memories, values, beliefs, and attitudes concerning the object.

We have now given a brief introduction to the stages of processing that enable you to arrive at a meaningful understanding of the perceptual world around you. In everyday life, perception seems to be entirely effortless. We will try to convince you that you actually do quite a bit of sophisticated processing, a lot of mental work, to arrive at this "illusion of ease."

◆ THE PROXIMAL AND DISTAL STIMULI

Imagine you are the person in **Figure 4.1A,** surveying a room from an easy chair. Some of the light reflected from the objects in the room enters your eyes and forms images on your retinas. **Figure 4.1B** shows what would appear to your left eye as you sit in the room. (The

<www.ablongman.com/gerrig17e>

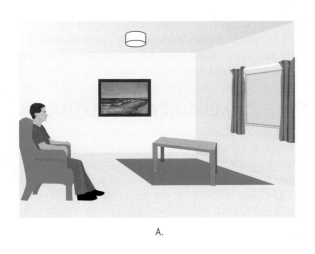

A.

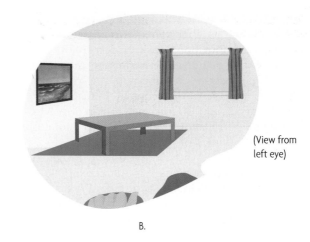

(View from left eye)

B.

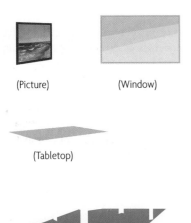

(Picture)   (Window)

(Tabletop)

(Rug)

C.

FIGURE 4.1

Interpreting Retinal Images

The major task of visual perception is to interpret or identify the distal stimulus, the actual object in the environment, using the information from the proximal stimulus, the retinal image produced by the object.

---

bump on the right is your nose, and the hand and knee at the bottom are your own.) How does this retinal image compare with the environment that produced it?

One very important difference is that the retinal image is *two-dimensional,* whereas the environment is *three-dimensional.* This difference has many consequences. For instance, compare the shapes of the physical objects in Figure 4.1A with the shapes of their corresponding retinal images (**Figure 4.1C**). The table, rug, window, and picture in the real-world scene are all rectangular, but only the image of the window actually produces a rectangle in your retinal image. The image of the picture is a trapezoid, the image of the tabletop is an irregular four-sided figure, and the image of the rug is actually three separate regions with more than 20 different sides! Here's our first perceptual puzzle: How do you manage to perceive all of these objects as simple, standard rectangles?

The situation is, however, even a bit more complicated. You can also notice that many parts of what you perceive in the room are not actually present in your

retinal image. For instance, you perceive the vertical edge between the two walls as going all the way to the floor, but your retinal image of that edge stops at the table top. Similarly, in your retinal image parts of the rug are hidden behind the table; yet this does not keep you from correctly perceiving the rug as a single, unbroken rectangle. In fact, when you consider all the differences between the environmental objects and the images of them on your retina, you may be surprised that you perceive the scene as well as you do.

The differences between a physical object in the world and its optical image on your retina are so profound and important that psychologists distinguish carefully between them as two different stimuli for perception. The physical object in the world is called the **distal stimulus** (distant from the observer) and the optical image on the retina is called the **proximal stimulus** (proximate, or near, to the observer).

The critical point of our discussion can now be restated more concisely: What you wish to *perceive* is the *distal stimulus*—the "real" object in the environment—

whereas the stimulus from which you must derive your information is the *proximal stimulus*—the image on the retina. The major computational task of perception can be thought of as the process of determining the distal stimulus from information contained in the proximal stimulus. This is true across perceptual domains. For hearing, touch, taste, and so on, perception involves processes that use information in the proximal stimulus to tell you about properties of the distal stimulus.

To show you how the distal stimulus and proximal stimulus fit with the three stages in perceiving, let's examine one of the objects in the scene from Figure 4.1: the picture hanging on the wall. In the sensory stage, this picture corresponds to a two-dimensional trapezoid in your retinal image; the top and bottom sides converge toward the right, and the left and right sides are different in length. This is the proximal stimulus. In the perceptual organization stage, you see this trapezoid as a rectangle turned away from you in three-dimensional space. You perceive the top and bottom sides as parallel, but receding into the distance toward the right; you perceive the left and right sides as equal in length. Your perceptual processes have developed a strong *hypothesis* about the physical properties of the distal stimulus; now it needs an identity. In the recognition stage, you identify this rectangular object as a picture. **Figure 4.2** is a flowchart illustrating this sequence of

events. The processes that take information from one stage to the next are shown as arrows between the boxes. By the end of this chapter, we will explain the interactions represented in this figure.

◆ REALITY, AMBIGUITY, AND ILLUSIONS

We have defined the task of perception as the identification of the distal stimulus from the proximal stimulus. Before we turn to some of the perceptual mechanisms that make this task successful, we want to discuss a bit more some other aspects of stimuli in the environment that make perception complex: *ambiguous* stimuli and perceptual *illusions*.

AMBIGUITY

A primary goal of perception is to get an accurate "fix" on the world. Survival depends on accurate perceptions of objects and events in your environment—is that motion in the trees a tiger?—that are not always easy to read. **Ambiguity** is an important concept in understanding perception because it shows that a single image at the sensory level can result in *multiple interpretations* at the perceptual and identification levels.

Figure 4.3 shows two examples of ambiguous figures. Each example permits two unambiguous but con-

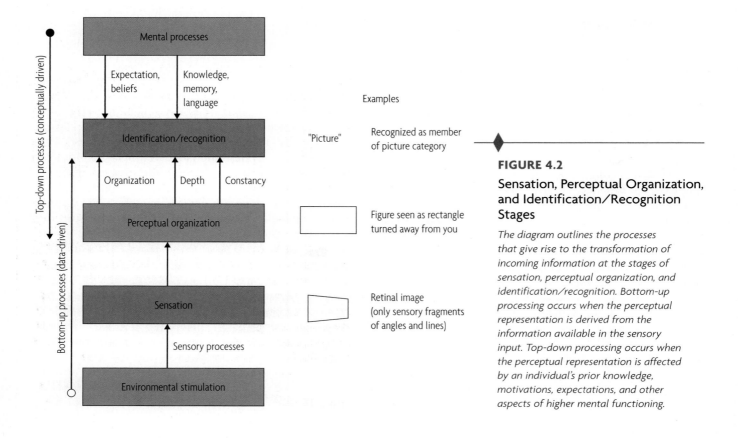

FIGURE 4.2

Sensation, Perceptual Organization, and Identification/Recognition Stages

The diagram outlines the processes that give rise to the transformation of incoming information at the stages of sensation, perceptual organization, and identification/recognition. Bottom-up processing occurs when the perceptual representation is derived from the information available in the sensory input. Top-down processing occurs when the perceptual representation is affected by an individual's prior knowledge, motivations, expectations, and other aspects of higher mental functioning.

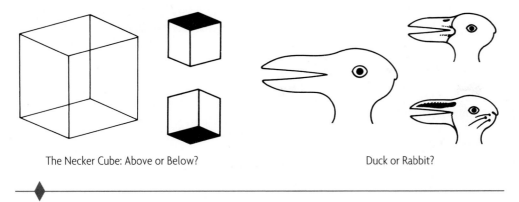

The Necker Cube: Above or Below?   Duck or Rabbit?

FIGURE 4.3

Perceptual Ambiguities

Each example allows two interpretations, but you cannot experience both at the same time. Do you notice your percept flipping back and forth between each pair of possibilities?

flicting interpretations. Look at each image until you can see the two alternative interpretations. Notice that once you have seen both of them, your perception flips back and forth between them as you look at the ambiguous figure. This perceptual *instability* of ambiguous figures is one of their most important characteristics.

The Necker cube presents an ambiguity in the perceptual organization stage. You have two different perceptions of the same objects in the environment. The Necker cube can be seen as a three-dimensional hollow cube either below you and angled to your left or above you and angled toward your right. The ambiguous alternatives are different physical arrangements of the object in three-dimensional space, both resulting from the same stimulus image.

The duck/rabbit figure is an example of ambiguity in the recognition stage. It is perceived as the same physical shape in both interpretations. The ambiguity arises in determining the kind of object it represents and in how best to classify it, given the mixed set of information available.

Many prominent artists have used perceptual ambiguity as a central creative device in their works. **Figure 4.4** presents *Slave Market with the Disappearing Bust of Voltaire,* by Salvador Dali. This work reveals a complex ambiguity in which a whole section of the picture must be radically reorganized and reinterpreted to allow perception of the "hidden" bust of the French philosopher-writer Voltaire. The white sky under the lower arch is Voltaire's forehead and hair; the white portions of the two ladies' dresses are his cheeks, nose, and chin. (If you have trouble seeing him, try squinting, holding the book at arm's length, or taking off your glasses.) Once you have seen the bust of Voltaire in this

picture, however, you will never be able to look at it without knowing where this Frenchman is hiding.

One of the most fundamental properties of normal human perception is the tendency to transform ambiguity and uncertainty about the environment into a clear interpretation that you can act upon with confidence. In a world filled with variability and change, your perceptual system must meet the challenges of discovering invariance and stability.

FIGURE 4.4

Ambiguity in Art

This painting by Salvador Dali is called Slave Market with the Disappearing Bust of Voltaire. *Can you find Voltaire? Dali is one of a large number of modern and contemporary artists who have exploited ambiguity in their work.*

ILLUSIONS

Ambiguous stimuli present your perceptual systems with the challenge of recognizing one unique figure out of several possibilities. One or another interpretation of the stimulus is correct or incorrect with respect to a particular context. When your perceptual systems actually deceive you into experiencing a stimulus pattern in a manner that is demonstrably incorrect, you are experiencing an **illusion.** The word *illusion* shares the same root as *ludicrous*—both stem from the Latin *illudere*, which means "to mock at." Illusions are shared by most people in the same perceptual situation because of shared physiology in sensory systems and overlapping experiences of the world. (As we shall explain in

Chapter 5, this sets illusions apart from hallucinations. Hallucinations are nonshared perceptual distortions that individuals experience as a result of unusual physical or mental states.) Examine the classic illusions in **Figure 4.5.** Although it is most convenient for us to present you with visual illusions, illusions also exist in other sensory modalities such as hearing (Bregman, 1981; Saberi, 1996; Shepard & Jordan, 1984) and taste (Todrank & Bartoshuk, 1991).

ILLUSIONS IN EVERYDAY LIFE

Illusions are also a basic part of your everyday life. Consider your day-to-day experience of your home planet, Earth. You've seen the sun "rise" and "set" even

A. Use a ruler to answer each question.

Which is larger: the brim or the top of the hat?

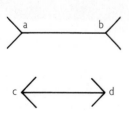

Top hat illusion

Is the diagonal line broken?

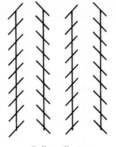

Poggendorf illusion

Which central circle is bigger?

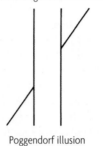

Ebbinghaus illusion

Which horizontal line is longer?

Müller–Lyer illusion

Are the vertical lines parallel?

Zöllner illusion

B. Which of the boxes are the same size as the standard box? Which are definitely smaller or larger? Measure them to discover a powerful illusory effect.

1.

2.

Standard

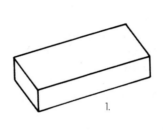

3.

4.

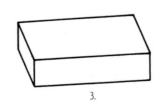

FIGURE 4.5

Five Illusions to Tease Your Brain

Each of these illusions represents circumstances in which perception is demonstrably incorrect. Researchers often use illusions to test their theories. These theories explain why perceptual systems that generally function quite accurately yield illusions in special circumstances.

though you know that the sun is sitting out there in the center of the solar system as decisively as ever. You can appreciate why it was such an extraordinary feat of courage for Christopher Columbus and other voyagers to deny the obvious illusion that Earth was flat and sail off toward one of its apparent edges. Similarly, when a full moon is overhead, it seems to follow you wherever you go even though you know the moon isn't chasing you. What you are experiencing is an illusion created by the great distance of the moon from your eye. When they reach Earth, the moon's light rays are essentially parallel and perpendicular to your direction of travel, no matter where you go.

People can control illusions to achieve desired effects. Architects and interior designers use principles of perception to create objects in space that seem larger or smaller than they really are. A small apartment becomes more spacious when it is painted with light colors and sparsely furnished with low, small couches, chairs, and tables in the center of the room instead of against the walls. Psychologists working with NASA in the U.S. space program have researched the effects of environment on perception in order to design space capsules that have pleasant sensory qualities. Set and lighting directors of movies and theatrical productions purposely create illusions on film and on stage.

Despite all of these illusions—some more useful than others—you generally do pretty well getting around the environment. That is why researchers typically study illusions to help explain how perception ordinarily works so well. The illusions themselves suggest, however, that your perceptual systems cannot perfectly carry out the task of recovering the distal stimulus from the proximal stimulus.

You now have an overview of your sensory and perceptual processes and some of the challenges those processes face. Let's begin to consider those processes in more detail.

PUT YOURSELF TO THE TEST

- What are some important stages within the overall process of perception?
- What is the relationship between proximal and distal stimuli?
- How do ambiguous stimuli and illusions demonstrate some of the challenges your sensory and perceptual processes face from external stimuli?

Sensory Knowledge of the World

Your experience of external reality must be relatively accurate and error free. If not, you couldn't survive. You need food to sustain you, shelter to protect you, interactions with other people to fulfill social needs, and awareness of danger to keep out of harm's way. To meet these needs, you must get reliable information about the world. The earliest psychological research on sensation examined the relationship between events in the environment and people's experience of those events.

◆ PSYCHOPHYSICS

How loud must a fire alarm at a factory be in order for workers to hear it over the din of the machinery? How bright does a warning light on a pilot's control panel have to be to appear twice as bright as the other lights? How much sugar do you need to put in a cup of coffee before it begins to taste sweet? To answer these questions, we must be able to measure the intensity of sensory experiences. This is the central task of **psychophysics,** the study of the relationship between physical stimuli and the behavior or mental experiences the stimuli evoke.

The most significant figure in the history of psychophysics was the German physicist **Gustav Fechner** (1801–1887). Fechner coined the term *psychophysics* and provided a set of procedures to relate the intensity of a physical stimulus—measured in physical units—to the magnitude of the sensory experience—measured in psychological units (Fechner, 1860/1966). Fechner's techniques are the same whether the stimuli are for light, sound, taste, odor, or touch: Researchers determine thresholds and construct psychophysical scales relating strength of sensation to strength of stimuli.

ABSOLUTE THRESHOLDS AND SENSORY ADAPTATION

What is the smallest, weakest stimulus energy that an organism can detect? How soft can a tone be, for instance, and still be heard? These questions refer to the **absolute threshold** for stimulation—the minimum amount of physical energy needed to produce a sensory experience. Researchers measure absolute thresholds by asking vigilant observers to perform detection tasks, such as trying to see a dim light in a dark room or trying to hear a soft sound in a quiet room. During a series of many trials the stimulus is presented at varying

Can you hear the tone? Hearing evaluation is usually done with an absolute threshold test. Why do these tests require multiple trials?

intensities, and on each trial the observers indicate whether they were aware of it. (If you've ever had your hearing evaluated, you participated in an absolute threshold test.)

The results of an absolute threshold study can be summarized in a **psychometric function:** a graph that shows the percentage of detections (plotted on the vertical axis) at each stimulus intensity (plotted on the horizontal axis). A typical psychometric function is shown in **Figure 4.6.** For very dim lights, detection is at 0 percent; for bright lights, detection is at 100 percent. If there were a single, true absolute threshold, you would

expect the transition from 0 to 100 percent detection to be very sharp, occurring right at the point where the intensity reached the threshold. But this does not happen, for at least two reasons: Viewers themselves change slightly each time they try to detect a stimulus (because of changes in attention, fatigue, and so on), and viewers sometimes respond even in the absence of a stimulus (the type of false alarm we will discuss shortly, when we describe signal detection theory). Thus, the psychometric curve is usually a smooth S-shaped curve, in which there is a region of transition from no detection to occasional detection to detection all the time.

Because a stimulus does not suddenly become clearly detectable at all times at a specific intensity, the operational definition of absolute threshold is *the stimulus level at which a sensory signal is detected half the time.* Thresholds for different senses can be measured using the same procedure, simply by changing the stimulus dimension. **Table 4.1** shows absolute threshold levels for several familiar natural stimuli.

Although it is possible to identify absolute thresholds for detection, it is also important to note that your sensory systems are more sensitive to *changes* in the sensory environment than to steady states. The systems have evolved so that they favor new environmental inputs over old through a process called adaptation. **Sensory adaptation** is the diminishing responsiveness of sensory systems to prolonged stimulus input. You may have noticed, for example, that sunshine seems less blinding after a while outdoors. People often have their most fortunate experiences of adaptation in the domain of smell: You walk into a room, and something really has a rank odor; over time, however, as your smell system adapts, the odor fades out of awareness.

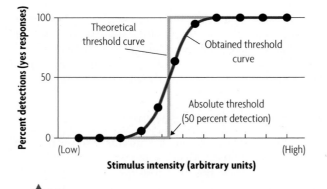

FIGURE 4.6

Calculation of Absolute Thresholds

Because a stimulus does not become suddenly detectable at a certain point, absolute threshold is defined as the intensity at which the stimulus is detected half of the time over many trials.

TABLE 4.1

Approximate Thresholds of Familiar Events

Sense Modality	Detection Threshold
Light	A candle flame seen at 30 miles on a dark, clear night
Sound	The tick of a watch under quiet conditions at 20 feet
Taste	One teaspoon of sugar in 2 gallons of water
Smell	One drop of perfume diffused into the entire volume of a three-room apartment
Touch	The wing of a bee falling on your cheek from a distance of 1 centimeter

<www.ablongman.com/gerrig17e>

Your environment is always full of a great diversity of sensory stimulation. The mechanism of adaptation allows you to notice, and react, more quickly to the challenges of new sources of information.

RESPONSE BIAS AND SIGNAL DETECTION THEORY

In our discussion so far, we have assumed that all observers are created equal. However, threshold measurements can also be affected by **response bias,** the systematic tendency for an observer to favor responding in a particular way because of factors unrelated to the sensory features of the stimulus. Suppose, for example, you are in an experiment in which you must detect a weak light. In the first phase of the experiment, the researcher gives you $5 when you are correct in saying, "Yes, a light was there." In the second phase, the researcher gives you $5 when you are correct in saying, "No, there wasn't any light." In each phase, you are penalized $2 any time you are incorrect. Can you see how this reward structure would create a shift in response bias from phase one to phase two? Wouldn't you say yes more often in the first phase—with the same amount of certainty that the stimulus was present?

Signal detection theory (SDT) is a systematic approach to the problem of response bias (Green & Swets, 1966). Instead of focusing strictly on sensory processes, signal detection theory emphasizes the process of making a *judgment* about the presence or absence of stimulus events. Whereas classical psychophysics conceptualized a single absolute threshold, SDT identifies two distinct processes in sensory detection: (1) an initial *sensory process,* which reflects the observer's sensitivity to the strength of the stimulus; and (2) a subsequent separate *decision process,* which reflects the observer's response biases.

If you decline a dinner invitation, will you be avoiding a dull evening (a correct rejection) or sacrificing the chance for a lifetime of love (a miss)?

SDT offers a procedure for evaluating both the sensory process and the decision processes at once. The measurement procedure is actually just an extension of the idea of catch trials. The basic design is given in **Figure 4.7.** A weak stimulus is presented in half the trials; no stimulus is presented in the other half. In each trial, observers respond by saying *yes* if they think the signal was present and *no* if they think it wasn't. As shown in matrix A of the figure, each response is scored as a hit, a miss, a false alarm, or a correct rejection, depending on whether a signal was, in fact, presented and whether the observer responded accurately.

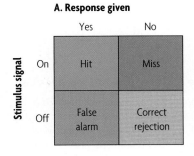
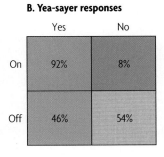
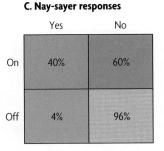

FIGURE 4.7

The Theory of Signal Detection

Matrix A shows the possible outcomes when a subject is asked if a target stimulus occurred on a given trial. Matrixes B and C show the typical responses of a yea-sayer *(biased toward saying yes) and a* nay-sayer *(biased toward saying no).*

An observer who is a *yea-sayer* (chronically answers *yes*) will give a high number of hits but will also have a high number of false alarms, as shown in matrix B. One who is a *nay-sayer* (chronically answers *no*) will give a lower number of hits but also a lower number of false alarms, as shown in matrix C. Working with the percentages of hits and false alarms, researchers use mathematical procedures to calculate separate measures of observers' sensitivity and response biases. This procedure makes it possible to find out whether two observers have the same sensitivity despite large differences in response criterion. By providing a way of separating sensory process from response bias, the theory of signal detection allows an experimenter to identify and separate the roles of the sensory stimulus and the individual's criterion level in producing the final response.

DIFFERENCE THRESHOLDS

Imagine you have been employed by a beverage company that wants to produce a cola product that tastes noticeably sweeter than existing colas, but (to save money) the firm wants to put as little extra sugar in the cola as possible. You are being asked to measure a **difference threshold,** the smallest physical difference between two stimuli that can still be recognized as a difference. To measure a difference threshold, you use pairs of stimuli and ask your observers whether they believe the two stimuli to be the same or different.

For the beverage problem, you would give your observers two colas on each trial, one of some standard recipe and one just a bit sweeter. For each pair, the individual would say *same* or *different.* After many such trials, you would plot a psychometric function by graphing the percent of *different* responses on the vertical axis as a function of the actual differences, plotted on the horizontal axis. The difference threshold is operationally defined as *the point at which the stimuli are recognized as different half of the time.* This difference threshold value is known as a **just noticeable difference,** or **JND.** The JND is a quantitative unit for measuring the magnitude of the psychological difference between any two sensations.

In 1834, **Ernst Weber** pioneered the study of JNDs and discovered the important relationship that we illustrate in **Figure 4.8.** This relationship is summarized as **Weber's law:** *The JND between stimuli is a constant fraction of the intensity of the standard stimulus.* Thus, the bigger or more intense the standard stimulus, the larger the increment needed to get a just noticeable difference. The formula for Weber's law is $\Delta I / I = k$, where I is the intensity of the standard; ΔI, or delta I, is the size of the increase that produces a JND. Weber found that each stimulus dimension has a characteristic value for this ratio. In this formula, k is that ratio, or *Weber's constant,* for the particular stimulus dimension. Weber's law provides a good approximation, but not a perfect fit to experimental data, of how the size of JND

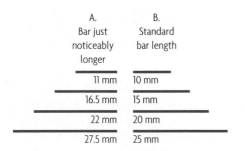

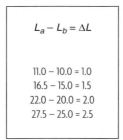

$$L_a - L_b = \Delta L$$

$$11.0 - 10.0 = 1.0$$
$$16.5 - 15.0 = 1.5$$
$$22.0 - 20.0 = 2.0$$
$$27.5 - 25.0 = 2.5$$

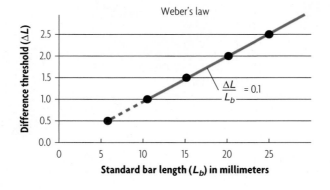

FIGURE 4.8

Just Noticeable Differences and Weber's Law

Suppose you are conducting an experiment in which you challenge participants to detect whether two bars are the same or different in length. The longer the standard bar, the greater the amount you must add (ΔL) to see a just noticeable difference. The difference threshold is the added length detected on half the trials. When these increments are plotted against standard bars of increasing length, the proportions stay the same—the amount added is always one-tenth of the standard length. The relationship is linear, producing a straight line on the graph. We can predict that the ΔL for a bar length of 5 will be 0.5.

increases with intensity (most problems with the law arise when stimulus intensities become extremely high).

You see in **Table 4.2** that Weber's constant (k) has different values for different sensory dimensions—smaller values mean that people can detect smaller differences. So this table tells you that you can differentiate two sound frequencies more precisely than light intensities, which, in turn, are detectable with a smaller JND than odor or taste differences are. Your beverage company would need a relatively large amount of extra sugar to produce a noticeably sweeter cola!

◆ FROM PHYSICAL EVENTS TO MENTAL EVENTS

Our review of psychophysics has made you aware of the central mystery of sensation: How do physical energies give rise to particular psychological experiences? How, for example, do the various physical wavelengths of light give rise to your experience of a rainbow? Before we consider specific sensory domains, we wish to give you an overview of the flow of information from physical events—waves of light and sound, complex chemicals, and so on—to mental events—your experiences of sights, sounds, tastes, and smells.

The conversion of one form of physical energy, such as light, to another form, such as neural impulses, is called **transduction.** Because all sensory information is transduced into identical types of neural impulses, your brain differentiates sensory experiences by devoting special areas of cortex to each sensory domain. For each domain, researchers try to discover how the transduction of physical energy into the electrochemical activity of the nervous system gives rise to sensations of different quality (red rather than green) and different quantity (loud rather than soft).

TABLE 4.2

Weber's Constant Values for Selected Stimulus Dimensions

Stimulus Dimension	Weber's Constant (k)
Sound frequency	0.003
Light intensity	0.01
Odor concentration	0.07
Pressure intensity	0.14
Sound intensity	0.15
Taste concentration	0.20

Sensory systems share the same basic flow of information. The trigger for any sensing system is the detection of an environmental event, or *stimulus.* Environmental stimuli are detected by specialized **sensory receptors.** Sensory receptors convert the physical form of the sensory signal into cellular signals that can be processed by the nervous system. These cellular signals contribute information to higher-level neurons that integrate information across different detector units. At this stage, neurons extract information about the basic qualities of the stimulus, such as its size, intensity, shape, and distance. Deeper into the sensory systems, information is combined into even more complex codes that are passed on to specific areas of the sensory and association cortex of the brain.

We move now to specific sensory domains.

PUT YOURSELF TO THE TEST

- ☛ What is the major goal of the field of psychophysics?
- ☛ How are absolute and difference thresholds measured?
- ☛ How does signal detection theory explain differences in people's performance on detection tasks?
- ☛ What role does transduction play in sensory processes?

The Visual System

Vision is the most complex, highly developed, and important sense for humans and most other mobile creatures. Animals with good vision have an enormous evolutionary advantage. Good vision helps animals detect their prey or predators from a distance. Vision enables humans to be aware of changing features in the physical environment and to adapt their behavior accordingly. Vision is also the most studied of all the senses.

◆ THE HUMAN EYE

The eye is the camera for the brain's motion pictures of the world (see **Figure 4.9**). A camera views the world through a lens that gathers and focuses light. The eye also gathers and focuses light—light enters the *cornea,* a transparent bulge on the front of the eye. Next it

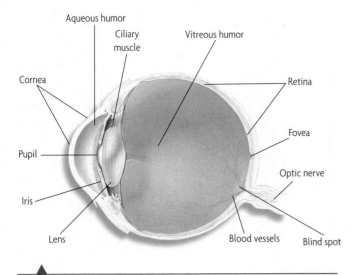

FIGURE 4.9

Structure of the Human Eye

The cornea, pupil, and lens focus light onto the retina. Nerve signals from the retina are carried to the brain by the optic nerve.

passes through the *anterior chamber,* which is filled with a clear liquid called the *aqueous humor.* The light then passes through the *pupil,* an opening in the opaque *iris.* To focus a camera, you move its lens closer to or farther from the object viewed. To focus light in the eye, a bean-shaped crystalline *lens* changes its shape, thinning to focus on distant objects and thickening to focus on near ones. To control the amount of light coming into a camera, you vary the opening of the lens. In the eye, the muscular disk of the iris changes the size of the pupil, the opening through which light passes into the eyeball. At the back of a camera body is the photosensitive film that records the variations in light that have come through the lens. Similarly, in the eye, light travels through the *vitreous humor,* finally striking the *retina,* a thin sheet that lines the rear wall of the eyeball.

As you can see, the features of a camera and the eye are very similar. Now let's examine the components of the vision process in more detail.

◆ THE PUPIL AND THE LENS

The pupil is the opening in the iris through which light passes. The iris makes the pupil dilate or constrict to control the amount of light entering the eyeball. Light passing through the pupil is focused by the lens on the retina; the lens reverses and inverts the light pattern as it does so. The lens is particularly important because of its variable focusing ability for near and far objects. The ciliary muscles can change the thickness of the lens and, hence, its optical properties in a process called **accommodation.**

People with normal accommodation have a range of focus from about 3 inches in front of their nose to as far as they can see. However, many people suffer from accommodation problems. For example, people who are nearsighted have their range of accommodation shifted closer to them with the consequence that they cannot focus well on distant objects; those who are farsighted have their range of accommodation shifted farther away from them so that they cannot focus normally on nearby objects. Aging also leads to problems in accommodation. The lens starts off as clear, transparent, and convex. As people age, however, the lens becomes more amber-tinted, opaque, and flattened, and it loses its elasticity. The effect of some of these changes is that the lens cannot become thick enough for close vision. When people age past the 45-year mark, the *near point*—the closest point at which they can focus clearly—gets progressively farther away.

◆ THE RETINA

You look with your eyes but see with your brain. The eye gathers light, focuses it, and starts a neural signal on its way toward the brain. The eye's critical function, therefore, is to convert information about the world from light waves into neural signals. This happens in the **retina,** at the back of the eye. Under the microscope, you can see that the retina has several highly organized layers of different types of neurons.

The basic conversion from light energy to neural responses is performed in your retina by *rods* and *cones*—receptor cells sensitive to light. These **photoreceptors** are uniquely placed in the visual system between the outer world, ablaze with light, and the inner world of

Visual acuity enables predatory animals to detect potential prey from a distance. What range of functions did evolution provide for the human visual system?

<www.ablongman.com/gerrig17e>

neural processing. Because you sometimes operate in near darkness and sometimes in bright light, nature has provided two ways of processing light, rods and cones (see **Figure 4.10**). The 120 million thin **rods** operate best in near darkness. The 7 million fat **cones** are specialized for the bright, color-filled day.

You experience differences between the functions of your rods and cones each time you turn off the lights to go to sleep at night. You have noticed many times that at first it seems as though you can't see much of anything in the dim light that remains, but over time your visual sensitivity improves again. You are undergoing the process of **dark adaptation**—the gradual improvement of the eyes' sensitivity after a shift in illumination from light to near darkness. Dark adaptation occurs because, as time passes in the dark, your rods become more sensitive than your cones; over time, your rods are able to respond to less light from the environment than your cones are.

Near the center of the retina is a small region called the **fovea,** which contains nothing but densely packed cones—it is rod-free. The fovea is the area of your sharpest vision—both color and spatial detail are most accurately detected there. Other cells in your retina are responsible for integrating information across regions of rods and cones. The **bipolar cells** are nerve cells that combine impulses from many receptors and send the results to ganglion cells. Each **ganglion cell** then integrates the impulses from one or more bipolar cells into a single firing rate. The cones in the central fovea send their impulses to the ganglion cells in that region while, farther out on the periphery of the retina, rods and cones converge on the same bipolar and ganglion cells. The axons of the ganglion cells make up the optic nerve, which carries this visual information out of the eye and back toward the brain.

Your **horizontal cells** and **amacrine cells** integrate information across the retina. Rather than send signals toward the brain, horizontal cells connect receptors to each other, and amacrine cells link bipolar cells to other bipolar cells and ganglion cells to other ganglion cells.

An interesting curiosity in the anatomical design of the retina exists where the optic nerve leaves each eye. This region, called the optic disk, or *blind spot,* contains no receptor cells at all. You do not experience blindness there, except under very special circumstances, for two reasons: First, the blind spots of the two eyes are positioned so that receptors in each eye register what is missed in the other; second, the brain "fills in" this region with appropriate sensory information from the surrounding area.

FIGURE 4.10
Retinal Pathways

This is a stylized and greatly simplified diagram showing the pathways that connect three of the layers of nerve cells in the retina. Incoming light passes through all these layers to reach the receptors, at the back of the eyeball, which are pointed away from the source of light. Note that the bipolar cells gather impulses from more than one receptor cell and send the results to ganglion cells. Nerve impulses (blue arrow) from the ganglion cells leave the eye via the optic nerve and travel to the next relay point.

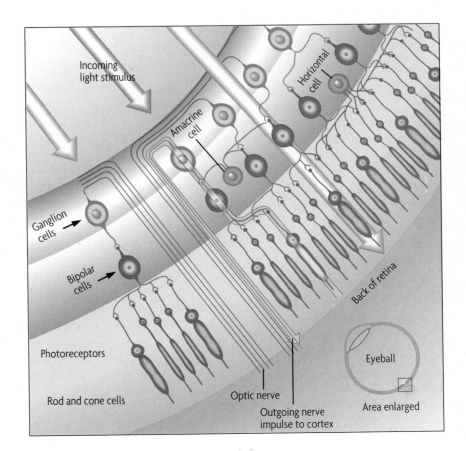

Incoming light stimulus

Horizontal cell

Amacrine cell

Ganglion cells

Bipolar cells

Back of retina

Photoreceptors

Rod and cone cells

Optic nerve

Outgoing nerve impulse to cortex

Eyeball

Area enlarged

To find your blind spot, you will have to look at **Figure 4.11** under special viewing conditions. Hold this book at arm's length, close your right eye, and fixate on the bank figure with your left eye as you bring the book slowly closer. When the dollar sign is in your blind spot, it will disappear, but you will experience no gaping hole in your visual field. Instead, your visual system fills in this area with the background whiteness of the surrounding area so you "see" the whiteness, which isn't there, while failing to see your money, which you should have put in the bank before you lost it!

For a second demonstration of your blind spot, use the same procedure to focus on the plus sign in Figure 4.4. As you pull the book closer to you, do you see the gap disappear and the line become whole?

◆ PROCESSES IN THE BRAIN

The ultimate destination of much visual information is the part of the occipital lobe of the brain known as primary **visual cortex.** However, most information leaving the retinas passes through other brain regions before it arrives at the visual cortex. Let's trace the pathways visual information takes.

The million axons of the ganglion cells that form each **optic nerve** come together in the *optic chiasma,* which resembles the Greek letter X (*chi,* pronounced *kye*). The axons in each optic nerve are divided into two bundles at the optic chiasma. Half of the fibers

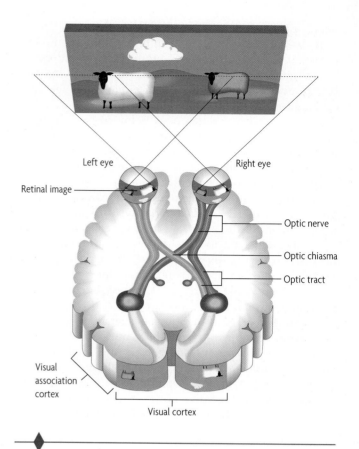

FIGURE 4.12

Pathways in the Human Visual System

The diagram shows the way light from the visual field projects onto the two retinas and the routes by which neural messages from the retina are sent to the two visual centers of each hemisphere.

FIGURE 4.11

Find Your Blind Spot

To find your blind spot, hold this book at arm's length, close your right eye, and fixate on the bank figure with your left eye as you bring the book slowly closer. When the dollar sign is in your blind spot, it will disappear, but you will experience no gaping hole in your visual field. Similarly, if you use the same procedure to focus on the plus sign, the line will appear whole when the gap is in your blind spot. In both cases, your visual system fills in the background whiteness of the surrounding area so you "see" the whiteness, which isn't there.

from each retina remain on the side of the body from which they originated. The axons from the inner half of each eye cross over the midline as they continue their journey toward the back of the brain (see **Figure 4.12**).

These two bundles of fibers, which now contain axons from both eyes, are renamed *optic tracts.* The optic tracts deliver information to two clusters of cells in the brain. Research supports the theory that visual analysis is separated into pathways for *pattern recognition*—how things look—and *place recognition*—where things are (Pasternak et al., 2003; Rao et al., 1997). The division into pattern and place recognition gives you an example of the way in which your visual system consists of several separate subsystems that analyze different aspects of the same retinal image. Although your final perception is of a unified visual scene, your vision of it is accomplished through a host of pathways in

<www.ablongman.com/gerrig17e>

your visual system that, under normal conditions, are exquisitely coordinated.

Pioneering work on how your visual system pieces together information from the world was done by **David Hubel** and **Torsten Wiesel,** sensory physiologists who won a Nobel Prize in 1981 for their studies of *receptive fields* of cells in the visual cortex. The **receptive field** of a cell is the area in the visual field from which it receives stimulation. As shown in **Figure 4.13,** Hubel and Wiesel discovered that cells at different levels of the visual system responded most strongly to different patterns of stimulation. For example, one type of cortical cell, *simple* cells, responded most strongly to bars of light in their "favorite" orientation (see Figure 4.13). *Complex* cells also each have a "favorite" orientation, but they require as well that the bar be moving. *Hypercomplex* cells require moving bars of a particular length or moving corners or angles. The cells provide types of information to higher visual centers in the brain that ultimately allow the brain to recognize objects in the visual world.

The advances in imaging techniques we described in Chapter 3 have enabled researchers to discover regions of the cortex that are specially responsive to even more complex environmental images.

PUTTING IDEAS TO THE TEST

Visual Processing of the Human Body

Take a moment to look at your hand. Now focus on any other object in the room. If a team of researchers is correct, one particular region of your brain just turned on and off as you shifted your focus from your hand—a body part—to an object from a different category (Downing et al., 2001). To test this hypothesis, the researchers collected fMRI data with the range of pictures shown in **Figure 4.14.** The fMRI images of the brain demonstrated that a region of the cortex on the boundary between the occipital and temporal lobes was selectively active to depictions of the human body (A–F). The exceptions to this finding were faces (G) and parts of faces (M). Other brain regions appear to handle the processing of human faces.

Humans are particularly important to other humans—that probably explains why particular brain regions are devoted to the processing of human faces and bodies. However, researchers still do not know if those regions have those special functions at birth or if those functions are the product of a lifetime of experience.

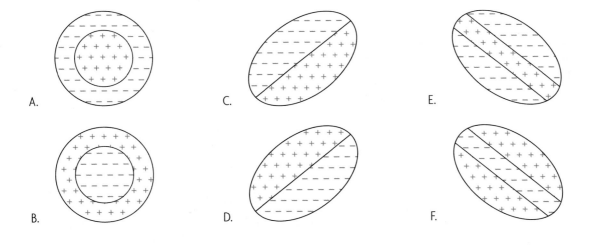

A. B. C. D. E. F.

FIGURE 4.13

Receptive Fields of Ganglion and Cortical Cells

The receptive field of a cell in the visual pathway is the area in the visual field from which it receives stimulation. The receptive fields of the ganglion cells in the retina are circular (A, B); those of the simplest cells in the visual cortex are elongated in a particular orientation (C, D, E, F). In both cases, the cell responding to the receptive field is excited by light in the regions marked with plus signs and inhibited by light in the regions marked with minus signs. In addition, the stimulus that most excites the cell is the one in which areas where light is excitatory (marked with plus signs) are illuminated, but areas where light is inhibitory (marked by minus signs) are in darkness.

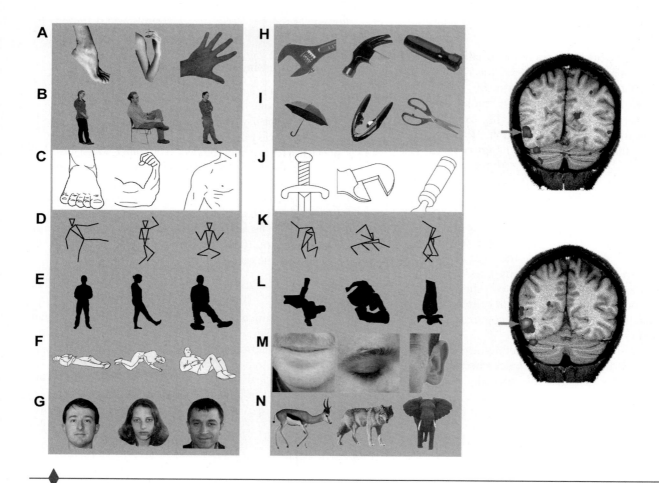

FIGURE 4.14

Cortical Regions for the Visual Processing of the Human Body

Researchers used fMRI to assess participants' brain responses to 19 different types of stimuli. One region of the cortex on the boundary between the occipital and temporal lobes became selectively active in response to all depictions of the human body (A–F). This region was not activated when participants viewed whole faces (G), objects (H–J) or scrambled bodies (K–L). The region became active at an intermediate level in response to face parts (M) and mammals (N).

You have now learned the basics of how visual information is distributed from the eyes to various parts of the brain. Researchers still have more to learn: There are roughly 30 anatomical subdivisions of primate visual cortex, and theories vary about the pattern of communication among those areas (Hilgetag et al., 1996). For now, we turn to particular aspects of the visual world. One of the most remarkable features of the human visual system is that your experiences of form, color, position, and depth are based on processing the same sensory information in different ways. How do the transformations occur that enable you to see these different features of the visual world?

◆ SEEING COLOR

Physical objects seem to have the marvelous property of being painted with color. You most often have the impression of brightly colored objects—red valentines, green fir trees, or blue robins' eggs—but your vivid experience of color relies on the rays of light these objects reflect onto your sensory receptors. Color is created when your brain processes the information coded in the light source.

<www.ablongman.com/gerrig17e>

Can Technology Restore Sight?

In December 1999 several news agencies reported that Stevie Wonder, the pop star who had been blind nearly from birth, was hoping to undergo an experimental surgical procedure that would restore his sight. In the procedure, developed by **Wentai Liu, Mark Humayun,** and their team of researchers (Liu et al., 2000), a small microchip is connected directly to the retina to replace the function of rods and cones that have been incapacitated by disease. Unfortunately, because of the length of time for which he has been blind, Wonder proved not to be a good candidate for this procedure. However, the technique holds out real promise for those individuals for whom more of the circuitry of the visual system is still intact.

Most blind people have become blind because the receptor cells in their retinas—the rods and cones—succumb to a degenerative disease. (Wonder's blindness was a consequence of too much oxygen being delivered to the incubator in which

he was placed shortly after birth.) Even when the sensory receptors cease to function, however, the other cells in the visual pathway—such as bipolar and ganglion cells—survive at high rates. Given the structure of the retina (see Figure 4.10), these other cells are accessible for direct electrical stimulation. The microchip developed by Liu, Humayun, and their colleagues does exactly that: It provides a pattern of electrical stimulation that replaces input from the nonfunctioning rods and cones.

The full system, known as the *multiple-unit artificial retina chipset* (MARC), has several components that function both outside and inside the eyeball. For example, a miniature video camera captures images from the environment. These images are processed and delivered to the microchip surgically implanted on the retina at the back of the eye. The microchip stimulates the ganglion cells in a grid that functions in a way comparable to the operation of a TV or computer

screen: Each element of the array—each *pixel*—can take on different values of gray to provide a range of visual sensations.

As you might infer, the MARC procedure will not restore full sight in the way implied by the articles about Stevie Wonder. The amount of information the device provides is quite limited compared to what you ordinarily obtain through your vast number of rods and cones. However, participants in experimental trials of the MARC have been able to identify simple images and shapes. The hope is that the MARC would restore visual function at least to the point at which people could navigate through their environment and read large-print texts. For the millions of people worldwide affected by diseases that cause degeneration of rods and cones, evolving technologies like MARC may very well provide an ingenious means to help preserve visual function.

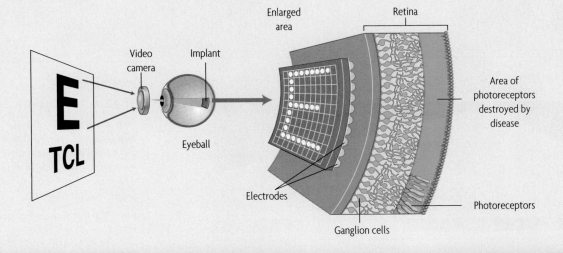

What three dimensions underlie experiences of color?

WAVELENGTHS AND HUES

The light you see is just a small portion of a physical dimension called the *electromagnetic spectrum* (see **Figure 4.15**). Your visual system is not equipped to detect other types of waves in this spectrum, such as X-rays, microwaves, and radio waves. The physical property that distinguishes types of electromagnetic energy, including light, is *wavelength,* the distance between the crests of two adjacent waves. Wavelengths of visible light are measured in *nanometers* (billionths of a meter). What you see as light is the range of wavelengths from 400 to about 700 nanometers. Light rays of particular physical wavelengths give rise to experiences of particular colors—for example, violet–blue at the lower end and red–orange at the higher end. Thus, light

is described physically in terms of wavelengths, not colors; colors exist only in your sensory system's interpretation of the wavelengths.

All experiences of color can be described in terms of three basic dimensions: hue, saturation, and brightness. **Hue** is the dimension that captures the qualitative experience of the color of a light. In pure lights that contain only one wavelength (such as a laser beam), the psychological experience of hue corresponds directly to the physical dimension of the light's wavelength. **Figure 4.16** presents the hues arranged in a color circle. Those hues perceived to be most similar are in adjacent positions. This order mirrors the order of hues in the spectrum. **Saturation** is the psychological dimension that captures the purity and vividness of color sensations. Undiluted colors have the most saturation; muted, muddy, and pastel colors have intermediate amounts of saturation; and grays have zero saturation. **Brightness** is the dimension of color experience that captures the intensity of light. White has the most brightness; black has the least. When colors are analyzed along these three dimensions, a remarkable finding emerges: Humans are capable of visually discriminating about 7 million different colors! However, most people can label only a small number of those colors.

Let's explain some facts about your everyday experience of color. At some point in your science education, you may have repeated Sir Isaac Newton's discovery that sunlight combines all wavelengths of light: You repeated Newton's proof by using a prism to separate sunlight into the full rainbow of colors. The prism shows that the right combination of wavelengths will

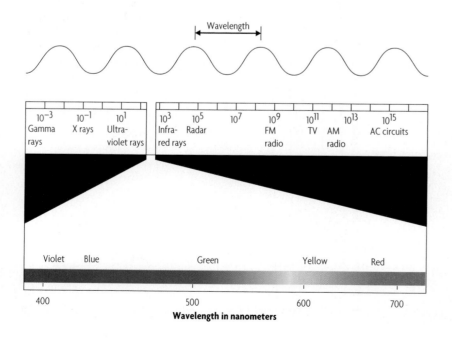

FIGURE 4.15

The Electromagnetic Spectrum

Your visual system can sense only a small range of wavelengths in the electromagnetic spectrum. You experience that range of wavelengths, which is enlarged in the figure, as the colors violet through red.

From "The Electromagnetic Spectrum," *Perception,* 3e by R. Sekular et al., pp. 27, 221, copyright © 1994 by the McGraw-Hill Companies. Reprinted by permission of the McGraw-Hill Companies.

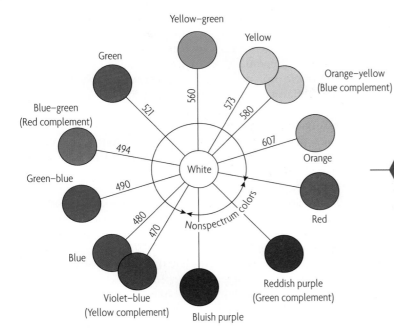

FIGURE 4.16
The Color Circle

Colors are arranged based on similarity. Complementary colors are placed directly opposite each other. Mixing complementary colors yields a neutral gray or white light at the center. The numbers next to each hue are the wavelength values for spectral colors, those colors within the regions of visual sensitivity. Nonspectral hues are obtained by mixing short and long spectral wavelengths.

yield white light. The combination of wavelengths is called *additive color mixture*. Take another look at Figure 4.16. Wavelengths that appear directly across from each other on the color circle—called **complementary colors**—will create the sensation of white light when mixed. Do you want to prove to yourself the existence of complementary colors? Consider **Figure 4.17.** The green–yellow–black flag should give you the experience of a *negative afterimage* (the afterimage is called "negative" because it is the opposite of the original color). For reasons that we will explain when we consider theories of color vision, when you stare at any color long enough to partially fatigue your photoreceptors, looking at a white surface will allow you to experience the complement of the original color.

You have probably noticed afterimages from time to time in your everyday exposure to colors. Most of your experience with colors, however, does not come from complementary lights. Instead, you have probably spent your time at play with colors by combining crayons or paints of different hues. The colors you see when you look at a crayon mark, or any other colored surface, are the wavelengths of light that are not absorbed by the surface. Although yellow crayon looks mostly yellow, it lets some wavelengths escape that give rise to the sensation of green. Similarly, blue crayon lets wavelengths escape that give rise to the sensations of blue and some green. When yellow and blue crayon are combined, yellow absorbs blue and blue absorbs yellow—the only wavelengths that are not absorbed look green! This phenomenon is called *subtractive color mixture*. The remaining wavelengths that are not absorbed—the wavelengths that are reflected—give the crayon mixture the color you perceive.

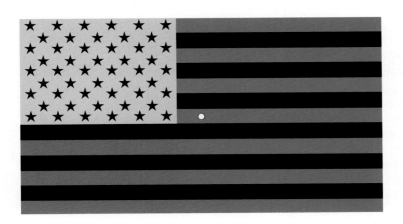

FIGURE 4.17
Color Afterimages

Stare at the dot in the center of the green, black, and yellow flag for at least 30 seconds. Then fixate on the center of a sheet of white paper or a blank wall. Try this aftereffect illusion on your friends.

Some of these rules about the experience of color do not apply to those people born with a color deficiency. *Color blindness* is the partial or total inability to distinguish colors. The negative afterimage effect of viewing the green, yellow, and black flag will not work if you are color-blind. Color blindness is usually a sex-linked hereditary defect associated with a gene on the X chromosome. Because males have a single X chromosome, they are more likely than females to show this recessive trait. Females would need to have a defective gene on both X chromosomes to be color-blind. An estimate for color blindness among Caucasian males is about 8 percent, but less than 0.5 percent among females (Coren et al., 1999).

Most color blindness involves difficulty distinguishing red from green, especially at weak saturations. More rare are people who confuse yellows and blues. Rarest of all are those who see no color at all, only variations in brightness. Let's now see how scientists have explained facts about color vision such as complementary colors and color blindness.

THEORIES OF COLOR VISION

The first scientific theory of color vision was proposed by **Sir Thomas Young** around 1800. He suggested that there were three types of color receptors in the normal human eye that produced psychologically primary sensations: red, green, and blue. All other colors, he believed, were additive or subtractive combinations of these three primaries. Young's theory was later refined and extended by **Hermann von Helmholtz** and came to be known as the Young-Helmholtz **trichromatic theory.**

Trichromatic theory provided a plausible explanation for people's color sensations and for color blindness (according to the theory, color-blind people had only one or two kinds of receptors). However, other facts and observations were not as well explained by the theory. Why did adaptation to one color produce color afterimages that had the complementary hue? Why did color-blind people always fail to distinguish pairs of colors: red and green or blue and yellow?

Answers to these questions became the cornerstones for a second theory of color vision proposed by **Ewald Hering** in the late 1800s. According to his **opponent-process theory,** all color experiences arise from three underlying systems, each of which includes two opponent elements: red versus green, blue versus yellow, or black (no color) versus white (all colors). Hering theorized that colors produced complementary afterimages because one element of the system became fatigued (from overstimulation) and thus increased the relative contribution of its opponent element. Acccording to Hering's theory, types of color blindness came in pairs

because the color system was actually built from pairs of opposites, not from single primary colors.

For many years, scientists debated the merits of the theories. Eventually, scientists recognized that the theories were not really in conflict; they simply described two different stages of processing that corresponded to successive physiological structures in the visual system (Hurvich & Jameson, 1974). We now know, for example, that there are, indeed, three types of cones. Although the three types each respond to a range of wavelengths, they are each *most* sensitive to light at a particular wavelength. The responses of these cone types confirm Young and Helmholtz's prediction that color vision relies on three types of color receptors. People who are color-blind lack one or more of these types of receptor cones.

We also now know that the retinal ganglion cells combine the outputs of these three cone types in accordance with Hering's opponent-process theory (De Valois & Jacobs, 1968). According to the contemporary version of opponent-process theory, as supported by **Leo Hurvich** and **Dorothea Jameson** (1974), the two members of each color pair work in opposition (are opponents) by means of neural inhibition. Some ganglion cells receive excitatory input from lights that appear red and inhibitory input from lights that appear green. Other cells in the system have the opposite arrangement of excitation and inhibition. Together, these two types of ganglion cells form the physiological basis of the red/green opponent-process system. Other ganglion cells make up the blue/yellow opponent system. The black/white system contributes to your perception of color saturation and brightness.

We turn now from the world of sight to the world of sound.

PUT YOURSELF TO THE TEST

- In what ways are the features of the eye similar to the features of a camera?
- What are the functions of the different types of the nerve cells in the retina?
- How do rods and cones differ in their functions?
- What have researchers learned about visual processing in the brain?
- What facts about color vision are captured by the contrasting theories?

Hearing

Hearing and vision play complementary functions in your experience of the world. You often hear stimuli before you see them, particularly if they take place behind you or on the other side of opaque objects such as walls. Although vision is better than hearing for identifying an object once it is in the field of view, you often see the object only because you have used your ears to point your eyes in the right direction. To begin our discussion of hearing, we describe the types of physical energy that arrive at your ears.

◆ THE PHYSICS OF SOUND

Clap your hands. Whistle. Tap your pencil on the table. Why do these actions create sounds? The reason is that they cause objects to vibrate. The vibrational energy is transmitted to the surrounding medium—usually air—as the vibrating objects push molecules of the medium back and forth. The resulting slight changes in pressure spread outward from the vibrating objects in the form of a combination of *sine waves* traveling at a rate of about 1,100 feet per second (see **Figure 4.18**). Sound cannot be created in a true vacuum (such as outer space) because there are no air molecules in a vacuum for vibrating objects to move.

A sine wave has two basic physical properties that determine how it sounds to you: frequency and amplitude. *Frequency* measures the number of cycles the wave completes in a given amount of time. A cycle, as indicated in Figure 4.18, is the left-to-right distance from the peak in one wave to the peak in the next wave. Sound frequency is usually expressed in *hertz* (Hz), which measures cycles per second. *Amplitude* measures the physical property of strength of the sound wave, as shown in its peak-to-valley height. Amplitude is defined in units of sound pressure or energy.

◆ PSYCHOLOGICAL DIMENSIONS OF SOUND

The physical properties of frequency and amplitude give rise to the three psychological dimensions of sound: pitch, loudness, and timbre. Let's see how these phenomena work.

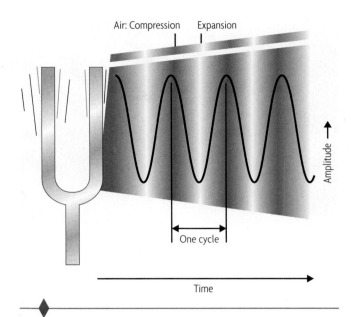

FIGURE 4.18

An Idealized Sine Wave

The two basic properties of sine waves are their frequency—the number of cycles in a fixed unit of time—and their amplitude—the vertical range of their cycles.

PITCH

Pitch is the highness or lowness of a sound determined by the sound's frequency; high frequencies produce high pitch, and low frequencies produce low pitch. The full range of human sensitivity to pure tones extends from frequencies as low as 20 Hz to frequencies as high as 20,000 Hz. (Frequencies below 20 Hz may be experienced through touch as vibrations rather than as sound.) You can get a sense of how big this range is by noting that the 88 keys on a piano cover only the range from about 30 to 4,000 Hz.

As you might expect from our earlier discussion of psychophysics, the relationship between frequency (the physical reality) and pitch (the psychological effect) is not a linear one. At the low end of the frequency scale, increasing the frequency by just a few hertz raises the pitch quite noticeably. At the high end of frequency, you require a much bigger increase in order to hear the difference in pitch. For example, the two lowest notes on a piano differ by only 1.6 Hz, whereas the two highest ones differ by 235 Hz. This is another example of the psychophysics of just noticeable differences.

What physical properties of sounds allow you to pick out the timbres of individual instruments from a musical ensemble?

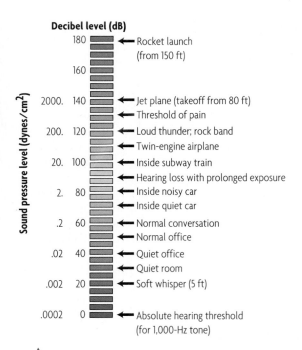

FIGURE 4.19

Decibel Levels of Familiar Sounds

This figure shows the range in decibels of the sounds to which you respond from the absolute threshold for hearing to the noise of a rocket launch. Decibels are calculated from sound pressure, which is a measure of a sound wave's amplitude level and generally corresponds to what you experience as loudness.

LOUDNESS

The **loudness,** or physical intensity, of a sound is determined by its amplitude; sound waves with large amplitudes are experienced as loud and those with small amplitudes as soft. The human auditory system is sensitive to an enormous range of physical intensities. At one limit, you can hear the tick of a wristwatch at 20 feet. This is the system's absolute threshold—if it were more sensitive, you would hear the blood flowing in your ears. At the other extreme, a jetliner taking off 100 yards away is so loud that the sound is painful. In terms of physical units of sound pressure, the jet produces a sound wave with more than a billion times the energy of the ticking watch.

Because the range of hearing is so great, physical intensities of sound are usually expressed in ratios rather than absolute amounts; sound pressure—the index of amplitude level that gives rise to the experience of loudness—is measured in units called decibels (dB). **Figure 4.19** shows the decibel measures of some representative natural sounds. It also shows the corresponding sound pressures for comparison. You can see that two sounds differing by 20 dB have sound pressures in a ratio of 10 to 1. Note that sounds louder than about 90 dB can produce hearing loss, depending on how long a person is exposed to them.

TIMBRE

The **timbre** of a sound reflects the components of its complex sound wave. Timbre is what sets apart, for example, the sound of a piano from the sound of a flute. A small number of physical stimuli, such as a tuning fork, produce pure tones consisting of a single sine wave. A *pure tone* has only one frequency and one amplitude. Most sounds in the real world are not pure tones. They are complex waves, containing a combination of frequencies and amplitudes.

The sounds that you call *noise* do not have the clear, simple structures of frequencies. Noise contains many frequencies that are not systematically related. For instance, the static noise you hear between radio stations contains energy at all audible frequencies; you perceive it as having no pitch because it has no fundamental frequency.

◆ THE PHYSIOLOGY OF HEARING

Now that you know something about the physical bases of your psychological experiences of sound, let's see how those experiences arise from physiological activity in the auditory system. First, we will look at the way the ear works. Then we will consider some theories about how pitch experiences are coded in the auditory system and how sounds are localized.

THE AUDITORY SYSTEM

You have already learned that sensory processes transform forms of external energy into forms of energy within your brain. For you to hear, as shown in **Figure 4.20,** four basic energy transformations must take place: (1) Airborne sound waves must get translated into *fluid* waves within the *cochlea* of the ear, (2) the fluid waves must then stimulate mechanical vibrations of the *basilar membrane*, (3) these vibrations must be converted into electrical impulses, and (4) the impulses must travel to the *auditory cortex*. Let's examine each of these transformations in detail.

In the first transformation, vibrating air molecules enter the ears (see Figure 4.20). Some sound enters the external canal of the ear directly and some enters after having been reflected off the *external ear,* or *pinna.* The sound wave travels along the canal through the outer ear until it reaches the end of the canal. There it encounters a thin membrane called the eardrum, or *tympanic membrane.* The sound wave's pressure variations set the eardrum into motion. The eardrum trans-mits the vibrations from the outer ear into the middle ear, a chamber that contains the three smallest bones in the human body: the *hammer,* the *anvil,* and the *stirrup.* These bones form a mechanical chain that transmits and concentrates the vibrations from the eardrum to the primary organ of hearing, the *cochlea,* which is located in the *inner ear.*

In the second transformation, which occurs in the cochlea, the airborne sound wave becomes "seaborne." The **cochlea** is a fluid-filled, coiled tube that has a membrane, known as the **basilar membrane,** running down its middle along its length. When the stirrup vibrates against the oval window at the base of the cochlea, the fluid in the cochlea causes the basilar membrane to move in a wavelike motion (hence, "seaborne").

In the third transformation, the wavelike motion of the basilar membrane bends the tiny hair cells connected

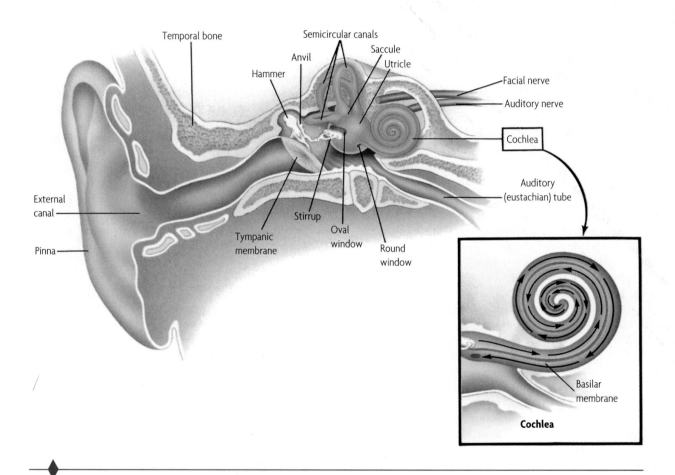

FIGURE 4.20

Structure of the Human Ear

Sound waves are channeled by the external ear, or pinna, through the external canal, causing the tympanic membrane to vibrate. This vibration activates the tiny bones of the inner ear—the hammer, anvil, and stirrup. Their mechanical vibrations are passed along from the oval window to the cochlea, where they set in motion the fluid in its canal. Tiny hair cells lining the coiled basilar membrane within the cochlea bend as the fluid moves, stimulating nerve endings attached to them. The mechanical energy is then transformed into neural energy and sent to the brain via the auditory nerve.

Sustained exposure to loud noise can lead to hearing loss. What can people do to avoid such losses?

to the membrane. The hair cells are the receptor cells for the auditory system. As the hair cells bend, they stimulate nerve endings, transforming the mechanical vibrations of the basilar membrane into neural activity.

Finally, in the fourth transformation, nerve impulses leave the cochlea in a bundle of fibers called the **auditory nerve.** These fibers meet in the *cochlear nucleus* of the brain stem. Similar to the crossing over of nerves in the visual system, stimulation from one ear goes to both sides of the brain. Auditory signals pass through a series of other nuclei on their way to the **auditory cortex,** in the temporal lobes of the cerebral hemispheres. Higher-order processing of these signals begins in the auditory cortex. (As you will learn shortly, other parts of the ear labeled in Figure 4.20 play roles in your other senses.)

The four transformations occur in fully functioning auditory systems. However, millions of people suffer from some form of hearing impairment. There are two general types of hearing impairment, each caused by a defect in one or more of the components of the auditory system. The less serious type of impairment is *conduction deafness,* a problem in the conduction of the air vibrations to the cochlea. Often in this type of impairment, the bones in the middle ear are not functioning properly, a problem that may be corrected in microsurgery by insertion of an

artificial anvil or stirrup. The more serious type of impairment is *nerve deafness,* a defect in the neural mechanisms that create nerve impulses in the ear or relay them to the auditory cortex. Damage to the auditory cortex can also create nerve deafness.

THEORIES OF PITCH PERCEPTION

To explain how the auditory system converts sound waves into sensations of pitch, researchers have outlined two distinct theories: place theory and frequency theory.

Place theory was initially proposed by Hermann von Helmholtz in the 1800s and was later modified, elaborated, and tested by **Georg von Békésy,** who won a Nobel Prize for this work in 1961. Place theory is based on the fact that the basilar membrane moves when sound waves are conducted through the inner ear. Different frequencies produce their most movement at particular locations along the basilar membrane. For high-frequency tones, the wave motion is greatest at the base of the cochlea, where the oval and round windows are located. For low-frequency tones, the greatest wave motion of the basilar membrane is at the opposite end. So place theory suggests that perception of pitch depends on the specific location on the basilar membrane at which the greatest stimulation occurs.

The second theory, **frequency theory,** explains pitch by the rate of vibration of the basilar membrane. This theory predicts that a sound wave with a frequency of 100 Hz will set the basilar membrane vibrating 100 times per second. The frequency theory also predicts that the vibrations of the basilar membrane will cause neurons to fire at the same rate, so that rate of firing is the neural code for pitch. One problem with this theory is that individual neurons cannot fire rapidly enough to represent high-pitched sounds, because none of them can fire more than 1,000 times per second. This limitation makes it impossible for one neuron to distinguish sounds above 1,000 Hz—which, of course, your auditory system can do quite well. The limitation might be overcome by the **volley principle,** which explains what might happen at such high frequencies. This principle suggests that several neurons in a combined action, or volley, fire at the frequency that matches a stimulus tone of 2,000 Hz, 3,000 Hz, and so on (Wever, 1949).

As with the trichromatic and opponent-process theories of color vision, the place and frequency theories each successfully account for different aspects of your experience of pitch. Frequency theory accounts well for coding frequencies below about 5,000 Hz. At higher frequencies, neurons cannot fire quickly and precisely enough to code a signal adequately, even in volley. Place theory accounts well for perception of pitch at frequencies above 1,000 Hz. Below 1,000 Hz, the entire basilar membrane vibrates so broadly that it cannot pro-

　　　　　　　　　　　　　　　　　　　　　　<www.ablongman.com/gerrig17e>

vide a signal distinctive enough for the neural receptors to use as a means of distinguishing pitch. Between 1,000 and 5,000 Hz, both mechanisms can operate. Thus a complex sensory task is divided between two systems that, together, offer greater sensory precision than either system alone could provide. We will next see that you also possess two converging neural systems to help you localize sounds in the environment.

SOUND LOCALIZATION

Suppose you are walking across campus and you hear someone call your name. In most cases, you can readily locate the spatial location of the speaker. This example suggests how efficiently your auditory system carries out the task of **sound localization**—you are able to determine the spatial origins of auditory events. You do so through two mechanisms: assessments of the relative timing and relative intensity of the sounds that arrive at each ear (Middlebrooks & Green, 1991; Phillips, 1993).

The first mechanism involves neurons that compare the relative times at which incoming sound reaches each ear. A sound occurring off to your right side, for example, reaches your right ear before your left (see point B in **Figure 4.21**). Neurons in your auditory system are specialized to fire most actively for specific time delays between the two ears. Your brain uses this information about disparities in arrival time to make precise estimates for the likely origins of a sound in space.

The second mechanism relies on the principle that a sound has a slightly greater intensity in the first ear at which it arrives—because your head itself casts a *sound shadow* that weakens the signal. These intensity differences depend on the relative size of the wavelength of a tone with respect to your head. Large-wavelength, low-frequency tones show virtually no intensity differences, whereas small-wavelength, high-frequency tones show measurable intensity differences. Your brain, once again, has specialized cells that detect intensity differences in the signals arriving at your two ears.

Why might bats have evolved the ability to use echolocation to navigate through their environment?

But what happens when a sound creates neither a timing nor an intensity difference? In Figure 4.21, a sound originating at point A would have this property. With your eyes closed, you cannot tell its exact location. So you must move your head—to reposition your ears—to break the symmetry and provide the necessary information for sound localization.

It's interesting to note that porpoises and bats use their auditory systems rather than their visual systems to locate objects in dark waters or dark caves. These species use *echolocation*—they emit high-pitched sounds that bounce off objects, giving them feedback about the objects' distances, locations, sizes, textures, and movements. In fact, one species of bat is able to use echolocation to differentiate between objects that are just 0.3 millimeters apart (Simmons et al., 1998).

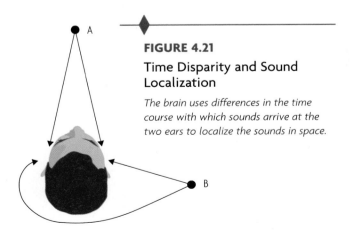

FIGURE 4.21

Time Disparity and Sound Localization

The brain uses differences in the time course with which sounds arrive at the two ears to localize the sounds in space.

PUT YOURSELF TO THE TEST

- What relationships exist between the physical and psychological dimensions of sounds?
- What four major energy transformations take place in the auditory system?
- How do the two theories of pitch perception combine to explain your auditory experiences?
- What two mechanisms allow you to localize sounds in space?

Your Other Senses

We have devoted the most attention to vision and hearing because scientists have studied them most thoroughly. However, your ability both to survive in and to enjoy the external environment relies on your full repertory of senses. We will close our discussion of sensation with brief analyses of several of your other senses.

◆ SMELL

You can probably imagine circumstances in which you'd be just as happy to give up your sense of smell: Did you ever have a family dog who lost a battle with a skunk? But to avoid that skunk experience, you'd also have to give up the smells of fresh roses, hot buttered popcorn, and sea breezes. Odors—both good and bad—first make their presence known by interacting with receptor proteins on the membranes of *olfactory cilia* (see **Figure 4.22**). It takes only eight molecules of a substance to initiate one of these nerve impulses, but at least 40 nerve endings must be stimulated before you can smell the substance. Once initiated, these nerve impulses convey odor information to the **olfactory bulb,** located just above the receptors and just below the frontal lobes of the cerebrum. Odor stimuli start the process of smell by stimulating an influx of chemical substances into ion channels in olfactory neurons, an event that, as you may recall from Chapter 3, triggers an action potential.

The significance of the sense of smell varies greatly across species. Smell presumably evolved as a system for detecting and locating food (Moncrieff, 1951). Humans seem to use the sense of smell primarily in conjunction with taste, to seek and sample food. However, for many species smell is also used to detect potential sources of danger. Dogs, rats, insects, and many other creatures for whom smell is central to survival have a far keener sense of smell than humans do. Relatively more of their brain is devoted to smell. Smell serves these species well because organisms do not have to come into direct contact with other organisms in order to smell them.

In addition, smell can be a powerful form of active communication. Members of many species communicate by secreting and detecting chemical signals called pheromones. **Pheromones** are chemical substances used within a given species to signal sexual receptivity, danger, territorial boundaries, and food sources (Luo et al., 2003). For example, male members of various insect species produce sex pheromones to alert females that they are available for mating (Farine et al., 1996; Minckley et al., 1991). We will revisit the topic of pheromones when we discuss both human and non-human sexual behaviors in Chapter 11.

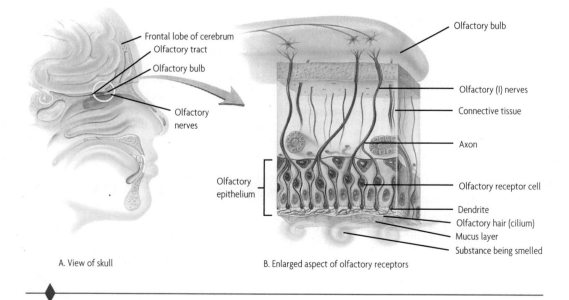

A. View of skull

B. Enlarged aspect of olfactory receptors

FIGURE 4.22

Receptors for Smell

The olfactory receptor cells in your nasal cavities are stimulated by chemicals in the environment. They send information to the olfactory bulb in your brain.

Why would a man with chronic sinus trouble be ill-advised to take up wine tasting?

◆ TASTE

Although food and wine gourmets are capable of making remarkably subtle and complex taste distinctions, many of their sensations are really smells, not tastes. Taste and smell work together closely when you eat. In fact, when you have a cold, food seems tasteless because your nasal passages are blocked and you can't smell the food. Demonstrate this principle for yourself: Hold your nose and try to tell the difference between foods of similar texture but different tastes, such as pieces of apple and raw potato. Some students living on campuses with notoriously bad food have reported that wearing nose plugs to meals makes everything taste uniformly bland—which is better than the usual taste!

The surface of your tongue is covered with *papillae,* which give it a bumpy appearance. Many of these papillae contain clusters of taste receptor cells called the *taste buds* (see **Figure 4.23**). Single-cell recordings of taste receptors show that individual receptor cells respond best to one of the four primary taste qualities: sweet, sour, bitter, and saline (salty) (Frank & Nowlis, 1989). In recent years, researchers have found receptors for a fifth basic taste quality, *umami* (Chaudhari, Landin, & Roper, 2000). Umami is the flavor of monosodium glutamate (MSG), the chemical that is often added to Asian foods and occurs naturally in foods rich in protein, such as meat, seafood, and aged cheese. Although receptor cells for the five qualities may produce small responses to other tastes, the "best" response most directly encodes quality. There appear to be separate transduction systems for each of the basic classes of taste (Bartoshuk & Beauchamp, 1994).

Taste receptors can be damaged by many things you put in your mouth, such as alcohol, cigarette smoke, and acids. Fortunately, your taste receptors get replaced every few days—even more frequently than smell receptors. Indeed, the taste system is the most resistant to damage of all your sensory systems; it is extremely rare for anyone to suffer a total, permanent taste loss (Bartoshuk, 1990).

◆ TOUCH AND SKIN SENSES

The skin is a remarkably versatile organ. In addition to protecting you against surface injury, holding in body fluids, and helping regulate body temperature, it contains nerve endings that produce sensations of pressure, warmth, and cold. These sensations are called the **cutaneous senses** (skin senses).

Because you receive so much sensory information through your skin, many different types of receptor cells operate close to the surface of the body. Each type of receptor responds to somewhat different patterns of contact with the skin (Sekuler & Blake, 2001). As two examples, *Meissner corpuscles* respond best when something rubs against the skin, and *Merkel disks* are most active when a small object exerts steady pressure against the skin. You may be surprised to learn that you have separate receptors for warmth and coolness. Rather than having one type of receptor that works like a thermometer, your brain integrates separate warm and cool signals to monitor changes in environmental temperature.

The skin's sensitivity to pressure varies tremendously over the body. For example, you are ten times more accurate in sensing the position of stimulation on your fingertips than on your back. The variation in sensitivity of different body regions is shown by the greater density of nerve endings in these regions and also by the greater amount of sensory cortex devoted to them. In Chapter 3, you learned that your sensitivity is greatest where you need it most—on your face, tongue, and hands. Precise sensory feedback from these parts of the body permits effective eating, speaking, and grasping.

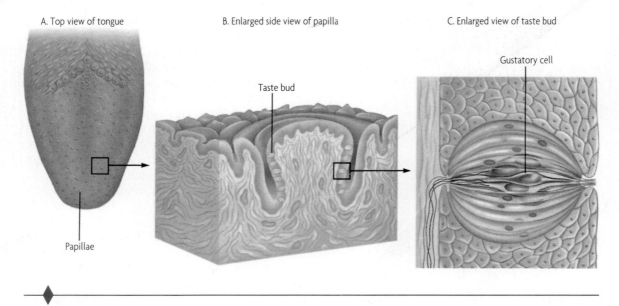

A. Top view of tongue   B. Enlarged side view of papilla   C. Enlarged view of taste bud

Gustatory cell

Taste bud

Papillae

FIGURE 4.23

Receptors for Taste

Part A shows the distribution of the papillae on the upper side of the tongue. Part B shows a single papilla enlarged so that the individual taste buds are visible. Part C shows one of the taste buds enlarged.

One aspect of cutaneous sensitivity plays a central role in human relationships: touch. Through touch, you communicate to others your desire to give or receive comfort, support, love, and passion. However, where you get touched or touch someone else makes a difference; those areas of the skin surface that give rise to erotic, or sexual, sensations are called *erogenous zones*. Other touch-sensitive erotic areas vary in their arousal potential for different individuals, depending on learned associations and the concentration of sensory receptors in the areas.

◆ THE VESTIBULAR AND KINESTHETIC SENSES

The next pair of senses we will describe may be entirely new to you because they do not have receptors you can see directly, like eyes, ears, or noses. Your **vestibular sense** tells you how your body—especially your head— is oriented in the world with respect to gravity. The receptors for this information are tiny hairs in fluid-filled sacs and canals in the inner ear. The hairs bend when the fluid moves and presses on them, which is what happens when you turn your head quickly. The *saccule* and *utricle* (shown in Figure 4.20) tell you about acceleration or deceleration in a straight line. The three canals, called the *semicircular canals,* are at right angles to each other and, thus, can tell you about motion in any direction. They inform you how your head is moving when you turn, nod, or tilt it.

People who lose their vestibular sense because of accidents or disease are initially quite disoriented and prone to falls and dizziness. However, most of these people eventually compensate by relying more heavily on visual information. *Motion sickness* can occur when the signals from the visual system conflict with those from the vestibular system. People feel nauseated when reading in a moving car because the visual signal is of a stationary object, while the vestibular signal is of movement. Drivers rarely get motion sickness because they are both seeing and feeling motion.

Whether you are standing erect, drawing pictures, or making love, your brain needs to have accurate information about the current positions and movement of your body parts relative to one another. The **kinesthetic sense** (also called *kinesthesis*) provides constant sensory feedback about what the body is doing during motor activities. Without it, you would be unable to coordinate most voluntary movements.

You have two sources of kinesthetic information: receptors in the joints and receptors in the muscles and tendons. Receptors that lie in the joints respond to pressures that accompany different positions of the limbs and to pressure changes that accompany movements of the joints. Receptors in the muscles and tendons respond to changes in tension that accompany muscle shortening and lengthening.

The brain often integrates information from your kinesthetic sense with information from touch senses. Your brain, for example, can't grasp the full meaning of

Why would riding in the front seat of a roller coaster be less likely to make you nauseated than riding in the rear?

the signals coming from each of your fingers if it doesn't know exactly where your fingers are in relation to one another. Imagine that you pick up an object with your eyes closed. Your sense of touch may allow you to guess that the object is a stone, but your kinesthetic sense will enable you to know how large it is.

◆ PAIN

Pain is the body's response to stimulation from harmful stimuli—those that are intense enough to cause tissue damage or threaten to do so. Are you entirely happy that you have such a well-developed pain sense? Your answer probably should be "yes and no." On the yes side, your pain sense is critical for survival. People born with congenital insensitivity to pain feel no hurt, but their bodies often become scarred and their limbs deformed from injuries that they could have avoided, had their brains been able to warn them of danger (Larner et al., 1994). Their experience shows that pain serves as an essential defense signal—it warns you of potential harm. On the no side, there are certainly times when you would be happy to be able to turn off your pain sense. More than 50 million people in the United States suffer from chronic, persistent pain. Medical treatment for pain and the workdays lost because of pain are estimated to cost more than $70 billion annually in the United States (Gatchel & Oordt, 2003).

Scientists have begun to identify the specific sets of receptors that respond to pain-producing stimuli. They have learned that some receptors respond only to temperature, others to chemicals, others to mechanical stimuli, and still others to combinations of pain-producing stimuli. This network of pain fibers is a fine meshwork that covers your entire body. Peripheral nerve fibers send pain signals to the central nervous system by two pathways: a fast-conducting set of nerve fibers that are covered with myelin and slower, smaller nerve fibers without any myelin coating. Starting at the spinal cord, the impulses are relayed to the thalamus and then to the cerebral cortex, where the location and intensity of the pain are identified, the significance of the injury is evaluated, and action plans are formulated.

Within your brain, *endorphins* have an impact on your experience of pain. Recall from Chapter 3 that pain-killing drugs such as morphine bind to the same receptor sites in the brain—the term *endorphin* comes from *endogenous* (self-produced) *morphines*. The release of endorphins within the brain controls your experience of pain. Researchers believe that endorphins are at least partially responsible for the pain-reducing effects of acupuncture and placebos (Fields & Levine, 1984; Murray, 1995; Watkins & Mayer, 1982).

Your emotional responses, context factors, and your interpretation of the situation can be as important as actual physical stimuli in determining how much pain you experience (Price, 2000; Turk & Okifuji, 2003). How are pain sensations affected by the psychological context? One theory about the way pain may be modulated is known as the **gate-control theory,** developed by Ronald Melzack (1973, 1980). This theory suggests that cells in the spinal cord act as neurological gates, interrupting and

What role does the kinesthetic sense play in the performance of skilled athletes?

Individuals taking part in religious rituals, such as walking on a bed of hot coals, are able to block out pain. What does that tell you about the relationship between the physiology and psychology of pain?

Organizational Processes in Perception

blocking some pain signals and letting others get through to the brain. Receptors in the skin and the brain send messages to the spinal cord to open or close those gates. Suppose, for example, you bump your shin on a table while running to answer the telephone. As you rub the skin around the bump, you send inhibitory messages to your spinal cord—closing the gates. Messages descending from the brain also can close the gates. If, for example, the phone call includes urgent news, your brain might close the gates to prevent you from experiencing the distraction of pain. In recent years, Melzack (1999) has proposed an updated *neuromatrix theory* of pain that incorporates the reality that people often experience pain with little or no physical cause: In these cases, the experience of pain originates wholly in the brain.

We've just seen that the way you perceive pain may reveal more about your psychological state than about the intensity of the pain stimulus: What you perceive may be different from, and even independent of, what you sense. This discussion of pain prepares you for the rest of the chapter, in which we discuss the perceptual processes that allow you to organize and label your experiences of the world.

PUT YOURSELF TO THE TEST

- What is the role of the olfactory bulb in your sense of smell?
- To what basic taste qualities do your taste buds respond?
- Why do you have several types of touch receptors?
- What are the purposes of the vestibular and kinesthetic senses?
- How does gate-control theory explain the relationship between the physiology and psychology of pain?

Imagine how confusing the world would be if you were unable to put together and organize the information available from the output of your millions of retinal receptors. You would experience a kaleidoscope of disconnected bits of color moving and swirling before your eyes. The processes that put sensory information together to give you the perception of coherence are referred to collectively as processes of perceptual organization.

We begin our discussion of perceptual organization with a description of the processes of *attention* that prompt you to focus on a subset of stimuli from your kaleidoscope of experience. We then examine the organizational processes first described by *Gestalt* theorists, who argued that what you perceive depends on laws of organization, or simple rules by which you perceive shapes and forms.

◆ ATTENTIONAL PROCESSES

Take a moment now to find ten things in your environment that had not been, so far, in your immediate awareness. Had you noticed a spot on the wall? Had you noticed the ticking of a clock? If you start to examine your surroundings very carefully, you will discover that there are literally thousands of things on which you could focus your **attention.** Generally, the more closely you attend to some object or event in the environment, the more you can perceive and learn about it.

DETERMINING THE FOCUS OF ATTENTION

What forces determine the objects that become the focus of your attention? The answer to this question has two components, which we will call goal-directed selection and stimulus-driven capture (Yantis, 1993). **Goal-directed selection** reflects the choices that you make about the objects to which you'd like to attend, as a function of your own goals. You are probably already comfortable with the idea that you can explicitly choose objects for particular scrutiny. **Stimulus-driven capture** occurs when features of the stimuli—objects in the environment—themselves automatically capture your attention, independent of your local goals as a perceiver. You've experienced stimulus-driven capture, for example, if you've ever been daydreaming at a stoplight while out for a drive. The stoplight's abrupt

Why Is Eating "Hot" Food Painful?

Leah Prebluda
George Washington University

Have you ever had this experience? You are eating a very "hot" dish in a Chinese or Mexican restaurant and you accidentally bite directly into a chili pepper. In just moments you go from enjoyment to intense pain. If this has happened, then you know that, in the realm of taste, there is a fine line between what gives pleasure and what gives pain. Let's explore this relationship.

Physiologically, it's easy to explain why hot pepper can cause you pain. On your tongue, your taste buds have associated with them pain fibers (Bartoshuk, 1993). Thus, the very same chemical that can stimulate the receptors in your taste buds can stimulate the closely allied pain fibers (Caterina et al., 2000). In the case of hot pepper, this chemical is *capsaicin*. If you want to enjoy a spicy meal, you have to keep the concentration of capsaicin in your meal sufficiently low so that your taste receptors are more active than your pain receptors.

But why, you might wonder, do different people have such obvious differences in their preferences for hot food? People often find it very difficult to understand how their friends can or cannot eat food that is very spicy. Again, we can look to physiology to explain these differences. The figure shows photographs of tongues from two individuals studied by **Linda Bartoshuk** and her colleagues. You can see that one tongue has considerably more taste buds than the other. If there are more taste buds, there will be more pain receptors. Therefore, people with more taste buds are more likely to get a strong pain response from capsaicin. The group of individuals who have more taste buds have been dubbed *supertasters* (Bartoshuk, 1993). They form a sharp contrast, in the extremes of their sensory experiences, to *nontasters*. For many taste sensations, these two groups are equivalent—you wouldn't know at most times whether you were a supertaster, a nontaster, or somewhere in between. The differences arise only for certain chemicals—capsaicin is an excellent example.

The variations in the density of taste buds on different people's tongues appear to be genetic (Bartoshuk, 1994). Women are much more likely to be supertasters than are men. Supertasters generally have more sensitivity to bitter chemicals—a sensory quality shared by most poisons. You can imagine that if women generally were responsible for nurturing and feeding offspring over the course of evolution, the children of women with greater taste sensitivity would be more likely to survive. Because taster status is genetic, you can find preference differences among children at very young ages (Anliker et al., 1991). Five- to seven-year-old supertasters preferred milk to cheddar cheese. This preference was reversed for nontasters. Why? The supertasters may perceive the milk as sweeter and the cheese as more bitter than do the nontasters. Thus, genetic differences may help explain why some young children have such strong (and vocal) taste preferences.

But let's return to the restaurant meal at which you have had your painful accident. What you might have noticed is that the sensation of pain fades over time. In this respect, the pain receptors in your mouth act like other sensory receptors: Over time, you adapt to a constant stimulus. That's good news! You should be glad that your sensory processes offer built-in relief.

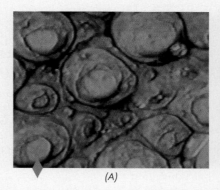

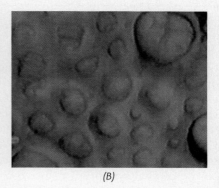

(A)   (B)

(A) The tongue of a supertaster. (B) The tongue of a nontaster.

change from red to green will often capture your attention even if you were not particularly focused on it.

You might wonder what the relationship is between these two processes: Research suggests that, at least under some circumstances, stimulus-driven capture wins out over goal-directed selection.

Competition Between Processes That Determine Focus of Attention

Researchers created visual displays that put goal-directed selection and stimulus-driven capture into competition (Theeuwes et al., 1998). As shown in Part A of **Figure 4.24,** each trial of an experiment began with a visual display of six gray circles filled with six dim figure eights. After one second, the display changed. In half the trials, as shown in Part B, all but one of the circles changed from gray to red. The participants' task was to shift their eyes to the remaining gray circle and respond whether the character inside was either a forward or a backward letter c. When they carry out this task, participants are using goal-directed selection: They are purposely shifting their attention to the remaining gray circle.

Now consider Part C of Figure 4.24. In this instance, which represents the remaining half of the trials, a new element is added to the visual array—a new red circle. New objects are the type of visual stimulus that typically engage stimulus-driven capture. Under ordinary circumstances, we'd expect participants to shift their eyes to that new object. However, in this particular experiment, the participants don't want their eyes to be pulled to that object: They are still asked to report only the contents of the single gray circle. So what happens? Can the participants stop themselves from moving their attention to the new red circle? In fact, on most occasions, the new object automatically drew the participants' attention—even though it was entirely irrelevant to the goal the experimenters had set for them.

You can recognize this phenomenon as stimulus-driven capture, because it works in the opposite direction of the perceiver's goals. Because, that is, the participants would perform the task better if they ignored the new red circle, they must be unable to ignore it (because experimental participants almost always prefer to perform as well as possible on the tasks researchers assign them). The important general conclusion is that your perceptual system is organized so that your attention is automatically drawn to objects that are new to an environment (Yantis & Jonides, 1996).

THE FATE OF UNATTENDED INFORMATION

If you have selectively attended to some subset of a perceptual display—by virtue of your own goals or of properties of the stimuli—what is the fate of the information to which you did *not* attend? Imagine listening to a lecture while people on both sides of you are engaged in conversations. How are you able to keep track of the lecture? What do you notice about the conversations? Could anything appear in the content of one or the other conversation to divert your attention from the lecture?

This constellation of questions was first explored by **Donald Broadbent** (1958), who suggested that the mind has only *limited capacity* to carry out complete processing. This limit requires that attention strictly regulate the flow of information from sensory input to con-

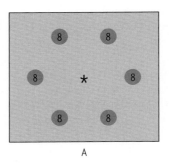

A

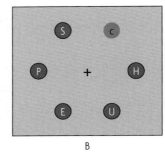 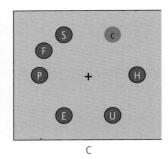

B   C

FIGURE 4.24

Processes That Select Attention

At the beginning of each trial of this experiment, participants viewed a display with six gray circles (Part A). When the display changed, the participants' task was to report whether the "c" in the one remaining gray circle was forward or backward. On half of the trials, the displays did not introduce new objects (Part B); on the other half of the trials, they did (Part C). Although the participants' goal was to attend to the single gray circle, the new objects—when they occurred—automatically drew their attention.

sciousness. The *filter theory* of attention asserted that the selection occurs early on in the process, before the input's meaning is accessed.

To test the filter theory, researchers re-created the real-life situation of multiple sources of input in the laboratory with a technique called **dichotic listening.** In this paradigm, a participant wearing earphones listens to two tape-recorded messages played at the same time—a different message is played into each ear. The participant is instructed to repeat only one of the two messages to the experimenter, while ignoring whatever is presented to the other ear. This procedure is called *shadowing* the attended message (see **Figure 4.25**).

The strongest form of filter theory was challenged when it was discovered that some listeners were recalling things they would not have been able to recall if attention had been totally filtering all ignored material (Cherry, 1953). Consider, for example, your own name. People often report that they hear their name being mentioned in a noisy room, even when they are engaged in their own conversation. This is often called the *cocktail party phenomenon.* Laboratory research has confirmed that people are especially likely to notice their own names among unattended information (Wood & Cowan, 1995a).

Researchers now believe that information in the unattended channel is processed to some extent—but not sufficiently to reach conscious awareness (Wood & Cowan, 1995b). Only if properties of the unattended information are sufficiently distinctive—by virtue, for example, of being a listener's name—will the information become the focus of conscious attention. (We will return to the relationship between attention and consciousness in Chapter 5.) The general rule is that unattended information will not make its presence known. You can see, therefore, why it's dangerous to let yourself become distracted from your immediate task or goal. If you fail to pay attention to some body of information—your professor's lecture, perhaps—the material won't just sink in of its own accord!

Let's suppose that you have focused your attention on some stimulus in the environment. It's time for your processes of perceptual organization to go to work.

◆ PRINCIPLES OF PERCEPTUAL GROUPING

Consider the image on the left in **Figure 4.26.** If you're like most people, you'll see a vase as *figure* against a black *ground.* A **figure** is seen as an objectlike region

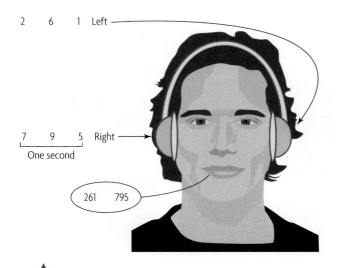

FIGURE 4.25

Dichotic Listening Task

A subject hears different digits presented simultaneously to each ear: 2 (left), 7 (right), 6 (left), 9 (right), 1 (left), and 5 (right). He reports hearing the correct sets—261 and 795. However, when instructed to attend only to the right-ear input, the subject reports hearing only 795.

in the forefront, and **ground** is seen as the backdrop against which the figures stand out. As you can see on the right of Figure 4.26, it's possible to change the relationship between figure and ground—to see two faces rather than one vase. One of the first tasks your perceptual processes carry out is to decide what in a scene counts as figure and what as ground.

How do your perceptual processes determine what should be gathered together into the figure? The principles of perceptual grouping were studied extensively by proponents of **Gestalt psychology,** such as **Kurt Koffka** (1935), **Wolfgang Köhler** (1947), and **Max Wertheimer** (1923). Members of this group maintained that psychological phenomena could be understood only when viewed as organized, structured *wholes* and not when broken down into primitive perceptual elements. The term *gestalt* roughly means "form," "whole," "configuration," or "essence." In their experiments, the Gestalt psychologists studied how perceptual arrays give rise to gestalts. By varying a single factor and observing how it affected the way people perceived the structure of the array, they were able to formulate a set of laws:

1. *The law of proximity.* People group together the nearest (most proximal) elements. That's why you see this display as five columns of objects instead of four rows.

2. *The law of similiarty.* People group together the most similar elements. That's why you see a square of O's against a field of X's rather than columns of mixed X's and O's.

```
X  X  X  X  X
X  O  O  O  X
X  O  O  O  X
X  O  O  O  X
X  X  X  X  X
```

3. *The law of good continuation.* People experience lines as continuous even when they are interrupted. That's what you interpret this display as

an arrow piercing the heart rather than as a design with three separate pieces.

4. *The law of closure.* People tend to fill in small gaps to experience objects as wholes. That's why you fill in the missing piece to perceive a whole circle.

5. *The law of common fate.* People tend to group together objects that appear to be moving in the same direction. That's why you experience this figure as alternating rows moving apart.

FIGURE 4.26

Figure and Ground

An initial step in perceptual grouping is for your perceptual processes to interpret part of a scene as a figure standing out against a ground.

◆ SPATIAL AND TEMPORAL INTEGRATION

All the Gestalt laws we have presented to you so far should have convinced you that a lot of perception consists of putting the pieces of your world together in the "right way." Often, however, you can't perceive an entire scene in one glance, or *fixation* (recall our discussion of attention). What you perceive at a given time is often a restricted glimpse of a large visual world extending in all directions to unseen areas of the environment. To get a complete idea of what is around you, you must combine information from fixations of different spatial locations—*spatial integration*—at different moments in time—*temporal integration.*

What may surprise you is that your visual system does not work very hard to create a moment-by-moment, integrated picture of the environment. Research suggests that your visual memory for each fixation on the world does not preserve precise details (Carlson-Radvansky & Irwin, 1995; Irwin, 1991; Simons, 2000). In fact, viewers are sometimes unable to detect when a whole object has changed from one fixation to the next.

PUTTING IDEAS TO THE TEST

What Did You Just See?

In one of a series of experiments, participants viewed for two seconds an array showing pictures of five familiar objects. Roughly four seconds later, the participants viewed a second array. In half of the trials, the second array was identical to the first. However, as shown in Part A of **Figure 4.27,** on the other half of the trials the second array differed from the first in one of three ways: One of the objects had changed identity (e.g., a *stapler* in the first array might be replaced by *keys* in the second array), two of the objects had switched their spatial position, or the whole set of objects was placed in a new configuration. Participants were challenged to judge whether the arrays were the *same* or *different*. You might imagine, on brief reflection, that this would be an easy task: How could you not notice that a *stapler* had turned into *keys?* However, as shown in Part B of Figure 4.27, performance for *identity* and *switch* changes was well below 100 percent correct. Participants were "blind" to a number of *very* obvious changes (Simons, 1996)!

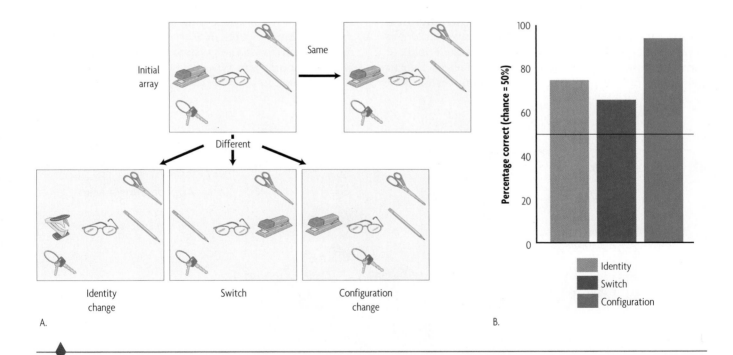

FIGURE 4.27

Change Blindness

(A) Experimental participants were asked to respond whether a second display was the "same as" or "different from" the initial array. (B) When the identity of an object was changed or two objects were switched, participants often were unable to detect the difference. Only when the whole configuration changed were participants nearly always correct.

Many people find this result surprising. How could it be that you have so few processing resources devoted to preserving the details of a scene over time—so that you wouldn't notice that a stapler has turned into a set of keys? Part of the answer might be that the world itself is generally a stable source of information (O'Regan, 1992). It is simply unnecessary to commit to memory information that remains steadily available in the external environment—and so you don't have processes that ordinarily allow you to do so.

◆ MOTION PERCEPTION

One type of perception that does require you to make comparisons across different glimpses of the world is motion perception. Consider the two images given in **Figure 4.28.** Suppose that this individual has stood still while you have walked toward him. The size of his image on your retina has expanded as you have drawn near. The rate at which this image has expanded gives you a sense of how quickly you have been approaching (Gibson, 1979).

As we noted, motion perception requires you to combine information from difference glimpses of the world. You can appreciate the consequences of how your perceptual processes combine those glimpses quite strongly when you experience the **phi phenomenon.** This phenomenon occurs when two stationary spots of light in different positions in the visual field are turned on and off alternately at a rate of about four to five times per second. This effect occurs on outdoor advertising signs and in disco light displays. Even at this relatively slow rate of alternation, it appears that a single light is moving back and forth between the two spots. There are multiple ways to conceive of the path that leads from the location of the first dot to the location of the second dot. Yet human observers normally see only the simplest path, a straight line (Cutting & Proffitt, 1982; Shepard, 1984). This straight-line rule is violated, however, when viewers are shown alternating views of a human body in motion. Then the visual system fills in the paths of normal biological motion (Shiffrar, 1994; Stevens et al., 2000).

◆ DEPTH PERCEPTION

Until now, we have considered only two-dimensional patterns on flat surfaces. Everyday perceiving, however, involves objects in three-dimensional space. Perceiving all three spatial dimensions is absolutely vital for you to approach what you want, such as interesting people and good food, and avoid what is dangerous, such as speeding cars and falling pianos. This perception requires accurate information about *depth* (the distance from you to an object) as well as about its *direction* from you. Your ears can help in determining direction, but they are not much help in determining depth. Your interpretation of depth relies on many different information sources about distance (often called *depth cues*)—among them binocular cues, motion cues, and pictorial cues.

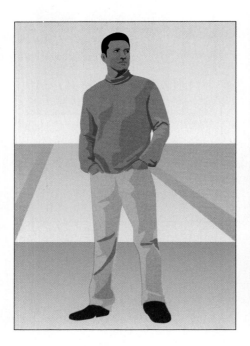

FIGURE 4.28

Approaching a Man

The size of an image expands on your retina as you draw nearer to the stimulus.

What makes you aware that the "protagonist" in this photo is moving—and in what direction is the motion?

BINOCULAR AND MOTION CUES

Have you ever wondered why you have two eyes instead of just one? The second eye is more than just a spare—it provides some of the best, most compelling information about depth. The two sources of binocular depth information are *retinal disparity* and *convergence*.

Because the eyes are about 2 to 3 inches apart horizontally, they receive slightly different views of the world. To convince yourself of this, try the following experiment. First, close your left eye and use the right one to line up your two index fingers with some small object in the distance, holding one finger at arm's length and the other about a foot in front of your face. Now, keeping your fingers stationary, close your right eye and open the left one while continuing to fixate on the distant object. What happened to the position of your two fingers? The second eye does not see them lined up with the distant object because it gets a slightly different view.

This displacement between the horizontal positions of corresponding images in your two eyes is called **retinal disparity.** It provides depth information because the amount of disparity, or difference, depends on the relative distance of objects from you (see **Figure 4.29**). For instance, when you switched eyes, the closer finger was displaced farther to the side than was the distant finger.

When you look at the world with both eyes open, most objects that you see stimulate different positions on your two retinas. If the disparity between corresponding images in the two retinas is small enough, the visual system is able to fuse them into a perception of a single object in depth. (However, if the images are too far apart, you actually see the double images, as when you cross your eyes.) When you stop to think about it, what your visual system does is pretty amazing: It takes two different retinal images, compares them for horizontal displacement of corresponding parts (binocular

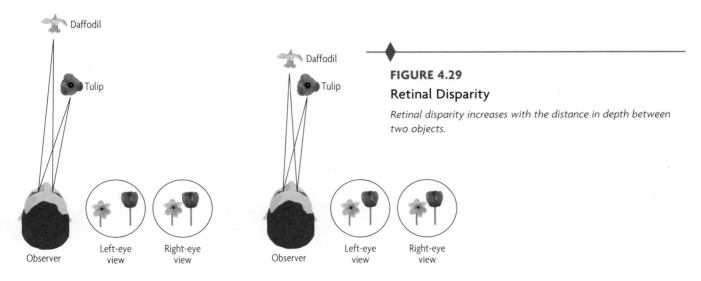

FIGURE 4.29

Retinal Disparity

Retinal disparity increases with the distance in depth between two objects.

disparity), and produces a unitary perception of a single object in depth. In effect, the visual system interprets horizontal displacement between the two images as depth in the three-dimensional world.

Other binocular information about depth comes from **convergence.** The two eyes turn inward to some extent whenever they are fixated on an object (see **Figure 4.30**). When the object is very close—a few inches in front of your face—the eyes must turn toward each other quite a bit for the same image to fall on both foveae. You can actually see the eyes converge if you watch a friend focus first on a distant object and then on one a foot or so away. Your brain uses information from your eye muscles to make judgments about depth. However, convergence information from the eye muscles is useful for depth perception only up to about 10 feet. At greater distances, the angular differences are too small to detect because the eyes are nearly parallel when you fixate on a distant object.

To see how *motion* is another source for depth information, try the following demonstration. As you did before, close one eye and line up your two index fingers with some distant object. Then move your head to the side while fixating on the distant object and keeping your fingers still. As you move your head, you see both your fingers move, but the close finger seems to move farther and faster than the more distant one. The fixated object does not move at all. This source of

information about depth is called **relative motion parallax.** Motion parallax provides information about depth because, as you move, the relative distances of objects in the world determine the amount and direction of their relative motion in your retinal image of the scene. Next time you are a passenger on a car trip, you should keep a watch out the window for motion parallax at work. Objects at a distance from the moving car will appear much more stationary than those closer to you.

PICTORIAL CUES

But suppose you had vision in only one eye. Would you not be able to perceive depth? In fact, further information about depth is available from just one eye. These sources are called pictorial cues because they include the kinds of depth information found in pictures. Artists who create images in what appear to be three dimensions (on the two dimensions of a piece of paper or canvas) make skilled use of pictorial cues.

Interposition, or *occlusion,* arises when an opaque object blocks out part of a second object (see **Figure 4.31**). Interposition gives you depth information indicating that the occluded object is farther away than the occluding one. Occluding surfaces also block out light, creating shadows that can be used as an additional source of depth information.

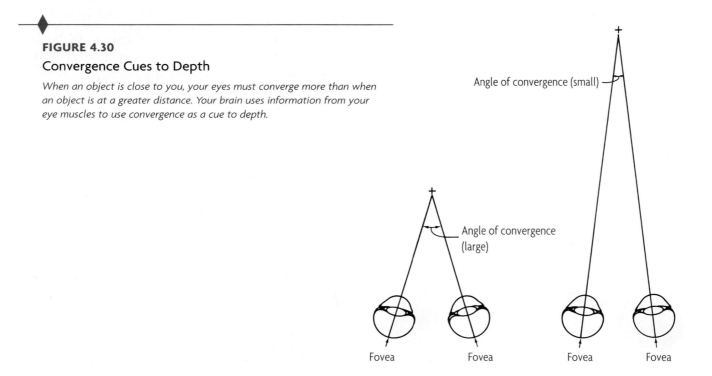

FIGURE 4.30

Convergence Cues to Depth

When an object is close to you, your eyes must converge more than when an object is at a greater distance. Your brain uses information from your eye muscles to use convergence as a cue to depth.

<www.ablongman.com/gerrig17e>

FIGURE 4.31

Interposition Cues to Depth

What visual cues tell you whether this woman is behind the bars?

Three more sources of pictorial information are all related to the way light projects from a three-dimensional world onto a two-dimensional surface such as the retina: relative size, linear perspective, and texture gradients. *Relative size* involves a basic rule of light projection: Objects of the same size at different distances project images of different sizes on the retina. The closest one projects the largest image and the farthest one the smallest image. This rule is called the *size/distance relation*. As you can see in **Figure 4.32,** if you look at an array with identical objects, you interpret the smaller ones to be farther away.

Linear perspective is a depth cue that also depends on the size/distance relation. When parallel lines (by definition separated along their lengths by the same distance) recede into the distance, they converge toward a point on the horizon in your retinal image (see **Figure 4.33**). Your visual system's interpretation of converging lines gives rise to the Ponzo illusion. The upper line looks longer because you interpret the converging sides according to linear perspective as parallel lines receding into the distance. In this context, you interpret the upper line as

FIGURE 4.33

The Ponzo Illusion

The converging lines add a dimension of depth, and, therefore, the distance cue makes the top line appear larger than the bottom line, even though they are actually the same length.

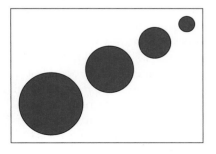

FIGURE 4.32

Relative Size as a Depth Cue

Objects that are closer project larger images on the retina. As a consequence, when you look at an array with identical objects, you interpret the smaller ones to be at a greater distance.

though it were farther away, so you see it as longer—a farther object would have to be longer than a nearer one for both to produce retinal images of the same size.

Texture gradients provide depth cues because the density of a texture becomes greater as a surface recedes in depth. The wheat field in **Figure 4.34** is an example of the way texture is used as a depth cue. You can think of this as another consequence of the size/distance relation. In this case, the units that make up the texture become smaller as they recede into the distance, and your visual system interprets this diminishing grain as greater distance in three-dimensional space.

By now, it should be clear that there are many sources of depth information. Under normal viewing conditions, however, information from these sources comes together in a single, coherent three-dimensional interpretation of the environment. You experience depth, not the different cues to depth that existed in the proximal stimulus. In other words, your visual system uses cues such as differential motion, interposition, and relative size automatically, without your conscious awareness, to make the complex computations that give you a perception of depth in the three-dimensional environment.

FIGURE 4.34

Examples of Texture as a Depth Cue

The wheat field is a natural example of the way texture can be used as a depth cue. Notice the way the wheat slants.

◆ PERCEPTUAL CONSTANCIES

To help you discover another important property of visual perception, we are going to ask you to play a bit with your textbook. Put your book down on a table, then move your head closer to it so that it's just a few inches away. Then move your head back to a normal reading distance. Although the book stimulated a much larger part of your retina when it was up close than when it was far away, didn't you perceive the book's size to remain the same? Now set the book upright and try tilting your head clockwise. When you do this, the image of the book rotates counterclockwise on your retina, but didn't you still perceive the book to be upright?

In general, you see the world as *invariant, constant,* and *stable* despite changes in the stimulation of your sensory receptors. Psychologists refer to this phenomenon as **perceptual constancy.** Roughly speaking, it means that you perceive the properties of the distal stimuli, which are usually constant, rather than the properties of proximal stimuli, which change every time you move your eyes or head. For survival, it is critical that you perceive constant and stable properties of objects in the world despite the enormous variations in the properties of the light patterns that stimulate your eyes. The critical task of perception is to discover *invariant* properties of your environment despite the variations in your retinal impressions of them. We will see how this works for size, shape, and orientation.

SIZE AND SHAPE CONSTANCY

What determines your perception of the size of an object? In part, you perceive an object's actual size on the basis of the size of its retinal image. However, the demonstration with your book shows that the size of the retinal image depends on both the actual size of the book and its distance from the eye. As you now know, information about distance is available from a variety of depth cues. Your visual system combines that information with retinal information about image size to yield a perception of an object size that usually corresponds to the actual size of the distal stimulus. **Size constancy** refers to your ability to perceive the true size of an object despite variations in the size of its retinal image.

If the size of an object is perceived by taking distance cues into account, then you should be fooled about size whenever you are fooled about distance. One such illusion occurs in the Ames room shown in **Figure 4.35.** In comparison to the child, the adult, looks quite short in the left corner of this room, but he looks enormous in the right corner. The reason for this illusion is that you perceive the room to be rectangular, with the two back corners equally distant from you. Thus, you perceive the child's actual size as being consistent

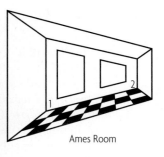

Ames Room

Viewer

FIGURE 4.35

The Ames Room

The Ames room is designed to be viewed through a peephole with one eye—that is the vantage point from which these photographs were taken. The Ames room is constructed from nonrectangular surfaces at odd angles in depth and height. However, with only the view from the peephole, your visual system interprets it as an ordinary room and makes some unusual guesses about the relative heights of the occupants.

with the size of the images on your retina in both cases. In fact, the child is not at the same distance, because the Ames room creates a clever illusion. It appears to be a rectangular room, but it is actually made from nonrectangular surfaces at odd angles in depth and height, as you can see in the drawings that accompany the photos. Any person on the right will make a larger retinal image, because he or she is twice as close to the observer. (By the way, to get the illusion you must view the display with a single eye through a peephole—that's the vantage point of the photographs in Figure 4.35. If you could move around while viewing the room, your visual system would acquire information about the unusual structure of the room.)

Another way that the perceptual system can infer objective size is by using prior knowledge about the characteristic size of similarly shaped objects. For instance, once you recognize the shape of a house, a tree, or a dog, you have a pretty good idea of how big

each is, even without knowing its distance from you. When past experience does not give you knowledge of what familiar objects look like at extreme distances, size constancy may break down. You have experienced this problem if you have looked down at people from the top of a skyscraper and thought that they resembled ants.

Shape constancy is closely related to size constancy. You perceive an object's actual shape correctly even when the object is slanted away from you, making the shape of the retinal image substantially different from that of the object itself. For instance, a rectangle tipped away projects a trapezoidal image onto your retina; a circle tipped away from you projects an elliptical image (see **Figure 4.36**). Yet you usually perceive the shapes accurately as a circle and a rectangle slanted away in space. When there is good depth information available, your visual system can determine an object's true shape simply by taking into account your distance from its different parts.

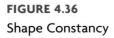

FIGURE 4.36

Shape Constancy

As a coin is rotated, its image becomes an ellipse that grows narrower and narrower until it becomes a thin rectangle, an ellipse again, and then a circle. At each orientation, however, it is still perceived as a circular coin.

LIGHTNESS CONSTANCY

Consider the photograph in **Figure 4.37.** When you look at the brick wall in this picture, you don't perceive some of the bricks to be light red and some of them to be dark red—instead, you perceive this as a wall in which all the bricks are equally light or dark, but some of them are in shadow (Goldstein, 1999). This is an example of lightness constancy: **Lightness constancy** is your tendency to perceive the whiteness, grayness, or blackness of objects as constant across changing levels of illumination.

As with the other constancies we have described, you experience lightness constancy quite frequently in everyday life. Suppose, for example, you are wearing a white T-shirt and walk from a dimly lit room outside into a bright sunny day. In bright sunshine, the T-shirt reflects far more light into your eyes than it does in the dim room, yet it looks about equally light to you in both contexts. In fact, lightness constancy works because the *percentage* of light an object reflects remains about the same even as the *absolute* amount of light changes. Your bright white T-shirt is going to reflect 80–90 percent of whatever light is available; your black jeans are going to reflect only about 5 percent of the available light. That's why—when you see them in the same context—the T-shirt will always look lighter than the jeans.

FIGURE 4.37

Lightness Constancy

Lightness constancy helps explain why you perceive all the bricks in the wall to be made of the same material.

In this section, we have described a number of organizational processes in perception. In the final section of the chapter, we consider the identification and recognition processes that give meaning to objects and events in the environment.

Identification and Recognition Processes

You can think of all the perceptual processes described so far as providing reasonably accurate knowledge about physical properties of the distal stimulus—the position, size, shape, texture, and color of objects in a three-dimensional environment. However, you would not know what the objects were or whether you had seen them before. Your experience would resemble a visit to an alien planet where everything was new to you; you wouldn't know what to eat, what to put on your head, what to run away from, or what to date. Your environment appears nonalien because you are able to recognize and identify most objects as things you have seen before and as members of the meaningful categories that you know about from experience. Identification and recognition attach meaning to what you perceive.

◆ BOTTOM-UP AND TOP-DOWN PROCESSES

When you identify an object, you must match what you see to your stored knowledge. Taking sensory data in from the environment and sending it toward the brain for extraction and analysis of relevant information is called bottom-up processing. **Bottom-up processing** is anchored in empirical reality and deals with bits of information and the transformation of concrete, physical features of stimuli into abstract representations. This type of processing is also called *data-driven processing,* because your starting point for identification is the sensory evidence you obtain from the environment—the data.

In many cases, however, you can use information you already have about the environment to help you make a perceptual identification. If you visit a zoo, for example, you might be a little more ready to recognize some types of animals than you otherwise would be. You are more likely to hypothesize that you are seeing a tiger there than you would be in your own backyard. When your expectations affect perception, the phenomenon is called top-down processing. **Top-down processing** involves your past experiences, knowledge, motivations, and cultural background in perceiving the world. With top-down processing, higher mental functioning influences how you understand objects and events. Top-down processing is also known as conceptually driven (or hypothesis-driven) processing because the concepts you have stored in memory affect interpretation of the sensory data. The importance of top-down processing can be illustrated by drawings known as droodles (Price, 1953/1980). Without the labels, these drawings are meaningless. However, once the drawings are identified, you can easily find meaning in them (see **Figure 4.38**).

For a more detailed example of top-down versus bottom-up processing, we turn to the domain of speech perception. You have undoubtedly had the experience of trying to carry on a conversation at a very loud party. Under those circumstances, it's probably true that not all of the physical signal you are producing arrives unambiguously at your acquaintance's ears: Some of what you had to say was almost certainly obscured by coughs, thumping music, or peals of laughter. Even so, people rarely realize that there are gaps in the physical signal they are experiencing. This phenomenon is known as *phonemic restoration* (Warren, 1970). As we explain more fully in Chapter 10, *phonemes* are the minimal, meaningful units of sound in a language; phonemic restoration occurs when people use top-down processes to fill in missing phonemes. Listeners often find it difficult to tell whether they are hearing a word that has a noise replacing part of the original speech signal or

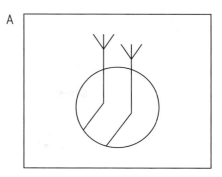

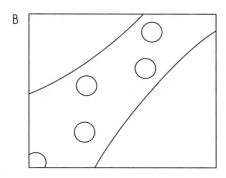

FIGURE 4.38

Droodles

What are these animals? Do you see in (A) an early bird who caught a very strong worm and in (B) a giraffe's neck? Each figure can be seen as representing something familiar to you, although this perceptual recognition usually does not occur until some identifying information is provided.

whether they are hearing a word with a noise just superimposed on the intact signal (see part A of **Figure 4.39**) (Samuel, 1981, 1991).

Part B of Figure 4.39 shows how bottom-up and top-down processes could interact to produce phonemic restoration (McClelland & Elman, 1986). Suppose part of what your friend says at a noisy party is obscured so that the signal that arrives at your ears is "I have to go home to walk my (noise)og." If noise covers the /d/, you are likely to think that you actually heard the full word *dog.* But why? In Figure 4.39, you see two of the types of information relevant to speech perception. We have the individual sounds that make up words, and the words themselves. When the sounds /o/ and /g/ arrive in this system, they provide information—in a bottom-up fashion—to the word level (we have given only a subset of the words in English that end with /og/). This provides you with a range of candidates for what your friend

A

The soldier's thoughts of the dangerous

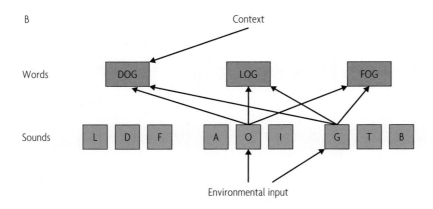

or { bat 🟊tle   (Noise added to signal; subject hears both "tle" and noise)
    { bat 🟊   (Noise replaces signal; subject hears only noise)

made him very nervous.

B

Context

Words   DOG   LOG   FOG

Sounds   L D F   A O I   G T B

Environmental input

FIGURE 4.39

Phonemic Restoration

(A) Even when a sound is replaced by noise, listeners tend to "hear" the missing information. (B) In this example, noise obscured the /d/ when your friend said "dog." Based only on the environmental input, your perceptual system can come up with several hypotheses: dog, log, fog, and so on. However, top-down information from the context—"I have to go home and walk my . . ."—supports the hypothesis that your friend said "dog."

might have said. Now top-down processes go to work—the context helps you select *dog* as the most likely word to appear in this utterance. When all of this happens swiftly enough—bottom-up identification of a set of candidate words and top-down selection of the likely correct candidate—you'll never know that the /d/ was missing. Your perceptual processes believe that the word was intact (Samuel, 1997). The next time you're in a noisy environment, you'll be glad your perceptual processes fill sounds in so efficiently!

◆ THE INFLUENCE OF CONTEXTS AND EXPECTATIONS

Early in the chapter, we noted that the world often gives you ambiguous information to perceive. Consider **Figure 4.40.** What do you make of it? Suppose we tell you that it's a view into our neighbor's back yard, showing a tree around which his dalmatian routinely sniffs? Now can you see a dog? (The dog's nose is roughly in the middle of the figure.) This is another top-down aspect of perception: Contexts and expectations can influence your hypotheses about what is out there in the world. Have you ever had the experience of seeing people you knew in places where you didn't expect to see them, such as in a different city or a different social group? It takes much longer to recognize them in such situations, and sometimes you aren't even sure that you really know them. The problem is not that they

look any different but that the *context* is wrong; you didn't *expect* them to be there. The spatial and temporal context in which objects are recognized provides an important source of information, because from the context you generate expectations about what objects you are and are not likely to see nearby.

FIGURE 4.40

An Ambiguous Picture

What do you see in this picture?

Perceptual identification depends on your expectations as well as on the physical properties of the objects you see—object identification is a constructive, interpretive process. Depending on what you already know, where you are, and what else you see around you, your identification may vary. Read the following words:

THE CAT

They say THE CAT, right? Now look again at the middle letter of each word. Physically, these two letters are exactly the same, yet you perceived the first as an H and the second as an A. Why? Clearly, your perception was affected by what you know about words in English. The context provided by T_E makes an H highly likely and an A unlikely, whereas the reverse is true of the context of C_T (Selfridge, 1955).

Researchers have often documented the effects of context and expectation on perception (and response) by studying set. **Set** is a temporary readiness to perceive or react to a stimulus in a particular way. There are three types of set: motor, mental, and perceptual. A *motor set* is a readiness to make a quick, prepared response. A runner trains by perfecting a motor set to come out of the blocks as fast as possible at the sound of the starting gun. A mental set is a readiness to deal with a situation, such as a problem-solving task or a game, in a way determined by learned rules, instructions, expectations, or habitual tendencies. A *mental set* can actually prevent you from solving a problem when the old rules don't seem to fit the new situation, as we'll see when we study problem solving in Chapter 9. A *perceptual set* is a readiness to detect a particular stimulus in a given context. A new mother, for example, is perceptually set to hear the cries of her child.

Often a set leads you to change your interpretation of an ambiguous stimulus. Consider these two series of words:

FOX; OWL; SNAKE; TURKEY; SWAN; D?CK

BOB; RAY; DAVE; BILL; HENRY; D?CK

Did you read through the lists? What word came to mind for D?CK in each case? If you thought DUCK and DICK, it's because the list of words created a set that directed your search of memory in a particular way.

All the effects of context on perception clearly require that your memory be organized in such a fashion that information relevant to particular situations becomes available at the right times. In other words, to generate appropriate (or inappropriate) expectations, you must be able to make use of prior knowledge stored in memory. Sometimes you "see" with your memory as much as you see with your eyes. In Chapter 7, we will discuss the properties of memory that make context effects on perception possible.

◆ FINAL LESSONS

To solidify all that you have learned in this chapter, we suggest that you take a look back at Figure 4.2—you now have the knowledge necessary to understand the whole flowchart. Examination of Figure 4.2 will also confirm that the important lesson to be learned from the study of perception is that a perceptual experience in response to a stimulus event is a response of the whole person. In addition to the information provided when your sensory receptors are stimulated, your final perception depends on who you are, whom you are with, and what you expect, want, and value. A perceiver often plays two different roles that we can compare to gambling and interior design. As a gambler, a perceiver is willing to bet that the present input can be understood in terms of past knowledge and personal theories. As a compulsive interior decorator, a perceiver is constantly rearranging the stimuli so that they fit better and are more coherent. Incongruity and messy perceptions are rejected in favor of those with clear, clean, consistent lines.

If perceiving were completely bottom-up, you would be bound to the same mundane, concrete reality of the here and now. You could register experience but not profit from it on later occasions, nor would you see the world differently under different circumstances. If perceptual processing were completely top-down, however, you could become lost in your own fantasy world of what you expect and hope to perceive. A proper balance between the two extremes achieves the basic goal of perception: to experience what is out there in a way that optimally serves your needs as a biological and social being, moving about and adapting to your physical and social environment.

PUT YOURSELF TO THE TEST

- ➤ What's the difference between bottom-up and top-down processing?
- ➤ How does phonemic restoration demonstrate the influence of top-down processing?
- ➤ What is the relationship between contexts and expectations?
- ➤ What are sets, and why do they have an impact on what you perceive?

Recapping Main Points

SENSING, ORGANIZING, IDENTIFYING, AND RECOGNIZING

- Perception is a three-stage process consisting of a sensory stage, a perceptual organization stage, and an identification and recognition stage.
- At the sensory level of processing, physical energy is detected and transformed into neural energy and sensory experience.
- At the organizational level, perceptual processes organize sensations into coherent images and give you perception of objects and patterns.
- At the level of identification and recognition, percepts of objects are compared with memory representations to be recognized as familiar and meaningful objects.
- The task of perception is to determine what the distal (external) stimulus is from the information contained in the proximal (sensory) stimulus.
- Ambiguity may arise when the same sensory information can be organized into different percepts.
- Knowledge about perceptual illusions can provide constraints on ordinary perceptual processes.

SENSORY KNOWLEDGE OF THE WORLD

- Psychophysics investigates psychological responses to physical stimuli. Researchers measure absolute thresholds and just noticeable differences between stimuli.
- Signal detection allows researchers to separate sensory acuity from response biases.
- Researchers in psychophysics have captured the relationship between physical intensity and psychological effect with mathematical functions.
- Sensation translates the physical energy of stimuli into neural codes via transduction.

THE VISUAL SYSTEM

- Photoreceptors in the retina, called rods and cones, convert light energy into neural impulses.
- Ganglion cells in the retina integrate input from receptors and bipolar cells. Their axons form the optic nerves that meet at the optic chiasma.
- Visual information is distributed to several different areas of the brain that process different aspects of the visual environment such as how things look and where they are.
- The wavelength of light is the stimulus for color.
- Color sensations differ in hue, saturation, and brightness.
- Color vision theory combines the trichromatic theory of three color receptors with the opponent-process theory of color systems composed of opponent elements

HEARING

- Hearing is produced by sound waves that vary in frequency, amplitude, and complexity.
- In the cochlea, sound waves are transformed into fluid waves that move the basilar membrane. Hairs on the basilar membrane stimulate neural impulses that are sent to the auditory cortex.
- Place theory best explains the coding of high frequencies, and frequency theory best explains the coding of low frequencies.
- To compute the direction from which the sound is arriving, two types of neural mechanisms compute the relative intensity and timing of sounds coming to each ear.

YOUR OTHER SENSES

- Smell and taste respond to the chemical properties of substances and work together when people are seeking and sampling food.
- Olfaction is accomplished by odor-sensitive cells deep in the nasal passages.
- Taste receptors are taste buds embedded in papillae, mostly in the tongue.
- The cutaneous (skin) senses give sensations of pressure and temperature.
- The vestibular sense gives information about the direction and rate of body motion.
- The kinesthetic sense gives information about the position of body parts and helps coordinate motion.
- Pain is the body's response to potentially harmful stimuli.

- The physiological response to pain involves sensory response at the site of the pain stimulus and nerve impulses moving between the brain and the spinal cord.

- Binocular, motion, and pictorial cues all contribute to the perception of depth.

- You tend to perceive objects as having stable size, shape, and lightness.

ORGANIZATIONAL PROCESSES IN PERCEPTION

- Both your personal goals and the properties of the objects in the world determine where you will focus your attention.

- The Gestalt psychologists provided several laws of perceptual grouping, including proximity, similarity, good continuation, closure, and common fate.

- Perceptual processes integrate over both time and space to provide an interpretation of the environment.

IDENTIFICATION AND RECOGNITION PROCESSES

- During the final stage of perceptual processing—identification and recognition of objects—percepts are given meaning through processes that combine bottom-up and top-down influences.

- Context, expectations, and perceptual sets may guide recognition of incomplete or ambiguous data in one direction rather than another equally possible one.

KEY TERMS

absolute threshold (p. 99)
accommodation (p. 104)
amacrine cells (p. 105)
ambiguity (p. 96)
attention (p. 122)
auditory cortex (p. 116)
auditory nerve (p. 116)
basilar membrane (p. 115)
bipolar cells (p. 105)
bottom-up processing (p. 135)
brightness (p. 110)
cochlea (p. 115)
complementary colors (p. 111)
cones (p. 105)
convergence (p. 130)
cutaneous senses (p. 119)
dark adaptation (p. 105)
dichotic listening (p. 125)
difference threshold (p. 102)
distal stimulus (p. 95)
figure (p. 125)
fovea (p. 105)
frequency theory (p. 116)
ganglion cells (p. 105)
gate-control theory (p. 121)
Gestalt psychology (p. 126)
goal-directed selection (p. 122)
ground (p. 126)
horizontal cells (p. 105)
hue (p. 110)

identification and recognition (p. 94)
illusion (p. 98)
just noticeable difference (JND) (p. 102)
kinesthetic sense (p. 120)
lightness constancy (p. 134)
loudness (p. 114)
olfactory bulb (p. 118)
opponent-process theory (p. 112)
optic nerve (p. 106)
pain (p. 121)
perception (p. 94)
perceptual constancy (p. 132)
perceptual organization (p. 94)
pheromones (p. 118)
phi phenomenon (p. 128)
photoreceptors (p. 104)
pitch (p. 113)
place theory (p. 116)
proximal stimulus (p. 95)
psychometric function (p. 100)
psychophysics (p. 99)
receptive field (p. 107)
relative motion parallax (p. 130)
response bias (p. 101)
retina (p. 104)
retinal disparity (p. 129)
rods (p. 105)
saturation (p. 110)
sensation (p. 94)

sensory adaptation (p. 100)
sensory receptors (p. 103)
set (p. 137)
shape constancy (p. 133)
signal detection theory (p. 101)
size constancy (p. 132)
sound localization (p. 117)
stimulus-driven capture (p. 122)
timbre (p. 114)
top-down processing (p. 135)
transduction (p. 103)
trichromatic theory (p. 112)
vestibular sense (p. 120)
visual cortex (p. 106)
volley principle (p. 116)
Weber's law (p. 102)

Mind, Consciousness, and Alternate States

As you begin reading this chapter, take a moment to think about a favorite past event. Now think about what you'd like to have happen tomorrow or the next day. Where did these memories of the past and projections into the future *come* from and when did they *arrive?* Although you obviously have a vast body of information stored in your brain, it is very unlikely that the thoughts we asked you to have were "in mind" just as you were sitting down to read your psychology text. Therefore, you might feel comfortable saying that the thoughts arrived in your consciousness—and that they came from some part of your brain that was not then conscious. But how did these particular thoughts come to mind? Did you actually consider several different memories or options for the future? That is, were you consciously aware of making a choice? Or did thoughts somehow just emerge—by virtue of some set of unconscious operations—into your consciousness?

This series of questions provides a preview of the major topics of Chapter 5. In this chapter, we will address a series of questions: What is ordinary conscious awareness?

What determines the contents of your consciousness? Why do you need consciousness? Can unconscious mental events really influence your thoughts, emotions, and behavior? How does consciousness change over the course of a day–night cycle, and how can you intentionally alter your state of consciousness? The budding psychologist in you should also want to know how aspects of mind can be studied scientifically. How can you externalize the internal, make public the private, and measure precisely subjective experiences?

Our analysis will begin with an exploration of the contents and functions of consciousness. Then we will shift to the regular mental changes experienced during daydreaming, fantasizing, sleeping, and night dreaming. Finally, we will look at how consciousness is altered dramatically by hypnosis, meditation, religious rituals, and drugs.

The Contents of Consciousness

W e must start by admitting that the term **consciousness** is ambiguous. We can use the term to refer to a general state of mind *or* to its specific contents. Sometimes you say you were "conscious" in contrast to being "unconscious" (for example, being under anesthesia or asleep); at other times, you say you were conscious—*aware*— of certain information or actions. There is, in fact, a certain consistency here—to be conscious of any particular information, you must be conscious. In this chapter, when we speak of the *contents* of consciousness, we mean the body of information of which you are aware.

◆ AWARENESS AND CONSCIOUSNESS

Some of the earliest research in psychology concerned the contents of consciousness. As psychology gradually diverged from philosophy in the 1800s, it became the science of the mind. Wundt and Titchener used introspection to explore the contents of the conscious mind, and William James observed his own stream of consciousness (see Chapter 1). In fact, on the very first page of his classic 1892 text, *Psychology*, James endorsed as a definition of psychology *"the description and explanation of states of consciousness as such."*

Your ordinary waking consciousness includes your perceptions, thoughts, feelings, images, and desires at a given moment—all the mental activity on which you are

Why is self-awareness considered such an important aspect of consciousness?

focusing your attention. You are conscious of both what you are doing and also of the fact that you are doing it. At times, you are conscious of the realization that others are observing, evaluating, and reacting to what you are doing. A *sense of self* comes out of the experience of watching yourself from this privileged "insider" position. Taken together, these various mental activities form the contents of consciousness—all the experiences you are consciously aware of at a particular time (Natsoulas, 1998).

We have defined the general types of information that *might* be conscious at a particular place and time, but what determines what is conscious right now? Were you, for example, aware of your breathing just now? Probably not; its control is part of *nonconscious processes*. Were you thinking about your last vacation or about the author of *Hamlet*? Again, probably not; control of such thoughts are part of *preconscious memories*. Were you aware of background noises, such as the ticking of a clock, the hum of traffic, or the buzzing of a fluorescent light? It would be difficult to be aware of all this and still pay full attention to the meaning of the material in this chapter; these stimuli are part of *unattended information*. Finally, there may be types of information that are *unconscious*—not readily accessible to conscious awareness—such as the set of grammatical rules that enable you to understand this sentence. Let's examine each of these types of awareness.

NONCONSCIOUS PROCESSES

There is a range of **nonconscious** bodily activities that rarely, if ever, impinge on consciousness. An example of nonconscious processes at work is the regulation of blood pressure. Your nervous system monitors physiological information to detect and act on changes continually, without your awareness. At certain times, some ordinarily nonconscious activities can be made conscious: You can, for example, choose to exercise conscious control over your pattern of breathing. Even so, your nervous system takes care of many important functions without requiring conscious resources.

PRECONSCIOUS MEMORIES

Memories accessible to consciousness only after something calls your attention to them are known as **preconscious memories.** The storehouse of memory is filled with an incredible amount of information, such as your general knowledge of language, sports, or geography and recollections of your personally experienced events. Preconscious memories function silently in the background of your mind until a situation arises in which they are consciously necessary (as when we asked you to call to mind a favorite past event). Memory will be discussed in detail in Chapter 7.

UNATTENDED INFORMATION

At any given time, you are surrounded by a vast amount of stimulation. As we described in Chapter 4, you can focus your attention only on a small part of it. What you focus on, in combination with the memories it evokes, will determine, to a large extent, what is in consciousness. Nevertheless, you sometimes have an unconscious representation of information that is not the focus of your attention. Recall this scenario from Chapter 4: At a noisy party, you try to focus attention on your attractive date and remain seemingly oblivious to a nearby conversation—until you overhear your name mentioned. Suddenly you are aware that you must have been monitoring the conversation—in some unconscious way—to detect that special signal amid the noise (Wood & Cowan, 1995a).

THE UNCONSCIOUS

You typically recognize the existence of *unconscious* information when you cannot explain some behavior by virtue of forces that were conscious at the time of the behavior. An initial theory of unconscious forces was developed by **Sigmund Freud,** who argued that certain life experiences—traumatic memories and taboo desires—are sufficiently threatening that special mental processes (that we will describe in Chapter 13) permanently banish them from consciousness. Freud believed that when the content of unacceptable ideas or motives is *repressed*—put out of consciousness—the strong feel-

At any given time, thoughts about your job, your parents, or your hungry pet may flow below the level of consciousness until something occurs to focus your attention on one of these topics. Why are these memories considered preconscious, not unconscious?

ings associated with the thoughts still remain and influence behavior. Freud's "discovery" of the unconscious contradicted a long tradition of Western thought. From the time the English philosopher John Locke (1690/1975) wrote his classic text on the mind, *An Essay Concerning Human Understanding,* most thinkers firmly believed that rational beings had access to all the activities of their own minds. Freud's initial hypothesis about the existence of unconscious mental processes was considered outrageous by his contemporaries (Dennett, 1987). (We will revisit Freud's ideas when we discuss the origin of your unique personality in Chapter 13.)

Many psychologists now use the term *unconscious* to refer to information and processes that are more benign than the types of thoughts Freud suggested must be repressed (Baars & McGovern, 1996; Westen, 1998). For example, many types of ordinary language processing rely on unconscious processes. Consider this sentence (Vu et al., 2000):

> *She investigated the bark.*

How did you interpret this sentence? Did you picture some woman looking after a dog or examining a tree? Because the word *bark* is ambiguous—and the sentence context provides little help—you can only guess at what the writer meant. Now consider the same sentence in a slightly larger context:

> *The botanist looked for a fungus. She investigated the bark.*

Did you find the sentence easier to understand in this context? If you did, it's because your unconscious language processes used the extra context to make a very swift choice between the two meanings of *bark.*

With this example, we demonstrate that processes that operate below the level of consciousness often affect your behavior—in this case, the ease with which you came to a clear understanding of the sentence. We have, thus, shifted subtly from discussing the contents of consciousness to discussing the functions of consciousness. Before we take up that topic in detail, however, we will briefly describe two ways in which the contents of consciousness can be studied.

◆ STUDYING THE CONTENTS OF CONSCIOUSNESS

To study consciousness, researchers have had to devise methodologies to make deeply private experiences overtly measurable. One method is a new variation on Wundt and Titchener's practice of introspection. Experimental participants are asked to speak aloud as they work through a variety of complex tasks. They report, in as much detail as possible, the sequence of thoughts they experience while they complete the tasks. The participants' reports, called **think-aloud protocols,** are used to document the mental strategies and representations of knowledge that the participants employ to do the task. These protocols also allow researchers to analyze the discrepancies between task performance and awareness of how it is carried out (Ericsson & Simon, 1993).

In the **experience-sampling method,** participants wear devices that signal them when they should provide reports about what they are feeling and thinking. For example, in one methodology, participants wear electronic pagers. A radio transmitter activates the pager at various random times each day for a week or more. Whenever the pager signals, participants may be asked to respond to questions such as "How well were you concentrating?" In this way, researchers can keep a running record of participants' thoughts, awareness, and focuses of attention as they go about their everyday lives (Hektner & Csikszentmihalyi, 2002). Consider an experiment that used palm-top computers to obtain experience samples.

PUTTING IDEAS TO THE TEST

Are There Cross-Cultural Differences in Reports of Well-Being?

A researcher provided 15 European American and 21 Asian (Japanese and Korean) students with palm-top computers (Oishi, 2003). At five random times during the day, the computers signaled the students to complete a survey that measured their sense of emotional well-being. These random samples allowed the researcher to calculate the proportion of time that each participant was experiencing overall positive moods while actually experiencing the day-to-day variations of life. At the end of the week-long experiment, the participants provided retrospective ratings by looking back over the week and noting the extent to which they had experienced positive moods. Mood ratings were combined so that higher numbers, on an 8-point scale, reflected more positive evaluations. **Figure 5.1** shows that the experience-sampling and retrospective measures yielded different conclusions. Whereas the Asians reported more positive moods while immersed in day-to-day experiences, they reported less positive moods when looking back on the week. Why might that be? The researcher suggested that European Americans and Asians have different cultural expectations of how satisfied they should be with their lives. Those cultural expectations had an impact on the retrospective judgments.

You can see from this example how important the experience-sampling measures were. If you just looked at the retrospective data, you might conclude that Asians have less happy lives. The day-to-day data argue strongly against that conclusion.

- What is the difference between *nonconscious* and *preconscious*?
- How has the concept of the unconscious been modified in the time since Freud's theories?
- What are some of the methods researchers use to study the contents of consciousness?

The Functions of Consciousness

When we address the question of the *functions* of consciousness, we are trying to understand why we *need* consciousness—what does it add to our human experience? In this section, we describe the importance of consciousness to human survival and social function.

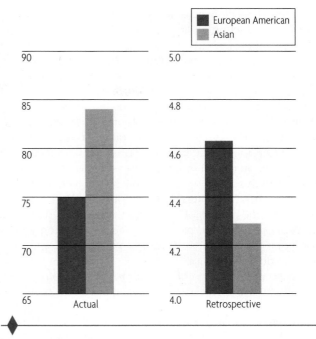

FIGURE 5.1

Cross-Cultural Measures of Well-Being

European Americans and Asians provided evaluations of their actual experiences of positive moods, based on random samples of their ongoing experience and retrospective reports looking back over a week's time. The Asians reported higher actual experiences of positive moods but were less positive when looking back on the week.

◆ THE USES OF CONSCIOUSNESS

Human consciousness was forged in the crucible of competition with the most hostile force in its evolutionary environment—other humans. The human mind may have evolved as a consequence of the extreme *sociability* of human ancestors, which was perhaps originally a group defense against predators and a means to exploit resources more efficiently. However, close group living then created new demands for cooperative as well as competitive abilities with other humans. Natural selection favored those who could think, plan, and imagine alternative realities that could promote both bonding with kin and victory over adversaries. Those who developed language and tools won the grand prize of survival of the fittest mind—and, fortunately, passed it on to us (Donald, 1995; McPhail, 1998).

Because consciousness evolved, you should not be surprised that it provides a range of functions that aid in the survival of the species (Baars, 1997; Baars &

McGovern, 1994; Cheney & Seyfarth, 1990; Ornstein, 1991). Consciousness also plays an important role in allowing for the construction of both personal and culturally shared realities.

AIDING SURVIVAL

From a biological perspective, consciousness probably evolved because it helped individuals make sense of environmental information and use that information in planning the most appropriate and effective actions. Usually, you are faced with a sensory-information overload. William James described the massive amount of information that strikes the sensory receptors as a "blooming, buzzing confusion" assailing you from all sides. Consciousness helps you adapt to your environment by making sense of this profusion of confusion in three ways.

First, consciousness reduces the flow of stimulus input by restricting what you notice and what you focus on. You might recognize this *restrictive* function of consciousness from the discussion of *attention* in Chapter 4. Consciousness helps you tune out much of the information that is not relevant to your immediate goals and purposes. Suppose you decide to take a walk to enjoy a spring day. You notice trees blooming, birds singing, and children playing. If, all at once, a snarling dog appears on the scene, you use consciousness to restrict your attention to that dog and assess the level of danger. The restrictive function also applies to information you draw from your internal storehouse of information. When, at the outset of this chapter, we asked you to think about a favorite past event, we were asking you to use your consciousness to restrict your mental attention to a single past memory.

A second function of consciousness is *selective storage*. Even within the category of information to which you consciously attend, not all of it has continuing relevance to your ongoing concerns. After your encounter with the snarling dog, you might stop yourself and think, "I want to remember not to walk down this block." Consciousness allows you to selectively store—commit to memory—information that you want to analyze, interpret, and act on in the future; consciousness allows you to classify events and experiences as relevant or irrelevant to personal needs by selecting some and ignoring others. When we consider memory processes in Chapter 7, we will see that not all the information you add to memory requires conscious processing. Still, conscious memories have different properties—and involve different brain regions—than other types of memories.

A third function of consciousness is to make you stop, think, and consider alternatives based on past knowledge and imagine various consequences. This *planning* function enables you to suppress strong desires when they conflict with moral, ethical, or practical concerns. With this kind of consciousness you can plan a route for your next walk that avoids that snarling dog. Because consciousness gives you a broad time perspective in which to frame potential actions, you can call on knowledge of the past and expectations for the future to influence your current decisions. For all these reasons, consciousness gives you great potential for flexible, appropriate responses to the changing demands in your life.

PERSONAL AND CULTURAL CONSTRUCTIONS OF REALITY

No two people interpret a situation in exactly the same way. Your *personal construction of reality* is your unique interpretation of a current situation based on your general knowledge, memories of past experiences, current needs, values, beliefs, and future goals. Each person attends more to certain features of the stimulus environment than to others precisely because his or her personal construction of reality has been formed from a selection of unique inputs. When your personal construction of reality remains relatively stable, your *sense of self* has continuity over time.

Individual differences in personal constructions of reality are even greater when people have grown up in different cultures, lived in different environments within a culture, or faced different survival tasks. The opposite is also true—because the people of a given culture share many of the same experiences, they often have similar constructions of reality. *Cultural constructions of reality* are ways of thinking about the world that are shared by most members of a particular group of people. When a member of a society develops a personal construction of reality that fits in with the cultural construction, it is affirmed by the culture and, at the same time, it affirms the cultural construction. You already saw one example of the impact of cultural on the construction of reality: Recall that Asian students reported retrospectively that their moods had been less positive than did their European American peers, despite their day-to-day experiences. In Chapter 13, we will describe more fully the relationship between the personal and the cultural sense of self.

◆ STUDYING THE FUNCTIONS OF CONSCIOUSNESS

Many functions of consciousness include implicit comparisons with what remains unconscious. That is, conscious processes often affect or are affected by unconscious processes. To study the functions of consciousness, researchers often study the relationship between conscious and unconscious influences on behavior. Researchers have developed a variety of ways to demonstrate that unconscious processes can affect conscious behavior (Nelson, 1996; Westen, 1998).

For example, researchers have used the *SLIP* (*S*poonerisms of *L*aboratory-*I*nduced *P*redisposition) technique to determine the way in which unconscious forces affect the probability of making a speech error (Baars et al., 1992). The SLIP procedure enables an experimenter to induce slips of the tongue by setting up expectations for certain patterns of sound. Thus, after pronouncing a series of word pairs like *ball doze, bell dark,* and *bean deck,* a participant might mispronounce *darn bore* as *barn door.* Experimenters can assess conscious or unconscious influences on the probability of such sound exchanges by altering circumstances external to the task. For instance, participants were more likely to make the error *bad shock* (from *shad bock*) when they believed they might receive a painful electric shock sometime during an experiment (Motley & Baars, 1979). Similarly, male participants who performed the SLIP task in the presence of a provocative female experimenter were more likely to err in producing *good legs* (from *lood gegs*). These results suggest an unconscious contribution to the production of speech errors.

Another way to study the functions of consciousness is to determine which of the many tasks you carry out a day-to-day basis require conscious intervention. To get a sense of these tasks, you can carry out a very simple experiment. Put your book down for a minute and try this:

- Try to find something that is red. Now try to find something that is magenta.
- Try to find something that is a square. Now try to find something that is round.
- Try to find something that is blue. Now try to find something that is both round and blue.

Which did you find harder in each case? Research suggests that you should find it easier to locate something magenta rather than something red (Treisman & Gormican, 1988), something square rather than something round (Kim & Cave, 1995), and something that is defined by one feature rather than two (Treisman & Sato, 1990). Why do you think that is so? You have just discovered some features of tasks that require less or more conscious attention.

We provide another example in **Figure 5.2.** In part A, try to find the yellow and blue item. In part B, try to find the yellow house with blue windows. Wasn't this second task much easier? Performance is much less affected by all the extra objects in the picture when the two colors are organized into *parts* and *wholes* (Wolfe et al., 1994). Could you feel your conscious attention being more engaged when we asked you to find the yellow and blue item? From results of this sort, researchers are assembling a global view of the circumstances in which consciousness functions.

We have seen how the contents and functions of consciousness are defined and studied. We turn now to ordinary and then extraordinary alterations in consciousness.

PUT YOURSELF TO THE TEST

- ➤ How are the restrictive and selective storage functions of consciousness related?
- ➤ In what ways does consciousness aid planning?
- ➤ How does consciousness contribute to personal and cultural constructions of reality?
- ➤ Why have researchers attempted to discriminate between conscious and unconscious processes?

A.   B.

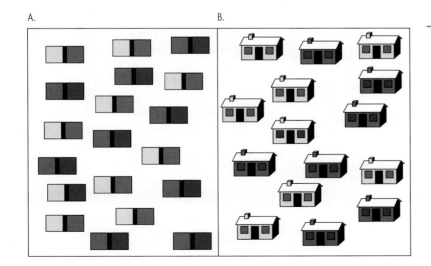

FIGURE 5.2

Search for the Conjunction of Two Colors

(A) Find the yellow and blue item. (B) Find the yellow house with blue windows. (A) Search is very inefficient when the conjunction is between the colors of two parts of a target. (B) However, search is much easier when the conjunction is between the color of the whole item and the color of one of its parts.

When Do Children Acquire Consciousness?
Michael Popper
Brandeis University

I t seems very likely that at some point in your life you've looked down into a crib at a newborn, or very young child, and wondered to yourself: "What's going on in this child's head?" Often, this question translates into an issue of consciousness: When does the child become conscious of him- or herself as a *self*? Research has suggested that children acquire, in turn, a subjective self and then an objective self (Lewis, 1991; 1999):

■ Children have acquired a *subjective self, or subjective self-awareness,* when they have come to the realization that they are separate from others. The child is able to *subject* the external world to conscious scrutiny.

■ Children have acquired an *objective self, or objective self-awareness,* when they can turn their consciousness on themselves—when they can make themselves the *object* of their own conscious analysis. Children are able to reflect on what they "know that they know" or "remember that they remember."

Classic research on children's acquisition of objective self-awareness has relied on their performance in front of mirrors. Researchers wondered, When do they realize that the image in the mirror is them? To answer this question, researchers asked mothers to put a small dot of rouge on their children's noses, without allowing the children to know that they were being marked—this is the *nose dot* test. Children understand some of the properties of

mirrors at a fairly young age. For example, by as early as 6 months, children will reach out and touch some parts of the image in the mirror. However, it isn't until about age 18 months that most children touch their noses in response to the dot of rouge (Bertenthal & Fischer, 1978). Apparently, it is not until that age that children can think (in some form), "That's me in the mirror—and what's that strange red mark on my nose?"

Even when children can pass the *nose dot* test, they are not finished acquiring a sense of self. Children must still acquire the idea of the objective self having a time component so they can think of themselves as continuously existing in the past, present, and future. An adaptation of the nose dot procedure allowed researchers to examine children's

acquisition of the temporal continuity of the self (Povinelli et al., 1996). In this study, children ranging in age from 30 to 42 months were videotaped while an experimenter secretly put a sticker in the child's hair. Some of the children were shown videotape of themselves with the sticker in a *live* recording: They could see the sticker in their hair while they were doing the things they were doing. The other half of the children watched a videotape after about a 3-minute *delay:* They were watching a tape of themselves, with a sticker in their hair, carrying out activities from the recent past. About two-thirds of the children in the *live* group reached up to the stickers, but only about one-third of the children did in the *delay* group. In fact, it was only at around age 4 years that children were reliably able to watch a delayed videotape of their activities and make a connection to the sticker. Apparently, it's reasonably difficult for children to reason from representations of the past—even the pretty immediate past—to what's happening now.

Do these results surprise you? If you've spent time with 2- and 3-year-old children, you know that they seem to have a pretty good idea of who they are and what they are up to. The research results suggest how much there really is for children to learn—and, therefore, how complex your adult experience of consciousness really is.

Although the daydreaming of a Little Leaguer may serve different functions than that of a major-league baseball player, daydreaming can have value for both. What functions does daydreaming fill in your day-to-day life?

Sleep and Dreams

Almost every day of your life you experience a rather profound change in consciousness: When you decide it's time to end your day, you will surrender yourself to sleep—and while you sleep you will undoubtedly dream. A third of your life is spent sleeping, with your muscles in a state of "benign paralysis" and your brain humming with activity. We begin this section by considering the general biological rhythms of wakefulness and sleeping. We then focus more directly on the physiology of sleeping. Finally, we examine the major mental activity that accompanies sleep—dreaming—and explore the role dreams play in human psychology.

◆ CIRCADIAN RHYTHMS

All creatures are influenced by nature's rhythms of day and night. Your body is attuned to a time cycle known as a **circadian rhythm:** Your arousal levels, metabolism, heart rate, body temperature, and hormonal activity ebb and flow according to the ticking of your internal clock. For the most part, these activities reach their peak during the day—usually during the afternoon—and hit their low point at night while you sleep. Research suggests that the clock your body uses is not exactly in synchrony with the clock on the wall: Without the corrective effects of external time cues, the human internal "pacemaker" establishes a 24.18-hour cycle (Czeisler et al., 1999). The exposure to sunlight that you get each day helps you make the small adjustment to a 24-hour cycle. Information about sunlight is gathered through your eyes, but receptors for regulation of circadian rhythms are not the same receptors as allow you to see the world (Menaker, 2003). For example, animals with-

out rods and cones (see Chapter 4) still sense light in a way that enables them to maintain their circadian rhythms (Freedman et al., 1999).

Changes that cause a mismatch between your biological clock and environmental clocks affect how you feel and act (Moore-Ede, 1993). Perhaps the most dramatic example of how such mismatches arise comes from long-distance air travel. When people fly across time zones, they may experience *jet lag,* a condition whose symptoms include fatigue, irresistible sleepiness, and subsequent unusual sleep–wake schedules. Jet lag occurs because the internal circadian rhythm is out of phase with the normal temporal environment (Redfern et al., 1994). For example, your body says it's 2 A.M.—and thus is at a low point on many physiological measures—when local time requires you to act as if it is noon. Jet lag, a special problem for flight crews, contributes to pilot errors that cause airplane accidents (Coleman, 1986).

What variables influence jet lag? The direction of travel and the number of time zones passed through are the most important variables. Traveling eastbound creates greater jet lag than does westbound flight, because your biological clock can be more readily extended than shortened, as required on eastbound trips (it is easier to stay awake longer than it is to fall asleep sooner). When healthy volunteers were flown back and forth between Europe and the United States, their peak performance on standard tasks was reached within two to four days after westbound flights but nine days after eastbound travel (Klein & Wegmann, 1974).

◆ THE SLEEP CYCLE

About a third of your circadian rhythm is devoted to that period of behavioral quiescence called *sleep.* Most of what is known about sleep concerns the electrical activities of the brain. The methodological breakthrough for the study of sleep came in 1937 with the application of a technology that records brain wave activity of the sleeper in the form of an electroencephalogram (EEG).

The EEG provided an objective, ongoing measure of the way brain activity varies when people are awake or asleep. With the EEG, researchers discovered that brain waves change in form at the onset of sleep and show further systematic, predictable changes during the entire sleep period (Loomis et al., 1937). The next significant discovery in sleep research was that bursts of **rapid eye movements (REM)** occur at periodic intervals during sleep (Aserinsky & Kleitman, 1953). The time when a sleeper is not showing REM is known as **non-REM (NREM) sleep.** We will see in a later section that REM and NREM sleep have significance for one of the night's major activities—dreaming.

Let us track your brain waves through the night. As you prepare to go to bed, an EEG records that your brain waves are moving along at a rate of about 14 cycles per second (cps). Once you are comfortably in bed, you begin to relax, and your brain waves slow down to a rate of about 8 to 12 cps. When you fall asleep, you enter your *sleep cycle*, each of whose stages shows a distinct EEG pattern. In Stage 1 sleep, the EEG shows brain waves of about 3 to 7 cps. During Stage 2, the EEG is characterized by *sleep spindles*, minute bursts of electrical activity of 12 to 16 cps. In the next two stages (3 and 4) of sleep, you enter into a very deep state of relaxed sleep. Your brain waves slow to about 1 to 2 cps, and your breathing and heart rate decrease. In a final stage, the electrical activity of your brain increases; your EEG looks very similar to those recorded during stages 1 and 2. It is during this stage that you will experience REM sleep, and you will begin to dream (see **Figure 5.3**). (Because the EEG pattern during REM sleep resembles that of an awake person, REM sleep was originally termed *paradoxical sleep*.)

Cycling through the first four stages of sleep, which are NREM sleep, requires about 90 minutes. REM sleep lasts for about 10 minutes. Over the course of a night's sleep, you pass through this 100-minute cycle four to six times (see **Figure 5.4**). With each cycle, the amount of time you spend in deep sleep (stages 3 and 4) decreases, and the amount of time you spend in REM sleep increases. During the last cycle, you may spend as much time as an hour in REM sleep. NREM sleep accounts for 75 to 80 percent of total sleep time, and REM sleep makes up 20 to 25 percent of sleep time.

Not all individuals sleep for the same amount of time. Although there is a genetic sleep need programmed into the human species, the actual amount of sleep each individual obtains is highly affected by conscious actions. People actively control sleep length in a number of ways, such as by staying up late or using alarm clocks. Sleep duration is also controlled by circadian rhythms; that is, when one goes to sleep influences sleep duration. Getting adequate amounts of NREM and REM sleep is only likely when you standardize your

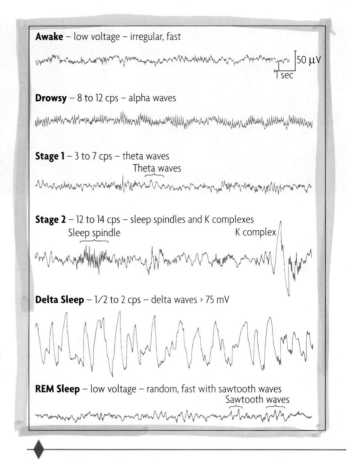

FIGURE 5.3

EEG Patterns Reflecting the Stages of a Regular Night's Sleep

Each sleep stage is defined by characteristic patterns of brain activity.

bedtime and rising time across the entire week, including weekends. In that way, the time you spend in bed is likely to correspond closely to the sleepy phase of your circadian rhythm.

Of further interest is the dramatic change in patterns of sleep that occurs over an individual's lifetime (shown in **Figure 5.5**). You started out in this world sleeping for about 16 hours a day, with nearly half of that time spent in REM sleep. By age 50, you may sleep only 6 hours and spend only about 20 percent of the time in REM sleep. Young adults typically sleep 7 to 8 hours, with about 20 percent REM sleep.

The change in sleep patterns with age doesn't mean that sleep isn't still quite important as you grow older. One study followed healthy older adults—those in their 60s through 80s—to see if there was a relationship between their sleep behaviors and how long they remained alive (Dew et al., 2003). The researchers

FIGURE 5.4

The Stages of Sleep

A typical pattern of the stages of sleep during a single night includes deeper sleep in the early cycles but more time in REM in the later cycles.

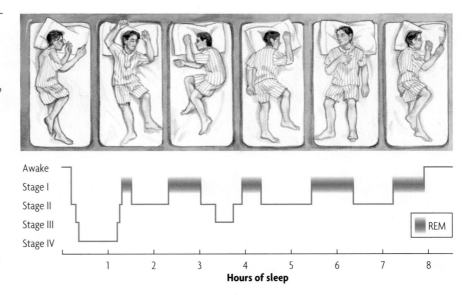

found that people who had higher sleep efficiency—a measure based on the amount of time they were asleep divided by the amount of time they spent in bed—were likely to live longer. This result leads directly to our next question: Why do people need sleep?

◆ WHY SLEEP?

The orderly progression of stages of sleep in humans and other animals suggests that there is an evolutionary basis and a biological need for sleep. People function quite well when they get the time-honored 7 to 8 hours of sleep a night (Harrison & Horne, 1996). Why do humans sleep so much and what functions do types of sleep (NREM and REM) serve?

The two most general functions for NREM sleep may be *conservation* and *restoration*. Sleep may have evolved because it enabled animals to conserve energy at times when there was no need to forage for food, search for mates, or work (Allison & Cicchetti, 1976; Cartwright, 1982; Webb, 1974). On the other hand, sleep also enables the body to engage in housekeeping functions

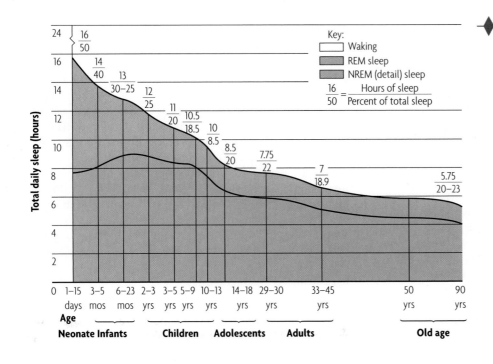

FIGURE 5.5

Patterns of Human Sleep over a Lifetime

The graph shows changes with age in total amounts of daily REM sleep and NREM sleep and percentage of REM sleep. Note that the amount of REM sleep decreases considerably over the years, and NREM diminishes less sharply.

What is the relationship between actual sleep patterns and people's perceptions of insomina?

and to *restore* itself in any of several ways. During sleep, neurotransmitters and neuromodulators may be synthesized to compensate for the quantities used in daily activities, and postsynaptic receptors may be returned to their optimal level of sensitivity (Porkka-Heiskanen et al., 1997; Rainnie et al., 1994). Research evidence also suggests that the brain's energy supply is replenished during NREM sleep (Benington & Heller, 1995).

If you were to be deprived of REM sleep for a night, you would have more REM sleep than usual the next night, suggesting that REM sleep also serves some necessary functions. A number of interesting, but not yet fully demonstrated, benefits have been attributed to REM sleep (Moffitt et al., 1993). For example, it appears that, during infancy, REM sleep is responsible for establishing the pathways between your nerves and muscles that enable you to move your eyes. REM sleep may establish functional structures in the brain, such as those involving the learning of motor skills. REM sleep may also play a role in the maintenance of mood and emotion, and it may be required for storing memories and fitting recent experiences into networks of previous beliefs or memories (Maquet, 2001; Siegel, 2001; Stickgold et al., 2001). On the physiological side, researchers have suggested that REM sleep may be necessary to restore the brain's balance after NREM sleep: The unusual type of brain activity characteristic of NREM sleep may, for example, change the balance of brain

function in ways that must be returned to normal by REM sleep (Benington & Heller, 1994).

◆ SLEEP DISORDERS

It would be nice if you could always take a good night's sleep for granted. Unfortunately, many people suffer from sleep disorders that pose a serious burden to their personal lives and careers. Disordered sleep can also have societal consequences. Of those individuals whose work schedules include night shifts, more than half nod off at least once a week on the job. Some of the world's most serious industrial accidents—Three Mile Island, Chernobyl, Bhopal, and the *Exxon Valdez* disaster— have occurred during late evening hours. People have speculated that these accidents occurred because key personnel failed to function optimally as a result of insufficient sleep. Because sleep disorders are important in many students' lives, we will review them here. As you read, remember that sleep disorders vary in severity. Similarly, their origins involve biological, environmental, and psychological forces.

INSOMNIA

When people are dissatisfied with their amount or quality of sleep, they are suffering from **insomnia.** This chronic failure to get adequate sleep is characterized by an inability to fall asleep quickly, frequent arousals during sleep, or early-morning awakening. In a recent poll, 48 percent of adults ages 18 and older reported that, in the past year, they experienced insomnia a few nights or more each week (National Sleep Foundation, 2003). Insomnia is a complex disorder caused by a variety of psychological, environmental, and biological factors (Spielman & Glovinsky, 1997). However, when insomniacs are studied in sleep laboratories, the objective quantity and quality of their actual sleep vary considerably, from disturbed sleep to normal sleep. Research has revealed that many insomniacs who complain of lack of sleep actually show completely normal physiological patterns of sleep—a condition described as *subjective insomnia*. For example, in one study 38 percent of the participants who reported that they suffered from insomnia actually had normal sleep (Edinger et al., 2000). Equally interesting, the same study showed detectable sleep disturbances in 43 percent of the participants who had no complaints of insomnia. The discrepancies may result from differences in the cognitions and emotions that surround sleep (Espie, 2002). People who experience insomnia—or those who only think they do—may be less able to banish intrusive thoughts and feelings from consciousness even while they are trying to sleep.

NARCOLEPSY

Narcolepsy is a sleep disorder characterized by periodic sleep during the daytime (Aldrich, 1992). It is often combined with *cataplexy,* muscle weakness or a loss of muscle control brought on by emotional excitement (such as laughing, anger, fear, surprise, or hunger) that causes the afflicted person to fall down suddenly. When they fall asleep, narcoleptics enter REM sleep almost immediately. This rush to REM causes them to experience—and be consciously aware of—vivid dream images or sometimes terrifying hallucinations. Narcolepsy affects about 1 of every 2,000 individuals. Because narcolepsy runs in families, scientists believe the disease has a genetic basis (Mignot, 1998). Narcolepsy often has a negative social and psychological impact on sufferers because of their desire to avoid the embarrassment caused by sudden bouts of sleep (Broughton & Broughton, 1994).

SLEEP APNEA

Sleep apnea is an upper-respiratory sleep disorder in which the person stops breathing while asleep. When this happens, the blood's oxygen level drops and emergency hormones are secreted, causing the sleeper to awaken and begin breathing again. Although most people have a few such apnea episodes a night, someone with sleep apnea disorder can have hundreds of such cycles every night. Sometimes apnea episodes frighten the sleeper, but often they are so brief that the sleeper fails to attribute accumulating sleepiness to them (Orr, 1997). Sleep apnea affects roughly 2 percent of adults (Sonnad et al., 2003).

Sleep apnea also occurs frequently among premature infants, who sometimes need physical stimulation to start breathing again. Because of their underdeveloped respiratory system, these infants must remain attached to monitors in intensive care nurseries as long as the problem continues.

SOMNABULISM

Individuals who suffer from **somnambulism,** or *sleepwalking,* leave their beds and wander while still remaining asleep. Sleepwalking is more frequent among children than among adults. For example, studies have found that about 7 percent of children sleepwalk (Nevéus et al., 2001) but only about 2 percent of adults do so (Ohayon et al., 1999). Sleepwalking is associated with NREM sleep. When monitored in a sleep laboratory, adult sleepwalkers demonstrated abrupt arousal—involving movement or speech—during stage 3 and stage 4 sleep (see Figure 5.3) in the first third of their night's sleep (Guilleminault et al., 2001). Contrary to popular conceptions, it is not particularly dangerous to wake sleepwalkers—they're just likely to be confused by the sudden awakening. Still, sleepwalking in itself can be dangerous because individuals are navigating in their environments without conscious awareness.

DAYTIME SLEEPINESS

The major complaint of the majority of patients evaluated at U.S. sleep disorder centers is excessive **daytime sleepiness.** Among a sample of 1,506 adults in the United States, 27 percent indicated that during a few days or more each month they are so sleepy that their daily activities are disturbed; 15 percent indicated that daytime sleepiness has a negative impact on their daily activities for a few days or more each *week* (National Sleep Foundation, 2003). Excessive sleepiness causes diminished alertness, delayed reaction times, and impaired performance on motor and cognitive tasks. In earlier research, nearly half the patients with excessive sleepiness reported having been involved in automobile accidents, and more than half have had job accidents, some serious (Roth et al., 1989).

In preparing *Sleep Alert,* a documentary film on this sleep deprivation disorder, psychologist **James Maas** reported that "there are some people who are literally walking zombies" (Maas, 1998). He learned of airline pilots who told of falling asleep on the job for short naps, only to find the rest of the crew napping when they awoke. According to Maas, as many as 30 percent of high school students fall asleep in class once a week.

Some degree of sleepiness is to be expected when individuals' lifestyles or job requirements prohibit them from getting sufficient nocturnal sleep. Excessive sleepiness, however, often has physiological roots, and sufferers should seek medical attention (White & Mitler, 1997).

◆ DREAMS: THEATER OF THE MIND

During every ordinary night of your life, you enter into the complex world of dreams. Once the province only of prophets, psychics, and psychoanalysts, dreams have become a vital area of study for scientific researchers. Much dream research begins in sleep laboratories, where experimenters can monitor sleepers for REM and NREM sleep. Although individuals report more dreams when they are awakened from REM periods—on about 82 percent of their awakenings—dreaming also takes place during NREM periods—on about 54 percent of awakenings (Foulkes, 1962). Dreaming associated with NREM states is less likely to contain story content that is emotionally involving. It is more akin to daytime thought, with less sensory imagery.

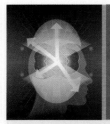

PSYCHOLOGY IN THE 21ST CENTURY

The 24/7 Lifestyle and Sleep

Ten or twenty years ago there was very little to do after midnight. When students had finished with their schoolwork, they could pretty much choose between watching late-night television or rolling into bed. By contrast, the last decade of the 20th century brought into existence the World Wide Web and, along with it, a 24/7 supply of stimulation. At any time of day or night, you can cruise the Web or join a chat room. You can finish your midnight snack in Berlin, Connecticut, at the same time you chat with someone eating an early breakfast in Berlin, Germany.

The growth of the Internet has amplified what we might characterize as many people's love–hate relationship with sleep. People love to sleep because being rested feels good (and being sleepy feels awful). As we've seen in this chapter, your body *needs* sleep to function effectively. However, people hate to sleep because there are so many enjoyable things to do while they are awake. The World Wide Web increases substantially the range of enjoyable things to do. Your textbook authors are willing to admit that they

have purposely lost sleep rather than discontinue cruising the Web.

From the point of view of many researchers, the 24/7 availability of the Web has only made a bad situation worse. They have been worried for several years that adolescents and college students do not get nearly enough sleep (Dement & Vaughan, 1999; Wolfson & Carskadon, 1998). Although experts recommend that everyone get 8 hours of sleep, a year-2000 poll carried out by the National Sleep Foundation (2000) suggests that the average 18- to 29-year-old never meets this standard. During weekdays, the average duration of sleep for individuals in this age range is 6.8 hours; on weekends, this increases to 7.8 hours.

How concerned are you about the amount of sleep you get? Research suggests that college students underestimate the negative consequences sleep deprivation has on their cognitive performance (Pilcher & Walters, 1997). You should take a moment to consider the reality that chronic sleep loss is likely

to be quite unfortunate for your college performance (Buboltz et al., 2002).

No doubt many college students lose sleep because of the stresses associated with studying for exams and writing papers (Murphy & Archer, 1996). However, 55 percent of the poll participants in the 18-to-29 range agreed to the statement that they "often stay up later than they should because they are watching TV or are on the Internet." Does this apply to you?

We are not trying to discourage you from using the Internet. We are simply offering the observation that new technologies often seem to bring with them new reasons for people to lose sleep. Sleepiness has many serious consequences: lower grades, work problems, and car accidents are just a few. So far, scientists have been able to invent pills that can stop you from sleeping—but none that can stop you from *needing* sleep. You should determine what personal steps you can take so that the 21st century doesn't become your Century of Sleeplessness.

Because dreams have such prominence in people's mental lives, virtually every culture has arrived at the same question: Do dreams have significance? The answer that has almost always emerged is yes. That is, most cultures encode the belief that, in one way or another, dreams have important personal and cultural meaning. We now review some of the ways in which cultures attach meaning to dreams.

FREUDIAN DREAM ANALYSIS

The most prominent dream theory in modern Western culture was originated by Sigmund Freud. Freud called dreams "transient psychoses" and models of "everynight madness." He also called them "the royal road to the unconscious." He made the analysis of dreams the cornerstone of psychoanalysis with his classic book *The Interpretation of Dreams* (1900/1965). Freud saw dream images as symbolic expressions of powerful unconscious, repressed wishes. These wishes appear in disguised form because they harbor forbidden desires, such as sexual yearning for the parent of the opposite sex. The two dynamic forces operating in dreams are, thus, the *wish* and the *censorship,* a defense against the wish. The censor transforms the hidden meaning, or **latent content,** of the dream into **manifest content,** which appears to the dreamer after a distortion process that Freud referred to as **dream work.** The manifest content is the acceptable version of the story; the latent content represents the socially or personally unacceptable version but also the true, "uncut" one.

According to Freud, the interpretation of dreams requires working backward from the manifest content to the latent content. To the psychoanalyst who uses dream analysis to understand and treat a patient's problems, dreams reveal the patient's unconscious wishes, the fears attached to those wishes, and the characteristic defenses the patient employs to handle the resulting psychic conflict between the wishes and the fears. Freud believed in both idiosyncratic—special to particular individuals—and universal meanings—many of a sexual nature—for the symbols and metaphors in dreams:

> *Boxes, cases, chests, cupboards and ovens represent the uterus, and also hollow objects, ships, and vessels of all kinds. Rooms in dreams are usually women; if the various ways in and out of them are represented, this interpretation is scarcely open to doubt. . . . A dream of going through a suite of rooms is a brothel or harem dream. . . . It is highly probable that all complicated machinery and apparatus occurring in dreams stand for the genitals (and as a rule male ones). . . . (Freud, 1900/1965, pp. 389–391)*

Freud's theory of dream interpretation related dream symbols to his explicit theory of human psychology.

Freud's emphasis on the psychological importance of dreams has pointed the way to contemporary examinations of dream content (Domhoff, 1996; Fisher & Greenberg, 1996).

NON-WESTERN APPROACHES TO DREAM INTERPRETATION

Many people in Western societies may never think seriously about their dreams until they become students of psychology or enter therapy. By contrast, in many non-Western cultures, dream interpretation is part of the very fabric of the culture (Lewis, 1995; Tedlock, 1987). Consider the daily practice of the Archur Indians of Ecuador (Schlitz, 1997, p. 2):

> *Like every other morning, the men [of the village] sit together in a small circle. . . . They share their dreams from the night before. This daily ritual of dream-sharing is vital to the life of the Archur. It is their belief that each individual dreams, not for themselves, but for the community as a whole. Individual experience serves collective action.*

During these morning gatherings, each dreamer tells his dream story and the others offer their interpretations, hoping to arrive at some consensus understanding of the meaning of the dream. Contrast the belief that individuals dream "for the community as a whole" with the view articulated by Freud, that dreams are the "royal road" to the individual unconscious.

In many cultures, specific groups of individuals are designated as possessing special powers to assist with dream interpretation. Consider the practices of Mayan Indians who live in various parts of Mexico, Guatemala, Belize, and Honduras. In the Mayan culture, *shamans* function as dream interpreters. In fact, among some subgroups of Mayans, the shamans are selected for these roles when they have dreams in which they are visited by deities who announce the shaman's calling. Formal instruction about religious rituals is also provided to these newly selected shamans by way of dream revelation. Although the shamans, and other religious figures, have special knowledge relevant to dream interpretation, ordinary individuals also recount and discuss dreams. Dreamers commonly wake their spouses in the middle of the night to narrate dreams; mothers in some communities ask their children each morning to talk about their dreams. In contemporary times, the Mayan people have been the victims of civil war in their homelands; many people have been killed or forced to flee. One important response, according to anthropologist **Barbara Tedlock,** has been "an increased emphasis on dreams and visions that enable them to stay in touch with their ancestors and the sacred earth on which they live" (Tedlock, 1992, p. 471).

The cultural practices of many non-Western groups with respect to dreams also reflect a fundamentally different time perspective. Freud's theory had dream interpretation looking backward in time, toward childhood experiences and repressed wishes. In many other cultures, dreams are believed instead to present a vision of the future (Basso, 1987). For example, among the people of the Ingessana Hills, a region along the border of Ethiopia and the Sudan, the timing of festivals is determined by dream visions (Jedrej, 1995). The keepers of religious shrines are visited in their dreams by their fathers and other ancestors who instruct them to "announce the festival." Other groups have culturally given systems of relationships between dream symbols and meanings. Consider these interpretations from the Kalapalo Indians of central Brazil (Basso, 1987, p. 104):

> When we dream we are burnt by fire, later we will be bitten by a wild thing, by a spider or a stinging ant, for example.
> When [we dream] we are making love to women, we will be very successful when we go fishing.
> When a boy is in seclusion and he dreams of climbing a tall tree, or another one sees a long path, they will live long. This would also be true if we dreamt of crossing a wide stream in a forest.

Note how each interpretation looks to the future. The future orientation of dream interpretation is an important component of a rich cultural tradition.

PHYSIOLOGICAL THEORIES OF DREAM CONTENT

The cornerstone of both Western and non-Western approaches to dream interpretation is that dreams provide information that is of genuine value to the person or community. This view has faced a challenge from biologically based theories. Recall that some researchers believe that you have a physiological need for REM sleep to offset the brain changes of NREM sleep (Benington & Heller, 1994). Are dreams merely the side effects of other brain activities—with no special meaning of their own? Consider the *activation-synthesis model* proposed by **J. Allan Hobson** and **Robert McCarley** (1977; Hobson, 1988). This model suggests that neural signals emerge from the brain stem and then stimulate areas of the brain's cortex. These electrical discharges occur automatically about every 90 minutes and stay activated for 30 minutes or so—accounting for the cyclic alternation of REM and NREM sleep periods. These discharges activate the forebrain and association areas of the cortex; at that point, they trigger memories and connections with the dreamer's past experiences. According to Hobson and McCarley's view, there are no logical connections, no intrinsic

meaning, and no coherent patterns to these random bursts of electrical "signals." More recent research suggests that dreams do not just arise from the brain stem. Instead, you experience dreams both because some brain regions are more active—for example, those regions associated with emotions—and because some are less active—for example, those regions associated with memories of specific life experiences (Stickgold et al., 2001).

However, studies of dream content still provide challenges to these physiologically based theories of dreams (Domhoff, 1999). Those studies suggest, first, that the content of dreams shows a good deal of continuity with dreamers' waking concerns. For example, research using experience-sampling methods suggested that girls were more likely than boys to be thinking about friends of both sexes, rather than just friends of their own sex (Richards et al., 1998). Dream studies with 9- to 15-year-olds demonstrate similar gender differences in dream content about peers (Strauch & Lederbogen, 1999). A second type of finding also challenges the suggestion that dreams are merely random signals: Across adulthood, the overall content of individuals' dreams stays very much the same. Dream expert **William Domhoff** (1999) suggests that this stability over years or decades requires broader regions of the brain to be involved in dream content than those that provide the random signals in physiological theories.

You might consider keeping your own dream log—try to write your dreams as soon as you wake up each morning—to see both how your own dreams relate to daily concerns and how your dream content changes or remains stable over time. Still, we should warn you that some people have more difficulty recalling dreams than other people do (Wolcott & Strapp, 2002). For example, it's easier to recall dreams if you wake up during a REM period or close to one. If you want to recall your dreams, you might consider changing the time for which you set your alarm. Also, people who have more positive attitudes toward dreaming appear to find it easier to recall their dreams. In that sense, the interest you show in your dreams by undertaking a dream log might help increase your ability to recall them.

Here's another interesting aspect of dreams: Over time, many people have reported that the solutions to important problems or interesting new ideas came to them in their dreams (Shepard, 1978). We offer a small number of examples. Friedrich Kekulé reported that he discovered the elusive chemical structure of benzene in a dream: A snakelike molecule chain suddenly grabbed its own tail, thus forming a ring. Elias Howe had a dream—he was being attacked with spears with holes through their points—that allowed him to perfect his invention of the sewing machine. Composers such as Mozart and Schumann have reported that important musical ideas came to them in their dreams.

NIGHTMARES

When a dream frightens you by making you feel helpless or out of control, you are having a *nightmare*. For most people nightmares are relatively infrequent. In one sample of 220 undergraduates who kept daily dream logs, the average frequency of nightmares (projected from a two-week sample period) was about 24 a year (Wood & Bootzin, 1990). However, some people experience nightmares more frequently, sometimes as often as every night. Children, for example, are more likely to experience nightmares than are adults (Mindell, 1997). Also, people who have experienced traumatic events, such as rape or war, may have repetitive nightmares that force them to relive some aspects of their trauma. College students who experienced a major earthquake in the San Francisco Bay area were about twice as likely to experience nightmares as were a matched group of students who hadn't experienced an earthquake—and, as you might imagine, many of the nightmares were about the devastating effects of earthquakes (Wood et al., 1992).

We can consider nightmares to be at the outer limit of ordinary consciousness. We turn now to circumstances in which individuals deliberately seek to go beyond those everyday experiences.

PUT YOURSELF TO THE TEST

- What is the relationship between circadian rhythms and jet lag?
- How does the balance of NREM and REM sleep change over the course of a night?
- What functions do researchers believe sleep serves?
- What are the symptoms of some major sleep disorders?
- How have different theories, from different cultures, explained the origins and consequences of dreams?

Altered States of Consciousness

In every culture, some people have been dissatisfied with ordinary transformations of their waking consciousness. They have developed practices that take them beyond familiar forms of consciousness to experiences of altered states of consciousness. Some of these practices are individual, such as taking recreational drugs. Others, such as certain religious practices, are shared attempts to transcend the normal boundaries of conscious experience. We survey a variety of such practices in which altered states of consciousness are induced by a range of procedures.

◆ LUCID DREAMING

Is it possible to be aware that you are dreaming while you are dreaming? Proponents of the theory of **lucid dreaming** have demonstrated that being consciously aware that one is dreaming is a learnable skill—perfected with regular practice—that enables dreamers to control the direction of their dreams (Gackenbach & LaBerge, 1988; LaBerge & DeGracia, 2000).

PUTTING IDEAS TO THE TEST

The Experimental Reality of Lucid Dreaming

Stephen LaBerge and his colleagues devised a methodology that enabled them to test the reality of reports of lucid dreaming. The demonstration relied on previous research that had shown that some of the eye movements of REM sleep correspond to the reported direction of the dreamer's gaze. The researchers therefore asked experienced lucid dreamers to execute distinctive patterns of *voluntary* eye movements when they realized that they were dreaming. The prearranged eye movement signals appeared on the polygraph records during REM, thus demonstrating that the participants had indeed been lucid during REM sleep (LaBerge et al., 1981).

A variety of methods have been used to induce lucid dreaming. For example, in some lucid dreaming research, sleepers wear specially designed goggles that flash a red light when they detect REM sleep. The participants have learned previously that the red light is a cue for becoming consciously aware that they are dreaming (LaBerge & Levitan, 1995). Once aware of dreaming, yet still not awake, sleepers move into a state of lucid dreaming in which they can take control of their dreams, directing them according to their personal goals and making the dreams' outcomes fit their current needs. The ability to have lucid dreams reportedly increases when sleepers firmly believe that such dreams are possible and regularly practice the induction techniques (LaBerge & Rheingold, 1990). Researchers such as Stephen LaBerge argue that gaining control over the "uncontrollable" events of dreams is healthy because it enhances self-confidence and generates positive experiences for the individual. However, some therapists who use dream analysis as part of their understanding of a patient's prob-

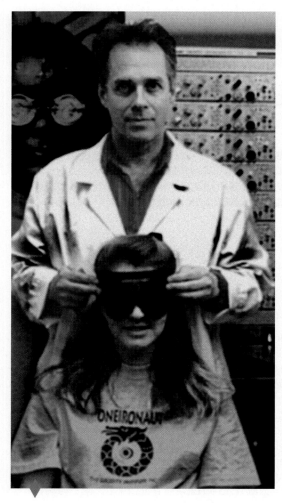

Researcher Stephen LaBerge adjusts the special goggles that will alert the sleeping participant that REM sleep is occurring. The individual is trained to enter into a state of lucid dreaming, being aware of the process and content of dream activity. If you had the ability to experience lucid dreaming, in what ways would you shape your dreams?

may in some cases give the *appearance* of being in a deeply relaxed, sleeplike state. (If people were really asleep, they could not respond to hypnosis.) A broad definition of hypnosis is that it is an alternative state of awareness characterized by the special ability some people have of responding to suggestion with changes in perception, memory, motivation, and sense of self-control. In the hypnotic state, participants experience heightened responsiveness to the hypnotist's suggestions—they often feel that their behavior is performed without intention or any conscious effort.

Researchers have often disagreed about the psychological mechanisms involved in hypnosis (Kirsch & Lynn, 1995, 1998). Some early theorists suggested that hypnotized individuals enter into a *trance* state, far different from waking consciousness. Others argued that hypnosis was nothing more than heightened motivation. Still others believed it to be a type of social role playing, a kind of *placebo* response of trying to please the hypnotist (see Chapter 2). In fact, research has largely ruled out the idea that hypnosis involves a special trancelike change in consciousness. However, even though nonhypnotized individuals can produce some of the same patterns of behavior that hypnotized individuals can, there appear to be some added effects of hypnosis—beyond motivational or placebo processes. After we discuss hypnotic induction and hypnotizability, we describe some of those effects.

HYPNOTIC INDUCTION AND HYPNOTIZABILITY

Hypnosis begins with a *hypnotic induction,* a preliminary set of activities that minimizes external distractions and encourages participants to concentrate only on suggested stimuli and believe that they are about to enter a special state of consciousness. Induction activities involve suggestions to imagine certain experiences or to visualize events and reactions. When practiced repeatedly, the induction procedure functions as a learned signal so that participants can quickly enter the hypnotic state. The typical induction procedure uses suggestions for deep relaxation, but some people can become hypnotized with an active, alert induction—such as imagining that they are jogging or riding a bicycle (Banyai & Hilgard, 1976).

Stage performances of hypnosis give the impression that the power of hypnosis lies with the hypnotist. However, the single most important factor in hypnosis is a participant's ability or "talent" to become hypnotized. **Hypnotizability** represents the degree to which an individual is responsive to standardized suggestions to experience hypnotic reactions. There are wide individual differences in susceptibility, varying from a complete lack of responsiveness to total responsiveness.

lems oppose such procedures because they feel that they distort the natural process of dreaming.

◆ HYPNOSIS

As portrayed in popular culture, hypnotists wield vast power over their witting or unwitting participants. Is this view of hypnotists accurate? What is hypnosis, what are its important features, and what are some of its valid psychological uses? The term **hypnosis** is derived from Hypnos, the name of the Greek god of sleep. Sleep, however, plays no part in hypnosis, except that people

Figure 5.6 shows the percentage of college-age individuals who presented various levels of hypnotizability the first time they were given a hypnotic induction test. What does it mean to have scored "high" or "very high" on this scale? When the test is administered, the hypnotist makes a series of posthypnotic suggestions, dictating the experiences each individual might have. When the hypnotist suggested that their extended arms had turned into bars of iron, highly hypnotizable individuals were likely to find themselves unable to bend those arms. With the appropriate suggestion, they were likely to brush away a nonexistent fly. As a third example, highly hypnotizable individuals probably couldn't nod their heads "no" when the hypnotist suggested they had lost that ability. Students who scored "low" on the hypnotizability scale experienced few if any of these reactions.

Hypnotizability is a relatively stable attribute. An adult's scores remain about the same when measured various times over a 10-year period (Morgan et al., 1974). In fact, when 50 men and women were retested 25 years after their college hypnotizability assessment, the results indicated a remarkably high correlation coefficient of .71 (Piccione et al., 1989). Children tend to be more suggestible than adults; hypnotic responsiveness peaks just before adolescence and declines thereafter. There is some evidence for genetic determinants of hypnotizability, because the scores of identical twins are more similar than are those of fraternal twins (Morgan et al., 1970). Although hypnotizability is relatively stable, it is not correlated with any personality trait such as gullibility or conformity (Fromm & Shor, 1979; Kirsch & Lynn, 1995). Rather, hypnotizability reflects a unique cognitive ability to become completely absorbed in an experience.

EFFECTS OF HYPNOSIS

In describing the way in which hypnotizability is measured, we already mentioned some of the standard effects of hypnosis: While under hypnosis, individuals respond to suggestions about motor abilities (for example, their arms become unbendable) and perceptual experiences (for example, they hallucinate a fly). How can we be sure, however, that these behaviors arise from special properties of hypnosis and not just a strong willingness on participants' part to please the hypnotist? To address this important question, researchers have often conducted experiments that contrast the performance of truly hypnotized individuals to that of *simulators*.

PUTTING IDEAS TO THE TEST

Hypnosis Is More Than Simulation

Two groups of students participated in an experiment. One group was truly hypnotized. The other group was instructed to *simulate* hypnosis: They were instructed by a first experimenter that it was their task to fool a second experimenter into believing that they were, in fact, hypnotized. Both groups were then exposed to a series of tones and asked to judge their loudness. An important part of the experiment was a *demand* instruction, in which the participants were told what they *should* experience (Reed et al., 1996, p. 143):

> *People who are exposed to the tone more than once tend to drift back into hypnosis, and this greatly reduces the intensity of the sound that they hear. You probably drifted back into hypnosis on this last trial, and for this reason, heard very little of the tone. Perhaps you didn't hear it at all.*

If all the effects of hypnosis can be attributed to participants' desire to respond correctly to experimenter demands, we would expect hypnotized and simulating participants to respond in the same way to this demand. In fact, they do not. Truly hypnotized individuals gave a wider variety of reports: They told something closer to their true experiences rather than inventing something they thought the experimenter wanted to hear (Reed et al., 1996).

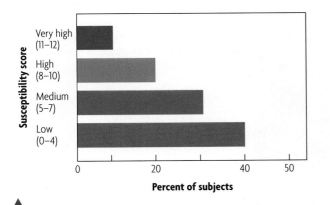

FIGURE 5.6

Level of Hypnosis at First Induction

The graph shows the results for 533 individuals hypnotized for the first time. Hypnotizability was measured on the Stanford Hypnotic Susceptibility Scale, which consists of 12 items.

In this case, simulators presumably guess incorrectly what they would be experiencing, were they truly hypnotized. From experiments of this type, we can learn exactly what independent contribution hypnosis makes to people's experiences.

An undisputed value of hypnosis is its ability to reduce pain (*hypnotic analgesia*). Your mind can amplify pain stimuli through anticipation and fear; you can diminish this psychological effect with hypnosis (Chaves, 1999). Pain control is accomplished through a variety of hypnotic suggestions: imagining the part of the body in pain as nonorganic (made of wood or plastic) or as separate from the rest of the body, thus taking one's mind on a vacation from the body and distorting time in various ways. People can control pain through hypnosis even when they banish all thoughts and images from consciousness (Hargadon et al., 1995). Hypnosis has proven especially valuable to surgery patients who cannot tolerate anesthesia, to mothers in natural childbirth, and to cancer patients learning to endure the pain associated with the disease and its treatment. Self-hypnosis (*autohypnosis*) is the best approach to controlling pain because patients can then exert control whenever pain arises. In a study of 86 women with metastatic cancer, those using self-hypnosis for pain control reported having only half as much pain as others (Spiegel et al., 1989).

One final note on hypnosis: The power of hypnosis does *not* reside in some special ability or skill of the hypnotist, but rather it resides in the relative hypnotizability of the person or persons being hypnotized. Being hypnotized does not involve giving up one's personal control; instead, the experience of being hypnotized allows an individual to learn new ways to exercise control that the hypnotist—as coach—can train the subject—as performer—to enact. You should keep all of this in mind if you watch a stage show in which people perform outlandish acts under hypnosis: Stage hypnotists make a living entertaining audiences by getting highly exhibitionist people to do things in public that most others could never be made to do. As used by researchers and therapists, hypnosis is a technique with the potential to allow you to explore and modify your sense of consciousness.

◆ MEDITATION

Many religions and traditional psychologies of the East work to direct consciousness away from immediate worldly concerns. They seek to achieve an inner focus on the mental and spiritual self. **Meditation** is a form of consciousness change designed to enhance self-knowledge and well-being by achieving a deep state of tranquility. During *concentrative* meditation, a person may focus on and regulate breathing, assume certain body positions (yogic positions), minimize external stimulation, generate specific mental images, or free the mind of all thought. By contrast, during *mindfulness* meditation, a person learns to let thoughts and memories pass freely through the mind without reacting to them.

Research has often focused on the ability of meditation to relieve the anxiety of those who must function in stress-filled environments (Anderson et al., 1999; Shapiro et al., 1998). For example, mindfulness meditation has served as the basis for mindfulness-based stress reduction (Kabat-Zinn, 1990). In one study, women suffering from heart disease were given eight weeks of training on mindfulness meditation; at the end of this intervention, the women reported consistently lower

How does meditation create an altered state of consciousness?

<www.ablongman.com/gerrig17e>

feelings of anxiety than they did before the study (Tacon et al., 2003). Women in the control group didn't experience improvement in their anxiety reports. Because feelings of anxiety play a role in the development of heart disease, this result provides evidence that the mind can help to heal the body. (We will return to this theme when we discuss health psychology in Chapter 12.)

Practicers of meditation have suggested that, when practiced regularly, some forms of meditation can heighten consciousness, help achieve *enlightenment* by enabling the individual to see familiar things in new ways, and free perception and thought from the restrictions of automatic, well-learned patterns. Some researchers have suggested that the regular practice of meditation moves the mind beyond the limits recognized by Western psychology—and may even result in increases in measured intelligence (IQ; see Chapter 9) and cognitive performance (Cranson et al., 1991). A foremost Buddhist teacher of meditation, Nhat Hanh (1991), recommends awareness of breathing and simple appreciation of your surroundings and minute daily acts as a path to psychological equilibrium.

◆ HALLUCINATIONS

Under unusual circumstances, a distortion in consciousness occurs during which an individual sees or hears things that are not actually present. **Hallucinations** are vivid perceptions that occur in the absence of objective stimulation; they are a mental construction of an individual's altered reality. They differ from illusions, which are perceptual distortions of real stimuli. Consider **Figure 5.7.** Most people see a triangle in this figure, although it is not "really" there. However, we would not want to call this a hallucination because the triangle "appears" as a consequence of the normal processes you use to perceive the world. You could not make this illusory triangle disappear by reminding yourself that it is not real. By contrast to illusions, hallucinations are individual experiences, not shared by others in a situation. Some hallucinations are short-lived; if individuals can swiftly demonstrate to themselves the unreality of a hallucination—by evaluating it against reality—the experience can come to an end. In some cases, however, individuals cannot dispel the "reality" of their hallucinations, and the hallucinations wield an influence on their lives (Siegel, 1992).

Hallucinations are fostered by heightened arousal, states of intense need, or the inability to suppress threatening thoughts. They also occur when the brain experiences an unusual type of stimulation—during, for example, high fevers, epileptic seizures, and migraine headaches—or in patients with severe mental disorders, who respond to private mental events as if they were

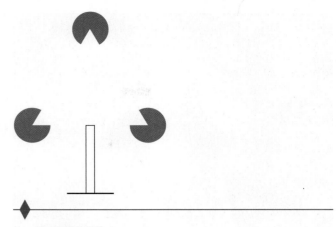

FIGURE 5.7

An Illusion, Not a Hallucination!

Although it is not really there, most people see a triangle in this Figure. When people hallucinate, they also have experiences that are not really there. However, the hallucinations arise from individuals' altered states of consciousness rather than from shared perceptual processes.

external sensory stimuli. Hallucinations are also frequently induced by psychoactive drugs, such as LSD and peyote, as well as by withdrawal from alcohol in severe cases of alcoholism (these hallucinations are known as *delirium tremens,* "the DTs"). These chemically induced hallucinations are prompted by direct effects of the drugs on the brain.

In some cultural or religious settings, hallucinations are a desirable and important occurrence (Siegel, 1992). In these circumstances, hallucinations are interpreted as mystical insights that confer special status on the visionary. So, in different settings, the same vivid perception of direct contact with spiritual forces may be deprecated as a sign of mental illness or respected as a sign of special gifts. Evaluation of such mental states often depends as much on the judgment of observers as on the content of the perceptual experience itself.

◆ RELIGIOUS ECSTASY

Meditation, prayer, fasting, and spiritual communication all contribute to intense *religious experiences.* For William James (1902), religious experiences constituted unique psychological experiences characterized by a sense of oneness and relatedness of events, of realness and vividness of experiences, and an inability to communicate, in ordinary language, the nature of the whole experience. For many people, religious experiences are clearly not part of their ordinary consciousness.

There are few religious experiences more intense than those of the Holy Ghost people of Appalachia.

The Holy Ghost people of Appalachia and other religious sects engage in practices such as snake handling to prove faith and achieve changes in consciousness. Rayford Dunn was bitten on the hand by this cottonmouth snake moments after this picture was taken in Kingston, Georgia. Although he behaved normally afterward—going out to eat and returning to church the next day to handle snakes again—some believers have died from poisonous snake bites. Have you ever been in a situation in which the strength of your beliefs led you to experience an altered state of consciousness?

Their beliefs and practices create a unique form of consciousness that enables them to do some remarkable things. At church services, they handle deadly poisonous snakes, drink strychnine poison, and handle fire. To prepare for these experiences, they listen to long sermons and participate in loud, insistent singing and wild spinning and dancing:

> *The enthusiasm may verge on violence. . . . Members wail and shake and lapse into the unintelligible, ecstatic "new tongues" of glossolalia [artificial speech with no linguistic content]. . . . The ecstasy spreads like contagion. . . . Their hands are definitely cold, even after handling fire. This would correspond with research in trance states involved in other religious cultures. It would also account for the vagueness of memory, almost sensory amnesia, that researchers have reported in serpent handlers as well as fire handlers. (Watterlond, 1983, pp. 53, 55)*

Psychological research on serpent-handling religious-group members has found them to be generally well-adjusted people who receive powerful social and psychological support from being part of the group.

Participating in the "signs of the spirits" gives them a "personal reward equaled in no other aspect of their lives" (Watterlond, 1983).

◆ MIND-ALTERING DRUGS

Since ancient times, people have taken drugs to alter their perception of reality. There is archaeological evidence for the uninterrupted use of sophora seed (mescal bean) for over 10,000 years in the southwestern United States and Mexico. The ancient Aztecs fermented mescal beans into a beer. From ancient times, individuals in North and South America also ingested *teonanacatl,* the *Psilocybe* mushroom also known as "the flesh of the gods," as parts of rituals. Small doses of these mushrooms produce vivid hallucinations.

In Western cultures, drugs are associated less with sacred communal rituals than with recreation. Individuals throughout the world take various drugs to relax, cope with stress, avoid facing the unpleasantness of current realities, feel comfortable in social situations, or experience an alternate state of consciousness. Over a hundred years ago, William James—whom we have cited several times as a founder of psychology in the United States—reported on his experiments with a mind-altering drug. After inhaling nitrous oxide, James explained that "the keynote of the experience is the tremendously exciting sense of intense metaphysical illumination. Truth lies open to the view in depth beneath depth of almost blinding evidence. The mind sees all the logical relations of being with an apparent subtlety and instantaneity to which its normal consciousness offer no parallel" (James, 1882, p. 186). Thus, James's interest in the study of consciousness extended to the study of self-induced alternate states.

As we shall see in Chapter 15, drugs that have an impact on individual's psychological states are often a critical aspect of the treatment of psychological disorders. In fact, as we indicate in **Table 5.1,** many types of drugs have important medical uses. Still, many individuals use drugs that are not prescribed to enhance physical or psychological health. In a 2001 survey of U.S. citizens, with nearly 70,000 respondents age 12 and older, 12.6 percent reported using one or more illicit drugs during the past year (Substance Abuse and Mental Health Services Administration [SAMHSA], 2003). The rate was much higher for people in their late teen years—32.8 percent of 16- to 17-year-olds and 36.8 percent of 18- to 20-year-olds reported some type of illicit drug use. In addition, 63.7 percent of the individuals in the sample consumed alcohol sometime in the year before the survey, and 29.1 percent smoked cigarettes. These figures support the importance of understanding the physiological and psychological consequences of drug use.

TABLE 5.1
Medical Uses of Psychoactive Drugs

Drug	Medical Uses
OPIATES (NARCOTICS)	
Morphine	Painkiller
Heroin	None
HALLUCINOGENS	
LSD	None
PCP (Phencyclidine)	Veterinary anesthetic
MDMA (Ecstasy)	Potential aid to psychotherapy
Cannabis (Marijuana)	Nausea associated with chemotherapy
DEPRESSANTS	
Barbiturates	Sedative, sleeping pill,
(for example, Seconal)	anesthetic, anticonvulsant
Benzodiazepines	Antianxiety, sedative, sleeping pill,
(for example, Valium)	anticonvulsant
Rohypnol	Sleeping pill
GHB	Treatment for narcolepsy
Alcohol	Antiseptic
STIMULANTS	
Amphetamines	Hyperkinesis, narcolepsy, weight control
Methamphetamines	None
Cocaine	Local anesthetic
Nicotine	Nicotine gum for cessation of smoking habit
Caffeine	Weight control, stimulant in acute respiratory failure, analgesic

DEPENDENCE AND ADDICTION

Psychoactive drugs are chemicals that affect mental processes and behavior by temporarily changing conscious awareness. Once in the brain, they attach themselves to synaptic receptors, blocking or stimulating certain reactions. By doing so, they profoundly alter the brain's communication system, affecting perception, memory, mood, and behavior. However, continued use of a given drug creates **tolerance**—greater dosages are required to achieve the same effect. (We describe some of the psychological roots of tolerance in Chapter 6.) Hand in hand with tolerance is **physiological dependence,** a process in which the body becomes adjusted to and dependent on the substance, in part because neurotransmitters are depleted by the frequent presence of the drug. The tragic outcome of tolerance and dependence is **addiction.** A person who is addicted requires the drug in his or her body and suffers painful

withdrawal symptoms (shakes, sweats, nausea, and, in the case of alcohol withdrawal, even death) if the drug is not present.

When an individual finds the use of a drug so desirable or pleasurable that a *craving* develops, with or without addiction, the condition is known as **psychological dependence.** Psychological dependence can occur with any drug. The result of drug dependence is that a person's lifestyle comes to revolve around drug use so wholly that his or her capacity to function is limited or impaired. In addition, the expense involved in maintaining a drug habit of daily—and increasing—amounts often drives an addict to robbery, assault, prostitution, or drug peddling.

VARIETIES OF PSYCHOACTIVE DRUGS

Common psychoactive drugs are listed in Table 5.1. (In Chapter 15, we will discuss other types of psychoactive drugs that are used to relieve mental illness.) We will briefly describe how each class of drugs achieves its physiological and psychological impact. We also note the personal and societal consequences of drug use.

The most dramatic changes in consciousness are produced by drugs known as *hallucinogens* or *psychedelics;* these drugs alter both perceptions of the external environment and inner awareness. As the name implies, these drugs often create hallucinations and a loss of the boundary between self and nonself. The three most common hallucinogens are *LSD, PCP,* and *MDMA* (more commonly known as *ecstasy*), which are synthesized in laboratories. Hallucinogenic drugs typically act in the brain by affecting the use of the chemical neurotransmitter serotonin (Aghajanian & Marek, 1999). For example, LSD binds very tightly to serotonin receptors so that neurons produce prolonged activation. Ecstasy causes nerve cells to release greater amounts of serotonin than normal so that, once again, serotonin receptors are overstimulated. Research suggests that repeated doses of ecstasy may cause damage to serotonin neurons. For example, even one year after they had ceased using the drug, former ecstasy users showed abnormalities in serotonin function (Gerra et al., 2000).

Cannabis is a plant with psychoactive effects. Its active ingredient is THC, found in both *hashish* (the solidified resin of the plant) and *marijuana* (the dried leaves and flowers of the plant). The experience derived from inhaling THC depends on its dose—small doses create mild, pleasurable highs, and large doses result in long hallucinogenic reactions. Regular users report euphoria, feelings of well-being, distortions of space and time, and, occasionally, out-of-body experiences. However, depending on the context, the effects may be negative—fear, anxiety, and confusion. Researchers have known for several years that *cannabinoids,* the active chemicals in marijuana, bind to specific receptors in the brain—these cannabinoid receptors are particularly common in the hippocampus, the brain region involved in memory. Only in the past decade, however, has research uncovered *anandamide,* a neurotransmitter that binds to the same receptors (Di Marzo et al., 1994; Stahl, 1998). That is, cannabinoids achieve their mind-altering effects at brain sites sensitive to anandamide, a naturally occurring substance in the brain. These naturally occurring cannabinoids function as neuromodulators. For example, they suppress the release of the neurotransmitter GABA (Wilson & Nicoll, 2002).

Opiates, such as *heroin* and *morphine,* suppress physical sensation and response to stimulation. The initial effect of an intravenous injection of heroin is a rush of pleasure—feelings of euphoria supplant all worries and awareness of bodily needs. Heroin use often leads to addiction. In Chapter 3, we noted that the brain contains endorphins (short for *endogenous morphines*) that generate powerful effects on mood, pain, and pleasure. Drugs like opium and morphine bind to the same receptor sites in the brain (Harrison et al., 1998; Reisine, 1995). Thus, both opiates and, as we described in the previous paragraph, marijuana achieve their effects because they have active components that have similar chemical properties to substances that naturally occur in the brain. When the neural receptors are artificially stimulated, the brain loses its subtle balance.

The *depressants* include *barbiturates* and, most notably, *alcohol.* These substances tend to depress (slow down) the mental and physical activity of the body by inhibiting or decreasing the transmission of nerve impulses in the central nervous system. Depressants achieve this effect, in part, by facilitating neural communication at synapses that use the neurotransmitter GABA (Delaney & Sah, 1999; Malizia & Nutt, 1995). GABA often functions to inhibit neural transmission, which explains depressants' inhibiting outcomes. In recent years, two depressants, *Rohypnol* (more commonly known as *roofies*) and *GHB,* have achieved reputations as "date rape drugs." Both substances can be manufactured as colorless liquids so that they can be added to alcohol or other beverages without detection. In that way, victims can be sedated and raped. In addition, Rohypnol causes amnesia, so that victims may not remember events that occurred while they were under the drug's influence.

Alcohol was apparently one of the first psychoactive substances used extensively by early humans. Under its influence, some people become silly, boisterous, friendly, and talkative; others become abusive and violent; still others become quietly depressed. Alcohol appears to stimulate the release of dopamine, which enhances feelings of pleasure. Also, as with other depressants, it appears to affect GABA activity (De Witte, 1996). At small dosages, alcohol can induce relaxation and slightly improve an adult's speed of reaction. However, the body can break down alcohol only at a slow rate, and large amounts consumed in a short time period overtax the central nervous system. Driving accidents and fatalities occur six times more often to individuals with 0.10 percent alcohol in their bloodstream than to those with half that amount. Another way alcohol intoxication contributes to accidents is by dilating the pupils of the eyes, thereby causing night vision problems. When the level of alcohol in the blood reaches 0.15 percent, there are gross negative effects on thinking, memory, and judgment, along with emotional instability and loss of motor coordination.

Excess consumption of alcohol is a major social problem in the United States. Alcohol-related automobile accidents are a leading cause of death among people between the ages of 15 and 25. When the amount and frequency of drinking interfere with job performance, impair social and family relationships, and create serious health problems, the diagnosis of *alcoholism* is appropriate. Physical dependence, tolerance, and addiction all develop with prolonged heavy drinking. For some individuals, alcoholism is associated with an inability to abstain from drinking. For others, alcoholism manifests itself as an inability to stop drinking once the person takes a few drinks. In a 2001 survey, 13.6 percent of 18- to 25-year-olds reported heavy drinking—defined as drinking five or more drinks on the same occasion on each of five or more days in a 1-month period (SAMHSA, 2003). However, for all ages, the average is much higher for men (9.2 percent) than women (2.6 percent).

Stimulants, such as *amphetamines, methamphetamines,* and *cocaine,* keep the drug user aroused and induce states of euphoria. Stimulants achieve their effects by increasing the brain levels of neurotransmitters such as norepinephrine, serotonin, and dopamine. For example, stimulants act in the brain to prevent the action of molecules that ordinarily remove dopamine from synapses (Giros et al., 1996). Long-term abuse of cocaine may produce changes in the brain systems that regulate the experience of pleasure (Gawin, 1991). Stimulants have three major effects that users seek: increased self-confidence, greater energy and hyperalertness, and mood alterations approaching euphoria. Heavy users experience frightening hallucinations and develop beliefs that others are out to harm them. These beliefs are known as *paranoid delusions.* A special danger with cocaine use is the contrast between euphoric highs and very depressive lows. This leads users to increase uncontrollably the frequency of drug use and the dosage.

Two stimulants that you may often overlook as psychoactive drugs are *caffeine* and *nicotine.* As you may

<www.ablongman.com/gerrig17e>

Why does alcohol remain the most popular way in which college students alter their consciousness?

know from experience, two cups of strong coffee or tea administer enough caffeine to have a profound effect on heart, blood, and circulatory functions and make it difficult for you to sleep. Nicotine, a chemical found in tobacco, is a sufficiently strong stimulant to have been used in high concentrations by Native American shamans to attain mystical states or trances. Unlike some modern users, however, the shamans knew that nicotine is addictive, and they carefully chose when to be under its influence. Like other addictive drugs, nicotine mimics natural chemicals released by the brain. In fact, research has uncovered common regions of brain activation for addiction to nicotine and cocaine (Pich et al., 1997). Chemicals in nicotine stimulate receptors that make you feel good whenever you have done something right—a phenomenon that aids survival. Unfortunately, nicotine teases those same brain receptors into responding as if it were good for you to be smoking. It's not. As you know, smoking is far from good for your health.

• • •

We began this chapter by asking you to remember your past and plan for your future. These ordinary activities allowed us nonetheless to pose some interesting questions about consciousness: Where did your thoughts come from? How did they emerge? When did they arrive? You've now learned some of the theories that apply to these questions and how it has been possible to test those theories. You've seen that consciousness ultimately allows you to have the full range of experiences that define you as human.

We also asked you to consider some increasingly less ordinary uses of consciousness. Why, we asked, do people become dissatisfied with their everyday working minds and seek to alter their consciousness in so many ways? Ordinarily, your primary focus is on meeting the immediate demands of tasks and situations facing you. However, you are aware of these reality-based constraints on your consciousness. You realize they limit the range and depth of your experience and do not allow you to fulfill your potential. Perhaps, at times, you long to reach beyond the confines of ordinary reality. You seek the uncertainty of freedom instead of settling for the security of the ordinary.

PUT YOURSELF TO THE TEST

- What is the major goal of lucid dreaming?
- How have hypnosis researchers demonstrated that hypnosis represents more than a willingness to please the hypnotist?
- What are some of the benefits that can be gained through meditation?
- What is the defining characteristic of hallucinations?
- What sets some religious experiences apart from ordinary consciousness?
- What is the relationship between physiological dependence and addiction?
- What are the physiological and psychological effects of major categories of drugs?

Recapping Main Points

THE CONTENTS OF CONSCIOUSNESS

- Consciousness is an awareness of the mind's contents.

- The contents of waking consciousness contrast with nonconscious processes, preconscious memories, unattended information, the unconscious, and conscious awareness.

- Research techniques such as think-aloud protocols and experience sampling are used to study the contents of consciousness.

THE FUNCTIONS OF CONSCIOUSNESS

- Consciousness aids your survival and enables you to construct both personal and culturally shared realities.

- Researchers have studied the relationship between conscious and unconscious processes.

SLEEP AND DREAMS

- Circadian rhythms reflect the operation of a biological clock.

- Patterns of brain activity change over the course of a night's sleep. REM sleep is signaled by rapid eye movements.

- The amount of sleep and relative proportion of REM to NREM sleep change with age.

- REM and NREM sleep serve different functions, including conservation and restoration.

- Sleep disorders such as insomnia, narcolepsy, and sleep apnea have a negative impact on people's ability to function during waking time. Daytime sleepiness is also a widespread, serious problem.

- Freud proposed that the content of dreams is unconscious material slipped by a sleeping censor.

- In other cultures, dreams are interpreted regularly, often by people with special cultural roles.

- Some dream theories have focused on biological explanations for the origins of dreams.

ALTERED STATES OF CONSCIOUSNESS

- Lucid dreaming is an awareness that one is dreaming, in an attempt to control the dream.

- Hypnosis is an alternate state of consciousness characterized by the ability of hypnotizable people to change perception, motivation, memory, and self-control in response to suggestions.

- Meditation changes conscious functioning by ritual practices that focus attention away from external concerns to inner experience.

- Hallucinations are vivid perceptions that occur in the absence of objective stimulation.

- In some cultural groups, people undergo intense religious experiences.

- Psychoactive drugs affect mental processes by temporarily changing consciousness as they modify nervous system activity.

- Among psychoactive drugs that alter consciousness are hallucinogens, opiates, depressants, and stimulants.

KEY TERMS

addiction (p. 163)

circadian rhythm (p. 149)

consciousness (p. 142)

daytime sleepiness (p. 153)

dream work (p. 155)

experience-sampling method (p. 144)

hallucinations (p. 161)

hypnosis (p. 158)

hypnotizability (p. 158)

insomnia (p. 152)

latent content (p. 155)

lucid dreaming (p. 157)

manifest content (p. 155)

meditation (p. 160)

narcolepsy (p. 153)

nonconscious (p. 143)

non-REM (NREM) sleep (p. 150)

physiological dependence (p. 163)

preconscious memories (p. 143)

psychoactive drugs (p. 163)

psychological dependence (p. 163)

rapid eye movements (REM) (p. 150)

sleep apnea (p. 153)

somnambulism (p. 153)

think-aloud protocols (p. 144)

tolerance (p. 163)

CHAPTER 6

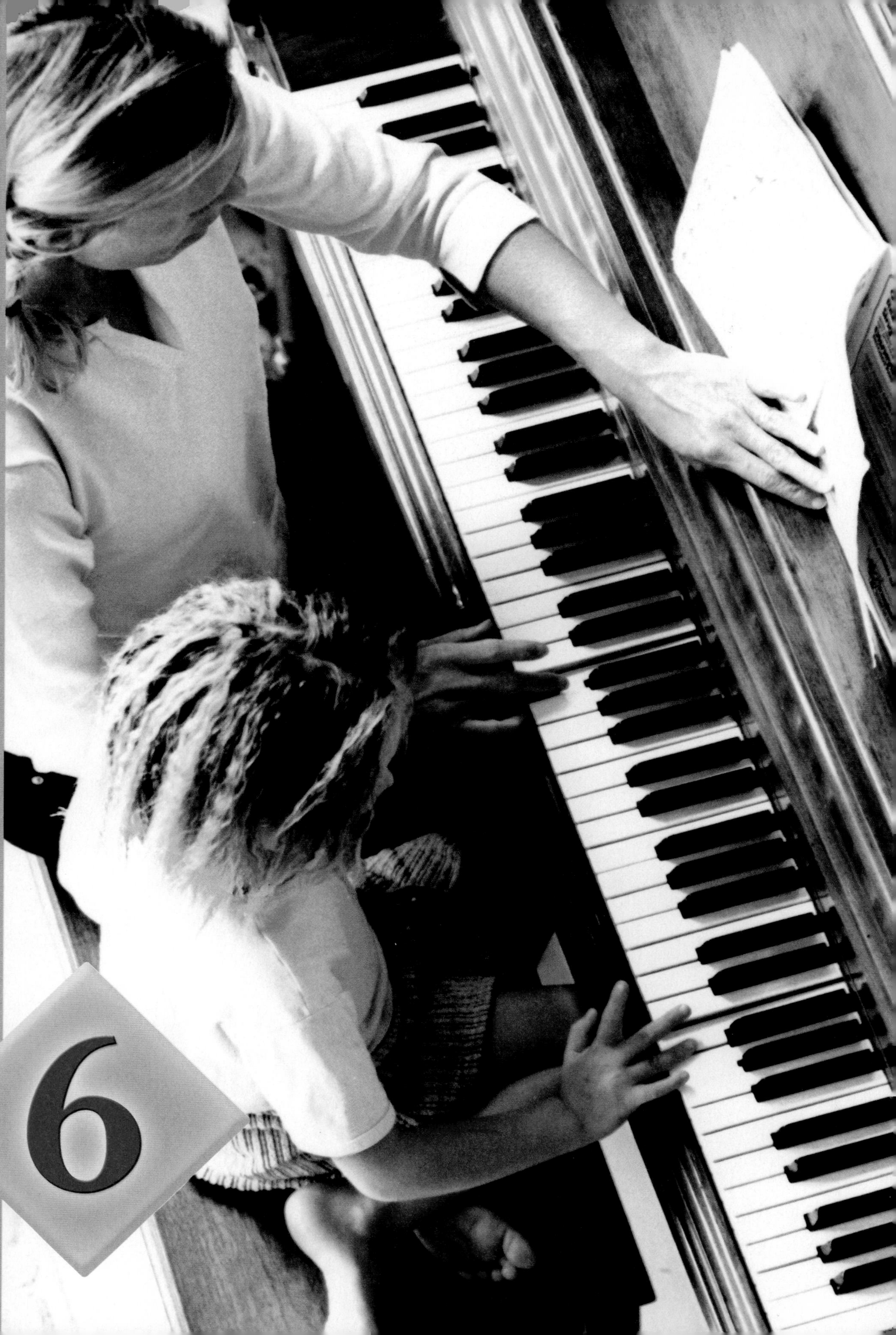

Learning and Behavior Analysis

I magine that you are in a movie theater, watching a horror film. As the hero approaches a closed door, the music on the movie's sound track grows dark and menacing. You suddenly feel the urge to yell, "Don't go through that door!" Meanwhile, you find that your heart is racing and that you are sweating all over the theater's upholstery. But why? If you think about this question formally, you might come to the answer, "I have learned an association between movie music and movie events—and that's what's making me nervous!" But had you ever thought about this relationship before? Probably not. Somehow, by virtue of sitting in enough movie theaters, you have learned the association without any particular thought. The main topic of Chapter 6 is the types of associations that you acquire effortlessly in your day-to-day experience.

Psychologists have long been interested in **conditioning,** or the ways in which events and behavior become associated with one another. In this chapter, we will examine two basic types of conditioning: classical conditioning and operant conditioning. As you shall see, each of these types of conditioning represents a different way in which organisms acquire and use information about the structure of their environments. For each of these forms of conditioning, we will describe both the basic mechanisms that govern its operation in the laboratory and applications to real-life situations.

Before we begin our study in earnest, let's consider the significance of learning from an *evolutionary perspective*. Learning is as much a product of your genetic endowment as any other aspect of your experience. Humans, like other organisms, inherit a particular *capacity* for learning. The capacity for learning varies among animal species according to their genetic blueprint. Some creatures, such as reptiles and amphibians, learn little from interactions with the environment. Their survival depends on living in a relatively constant habitat, in which their innate responses to specific environmental events bring them to what they need or take them away from what they must avoid. For example, frogs don't need to learn how to catch flies: The frog is born with cells in its brain that serve as "fly detectors"; these cells cause the frog to flick its tongue in response to appropriate stimuli in the environment.

For other animals including humans, genes play much less of a role in determining specific behavior–environment interactions and allow for greater *plasticity*, or variability, in learning. These animals are able to learn according to the ways in which their behavior produces changes in their environment. Thus, unlike the frog, your brain didn't come pre-equipped with cells that allow you to locate specific types of food in the environment. Rather, you inherited the capacity to learn how to acquire all types of food. Whether that capacity is realized—and to what extent—depends on your personal experiences.

The Study of Learning

To begin our exploration of learning, we will first define learning itself and then offer a brief sketch of the history of psychological research on the topic.

◆ WHAT IS LEARNING?

Learning is a process that results in a relatively consistent change in behavior or behavior potential and is based on experience. Let's look more closely at the three critical parts of this definition.

How does consistent form in ballet dancers fit the definition of learning?

A CHANGE IN BEHAVIOR OR BEHAVIOR POTENTIAL

It is obvious that learning has taken place when you are able to demonstrate the results, such as when you drive a car or use a microwave oven. You can't directly observe learning itself—you can't ordinarily see the changes in your brain—but learning is apparent from improvements in your *performance*. Often, however, your performance doesn't show everything that you have learned. Sometimes, too, you have acquired general attitudes, such as an *appreciation* of modern art or an *understanding* of Eastern philosophy, that may not be apparent in your measurable actions. In such instances, you have achieved a potential for behavior change, because you have learned attitudes and values that can influence the kinds of books you read or the way you spend your leisure time. This is an example of the **learning-performance distinction**—the difference between what has been learned and what is expressed, or performed, in overt behavior.

A RELATIVELY CONSISTENT CHANGE

To qualify as learned, a change in behavior or behavior potential must be relatively consistent over different occasions. Thus, once you learn to swim, you will probably always be able to do so. Note that consistent changes are not always permanent changes. You may, for example, have become quite a consistent dart thrower when you practiced every day. If you gave up the sport, however, your skills might have deteriorated toward their original level. But if you have learned once to be a championship dart thrower, it ought to be easier for you to learn a second time. Something has been "saved" from your prior experience. In that sense, the change may be permanent.

A PROCESS BASED ON EXPERIENCE

Learning can take place only through experience. Experience includes taking in information (and evaluating and transforming it) and making responses that affect the environment. Learning consists of a response influenced by the lessons of memory. Learned behavior does not include changes that come about because of physical maturation or brain development as the organism ages, nor those caused by illness or brain damage. Some lasting changes in behavior require experience following maturational readiness. For example, consider the timetable that determines when an infant is ready to crawl, stand, walk, run, and be toilet trained. No amount of training or practice will produce those behaviors before the child has matured sufficiently. Psychologists are especially interested in discovering what aspects of behavior can be changed through experience and how such changes come about.

◆ BEHAVIORISM AND BEHAVIOR ANALYSIS

Much of modern psychology's view of learning finds its roots in the work of **John Watson** (1878–1958). Watson founded the school of psychology known as *behaviorism*. For nearly 50 years, American psychology was dominated by the behaviorist tradition expressed in Watson's 1919 book, *Psychology from the Standpoint of a Behaviorist*. Watson argued that introspection—people's verbal reports of sensations, images, and feelings—was *not* an acceptable means of studying behavior because it was too subjective. How could scientists verify the accuracy of such private experiences? But once introspection has been rejected, what should the subject matter of psychology be? Watson's answer was *observable behavior*. In Watson's words, "States of consciousness, like the so-called phenomenon of spiritualism, are not objectively verifiable and for that reason can never become data for science" (Watson, 1919, p. 1). Watson also defined the chief goal of psychology as "the prediction and control of behavior" (Watson, 1913, p. 158).

B. F. Skinner (1904–1990) adopted Watson's cause and expanded his agenda. Over time, Skinner formulated a position known as *radical behaviorism*. Skinner acknowledged that evolution provided each species with a repertory of behaviors. He argued, most famously in the popular book *Beyond Freedom and Dignity*

B. F. Skinner expanded on Watson's ideas and applied them to a wide spectrum of behavior. Why did Skinner's psychology focus on environmental events rather than internal states?

(1972), that all behavior beyond that repertory could be understood as the products of simple forms of learning.

Skinner began the research that would lead him to formulate this position when, after reading Watson's 1924 book, *Behaviorism,* he began his graduate study in psychology at Harvard. Skinner embraced Watson's complaint against internal states and mental events. However, Skinner focused not so much on their legitimacy as data as on their legitimacy as *causes of behavior* (Skinner, 1990). In Skinner's view, mental events, such as thinking and imagining, do not cause behavior. Rather, they are examples of behavior that are caused by environmental stimuli. Suppose that we deprive a pigeon of food for 24 hours, place it in an apparatus where it can obtain food by pecking a small disk, and find that it soon does so. Skinner would argue that the animal's behavior can be fully explained by environmental events—deprivation and the use of food as reinforcement. The subjective feeling of hunger, which cannot be directly observed or measured, is not a cause of the behavior, but the result of deprivation. It adds nothing to our account to say that the bird pecked the disk because it was hungry or because it wanted to get the food. To explain what the bird does, you need not understand anything about its inner psychological states—you need only understand the simple principles of learning that allow the bird to acquire the association between behavior and reward. This is the essence of Skinner's brand of behaviorism (Delprato & Midgley, 1992).

This brand of behaviorism originated by Skinner served as the original philosophical cornerstone of **behavior analysis,** the area of psychology that focuses on discovering environmental determinants of learning and behavior (Grant & Evans, 1994). In general, behavior analysts attempt to discover regularities in learning that are universal, occurring in all types of animal species, including humans, under comparable situations. These researchers generally assume that elementary processes of learning are *conserved across species*—that is, across all animal species, these processes are comparable in their basic features. That is why studies with nonhuman animals have been so critical to progress in this area. Complex forms of learning represent combinations and elaborations of simpler processes and not qualitatively different phenomena. In the sections that follow, we describe classical conditioning and operant conditioning—two simple forms of learning that give rise to quite complex behaviors.

PUT YOURSELF TO THE TEST

- What are the three parts of the definition of learning?
- Why did Watson and Skinner emphasize the importance of observable behaviors rather than mental events?
- What is the major goal of behavior analysis?
- What does it mean for forms of learning to be conserved across species?

Classical Conditioning: Learning Predictable Signals

Imagine once more that you are watching that horror movie. Why do you start to sweat when the sound track signals trouble for the hero? Somehow your body has learned to produce a physiological response (a racing heart) when one environmental event (for example, scary music) is associated with another (scary visual events). This type of learning is known as **classical conditioning,** a basic form of learning in which one stimulus or event predicts the occurrence of another stimulus or event. The organism learns a new *association* between two stimuli—a stimulus that did not previously elicit the response and one that naturally elicited the response. As you shall see, the innate capacity to quickly associate pairs of events in your environment has profound behavioral implications.

◆ PAVLOV'S SURPRISING OBSERVATION

The first rigorous study of classical conditioning was the result of what may well be psychology's most famous accident. The Russian physiologist **Ivan Pavlov** (1849–1936) did not set out to study classical conditioning or any other psychological phenomenon. He happened on classical conditioning while conducting research on digestion, for which he won a Nobel Prize in 1904.

Pavlov had devised a technique to study digestive processes in dogs by implanting tubes in their glands and digestive organs to divert bodily secretions to containers outside their bodies so that the secretions could be measured and analyzed. To produce these secretions, Pavlov's assistants put meat powder into the dogs' mouths. After repeating this procedure a number of times, Pavlov observed an unexpected behavior in his dogs—they salivated *before* the powder was put in their mouths! They would start salivating at the mere sight of the food and, later, at the sight of the assistant who brought the food or even at the sound of the assistant's footsteps. Indeed, any stimulus that regularly preceded the presentation of food came to elicit salivation. Quite by accident, Pavlov had observed that learning may result from two stimuli becoming associated with each other.

Fortunately, Pavlov had the scientific skills and curiosity to begin a rigorous attack on this surprising phenomenon. He ignored the advice of the great physiologist of the time, Sir Charles Sherrington, that he should give up his foolish investigation of "psychic" secretions. Instead, Pavlov abandoned his work on digestion and, in so doing, changed the course of psychology forever (Pavlov, 1928). For the remainder of

Physiologist Ivan Pavlov (shown here with his research team) observed classical conditioning while conducting research on digestion. What were some of Pavlov's major contributions to the study of this form of learning?

Pavlov's life, he continued to search for the variables that influence classically conditioned behavior. Classical conditioning is also called *Pavlovian conditioning* because of Pavlov's discovery of the major phenomena of conditioning and his dedication to tracking down the variables that influence it.

Pavlov's considerable research experience allowed him to follow a simple and elegant strategy to discover the conditions necessary for his dogs to be conditioned to salivate. As shown in **Figure 6.1,** dogs in his experiments were first placed in a restraining harness. At regular intervals, a stimulus such as a tone was presented, and a dog was given a bit of food. Importantly, the tone had no prior meaning for the dog with respect to food or salivation. As you might imagine, the dog's first reaction to the tone was only an *orienting response*—the dog pricked its ears and moved its head to locate the source of the sound. However, with *repeated pairings* of the tone and the food, the orienting response stopped and salivation began. What Pavlov had observed in his earlier research was no accident: The phenomenon could be replicated under controlled conditions. Pavlov demonstrated the generality of this effect by using a variety of other stimuli ordinarily neutral with respect to salivation, such as lights and ticking metronomes.

The main features of Pavlov's classical conditioning procedure are illustrated in **Figure 6.2.** At the core of classical conditioning are reflex responses. A **reflex** is an unlearned response—such as salivation, pupil contraction, knee jerks, or eye blinking—that is naturally elicited by specific stimuli that are biologically relevant for the organism. Any stimulus, such as the food powder used in Pavlov's experiments, that naturally elicits a reflexive behavior is called an **unconditioned stimulus (UCS),** because learning is not a necessary condition for the stimulus to control the behavior. The behavior elicited by the unconditioned stimulus is called the **unconditioned response (UCR).**

In a typical classical conditioning experiment, a *neutral stimulus*—a stimulus, such as a light or a tone, that ordinarily has no meaning in the context of the UCS–UCR reflex—is repeatedly paired with the unconditioned stimulus so that the UCS predictably follows the neutral stimulus. The neutral stimulus, like the tone used in Pavlov's experiment, paired with the unconditioned stimulus is called the **conditioned stimulus (CS),** because its power to elicit behavior like the UCR is *conditioned* on its association with the UCS. After several trials, the CS will produce a response called the **conditioned response (CR).** Often, the conditioned response is similar to the unconditioned response. For Pavlov's dogs, both responses were salivation. In some cases, however, the CR is more dissimilar to the UCR: The conditioned response is whatever response the conditioned stimulus elicits as a product of learning. Let's review. Nature provides the UCS–UCR connections, but the learning produced by classical conditioning creates the CS–CR connection. The conditioned stimulus acquires some of the power to influence behavior that was originally limited to the unconditioned stimulus. Let's now look in more detail at the basic processes of classical conditioning.

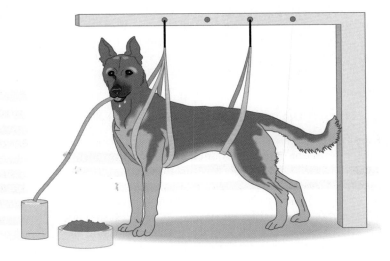

FIGURE 6.1
Pavlov's Original Procedure

In his original experiments, Pavlov used a variety of stimuli such as tones, bells, lights, and metronomes to serve as neutral stimuli. The experimenter presented one of these neutral stimuli and then the food powder. The dog's saliva was collected through a tube.

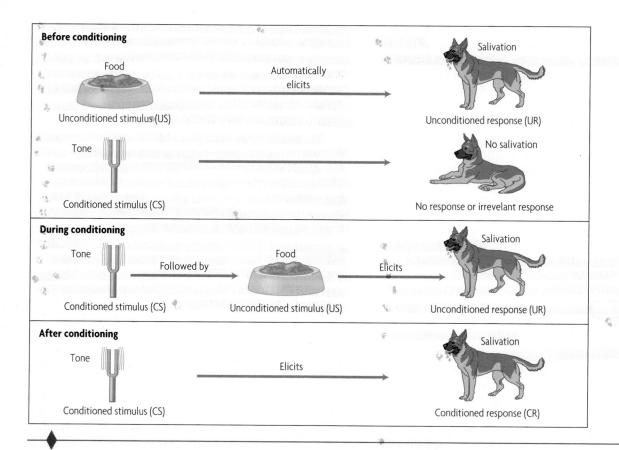

FIGURE 6.2

Basic Features of Classical Conditioning

Before conditioning, the unconditioned stimulus (UCS) naturally elicits the unconditioned response (UCR). A neutral stimulus, such as a tone, has no eliciting effect. During conditioning, the neutral stimulus is paired with the UCS. Through its association with the UCS, the neutral stimulus becomes a conditioned stimulus (CS) and elicits a conditioned response (CR) that is similar to the UCR.

◆ PROCESSES OF CONDITIONING

How does the relative timing of the UCS and CS affect the success of classical conditioning? How fragile is the learning? How precise are the associations? In this section, we review answers to these questions that have emerged from hundreds of different studies across a wide range of animal species.

ACQUISITION AND EXTINCTION

Figure 6.3 displays a hypothetical classical conditioning experiment. The first panel displays **acquisition,** the process by which the CR is first elicited and gradually increases in frequency over repeated trials. In general, the CS and UCS must be paired several times before the CS reliably elicits a CR. With systematic CS–UCS pairings, the CR is elicited with increasing frequency, and the organism may be said to have acquired a conditioned response.

In classical conditioning, as in telling a good joke, *timing* is critical. The CS and UCS must be presented closely enough in time to be perceived by the organism as being related. (We will describe an exception to this rule in a later section on *taste-aversion learning*.) Researchers have studied four temporal patterns between the two stimuli, as shown in **Figure 6.4** (Hearst, 1988). The most widely used type of conditioning is called *delay conditioning,* in which the CS comes on prior to and stays on at least until the UCS is presented. In *trace conditioning,* the CS is discontinued or turned off before the UCS is presented. *Trace* refers to the memory that the organism is assumed to have of the CS, which is no longer present when the UCS appears. In *simultaneous conditioning,* both the CS and UCS are presented at the same time. Finally, in the case of *backward conditioning,* the CS is presented after the UCS.

Conditioning is usually most effective in a delayed conditioning paradigm, with a short interval between

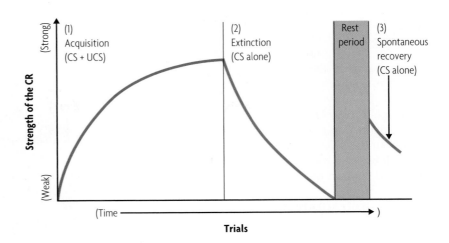

FIGURE 6.3

Acquisition, Extinction, and Spontaneous Recovery in Classical Conditioning

During acquisition (CS + UCS), the strength of the CR increases rapidly. During extinction, when the UCS no longer follows the CS, the strength of the CR drops to zero. The CR may reappear after a brief rest period, even when the UCS is still not presented. The reappearance of the CR is called spontaneous recovery.

the onsets of the CS and UCS. However, the exact time interval between the CS and the UCS that will produce optimal conditioning depends on several factors, including the intensity of the CS and the response being conditioned. Let's focus on the response being conditioned. For muscular responses, such as eye blinks, a short interval of a second or less is best. For visceral responses, such as heart rate and salivation, however, longer intervals of 5 to 15 seconds work best. Conditioned fear usually requires a longer interval still, of many seconds or even minutes, to develop.

Conditioning is generally poor with a simultaneous procedure and very poor with a backward procedure. Evidence of backward conditioning may appear after a few pairings of the UCS and CS but disappear with extended training as the animal learns that the CS is followed by a period free of the UCS. In both cases, con-

ditioning is weak because the CS does not actually predict the onset of the UCS. (We will return to the importance of predictability, or contingency, in the next section.)

But what happens when the CS (for example, the tone) no longer predicts the UCS (the food powder)? Under those circumstances, the CR (salivation) becomes weaker over time and eventually stops occurring. When the CR no longer appears in the presence of the CS (and the absence of the UCS), the process of **extinction** is said to have occurred (see Figure 6.3, panel 2). Conditioned responses, then, are not necessarily a permanent aspect of the organism's behavioral repertory. However, the CR will reappear in a weak form when the CS is presented alone again (see Figure 6.3, panel 3). Pavlov referred to this sudden reappearance of the CR after a rest period, or time-out, without further exposure to the UCS as **spontaneous recovery.**

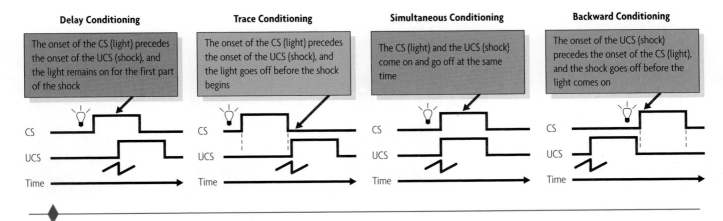

FIGURE 6.4

Four Variations of the CS–UCS Temporal Arrangement in Classical Conditioning

Researchers have explored the four possible timing arrangements between the CS and UCS. Conditioning is generally most effective in a delay conditioning paradigm with a short interval between the onsets of the CS and UCS.

From Robert A. Baron, *Psychology*, 5e. Published by Allyn & Bacon, Boston, MA. Copyright © 2001 by Pearson Education. Reprinted by permission of the publisher.

When the original pairing is renewed, postextinction, the CR becomes rapidly stronger. This more rapid relearning is an instance of *savings:* Less time is necessary to reacquire the response than to acquire it originally. Thus, some of the original conditioning must be retained by the organism even after experimental extinction appears to have eliminated the CR. In other words, extinction has only weakened performance, not wiped out the original learning—this is why we made a distinction between learning and performance in our original definition of learning.

STIMULUS GENERALIZATION

Suppose we have taught a dog that presentation of a tone of a certain frequency predicts food powder. Is the dog's response specific to only that stimulus? If you think about this question for a moment, you will probably not be surprised that the answer is no. In general, once a CR has been conditioned to a particular CS, similar stimuli may also elicit the response. For example, if conditioning was to a high-frequency tone, a slightly lower tone could also elicit the response. A child bitten by a big dog is likely to respond with fear even to smaller dogs. This automatic extension of responding to stimuli that have never been paired with the original UCS is called **stimulus generalization.** The more similar the new stimulus is to the original CS, the stronger the response will be. When response strength is measured for each of a series of increasingly dissimilar stimuli along a given dimension, as shown in **Figure 6.5,** a *generalization gradient* is found.

The existence of generalization gradients should suggest to you the way classical conditioning serves its function in everyday experience. Because important

Why might a child who has been frightened by one dog develop a fear response to all dogs?

stimuli rarely occur in exactly the same form every time in nature, stimulus generalization builds in a similarity safety factor by extending the range of learning beyond the original specific experience. With this feature, new but comparable events can be recognized as having the same meaning, or behavioral significance, despite apparent differences. For example, even when a predator makes a slightly different sound or is seen from a

---

FIGURE 6.5

Stimulus Generalization Gradients

After conditioning to a medium green stimulus, the subject responds almost as strongly to stimuli of similar hues, as shown by the flat generalization gradient in panel A. When the subject is exposed to a broader range of colored stimuli, responses grow weaker as the color becomes increasingly dissimilar to the training stimulus. The generalization gradient becomes very steep, as shown in panel B. The

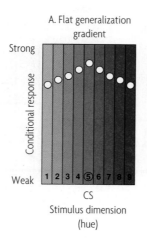

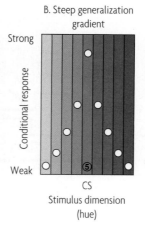

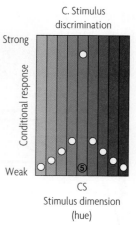

experimenter could change the generalization gradient shown in panel A to resemble the one in panel C by giving the subject discrimination training. In this case, the medium green stimulus would be continually paired with the UCS, but stimuli of all other hues would not.

From *Principles and Methods of Psychology* by Robert B. Lawson, Stephen G. Goldstein, & Richard E. Musty, copyright © 1975 by Oxford University Press, Inc. Used by permission of Oxford University Press, Inc.

different angle, its prey can still recognize and respond to it quickly.

STIMULUS DISCRIMINATION

In some circumstances, however, it is important that a response be made to only a very small range of stimuli. An organism should not, for example, exhaust itself by fleeing too often from animals that are only superficially similar to its natural predators. **Stimulus discrimination** is the process by which an organism learns to respond differently to stimuli that are distinct from the CS on some dimension (for example, differences in hue or in pitch). An organism's discrimination among similar stimuli (tones of 1,000; 1,200; and 1,500 Hz, for example) is sharpened with discrimination training in which only one of them (1,200 Hz, for example) predicts the UCS and in which the others are repeatedly presented without it. Early in conditioning, stimuli similar to the CS will elicit a similar response, though not quite as strong. As discrimination training proceeds, the responses to the other, dissimilar stimuli weaken: The organism gradually learns which event-signal predicts the onset of the UCS and which signals do not.

For an organism to perform optimally in an environment, the processes of generalization and discrimination must strike a balance. You don't want to be overselective—it can be quite costly to miss the presence of a predator—nor do you want to be overresponsive—you don't want to be fearful of every shadow. Classical conditioning provides a mechanism that allows creatures to react efficiently to the structure of their environments (Garcia, 1990).

◆ FOCUS ON ACQUISITION

In this section, we will examine more closely the conditions that are necessary for classical conditioning to take place: So far, we have *described* the acquisition of classically conditioned responses, but we have not yet *explained* it. Pavlov believed that classical conditioning resulted from the mere pairing of the CS and the UCS. In his view, if a response is to be classically conditioned, the CS and the UCS must occur close together in time— that is, be *temporally contiguous*. As we shall now see, contemporary research has modified that view.

Pavlov's theory dominated classical conditioning until the mid-1960s, when **Robert Rescorla** (1966) conducted a very telling experiment using dogs as subjects. Rescorla designed an experiment that contrasted circumstances in which a tone (the CS) and a shock (the UCS) were merely contiguous—which, if Pavlov was correct, would be sufficient to produce classical conditioning—versus circumstances in which, additionally, the tone reliably predicted the presence of the shock.

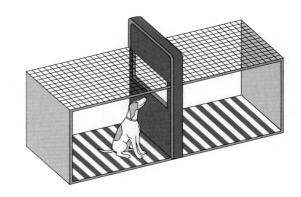

FIGURE 6.6

A Shuttlebox

Rescorla used the frequency with which dogs jumped over a barrier as a measure of fear conditioning.

CLASSIC
PUTTING IDEAS TO THE TEST

Contingency Matters

In the first phase of the experiment, Rescorla trained dogs to jump a barrier from one side of a shuttlebox to the other to avoid an electric shock delivered through the grid floor (see **Figure 6.6**). If the dogs did not jump, they received a shock; if they did jump, the shock was postponed. Rescorla used the frequency with which dogs jumped the barrier as a measure of fear conditioning.

When the dogs were jumping across the barrier regularly, Rescorla divided his subjects into two groups and subjected them to another training procedure. To the random group, the UCS (the shock) was delivered randomly and independently of the CS (the tone) (see **Figure 6.7**). Although the CS and the UCS often occurred close together in time—they were, by chance, temporally contiguous—the UCS was as likely to be delivered in the absence of the CS as it was in its presence. Thus, the CS had no predictive value. For the contingency group, however, the UCS always followed the CS. Thus, for this group, the sounding of the tone was a reliable predictor of the delivery of the shock.

Once this training was complete, the dogs were put back into the shuttlebox, but this time with a twist. Now the tone used in the second training procedure occasionally sounded, signaling shock. What happened? **Figure 6.8** indicates that dogs exposed to the *contingent* (predictable) CS–UCS relation jumped more frequently in the presence of the tone than did dogs exposed only to the *contiguous* (associated) CS–UCS relation. Contingency was critical for the signal to serve the dogs as a successful cue for the shock.

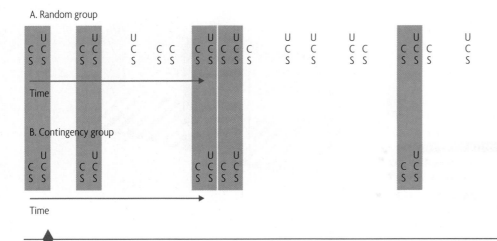

A. Random group

Time

B. Contingency group

Time

FIGURE 6.7

Rescorla's Procedure for Demonstrating the Importance of Contingency

For the random group, 5-second tones (the CS) and 5-second shocks (the UCS) were distributed randomly through the experimental period. For the contingency group, the dogs experienced only the subset of tones and shocks that occurred in a predictive relationship (the onset of the CS preceded the onset of the UCS by 30 seconds or less). Only the dogs in the contingency group learned to associate the CS with the UCS.

Thus, in addition to the CS being contiguous—occurring close in time—with the UCS, the CS must also *reliably predict* the occurrence of the UCS in order for classical conditioning to occur (Rescorla, 1988). This finding makes considerable sense. After all, in natural situations, where learning enables organisms to adapt to changes in their environment, stimuli come in clusters and not in neat, simple units, as they do in laboratory experiments.

There's one last requirement for a stimulus to serve as a basis for classical conditioning: It must be *informative* in the environment. Consider an experimental situation in which rats have learned that a tone predicts a shock. Now, a light is added into the situation so that both the light and tone precede the shock. However, when the light is subsequently presented alone, the rats do not appear to have learned that the light predicts the shock (Kamin, 1969). For these rats, the previous conditioning to the tone in the first phase of the experiment *blocked* any subsequent conditioning that could occur to the light. From the rat's point of view, the light may as well not have existed; it provided no additional information beyond that already given by the tone.

The requirement of informativeness explains why conditioning occurs most rapidly when the CS stands out against the many other stimuli that may also be present in an environment. A stimulus is more readily noticed the more *intense* it is and the more it *contrasts* with other stimuli. If you wish to generate good conditioning, you should present either a strong, novel stimulus in an unfamiliar situation or a strong, familiar stimulus in a novel context.

You can see that classical conditioning is more complex than even Pavlov originally realized. A neutral stimulus will become an effective CS only if it is both appropriately contingent and informative. But now let's shift your attention a bit. We want to identify real-life situations in which classical conditioning plays a role.

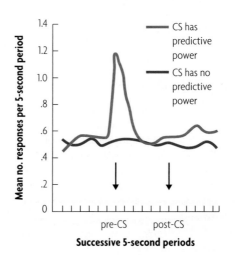

FIGURE 6.8

The Role of Contingency in Classical Conditioning

Rescorla demonstrated that dogs trained under the contingent CS–UCS relation showed more jumping (and thus conditioned fear) than did dogs trained under the contiguous but non-contingent CS–UCS relation. The arrows indicate the onset and offset of the CS tone.

◆ APPLICATIONS OF CLASSICAL CONDITIONING

Your knowledge of classical conditioning can help you understand significant everyday behavior. In this section, we will help you recognize some real-world instances of emotions and preferences as the products of this form of learning. We also explore the role classical conditioning plays in the unfolding of drug addiction.

EMOTIONS AND PREFERENCES

Earlier we asked you to think about your experience at a horror movie. In that case, you (unconsciously) learned an association between scary music (the CS) and certain likely events (the UCS—the kinds of things that happen in horror movies that cause reflexive revulsion). If you pay careful attention to events in your life, you will discover that there are many circumstances in which you can't quite explain why you are having such a strong emotional reaction or why you have such a strong preference about something. You might take a step back and ask yourself, Is this the product of classical conditioning?

Consider these situations (Rozin & Fallon, 1987; Rozin et al., 1986):

- Do you think you'd be willing to eat fudge that had been formed into the shape of dog feces?

- Do you think you'd be willing to drink a sugar-water solution if the sugar was drawn from a container that you knew was incorrectly labeled poison?

- Do you think you would be willing to drink apple juice into which a sterilized cockroach had been dipped?

How do processes of classical conditioning help explain people's fear responses at horror movies?

How did John Watson and Rosalie Rayner condition Little Albert to fear small, furry objects?

If each of these situations makes you say "No way!" you are not alone. The classically conditioned response—"This is disgusting" or "This is dangerous"—wins out over the knowledge that the stimulus is really okay. Because classically conditioned responses are not built up through conscious thought, they are also hard to eliminate through conscious reasoning!

One of the most extensively studied real-world products of classical conditioning is *fear conditioning*. In the earliest days of behaviorism, John Watson and his colleague Rosalie Rayner sought to prove that many fear responses could be understood as the pairing of a neutral stimulus with something naturally fear-provoking. To test their idea, they experimented on an infant who came to be called Little Albert.

CLASSIC
PUTTING IDEAS TO THE TEST

Little Albert's Acquired Fear

Watson and Rayner (1920) trained Albert to fear a white rat he had initially liked, by pairing its appearance with an aversive UCS—a loud noise just behind him created by striking a large steel bar with a hammer. The unconditioned startle response and the emotional distress to the noxious noise formed the basis of Albert's learning to react with fear to the appearance of the white rat. His fear was developed in just seven conditioning trials. The emotional conditioning was then extended to behavioral conditioning when Albert learned to escape from the feared stimulus. The infant's learned fear then generalized to other furry objects, such as a rabbit, a dog, and even a Santa Claus mask! (Albert's mother, a wet nurse at the hospital where the study was conducted, took him away before the researchers could remove the experimentally conditioned fear. So we don't know whatever happened to Little Albert [Harris, 1979].)

We know now that conditioned fear is highly resistant to extinction. A single traumatic event can condition you to respond with strong physical, emotional, and cognitive reactions—perhaps for a lifetime. For example, one of our friends was in a bad car accident during a rainstorm. Now every time it begins to rain while he is driving, he becomes panic-stricken, sometimes to the extent that he has to pull over and wait out the storm. On one occasion, this rational, sensible man even crawled into the back seat and lay on the floor, face down, until the rain subsided. We will see in Chapter 15 that therapists have designed treatments for these types of fears that are intended to counter the effects of classical conditioning.

We don't want to leave you with the impression that only negative responses are classically conditioned. In fact, we suspect that you will also be able to interpret responses of happiness or excitement as instances of classical conditioning. Certainly, toilers in the advertising industry hope that classical conditioning works as a positive force. They strive, for example, to create associations in your mind between their products (for example, blue jeans, sports cars, and soda pop) and passion. They expect that elements of their advertisements—"sexy" individuals or situations—will serve as the UCS to bring about the UCR—feelings of sexual arousal. The hope then is that the product itself will be the CS, so that the feelings of arousal will become associated with it. To find more examples of the classical conditioning of positive emotions, you should monitor your life for circumstances in which you have a rush of good feelings when you return, for instance, to a familiar location.

How do advertisers exploit classical conditioning to make you feel "passion" toward their products?

LEARNING TO BE A DRUG ADDICT

Consider this scenario. A man's body lies in a Manhattan alley, a half-empty syringe dangling from his arm. Cause of death? The coroner called it an overdose, but the man had ordinarily shot up far greater doses than the one that had supposedly killed him. This sort of incident baffled investigators. How could an addict with high drug tolerance die of an overdose when he didn't even get a full hit?

Some time ago, Pavlov (1927) and later his colleague Bykov (1957) pointed out that tolerance to opiates can develop when an individual anticipates the pharmacological action of a drug. Contemporary researcher **Shepard Siegel** refined these ideas. Siegel suggested that the setting in which drug use occurs acts as a conditioned stimulus for a situation in which the body learns to protect itself by preventing the drug from having its usual effect. When people take drugs, the drug (UCS) brings about certain physiological responses to which the body responds with countermeasures intended to reestablish homeostasis (see Chapter 3). The body's countermeasures to the drug are the unconditioned response (UCR). Over time, this *compensatory response* also becomes the conditioned response. That is, in settings ordinarily associated with drug use (the CS), the body physiologically prepares

Years after World War II was over, navy veterans still responded as if to current danger signals when exposed to auditory stimuli resembling former battleship gongs. How does classical conditioning explain this response?

<www.ablongman.com/gerrig17e>

itself (the CR) for the drug's expected effects. Tolerance arises because, in that setting, the individual must consume an amount of the drug that overcomes the compensatory response before starting to get any "positive" effect. Increasingly larger doses are needed as the conditioned compensatory response itself grows.

Siegel tested these ideas in his laboratory by creating tolerance to heroin in laboratory rats.

CLASSIC

PUTTING IDEAS TO THE TEST

Conditioned Aspects of Drug Tolerance

In one study, Siegel and his colleagues classically conditioned rats to expect heroin injections (UCS) in one setting (CS$_1$) and dextrose (sweet sugar) solution injections in a different setting (CS$_2$) (Siegel et al., 1982). In the first phase of training, all rats developed heroin tolerance. On the test day, all animals received a larger-than-usual dose of heroin—nearly twice the previous amount. Half of them received it in the setting where heroin had previously been administered; the other half received it in the setting where dextrose solutions had been given during conditioning. Twice as many rats died in the dextrose-solution setting as in the usual heroin setting— 64 percent versus 32 percent!

Presumably, those receiving heroin in the usual setting were more prepared for this potentially dangerous situation, because the context (CS$_1$) brought about a physiological response (CR) that countered the drug's typical effects (Poulos & Cappell, 1991).

To find out if a similar process might operate in humans, Siegel and a colleague interviewed heroin addicts who had come close to death from supposed overdoses. In seven out of ten cases, the addicts had been shooting up in a new and unfamiliar setting (Siegel, 1984). Although this natural experiment provides no conclusive data, it suggests that a dose for which an addict has developed tolerance in one setting may become an overdose in an unfamiliar setting. This analysis allows us to suggest that the addict we invoked at the beginning of this section died because he had never shot up before in that alley.

Although we have mentioned research with heroin, classical conditioning is an important component to tolerance for a variety of drugs (Goodison & Siegel, 1995; Poulos & Cappell, 1991; Siegel, 1999). Thus, the same principles Pavlov observed for dogs, bells, and salivation help explain some of the mechanisms underlying human drug addiction.

PUT YOURSELF TO THE TEST

- What is the role of reflexive behaviors in classical conditioning?
- What are the UCS, UCR, CS, and CR?
- What are the concepts of generalization and discrimination?
- Why is contingency so important to classical conditioning?
- What is the impact of classical conditioning on preferences, emotions, and drug tolerance?

Operant Conditioning: Learning About Consequences

Let's return to the movie theater. The horror film is now over, and you peel yourself off your seat. The friend with whom you saw the movie asks you if you're hoping that a sequel will be made. You respond, "I've learned that I shouldn't go to horror films." You're probably right, but what kind of learning is this? Once again our answer begins around the turn of the 20th century.

◆ THE LAW OF EFFECT

At about the same time that Pavlov was using classical conditioning to induce Russian dogs to salivate to the sound of a bell, **Edward L. Thorndike** (1898) was watching American cats trying to escape from puzzle boxes (see **Figure 6.9**). Thorndike reported his observations and inferences about the kind of learning he believed was taking place in his subjects. The cats at first only struggled against their confinement, but once some "impulsive" action allowed them to open the door "all the other unsuccessful impulses [were] stamped out and the particular impulse leading to the successful act [was] stamped in by the resulting pleasure" (Thorndike, 1898, p. 13).

What had Thorndike's cats learned? According to Thorndike's analysis, learning was an association between stimuli in the situation and a response that an animal learned to make: a *stimulus–response (S–R) connection*. Thus, the cats had learned to produce an appropriate response (for example, clawing at a button or loop) that in these stimulus circumstances (confinement in the puzzle box) led to a desired outcome (momentary freedom). Note that the learning of these S–R connections occurred gradually and automatically

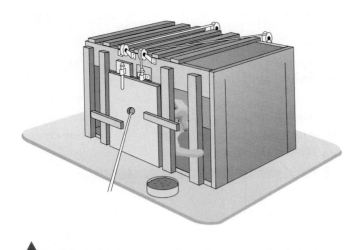

FIGURE 6.9

A Thorndike Puzzle Box

To get out of the puzzle box and obtain food, Thorndike's cat had to manipulate a mechanism to release a weight that would then pull the door open.

in a mechanistic way as the animal experienced the consequences of its actions through blind *trial and error*. Gradually, the behaviors that had satisfying consequences increased in frequency; they eventually became the dominant response when the animal was placed in the puzzle box. Thorndike referred to this relationship between behavior and its consequences as the **law of effect:** A response that is followed by satisfying consequences becomes more probable and a response that is followed by dissatisfying consequences becomes less probable.

◆ EXPERIMENTAL ANALYSIS OF BEHAVIOR

B. F. Skinner embraced Thorndike's view that environmental consequences exert a powerful effect on behavior. Skinner outlined a program of research whose purpose was to discover, by systematic variation of stimulus conditions, the ways that various environmental conditions affect the likelihood that a given response will occur:

> *A natural datum in a science of behavior is the probability that a given bit of behavior will occur at a given time. An experimental analysis deals with that probability in terms of frequency or rate of responding. . . . The task of an experimental analysis is to discover all the variables of which probability of response is a function. (Skinner, 1966, pp. 213–214)*

Skinner's analysis was experimental rather than theoretical—theorists are guided by derivations and predictions about behavior from their theories, but empiricists, such as Skinner, advocate the bottom-up approach. They start with the collection and evaluation of data within the context of an experiment and are not theory driven.

To analyze behavior experimentally, Skinner developed **operant conditioning** procedures, in which he manipulated the *consequences* of an organism's behavior in order to see what effect they had on subsequent behavior. An **operant** is any behavior that is *emitted* by an organism and can be characterized in terms of the observable effects it has on the environment. Literally, *operant* means *affecting the environment,* or operating on it (Skinner, 1938). Operants are *not elicited* by specific stimuli, as classically conditioned behaviors are. Pigeons peck, rats search for food, babies cry and coo, some people gesture while talking, and others stutter. The probability of these behaviors occurring in the future can be increased or decreased by manipulating the effects they have on the environment. If, for example, a baby's coo prompts desirable parental contact, the baby will coo more in the future. Operant condi-

What environmental contingencies might cause babies to smile more often?

<www.ablongman.com/gerrig17e>

tioning, then, modifies the probability of different types of operant behavior as a function of the environmental consequences they produce.

To carry out his new experimental analysis, Skinner invented an apparatus that allowed him to manipulate the consequences of behavior, the *operant chamber.* **Figure 6.10** shows how the operant chamber works. When, after having produced an appropriate behavior defined by the experimenter, a rat presses a lever, the mechanism delivers a food pellet. This device allows experimenters to study the variables that allow rats to learn—or not to learn—the behaviors they define. For example, if a lever press produces a food pellet only after a rat has turned a circle in the chamber, the rat will swiftly learn (through a process called *shaping* that we will consider shortly) to turn a circle before pressing the lever.

In many operant experiments, the measure of interest is how much of a particular behavior an animal carries out in a period of time. Researchers record the pattern and total amount of behavior emitted in the course of an experiment. This methodology allowed Skinner to study the effect of reinforcement contingencies on animals' behavior.

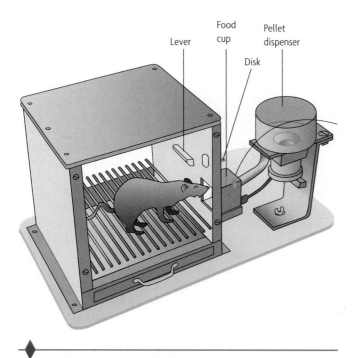

FIGURE 6.10

Operant Chamber

In this specially designed apparatus, typical of those used with rats, a press on the lever may be followed by delivery of a food pellet.

♦ REINFORCEMENT CONTINGENCIES

A **reinforcement contingency** is a consistent relationship between a response and the changes in the environment that it produces. Imagine, for example, an experiment in which a pigeon's pecking a disk (the response) is generally followed by the presentation of grain (the corresponding change in the environment). This consistent relationship, or reinforcement contingency, will usually be accompanied by an increase in the rate of pecking. For delivery of grain to increase *only* the probability of pecking, it must be contingent *only* on the pecking response—the delivery must occur regularly after that response but not after other responses, such as turning or bowing. Based on Skinner's work, modern behavior analysts seek to understand behavior in terms of reinforcement contingencies. Let's take a closer look at what has been discovered about these contingencies.

POSITIVE AND NEGATIVE REINFORCERS

Suppose you are now captivated by the idea of getting your pet rat to turn a circle in its cage. To increase the probability of circle-turning behavior, you would want to use a *reinforcer.* A **reinforcer** is any stimulus that—when made contingent on a behavior—increases the probability of that behavior over time. *Reinforcement* is the delivery of a reinforcer following a response.

Reinforcers are always defined empirically—in terms of their effects on changing the probability of a response. If you look out at the world, you can probably find three classes of stimuli: those toward which you are neutral, those that you find *appetitive* (you have an "appetite" for them), and those that you find *aversive* (you seek to avoid them). It should be clear that the compositions of these classes of stimuli will not be the same for all individuals: What is appetitive or aversive is defined by the behavior of the individual organism. Consider the strawberry. Although many people find strawberries quite delicious, one of your authors finds strawberries virtually inedible. If you intend to use strawberries to change that author's behavior, it's important to know that—for him—they are aversive rather than appetitive.

When a behavior is followed by the delivery of an appetitive stimulus, the event is called **positive reinforcement.** Your pet rat will turn circles if a consequence of circle turning is the delivery of desirable food. Humans will tell jokes if a consequence of their joke telling is a type of laughter they find pleasurable.

When a behavior is followed by the removal of an aversive stimulus, the event is called **negative reinforcement.** Your author, for example, would be more likely to perform a behavior if it would allow him to cease eating strawberries. There are two general types of learning circumstances in which negative reinforcement applies. In *escape conditioning*, animals learn that a response will allow them to escape from an aversive stimulus. Raising an umbrella during a downpour is a common example of escape conditioning. You learn to use an umbrella to escape the aversive stimulus of getting wet. In *avoidance conditioning*, animals learn responses that allow them to avoid aversive stimuli before they begin. Suppose your car has a buzzer that sounds when you fail to buckle your seat belt. You will learn to buckle up to avoid the aversive noise.

To distinguish clearly between positive and negative reinforcement, try to remember the following: Both positive reinforcement and negative reinforcement *increase* the probability of the response that precedes them. Positive reinforcement increases response probability by the presentation of an appetitive stimulus following a response; negative reinforcement does the same in reverse, through the removal, reduction, or prevention of an aversive stimulus following a response.

You should recall that for classical conditioning, when the unconditioned stimulus is no longer delivered, the conditioned response suffers extinction. The same rule holds for operant conditioning—if reinforcement is withheld, **operant extinction** occurs. Thus, if a behavior no longer produces predictable consequences, it returns to the level it was at before operant conditioning—it is extinguished. You can probably catch your own behaviors being reinforced and then *extinguished*. Have you ever had the experience of dropping a few coins into a soda machine and getting nothing in return? If you kicked the machine one time and your soda came out, the act of kicking would be reinforced. However, if the next few times your kicking produced no soda, kicking would quickly be extinguished.

POSITIVE AND NEGATIVE PUNISHMENT

You are probably familiar with another technique for decreasing the probability of a response—punishment. A **punisher** is any stimulus that—when it is made contingent on a response—decreases the probability of that response over time. *Punishment* is the delivery of a punisher following a response. Just as we could identify positive and negative reinforcement, we can identify positive punishment and negative punishment. When a behavior is followed by the delivery of an aversive stimulus, the event is called **positive punishment** (you can remember *positive,* because something is added to the situation). Touching a hot stove, for example, produces pain that punishes the preceding response so that you are less likely next time to touch the stove. When a behavior is followed by the removal of an appetitive stimulus, the event is referred to as **negative punishment** (you can remember *negative,*

because something is subtracted from the situation). Thus, when a parent withdraws a child's allowance after she hits her baby brother, the child learns not to hit her brother in the future. Which kind of punishment explains why you might stay away from horror movies?

Although punishment and reinforcement are closely related operations, they differ in important ways. A good way to differentiate them is to think of each in terms of its effects on behavior. Punishment, by definition, always *reduces* the probability of a response occurring again; reinforcement, by definition, always *increases* the probability of a response recurring. For example, some people get severe headaches after drinking caffeinated beverages. The headache is the stimulus that positively punishes and reduces the behavior of drinking coffee. However, once the headache is present, people often will take aspirin or another pain reliever to eliminate the headache. The aspirin's analgesic effect is the stimulus that negatively reinforces the behavior of ingesting aspirin.

You are now acquainted with the four basic ways to change the probability of a behavior. **Figure 6.11** shows how you might use them with respect to behaviors in your own life.

DISCRIMINATIVE STIMULI AND GENERALIZATION

You are unlikely to want to change the probability of a certain behavior at all times. Rather, you may want to change the probability of the behavior in a particular context. For example, you often want to increase the probability that a child will sit quietly in class without changing the probability that he or she will be noisy and active during recess. Through their associations with reinforcement or punishment, certain stimuli that precede a particular response—**discriminative stimuli**—come to set the context for that behavior. Organisms learn that, in the presence of some stimuli but not of others, their behavior is likely to have a particular effect on the environment. For example, in the presence of a green street light, the act of crossing an intersection in a motor vehicle is reinforced. When the light is red, however, such behavior may be punished—it may result in a traffic ticket or an accident. Skinner referred to the sequence of discriminative stimulus–behavior–consequence as the **three-term contingency** and believed that it could explain most human action (Skinner, 1953). **Table 6.1** describes how the three-term contingency might explain several different kinds of human behavior.

Under laboratory conditions, manipulating the consequences of behavior in the presence of discriminative stimuli can exert powerful control over that behavior. For example, a pigeon might be given grain after pecking a disk in the presence of a green light but not a red light.

FIGURE 6.11

Operant Conditioning in Your Life

We want to give you the opportunity to develop your own application for positive and negative reinforcement and positive and negative punishment. Begin by choosing a behavior.

A behavior (of your own, or of someone else) that you'd like to increase in frequency:

Or a behavior that you'd like to decrease in frequency:

Fill in your plan of action for each cell. For example, suppose a behavior you would choose to decrease is your roommate's "staying on the phone" behavior. You might fill in "I would deliver a candy bar each time a phone call lasted less than two minutes" in cell 1 or "I would start slapping my roommate each time a phone call began and only stop when the call was over" in cell 4 (in which case, you'd actually be trying to increase your roommate's "stay off the phone" behavior). Note that, in real life, you might not be able to carry out the actions you invent for each cell!

	APPETITIVE STIMULUS	**AVERSIVE STIMULUS**
DELIVER	Positive reinforcement (1)	(2) Positive punishment
REMOVE	Negative punishment (3)	(4) Negative reinforcement

The green light is a discriminative stimulus that sets the occasion for pecking; the red is a discriminative stimulus that sets the occasion for not pecking. Organisms learn quickly to discriminate between these conditions, responding regularly in the presence of one stimulus and not responding in the presence of the other. By manipulating the components of the three-term contingency, you can constrain a behavior to a particular context.

Organisms also generalize responses to other stimuli that resemble the discriminative stimulus. Once a response has been reinforced in the presence of one discriminative stimulus, a similar stimulus can become a discriminative stimulus for that same response. For example, pigeons trained to peck a disk in the presence of a green light will also peck the disk in the presence of lights that are lighter or darker shades of green than the original discriminative stimulus. Similarly, you generalize to different shades of green on stop lights as a discriminative stimulus for your "resume driving" behavior.

USING REINFORCEMENT CONTINGENCIES

Are you ready to put your new knowledge of reinforcement contingencies to work? Here are some considerations you might have:

- *How can you define the behavior that you would like to reinforce or eliminate?* You must always carefully target the specific behavior whose probability you would like to change. Reinforcement should be contingent on exactly that behavior. When reinforcers are presented noncontingently, their presence has little effect on behavior. For example, if a parent praises bad work as well as good efforts, a child will not learn to work harder in school—but, because of the positive reinforcement, other behaviors are likely to increase. (What might those be?)

- *How can you define the contexts in which a behavior is appropriate or inappropriate?*

TABLE 6.1

The Three-Term Contingency: Relationships Among Discriminative Stimuli, Behavior, and Consequences

	Discriminative Stimulus	Emitted Response	Stimulus Consequence
1. Positive reinforcement: A response in the presence of an effective signal produces the desired consequence. This response increases.	Soft-drink machine	Put coin in slot	Get drink
2. Negative reinforcement (escape): An aversive situation is escaped from by an operant response. This escape response increases.	Heat	Fan oneself	Escape from heat
3. Positive punishment: A response is followed by an aversive stimulus. The response is eliminated or suppressed.	Attractive matchbox	Play with matches	Get burned or get caught and spanked
4. Negative punishment: A response is followed by the removal of an appetitive stimulus. The response is eliminated or suppressed.	Brussels sprouts	Refusal to eat them	No dessert

Remember that you rarely want to allow or disallow every instance of a behavior. We suggested earlier, for example, that you might want to increase the probability that a child will sit quietly in class without changing the probability that he or she will be noisy and active during recess. You must define the discriminative stimuli and investigate how broadly the desired response will be generalized to similar stimuli. If, for example, the child learned to sit quietly in class, would that behavior generalize to other "serious" settings?

- *Have you unknowingly been reinforcing some behaviors?* Suppose you want to eliminate a behavior. Before you turn to punishment as a way of reducing its probability (more on that in the Psychology in Your Life box), you should try to determine whether you can identify reinforcers for that behavior. If so, you can try to extinguish the behavior by eliminating those reinforcers. Imagine, for example, that a young boy throws a large number of tantrums. You might ask yourself, "Have I been reinforcing those tantrums by paying the boy extra attention when he screams?" If so,

you can try to eliminate the tantrums by eliminating the reinforcement. Even better, you can combine extinction with positive reinforcement of more socially approved behaviors.

It's important to be aware that the reinforcers parents produce can make children's conduct problems, such as tantrums, more likely. In fact, parenting research has identified unknowing reinforcement as one cause of serious behavior problems in children. For example, **Gerald Patterson** and his colleagues (Patterson, 2002; Reid et al., 2002) have outlined a *coercion model* for antisocial behavior. Family observations suggest that children are put at risk when their parents issue threats in response to small misbehaviors (e.g., whining, teasing, or yelling) without following through. At some moments, however, these parents would issue harsh or explosive discipline toward the same behaviors. The children appear to learn the lesson that relatively large acts of aggressive and coercive behavior are appropriate and necessary for achieving goals—leading to a cycle of increase in the severity of the children's antisocial behavior.

How can parents use reinforcement contingencies to affect their children's behavior?

Behavior analysts assume that any behavior that persists does so because it results in reinforcement. Any behavior, they argue—even irrational or bizarre behavior—can be understood by discovering what the reinforcement or payoff is. For example, symptoms of mental or physical disorders are sometimes maintained because the person gets attention and sympathy and is excused from normal responsibilities. These *secondary gains* reinforce irrational and sometimes self-destructive behavior. Can you see how shy behaviors can be maintained through reinforcement, even though the shy person would prefer not to be shy? It is, of course, not always possible to know what reinforcers are at work in an environment. However, as a behavior becomes more or less probable, you might try to carry out a bit of behavior analysis.

One final thought. It's often the case that real-life situations will involve intricate combinations of reinforcement and punishment. Suppose, for example, parents use negative punishment by grounding a teenager for two weeks when he stays out past curfew. To soften up his parents, the teen helps more than usual around the house. Assuming his helping behavior appeals to the parents, the teen is trying to reinforce his parents' "reducing the sentence" behavior. If this strategy succeeds in changing the punishment to only one week, the teen's helping behavior will have been negatively reinforced—because helping led to the removal of the aversive stimulus of being grounded. Whenever the teen is grounded again (a discriminative stimulus), his helping behavior should be more likely. Do you see how all the contingencies fit together to change both the teen's and the parents' behaviors?

We have recommended that, as much as possible, you use positive reinforcement to change behaviors. Let's now take a look at the ways in which various objects and activities may come to function as reinforcers.

◆ PROPERTIES OF REINFORCERS

Reinforcers are the power brokers of operant conditioning—they change or maintain behavior. Reinforcers have a number of interesting and complex properties. They can be learned through experience rather than be biologically determined and can be activities rather than objects. In some situations, even ordinarily powerful reinforcers may not be enough to change a dominant behavior pattern (in this case, we would say that the consequences were not actually reinforcers).

CONDITIONED REINFORCERS

When you came into the world, there were a handful of **primary reinforcers,** such as food and water, whose reinforcing properties were biologically determined. Over time, however, otherwise neutral stimuli have become associated with primary reinforcers and now function as **conditioned reinforcers** for operant responses. Conditioned reinforcers can come to serve as ends in themselves. In fact, a great deal of human behavior is influenced less by biologically significant primary reinforcers than by a wide variety of conditioned reinforcers. Money, grades, smiles of approval, gold stars, and various kinds of status symbols are among the many potent conditioned reinforcers that influence much of your behavior.

Virtually any stimulus can become a conditioned reinforcer by being paired with a primary reinforcer. In one experiment, simple tokens were used with animal learners.

CLASSIC
PUTTING IDEAS TO THE TEST

Conditioned Reinforcers for Chimps

With raisins as primary reinforcers, chimps were trained to solve problems. Then tokens were delivered along with the raisins. When only the tokens were presented, the chimps continued working for their "money" because they could later deposit the hard-earned tokens in a "chimp-o-mat" designed to exchange tokens for the raisins (Cowles, 1937).

D o you believe the old adage "Spare the rod, spoil the child"—that children who are not occasionally spanked, for example, will end up being spoiled? If you believe this adage, you are similar to the majority of parents in the United States. In one sample of 991 parents, 35 percent reported using some form of corporal punishment (e.g., spanking, slapping) on their 1- to 2-year-olds and 94 percent had used corporal punishment on their 3- to 4-year-olds (Straus & Stewart, 1999). In another sample of 449 parents, 93 percent of them had themselves been spanked—and 87 percent of them approved of it as a form of punishment (Buntain-Ricklefs et al., 1994). You can see that spanking is quite common, and people generally approve of it as a form of punishment. But what are the consequences for children who are spanked?

Researchers have begun to answer this question by examining the link between parents' use of physical punishment and children's aggressive behavior. Contrary to popular wisdom, what many theorists believe is that parents' physical aggression toward their children—even in the context of trying to correct inappropriate behavior—serves as a *model* for children's own responses to situations in which they wish to control other individuals' behavior. That is, children learn from their parents to use physical aggression. (We will have more to say about learning from models in a later section entitled "Observational Learning.") How might this idea be tested? In one study, involving 273 kindergarten children in Indiana and Tennessee, parents were asked to

Spare the Rod, Spoil the Child?
Marla Ranieri
Stanford University

fill out self-reports about the types of physical punishment they used with their children (Strassberg et al., 1994). We're going to focus on the children's mothers. About 6 percent of the children had mothers who did not use physical punishment. Sixty-eight percent of the children were spanked by their mothers. The remaining 26 percent received more intense forms of physical punishment: Their mothers hit them with fists or closed hands or beat them up.

About 6 months after the mothers reported on their forms of physical punishment, the children were observed interacting with peers in school. The researchers recorded the children's acts of aggression toward their peers— instances, for example, in which they bullied or became angry and hit another child. Based on these observations, each child earned a score for aggressive acts per hour. The accompanying figure presents the results. As you can see, the more intense the form of the mother's physical punishment, the more aggressive the child. These data suggest rather strongly that children are learning an aggressive style from their parents. You might be thinking: Maybe kids are being spanked or hit because they were *already* aggressive children. Other developmental evidence suggests that this isn't the case (Chess & Thomas, 1984).

Suppose, even so, that there is some truth to the idea that "bad" kids are getting more physical punishment. This study makes it clear that physical punishment is not having the presumably intended effect of teaching bad kids to be better (Mahoney et al., 2000).

If we haven't already convinced you that physical punishment is not an effective parenting strategy, let us report the results from one more study. This analysis was based on a subset of data from an ambitious project that studied 6,002 U.S. families to establish patterns and consequences of family violence. In this instance, the researchers were interested in physical punishment people received during their teenage years as it related to later life outcomes (Straus & Kantor, 1994). The results were quite dramatic. Roughly 50 percent of the sample reported having been physically punished as teenagers (58 percent of the boys and 44 percent of the girls). Those individuals who were physically punished were more likely to experience a host of later problems: They were put at risk for depression, suicide, alcohol abuse, physical abuse of their children, and (for men) wife beating. The researchers conclude that "ending all use of spanking and other corporal punishment can make an important contribution to primary prevention of physical abuse of children and spouses, depression, suicide, and drinking problems" (p. 558). This conclusion is worth serious consideration.

We hope to have convinced you, based on concrete research results, that spanking children is not an appropriate or effective parenting technique. Note, however, that our intention is not

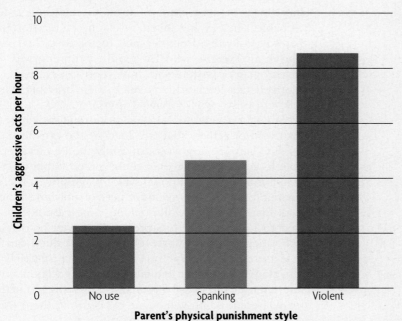

Physical Punishment and Children's Aggression

Children who are spanked by their mothers commit more aggressive acts in the classroom than do their peers who are not spanked. The most aggressive children are those whose mothers use violent punishment—hitting with a fist, closed hand, or object or beating up their children.

to rule out all forms of punishment. There may well be situations in which, to stop a child's undesirable actions swiftly enough, punishment may become the only alternative. Research shows that punishment should meet a number of conditions (Walters & Grusec, 1977). Punishment should:

- be swift and brief
- be administered right after the response occurs
- be limited in intensity
- be a response to specific undesirable behaviors and never to the person's character
- be limited to the situation in which the response occurs
- consist of penalties instead of physical pain

But beware: The reason many parents use punishment too often is that it can stop a child's unwanted behavior immediately. Because the parents achieve their short-term goal, the children's immediate response reinforces the parents' punishing behavior (Grant & Evans, 1994). But the lesson here is "short-term gain, long-term pain." Parents must patiently forgo that immediate reinforcement to act in the better, long-term interest of their children.

Inedible tokens can be used as conditioned reinforcers.
In one study, chimps deposited tokens in a "chimp-o-mat"
in exchange for raisins. What types of conditioned
reinforcers function in your life?

Suppose you need to get a child to do something. You don't want to pay her or give her a gold star, so instead you strike this bargain: "When you finish your homework, you can play with your video game." Your use of "video game playing" in these circumstances is in keeping with the *Premack principle,* named after its discoverer, **David Premack** (1965). The Premack principle suggests that a more probable activity (that is, a behavior with a higher probability of occurring under ordinary circumstances) can be used to reinforce a less probable one. In his initial research, Premack found that water-deprived rats learned to increase their running in an exercise wheel when their running was followed by an opportunity to drink. Conversely, exercise-deprived rats learned to increase their drinking when that response was followed by a chance to run. According to the Premack principle, a reinforcer may be any event or activity that is valued by the organism.

You can see how you can apply the Premack principle to get children to engage in low-probability activities. For a socially outgoing child, playing with friends can reinforce the less pleasant task of finishing homework first. For a shy child, reading a new book can be used to reinforce the less-preferred activity of playing with other children. Whatever activity is valued can be used as a reinforcer and thus increase the probability of engaging in an activity that is not currently valued. Over time, there is the possibility that the less favored activities will come to be valued, as exposure to them leads to discovery of their intrinsic worth.

◆ SCHEDULES OF REINFORCEMENT

What happens when you cannot, or do not want to, reinforce your pet on every occasion when it performs a special behavior? Consider a story about the young B. F. Skinner. It seems that one weekend he was secluded in his laboratory with not enough of a food-reward supply for his hardworking rats. He economized by giving the rats pellets only after a certain interval of time—no matter how many times they pressed in between, they couldn't get any more pellets. Even so, the rats responded as much with this *partial reinforcement schedule* as they had with continuous reinforcement. And what do you predict happened when these animals underwent extinction training and their responses were followed by no pellets at all? The rats whose lever pressing had been partially reinforced continued to respond longer and more vigorously than did the rats who had gotten payoffs after every response. Skinner was onto something important!

The discovery of the effectiveness of partial reinforcement led to extensive study of the effects of dif-

Teachers and experimenters often find conditioned reinforcers more effective and easier to use than primary reinforcers because (1) few primary reinforcers are available in the classroom, whereas almost any stimulus event that is under control of a teacher can be used as a conditioned reinforcer; (2) they can be dispensed rapidly; (3) they are portable; and (4) their reinforcing effect may be more immediate, because it depends only on the perception of receiving them and not on biological processing, as in the case of primary reinforcers.

In some institutions, such as psychiatric hospitals or drug treatment programs, *token economies* have been set up based on these principles. Desired behaviors (grooming or taking medication, for example) are explicitly defined, and token payoffs are given by the staff when the behaviors are performed. These tokens can later be exchanged by the patients for a wide array of rewards and privileges (Kazdin, 1994; Martin & Pear, 1999). These systems of reinforcement are especially effective in modifying patients' behaviors regarding self-care, upkeep of their environment, and, most important, frequency of their positive social interactions.

<www.ablongman.com/gerrig17e>

ferent **schedules of reinforcement** on behavior (see **Figure 6.12**). You have experienced different schedules of reinforcement in your daily life. When you raise your hand in class, the teacher sometimes calls on you and sometimes does not; some slot machine players continue to put coins in the one-armed bandits even though the reinforcers are delivered only rarely. In real life or in the laboratory, reinforcers can be delivered according to either a *ratio schedule,* after a certain number of responses, or an *interval schedule,* after the first response following a specified interval of time. In each case, there can be either a constant, or *fixed,* pattern of reinforcement or an irregular, or *variable,* pattern of reinforcement, making four major types of schedules in all. So far you've learned about the **partial reinforcement effect:** Responses acquired under schedules of partial reinforcement are more resistant to extinction than those acquired with continuous reinforcement. Let's see what else researchers have discovered about different schedules of reinforcement.

FIXED-RATIO (FR) SCHEDULES

In **fixed-ratio schedules,** the reinforcer comes after the organism has emitted a fixed number of responses. When reinforcement follows one response, the schedule is called an FR-1 schedule (this is the original continuous reinforcement schedule). When reinforcement follows only every twenty-fifth response, the schedule is an FR-25 schedule. FR schedules generate high rates of responding because there is a direct correlation between responding and reinforcement—a pigeon can get as much food as it wants in a period of time if it pecks often enough. Figure 6.12 shows that FR schedules produce a pause after each reinforcer. The higher the ratio, the longer the pause after each reinforcement. Stretching the ratio too thin by requiring a great many responses for reinforcement without first training the animal to emit that many responses may lead to extinction. Many salespeople are on FR schedules: They must sell a certain number of units before they can get paid.

VARIABLE-RATIO (VR) SCHEDULES

In a **variable-ratio schedule,** the average number of responses between reinforcers is predetermined. A VR-10 schedule means that, on average, reinforcement follows every tenth response, but it might come after only 1 response or after 20 responses. Variable-ratio schedules generate the highest rate of responding and the greatest resistance to extinction, especially when the VR value is large. Suppose you start a pigeon with a low VR value (for example, VR-5) and then move it toward a higher value. A pigeon on a VR-110 schedule will respond with up to 12,000 pecks per hour and will continue responding for hours even with no reinforcement.

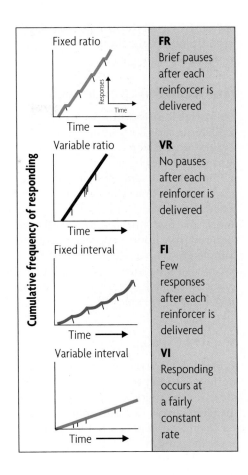

FIGURE 6.12

Reinforcement Schedules

These different patterns of behavior are produced by four simple schedules of reinforcement. The hash marks indicate when reinforcement is delivered.

Gambling would seem to be under the control of VR schedules. The response of dropping coins in slot machines is maintained at a high, steady level by the payoff, which is delivered only after an unknown, variable number of coins has been deposited. VR schedules leave you guessing when the reward will come—you gamble that it will be after the next response, not many responses later (Rachlin, 1990).

FIXED-INTERVAL (FI) SCHEDULES

On a **fixed-interval schedule,** a reinforcer is delivered for the first response made after a fixed period of time. On an FI-10 schedule, the subject, after receiving reinforcement, will have to wait 10 seconds before another response can be reinforced—irrespective of the number of responses. Response rates under FI schedules show a scalloped pattern. Immediately after each reinforced response, the animal makes few if any responses. As the payoff time approaches, the animal responds more and more. A monthly paycheck puts you on an FI schedule.

VARIABLE-INTERVAL (VI) SCHEDULES

For **variable-interval schedules,** the average interval is predetermined. For example, on a VI-20 schedule, reinforcers are delivered at an average rate of 1 every 20 seconds. This schedule generates a moderate but very stable response rate. Extinction under VI schedules is gradual and much slower than under fixed-interval schedules. In one case, a pigeon pecked 18,000 times during the first 4 hours after reinforcement stopped and required 168 hours before its responding extinguished completely (Ferster & Skinner, 1957). You have experienced a VI schedule if you've taken a course with a professor who gave occasional, irregularly scheduled pop quizzes. Did you study your notes each day before class?

◆ SHAPING

As parts of experiments, we have spoken of rats pressing levers to get food. However, even lever pressing is a learned behavior. When a rat is introduced to an operant chamber, it is quite unlikely that it will ever press the lever spontaneously; the rat has learned to use its paws in many ways, but it probably has never pressed a lever before. How should you go about training the rat to perform a behavior that it would rarely, if ever, produce on its own? You've settled on a reinforcer, food, and a schedule of reinforcement, FR-1—now what? To train new or complex behaviors, you will want to use a method called **shaping by successive approximations**—in which you reinforce any responses that successively approximate and ultimately match the desired response.

Here's how you'd do it. First, you deprive the rat of food for a day. (Without deprivation, food is not likely to serve as a reinforcer.) Then you systematically make food pellets available in the food hopper in an operant chamber so that the rat learns to look there for food. Now you can begin the actual shaping process by making delivery of food contingent on specific aspects of the rat's behavior, such as orienting itself toward the lever. Next, food is delivered only as the rat moves closer and closer to the lever. Soon the requirement for reinforcement is actually to touch the lever. Finally, the rat must depress the lever for food to be delivered. In small increments, the rat has learned that a lever press will produce food. Thus, for *shaping* to work, you must define what constitutes progress toward the target behavior and use *differential reinforcement* to refine each step along the way.

Let's look at another example, in which shaping was used to improve the performance of a Canadian pole vaulter who was an international competitor.

Shaping Improves Athletic Performance

A 21-year-old university pole vaulter sought a research team's assistance to help him correct a technical problem with his vaulting technique (Scott et al., 1997). The vaulter's particular problem was that he didn't sufficiently extend his arms (holding the pole) above his head before he planted the pole to lift himself off. At the beginning of the intervention, the vaulter's average hand-height at takeoff was calculated as 2.25 meters. The goal was set to use a shaping procedure to help him achieve his physical potential of 2.54 meters. A photoelectric beam was set up so that, when the vaulter achieved a desired extension, the beam was broken and equipment produced a beep. The beep served as a conditioned positive reinforcer. At first, the beam was set at 2.30 meters but, once the vaulter was able to reach that height with 90 percent success, the beam was moved to 2.35 meters. Further success brought further increments of 2.40, 2.45, 2.50, and 2.52 meters. In that way, the vaulter's behavior was successfully shaped toward the desired goal.

You can imagine how difficult it would have been for the vaulter to show spontaneous improvement of 0.27 meters. (That's about $10\frac{1}{2}$ inches.) The shaping procedure allowed him to achieve that gain through successive approximations to the desired behavior.

Let's return to your rat. Recall that we suggested you might wish to teach it to turn circles in its cage. Can you devise a plan, using shaping, to bring about this behav-

This woman, Sue Strong, was assisted by a monkey who had been operantly shaped to comb her hair, feed her, turn book pages, and make other responses she could not do for herself because of paralysis. For each of these behaviors, can you think through the successive approximations you would reinforce to arrive at the end point?

ior? What you need to think about is what each successive approximation would be. At the beginning, for example, you might reinforce the rat if it just turned its head in a particular direction. Next, you would let the rat obtain a food pellet only if it turned its whole body in the right direction. What might you do after that?

The two forms of learning we have examined so far—classical conditioning and operant conditioning—have most often been studied with the assumption that processes of learning were consistent across all animals. In fact, we have cited examples from dogs, cats, rats, mice, pigeons, and humans to show exactly such consistency. However, researchers have come to understand that learning is modified in many situations by the particular biological and cognitive capabilities of individual species. We turn now to the processes that limit the generality of the laws of learning.

PUT YOURSELF TO THE TEST

- What is the law of effect?
- What impact do reinforcers and punishers have on a behavior?
- What is the role of discriminative stimuli in operant conditioning?
- What are the consequences of different schedules of reinforcement?
- How does the shaping procedure bring about changes in behavior?

Biology and Learning

The contemporary view that a single, general account of the associationist principles of learning is common to humans and all animals was first proposed by English philosopher **David Hume** in 1748. Hume reasoned that "any theory by which we explain the operations of the understanding, or the origin and connexion of the passions in man, will acquire additional authority, if we find that the same theory is requisite to explain the same phenomena in all other animals" (Hume, 1748/1951, p. 104).

The appealing simplicity of such a view has come under scrutiny since the 1960s as psychologists have discovered certain constraints, or limitations, on the generality of the findings regarding conditioning (Bailey & Bailey, 1993; Garcia, 1993; Todd & Morris, 1992, 1993). In Chapter 3, we familiarized you with the idea that animals have evolved in response to the need for survival:

We can explain many of the differences among species as adaptations to the demands of their particular environmental niches. The same evolutionary perspective applies to a species' capacity for learning (Leger, 1992). **Biological constraints on learning** are any limitations on learning imposed by a species' genetic endowment. These constraints can apply to the animal's sensory, behavioral, and cognitive capacities. We will examine two areas of research that show how behavior–environment relations can be biased by an organism's genotype: instinctual drift and taste-aversion learning.

◆ INSTINCTUAL DRIFT

You have no doubt seen animals performing tricks on television or in the circus. Some animals play baseball or Ping-Pong, and others drive tiny race cars. For years, **Keller Breland** and **Marion Breland** used operant conditioning techniques to train thousands of animals from many different species to perform a remarkable array of behaviors. The Brelands had believed that general principles derived from laboratory research using virtually any type of response or reward could be directly applied to the control of animal behavior outside the laboratory.

At some point after training, though, some of the animals began to "misbehave." For example, a raccoon was trained to pick up a coin, put it into a toy bank, and collect an edible reinforcer. The raccoon, however, would not immediately deposit the coin. Even worse, when there were two coins to be deposited, conditioning broke down completely—the raccoon would not give up the coins at all. Instead, it would rub the coins together, dip them into the bank, and then pull them back out. But is this really so strange? Raccoons often engage in rubbing and washing behaviors as they remove the outer shells of a favorite food, crayfish. Similarly, when pigs were given the task of putting their hard-earned tokens into a large piggy bank, they instead would drop the coins onto the floor, root (poke at) them with their snouts, and toss them into the air. Again, should you consider this strange? Pigs root and shake their food as a natural part of their inherited food-gathering repertory.

These experiences convinced the Brelands that, even when animals have learned to make operant responses perfectly, the "learned behavior drifts toward instinctual behavior" over time. They called this tendency **instinctual drift** (Breland & Breland, 1951, 1961). The behavior of their animals is not explainable by ordinary operant principles, but it is understandable if you consider the species-specific tendencies imposed by an inherited genotype. These tendencies override the changes in behavior brought about by operant conditioning.

The bulk of traditional research on animal learning focused on arbitrarily chosen responses to conveniently available stimuli. The Brelands' theory and demonstration

How could you use operant conditioning techniques to teach an animal friend to waterski?

of instinctual drift makes it evident that not all aspects of learning are under the control of the experimenters' reinforcers. Behaviors will be more or less easy to change as a function of an animal's normal, genetically programmed responses in its environment. Conditioning will be particularly efficient when you can frame a target response as biologically relevant. For example, what change might you make to get the pigs to place their tokens in a bank? If the token was paired with a water reward for a thirsty pig, it would then not be rooted as food but would be deposited in the bank as a valuable commodity—dare we say a liquid asset?

◆ TASTE-AVERSION LEARNING

Your authors have a pair of confessions to make: One of us still gets a bit queasy at the thought of eating pork and beans; the other has the same response, alas, to popcorn. Why? In each case, we became violently ill after eating one of these foods. Although it's unlikely that it was the food itself that made us sick—and we have tried valiantly, particularly for the popcorn, to con-

vince ourselves of that fact—we nonetheless have this queasy response. We can look to nonhuman animals for a clue to why this is so.

Suppose we asked you to devise a strategy for tasting a variety of unfamiliar substances. If you had the genetic endowment of rats, you would be very cautious in doing so. When presented with a new food or flavor, rats take only a very small sample. Only if it fails to make them sick will they go back for more. To flip that around, suppose we include a substance with the new flavor that does make the rats ill—they'll never consume that flavor again. This phenomenon is known as **taste-aversion learning.** You can see why having this genetic capacity to sample and learn which foods are safe and which are toxic could have great survival value.

Taste-aversion learning is an enormously powerful mechanism. Unlike most other instances of classical conditioning, taste aversion is learned with only one pairing of a CS (the novel flavor) and its consequences (the result of the underlying UCS—the element that actually brings about the illness). This is true even with a long interval, 12 hours or more, between the time the rat consumes the substance and the time it becomes ill. Finally, unlike many classically conditioned associations that are quite fragile, this one is permanent after one experience. Again, to understand these violations of the norms of classical conditioning, you should consider how dramatically this mechanism aids survival.

John Garcia, the psychologist who first documented taste-aversion learning in the laboratory, and his colleague Robert Koelling used this phenomenon to demonstrate that, in general, animals are biologically prepared to learn certain associations. The researchers discovered that some CS–UCS combinations can be classically conditioned in particular species of animals, but others cannot.

Why are there some behaviors raccoons cannot learn to perform?

Matches Between Stimuli and Consequences

In phase 1 of Garcia and Koelling's experiment, thirsty rats were first familiarized with the experimental situation in which licking a tube produced three CSs: saccharin-flavored water, noise, and bright light. In phase 2, when the rats licked the tube, half of them received only the sweet water and half received only the noise, light, and plain water. Each of these two groups was again divided: Half of each group was given electric shocks that produced pain, and half was given X-ray radiation that produced nausea and illness.

The amount of water drunk by the rats in phase 1 was compared with the amount drunk in phase 2, when pain and illness were involved (see **Figure 6.13**). Big reductions in drinking occurred when flavor was associated with illness (taste aversion) and when noise and light were associated with pain. However, there was little change in behavior under the other two conditions—when flavor predicted pain or when the "bright-noisy water" predicted illness.

The pattern of results suggests that rats have an inborn bias to associate particular stimuli with particular consequences (Garcia & Koelling, 1966). Some instances of conditioning, then, depend not only on the relationship between stimuli and behavior but also on the way an organism is genetically predisposed toward stimuli in its environment (Barker et al., 1978). Animals appear to have encoded, within their genetic inheritance, the types of sensory cues—taste, smell, or appearance—that are most likely to signal dimensions of reward or danger. Taste-aversion learning is an example of what researchers call *biological preparedness:* A particular species has evolved so that the members of the species require less learning experience than normal to acquire a conditioned response. Experimenters who try arbitrarily to break these genetic links will look forward to little success. (In Chapter 14, we will see that researchers believe humans are biologically prepared to acquire intense fears—known as *phobias*—to stimuli such as snakes and spiders that provided dangers over the course of human evolution.)

Researchers have put knowledge of the mechanisms of taste-aversion learning to practical use. To stop coyotes from killing sheep (and sheep ranchers from shooting coyotes), John Garcia and colleagues have put toxic lamb burgers wrapped in sheep fur on the outskirts of fenced-in areas of sheep ranches. The coyotes who eat these lamb burgers get sick, vomit, and develop an instant distaste for lamb meat. Their subsequent disgust at the mere sight of sheep makes them back away from the animals instead of attacking.

One of the most serious instances of taste aversions in humans occurs when cancer patients become unable to tolerate normal foods in their diets. Their aversions are, in part, a consequence of their chemotherapy treatments, which often follow meals and which produce nausea.

Taste Aversions in Breast Cancer Patients

A group of 22 women undergoing treatments for breast cancer provided reports on their food preferences over the course of eight sessions of chemotherapy, each separated by three weeks. The women reported everything they had eaten in the 24-hour periods before and after chemotherapy. They rated each type of food and beverage on a scale from 1 (dislike very much) to 9 (like very much). The researchers considered an aversion to have formed if a participant's rating dropped by 4 points over the course of chemotherapy. Overall, 46 percent of the women developed an aversion to at least one food. However, those aversions formed in the first two sessions of therapy were short-lived. The researchers speculated that, unlike rats and other animals that acquire taste aversions, these women were able to reason that "the chemotherapy caused nausea, not the food." If they tried the food again, the women provided themselves with extinction trials that extinguished the conditioned aversion (Jacobsen et al., 1993).

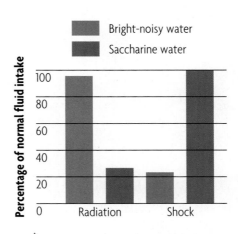

FIGURE 6.13

Inborn Bias

Results from Garcia and Koelling's study (1966) showed that rats possess an inborn bias to associate certain cues with certain outcomes. Rats avoided saccharin-flavored water when it predicted illness but not when it predicted shock. Conversely, rats avoided the "bright-noisy water" when it predicted shock but not when it predicted illness.

By showing that aversions are acquired through the mechanisms of classical conditioning, researchers can devise means to counteract them (Bernstein, 1991). Researchers have arranged, for example, for children with cancer not to be given meals just before chemotherapy. They've also created "scapegoat" aversions. The children are given candies or ice cream of unusual flavors to eat before the treatments so that the taste aversion becomes conditioned only to those special flavors and not to the flavors they generally like. Researchers have uncovered other aspects of patients' experiences of chemotherapy that are the product of classical conditioning. Many patients, for example, begin to experience nausea before the chemotherapy sessions—the clinic settings in which they receive treatment begin to function as a conditioned stimulus (Tomoyasu et al., 1996). (This effect should remind you

How have researchers used taste-aversion conditioning to prevent coyotes from killing sheep?

of the studies on drug tolerance.) Once again, understanding the roots of such effects in conditioning allows researchers to design treatments to counteract them.

You have now seen why modern behavior analysts must be attentive to the types of responses each species is best suited to learn (Todd & Morris, 1992). If you want to teach an old dog new tricks, you're best off adapting the tricks to the dog's genetic behavioral repertory! Our survey of learning is not complete, however, because we have not yet dealt with types of learning that might require more complex cognitive processes. We turn now to those types of learning.

PUT YOURSELF TO THE TEST

➤ In what circumstances might you observe instinctual drift?

➤ What makes taste-aversion learning unusual as a conditioned response?

➤ Why does taste aversion occur in circumstances of cancer treatment?

Cognitive Influences on Learning

Our reviews of classical and operant conditioning have demonstrated that a wide variety of behaviors can be understood as the products of simple learning processes. You might wonder, however, if there are certain classes of learning that require more complex, more cognitive types of processes. *Cognition* is any mental activity involved in the representation and processing of knowledge, such as thinking, remembering, perceiving, and language use. In this section, we look at forms of learning in animals and humans that cannot be explained only by principles of classical or operant conditioning. We suggest, therefore, that the behaviors are partially the product of cognitive processes.

◆ ANIMAL COGNITION

In this chapter, we have emphasized that, species-specific constraints aside, rules of learning acquired from research on rats and pigeons apply as well to dogs, monkeys, and humans. Researchers who study

animal cognition have demonstrated that it is not only classical and operant conditioning that generalizes across species (Wasserman, 1993, 1994). In his original formulation of the theory of evolution, Charles Darwin suggested that cognitive abilities evolved along with the physical forms of animals. In this section, we will describe two impressive types of animal performance that indicate further continuity in the cognitive capabilities of nonhuman and human animals.

COGNITIVE MAPS

Edward C. Tolman (1886–1959) pioneered the study of cognitive processes in learning by inventing experimental circumstances in which mechanical, one-to-one associations between specific stimuli and responses could not explain animals' observed behavior. Consider the maze shown in **Figure 6.14.** Tolman and his students demonstrated that, when an original goal path is blocked in a maze, a rat with prior experience in the

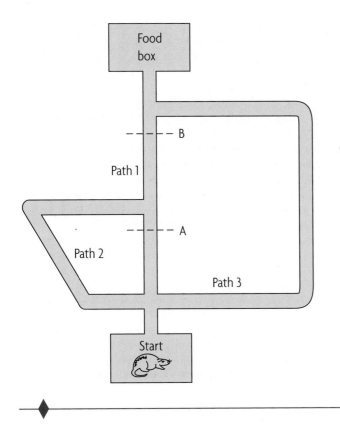

FIGURE 6.14

Use of Cognitive Maps in Maze Learning

Subjects preferred the direct path (Path 1) when it was open. With a block at A, they preferred Path 2. When a block was placed at B, the rats usually chose Path 3. Their behavior seemed to indicate that they had a cognitive map of the best way to get the food.

maze will take the shortest detour around the barrier, even though that particular response was never previously reinforced (Tolman & Honzik, 1930). The rats, therefore, behaved as if they were responding to an internal **cognitive map**—a representation of the overall layout of the maze—rather than blindly exploring different parts of the maze through trial and error (Tolman, 1948). Tolman's results showed that conditioning involves more than the simple formation of associations between sets of stimuli or between responses and reinforcers. It includes learning and representing other facets of the total behavioral context.

Research in Tolman's tradition has consistently demonstrated an impressive capacity for spatial memory in birds, bees, rats, humans, and other animals (Benhamou & Poucet, 1996; Olton, 1992). To understand the efficiency of spatial cognitive maps, consider the functions they serve (Poucet, 1993):

- Animals use spatial memory to recognize and identify features of their environments.
- Animals use spatial memory to find important goal objects in their environments.
- Animals use spatial memory to plan their route through an environment.

You can see these different functions of cognitive maps at work in the many species of birds that store food over a dispersed area but are able to recover that food with great accuracy when they need it:

> *Clark's nutcracker is the champion among food storers that have been studied. In the late summer, these birds bury up to 6,000 caches of pine seeds on mountainsides in the American Southwest. They recover the seeds as late as the next spring, when the cached food supports exceptionally early breeding. (Shettleworth, 1993, p. 180)*

The birds are not just roaming their environment and coming on the seeds through good fortune. They return, with up to 84 percent accuracy, to the thousands of locations at which they buried their seeds (Kamil & Balda, 1990). They are also able to discriminate sites that still have seeds from those that have been emptied (Kamil et al., 1993). Bird species that depend heavily on cached seeds for their food supply outperform other, even closely related, species on laboratory spatial memory tasks (Balda et al., 1997; Olson et al., 1995). No differences correlated with caching behavior are found when the species are compared on nonspatial memory tasks. Note that these birds' caching behaviors are not reinforced when they initially bury their seeds. Only if their cognitive maps remained accurate over the winter can they later recover the seeds and survive to reproduce.

The Far Side® by Gary Larson © 1986 FarWorks, Inc. All Rights Reserved. Used with permission.

© 1986 FarWorks, Inc. All Rights Reserved/Dist. by Creators Syndicate

"Stimulus, response! Stimulus, response!
Don't you ever *think?*"

CONCEPTUAL BEHAVIOR

We have seen that cognitive maps, in part, help animals preserve details of the spatial locations of objects in their environments. But what other cognitive processes can animals use to find structure, or categories of experiences, in the diverse stimuli they encounter in their environments? In Chapter 10, we will suggest that one of the challenges of language acquisition is for children to form generalizations about new *concepts* and *categories* they are learning, like the words *dog* and *tree*. Human children, however, are not the only animals capable of facing this challenge. Researchers have demonstrated that pigeons as well have the cognitive ability to make use of *conceptual* distinctions.

Pigeons Make Judgments Based on Category Structure

Edward Wasserman and his colleagues (1992) presented pigeons with color photographs of people, flowers, cars, and chairs. For each pigeon, the set of four concepts was divided into two larger categories (see **Figure 6.15**). For example, one pigeon might receive food if it pecked an orange key after viewing a person or a car and if it pecked a red key after viewing a flower or a chair. The pigeons learned to make the appropriate responses around 80 percent of the time or better. In a second training phase of the experiment, the pigeon was trained to provide a new response to the members of one smaller category from each of these larger categories. Thus, the pigeon might be required to peck a green key when it saw a person and a white key when it saw a chair. Once again, performance on this task was about 80 percent accurate or better.

Now what happens when the pigeons are shown a flower or a car and must choose between the green and white keys? They have no history of reinforcement that links these stimuli to these responses, so we can't predict behavior based on simple learning processes. But what would you do if we put you in this situation? In the first phase of the experiment, you would have learned that, for example, flowers and chairs go together. In the second phase of the experiment, you would have learned that you should provide one of two responses to each photo of a flower. When confronted with a chair, and the same choice of responses, you would probably try the response that had applied to flowers. That is, in fact, what pigeons largely did as well. On 60 to 70 percent of test trials, they used "category" information to emit a previously unreinforced behavior.

	Stimulus	Reinforced response
Training phase 1	People and cars	Orange key press
	Flowers and chairs	Red key press
Training phase 2	People	Green key press
	Chairs	White key press
	Stimulus	**Category response**
Test phase	Cars	Green key press
	Flowers	White key press

FIGURE 6.15

Concept Learning in Pigeons

The first training phase teaches the pigeons which concepts go together into the same larger category. The second training phase teaches a new response for one group within each category. The test phase demonstrates generalization to the other members of the newly acquired large categories. (This is one example of the different combinations of stimuli and responses presented to different pigeons.)

We already saw that generalization occurs in classical and operant conditioning based on the *perceptual similarity* of stimuli. In this experiment by Wasserman and colleagues, the generalization did not involve perceptual similarity—chairs and flowers, for example, don't look much alike. Instead, the grounds for generalization was the *cognitive similarity* brought about by the newly acquired conceptual structure. Further research suggests that pigeons are able to acquire the abstract concepts of *same* and *different:* They are able to produce distinctive responses when the elements of a test array are all the same (for example, 16 identical pictures of train engines) versus all different (for example, 16 varied pictures) (Young & Wasserman, 2001; Young et al., 1997).

We will devote Chapters 7 and 8 to an analysis of cognitive processes in humans. The experiments we have described here, however, should convince you that humans are not the only species with impressive and useful cognitive capabilities. Before we conclude this chapter, let's move to another type of learning that requires cognitive processes.

◆ OBSERVATIONAL LEARNING

To introduce this further type of learning, we'd like you to return for a moment to the comparison of rats' and humans' approaches to sampling new foods. The rats are almost certainly more cautious than you are, but that's largely because they are missing an invaluable source of information—input from other rats. When you try a new food, it's almost always in a context in which you have good reason to believe that other people have eaten and enjoyed the food. The probability of your "food-eating behavior" is thus influenced by your knowledge of patterns of reinforcement for other individuals. This example illustrates your capacity to learn via *vicarious reinforcement* and *vicarious punishment*. You can use your cognitive capacities for memory and reasoning to change your own behaviors in light of the experience of others.

In fact, much *social learning* occurs in situations where learning would not be predicted by traditional conditioning theory, because a learner has made no active response and has received no tangible reinforcer. The individual, after simply watching another person exhibiting behavior that was reinforced or punished, later behaves in much the same way, or refrains from doing so. This is known as **observational learning.** Cognition often enters into observational learning in the form of expectations. In essence, after observing a model, you may think: If I do exactly what she does, I will get the same reinforcer or avoid the same punisher. A younger child may be better behaved than his older sister because he has learned from the sister's mistakes.

This capacity to learn from watching as well as from doing is extremely useful. It enables you to acquire large, integrated patterns of behavior without going through the tedious trial-and-error process of gradually eliminating wrong responses and acquiring the right ones. You can profit immediately from the mistakes and successes of others. Researchers have demonstrated that observational learning is not special to humans. Among other species, pigeons (Zentall et al., 1996), zebra danio fish (Hall & Suboski, 1995), and even octopuses (Fiorito & Scotto, 1992) are capable of changing their behavior after observing the performance of another member of their species.

A classic demonstration of human observational learning occurred in the laboratory of **Albert Bandura.** After watching adult models punching, hitting, and kicking a large plastic BoBo doll, the children in the experiment later showed a greater frequency of the same behaviors than did children in control conditions who had not observed the aggressive models (Bandura et al., 1963). Subsequent studies showed that children imitated such behaviors just from watching filmed sequences of models, even when the models were cartoon characters.

There is little question now that we learn much—both prosocial (helping) and antisocial (hurting) behaviors—through observation of models, but there are many possible models in the world. What variables are important in determining which models will be most likely to influence you? Research has yielded the following general conclusions (Baldwin & Baldwin, 1973; Bandura, 1977). A model's observed behavior will be most influential when

- it is seen as having reinforcing consequences
- the model is perceived positively, liked, and respected
- there are perceived similarities between features and traits of the model and the observer
- the observer is rewarded for paying attention to the model's behavior
- the model's behavior is visible and salient—it stands out as a clear figure against the background of competing models
- it is within the observer's range of competence to imitate the behavior

To understand this list of findings, you should imagine yourself in modeling situations and see how each item in the list would apply. Imagine, for example, you are watching someone who is learning how to parachute jump. Or consider how someone might learn to be a "good" gang member by observing his or her friends.

Because people learn so efficiently from models, you can understand why a good deal of psychological research has been directed at the behavioral impact of television: Are viewers affected by what they see being rewarded and punished on TV? Attention has focused on the link between televised acts of violence—murder, rape, assault, robbery, terrorism, and suicide—and children's and adolescents' subsequent behavior. Does exposure to acts of violence foster imitation? The conclusion from psychological research is yes—it does for some people, and particularly in the United States (Comstock & Scharrer, 1999).

From top to bottom: Adult models aggression; boy imitates aggression; girl imitates aggression. What does this experiment demonstrate about the role models play in learning?

Childhood TV Viewing and Adult Aggression

This project began in 1977, when a team of researchers measured two years of television viewing for 557 children starting in either first or third grade. In particular, the researchers obtained measures of the extent to which the children watched TV shows with violent content. Fifteen years later, the researchers were able to conduct interviews with 329 of those children, who were now 20 to 22 years old (Huesmann et al., 2003). The researchers sought to determine whether there would be a relationship between the amount of television violence the individuals viewed in childhood and their level of aggression as young adults. Their adult level of aggression was measured both through their own self-reports and through the reports of others, such as spouses. As shown in **Figure 6.16**, the men and women who had watched the most violent TV as children also displayed the highest adult levels of aggression. These data suggest that early TV viewing of violence causes later aggression. You might wonder, however, if the causality works in the opposite direction: Could it be that the children destined to be aggressive were already more interested in violent content as children? Fortunately, the researchers collected data that allowed them to argue against this possibility. For example, the data found only a small relationship between childhood aggression and the individuals' viewing of TV violence as adults.

This study argues strongly that children who watch violent TV are at risk to become overly aggressive as adults.

Several decades of research have demonstrated three ways in which television violence has a negative impact on viewers' lives (Smith & Donnerstein, 1998). First, as we have just seen, the viewing of television violence brings about, through the mechanisms of observational learning, increases in aggressive behavior. This causal association has particularly important implications for children: Aggressive habits born of heavy television viewing early in life may serve as the basis for antisocial behavior later in life. Second, the viewing of television violence leads viewers to overestimate the occurrences of violence in the everyday world. Television viewers may be unduly afraid of becoming victims of real-world violence. Third, the viewing of television violence may

bring about *desensitization,* a reduction in both emotional arousal and distress at viewing violent behavior.

Note that research has also shown that children can learn prosocial, helping behaviors when they watch television programs that provide prosocial behavioral models (Rosenkoetter, 1999; Singer & Singer, 1990). You should take seriously the idea that children learn from the television they watch. As a parent or caretaker, you may want to help children select appropriate televised models.

An analysis of observational learning acknowledges both that principles of reinforcement influence behavior and that humans have the capacity to use their cognitive processes to change behaviors with vicarious rewards and punishment. This approach to the understanding of human behavior has proven very powerful. In Chapter 15, we will look at successful programs of therapy that have emerged from the cognitive modification of maladaptive patterns of behavior.

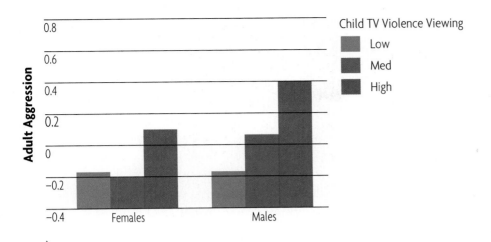

FIGURE 6.16

TV Violence and Aggression

For both men and women, those individuals who had viewed the most violent TV as children also displayed the most aggression as adults. The measure of aggression is a composite score that reflects the individuals' self-ratings and ratings of them by others. Higher scores indicate higher levels of aggression.

Why might observation of models encourage children to engage in prosocial behavior?

Let's close this chapter by calling back to mind a visit to a horror movie. How can behavior analysis explain your experiences? If you went to the movie because of a friend's recommendation, you have succumbed to vicarious reinforcement. If you made it to the theater, despite having to forgo your normal route, you have shown evidence of a cognitive map. If the sound of scary music made you fear for the hero's well-being, you felt the effects of classical conditioning. If your failure to enjoy the film made you vow never to see a horror movie again, you have discovered the effect a punisher has on your subsequent behavior.

Are you ready to return to the theater?

PUT YOURSELF TO THE TEST

- What conclusions have researchers drawn from Tolman's pioneering research?
- Why do some species have spatial memory that is particularly well developed?
- What evidence suggests that pigeons can make conceptual distinctions?
- In what circumstances do vicarious reinforcement and punishment operate?
- What mechanisms explain why viewing of TV violence might be a cause of aggressive behavior?

Recapping Main Points

THE STUDY OF LEARNING

- Learning entails a relatively consistent change in behavior or behavior potential based on experience.
- Behaviorists believe that much behavior can be explained by simple learning processes.
- They also believe that many of the same principles of learning apply to all organisms.

CLASSICAL CONDITIONING: LEARNING PREDICTABLE SIGNALS

- In classical conditioning, first investigated by Pavlov, an unconditioned stimulus (UCS) elicits an unconditioned response (UCR). A neutral stimulus paired with the UCS becomes a conditioned stimulus (CS), which elicits a response, called the conditioned response (CR).
- Extinction occurs when the UCS no longer follows the CS.
- Stimulus generalization is the phenomenon whereby stimuli similar to the CS elicit the CR.
- Discrimination learning narrows the range of CSs to which an organism responds.
- For classical conditioning to occur, there must be a contingent and informative relationship between the CS and UCS.
- Classical conditioning explains many emotional responses and drug tolerance.

OPERANT CONDITIONING: LEARNING ABOUT CONSEQUENCES

- Thorndike demonstrated that behaviors that bring about satisfying outcomes tend to be repeated.
- Skinner's behavior analytic approach centers on manipulating contingencies of reinforcement and observing the effects on behavior.
- Behaviors are made more likely by positive and negative reinforcement. They are made less likely by positive and negative punishment.

- Contextually appropriate behavior is explained by the three-term contingency of discriminative stimulus-behavior-consequence.
- Primary reinforcers are stimuli that function as reinforcers even when an organism has not had previous experience with them. Conditioned reinforcers are acquired by association with primary reinforcers.
- Probable activities function as positive reinforcers.
- Behavior is affected by schedules of reinforcement that may be varied or fixed and delivered in intervals or in ratios.
- Complex responses may be learned through shaping.

BIOLOGY AND LEARNING

- Research suggests that learning may be constrained by the species-specific repertoires of different organisms.
- Instinctual drift may overwhelm some response–reinforcement learning.
- Taste-aversion learning suggests that species are genetically prepared for some forms of associations.

COGNITIVE INFLUENCES ON LEARNING

- Some forms of learning reflect more complex processes than those of classical or operant conditioning.
- Animals develop cognitive maps to enable them to function in a complex environment.
- Conceptual behavior allows animals to form generalizations about the structure of the environment.
- Behaviors can be vicariously reinforced or punished. Humans and other animals can learn through observation.

<www.ablongman.com/gerrig17e>

KEY TERMS

acquisition (p. 174)

animal cognition (p. 197)

behavior analysis (p. 171)

biological constraints on learning
(p. 193)

classical conditioning (p. 172)

cognitive map (p. 197)

conditioned reinforcers (p. 187)

conditioned response (CR) (p. 173)

conditioned stimulus (CS) (p. 173)

conditioning (p. 169)

discriminative stimuli (p. 184)

extinction (p. 175)

fixed-interval schedule (p. 191)

fixed-ratio schedule (p. 191)

instinctual drift (p. 193)

law of effect (p. 182)

learning (p. 170)

learning-performance distinction
(p. 170)

negative punishment (p. 184)

negative reinforcement (p. 183)

observational learning (p. 199)

operant (p. 182)

operant conditioning (p. 182)

operant extinction (p. 184)

partial reinforcement effect (p. 191)

positive punishment (p. 184)

positive reinforcement (p. 183)

primary reinforcers (p. 187)

punisher (p. 184)

reflex (p. 173)

reinforcer (p. 183)

reinforcement contingency (p. 183)

schedules of reinforcement (p. 191)

shaping by successive approximations
(p. 192)

spontaneous recovery (p. 175)

stimulus discrimination (p. 177)

stimulus generalization (p. 176)

taste-aversion learning (p. 194)

three-term contingency (p. 184)

unconditioned response (UCR)
(p. 173)

unconditioned stimulus (UCS)
(p. 173)

variable-interval schedule (p. 192)

variable-ratio schedule (p. 191)

Memory

As you begin this chapter on memory processes, we'd like you to take a moment to recover your own earliest memory. How long ago did the memory originate? How vivid a scene do you recall? Has your memory been influenced by other people's recollections of the same event?

Now, a slightly different exercise. We'd like you to imagine what it would be like if you suddenly had no memory of your past—of the people you have known or of events that have happened to you. You wouldn't remember your mother's face, or your tenth birthday, or your senior prom. Without such "time anchors," how would you maintain a sense of who you are—of your self-identity? Or suppose you lost the ability to form any new memories. What would happen to your most recent experiences? Could you follow a conversation or untangle the plot of a TV show? Everything would vanish, as if events had never existed, as if you had never had any thoughts in mind. Is there any activity you can think of that is not influenced by memory?

If you have never given much thought to your memory, it's probably because it tends to do its job reasonably well—you take it for granted, alongside other bodily processes, like digestion or breathing. But as with stomachaches or allergies, the times you notice your memory are likely to be the times when something goes wrong: You forget your car keys, an important date, lines in a play, or the answer to an examination question that you know you "really knew." There's no reason you shouldn't find these occasions irritating, but you should also reflect for a moment on the estimate that the average human brain can store 100 trillion bits of information. The task of managing such a vast array of information is a formidable one. Perhaps you shouldn't be too surprised when an answer is sometimes not available when you need it!

Our goal in this chapter is to explain how you usually remember so much, and why you forget some of what you have known. We will explore how you get your everyday experiences into and out of memory. You will learn what psychology has discovered about different types of memories and about how those memories work. We hope that in the course of learning the many facts of memory, you will gain an appreciation for how wonderful memory is.

How are actors and actresses able to remember all the different aspects—movements, expressions, and words—of their performances?

One last thing: Because this is a chapter on memory, we're going to put your memory immediately to work. We'd like you to remember the number 43. Do whatever you need to do to remember 43. And yes, there will be a test!

What Is Memory?

To begin, we will define **memory** as the capacity to store and retrieve information. In this chapter, we will describe memory as a type of *information processing*. The bulk of our attention, therefore, will be trained on the flow of information in and out of your memory systems. Our examination of the processes that guide the acquisition and retrieval of information will enable you to refine your sense of what *memory* means. Our discussion starts with the earliest formal body of research on memory, published in 1885. We will then introduce you to distinctions among types of memories, carved out by contemporary researchers.

◆ EBBINGHAUS QUANTIFIES MEMORY

See if this statement rings true: "Facts crammed at examination time soon vanish, if they were not sufficiently grounded by other study and later subjected to a sufficient review." In other words, if you cram for a test, you're not likely to remember very much a few days later. This astute, and very contemporary, observation was made in 1885 by the German psychologist **Hermann Ebbinghaus,** who outlined a series of such phenomena to motivate his new science of memory. Ebbinghaus's observations added up to a convincing argument in favor of an empirical investigation of memory. What was needed was a methodology, and Ebbinghaus invented a brilliant one. Ebbinghaus used nonsense syllables—meaningless three-letter units consisting of a vowel between two consonants, such as *CEG* or *DAX.* He used nonsense syllables, rather than meaningful words, like DOG, because he hoped to obtain a "pure" measure of memory—one uncontaminated by previous learning or associations that a person might bring to the experimental memory task. Not only was Ebbinghaus the researcher, he was also his own subject. He performed the research tasks himself and measured his own performance. The task he assigned himself was memorization of lists of varying length. Ebbinghaus chose to use *rote learning,* memorization by mechanical repetition, to perform the task.

<www.ablongman.com/gerrig17e>

Ebbinghaus started his studies by reading through the items one at a time until he finished the list. Then he read through the list again in the same order, and again, until he could recite all the items in the correct order—the *criterion performance*. Then he distracted himself from rehearsing the original list by forcing himself to learn many other lists. After this interval, Ebbinghaus measured his memory by seeing how many trials it took him to *relearn* the original list. If he needed fewer trials to relearn it than he had needed to learn it initially, information had been *saved* from his original study. (This concept should be familiar from Chapter 6. Recall that there is often a savings when animals relearn a conditioned response.)

Ebbinghaus's Forgetting Curve

For example, if Ebbinghaus took 12 trials to learn a list and 9 trials to relearn it several days later, his savings score for that elapsed time would be 25 percent (12 trials – 9 trials = 3 trials; 3 trials ÷ 12 trials = 0.25, or 25 percent). Using savings as his measure, Ebbinghaus recorded the degree of memory retained after different time intervals. The curve he obtained is shown in **Figure 7.1**. As you can see, he found a rapid initial loss of memory, followed by a gradually declining rate of loss. Ebbinghaus's curve is typical of results from experiments on rote learning.

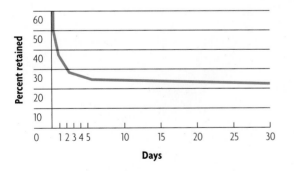

FIGURE 7.1

Ebbinghaus's Forgetting Curve

The curve shows how many nonsense syllables are remembered by individuals using the savings method when tested over a 30-day period. The curve decreases rapidly and then reaches a plateau of little change.

Following Ebbinghaus's lead, psychologists studied verbal learning for many decades by observing participants attempting to learn and recall nonsense syllables. By studying memory in as "pure" a form as possible, uncontaminated by meaning, researchers hoped to find basic principles that would shed light on more complex examples of remembering. Researchers still aspire to discover those basic principles, but they have also turned to the study of memory for meaningful material—the type of information you commit to memory on a day-to-day basis.

◆ TYPES OF MEMORIES

When you think about memory, what is most likely to come to mind at first are situations in which you use your memory to recall (or try to recall) specific events or information: your favorite movie, the dates of World War II, or your student ID number. In fact, one of the important functions of memory is to allow you to have conscious access to the personal and collective past. But memory does much more for you than that. It also enables you to have effortless continuity of experience from one day to the next. When you drive in a car, for example, it is this second function of memory that makes the stores along the roadside seem familiar. In defining types of memories, we will make plain to you how hard your memory works to fulfill these functions, often outside of conscious awareness.

IMPLICIT AND EXPLICIT MEMORY

Consider **Figure 7.2.** What's wrong with this picture? It probably strikes you as unusual that there's a bunny rabbit in the kitchen. But where does this feeling come from? You probably didn't go through the objects in the picture one by one and ask yourself, "Does the refrigerator belong?" "Do the cabinets belong?" Rather, the rabbit jumps out at you as being out of place.

This simple example allows you to understand the difference between **explicit** and **implicit uses of memory.** Your discovery of the rabbit is implicit, because your memory processes brought past knowledge of kitchens to bear on your interpretation of the picture without any particular effort on your part. Suppose now we asked you, "What's missing from the picture?" To answer this second question, you probably have to put explicit memory to work. What appears in the typical kitchen? What's missing? (Did you think of the sink or the stove?) Thus, when it comes to using knowledge stored in memory, sometimes the use will be implicit—the information becomes available without any conscious effort—and sometimes it will be explicit—you make a conscious effort to recover the information.

We can make the same distinction when it comes to the initial acquisition of memories. How do you

Did you think right away, "What's a bunny doing in the kitchen?" If the bunny immediately jumped out at you, it is because your memory processes performed an analysis of the scene outside of consciousness and delivered the bunny as the odd element.

know what should appear in a kitchen? Did you ever memorize a list of what appears there and what the appropriate configuration should be? Probably not. Rather, it's likely that you acquired most of this knowledge without conscious effort. By contrast, you probably learned the names of many of the objects in the room explicitly. As we shall see in Chapter 10, to learn the association between words and experiences, your younger self needed to engage in explicit memory processes. You learned the word *refrigerator* because someone called your explicit attention to the name of that object.

The distinction between implicit and explicit memory greatly expands the range of questions researchers must address about memory processes (Bowers & Marsolek, 2003; Buchner & Wippich, 2000). In the tradition established by Ebbinghaus, most research concerned the explicit acquisition of information. Experimenters most frequently provided participants with new information to retain, and theories of memory were directed to explaining what participants could and could not remember under those circumstances. However, as you will see in this chapter, researchers have now devised methods for studying implicit memory as well. Thus, we can give you a more complete account of the variety of uses to which you put your memory. We can acknowledge that most circumstances in which you encode or retrieve information represent a mix of implicit and explicit uses of memory. Let's turn now to a second dimension along which memories are distributed.

DECLARATIVE AND PROCEDURAL MEMORY

Can you whistle? Go ahead and try. Or if you can't whistle, try snapping your fingers. What kind of memory allows you to do these sorts of things? You probably

remember having to learn these skills, but now they seem effortless. The examples we gave before of both implicit and explicit memories all involved the recollection of *facts* and *events,* which is called **declarative memory.** Now we see that you also have memories for *how to do things,* which is called **procedural memory.** Because the bulk of this chapter will be focused on how

◆

Why does pretending to dial a phone number help you to remember it?

you acquire and use facts, let's take a moment now to consider how you acquire the ability to do things.

Procedural memory refers to the way you remember how things get done. It is used to acquire, retain, and employ perceptual, cognitive, and motor skills. Theories of procedural memory most often concern themselves with the time course of learning (Anderson, 1996; Anderson et al., 1999): How do you go from a conscious list of declarative facts about some activity to unconscious, automatic performance of that same activity? And why is it that after learning a skill, you often find it difficult to go back and talk about the component declarative facts?

We can see these phenomena at work in even the very simple activity of dialing a phone number that, over time, has become highly familiar. At first, you probably had to think your way through each digit, one at a time. You had to work through a list of declarative facts:

> First, I must dial 2,
>
> Next, I must dial 0,
>
> Then I dial 7,
>
> and so on.

However, when you began to dial the number often enough, you could start to produce it as one unit—a swift sequence of actions on the touch-tone pad. The process at work is called *knowledge compilation* (Anderson, 1987). As a consequence of practice, you are able to carry out longer sequences of the activity without conscious intervention. But you also don't have conscious access to the content of these compiled units: Back at the telephone, it's not uncommon to find someone who can't actually remember the phone number without pretending to dial it. In general, knowledge compilation makes it hard to share your procedural knowledge with others. You may have noticed this if your parents tried to teach you to drive. Although they may be good drivers themselves, they may not have been very good at communicating the content of compiled good-driving procedures.

You may also have noticed that knowledge compilation can lead to errors. If you are a skilled typist, you've probably suffered from the *the* problem: As soon as you hit the *t* and the *h* keys, your finger may fly to the *e*, even if you're really trying to type *throne* or *thistle*. Once you have sufficiently committed the execution of *the* to procedural memory, you can do little else but finish the sequence. Without procedural memory, life would be extremely laborious—you would be doomed to go step by step through every activity. However, each time you mistakenly type *the,* you can reflect on the trade-off between efficiency and potential error. Let's continue now to an overview of the basic processes that apply to all these different types of memory.

◆ AN OVERVIEW OF MEMORY PROCESSES

No matter what the category of memory, being able to use knowledge at some later time requires the operation of three mental processes: encoding, storage, and retrieval. **Encoding** is the initial processing of information that leads to a representation in memory. **Storage** is the retention over time of encoded material. **Retrieval** is the recovery at a later time of the stored information. Simply put, encoding gets information in, storage holds it until you need it, and retrieval gets it out. Let's now expand on these ideas.

Encoding requires that you form *mental representations* of information from the external world. You can understand the idea of mental representations if we draw an analogy to representations outside your head. Imagine we wanted to know something about the best gift you got at your last birthday party. (Let's suppose it's not something you have with you.) What could you do to inform us about the gift? You might describe the properties of the object. Or you might draw us a picture. Or you might pretend that you're using the object. In each case, these are representations of the original object. Although none of the representations is likely to be quite as good as having the real thing present, they should allow us to acquire knowledge of the most important aspects of the gift. Mental representations work much the same way. They preserve important features of past experiences in a way that enables you to *re-present* those experiences to yourself.

If information is properly encoded, it will be retained in *storage* over some period of time. Storage requires both short- and long-term changes in the structures of your brain. At the end of the chapter, we will see how researchers are attempting to locate the brain structures that are responsible for storing new and old memories. We will also see what happens in cases of extreme amnesia, where individuals become incapable of storing new memories.

Retrieval is the payoff for all your earlier effort. When it works, it enables you to gain access—often in a split second—to information you stored earlier. Can you remember what comes before storage: decoding or encoding? The answer is simple to retrieve now, but will you still be able to retrieve the concept of encoding as swiftly and with as much confidence when you are tested on this chapter's contents days or weeks from now? Discovering how you are able to retrieve one specific bit of information from the vast quantity of information in your memory storehouse is a challenge facing psychologists who want to know how memory works and how it can be improved.

Although it is easy to define encoding, storage, and retrieval as separate memory processes, the interaction among the three processes is quite complex. For example, to be able to encode the information that you have seen a tiger, you must first retrieve from memory information about the concept *tiger*. Similarly, to commit to memory the meaning of a sentence such as "He's as honest as Benedict Arnold," you must retrieve the meanings of each individual word, retrieve the rules of grammar that specify how word meanings should be combined in English, and retrieve cultural information that specifies exactly how honest Benedict Arnold—a famous Revolutionary War traitor—was.

We are now ready to look in more detail at the encoding, storage, and retrieval of information. Our discussion will start with short-lived types of memories, beginning with sensory memory, and then move to the more permanent forms of long-term memory (see **Figure 7.3**). We will give you an account of how you remember and why you forget. Our plan is to make you forever self-conscious about all the ways in which you use your capacity for memory. We hope this will even allow you to improve some aspects of your memory skills.

PUT YOURSELF TO THE TEST

- What important contributions did Ebbinghaus make to memory research?

- What makes uses of memory explicit versus implicit?

- What types of memories are declarative versus procedural?

- What are the relationships among encoding, storage, and retrieval?

Sensory Memory

Let's begin with a demonstration of the impermanence of some memories. In **Figure 7.4** we have provided you with a reasonably busy visual scene. We'd like you to take a quick look at it—about 10 seconds—and then cover it up. Suppose we now ask you a series of questions about the scene:

1. What tool is the little boy at the bottom holding?
2. What is the middle man at the top doing?
3. In the lower right-hand corner, does the woman's umbrella handle hook to the left or to the right?

To answer these questions, wouldn't you be more comfortable if you could go back and have an extra peek at the picture?

Fortunately, the opportunity to have an "extra peek" at the sensory world is built into your memory processes through the operation of **sensory memory** systems: Each sensory memory preserves accurate representations of the physical features of sensory stimuli for a few seconds or less. These memories extend the availability of information acquired from the environment. To make this idea more concrete for you, we will describe research on sensory memory for vision and hearing.

◆ ICONIC MEMORY

Researchers have labeled sensory memory in the visual domain **iconic memory** (Neisser, 1967). Iconic memory allows very large amounts of information to be stored for very brief durations. A visual memory, or icon, lasts about half a second. Iconic memory was first revealed in experiments that required participants to retrieve information from visual displays that were exposed for only one-twentieth of a second.

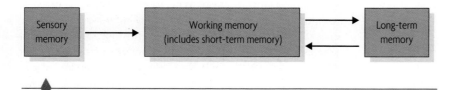

FIGURE 7.3
The Flow of Information In and Out of Long-Term Memory

Memory theories describe the flow of information to and from long-term memory. The theories address initial encodings of information in sensory and working memory, the transfer of information into long-term memory for storage, and the transfer of information from long-term memory to working memory for retrieval.

<www.ablongman.com/gerrig17e>

How Much Can You Remember from This Scene?

After viewing this scene for about 10 seconds, cover it up and try to answer the questions in the text. Under ordinary circumstances, iconic memory preserves a glimpse of the visual world for a brief time after the scene has been removed.

CLASSIC

PUTTING IDEAS TO THE TEST

Iconic Memory

George Sperling (1960, 1963) presented participants with arrays of three rows of letters and numbers.

> 7 1 V F
> X L 5 3
> B 4 W 7

Participants were asked to perform two different tasks. In a *whole-report procedure*, they tried to recall as many of the items in the display as possible. Typically, they could report only about four items. Other participants underwent a *partial-report proce-dure*, which required them to report only one row rather than the whole pattern. A signal of a high, medium, or low tone was sounded immediately after the presentation to indicate which row the participants were to report. Sperling found that regardless of which row he asked for, the participants' recall was quite high.

Because participants could accurately report any of the three rows in response to a tone, Sperling concluded that all of the information in the display must have gotten into iconic memory. That is evidence for its large capacity. At the same time, the difference between the whole- and partial-report procedures suggests that the information fades rapidly: The participants in the whole-report procedure were unable to recall all the information present in the icon. This second point was reinforced by experiments in which the identification signal was slightly delayed. **Figure 7.5** shows that as the delay interval increases from zero seconds to one second, the number of items accurately reported declines steadily. Researchers have measured quite accurately the time course with which information must be transferred from the fading icon (Becher et al., 2000; Gegenfurtner & Sperling, 1993). To take advantage of the "extra peek" at the visual world, your memory processes must very quickly transfer information to more durable stores.

Note that iconic memory is not the same as the "photographic memory" that some people claim to

FIGURE 7.5

Recall by the Partial-Report Method

The solid line shows the average number of items recalled using the partial-report method, both immediately after presentation and at four later times. For comparison, the dotted line shows the number of items recalled by the whole-report method. (Adapted from Sperling, 1960.)

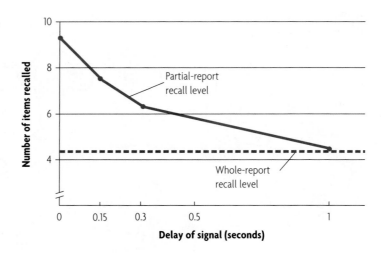

have. The technical term for "photographic memory" is *eidetic imagery:* People who experience eidetic imagery are able to recall the details of a picture, for periods of time considerably longer than iconic memory, as if they were still looking at a photograph. "People" in this case really means children: Researchers have estimated that roughly 8 percent of preadolescent children are eidetickers, but virtually no adults (Neath, 1998). No satisfactory theory has been proposed for why eidetic imagery fades over time (Crowder, 1992). However, if you are reading this book as a high school or college student, you almost certainly have iconic memory but not eidetic images.

◆ ECHOIC MEMORY

Sensory memory for sounds is called **echoic memory.** Just like iconic memory, echoic memory briefly preserves more information than participants can report before it fades away (Crowder & Morton, 1969; Darwin et al., 1972). Echoic memories, however, last longer than iconic memories, perhaps for as long as 5 to 10 seconds. The longer duration of echoic memories may be related to the way in which sounds unfold over time. For example, when you are trying to understand a spoken sentence, increments of sound arrive at your ear one after the other. Echoic memory may help you to gather those increments into coherent wholes.

Research on echoic memory has illustrated another important property of sensory memories: They are easily displaced by new information. If someone reads a list of words to you, each new word will displace the former word in echoic memory. Researchers originally believed that the *physical* similarity of sounds determined whether one stimulus would displace another in echoic memory (Crowder, 1976). However, we know now that the way a listener categorizes an auditory

stimulus also matters (Ayres et al., 1979). As you listen to the world, you divide the stream of information arriving at your ears into units—you determine which sounds go together to form a whole. Echoic memory depends on how you group auditory experiences (LeCompte & Watkins, 1995).

PUTTING IDEAS TO THE TEST

Categorization Influences Echoic Memory

Students participated in a memory experiment in which lists of letters were followed by a *suffix.* The suffix was always the same physical stimulus—it sounded like a sheep's *baa.* However, in one case, participants were led to believe that it was genuinely an animal sound, while in another case, participants believed that it was a *baa* produced by a human trying to sound like a sheep (as it really was). The suffix served to displace information in echoic memory only when the participants believed it to be produced by a human (Neath et al., 1993).

Remember that the actual physical sound was the same in both cases. But only when the participants categorized the list (letters read by a human) and the *baa* (a noise produced by the human) in the same way was echoic memory disrupted. Thus, even at the earliest stages of the encoding and storage of memories, your *interpretation* of the world becomes important.

You might wonder why sensory memories have the two basic properties of being short-lived and easily displaced. The answer is that these properties fit the facts of your interactions with the environment. You are constantly experiencing new visual and auditory stimula-

<www.ablongman.com/gerrig17e>

tion. This new information must also be processed. Sensory memories are durable enough to give you a sense of the continuity of your world but not sufficiently strong to interfere with new sensory impressions. We now turn to the types of memory processes that enable you to form more durable memories.

PUT YOURSELF TO THE TEST

➤ What is the major purpose of sensory memories?
➤ What have researchers learned about the capacity and duration of iconic memory?
➤ Why are most echoic memories so easily displaced?

Short-Term Memory and Working Memory

Before you began to read this chapter, you may not have been aware that you had iconic or echoic memory. It is very likely, however, that you were aware that there are some memories that you possess only for the short term. Consider the common occurrence of consulting a telephone book to find a friend's number and then remembering the number just long enough to dial it. If the number turns up busy, you often have to go right back to the phone book. When you consider this experience, it's easy to understand why researchers have hypothesized a special type of memory called **short-term memory (STM).**

You shouldn't think of short-term memory as a particular place that memories go to, but rather as a built-in mechanism for focusing cognitive resources on some small set of mental representations (Cowan, 1993; Shiffrin, 1993). But the resources of STM are fickle. As even your experience with phone numbers shows, you have to take some special care to ensure that memories become encoded into more permanent forms. We will largely focus on the types of short-term memory resources that lead to the acquisition of explicit memories. This focus is necessary because researchers have only just begun to study short-term representations for implicit memories (McKone & Trynes, 1999). Preliminary findings suggest that implicit memories may also pass through a state in which they draw extra short-term resources before passing into more long-term forms of memory.

In this section, we also consider a broader concept of the types of memory processes that provide a foundation for the moment-by-moment fluidity of thought and action: **working memory.** As we shall see, working memory is the memory resource that you use to accomplish tasks such as reasoning and language comprehension. Suppose you are trying to remember a phone number while you search for a pencil and pad, to write it down. Whereas your short-term memory processes allow you to keep the number in mind, your more general working memory resource allows you to execute the mental operations to accomplish an efficient search. Let's begin with short-term memory.

◆ THE CAPACITY LIMITATIONS OF STM

The major features of short-term memories are an immediate consequence of the vast amount of information you could potentially make the focus of consciousness. There is always a great amount of new information available. In Chapter 4, we described how your attentional resources are devoted to selecting the objects and events in the external world on which you will expend your mental resources. Just as there are limits on your capacity to attend to more than a small sample of the available information, there are limits on your ability to keep more than a small sample of information active in STM. The limited capacity of STM enforces a sharp focus of mental attention.

To estimate the capacity of STM, researchers at first turned to tests of *memory span*. At some point in your life, you have probably been asked to carry out a task like this one:

> Read the following list of random numbers once, cover them, and write down as many as you can in the order they appear.
>
> 8 1 7 3 4 9 4 2 8 5
>
> How many did you get correct?
>
> Now read the next list of random letters and perform the same memory test.
>
> J M R S O F L P T Z B
>
> How many did you get correct?

If you are like most individuals, you probably could recall somewhere in the range of five to nine items. **George Miller** (1956) suggested that seven (plus or minus two) was the "magic number" that characterized people's memory performance on random lists of letters, words, numbers, or almost any kind of meaningful, familiar item.

Tests of memory span, however, overestimate the true capacity of STM because participants are able to use other sources of information to carry out the task. Remember, for example, that echoic memory will help you to improve your recall on the last few items of a list that is read aloud (at least if there is no suffix). When other sources of memory are factored out, researchers have estimated the pure contribution of STM to your seven (or so) item memory span to be only between two and four items (Crowder, 1976). But if that's all the capacity you have to commence the acquisition of new memories, why don't you notice your limitations more often?

◆ ACCOMMODATING TO STM CAPACITY

Despite the capacity limitations of STM, you function efficiently for at least two reasons. First, the encoding of information in STM can be enhanced through rehearsal and chunking. Second, the retrieval of information from STM is quite rapid.

REHEARSAL

You probably know that a good way to keep your friend's telephone number in mind is to keep repeating the digits in a cycle in your head. This memorization technique is called *maintenance rehearsal*. The fate of unrehearsed information was demonstrated in an ingenious experiment.

Without Rehearsal, Short-Term Memory Fades

Participants heard three consonants, such as F, C, and V. They had to recall those consonants when given a signal after a variable interval of time, ranging from 3 to 18 seconds. To prevent rehearsal, a *distractor task* was put between the stimulus input and the recall signal—the participants were given a three-digit number and told to count backward from it by 3's until the recall signal was presented. Many different consonant sets were given, and several short delays were used over a series of trials with a number of participants.

As shown in **Figure 7.6**, recall became increasingly poorer as the time required to retain the information became longer. After even 3 seconds, there was considerable memory loss, and by 18 seconds, loss was nearly total. In the absence of an opportunity to rehearse the information, short-term recall was impaired with the passage of time (Peterson & Peterson, 1959).

Performance suffered because information could not be rehearsed. It also suffered because of interference from the competing information of the distractor task.

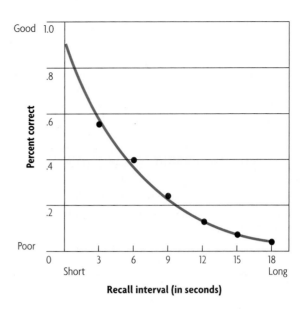

◆

FIGURE 7.6

Short-Term Memory Recall Without Rehearsal

When the interval between stimulus presentation and recall was filled with a distracting task, recall became poorer as the interval grew longer.

What role does short-term memory play when you punch in your ATM password?

(We will discuss interference as a cause of forgetting later in this chapter.) You may have noticed how often a new acquaintance says his or her name—and then you immediately forget it. One of the most common reasons for this is that you are distracted from performing the type of rehearsal you need to carry out to acquire a new memory. As a remedy, try to encode and rehearse a new name carefully before you continue with a conversation.

Our conclusion so far is that rehearsal will help you to keep information from fading out of STM. But suppose the information you wish to acquire is, at least at first, too cumbersome to be rehearsed? You might turn to the strategy of chunking.

CHUNKING

A *chunk* is a meaningful unit of information (Anderson, 1996). A chunk can be a single letter or number, a group of letters or other items, or even a group of words or an entire sentence. For example, the sequence 1–9–8–4 consists of four digits that could exhaust your STM capacity. However, if you see the digits as a year or the title of George Orwell's book *1984,* they constitute only one chunk, leaving you much more capacity for other chunks of information. **Chunking** is the process of reconfiguring items by grouping them on the basis of similarity or some other organizing principle, or by combining them into larger patterns based on information stored in long-term memory (Baddeley, 1994).

See how many chunks you find in this sequence of 20 numbers: 19411917186518121776. You can answer "20" if you see the sequence as a list of unrelated digits, or "5" if you break down the sequence into the dates of major wars in U.S. history. If you do the latter, it's easy for you to recall all the digits in proper sequence after one quick glance. It would be impossible for you to remember them all from a short exposure if you saw them as 20 unrelated items.

Your memory span can always be greatly increased if you can discover ways to organize an available body of information into smaller chunks. A famous subject, S. F., was able to memorize 84 digits by grouping them as racing times (S. F. was an avid runner):

The Benefits of Chunking

S. F.'s memory protocols provided the key to his mental wizardry. Because he was a long-distance runner, S. F. noticed that many of the random numbers could be grouped into running times for different distances. For instance, he would recode the sequence 3, 4, 9, 2, 5, 6, 1, 4, 9, 3, 5 as 3:49.2, near record mile; 56:14, 10-mile time; 9:35, slow 2 miles. Later, S. F. also used ages, years of memorable events, and special numerical patterns to chunk the random digits. In this way, he was able to use his long-term memory to convert long strings of random input into manageable and meaningful chunks. S. F.'s memory for letters was still about average, however, because he had not developed any chunking strategies to recall alphabet strings (Chase & Ericsson, 1981; Ericsson & Chase, 1982).

Like S. F., you can structure incoming information according to its personal meaning to you (linking it to the ages of friends and relatives, for example); or you can match new stimuli with various codes that have

How can you put chunking to good use while listening to a lecture?

been stored in your long-term memory. Even if you can't link new stimuli to rules, meanings, or codes in your long-term memory, you can still use chunking. You can simply group the items in a rhythmical pattern or temporal group (181379256460 could become 181, pause, 379, pause, 256, pause, 460). You know from everyday experience that this grouping principle works well for remembering telephone numbers.

RETRIEVAL FROM STM

Rehearsal and chunking both relate to the way in which you encode information to enhance the probability that it will remain or fit in STM. Even without these strategic measures, however, it turns out that retrieval from STM is very efficient. In a series of classic studies, **Saul Sternberg** (1966, 1969) invented a task that enabled him to demonstrate the great speed with which participants could assess which information was in short-term focus.

CLASSIC
PUTTING IDEAS TO THE TEST

Efficient Retrieval from STM

On each of many trials, participants were given a memory set consisting of from one to six items—for instance, the digits 5, 2, 9, 4, and 6. From trial to trial, the list would vary in terms of which digits and how many were shown. After presenting each set, Sternberg immediately offered a single test "probe"—a digit that the participants would determine either had or had not been a part of the memory set just shown. The dependent variable was *speed of recognition*. How quickly could participants press a *yes* button to indicate that they had seen the test item in the memory set or a *no* button to indicate they were sure that they had not seen it? Sternberg calculated that it took about 400 milliseconds to encode the test stimulus and make a response and then about 35 milliseconds more to compare the stimulus to each item in the memory set. In a single second, a person could make about 30 such comparisons. Retrieval from STM proved to be extremely efficient.

Although different theories have been offered to explain Sternberg's results (Ratcliff, 1978; Townsend, 1971, 1990), they all agree that retrieval from STM is very swift. Let's draw some conclusions from this finding by making an analogy to a vast research library. Given the abundance of volumes in the library (the abundance of sensory impressions available to you), you would probably be dismayed to discover that the library allowed you to borrow only three books at any given time (the limitations of STM). But suppose each patron could access the information in a book with lightning speed (the speed of retrieval from STM). With this high level of performance, you would use the library and only rarely become aware of the three-book rule. Your short-term memory provides the same trade-off between capacity and efficiency of processing.

◆ WORKING MEMORY

Our focus so far has been on short-term memory, and specifically the role that STM plays in the explicit acquisition of new memories. However, as we suggested earlier, you need more memory resources on a moment-by-moment basis than those that allow you to acquire facts. For example, you also need to be able to retrieve preexisting memories. At the start of this chapter, we asked you to commit a number to memory. Can you remember now what it was? If you can remember (if not, peek), you have made your mental representation of that memory active once more—that's another memory function. If we ask you to do something more complicated—suppose we ask you to toss a ball from hand to hand while you count backwards by 3's from 132—you'll put even more demands on your memory resources. Based on an analysis of the memory *functions* you require to navigate through life, researchers have articulated theories of working memory that subsume the "classic" short-term memory (Healy & McNamara, 1996). **Alan Baddeley** and his colleagues (Baddeley, 1986, 1992; Baddeley & Andrade, 2000) have provided evidence for three components of working memory:

- A *phonological loop*. This resource holds and manipulates speech-based information. The phonological loop overlaps most with short-term memory, as we have described it in the earlier sections. When you rehearse a telephone number by "listening" to it as you run it through your head, you are making use of the phonological loop.

- A *visuospatial sketchpad*. This resource performs the same types of functions as the phonological loop for visual and spatial information. If, for example, someone asked you how many desks there are in your psychology classroom, you might use the resources of the visuospatial sketchpad to form a mental picture of the classroom and then estimate the number of desks from that picture.

- The *central executive*. This resource is responsible for controlling attention and coordinating information from the phonological loop and the visuospatial sketchpad. Any time you carry out a task that requires a combination of mental processes— imagine, for example, you are asked to describe a picture from memory—you rely on the central executive function to apportion your mental

<www.ablongman.com/gerrig17e>

In what ways is retrieval from STM analogous to retrieval from a vast research library?

TABLE 7.1

A Test for Working Memory Span

Read these sentences aloud, and then (without looking back) try to recall the final words of each sentence.

He had patronized her when she was a schoolgirl and teased her when she was a student.

He had an elongated skull which sat on his shoulders like a pear on a dish.

The products of digital electronics will play an important role in your future.

The taxi turned up Michigan Avenue where they had a clear view of the lake.

When at last his eyes opened, there was no gleam of triumph, no shade of anger.

Source: Daneman & Carpenter, 1980.

resources to different aspects of the task (we return to this idea in Chapter 8).

The incorporation of short-term memory into the broader context of working memory should help reinforce the idea that STM is not a place but a process. To do the work of cognition—to carry out cognitive activities like language processing or problem solving—you must bring a lot of different elements together in quick succession. You can think of working memory as short-term special focus on the necessary elements. If you wish to get a better look at a physical object, you can shine a brighter light on it; working memory shines a brighter mental light on your mental objects—your memory representations. Working memory also coordinates the activities required to take action with respect to those objects.

Researchers have demonstrated that working memory capacity differs among individuals (Engle, 2002; Jenkins et al., 1999). One common measure of these differences is *working memory span*. To determine working memory span, researchers may ask participants to read aloud a series of sentences and then recall the final words. We've given you some sentences to try in **Table 7.1.** It's really not so easy! People are usually considered to be *high span* if they can recall 4 or more words and *low span* if they recall 2.5 or fewer—these are averages across several trials and sets of sentences, so you won't have gotten much information about yourself just by trying Table 7.1. Because working memory span is a measure of the resources individuals have available to carry out short-term cognitive processes, researchers can use it to predict performance on a variety of tasks.

PUTTING IDEAS TO THE TEST

Working Memory Span Affects Memory for Texts

Researchers identified groups of high-, middle-, and low-span individuals. Each participant was asked to read a story about a "fine old home" from either the perspective of a potential homebuyer or a potential burglar. The story contained facts that were more relevant to one or the other perspective: for example, a leaky roof versus a coin collection. The researchers were interested in how much readers' memory representations were affected by the perspective from which they read the story. Participants were asked to recall the story twice: once from their original perspective (that is, homebuyer or burglar) and then a second time from the switched perspective (that is, "now imagine that you're a …"). High-span readers were able to produce a good deal of information from the "other" perspective; other readers were not (Lee-Sammons & Whitney, 1991).

The researchers concluded that low- and middle-span readers used the perspective to make *choices* about which story information to process extensively; high-span readers were able to process information both relevant and irrelevant to their perspective. Experiments that measure working memory span help to define the ways in which different individuals expend their memory resources.

A final note on working memory: Working memory helps maintain your psychological present. It is what sets a context for new events and links separate episodes together into a continuing story. It enables you to maintain and continually update your representation of a changing situation and to keep track of topics during a conversation. All of this is true because working memory serves as a conduit for information coming and going to long-term memory. Let's turn our attention now to the types of memories that can last a lifetime.

PUT YOURSELF TO THE TEST

- What is the primary function of short-term memory (STM)?
- How do rehearsal and chunking allow you to accommodate to STM capacity?
- How efficient is retrieval from STM?
- What are the components of working memory?
- What are the consequences of individual differences in working memory?

Long-Term Memory: Encoding and Retrieval

How long can memories last? At the chapter's outset, we asked you to recall your own earliest memory. How old is that memory? Fifteen years? Twenty years? Longer? When psychologists speak of *long-term memory,* it is with the knowledge that memories will often last a lifetime. Therefore, whatever theory explains how memories are acquired for the long term must also explain how they can remain accessible over the life course. **Long-term memory (LTM)** is the storehouse of all the experiences, events, information, emotions, skills, words, categories, rules, and judgments that have been acquired from sensory and short-term memories. LTM constitutes each person's total knowledge of the world and of the self.

Psychologists know that it is often easier to acquire new long-term information when an important conclusion is stated in advance. With that conclusion in place, you have a framework for understanding the incoming information. For memory, the conclusion we will reach is this: Your ability to remember will be greatest when there is a good match between the circumstances in which you encoded information and the circumstances in which you attempt to retrieve it. We will see over the next several sections what it means to have a "good match."

◆ CONTEXT AND ENCODING

To begin our exploration of the match between encoding and retrieval, we want you to consider a phenomenon that you might call "context shock." You see someone across a crowded room, and you know that you know the person but you just can't place her. Finally, after staring for longer than is absolutely polite, you remember who it is—and you realize that the difficulty is that the person is entirely in the wrong context. What is the woman who delivers your mail doing at your best friend's party? Whenever you have this type of experience, you have rediscovered the principle of **encoding specificity:** Memories emerge most efficiently when the context of retrieval matches the context of encoding. Let's see how researchers have demonstrated that principle.

ENCODING SPECIFICITY

What are the consequences of learning information in a particular context? Endel Tulving and Donald Thomson (1973) first demonstrated the power of encoding specificity by reversing the usual performance relationship between recall and recognition.

CLASSIC
PUTTING IDEAS TO THE TEST

Encoding Specificity Affects Recall and Recognition

Participants were asked to learn pairs of words like *train–black,* but they were told that they would be responsible for remembering only the second word of the pair. In a subsequent phase of the experiment, participants were asked to generate four free associates to words like *white.* Those words were chosen so that it was likely that the original to-be-remembered words (like *black*) would be among the associates. The participants were then asked to check off any words on their associates lists that they recognized as to-be-remembered words from the first phase of the experiment. They were able to do so 54 percent of the time. However, when the participants were later given the first words of the pair, like *train,* and asked to recall the associate, they were 61 percent accurate.

Why was recall better than recognition? Tulving and Thomson suggested that what mattered was the change in context. After the participants had studied the word *black* in the context of *train,* it was hard to recover the memory representation when the context was changed to *white.* Given the significant effect of even these minimal contexts, you can anticipate that richly organized real-life contexts would have an even greater effect on your memory.

<www.ablongman.com/gerrig17e>

Researchers have been able to demonstrate rather remarkable effects of context on memory. In one experiment, scuba divers learned lists of words either on a beach or under water. They were then tested for retention of those words, again in one of those two contexts. Performance was nearly 50 percent better when the context at encoding and recall matched—even though the material had nothing at all to do with water or diving (Gooden & Baddeley, 1975). Similarly, people performed better on memory tasks when the tempo of background music remained the same between encoding and recall (Balch & Lewis, 1996). In another study, memory performance was much improved when the smell of chocolate was present at both encoding and recall (Schab, 1990). This research on context-dependent memory with odors has been extended to suggest that the odor must be *distinctive* in the environment.

After receiving a traffic warning from this man, why might you not recognize him if you ran into him at a party?

PUTTING IDEAS TO THE TEST

Distinctive Odors Serve as Cues

What odors are sufficiently distinctive to foster context-dependent memories? A pair of experiments used a scent *novel* for the participants (*osmanthus*, "an unusual, Asian, floral-fruity scent"; Herz, 1997, p. 375), a familiar scent that was *inappropriate* for a research laboratory (*peppermint*), and a familiar scent *appropriate* for the laboratory (*clean fresh pine*). The hypothesis tested was that only the two odors that called attention to themselves in the environment—by virtue of being novel or inappropriate—would be used for encoding. The results bore out this prediction. Although the encoding and retrieval sessions were 48 hours apart, participants were able to remember reliably more words (from a 20-item list) when the odor in the laboratory room was the same at retrieval as at encoding—but only for osmanthus and peppermint (Herz, 1997).

These studies suggest that not all environmental odors are sufficiently distinctive to provide context for memory encoding. What is distinctive, of course, will vary from context to context. In a candy shop, peppermint might lose its power as a distinctive element of the context.

THE SERIAL POSITION EFFECT

We can also use changes in context to explain one of the classic effects in memory research: the **serial position effect.** Suppose we required you to learn a list of unrelated words. If we asked you to recall those words in order, your data would almost certainly conform to

the pattern shown in **Figure 7.7:** You would do very well on the first few words (the **primacy effect**) and very well on the last few words (the **recency effect**) but rather poorly on the middle part of the list. Figure 7.7 shows the generality of this pattern when students are asked to try to remember word lists of varying lengths (6, 10, and 15 words) using either *serial recall* ("Recite the words in the order you heard them") or *free recall* ("Recite as many words as you can") (Jahnke, 1965). Researchers have found primacy and recency in a wide variety of test situations (Crowder, 1976; Neath, 1993). What day is it today? Do you believe that you would be almost a second faster to answer this question at the beginning or end of the week than in the middle (Koriat & Fischoff, 1974)?

The role context plays in producing the shape of the serial position curve has to do with the **contextual distinctiveness** of different items on a list, different experiences in your life, and so on (Knoedler et al., 1999; Marks & Crowder, 1997; Neath & Knoedler, 1994). To understand contextual distinctiveness, you can ask the question, "How different were the contexts in which I learned this information from the context in which I will try to recall it?" Let's focus on recency. **Figure 7.8** is a visual representation of distinctiveness. Imagine, in part A, that you are looking at train tracks. What you can see is that they look as if they clump together at the horizon—even though they are equally spaced apart.

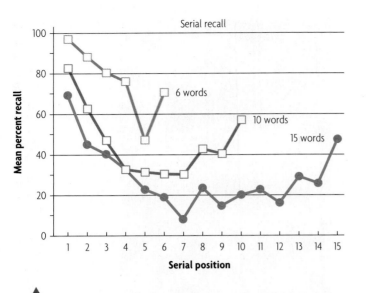

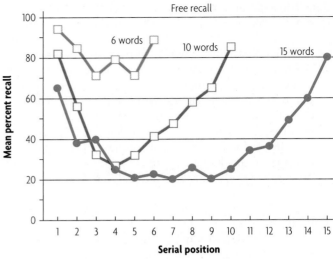

FIGURE 7.7

The Serial Position Effect

This figure shows the generality of the serial position effect. Students were asked to try to remember word lists of varying lengths (6, 10, and 15 words) using either serial recall ("Recite the words in the order you heard them") or free recall ("Recite as many words as you can"). Each curve shows better memory for both the beginning (the primacy effect) and end (the recency effect) of the list.

We could say that the nearest tracks stand out most—are most distinctive—from your context. Imagine now that you are trying to remember the last ten movies you've seen. The movies are like the train tracks. Under most circumstances, you should remember the last movie best, because you share the most overlapping context with the experience—it is "closest" to the context of your current experiences. This logic suggests that "middle" information will become more memorable if it is made more distinctive. The idea with respect to our analogy, as shown in part B of Figure 7.8, is to make the train tracks seem equally far apart.

FIGURE 7.8

Contextual Distinctiveness

You can think of items you put into memory as train tracks. In part A, you can imagine that memories farther back in time become blurred together, just like train tracks in the distance. In part B, you see that one way to combat this effect is to make the earlier tracks physically farther apart, so the distances look proportional. Similarly, you can make early memories more distinctive by moving them apart psychologically.

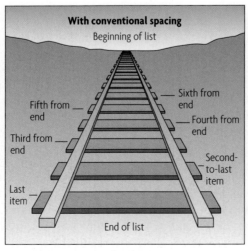

Part A

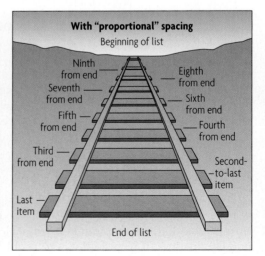

Part B

<www.ablongman.com/gerrig17e>

Making List Items More Distinctive in Context

To make the train tracks seem evenly spaced, engineers would have to make the more distant ones actually be farther apart. Researchers have used the same logic for a memory test, by exploiting the analogy between space and time. They had participants try to learn lists of letters, but they manipulated how far apart in time the letters were made to seem. This manipulation was accomplished by asking participants to read out some number of random digits that appeared on a computer screen between the letters. In the *conventional* condition (like part A of Figure 7.8), each pair of letters was separated by two digits. In the *proportional* condition (like part B), the first pair had four digits and the last pair had zero digits; this should have the effect of making the early digits more distinctive, just like moving distant train tracks farther apart. Participants, in fact, showed better memory for early items on the list when those items had been made more separate (Neath & Crowder, 1990).

This experiment suggests that the standard recency effect arises because the last few items are almost automatically distinctive. The same principle may explain primacy—each time you begin something new, your activity establishes a new context. In that new context, the first few experiences are particularly distinctive. Thus, you can think of primacy and recency as two views of the same set of train tracks—one from each end!

◆ RETRIEVAL CUES

As we continue our exploration of encoding and retrieval, this is a good time to put your memory to work. We will attempt to replicate classic memory experiments by asking you to learn some word pairs. Keep working at it until you can go through the six pairs three times in a row without an error.

> Apple–Boat
> Hat–Bone
> Bicycle–Clock
> Mouse–Tree
> Ball–House
> Ear–Blanket

Now that you've committed the pairs to memory, we want to make the test more interesting. We need to do something to give you a *retention interval*—a period of time over which you must keep the information in memory. Let's spend a moment, therefore, discussing some of the procedures we might use to test your mem-

ory. You might assume that you either know something or you don't and that any method of testing what you know will give the same results. Not so. Let's consider two tests for explicit memory, recall and recognition.

When you **recall,** you reproduce the information to which you were previously exposed. "What is the serial position effect?" is a recall question. **Recognition** refers to the realization that a certain stimulus event is one you have seen or heard before. "Which is the term for a visual sensory memory: (1) echo; (2) engram; (3) icon; or (4) abstract code?" is a recognition question. You can relate recall and recognition to your day-to-day experiences of explicit memory. When trying to identify a criminal, the police would be using a recall method if they asked the victim to describe, from memory, some of the perpetrator's distinguishing features: "Did you notice anything unusual about the attacker?" They would be using the recognition method if they showed the victim photos, one at a time, from a file of criminal suspects or if they asked the victim to identify the perpetrator in a police lineup.

Let's now use these two procedures to test you on the word pairs you learned a few moments ago. What words finished the pairs?

Hat–?	Bicycle–?	Ear–?

Can you select the correct pair from these possibilities?

Apple–Baby	Mouse–Tree	Ball–House
Apple–Boat	Mouse–Tongue	Ball–Hill
Apple–Bottle	Mouse–Tent	Ball–Horn

Was the recognition test easier than the recall test? It should be. Let's try to explain this result with respect to retrieval cues.

Retrieval cues are the stimuli available as you search for a particular memory. These cues may be provided externally, such as questions on a quiz ("What memory principles do you associate with the research of Sternberg and Sperling?"), or generated internally ("Where have I met her before?"). Each time you attempt to retrieve an explicit memory, you do so for some purpose, and that purpose often supplies the retrieval cue. It won't surprise you that memories can be easier or harder to retrieve depending on the quality of the retrieval cue. If a friend asks you, "Who's the one Roman emperor I can't remember?" you're likely to be involved in a guessing game. If she asks instead, "Who was the emperor after Claudius?" you can immediately respond "Nero."

Let's return to recall and recognition. Both memory tests require a search using cues. The cues for recognition, however, are much more useful. For recall, you have to hope that the cue alone will help you locate the information. For recognition, part of the work has been done for you. When you look at the pair *Mouse–Tree,* you only have to answer yes or no to "Did I have this experience?" rather than, in response to *Mouse—?* "What was the experience I had?" In this light, you can see that we made the recognition test reasonably easy for you. Suppose we had given you, instead, recombinations of the original pairs. Which of these are correct?

Hat–Clock   Ear–Boat

Hat–Bone   Ear–Blanket

Now you must recognize not just that you saw the word before, but that you saw it in a particular context. (We will return to the idea of context shortly.) If you are a veteran of difficult multiple-choice exams, you have come to learn how tough even recognition situations can be. However, in most cases, your recognition performance will be better than your recall, because retrieval cues are more straightforward for recognition. Let's look at some other aspects of retrieval cues.

EPISODIC AND SEMANTIC MEMORIES

We have already made a pair of distinctions about types of memories. You have implicit and explicit memories and declarative and procedural memories. We can define another dimension along which declarative memories differ with respect to the cues that are necessary to retrieve them from memory. Canadian psychologist **Endel Tulving** (1972) first proposed the distinction between *episodic* and *semantic* types of declarative memories.

Episodic memories preserve, individually, the specific events that you have personally experienced. For example, memories of your happiest birthday or of your first kiss are stored in episodic memory. To recover such memories, you need retrieval cues that specify something about the time at which the event occurred and something about the content of the events. Depending on how the information has been encoded, you may or may not be able to produce a specific memory representation for an event. For example, do you have any specific memories to differentiate the tenth time ago you brushed your teeth from the eleventh time ago?

Everything you know, you began to acquire in some particular context. However, there are large classes of information that, over time, you encounter in many different contexts. These classes of information come to be available for retrieval without reference to their multiple times and places of experience. These **semantic memories** are generic, categorical memories, such as the meanings of words and concepts. For most people, facts like the formula $E = MC^2$ and the capital of France don't require retrieval cues that make reference to the episodes, the original learning contexts, in which the memory was acquired.

Of course, this doesn't mean that your recall of semantic memories is foolproof. You know perfectly well that you can forget many facts that have become

Events of personal importance, like seeing a good friend for the first time after a year's separation, are retained in episodic *memory. What types of information from* semantic *memory might contribute to a reunion?*

dissociated from the contexts in which you learned them. A good strategy when you can't recover a semantic memory is to treat it like an episodic memory again. By thinking to yourself, "I know I learned the names of the Roman emperors in my Western civilization course," you may be able to provide the extra retrieval cues that will shake loose a memory.

INTERFERENCE

When we asked you to learn the paired associates earlier, we were really asking you to acquire new episodic memories. Suppose, now, we ask you to acquire another set of episodic memories. Once again, keep working on these word pairs until you can repeat them three times in a row without an error.

Apple–Robe

Hat–Circle

Bicycle–Roof

Mouse–Magazine

Ball–Baby

Ear–Penny

How did it go? Examine the list. You can see what we've done—each old prompt is paired with a new response. Was it harder for you to learn these new pairs? Do you think it would now be harder for you to recall the old ones? (Go ahead and try.) The answer in both cases is typically "yes." This brief exercise should give you a sense of how memories can compete—or provide *interference*—with each other.

<www.ablongman.com/gerrig17e>

PEANUTS reprinted by permission of United Feature Syndicate, Inc.

We have already given you a real-life example of the problem of interference when we asked you to try to differentiate your recollections of your episodes of toothbrushing. All of the specific memories interfere with each other. **Proactive interference** (*proactive* means "forward acting") refers to circumstances in which information you have acquired in the past makes it more difficult to acquire new information (see **Figure 7.9**). **Retroactive interference** (*retroactive* means "backward acting") occurs when the acquisition of new information makes it harder for you to remember older information. The word lists we've provided demonstrate both

of these types of interference. You've also experienced both proactive and retroactive interference if you've ever moved and had to change your phone number. At first, you probably found it hard to remember the new number—the old one kept popping out (proactive interference). However, after finally being able to reliably reproduce the new one, you may have found yourself unable to remember the old number—even if you had used it for years (retroactive interference).

As with many other memory phenomena, Hermann Ebbinghaus was the first researcher to document interference rigorously through experiments. Ebbinghaus, after learning dozens of lists of nonsense syllables, found himself forgetting about 65 percent of the new ones he was learning. Fifty years later, students at Northwestern University who studied Ebbinghaus's lists had the same experience—after many trials with many lists, what the students had learned earlier interfered proactively with their recall of current lists (Underwood, 1948, 1949).

Remember that the conclusion we are working toward is that the match between encoding and retrieval is critical. From these last two sections, you can see how the pieces fit together to reach that conclusion: The context in which you attempt to retrieve a memory itself acts as a source of retrieval cues. When there is a mismatch between the contexts of encoding and retrieval, the cues provided in the retrieval context cannot help (and may even hurt) your attempt to find the memory you seek.

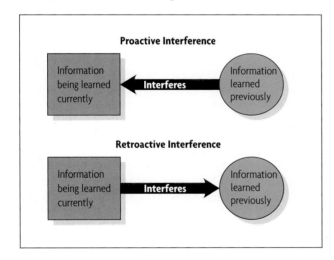

FIGURE 7.9

Proactive and Retroactive Interference

Proactive and retroactive interference help explain why it can be difficult to encode and retrieve memories. What you have learned in the past can make it more difficult for you to encode new information (proactive interference). What you are learning now can make it more difficult for you to retrieve old information (retroactive interference).

From Robert A. Baron, *Psychology*, 5e. Published by Allyn & Bacon, Boston, MA. Copyright © 2001 by Pearson Education. Reprinted by permission of the publisher.

◆ THE PROCESSES OF ENCODING AND RETRIEVAL

We have seen so far that a match between the context of encoding and of retrieval is beneficial to good memory performance. We will now refine this conclusion somewhat by considering the actual processes that are used to get information to and from long-term memory. We will see that memory functions best when encoding and retrieval processes make a good match as well.

LEVELS OF PROCESSING

Let's begin with the idea that the type of processing you perform on information—the type of attention you pay to information at time of encoding—will have an influence on your memory for the information. **Levels-of-processing theory** suggests that the deeper the level at which information was processed, the more likely it is to be committed to memory (Craik & Lockhart, 1972; Lockhart & Craik, 1990). If processing involves more analysis, interpretation, comparison, and elaboration, it should result in better memory.

The depth of processing is often defined by the types of judgments participants are required to make with respect to experimental materials. Consider the word *GRAPE*. We could ask you to make a physical judgment—is the word in capital letters? Or a rhyme judgment—does the word rhyme with *tape?* Or a meaning judgment—does the word represent a type of fruit? Do you see how each of these questions requires you to think a little bit more deeply about *GRAPE?* In fact, the deeper the original processing participants carry out, the more words they remember (Lockhart & Craik, 1990).

A difficulty of the levels-of-processing theory, however, is that researchers have not always been able to specify exactly what makes certain processes "shallow" or "deep." Even so, results of this sort confirm that the way in which information is committed to memory—the mental processes that you use to encode information—has an effect on whether you can retrieve that information later. However, so far we have discussed only explicit memory. We will now see that the match between processes at encoding and retrieval is particularly critical for implicit memory.

PROCESSES AND IMPLICIT MEMORY

Earlier, we defined the explicit versus implicit dimension for memories as a distinction that applies both at encoding and at retrieval (Bowers & Marsolek, 2003). Under many circumstances, for example, you will retrieve implicitly memories that you originally encoded explicitly. This is true when you greet your best friend by name without having to expend any particular mental effort. Even so, implicit memories are often most robust when there is a strong match between the processes at implicit encoding and the processes at implicit retrieval. This perspective is called **transfer-appropriate processing:** Memory is best when the type of processing carried out at encoding *transfers* to the processes required at retrieval (Roediger et al., 2002). To support this perspective, we will first describe some of the methodologies that are used to demonstrate implicit memories. Then we will show how the match between encoding and retrieval processes matters.

Let's consider a typical experiment in which implicit memory is assessed. The researchers presented students with lists of concrete nouns and asked them to judge the pleasantness of each word on a 1 (least pleasant) to 5 (most pleasant) scale (Rajaram & Roediger, 1993). The pleasantness ratings required participants to think about the meaning of a word without explicitly committing it to memory. After this study phase, participants' memory was assessed using one of four implicit memory tasks (suppose that a word on one list was *unicorn*):

- *Word fragment completion.* The participant is given fragments of a word, like _ni_or_, and asked to complete the fragments with the first word that comes to mind.

- *Word stem completion.* The participant is asked to complete a stem, like *uni_____*, with the first word that comes to mind.

- *Word identification.* Words are flashed on a computer screen in such a fashion that participants cannot see them clearly. They must try to guess each word that is flashed. In this case, one of the words would be *unicorn.*

- *Anagrams.* Participants are given a scrambled word, like *corunni,* and asked to give the first unscrambled word that comes to mind.

Just like our example with *unicorn,* correct responses to each of the tasks can be provided by words from the earlier lists. What is critical, however, is that the experimenters have not called attention to the relationship between the words on the earlier list and appropriate responses on these new tasks—that's why the use of memory is implicit.

To assess the degree of implicit memory, the researchers compared the performance of participants who had seen a particular word, like *unicorn,* on the pleasantness lists with those who had not. **Figure 7.10** plots the improvement brought about by implicit memory for a word—percent correct when the word had appeared on the participant's list minus percent correct when it had not. (Different participants experienced different word lists.) You can see that for each task, there was an advantage to having seen a word before, even though participants had been asked only to say whether the word had a pleasant meaning. This advantage is known as **priming,** because the first experience of the word *primes* memory for later experiences. For some memory tasks, like word fragment completion, researchers have found priming effects lasting a week and beyond (Sloman et al., 1988).

Let's turn now to the nature of the match between encoding and retrieval. The four implicit memory tests we've mentioned so far all rely on a *physical* match between the original stimulus and the information given at test. In a sense, whatever processes allow you to encode *unicorn* also make that word available when you are asked to complete the stem *uni_____*, and so on. We can, however, introduce another test, *general*

<www.ablongman.com/gerrig17e>

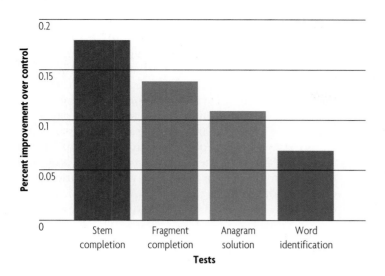

FIGURE 7.10

Priming on Implicit Memory Tests

Priming indicates improvement on the various tasks over performance on control words. Some implicit memory tests demonstrate that priming can last a week or more.

knowledge, that relies on *meaning* or *concepts* instead of on a physical match. Imagine we gave you the question, "What mythological creature had a single horn?" You might very well say unicorn. However, if you became more likely to say unicorn because you had seen the word on an earlier list, in a different context, that would be evidence of implicit memory.

Using two different types of implicit memory tests based on priming—by physical features or by meaning—we can look for a relationship between encoding and retrieval.

PUTTING IDEAS TO THE TEST

Priming Occurs When Processes Match

Memory researchers designed a levels-of-processing experiment to demonstrate that different implicit memories rely on different types of processes. Participants were asked to respond to each word on a list. For *deep* judgments, they responded to the words' meanings—for example, "Can you buy this?" For *shallow* judgments, they responded to the words' physical features—for example, "Does this word contain a 'c'?" The researchers assessed implicit memory by using general knowledge questions and word fragment completion. Let's examine the tasks with an eye to transfer-appropriate processing. The deep judgments engage conceptual processes at encoding, but the shallow judgments do not. The general knowledge questions engage conceptual processes at retrieval, but word fragment completion does not. Accordingly, the researchers predicted that they should find a priming advantage for deep judgments when processes at encoding and retrieval matched (deep judgments with general knowledge questions) than when they mismatched (deep judgments with fragment completion). The results confirmed the prediction (Hamilton & Rajaram, 2001).

This type of research supports the idea of transfer-appropriate processing: If you use a certain type of processing—for example, physical or meaning analysis—to encode information, you will retrieve that information most efficiently when the processing uses the same type of analysis (Park & Gabrieli, 1995; Rajaram et al., 1998; Weldon et al., 1995). Earlier we made this assertion: Your ability to remember will be greatest when there is a good match between the circumstances in which you encode information and the circumstances in which you attempt to retrieve it. This section provided the research evidence for this assertion. Let's now see how we can put theories of encoding and retrieval further to work for you.

◆ IMPROVING MEMORY FOR UNSTRUCTURED INFORMATION

After reading this whole section, you should have some concrete ideas about how you could improve your everyday memory performance—how you can remember more and forget less. (The Psychology in Your Life box, later in the chapter, will help you solidify those ideas with respect to school work.) You know, especially, that you're best off trying to recover a piece of information in the same context, or by performing the same types of mental tasks, as when you first acquired it. But there's a slightly different problem with which we still must give you some help. It has to do with encoding unstructured or arbitrary collections of information.

For example, imagine that you are working as a clerk in a store. You must try to commit to memory the several items that each customer wants: "The woman in the green blouse wants hedge clippers and a garden hose. The man in the blue shirt wants a pair of pliers, six quarter-inch screws, and a paint scraper." This scenario, in fact, comes very close to the types of experiments in which researchers ask you to memorize paired associates. How did you go about learning the word pairs we presented earlier? The task probably was somewhat of a chore, because the pairs were not particularly meaningful for you—and information that isn't meaningful is hard to remember. To find a way to get the right items to the right customer, you need to make associations seem less arbitrary. Let's explore *elaborative rehearsal* and *mnemonics.*

ELABORATIVE REHEARSAL

A general strategy for improving encoding is called **elaborative rehearsal.** The basic idea of this technique is that while you are rehearsing information—while you are first committing it to memory—you elaborate on the material to enrich the encoding. One way to do this is to invent a relationship that makes an association seem less arbitrary. For example, if you wanted to remember the pair *Mouse–Tree,* you might conjure up an image of a mouse scurrying up a tree to look for cheese. Recall is enhanced when you encode separate bits of information into this type of miniature story line. Can you imagine, in the clerk situation, swiftly making up a story to link each customer with the appropriate items? (It will work with practice.) You may have already guessed that it is also often helpful to supplement your story line with a mental picture—a visual image—of the scene you are trying to remember. Visual imagery can enhance your recall because it gives you codes for both verbal and visual memories simultaneously (Paivio, 1995).

Elaborative rehearsal can also help save you from what has been called the *next-in-line effect:* When, for example, people are next in line to speak, they often can't remember what the person directly before them said. If you've ever had a circle of people each give his or her name, you're probably well acquainted with this effect. What was the name of the person directly in front of you? The origin of this effect appears to be a shift in attention toward preparing to make your own remarks or to say your own name (Bond et al., 1991). To counter this shift, you should use elaborative rehearsal. Keep your attention focused on the person in front of you and enrich your encoding of his or her name: "*Julie*—her hair is truly unruly."

MNEMONICS

Another memory-enhancing option is to draw on special mental strategies called *mnemonics* (from the Greek word meaning "to remember"). **Mnemonics** are devices that encode a long series of facts by associating them with familiar and previously encoded information. Many mnemonics work by giving you ready-made retrieval cues that help organize otherwise arbitrary information.

Consider the *method of loci,* first practiced by ancient Greek orators. The singular of *loci* is *locus,* and it means "place." The method of loci is a means of remembering the order of a list of names or objects—or, for the orators, the individual sections of a long speech—by associating them with some sequence of places with which you are familiar. To remember a grocery list, you might mentally put each item sequentially along the route you take to get from home to school. To remember the list later, you mentally go through

How might a waiter or waitress use elaborative rehearsal or mnemonics to get the right meals to the right customers?

<www.ablongman.com/gerrig17e>

your route and find the item associated with each spot (see **Figure 7.11**).

The *peg-word method* is similar to the method of loci, except that you associate the items on a list with a series of cues rather than with familiar locations. Typically, the cues for the peg-word method are a series of rhymes that associate numbers with words. For example, you might memorize "one is a *bun*," "two is a *shoe*," "three is a *tree*," and so on. Then you would associate each item on your list interacting with the appropriate cue. Suppose a history professor asked you to memorize, in order, the rulers of the Roman empire. You might have Augustus eating a platter of buns, Tiberius wearing oversized shoes, Caligula sitting in a tree, and so on. You can see that the key to learning arbitrary information is to encode the information in such a fashion that you provide yourself with efficient retrieval cues.

◆ METAMEMORY

Suppose you're in a situation in which you'd really like to remember something. You're doing your best to use retrieval cues that reflect the circumstances of encoding, but you just can't get the bit of information to emerge. Part of the reason you're expending so much effort is that you're sure that you are in possession of the information. But are you correct to be so confident about the contents of your memory? Questions like this one—about how your memory works or how you know what information you possess—are questions of **metamemory.** One major question on metamemory has been when and why *feelings-of-knowing*—the subjective sensations that you do have information stored in memory—are accurate.

Research on feelings-of-knowing was pioneered by **J. T. Hart** (1965), who began his studies by asking students a series of general knowledge questions. Suppose,

Bread

Orange juice

Ice cream

Bananas

FIGURE 7.11
The Method of Loci

In the method of loci, you associate the items you wish to remember (such as the items on a grocery list) with locations along a familiar path (such as your route to and from school).

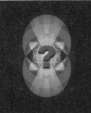

How Can Memory Research Help You Prepare for Exams?
Danielle Stead
University of Rhode Island

Among the most frequent questions students ask after they've read about memory research are, "How can I put the information to immediate use? How will this research help me prepare for my next exam?" Let's see what types of advice we can generate from the research conclusions:

■ *Encoding specificity.* As you'll recall, the principle of encoding specificity suggests that the context of retrieval should match the context of encoding. In school settings, "context" often will mean "the context of other information." If you always study material in the same context, you may find it difficult to retrieve it in a different context—so, if a professor's questions approach a topic in a slightly unusual way, you might be entirely at a loss. As a remedy, you should change contexts even while you study. Rearrange the order of your notes. Ask yourself questions that mix different topics together. Try to make your own novel combinations. But if you get stuck while you're taking an exam, try to generate as many retrieval cues as you can that reinstate the original context: "Let's see. We heard about this in the same lecture we learned about short-term memory . . ."

■ *Serial position.* You know from the serial position curve that, under very broad circumstances, information presented in the "middle" is least well remembered. In fact, college students fail more exam items on material from the middle of a lecture than on material from the start or end of the lecture

(Holen & Oaster, 1976; Jensen, 1962). When you're listening to a lecture, you should remind yourself to pay special attention in the middle of the session. When it comes time to study, you should devote some extra time and effort to that material—and make sure not to study the material in the same order each time. You might also note that the chapter you're reading now is about at the middle of *Psychology and Life.* If you have a final examination that covers all the course material, you're going to want to make an especially careful review of this chapter.

■ *Elaborative rehearsal and mnemonics.* Sometimes when you study for exams, you will feel as if you are trying to acquire "unstructured information." You might, for example, be asked to memorize the functions of different parts of

the brain. Under these circumstances, you need to find ways to provide the structure yourself. Try to form visual images or make up sentences or stories that use the concepts in creative ways. One of your authors still remembers his mnemonic from introductory psychology to remember the function of the *ventromedial hypothalamus,* which is often abbreviated VMH: Very Much Hungry (however, as you will learn in Chapter 11, research in the 25 intervening years has made that mnemonic less accurate). Elaborative rehearsal allows you to use what you know already to make new material more memorable.

■ *Metamemory.* Research on metamemory suggests that people generally have good intuitions about what they know and what they don't know. If you are in an exam situation in which there is time pressure, you should allow those intuitions to guide how you allocate your time. You might, for example, read the whole test over quickly and see which questions give you the strongest feelings-of-knowing. If you are taking an exam on which you lose points for giving wrong answers (which happens, for example, on SAT and some GRE exams), you should be particularly attentive to your metamemory intuitions, so you can avoid answering those questions on which you "sense" you are most likely to be incorrect.

We hope you now have several concrete ideas about how memory research can help you to prepare for your next exam!

for example, we asked you, "What planet is the largest in our solar system?" Do you know the answer? If you don't, how would you respond to this question: "Even though I don't remember the answer now, do I know the answer to the extent that I could pick the correct answer from among several wrong answers?" This was the question Hart put to his participants. He allowed them to give ratings from 1, to say they were quite sure they wouldn't choose correctly on the multiple choice, to 6, to say they were quite sure they would choose correctly. What would your rating be? Now here are your alternatives:

a. Pluto
b. Venus
c. Earth
d. Jupiter

If you made an accurate feeling-of-knowing judgment, you should have been less likely to get the correct answer, d, if you gave a 1 rating than if you gave a 6. (Of course, to have a fair test, we'd want to give you a long series of questions.) Hart found that when participants gave 1 ratings, they answered the questions correctly only 30 percent of the time, whereas 6 ratings predicted 75 percent success. That's pretty impressive evidence that feelings-of-knowing can be accurate.

Research on metamemory focuses on both the processes that give rise to feelings-of-knowing and on how their accuracy is ensured (Koriat & Levy-Sadot, 1999; Metcalfe, 2000):

- The *cue familiarity hypothesis* suggests that people base their feelings-of-knowing on their familiarity with the retrieval cue. Suppose you were asked, "What is the last name of the composer of the 'Maple Leaf Rag'?" If you have prior familiarity with the "Maple Leaf Rag," you might think that you probably would be able to recognize the correct alternative when given the multiple choice (Metcalfe et al., 1993; Reder & Ritter, 1992; Schwartz & Metcalfe, 1992).

- The *accessibility hypothesis* suggests that people base their judgments on the accessibility, or availability, of partial information from memory. Thus, if the question "What is the last name of the composer of the 'Maple Leaf Rag'?" calls quite easily to mind information you believe to be related to the correct answer, you are likely to think that you will be able to recognize the correct answer as well (Koriat, 1993, 1995).

Both of these theories have obtained empirical support—and both suggest that you can generally trust your instincts when you believe that you know something. (Later in the chapter, we will describe research on eyewitness testimony, which provides some exceptions to this general rule.)

You have now learned quite a bit about how you get information in and out of memory. You know what we mean by a "good match" between the circumstances of encoding and of retrieval. In the next section, we will shift our focus from your memory processes to the content of your memories.

PUT YOURSELF TO THE TEST

- What is the encoding specificity principle?
- How have researchers explained primacy and recency effects?
- With respect to retrieval cues, why is recall generally more difficult than recognition?
- What properties define semantic versus episodic memories?
- Under what circumstances do proactive and retroactive interference arise?
- Why do the levels-of-processing and transfer-appropriate processing approaches emphasize the importance of memory processes?
- What types of information have an impact on feelings-of-knowing?

Structures in Long-Term Memory

In most of our examples so far, we have asked you to try to acquire and retrieve isolated or unrelated bits of information. What you mostly have represented in memory, however, are large bodies of *organized knowledge*. Recall, for example, that we asked you to consider whether *grape* is a fruit. You could say *yes* very quickly. How about *porcupine*? Is it a fruit? How about *tomato*? In this section, we will examine how the difficulty of these types of judgments relates to the way information is structured in memory. We will also discuss how memory organization allows you to make a best guess at the content of experiences you can't remember exactly.

◆ MEMORY STRUCTURES

An essential function of memory is to draw together similar experiences, to enable you to discover patterns in your interactions with the environment. (Recall a similar description, in Chapter 4, on the functions of perception.) You live in a world filled with countless individual events, from which you must continually extract information to combine them into a smaller, simpler set that you can manage mentally. But apparently you don't need to expend any particular conscious effort to find structure in the world. Just as we suggested when we defined the implicit acquisition of memories, it's unlikely that you ever formally thought to yourself something like, "Here's what belongs in a kitchen." It is through ordinary experience in the world that you have acquired mental structures to mirror environmental structures. Let's look at the types of memory structures you have formed in your moment-by-moment experience of the world.

CATEGORIZATION AND CONCEPTS

We will begin by previewing one of the topics we will discuss in Chapter 10—the mental effort a child must go through to acquire the meaning of a word, such as *doggie*. For this word to have meaning, the child must be able to store each instance in which the word *doggie* is used, as well as information about the context. In this way, the child finds out what common core experience—

How does the formation of categories—such as what constitutes a healthy head of lettuce, a sweet melon, or a flavorful tomato—help you make daily decisions like what to buy for dinner?

a furry creature with four legs—is meant by *doggie*. The child must acquire the knowledge that *doggie* applies not just to one particular animal, but to a whole category of creatures. This ability to *categorize* individual experiences—to take the same action toward them or give them the same label—is one of the most basic abilities of thinking organisms (Mervis & Rosch, 1981).

The mental representations of the categories you form are called **concepts.** The concept *doggie,* for example, names the set of mental representations of experiences of dogs that a young child has gathered together in memory. (As we shall see in Chapter 10, if the child hasn't yet refined his or her meaning for *doggie,* the concept might also include features that adults wouldn't consider to be appropriate.) You have acquired a vast array of concepts. You have categories for *objects* and *activities,* such as *barns* and *baseball.* Concepts may also represent *properties,* such as *red* or *large; abstract ideas,* such as *truth* or *love;* and *relations,* such as *smarter than* or *sister of.* Each concept represents a summary unit for your experience of the world.

PROTOTYPES

Given the number of dogs you've seen in your life, what exactly do you think about when, for example, you read a sentence like, "The dog buried the bone"? Do you call to mind some particular dog? Or do you envision some typical dog, averaged across all the dogs you have experienced—your **prototype** for a dog? Let's look at an experiment that helps to address these questions.

CLASSIC
PUTTING IDEAS TO THE TEST

The Formation of Prototypes

Participants were shown a set of exemplar faces that varied, to different degrees, from prototype faces (*exemplars* are examples of the members of a category; see **Figure 7.12**). Then they saw a second group of faces: some of the original exemplar faces; some new ones that were made to differ from the prototype; and the prototype face, which they had never actually seen. The participants' task was to rate their confidence in having seen each face before, during the first presentation.

Three results clearly emerged, as seen in the graph in Figure 7.12. Recall confidence was equally high for all the old items, even if they had only a 25 percent similarity to the prototype. The new items were confidently identified as unfamiliar to the extent that they differed from the prototype. Finally, the highest level of confidence was for the prototype face itself—although the participants had never seen it before (Solso & McCarthy, 1981).

<www.ablongman.com/gerrig17e>

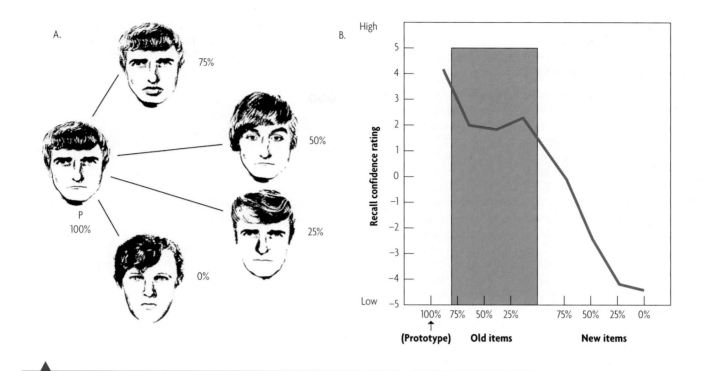

FIGURE 7.12

(A) Prototype Face and Exemplar Faces
(B) Confidence Ratings for Prototype, Old Items, and New Items

(A) The 75-percent face has all the features of the prototype face except the mouth; the 50-percent face has different hair and eyes; the 25-percent face has only the eyes in common; and the 0-percent face has no features in common. (B) Participants were asked to rate how confident they were that they had previously seen a face. Confidence was highest for the prototype face—which they had never actually seen. Confidence was equivalent for old faces. For new faces, participants' confidence dropped as the face grew more different from the prototype.

In this experiment, participants acted as if they had averaged together all the exemplar faces they had seen to construct the prototypical face.

The prototypes you have for categories are derived from all your experiences with members of that category. For that reason, your prototype shifts subtly every time you encounter a new exemplar of a category. Consequently, researchers believe that you do not actually have a specific mental representation of the prototype for a particular category. Rather, the prototype emerges as an average across your pool of exemplars (Hintzman, 1986; Nosofsky et al., 1992). For example, all the dogs you have encountered to this moment contribute to your notion of the prototypical dog. Moreover, if you go for a walk today and see a dog or two, your prototype will change just the slightest bit.

Being able to find the prototype for a category like *dog* also allows you to recognize some category members as more or less typical—the more features the members share with the prototypical member of the category, the more typical they are likely to be. You can develop this intuition if you think about a category like *bird*. What makes a robin a typical bird, but an ostrich or a penguin atypical? The answer has to do with the degree of match of these creatures to all the other entities that you have classified in memory as birds. The degree of typicality of a category member—the extent to which something matches your prototype—has real-life consequences. Research has shown, for example, that people respond more quickly to typical members of a category than to its more unusual ones. Your reaction time to determine that a robin is a bird would be quicker than your reaction time to determine that an ostrich is a bird (Rosch et al., 1976). This effect arises, once again, because you maintain in memory your history of experiences with the members of the category *bird*. It is easier to find robin experiences than ostrich experiences (unless, of course, you have spent your life among ostriches).

HIERARCHIES AND BASIC LEVELS

Concepts, and their prototypes, do not exist in isolation. As shown in **Figure 7.13,** concepts can often be arranged into meaningful organizations. A broad category like *animal* has several subcategories, such as *bird* and *fish,* which in turn contain exemplars such as *canary, ostrich, shark,* and *salmon.* The animal category is itself a subcategory of the still larger category of *living beings.* Concepts are also linked to other types of information: You store the knowledge that some birds are *edible,* some are *endangered,* some are *national symbols.*

There seems to be a level in such hierarchies at which people best categorize and think about objects. This has been called the **basic level** (Rosch, 1973, 1978). For example, when you buy an apple at the grocery store, you could think of it as a *piece of fruit*—but that seems imprecise—or a *Golden Delicious*—but that seems too specific or picayune. The basic level is just *apple.* If you were shown a picture of such an object, that's what you'd be likely to call it. You would also be

faster to say that it was an apple than that it was a piece of fruit (Rosch, 1978). The basic level emerges pretty much through the same forces that give rise to the prototype. You have more experience with the term *apple* than with its more or less specific alternatives. If you became an apple grower, however, your basic level would probably shift lower in the hierarchy.

SCHEMAS

We have seen that concepts are the building blocks of memory hierarchies. They also serve as building blocks for more complex mental structures. Recall Figure 7.2. Why did you instantly know that the rabbit didn't belong in the kitchen? We suggested earlier that this judgment relied on implicit memory—but we didn't say what type of memory structure you were using. Clearly, what you need is some representation in memory that combines the individual concepts of a kitchen—your knowledge about ovens, sinks, and refrigerators—into a larger unit. We call that larger unit a schema. **Schemas** are conceptual frameworks, or clusters of knowledge, regarding objects, people, and situations. Schemas are "knowledge packages" that encode complex generalizations about your experi-

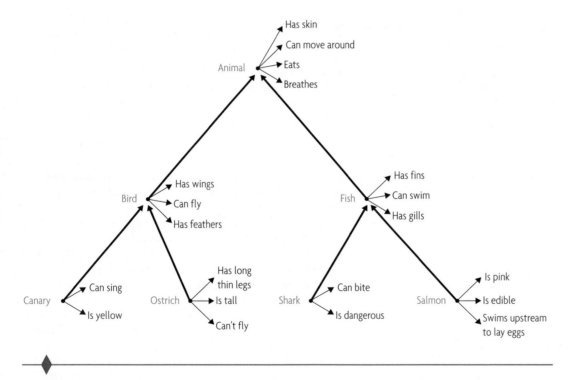

FIGURE 7.13

Hierarchically Organized Structure of Concepts

The category animal *can be divided into subcategories such as* bird *and* fish; *similarly, each subcategory can be further divided. Some information (such as* has skin*) applies to all concepts in the hierarchy; other information (such as* can sing*) applies only to concepts at lower levels (for example, a* canary*).*

ence of the structure of the environment. You have schemas for kitchens and bedrooms, race car drivers and professors, surprise parties and graduations. In later chapters, we'll provide more illustrations of the types of schemas that shape your day-to-day experiences. For example, in Chapter 10 we'll see that the attachment relationships children form with their parents provide schemas for later social interactions. In Chapter 13, we'll see that you possess a *self-schema*—a memory structure that allows you to organize information about yourself.

One thing you may have guessed is that your schemas do not include all the individual details of all your varied experiences. Just as a prototype is the average of your experiences of a category, a schema represents your average experience of situations in the environment. Thus, also like prototypes, your schemas are not permanent but shift with your changing life events. Your schemas also include only those details in the world to which you have devoted sufficient attention. For example, when asked to draw the information on the head sides of U.S. coins, college students virtually never filled in the word *Liberty,* although it appears on every coin (Rubin & Kontis, 1983). Check a coin! Thus, your schemas provide an accurate reflection of what you've *noticed* about the world. Let's now look at all the ways in which you use your concepts and schemas.

◆ USING MEMORY STRUCTURES

Let's consider a couple of instances of memory structures in action. You already saw that your schema for kitchen enables you to determine that the bunny just doesn't belong. For a second example, think back to Chapter 4, where we discussed how prior knowledge has an effect on interpretations of ambiguous stimuli. Do you remember **Figure 7.14?** Do you see a duck or a rabbit? Let's suppose we give you the expectation that you're going to see a duck. If you match the features of the picture against your schematic expectations for the features of a duck, you're likely to be reasonably con-

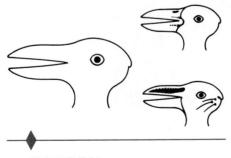

FIGURE 7.14
Recognition Illusion

Duck or rabbit?

tent. The same thing would happen if we told you to expect a rabbit. You use information from memory to generate—and confirm—expectations.

You also have memory structures that influence what you perceive and remember about people (Cantor & Mischel, 1979; Levy et al., 1999). For example, you have probably acquired the concepts of dentists, cult leaders, environmentalists, and used-car salespeople. If a person you do not know is described as belonging to one of these categories, your stereotypes may lead you to assume that the person has particular personality characteristics or behaves in a particular way. Social psychologists have demonstrated that even the words a language makes available can influence this interpersonal use of concepts.

PUTTING IDEAS TO THE TEST

Stereotypes Across Languages

The researchers created descriptions of four individuals, two of whom could easily be labeled by personality-type terms in English, but not in Chinese, and two of whom could easily be labeled in Chinese, but not in English. Consider the term *shì gù*. In Chinese, this term captures an individual who is "worldly, experienced, socially skillful, devoted to his or her family, and somewhat reserved" (Hoffman et al., 1986, p. 1098). In English, no single term or phrase applies to this whole collection of traits. Similarly, no single phrase in Chinese captures the English stereotype of the *artistic type.*

Chinese–English bilinguals read the descriptions in either Chinese or English (half read each description in each language). The researchers predicted that the availability or unavailability of an organized concept in a language would determine whether participants' reasoning was guided by their stereotypes. This expectation was borne out. The impressions participants wrote down for each character were considerably more congruent with a stereotype when the language of processing matched the language in which a concept label was available. For example, a participant might infer that an *artistic-type* person would be *unreliable*—but only when reading the description in English, the language that has the information *artistic* and *unreliable* drawn together as a concept (Hoffman et al., 1986).

This research demonstrates that the availability of memory structures can influence the way you think about the world: Your past experiences color your present experiences and change your expectations for the future. You will see shortly that, for much the same reasons, concepts and schemas can sometimes work against accurate memory.

◆ REMEMBERING AS A RECONSTRUCTIVE PROCESS

Let's turn now to another important way in which you use memory structures. In many cases, when you are asked to remember a piece of information, you can't remember the information directly. Instead, you *reconstruct* the information based on more general types of stored knowledge. To experience **reconstructive memory**, consider this trio of questions:

- Did Chapter 3 have the word *the* in it?
- Did 1991 contain the day July 7?
- Did you breathe yesterday between 2:05 and 2:10 P.M.?

You probably were willing to answer "Yes!" to each of these questions without much hesitation, but you almost certainly don't have specific, episodic memories to help you (unless, of course, something happened to fix these events in memory—perhaps July 7 is your birthday or you crossed out all the *the*'s in Chapter 3 to curb your boredom). To answer these questions, you must use more general memories to reconstruct what is likely to have happened. Let's examine this process of reconstruction in a bit more detail.

THE ACCURACY OF RECONSTRUCTIVE MEMORY

If people reconstruct some memories, rather than recovering a specific memory representation for what happened, then you might expect that you could find occasions on which the reconstructed memory differed from the real occurrence—distortions. One of the most impressive demonstrations of memory distortions is also the oldest. In his classic book *Remembering: A Study in Experimental and Social Psychology* (1932), **Sir Frederic Bartlett** undertook a program of research to demonstrate how individuals' prior knowledge influenced the way they remembered new information. Bartlett studied the way British undergraduates remembered stories whose themes and wording were taken from another culture. His most famous story was "The War of the Ghosts," an American Indian tale.

Bartlett found that his readers' reproductions of the story were often greatly altered from the original. The distortions Bartlett found involved three kinds of reconstructive processes:

- *Leveling*—simplifying the story.
- *Sharpening*—highlighting and overemphasizing certain details.
- *Assimilating*—changing the details to better fit the participant's own background or knowledge.

Thus, readers reproduced the story with words familiar in their culture taking the place of those unfamiliar:

Boat might replace *canoe* and *go fishing* might replace *hunt seals*. Bartlett's participants also often changed the story's plot to eliminate references to supernatural forces that were unfamiliar in their culture.

Following Bartlett's lead, contemporary researchers have demonstrated a variety of memory distortions that occur when people use constructive processes to reproduce memories (Bergman & Roediger, 1999). For example, one team of researchers produced what they called a "soap opera" effect in story recall (Owens et al., 1979). Here's an example of an episode from one of their stories:

> *Nancy arrived at the cocktail party. She looked around the room to see who was there. She went to talk to her professor. She felt she had to talk to him but was a little nervous about just what to say. A group of people started to play charades. Nancy went over and had some refreshments. The hors d'oeuvres were good but she wasn't interested in talking to the rest of the people at the party. After a while, she decided she'd had enough and left the party.*

Imagine how different it would have been to read that excerpt if you had been among the half of the participants who read this extra introduction to the story:

> *Nancy woke up feeling sick again and she wondered if she really were pregnant. How would she tell the professor she had been seeing? And the money was another problem.*

Suppose, while you were at this barbecue, someone told you the man on your left was a millionaire. How would this affect your memories for his actions at the barbecue? What if you had been told he only had delusions of being a millionaire?

<www.ablongman.com/gerrig17e>

You might go back now and reread the story excerpt. For the original participants, the presence or absence of the introduction had a dramatic effect on memory performance. When asked to recall the story or to recognize statements from it, readers who had read the extra introductory material—and, thereby, called to mind a schema for an "unwanted pregnancy"—were much more likely to produce or recognize invented statements related to Nancy's pregnancy. The participants' use of the schema led to predictable distortions.

An important aspect of the process of memory reconstruction is that people often piece memories together from a variety of sources. However, people are not always accurate at recalling the original sources for various components of their memories (Mitchell & Johnson, 2000). In fact, researchers have demonstrated that individuals will sometimes come to believe that they actually carried out actions that they, in fact, only accomplished in their imaginations.

PUTTING IDEAS TO THE TEST

When Imagination Becomes Action

A group of 210 college students participated in an experiment that had three sessions. In session 1, the students sat at a table that was covered with an array of objects. The experimenter read statements to the students that described actions that could be carried out with the objects. Some of those actions were ordinary (e.g., flip the coin) whereas some were bizarre (e.g., sit on the dice). The students were asked actually to perform half of the actions (both ordinary and bizarre), but they were asked only to imagine performing the rest. Session 2 took place 24 hours later. In that second session, the students were asked only to imagine performing actions—including some from the day before—up to five times. In session 3, which took place two weeks after session 2, the students were asked to think back to the first session. They were asked to recall whether they had actually performed each action or only imagined doing it. For both ordinary and bizarre actions, the same rule held true: The more times in session 2 the students had imagined carrying out an action, the more likely they were to remember actually having performed the action—even when they never had done so (Thomas & Loftus, 2002).

Can you find applications of this result in your own life? Suppose you keep reminding yourself to set your alarm clock before you go to bed. Each time you remind yourself, you form a picture in your head of the steps you must go through. If you imagine setting the clock often enough, you might mistakenly come to believe that you actually did so!

It is important to keep in mind, however, that just as in Chapter 4, when we discussed perceptual illusions, psychologists often infer the normal operation of processes by demonstrating circumstances in which the processes lead to errors. You can think of these memory distortions as the consequences of processes that usually work pretty well. In fact, a lot of the time, you don't need to remember the exact details of a particular episode. Reconstructing the gist of events will serve just fine. There is, however, at least one real-life domain in which you are always held responsible for *exactly* what happened. Let's turn now to eyewitness memory.

EYEWITNESS MEMORY

A witness in a courtroom swears "to tell the truth and nothing but the truth." Throughout this chapter, however, we have seen that whether a memory is accurate or inaccurate depends on the care with which it was encoded and the match of the circumstances of encoding and retrieval. Because researchers understand that people may not be able to report "the truth," even when they genuinely wish to do so, they have focused a good deal of attention on the topic of *eyewitness memory*. The goal is to help the legal system discover the best methods for ensuring the accuracy of witnesses' memories.

Influential studies on eyewitness memory were carried out by **Elizabeth Loftus** (1979; Wells & Loftus, 2003) and her colleagues. The general conclusion from their research was that eyewitnesses' memories for what they had seen were quite vulnerable to distortion from *postevent information*. For example, participants in one study were shown a film of an automobile accident and were asked to estimate the speeds of the cars involved (Loftus & Palmer, 1974). However, some participants were asked, "How fast were the cars going when they smashed into each other?" while others were asked, "How fast were the cars going when they contacted each other?" *Smash* participants estimated the cars' speed to have been over 40 miles per hour; *contact* participants estimated the speed at 30 miles per hour. About a week later, all the eyewitnesses were asked, "Did you see any broken glass?" In fact, no broken glass had appeared in the film. However, about a third of the *smash* participants reported that there had been glass, while only 14 percent of the *contact* eyewitnesses did so. Thus, postevent information had a substantial effect on what eyewitnesses reported they had experienced.

Postevent information can impair eyewitness memories even when the witnesses are made explicitly aware that the experimenter has attempted to mislead them.

What postevent factors make it difficult for eyewitnesses to make accurate reports of events?

Memory Reports Are Influenced by Postevent Information

In one experiment, participants viewed a slide show of an office theft. The slide show was accompanied by a tape recording of a woman's voice describing the sequence of events. Immediately after the slide show, the participants heard the woman describe the events again. However, this postevent narrative contained misinformation. For example, for participants who had seen *Glamour* magazine, the tape mentioned *Vogue* instead. Forty-eight hours later, the researcher tested his participants' memory for the information pictured in the slides, but he explicitly informed them that there was no question on the memory test for which the correct answer was mentioned in the postevent narrative. Thus, if participants were able to make a clear distinction in memory between the original events and the postevent information, they should have remained unaffected by that postevent information. That was not the case. Even with fair warning, participants often recalled postevent misinformation rather than real memories (Lindsay, 1990).

The participants had been unable to discriminate between the original sources—event or postevent—of the memory representations (Johnson et al., 1993; Weingardt et al., 1995). As you might expect, when people are repeatedly exposed to the misleading postevent information, they become even more likely to report false memories as real (Mitchell & Zaragoza, 1996). Although some controversy still surrounds the psychological mechanisms that give rise to this memory performance (Lindsay, 1993; Loftus, 1992; Schreiber &

Sergent, 1998), the potential for eyewitnesses' reports to be altered in response to postevent information has now been firmly established. This research reinforces the idea that your memories are often collages, reconstructed from different elements of your past experiences.

We have now considered several important features of the encoding, storage, and retrieval of information. In the final section of the chapter, we discuss the brain bases of these memory functions.

- How are the prototypes of categories formed?
- What types of information may be encoded in hierarchies?
- How do schemas function in everyday experience?
- Under what circumstances are memories reconstructed?
- What does eyewitness research indicate about memory accuracy?

Biological Aspects of Memory

The time has come, once again, for us to ask you to recall the number you committed to memory at the beginning of the chapter. Can you still remember it? What was the point of this exercise? Think for a minute about biological aspects of your ability to

<www.ablongman.com/gerrig17e>

Understanding Alzheimer's Disease

In recent years, researchers have acquired a deeper understanding of how memories are formed in the brain. This knowledge has allowed for focused attention on *Alzheimer's disease*—a biological condition in which memory function gradually breaks down. This disease afflicts about 10 percent of Americans over age 65 and perhaps 50 percent of those over 85 (Evans et al., 1989). Alzheimer's disease onset is deceptively mild—in early stages the only observable symptom may be memory impairment. However, its course is one of steady deterioration. Individuals with Alzheimer's disease may show gradual personality changes, such as apathy, lack of spontaneity, and withdrawal from social interactions. In advanced stages, people with Alzheimer's disease may become completely mute and inattentive, even forgetting the names of their spouse and children.

The symptoms of Alzheimer's disease were first described in 1906 by the German psychiatrist Alois Alzheimer. In those earliest investigations, Alzheimer noted that the brains of individuals who had died from the disease contained unusual tangles of neural tissue and sticky deposits called plaques. Still, Alzheimer could not determine whether those brain changes were the cause of the disease or its products. (As you might recall from Chapter 2, correlation does not necessarily imply causation.) Only in the past 10 to 15 years have researchers been able to assemble the evidence that the plaques themselves cause the brain to deteriorate (Esler & Wolfe, 2001; Hardy & Selkoe, 2002). The plaques are formed from a substance called *amyloid β-peptide (Aβ)*. Ordinary processes in the human brain that aid in the growth and maintenance of neurons create Aβ as a by-product. Normally, Aβ dissolves in the fluid surrounding neurons, without any consequences. However, in Alzheimer's disease, Aβ becomes deadly to neurons: Aβ forms plaques and causes brain cells to self-destruct (Marx, 2001).

This understanding of the role of Aβ in the progress of Alzheimer's disease has led to important recent breakthroughs. For example, researchers are beginning to improve their ability to diagnose the disease. As we shall see in Chapter 10, human aging is accompanied by some ordinary changes in memory function. To make a timely diagnosis of Alzheimer's disease, doctors need a way to determine whether older adults' memory impairments are something more than ordinary change. For most of the past hundred years that was a difficult task. Alzheimer's disease could be definitively diagnosed only when doctors could see the patients' brains—something that was not possible while the patients were living. However, researchers have begun to develop applications of PET scans (see Chapter 3) that enable them to detect the presence of Aβ in the living brain (Helmuth, 2002a). The key advance was the manufacture of a radioactive marker that attaches itself to the Aβ plaques. This radioactive marker becomes visible through PET scans—providing a mechanism for early diagnosis of ominous patterns of Aβ in the brain.

Early diagnosis would allow early treatment, with the goal of minimizing the negative impact of the disease. Although scientists are pursuing a number of preventive measures and treatments, several lines of research once again focus on Aβ (Hardy & Selkoe, 2002; Helmuth, 2002b). For example, researchers are seeking methods to interrupt the biochemical processes that produce Aβ in the first place. They are also exploring techniques to destroy the Aβ plaques once they have begun to form. Taken together, these approaches hold out great hope that Alzheimer's disease will be less devastating for future generations.

---

look at an arbitrary piece of information and commit it instantly to memory. How can you do that? To encode a memory requires that you instantly change something inside your brain. If you wish to retain that memory for at least the length of a chapter, the change must have the potential to become permanent. Have you ever wondered how this is possible? Our excuse for having you recall an arbitrary number was so that we could ask you to reflect on how remarkable the biology of memory really is. Let's take a closer look inside the brain.

◆ SEARCHING FOR THE ENGRAM

Let's consider your memory for the number 43 or, more specifically, your memory that the number 43 was the number we asked you to remember. How could we determine where in your brain that memory resides? **Karl Lashley** (1929, 1950), who performed pioneering work on the anatomy of memory, referred to this question as the search for the **engram,** the physical memory representation. Lashley trained rats to learn mazes, removed varying-size portions of their cortexes, and then retested their memories for the mazes. Lashley found that memory impairment from brain lesioning was proportional to the amount of tissue removed. The impairment grew worse as more of the cortex was damaged. However, memory was not affected by *where* in the cortex the tissue was removed. Lashley concluded that the elusive engram did not exist in any localized regions but was widely distributed throughout the entire brain.

Perhaps Lashley could not localize the engram partly because of the variety of types of memories that are called into play even in an apparently simple situation. Maze learning, in fact, involves complex inter-actions of spatial, visual, and olfactory signals. Neuroscientists now believe that memory for complex sets of information is distributed across many neural systems, even though discrete types of knowledge are separately processed and localized in limited regions of the brain (Markowitsch, 2000; Rolls, 2000).

Four major brain structures are involved in memory:

- The *cerebellum*, essential for procedural memory, memories acquired by repetition, and classically conditioned responses.

- The *striatum*, a complex of structures in the forebrain; the likely basis for habit formation and for stimulus-response connections.

- The *cerebral cortex*, responsible for sensory memories and associations between sensations.

- The *amygdala* and *hippocampus*, largely responsible for declarative memory of facts, dates, and names and also for memories of emotional significance.

Other parts of the brain, such as the thalamus, the basal forebrain, and the prefrontal cortex, are involved also as way stations for the formation of particular types of memories (see **Figure 7.15**).

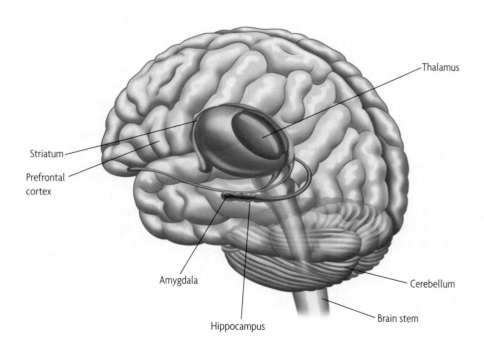

Thalamus

Striatum

Prefrontal cortex

Amygdala

Hippocampus

Cerebellum

Brain stem

FIGURE 7.15

Brain Structures Involved in Memory

This simplified diagram shows some of the main structures of the brain that are involved in the formation, storage, and retrieval of memories.

In Chapter 3, we focused directly on brain anatomy. Here, let's take a look at the methods that neuroscientists use to draw conclusions about the role of specific brain structures for memory. We will examine two types of research. First, we consider the insights generated by "experiments of nature"—circumstances in which individuals who have suffered brain damage volunteer to further memory research. Second, we describe the ways in which researchers are applying new brain imaging techniques to improve their understanding of memory processes in the brain.

◆ AMNESIA

In 1960, Nick A., a young Air Force radar technician, experienced a freak injury that permanently changed his life. Nick had been sitting at his desk while his roommate played with a miniature fencing foil. Then, suddenly, Nick stood up and turned around—just as his buddy happened to lunge with the sword. The foil pierced Nick's right nostril and continued to cut into the left side of his brain. The accident left Nick seriously disoriented. His worst problem was **amnesia,** the failure of memory over a prolonged period. Because of Nick's amnesia, he forgets many events immediately after they happen. After he reads a few paragraphs of writing, the first sentences slip from his memory. He cannot remember the plot of a television show unless, during commercials, he actively thinks about and rehearses what he was just watching.

The particular type of amnesia from which Nick suffers is called *anterograde* amnesia. This means that Nick can no longer form explicit memories for events that occur after the time at which he suffered physical damage. Other patients suffer from *retrograde* amnesia. In those cases, brain damage prevents access to memories that preceded the moment of injury. If you've ever had the misfortune of receiving a sharp blow to the head (during, for example, a car crash), you're likely to have experienced retrograde amnesia for the events leading up to the accident.

Researchers are grateful to patients like Nick for allowing themselves to be studied as "experiments of nature." By relating the locus of brain injuries like Nick's to patterns of performance deficit, researchers have begun to understand the mapping between the types of memories we have introduced you to in this chapter and regions of the brain (Mayes, 2000; Squire et al., 1989). Nick still remembers how to do things—his procedural knowledge appears to be intact even in the absence of declarative knowledge. So, for example, he remembers how to mix, stir, and bake the ingredients in a recipe, but he forgets what the ingredients are.

The selective impairment of explicit memory of the sort demonstrated by Nick strongly suggests that different regions of the brain are involved for different types of encoding and retrieval. For that reason, damage to a single brain region may impair one memory process but not another. Researchers have demonstrated this type of dissociation by contrasting explicit and implicit uses of memory.

PUTTING IDEAS TO THE TEST

Amnesia Spares Implicit Memory

Fifteen amnesic and 12 control individuals participated in a study that assessed their explicit and implicit memory ability (Goshen-Gottstein et al., 2000). In the experiment, the participants viewed word pairs such as *purse–sauce*. Their task was to create a meaningful sentence for each pair that kept the words in their original order (e.g., a participant might think, "I filled the purse with sauce"). Later, the participants performed explicit and implicit memory tasks. For the explicit task, participants were again presented with pairs of words. They were asked to indicate whether they had previously seen both words from the pair. By comparison to the control individuals, the amnesics performed quite poorly on this explicit task. For the implicit memory task, the participants also saw pairs of words. However, in this case they were asked to indicate whether both letter strings were legitimate words in the English language. On this implicit task, amnesics performed as well as the controls. Although the amnesics couldn't explicitly remember that they had seen words like *purse* and *sauce* paired together, their earlier experience of creating sentences with the words still improved performance on the implicit task.

The knowledge that certain forms of brain damage selectively impair explicit but not implicit memory allows researchers to isolate the specific contributions of the two types of memory to encoding and retrieval. Consider, for example, the ways in which people form new verbal associations of the type conveyed in a sentence such as "*medicine* cured *hiccup*." We know, because of the type of research we just described, that individuals with amnesia can acquire knowledge of individual words outside of explicit awareness—but can they also acquire knowledge of associations between words? One answer, from research with an individual known as C. V., whose amnesia stems from damage to the part of his temporal lobe called the medial temporal lobe, is no (Rajaram & Coslett, 2000). Although C. V. provided evidence of *perceptual* implicit memory, he provided no evidence of *conceptual* implicit memory (see page 225). This result suggests that, without explicit memory function, you cannot encode certain types of associations. Studies of this type allow researchers to gain a better understanding of both the brain bases of memory and the organization of memory processes.

◆ BRAIN IMAGING

Psychologists have gained a great deal of knowledge about the relationship between anatomy and memory from the amnesic patients who generously serve as participants in these experiments. However, the advent of brain imaging techniques has enabled researchers to study memory processes in individuals without brain damage (Nyberg & Cabeza, 2000). (You may want to review the section on imaging techniques in Chapter 3.) For example, using positron-emission tomography (PET), Endel Tulving and his colleagues (Nyberg et al., 1996; Tulving et al., 1994) have identified a difference in activation between the two brain hemispheres in the encoding and retrieval of episodic information. Their studies parallel standard memory studies, except that the participants' cerebral blood flow is monitored through PET scans during encoding or retrieval. These researchers discovered disproportionately high brain activity in the left prefrontal cortex (see Figure 7.15) for encoding of episodic information and in the right prefrontal cortex for retrieval of episodic information. Thus, the processes show some anatomical distinctions in addition to the conceptual distinctions made by cognitive psychologists.

Research with functional magnetic resonance imaging (fMRI) has also provided remarkable detail about the way that memory operations are distributed in the brain (Gabrieli et al., 1996, 1997). Consider two types of responses you might make to a word, such as *LOVE*. You could respond to *semantic* (meaning) aspects of a word—is it abstract or concrete? Or, you could respond to *perceptual* aspects of a word—is it in upper- or lowercase letters? As shown in **Figure 7.16,** fMRI scans reveal greater activation in an area of the left prefrontal cortex (the nonmotor part of the frontal cortex) for semantic than for perceptual encoding (Gabrieli et al., 1996). This region of cortex may be particularly activated for semantic encoding because of the link to language functions in the left hemisphere (see Chapter 3).

Further studies with fMRI have begun to identify the specific brain regions that are activated when new memories are formed (Brewer et al., 1998; Wagner et al., 1998). In these studies, participants were asked to

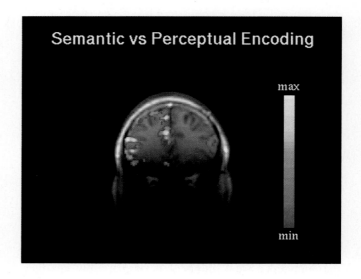

FIGURE 7.16

Encoding Operations in the Brain

The figure displays regions of the brain that show extra activity for the semantic task relative to the perceptual task. Note especially the high activity in the left prefrontal cortex—the region of the frontal lobe not involved in motor control—for the semantic task.

view scenes or words and make simple judgments (for example, whether the word represents something abstract or concrete). While they performed these tasks, the participants were undergoing fMRI scans to reveal regions of brain activation. Those fMRI scans uncovered a fascinating pattern: The more strongly that areas in prefrontal cortex and parahippocampal cortex (a part of cortex close to the hippocampus) were lit up during the scans, the better the participants were later able to recognize the scenes or words. This new research captures the biological basis for the birth of new memories in the cortex.

Historically, it has been difficult for researchers to obtain brain images of some of the most important subcortical regions involved in memory processes. For example, as you can see in Figure 7.15, the hippocampus is rolled into a small, tight spiral deep within the brain. However, recent breakthroughs in fMRI have provided some of the first images of the particular regions of the hippocampus that are at work while people learn and recall new associations.

Encoding and Retrieval in the Hippocampus

While lying in an MRI device, participants took part in a memory experiment. The participants viewed pictures of strangers' faces paired with names (e.g., Janet). This task was meant to reflect the types of new associations between faces and names people need to learn in everyday life. The brain scans showed a remarkable pattern of activity (see **Figure 7.17**). One pair of regions within the hippocampus—areas two and three of the *cornu ammonis* (abbreviated CA23) and the *dentate gyrus* (DG)—showed a high level of activity during initial encoding. Once, however, the participants had learned the associations, these subregions became less active. Another subregion—known as the *subiculum*—became active just for the retrieval of the new associations between faces and names rather than for their encoding (Zeineh et al., 2003).

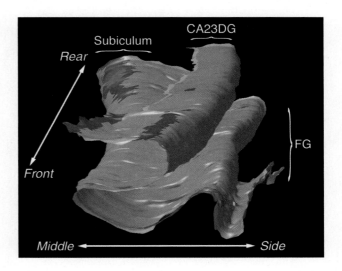

FIGURE 7.17

Regions of the Hippocampus Involved in Encoding and Retrieval

The regions shown in red—areas two and three of the cornu ammonis *(CA23) and the* dentate gyrus (DG)—*are particularly active during encoding of new associations. The region shown in blue—the* subiculum—*is particularly active during recall. The region shown in purple—the* fusiform gyrus (FG)—*is active for both encoding and retrieval, which suggests that the activation is not related to learning or recall in particular.*

Source: Zeineh et al., 2003.

Unless you pursue studies in cognitive neuroscience, you needn't worry why it is that the dentate gyrus handles encoding and the subiculum handles retrieval. Instead, studies of this sort should give you a strong sense of the link between the memory processes labeled in cognitive psychological models (e.g., encoding and retrieval) and comparable operations in the brain.

The results from imaging studies illustrate why researchers from different disciplines must work closely together in the quest for a full understanding of memory processes. Psychologists provide the data on human performance that become fuel for neurophysiologists' detection of specialized brain structures. At the same time, the realities of physiology constrain psychologists' theories of the mechanisms of encoding, storage, and retrieval. Through shared effort, scientists in these fields of research provide great insight into the operation of memory processes.

- What did Karl Lashley discover when he made his search for the engram?
- What have studies with amnesic individuals demonstrated about the brain bases of explicit and implicit memories?
- How have brain imaging procedures aided in the search for the engram?
- What has been learned about the brain bases of encoding and retrieval?

◆ Recapping Main Points

WHAT IS MEMORY?

- Cognitive psychologists study memory as a type of information processing.
- Memories involving conscious effort are explicit. Unconscious memories are implicit.
- Declarative memory is memory for facts; procedural memory is memory for how to perform skills.
- Memory is often viewed as a three-stage process of encoding, storage, and retrieval.

SENSORY MEMORY

- Sensory memory systems have large capacity but very short duration.
- Iconic memory momentarily preserves the visual world.
- Echoic memory holds auditory stimuli.

SHORT-TERM MEMORY AND WORKING MEMORY

- Short-term memory (STM) has a limited capacity and lasts only briefly without rehearsal.
- Maintenance rehearsal can extend the presence of material in STM indefinitely.
- STM capacity can be increased by chunking unrelated items into meaningful groups.
- Retrieval from STM is very efficient.
- The broader concept of working memory includes STM.
- The three components of working memory provide the resources for moment-by-moment experiences of the world.

LONG-TERM MEMORY: ENCODING AND RETRIEVAL

- Long-term memory (LTM) constitutes your total knowledge of the world and of yourself. It is nearly unlimited in capacity.

- Your ability to remember information relies on the match between circumstances of encoding and retrieval.
- Similarity in context between learning and retrieval aids retrieval.
- The serial position curve is explained by distinctiveness in context.
- Retrieval cues allow you to access information in LTM.
- Episodic memory is concerned with memory for events that have been personally experienced. Semantic memory is memory for the basic meaning of words and concepts.
- Interference occurs when retrieval cues do not lead uniquely to specific memories.
- Information processed more deeply is typically remembered better.
- For implicit memories, it is important that the processes of encoding and retrieval be similar.
- Memory performance can be improved through elaborative rehearsal and mnemonics.
- In general, feelings-of-knowing accurately predict the availability of information in memory.

STRUCTURES IN LONG-TERM MEMORY

- Concepts are the memory building blocks of thinking. They are formed when memory processes gather together classes of objects or ideas with common properties.
- Prototypes represent the average exemplar of a concept.
- Concepts are often organized in hierarchies, ranging from general, to basic level, to specific.
- Schemas are more complex cognitive clusters.
- All these memory structures are used to provide expectations and a context for interpreting new information.
- Remembering is not simply recording but is a constructive process.
- Past experiences affect what you remember.

New information can bias recall, making eyewitness memory unreliable when contaminated by postevent input.

BIOLOGICAL ASPECTS OF MEMORY

Different brain structures (including the hippocampus, the amygdala, the cerebellum, and the cerebral cortex) have been shown to be involved in different types of memories.

Experiments with individuals with amnesia have helped investigators understand how different types of memories are acquired and represented in the brain.

Brain imaging techniques have extended knowledge about the brain bases of memory encoding and retrieval.

KEY TERMS

amnesia (p. 239)

basic level (p. 232)

chunking (p. 215)

concepts (p. 230)

contextual distinctiveness (p. 219)

declarative memory (p. 208)

echoic memory (p. 212)

elaborative rehearsal (p. 226)

encoding (p. 209)

encoding specificity (p. 218)

engram (p. 238)

episodic memories (p. 222)

explicit uses of memory (p. 207)

iconic memory (p. 210)

implicit uses of memory (p. 207)

levels-of-processing theory (p. 224)

long-term memory (LTM) (p. 218)

memory (p. 206)

metamemory (p. 227)

mnemonics (p. 226)

primacy effect (p. 219)

priming (p. 224)

proactive interference (p. 223)

procedural memory (p. 208)

prototype (p. 230)

recall (p. 221)

recency effect (p. 219)

recognition (p. 221)

reconstructive memory (p. 234)

retrieval (p. 209)

retrieval cues (p. 221)

retroactive interference (p. 223)

schemas (p. 232)

semantic memories (p. 222)

sensory memory (p. 210)

serial position effect (p. 219)

short-term memory (STM) (p. 213)

storage (p. 209)

transfer-appropriate processing (p. 224)

working memory (p. 213)

Cognitive Processes

I t is midnight. There's a knock on your door. When you answer, no one is there, but you see an envelope on the floor. Inside the envelope is a single sheet of paper with a handwritten message: "The cat is on the mat." What do you make of this?

You must now begin to engage a variety of cognitive processes. You will need language processes to put together some basic meanings for the words, but what then? Can you find any episode in memory to which these words are relevant? (Recall that in Chapter 7 we discussed memory as a type of cognitive processing.) If you can't, you'll have to give other types of thought to the matter. Is the message a code? What kind of code? Whom do you know who might encode a message? Does the fate of civilization rest in your hands?

Perhaps we're getting a bit carried away, but we want to make plain to you what kinds of activities count as **cognitive processes** and why they might interest you. The capacity to use language and to think in abstract ways has often been cited as the essence of the human experience. You tend to take cognition for granted because it's an activity you do continually during your waking hours. Even so, when a carefully crafted speech wins your vote or when you read a detective story in which the sleuth combines a few scraps of apparently trivial clues into a brilliant solution to a crime, you are forced to acknowledge the intellectual triumph of cognitive processes.

Cognition is a general term for all forms of knowing: As shown in **Figure 8.1,** the study of cognition is the study of your mental life. (Note that Chapter 4 already discussed some of the topics shown in Figure 8.1.) Cognition includes both contents and processes. The *contents* of cognition are *what* you know—concepts, facts, propositions, rules, and memories: "A dog is a mammal." "A red light means stop." "I first left home at age 18." Cognitive *processes* are *how* you manipulate these mental contents—in ways that enable you to interpret the world around you and to find creative solutions to your life's dilemmas.

Within psychology, the study of cognition is carried out by researchers in the field of **cognitive psychology.** Over the past three decades, the field of cognitive psychology has been supplemented by the interdisciplinary field of **cognitive science** (see **Figure 8.2**). Cognitive science focuses the collected knowledge of several academic specialties on the same theoretical issues. It benefits the practitioners of each of these fields to share their data and insights. You saw this cognitive science philosophy at work in Chapter 7, when we described how studies of the biology of memory can be used to con-

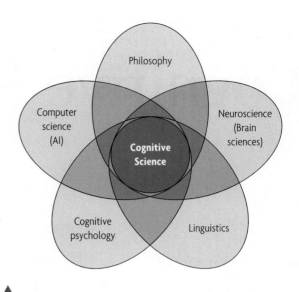

FIGURE 8.2

The Domain of Cognitive Science

The domain of cognitive science occupies the intersection of philosophy, neuroscience, linguistics, cognitive psychology, and computer science (artificial intelligence).

strain—limit and refine—theories of memory processes. Many of the theories we will describe in this chapter have similarly been shaped through the interactions of researchers from a number of disciplinary perspectives.

We will begin our study of cognition with a brief description of the ways in which researchers try to measure the inner, private processes involved in cognitive functioning. Then we will examine, at some length, topics in cognitive psychology that generate much basic research and practical application: language use, visual cognition, problem solving, reasoning, and judging and decision making.

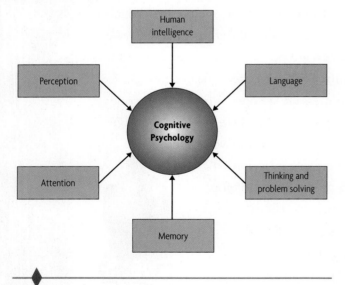

FIGURE 8.1

The Domain of Cognitive Psychology

Cognitive psychologists study higher mental functions with particular emphasis on the ways in which people acquire knowledge and use it to shape and understand their experiences in the world.

From Solso, Robert L., *Cognitive Psychology* 3e © 1991. Published by Allyn & Bacon, Boston, MA. Copyright © 2003 by Pearson Education. Reprinted by permission of the publisher.

Studying Cognition

How can you study cognition? The challenge, of course, is that it goes on inside the head. You can see the input—for example, a note that says, "Call me"—and experience the output—you make a phone call—but how can you determine the series of mental steps that connected the note to your response? How, that is, can you reveal what hap-

<www.ablongman.com/gerrig17e>

pened in the middle—the cognitive processes and the mental representations on which your action relies? In this section, we describe the types of logical analyses that have made possible the scientific study of cognitive psychology.

◆ DISCOVERING THE PROCESSES OF MIND

One of the fundamental methodologies for studying mental processes was devised, in 1868, by the Dutch physiologist **F. C. Donders.** To study the "speed of mental processes," Donders invented a series of experimental tasks that he believed were differentiated by the mental steps involved for successful performance (Lachman et al., 1979). **Table 8.1** provides a paper-and-pencil experiment that follows Donders's logic. Before reading on, please take a moment to complete each task.

How long did you take to do task 1? Suppose you wanted to give a list of the steps you carried out to perform the task. It might look something like this:

a. Determine whether a character is a capital letter or a small letter.

b. If it is a capital letter, draw a C on top.

◆

TABLE 8.1
Donders's Analysis of Mental Processes

Note how long (in seconds) it takes you to complete each of these three tasks. Try to complete each task accurately, but as quickly as possible.

Task 1: Draw a C on top of all the capitalized letters:
TO Be, oR noT To BE: tHAT Is thE qUestioN:
WhETher 'Tis noBlEr In tHE MINd tO SuFfER
tHe SLings AnD ARroWS Of OUtrAgeOUs forTUNe,
or To TAke ARmS agaINST a sEa Of tROUBleS,
AnD by oPPOsinG END theM.   TIME: _____

Task 2: Draw a V on top of the capitalized vowels and a C on top of the capitalized consonants:
TO Be, oR noT To BE: tHAT Is thE qUestioN:
WhETher 'Tis noBlEr In tHE MINd tO SuFfER
tHe SLings AnD ARroWS Of OUtrAgeOUs forTUNe,
or To TAke ARmS agaINST a sEa Of tROUBleS,
AnD by oPPOsinG END theM.   TIME: _____

Task 3: Draw a V on top of all the capitalized letters:
TO Be, oR noT To BE: tHAT Is thE qUestioN:
WhETher 'Tis noBlEr In tHE MINd tO SuFfER
tHe SLings AnD ARroWS Of OUtrAgeOUs forTUNe,
or To TAke ARmS agaINST a sEa Of tROUBleS,
AnD by oPPOsinG END theM.   TIME: _____

How long did you take for task 2? When we have used this exercise, students have often taken an additional half minute or more. You can understand why, once we spell out the necessary steps:

a. Determine whether a character is a capital letter or a small letter.

b. Determine whether each capital letter is a vowel or a consonant.

c. If it is a consonant, draw a C on top. If it is a vowel, draw a V.

Thus, going from task 1 to task 2, we add two mental steps, which we can call *stimulus categorization* (vowel or consonant?) and *response selection* (draw a C or draw a V). Task 1 requires one stimulus categorization step. Task 2 requires two such categorizations. Task 2 also requires selecting between two responses. Because task 2 requires you to do everything you did for task 1 and more, it takes you more time. That was Donders's fundamental insight: Extra mental steps will often result in more time to perform a task.

(You may be wondering why we included task 3. This is a necessary procedural control for the experiment. We have to ensure that the time difference between tasks 1 and 2 does not stem from the fact that it takes much longer to draw V's than to draw C's. Task 3 should still be much swifter than task 2. Was it?)

Researchers still follow Donders's basic logic. They frequently use *reaction time*—the amount of time it takes experimental participants to perform particular tasks—as a way of testing specific accounts of how some cognitive process is carried out. Donders's basic premise that extra mental steps will result in extra time is still fundamental to a great deal of cognitive psychological research. Let's see how this successful idea has been developed over the past 135 years.

◆ MENTAL PROCESSES AND MENTAL RESOURCES

When cognitive psychologists break down high-level activities, like language use or problem solving, into their component processes, they often act as if they are playing a game with blocks. Each block represents a different component that must be carried out. The goal is to determine the shape and size of each block and to see how the blocks fit together to form the whole activity. For the Donders tasks, you saw that the blocks can be laid out in a row (see **Figure 8.3,** part A). Each step comes directly after another. The block metaphor allows you to see that we could also stack the blocks so that more than one process occurs simultaneously (part B). These two pictures illustrate the distinction between **serial** and **parallel processes.** Processes are *serial*

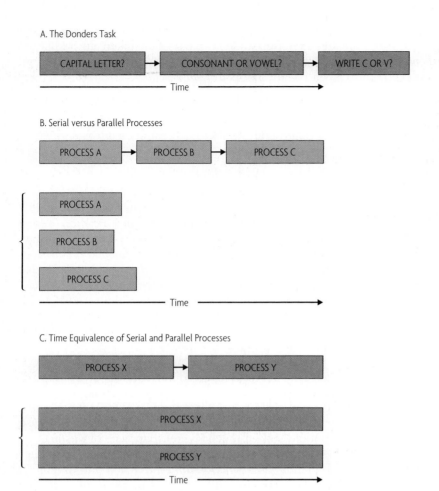

A. The Donders Task

| CAPITAL LETTER? | → | CONSONANT OR VOWEL? | → | WRITE C OR V? |

—— Time ——→

B. Serial versus Parallel Processes

| PROCESS A | → | PROCESS B | → | PROCESS C |

PROCESS A

PROCESS B

PROCESS C

—— Time ——→

C. Time Equivalence of Serial and Parallel Processes

| PROCESS X | → | PROCESS Y |

PROCESS X

PROCESS Y

—— Time ——→

◆

FIGURE 8.3

Breaking Down High-Level Cognitive Activities

Cognitive psychologists attempt to determine the identity and organization of the mental processes that are the building blocks of high-level cognitive activities.
(A) Our version of the Donders task requires that at least three processes be carried out one after the other.
(B) Some processes are carried out serially, in sequence; others are carried out in parallel, all at the same time.
(C) The time taken to perform a task does not always allow researchers to conclude whether serial or parallel processes were used.

when they take place one after the other. Suppose you're in a restaurant and you need to decide what to order. You focus on entries one at a time and then judge whether they qualify as "yes," "no," or "maybe." For each entry, your judgment processes follow your reading processes. Processes are *parallel* when they overlap in time. When it comes time to place your order, the language processes that enable you to understand the waiter's question (e.g., "What can I get for you?") are likely to operate at the same time as the processes that allow you to formulate your reply (e.g., "I'd like the osso buco"). That's why you're ready to respond as soon as the waiter finishes his question.

Cognitive psychologists often use reaction times to determine whether processes are carried out in parallel or serially. However, the examples in part C of Figure 8.3 should convince you that this is a tricky business. Imagine that we have a task that we believe can be broken down into two processes, *X* and *Y*. If the only information we have is the total time needed to complete the process, we can never be sure if processes *X* and *Y* happen side by side or one after the other.

Much of the challenge of research in cognitive psychology is to invent task circumstances that allow the experimenter to determine which of many possible configurations of blocks is correct. In task 2 of the exercise you just did, we could be reasonably certain that the processes were serial, because some activities logically required others. For example, you couldn't execute your response (prepare to draw a C or a V) until you had determined what the response might be.

In many cases, theorists try to determine if processes are serial or parallel by assessing the extent to which the processes place demands on *mental resources*. Suppose, for example, you are walking to class with a friend. Ordinarily, it should be easy for you to walk a straight path at the same time you carry on a conversation—your navigation processes and your language processes can go on in parallel. But what would happen if you suddenly get to a patch of sidewalk that's dotted with puddles? As you pick your way among the puddles, you may have to stop talking. Now your navigation processes require extra resources for planning, and your language processes are momentarily squeezed out.

Why is it difficult to carry on a conversation while you are trying to avoid puddles?

A key assumption in this example is that you have *limited* processing resources that must be spread over different mental tasks (Logan, 2002). Your *attentional processes* are responsible for distributing these resources. In Chapter 4, we discussed attention as the set of processes that allow you to select, for particular scrutiny, some small subset of available perceptual information. Our use of *attention* here preserves the idea of selectivity. The decision now, however, concerns which mental processes will be selected as the recipients of processing resources.

We have one more complication to add: Not all processes put the same demands on resources. We can, in fact, define a dimension that goes from processes that are *controlled* to those that are *automatic* (Shiffrin & Schneider, 1977). **Controlled processes** require attention; **automatic processes** generally do not. It is often difficult to carry out more than one controlled process at a time, because they require more resources; automatic processes can often be performed alongside other tasks without interference.

We want to give you an example of an automatic process. To get started, take a moment to carry out the task in **Table 8.2.** Did you find List A somewhat harder than List B?

You Can't Ignore the "Meaning" of Numbers

Experimental participants were asked to make the types of judgments illustrated in Table 8.2. The pattern of results suggested that people find it harder to respond *different* when the numbers are close together (for example, 1–2) than when they are far apart (for example, eight–one) irrespective of whether the numbers are rendered as arabic numerals or written out. Note that list A had "close" different pairs and list B had "far" different pairs, so you should have found it somewhat harder to complete list A. But why should the closeness of the numbers matter for a judgment of *physical* similarity? *One–two* and *one–nine* are about equal on the dimension of *physical* dissimilarity. The researchers suggested that when you look at *2* or *two*, you can't help but think of the quantity it represents—even when the quantity, in this case, impairs performance on the task you've been asked to carry out. That is, you *automatically* access the meaning of a number, even when you don't need (or want) to do so (Dehaene & Akhavein, 1995).

This number task illustrates that automatic processes rely heavily on the efficient use of memory (Logan, 1988, 1992). Whether the object in the environment is *2* or *two,* your memory processes swiftly provide information about quantity.

TABLE 8.2
Number Processing

Your task is to put a check mark on top of the pairs of numbers that are *physically different,* in either numbers or words (that is, you would check both *4–6* and *four–six*). Try to judge which list is harder.

List A

8–8	nine–eight	1–2	eight–eight
2–1	8–9	9–9	2–2
two–two	one–two	nine–nine	eight–nine
one–one	1–1	two–one	9–8

List B

1–1	nine–two	one–one	nine–nine
2–9	eight–two	9–9	1–9
eight–one	8–8	eight–eight	nine–one
2–2	1–8	2–8	two–two

The number task also illustrates the way in which tasks that first involved controlled processes can become automatic with sufficient practice. You probably remember, as a small child, having to learn how numbers work. Now, the association between numbers and the quantities they represent has become so automatic, you can't shut off the association. You can probably think of other instances in which you've practiced enough to make tasks automatic. Did you learn to play an instrument? Can you type without looking at the keyboard?

Let's apply this knowledge of controlled and automatic processes back to the situation of walking and talking. When you are walking a straight route, you feel little interference between the two activities, suggesting that maintaining your path and planning your utterances are each relatively automatic activities. The situation changes, however, when the puddles force you to choose between a greater number of options for your path. Now you must select where to go and what to say. Because you can't make both choices simultaneously, you have hit an attentional *bottleneck* (Pashler, 1992, 1994). This example shows why controlled and automatic processes are defined along a dimension, rather than constituting strict categories. When circumstances become challenging, what before seemed automatic now requires controlled attention. Thus, processes may require more or less attention, depending on the context.

Before we leave this discussion of the distinction between controlled and automatic processes, we want to take a moment to look into your brain. Recall that in Chapter 1, we defined *cognitive neuroscience* as the field that attempts to understand the brain processes that underlie higher cognitive functions. Cognitive neuroscientists often examine the processing distinctions that emerge in cognitive psychological theories, to see if those distinctions are paralleled by activity in the brain. Consider **Figure 8.4.** This figure shows the results of a study that used fMRI scans to compare brain activity during automatic and controlled processing (Rossell et al., 2001). The experiment focused on the relationships among word meanings. Participants read one word (e.g., *lemon*). Then, after some gap in time, the participants viewed two letter strings and had to indicate which of the two formed a word of English (e.g., *pear* or *poike*). With a brief time gap, this task relies on automatic processes—because *lemon* immediately makes people think of *pear*. With a longer gap, however, people begin to use controlled effort to anticipate what words might come next. As you can see in Figure 8.4, the two versions of the task yield greater activity in different areas of a brain structure known as the *anterior cingulate cortex (ACC)*. The ACC plays a role in a wide range of cognitive and emotional

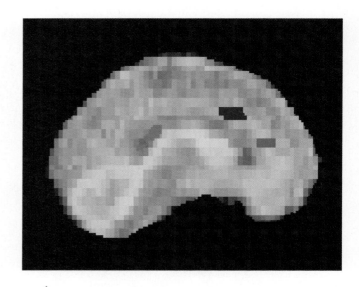

FIGURE 8.4

Automatic and Controlled Processes in the Brain

Different regions of anterior cingulate cortex were relatively more active when a task involved automatic processes (shown in red) versus controlled processes (shown in blue).

processes (Bush et al., 2000). Each new experimental result—such as this outcome for controlled and automatic processes—helps generate a greater understanding of how the brain processes information.

You now know a lot about the logic of mental processes. To explain how complex mental tasks are carried out, theorists propose models that combine serial and parallel and controlled and automatic processes. The goal of much cognitive psychological research is to invent experiments that confirm each of the components of such models. Now that you understand some of the logic behind cognitive psychological research into mental processes, it is time to move to more specific domains in which you put cognitive processes to work. We begin with language use.

PUT YOURSELF TO THE TEST

- How did Donders's program of research seek to identify the building blocks of cognition?
- What is the distinction between serial and parallel processes?
- What is the relationship of controlled and automatic processes to attentional resources?

Language Use

Let's return to the message you received at midnight, "The cat is on the mat." What could we do to change the situation so that this message immediately made sense to you? The easiest step we could take would be to introduce appropriate background knowledge. Suppose you are a secret agent who always gets instructions in this curious fashion. You might know that "the cat" is your contact and that "on the mat" means in the wrestling arena. Off you go.

But you don't have to be a spy for "The cat is on the mat" to take on a variety of meanings:

- Suppose your cat waits on a mat by the door when she wants to be let out. When you say to your roommate, "The cat is on the mat," you use those words to communicate, "Could you get up and let the cat out?"

- Suppose your friend is worried about pulling the car out of the driveway because she's uncertain where the cat is. When you say, "The cat is on the mat," you use those words to communicate, "It's safe to pull out of the driveway."

- Suppose you are trying to have a race between your cat and your friend's dog. When you say, "The cat is on the mat," you use those words to communicate, "My cat won't race!"

These examples illustrate the difference between *sentence meaning*—the generally simple meaning of the combined words of a sentence—and *speaker's meaning*—the unlimited number of meanings a speaker can communicate by putting a sentence to good use (Grice, 1968). When psychologists study language use, they want to comprehend both the *production* and the *understanding* of speakers' meaning:

- How do speakers produce the right words to communicate the meaning they intend?

- How do listeners recover the messages the speakers wished to communicate?

We will examine each of these questions in turn.

◆ LANGUAGE PRODUCTION

Look at **Figure 8.5.** Try to formulate a few sentences about this picture. What did you think to say? Suppose now we asked you to redescribe the person for someone who was blind. How would your description

FIGURE 8.5

Language Production

How would you describe this character to a friend? How might your description change if your friend were blind?

change? Does this second description seem to require more mental effort? The study of **language production** concerns both what people say—what they choose to say at a given time—and the processes they go through to produce the message. Note that language users need not produce language out loud. Language production also includes both signing and writing. For convenience, however, we will call language producers *speakers* and language understanders *listeners*.

AUDIENCE DESIGN

We asked you to imagine the different descriptions you'd give of Figure 8.5 to a sighted and a blind person as a way of getting you to think about **audience design** in language production. Each time you produce an utterance, you must have in mind the audience to whom the utterance will be directed, and what knowledge you share with members of that audience (Clark, 1996; Clark & Van Der Wege, 2002). For example, it won't do you the least bit of good to say, "The cat is on the mat" if your listener does not know that the cat sits on the mat only when she wishes to be let out. An overarching rule of audience design, the *cooperative principle,* was first proposed by the philosopher **H. Paul Grice** (1975). Grice phrased the cooperative principle as an instruction to speakers that they should produce utterances appropriate to the setting and meaning of the ongoing conversation. To expand on this instruction, Grice defined four maxims that cooperative speakers

live by. In **Table 8.3,** we present each of those maxims, as well as an invented conversation that illustrates the effect the maxims have on moment-by-moment choices in language production.

As you can see from Table 8.3, being a cooperative speaker depends, in large part, on having accurate expectations about what your listener is likely to know and understand. Thus, you certainly wouldn't tell a friend "I'm having lunch with Alex" if you didn't have good reason to believe that your friend knew who Alex

TABLE 8.3
Grice's Maxims in Language Production

1. *Quantity:* Make your contribution as informative as is required (for the current purposes of the exchange). Do not make your contribution more informative than is required.

   The consequence for the speaker: You must try to judge how much information your audience really needs. Often this judgment will require you to assess what your listener is likely to know already.

2. *Quality:* Try to make your contribution one that is true. Do not say what you believe to be false. Do not say that for which you lack adequate evidence.

   The consequence for the speaker: When you speak, listeners will assume that you can back up your assertions with appropriate evidence. As you plan each utterance, you must have in mind the evidence on which it is based.

3. *Relation:* Be relevant.

   The consequence for the speaker: You must make sure that your listeners will see how what you are saying is relevant to what has come before. If you wish to shift the topic of conversation—so that your utterance is not directly relevant—you must make that clear.

4. *Manner:* Be perspicacious. Avoid obscurity of expression. Avoid ambiguity. Be brief. Be orderly.

   The consequence for the speaker: It is your responsibility to speak in as clear a manner as possible. Although you will inevitably make errors, as a cooperative speaker you must ensure that your listeners can understand your message.

In this conversation, can you see how Chris follows (or violates) Grice's maxims?

What Is Said	What Chris Might Be Thinking
Pat: *Have you ever been to New York City?* Chris: *I was there once in 1992.*	I don't know why Pat is asking me this question, so I probably should say a little more than just "yes."
Pat: *I'm supposed to visit, but I'm worried about being mugged.* Chris: *I think a lot of areas are safe.*	I can't say that he shouldn't worry, because he won't believe me. What can I say that will sound true but make him feel okay?
Pat: *How was your hotel?* Chris: *We didn't stay overnight.*	If I say, "We didn't stay in a hotel," that might suggest we stayed somewhere else. I need to say something relevant that will make clear why I can't answer the question.
Pat: *Would you like to go to New York with me?* Chris: *I'd have to find a way to see if it would be possible for me to leave without it being too impossible.* Pat: *Huh?* Chris: *Well . . .*	I don't want to go, but I don't want to seem rude. Will Pat notice that I'm being evasive in my response? Trapped.

 <www.ablongman.com/gerrig17e>

Among ichthyologists, this is a Choerodon fasciatus. *What would you call it if you were talking or writing about it to a friend?*

Community Membership Affects Language Production

Researchers created circumstances in which unacquainted students were asked to perform a matching task. The *director* had 16 New York City postcards in front of her, laid out in a 4-by-4 array. She had to describe the sights pictured in the postcards so that the *matcher* could recreate the correct 4-by-4 ordering of the pictures. Although the director and the matcher couldn't see each other, they could converse freely. As a consequence, the directors were quickly able to determine whether their matchers were "experts" or "novices" about New York. When they discovered that they were talking to a fellow New Yorker, they were much more likely to use a proper name to pinpoint a postcard—"it's the Citicorp building"—than to give a roundabout description—"it's the tall building with a triangular top" (Isaacs & Clark, 1987).

was. You also must assure yourself that, of all the Alexes your friend might know and that she knows that you know, only one would come to mind as the specific Alex you would mention in these circumstances. More formally, we can say that there must be some Alex who is prominent in the *common ground*—common knowledge—you share with your friend. **Herbert Clark** and Catherine Marshall (1981) suggested that judgments of common ground are based on three sources of evidence:

- *Community membership.* Language producers often make strong assumptions about what is likely to be mutually known based on shared membership in communities of various sizes.

- *Linguistic copresence.* Language producers often assume that information contained in earlier parts of a conversation (or in past conversations) is part of the common ground.

- *Physical copresence.* Physical copresence exists when a speaker and a listener are directly in the physical presence of objects or situations. This includes both the setting of the conversation and all the people around the conversationalists.

Thus, your use of Alex in "I'm having lunch with Alex" might succeed because your friend and you are part of a small community (for example, roommates) that includes only one Alex (community membership). Or it might succeed because you've introduced the existence of Alex earlier in the conversation (linguistic copresence). Or Alex might be standing right there in the room (physical copresence).

Let's focus a bit more on community membership. Suppose you are meeting a date for the first time. If you want to be a cooperative conversationalist, one of the first things you must do is to determine the communities to which that individual belongs.

Thus, speakers adjusted their utterances based on their expectations about what the listener would be able to understand. On the whole, people are pretty accurate at guessing what members of their own communities are likely to know—although they tend to err in the direction of believing other people know the same things they do (Fussell & Krauss, 1992). The accurate guesses make possible appropriate adjustments in language production.

Next time a stranger stops you on the street to ask for directions, pay attention to what you do to figure out how much common ground you share. Do you ask specific questions (for example, "Do you know where the town hall is?")? Do you try to make your best guess from what the stranger is wearing (for example, a campus sweatshirt) or how he or she talks (for example, with a Southern accent in a Midwestern town)?

Our discussion so far has focused on language production at the level of the message: How you shape what you wish to say will depend on the audience to whom you are speaking. Let's turn now to a discussion of the mental processes that allow you to produce these messages.

SPEECH EXECUTION AND SPEECH ERRORS

Would you like to be famous for tripping over your tongue? Consider the Reverend W. A. Spooner of Oxford University, who lent his name to the term *spoonerism:* an exchange of the initial sounds of two or more words in a phrase or sentence. Reverend Spooner came by this honor honestly. When, for example, he was tongue-lashing a lazy student for wasting the term,

Reverend Spooner said, "You have tasted the whole worm!" A spoonerism is one of the limited types of speech errors that language producers make. These errors give researchers insight into the planning that goes on as speakers produce utterances. As you can see in **Table 8.4,** you need to plan an utterance at a number of different levels, and speech errors give evidence for each of those levels (Bock & Levelt, 1994; Rapp & Goldrick, 2000). What should impress you about all these examples of errors is that they are not just random—they make sense given the structure of spoken English. Thus, a speaker might exchange initial consonants—"tips of the slung" for "slips of the tongue"—but would never say, "tlips of the sung," which would violate the rule of English that "tl" does not occur as an initial sound (Fromkin, 1980).

Given the importance of speech errors to developing theoretical models of speech production, researchers have not always been content just to wait around for errors to happen naturally. Instead, researchers have explored a number of ways to produce artificial errors in controlled experimental settings (Bock, 1996). Those techniques have yielded insights into both the processes and representations that underlie fluent speech production:

- *Processes.* Recall, from Chapter 5, the SLIP (for "spoonerisms of laboratory-induced predisposition") technique that encourages participants to produce spoonerisms (Baars, 1992). In this procedure, participants are asked to read silently lists of word pairs that provide models for the phonetic structure of a target spoonerism: *ball doze, bash door, bean deck, bell dark.* They then are required to pronounce out loud a word pair like *darn bore,* but under the influence of the earlier pairs it will sometimes come out *barn door.*

With this technique, researchers can study the factors that affect the likelihood that speakers will produce errors. For example, a spoonerism is more likely when the error will still result in real words (Baars et al., 1975; Stemberger, 1992). Thus an error on *darn bore* (to produce *barn door*) is more likely than an error on *dart board* (to produce *bart doard*). Findings like this one suggest that while you are producing utterances, some of your cognitive processes are devoted to detecting and editing potential errors. Those processes are reluctant to let you pronounce sounds like *doard,* which are not real English words.

- *Representations.* Another procedure required participants to read pairs of idioms (like *shoot the breeze* and *raise the roof*). After a two-second interval, they were asked to produce one of the idioms from memory, as swiftly as possible. Under this time pressure, participants sometimes produced *blends* of the two idioms, such as *kick the maker* (from *kick the bucket* and *meet your maker*). These blend errors were most likely when the two idioms shared the same underlying meaning (as with *kick the bucket* and *meet your maker*) rather than when they differed in meaning (as with *shoot the breeze* and *raise the roof*). This result suggests that representations of idioms with similar meanings are linked in memory: As you begin to produce one idiom, a representational link to another with similar meaning may lead to a blend error (Cutting & Bock, 1997). That's the way the cookie bounces!

We have now looked at some of the forces that lead speakers to produce particular utterances and at some of the processes that allow them to do so. We turn next to the listeners, who are responsible for understanding what speakers intend to communicate.

◆ **LANGUAGE UNDERSTANDING**

Suppose a speaker has produced the utterance "The cat is on the mat." You already know that, depending on the context, this utterance can be used to communicate any number of different meanings. How, as a listener, do you settle on just one meaning? We will begin this

---

◆———————————————————

TABLE 8.4
Errors in Planning Speech Production

Types of planning:

- Speakers must choose the content words that best fit their ideas.

    If the speaker has two words in mind, such as *grizzly* and *ghastly,* a blend like *grastly* might result.

- Speakers must put the chosen words in the right places in the utterance.

    Because speakers plan whole units of their utterances while they produce them, content words will sometimes become misplaced.

    a tank of gas → a gas of tank

    wine is being served at dinner → dinner is being served at wine

- Speakers must fill in the sounds that make up the words they wish to utter.

    Once again, because speakers plan ahead, sounds will sometimes get misplaced.

    left hemisphere → heft lemisphere

    pass out → pat ous

<www.ablongman.com/gerrig17e>

discussion of language understanding by considering more fully the problem of the ambiguity of meaning.

RESOLVING AMBIGUITY

What does the word *bank* mean? You can probably think of at least two meanings, one having to do with rivers and the other having to do with money. Suppose you hear the utterance "He came from the bank." How do you know which meaning is intended? You need to be able to resolve the *lexical ambiguity* between the two meanings. (*Lexical* is related to *lexicon,* a synonym for *dictionary.*) If you think about this problem, you'll realize that you have some cognitive processes that allow you to use surrounding context to eliminate the ambiguity—to *disambiguate*—the word. Have you been talking about rivers or about money? That broader context should enable you to choose between the two meanings. But how?

Before we answer that question, we'd like to introduce another type of ambiguity. What does this sentence mean: "The mother of the boy and the girl will arrive soon?" You may detect only one meaning right off, but there is a *structural ambiguity* here (Akmajian et al., 1990). Take a look at **Figure 8.6**. Linguists often represent the structure of sentences with tree diagrams to show how the various words are gathered together into grammatical units. In part A, we've shown you an analysis of "The cat is on the mat." The structure is pretty simple: a noun phrase made up of an article and a noun, plus a verb phrase made up of a verb and a prepositional phrase. In the other two parts, you see the more complex structures for the two different meanings of "The mother . . ." In part B, the analysis shows that the whole phrase "of the boy and the girl" applies to the mother. One person—the mother of two children—will arrive soon. In part C, the analysis shows that there are

Structure A

Structure B

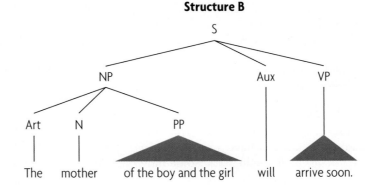

Art = article
Aux = auxiliary
NP = noun phrase
PP = prepositional phrase
S = sentence
VP = verb phrase

Structure C

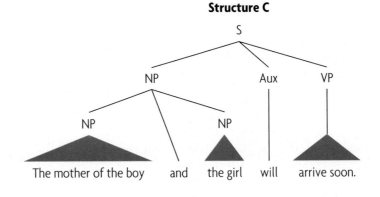

FIGURE 8.6

Sentence Structures

Linguists use tree diagrams to display the grammatical structure of sentences. Part A shows the structure of "The cat is on the mat." Parts B and C show that the sentence "The mother of the boy and the girl will arrive soon" can be represented by two different structural analyses. Who will arrive soon, one person (structure B) or two (structure C)?

Now that you are looking at a picture of a dancing couple, what comes to mind when you think of the word ball?

two noun phrases, "the mother of the boy" and "the girl." There are two people, both of whom will arrive soon. Which understanding of the sentence did you come to when you first read it? Now that you can see that two meanings are possible, we arrive at the same question we did for lexical ambiguity: How does prior context enable you to settle on one meaning when more than one is possible?

Let's return to lexical ambiguity (an ambiguity of word meaning). Consider this sentence:

Nancy watched the ball.

When you read this sentence, how do you interpret the word *ball*? If you imagine that you have a dictionary in your head, your entry for ball might look something like this:

Definition 1. A round object used in a game or sport

Definition 2. A large formal event for dancing

The sentence "Nancy watched the ball" contains no information that allows you to choose between these two definitions. In fact, research suggests that both definitions become accessible in memory after you read this type of sentence (Vu et al., 1998). You need help from surrounding context to determine which ball is which. But how does context help you decide among meanings? Research suggests that context provides a variety of types of evidence (Vu et al., 1998, 2000). Consider these examples:

1. She catered the ball.
2. The juggler watched the ball.
3. The debutante sat by the door. She watched the ball.

In example 1, the verb *catered* helps specify which definition of *ball* is appropriate; in example 2, the noun *juggler* does the work. In example 3, the first sentence

evokes a scenario that creates a storylike context for the second sentence, "She watched the ball."

These examples suggest that you put various types of evidence to swift and efficient use each time you encounter an ambiguous word: Context immediately affects listeners' consideration of the meanings of ambiguous words (Gorfein, 2001). Context wields a similar influence on structural ambiguities (MacDonald, 1993; Shapiro et al., 1993; Trueswell, 1996). Contextual information speeds decisions when you must choose among different possible grammatical structures.

The overall conclusion you can draw is that your language processes use context powerfully and efficiently to resolve ambiguities. In a way, this shows that there is a good match between production and understanding. When we discussed language production, we emphasized audience design—the processes by which speakers try to make their utterances appropriate in the current context. Our analysis of understanding suggests that listeners expect speakers to have done their jobs well. Under those circumstances, it makes sense for listeners to let context guide their expectations about what speakers will have meant.

THE PRODUCTS OF UNDERSTANDING

Our discussion of ambiguity resolution focused on the *processes* of understanding. In this section, we shift our attention to the *products* of understanding. The question now is: What *representations* result in memory when listeners understand utterances or texts? What, for example, would be stored in memory when you hear our old standby "The cat is on the mat"? Research has suggested that meaning representation begins with basic units called *propositions* (Clark & Clark, 1977; Kintsch, 1974). Propositions are the main ideas of utterances. For "The cat is on the mat," the main idea is that something is on something else. When you read the utterance, you will extract the proposition *on* and understand the relationship that it expresses between *the cat* and *the mat.* Often propositions are written like this: *ON (cat, mat).* Many utterances contain more than one proposition. Consider "The cat watched the mouse run under the sofa." We have as the first component proposition *UNDER (mouse, sofa).* From that, we build up *RUN (mouse, UNDER (mouse, sofa)).* Finally, we get to *WATCH (cat, RUN (mouse, UNDER (mouse, sofa))).*

How can we test whether your mental representations of meaning really work this way? Some of the earliest experiments in the psychology of language were devoted to showing the importance of propositional representations in understanding (Kintsch, 1974). Research has shown that if two words in an utterance belong to the same proposition, they will be represented together in memory even if they are not close together in the actual sentence.

<www.ablongman.com/gerrig17e>

Propositions Structure Memory

Consider the sentence "The mausoleum that enshrined the tzar overlooked the square." Although *mausoleum* and *square* are far apart in the sentence, a propositional analysis suggests that they should be gathered together in memory in the proposition *OVERLOOKED (mausoleum, square)*. To test this analysis, researchers asked participants to read lists of words and say whether each had appeared in the sentence. Some participants saw *mausoleum* directly after *square* on the list. Other participants saw *mausoleum* after a word from another proposition. The response "Yes, I saw *mausoleum*" was swifter when *mausoleum* came directly after *square* than when its predecessor came from another proposition. This finding suggests that the concepts *mausoleum* and *square* had been represented together in memory (Ratcliff & Mckoon, 1978).

Have you ever noticed how hard it is to remember *exactly* what someone said? You might, for example, have tried to remember a line from a movie word-for-word—but you realized when you got home that you could only remember the general sense of what was said. This experiment indicates why word-for-word memory isn't so good: Because one of the main operations your language processes carry out is the extraction of propositions, the exact form with which those propositions were rendered gets lost pretty quickly (for example, "The cat chased the mouse" versus "The mouse was chased by the cat").

Not all the propositions listeners store in memory are made up of information directly stated by the speaker. Often listeners fill gaps with **inferences**—logical assumptions made possible by information in memory. Consider this pair of utterances:

I'm heading to the deli to meet Donna.

She promised to buy me a sandwich for lunch.

To understand how these sentences go together, you must draw at least two important inferences. You must figure out both who *she* is in the second sentence and how going to a deli is related to a promise to buy a sandwich. Note that a friend who actually uttered this pair of sentences would be confident you could figure these things out. You'd never expect to hear this:

I'm heading to the deli to meet Donna. She—and by *she* I mean Donna—promised to buy me a sandwich—and a *deli* is a place where you can buy a sandwich—for lunch.

Speakers count on listeners to draw inferences of this sort.

A great deal of research has been directed toward determining what types of inferences listeners draw on a regular basis (Gerrig & Egidi, 2003; Graesser et al., 1994; McKoon & Ratcliff, 1992). The number of potential inferences after any utterance is unlimited. For example, because you know that Donna is likely to be a human, you could infer that she has a heart, a liver, a pair of lungs, and so on (and on), but it's unlikely that you would feel compelled to call any of those (perfectly valid) inferences to mind when you heard "I'm heading to the deli to meet Donna." Research suggests, in fact, that listeners are reasonably conservative in the inferences they draw. Consider this sentence:

The architect stabbed the man.

When explicitly asked to name what instrument this sentence made them think of, participants most often said *knife*. However, researchers found no evidence that participants, in natural circumstances of reading, called the concept *knife* to mind, or other instruments in similar sentences (Dosher & Corbett, 1982). This finding suggests that you do not automatically draw even some inferences that are pretty safe bets—for instance, that someone who was stabbed was stabbed with a knife. Most of the inferences you habitually draw are like the ones we illustrated before—inferences that capture the relationship between *Donna* and *she* and between *deli* and *sandwich*. These inferences help you form a coherent representation of the information the speaker wishes you to understand; they do not elaborate on it.

Our discussion of language use has demonstrated how much work a speaker does to produce the right sentence at the right time and how much work a listener does to figure out exactly what the speaker meant. You usually aren't aware of all this work! Does this give you a greater appreciation for the elegant design of your cognitive processes?

◆ LANGUAGE, THOUGHT, AND CULTURE

Have you had the opportunity to learn more than one language? If so, do you believe that you *think* differently in the two languages? Does language affect thought? This question is one that researchers have addressed in a variety of ways. Let us give you a cross-linguistic example to make this question more concrete. Imagine a scene in which a child has watched her father throw a ball. If the child were an English speaker, she might utter the sentence, "Daddy threw the ball." If, by contrast, the child were a Turkish speaker, she would say, "Topu babam atti." Is this just a different collection of words for the same idea? Not entirely: the *-ti* suffix at the end of the Turkish sentence indicates that the event was witnessed by the speaker; if the event

Y ou have almost certainly seen a movie or television show in which a nonhuman animal carries out a vigorous conversation with a human. Do you remember Mr. Ed, the talking horse? Could this happen in real life? Beginning as early as the 1920s, psychologists tried to address this question by attempting to teach language to chimpanzees. Chimps don't have the appropriate vocal apparatus to produce spoken language, so researchers had to devise other methods of communication. For example, a chimp named Washoe was taught a highly simplified version of American Sign Language (Gardner & Gardner, 1969); a chimp named Sarah was taught to manipulate symbols (which stood for concepts like *apple* and *give*) on a magnetic board (Premack, 1971). The results of these experiments inspired great controversy (Seidenberg & Petitto, 1979). Skeptics asked whether the chimps' occasional combinations of gestures or symbols (for example, *Washoe sorry, You more drink*) constituted any meaningful kind of language use. They also wondered whether most of the meaning attributed to the chimps' utterances wasn't arising in the heads of the humans rather than in the heads of the chimps.

In recent years, **Sue Savage-Rumbaugh** and her colleagues (Savage-Rumbaugh et al., 1998) have conducted research that has provided more solid insights into the language capabilities of chimps. Savage-Rumbaugh works primarily with *bonobos,* a species of great ape that is evolutionarily nearer to humans even than common chimpanzees. Rather remarkably, two of the bonobos in her studies, Kanzi and Mulika, acquired the meanings of plastic symbols *spontaneously:* They received no

Can Nonhuman Animals Learn Language?
Megan Mulloy
Santa Clara University

explicit training; rather, they acquired the symbols by observing others (humans and bonobos) using them to communicate. Moreover, Kanzi and Mulika are able to understand some *spoken* English. For example, when Kanzi hears a spoken word, he is able to locate either the symbol for the word or a photograph of the object. This group of researchers has also raised a bonobo and a common chimpanzee together—giving them early language experiences that closely match the circumstances in which humans acquire language (see Chapter 10). This project has demonstrated that even the common chimpanzee, Panpanzee, can acquire the meanings of some spoken English words—although not as many as her companion bonobo, Panbanisha (Brakke & Savage-Rumbaugh, 1995).

The results with bonobos are fascinating. However, there is much more to language than just the use of words. Consider *audience design.* Could non-

human animals modify their messages based on what members of their audience know? Researchers have set out to answer this question. For example, **Dorothy Cheney** and **Robert Seyfarth** (1990) have done extensive research on the communicative capabilities of *vervet monkeys.* Vervet monkeys make distinct *calls* to signal the presence of different dangers, such as leopards, eagles, and snakes. These monkeys are able to modify their calls depending on their audience: Female monkeys gave alarms at much higher rates when they were with their own offspring than when they were with monkeys unrelated to them. However, the vervets do not modify their calls based on what their audience *knows:* In an experimental setting, mother vervets produced the same calls irrespective of whether their offspring had also witnessed the events that evoked the calls. In fact, researchers have suggested that humans may be the only species that can modify its behavior based on someone else's knowledge (Karin-D'Arcy & Povinelli, 2002; Povinelli & Prince, 1998).

You can see from this review that chimpanzees and bonobos possess some but not all of the cognitive capabilities necessary for humanlike language performance.

Some bonobos have learned the meanings of words without explicit training. What other abilities must these animals demonstrate before it can be said that they have genuinely acquired a human language?

The Dani people of Papua New Guinea speak a language with only two basic color terms—they make a distinction between black and white (or light and dark). English, by comparison, has 11 basic color terms. Could this language difference affect the way people experience the world?

hadn't been witnessed by the speaker, a different suffix (*miş*) would be added to *at* (which is the equivalent of *threw*) to form *atmiş*. As an English speaker, you are not required to divide the world into events you witnessed yourself versus those you learned about through other sources; as a Turkish speaker, you would be (Slobin, 1982; Slobin & Aksu, 1982). Could it be the case that the different grammatical requirements of these two languages would affect, in very basic ways, the manner in which people think about the world? No one knows the answer to this specific question about English and Turkish—would you like to carry out appropriate research?—but this distinction provides a good example of why people have so often been intrigued by the question of language's potential influence on thought.

Scholarly work on this question was originated by **Edward Sapir** and his student **Benjamin Lee Whorf,** whose cross-linguistic explorations led them to the somewhat radical conclusion that differences in language would create differences in thought. Here's how Sapir put it:

> We see and hear and otherwise experience very largely as we do because the language habits of our community predispose certain choices of interpretation. (Sapir, 1941/1964, p. 69)

For Sapir and Whorf, this conclusion emerged directly from relationships they believed to exist in their own data. From the hypotheses that Sapir and Whorf proposed, the one that has received the most attention is called *linguistic relativity* (Brown, 1976). According to this hypothesis, the structure of the language an individual speaks has an impact on the way in which that individual thinks about the world. Contemporary researchers in psychology, linguistics, and anthropology

have attempted to create rigorous tests of these ideas (Gumperz & Levinson, 1996; Oezgen & Davies, 2002). Let's look at a particular domain in which researchers have demonstrated an impact of language on thought.

You may be surprised to learn that languages of the world differ with respect to the number of basic color terms they use. As determined by linguistic analysis, English has 11 *(black, white, red, yellow, green, blue, brown, purple, pink, orange,* and *gray);* some languages of the world, such as the language spoken by the Dani people of Papua New Guinea, have only 2, a simple distinction between *black* and *white* (or *light* and *dark*) (Berlin & Kay, 1969). Whorf had suggested that language users "dissect nature along the lines laid down by [their] native languages" (1956, p. 213): Researchers speculated that the number of color terms (for example, 2 versus 11) might influence the ways in which speakers of different languages were able to think about colors.

Language Affects Color Judgments

Researchers asked participants to examine triads of color chips all taken from the blue-green continuum. The participants' task was to indicate which of the three hues was most different from the other two. The two groups of participants were speakers of English, a language that includes a lexical distinction between blue and green, and speakers of Tarahumara, a language of Northern Mexico that has only a single lexical item, *siyóname,* that covers both green and blue hues. The researchers suggested that, if the Sapir-Whorf hypothesis is correct, "colors near the *green–blue* boundary will be subjectively pushed apart by English speakers precisely because English has the words *green* and *blue,* while Tarahumara speakers, lacking the lexical distinction, will show no comparable distortion" (Kay & Kempton, 1984, p. 68). The data strongly bore out this prediction: In their judgments of the color triads, English speakers distorted the interhue distances whereas Tarahumara speakers did not.

A second team of researchers carried out a similar study contrasting speakers of English with speakers of Setswana (Davies et al., 1998). Setswana is a language spoken in Botswana, in southern Africa, that has five basic color terms (versus the 11 in English). For the most part, the speakers of English and Setswana made similar judgments when evaluating the triads of color chips. However, the researchers were able to find instances in which the participants' choices were most easily attributed to differences in the languages they spoke. The results provide support for the claim of linguistic relativity—that language may, in some circumstances, have an impact on thought.

There are thousands of languages in the world, which provide many interesting distinctions: As we indicated for the English–Turkish example with which we started, many interesting hypotheses about the link between language and thought have yet to be tested (Gerrig & Banaji, 1994; Hunt & Agnoli, 1991; Smith, 1996). It is likely to be the case that very many of the lexical and grammatical differences—differences in words and structures—between languages will have no effect on thought. Even so, as we describe cultural differences throughout *Psychology and Life,* it is worth keeping an open mind about linguistic relativity. Given the many situations in which members of different cultures speak very different languages, we can wonder to what extent language plays a causal role in bringing about cultural differences.

Let's turn now from circumstances in which meaning is communicated through words to those in which meaning relies also on pictures.

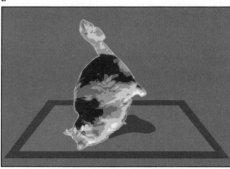

FIGURE 8.7
Visual Representations
Are both of these cats on the mat?

PUT YOURSELF TO THE TEST

- What is the relationship between the cooperative principle and audience design?
- Why do researchers study speech errors to learn about language production?
- Why is ambiguity an important problem for language comprehension?
- What are some of the products of language comprehension?
- How have researchers tested the hypothesis of linguistic relativity?

Visual Cognition

I n **Figure 8.7,** we give you two choices for visual representations of the sentence "The cat is on the mat." Which one seems right? If you think in terms of language-based propositions, each alternative captures the right meaning—the cat *is* on the mat. Even so, you're probably happy only with option A, because

it matches the scene you likely called to mind when you first read the sentence (Searle, 1979b). How about option B? It probably makes you somewhat nervous because it seems as if the cat is going to tip right over. This anxious feeling must arise because you can think with pictures. In a sense, you can *see* exactly what's going to happen. In this section, we will explore some of the ways in which visual images and visual processes contribute to the way you think.

◆ USING VISUAL REPRESENTATIONS

History is full of examples of famous discoveries apparently made on the basis of mental imagery (Shepard, 1978). Recall F. A. Kekulé, whom we mentioned in Chapter 5. Kekulé, the discoverer of the chemical structure of benzene, often conjured up mental images of dancing atoms that fastened themselves into chains of molecules. His discovery of the benzene ring occurred in a dream in which a snakelike molecule chain suddenly grabbed its own tail, thus forming a ring. Michael

<www.ablongman.com/gerrig17e>

Faraday, who discovered many properties of magnetism, knew little about mathematics, but he had vivid mental images of the properties of magnetic fields. Albert Einstein claimed to have thought entirely in terms of visual images, translating his findings into mathematical symbols and words only after the work of visually based discovery was finished.

We have given you these examples to encourage you to try to indulge in visual thinking. But even without trying, you regularly use your capabilities for manipulating visual images. Consider a classic experiment in which participants were asked to transform images in their heads.

You put this ability for mental rotation to very good use. You often see objects in the environment from unfamiliar points of view. Mental rotation allows you to transform the image to one that matches representations stored in memory (Lloyd-Jones & Luckhurst, 2002). For example, in Figure 8.7, you almost certainly had to rotate the image (or did you just tilt your head?) to recognize the object as a cat on a mat.

You can also use visual images to answer certain types of questions about the world. Suppose, for example, we asked you whether a golf ball is bigger than a Ping-Pong ball. If you can't retrieve that fact directly from memory, you might find it convenient to form a visual image of them side by side. This use of an image, once again, has much in common with the properties of real visual perception.

Mental Rotation Is like Physical Rotation

Researchers presented students with examples of the letter R and its mirror image that had been rotated various amounts, from 0 to 180 degrees (see **Figure 8.8**). As the letter appeared, the student had to identify it as either the normal R or its mirror image. The reaction time taken to make that decision was longer in direct proportion to the amount the figure had been rotated. This finding indicated that a subject was imagining the figure in his or her "mind's eye" and rotating the image into an upright position at some fixed rate before deciding whether the figure was an R or a mirror image. The consistency of the rate of rotation suggested that the process of mental rotation was very similar to the process of physical rotation (Shepard & Cooper, 1982).

Scanning Visual Images

In one study, participants first memorized pictures of complex objects, such as a motorboat (see **Figure 8.9**). Then they were asked to recall their visual images of the boat and focus on one spot—for example, the motor. When asked if the picture contained another object—a windshield or an anchor, for example (both were present)—they took longer to "see" the anchor than the windshield, which was closer to the motor than the anchor was. The reaction time difference provides evidence that people scan visual images as if they were scanning real objects (Kosslyn, 1980).

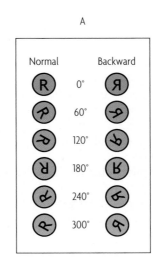

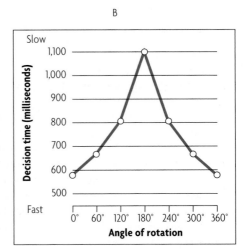

FIGURE 8.8

Rotated R Used to Assess Mental Imagery

Participants presented with these figures in random order were asked to say, as quickly as possible, whether each figure was a normal R or a mirror image. The more the figure was rotated from upright, the longer the reaction time was.

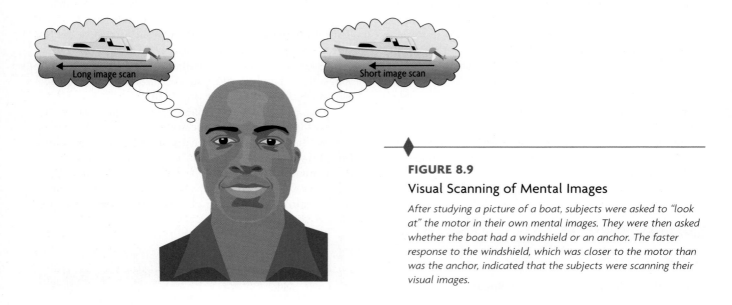

FIGURE 8.9

Visual Scanning of Mental Images

After studying a picture of a boat, subjects were asked to "look at" the motor in their own mental images. They were then asked whether the boat had a windshield or an anchor. The faster response to the windshield, which was closer to the motor than was the anchor, indicated that the subjects were scanning their visual images.

There are, of course, limits to the use of your visual imagination. Consider this problem:

> *Imagine that you have a large piece of blank paper. In your mind, fold it in half (making two layers), fold it in half again (four layers), and continue folding it over 50 times. About how thick is the paper when you are done? (Adams, 1986)*

The actual answer is about 50 million miles ($2^{50} \times 0.028$ inches, the thickness of a piece of paper), approximately half the distance between Earth and the sun. Your estimate was probably considerably lower. Your mind's eye was overwhelmed by the information you asked it to represent.

◆ COMBINING VERBAL AND VISUAL REPRESENTATIONS

Our discussion so far has largely focused on the types of visual representations that you form by committing to memory—or in the case of imagery, retrieving from memory—visual stimuli from the environment. However, you often form visual images based on verbal descriptions. You can, for example, create a mental picture of a cat with three tails, although you've almost certainly never seen one. The verbal description enables you to form a visual representation. Your ability to produce a mental image of a verbal scene is particularly useful when you read works of fiction that involve spatial details. Consider this passage from the James Bond short story "From a View to a Kill":

> *The clearing was about as big as two tennis courts and floored in thick grass and moss. There was one large patch of lilies of the valley and, under the bordering trees, a scattering of bluebells. To one side there was a low mound . . . completely surrounded and covered with brambles and briar roses now thickly in bloom. Bond walked round this and gazed in among the roots, but there was nothing to see except the earthy shape of the mound. (Fleming, 1959, pp. 19–20)*

Did you try to imagine the scene—and help Bond search for danger? (He will find it.) When you read, you can form a *spatial mental model* to keep track of the whereabouts of characters (Zwaan & Radvansky, 1998). Researchers have often focused on the ways in which spatial mental models capture properties of real spatial experiences (Rinck et al., 1997).

Suppose, for example, you read a passage of a text that places you in the middle of an interesting environment.

> *You are hob-nobbing at the opera. You came tonight to meet and chat with interesting members of the upper class. At the moment, you are standing next to the railing of a wide, elegant balcony overlooking the first floor. Directly behind you, at your eye level, is an ornate lamp attached to the balcony wall. The base of the lamp, which is attached to the wall, is gilded in gold. (Franklin & Tversky, 1990, p. 65)*

In a series of experiments, readers studied descriptions of this sort that vividly described the layout of objects around the viewer (Franklin & Tversky, 1990). The researchers wished to show that readers were faster or slower to access information about the scene, depending on where the objects were in the mental space around them. Readers, for example, were quicker to say what object was in front of them in the scene than what object was behind them, even though all objects were introduced equally carefully in the stories (see **Figure 8.10**). It's easiest to understand this result if you believe that the representation you form while reading actually places you, in some sense, in the scene. You are able to transform a verbal experience into a visual, spatial experience.

In general, when you think about the world around you, you are almost always combining visual and verbal representations of information. To prove that to yourself, you can take a minute to draw a map of the world. Go ahead—make a sketch! How do you go about doing this? Some of the things you draw in are probably based on visual experiences—you know the overall shape of Africa only because you have seen it represented in the past. Other features of your drawing will probably rely on verbal information—you are likely to remember that Japan is made up of several islands, even if you don't have a visual representation of quite where they go. In one study, nearly 4,000 students from 71 cities in 49 countries were asked to carry out the task of drawing a world map (Saarinen, 1987). The goal of the study was to broaden understanding of cultural differences in the way the world is visualized and to promote world peace. The study found that the majority of maps had a Eurocentric worldview. Europe was placed in the center of the map and the other countries were arranged around it, probably due to the dominance for many centuries of Eurocentric representations in geography books. However, the study also yielded many instances of culture-biased maps, such as the one by a

FIGURE 8.10

Spatial Mental Models

You can use imagination to project yourself into the middle of a scene. Just as if you were really standing in the room, you would take less time to say what is in front of you (the lamp) than what is behind you (the bust).

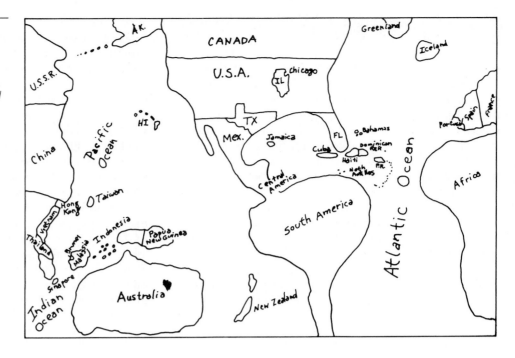

FIGURE 8.11

A Chicagocentric View of the World

How does this view of the world compare with yours?

Chicago student, in **Figure 8.11,** and that of an Australian student, in **Figure 8.12.** These maps show what happens when a verbal perspective—My home should be in the middle!—is imposed on a visual representation.

In this section, we have seen that you have visual processes and representations to complement your verbal abilities. These two types of access to information give you extra help in dealing with the demands and tasks of your life. We turn now to domains in which you put both visual and verbal representations to use in coping with your life's complexities: *problem solving* and *reasoning*.

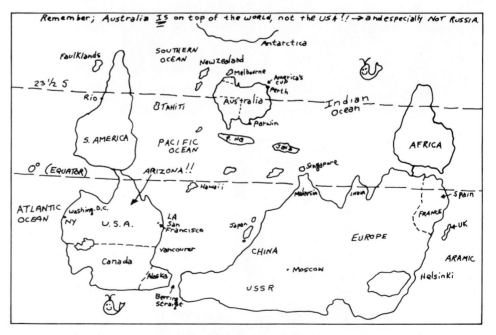

FIGURE 8.12

An Australocentric View of the World

Look at this view of the world. Now who's down under?

Both figures from Solso, Robert L., *Cognitive Psychology*, 3e © 1991. Published by Allyn & Bacon, Boston, MA. Copyright © 2003 by Pearson Education. Reprinted by permission of the publisher.

- In what ways is mental rotation similar to physical rotation?
- What are some circumstances in which people are likely to use mental rotation?
- What properties of visual images make them comparable to real acts of perception?
- How do people combine verbal and visual information?

Problem Solving and Reasoning

Let's return for a minute to your mysterious message, "The cat is on the mat." If you've come to understand the message, what do you do next? For those of you whose lives are less filled with mystery, consider a more common situation: You've accidentally locked yourself out of your home, room, or car. Again, what do you do next? For both situations, reflect on the types of mental steps you might take to overcome your difficulty. Those mental steps will almost certainly include the cognitive processes that make up **problem solving** and **reasoning.** Both of these activities require you to combine current information with information stored in memory to work toward some particular goal: a conclusion or a solution. We will look at aspects of problem solving and at two types of reasoning, deductive and inductive.

◆ PROBLEM SOLVING

What goes on four legs in the morning, on two legs at noon, and on three legs in the twilight? According to Greek mythology, this was the riddle posed by the Sphinx, an evil creature who threatened to hold the people of Thebes in tyranny until someone could solve the riddle. To break the code, Oedipus had to recognize elements of the riddle as metaphors. Morning, noon, and twilight represented different periods in a human life. A baby crawls and so (effectively) has four legs, an adult walks on two legs, and an older person walks on two legs but uses a cane, making a total of three legs. Oedipus's solution to the riddle was *humans.*

Although your daily problems may not seem as monumental as the one faced by young Oedipus, problem-solving activity is a basic part of your everyday exis-

tence. You continually come up against problems that require solutions: how to manage work and tasks within a limited time frame, how to succeed at a job interview, how to break off a relationship, and so on. Many problems involve discrepancies between what you know and what you need to know. When you solve a problem, you reduce that discrepancy by finding a way to get the missing information. To get into the spirit of problem solving, try the problems in **Figure 8.13.** After you're done, we'll see how psychological research can shed light on your performance—and, perhaps, provide some suggestions about how to improve it.

PROBLEM SPACES AND PROCESSES

How do you define a problem in real-life circumstances? You usually perceive the difference between your current state and a desired goal: for example, you are broke, and you'd like to have some money. You are also usually aware of some of the steps you would be able (or willing) to take to bridge the gap: You will try to get a part-time job, but you won't become a pickpocket. The formal definition of a *problem* captures these three elements (Newell & Simon, 1972). A problem is defined by (1) an *initial state*—the incomplete information or unsatisfactory conditions you start with; (2) a *goal state*—the information or state of the world you hope to obtain; and (3) a *set of operations*—the steps you may take to move from an initial state to a goal state. Together, these three parts define the **problem space.** You can think of solving a problem as walking through a maze (the problem space) from where you are (the initial state) to where you want to be (the goal state), making a series of turns (the allowable operations).

Much of the initial difficulty in solving a problem will arise if any of these elements are not well defined (Simon, 1973). A *well-defined problem* is similar to a textbook problem in which the initial state, the goal state, and the operations are all clearly specified. Your task is to discover how to use allowable, known operations to get the answer. By contrast, an *ill-defined problem* is similar to designing a home, writing a novel, or finding a cure for AIDS. The initial state, the goal state, and/or the operations may be unclear and vaguely specified. In such cases, the problem solver's first task is to work out, as much as possible, exactly what the problem is—to make explicit a beginning, an ideal solution, and the possible means to achieve it.

As you know from your own experience, even when the initial and goal states are well defined, it can still be difficult to find the right set of operations to get from the beginning to the end. If you think back to your experience in math classes, you know that this is true. Your teacher gave you a formula like $x^2 + x - 12 = 0$

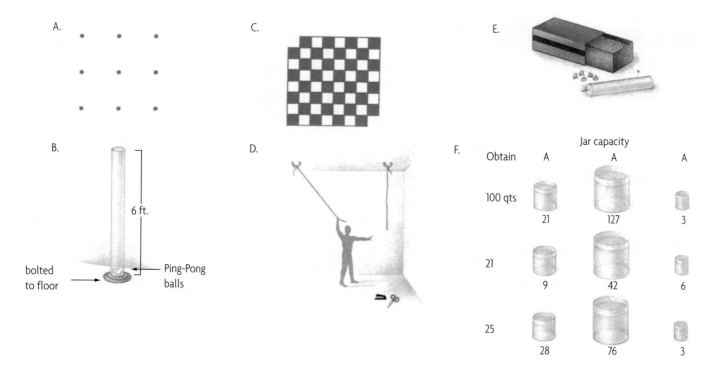

(A) Can you connect all the dots in the pattern by drawing four straight, connected lines without lifting your pen from the paper?

(B) A prankster has put 3 Ping-Pong balls into a 6-foot-long pipe that is standing vertically in the corner of the physics lab, fastened to the floor. How would you get the Ping-Pong balls out?

(C) The checkerboard shown has had 2 corner pieces cut out, leaving 62 squares. You have 31 dominoes, each of which covers exactly 2 checkerboard squares. Can you use them to cover the whole checkerboard?

(D) You are in the situation depicted and given the task of tying the 2 strings together. If you hold one sting, the other is out of reach. Can you do it?

(E) You are given the objects shown (a candle, tacks, matches in a matchbox). The task is to mount a lighted candle on a door. Can you do it?

(F) You are given 3 "water-jar" problems. Using only the 3 containers (water supply is unlimited), can you obtain the exact amount specified in each case?

FIGURE 8.13

Can You Solve It? (Part I)

Try to solve each of these problems (the answers are given in Figure 8.14 on page 268, but don't look until you try to solve them all).

and asked you to solve for possible values of x. What do you do next? To solve this algebra problem, you can use an **algorithm:** a step-by-step procedure that always provides the right answer for a particular type of problem. If you apply the rules of algebra correctly, you are guaranteed to obtain the correct values of x (i.e., 3 and -4). If you've ever forgotten the combination to a lock, you may also have engaged in behavior guided by an algorithm. If you try solutions systematically (e.g., 1, 2, 3; 1, 2, 4) you will definitely arrive at the right combination—though you may be at it for a good long while! Because well-defined problems have clear initial states and goal states, algorithms are more likely to be available for them than for ill-defined problems. When algorithms are unavailable, problem solvers often rely on **heuristics,** which are strategies or "rules of thumb." Suppose, for example, you are reading a mystery and

you'd like to solve the problem of who murdered an e-commerce tycoon. You might rule out the possibility that "the butler did it," because you use the heuristic that authors wouldn't use such a trite plot line. As we shall see shortly, heuristics are also a critical aspect of *judgment* and *decision making.*

Researchers have been interested in understanding the way people apply both algorithms and heuristics as they make their way through a problem space. To study the steps problem solvers take, researchers have often turned to **think-aloud protocols.** In this procedure, participants are asked to verbalize their ongoing thoughts (Ericsson & Simon, 1993). For example, a pair of researchers were interested in capturing the mental processes that enable participants to solve the mutilated checkerboard problem that is part C of Figure 8.13 (Kaplan & Simon, 1990). Here is one of their participants

<www.ablongman.com/gerrig17e>

How do scientists approach the ill-defined problem of curing AIDS?

having the crucial breakthrough that the problem cannot be solved with only horizontal and vertical placement of pieces (the checkerboard was pink and black):

> *So you're leaving . . . it's short—how many, you're leaving uhhhh . . . there's more pinks than black, and in order to complete it you'd have to connect two pinks but you can't because they are diagonally . . . is that getting close? (Kaplan & Simon, 1990, p. 388)*

The solver has just realized that the goal cannot be accomplished if the dominoes can just be placed horizontally or vertically. Researchers have often used participants' own accounts of their thinking as the starting point for more formal models of problem solving (Simon, 1979, 1989).

IMPROVING YOUR PROBLEM SOLVING

What makes problem solving hard? If you reflect on your day-to-day experience, you might come up with the answer "There are too many things to consider all at once." Research on problem solving has led to much the same conclusion. What often makes a problem difficult to solve is that the mental requirements for solving a particular problem overwhelm processing resources (Kotovsky et al., 1985; Kotovsky & Simon, 1990). To solve a problem, you need to plan the series of operations you will take. If that series becomes too complex, or if each operation itself is too complex, you may be unable to see your way through from the initial state to the goal state. How might you overcome this potential limitation?

An important step in improving problem solving is to find a way to represent a problem so that each operation is possible, given your processing resources. If you must habitually solve similar problems, a useful procedure is to practice each of the components of the solution so that, over time, those components require fewer resources (Kotovsky et al., 1985). Suppose, for example, you were a cab driver in New York City and were faced with daily traffic jams. You might mentally practice your responses to jams at various points in the city, so that you'd have ready solutions to components of the overall problem of getting your fare from a pickup spot to a destination. By practicing these component solutions, you could keep more of your attention on the road!

You can see an extreme example of the ability to apply past solutions to current problems in the extraordinary performance of world champion chess master Gary Kasparov. Kasparov is able to simultaneously beat several human opponents by recognizing weaknesses in configurations of chess pieces and applying appropriate, practiced solutions (Gobet & Simon, 1996).

Sometimes, finding a useful representation means finding a whole new way to think about the problem. Read the puzzle given in **Table 8.5.** How would you go

TABLE 8.5
The Monk Puzzle

One morning, exactly at sunrise, a Buddhist monk began to climb a tall mountain. A narrow path, no more than a foot or two wide, spiraled around the mountain to a glittering temple at the summit. The monk ascended at varying rates of speed, stopping many times along the way to rest and eat dried fruit he carried with him. He reached the temple shortly before sunset. After several days of fasting and meditation, he began his journey back along the same path, starting at sunrise and again walking at variable speeds with many pauses along the way. His average speed descending was, of course, greater than his average climbing speed. Prove that there is a spot along the path that the monk will occupy on both trips at precisely the same time of day.

See a "proof" for the Monk Puzzle in Figure 8.15.

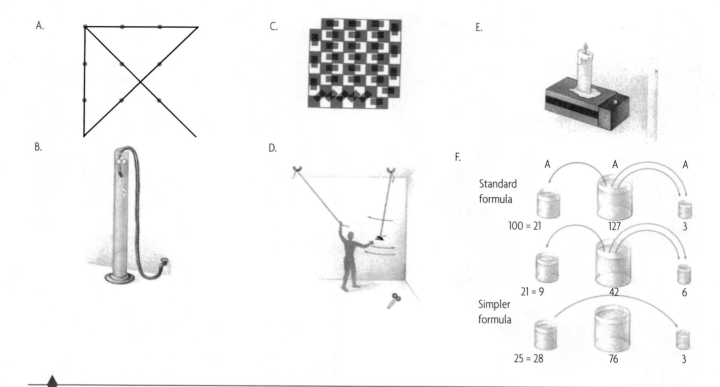

FIGURE 8.14

Can You Solve It? (Part II)

Here are the solutions to the problems. How did you do? As the section on problem solving and reasoning unfolds, we will talk about what makes these problems hard.

about offering this proof? Think about it for a few minutes before you read on. How well did you do? If the word *proof* suggested to you something mathematical, you probably didn't make much progress. A better way to think about the problem is to imagine two monks, one starting at the top and another starting at the bottom (Adams, 1986). As one climbs and one descends, it's clear that they will pass at some point along the mountain, right (see **Figure 8.15**)? Now replace the pair of monks with just the one—conceptually it's the same—and there's your proof. What makes this problem suddenly very easy is using the right sort of representation: visual rather than verbal or mathematical.

If you go back to the problems in Figure 8.13 you have other good examples of the importance of an appropriate representation of the problem space. To get the Ping-Pong balls out of the pipe, you had to realize that the solution did not involve reaching into the pipe. To connect the two strings, you had to see one of the tools on the floor as a weight. To mount the candle on the door, you had to alter your usual perspective and perceive the matchbox as a platform instead of as a container, and you had to perceive the candle as a tool as well as the object to be mounted on the door. The last

two problems show a phenomenon called functional fixedness (Duncker, 1945; Maier, 1931). **Functional fixedness** is a mental block that adversely affects problem solving by inhibiting the perception of a new function for an object that was previously associated with some other purpose. Whenever you are stuck on a problem, you should ask yourself, "How am I representing the problem? Are there different or better ways that I can think about the problem or components of its solution?" If words don't work, try drawing a picture. Or try examining your assumptions, and see what "rules" you can break by making novel combinations.

Often, when you try to solve problems, you engage in special forms of thinking that are called reasoning. Let's turn now to a first type of reasoning you use to solve problems, deductive reasoning.

◆ DEDUCTIVE REASONING

Suppose you are on your way to a restaurant and you want to pay for your meal with your only credit card, American Express. You call the restaurant and ask, "Do you accept American Express?" The restaurant's hostess replies, "We accept all major credit cards." You can now

<www.ablongman.com/gerrig17e>

FIGURE 8.15

A

B

A "Proof" for the Monk Puzzle

Panel A shows two monks, one who starts at the bottom of the mountain and one who starts at the top. Panel B shows that they must meet at some time during the day. Replace the two monks with a single monk, and you have your proof!

safely conclude that they accept American Express. To see why, we can reformulate your interchange to fit the structure of the *syllogism,* introduced by the Greek philosopher Aristotle over 2,000 years ago:

> *Premise 1.* The restaurant accepts all major credit cards.
>
> *Premise 2.* American Express is a major credit card.
>
> *Conclusion.* The restaurant accepts American Express.

Aristotle was concerned with defining the logical relationships between statements that would lead to *valid* conclusions. **Deductive reasoning** involves the correct application of such logical rules. We gave the credit-card example to show that you are quite capable of drawing conclusions that have the form of logical, deductive proofs. Even so, psychological research has focused on the question of whether you actually have the formal rules of deductive reasoning represented in your mind (Schaeken et al., 2000). This body of research suggests that you may have some general, abstract sense of formal logic, but your real-world deductive reasoning is affected both by the specific knowledge you possess about the world and the representational resources you can bring to bear on a particular reasoning problem. Let's expand on these conclusions.

How does knowledge influence deductive reasoning? Consider this syllogism:

> *Premise 1.* All things that have a motor need oil.
>
> *Premise 2.* Automobiles need oil.
>
> *Conclusion.* Automobiles have motors.

Is this a valid conclusion? According to the rules of logic, it is *not,* because Premise 1 leaves open the possibility

that some things that don't have motors will also need oil. The difficulty is that what is invalid in a logic problem is not necessarily untrue in real life. That is, if you take Premises 1 and 2 to be all the information in your possession—as you should if you accept this simply as an exercise in formal logic—the conclusion is not valid. Even so, when participants judge whether the conclusion "follows logically from the premises," they are much more inclined to say yes when the conclusion considers *automobiles* than they are when the nonsense term *oppobines* is substituted (Markovitz & Nantel, 1989).

This result illustrates a general **belief-bias effect**—people tend to judge as valid those conclusions for

which they can construct a reasonable real-world model and as invalid those for which they cannot (Evans et al., 1983; Janis & Frick, 1943; Newstead et al., 1992). More specifically, if there is a believable conclusion that is consistent with people's mental representations of a problem, they tend to accept that conclusion. In this case, knowledge about automobiles makes it hard to reject the conclusion as invalid. However, when participants were given just the two premises and asked to generate their own conclusions, about half were able to correctly state that no valid conclusion could be reached (that is, based on the two premises, you can't determine whether automobiles have motors). Thus, the belief bias may have a smaller effect on your actual reasoning processes than on your ability to judge someone else's conclusions (Rips, 1990). Formal instruction on logical reasoning, of the sort you are obtaining now, also helps reduce belief bias (Evans et al., 1994).

Experience also improves your reasoning ability. You can see this to be true if you compare performance on an abstract reasoning task with that on a version of the same task that allows you to apply real-world knowledge. Imagine that you are given the array of four cards pictured in **Figure 8.16,** which have printed on them *A, D, 4,* and *7.* Your task is to determine which cards you must turn over to test the rule "If a card has a vowel on one side, then it has an even number on the other side" (Johnson-Laird & Wason, 1977). What would you do? Most people say that they would turn over the *A,* which is correct, and the *4*—which is incorrect. No matter what character appears on the flip side of the *4,* the rule will not be invalidated. (Can you see why that is true?) Instead, you must flip the *7.* If you were to find a vowel there, you would have invalidated the rule.

The original research on this task, which is often called the *Wason selection task,* prompted doubts about people's ability to reason effectively. This negative view, however, has been modified in two ways. First, researchers have suggested that participants may follow a nondeductive strategy of examining the cards that will allow them to *confirm* rather than *disconfirm* the generality of the relationship stated in the rule. Although this strategy may lead to the appearance of faulty deductive reasoning, it is a reasonable real-world strategy for learning about associations and making decisions (Oaksford & Chater, 1994; Oaksford et al., 1997).

Second, deductive reasoning is improved when participants are able to apply their real-world knowledge to the Wason task (Holyoak & Spellman, 1993). Suppose you were asked to perform what is a logically comparable task, on the lower set of cards in Figure 8.16. In this case, however, you are asked to evaluate the rule "If a customer is to drink an alcoholic beverage, then she *must* be at least 18" (Cheng & Holyoak, 1985). Now you can probably see immediately which are the correct

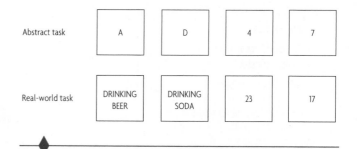

FIGURE 8.16

Abstract Versus Real-World Reasoning

In the top row, you are required to say which cards you must turn over to test the rule "If a card has a vowel on one side, then it has an even number on the other side." In the bottom row, you must say which cards you need to turn over to test the rule "If a customer is to drink an alcoholic beverage, then she must be at least 18." People typically do better on the second task, which allows them to use real-world strategies.

cards to turn over: *17* and *drinking beer.* When the problem is familiar in real life, you can make use of a *pragmatic reasoning schema.* As we described in Chapter 7, you derive schemas over the course of your experience in the environment. You have had a good deal of experience in *permission* situations—recall all the times you were given conditions like, "You can't watch television unless you do your homework." Through all those interactions, you derive a reasoning schema. The real-life situation linking age to drinking calls to mind this schema; the arbitrary situation linking even numbers and vowels does not. As a consequence, the arbitrary reasoning task underestimates your ability to make correct deductions.

Note that recent research has proposed an alternative to the view that people *acquire* a schema with respect to permissions. In a version of the card-turning task adapted for children, participants as young as 3 years old could reason successfully about what was and was not permitted by a rule. This result suggests that reasoning about permission situations may be innate (Cummins, 1996). That is, the ability to determine when actions do not follow social norms may be part of the genetic package you inherited as a member of the highly social human species (Cummins, 1999).

To begin this section on deductive reasoning, we described a situation in which you drew a valid deductive inference about your ability to use your American Express card to buy a meal. Unfortunately, life provides many occasions on which you cannot be so certain that you have drawn valid inferences from valid premises. We turn now to a version of the restaurant scenario that requires you to use a different form of reasoning.

<www.ablongman.com/gerrig17e>

◆ INDUCTIVE REASONING

Let's suppose that you have arrived outside the restaurant and only then think to check to see if you have enough cash. Once again you find that you'll want to use your American Express card, but there's no helpful sign on the outside. You peek through the restaurant's windows and see well-dressed clientele. You look at the expensive prices on the menu. You consider the upscale quality of the neighborhood. All these observations lead you to believe that the restaurant is likely to take your credit card. This is not deductive reasoning, because your conclusion is based on probabilities rather than logical certainties. Instead, this is **inductive reasoning**—a form of reasoning that uses available evidence to generate likely, but not certain, conclusions.

Although the name might be new, we have already described to you several examples of inductive reasoning. We saw repeatedly, in Chapters 4 and 7, that people use past information stored as schemas to generate expectations about the present and future. You are using inductive reasoning, for example, if you decide that a certain odor in the air indicates that someone is making popcorn; you are using inductive reasoning if you agree that the words on this page are unlikely to suddenly become invisible (and that, if you study, your knowledge of this material won't become invisible on test day). Finally, earlier in this chapter, we discussed the types of inferences people draw when they use language. Your belief that *she* must be *Donna* in the sequence of utterances we gave you relies on inductive inference.

In real-life circumstances, much of your problem-solving ability relies on inductive reasoning. Return to our opening example: You have accidentally locked yourself out of your home, room, or car. What should you do? A good first step is to call up from memory solutions that worked in the past. This process is called *analogical problem solving:* You establish an analogy between the features of the current situation and the features of previous situations (Holyoak & Nisbett, 1988; Holyoak & Thagard, 1997). In this case, your past experiences of "being locked out" may have allowed you to form the *generalization* "find other people with keys" (Ross & Kennedy, 1990). With that generalization in hand, you can start to figure out who those individuals might be and how to find them. This task might require you to retrieve the method you developed for tracking down your roommates at their afternoon classes. If this problem seems easy to you, it's because you have grown accustomed to letting your past inform your present: Inductive reasoning allows you to access tried-and-true methods that speed current problem solving.

We have one caution to add about inductive reasoning. Often a solution that has worked in the past can be reused for a successful solution. But sometimes you must recognize that reliance on the past can hamper your problem-solving ability when there is a critical difference between the old and current situations. The water-jar problem given in Figure 8.13 is a classic example of circumstances in which reliance on the past may cause you to miss a solution to a problem (Luchins, 1942). If you had discovered, in the first two problems in part F, the conceptual rule that $B - A - 2(C) = answer$, you probably tried the same formula for the third problem and found it didn't work. Actually, simply filling jar A and pouring off enough to fill jar C would have left you with the right amount. If you were using your initial formula, you probably did not notice this simpler possibility— your previous success with the other rule would have given you a mental set. A **mental set** is a preexisting state of mind, habit, or attitude that can enhance the quality and speed of perceiving and problem solving under some conditions. However, the same set may inhibit or distort the quality of your mental activities at times when old ways of thinking and acting are nonproductive in new situations. When you find yourself frustrated in a problem-solving situation, you might take a step back and ask yourself, "Am I allowing past successes to narrow my focus too much?" Try to make your problem solving more creative by considering a broader spectrum of past situations and past solutions.

Before we leave this discussion of reasoning, we're going to turn once more to your brain. In this section, we've made a rather strong distinction between deductive and inductive reasoning. Research suggests that separation also exists in the way your brain accomplishes the two types of reasoning.

PUTTING IDEAS TO THE TEST

The Brain Bases of Deductive and Inductive Reasoning

Participants carried out two types of reasoning tasks while their brains were undergoing PET scans. As shown in the top portion of **Figure 8.17**, one type of problem required deduction. Participants viewed classic syllogisms and assessed whether the conclusions were valid or not. A second type of problem provided premises that left conclusions uncertain. For that reason, the problems required participants to engage in inductive reasoning. Participants indicated whether the arguments were more likely to be true than false. As shown in the bottom portion of Figure 8.17, the two types of reasoning brought about different patterns of activation. The data are easy to summarize: Deductive reasoning produced greater activation in the right hemisphere; inductive reasoning produced greater activation in the left hemisphere (Parsons & Osherson, 2001).

Deductive reasoning:	Inductive reasoning:
Either he likes country music or he listens to opera.	If he is either an accountant or a librarian he listens to opera.
He does not like country music.	He listens to opera.
He listens to opera.	He is an accountant.
Is the conclusion valid?	**Is the conclusion more likely to be true than false?**

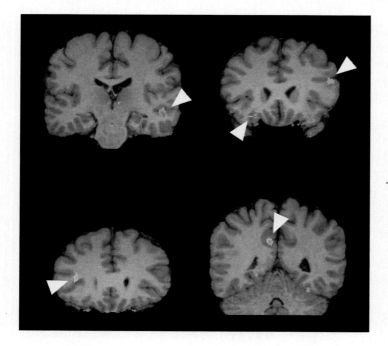

FIGURE 8.17

Reasoning in the Brain

When students were asked to carry out deductive reasoning, brain structures on the right sides of their brain were relatively more active. (Those areas are shown in green.) When students were asked to carry out inductive reasoning, brain structures on the left sides of their brain were relatively more active. (Those areas are shown in yellow.)

To make sense of this result, you should think back to Chapter 3. Recall that your left hemisphere plays a large role in language processing whereas your right hemisphere does not. The results of this study on reasoning suggest that deductive reasoning involves a type of logical analysis that is relatively independent of language. Inductive reasoning calls upon the language-based comprehension and inferencing processes we described earlier in the chapter.

In this section, we have examined a range of types of problem solving and reasoning—and have suggested, in each case, concrete steps you can take to improve your performance in real-world circumstances. We follow the same strategy in the final section of the chapter. We describe some major research findings on the processes of *judgment* and *decision making* and then suggest how you can apply those findings to important situations in your life.

PUT YOURSELF TO THE TEST

- How do algorithms and heuristics function in the domain of problem solving?
- What measures can you take to improve your problem-solving ability?
- What factors affect your ability to engage in accurate deductive reasoning?
- What role does memory play in inductive reasoning?

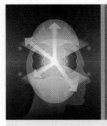

Expert Systems and Medicine

If you've ever had a serious consultation with a medical professional, you've been a participant in a situation in which an individual's ability to reason and problem-solve matters enormously. The person responsible for your health must try to identify the pattern that underlies your constellation of symptoms and infer an underlying cause. Based on his or her causal inferences, the individual must prescribe a plan of action. Given the complexities of this process—just think how hard it is even for you to describe your symptoms accurately, in a way that someone else can understand—it won't surprise you to learn that cognitive scientists have been involved for several years in efforts to provide computer programs that assist doctors and other health-care personnel with diagnosis and treatment planning.

The programs that these researchers have developed are called *expert systems:* An expert system is a computer program that simulates experts' problem-solving performance with respect to an organized body of knowledge. Expert systems represent one application of research in *artificial intelligence (AI).* The general goal of AI research is to build computer programs that exhibit intelligent behavior. For many researchers, a particular aim is to create computer programs that can assume some of the burdens of human cognition. Expert systems in medicine have that property.

Consider *MYCIN,* a system developed in the mid-1970s that laid the groundwork for much of the research in this area. MYCIN was intended to assist with the diagnosis and treatment of infectious diseases (Shortliffe, 1976). At the heart of MYCIN was a series of "if-then" rules—rules that related premises to conclusions—that captured heuristic knowledge (i.e., the "rules of thumb") used by experts in this field. As in real medical diagnosis, MYCIN was able to convey the confidence with which premises (e.g., the results of patients' blood tests) are related to particular conclusions (e.g., a diagnosis or a treatment recommendation). The program would also, if asked, reveal the line of reasoning it used to arrive at an ultimate conclusion. Although MYCIN was never implemented in a medical setting, the programs designed by contemporary researchers retain the same basic philosophy of providing users with an understanding of the "reasoning" behind the system's recommendations (Chae, 1998; Hudson & Cohen, 2000).

The ability of these programs to capture reasoning processes is, in fact, an important component of their success or failure. Take the perspective of a doctor interacting with a medical expert system. As a doctor, you might be reluctant to accept the idea that any computer program could outperform your long years of study. What is important to remember, however, is that expert systems gather together the knowledge of experts in a field. Moreover, these systems incorporate not just facts but the way in which experts reason with respect to those facts. Current research is intended to develop expert systems that provide even more systematic explanations for why a set of facts should lead a health-care provider to a particular set of conclusions (Chandrasekaran & Mittal, 1999).

Now shift your perspective from doctor to patient. As the 21st century leads to greater improvements in expert systems, it is not unlikely that you will observe a health-care provider entering your case into a computer. You should feel pleased if the doctor is taking a moment to supplement his or her own reasoning skills with those of the collected experts in a field.

Judgment and Decision Making

For a final time, we're back to "The cat is on the mat." Let's engage the processes of *judgment* and *decision making*. How likely is it that the message was just a prank? How likely is it that the message has some real importance that has eluded you? Should you just give up and go to sleep?

This series of questions illustrates one of the great truths of your day-to-day experience: You live in a world filled with *uncertainty*. Here are some more questions, of a sort that will be entirely familiar. Should you spend $9 on a movie you may or may not enjoy? Before an exam, would you be better off studying your notes or rereading the chapter? Are you ready to commit yourself to a long-term relationship? Because you can only guess at the future, and because you almost never have full knowledge of the past, very rarely can you be completely certain that you have made a correct judgment or decision. Thus, the processes of judgment and decision making must operate in a way that allows you to deal efficiently with uncertainty. As **Herbert Simon,** one of the founding figures of cognitive psychology, put it: because "human thinking powers are very modest when compared with the complexities of the environments in which human beings live" they must be content "to find 'good enough' solutions to their problems and 'good enough' courses of action" (1979, p. 3). In this light, Simon suggested that thought processes are guided by *bounded rationality*. Your judgments or decisions might not be as good—as "rational"—as they always could be, but you should be able to see how they result from your applying limited resources to situations that require swift action.

Before we move to a closer analysis of the products of bounded rationality, let's quickly distinguish between the two processes of judgment and decision making. **Judgment** is the process by which you form opinions, reach conclusions, and make critical evaluations of events and people. You often make judgments spontaneously, without prompting. **Decision making** is the process of choosing between alternatives, selecting and rejecting available options. Judgment and decision making are interrelated processes. For example, you might meet someone at a party and, after a brief discussion and a dance together, *judge* the person to be intelligent, interesting, honest, and sincere. You might then *decide* to spend most of your party time with that person and to arrange a date for the next weekend; decision making is more closely linked to behavioral actions. Let's turn now to research on these two types of thinking.

◆ HEURISTICS AND JUDGMENT

What's the best way to make a judgment? Suppose, for example, you are asked whether you enjoyed a movie. To answer this question, you could fill out a chart with two columns, "What I liked about the movie" and "What I didn't like about the movie," and see which column came out longer. To be a bit more accurate, perhaps you'd weight the entries in each list according to their importance (thus, you might weight "the actors' performances" as more important on the plus side than "the blaring sound track" on the minus side). If you went through this whole procedure, you'd probably be pretty confident of your judgment—but you know already that this is an exercise you rarely undertake. In real-life circumstances, you have to make judgments frequently and rapidly. You don't have the time—and often you don't have sufficient information—to use such a formal procedure. What do you do instead? An answer to this question was pioneered by **Amos Tversky** and **Daniel Kahneman,** who argued that people's judgments rely on heuristics rather than on formal methods of analysis. As we noted in our discussion of problem solving, heuristics are informal rules of thumb that provide shortcuts, reducing the complexity of making judgments.

How do you demonstrate that people are using these mental rules of thumb? As you will soon see, researchers have most often opted to show the circumstances in which the shortcuts lead people to make errors. The logic of these experiments should sound familiar to you by now: Just as you can understand perception by studying perceptual illusion and memory by studying memory failures, you can understand judgment processes by studying judgment errors (Kahneman, 1991). As in those other domains, you have to be careful not to mistake the method for the conclusion. Even though there is a wide range of situations in which psychologists can show that your perceptual processes can be fooled, you rarely walk into walls. Similarly, despite the errors that arise because your judgment making is implemented by heuristics, you rarely bump against the wall of cognitive limitations.

Does this mean you should be entirely comfortable with these types of errors? Here the analogy to perception breaks down to some extent. Most perceptual illusions are immune to learning. You're always going to perceive the lengths of the lines of the Müller-Lyer illusion (see Chapter 4) to be different, no matter how much you learn about it. By comparison, knowing about judgmental heuristics can enable you to avoid

<www.ablongman.com/gerrig17e>

If you were in a happy mood, would you be more likely to remember good times from your younger days?

would begin with the letter *k* (for example, *kangaroo*) or have *k* in third position (for example, *duke*)? If you are like the participants in a study by Tversky and Kahneman (1973), then you probably judged that *k* is found more often at the beginning of words. In fact, *k* appears about twice as often in the third position.

Why do most people believe that *k* is more likely to appear in first position? The answer has to do with the *availability* of information from memory. It's much easier to think of words that begin with *k* than to think of those in which *k* comes third. Your judgment, thus, arises from use of the **availability heuristic:** You base your judgment on information that is readily available in memory. This heuristic makes sense, because much of the time what is available from memory will lead to accurate judgments. If, for example, you judge bowling to be a less dangerous sport than hang gliding, availability is serving you well. Trouble only arises either when (1) memory processes give rise to a biased sample of information or (2) the information you've stored in memory is not accurate. Let's look at an example of each of these potential problems.

The *k* question is a good example of circumstances in which your memory processes can make an availability-based judgment inaccurate. Given the way words are organized in memory, it's simply easier to find words that begin with a particular letter. Let's consider another case that is closer to the judgments you make in everyday life.

some types of errors. Although general intellectual skills provide no defense against these errors—even the most gifted judgment makers err under some circumstances—specific training can help. Throughout this section, we will point out the ways in which you can improve your judgment making. Let's turn now to three heuristics: availability, representativeness, and anchoring.

AVAILABILITY HEURISTIC

We'll begin by asking you to make a rather trivial judgment. (We know you're likely to give the wrong answer, and we don't want to embarrass you about something important.) If we were to give you a brief excerpt from a novel, do you believe more words in the excerpt

Mood Affects the Availability of Memories

Researchers wanted to demonstrate how people's moods influenced their judgments about the likelihood that certain fates would befall them. Participants in their study read statements that put them in either measurably happy or unhappy moods. They then were asked to think of past instances of happy or unhappy events—for example, a welcome invitation or a painful injury—and to estimate how likely it would be that events of this type would happen to them again in the next six months. The participants' ability to recall past events was strongly predicted by their mood—and the availability of mood-congruent memories predicted judgments about the future. Thus, participants in a happy mood found it easier to recall happy events. But, also, the availability of those happy events led participants to judge that more happy events, and fewer unhappy events, would occur in the future (Macleod & Campbell, 1992).

This experiment demonstrates how easily judgments can be affected by the type of information that is—for whatever reasons—easily available from memory. You see the implications for your day-to-day life. If you are making important judgments about your future, you should factor in the way mood affects the information available to you. More generally, when it's time to make an important judgment, you can ask yourself, "Is there anything special about my frame of mind that will bias the information coming out of memory?"

A second difficulty with availability as a judgment heuristic arises when the information you have stored in memory has a bias to it. For example, one study examined the relationship between people's television viewing and their estimates about the typical wealth of U.S. citizens (O'Guinn & Shrum, 1997). People who watched more television shows like *Dynasty* and *Dallas* were also more likely to estimate greater numbers of U.S. households that have hot tubs or employ servants. The researchers' explanation for this correlation was that the television programs make unrealistic images of great wealth easily available to heavy viewers. As a second example, consider people's judgments of the populations of various countries (Brown & Siegler, 1992). See if you can order these four countries from smallest to largest population:

a. Sweden

b. Indonesia

c. Israel

d. Nigeria

Researchers demonstrated that, in general, the more participants knew about a country, the higher their population estimates. Furthermore, there was a sizable correlation between participants' rated knowledge about a country and the number of times it had been mentioned in *New York Times* articles in a given year. (The right answer, by the way, is Israel, Sweden, Nigeria, Indonesia. Did availability lead you astray?)

Clearly, you shouldn't feel bad about your cognitive processes because the media have provided you with a flawed database. Even so, you can combat this effect of availability by examining the sources of your information before you make important judgements. How do you know what you think you know?

REPRESENTATIVENESS HEURISTIC

When you make judgments based on the **representativeness heuristic,** you assume that if something has the characteristics considered typical of members of a category, it is, in fact, a member of that category. This heuristic will seem familiar to you because it captures the idea that people use past information to make judgments about similar circumstances in the present. That is the essence of inductive reasoning. Under most circumstances—as long as you have unbiased ideas about the features and categories that go together—making judgments along the lines of similarity will be quite reasonable. Thus, if you are deciding whether to begin a new activity like hang gliding, it makes sense to determine how representative that sport is of the category of activities you have previously enjoyed. Representativeness will lead you astray, however, when it causes you to ignore other types of relevant information, as you will now see (Kahneman & Tversky, 1973).

Consider, for example, the description of a successful attorney, given in **Figure 8.18.**

FIGURE 8.18

Using the Representativeness Heuristic

When asked to choose the attorney's favorite sport, the representativeness heuristic leads most people to choose "tennis." However, as shown in the bottom part of the figure, the more probable answer is "a ball game," because that includes within it "tennis."

A successful Jerusalem attorney. Colleagues say his whims prevent him from being a team worker, attributing his success to competitiveness and drive. Slim and not tall, he watches his body and is vain. Spends several hours a week on his favorite sport. What sport is that?

a. Fast walking
b. A ball game
c. Tennis
d. A track and field sport

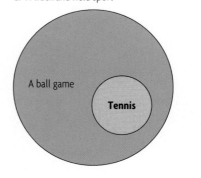

The more inclusive category <u>must</u> be more probable.

<www.ablongman.com/gerrig17e>

Representativeness Affects Judgments

In one experiment, researchers provided their participants with a list of options, including those in Figure 8.18, and gave them the chance to win $45—real money—by ranking the correct option as number 1. Which option seems correct to you? If you're like a majority of the original participants, you'll lose the $45 because you'll say *tennis* rather than *a ball game*. The lower part of Figure 8.18 shows why *tennis* could never be as good a bet: it is included within the category *a ball game*. Participants judge *tennis* to be a better answer because it seems to have all the features of the sport the attorney is likely to play. However, this judgment by representativeness causes participants to neglect another sort of information—category structure. In this case, the measurable cost is $45 (Bar-Hillel & Neter, 1993).

The implication for your day-to-day life is that you should not be fooled into grabbing at a representative alternative before you consider the structure of all the alternatives.

Let's look at a second representativeness example that also might affect the bets you make. Suppose you were given the opportunity to play in a lottery. To win, you must match the three numbers the state draws in the exact order. Which of these numbers would you feel most comfortable betting on?

859	101	333
574	948	772

The question we are really asking you is: Which of these numbers strikes you as most representative of the numbers that win these kinds of lotteries? If you are like most bettors, you will avoid playing numbers that have repeated digits—because those numbers do not seem representative of a random sequence. In fact, 27 percent of the time a three-digit number—with each digit drawn randomly from the pool 0 to 9—will have a repeated numeral. Nevertheless, among individuals who took part in the Indiana Pick-3 lottery in a 15-day period, only 12.6 percent chose to play a number with a repeated digit (Holtgraves & Skeel, 1992). You should be wary, in general, of the way that most gambling situations are constructed. Most often the hope is that you will be guided by representativeness—so you'll choose the options that look like they're more likely to win—rather than by a careful consideration of the odds.

ANCHORS AWEIGH!

To introduce you to a third heuristic, we need you to try a thought experiment. First take five seconds to estimate the following mathematical product and write down your answer:

$$1 \times 2 \times 3 \times 4 \times 5 \times 6 \times 7 \times 8 = \underline{\qquad}$$

In five seconds, you can probably make only a couple of calculations. You get a partial answer, perhaps 24, and then adjust up from there. Now try this series of numbers:

$$8 \times 7 \times 6 \times 5 \times 4 \times 3 \times 2 \times 1 = \underline{\qquad}$$

Even if you notice that this is the same list in reverse, you can see how the experience of carrying out the multiplication would feel quite different. You'd start with 8×7, which is 56, and then attempt 56×6, which already feels quite large. Once again, you can only make a partial guess and then adjust upward. When Tversky and Kahneman (1974) gave these two arrangements of the identical problem to experimental participants, the 1 to 8 order produced median estimates of 512, and the 8 to 1 group produced estimates of 2,250 (*the real answer is 40,320*). Apparently, when participants adjusted up from their five-second estimates, the higher partial solutions led to higher estimates.

Performance on this simple multiplication task provides evidence for an anchoring bias. When you judge the probable value of some event or outcome, a bias based on the **anchoring heuristic** is an insufficient adjustment—either up or down—from an original starting value. In other words, your judgment is "anchored" too firmly to an original guess. The use of an anchor is not costly when the original estimate consists of information genuinely relevant to the judgment at hand. However, people show a strong tendency to be influenced by an anchor, even when the information is clearly of little or no use.

Arbitrary Anchors Change Estimates

In one study, students in experimental conditions were given an arbitrary identification number (in the range 1,928 to 1,935) that they were instructed to copy onto their questionnaires. (Students in the control group did not receive a number.) The students' attention was called to the number in one of several ways (for example, they were asked to check whether it was higher than 1,940), but the identification numbers were clearly defined as irrelevant to any other answer. Subsequently, the students were asked to estimate the number of physicians listed in the local Yellow Pages. The responses were clearly affected by the totally irrelevant, arbitrary anchor. Students who had their attention called to the arbitrary identification number gave much higher estimates than did students in the control group—631 versus 219. Even when students were specifically warned that the ID number might affect their judgments, they still increased their estimates to 539—well over the control group's 219 estimate (Wilson et al., 1996)!

This last result should give you particular pause: Even a warning didn't help. Salespeople often use anchoring when they are trying to convince you to buy a product. Suppose, for example, you are thinking of buying a new stereo. A salesperson might say, "You'd expect to pay $1,000 or $2,000, wouldn't you?" Once you are anchored on that high estimate, the real price (perhaps $599.99) seems like a good deal. We'd like to think that reading this section will help you to avoid negative anchoring effects, but you are now forewarned that you must be very, very careful.

You employ judgmental heuristics like availability, representativeness, and anchoring because, in most situations, they allow you to make efficient, acceptable judgments. In a sense, you are doing the best you can, given the uncertainties of situations and constraints on your processing resources. We have shown you, however, that heuristics can lead to errors. You should try to use this knowledge to examine your own thought processes when the time comes to make important judgments. You should be especially critical when you feel others might be trying to bias your judgments. Let's move now to the decisions you make, often on the basis of those judgments.

◆ THE PSYCHOLOGY OF DECISION MAKING

Let us begin with a powerful example of the way that psychological factors affect the decisions people make.

Consider the problem given in part 1 of **Table 8.6.** Read the instructions, and then make your choice between Spot A and Spot B. Now read the version of the problem given in part 2. Would you like to change your choice?

In an experiment, students read one version of this problem (Shafir, 1993). When they were asked in part 1 which option they preferred, 67 percent of the students opted for Spot B. However, when students were asked in part 2 to cancel an option, this figure fell to 52 percent (that is, 48 percent said they would cancel Spot B). Why is this change odd? If you take a close look at the "prefer" and "cancel" versions of the problem, you will see that there is no difference in the information available in the two cases. On first pass, you might expect that the same information would lead to the same decision. But that's not what people do. It seems that the "prefer" question focuses people's attention on positive features of options—you're gathering evidence in favor of something—whereas the "cancel" question focuses attention on negative features of options—you're gathering evidence against something. Your decision may shift.

This straightforward example demonstrates that the way in which a question is phrased can have great consequences for the decision you will make (Slovic, 1995). This is why you need to understand the psychological aspects of decision making: You need to be able to test your own decisions to see whether they hold up under careful analysis. In this case, you might ask yourself, "How would my choice change if I were asked to reject an option rather than to choose one?" If you find that

TABLE 8.6
The Effect of Psychological Factors on Decision Making

Part 1: Prefer Version	Part 2: Cancel Version
1. Imagine that you are planning a week vacation in a warm spot over spring break. You currently have two options that are reasonably priced. The travel brochure gives only a limited amount of information about the two options. Given the information available, which vacation spot would you prefer?	2. Imagine that you are planning a week vacation in a warm spot over spring break. You currently have two options that are reasonably priced, but you can no longer retain your reservation for both. The travel brochure gives only a limited amount of information about the two options. Given the information available, which reservation do you decide to cancel?
Spot A average weather average beaches medium-quality hotel medium-temperature water average nightlife	Spot A average weather average beaches medium-quality hotel medium-temperature water average nightlife
Spot B lots of sunshine gorgeous beaches and coral reefs ultramodern hotel very cold water very strong winds no nightlife	Spot B lots of sunshine gorgeous beaches and coral reefs ultramodern hotel very cold water very strong winds no nightlife

your top preference is also your top candidate for rejection, you will have learned that the option has both many positive and many negative features. Now ask, "Is that acceptable?" This is a key step in developing your critical thinking skills.

THE FRAMING OF DECISIONS

One of the most natural ways to make a decision is to judge which option will bring about the biggest gain or which option will bring about the smallest loss. Thus, if we offer you $5 or $10, you will feel very little uncertainty that the better option is $10. What makes the situation a bit more complicated, however, is that the perception of a gain or a loss often depends on the way in which a decision is *framed*. A **frame** is a particular description of a choice. Suppose, for example, you were asked how happy you would be to get a $1,000 raise in your job. If you were expecting no raise at all, this would seem like a great gain, and you'd probably be quite happy. But suppose you'd been told several times to expect a raise of $10,000. Now how do you feel? Suddenly, you may feel as if you've lost money, because the $1,000 is less than what you had expected. You're not happy at all! In either case, you'd be getting $1,000 more a year—objectively, you'd be in exactly the same position—but the psychological effect is very different. That's why *reference points* are important in decision making (Kahneman, 1992). What seems like a gain or a loss will be determined in part by the expectations—a $0 raise or a $10,000 raise—to which a decision maker refers. (The decision, in this case, might be whether to stay in the job.)

Let's now take a look at a slightly more complex example in which framing has a sizable impact on the decisions people make. In **Table 8.7,** you are asked to imagine making a choice between surgery and radiation for treatment of lung cancer. First, read the *survival* frame for the problem and choose your preferred treatment; then read the *mortality* frame and see if you feel like changing your preference. Note that the data are objectively the same in the two frames. The only difference is whether statistical information about the consequences of each treatment is presented in terms of survival rates or of mortality rates. When this decision was presented to participants, the focus on relative gains and losses had a marked effect on choice of treatment. Radiation therapy was chosen by only 18 percent of the participants who were given the survival frame, but by 44 percent of those given the mortality frame. This framing effect held equally for a group of clinic patients, statistically sophisticated business students, and experienced physicians (McNeil et al., 1982).

What makes this example important is that it mirrors the uncertainty you frequently have in real life.

The Framing of Romance

Suppose you have been in a relationship for six months. How do you decide whether the relationship has a healthy future? Researchers demonstrated that framing has an impact on students' level of relationship optimism (Knee & Boon, 2001). At the outset of the study, the participants were informed that most undergraduates value partners who have honesty, humor, and intelligence. The participants were then asked to imagine a hypothetical partner who embodied a subset of those features. In the *gain* version of the description, the students were told that their partners possessed two of the three features (e.g., honesty and humor). In the *loss* version of the description, the students were told their partners lacked one of the three features (e.g., intelligence). You can see that these two descriptions yield the same individual (e.g., in either case he or she is honest and funny, but not intelligent). Still, when students rated their impressions of the future success of the relationship, they were consistently less optimistic with the *loss* description than with the *gain* description.

You can see how a small change in framing could have a large impact on how you think about your future. This result should encourage you to try to think about important decisions with *both* a gain frame and a loss frame.

TABLE 8.7
The Effect of Framing

Survival frame

Surgery. Of 100 people having surgery, 90 live through the postoperative period, 68 are alive at the end of the first year, and 34 are alive at the end of five years.

Radiation therapy. Of 100 people having radiation therapy, all live through the treatment, 77 are alive at the end of one year, and 22 are alive at the end of five years.

What do you choose: surgery or radiation?

Mortality frame

Surgery. Of 100 people having surgery, 10 die during surgery or the postoperative period, 32 die by the end of one year, and 66 die by the end of five years.

Radiation therapy. Of 100 people having radiation therapy, none dies during treatment, 23 die by the end of one year, and 78 die by the end of five years.

What do you choose: surgery or radiation?

In what ways can salespeople frame their products to get prospective customers to consider them in a positive light?

Suppose, for example, you are going to buy a new car. The salesperson will be inclined to frame everything as a gain: "Seventy-eight percent of the Xenons require no repairs in the first year!" You can reframe that to "Twenty-two percent require some repairs in the first year!" Would the new frame change how you feel about the situation? It's an exercise worth trying in real life.

The car salesperson is a good example of a situation in which someone is trying to frame information in a fashion that will have a desired effect on your decision. This, of course, is a regular part of your life. For example, as each election approaches, the opposing candidates compete to have their framings of themselves and of the issues prevail among the voters. One candidate might say, "I believe in sticking with policies that have been successful." His opponent might counter, "He is afraid of new ideas." One candidate might say, "That policy will bring about economic growth." Her opponent might counter, "That policy will bring about environmental destruction." Often both claims are true—the same policy often will bring about both economic good and environmental harm. In this light, whichever frame seems more compelling may be largely a matter of personal history (Tversky & Kahneman, 1981; Vaughan & Seifert, 1992). Thus, your knowledge of framing effects can help you understand how people can come to such radically different decisions when they are faced with exactly the same evidence. If you want to understand other people's actions, try to think about how those individuals have framed a decision.

DECISION AVERSION

Let's suppose that you have worked hard to evaluate a choice from the perspective of different frames. What happens next? You might discover that you have created a situation for yourself in which you will experience **decision aversion:** You might find that you will try hard to avoid making any decision at all. In **Table 8.8,** we provide an example of circumstances that can bring about an increasing unwillingness to make a decision. Consider the scenario in part A. Which would you choose? Researchers found that only 34 percent of their participants said they would wait for more information (Tversky & Shafir, 1992). Now consider the slightly altered scenario given in part B. Do you want to change your choice? In fact, 46 percent of the participants who read this version said they would wait for new information. How could this be? Ordinarily, you would expect that adding an option would decrease the share of the other options. If, for example, a third candidate enters a political race, you would expect that candidate to pull votes away from the original pair. Here, however, the addition of a third possibility increases the share of one of the original choices by 12 percent. What's going on?

The key to obtaining this effect is to make the decision hard. When the researchers tested participants on a version of the problem that provided a low-quality CD player as an extra option, only 24 percent said they would wait for more information—a decrease rather than an increase—which reflects the ease of choosing the Sony. The decision between the less expensive Sony model and the top-quality Aiwa, however, is hard.

TABLE 8.8
Decision Aversion

A. Suppose you are considering buying a compact disk (CD) player, and have not yet decided what model to buy. You pass by a store that is having a 1-day clearance sale. They offer a popular SONY player for just $99, well below the list price. Do you

　1. buy the SONY player

　2. wait until you learn more about the various models

B. Suppose you are considering buying a compact disk (CD) player, and have not yet decided what model to buy. You pass by a store that is having a 1-day clearance sale. They offer a popular SONY player for just $99, and a top-of-the-line AIWA player for just $159, both well below the list price. Do you

　1. buy the AIWA player

　2. buy the SONY player

　3. wait until you learn more about the various models

<www.ablongman.com/gerrig17e>

It's convenient to put the hard decision off, to wait for more information.

Although there are some individual differences, the general tendency to avoid tough decisions is very powerful in most people. Several psychological forces are at work (Anderson, 2003; Beattie et al., 1994):

- People don't like to make decisions that will cause some people to have more and some people to have less of some desired good.
- People are able to anticipate the regret they will feel if the option they choose turns out worse than the option they didn't choose.
- People don't like to be accountable for decisions that lead to bad outcomes.
- People don't like to make decisions for other people.

We can turn this last principle around to define circumstances in which people are *decision seeking:* As much as people are averse to making decisions, they are generally happier to make them themselves than to let other people do so for them. This is something you should bear in mind. Try to avoid letting other people make important decisions for you. Try, as well, not to convince yourself that a decision is so hard that you can't make it at all. In most circumstances, you can count on your cognitive processes to provide you with accurate judgments. Use those judgments to make appropriate choices!

Throughout this chapter, we've asked you to imagine the mysterious midnight message, "The cat is on the mat." Our goal has been to get you to consider your many types of cognitive processing—language use, visual cognition, problem solving, reasoning, judging, and deciding. Now that this chapter has come to an end, we hope that the example will stick with you—so that you'll never take your cognitive processes for granted. Every chance you get, give some thought to your thought, reason about your reasoning, and so on. You will be reflecting on the essence of the human experience.

PUT YOURSELF TO THE TEST

- Why do people rely on heuristics when they are making judgments?
- In what real-life circumstances do availability, representativeness, and anchoring play a role?
- Why do frames play such a large role in the psychology of decision making?
- Why do people experience decision aversion?

Recapping Main Points

STUDYING COGNITION

- Cognitive psychologists study the mental processes and structures that enable you to perceive, use language, reason, solve problems, and make judgments and decisions.
- Researchers use reaction time measures to break up complex tasks into underlying mental processes.

LANGUAGE USE

- Language users both produce and understand language.
- Speakers design their utterances to suit particular audiences.
- Speech errors reveal many of the processes that go into speech planning.
- Much of language understanding consists of using context to resolve ambiguities.
- Memory representations of meaning begin with propositions supplemented with inferences.
- The language individuals speak may play a role in determining how they think.

VISUAL COGNITION

- Visual representations can be used to supplement propositional representations.
- Visual representations allow you to think about visual aspects of your environment.
- People form visual representations that combine verbal and visual information.

PROBLEM SOLVING AND REASONING

- Problem solvers must define initial state, goal state, and the operations that get them from the initial to the goal state.
- Deductive reasoning involves drawing conclusions from premises based on rules of logic.
- Inductive reasoning involves inferring a conclusion from evidence based on its likelihood or probability.

JUDGMENT AND DECISION MAKING

- Much of judgment and decision making is guided by heuristics—mental shortcuts that can help individuals reach solutions quickly.
- Availability, representativeness, and anchoring can all lead to errors when they are misapplied.
- Decision making is affected by the way in which different options are framed.
- Because of psychological forces, people have a tendency to avoid making difficult decisions.

<www.ablongman.com/gerrig17e>

KEY TERMS

algorithm (p. 266)

anchoring heuristic (p. 277)

audience design (p. 251)

automatic processes (p. 249)

availability heuristic (p. 275)

belief-bias effect (p. 269)

cognition (p. 246)

cognitive processes (p. 245)

cognitive psychology (p. 246)

cognitive science (p. 246)

controlled processes (p. 249)

decision aversion (p. 280)

decision making (p. 274)

deductive reasoning (p. 269)

frame (p. 279)

functional fixedness (p. 268)

heuristics (p. 266)

inductive reasoning (p. 271)

inferences (p. 257)

judgment (p. 274)

language production (p. 251)

mental set (p. 271)

parallel processes (p. 247)

problem solving (p. 265)

problem space (p. 265)

reasoning (p. 265)

representativeness heuristic (p. 276)

serial processes (p. 247)

think-aloud protocols (p. 266)

9

Intelligence and Intelligence Assessment

Suppose you were asked to define the word *intelligence*. What types of behaviors would you include in your definition? Think back on your own experiences. What was it like when you first started school? What was it like when you labored at your first job? It's very likely that you heard your behaviors labeled as intelligent or unintelligent—smart or not so smart—in those and other situations. When those labels are applied in casual conversation, they have relatively few consequences. However, there are many settings in which it matters whether your behaviors are considered intelligent or not. For example, if you grew up in the United States, it is likely that your "potential" was measured at an early age. In most school districts, teachers and administrators attempt, very early in your life, to measure your *intelligence*. The goal, most often, is to match students with classroom work that makes appropriate demands. However, as you've almost certainly observed, people's lives often seem to be affected by intelligence testing in areas well outside the classroom.

In this chapter, we will examine the foundations and uses of intelligence assessment. We will review the contributions psychologists have made to the understanding of individual differences in the areas of intelligence. We will also discuss the types of controversies that almost inevitably arise when people begin to interpret these differences. Our focus will be on how intelligence tests work, what makes any test useful, and why they do not always do the job they were intended to do. Finally, we will conclude on a personal note, by considering the role of psychological assessment in society.

We begin now with a brief overview of the general practice of psychological assessment.

What Is Assessment?

Psychological assessment is the use of specified testing procedures to evaluate the abilities, behaviors, and personal qualities of people. Psychological assessment is often referred to as the measurement of *individual differences,* because the majority of assessments specifies how an individual is different from or similar to other people on a given dimension. Before we examine in detail the basic features of psychological testing, let's outline the history of assessment. This historical overview will help you to understand both the uses and limitations of assessment, as well as prepare you to appreciate some current controversies.

◆ HISTORY OF ASSESSMENT

The development of formal tests and procedures for assessment is a relatively new enterprise in Western psychology, coming into wide use only in the early 1900s. However, long before Western psychology began to devise tests to evaluate people, assessment techniques were commonplace in ancient China. In fact, China employed a sophisticated program of civil service testing over 4,000 years ago—officials were required to demonstrate their competence every third year at an oral examination. Two thousand years later, during the Han Dynasty, written civil service tests were used to measure competence in the areas of law, the military, agriculture, and geography. During the Ming Dynasty (A.D. 1368–1644), public officials were chosen on the basis of their performance at three stages of an objective selection procedure. During the first stage, examinations were given at the local level. The 4 percent who passed these tests had to endure the second stage: nine days and nights of essay examinations on the classics. The 5 percent who passed the essay exams were allowed to complete a final stage of tests conducted at the nation's capital.

China's selection procedures were observed and described by British diplomats and missionaries in the early 1800s. Modified versions of China's system were soon adopted by the British and later by the Americans for the selection of civil service personnel (Wiggins, 1973).

The key figure in the development of Western intelligence testing was an upper-class Englishman, **Sir Francis Galton.** His book *Hereditary Genius,* published in 1869, greatly influenced subsequent thinking on the methods, theories, and practices of testing. Galton, a half cousin to Charles Darwin, attempted to apply Darwinian evolutionary theory to the study of human abilities. He was interested in how and why people differ in their abilities. He wondered why some people were gifted and successful—like him—while many others were not.

Galton was the first to postulate four important ideas about the assessment of intelligence. First, differences in intelligence were *quantifiable* in terms of degrees of intelligence. In other words, numerical values could be assigned to distinguish among different people's levels of intelligence. Second, differences among people formed a *bell-shaped curve,* or *normal distribution.* On a bell-shaped curve, most people's scores cluster in the middle and fewer are found toward

What important ideas about the assessment of intelligence are credited to Sir Francis Galton (1822–1911)?

the two extremes of genius and mental deficiency (we return to the bell-shaped curve later in the chapter). Third, intelligence, or mental ability, could be measured by objective tests, tests on which each question had only one "right" answer. And fourth, the precise extent to which two sets of test scores were related could be determined by a statistical procedure he called *co-relations,* now known as *correlations*. These ideas proved to be of lasting value.

Unfortunately, Galton postulated a number of ideas that proved considerably more controversial. He believed, for example, that genius was inherited. In his view, talent, or eminence, ran in families; nurture had only a minimal effect on intelligence. In his view, intelligence was related to Darwinian species' fitness and, somehow, ultimately to one's moral worth. Galton attempted to base public policy on the concept of genetically superior and inferior people. He started the *eugenics* movement, which advocated improving the human species by applying evolutionary theory to encouraging biologically superior people to interbreed while discouraging biologically inferior people from having offspring. Galton wrote, "There exists a sentiment, for the most part quite unreasonable, against the gradual extinction of an inferior race" (Galton, 1883/1907, p. 200).

These controversial ideas were endorsed and extended later by many who argued forcefully that the intellectually superior race should propagate at the expense of those with inferior minds. Among the proponents of these ideas were American psychologists Goddard and Terman, whose theories we review later, and, of course, Nazi dictator Adolf Hitler. We will also see later in the chapter that remnants of these elitist ideas are still being proposed today.

Sir Francis Galton's work created a context for contemporary intelligence assessment. Let's now see what features define circumstances of formal assessment.

◆ BASIC FEATURES OF FORMAL ASSESSMENT

To be useful for classifying individuals or for selecting those with particular qualities, a **formal assessment** procedure should meet three requirements. The assessment instrument should be (1) reliable, (2) valid, and (3) standardized. If it fails to meet these requirements, we cannot be sure whether the conclusions of the assessment can be trusted. Although this chapter focuses on intelligence assessment, formal assessment procedures apply to all types of psychological testing. To ensure that you'll understand the broad application of these principles, we will draw on examples both from intelligence testing and other domains of psychological assessment.

RELIABILITY

Reliability is the extent to which an assessment instrument can be trusted to give consistent scores. If you stepped on your bathroom scale three times in the same morning and it gave you a different reading each time, the scale would not be doing its job. You would call it *unreliable* because you could not count on it to give consistent results. Of course, if you ate a big meal in between two weighings, you wouldn't expect the scale to produce the same result. That is, a measurement device can be considered reliable or unreliable only to the extent that the underlying concept it is measuring should remain unchanged.

One straightforward way to find out if a test is reliable is to calculate its **test–retest reliability**—a measure of the correlation between the scores of the same people, on the same test, given on two different occasions. A perfectly reliable test will yield a correlation coefficient of +1.00. This means that the identical pattern of scores emerges both times. The same people who got the highest and lowest scores the first time do so again. A totally unreliable test results in a 0.00 correlation coefficient. That means there is no relationship between the first set of scores and the second set. Someone who initially got the top score gets a completely different score the second time. As the correlation coefficient moves higher (toward the ideal of +1.00), the test is increasingly reliable.

There are two other ways to assess reliability. One is to administer alternate, **parallel forms** of a test instead of giving the same test twice. Using parallel forms reduces the effects of direct practice of the test questions, memory of the test questions, and the desire of an individual to appear consistent from one test to the next. Reliable tests yield comparable scores on parallel forms of the test. The other measure of reliability is the

◆ *The wrong way to measure split-half reliability.*

internal consistency of responses on a single test. For example, we can compare a person's score on the odd-numbered items of a test with the score on the even-numbered items. A reliable test yields the same score for each of its halves. It is then said to have high internal consistency on this measure of **split-half reliability.**

In most circumstances, not only should the measurement device itself be reliable, but so should the method for using the device. Suppose researchers wished to observe children in a classroom in order to assess different levels of aggressive play. The researchers might develop a *coding scheme* that would allow them to make appropriate distinctions. The scheme would be reliable to the extent that all the people who viewed the same behavior would give highly similar ratings to the same children. This is one of the reasons that quite a bit of training is required before individuals can carry out accurate psychological assessment. They must learn to apply systems of distinctions in a reliable fashion.

The researchers who develop and administer assessment devices work hard to ensure reliability. Did you take the SAT I exam for college admissions? You may not know this, but one section of the exam you took did not have an impact on your score. The questions on this unscored section were most likely being considered for future exams. The researchers who develop the exam can compare performance on the scored questions to performance on the unscored questions to ensure that people's scores on future exams are comparable to the scores on the exam that you took. For that reason, if you took the SAT I, you provided some of the information that helps to make the test reliable.

VALIDITY

The **validity** of a test is the degree to which it measures what an assessor intends it to measure. A valid test of intelligence measures that trait and predicts performance in situations where intelligence is important. Scores on a valid measure of creativity reflect actual creativity, not drawing ability or moods. In general, then, validity reflects a test's ability to make accurate predictions about behaviors or outcomes related to the purpose or design of the test. Three important types of validity are *face validity, criterion validity,* and *construct validity.*

The first type of validity is based on the surface *content* of a test. When test items appear to be directly related to the attribute of interest, the test has **face validity.** Face-valid tests are very straightforward—they simply ask what the test maker needs to know: How anxious do you feel? Are you creative? The person taking the test is expected to answer accurately and honestly. Unfortunately, face validity is often not sufficient to ensure accurate measurement. First, people's perceptions of themselves may not be accurate, or they

may not know how they should rate themselves in comparison to other people. Second, a test that too obviously measures some attribute may allow test takers to manipulate the impression they make. Consider the classic case of institutionalized mental patients who did not want to be released from their familiar, structured environment.

CLASSIC

PUTTING IDEAS TO THE TEST

Patients Manipulate Psychiatrists' Assessments

These long-term schizophrenic patients were interviewed by the staff about how disturbed they were. When they were given a *transfer* interview to assess if they were well enough to be moved to an open ward, these patients gave generally positive self-references. However, when the purpose of the interview was to assess their suitability for *discharge,* the patients gave more negative self-references, because they did not want to be discharged. Psychiatrists who rated the interview data, without awareness of this experimental variation in the purpose of the interview, judged those who gave more negative self-references as more severely disturbed and recommended against their discharge. So the patients achieved the assessment outcome they wanted. The psychiatrists' assessment may also have been influenced by their perspective that anyone who wanted to stay in a mental hospital must be very disturbed (Braginsky & Braginsky, 1967).

This example makes it particularly clear that test givers cannot rely only on measures that have face validity. Let's consider other types of validity that overcome some of these limitations.

To assess the **criterion validity** (also known as **predictive validity**) of a test, psychologists compare a person's score on the test with his or her score on some other standard, or *criterion,* associated with what the test measures. For example, if a test is designed to predict success in college, then college grades would be an appropriate criterion. If the test scores correlate highly with college grades, then the test has criterion validity. A major task of test developers is to find appropriate, measurable criteria. Once criterion validity has been demonstrated for an assessment device, researchers feel confident using the device to make future predictions.

The conditions under which a test is valid may be very specific, so it is always important to ask about a test, "For what purpose is it valid?" Knowing which other measures a test does and does not correlate with

How would you feel if someone used your adult height to assess intelligence? The measure would be reliable, but would it be valid?

may reveal something new about the measures, the construct, or the complexity of human behavior. For example, suppose you design a test to measure the ability of medical students to cope with stress. You then find that scores on that test correlate well with students' ability to cope with classroom stress. You presume your test will also correlate with students' ability to deal with stressful hospital emergencies, but you discover it does not. Because you have demonstrated some validity, you have learned something both about your test—the circumstances in which it is valid—and about your construct—different categories of stressors have different consequences. You would then modify your test to take account of the kinds of special stressors found in hospital emergencies.

Consider for a moment the relationship between validity and reliability. While reliability is measured by the degree to which a test correlates with itself (administered at different times or using different items), validity is measured by the degree to which the test correlates with something external to it (another test, a behavioral criterion, or judges' ratings). Usually, a test that is not reliable is also not valid, because a test that cannot predict itself will be unable to predict anything else. For example, if your class took a test of aggressiveness today and scores were uncorrelated with scores from a parallel form of the test tomorrow (demonstrating unreliability), it is unlikely that the scores from either day would predict which students had fought or argued most frequently over a week's time: After all, the two sets of test scores would not even make the same prediction! On the other hand, it is quite possible for a test to be highly reliable without being valid. Suppose, for example, we decided

to use your adult height as a measure of intelligence. Do you see why that would be reliable but not valid?

NORMS AND STANDARDIZATION

So we have a reliable and valid test, but we still need *norms* to provide a context for interpreting different test scores. Suppose, for example, you get a score of 18 on a test designed to reveal how depressed you are. What does that mean? Are you a little depressed, not at all depressed, or about averagely depressed? To find out what your score means, you would want to compare your individual score with typical scores, or statistical **norms,** of other students. You would check the test norms to see what the usual range of scores is and what the average is for students of your age and sex. That would provide you with a context for interpreting your depression score.

You probably encountered test norms when you received your scores on aptitude tests, such as the SAT I. The norms told you how your scores compared with those of other students and helped you interpret how well you had done relative to that *normative population.* Group norms are most useful for interpreting individual scores when the comparison group shares important qualities with the individuals tested, such as age, social class, culture, and experience.

For norms to be meaningful, everyone must take the same test under standardized circumstances. **Standardization** is the administration of a testing device to all persons, in the same way, under the same conditions. The need for standardization sounds obvious, but it does not always occur in practice. Some people may be allowed more time than others, be given clearer or more detailed instructions, be permitted to ask questions, or be motivated by a tester to perform better. Consider the experience of one of your authors:

As a graduate student at Yale, I administered a scale to assess children's degree of test anxiety in grade-school classes. Before starting, one teacher told her class, "We're going to have some fun with this new kind of question game this nice man will play with you." A teacher in another classroom prepared her class for the same assessment by cautioning, "This psychologist from Yale University is going to give you a test to see what you are thinking; I hope you will do well and show how good our class is!" (Zimbardo, personal communication, 1958)

Could you directly compare the scores of the children in these two classes on this "same" test? The answer is no, because the test was not administered in a standardized way. In this case, the children in the second class scored higher on test anxiety. (You're probably not surprised!) When procedures do not include explicit instructions about the way to administer the test or the way to score the results, it is difficult to interpret what a given test score means or how it relates to any comparison group.

We have now reviewed some of the concerns researchers have when they construct a test and find out whether it is indeed testing what they wish to test. They must assure themselves that the test is reliable and valid. They must also specify the standard conditions under which it should be administered, so that resulting norms have meaning. Therefore, you should evaluate any test score you get in terms of the test's reliability and validity, the norms of performance, and the degree of standardization of the circumstances in which you took the test.

We are now ready to turn to the measurement of intelligence.

PUT YOURSELF TO THE TEST

- ➤ What is the purpose of psychological assessment?
- ➤ What concepts with respect to intelligence assessment did Sir Francis Galton originate?
- ➤ What are some of the ways in which reliability is assessed?
- ➤ What are some different types of validity?
- ➤ Why are norms and standardization important for psychological assessment?

Intelligence Assessment

How intelligent are you or your friends? To answer this question, you must begin by defining **intelligence.** Doing so is not an easy task, but a group of 52 intelligence researchers concurred on this general definition: "Intelligence is a very general mental capability that, among other things, involves the ability to reason, plan, solve problems, think abstractly, comprehend complex ideas, learn quickly and learn from experience" (Gottfredson, 1997a, p. 13). Given this range of capabilities, it should be clear immediately why controversy has almost always surrounded how intelligence is measured. The way in which theorists conceptualize intelligence and higher mental functioning greatly influences the way they try to assess it (Sternberg, 1994). Some psychologists believe that human intelligence can be quantified and reduced to a single score. Others argue that intelligence has many components that should be separately assessed. Still others say that there are actually several distinct kinds of intelligence, across different domains of experience.

In this section, we will describe how tests of intelligence mesh with these different conceptions of intelligence. Let's begin by considering the historical context in which interest in intelligence and intelligence testing first arose.

◆ THE ORIGINS OF INTELLIGENCE TESTING

The year 1905 marked the first published account of a workable intelligence test. **Alfred Binet** had responded to the call of the French minister of public instruction for the creation of more effective teaching methods for developmentally disabled children. Binet and his colleague Théophile Simon believed that measuring a child's intellectual ability was necessary for planning an instructional program. Binet attempted to devise an objective test of intellectual performance that could be used to classify and separate developmentally disabled from normal schoolchildren. He hoped that such a test would reduce the school's reliance on the more subjective, and perhaps biased, evaluations of teachers.

To *quantify*—measure—intellectual performance, Binet designed age-appropriate problems or test items on which many children's responses could be compared. The problems on the test were chosen so that they could be scored objectively as correct or incorrect,

---

could vary in content, were not heavily influenced by differences in children's environments, and assessed judgment and reasoning rather than rote memory (Binet, 1911).

Children of various ages were tested, and the average score for normal children at each age was computed. Then each individual child's performance was compared with the average for other children of his or her age. Test results were expressed in terms of the average age at which normal children achieved a particular score. This measure was called the **mental age.** For instance, when a child's score equaled the average score of a group of 5-year-olds, the child was said to have a *mental age* of 5, regardless of his or her actual **chronological age,** the number of years since birth.

There are four important features of Binet's approach. First, he interpreted scores on his test as an estimate of *current performance* and not as a measure of *innate intelligence.* Second, he wanted the test scores to be used to identify children who needed special help and not to *stigmatize* them. Third, he emphasized that training and opportunity could affect intelligence, and he sought to identify areas of performance in which special education could help disadvantaged children. Finally, he constructed his test empirically—he collected data to see if it was valid—rather than tying it to a particular theory of intelligence.

Binet's successful development of an intelligence test had great impact in the United States. A unique combination of historical events and social-political forces had prepared the United States for an explosion of interest in assessing mental ability. At the beginning of the 20th century, the United States was a nation in turmoil. As a result of global economic, social, and political conditions, millions of immigrants entered the country. New universal education laws flooded schools with students. Some form of assessment was needed to identify, document, and classify immigrant adults and schoolchildren (Chapman, 1988). When World War I began, millions of volunteers marched into recruiting stations. Recruiters needed to determine who of these many people had the ability to learn quickly and benefit from special leadership training. New nonverbal, group-administered tests of mental ability were used to evaluate over 1.7 million recruits. A group of prominent psychologists, including Lewis Terman, Edward Thorndike, and Robert Yerkes, responded to the wartime emergency and designed these tests in only one month's time (Lennon, 1985).

One consequence of this large-scale testing program was that the American public came to accept the idea that intelligence tests could differentiate people in terms of leadership ability and other socially important characteristics. This acceptance led to the widespread use of tests in schools and industry. Assessment was seen as a way to inject order into a chaotic society and as an inexpensive, democratic way to separate those who could benefit from education or military leadership training from those who could not. To facilitate the wide-scale use of intelligence testing, researchers strove for more broadly applicable testing procedures.

◆ IQ TESTS

Although Binet began the standardized assessment of intellectual ability in France, U.S. psychologists soon took the lead. They also developed the IQ, or intelligence quotient. The IQ was a numerical, standardized measure of intelligence. Two families of individually administered IQ tests are used widely today: the Stanford–Binet scales and the Wechsler scales.

THE STANFORD–BINET INTELLIGENCE SCALE

Stanford University's **Lewis Terman,** a former public school administrator, appreciated the importance of Binet's method for assessing intelligence. He adapted Binet's test questions for U.S. schoolchildren, he standardized the administration of the test, and he developed age-level norms by giving the test to thousands of children. In 1916, he published the Stanford Revision of the Binet Tests, commonly referred to as the *Stanford–Binet Intelligence Scale* (Terman, 1916).

With his new test, Terman provided a base for the concept of the **intelligence quotient,** or **IQ** (a term coined by William Stern, 1914). The IQ was the ratio of mental age to chronological age multiplied by 100 to eliminate decimals:

$$\text{IQ} = \text{mental age} \div \text{chronological age} \times 100$$

A child with a chronological age of 8 whose test scores revealed a mental age of 10 had an IQ of 125 ($10 \div 8 \times 100 = 125$), while a child of that same chronological age who performed at the level of a 6-year-old had an IQ of 75 ($6 \div 8 \times 100 = 75$). Individuals who performed at the mental age equivalent to their chronological age had IQs of 100. Thus, the score of 100 was considered to be the average IQ.

The new Stanford–Binet test soon became a standard instrument in clinical psychology, psychiatry, and educational counseling. The Stanford–Binet contains a series of subtests, each tailored for a particular mental age. Since it was first introduced, the Stanford–Binet has undergone a series of revisions (Terman & Merrill, 1937, 1960, 1972; Thorndike et al., 1986). Through those revisions, the range of the test has been extended to measure the IQ of very young children and very intelligent adults. In addition, the revisions have provided updated norms for age-appropriate average scores. The most recent, fifth edition of the Stanford–Binet test provides IQ estimates for individuals in the normal range of performance as well as for those individuals who are either mentally impaired or mentally gifted (Roid, 2003).

David Wechsler of Bellevue Hospital in New York set out to correct the dependence on verbal items in the assessment of adult intelligence. In 1939, he published the Wechsler–Bellevue Intelligence Scale, which combined verbal subtests with nonverbal, or performance, subtests. Thus, in addition to an overall IQ score, people were given separate estimates of verbal IQ and nonverbal IQ. After a few changes, the test was retitled the *Wechsler Adult Intelligence Scale*—the WAIS in 1955. Today, you would take the WAIS-III (Wechsler, 1997).

The WAIS-III has 14 subtests that span *verbal* and *performance* aspects of IQ. **Table 9.1** provides examples of the types of questions you would find on the test. The verbal subtests cover areas such as vocabulary and comprehension. The performance subtests involve manipulation of materials and have little or no verbal content. If you were to take the WAIS-III, you would perform the full range of subtests, and receive 3 scores: a Verbal IQ, a Performance IQ, and an overall, or Full Scale, IQ.

The WAIS-III is designed for people age 16 years and older, but similar tests have been developed for children. *The Wechsler Intelligence Scale for Children— Third Edition* (WISC-III; Wechsler, 2003) is suited for children ages 6 to 16, and the *Wechsler Preschool and Primary Scale of Intelligence—Revised* (WPPSI-III; Wechsler, 2002) for children ages $2\frac{1}{2}$ to $7\frac{1}{4}$ years. The recent revisions of both of these tests have made the materials more colorful, more contemporary, and more enjoyable for children.

TABLE 9.1

Questions and Problems Similar to Those on the WAIS-III

Verbal Subtests	
Information	Who wrote *The Great Gatsby*?
Comprehension	What does it mean when people say "Birds of a feather flock together"?
Arithmetic	If you paid $8.50 for a movie ticket and $2.75 for a bucket of popcorn, how much change would you have left from a $20 bill?
Similarities	In what ways are airplanes and submarines alike?
Digit span	Repeat the following numbers: 3 2 7 5 9.
Vocabulary	What does *emulate* mean?

Performance Subtests	
Digit symbol-coding	The examiner presents a key that matches digits (e.g., 1, 2, 3) with symbols (e.g., Φ,Θ,∀). The test taker uses the key to complete a chart that gives just digits or symbols.
Picture completion	The test taker examines a picture and says what is missing (e.g., a horse without a mane).
Block design	The test taker uses patterned blocks to reproduce designs provided by the examiner.
Picture arrangement	The test taker puts a series of cartoonlike pictures into order so that they tell a story.
Object assembly	The examiner gives the test taker a set of cardboard puzzle pieces. The test taker arranges the pieces to form a picture of a common object.

FIGURE 9.1

Intelligence Testing

A psychologist administers an intelligence test to a 4-year-old child. The performance part of the test includes sorting an array of colored candy. Why is performance an important component of an IQ assessment?

The WAIS-III, the WISC-IV, and the WPPSI-III form a family of intelligence tests that yield a Verbal IQ, a Performance IQ, and a Full Scale IQ at all age levels. In addition, they provide comparable subtest scores that allow researchers to track the development over time of more specific intellectual abilities. For this reason, the Wechsler scales are particularly valuable when the same individual is to be tested at different ages—for example, when a child's progress in response to different educational programs is monitored.

INTERPRETING IQ SCORES

IQ scores are no longer derived by dividing mental age by chronological age. If you took the test today, your score would be added up and directly compared with the scores of other people your age. An IQ of 100 is "average" and would indiate that 50 percent of those your age had earned lower scores (see **Figure 9.2**). Scores between 90 and 110 are now labeled "normal," and those above 120 are "superior."

When individuals below the age of 18 obtain valid IQ scores of 70 to 75 or below, they meet one criterion for a classification of **mental retardation.** However, as shown in **Table 9.2,** to be considered mentally retarded, individuals must also demonstrate limitations in their ability to bring *adaptive skills* to bear on life tasks (American Association on Mental Retardation [AAMR], 1992). In earlier times, IQ scores were used to classify mental retardation as "mild," "moderate," "severe," and "profound" (see Figure 9.2). However, the contemporary emphasis on adaptive skills has prompted experts to abandon that terminology in favor

TABLE 9.2

Diagnosis of Mental Retardation

Mental retardation is diagnosed if:

- The individual's IQ is approximately 70 to 75 or below.

- There are significant disabilities in two or more adaptive skill areas:
  Communication. Skills related to the ability to comprehend and express information through linguistic means and nonlinguistic means (for example, facial expressions).
  Self-care. Skills involved in toileting, eating, dressing, hygiene, and grooming.
  Home living. Skills related to functioning within a home, such as housekeeping and daily scheduling.
  Social. Skills related to social exchanges with other individuals.
  Community use. Skills related to the appropriate use of community resources, such as shopping in grocery stores and using public transportation.
  Self-direction. Skills relating to making choices and seeking appropriate assistance.
  Health and safety. Skills relating to maintaining one's health and safety.
  Functional academics. Skills relating to the acquisition of academic subjects (such as reading and mathematics) that contribute to the goal of independent living.
  Leisure. Skills related to the development of leisure and recreational interests.
  Work. Skills related to holding a part- or full-time job or jobs.

- The age of onset is below 18.

Source: Adapted from American Association on Mental Retardation, 1992, pp. 24, 40–41.

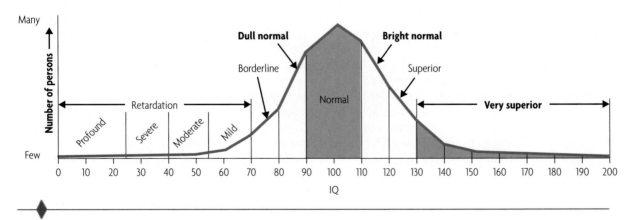

FIGURE 9.2

Distribution of IQ Scores Among a Large Sample

IQ scores are normed so that a score of 100 is the population average (as many people score below 100 as score above 100). Scores between 90 and 110 are labeled normal. Scores above 120 are considered to be superior or very superior; scores below 70 represent increasing levels of mental disability.

From *Wechsler's Measurement and Appraisal of Adult Intelligence,* 5e by Joseph D. Matarazzo, copyright © 1972 by Oxford University Press, Inc. Used by permission of Oxford University Press, Inc.

of more precise descriptions such as "a person with mental retardation with extensive supports needed in the areas of social skills and self-direction" or "a person with mental retardation who needs limited supports in communication and social skills" (AAMR, 1992, p. 34).

IQ scores give general information about how well people are able to perform—with respect to age-appropriate norms—on a variety of verbal and nonverbal tasks. In some instances, there is cause for concern when IQ scores and performance fail to match up. People who present a sufficiently large discrepancy between their achievement and their measured IQ might be diagnosed with a **learning disorder.** Before clinicians diagnose a learning disorder, they need to rule out other factors that can lead to poor performance such as low motivation, mediocre teaching, or physical problems (e.g., visual

deficits). Many schools provide special assistance to students who have been diagnosed with learning disorders.

PUT YOURSELF TO THE TEST

◆ Why did intelligence testing arise from Alfred Binet's work?

◆ What measures were originally used to compute the intelligence quotient?

◆ What are important properties of the Stanford–Binet and WAIS-III tests?

◆ How is mental retardation assessed?

◆ How are learning disorders assessed?

PSYCHOLOGY IN THE 21ST CENTURY

Assessment on the World Wide Web

After reading a chapter on intelligence, students often wonder how they would do if they took an IQ test. Nowadays, it's pretty easy for you to visit one of several Web sites to click through a test and get some IQ score. Do the numbers you get mean much of anything? We'll answer that question by reviewing some of the concepts we've introduced in this chapter.

To give our analysis, we needed some data—so we asked a friend, whom we'll call Poindexter, to take some online IQ tests for us. The first site he visited had four different tests, which gave us the opportunity to assess reliability. Recall that reliability is about consistency: Does each test, which claims to be measuring the same thing, yield very nearly the same score? In fact, Poindexter's four scores were 116, 117, 129, and 130. If you refer back to Figure 9.2, you'll see that all these scores indicate that Poindexter is above average (how nice for Poindexter), but two

place him in "bright normal" and two place him right at the border of "superior" and "very superior." These supposed IQ tests are not particularly reliable.

If the tests aren't reliable, they can't be valid. But let's suppose they were reliable. Let's consider why, in any case, we'd be concerned about their validity: To what extent do the tests measure what they're supposed to measure? The IQ scores at the site Poindexter visited were calculated by comparing his performance (the number he got right out of 20 questions) to the performance of those individuals who had preceded him to the site. By assuming a bell-shaped distribution like the one shown in Figure 9.2, the site estimates IQ. Can you see the problems here? First, we have no reason to believe that, for the people who visit this site, the average IQ (measured by a traditional, reliable off-line test) would be, as it should be, 100. Doesn't it seem likely that there would be self-selection among the

people who would take IQ tests on the Web? Second, we have no reason to believe that everyone took the tests under the same standard circumstances. For example, the tests rely somewhat on vocabulary questions. How can we be sure that people didn't pull out a handy dictionary (or access one online) to enhance their scores? ("Look, Ma, I always told you I was a genius!")

The World Wide Web provides a vast number of opportunities for you to assess IQ as well as other performance and personality constructs. You should use the knowledge you've gained in this chapter to do your own careful assessment of the reliability and validity of any scores you obtain on the Web.

Meanwhile, Poindexter has become something of an online IQ addict. His best score so far is a 159 on a "European IQ test." Poindexter is convinced that 159 is a valid measure of his IQ. Are you convinced too?

Theories of Intelligence

So far, we have seen some of the ways in which intelligence has been measured. You are now in a position to ask yourself: Do these tests capture everything that is meant by the word *intelligence*? Do these tests capture all abilities you believe constitute your own intelligence? To help you to think about those questions, we now review theories of intelligence. As you read about each theory, ask yourself whether its proponents would be comfortable using IQ as a measure of intelligence.

◆ PSYCHOMETRIC THEORIES OF INTELLIGENCE

Psychometric theories of intelligence originated in much the same philosophical atmosphere that gave rise to IQ tests. **Psychometrics** is the field of psychology that specializes in mental testing in any of its facets, including personality assessment, intelligence evaluation, and aptitude measurement. Thus, psychometric approaches are intimately related to methods of testing. These theories examine the *statistical relationships* between different measures of ability, such as the 14 subtests of the WAIS-III, and then make inferences about the nature of human intelligence on the basis of those relationships. The technique used most frequently is called *factor analysis,* a statistical procedure that detects a smaller number of dimensions, clusters, or factors within a larger set of independent variables. The goal of factor analysis is to identify the basic psychological dimensions of the concept being investigated. Of course, a statistical procedure only identifies statistical regularities; it is up to psychologists to suggest and defend interpretations of those regularities.

Charles Spearman carried out an early and influential application of factor analysis in the domain of intelligence. Spearman discovered that the performance of individuals on each of a variety of intelligence tests was highly correlated. From this pattern he concluded that there is a factor of *general intelligence,* or **g,** underlying all intelligent performance (Spearman, 1927). Each individual domain also has associated with it specific skills that Spearman called *s.* For example, a person's performance on tests of vocabulary or arithmetic depends both on his or her general intelligence and on domain-specific abilities.

Raymond Cattell (1963), using more advanced factor analytic techniques, determined that general intel-

ligence can be broken down into two relatively independent components, which he called crystallized and fluid intelligence. **Crystallized intelligence** involves the knowledge a person has already acquired and the ability to access that knowledge; it is measured by tests of vocabulary, arithmetic, and general information. **Fluid intelligence** is the ability to see complex relationships and solve problems; it is measured by tests of block designs and spatial visualization in which the background information needed to solve a problem is included or readily apparent. Crystallized intelligence allows you to cope well with your life's recurring, concrete challenges; fluid intelligence helps you attack novel, abstract problems.

J. P. Guilford (1961) used factor analysis to examine the demands of many intelligence-related tasks. His *structure of intellect* model specifies three features of intellectual tasks: the *content,* or type of information; the *product,* or form in which information is represented; and the *operation,* or type of mental activity performed.

As shown in **Figure 9.3,** there are five kinds of content in this model—visual, auditory, symbolic, semantic,

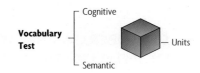

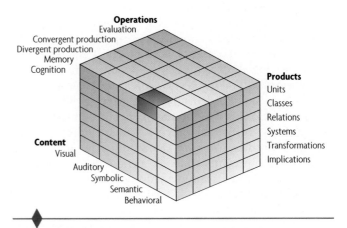

FIGURE 9.3

The Structure of Intellect

In his structure of intellect model, J. P. Guilford specified three features of intellectual tasks; the content, or type of information; the product, or form in which information is represented; and the operation, or type of mental activity performed. Each task performed by the intellect can be identified according to the particular types of content, products, and operations involved. For example, a test of vocabulary would assess your ability for cognition of units with semantic content.

and behavioral; six kinds of products—units, classes, relations, systems, transformations, and implications; and five kinds of operations—evaluation, convergent production, divergent production, memory, and cognition. Each task performed by the intellect can be identified according to the particular types of content, products, and operations involved. Further, Guilford believes that each content-product-operation combination (each small cube in the model) represents a distinct mental ability. For example, as Figure 9.3 shows, a test of vocabulary would assess your ability for *cognition* of *units* with *semantic content*. Learning a dance routine, on the other hand, requires *memory* for *behavioral systems*.

This theoretical model is analogous to a chemist's periodic table of elements. By means of such a systematic framework, intellectual factors, like chemical elements, may be postulated before they are discovered. In 1961, when Guilford proposed his model, nearly 40 intellectual abilities had been identified. Researchers have since accounted for over 100, which shows the predictive value of Guilford's conception of intelligence (Guilford, 1985).

Since Guilford, many psychologists have broadened their conceptions of intelligence to include much more than performance on traditional IQ tests. We now examine two types of theories that go beyond IQ.

◆ STERNBERG'S TRIARCHIC THEORY OF INTELLIGENCE

Robert Sternberg (1985, 1999) also stresses the importance of cognitive processes in problem solving as part of his more general theory of intelligence. Sternberg outlines a triarchic—three-part—theory. His three types of intelligence, analytical, creative, and practical, all represent different ways of characterizing effective performance.

Analytical intelligence provides the basic information-processing skills that people apply to life's many familiar tasks. This type of intelligence is defined by the components, or mental processes, that underlie thinking and problem solving. Sternberg identifies three types of components that are central to information processing: (1) knowledge acquisition components, for learning new facts; (2) performance components, for problem-solving strategies and techniques; and (3) metacognitive components, for selecting strategies and monitoring progress toward success. To put some of your analytical intelligence to work, we'd like you now to try the exercise in **Table 9.3.**

How did you do on the anagrams? To solve these anagrams, you mostly needed to use performance components and metacognitive components. The performance components are what allowed you to manipulate the letters in your head; the metacognitive components are what allowed you to have strategies for finding solutions. Consider T-R-H-O-S. How did you

---

TABLE 9.3
Using Analytical Intelligence

The following is a list of *anagrams*—scrambled words. As quickly as possible, try to find a solution for each anagram (Sternberg, 1986).

1. H-U-L-A-G   _____
2. P-T-T-M-E   _____
3. T-R-H-O-S   _____
4. T-N-K-H-G-I   _____
5. T-E-W-I-R   _____
6. L-L-A-O-W   _____
7. R-I-D-E-V   _____
8. O-C-C-H-U   _____
9. T-E-N-R-E   _____
10. C-I-B-A-S   _____

Turn to page 312 for the solutions.

mentally transform that into SHORT? A good strategy to get started is to try consonant clusters that are probable in English—such as S-H and T-H. Selecting strategies requires metacognitive components; carrying them out requires performance components. Note that a good strategy will sometimes fail. Consider T-N-K-H-G-I. What makes this anagram hard for many people is that K-N is not a very likely combination to start a word, whereas T-H is. Did you stare at this anagram for a while, trying to turn it into a word beginning with T-H?

By breaking down various tasks into their components, researchers can pinpoint the processes that differentiate the performance outcomes of individuals with different IQs. For example, researchers might discover that the metacognitive components of high-IQ students prompt them to select different strategies to solve a particular type of problem than do their lower-IQ peers. The difference in strategy selection accounts for the high-IQ students' greater problem-solving success.

Creative intelligence captures people's ability to deal with two extremes: novel versus very routine problems. Suppose, for example, a group of individuals found themselves stranded after an accident. You would credit with intelligence the person in the group who could most quickly help the group find its way home. In other circumstances, you would recognize as intelligent the behavior of someone who was able to perform routine tasks automatically. If, for example, a group of people carried out the same tasks day after day, you would be most impressed by the individual who could complete the tasks successfully with the least amount of "new" thought.

To what extent does the ability to handicap races correlate with intelligence as it is traditionally measured?

Practical intelligence is reflected in the management of day-to-day affairs. It involves your ability to *adapt* to new and different contexts, *select* appropriate contexts, and effectively *shape* your environment to suit your needs. Practical intelligence is what people sometimes call *street smarts* or *business sense*. Research has shown that people can have high practical intelligence without having high IQs.

CLASSIC
PUTTING IDEAS TO THE TEST

Practical Intelligence at the Race Track

Researchers approached "regulars" at a race track to assess the relationship between IQ and success at making predictions about horse races. A group of 30 men was divided into experts and nonexperts, based on their performance at predicting which horses would have the best odds at race time. Although the two groups both had average IQs, right around 100, and there was almost no correlation between IQ and expertise, experts correctly chose the top horse 93 percent of the time, versus 33 percent for nonexperts. The researchers went on to show that the experts were making their quite accurate judgments in a way that mimicked complex statistical procedures (Ceci & Liker, 1986).

Because each horse presents a new combination of variables along a variety of dimensions (lifetime speed, lifetime earnings, track conditions, jockey ability, and several others), the experts' success can't be attributed just to repetition of familiar situations. Rather, they had developed impressive abilities specifically suited to their environment.

◆ GARDNER'S MULTIPLE INTELLIGENCES AND EMOTIONAL INTELLIGENCE

Howard Gardner (1983, 1996) has also proposed a theory that expands the definition of intelligence beyond those skills covered on an IQ test. Gardner identifies numerous intelligences that cover a range of human experience. The value of any of the abilities differs across human societies, according to what is needed by, useful to, and prized by a given society. As shown in **Table 9.4,** Gardner identified eight intelligences.

Gardner argues that Western society promotes the first two intelligences, while non-Western societies often value others. For example, in the Caroline Island of Micronesia, sailors must be able to navigate long distances without maps, using only their spatial intelligence and bodily kinesthetic intelligence. Such abilities count more in that society than the ability to write a term paper. In Bali, where artistic performance is part of everyday life, musical intelligence and talents involved in coordinating intricate dance steps are highly valued. Interpersonal intelligence is more central to collectivist societies such as Japan, where cooperative action and communal life are emphasized, than it is in individualistic societies such as the United States (Triandis, 1990).

Assessing these kinds of intelligence demands more than paper-and-pencil tests and simple quantified measures. Gardner's theory of intelligence requires that the individual be observed and assessed in a variety of life situations as well as in the small slices of life depicted in traditional intelligence tests.

In recent years, researchers have begun to explore a type of intelligence—*emotional intelligence*—that is related to Gardner's concepts of *interpersonal* and *intrapersonal* intelligence (see Table 9.4). **Emotional intelligence** is defined as having four major components (Mayer & Salovey, 1997; Mayer et al., 2000):

- The ability to perceive, appraise, and express emotions accurately and appropriately
- The ability to use emotions to facilitate thinking
- The ability to understand and analyze emotions and to use emotional knowledge effectively
- The ability to regulate one's emotions to promote both emotional and intellectual growth

This definition reflects a new view of the positive role of emotion as it relates to intellectual functioning—emotions can make thinking more intelligent, and people can think intelligently about their emotions and those of others.

Researchers have begun to demonstrate that emotional intelligence has important consequences for everyday life.

TABLE 9.4

Gardner's Eight Intelligences

Intelligence	End States	Core Components
Logical–mathematical	Scientist Mathematician	Sensitivity to, and capacity to discern, logical or numerical patterns; ability to handle long chains of reasoning.
Linguistic	Poet Journalist	Sensitivity to the sounds, rhythms, and meanings of words; sensitivity to the different functions of language.
Naturalist	Biologist Environmentalist	Sensitivity to the differences among diverse species; abilities to interact subtly with living creatures.
Musical	Composer Violinist	Abilities to produce and appreciate rhythm, pitch, and timbre; appreciation of the forms of musical expressiveness.
Spatial	Navigator Sculptor	Capacities to perceive the visual-spatial world accurately and to perform transformations on one's initial perceptions.
Bodily kinesthetic	Dancer Athlete	Abilities to control one's body movements and to handle objects skillfully.
Interpersonal	Therapist Salesperson	Capacities to discern and respond appropriately to the moods, temperaments, motivations, and desires of other people.
Intrapersonal	Person with detailed, accurate self-knowledge	Access to one's own feelings and the ability to discriminate among them and draw upon them to guide behavior; knowledge of one's own strengths, weaknesses, desires, and intelligences.

PUTTING IDEAS TO THE TEST

Emotional Intelligence and Everyday Well-Being

Take a moment to review the components of the definition of emotional intelligence. Can you see how people who have more of these abilities would also be better able to cope with day-to-day hassles? A pair of researchers tested the hypothesis that people high in EQ would cope better and therefore have a greater sense of psychological well-being (Slaski & Cartwright, 2002). The sample they used were middle managers working for a major retailer in England. These men and women had jobs that were reasonably demanding. Each manager completed an assessment device that measured EQ. They also reported on aspects of well-being, such as their level of psychological distress, their morale, and their quality of working life. Finally, each manager's supervisor rated his or her job performance. The researchers divided the managers into a low-EQ group and a high-EQ group. The results were quite dramatic. By comparison to the low-EQ group, the high-EQ managers reported less psychological distress, higher morale, and better quality of working life. Their bosses also rated the high-EQ group as better managers.

You can probably see how all the pieces fit together. People whose emotional intelligence allows them to experience low distress and good morale are also more likely to be effective in their jobs. The same researchers are now trying to implement a training program to improve the emotional intelligence of the low-EQ managers.

Our review of intelligence testing and theories of intelligence sets the stage for a discussion of the societal circumstances that make the topic of intelligence so controversial.

PUT YOURSELF TO THE TEST

- Why did Spearman come to believe in *g*, general intelligence?
- How do researchers in the psychometric tradition find the components of intelligence?
- What are the three types of intelligence in Sternberg's triarchic theory?
- What are the eight types of intelligence in Gardner's theory?
- What role does emotional intelligence play in day-to-day life?

Do Theories of Intelligence Matter?

Jennifer Trebby

Brown University

When students learn about Sternberg's triarchic intelligences and Gardner's multiple intelligence, they often have this response: It's nice to say that other things matter besides classic academic intelligence, but do these theories really have an impact beyond an introductory psychology textbook? In fact, both Gardner (1999a) and Sternberg (Sternberg & Grigorenko, 2000) are heavily involved with the reform of educational practice. Their quest is to export their insights about intelligence from research settings directly into classrooms.

Let's focus on a classroom study that grew out of both Gardner's and Sternberg's theories (Williams et al., 2002). The study involved several hundred fifth- and sixth-graders in schools in Connecticut and Massachusetts. The purpose of the study was to improve the students' school performance by providing them with a special curriculum—the *practical intelligence for school* (PIFS) curriculum—that emphasized practical intelligence. Recall that practical intelligence relates to people's ability to manage their day-to-day tasks. The curriculum embodied five themes that helped students acquire practical intelligence for school:

- *Knowing why.* Students were asked to consider the purposes of schoolwork (e.g., What is the point of homework?) and the relationship of schoolwork to life outside school (e.g., How do tests in school help prepare you for the tests adults face in their work?).

- *Knowing self.* Students were encouraged to think about their strengths and weaknesses with respect to schoolwork and other aspects of life; they were encouraged to imagine how they would take advantage of their strengths and work around their weaknesses.

- *Knowing differences.* Students were encouraged to consider why different working styles might be necessary for different types of assignments (e.g., completing math problems versus writing an essay).

- *Knowing process.* Students were encouraged to develop an awareness of the types of problems that arise in academic settings and the processes and resources that are available to overcome those problems.

- *Revisiting.* Students were encouraged to consider the benefits of reviewing their work by rereading texts, revising writing, reworking problems, and so on.

Can you see how each of these themes could help students develop practical intelligence with respect to school success?

The students received pretests of their abilities in October and posttests of their abilities in June. Those pre- and posttests assessed improvement in a variety of domains, such as reading, writing, and homework quality. Students who had been exposed to the PIFS curriculum showed considerable improvement across the year. You might wonder if the improvement came about just because of ordinary classroom activities unrelated to the PIFS curriculum. To address that issue, the research team also assessed the progress of a control group who hadn't experienced the PIFS curriculum. The students in the control group also showed improvement, but not to the same extent as the PIFS students. For example, in the Connecticut sample one group of PIFS students showed a 17 percent greater improvement in a measure of reading and writing ability than did the control-group students. Similarly, in the Massachusetts sample a PIFS group showed 18 percent greater improvement in writing than did the control-group students. The curriculum that focused on practical intelligence allowed students to show greater improvement on classic academic tasks such as reading and writing.

Take a look back at the five themes embodied in the PIFS curriculum. How much have you thought about each of these themes? Can you see how ideas from a theory of intelligence—*practical* intelligence is different from *analytical* intelligence—generate a successful approach to lessons in the classroom?

The Politics of Intelligence

We have seen that contemporary conceptions of intelligence reject the narrow linking of a score on an IQ test with a person's intelligence. Even so, IQ tests remain the most frequent measure of "intelligence" in Western society. Because of the prevalence of IQ testing and the availability of IQ scores, it becomes easy to compare different groups according to their "average" IQ. In the United States, such ethnic and racial group comparisons have often been used as evidence for the innate, genetic inferiority of members of minority groups. We will briefly examine the history of this practice of using IQ test scores to index the alleged mental inferiority of certain groups. Then we will look at current evidence on the nature and nurture of intelligence and IQ test performance. You will see that this is one of the most politically volatile issues in psychology, because public policies about immigration quotas, educational resources, and more may be based on how group IQ data are interpreted.

◆ THE HISTORY OF GROUP COMPARISONS

In the early 1900s, psychologist **Henry Goddard** advocated mental testing of all immigrants and the *selective exclusion* of those who were found to be "mentally defective." Such views may have contributed to a hostile national climate against admission of certain immigrant groups (Zenderland, 1998). Indeed, Congress passed the 1924 Immigration Restriction Act, which made it national policy to administer intelligence tests to immigrants as they arrived at Ellis Island in New York Harbor. Vast numbers of Jewish, Italian, Russian, and immigrants of other nationalities were classified as "morons" on the basis of IQ tests. Some psychologists interpreted these statistical findings as evidence that immigrants from southern and eastern Europe were genetically inferior to those from the hardy northern and western European stock (see Ruch, 1937). However, these "inferior" groups were also least familiar with the dominant language and culture, embedded in the IQ tests, because they had immigrated most recently. (Within a few decades, these group differences completely disappeared from IQ tests, but the theory of racially inherited differences in intelligence persisted.)

Goddard (1917) and others then went beyond merely associating low IQ with hereditary racial and ethnic origins. They added moral worthlessness, mental deficiency, and immoral social behavior to the mix of negatives related to low IQ. Evidence for their view came from case studies of infamous families. Consider the *Kallikak* family, a family with one "good seed" side and one "bad seed" side to its family tree. (In his study, Goddard renamed the family Kallikak, which means good–bad in Greek.) Martin Kallikak was a Revolutionary War soldier who had an illegitimate son with a woman described as developmentally disabled. Their union eventually produced 480 descendants. Goddard classified 143 of them as "defective" and only 46 as normal. He found crime, alcoholism, mental disorders, and illegitimacy common among the rest of the family members. By contrast, when Martin Kallikak later married a "good woman," their union produced 496 descendants, only three of whom were classified as "defective." Goddard also found that many offspring from this high-quality union had become "eminent" (Goddard, 1914). Goddard came to believe that heredity determined intelligence, genius, and eminence on the positive side. On the negative side, he arrayed delinquency, alcoholism, sexual immorality, developmental disability, and maybe even poverty (McPherson, 1985).

Goddard's genetic inferiority argument was further reinforced by the fact that, on the World War I Army Intelligence tests, African Americans and other racial minorities scored lower than the white majority. Louis Terman, who as we saw promoted IQ testing in the

Why were IQ tests given to immigrants as they arrived at Ellis Island? How were these tests used to draw conclusions about genetic inferiority?

United States, commented in this unscientific manner on the data he had helped collect on U.S. racial minorities:

> *Their dullness seems to be racial. . . . There seems no possibility at present of convincing society that they should not be allowed to reproduce, although from a eugenics point of view, they constitute a grave problem because of their unusually prolific breeding. (Terman, 1916, pp. 91–92)*

The names have changed, but the problem remains the same. In the United States today, African Americans and Latinos score, on average, lower than Asian Americans and whites on standardized intelligence tests. Of course, there are individuals in all groups who score at the highest (and the lowest) extremes of the IQ scale. How should these group differences in IQ scores be interpreted? One tradition has been to attribute these differences to genetic inferiority (nature). After we discuss the evidence for genetic differences in IQ, we will consider a second possibility, that differences in envi-

ronments (nurture) exert a significant impact on IQ. The validity of either explanation, or some combination of them, has important social, economic, and political consequences.

◆ HEREDITY AND IQ

How can researchers assess the extent to which intelligence is genetically determined? Any answer to this question requires that the researcher choose some measure as an index of intelligence. Thus, the question becomes not whether "intelligence," in the abstract, is influenced by heredity but, in most cases, whether IQs are similar within family trees. To answer this more limited question, researchers need to tease apart the effects of shared genes and shared environment. One method is to compare functioning in identical twins (monozygotic), fraternal twins (dizygotic), and relatives with other degrees of genetic overlap. **Figure 9.4** presents correlations between IQ scores of individuals on the basis of their degree of genetic relationship (Plomin &

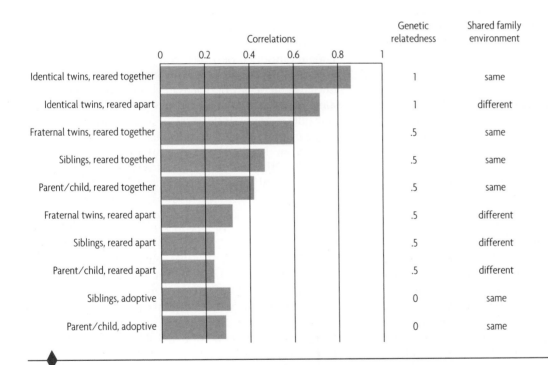

FIGURE 9.4

IQ and Genetic Relationship

This figure presents the correlations between the IQ scores of identical (monozygotic) and fraternal (dizygotic) twins reared together (in the same home environments) or reared apart (in different home environments). For comparison, it also includes data for siblings (brothers and sisters) and parents and children, both biological and adoptive. The data demonstrate the importance of both genetic factors (the numbers under "genetic relatedness" specify the overlap of genetic material) and environmental factors. For example, identical twins show higher correlations between their IQs than do fraternal twins—a genetic influence. However, both types of twins show higher correlations when raised together—an environmental influence.

This photo shows Nobel Prize winning Chemist Marie Curie with her daughters Irene (on the left) and Eve (on the right). Irene also won a Nobel Prize in Chemistry and Eve became a famous author. Why do families like this one encourage researchers to attempt to understand the impact of heredity and environment on IQ?

Petrill, 1997). As you can see, the greater the genetic similarity, the greater the IQ similarity. (You should note in these data that the impact of environment is also revealed in the greater IQ similarities among those who have been reared together.)

Researchers use results of this sort to try to estimate the *heritability* of IQ. A **heritability estimate** of a particular trait, such as intelligence, is based on the proportion of the variability in test scores on that trait that can be traced to genetic factors. The estimate is found by computing the variation in all the test scores for a given population (college students or psychiatric patients, for example) and then identifying what portion of the total variance is due to genetic or inherited factors. This is done by comparing individuals who have different degrees of genetic overlap. Researchers who have reviewed the variety of studies on heritability of IQ conclude that about 50 percent of the variance in IQ scores is due to genetic makeup (Grigordenko, 2000; Neisser et al., 1996; Plomin & Petrill, 1997).

What is perhaps even more interesting, however, is that heritability *increases* across the life span: Heritability is about 40 percent for 4- to 6-year-olds but increases to about 60 percent in early adulthood and to about 80 percent in older adults! Many people are surprised by this result, because it seems that environments should have more, not less, of an effect as people get older. Here's

how researchers explain this counterintuitive finding: "It is possible that genetic dispositions nudge us toward environments that accentuate our genetic propensities, thus leading to increased heritability throughout the life span" (Plomin & Petrill, 1997, p. 61).

Let's return now to the point at which genetic analysis becomes controversial: test score differences between African Americans and white Americans. Although several decades ago, the gap was 15 IQ points, the scores of whites and blacks have been converging over time, so that on a number of contemporary indicators the gap is between 7 and 10 points (Nisbett, 1995, 1998; Williams & Ceci, 1997). Although the close in the gap suggests environmental influences, the lingering difference has prompted many people to suggest that there are unbridgeable genetic differences between the races (Hernnstein & Murray, 1994). However, even if IQ is highly heritable, does this difference reflect genetic inferiority of individuals in the lower-scoring group? The answer is no. Heritability is based on an estimate *within* one given group. It cannot be used to interpret differences *between* groups, no matter how large those differences are on an objective test. Heritability estimates pertain only to the average in a given population of individuals. Even though we know that height, for instance, has a high heritability estimate (about 90 percent), you cannot determine how much of your height is due to genetic influences. The same argument is true for IQ; despite high heritability estimates, we cannot determine the specific genetic contribution to any individual's IQ or to mean IQ scores among groups. The fact that on an IQ test one racial or ethnic group scores lower than another group does not mean that the difference between these groups is genetic in origin, even if the heritability estimate for IQ scores is high as assessed within a group.

Another reason that genetic makeup cannot be wholly responsible for group differences in IQ has to do with the *relative* sizes of the differences. There is much overlapping in the distribution of each group's scores despite mean differences: the difference between groups is small compared with the differences among the scores of individuals within each group (Loehlin, 2000; Suzuki & Valencia, 1997). In general, the differences between the gene pools of different racial groups are minute compared with the genetic differences among individual members of the same group (Gould, 1981; Zuckerman, 1990). Furthermore, in the United States, race is often more of a *social* construct than a *biological* construct. Consider the remarkable young golfer Tiger Woods, who has often been labeled—and discriminated against—as African American even though his actual heritage is much more complex (his ancestors were white, black, Thai, Chinese, and Native American). Woods provides an excellent example of

Tiger Woods has ancestors who were white, African American, Thai, Chinese, and Native American. Why is he most often described as African American? What does that suggest about the construct of race in the United States?

circumstances in which social judgments do not follow biological reality. As such, there is great danger in treating IQ differences among socially distinct groups as if those differences conform to underlying biology (Cohen, 2002; Suzuki & Valencia, 1997).

Researchers have found ways to put this perspective to a test in a series of studies in which the degree of white or European parentage among blacks is determined. In the United States, the "black" population is estimated to be about 20 to 30 percent European through intermarriages. Does it make a difference in IQ if a "black" person has more or less European genetic stock? The genetic argument holds that it does, but the data suggest the correlation of degree of European ancestry with IQ is very low (on the order of only .15 across many studies). This is true whether skin color or blood groups are used as the index of racial mixture. Comparisons of German children fathered by African American GI fathers and white GI fathers show no difference in their IQ scores. In addition, children of "black–white" unions have IQs that are seven points higher if the mother is white. This difference is most likely due to the greater contribution of mothers than fathers to a child's intellectual socialization, and, of course, cannot be due to any genetic factor, because each parent contributes equally to the genes of the offspring (Loehlin, 2000; Nisbett, 1998).

Surely genetics plays a sizable role in influencing individuals' scores on IQ tests, as it does on many other traits and abilities. We have argued, however, that heredity does not constitute an adequate explanation for IQ

differences between racial and ethnic groups. It has a necessary, but not sufficient, role in our understanding of such performance effects. Let's turn now to the role the environment may play in creating the IQ gap.

◆ ENVIRONMENTS AND IQ

Because heritability estimates are less than 1.0, we know that genetic inheritance is not solely responsible for anyone's IQ. Environments must also affect IQ. But how can we assess what aspects of the environment are important influences on IQ? What features of your environment affect your potential to score well on an IQ test (Beiser & Gotowiec, 2000; Ceci, 1999; Rowe, 1997; Suzuki & Valencia, 1997)? Environments are complex stimulus packages that vary on many dimensions, both physical and social, and may be experienced in different ways by those within them. Even children in the same family setting do not necessarily share the same critical, psychological environment. Think back to growing up in your family. If you had siblings, did they all get the same attention from parents, did conditions of stress change over the course of time, did the family's financial resources change, did your parents' marital status change? It is obvious that environments are made up of many components that are in a dynamic relationship and that change over time. So it becomes difficult for psychologists to say what kinds of environmental conditions—attention, stress, poverty, health, war, and so on—actually have an impact on IQ.

Researchers have most often focused on more global measures of environment, like the socioeconomic status of the family. For example, in a large-scale longitudinal study of more than 26,000 children, the best predictors of a child's IQ at age 4 were the family's socioeconomic status and the level of the mother's education. This was equally true for African American and Caucasian children (Broman et al., 1975). Similarly, **Figure 9.5** shows an overall impact of social class on IQ.

Why does social class affect IQ? Wealth versus poverty can affect intellectual functioning in many ways, health and educational resources being two of the most obvious. Poor health during pregnancy and low birth weight are solid predictors of a child's lowered mental ability. Children born into impoverished families often suffer from poor nutrition, many going to school hungry, thus less able to concentrate on learning tasks. Furthermore, impoverished homes may suffer from a lack of books, written media, computers, and other materials that add to one's mental stimulation. The "survival orientation" of poor parents, especially in single-parent families, that leaves parents little time or energy to play with and intellectually stimulate their children is detrimental to performance on tasks such as those on standard IQ tests.

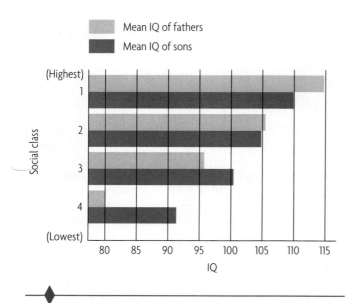

Mean IQ of fathers
Mean IQ of sons

FIGURE 9.5

The Relationship Among Heredity, Environment, and IQ

This chart shows evidence for the contribution of heredity and environment to IQ scores. There are similar IQs for fathers and sons (influence of heredity), but the IQs of both fathers and sons are related to social class (influence of environment).

Researchers have spent the past 40 years developing programs intended to counteract the effects of impoverished environments. The Head Start program was first funded by the federal government in 1965 to address the "physical health, developmental, social, educational, and emotional needs of low-income children and to increase the capacity of the families to care for their children, through empowerment and supportive services" (Kassebaum, 1994, p. 123). The idea of Head Start was not to move children to privileged environments but to improve the environments into which they were born. Children are exposed to special preschool education, they receive decent daily meals, and their parents are given advice on health and other aspects of child rearing. Early assessments of Head Start's effects focused narrowly on improvement on IQ tests and other achievement measures. In fact, after children had been in the program only a few weeks, their IQ scores rose by 10 points. Unfortunately, after they left the program, these IQ gains tended to fade away (Barnett, 1998; Zigler & Muenchow, 1992; Zigler & Styfco, 1994). This pattern yields two lessons: IQ can be affected by the environment, but the enriched environment must be sustained. In any case, more recent assessments of Head Start have overcome the earlier narrow focus on IQ.

The empirical literature . . . delivers good news and bad news. The bad news is that neither Head Start nor any preschool program can inoculate children against the ravages of poverty. Early intervention simply cannot overpower the effects of poor living conditions, inadequate nutrition and health care, negative role models, and substandard schools. But good programs can prepare children for school and possibly help them develop better coping and adaptation skills

The personal attention children receive can affect their intelligence. In the "separate but equal" schoolroom of 1940s Tennessee shown (at left), African American children received little attention. In contrast, the parent shown (at right) is deeply involved in her child's education. How do these types of environmental differences affect IQ?

<www.ablongman.com/gerrig17e>

that will enable better life outcomes, albeit not perfect ones. (Zigler & Styfco, 1994, p. 129)

If we use a broader definition of intelligence that goes beyond just verbal and performance tasks on IQ tests, the influence of environment factors becomes clear. An enriched, supportive environment is a good predictor of successful and enhanced intellectual, scholastic, and situationally adaptive performance.

◆ CULTURE AND THE VALIDITY OF IQ TESTS

People would probably care much less about IQ scores if they didn't allow for such useful predictions: Extensive research shows that IQ scores are valid predictors of school grades from elementary school through college, of occupational status, and of performance in many jobs (Brody, 1997b; Gottfredson, 1997b). These patterns of results suggest that IQ tests validly measure intellectual abilities that are very basic and important toward the types of success that are valued in Western cultures—intelligence, as measured by IQ, directly affects success. IQ distinctions can also affect academic and job performance indirectly by changing one's motives and beliefs. Those with higher IQ scores are likely to have had more success experiences in school, become more motivated to study, develop an achievement orientation, and become optimistic about their chances of doing well. Also, children scoring low on IQ tests may get "tracked" into schools, classes, or programs that are inferior and may even be stigmatizing to the students' sense of self-competence. In this way, IQ can be affected by environment and, in turn, can create new environments for the child—some better, some worse. IQ assessment may thus become destiny—whatever the child's underlying genetic endowment for intelligence.

Even though IQ tests have proven to be valid for mainstream uses, many observers still question their validity for comparisons among different cultural and racial groups (Greenfield, 1997; Samuda, 1998; Serpell, 2000). Many forms of tests and testing may not match cultural notions of intelligence or appropriate behavior. Consider one case of negative evaluations in the classroom:

> *When children of Latino immigrant parents go to school, the emphasis on understanding rather than speaking, on respecting the teacher's authority rather than expressing one's own opinions leads to negative academic assessment. . . . Hence, a valued mode of communication in one culture—respectful listening—becomes the basis for a rather sweeping negative evaluation in the*

school setting where self-assertive speaking is the valued mode of communication. (Greenfield, 1997, p. 1120)

These immigrant children must learn how they must behave in U.S. classrooms to make their teachers believe they are intelligent.

One of the standard concerns about IQ tests is that they are biased toward or against members of different cultures: Critics have argued that group differences in IQ scores are caused by systematic bias in the test questions, making them invalid and unfair for minorities. But even when tests are made more "culture-fair," there remains a racial gap (Neisser et al., 1996). In fact, the issue may be more a problem of the *context* of the test rather than the *content* of the test. **Claude Steele** (1997; Steele & Aronson, 1995, 1998) has argued that people's performance on ability tests is influenced by **stereotype threat** (also known as *stereotype vulnerability*)—the threat of being at risk for confirming a negative stereotype of one's group. Steele's research suggests that the belief that a negative stereotype is relevant in a situation can function to bring about the poor performance encoded in the stereotype.

PUTTING IDEAS TO THE TEST

The Implications of Stereotype Threat

In one study, black and white undergraduates tried to answer very difficult verbal questions of the type found on the Graduate Record Exam. Half of the students were led to believe that performance on the questions was *diagnostic* of their intellectual ability; the other half were only told that the experiment concerned psychological factors involved in solving problems. The theory of stereotype threat suggests that only students for whom the threat of the stereotype is called into action by the situation—the black students in the *diagnostic* condition—will perform less well on the questions. As you can see in part A of **Figure 9.6,** the results confirmed this prediction. When the black students believed performance could be used to diagnose their intelligence, they performed less well (Steele & Aronson, 1995). The logic of stereotype threat applies to any group for whom there is a stereotype of inferior performance. For example, stereotypes suggest that women are less able at math than are men. As shown in part B of Figure 9.6, a difficult math test produced gender differences only when students had been told that it would (Steele, 1997). That is, prior to attempting the problems, students in the *gender-difference* condition had been told that the test had, in the past, produced gender differences—and so it did, for them.

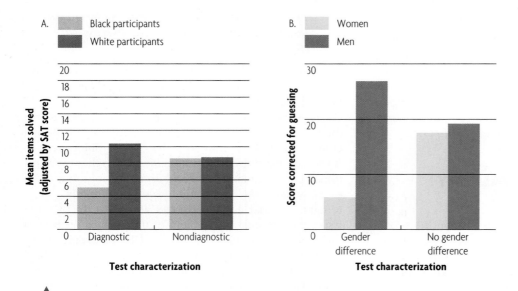

A. Black participants / White participants

B. Women / Men

FIGURE 9.6

Stereotype Threat

Stereotype threat occurs when people believe a negative stereotype is relevant to the current testing situation. (A) One study examined the stereotype that African Americans score poorly on intelligence tests. Half of a sample of black and white students were led to believe that a test was diagnostic of their intellectual ability; the other half did not receive this information. When black students believed that the test was diagnostic, their performance was impaired. (Participants' SAT scores were used to eliminate preexisting differences between their expected performance.) (B) A second study examined the stereotype that women score poorly on mathematics exams. Half of a sample of male and female students were told that a math test had previously produced gender differences; the other half did not receive this information. When women believed that the test would produce gender differences, their performance was impaired.

Note that in each of these studies what matters is how the test takers define the situation. Only when people believe the situation is relevant to the stereotype—because, for example, they believe that the test measures intelligence—does knowledge of the stereotype impair performance. Do you think it would be possible to measure IQ without invoking stereotype threat? If not, researchers may never be able to determine "real" performance.

One final thought on intelligence and culture. Taken as a whole, the United States demonstrates a cultural bias toward genetic explanations of individual differences. **Harold Stevenson** and his colleagues (1993) spent several years tracking the mathematics achievement of Chinese, Japanese, and U.S. children. In 1980, Asian children on the average vastly outperformed their U.S. peers. In 1990, the gap remained: "Only 4.1% of the Chinese children and 10.3% of the Japanese children . . . had scores as low as those of the average American child" (p. 54). Are Asian children genetically superior? In fact, people in the United States are more likely to answer yes. When Stevenson and his colleagues asked Asian and U.S. students, teachers, and parents to contrast the importance of "studying hard" versus "innate

intelligence," Asian respondents emphasized hard work. U.S. respondents emphasized innate ability. Do you see how this perspective could lead to the conclusion by Americans that Asians must be genetically superior in mathematics? Because such beliefs have public policy implications—how much money should be expended on teaching mathematics if Americans cannot learn math anyway?—it is important to examine rigorous research to sort out what can and cannot be changed with respect to intellectual performance.

PUT YOURSELF TO THE TEST

◆ Under what circumstances did Goddard and others begin to make IQ comparisons among groups?

◆ Why is it inappropriate to use heritability estimates to make claims about racial differences in IQ?

◆ What types of research demonstrate the impact of environments on IQ?

◆ What are the implications of the concept of stereotype threat for the cultural fairness of IQ and other performance tests?

 <www.ablongman.com/gerrig17e>

Creativity

Before we leave the area of intelligence and its assessment, we wish to turn to the topic of creativity. **Creativity** is an individual's ability to generate ideas or products that are both *novel* and *appropriate* to the circumstances in which they were generated (Sternberg & Lubart, 1999). Consider the invention of the wheel. The device was novel because no one before its unknown inventor had seen the application of rolling objects. It was appropriate because the use to which the novel object could be put was very clear. Without appropriateness, new ideas or objects are often considered strange or irrelevant.

Our discussion of creativity falls within a chapter on intelligence because many people believe that there is a strong relationship between intelligence and creativity. To determine if this is the case, we need to be able first to test creativity and then to determine the relationship between creativity and intelligence. Thus, we first discuss methods for judging ideas or products to be creative and then look at the link to intelligence. Next, we look at situations of exceptional creativity and evaluate the relationship between creativity and madness. We will see what lessons you can learn from people who are possessed of exceptional creative abilities.

◆ ASSESSING CREATIVITY AND THE LINK TO INTELLIGENCE

How might you go about rating individuals as (relatively) creative or uncreative? Many approaches focus on **divergent thinking,** which is defined as the ability to generate a variety of unusual solutions to a problem. Questions that test divergent thinking give the test taker the opportunity to demonstrate *fluid* (swift) and *flexible* thinking (Torrance, 1974; Wallach & Kogan, 1965):

- Name all the things you can think of that are square.

- List as many white, edible things as you can in three minutes.

- List all the uses that you can think of for a *brick*.

Responses are scored along such dimensions as *fluency,* the overall number of distinct ideas; *uniqueness,* the number of ideas that were given by no other person in an appropriate sample; and *unusualness,* the number of ideas that were given by, for example, less than 5 percent of a sample (Runco, 1991).

When creativity is assessed in this fashion, the test provides a performance index that can be correlated with other measures. On many occasions, researchers have evaluated the relationship between measures of divergent thinking and IQ. A common pattern has emerged: There is a weak or moderate correlation between the two measures up to an IQ level of about 120; above 120, the correlation decreases (Sternberg & O'Hara, 1999). Why might this be so? One researcher suggests that "intelligence appears to enable creativity to some extent but not to promote it" (Perkins, 1988, p. 319). In other words, a certain level of intelligence gives a person the opportunity to be creative, but the person may not avail himself or herself of that opportunity.

Creativity researchers have often been concerned that divergent-thinking tests are too closely tied to the tradition of intelligence testing and to IQ tests themselves (which may explain the correlations up into the 120 IQ range) (Lubart, 1994). A different approach to judging some individuals as creative or uncreative is to ask them specifically to generate a creative product—a drawing, a poem, or a short story. Judges then rate the creativity of each of the products. Consider the two photographs shown in **Figure 9.7.** Which do you think is more creative? Could you explain why you think so? Do you think your friends would agree? Research has shown that agreement is quite high when judges rank products for creativity (Amabile, 1983). People can be reliably identified across judges as being high or low in creativity.

◆ EXCEPTIONAL CREATIVITY AND MADNESS

There are some exceptional individuals who would emerge from assessments of creativity as almost off the scale. Whom do you think of when you are asked to name someone who is exceptionally creative? Your answer is likely to depend partly on your own areas of expertise and your own preferences. Psychologists might nominate Sigmund Freud. Those people interested in fine art, music, or dance might mention Pablo Picasso, Igor Stravinsky, or Martha Graham. Is it possible to detect the commonalities in the personalities or backgrounds of such individuals that could be predictive of exceptional creativity? Howard Gardner (1993) chose a selection of individuals whose extraordinary abilities were relevant to the eight types of intelligence we described earlier, including Freud, Picasso, Stravinsky, and Graham. Gardner's analysis allows him to yield a portrait of the life experiences of the *exemplary creator,* whom he dubs E.C.:

> *E.C. discovers a problem area or realm of special interest, one that promises to [lead] into*

(A)   (B)

FIGURE 9.7

Making Judgments About Creativity

Hypothetical photography class assignment: Take the best picture you can of (A) a noncreative response. (B) A creative response.

uncharted waters. This is a highly charged moment. At this point E.C. becomes isolated from her peers and must work mostly on her own. She senses that she is on the verge of a breakthrough that is as yet little understood, even by her. Surprisingly, at this crucial moment, E.C. craves both cognitive and affective support, so that she can retain her bearings. Without such support, she might well experience some kind of breakdown. (Gardner, 1993, p. 361)

What lessons are there for you in tales of exceptional creativity that would allow you to be more creative? You can emulate a pattern of *risk taking.* Highly creative individuals are willing to go into "uncharted waters" (Gardner, 1993; Sternberg & Lubart, 1996). There is a pattern of *preparation.* Highly creative individuals typically have spent years acquiring expertise in the domains in which they will excel (Weisberg, 1986). There is a pattern of *intrinsic motivation.* Highly creative individuals pursue their tasks because of the enjoyment and satisfaction they take in the products they generate (Collins & Amabile, 1999). If you can bring all these factors together in your own life, you should be able to increase your personal level of creative performance.

Before we leave the topic of creativity, we want to consider one of the most common stereotypes of exemplary creators: their life experiences border on—or include the experience of—madness. The idea that great creativity is intimately related to madness has a history that has been traced as far back as Plato (Kessel,

1989). In more modern times, Kraepelin (1921) argued that the manic phases of individuals who suffer from "manic-depressive insanity," or bipolar disorder, provide a context of free-flowing thought processes that facilitate great creativity. Mania, as we will see in Chapter 15, is characterized by periods of endurig excitedness; the person generally acts and feels elated and expansive. There is little doubt that many great figures in the arts and humanities have suffered from such mood disorders (Keiger, 1993). But how can researchers determine whether these individuals' actual thought processes were affected by their mental illness?

PUTTING IDEAS TO THE TEST

Creativity and Mania

To answer this question, creativity research **Robert Weisberg** (1994, 1996) examined the artistic output of the composer Robert Schumann, who was diagnosed with bipolar disorder. Part of the data seems consistent with a proposed link between mania and creativity. Schumann produced considerably more compositions in manic years (an average of 12.3) than in years when he was suffering from the other extreme, depression (an average of 2.7). The link broke down, however, when Weisberg factored in *quality.* The works composed in the years of mania were no higher in quality than those composed in years of depression.

Art historians have often speculated that Vincent Van Gogh's creativity as an artist was influenced by mental illness. What, in general, have researchers discovered about the link between creativity and madness?

Weisberg's study suggests that madness (in the form of mania) may largely affect motivation. The individual rides the wave of mania to create a great output of work. If the person has a certain level of talent, some, but not all, of that work will reach brilliance—but at a rate no higher than at other times in the artist's life. In general, careful reviews of historical cases find few links between creativity and madness (Rothenberg, 2001). Expert **Albert Rothenberg** concluded, "It is a false and romantic notion that people have to undergo suffering themselves in order to be able to understand the human concerns and suffering of others" (Rothenberg, 1990, p. 164).

You have now learned some of the ways in which psychologists assess and interpret individual differences in intelligence and creativity. However, as you are certainly aware, there is much more to understanding people than just knowing how intelligent or creative they are. In the next section, we discuss the ways in which psychologists obtain information about the range of personality attributes that make each individual unique.

PUT YOURSELF TO THE TEST

➤ How is creativity measured?

➤ What is the relationship between IQ and creativity?

➤ What do tales of exceptional creativity teach about becoming more creative?

➤ What have researchers learned about the link between mental illness and creativity?

Assessment and Society

The primary goal of psychological assessment is to make accurate assessments of people that are as free as possible of errors of assessors' judgments. This goal is achieved by replacing subjective judgments of teachers, employers, and other evaluators with more objective measures that have been carefully constructed and are open to critical evaluation. This is the goal that motivated Alfred Binet in his pioneering work. Binet and others hoped that testing would help democratize society and minimize decisions based on arbitrary criteria of sex, race, nationality, privilege, or physical appearance. However, despite these lofty goals, there is no area of psychology more controversial than assessment. Three ethical concerns that are central to the controversy are the fairness of test-based decisions, the utility of tests for evaluating education, and the implications of using test scores as labels to categorize individuals.

Critics concerned with the fairness of testing practices argue that the costs or negative consequences may be higher for some test takers than for others (Bond, 1995). The costs are quite high, for example, when tests on which minority groups receive low scores are used to keep them out of certain jobs. In some cities, applicants for civil service janitor jobs must pass a verbal test, rather than a more appropriate test of manual skills. According to researcher William Banks, this is a strategy unions use to keep minorities from access to jobs (1990). Sometimes, minority group members test poorly because their scores are evaluated relative to inappropriate norms. In addition, arbitrary cutoff scores that favor applicants from one group may be used to make selection decisions, when, in reality, a lower cutoff score that is fairer would produce just as many correct hiring decisions. In addition, overreliance on testing may make personnel selection an automatic attempt to fit people into available jobs. Instead, sometimes society might benefit more by changing job descriptions to fit the needs and abilities of people.

A second ethical concern is that testing not only helps evaluate students; it may also play a role in the shaping of education. The quality of school systems and the effectiveness of teachers are frequently judged on the basis of how well their students score on standardized achievement tests. Local support of the schools through tax levies, and even individual teacher salaries, may ride on test scores. The high stakes associated with

When schools are rewarded for high scores on standardized tests, are teachers likely to place more emphasis on test-taking skills than on broader learning goals?

test scores have led to cheating scandals in several school districts (Kantrowitz & McGinn, 2000). For example, in Potomac, Maryland, an elementary school principal resigned when strong evidence suggested that fifth-graders at her school had been given several types of assistance, including extra time and second chances, to improve their test scores (Thomas & Wingert, 2000). The evidence against the school had come from the students themselves. The 10-year-olds reported to their parents that they had been asked or allowed to cheat: They wondered why the adults at the school had insisted that they do so. These circumstances illustrate how damaging it can be when test scores are taken to matter more than education.

A third ethical concern is that test outcomes can take on the status of unchangeable labels. People too often think of themselves as being an IQ of 110 or a B student, as if the scores were labels stamped on their foreheads. Such labels may become barriers to advancement as people come to believe that their mental and personal qualities are fixed and unchangeable—that they cannot improve their lot in life. For those who are negatively assessed, the scores can become self-imposed motivational limits that lower their sense of self-efficacy and restrict the challenges they are willing to tackle. That is another insidious consequence of pronounce-

ments about group deficiencies in IQ. Those stigmatized publicly in this way come to believe what the "experts" are saying about them, and so disidentify with schools and education as means to improve their lives.

This tendency to give test scores a sacred status has societal as well as personal implications. When test scores become labels that identify traits, states, maladjustment, conflict, and pathology within an individual, people begin to think about the "abnormality" of individual children rather than about educational systems that need to modify programs to accommodate all learners. Labels put the spotlight on deviant personalities rather than on dysfunctional aspects of their environment. In societies that have an individualistic orientation, like the United States, people are all too ready to misattribute success and failure to the person, while underestimating the impact of the behavioral setting. We blame the victim for failure and thereby take society off the hook; we give credit to the person for success and thereby do not recognize the many societal influences that made it possible. We need to recognize that what people are now is a product of where they've been, where they think they are headed, and what situation is currently influencing their behavior.

We'd like to conclude this chapter on a personal note from Phil Zimbardo, one that may have some inspirational value to students who do not do well on objective tests:

Although I have gone on to have a successful career as a professional psychologist, the relevant tests I took many years ago would have predicted otherwise. Despite being an Honors undergraduate student, who graduated Summa Cum Laude, I got my only C grade in Introductory Psychology, where grades were based solely on multiple-choice exams. I was initially rejected for graduate training at Yale University; then I became an alternate, and finally, I was accepted reluctantly. This was in part because my GRE math scores were below the psychology department's criterion cutoff level. But I later discovered that it was also due in part to the false assumption of some faculty that I must be Negro—on the basis of the pattern of my answers and other "evidence" revealed in my application and tests. Such data negatively colored their judgments of my potential for a career in psychology. Fortunately, some others were willing to give me a chance when one of their respectable admits (Gordon Bower, now a famous psychologist) went elsewhere to start his graduate training.

Successful performance in a career and in life requires much more than the skills, abilities, *and traits measured by standardized tests. While the best tests perform the valuable function of predicting how well people will do on the average, there may be decisional error for any given individual. People can override the pessimistic predictions of their tests scores when ambition, imagination, hope, personal pride, and intense effort empower their performance. Perhaps it is vital to know when you should believe more in yourself than in the results of a test.*

PUT YOURSELF TO THE TEST

- Why might assessment have negative consequences for particular groups of individuals?
- Why do people worry that assessment plays a role in shaping educational practices?
- Why might test scores become labels that have broad consequences?

Recapping Main Points

WHAT IS ASSESSMENT?

- Psychological assessment has a long history, beginning in ancient China. Many important contributions were made by Sir Francis Galton.
- A useful assessment tool must be reliable, valid, and standardized. A reliable measure gives consistent results. A valid measure assesses the attributes for which the test was designed.
- A standardized test is always administered and scored in the same way; norms allow a person's score to be compared with the averages of others of the same age, sex, and culture.

INTELLIGENCE ASSESSMENT

- Binet began the tradition of objective intelligence testing in France in the early 1900s. Scores were given in terms of mental ages and were meant to represent children's current level of functioning.
- In the United States, Terman created the Stanford–Binet Intelligence Scale and popularized the concept of IQ.
- Wechsler designed special intelligence tests for adults, children, and preschoolers.

THEORIES OF INTELLIGENCE

- Psychometric analyses of IQ suggest that several basic abilities, such as fluid and crystallized aspects of intelligence, contribute to IQ scores.
- Contemporary theories conceive of and measure intelligence very broadly by considering the skills and insights people use to solve the types of problems they encounter.
- Sternberg differentiates analytical, creative, and practical aspects of intelligence.
- Gardner identifies eight types of intelligence that both include and go beyond the types of intelligence assessed by standard IQ measures. Recent research has focused on emotional intelligence.

THE POLITICS OF INTELLIGENCE

- Almost from the outset, intelligence tests have been used to make negative claims about ethnic and racial groups.
- Because of the reasonably high heritability of IQ, some researchers have attributed the lower scores of some racial and cultural groups to innate inferiority.
- Environmental disadvantages and stereotype threat appear to explain the lower scores of certain groups. Research shows that group differences can be affected through environmental interventions.

CREATIVITY

- Creativity is often assessed using tests of divergent thinking.
- Exceptionally creative people take risks, prepare, and are highly motivated.
- A link between madness and creativity has not been confirmed.

ASSESSMENT AND SOCIETY

- Though often useful for prediction and as an indication of current performance, test results should not be used to limit an individual's opportunities for development and change.
- When the results of an assessment will affect an individual's life, the techniques used must be reliable and valid for that individual and for the purpose in question.

Solutions to the anagrams in Table 9.3:

1. laugh		6. allow	
2. tempt		7. drive	
3. short		8. couch	
4. knight		9. enter	
5. write		10. basic	

KEY TERMS

chronological age (p. 291)

creativity (p. 307)

criterion validity (p. 288)

crystallized intelligence (p. 295)

divergent thinking (p. 307)

emotional intelligence (p. 297)

EQ (p. 298)

face validity (p. 288)

fluid intelligence (p. 295)

formal assessment (p. 287)

g (p. 295)

heritability estimate (p. 302)

intelligence (p. 290)

intelligence quotient (IQ) (p. 291)

internal consistency (p. 288)

learning disorders (p. 294)

mental age (p. 291)

mental retardation (p. 293)

norms (p. 289)

parallel forms (p. 287)

predictive validity (p. 288)

psychological assessment (p. 286)

psychometrics (p. 295)

reliability (p. 287)

split-half reliability (p. 288)

standardization (p. 289)

stereotype threat (p. 305)

test–retest reliability (p. 287)

validity (p. 288)

Human Development Across the Life Span

I magine you are holding a newborn baby. How might you predict what this child will be like as a 1-year-old? At 5 years? At 15? At 50? At 70? At 90? Your predictions would almost certainly consist of a mixture of the general and the specific—the child is extremely likely to learn a language but might or might not be a gifted author. Your predictions would also rely on considerations of heredity and of environment—if both of the child's parents were gifted authors, you might be willing to guess that the child would also show literary talent; if the child was educated in an enriched environment, you might predict that the child's accomplishments would exceed those of the parents. In this chapter, we describe the theories of developmental psychology that enable us to think systematically about the types of predictions we can make for the life course of a newborn child.

Developmental psychology is the area of psychology that is concerned with changes in physical and psychological functioning that occur from conception across the entire life span. The task of developmental psychologists is to find out how and why organisms change over time—to document and explain

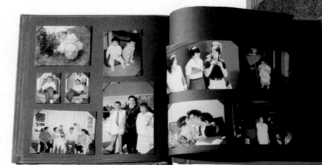

development. Investigators study the time periods in which different abilities and functions first appear and observe how those abilities are modified. The basic premise is that mental functioning, social relationships, and other vital aspects of human nature develop and change throughout the entire life cycle. **Table 10.1** presents a rough guide to the major periods of the life span.

In this chapter we will provide a general account of how researchers document development and the theories they use to explain patterns of change over time. We will then divide your life experiences into different domains and trace development in each domain. Early in the chapter, we focus on physical, cognitive, and language development. We then shift our attention to the changing nature of social relationships over the life span as well as the specific tasks individuals face at different moments in their lives. Let's begin now with the question of what it means to study development.

Studying Development

Suppose we ask you to make a list of all the ways in which you believe you have changed in the last year. What sorts of things would you put on the list? Have you undertaken a new physical fitness program? Or have you let an injury heal? Have you developed a range of new hobbies? Or have you decided to focus on just one interest? Have you developed a new circle of friends? Or have you become particularly close

◆

TABLE 10.1

Stages in Life Span Development

Stage	Age Period
Prenatal	Conception to birth
Infancy	Birth at full term to about 18 months
Early childhood	About 18 months to about 6 years
Middle childhood	About 6 years to about 11 years
Adolescence	About 11 years to about 20 years
Early adulthood	About 20 years to about 40 years
Middle adulthood	About 40 years to about 65 years
Late adulthood	About 65 years and older

to one individual? When we describe development, we will conceptualize it in terms of *change.* We have asked you to perform this exercise of thinking about your own changes to make the point that change almost always involves trade-offs.

Often people conceptualize the life span as mostly *gains*—changes for the better—in childhood and mostly *losses*—changes for the worse—over the course of adulthood. However, the perspective on development we will take here emphasizes that *options,* and therefore gains and losses, are features of all development (Dixon, 1999; Uttal & Perlmutter, 1989). When, for example, people choose a lifetime companion, they give up variety but gain security. When people retire, they give up status but gain leisure time.

It is also important that you not think of development as a *passive* process. You will see that many developmental changes require an individual's *active* engage-

In a longitudinal design, observations are made of the same individual at different ages, often for many years. This well-known woman might be part of a longitudinal study of British children born in 1926. How might she be similar to and different from other children in that cohort?

A drawback of cross-sectional research is the cohort effect. What differences might exist between these two groups of women as a result of the eras in which they have lived?

ment with his or her environment (Bronfenbrenner, 1999; Bronfenbrenner & Ceci, 1994).

To document change, a good first step is to determine what an average person is like—in physical appearance, cognitive abilities, and so on—at a particular age. **Normative investigations** seek to describe a characteristic of a specific age or developmental stage. By systematically testing individuals of different ages, researchers can determine developmental landmarks. These data provide *norms,* standard patterns of development or achievement, based on observation of many people.

Normative standards allow psychologists to make a distinction between **chronological age**—the number of months or years since a person's birth—and **developmental age**—the chronological age at which most people show the particular level of physical or mental development demonstrated by that child. A 3-year-old child who has verbal skills typical of most 5-year-olds is said to have a developmental age of 5 for verbal skills. Norms provide a standard basis for comparison both between individuals and between groups.

Developmental psychologists use several types of research designs to understand possible mechanisms of change. In a **longitudinal design,** the same individuals are repeatedly observed and tested over time, often for many years. Researchers might, for example, test the same children several times weekly over the course of a few months to catch, as closely as possible, the moment at which each child begins to use a mature strategy to solve arithmetic problems (Siegler & Crowley, 1991). By isolating the moment of change, researchers can gain a better understanding of what circumstances must precede the change. Researchers also often use longitudinal designs to study *individual differences.* To understand the life outcomes of different people, researchers may assess a range of potential causal factors early in life and see how those factors influence each individual's life course.

A general advantage of longitudinal research is that, because the participants have lived through the same socioeconomic period, age-related changes cannot be confused with variations in differing societal circumstances. A disadvantage, however, is that some types of generalizations can be made only to the same *cohort,* the group of individuals born in the same time period as the research participants. Also, longitudinal studies are costly because it is difficult to keep track of the participants over extended time, and data are easily lost due to participants' quitting or disappearing.

Most research on development uses a **cross-sectional design,** in which groups of participants, of different chronological ages, are observed and compared at one and the same time. A researcher can then draw conclusions about behavioral differences that may be related to age changes. Researchers might, for example, study changes in the ways friends provide social support across the teenage years by having pairs of 11-, 15-, and 19-year-olds engage in the same laboratory task (Denton & Zarbatany, 1996). A disadvantage of cross-sectional designs comes from comparing individuals who differ by year of birth as well as by chronological age. Age-related changes are confounded by differences in the social or political conditions experienced by different birth cohorts. Thus a study comparing samples of 10- and 18-year-olds now might find that the participants differ from 10- and 18-year-olds who grew up in the 1970s, in ways related to their different eras as well as to their developmental stages.

Each methodology gives researchers the opportunity to document change from one age to another. Researchers use these methodologies to study development in each of several domains. As we now consider some of those domains—physical, cognitive, and social development—you'll come to appreciate and understand some of the vast changes you've already experienced.

- Why is it important to conceptualize development across the full life span with respect to both gains and losses?
- What is the distinction between chronological age and developmental age?
- What are some of the advantages and disadvantages of longitudinal research?
- What are some of the advantages and disadvantages of cross-sectional research?

Physical Development Across the Life Span

Many of the types of development we describe in this chapter require some special knowledge to detect. For example, you might not notice landmarks in social development until you read about them here. We will begin, however, with a realm of development in which changes are often plainly visible to the untrained eye: **physical development.** There is no doubt that you have undergone enormous physical change since you were born. Such changes will continue until the end of your life. Because physical changes are so numerous, we will focus on the types that have an impact on psychological development.

◆ PRENATAL AND CHILDHOOD DEVELOPMENT

You began life with unique genetic potential: At the moment of conception a male's sperm cell fertilized a female's egg cell to form the single-cell **zygote;** you received half of the 46 chromosomes found in all normal human body cells from your mother and half from your father. In this section, we outline physical development in the *prenatal period,* from the moment of conception until the moment of birth. We also describe some of the sensory abilities children have obtained even before birth. Finally, we describe the important physical changes that you experienced during childhood.

PHYSICAL DEVELOPMENT IN THE WOMB

The earliest behavior of any kind is the heartbeat. It begins in the *prenatal period,* before birth, when the embryo is about 3 weeks old and a sixth of an inch

long. Responses to stimulation have been observed as early as the sixth week, when the embryo is not yet an inch long. Spontaneous movements are observed by the eighth week (Carmichael, 1970; Humphrey, 1970).

After the eighth week, the developing embryo is called a *fetus.* The mother feels fetal movements in about the sixteenth week after conception. At this point, the fetus is about 7 inches long (the average length at birth is 20 inches). As the brain grows in utero, it generates new neurons at the rate of 250,000 per minute, reaching a full complement of over 100 billion neurons by birth (Cowan, 1979). In humans and many other mammals, most of this cell proliferation and migration of neurons to their correct locations take place prenatally, while the development of the branching processes of axons and dendrites largely occurs after birth (Kolb, 1989). The sequence of brain development, from 30 days to 9 months, is shown in **Figure 10.1.**

During the first months of pregnancy, environmental factors such as malnutrition, infection, radiation, or drugs can prevent the normal formation of organs and body structures. For example, when mothers are infected with rubella (German measles) two to four weeks after conception, the probability is roughly 50 percent that the child will suffer negative consequences such as mental retardation, eye damage, deafness, or heart defects. If exposure occurs at other times, the probability of adverse effects is much lower (e.g., 22 percent in the second month; 8 percent in the third month) (Murata et al., 1992). Similarly, mothers who consume certain substances, like alcohol, during sensitive periods put their unborn children at risk for brain

As the brain grows in the developing fetus, it generates 250,000 new neurons per minute. What must the brain be prepared to do, as soon as the child enters the world?

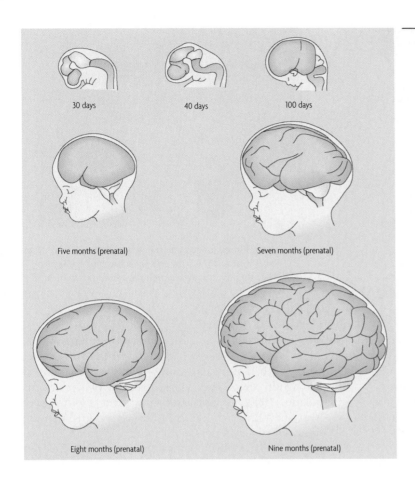

FIGURE 10.1

The Development of the Human Brain

During the nine months before birth, the brain reaches its complement of over 100 billion neurons.

30 days

40 days

100 days

Five months (prenatal)

Seven months (prenatal)

Eight months (prenatal)

Nine months (prenatal)

damage and other impairments (Mattson et al., 2001; Randall, 2001). Facial abnormalities, for example, are most likely to arise from mothers' drinking in the first two months of pregnancy (Coles, 1994). Pregnant women who smoke also put their children at risk, particularly in the second half of pregnancy. Smoking during pregnancy increases the risk of miscarriage, premature births, and low-birth-weight babies. In fact, women who are exposed to secondhand smoke during pregnancy are also more likely to have babies with low birth weights (Dejin-Karlsson et al., 1998).

Some substances may bring about damage at virtually any time during pregnancy. Cocaine, for example, travels through the placenta and can affect fetal development directly. In adults, cocaine causes blood vessels to constrict; in pregnant women, cocaine restricts placental blood flow and oxygen supply to the fetus. If severe oxygen deprivation results, blood vessels in the fetus's brain may burst. Such prenatal strokes can lead to lifelong mental handicaps (Koren et al., 1998; Singer et al., 2002). Research suggests that the brain systems most damaged by cocaine are those responsible for controlling attention: Children exposed to cocaine in the womb may spend their lives overcome by the distractions of irrelevant sights and sounds.

We use these examples to emphasize that nature and nurture interact to shape body and brain even before a child is born.

BABIES PREWIRED FOR SURVIVAL

What capabilities are programmed into this body and brain at birth? We are accustomed to thinking about newborns as entirely helpless. John Watson, the founder of behaviorism, described the human infant as "a lively, squirming bit of flesh, capable of making a few simple responses." If that sounds right, you might be surprised to learn that, moments out of the womb, infants reveal remarkable abilities to obtain information through their senses and react to it. They might be thought of as *prewired for survival,* well suited to respond to adult caregivers and to influence their social environments.

For example, infants can hear even before birth. Researchers have demonstrated that what infants hear while in the womb has consequences. Newborns prefer to listen to their mothers' voices rather than the voices of other women (Spence & DeCasper, 1987; Spence & Freeman, 1996). In fact, the most recent research suggests that children recognize their mothers' voices even before they are born.

Voice Recognition in the Womb

A team of researchers recruited mothers-to-be at a hospital in southeast China (Kisilevsky et al., 2003). On average, the mothers had been pregnant for 38.4 weeks, which meant that the fetuses were full-term. The mothers were asked to tape-record a two-minute poem. The recordings of the poem were played to the fetuses through a loudspeaker that was poised about 4 inches above the mothers' abdomens. Half the fetuses were played the poem read in their own mothers' voice; the other half heard the poem read by someone else's mother. The researchers monitored fetal heart rate. The results were quite dramatic: Fetal heart rate increased in response to the mothers' voice and decreased in response to the strangers' voices!

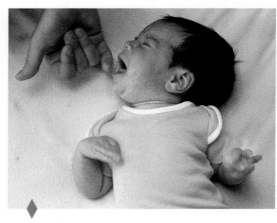

When something touches a newborn's cheek, the rooting reflex prompts the baby to seek something to suck. In what other ways are children prewired for survival?

Given these strong results favoring mothers, you might wonder whether children also respond more to their fathers' voices. Unfortunately, research so far indicates that children don't seem to have enough auditory experience with their dads. Newborns show no preference for their fathers' voices (DeCasper & Prescott, 1984). Even at age 4 months, infants still do not prefer their father's voice to a stranger's voice (Ward & Cooper, 1999).

Infants also put their visual systems to work almost immediately: A few minutes after birth, a newborn's eyes are alert, turning in the direction of a voice and

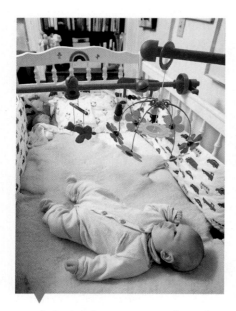

Early on, infants can perceive large objects that display a great deal of contrast. What visual experiences do newborns find particularly appealing?

searching inquisitively for the source of certain sounds. Even so, vision is less well developed than the other senses at birth. The visual acuity of adults is roughly 40 times better than the visual acuity of newborns (Sireteanu, 1999). Visual acuity improves rapidly over the first six months of a baby's life. Newborns also are ill equipped to experience the world in three dimensions: It is only at about 4 months of age that children are able to combine information from their two eyes to perceive depth. Good vision—sensitivity to contrast, visual acuity, and color discrimination—requires that a great many photoreceptor cells function in the center of the eye's receptive area and that the optics of the eye develop appropriately (see Chapter 4). Many of these components have yet to mature in the infant's visual system. Good vision also requires that numerous connections between neurons in the brain's visual cortex be made in response to visual experience (Maurer et al., 1999). At birth, not enough of these connections are laid down.

Even without perfect vision, however, children have visual preferences. Pioneering researcher **Robert Fantz** (1963) observed that babies as young as 4 months old preferred looking at objects with contours rather than those that were plain, complex ones rather than simple ones, and whole faces rather than faces with features in disarray. More recent research has confirmed that children prefer human faces to visually similar displays right from birth (Valenza et al., 1996). In fact, by age 4 days, newborns have stored important information about their environment (Pascalis et al., 1995): features of their mother's face. You can see why we characterized infants as "prewired for survival."

Once children start to move around in their environment, they quickly acquire other perceptual capabilities. For example, classic research by **Eleanor Gibson** and **Richard Walk** (1960) examined how children respond to depth information. This research used an apparatus called a *visual cliff.* The visual cliff had a board running across the middle of a solid glass surface. As shown in **Figure 10.2,** checkerboard cloth was used to create a deep end and a shallow end. In their original research, Gibson and Walk demonstrated that children would readily leave the center board to crawl across the shallow end, but they were reluctant to crawl

across the deep end. Subsequent research has demonstrated that fear of the deep end depends on crawling experience: Children who have begun to crawl experience fear of the deep end, whereas their noncrawling same-age peers do not (Campos et al., 1992). Thus, wariness of heights is not quite "prewired," but it develops quickly as children begin to explore the world under their own power.

GROWTH AND MATURATION IN CHILDHOOD

Newborn infants change at an astonishing rate but, as shown in **Figure 10.3,** physical growth is not equal across all physical structures. You've probably noticed that babies seem to be all head. At birth, a baby's head is already about 60 percent of its adult size and measures a quarter of the whole body length (Bayley, 1956). An infant's body weight doubles in the first six months and triples by the first birthday; by the age of 2, a child's trunk is about half of its adult length. Genital tissue shows little change until the teenage years and then develops rapidly to adult proportions.

For most children, physical growth is accompanied by the maturation of motor ability. **Maturation** refers to the process of growth typical of all members of a species who are reared in the species's usual habitat. The characteristic maturational sequences newborns experience are determined by the interaction of inherited biological boundaries and environmental inputs. For example, in the sequence for locomotion, as shown

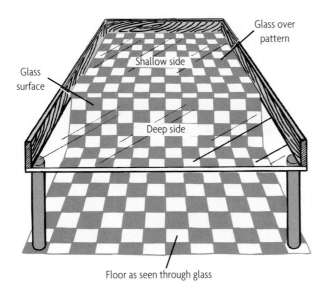

FIGURE 10.2

The Visual Cliff

Once children have gained experience crawling around their environment, they show fear of the deep side of the visual cliff.

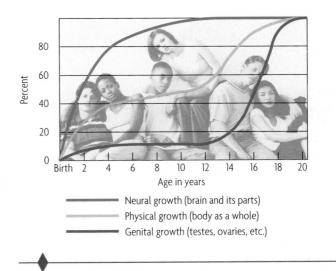

FIGURE 10.3

Growth Patterns Across the First Two Decades of Life

Neural growth occurs very rapidly in the first year of life. It is much faster than overall physical growth. By contrast, genital maturation does not occur until adolescence.

What effect does a cradleboard have on the infant's ability to learn to walk?

in **Figure 10.4,** a child learns to walk without special training. This sequence applies to the great majority of babies; a minority of children skip a step or develop their own original sequences. Even so, in cultures in which there is less physical stimulation, children begin to walk later. The Native American practice of carrying babies in tightly bound back cradles retards walking, but, once released, the child goes through the same sequence. Therefore, you can think of all unimpaired newborn children as possessing the same potential for physical maturation.

◆ PHYSICAL DEVELOPMENT IN ADOLESCENCE

The first concrete indicator of the end of childhood is the *pubescent growth spurt*. At around age 10 for girls and age 12 for boys, growth hormones flow into the bloodstream. For several years, the adolescent may grow three to six inches a year and gain weight rapidly as well. The adolescent's body does not reach adult proportions all at once. Hands and feet grow to full adult size first. The arms and legs come next, with the torso

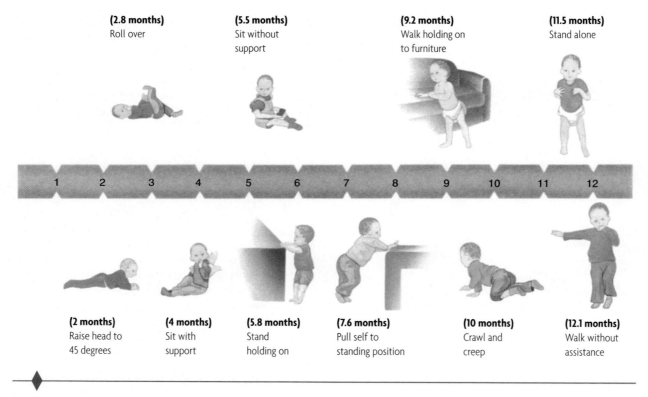

(2.8 months) Roll over

(5.5 months) Sit without support

(9.2 months) Walk holding on to furniture

(11.5 months) Stand alone

1 2 3 4 5 6 7 8 9 10 11 12

(2 months) Raise head to 45 degrees

(4 months) Sit with support

(5.8 months) Stand holding on

(7.6 months) Pull self to standing position

(10 months) Crawl and creep

(12.1 months) Walk without assistance

FIGURE 10.4

Maturational Timetable for Locomotion

The development of walking requires no special teaching. It follows a fixed, time-ordered sequence that is typical of all physically capable members of our species.

developing most slowly. Thus an individual's overall shape changes several times over the teenage years.

Another important process that occurs during adolescence is **puberty,** which brings about sexual maturity. (The Latin word *pubertas* means "covered with hair" and signifies the growth of hair on the arms and legs, under the arms, and in the genital area.) Puberty for males brings about the production of live sperm, while for girls it leads to **menarche,** the onset of menstruation. In the United States, the average time for menarche is between the ages of 12 and 13, although the normal range extends from 11 to 15. For boys, the production of live sperm first occurs, on average, between the ages of 12 and 14, but again there is considerable variation in this timing. These physical changes often bring about an awareness of sexual feelings. In Chapter 11, we will discuss the onset of sexual motivation.

Some other important physical changes happen inside adolescents' brains. Researchers once thought that most brain growth was over within the first few years of life. However, recent studies using brain imaging techniques have demonstrated a growth spurt within the adolescent brain (Sowell et al., 2002). The areas of the brain that undergo the greatest change from

Why do researchers give the advice "Use it or lose it?"

puberty into young adulthood are the *frontal lobes*—the areas responsible for planning and regulation of emotions. The new growth beginning around ages 10 to 12 is followed by pruning of unused connections through about age 20. This pruning process leaves individuals with efficient and well-organized adult brains.

With the passing of adolescence, your body once again reaches a period of the life span in which biological change is comparatively minimal. You may affect your body in a variety of ways—by diet and exercise, for example—but the next striking set of changes that are consistent consequences of aging occurs in middle and late adulthood.

◆ PHYSICAL CHANGES IN ADULTHOOD

Some of the most obvious changes that occur with age concern your physical appearance and abilities. As you grow older, you can expect your skin to wrinkle, your hair to thin and gray, and your height to decrease an inch or two. You can also expect some of your senses to become less acute. These changes do not appear suddenly at age 65. They occur gradually, beginning as soon as early adulthood. However, before we describe some common age-related changes, we want to make a more general point: Many physical changes arise not from aging but from *disuse;* research supports a general belief in the maxim "Use it or lose it." Older adults who maintain (or renew) a program of physical fitness may experience fewer of the difficulties that are often thought to be inevitable consequences of aging. (Note that we will reach exactly the same conclusion when we discuss cognitive and social aspects of middle and late adulthood.) Let's now look, however, at some changes that are largely unavoidable and frequently have an impact on the way adults think about their lives.

VISION

The vast majority of people over 65 experiences some loss of visual function (Carter, 1982; Pitts, 1982). With age, the lenses of people's eyes become yellowed and less flexible. The yellowing of the lens is thought to be responsible for diminished color vision experienced by some older people. Colors of lower wavelengths—violets, blues, and greens—are particularly hard for some older adults to discriminate. The rigidity of the lens can make seeing objects at close range difficult. Lens rigidity also affects dark adaptation, making night vision a problem for older people. Many normal visual changes can be aided with corrective lenses.

HEARING

Hearing loss is common among those 60 and older. The average older adult has difficulty hearing high-frequency sounds (Corso, 1977). This impairment is usually greater for men than for women. Older adults can have a hard time understanding speech—particularly that spoken by high-pitched voices. (Oddly enough, with age, people's speaking voices increase in pitch due to stiffening of the vocal cords.) Deficits in hearing can be gradual and hard for an individual to notice until they are extreme. In addition, even when individuals become aware of hearing loss, they may deny it, because it is perceived as an undesirable sign of aging. Some of the physiological aspects of hearing loss can be overcome with the help of hearing aids. You should also be aware, as you grow older or interact with older adults, that it helps to speak in low tones, enunciate clearly, and reduce background noise.

REPRODUCTIVE AND SEXUAL FUNCTIONING

We saw that puberty marks the onset of reproductive functioning. In middle and late adulthood, reproductive capacity diminishes. Around age 50, most women experience *menopause,* the cessation of menstruation and ovulation. For men, changes are less abrupt, but the quantity of viable sperm falls off after age 40, and the volume of seminal fluid declines after age 60. Of course, these changes are relevant primarily to reproduction. Increasing age and physical change do not necessarily impair other aspects of sexual experience (Levine, 1998; Levy, 1994). Indeed, sex is one of life's healthy pleasures that can enhance successful aging because it is arousing, provides aerobic exercise, stimulates fantasy, and is a vital form of social interaction.

Older adults can and do enjoy the many benefits of intimacy and sexual relationships. Why does this image clash with stereotypes of late adulthood?

You have had a brief review of the landmarks of physical development. Against that background, let's turn now to the ways in which you developed an understanding of the world around you.

PUT YOURSELF TO THE TEST

◆ To what extent can children be affected by prenatal environmental factors?

◆ What evidence suggests that babies are "prewired for survival"?

◆ How is maturation defined?

◆ What are the changes in body and brain that affect adolescents?

◆ What are some of the important physical changes that accompany adulthood?

Cognitive Development Across the Life Span

How does an individual's understanding of physical and social reality change across the life span? **Cognitive development** is the study of the processes and products of the mind as they emerge and change over time. Because researchers have been particularly fascinated by the earliest emergence of cognitive capabilities, we will focus much of our attention on the earliest stages of cognitive development. However, we will also describe some of the discoveries researchers have made about cognitive development across the adult years.

As we begin this discussion of cognitive development, we want to remind you of a distinction we introduced in Chapter 3—*nature versus nurture.* The question is how best to account for the profound differences between a newborn and, for example, a 10-year-old: To what extent is such development determined by heredity (nature), and to what extent is it a product of learned experiences (nurture)? The debate concerning nature and nurture has a long history among philosophers, psychologists, and educators. On one side of this debate are those who believe that the human infant is born without knowledge or skills and that experience, in the form of human learning, etches messages on the blank tablet (in Latin, the *tabula rasa*) of the infant's unformed mind. This view, originally proposed by British philosopher **John Locke,** is known as *empiricism.* It credits human

<www.ablongman.com/gerrig17e>

development to experience. Empiricists believe that what directs human development is the stimulation people receive as they are *nurtured.* Among the scholars opposing empiricism was French philosopher **Jean-Jacques Rousseau.** He argued the *nativist* view that *nature,* or the evolutionary legacy that each child brings into the world, is the mold that shapes development. Our discussion of cognitive development should lead you to see that there is truth to both sides of the debate. Children have innate preparation to learn from their experiences in the world.

We begin our discussion of cognitive development with the pioneering work of the late Swiss psychologist Jean Piaget.

◆ PIAGET'S INSIGHTS INTO MENTAL DEVELOPMENT

For nearly 50 years, **Jean Piaget** (1929, 1954, 1977) developed theories about the ways that children think, reason, and solve problems. Perhaps Piaget's interest in cognitive development grew out of his own intellectually active youth: Piaget published his first article at age 10 and was offered a post as a museum curator at age 14 (Brainerd, 1996). Piaget used simple demonstrations and sensitive interviews with his own children and with other children to generate complex theories about early mental development. His interest was not in the amount of information children possessed but in the ways their thinking and inner representations of physical reality changed at different stages in their development.

BUILDING BLOCKS OF DEVELOPMENTAL CHANGE

Piaget gave the name **schemes** to the mental structures that enable individuals to interpret the world. Schemes are the building blocks of developmental change. Piaget characterized the infant's initial schemes as *sensorimotor intelligence*—mental structures or programs that guide sensorimotor sequences, such as sucking, looking, grasping, and pushing. With practice, elementary schemes are combined, integrated, and differentiated into ever-more-complex, diverse action patterns, as when a child pushes away undesired objects to seize a desired one behind him or her. According to Piaget, two basic processes work in tandem to achieve cognitive growth—assimilation and accommodation. **Assimilation** modifies new environmental information to fit into what is already known; the child accesses existing schemes to structure incoming sensory data. **Accommodation** restructures or modifies the child's existing schemes so that new information is accounted for more completely.

Consider the transitions a baby must make from sucking at a mother's breast, to sucking the nipple of a bottle, to sipping through a straw, and then to drinking from a cup. The initial sucking response is a reflex action present at birth, but it must be modified somewhat so that the child's mouth fits the shape and size of the mother's nipple. In adapting to a bottle, an infant still uses many parts of the sequence unchanged (assimilation) but must grasp and draw on the rubber nipple somewhat differently from before and learn to hold the bottle at an appropriate angle (accommodation). The steps from bottle to straw to cup require more accommodation but continue to rely on earlier skills. Piaget saw cognitive development as the result of exactly this sort of interweaving of assimilation and accommodation. The balanced application of assimilation and accommodation permits children's behavior and knowledge to become less dependent on concrete external reality, relying more on abstract thought.

STAGES IN COGNITIVE DEVELOPMENT

Piaget believed that children's cognitive development could be divided into a series of four ordered, discontinuous stages (see **Table 10.2**). All children are assumed to progress through these stages in the same sequence, although one child may take longer to pass through a given stage than another.

Sensorimotor Stage The sensorimotor stage extends roughly from birth to age 2. In the early months, much of an infant's behavior is based on a limited array of inborn schemes, like sucking, looking, grasping, and pushing. During the first year, sensorimotor sequences

TABLE 10.2
Piaget's Stages of Cognitive Development

Stage/Ages	Characteristics and Major Accomplishments
Sensorimotor (0–2)	Child begins life with small number of sensorimotor sequences. Child develops object permanence and the beginnings of symbolic thought.
Preoperational (2–7)	Child's thought is marked by egocentrism and centration. Child has improved ability to use symbolic thought.
Concrete operations (7–11)	Child achieves understanding of conservation. Child can reason with respect to concrete, physical objects.
Formal operations (11→)	Child develops capacity for abstract reasoning and hypothetical thinking.

Piaget observed that the typical 6-month-old will attend to an attractive toy (left) but will quickly lose interest if a screen blocks the toy from view (right). What understanding about objects will the child achieve by age 2?

are improved, combined, coordinated, and integrated (sucking and grasping, looking and manipulating, for example). They become more varied as infants discover that their actions have an effect on external events.

The most important cognitive acquisition of the infancy period is the ability to form mental representations of absent objects—those with which the child is not in direct sensorimotor contact. **Object permanence** refers to children's understanding that objects exist and behave independently of their actions or awareness. In the first months of life, children follow objects with their eyes, but, when the objects disappear from view, they turn away as if the objects had also disappeared from their minds. At around 3 months of age, however, they keep looking at the place where the objects had disappeared. Between 8 and 12 months, children begin to search for those disappearing objects. By age 2 years, children have no remaining uncertainty that "out of sight" objects continue to exist (Flavell, 1985).

Preoperational Stage The preoperational stage extends roughly from 2 to 7 years of age. The big cognitive advance in this developmental stage is an improved ability to represent mentally objects that are not physically present. Except for this development, Piaget characterizes the preoperational stage according to what the child *cannot* do. For example, Piaget believed that young children's preoperational thought is marked by **egocentrism,** the child's inability to take the perspective of another person. You have probably noticed egocentrism if you've heard a 2-year-old's conversations with other children. Children at this age often seem to be talking to themselves rather than interacting.

Preoperational children also experience **centration**— the tendency to have their attention captured by the more perceptually striking features of objects. Centration is illustrated by Piaget's classic demonstration of a child's inability to understand that the amount of a liquid does not change as a function of the size or shape of its container.

Piaget Demonstrates Centration

When an equal amount of lemonade is poured into two identical glasses, children of ages 5 and 7 report that the glasses contain the same amount. When, however, the lemonade from one glass is poured into a tall, thin glass, their opinions diverge. The 5-year-olds know that the lemonade in the tall glass is the same lemonade, but they report that it now is *more*. The 7-year-olds correctly assert that there is no difference between the amounts.

In Piaget's demonstration, the younger children center on a single, perceptually salient dimension—the height of the lemonade in the glass. The older children take into account both height and width and correctly infer that appearance is not reality.

Concrete Operations Stage The concrete operations stage goes roughly from 7 to 11 years of age. At this stage, the child has become capable of *mental operations,* actions performed in the mind that give rise to logical thinking. The preoperational and concrete operations stages are often put in contrast because children in the concrete operation stage are now capable of what they failed earlier on. Concrete operations allow children to replace physical action with mental action. For example, if a child sees that Adam is taller than Zara and, later, that Zara is taller than Tanya, the child can reason that Adam is the tallest of the three—without physically manipulating the three individuals. However, the child still cannot draw the appropriate inference ("Adam is tallest") if the problem is just stated with a verbal description. This inability to determine relative

This 5-year-old girl is aware that the two containers have the same amount of colored liquid. However, when the liquid from one is poured into a taller container, she indicates that there is more liquid in the taller one. She has not yet grasped the concept of conservation, which she will understand by age 6 or 7. Why wouldn't the 5-year-old child understand the concept, even if she were told the right answer?

heights (and solve similar problems) without direct, physical observation suggests that abstract thought is still in the offing in the period of concrete operations.

The lemonade study illustrates another hallmark of the concrete operations period. The 7-year-olds have mastered what Piaget called **conservation:** They know that the physical properties of objects do not change when nothing is added or taken away, even though the objects' appearance changes. **Figure 10.5** presents examples of Piaget's tests of conservation for different

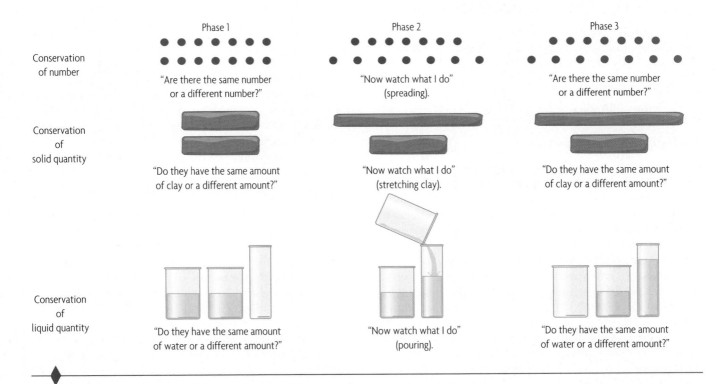

FIGURE 10.5

Tests of Conservation

dimensions. One of the newly acquired operations children can bring to bear on conservation tasks is reversibility. *Reversibility* is the child's understanding that both physical actions and mental operations can be reversed: The child can reason that the amount of lemonade *can't* have changed, because when the physical action is reversed—when the lemonade is poured back into the original glass—the two volumes will once again look identical.

Formal Operations Stage The formal operations stage covers a span roughly from age 11 on. In this final stage of cognitive growth, thinking becomes abstract. Adolescents can see how their particular reality is only one of several imaginable realities, and they begin to ponder deep questions of truth, justice, and existence. They seek answers to problems in a systematic fashion: Once they achieve formal operations, children can start to play the role of scientist, trying each of a series of possibilities in careful order. Adolescents also begin to be able to use the types of advanced deductive logic we described in Chapter 8. Unlike their younger siblings, adolescents have the ability to reason from abstract premises ("If A, then B" and "not B") to their logical conclusions ("not A").

◆ CONTEMPORARY PERSPECTIVES ON EARLY COGNITIVE DEVELOPMENT

Piaget's theory remains the classic reference point for the understanding of cognitive development (Flavell, 1996; Lourenço & Machado, 1996; Scholnick et al., 1999). However, contemporary researchers have come up with more flexible ways of studying the development of the child's cognitive abilities.

ADVANCES IN RESEARCH METHODS

We've already detailed some of the tasks Piaget used to draw conclusions about cognitive development. However, contemporary researchers have developed innovative techniques that have allowed them to reevaluate some of Piaget's conclusions. Consider object permanence, which Piaget suggested was the major accomplishment of the 2-year-old child. Contemporary research techniques suggest that infants as young as 3 months old, and perhaps younger, have already developed aspects of this concept. They apparently understand the basic principle that solid objects cannot pass through other solid objects. This important finding has been shown with different tasks devised by researcher **Renée Baillargeon** (Buy-ay-zhon) (1987a, 1987b; Baillargeon & DeVos, 1991). During one task, infants demonstrated surprise when observing sequences of events that were impossible.

Infants Contemplate Impossible Events

The infants sat in front of a large display box. Directly before them was a small screen; to the left of the screen was a long ramp. The infants watched the following event: The screen was raised (so the infants could see there was nothing behind it) and then lowered; a toy car was pushed onto the ramp; the car rolled down the ramp and across the display box, disappearing as it shot behind the screen, reappearing at the end of the screen, and finally exiting the display box to the right (see **Figure 10.6**).

After the infants became habituated to this event, they saw two test events. *Habituation* reflects a weakened response when a stimulus is repeated over time. In both test events, a box was revealed when the screen was raised, but the location of the box differed. In the *possible event,* the box was placed at the back of the display box, behind the tracks of the car, so the car could roll freely through the display. In the *impossible event,* the box was placed on top of the tracks so that it blocked the car's path. Even so, during the event, the car appeared to roll freely across the display. The infants looked longer at the "impossible" event, suggesting that it surprised—dishabituated—them (Baillargeon, 1986).

We can't take the infants' surprise as evidence that they have acquired the full concept of object permanence—they may only know that *something* is wrong without knowing exactly what that something is (Lourenço & Machado, 1996). Even so, Baillargeon's research suggests that even very young children have acquired important knowledge of the physical world.

CHILDREN'S FOUNDATIONAL THEORIES

Piaget's theory is built around stages in which landmark changes take place in children's ways of thinking. More recently, researchers have explored the idea that changes occur separately, in each of several major domains, as children develop **foundational theories**—frameworks for initial understanding—to explain their experiences of the world (Gelman & Raman, 2002; Wellman & Inagaki, 1997). For example, children accumulate their experiences of the properties of mental states into a *theory of mind,* or naive psychology. By doing so, they are better able to understand the thought processes of themselves and others.

Researchers have formally studied the development of scientific concepts, such as the way in which children project biological properties from one species to another. When asked which of a series of animals sleep or have bones, 4-year-old children were inclined to make their judgments based on their perceptions of the similarity of the animal to humans (Carey, 1985). For example, more 4-year-olds attributed these properties (i.e., "sleep" and "have bones") to dogs than they did to fish, and attributions to fish were, in turn, greater than those to flies. Over time, children must replace a theory based on similarity to humans with one that acknowledges more structure in the animal kingdom—for example, they must acquire the formal distinction between *vertebrates* and *invertebrates* that defines which types of animals have bones. Similarly, 3- and 4-year-old children understand that what is inside objects affects their functions—although they have no clear idea what those insides are (Gelman, 2003; Gelman & Wellman, 1991). Thus, although 3- and 4-year-olds aren't entirely sure what kinds of things are inside dogs, they are quite certain that a dog would cease to be a dog if you removed whatever is inside. In each domain, you see that children begin to develop a general theory and then use a range of new experiences to provide successive refinements.

SOCIAL AND CULTURAL INFLUENCES ON COGNITIVE DEVELOPMENT

Another focus of contemporary research is on the role of social interactions in cognitive development. Much of this research has its origins in the theories of Russian psychologist **Lev Vygotsky.** Vygotsky argued that children develop through a process of **internalization:** They absorb knowledge from their social context that has a major impact on how cognition unfolds over time.

The social theory that Vygotsky pioneered has found support in cross-cultural studies of development. As Piaget's theory initially seized the attention of developmental researchers, many of them sought to use his tasks to study the cognitive achievements of children in diverse cultures (Rogoff, 2003; Rogoff & Chavajay, 1995). These studies began to call into question the universality of Piaget's claims because, for example, people in many cultures failed to show evidence that they had acquired formal operations. Late in his life, Piaget himself began to speculate that the specific achievements he characterized as formal operations may rely more on the particular type of science education children obtain rather than on an unfolding of biologically predetermined stages of cognitive development (Lourenço & Machado, 1996).

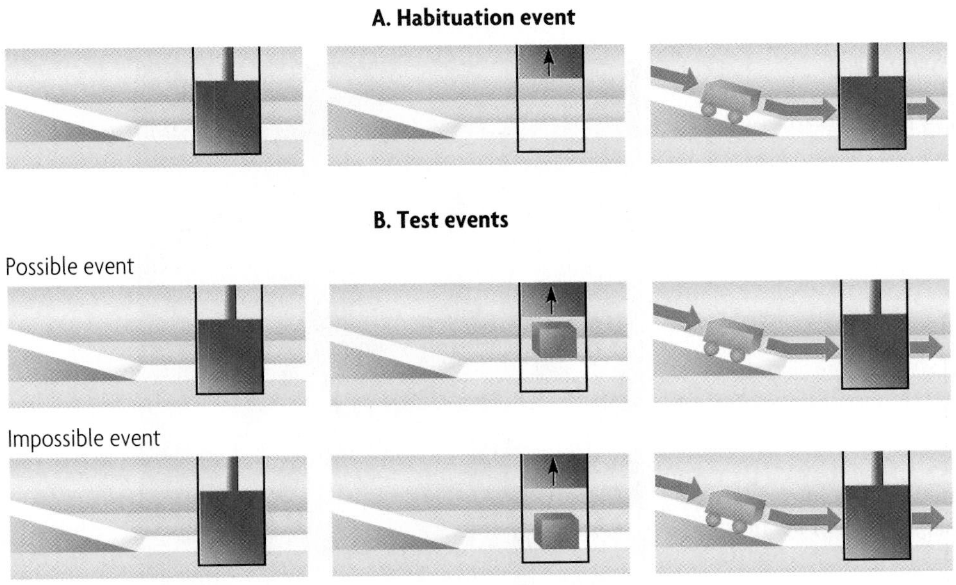

A. Habituation event

B. Test events

Possible event

Impossible event

FIGURE 10.6

A Schematic Representation of Habituation and Test Events

In the habituation phase, infants' interest in the event diminished over time. In the test case, their interest was recaptured by the impossible event.

How do children begin to form generalizations about the world based on what they have experienced and observed?

Vygotsksy's concept of internalization helps to explain the effect culture has on cognitive development. Children's cognition develops to perform culturally valued functions (Serpell & Boykin, 1994; Serpell, 2000). Piaget, for example, invented tasks that reflected his own preconceptions about appropriate and valuable cognitive activities. Other cultures prefer their children to excel in other ways. If Piaget's children had been evaluated with respect to their understanding of the cognitive complexities of weaving, they probably would have appeared to be retarded in their development relative to Mayan children in Guatemala (Rogoff, 1990). Cross-cultural studies of cognitive development have quite often demonstrated that type of schooling plays a large role in determining children's achievement on Piagetian tasks (Rogoff & Chavajay, 1995). Psychologists must use these types of findings to sort out the nature and nurture of cognitive development.

The developmental changes we have documented so far are very dramatic. It's easy to tell that a 12-year-old has all sorts of cognitive capabilities unknown to a 1-year-old. We now shift to the more subtle changes that take place throughout adulthood.

◆ COGNITIVE DEVELOPMENT IN ADULTHOOD

As we have traced cognitive development across childhood into adolescence, "change" has usually meant "change for the better." When we arrive at the period of late adulthood, though, cultural stereotypes suggest that "change" means "change for the worse" (Parr & Siegert, 1993). However, even when people believe that the course of adulthood brings with it general decline, they still anticipate certain types of gains very late into life (Dixon, 1999). We will look at intelligence and memory to see the interplay of losses and gains.

INTELLIGENCE

There is little evidence to support the notion that general cognitive abilities decline among the healthy elderly. Only about 5 percent of the population experiences major losses in cognitive functioning. When age-related decline in cognitive functioning occurs, it is usually limited to only some abilities. When intelligence is separated into the components that make up your verbal abilities *(crystallized intelligence)* and those that are part of your ability to learn quickly and thoroughly *(fluid intelligence),* fluid intelligence shows the greater decline with age (Baltes & Staudinger, 1993; Singer et al., 2003). Much of the decrease in fluidity has been attributed to a general slowing down of processing speed: Older adults' performance on intellectual tasks

Many prominent figures, such as Nelson Mandela, continue to make important professional contributions through their 70s and beyond. How can some aspects of intellectual performance be kept from decline through late adulthood?

   <www.ablongman.com/gerrig17e>

that require many mental processes to occur in small amounts of time is greatly impaired (Salthouse, 1996).

But all change is not in the direction of poorer functioning. For instance, psychologists are now exploring age-related gains in **wisdom**—expertise in the fundamental practices of life (Baltes & Kunzmann, 2003; Baltes & Staudinger, 2000). **Table 10.3** presents some of the types of knowledge that define wisdom (Smith & Baltes, 1990). You can see that each type of knowledge is best acquired over a long and thoughtful life. Furthermore, individuals vary greatly in their later-life intellectual performance. Research indicates that older adults who pursue high levels of environmental stimulation tend to maintain high levels of cognitive abilities.

TABLE 10.3
Features of Wisdom

- *Rich factual knowledge.* General and specific knowledge about the conditions of life and its variations

- *Rich procedural knowledge.* General and specific knowledge about strategies of judgment and advice concerning life matters

- *Life span contextualism.* Knowledge about the contexts of life and their temporal (developmental) relationships

- *Uncertainty.* Knowledge about the relative indeterminacy and unpredictability of life and ways to manage it

---

PUTTING IDEAS TO THE TEST

When Professors Grow Old

A group of 22 senior professors, ages 60 to 71, from the University of California, Berkeley, were compared in their intellectual functioning to their younger colleagues (ages 30 to 59) and to a control group of older adults in the same age range. The professors performed a variety of tests that tapped different aspects of cognitive functioning. On some of the tests—for example, paired associate learning (see Chapter 7)—the senior professors showed typical patterns of age-related impairment. However, on other measures, the senior professors kept pace with their younger colleagues. For example, they were equally able to listen to tape recordings of brief stories and recall information from those stories. The control group of older adults showed typical age-related impairment on this task. How can we explain preserved function for the professors? The researchers suggest that the professors' occupation, which requires them to maintain a high level of mental activity, may protect them from some typical losses of aging (Shimamura et al., 1995).

Does this finding make you want to become a college professor? Other studies suggest that you need not go to that extreme. The important conclusion is that you should keep your mind at work. **Warner Schaie** and his colleagues have even been able to demonstrate that training programs can reverse older adults' decline in some cognitive abilities (Schaie, 1994; Schaie & Willis, 1986). It appears that disuse, rather than decay, may be responsible for the deficits in intellectual performance that are not related to processing speed (Hultsch et al., 1999). As promised, we have again arrived at the conclusion that "Use it or lose it (or seek training to get it back)" is an appropriate motto for the wise older adult.

How can older adults cope successfully with whatever changes inevitably accompany increasing age? Successful aging might consist of making the most of gains while minimizing the impact of the normal losses that accompany aging. This strategy for successful aging, proposed by psychologists **Paul Baltes** and **Margaret Baltes,** is called **selective optimization with compensation** (Baltes et al., 1992; Freund & Baltes, 1998). *Selective* means that people scale down the number and extent of their goals for themselves. *Optimization* refers to people exercising or training themselves in areas that are of highest priority to them. *Compensation* means that people use alternative ways to deal with losses—for example, choosing age-friendly environments. Let's consider an example:

> *When the concert pianist [Arthur] Rubinstein was asked, in a television interview, how he managed to remain such a successful pianist in his old age, he mentioned three strategies: (1) In old age he performed fewer pieces, (2) he now practiced each piece more frequently, and (3) he produced more ritardandos [slowings of the tempo] in his playing before fast segments, so that the playing speed sounded faster than it was in reality. These are examples of selection (fewer pieces), optimization (more practice), and compensation (increased use of contrast in speed). (Baltes, 1993, p. 590)*

MEMORY

A common complaint among the elderly is the feeling that their ability to remember things is not as good as it used to be. On a number of tests of memory, adults over 60 *do* perform worse than young adults in their 20s (Craik, 1994; Hultsch et al., 1998). People experience memory deficits with advancing age, even when they have been highly educated and otherwise have good intellectual skills (Zelinski et al., 1993). Aging does *not* seem to diminish elderly individuals' ability to access their general knowledge store and personal information about events that occurred long ago. In a study of name and face recognition, middle-aged adults could identify 90 percent of their high school classmates in yearbooks 35 years after graduation, while older adults were still able to recognize 70 to 80 percent of their classmates some 50 years later (Bahrick et al., 1975). However, aging affects the processes that allow new information to be effectively organized, stored, and retrieved (Craik, 1994; Giambra & Arenberg, 1993).

As yet, researchers have been unable to develop a wholly adequate description of the mechanisms that underlie memory impairment in older adults (Craik, 1999). Some theories focus on differences between older and younger people in their efforts to organize and process information. Other theories point to elderly people's reduced ability to pay attention to information. Another type of theory looks to neurobiological changes in the brain systems that produce the physical memory traces. Note that these brain changes are not the same as the abnormal tangles of neural tissue and plaques that cause the memory loss of Alzheimer's disease (see Chapter 7). Researchers also believe that older adults' performance may be impaired by their very belief that their memory will be poor (Hertzog et al., 1990; Levy & Langer, 1994). Researchers continue to evaluate the relative contributions of each of these factors.

Let's now narrow our focus from general cognitive development to the more specific topic of the acquisition of language.

PUT YOURSELF TO THE TEST

◆ In Piaget's theory, what is the relationship between assimilation and accommodation?

◆ What aspects of cognitive development define each of Piaget's four stages?

◆ Why have advances in methods led to Piaget's ideas?

◆ Why do researchers believe some aspects of cognitive development occur within specific domains of knowledge?

◆ How has cross-cultural research changed some views of cognitive development?

◆ What are the gains and losses associated with adulthood and cognitive processes?

Acquiring Language

Here's a remarkable fact: By the time they are 6 years old, children can analyze language into its units of sound and meaning, use the rules they have discovered to combine sounds into words and words into meaningful sentences, and take an active part in coherent conversations. Children's remarkable language accomplishments have prompted most researchers to agree that the ability to learn language is biologically based—that you are born with an innate language capacity (Pinker, 1994). Even so, depending on where a child happens to be born, he or she may end up as a native speaker of any one of the world's 4,000 different languages. In addition, children are prepared to learn both spoken languages and gestural languages, like American Sign Language. This means that the innate predisposition to learn language must be both quite strong and quite flexible (Meier, 1991).

To explain how it is that infants are such expert language learners, we will describe the evidence that supports the claim of an innate language capacity. We will, however, also discuss the role that the environment plays—after all, children learn the particular languages that are being used in the world around them. **Table 10.4** outlines the various types of knowledge children must acquire for their particular signed or spoken language. You might review the language use section of Chapter 8 (pages 251 to 260) to remind yourself how adults put all these types of knowledge to use in fluent conversation.

◆ PERCEIVING SPEECH AND PERCEIVING WORDS

Imagine you are a newborn child, hearing a buzz of noise all around you. How do you start to understand that some of those sounds are relevant to communicating with other people? A child's first step in acquiring a particular language is to take note of the sound contrasts that are used meaningfully in that language. (For signed languages, the child must attend to contrasts in, for example, hand positions.) Each spoken language samples from the set of possible distinctions that can be produced by the human vocal tract; no language uses all of the speech–sound contrasts that can be made. The minimal meaningful units in a language are known as

phonemes. There are about 45 distinct phonemes in English. Imagine you heard someone speak the words *right* and *light*. If you are a native speaker of English, you would have no trouble hearing the difference—/r/ and /l/ are different phonemes in English. If, however, your only language experience was with Japanese, you would not be able to hear the difference between these two words, because /r/ and /l/ are not distinct phonemes in Japanese. Do English speakers acquire the ability to make this distinction, or do Japanese speakers lose it?

To answer this type of question, researchers needed to develop methods to obtain linguistic information from prelinguistic children.

PUTTING IDEAS TO THE TEST

Could You Perceive Hindi at Birth?

Using principles of operant conditioning we described in Chapter 5, researchers condition infants to turn their head toward a sound source when they detect a change from one speech sound to another. The reward that reinforces this behavior is an illuminated box that contains a clapping and drumming toy animal. The procedure ensures that, if the children detect changes, they are very likely to turn toward the sound source. To measure the children's ability to perceive a distinction, researchers monitor how frequently the children turn their heads when a change is present.

Janet Werker and her colleagues (Werker, 1991; Werker & Lalond, 1988) have used this technique to examine the innate basis of speech perception abilities—a version of the /r/–/l/ question we posed earlier. Werker studied sound distinctions that are used in Hindi, but not in English—distinctions that make it difficult for adult English speakers to learn Hindi. Werker and her colleagues measured the ability of infants learning English or Hindi, as well as adults who spoke English or Hindi, to hear the differences between the Hindi phonemes. She found that all the infants, regardless of which language they were learning, could hear the differences until the age of 8 months. However, of the infants older than 8 months and of the adults, only the Hindi speakers or speakers-to-be could hear the Hindi contrasts.

Research of this type strongly suggests that you started out with an innate ability to perceive sound contrasts that are important for spoken languages. However, you swiftly lose the ability to perceive some of the contrasts that are not present in the language you begin to acquire (Werker & Tees, 1999).

TABLE 10.4
The Structure of Language

Grammar is the field of study that seeks to describe the way language is structured and used. It includes several domains:

Phonology—the study of the sounds that are put together to form words.

A **phoneme** is the smallest unit of speech that distinguishes between any two utterances. For example, *b* and *p* distinguish *bin* from *pin*.

Phonetics is the study and classification of speech sounds.

Syntax—the way in which words are strung together to form sentences. For example, subject *(I)* + verb *(like)* + object *(you)* is standard English word order.

A **morpheme** is the minimum distinctive unit of grammar that cannot be divided without losing its meaning. The word *bins* has two morphemes, *bin* and *s*, indicating the plural.

Semantics—the study of the meanings of words and their changes over time.

Lexical meaning is the dictionary meaning of a word. Meaning is sometimes conveyed by the *context* of a word in a sentence ("Run *fast*" versus "Make the knot *fast*") or the *inflection* with which it is spoken (try emphasizing different words in *white house cat*).

Pragmatics—rules for participation in conversations; social conventions for communicating, sequencing sentences, and responding appropriately to others.

Along with this biological head start for speech perception, many children also get an environmental head start. When adults in many cultures speak to infants and young children, they use a special form of language that differs from adult speech: an exaggerated, high-pitched intonation known as **child-directed speech,** or less formally as *motherese* or *parentese*. The features that define child-directed speech appear in many but not all cultures (Fernald & Morikawa, 1993; Kitamura et al., 2002). Child-directed speech may help infants acquire language by keeping them interested in and attentive to the things that their parents say to them. The sound patterns of child-directed speech also emphasize emotional content, which might help forge an emotional bond between infants and their caregivers (Trainor et al., 2000).

At what age are children able to perceive the repetition of patterns of sounds—words—within the stream of speech directed to them? This is the first big step toward acquiring language: You can't learn that *doggie* has something to do with the shaggy thing in the corner until you recognize that the sound pattern *doggie* seems to recur in that shaggy thing's presence. Infants, on average, appear to gain the insight that repeated sounds have significance somewhere between ages 6 and $7\frac{1}{2}$ months (Jusczyk, 2003; Jusczyk & Aslin, 1995). For one special word, however, the breakthrough comes a couple of months early: Children at age $4\frac{1}{2}$ months already show a recognition preference for their own names (Mandel et al., 1995)!

◆ LEARNING WORD MEANINGS

Once you could detect the co-occurrence of sounds and experiences, you were prepared to start learning word meanings. There's no denying that children are excellent word learners. At around 18 months, children's word learning often takes off at an amazing rate. Researchers have called this phase the *naming explosion* because children begin to acquire new words, especially names for objects, at a rapidly increasing rate (see **Figure 10.7**). By the age of 6, the average child is estimated to understand 14,000 words (Templin, 1957). Assuming that most of these words are learned between the ages of 18 months and 6 years, this works out to about nine new words a day or almost one word per waking hour (Carey, 1978). How is this possible?

Imagine a straightforward situation in which a child and her father are walking through a park and the father points and says, "That's a doggie." The child must

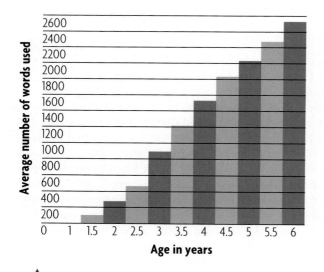

FIGURE 10.7

Children's Growth in Vocabulary

The number of words a child can use increases rapidly between the ages of 18 months and 6 years. This study shows children's average vocabularies at intervals of six months.

(Source: B. A. Moskowitz, 1978. The acquisition of language. Scientific American, Inc. All rights reserved. Reprinted by permission.)

decide to which piece of the world *doggie* applies. This is no easy feat (Quine, 1960). Perhaps *doggie* means "any creature with four legs" or "the animal's fur" or "the animal's bark" or any of the other large set of meanings that will be true each time someone points toward a dog. Given all the possibilities, how are children able to fix the meanings of individual words?

Researchers suggest that children act like scientists—developing *hypotheses* about what each new word might mean. You can, for example, see children's scientific minds actively at work when they *overextend* words, using them incorrectly to cover a wide range of objects. They may use the word *doggie* to refer to all animals, or the word *moon* to refer to all round objects, including clocks and coins. Other times, children might *underextend* a word—believing, for example, that *doggie* refers only to their own family dog.

The view that children form hypotheses, however, does not explain how children acquire particular meanings in particular contexts. Researchers have suggested that children's hypotheses are guided by expectations such as the *principle of contrast*. This principle suggests that differences in *forms* signal differences in *meaning*: When children hear new words, they should look for meanings that contrast with those for the words they already know (Clark, 2003). Suppose, for example, a father and daughter are watching a TV scene in which a kangaroo is jumping. The child knows the word *jump* but not the word *kangaroo*. Suppose the parent says, "Kangaroo!" What might happen next? Because the child knows *jump*, she supposes that her parent would just say *jump* if *kangaroo* just meant "jump"—different forms should signal contrasts in meaning. The child can now hypothesize that *kangaroo* must label the object rather than the action. She is on her way to acquiring a meaning for *kangaroo*. If you've spent time around small children, you've probably noticed the principle of contrast at work. For example, a child will often become upset if his mother calls his fire *engine* a fire *truck!*

◆ ACQUIRING GRAMMAR

To explain how children acquire meanings, we characterized children as scientists whose hypotheses are constrained by innate principles. We can use the same analogy to describe how children acquire the rules by which units of meaning are combined into larger units—in other words, grammar. The challenge for the child is that different languages follow different rules. For example, in English the typical ordering of units in a sentence is subject-verb-object, but in Japanese the ordering is subject-object-verb. Children must discover what order is present in the language being used around them. How do they do that?

Most researchers now believe that a large part of the answer resides in the human genome. Linguist **Noam Chomsky** (1965, 1975), for example, argued that children are born with mental structures that facilitate the comprehension and production of language. Some of the best evidence for such a biological basis for grammar comes from children who acquire complete grammatical structure in the absence of well-formed input. For example, researchers have studied deaf children whose hearing loss was sufficiently severe that they could not acquire spoken language but whose parents did not expose them to full-fledged signed languages such as American Sign Language (Goldin-Meadow, 2003). These children began to invent signing systems of their own and—despite the lack of environmental support for these invented languages—the gestural systems came to have regular, grammatical structure: "With or without an established language as a guide, children appear to be 'ready' to seek structure at least at word and sentence levels when developing systems for communication" (Goldin-Meadow & Mylander, 1990, p. 351).

But how can researchers go about specifying exactly what knowledge is innately given? The most productive approach to this question is to study language acquisition across many languages—*cross-linguistically.* By examining what is hard and what is easy for children to acquire across the world's many languages, researchers can determine what aspects of grammar are most likely to be supported by innate predispositions.

Here we arrive back at the child as scientist. Children bring innate constraints to the task of learning a particular language. **Dan Slobin** has defined these guidelines as a set of *operating principles* that together constitute the child's **language-making capacity.** According to Slobin's (1985) theory, the operating principles take the form of directives to the child. Here, for example, is an operating principle that helps children discover the words that go together to form a grammatical unit: "store together ordered sequences of word classes and functor classes that co-occur in the expression of a particular proposition type, along with a designation of the proposition type" (p. 1252). In simpler language, this operating principle suggests that children must keep track of the relationship between the order in which words appear and the meanings they express. Slobin derived the operating principles by summarizing across the data provided by a large number of other researchers, who examined a variety of different languages. We will, however, use English examples to demonstrate the principles at work.

Consider what English-speaking children can do when they begin, at about age 2, to use combinations of words—the *two-word stage.* Children's speech at this point has been characterized as *telegraphic* because it is filled with short, simple sequences using mostly nouns and verbs. Telegraphic speech lacks function words, such

Children develop linguistic fluency by listening to the speech patterns of those around them. What are the roles of nature and nurture in the acquisition of grammar?

as *the, and,* and *of,* which help express the relationships between words and ideas. For example, "Allgone milk" is a telegraphic message.

For adults to understand two-word utterances, they must know the context in which the words are spoken. "Tanya ball," for example, could mean, among other things, "Tanya wants the ball" or "Tanya throws the ball." Even so, children at the two-word stage show evidence that they have already acquired some knowledge of the grammar of English. Operating principles allow them to discover that word order is important in English and that the three critical elements are actor-action-object (subject-verb-object), arranged in that order. Evidence for this "discovery" comes when children misinterpret a sentence such as "Mary was followed by her little lamb to school" as *Mary* (actor) *followed* (action) *her lamb* (object) (see **Figure 10.8**). Over time, children must apply other operating principles to discover that there are exceptions to the actor-action-object rule.

Consider now an operating principle, which Slobin calls *extension,* that requires children to try to use the same unit of meaning, or *morpheme,* to mark the same concept. Examples of such concepts are possession, past tense, and continuing action. In English, each of these concepts is expressed by adding a grammatical morpheme to a content word, such as *-'s* (e.g., Maria*'s*), *-ed* (e.g., call*ed*), and *-ing* (e.g., laugh*ing*). Note how the addition of each of these sounds to a noun or verb changes its meaning.

Children use operating principles like extension to form hypotheses about how these morphemes work. Because, however, this principle requires that the child try to mark all cases in the same way, the error of

FIGURE 10.8

Acquiring Grammar

Many toddlers would interpret "Mary was followed by the lamb" and "Mary followed the lamb" to have identical meanings.

overregularization often results. For example, once children learn the past-tense rule (adding -*ed* to the verb), they add -*ed* to all verbs, forming words such as *doed* and *breaked*. As children learn the rule for plurals (adding the sound -*s* or -*z* to the end of a word), they again overextend the rule, creating words such as *foots* and *mouses*. Overregularization is an especially interesting error, because it usually appears *after* children have learned and used the correct forms of verbs and nouns. The children first use the correct verb forms (for example, *came* and *went*), apparently because they learned them as separate vocabulary items; but when they learn the general rule for the past tense, they extend it even to verbs that are exceptions to the rule—words that they previously used correctly. Over time, children use other operating principles to overcome this temporary overapplication.

Children's acquisition of language has a major impact on their ability to participate in social interactions. You should keep them in mind as we shift our focus now to social development across the life span.

PUT YOURSELF TO THE TEST

- What does research with infants suggest about children's ability to perceive language sounds?
- Why is it necessary for children to create hypotheses about word meanings?
- What is meant by the language-making capacity?
- What role do operating principles play in children's acquisition of grammar?

Social Development Across the Life Span

We have seen so far how radically you change as a physical and cognitive being from birth to older adulthood. In this section of the chapter we explore **social development:** how individuals' social interactions and expectations change across the life span. We will see that social and cultural environment interacts with biological aging to provide each period of the life span with its own special challenges and rewards.

As we discuss social development, it is particularly important for you to consider the way in which culture and environment affect certain aspects of our lives. For example, people who live in circumstances of economic hardship undergo types of stresses that are absent from the "normal" course of development (Crockett & Silbereisen, 2000; Leventhal & Brooks-Gunn, 2000). Current trends in the United States and in other countries throughout the world make it imperative for developmental psychologists to consider the difficult circumstances in which many children, adolescents, and adults are forced to live—circumstances that continually put their sanity, safety, and survival at risk (Dryfoss, 1990; Huston et al., 1994; Ladd & Cairns, 1996). U.S. culture also enforces different outcomes for men and for women and for individuals who belong to minority groups. For example, elderly women are more often economically disadvantaged than elderly men; elderly African American women are worse off even than elderly white women (Carstensen & Pasupathi, 1993). These differences are direct products of structural inequities in contemporary U.S. society.

When we draw conclusions about the "average" life course, you should keep in mind that culture dictates that some individuals will depart from this average; as we describe the psychological challenges facing the "ordinary" individual, bear in mind that many individuals face extraordinary challenges. It is the role of researchers to document the impact of contemporary problems—and to design interventions to alleviate their harshest consequences. Major reforms are clearly needed to institute and coordinate better health care, welfare programs, and social policy. Psychologists will play a role in helping to define what is in the best interest of families and their children (Scarr & Eisenberg, 1993). As we discuss social development, we will have several opportunities to revisit the impact of culture.

As you read the remainder of this chapter, you should keep in mind how the tasks of life are jointly determined by a biological accumulation of years and a social accumulation of cultural experiences. To begin our discussion of social development, we describe Erik

Erikson's life span theory, which makes explicit the challenges and rewards in each of life's major periods.

◆ ERIKSON'S PSYCHOSOCIAL STAGES

Erik Erikson (1963), who was trained by Sigmund Freud's daughter, Anna Freud, proposed that every individual must successfully navigate a series of **psychosocial stages,** each of which presented a particular conflict or crisis. Erikson identified eight stages in the life cycle. At each stage, a particular crisis comes into focus, as shown in **Table 10.5.** Although each conflict never completely disappears, it needs to be sufficiently resolved at a given stage if an individual is to cope successfully with the conflicts of later stages.

In Erikson's first stage an infant needs to develop a basic sense of *trust* in the environment through interaction with caregivers. Trust is a natural accompaniment to a strong attachment relationship with a parent who provides food, warmth, and the comfort of physical closeness. But a child whose basic needs are not met, who experiences inconsistent handling, lack of physical closeness and warmth, and the frequent absence of a caring adult, may develop a pervasive sense of mistrust, insecurity, and anxiety.

TABLE 10.5
Erikson's Psychosocial Stages

Approximate Age	Crisis	Adequate Resolution	Inadequate Resolution
$0-1\frac{1}{2}$	Trust vs. mistrust	Basic sense of safety	Insecurity, anxiety
$1\frac{1}{2}-3$	Autonomy vs. self-doubt	Perception of self as agent capable of controlling own body and making things happen	Feelings of inadequacy to control events
3–6	Initiative vs. guilt	Confidence in oneself as initiator, creator	Feelings of lack of self-worth
6–puberty	Competence vs. inferiority	Adequacy in basic social and intellectual skills	Lack of self-confidence, feelings of failure
Adolescent	Identity vs. role confusion	Comfortable sense of self as a person	Sense of self as fragmented; shifting, unclear sense of self
Early adult	Intimacy vs. isolation	Capacity for closeness and commitment to another	Feeling of aloneness, separation; denial of need for closeness
Middle adult	Generativity vs. stagnation	Focus of concern beyond oneself to family, society, future generations	Self-indulgent concerns; lack of future orientation
Later adult	Ego-integrity vs. despair	Sense of wholeness, basic satisfaction with life	Feelings of futility, disappointment

Erik Erikson's psychosocial stage model is a widely used tool for understanding human development over the life span. What crisis did Erikson suggest dominates individuals of your age?

With the development of walking and the beginnings of language, there is an expansion of a child's exploration and manipulation of objects (and sometimes people). With these activities should come a comfortable sense of *autonomy* and of being a capable and worthy person. Excessive restriction or criticism at this second stage may lead instead to self-doubts, while demands beyond the child's ability, as in too-early or too-severe toilet training, can discourage the child's efforts to persevere in mastering new tasks.

Toward the end of the preschool period, a child who has developed a basic sense of trust, first in the immediate environment and then in himself or herself, can now *initiate* both intellectual and motor activities. The ways that parents respond to the child's self-initiated activities either encourage the sense of freedom and self-confidence needed for the next stage or produce guilt and feelings of being an inept intruder in an adult world.

During the elementary school years, the child who has successfully resolved the crises of the earlier stages is ready to go beyond random exploring and testing to the systematic development of *competencies*. School and sports offer arenas for learning intellectual and motor skills, and interaction with peers offers an arena for developing social skills. Successful efforts in these pursuits lead to feelings of competence. Some youngsters, however, become spectators rather than performers or experience enough failure to give them a sense

of inferiority, leaving them unable to meet the demands of the next life stages.

Erikson believed that the essential crisis of adolescence is discovering one's true *identity* amid the confusion created by playing many different roles for the different audiences in an expanding social world. Resolving this crisis helps the individual develop a sense of a coherent self; failing to do so adequately may result in a self-image that lacks a central, stable core.

The essential crisis for the young adult is to resolve the conflict between *intimacy* and *isolation*—to develop the capacity to make full emotional, moral, and sexual commitments to other people. Making that kind of commitment requires that the individual compromise some personal preferences, accept some responsibilities, and yield some degree of privacy and independence. Failure to resolve this crisis adequately leads to isolation and the inability to connect to others in psychologically meaningful ways.

The next major opportunity for growth, which occurs during adult midlife, is known as *generativity*. People in their 30s and 40s move beyond a focus on self and partner to broaden their commitments to family, work, society, and future generations. Those people who haven't resolved earlier developmental tasks are still self-indulgent, question past decisions and goals, and pursue freedom at the expense of security.

The crisis in later adulthood is the conflict between *ego-integrity* and *despair*. Resolving the crises at each of the earlier stages prepares the older adult to look back without regrets and to enjoy a sense of wholeness. When previous crises are left unresolved, aspirations remain unfulfilled, and the individual experiences futility, despair, and self-depreciation.

You will see that Erikson's framework is very useful for tracking individuals' progress across the life span. We begin with childhood.

◆ SOCIAL DEVELOPMENT IN CHILDHOOD

Children's basic survival depends on forming meaningful, effective relationships with other people. **Socialization** is the lifelong process through which an individual's behavior patterns, values, standards, skills, attitudes, and motives are shaped to conform to those regarded as desirable in a particular society. This process involves many people—relatives, friends, teachers—and institutions—schools, houses of worship—that exert pressure on the individual to adopt socially approved values and standards of conduct. The family, however, is the most influential shaper and regulator of socialization. The concept of family itself is being transformed to recognize that many children grow up in circumstances that include either less (a single parent) or more (an extended household) than a mother, father, and siblings. Whatever the configuration, though, the family helps the individual form basic patterns of responsiveness to others—and these patterns, in turn, become the basis of the individual's life-long style of relating to other people.

ATTACHMENT

Social development begins with the establishment of a close emotional relationship between a child and a mother, father, or other regular caregiver. This intense, enduring, social–emotional relationship is called **attachment.** Because children are incapable of feeding or protecting themselves, the earliest function of attachment is to ensure survival. In some species, the infant automatically becomes *imprinted* on the first moving object it sees or hears (Johnson & Gottlieb, 1981). **Imprinting** occurs rapidly during a critical period of development and cannot easily be modified. The automaticity of imprinting can sometimes be problematic. Ethologist **Konrad Lorenz** demonstrated that young geese raised by a human will imprint on the human instead of on one of their own kind. In nature, fortunately, young geese mostly see other geese first.

Human infants rely less on instinctive attachment behaviors. Although many hospitals try to foster attachment by placing newborn babies on the mother's stomach, humans rely on more complex signals to solidify adult–child bonding. Infants' *proximity-promoting signals*—such as smiling, crying, and vocalizing—appear to be behaviors built in to signal others to respond to them (Campos et al., 1983). Ten-month-old infants, for example, use smiles selectively to produce an effect on their audience (Jones et al., 1991). Successful attachment, of course, depends not only on an infant's ability to emit signals such as smiles but also on an adult's tendency to respond to the signals. Who can resist a baby's smile? According to **John Bowlby** (1973), an influential theorist on human attachment, infants and adults are biologically predisposed to form attachments.

One of the most widely used research procedures for assessing attachment is the *Strange Situation Test,* developed by **Mary Ainsworth** and her colleagues (Ainsworth et al., 1978). In the first of several standard episodes, the child is brought into an unfamiliar room filled with toys. With the mother present, the child is encouraged to explore the room and to play. After several minutes, a stranger comes in, talks to the mother, and approaches the child. Next, the mother exits the room. After this brief separation, the mother returns, there is a reunion with her child, and the stranger leaves. The researchers record the child's behaviors at separation and reunion. Researchers have found that

Konrad Lorenz, the researcher who pioneered the study of imprinting, graphically demonstrates what can happen when young animals become imprinted on someone other than their mother. Why is imprinting important for many animal species?

children's responses on this test fall into three general categories (Ainsworth et al., 1978):

- *Securely attached* children show some distress when the parent leaves the room; seek proximity, comfort, and contact upon reunion; and then gradually return to play.
- *Insecurely attached–avoidant* children seem aloof and may actively avoid and ignore the parent upon her return.
- *Insecurely attached–ambivalent/resistant* children become quite upset and anxious when the parent leaves; at reunion, they cannot be comforted, and they show anger and resistance to the parent but, at the same time, express a desire for contact.

In middle-class United States samples, about 70 percent of babies are classified as securely attached; among the insecurely attached children, about 20 percent are classified as avoidant and 10 percent as resistant. Cross-cultural research on attachment relationships—in countries as diverse as Sweden, Israel, Japan, and China—reveals reasonable consistency in the prevalence of types of attachments (van IJzendoorn & Kroonenberg, 1988). In every country, the majority of children are securely attached; most of the cultural differences occur with respect to the prevalence of different types of insecure attachments. Researchers also find a high rate of agreement between attachment classifications made in the Strange Situation and those based on naturalistic observation of children and mothers in their homes (Pederson & Moran, 1996).

Why is it important for a child to develop a secure attachment to a parent or other caregiver?

Categorizations based on the Strange Situation Test have proven to be highly predictive of a child's later behavior in a wider variety of settings—particularly the overall division between children who are securely and insecurely attached. For example, longitudinal research revealed that children who showed secure or insecure behavior in the Strange Situation at 15 months differed widely in their school behavior at age 8 to 9 years (Bohlin et al., 2000). Those children who had been securely attached at 15 months were more popular and less socially anxious than their peers who had been insecurely attached. Similar continuity from the quality of attachment to later years has been demonstrated in 10-year-olds (Urban et al., 1991) and adolescents (Weinfield et al., 1997). This suggests that the quality of attachment, as revealed in the Strange Situation, really does have long-term importance (Stams et al., 2002). We will see in Chapter 16 that researchers also use attachment measures to predict the quality of adults' loving relationships.

You may wonder *why* the attachment relationship matters so late into life. Beginning with John Bowlby (1973), theorists have suggested that the experiences that give rise to an attachment relationship provide individuals with a lifelong schema for social relationships called an *internal working model* (Bretherton, 1996). An internal working model is a memory structure that gathers together a child's history of interactions with his or her caretakers—the interactions that yielded a particular pattern of attachment. The internal working model provides a template with respect to which an individual generates expectations about future social interactions. Individuals with secure attachments expect to have social relationships in which people are available to them and treat them as worthy of care; individuals with insecure attachments expect to have social relationships in which other people are unresponsive and unavailable. As we shall see in Chapter 16, people's expectations about social interactions can have an impact on how those interactions come to pass. For that reason, expectations based on internal working models help explain the importance of attachment relationships across the life span.

We have seen that attachment relationships are quite important in young lives. Secure attachment to adults who offer dependable social support enables the child to learn a variety of prosocial behaviors, to take risks, to venture into novel situations, and to seek and accept intimacy in personal relationships. We turn now to the question of what parents can do to help bring about these critical secure attachments.

PARENTING STYLES AND PARENTING PRACTICES

Children bring individual temperaments to their interactions with their parents: Parents with more than one child often note how different their children seemed from their very earliest days. Children's temperaments may make parents' best (or worst) efforts at parenting have unexpected consequences. Researchers recognize that children's temperaments and parents' behaviors each influence the other to yield developmental outcomes such as the quality of attachment relationships: As much as parents change their children, children change their parents (Collins et al., 2000).

Even so, researchers have located a **parenting style** that is generally most beneficial. This style resides at the intersection of the two dimensions of *demandingness* and *responsiveness* (Maccoby & Martin, 1983): "Demandingness refers to the parent's willingness to act as a socializing agent, whereas responsiveness refers to the parent's recognition of the child's individuality" (Darling & Steinberg, 1993, p. 492). As shown in **Figure 10.9,** *authoritative* parents make appropriate demands on their children—they demand that their children conform to appropriate rules of behavior—but are also responsive to their children—they keep channels of communication open to foster their children's ability to regulate themselves (Gray & Steinberg, 1999). This authoritative style is most likely to produce an effective parent–child bond. The contrast, as seen in Figure 10.9, is to parenting styles that are *authoritarian*—parents apply discipline with little attention to the child's autonomy—or *indulgent*—parents are responsive, but they fail to help children learn

     <www.ablongman.com/gerrig17e>

FIGURE 10.9

A Classification of Parenting Styles

Parenting styles can be classified with respect to the two dimensions of demandingness— the parent's willingness to act as a socializing agent—and responsiveness—the parent's recognition of the child's individuality. The authoritative style is most likely to produce an effective parent–child bond.

	Parent's responsiveness	
	Accepting Responsive Child-centered	*Rejecting Unresponsive Parent-centered*
Demanding, controlling	Authoritative-reciprocal High in bidirectional communication	Authoritarian Power assertive
Undemanding, low in control attempts	Indulgent	Neglecting, ignoring, indifferent, uninvolved

Parent's demandingness

about the structure of social rules in which they must live—or *neglecting*—parents neither apply discipline nor are they responsive to their children's individuality.

Even parents with the same overall styles put different priorities on the *socialization goals* they consider important for the children. **Parenting practices** arise in response to particular goals (Darling & Steinberg, 1993). Thus authoritative parents who wish their children to do well in school may create a home environment in which the children come to understand why their parents value that as a goal—and may strive to do well in school because they are effectively socialized toward that goal. However, because not all authoritative parents value school success, you could not predict children's school performance based only on their parents' style (Steinberg et al., 1992). Parents' general attitudes and specific behaviors are both important for charting their children's life course.

A close interactive relationship with loving adults is a child's first step toward healthy physical growth and normal socialization. As the original attachment to the primary caregiver extends to other family members, they too become models for new ways of thinking and behaving. From these early attachments, children develop the ability to respond to their own needs and to the needs of others.

CONTACT COMFORT AND SOCIAL EXPERIENCE

What do children obtain from the attachment bond? Sigmund Freud and other psychologists argued that babies become attached to their parents because the parents provide them with food—their most basic physical need. This view is called the *cupboard theory* of attachment. If the cupboard theory were correct, children should thrive as long as they are adequately fed. Does this seem right?

Harry Harlow (1965) did not believe that the cupboard theory explained the importance of attachment. He set out to test the cupboard theory against his own hypothesis that infants might also attach to those who provide **contact comfort** (Harlow & Zimmerman, 1958). Harlow separated macaque monkeys from their mothers at birth and placed them in cages, where they had access to two artificial "mothers": a wire one and a terry cloth one. Harlow found that the baby monkeys nestled close to the terry cloth mother and spent little time on the wire one. They did this even when only the wire mother gave milk! The baby monkeys also used the cloth mother as a source of comfort when frightened and as a base of operations when exploring new stimuli. When a fear stimulus (for example, a toy bear beating a drum) was introduced, the baby monkeys would run to the cloth mother. When novel and intriguing stimuli were introduced, the baby monkeys would gradually venture out to explore and then return to the terry cloth mother before exploring further.

Further studies by Harlow and his colleagues found that the monkeys' formation of a strong attachment to the mother substitute was not sufficient for healthy social development. At first, the experimenters thought the

When psychologists first began to study social development, many of the infants on whom they based their conclusions stayed home full time with their mothers. However, societal constraints have shifted over the last few decades, making it necessary for much larger numbers of mothers to work outside the home. As a consequence, many children spend long hours of even the earliest part of their lives outside the influence of their parents. Researchers have reacted to this shift by addressing a pair of questions: In what ways is day care better or worse for the developing child? What is the optimal form of day care?

We have already provided the context in which you can interpret the first question: If the attachments between children and mothers are so critical, shouldn't anything that disrupts the formation of those attachments—such as day care—be necessarily bad for the children? The answer to this question is, "On balance, *no*" (Scarr, 1998). To arrive at this answer, researchers typically made comparisons between children who stayed at home and those who were placed in day care, on measures of both intellectual and social development. Researchers have found that children placed in day care are often at an *advantage* with respect to these measures, primarily because day care provides more opportunities (Burchinal et al., 1997; Clarke-Stewart, 1991, 1993). Intellectual development can benefit from a greater range of educational and play activities; social development can benefit from a wider variety of social interactions than would be available in the home.

There are two reasons, however, that the answer "no" must be qualified by "on

How Does Day Care Affect Children's Development?
Christine Halsey
Boston College

balance." One is that there are individual differences in the way children respond to care outside the home. The second is that day care takes many forms. Researchers, therefore, have turned their attention away from the "better or worse" question toward the issue of what constitutes quality care for particular children (Sagi et al., 2002; Zaslow, 1991).

Alison Clarke-Stewart (1993), an expert on day care, has summarized the research literature to provide a series of guidelines for quality day care. Some of her recommendations relate to the physical comfort of the children:

- The day-care center should be physically comfortable and safe.

- There should be at least one caretaker for every six or seven children (more for children under age 3).

Other recommendations cover educational and psychological aspects of the day-care curriculum:

- Children should have a free choice of activities intermixed with explicit lessons.

- Children should be taught social problem-solving skills.

Clarke-Stewart has also suggested that day-care providers should share the qualities of good parents:

- Caregivers should be responsive to the children's needs and actively involved in their activities.

- Caregivers should not put undue restrictions on the children.

- Caregivers should have sufficient flexibility to recognize differences among the needs of individual children.

If these guidelines are followed, quality day care can be provided to all children whose parents work outside the home. For day care to be truly effective, however, there will have to be changes in the general attitudes of society. First, people must accept the reality that increasing numbers of children will be experiencing day care—and society must direct its resources toward the goal of making all day care quality day care (Fuller et al., 1996; Scarr et al., 1990). Second, people must work to eliminate the stigma associated with "working motherhood" and day care itself (Hoffman, 1989). As psychologists spread the message that day care does not harm, and may even enhance, children's development, parents should feel less distress about the necessity of a dual-career family. Such a reduction in stress could only improve the child's overall psychological environment.

How did Harlow demonstrate the importance of contact comfort for normal social development?

monkeys and for maintaining a high social status in the group. Let's see now what lessons research with monkeys holds for human deprivation.

HUMAN DEPRIVATION

Tragically, human societies have sometimes created circumstances in which children are deprived of contact comfort. Many studies have shown that a lack of close, loving relationships in infancy affects physical growth and even survival. In 1915, a doctor at Johns Hopkins Hospital reported that, despite adequate physical care, 90 percent of the infants admitted to orphanages in Baltimore died within the first year. Studies of hospitalized infants over the next 30 years found that, despite adequate nutrition, the children often developed respiratory infections and fevers of unknown origin, failed to gain weight, and showed general signs of physiological deterioration (Bowlby, 1969; Sherrod et al., 1978). Another study of infants in foundling homes in the United States and Canada reported evidence of severe emotional and physical disorders as well as high mortality rates, despite good food and medical care (Spitz & Wolf, 1946).

Negative environments also affect social development. In one study of ten abused toddlers, ages 1 to 3 years, researchers found that the children did not respond appropriately when a peer was in distress. When another child is upset and crying, toddlers will normally show concern, empathy, or sadness. By contrast, the abused children were more likely to respond with fear, anger, or physical attacks (Main & George, 1985). Another study examined the relationship between childhood and adolescent physical and sexual abuse and later-life mental health outcomes. In a sample of 375 young adults, nearly 11 percent reported having endured some type of abuse. Of that group, about 80 percent presented symptoms of one or more psychiatric disorders (Silverman et al., 1996).

Instances of child abuse provide psychologists with a very important agenda: to determine what types of interventions are in the best interest of the child. In the United States, roughly 500,000 children and youths have been removed from their homes and placed in some type of government-funded setting (e.g., a foster home or group residence) (Shealy, 1995). Are these children always happy to be removed from their abusive homes? The answer is complex, because even abused children have often formed an attachment to their caretakers: The children may retain loyalty to their natural family and hope that everything could be put right if they were allowed to return. This is one reason that much research attention is focused on designing intervention programs to reunite families (Gillespie et al., 1995; Leathers, 2002).

young monkeys with terry cloth mothers were developing normally, but a very different picture emerged when it was time for the female monkeys who had been raised in this way to become mothers. Monkeys who had been deprived of chances to interact with other responsive monkeys in their early lives had trouble forming normal social and sexual relationships in adulthood.

Primate researcher **Stephen Suomi** (1999; Champoux et al., 1995) has shown that putting emotionally vulnerable infant monkeys in the foster care of supportive mothers virtually turns their lives around. Suomi notes that monkeys put in the care of mothers known to be particularly loving and attentive are transformed from marginal members of the monkey troop into bold, outgoing young males who are among the first to leave the troop at puberty to work their way into a new troop. This *cross-fostering* gives them coping skills and information essential for recruiting support from other

In this section, you have seen how experiences during childhood have an impact on later social development. We now shift our focus to later periods of life, beginning with adolescence.

◆ SOCIAL DEVELOPMENT IN ADOLESCENCE

Earlier in the chapter, we defined adolescence by physical and cognitive changes. In this section, those changes will serve as background to social experiences. Because the individual has reached a certain level of physical and mental maturity, new social and personal challenges present themselves. We will first consider the general experience of adolescence and then turn to the individual's changing social world.

THE EXPERIENCE OF ADOLESCENCE

The traditional view of adolescence predicts a uniquely tumultuous period of life, characterized by extreme mood swings and unpredictable, difficult behavior: "storm and stress." This view can be traced back to Romantic writers of the late eighteenth and early nineteenth centuries, such as Goethe. The storm-and-stress conception of adolescence was strongly propounded by **G. Stanley Hall,** the first psychologist of the modern era to write at length about adolescent development (1904). Following Hall, the major proponents of this view have been psychoanalytic theorists working within the Freudian tradition (for example, Blos, 1965; Freud, 1946, 1958). Some of them have argued that not only is extreme turmoil a normal part of adolescence but that failure to exhibit such turmoil is a sign of arrested development. **Anna Freud** wrote that "to be normal during the adolescent period is by itself abnormal" (1958, p. 275).

Two early pioneers in cultural anthropology, **Margaret Mead** (1928) and **Ruth Benedict** (1938), argued that the storm-and-stress theory is not applicable to many non-Western cultures. They described cultures in which children gradually take on more and more adult responsibilities without any sudden stressful transition or period of indecision and turmoil. It was not until large studies were undertaken of representative adolescents in Western society, however, that the turmoil theory finally began to be widely questioned within psychology. The results of such studies have been consistent: Few adolescents experience the inner turmoil and unpredictable behavior ascribed to them (Offer & Schonert-Reichl, 1992). **Table 10.6** summarizes key findings from a study of

the psychological adjustment of over 20,000 adolescents (Offer et al., 1981a).

Unfortunately, those adolescents who experience maladjustment are likely to continue doing so as they move into adulthood (Mahoney et al., 2001; Offer et al., 1998). Consider the following research that points to a strong link between adolescent conduct problems and subsequent adult criminality.

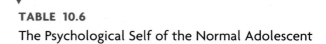

PUTTING IDEAS TO THE TEST

Consequences of Adolescent Aggressiveness

A large-scale longitudinal study of adolescents (ages 10 to 13) attending school in a typical Swedish town compared their conduct status (from teachers' reports) and biological functioning with the likelihood of their having criminal records or other adjustment problems as young adults (ages 18 to 26). Among the boys, those who showed early aggressiveness and restlessness (hyperactivity) were significantly more likely to develop into adults who would commit registered criminal offenses. In addition, a more severe pattern of early maladjustment was correlated with other adult adjustment problems as well, such as alcohol abuse and being under psychiatric care. **Figure 10.10** shows the extent to which early aggressiveness is linked to adult criminality (Magnusson, 1987; Magnusson & Bergman, 1990).

TABLE 10.6

The Psychological Self of the Normal Adolescent

Item	Percentage of Adolescents Endorsing Each Item
I feel relaxed under normal circumstances.	91
I enjoy life.	90
Usually I control myself.	90
I feel strong and healthy.	86
Most of the time I am happy.	85
Even when I am sad I can enjoy a good joke.	83

<www.ablongman.com/gerrig17e>

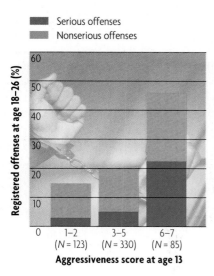

Registered offenses at age 18–26 (%)

60
50
40
30
20
10
0

1–2   3–5   6–7
(N = 123)   (N = 330)   (N = 85)

Aggressiveness score at age 13

FIGURE 10.10

Adolescent Aggression annd Adult Criminality

This chart shows the number of individuals who achieved various ratings of aggressiveness at the age of 13 and the percentages of those individuals who were registered for criminal offenses at the ages of 18 to 26. An offense was regarded as serious if the expected legal sanction was at least one month imprisonment according to Swedish law.

Adolescent problems should not, therefore, be incorrectly attributed to the myth of "storm and stress." Particularly because adolescents are at high risk for suicide (Garland & Zigler, 1993), signs of disturbance should be treated with sincere attention by all those in contact with such adolescents.

Now that we've considered the general adolescent experience, let's shift to aspects of identity formation in adolescence. In Erikson's description of the life span, the essential task of adolescence is to discover one's true identity. We will see the roles that social relationships and future goals play in the formation of this sense of identity.

SOCIAL RELATIONSHIPS

Much of the study of social development in adolescence focuses on the changing roles of family (or adult caretakers) and friends (Bukowski et al., 1998; Galambos et al., 2003). We have already seen that attachments to adults form soon after birth. Children also begin to have friends at very young ages. Adolescence, however, marks the first period in which peers appear to compete with parents to shape a person's attitudes and behaviors.

Through interaction with peers, adolescents gradually define the social component of their developing identities, determining the kinds of people they choose to be and the kinds of relationships they choose to pursue (Berndt, 1992; Hartup, 1996). For this reason, adolescents and their friends are often tightly clustered—for example, with respect to their patterns of drug use (Allen et al., 2003; Dinges & Oetting, 1993).

Parents and their adolescent children must also weather a transition in their relationship from one in which a parent has unquestioned authority to one in which the adolescent is granted reasonable independence, or *autonomy*, to make important decisions (Allen & Land, 1999; Holmbeck & O'Donnell, 1991). This transition can be difficult for parents who wish to acknowledge an adolescent's progress toward adulthood by allowing dissent—without allowing improper choices to compromise his or her future.

PUTTING IDEAS TO THE TEST

Adolescent–Parent Conflicts in Hong Kong

Are the types of conflicts adolescents have with their parents consistent across cultures? Researchers were interested in studying conflicts among Chinese adolescents in Hong Kong, because Chinese culture puts relatively less emphasis on *autonomy* than do Western cultures. (We will expand on this cultural difference in later chapters.) Seventh, ninth, and twelfth graders were asked to generate lists of actual conflicts they had had with their parents, as well as the frequency and severity of those conflicts. The students were also asked to provide justifications for their positions in the conflicts: "Why do you think it is OK for you to do (not do) [this activity]?" The data revealed impressive consistency with the experiences of their Western peers—these Chinese adolescents tended to have conflicts of moderate frequency and severity, mostly with their mothers, about everyday issues such as using the telephone and watching TV. Furthermore, the adolescents' justifications for the conflicts largely reflected the need to assert autonomy or forge an individual identity by making their own decisions. Thus, even in a culture that relatively de-emphasizes individual autonomy, adolescents' conflicts with their parents still often center on the desire to establish a unique identity (Yau & Smetana, 1996).

This study reinforces the idea that parent–child relationships will undergo changes over the period of adolescence as children become less reliant on their parents' authority. Although friendships change somewhat over the adolescent years (Shulman, 1993), these changes reflect greater mutual dependence between friends rather than changes in the equality of the relationship. Parent–child relationships thus may have more built-in potential for conflict than peer relationships.

Identity development ultimately requires the adolescent to establish independent commitments that are sensitive to parental and peer environments but are not mere reflections of either. What is important is that adolescents find some consistent sources of social support in their environment (DuBois et al., 2002; Fuligni, 1997). Such social support will enable the adolescent to plan for the future, the topic to which we now move.

FUTURE GOALS

Adolescence is the period in which individuals are expected to begin to answer seriously the ever-present question, "What are you going to be when you grow up?" The "What are you going to be?" question itself reflects the common assumption that individuals' identities are fixed, in part, by their goals. The selection, for example, of a future occupation involves tasks central to identity formation: appraisal of one's abilities and interests, awareness of realistic alternatives, and the ability to make and follow through on a choice. Adolescents have concerns about the future at both the personal and societal levels: They worry about their occupations and families as well as global threats of economic collapse or nuclear war (Nurmi, 1991). They also have a keen sense of how their futures should unfold with age. First, educational goals must be met, followed by occupational goals, and finally family goals. At each juncture, goals are shaped by the constraints of gender roles and family context and available resources.

Of course, not all adolescents have the same expectations about what the future will hold. Researchers have studied the social and personal processes that help define how adolescents set goals for themselves.

The Social Context of Aspirations and Expectations

A group of researchers examined the occupational aspirations and expectations for boys from low-income and middle-income settings: *Aspirations* refer to the job the boys would have if they could have "any job they wanted" when they grew up; *expectations* refer to the job the boys thought they would "probably get" when they grew up. Data were collected from boys in grades 2, 4, 6, and 8 who attended schools either in poor minority neighborhoods or affluent white neighborhoods. **Figure 10.11** displays aspirations and expectations with respect to white-collar occupations (e.g., lawyers or doctors). Although it may not be surprising that inner-city children had lower expectations, note that they also had lower aspirations across this age range. That is, the inner city children didn't even admit to wanting jobs that they didn't believe they could obtain (Cook et al., 1996).

How much influence do peers have during adolescence?

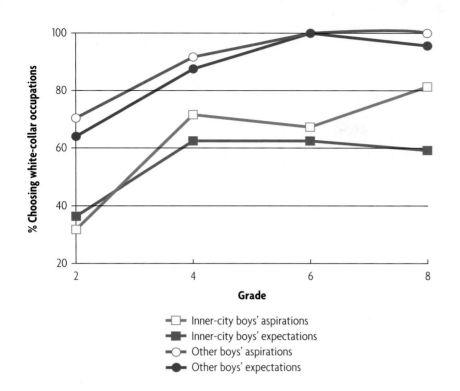

FIGURE 10.11

Career Aspirations and Expectations

Boys from low-income (inner-city boys) and middle-income (other boys) settings were asked what type of job they would most like to have—their aspirations—and what type of job they thought they would really obtain—their expectations. The results show that the inner-city boys not only have lower expectations, but they also have less ambitious aspirations.

Clearly, if adolescents do not aspire to jobs they will not obtain them. What can be done to change inner-city children's aspirations and expectations? The data from this study suggested that children's expectations were very much influenced by their educational expectations—how far they believed they could get in school. To change these inner-city students' sense of their futures could, therefore, ultimately require educational reforms that would enable all students to believe in the importance and efficacy of their schoolwork.

Choices about educational and occupational goals made in later adolescence can have a profound effect on future options. But, as with all aspects of identity, goal formation is best conceived of in the context of the whole life cycle. The key is a flexibility and a willingness to explore new directions based on a sense of self-confidence developed during successful negotiation through the demands of adolescence. These successes in adolescence set the stage for adult development.

◆ SOCIAL DEVELOPMENT IN ADULTHOOD

Erikson defined two tasks of adulthood to be intimacy and generativity. Freud identified the needs of adulthood to be *Lieben und Arbeiten,* or love and work. Abraham Maslow (1968, 1970) described the needs of

this period of life as love and belonging, which, when satisfied, develop into the needs for success and esteem. Other theorists label these needs as affiliation or social acceptance and achievement or competence needs. The shared core of these theories is that adulthood is a time in which both social relationships and personal accomplishments take on special priority. In this section, we track these themes across the breadth of adulthood.

INTIMACY

Erikson described **intimacy** as the capacity to make a full commitment—sexual, emotional, and moral—to another person. Intimacy, which can occur in both friendships and romantic relationships, requires openness, courage, ethical strength, and usually some compromise of one's personal preferences. Research has consistently confirmed Erikson's supposition that social intimacy is a prerequisite for a sense of psychological well-being across the adult life stages (Fernandez-Ballesteros, 2002; Ishii-Kuntz, 1990). **Figure 10.12** demonstrates that interactions with family and friends trade off over this long span of years to provide a fairly constant level in people's reports of their own well-being. The changes in these sources of support reflect, in part, the life events that are typically correlated with each age. Let's examine these correlations.

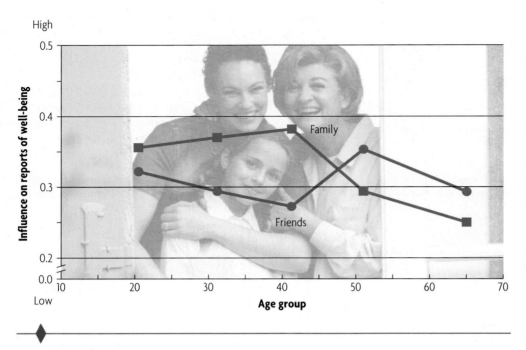

High

FIGURE 10.12

The Effects of Social Interaction on Well-Being

Across the life span, social interactions with family and friends trade off to provide a fairly constant level of individuals' reports of well-being.

Young adulthood is the period in which many people enter into marriage or other stable relationships. The group that counts as family thus will ordinarily grow larger. Historically, most research on relationships and families across adulthood focused on the "standard" configurations of a mother, father, and a house full of children. However, as the realities of people's families have changed, researchers have tried to document and understand the consequences of those changes (Mason et al., 1998). For example, studies now focus on the ways in which homosexual couples enter into and sustain long-term relationships (James & Murphy, 1998). Research suggests that the strategies heterosexuals and homosexuals use to maintain relationships over time have much in common: Both types of couples try to remain close by, for example, sharing tasks and activities together (Haas, 2003; Haas & Stafford, 1998). However, to combat a lack of social acceptance for gay and lesbian relationships, homosexual couples also need to take special measures to maintain relationships, such as being publicly "out" as a couple. Some heterosexual couples also must persevere in the face of continuing barriers to social acceptance; research suggests that interracial couples also face types of prejudices that have a negative impact on the ability

of relationships to endure (Chan & Wethington, 1998; Gaines & Agnew, 2003).

Each of these types of relationships increases the role of family in adults' social lives. Families also grow when individuals decide to include children in their lives. What may surprise you, however, is that the birth of children can often pose a threat to the overall happiness of a couple. Why might that be? Researchers have focused on differences in the way that men and women make the transition to parenthood in heterosexual relationships (Cowan & Cowan, 1998, 2000). In contemporary Western society, marriages are more often founded on notions of equality between men and women than was true in the past. However, children's births can have the effect of pushing husbands and wives in the direction of more traditional gender roles. The wife may feel too much of the burden of child care; the husband may feel too much pressure to support a family. The net effect may be that, following the birth of a child, the marriage changes in ways that both spouses find to be negative (Cowan et al., 1985). Although research on gay male and lesbian couples raising children is far more limited, that research suggests that, as you might expect, concerns about gender roles with respect to parenting have

Statistically speaking, which spouse is likely to outlive the other? What effect might the quality of the marriage have on this outcome?

Predicting Who Will Divorce

In 1983, researchers began a longitudinal study of married couples. After following the couples for 14 years, the researchers were able to form some generalizations about why some of the couples remained married while some had been divorced (Gottman & Levenson, 2000). During the initial data collection in 1983, the couples visited the laboratory to have conversations on a neutral topic (events of the day) and a conflictual topic (each couple's area of continuing disagreement). Trained research assistants viewed tapes of these conversations and evaluated the extent of positive and negative affect—emotional content—the spouses expressed toward each other. Some couples discussed difficult topics with a sense of humor whereas other couples discussed similar topics with put-downs and complaints. The affective content of their discussions was highly predictive of the couples' fates. From the sample of 79 couples, 11 percent got divorced relatively early—after, on average, 7.4 years after marriage. On the whole, those couples had shown high levels of *negative* affect in their discussions of conflictual topics. There were also 16 percent of the couples who divorced relatively late—after, on average, 13.9 years. On the whole, those had shown low levels of *positive* affect toward each other.

less of a negative impact on homosexual relationships (Patterson, 2002).

For many heterosexual couples, satisfaction with the marriage continues to decline because of conflicts as the child or children pass through their adolescent years. Contrary to the cultural stereotype, many parents look forward to the time when their youngest child leaves home and leaves them with an "empty nest" (White & Edwards, 1990). Parents may enjoy their children most when they are no longer under the same roof (Levenson et al., 1993). Have we discouraged you from having children? We certainly hope not! Our goal, as always, is to make you aware of research that can help you anticipate and interpret the patterns in your own life.

If marriages are, on the whole, happier when the spouses reach late adulthood, should everyone try to stay married late into life? Researchers would like to be able to determine which couples are fundamentally mismatched—with respect, for example, to their patterns of interactions—and which couples could avoid being among the approximately two-thirds of marriages that now end in divorce (Gottman, 1994; Karney & Bradbury, 1995).

Why did this pattern emerge? The researchers suggested that "intense marital conflict likely makes it difficult to stay in the marriage for long, but its absence makes marriage somewhat more acceptable. Nonetheless, the absence of positive affect takes its toll" (Gottman & Levenson, 2000, p. 743). You can probably find both types of relationships around you: Those in which couples fight constantly and those in which couples are calm but do not respond positively to each other.

When individuals stay together late into life, one member of the couple most often must cope with the death of a spouse. When we contemplate the death of a spouse or partner, we have come back to one reason that the balance of social interactions shifts somewhat from family to friends late in life (see Figure 10.12). A stereotype about late adulthood is that individuals become more socially isolated. While it is true that older individuals may interact socially with fewer people, the nature of those interactions changes so that intimacy needs continue to be met. This trade-off is captured by the **selective social interaction theory.** This view suggests that, as people age, they become more selective in choosing social partners who satisfy their emotional needs. According to **Laura Carstensen** (1991, 1998), selective interaction may be a practical means by which people can regulate their emotional experiences and conserve their physical energy. Older adults remain vitally involved with some people—particularly family members and longtime friends.

Let's conclude this section where we began, with the idea that social intimacy is a prerequisite for psychological well-being. What matters most is not the quantity of social interaction but the quality (particularly, in U.S. culture, for women). As you grow into older adulthood, you will begin to protect your need for intimacy by selecting those individuals who provide the most direct emotional support.

Let's turn now to a second aspect of adult development, generativity.

GENERATIVITY

Those people who have established an appropriate foundation of intimate relationships are most often able to turn their focus to issues of **generativity.** This is a commitment beyond oneself to family, work, society, or future generations—typically a crucial step in development in one's 30s and 40s (McAdams & de St. Aubin, 1998). An orientation toward the greater good allows adults to establish a sense of psychological well-being that offsets any longing for youth.

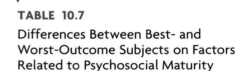

CLASSIC
PUTTING IDEAS TO THE TEST

Life Outcomes and Generativity

George Vaillant studied the personality development of 95 highly intelligent men through interviews and observations over a 30-year period following their graduation from college in the mid-1930s. Many of the men showed great changes over time, and their later behavior was often quite different from their behavior in college. The interviews covered the topics of physical health, social relationships, and career achievement. At the end of the 30-year period, the 30 men with the best outcomes and the 30 with the worst outcomes were identified and compared (see **Table 10.7**). By middle life, the best-outcome men were carrying out generativity tasks, assuming responsibility for others, and contributing in some way to the world. Their maturity even seemed to be associated with the adjustment of their children—the more mature fathers were better able to give children the help they needed in adjusting to the world (Vaillant, 1977).

This study illustrates the prerequisites for generativity: For the best-outcome men, other aspects of their lives were sufficiently stable to allow them to direct their resources outwards, toward generations to come. When asked what it means to be well adjusted, middle-aged adults (average age 52) and older adults (average age 74) gave the same response as their most frequent answer. Both groups suggested that adjustment relies on being "others oriented"—on being a caring, compassionate person and having good relationships (Ryff, 1989). This is the essence of generativity.

Let us also note that most older adults looking back on their lives do so with a degree of well-being that is unchanged from earlier years of adulthood (Carstensen & Freund, 1994). As we have seen with respect to social relationships, late adulthood is a time when goals are shifted; priorities change when the future does not apparently flow as freely. Across that change in priorities, however, older adults preserve their sense of the value of their lives. Erikson defined the last crisis of adulthood to be the conflict between ego-integrity and despair. The data suggest that few adults look back over their lives with despair. Most older adults review their

TABLE 10.7

Differences Between Best- and Worst-Outcome Subjects on Factors Related to Psychosocial Maturity

	Best Outcomes (30 Men)	Worst Outcomes (30 Men)
Personality integration rated in bottom fifth percentile during college	0%	33%
Dominated by mother in adult life	0%	40%
Bleak friendship patterns at 50	0%	57%
Failure to marry by 30	3%	37%
Pessimism, self-doubt, passivity, and fear of sex at 50	3%	50%
Childhood environment poor	17%	47%
Current job has little supervisory responsibility	20%	93%
Subjects whose career choice reflected identification with father	60%	27%
Children's outcome described as good or excellent	66%	23%

<www.ablongman.com/gerrig17e>

lives—and look to the future—with a sense of wholeness and satisfaction.

THE CULTURAL CONSTRUCTION OF LATE ADULTHOOD

Our review of research on the long period of adulthood has emphasized continuities rather than discontinuities; there is no moment at which an individual suddenly becomes old. Even so, it is clear that there are strong cultural beliefs and expectations about the last periods of life (Nelson, 2002). Researchers have documented these expectations by gathering evidence of the stereotypes college-age adults have about the members of their grandparents' generation. These studies suggest that young adults have more than one stereotype of older adults (Hummert, 1999). Attitudes toward older adults vary with these stereotypes. Young adults have relatively positive attitudes toward a "perfect grandparent" and relatively negative attitudes toward a "despondent" older person. Even so, the overall stereotype is negative, particularly with respect to declines in physical attractiveness and mental competence (Kite & Wagner, 2002).

One consequence of this negative stereotype is the particular prejudice against older people, called **ageism.** Ageism leads to discrimination against the elderly that limits their opportunities, isolates them, and fosters negative self-images. Psychologists themselves are often guilty of ageism in the language they use (Schaie, 1993). A survey of 139 undergraduate texts written over 40 years revealed that many failed to cover late adulthood or presented stereotypical views of the elderly (Whitbourne & Hulicka, 1990). But a more dramatic instance of ageism is shown in the personal experiences of a reporter who deliberately "turned old" for a while.

PUTTING IDEAS TO THE TEST

The Experience of Ageism

Pat Moore disguised herself as an 85-year-old woman and wandered the streets of over 100 American cities to discover what it means to be old in the United States. Clouded contact lenses and earplugs diminished her vision and hearing; bindings on her legs made walking difficult; and taped fingers had the dexterity of arthritic ones. This "little old lady" struggled to survive in a world designed for the young, strong, and agile. She couldn't open jars, hold pens, read labels, or climb up bus steps. The world of speed, noise, and shadows frightened her. When she needed assistance, few ever offered it. She was often ridiculed for being old and vulnerable and was even violently attacked by a gang of adolescents (Moore, 1990).

Moore's experience reinforces the idea that society, in both the physical and social sense, conspires against the elderly.

We have worked our way through the life span by considering social and personal aspects of childhood, adolescence, and adulthood. To close out the chapter, we will trace two particular domains in which experience changes over time, the domains of gender development and moral development.

PUT YOURSELF TO THE TEST

- What eight crises define the life span in Erikson's theory?
- Why is the quality of children's attachment to their caregivers important to social development?
- What styles of parenting produce effective bonds between children and caregivers?
- What are some consequences of deprivation on social development?
- How do social relationships and future goals affect social development in adolescence?
- What consequences do intimacy and generativity have for social development in adulthood?
- Why does ageism have an impact on people's life experiences?

Gender Development

One type of information most children acquire early on is that there are two categories of people in their social world, males and females. Note that, at first, the differences children perceive are entirely social: They begin to sense sex differences well before they understand anything about anatomy. As an adult who both knows about anatomy and understands that sex differences are more than just physical, you can begin to consider why these differences arise. Which differences are indirect consequences of biology? Which are products of socialization? How do boys and girls learn the different expectations their culture has for them?

◆ SEX AND GENDER

Biologically based characteristics that distinguish males and females are referred to as **sex differences.** These characteristics include different reproductive functions and differences in hormones and anatomy. These differences are universal, biologically determined, and unchanged by social influence. Over time, they have also led to the development of some traditional social roles (Wood & Eagly, 2002). For example, because women can breast-feed their babies, prehistoric peoples may have determined that women should also remain close to home, caring for children, while the men hunted for food.

Sex differences may also explain the finding that, after infancy, boys are more physically active and aggressive than girls. All over the world, boys are more likely than girls to engage in rough play. This difference is partly related to sex hormones—biological factors can create behavioral dispositions (Alexander, 2003; Collaer & Hines, 1995). Researchers know that sex hormones affect social play, because observations of young male and female rats and monkeys reveal the same behavioral differences found in humans (Meany et al., 1988). Male animals engage in vigorous forms of physical play that require gross motor activity. Female animals engage in activities that require precise motor skills.

In contrast to biological sex, **gender** is a psychological phenomenon referring to learned, sex-related behaviors and attitudes. Cultures vary in how strongly gender is linked to daily activities and in the amount of tolerance for what is perceived as cross-gender behavior. **Gender identity** is an individual's sense of maleness or femaleness; it includes awareness and acceptance of one's sex. This awareness develops at quite a young age: 10- to

How do children form the belief that kitchen work is women's work?

14-month-old children already demonstrate a preference for a video showing the abstract movements of a child of the same sex (Kujawski & Bower, 1993). **Gender roles** are patterns of behavior regarded as appropriate for males and females in a particular society. They provide the basic definitions of masculinity and femininity.

Researchers who study differences between males and females often try to determine which differences should be attributed to nature and nurture—that is, which differences follow from underlying biology and which are consequences of the way in which boys and girls are socialized in particular cultures. Note that young children themselves appear to believe that biology is destiny.

PUTTING IDEAS TO THE TEST

Children's Understanding of Sex Differences

Groups of children ages 4, 5, 8, 9, and 10 were asked to make predictions about a 10-year-old character named Chris or Pat. The children all believed that the character had been brought up on a beautiful island. However, some of the children were told that Chris or Pat was raised on that isolated island entirely by members of the same sex (e.g., Chris was a boy and all of his caretakers were also male) or entirely by members of the opposite sex (e.g., Chris was a boy and all of his caretakers were female). How did the environment affect the 4- to 10-year-olds' predictions about Chris or Pat's sex-stereotyped behavior? Until age 9, children believed that sex-stereotyped behavior would emerge regardless of the social context. For example, the younger children thought it was equally likely that boy Chris would want to be a firefighter and girl Chris would want to be a nurse, no matter who raised him or her. The older children's judgments were, by contrast, sensitive to the context in which the child was raised: Now Chris's career choice was influenced by his or her caretakers' sex as well as his or her own (Taylor, 1996).

These results suggest that children underestimate the effects environments have on the ways in which boys and girls become different. They are also consistent with the finding that children between the ages of 2 and 6 seem to have more extreme and inflexible perceptions of gender than do adults (Stern & Karraker, 1989). When shown infants dressed in neutral clothing, children of this age are much more consistently affected in their judgments about the infant by an arbitrary label of "male" or "female" than are adults. Younger children's extreme reactions may be linked to the fact that they are at an age when they are trying to establish their own

How do parents and peers influence children's acquisition of gender roles?

Parents are not the only socializers of gender roles. **Eleanor Maccoby** (1998) argues, for example, that parents do not merely stamp in gender roles. She has found evidence that play styles and toy preferences are not, in fact, highly correlated with parental preferences or roles. Young children are segregationists—they seek out peers of the same sex even when adults are not supervising them or in spite of adult encouragement for mixed-group play. Maccoby believes that many of the differences in gender behavior among children are the results of peer relationships.

The Structure of Boys' and Girls' Play

To understand the effects of peer relationships and the acquisition of gender roles, researchers have begun to carry out detailed analyses of the ways in which boys' and girls' play differs. One study examined the extent to which 4- and 6-year-old children in same-sex groups played with one other child—that is, in *dyads*—or engaged in activities involving a larger group of children. The researchers videotaped children at play and then categorized all the children's interactions. The results revealed that boys and girls are equally likely to play in dyads, although the girls were more likely to play with each peer for a longer period of time (i.e., boys had more different partners), perhaps because girls have longer attention spans. Among these children, only the 6-year-old boys were likely to engage in activities that involved the whole group (Benenson et al., 1997).

gender identity. They appear, on the whole, to be much more attuned to the "scripts" for gender-appropriate behavior than are their older siblings (Levy & Fivush, 1993).

We have suggested that gender roles are acquired in a cultural context. Let's now consider some of the forces that give rise to those roles.

◆ THE ACQUISITION OF GENDER ROLES

Much of what people consider masculine or feminine is shaped by culture (Leaper, 2000). Many researchers have suggested that gender-role socialization begins at birth. In one study, parents described their newborn daughters, using words such as *little, delicate, beautiful,* and *weak*. By contrast, parents described their newborn sons as *firm, alert, strong,* and *coordinated*. The babies actually showed no differences in height, weight, or health (Rubin et al., 1974). Parents dress their sons and daughters differently, give them different kinds of toys to play with, and communicate with them differently. For children as young as 18 months, parents tend to respond more positively when their children play with sex-appropriate toys. For example, in one experiment fathers gave fewer positive reactions to boys engaging in play with toys typical for girls (Fagot & Hagan, 1991). In general, children receive encouragement from their parents to engage in sex-typed activities (Lytton & Romney, 1991; Witt, 1997).

The researchers did not offer a full explanation for why 6-year-old boys, but not 6-year-old girls, shift to group play. As always, it's difficult to know whether it is something biological (is it a sex difference?) or something about the expectations adults bring to boys' and girls' play (is it a gender difference?). Even when girls do begin to play in groups, the groups are different. Boys' groups, for example, are more concerned with dominance—who has power over whom—than are girls' groups; girls' groups are typically more interested in consensus than power. Accordingly, boys and girls grow up in different psychological environments that shape their views of the world and their ways of dealing with problems.

We have briefly considered how and why it is that boys and girls experience social development in different fashions. In the next section you will see that some researchers believe that gender also has an impact on moral development.

➤ What is the difference between sex and gender?

➤ What is the relationship between gender identity and gender roles?

➤ How do parents influence the acquisition of gender roles?

➤ How do peers influence the acquisition of gender roles?

Moral Development

So far we have seen how important it is, across the life span, to develop close social relationships. Let's now consider another aspect of what it means to live as part of a social group: On many occasions you must judge your behavior according to the needs of society, rather than just according to your own needs. This is the basis of *moral behavior.* **Morality** is a system of beliefs, values, and underlying judgments about the rightness or wrongness of human acts. Society needs children to become adults who accept a moral value system and whose behavior is guided by moral principles (Killen & Hart, 1999). As you know, however, what constitutes moral and immoral behavior in particular situations can become a matter of heated public debate. Perhaps it is no coincidence, therefore, that the study of moral development has also proved to be controversial. The controversy begins with the foundational research of Lawrence Kohlberg.

◆ KOHLBERG'S STAGES OF MORAL REASONING

Lawrence Kohlberg (1964, 1981) founded his theory of moral development by studying *moral reasoning*—the judgments people make about what courses of action are correct or incorrect in particular situations. Kohlberg's theory was shaped by the earlier insights of Jean Piaget (1965), who sought to tie the development of moral judgment to a child's general cognitive development. In Piaget's view, as the child progresses through the stages of cognitive growth, he or she assigns differing relative weights to the *consequences* of an act and to the actor's

intentions. For example, to the preoperational child, someone who breaks ten cups accidentally is "naughtier" than someone who breaks one cup intentionally. As the child gets older, the actor's intentions weigh more heavily in the judgment of morality.

Cognitive Development and Moral Reasoning

Children ages 3, 4, and 5 years old were asked to make moral judgments about people's behavior that varied along three dimensions: actions, outcomes, and intentions. The *actions* were defined as either positive or negative within a particular scenario (e.g., petting versus hitting an animal) as were the *outcomes* (e.g., the animal either cried or smiled). To vary *intentions,* the experimenters described some behaviors as intentional and others as accidental (e.g., the actor hit the pet either on purpose or by mistake). The children were asked to rate the *acceptability* of the behavior by choosing one of a series of five faces that represented values from "really, really bad" to "really, really good." The younger children based their acceptability ratings almost entirely on the outcome; only the 5-year-olds took intention into account. However, when children were asked whether the actor should be *punished,* more younger children took the actor's intention into account (Zelazo et al., 1996).

These results suggest that as children become more sophisticated cognitively, they are able to shift their focus from just outcomes to consideration of both outcomes and intentions together. However, the difference between acceptability judgments and punishment judgments suggests that some types of moral judgments allow children to consider more factors at an earlier age. As we saw earlier in the chapter, what children are specifically asked to do determines, in part, how "mature" they seem.

Kohlberg expanded Piaget's view to define stages of moral development. Each stage is characterized by a different basis for making moral judgments (see **Table 10.8**). The lowest level of moral reasoning is based on self-interest, while higher levels center on social good, regardless of personal gain. To document these stages, Kohlberg used a series of dilemmas that pit different moral principles against one another:

In one dilemma, a man named Heinz is try-ing to help his wife obtain a certain drug needed to treat her cancer. An unscrupulous druggist will only sell it to Heinz for ten times more than

TABLE 10.8

Kohlberg's Stages of Moral Reasoning

Levels and Stages	Reasons for Moral Behavior
I Preconventional morality	
Stage 1 Pleasure/pain orientation	To avoid pain or not to get caught
Stage 2 Cost–benefit orientation; reciprocity—an eye for an eye	To get rewards
II Conventional morality	
Stage 3 Good-child orientation	To gain acceptance and avoid disapproval
Stage 4 Law and order orientation	To follow rules, avoid censure by authorities
III Principled morality	
Stage 5 Social contract orientation	To promote the society's welfare
Stage 6 Ethical principle orientation	To achieve justice and avoid self-condemnation
Stage 7 Cosmic orientation	To be true to universal principles and feel oneself part of a cosmic direction that transcends social norms

what the druggist paid. This is much more money than Heinz has and more than he can raise. Heinz becomes desperate, breaks into the druggist's store, and steals the drug for his wife. Should Heinz have done that? Why? An interviewer probes the participant for the reasons for the decision and then scores the answers.

The scoring is based on the *reasons* the person gives for the decision, not on the decision itself. For example, someone who says that the man should steal the drug because of his obligation to his dying wife or that he should not steal the drug because of his obligation to uphold the law (despite his personal feelings) is expressing concern about meeting established obligations and is scored at Stage 4.

Four principles govern Kohlberg's stage model: (1) an individual can be at only one stage at a given time; (2) everyone goes through the stages in a fixed order; (3) each stage is more comprehensive and complex than the preceding; and (4) the same stages occur in every culture. Kohlberg inherited much of this stage philosophy from Piaget, and, in fact, the progression from Stages 1 to 3 appears to match the course of normal cognitive development. The stages proceed in order, and each can be seen to be more cognitively sophisticated than the preceding. Almost all children reach Stage 3 by the age of 13.

Much of the controversy with Kohlberg's theory occurs beyond Stage 3. In Kohlberg's original view, people would continue their moral development in a steady progression beyond level 3. However, not all people attain Stages 4 to 7. In fact, many adults never

reach Stage 5, and only a few go beyond it. The content of Kohlberg's later stages appears to be subjective, and it is hard to understand each successive stage as more comprehensive and sophisticated than the preceding. For example, "avoiding self-condemnation," the basis for moral judgments at Stage 6, does not seem obviously more sophisticated than "promoting society's welfare," the basis for Stage 5. Furthermore, the higher stages are not found in all cultures (Eckensberger & Zimba, 1997). We turn now to extended contemporary critiques of Kohlberg's theory that arise from considerations of gender and culture.

◆ GENDER AND CULTURAL PERSPECTIVES ON MORAL REASONING

Most critiques of Kohlberg's theory take issue with his claims of universality: Kohlberg's later stages have been criticized because they fail to recognize that adult moral judgments may reflect different, but equally moral, principles. In a well-known critique, **Carol Gilligan** (1982) pointed out that Kohlberg's original work was developed from observations only of boys. She argued that this research approach overlooked potential differences between the habitual moral judgments of men and women. Gilligan proposed that women's moral development is based on a standard of *caring for others* and progresses to a stage of self-realization, whereas men base their reasoning on a standard of *justice*. Thus

Gilligan's theory broadens Kohlberg's ideas about the range of considerations that may be relevant to moral judgments beyond childhood. Although we can value this contribution, research has suggested that she is incorrect to identify unique styles of moral reasoning for men and women. Let's examine the evidence.

Some studies have indicated that women mold their moral decisions to maintain harmony in their social relationships, whereas men refer more to fairness (Lyons, 1983). Even so, researchers continue to dispute whether gender differences in moral reasoning really exist at all (Jaffee & Hyde, 2000). Although men and women may arrive at their adult levels of moral development through different processes, the actual judgments they make as adults are highly similar (Boldizar et al., 1989). One possibility is that the gender differences are really consequences of the different types of social situations that arise in the lives of men and women. When asked to reason about the same moral dilemmas, men and women gave highly similar patterns of care and justice responses (Clopton & Sorell, 1993).

We can thus characterize adult reasoning about moral dilemmas as a mix between considerations of justice and considerations of caring. This mix will remain in place over most of the life span. However, as you might expect, moral judgments are affected by general changes in adult cognition. One relevant change of late adulthood is that individuals shift the grounds for their judgments away from the details of specific situations toward the use of general principles. Consequently, moral judgments come to be based more on general societal concerns—for example, "What is the law?"—than on particular dilemmas—for example, "Should an exception be made in this case?" (Pratt et al., 1988).

Note that debates about gender differences in moral reasoning have still mostly been carried out with respect to moral reasoning in Western cultures. Cross-cultural research has provided an important critique of this whole body of research: Comparisons between cultures suggest that it is not even possible to make universal claims about the set of situations to which moral judgments are relevant. Consider this situation: You see a stranger at the side of the road with a flat tire. Should you stop to help? Suppose you say no. Is that immoral? If you have grown up in the United States, you probably think helping, under these circumstances, is a matter of personal choice—so it isn't immoral; on the other hand, if you had grown up as a Hindu in India, a culture that puts considerably more emphasis on interdependence and mutual assistance, you probably *would* view a failure to help as immoral (Miller et al., 1990).

Let's consider a study that made cross-cultural comparisons of moral reasoning:

Justice Versus Interpersonal Responsibilities

Participants for a study on moral judgments were recruited from two locations: New Haven, Connecticut, and Mysore, in southern India. These representatives of Western and Hindu cultures were asked to respond to scenarios that made a contrast between *justice* and *interpersonal responsibility.* Suppose, for example, the only way you could deliver the wedding rings to your best friend's wedding was to steal money for a train ticket. The principle of *justice* suggests that you shouldn't steal; the principle of *interpersonal responsibility* suggests that you should honor your interpersonal commitment. If you grew up in a Western culture, you probably don't think of interpersonal responsibility in moral terms: It would be unfortunate, but not immoral, to fail to deliver the wedding rings. However, we noted just earlier that members of the Hindu culture in India do generally consider interpersonal commitments to have a moral character. As a consequence, the researchers predicted that Indian respondents would be more likely to favor interpersonal responsibility than would United States respondents. As shown in **Figure 10.13,** at three different ages Indian respondents were more likely to choose the options that favored interpersonal responsibility (Miller & Bersoff, 1992).

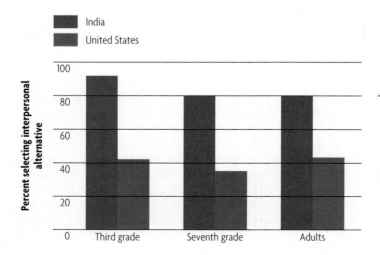

FIGURE 10.13

Cross-Cultural Responses to Moral Dilemmas

Schoolchildren and adults in India and the United States were asked to choose which courses of action they thought characters should take to resolve moral dilemmas. The participants from India were much more likely to favor interpersonal responsibility options over justice options.

<www.ablongman.com/gerrig17e>

You can see from this example the role that culture plays in defining what is moral or immoral. If you've grown up in the United States, you are probably surprised how strongly individuals from India believe that the commitment to the friend must be honored—it is better to steal than to fail to deliver the rings. Note that this difference in cultural norms most likely applies beyond the two countries of the United States and India. As we shall explore more fully in later chapters, the United States and India are typical of Western and non-Western countries with respect to their emphasis on the individual good versus the collective good.

PUT YOURSELF TO THE TEST

- What are the important changes across the stages of Kohlberg's theory?
- What are some criticisms of Kohlberg's stage theory?
- Does research support claims about gender differences in moral reasoning?
- Why does moral reasoning differ across cultures?

Learning to Age Successfully

Let us now review some of the themes of this chapter, to form a prescription for successful aging. Early in the chapter, we encouraged you to think of development as a type of change that always brings with it gains and losses. In this light, the trick to prospering across the life span is to solidify one's gains and minimize one's losses. We saw that the rule "use it or lose it" applies in both physical and cognitive domains of life. Many of the changes that are stereotypically associated with aging are functions of disuse rather than decay. Our first line of advice is straightforward: Keep at it!

We also suggested that part of successful aging means to employ *selective optimization with compensation* (Baltes et al., 1992; Freund & Baltes, 1998). As you may recall, *selective* means that people choose the most appropriate goals for themselves. *Optimization* refers to people's exercising or training themselves in areas that are of highest priority to them. *Compensation* refers to the alternative ways that people use to deal with losses. In this chapter, we saw another good example of this process when we considered the way in which social relationships change during adulthood. Older adults select the goal of having friends who provide optimal levels of emotional support; the choice of friends must change over time to compensate for deaths or other disruptions (Carstensen, 1998; Lang & Carstensen, 1994). Although the selective optimization perspective originated in research on the aging process, it is a good way to characterize the choices you must make throughout your life span. You should always try to select the goals most important to you, optimize your performance with respect to those goals, and compensate when progress toward those goals is blocked. That's our final bit of advice about life span development. We hope you will age wisely and well.

Recapping Main Points

STUDYING DEVELOPMENT

- Researchers collect normative, longitudinal, and cross-sectional data to document change.

PHYSICAL DEVELOPMENT ACROSS THE LIFE SPAN

- Environmental factors can affect physical development while a child is still in the womb.
- Newborns and infants possess a remarkable range of capabilities: They are prewired for survival.
- Through puberty, adolescents achieve sexual maturity.
- Some physical changes in late adulthood are consequences of disuse, not inevitable deterioration.

COGNITIVE DEVELOPMENT ACROSS THE LIFE SPAN

- Piaget's key ideas about cognitive development include development of schemes, assimilation, accommodation, and the four-stage theory of discontinuous development. The four stages are sensorimotor, preoperational, concrete operational, and formal operational.
- Many of Piaget's theories are now being altered by ingenious research paradigms that reveal infants and young children to be more competent than Piaget had thought.
- Researchers suggest that children develop foundational theories, which change over time, in different psychological and physical domains.
- Cross-cultural research has questioned the universality of cognitive developmental theories.
- Age-related declines in cognitive functioning are typically evident in only some abilities. Research suggests that some cognitive deficits are caused by disuse rather than inevitable decay.
- Successful cognitive aging can be defined as people optimizing their functioning in select domains that are of highest priority to them and compensating for losses by using substitute behaviors.

ACQUIRING LANGUAGE

- Many researchers believe that humans have an inborn language-making capacity. Even so, interactions with adult speakers is an essential part of the language acquisition process.
- Like scientists, children develop hypotheses about the meanings and grammar of their language. These hypotheses are often constrained by innate principles.

SOCIAL DEVELOPMENT ACROSS THE LIFE SPAN

- Social development takes place in a particular cultural context.
- Departures from the typical course of developmental change are often products of culturally determined environments.
- Erik Erikson conceptualized the life span as a series of crises with which individuals must cope.
- Socialization is the process whereby children acquire values and attitudes that conform to those considered desirable in society.
- Socialization begins with an infant's attachment to a caregiver.
- Failure to make this attachment leads to numerous physical and psychological problems.
- Lack of nurturing relationships in childhood can impair social development.
- Research shows that most adolescents are satisfied with their lives.
- Adolescents must develop a personal identity by forming comfortable social relationships with parents and peers and by choosing future goals.
- The central concerns of adulthood are organized around the needs of intimacy and generativity.
- People become less socially active as they grow older because they selectively maintain only those relationships that matter most to them emotionally.
- People assess their lives, in part, by their ability to contribute positively to the lives of others.
- Negative stereotypes of older adults lead to ageism.

GENDER DEVELOPMENT

- Gender is a psychological phenomenon referring to learned sex-related behavior and attitudes.
- Gender-role socialization begins at birth. A variety of socializing agents reinforce gender stereotypes.

MORAL DEVELOPMENT

- Kohlberg defined stages of moral development.
- Subsequent research has evaluated gender and cultural differences in moral reasoning.
- Different cultures have different standards for what types of situations and behaviors count as moral or immoral.

KEY TERMS

accommodation (p. 325)

ageism (p. 351)

assimilation (p. 325)

attachment (p. 339)

centration (p. 326)

child-directed speech (p. 333)

chronological age (p. 317)

cognitive development (p. 324)

conservation (p. 327)

contact comfort (p. 341)

cross-sectional design (p. 317)

developmental age (p. 317)

developmental psychology (p. 315)

egocentrism (p. 326)

foundational theories (p. 328)

gender (p. 352)

gender identity (p. 352)

gender roles (p. 352)

generativity (p. 350)

imprinting (p. 339)

internalization (p. 329)

intimacy (p. 347)

language-making capacity (p. 335)

longitudinal design (p. 317)

maturation (p. 321)

menarche (p. 323)

morality (p. 354)

normative investigations (p. 317)

object permanence (p. 326)

overregularization (p. 336)

parenting practices (p. 341)

parenting style (p. 340)

physical development (p. 318)

phonemes (p. 333)

psychosocial stages (p. 337)

puberty (p. 323)

schemes (p. 325)

selective optimization with compensation (p. 331)

selective social interaction theory (p. 349)

sex differences (p. 352)

social development (p. 336)

socialization (p. 338)

wisdom (p. 331)

zygote (p. 318)

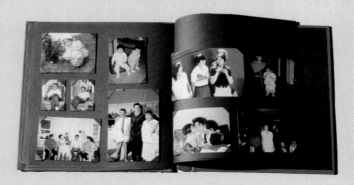

II

Motivation

Your alarm clock went off this morning. You would have loved to hit the snooze button to get a few extra minutes of sleep, but you dragged yourself right out of bed. Why? Were you desperately hungry? Did you have to complete some important assignment? Had you made a date with someone who has captured your heart? When you consider the question "Why did I get out of bed this morning?" you have arrived directly at the core question of *motivation*: What makes you act as you do? What makes you persistently try to attain some goals despite the high effort, pain, and financial costs involved? Why, on the other hand, do you sometimes procrastinate too long before attempting to achieve other goals or give in and quit too soon?

Your day-to-day life is filled with circumstances in which people invoke motivational factors to explain events that do and do not take place. You may hear a boss tell her salespeople, "You've got to try harder to sell!" Your friend may reveal that she failed an exam because the professor never motivated her enough. You may read a mystery story and try to figure out the motive for a crime—and by doing so, satisfy your own goal of beating the detective to the identity of the murderer. Like millions of other viewers worldwide, you may glue yourself to soap operas each day to peer into cauldrons of seething motives like greed, power, and lust.

It is the task of psychological researchers to bring theoretical rigor to such examples of motivation. How might motivational states affect the outcome of a sports competition or an exam? Why do some people become overweight and others starve themselves to death? Are our sexual behaviors determined by our genetic heritage? In this chapter, you will learn that human actions are motivated by a variety of needs—from fundamental physiological needs like hunger and thirst to psychological needs like personal achievement. But you will see that physiology and psychology are often not easy to separate. Even a seemingly biological drive such as hunger competes with an individual's need for personal control and social acceptance to determine patterns of eating.

We begin the chapter by providing you with a framework to understand general issues about the nature and study of motivation. In the second part of the chapter, we will look in depth at three types of motivation, each important in a different way and each varying in the extent to which biological and psychological factors operate. These three are hunger, sex, and personal achievement.

Understanding Motivation

Motivation is the general term for all the processes involved in starting, directing, and maintaining physical and psychological activities. The word *motivation* comes from the Latin *movere,* which means "to move." All organisms move toward some stimuli and activities and away from others, as dictated by their appetites and aversions. Theories of motivation explain both the general patterns of "movement" of each animal species, including humans, and the personal preferences and performances of the individual members of each species. Let's begin our analysis of motivation by considering the different ways in which motivation has been used to explain and predict species and individual behavior.

What different motivational questions might be asked of this individual's behavior?

◆ FUNCTIONS OF MOTIVATIONAL CONCEPTS

Psychologists have used the concept of motivation for five basic purposes:

- *To relate biology to behavior.* As a biological organism, you have complex internal mechanisms that regulate your bodily functioning and help you survive. Why did you get out of bed this morning? You may have been hungry, thirsty, or cold. In each case, internal states of deprivation trigger bodily responses that motivate you to take action to restore your body's balance.

- *To account for behavioral variability.* Why might you do well on a task one day and poorly on the same task another day? Why does one child do much better at a competitive task than another child with roughly the same ability and knowledge? Psychologists use motivational explanations when the variations in people's performance in a constant situation cannot be traced to differences in ability, skill, practice, or chance. If you were willing to get up early this morning to get in some extra studying but your friend was not, we would be comfortable describing you as in a different motivational state than your friend.

- *To infer private states from public acts.* You see someone sitting on a park bench, chuckling. How

<www.ablongman.com/gerrig17e>

can you explain this behavior? Psychologists and laypersons are alike in typically moving from observing some behavior to inferring some internal cause for it. People are continually interpreting behavior in terms of likely reasons for why it occurred as it did. The same rule applies to your own behaviors. You often seek to discover whether your own actions are best understood as internally or externally motivated.

- *To assign responsibility for actions.* The concept of personal responsibility is basic in law, religion, and ethics. Personal responsibility presupposes inner motivation and the ability to control your actions. People are judged less responsible for their actions when (1) they did not intend negative consequences to occur, (2) external forces were powerful enough to provoke the behaviors, or (3) the actions were influenced by drugs, alcohol, or intense emotion. Thus, a theory of motivation must be able to discriminate among the different potential causes of behavior.

- *To explain perseverance despite adversity.* A final reason psychologists study motivation is to explain why organisms perform behaviors when it might be easier not to perform them. Motivation gets you to work or class on time even when you're exhausted. Motivation helps you persist in playing the game to the best of your ability even when you are losing and realize that you can't possibly win.

You now have a general sense of the circumstances in which psychologists might invoke the concept of motivation to explain and predict behavior. Before we turn to specific domains of experience, let's consider general sources of motivation.

◆ SOURCES OF MOTIVATION

In 1999, cyclist Lance Armstrong won the Tour de France—completing one of the most remarkable comebacks in sports history. In 1996, Armstrong had been diagnosed with testicular cancer that had spread to his lungs and brain. After enduring aggressive chemotherapy, Armstrong chose to go back into training. Within three years, he was victorious in his sport's most prestigious event. As of 2003, Armstrong had won the Tour de France five times in a row. Detractors had claimed that the field he beat in 1999 was weak; his four additional victories by 2003 proved that he could repeatedly beat the world's best cyclists.

Could you do what Lance Armstrong did? Could you come back from a serious illness to challenge your body again? Do you think that whatever motivated his

What combination of internal and external motivational forces may have helped cyclist Lance Armstrong to overcome cancer and win the Tour de France?

behavior was something *internal* to him? Would it take a special set of life experiences for someone to persevere in this manner? Or was it something *external,* something about the situation? Would many or most people behave in this way if they were put in the same situation? Or does his behavior represent an *interaction* of aspects of the person and features of the situation? To help you think about the sources of motivation, we will explore this distinction between internal and external forces. Let's begin with theories that explain certain types of behavior as arising from internal, biological drives.

DRIVES AND INCENTIVES

Some forms of motivation seem very basic: If you feel hungry, you eat; if you feel thirsty, you drink. The theory that much important behavior was motivated by internal drives was most fully developed by theorist **Clark Hull** (1943, 1952). In Hull's view, **drives** are internal states that arise in response to an animal's physiological needs. Organisms seek to maintain a state of equilibrium, or **homeostasis,** with respect to biological conditions such as the body's temperature and energy supply (see Chapter 3, p. 70). Drives are aroused when deprivation creates disequilibrium or *tension.* These drives activate the organism toward *tension reduction;* when the drives are satisfied or reduced—when homeostasis is restored—the organism ceases to act. Thus, according to Hull, when an animal has been deprived of food for many hours, a state of hunger is aroused that motivates food-seeking and eating behaviors. The animal's responses that have led to the food goal will be reinforced because they are associated with the tension reduction that eating produces.

Can tension reduction explain all motivated behavior? Apparently not. Consider groups of rats that have been deprived of food or water. Tension reduction would predict that they would eat or drink at their first opportunity. However, when such rats were placed in a novel environment with plenty of opportunities everywhere to eat or drink, they chose to explore instead. Only after they had first satisfied their curiosity did they begin to satisfy their hunger and thirst (Berlyne, 1960; Fowler, 1965; Zimbardo & Montgomery, 1957). In another series of studies, young monkeys spent much time and energy manipulating gadgets and new objects in their environment, apparently for the sheer pleasure of "monkeying around," without any external rewards (Harlow et al., 1950).

These experiments demonstrate that behavior is not only motivated by internal drives: Behavior is also motivated by **incentives**—external stimuli or rewards that do not relate directly to biological needs. When the rats or monkeys were attuned to objects in the environment rather than to their own internal states, they demonstrated that their behavior was controlled by incentives. Human behavior is also controlled by a variety of incentives. Why do you stay up late cruising the Web instead of getting a good night's sleep? Why do you watch a movie that you know will make you feel anxious or frightened? Why do you eat junk food at a party even when you're already feeling full? In each case, elements of the environment serve as incentives to motivate your behavior.

You can see already that behaviors find their origins in a mixture of internal and external sources of motivation. Even though rats might feel biological pressure to eat or drink, they also indulge an impulse to explore a new environment. We turn now to a contemporary approach to motivation that specifically examines competing motivational states, *reversal theory*.

REVERSAL THEORY

In recent years, **Michael Apter** (1989, 2001) and his colleagues have developed a new theory that also rejects the idea of motivation as tension reduction. Instead, the theory hypothesizes four pairs of *metamotivational states*: states that give rise to distinct patterns of motivation. As shown in **Table 11.1,** the pairs are placed in opposition. The theory claims that, at any given time, only one of the two states in each pair can be operative. If you work your way through the table, you'll see how each pair defines motivational states that are incompatible. For example, imagine you are in some work-related situation. At a given moment, are you motivated to fit in or to be independent? Are you motivated to be focused on your own feelings or focused on others' feelings? This theory is known as

---

TABLE 11.1

Principal Characteristics of the Four Pairs of Metamotivational States

Telic	Paratelic
Serious	Playful
Goal-oriented	Activity-oriented
Prefers planning ahead	Living for the moment
Anxiety-avoiding	Excitement-seeking
Desires progress—achievement	Desires fun and enjoyment

Conformist	Negativistic
Compliant	Rebellious
Wants to keep to rules	Wants to break rules
Conventional	Unconventional
Agreeable	Angry
Desires to fit in	Desires to be independent

Mastery	Sympathy
Power-oriented	Care-oriented
Sees life as struggle	Sees life as cooperative
Tough-minded	Sensitive
Concerned with control	Concerned with kindness
Desires dominance	Desires affection

Autic	Alloic
Primary concern with self	Primary concern with others
Self-centered	Identifying with other(s)
Focus on own feelings	Focus on others' feelings

Note: The terms *telic* and *paratelic* are derived from the ancient Greek word *telos,* meaning *"goal."* The terms *autic* and *alloic* are based on Greek words meaning *"self"* and *"other."*

---

reversal theory because it seeks to explain human motivation in terms of *reversals* from one to the other of the opposing states. Consider the contrast between the *paratelic* and the *telic* states. You are in a paratelic state when you engage in an activity with no goal beyond enjoying that particular activity; you are in a telic state when you engage in an activity that is important to you beyond the moment. For example, you are probably in a telic state right now as you read your textbook—you wish to acquire the material so you can do well on an exam. If, however, you take a break from studying to eat a snack or listen to a new CD, you have

<www.ablongman.com/gerrig17e>

almost certainly gone into a paratelic state. Reversal theory, in fact, suggests that you are always in one or the other state but never both simultaneously.

At times, you have probably become very aware of the types of reversals predicted by this theory. One particularly dramatic form of reversal occurs in people who engage in high-risk activities, such as parachuting.

An Anxiety-to-Excitement Reversal

Why would people voluntarily jump out of airplanes—and claim to do it for fun? It is hard to understand this behavior with respect to tension reduction because the anticipation of jumping out of an airplane increases, rather than reduces, tension. Reversal theory, however, suggests that the experience of parachuting presents a switch from a telic to a paratelic state. In the telic state, high arousal—of the type that would be experienced as you contemplate jumping out of an airplane—leads to feelings of anxiety; in the paratelic state, high arousal is experienced as great excitement. Thus, a reversal from the telic to the paratelic state at the same level of arousal would create an immediate shift from great anxiety to great pleasure. To verify the existence of this immediate shift, researchers gathered data from members of two parachuting clubs. Members of the clubs reported on their feelings of anxiety and excitement in the time before, during, and after their leaps. The data showed a clear reversal: Moments before the leap, they were anxious (but not excited); moments after the parachute opened, they were excited (but not anxious). The arousal did not go away—it took on a different meaning as the parachuter reversed from the telic to the paratelic state (Apter & Batler, 1997).

Do you see how reversal theory explains the self-reports of these parachuters?

Reversal theory provides an interesting general approach to motivation. We move now to a different tradition of research on motivation, one that focuses on species-specific *instinctual* behaviors.

INSTINCTUAL BEHAVIORS AND LEARNING

Why do organisms behave the way they do? Part of the answer is that some aspects of a species's behavior are governed by **instincts,** preprogrammed tendencies that are essential for the survival of their species. Instincts provide repertoires of behavior that are part of each animal's genetic inheritance. Salmon swim thousands of miles back to the exact stream where they were spawned, leaping up waterfalls until they come to the right spot, where the surviving males and females engage in ritualized courtship and mating. Fertilized eggs are deposited, the parents die, and, in time, their young swim downstream to live in the ocean until, a few years later, it is time for them to return to complete their part in this continuing drama. Similarly remarkable activities can be reported for most species of animals. Bees communicate the location of food to other bees, army ants go on highly synchronized hunting expeditions, birds build nests, and spiders spin complex webs—exactly as their parents and ancestors did.

Early theories of human function tended to overestimate the importance of instincts for humans. **William James,** writing in 1890, stated his belief that humans rely even more on instinctual behaviors than other animals (although human instincts were generally not carried out with fixed-action patterns). In addition to the biological instincts humans share with animals, a host of social instincts, such as sympathy, modesty, sociability, and love, come into play. For James, both human and animal instincts were *purposive*—they served important purposes, or functions, in the organism's adaptation to its environment.

Instinctive behaviors, like the argiope spider's proclivity to build an elaborate capture thread into its web, are motivated by genetic inheritance. What instincts have theorists attributed to the human species?

Sigmund Freud (1915) proposed that humans experience drive states arising from life instincts (including sexuality) and death instincts (including aggression). He believed that instinctive urges direct *psychic energy* to satisfy bodily needs. Tension results when this energy cannot be discharged; this tension drives people toward activities or objects that will reduce the tension. For example, Freud believed that the life and death instincts operated largely below the level of consciousness. However, their consequences for conscious thoughts, feelings, and actions were profound, because of the way the instincts motivated people to make important life choices (we will expand on these ideas in Chapter 13).

By the 1920s, psychologists had compiled lists of over 10,000 human instincts (Bernard, 1924). At this same time, however, the notion of instincts as universal explanations for human behavior was beginning to stagger under the weight of critical attacks. Cross-cultural anthropologists, such as **Ruth Benedict** (1959) and **Margaret Mead** (1939), found enormous behavioral variation between cultures. Their observations contradicted theories that considered only the universals of inborn instincts.

Most damaging to the early instinct notions, however, were behaviorist empirical demonstrations that important behaviors and emotions were learned rather than inborn. These types of demonstrations should be familiar to you from Chapter 6. We saw there that human and nonhuman animals alike are highly sensitive to the ways in which stimuli and responses are associated in the environment. If you want to explain why one animal performs a behavior and another does not, you may need to know nothing more than that one animal's behavior was reinforced and the other's was not. Under those circumstances, you don't need a separate account of motivation at all (that is, it would be a mistake to say that one animal is "motivated" and the other is not).

Recall, however, that in Chapter 6 we also saw that the types of behaviors animals will most readily learn are determined, in part, by species-specific instincts (see page 193). That is, each animal displays a combination of learned and instinctive behaviors. Thus, if you are asked to explain or predict an animal's behavior, you will want to know two things: first, something about the history of its species—what adaptive behaviors are part of the organism's genetic inheritance?—and second, something about the personal history of the animal—what unique set of environmental associations has the organism experienced? In these cases, motivation resides in the effects history has on current behavior.

One final look back to Chapter 6: We saw there that cognitively oriented researchers have challenged the belief that instincts and reinforcement history are suffi-

cient to explain all the details of an animal's behavior. Let's turn now to the role of expectations and cognition in motivation.

EXPECTATIONS AND COGNITIVE APPROACHES TO MOTIVATION

Consider *The Wizard of Oz* as a psychological study of motivation. Dorothy and her three friends work hard to get to the Emerald City, overcoming barriers, persisting against all adversaries. They do so because they expect the Wizard to give them what they are missing. Instead, the wonderful (and wise) Wizard makes them aware that they, not he, always had the power to fulfill their wishes. For Dorothy, *home* is not a place but a feeling of security, of comfort with people she loves; it is wherever her heart is. The courage the Lion wants, the intelligence the Scarecrow longs for, and the emotions the Tin Man dreams of are attributes they already possess. They need to think about these attributes not as internal conditions but as positive ways in which they are already relating to others. After all, didn't they demonstrate those qualities on the journey to Oz, a journey motivated by little more than an *expectation,* an idea about the future likelihood of getting something they wanted? The Wizard of Oz was clearly among the first cognitive psychologists, because he recognized the importance of people's thought processes in determining their goals and behaviors to reach them.

Contemporary psychologists use cognitive analyses to explore the forces that motivate a variety of personal and social behaviors. These psychologists share the Wizard's point of view that significant human motivation comes not from objective realities in the external world but from subjective interpretations of reality. The reinforcing effect of a reward is lost if you don't perceive that your actions obtained it. What you do now is often controlled by what you think was responsible for your past successes and failures, by what you believe is possible for you to do, and by what you anticipate the outcome of an action will be. Cognitive approaches explain why human beings are often motivated by expectations of future events.

The importance of *expectations* in motivating behavior was developed by **Julian Rotter** (1954) in his **social-learning theory** (we touched on social learning in our discussion of observational learning in Chapter 6). For Rotter, the probability that you will engage in a given behavior (studying for an exam instead of partying) is determined by your *expectation* of attaining a goal (getting a good grade) that follows the activity and by the *personal value* of that goal. A *discrepancy* between expectations and reality can motivate an individual to perform corrective behaviors (Festinger, 1957;

<www.ablongman.com/gerrig17e>

Lewin, 1936). For example, if you find that your own behaviors do not match the standards or values of a group to which you belong, you might be motivated to change your behaviors to achieve a better fit with the group.

How do expectations relate to internal and external forces of motivation? **Fritz Heider** (1958) postulated that the outcome of your behavior (a poor grade, for example) can be attributed to *dispositional forces,* such as lack of effort or insufficient intelligence, or to *situational forces,* such as an unfair test or a biased teacher. These attributions influence the way you will behave. You are likely to try harder next time if you see your poor grade as a result of your lack of effort, but you may give up if you see it as resulting from injustice or lack of ability (Dweck, 1975). Thus, the identification of a source of motivation as internal or external may depend, in part, on your own subjective interpretation of reality.

Let's review the various sources of motivation. We began with the observation that researchers can differentiate internal and external factors that bring about behaviors. Drives, instincts, and histories of learning are all internal sources of motivation that affect behaviors in the presence of appropriate external stimuli. Once organisms begin to think about their behaviors—something humans are particularly prone to do—expectations about what should or should not happen also begin to provide motivation. Thinking animals can choose to attribute some motivations to themselves and others to the outside world.

We have now given you a general framework for understanding motivation. In the remainder of the chapter, we will take a closer look at three different types of behaviors that are influenced by interactions of motives: eating, sexual performance, and personal achievement.

PUT YOURSELF TO THE TEST

➥ What are five functions of motivational concepts?

➥ Why do theories often make a distinction between internal and external sources of motivation?

➥ What is the relationship between drives and incentives?

➥ Why does reversal theory organize motivation into opposing states?

➥ How do instincts help determine species's behaviors?

➥ What is the role of expectations in cognitive theories of motivation?

Eating

We'd like to ask you to make a prediction. We are about to offer a slice of pizza to a student enrolled in an introductory psychology course. How likely do you think it is that the student will eat the slice of pizza? Are you willing to make a guess? Your response should probably be, "I need more information." In the last section, we gave you a way of organizing the extra information you need to acquire before making such a prediction. You would want to know about *internal* information. How much has the student eaten already? Is the student trying to diet? You would also want to know about *external* information. Is the pizza tasty? Are friends there to share the pizza and conversation? You can see already that we have some work to do to explain the types of forces that might influence even a simple outcome, such as whether someone is going to eat a slice of pizza. Let's begin with some of the physiological processes that evolution has provided to regulate eating.

◆ THE PHYSIOLOGY OF EATING

When does your body tell you it's time to eat? You have been provided with a variety of mechanisms that contribute to your physical sense of hunger or satiety (Logue, 1991). To regulate food intake effectively, organisms must be equipped with mechanisms that accomplish four tasks: (1) detect internal food need, (2) initiate and organize eating behavior, (3) monitor the quantity and quality of the food eaten, and (4) detect when enough food has been consumed and stop eating. Researchers have tried to understand these processes by relating them either to *peripheral* mechanisms in different parts of the body, such as stomach contractions, or to *central* brain mechanisms, such as the functioning of the hypothalamus. Let's look at these processes in more detail.

PERIPHERAL RESPONSES

Where do sensations of hunger come from? Does your stomach send out distress signals to indicate that it is empty? A pioneering physiologist, **Walter Cannon** (1934), believed that gastric activity in an empty stomach was the sole basis for hunger. To test this hypothesis, Cannon's intrepid student A. L. Washburn trained himself to swallow an uninflated balloon attached to a rubber tube. The other end of the tube was attached to a device that recorded changes in air pressure. Cannon then inflated the balloon in Washburn's stomach. As the student's stomach contracted, air was expelled from the balloon and activated the recording device. Reports of Washburn's hunger pangs were correlated with periods when the record showed his stomach was severely contracted but not when the record showed his stomach was distended. Cannon thought he had proved that stomach cramps were responsible for hunger (Cannon & Washburn, 1912).

Although Cannon and Washburn's procedure was ingenious, later research showed that stomach contractions are not even a necessary condition for hunger. Injections of sugar into the bloodstream will stop the stomach contractions but not the hunger of an animal with an empty stomach. Human patients who have had their stomachs entirely removed still experience hunger pangs (Janowitz & Grossman, 1950), and rats without stomachs still learn mazes when rewarded with food (Penick et al., 1963). So, although sensations originating in the stomach may play a role in the way people usually experience hunger, they do not fully explain how the body detects its need for food and is motivated to eat.

Your empty stomach may not be necessary to feel hungry, but does a "full" stomach terminate eating? Research has shown that gastric distension caused by food—but not by an inflated balloon—will cause an individual to end a meal (Logue, 1991). Thus, the body is sensitive to the source of pressure in the stomach. The oral experience of food also provides a peripheral source of *satiety* cues—cues relevant to feelings of satiation or fullness. You may have noticed that you become less enthusiastic about the tastes of even your favorite foods over the course of a meal, a phenomenon called *sensory-specific satiety* (Raynor & Epstein, 2001). Foods high in calories and high in protein produce more satiety than do low-calorie and low-protein food (Johnson & Vickers, 1993; Vandewaters & Vickers, 1996). This immediate reduction in "liking" for these types of foods may be one way in which your body regulates intake. However, the "specific" in sensory-specific satiety means that the satiety applies most directly to the actual foods that are eaten. When people are given the opportunity to eat a series of foods with different tastes, rather than sticking with a single, even favorite taste, they eat more food (Rolls et al., 1981). Therefore, variety in food tastes—as is common in many multicourse meals—might counteract other bodily indications that you've already had enough to eat.

Let's turn now to the brain mechanisms involved in eating behaviors, where information from peripheral sources is gathered together.

CENTRAL RESPONSES

As is often the case, simple theories about the brain centers for the initiation and cessation of eating have given way to more complex theories. The earliest theories of the brain control of eating were built around observations of the *lateral hypothalamus (LH)* and the *ventromedial hypothalamus (VMH)*. (The location of the hypothalamus is shown in Figure 3.12 on page 71.) Research showed that if the VMH was lesioned (or the LH stimulated), the animal consumed more food. If the procedure was reversed, so that the LH was lesioned (or the VMH stimulated), the animal consumed less food. These observations gave rise to the *dual-center model,* in which the LH was thought to be the "hunger center" and the VMH the "satiety center."

Over time, however, the data failed to confirm this theory (Martin et al., 1991; Rolls, 1994). For example, rats with VMH lesions only overeat foods they find palatable; they strongly avoid foods that don't taste good. Thus, the VMH could not just be a simple center for signaling "eat more" or "don't eat more"—the signal depends on the type of food. In fact, destruction of the VMH may, in part, have the effect of exaggerating ordinary reflex responses to food (Powley, 1977). If the rat's reflex response to good-tasting food is to eat it, its exaggerated response will be to overeat. If the rat reflexively avoids bad-tasting food by gagging or vomiting, its exaggerated response could keep the rat from eating altogether.

Let's focus on how the VMH and LH carry out the tasks assigned to them by the brain. Some of the most important information the VMH and LH use to regulate

Why do people tend to eat more food when a variety of tastes are available?

<www.ablongman.com/gerrig17e>

eating comes from your bloodstream (Woods et al., 1998). Sugar (in the form of glucose in the blood) and fat are the energy sources for metabolism. The two basic signals that initiate eating come from receptors that monitor the levels of sugar and fat in the blood. When stored glucose is low or unavailable for metabolism, signals from liver cell receptors are sent to the LH, where neurons acting as glucose detectors change their activity in response to this information. Other hypothalamic neurons may detect changes in free fatty acids and insulin levels in the blood. Together, these neurons appear to activate appetitive systems in the lateral zone of the hypothalamus and initiate eating behavior. Signals that the blood has a high level of glucose or fatty acids are used by the VMH to terminate eating behaviors.

We have seen so far that you have body systems that are dedicated to getting you to start and to stop eating. You almost certainly know, however, from an enormous amount of personal experience, that your need for food depends on more than just the cues generated by your body. Let's look now at psychological factors that motivate you to eat more food or less food.

◆ THE PSYCHOLOGY OF EATING

You know now that your body is equipped with a variety of mechanisms that regulate the amount of food you eat. But do you eat only in response to hunger? You are likely to respond, "Of course not!" If you think back over the last couple of days, you can probably recall several occasions on which when and what you ate had little to do with hunger. For example, people in the United States typically eat three daily meals at set times; the timing of those meals relies more on social norms than on body cues. Moreover, people often choose what to eat based on social or cultural norms. Would you say yes if you were offered a free lobster dinner? Your answer might depend on whether, for example, you are an observant Jew (in which case you would say no) or a vegetarian (in which case your answer would still depend on whether you are the type of vegetarian who eats seafood). These examples suggest immediately why eating is not just about paying heed to your body's cues.

Beyond social and cultural constraints, why else might your eating be relatively insensitive to feelings of hunger? If you are like most people, you spend quite a bit of time thinking about the consequences of what you eat for your body shape and size. To discuss the psychology of eating, we will focus largely on circumstances in which people try to exercise control over these consequences—to try to reshape their bodies in response to their perceptions of some personal or societal ideal.

In the next section, we will explore some of the roots and consequences of obesity and dieting. We then describe how eating disorders may arise as an extreme response to concerns about body image and weight.

OBESITY AND DIETING

Psychologists have spent a good deal of time considering circumstances that have given rise to what has often been labeled an "epidemic" of obesity. To determine who is overweight and who is obese, researchers often turn to a measure called *body mass index (BMI)*. To calculate BMI, one divides an individual's weight in kilograms by the square of height in meters. For example, someone who weighed 154 lbs and was 5'7" would have a BMI of 24.2. (154 lbs = 69.8 kilograms. 5'7" = 1.70 meters. $69.8/(1.70)^2 = 24.2$. You can also use Google to find a BMI calculator on the Web.) In most instances, individuals who have BMIs between 25 to 29.9 are considered overweight. Those individuals with BMIs 30 and above are considered obese. By those standards, roughly 45 percent of adult men and 29 percent of adult women in the United States are overweight. An additional 21 percent of both men and women are obese (Mokdad et al., 2003). These obesity rates have risen 71 percent since 1991.

These figures suggest why there's a certain urgency to answer the question, Why do people become overweight? It probably will not surprise you, as you have seen throughout *Psychology and Life,* that the answer lies partly in nature and partly in nurture. This chapter's Psychology in the 21st Century box describes the strong case for "nature": Some people have a genetic predisposition toward obesity. However, even a biological predisposition may not be enough to "cause" a particular person to become overweight. What matters, in addition, is the way in which an individual *thinks* about food and eating behaviors. Early research on psychological aspects of eating focused on the extent to which overweight individuals are attentive to their bodies' internal hunger cues versus food in the external environment (Schachter, 1971a). The suggestion was that, when food is available and prominent, overweight individuals ignore the cues their bodies give them. This theory proved to be insufficient, however, because weight itself does not always predict eating patterns. That is, not all people who are overweight have the same psychological makeup with respect to eating behaviors. Let's see why.

Janet Polivy and **Peter Herman** have proposed that the critical dimension that underlies the psychology of eating behaviors is *restrained* versus *unrestrained* eating (Polivy & Herman, 1999). *Restrained* eaters put constant limits on the amount of food they will let

Genes and Obesity

The 21st century began with a remarkable announcement from the world of science: Researchers on the *Human Genome Project* reported that they were very close to providing an initial mapping of the chemical bases of the human genome. The ultimate goal of this project is to provide a complete account of the genes that make up that genome. The Human Genome Project has increased scientists' beliefs that they will be able to understand the genetic bases of a large range of disorders that impair the quality of individuals' lives.

One such disorder with a genetic basis is *obesity*. Researchers have provided ample evidence that people are born with innate tendencies to be lighter or heavier. For example, studies of identical twins have revealed great similarity in their overall weight (Allison et al., 1994; Stunkard et al., 1990). Part of this similarity may be explained by the finding that the rate at which an individual's body burns calories to maintain basic functions, the individual's *resting metabolic rate*, is also highly heritable (Bouchard et al., 1989). Thus, some people are innately predisposed to

burn a lot of calories just through ordinary day-to-day activities; others are not. Those who are not are more at risk for weight gain.

Recently, researchers have discovered some of the actual genetic mechanisms that may predispose some individuals to obesity (Gura, 2000; Marx, 2003). For example, a gene has been isolated that appears to control signals to the brain that enough fat has been stored in the body in the course of a meal—so the individual should stop eating (Zhang et al., 1994). If this gene, called *leptin*, is inactive, the individual will continue to eat, with obesity as a potential result. In fact, researchers have discovered small populations of obese individuals with mutations in this gene; the mutation appears to explain their obesity (Jackson et al., 1997; Montague et al., 1997). Because these mutations are extremely rare, they cannot account for the vast majority of cases of obesity. Even so, the confirmation that leptin plays a roll in weight regulation has encouraged researchers' efforts to identify and understand other weight-related genes.

This genetic research holds out the promise of innovative solutions to obesity. Researchers hope, for example, that an understanding of the link between genes and weight regulation will enable them to provide new drug treatments (Campfield et al., 1998; Gura, 2003). Some of the early efforts have been discouraging: Research manipulating leptin has yet to show a great impact on weight loss. However, given constant leaps forward in genetic understanding, scientists continue to form new hypotheses about how they might intervene in the body's mechanisms for weight regulation (Gura, 2000). Nonetheless, even the most optimistic researchers provide words of caution: "Innovative drugs will be most effective when they are used as adjuncts to, rather than substitutes for, lifestyle changes to improve the metabolic fitness, health, and quality of life for obese individuals" (Campfield et al., 1998, p. 1387). Put another way, no matter how much we come to understand *nature*, we must always be aware that *nurture* still plays a critical role in our life outcomes.

themselves eat: They are chronically on diets; they constantly worry about food. Although obese people may be more likely to report these kinds of thoughts and behaviors, individuals can be restrained eaters whatever their body size. How do people gain weight if they are constantly on a diet? Research suggests that when restrained eaters become *disinhibited*—when life circumstances cause them to let down their restraints—

they tend to indulge in high-calorie binges. Unfortunately, many types of life circumstances appear to lead restrained eaters to become disinhibited. Disinhibition will occur, for example, when restrained eaters are made to feel stress about their capabilities and self-esteem (Greeno & Wing, 1994; Tanofsky-Kraff et al., 2000). In fact, one type of stress is the *anticipation* of being on a strict diet.

The Effects of Anticipated Diets on Restrained and Unrestrained Eaters

Based on self-evaluations of their behaviors and thoughts with respect to food and dieting, female college students were classified as either restrained (17 women) or unrestrained (24 women) eaters. The students were told they were taking part in a study "investigating the effects of food deprivation on taste perception" (Urbszat et al., 2002, p. 398). When they arrived for the experiment, half of the students were asked to undertake a low-calorie diet—approved by "the Canadian Government and the University of Toronto"—for one week. Participants in both the *diet* and *no-diet* conditions were then asked to perform taste tests on three plates of cookies. The participants believed that these taste tests were the baseline data for the study of taste perception. In fact, the researchers were measuring the total grams of cookies each participant consumed. The results of the study are shown in **Figure 11.1.** For unrestrained eaters, it made no difference whether they were anticipating a strict diet. However, for the restrained eaters, anticipation of the diet led them to eat more than twice as much of the cookies.

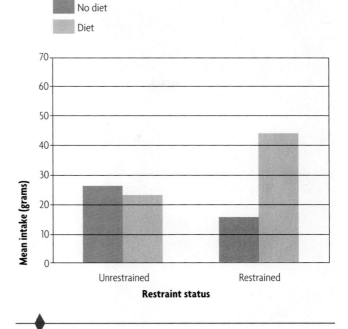

FIGURE 11.1

The Effects of Anticipated Diets

Restrained and unrestrained eaters sampled cookies to rate their taste. Half of the women in each group had agreed to undertake a reduced-calorie diet for one week. For unrestrained eaters, the amount of cookies (in grams) they ate while making the taste ratings was unaffected by the anticipation of a diet. However, those restrained eaters who anticipated dieting ate more than twice as much as their no-diet peers.

This result suggests why diets are often unsuccessful for restrained eaters. As the researchers note, their diets can be broken even "by the prospect of not being able to eat forbidden food" (Urbszat et al., 2002, p. 399).

You see now why it might be difficult for people to lose weight once they have become overweight. Many overweight people report themselves as constantly on diets—they are often restrained eaters. If stressful life events occur that cause these eaters to become disinhibited, binge eating can easily lead to weight gain. Thus, the psychological consequences of being constantly on a diet can, paradoxically, create circumstances that are more likely to lead to weight gain than to weight loss. In the next section, we will see how these same psychological forces can lead to health- and life-threatening eating disorders.

EATING DISORDERS AND BODY IMAGE

One finding about body image is that the group of people who believe themselves to be overweight is larger than the group of people who are actually overweight (Brownell & Rodin 1994). When the disparity between people's perceptions of their body image and their actual size becomes too large, they may be at risk for

eating disorders. **Anorexia nervosa** is diagnosed when an individual weighs less than 85 percent of her or his expected weight, but still expresses an intense fear of becoming fat (*DSM-IV*, 1994). The behavior of people diagnosed with **bulimia nervosa** is characterized by binges—periods of intense, out-of-control eating—followed by measures to purge the body of the excess calories—self-induced vomiting, misuse of laxatives, fasting, and so on (*DSM-IV*, 1994). Sufferers from anorexia nervosa may also binge and then purge as a way of minimizing calories absorbed. Both of these syndromes can have serious medical consequences. In the worst cases, sufferers may starve to death.

The prevalence of anorexia among women in late adolescence and early adulthood is about 0.5 to 1.0 percent (*DSM-IV*, 1994). From 1 to 3 percent of the women in this same age group suffer from bulimia (*DSM-IV*, 1994; Rand & Kuldau, 1992). Women suffer from both diseases at approximately ten times the rate of men.

What do these photographs of Courtney Cox and Marilyn Monroe suggest about changes over time in how thin women must be for the media to promote them as sexy?

Why do people begin to starve themselves to death, and why are most of those people women? There is some evidence that a predilection toward eating disorders may be genetically transmitted (Kortegaard et al., 2001). Much research attention, however, has focused on women's expectations for their ideal weight as generated by society and the media (Durkin & Paxton, 2002; Wertheim et al., 1997). For example, many of the magazines that are marketed specifically to women put great emphasis on weight loss; the same is not true for the magazines that men read (Andersen & DiDomenico, 1992). Thus, women may get more cultural support for their belief that they are overweight than do men. The belief that eating disorders follow, in part, from cultural forces has also received support from a number of analyses that have demonstrated important cultural differences.

PUTTING IDEAS TO THE TEST

Cross-Cultural Perceptions of Body Size

A sample of 219 students from the University of Vermont and 349 students from the University of Ghana were asked a number of questions about their eating and dieting practices. These surveys revealed, for example, that although roughly the same number of the college-age men in the two countries had ever been on a diet (U.S., 5.3 percent; Ghana, 6.1 percent) considerably more U.S. women (43.5 percent) had undertaken diets than had Ghanian women (13.3 percent). The students were also asked to choose which of the figures from **Figure 11.2** best represented what they considered to be the ideal male and female bodies. The students' average ratings are presented in **Figure 11.3**. What you can see is that the ratings for men are pretty consistent across raters (that is, men and women) and countries. Compare the average ratings to those in Figure 11.2. The "ideal" male lies between M5 and M6, but closer to M5. However, the ratings for the ideal woman's body differed from the United States to Ghana by about a full point. Students in the United States idealized a body a bit slimmer than F5; Ghanians chose something closer to F6 (Cogan et al., 1996).

How might these differences be explained? The researchers suggest that in Ghana, as well as in other African countries, not everyone can *afford* to be overweight: "fat is associated with wealth and abundance" (Cogan et al., 1996, p. 98). As you can see in Figure 11.3, the positive association between size and prosperity is particularly applied to women, and particularly by Ghanian men.

Within the United States, it is equally easy to find group differences in judgments about body size. For

<www.ablongman.com/gerrig17e>

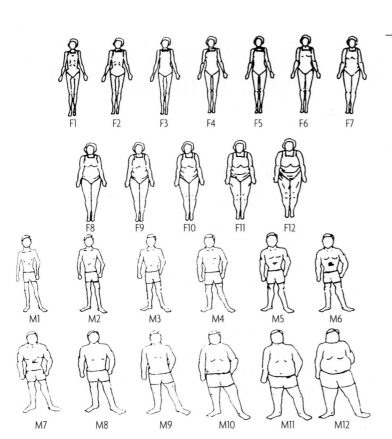

FIGURE 11.2

Judgments of Body Size

Which picture do you believe best represents the United States' ideal for a woman? For a man?

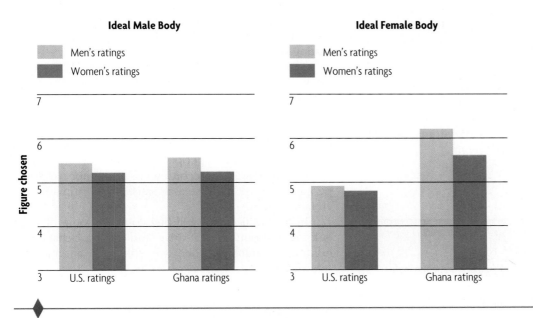

FIGURE 11.3

Cross-Cultural Perceptions of Body Size

Students from the University of Vermont and the University of Ghana indicated which of the figures from Figure 11.2 best represented what they considered to be the ideal male and female bodies. The students' ratings for male bodies are largely consistent across raters (that is, men and women) and countries. However, the ratings for the ideal woman's body differed from the United States to Ghana by about a full point. Ghanian men gave even higher ratings than Ghanian women.

example, surveys of large groups of adolescent girls consistently reveal that African American girls are more comfortable with their body sizes than are white adolescent girls (Parker et al., 1995; Rand & Kuldau, 1990; Rucker & Cash, 1992). Similarly, when black and white college women rated photographs of thin, average, and large models, only the white women rated the large models lower (compared to the thin and average models) on dimensions such as attractiveness, intelligence, and popularity (Hebl & Heatherton, 1998).

Against this background, you will probably not be surprised to learn that white females are also more likely to suffer from eating disorders than are African American females. One study involved 985 white women and 1,061 African American women who were all about 21 years of age (Striegel-Moore et al., 2003). In those groups, 1.5 percent of the white women had suffered from anorexia nervosa at some point in their lives; no African American women had experienced that disorder. Bulimia nervosa had affected 2.3 percent of the white women but only 0.4 percent of the African American women. Fewer studies have examined other racial and ethnic groups, but evidence to date suggests that eating disturbances are also less frequent in Asian Americans than whites but equally common among Hispanic females as among whites. For each of these findings, researchers try to draw a link between cultural values about body size and dieting behaviors.

A final note: Right now, you're likely to be part of a particular culture that promotes eating disorders. Women in high school and college tend to suffer from anorexia or bulimia more than do nonstudents. In college settings, women may solve the tension between wanting to look attractive and wanting to eat and drink with their friends by bingeing—enjoying the party—and then purging—eliminating the calories (Rand & Kuldau, 1992). You should be aware that college life provides this dangerous potential.

PUT YOURSELF TO THE TEST

- What are some of the peripheral responses that contribute to feelings of hunger?
- What role does the hypothalamus play in the regulation of eating?
- What is the importance of restrained eating to dieting and obesity?
- How do cultural norms affect the development of eating disorders?

Sexual Behaviors

Your body physiology makes it essential that you think about food every day. But what about sex? It's easy to define the biological function of sex—reproduction—but does that explain the frequency with which you think about sexual behaviors? When asked how often they think about sex, 54 percent of adult men and 19 percent of adult women report they think about sex at least once every day (Michael et al., 1994). How can we explain the frequency with which people think about sex? How do thoughts about sex relate to sexual behaviors?

The question of motivation, once again, is the question of why people carry out certain ranges of behavior. As we already acknowledged, sexual behaviors are biologically necessary only for reproduction. Thus, while eating is essential to individual survival, sex is not. Some animals and humans remain celibate for a lifetime without apparent detriment to their daily functioning. But reproduction is crucial to the survival of the species as a whole. To ensure that effort will be expended toward reproduction, nature has made sexual stimulation intensely pleasurable. An orgasm serves as the ultimate reinforcer for the energy expended in mating.

This potential for pleasure gives to sexual behaviors motivating power well beyond the need for reproduction. Individuals will perform a great variety of behaviors to achieve sexual gratification. But some sources of sexual motivation are external. Cultures establish norms or standards for what is acceptable or expected sexual behavior. While most people may be motivated to perform behaviors that accord with those norms, some people achieve their sexual satisfaction primarily by violating them.

In this section, we will first consider some of what is known about the sex drive and mating behavior in nonhuman animals. Then we shift our attention to selected issues in human sexuality.

◆ NONHUMAN SEXUAL BEHAVIORS

The primary motivation for sexual behaviors in nonhuman animals is reproduction. For species that use sex as a means of reproduction, evolution has generally provided two sexual types, males and females. The female produces relatively large eggs (which contain the energy store for the embryo to begin its growth), and the male produces sperm that are specialized for motility (to move into the eggs). The two sexes must synchronize their activity so that sperm and egg meet under the appropriate conditions, resulting in conception.

Sexual arousal is determined primarily by physiological processes. Animals become receptive to mating largely in response to the flow of hormones controlled by the pituitary gland and secreted from the *gonads,* the sex organs. In males, these hormones are known as *androgens,* and they are continuously present in sufficient supply so that males are hormonally ready for mating at almost any time. In the females of many species, however, the sex hormone *estrogen* is released according to regular time cycles of days or months, or according to seasonal changes. Therefore, the female is not always hormonally receptive to mating.

These hormones act on both the brain and genital tissue and often lead to a pattern of predictable *stereotyped sexual behavior* for all members of a species. If, for example, you've seen one pair of rats in their mating sequence, you've seen them all. The receptive female rat darts about the male until she gets his attention. Then he chases her as she runs away. She stops suddenly and raises her rear, and he enters her briefly, thrusts, and pulls out. She briefly escapes him and the chase resumes—interrupted by 10 to 20 intromissions before he ejaculates, rests awhile, and starts the sex chase again. Apes also copulate only briefly (for about 15 seconds). For sables, copulation is slow and long, lasting for as long as eight hours. Predators, such as lions, can afford to indulge in long, slow copulatory rituals—as much as every 30 minutes over four consecutive days. Their prey, however, such as antelope, copulate for only a few seconds, often on the run (Ford & Beach, 1951).

Sexual arousal is often initiated by stimuli in the external environment. In many species, the sight and sound of ritualized display patterns by potential partners is a necessary condition for sexual response. Furthermore, in species as diverse as sheep, bulls, and rats, the novelty of the female partner affects a male animal's behavior. A male that has reached sexual satiation with one female partner may renew sexual activity when a new female is introduced (Dewsbury, 1981). Touch, taste, and smell can also serve as external stimulants for sexual arousal. As we described in Chapter 4, some species secrete chemical signals, called *pheromones,* that attract suitors, sometimes from great distances (Farine et al., 1996; Luo et al., 2003). In many species, the female emits pheromones when her fertility is optimal (and hormone level and sexual interest are peaking). These secretions are unconditioned stimuli for arousal and attraction in the males of the species, who have inherited the tendency to be aroused by the stimuli. When captive male rhesus monkeys smell the odor of a sexually receptive female in an adjacent cage, they respond with a variety of sex-related physiological changes, including an increase in the size of their testes (Hopson, 1979).

Although sexual response in nonhuman animals is largely determined by innate biological forces, this still leaves room for "cultural" aspects to affect choices of mate. Consider the sailfin molly.

PUTTING IDEAS TO THE TEST

Mate-Choice Copying in Sailfin Mollies

Under most circumstances, the female sailfin mollies from the Comal River in Texas show a mating preference for larger males. However, what happens when a female sailfin molly observes another female showing a preference for a smaller male? To answer this question, researchers arranged a set of tanks so that female sailfin mollies swam in a large tank that had two smaller tanks at each end (Witte & Noltemeir, 2002). In the initial phase of the experiment, a large and a small male fish were put into small tanks at either end. As seen in **Figure 11.4,** the females spent considerably more time swimming in proximity to the larger male. In the second phase of the experiment, a second female was placed in another small tank so that she appeared to be swimming near the smaller of the two males. The original female had 20 minutes to observe the second female fraternizing with the smaller male. In the final phase of the experiment, the researchers removed the second female and again observed the original females' preferences. As seen in Figure 11.4, in the second preference test the pattern had largely reversed. The female sailfin mollies were now spending most of their time swimming near the smaller males.

What factors determine the sexual behaviors of most species?

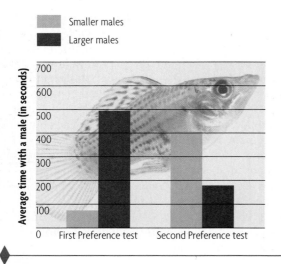

Smaller males
Larger males

FIGURE 11.4

Female Sailfin Mollies' Mate Selection

*Researchers calculated how long female sailfin mollies swam
in proximity to larger versus smaller male fish. In the first
preference test, the females spent much more time swimming
near the larger fish. Next, the original females observed a second
female swim close to the smaller male for 20 minutes. In the
second preference test, which took place after those 20 minutes,
the original females reversed their original pattern to spend
more time close to the smaller males.*

Are you surprised to learn that innocent fish swimming in
aquariums are paying attention to which other fish have
been judged desirable and undesirable? This experiment
sets the stage for our discussion of human sexuality. We
will soon see that researchers believe that human sexual
response is also shaped both by our evolutionary history
and the preferences of those around us.

◆ HUMAN SEXUAL AROUSAL AND RESPONSE

Hormonal activity, so important in regulating sexual
behavior among other animal species, has little effect on
sexual receptiveness or gratification in the vast majority
of men and women (Bancroft, 1978). In women, hormones play an important role in controlling the cycles of
ovulation and menstruation. However, individual differences in hormone levels, within normal limits, are not
predictive of the frequency or quality of sexual activity.
For men, the hormone *testosterone* is necessary for sexual arousal and performance. Most healthy men from
ages 18 to at least 60 have sufficient testosterone levels
to experience normal sex drives. Once again, individual
variation in these levels among men, within normal limits, is not related to sexual performance.

Sexual arousal in humans is the motivational state
of excitement and tension brought about by physiological and cognitive reactions to erotic stimuli. *Erotic stim-*

uli, which may be physical or psychological, give rise
to sexual excitement or feelings of passion. Sexual
arousal induced by erotic stimuli is reduced by sexual
activities that are perceived by the individual as satisfying, especially by achieving orgasm.

Researchers have studied sexual practices and sexual responses in nonhuman animals for several decades,
but for many years studies of similar behaviors in
humans were off limits. **William Masters** and **Virginia
Johnson** (1966, 1970, 1979) broke down this traditional
taboo. They legitimized the study of human sexuality by
directly observing and recording, under laboratory conditions, the physiological patterns involved in ongoing
human sexual performance. By doing so, they explored
not what people said about sex but how individuals
actually reacted or performed sexually.

For their direct investigation of the human response
to sexual stimulation, Masters and Johnson conducted
controlled laboratory observations of thousands of volunteer males and females during tens of thousands of sexual
response cycles of intercourse and masturbation. Four of
the most significant conclusions drawn from this research
are that (1) men and women have similar patterns of sexual response; (2) although the sequence of phases of the
sexual response cycle is similar in the two sexes, women
are more variable, tending to respond more slowly but
often remaining aroused longer; (3) many women can
have multiple orgasms, whereas men rarely do in a
comparable time period; and (4) penis size is generally
unrelated to any aspect of sexual performance (except
in the male's attitude toward having a large penis).

Four phases were found in the human sexual response cycle: excitement, plateau, orgasm, and resolution (see **Figure 11.5**).

- In the excitement phase (lasting from a few minutes to more than an hour), there are vascular
(blood vessel) changes in the pelvic region. The
penis becomes erect and the clitoris swells; blood
and other fluids become congested in the testicles
and vagina; a reddening of the body, or sex flush,
occurs.

- During the plateau phase, a maximum (though
varying) level of arousal is reached. There are rapidly increased heartbeat, respiration, and blood
pressure, increased glandular secretions, and both
voluntary and involuntary muscle tension throughout the body. Vaginal lubrication increases, and
the breasts swell.

- During the orgasm phase, males and females
experience a very intense, pleasurable sense of
release from the sexual tension that has been
building. Orgasm is characterized by rhythmic
contractions that occur approximately every eight-
tenths of a second in the genital areas. Respiration
and blood pressure reach very high levels in both

<www.ablongman.com/gerrig17e>

men and women, and heart rate may double. In men, throbbing contractions lead to ejaculation, an "explosion" of semen.

- During the resolution phase, the body gradually returns to its normal preexcitement state, with both blood pressure and heartbeat slowing down. After one orgasm, most men enter a refractory period, lasting anywhere from a few minutes to several hours, during which no further orgasm is possible. With sustained arousal, some women are capable of multiple orgasms in fairly rapid succession.

Although Masters and Johnson's research focused on the physiology of sexual response, perhaps their most important discovery was the central significance of *psychological* processes in both arousal and satisfaction. They demonstrated that problems in sexual response often have psychological, rather than physiological, origins and can be modified or overcome through therapy. Of particular concern is the inability to complete the response cycle and achieve gratification. Often the source of the inability is a preoccupation with personal problems, fear of the consequences of sexual activity, anxiety about a partner's evaluation of one's sexual performance, or unconscious guilt or negative thoughts. However, poor nutrition, fatigue, stress, and excessive use of alcohol or drugs can also diminish sexual drive and performance.

We have now reviewed some physiological aspects of human sexuality and sexual arousal. But we have not yet considered the forces that give rise to *differences* in sexual expression. We begin with the idea that the goal of reproduction ensures different patterns of sexual behavior for men and for women.

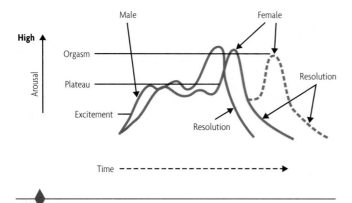

FIGURE 11.5

Phases of Human Sexual Response

The phases of human sexual response in males and females have similar patterns. The primary differences are in the time it takes for males and females to reach each phase, and in the greater likelihood that females will achieve multiple orgasms.

Although sex fulfills the biological function of reproduction, most humans engage in sex many more times than they reproduce. Even so, how does the evolutionary perspective explain contemporary sexual strategies?

◆ THE EVOLUTION OF SEXUAL BEHAVIORS

For nonhuman animals, we have already seen that the pattern of sexual behaviors was largely fixed by evolution. The main goal is reproduction—preservation of the species—and sexual behaviors are highly ritualized and stereotyped. Can the same claim be made for general patterns of human sexual behaviors?

Evolutionary psychologists have explored the idea that men and women have evolved to have different *strategies* that underlie sexual behavior (Buss, 1999; Wright, 1994). To describe these strategies, we have to remind you of some of the realities of human reproduction. Human males could reproduce hundreds of times a year if they could find enough willing mates. To produce a child, all they need to invest is a teaspoon of sperm and a few minutes of intercourse. Women can reproduce at most about once a year, and each child then requires a huge investment of time and energy. (Incidentally, the world record for the number of times a woman has given birth falls short of 50, but men have fathered many more children. A Moroccan despot, King Ismail the Blood-Thirsty, had over 700 children, and the first emperor of China is said to have fathered over 3,000; both had large harems.)

Thus, when reproduction is a goal, eggs are the limited resource and males compete for opportunities to fertilize them. The basic problem facing a male animal is to maximize the number of offspring he produces, by mating with the largest number of females possible. But the basic problem facing a female animal is to find a high-quality male to ensure the best, healthiest offspring from her limited store of eggs. Furthermore, human offspring take so long to mature and are so helpless while growing that substantial **parental investment** is required (Trivers, 1972; Wright, 1994). Mothers and fathers must spend time and energy raising the children—unlike fish or spiders, which simply lay eggs and depart. Females thus have the problem of selecting not just the biggest, strongest, smartest, highest-status, most thrilling mate but also the most loyal, committed partner to help raise their children.

One evolutionary psychologist, **David Buss** (1999; Buss & Schmitt, 1993), has suggested that men and women evolved different strategies, emotions, and motivations for *short-term mating* versus *long-term mating*. The male strategy of seducing and abandoning— showing signs of loyalty and commitment and then leaving—is a short-term strategy. The male strategy of staying committed to the female and investing in the offspring is a long-term strategy. The female strategy of attracting a loyal male who will stay to help raise her children is a long-term strategy. There is some controversy about whether women have evolved short-term mating strategies. Some argue that indiscriminate sex never pays for women in an evolutionary sense—they can get pregnant without assurance of male investment later. Women do seem less interested in casual sex than men (Buss & Schmitt, 1993; Schmidt et al., 2001). Others argue that short-term mating with many men—especially older, rich men—in exchange for immediate rewards may pay off by assuring short-term survival.

Researchers have provided a variety of types of evidence to support predictions of evolutionary theory. Consider studies that examined how women's judgments of the attractiveness of male faces was affected by the possibility of conception.

PUTTING IDEAS TO THE TEST

Women's Preferences for Males' Faces

Which male faces will a particular woman find attractive? A team of researchers hypothesized that the answer to this question depends, in part, on the phase of the woman's menstrual cycle (Penton-Voak et al., 1999; Penton-Voak & Perrett, 2000). The male faces used in the experiments were computer manipulated to provide a range from those that looked relatively more masculine to those that looked relatively more feminine. When asked to choose the most attractive face for a "long-term relationship," women preferred those faces that looked relatively more feminine: Apparently the more feminine faces implied that the man would be a reliable partner for the long term. However, choices for "short-term relationships" depended on the women's menstrual phases. Those women who were in the part of their menstrual cycle that put them at risk for conception shifted their choices to faces that were relatively more masculine looking. Apparently, the possibility of pregnancy shifted the women's preferences from faces that signaled "good provider" to those that signaled "good genes."

This research examined preferences, rather than actual sexual behavior. Even so, it illustrates how important aspects of human lives may be guided by our evolutionary history.

Although research supports many of the predictions of the evolutionary account of human sexual behaviors, other theorists believe that the account greatly underestimates the role of culture (Angier, 1999; Baumeister & Twenge, 2002). For example, women demonstrate greater *erotic plasticity* than men: Women show greater variation in sexual responses and sexual behaviors than men do (Baumeister, 2000). These variations appear, in large part, to be a consequence of cultural constraints (Hyde & Durik, 2000). Consider the "sexual revolution" of the 1960s: Changes in sexual behavior were brought about by women's increased willingness to engage in casual sexual relations. What had changed was not, of course, women's evolutionary history but, rather, cultural attitudes toward the expression of sexuality.

Although the evolutionary approach explains some aspects of human sexual behavior, the critique calls attention to variability imposed by culture. Norms of sexual behavior are highly sensitive to time and place. We turn now to sexual norms.

◆ SEXUAL NORMS

What is an average sex life like? Scientific investigation of human sexual behavior was given the first important impetus by the work of **Alfred Kinsey** and his colleagues beginning in the 1940s (1948, 1953). They interviewed some 17,000 Americans about their sexual behavior and revealed—to a generally shocked public—that certain behaviors, previously considered rare and even abnormal, were actually quite widespread—or at least were reported to be. In recent years, researchers have conducted surveys about sexual practices with great regularity. The results are often widely trumpeted by the media. In **Table 11.2,** we have provided you with some data from one major effort (Michael et al., 1994). The researchers asked a wide range of questions. We have given you only a small sample of the responses. Can you spot any interesting trends? You might find it noteworthy, for example, that people age 55 to 59 are much more likely to have stuck with one partner since age 18 than are those age 25 to 29. This outcome suggests that the norms for sexual behavior have changed over the past several decades.

These sexual norms are part of what you acquire as a member of a culture. We already suggested that some general "male" and "female" aspects of sexual behavior may be products of the evolution of the human species. Even so, different cultures define ranges of behavior that are considered to be appropriate for expressing sexual impulses. **Sexual scripts** are socially learned programs

TABLE 11.2

Sexual Activity of Adult Americans, 1994*

	NUMBER OF SEXUAL PARTNERS SINCE AGE 18 (PERCENTAGE IN EACH CATEGORY)			
	0	**1**	**2–10**	**10 or More**
Men	3	26	44	33
Women	3	31	56	9
Ages 25–29	2	25	53	19
Ages 55–59	1	40	43	15
High school education	3	30	49	17
College education	2	24	50	24

	FREQUENCY OF SEXUAL ACTIVITY IN THE PAST 12 MONTHS (PERCENTAGE IN EACH CATEGORY)			
	Not at All	**A Few Times per Year**	**A Few Times per Month**	**Two or More Times per Week**
Men	14	16	37	34
Women	10	18	36	37
Men				
Ages 25–29	7	15	31	47
Ages 55–59	11	22	43	23
Women				
Ages 25–29	5	10	38	47
Ages 55–59	30	22	35	13
Men				
High school	10	15	34	41
Some college	9	18	38	35
Women				
High school	11	16	38	36
Some college	14	17	37	33

*Based on a random survey sample of 3,432 adults, age 18 and older.

of sexual responsiveness that include prescriptions, usually unspoken, of what to do; when, where, and how to do it; with whom, or with what, to do it; and why it should be done (Laumann & Gagnon, 1995). Different aspects of these scripts are assembled through social interaction over your lifetime. The attitudes and values embodied in your sexual script are an external source of sexual motivation: The script suggests the types of behaviors you might or should undertake.

Scripts are combinations of prescriptions generated by social norms (what is proper and accepted), individual expectations, and preferred sequences of behavior from past learning. Your sexual scripts include scenarios not only of what you think is appropriate on your part but also of your expectations for a sexual partner. When they are not recognized, discussed, or synchronized,

differing scripts can create problems of adjustment between partners.

Let's focus more specifically on the sexual practices of college students. Researchers have often been interested in understanding *sexual risk taking:* circumstances in which individuals engage in sexual practices that ignore the risk of pregnancy or sexually transmitted diseases. Given our discussion of evolution and sex differences, you may not be surprised to learn that, on the whole, men are more likely than women to engage in risky behaviors (Poppen, 1995). In one sample of college students, more men than women report that they have gone to bars to meet prospective sex partners (77 vs. 14 percent) and that they have had sex with someone they have just met (47 vs. 24 percent). In addition, slightly more men than women reported having

How might instances of sexual harassment arise from conflicting sexual scripts?

had sex without some form of contraception (78 vs. 64 percent).

Research into the sexual experience of college students has revealed another area in which male and female sexual scripts come into devastating conflict: *rape*. In one study, researchers asked 4,446 women at 2- or 4-year colleges and universities to provide information about their experiences of sexual aggression in 7 months of a school year (Fisher et al., 2000). In that reference period, 1.1 percent of the women had experienced attempted rape and 1.7 percent had experienced completed rape. The researchers extended those numbers to estimate the likelihood that a woman would experience an attempted or completed rape during her college career: They concluded that the number of victimized women might climb to 20 to 25 percent. The researchers also examined a particular type of rape: **date rape.** Date rape applies to circumstances in which someone is coerced into sexual activity by a social acquaintance. For this sample of women, 12.8 percent of completed rapes and 35.0 percent of attempted rapes occurred on dates.

When asked to say who was responsible for a date rape, males surveyed tend to blame the victim (that is, the woman who was raped) more than females do (Bell et al., 1994; Ryckman et al., 1998). Studies of date rape reveal that women's and men's sexual scripts differ significantly with respect to the incidence of *token resistance*—a woman's mild resistance to sexual advances despite the intention, ultimately, to allow sexual intercourse. Very few women—about 5 percent—report engaging in token resistance, but about 60 percent of men say that they have, at least once, *experienced* token resistance (Marx & Gross, 1995). The difference between those two figures likely includes many incidents of date rape. Research suggests that some men come to believe that token resistance is part of a sexual game; resistance

doesn't signal genuine distress on a woman's part. It is important for men to understand that women, in fact, rarely report themselves to be playing that game—resistance is real.

Throughout most of our discussion of sexual motivation, we have been ignoring a major category of sexual experience: homosexuality. We conclude this section on sexual motivation with a discussion of lesbians and gay men. This discussion will give us another opportunity to see how sexual behavior is controlled by the interplay of internal and external motivational forces.

◆ HOMOSEXUALITY

Our discussion so far has focused on the motivations that cause people to perform a certain range of sexual behaviors. In this same context we can discuss the existence of homosexuality. That is, rather than presenting homosexuality as a set of behaviors that is "caused" by a deviation from heterosexuality, our discussion of sexual motivation should allow you to see that all sexual behavior is "caused." In this view, homosexuality and heterosexuality result from similar motivational forces. Neither of them represents a motivated departure from the other.

Most surveys of sexual behavior have tried to obtain an accurate estimate of the incidence of homosexuality. In his early research, Alfred Kinsey found that 37 percent of men in his sample had had at least some homosexual experience and that about 4 percent were exclusively homosexual (percentages for women were somewhat smaller). More recent surveys have tried to capture the distinction between having homosexual desires and acting on them. Michael and colleagues (1994) found that about 4 percent of women in their sample were sexually attracted to individuals of the same gender, but only 2 percent of the sample had actually had sex with another woman in the past year. Similarly, 6 percent of the men in their survey were sexually attracted to other men, but again only 2 percent of the sample had actually had sex with another man in the past year. Are these figures correct? As long as there is societal hostility directed toward acting on homosexual desires, it may be impossible to get entirely accurate estimates of the incidence of homosexuality because of people's reluctance to confide in researchers.

In this section we consider the origins of homosexuality and heterosexuality. We also review research on societal and personal attitudes toward homosexual behavior.

THE NATURE AND NURTURE OF HOMOSEXUALITY

After our discussion of evolution and sexual behaviors, it should not surprise you to learn that research evidence suggests that sexual preference has a genetic compo-

<www.ablongman.com/gerrig17e>

What evidence suggests that sexual orientation has a genetic component?

nent. As is often the case, researchers have made this assertion based on studies that compare concordance rates of *monozygotic* (MZ) twins (those who are genetically identical) and *dizygotic* (DZ) twins (those who, like siblings, share only half their genes). When both members of a pair of twins have the same orientation—homosexual or heterosexual—they are concordant. If one twin is homosexual and the other is heterosexual, they are discordant. Studies of both gay men and lesbians have demonstrated considerably higher concordance rates for MZ than for DZ twins (Bailey & Pillard, 1991; Bailey et al., 1993). In these studies, the experimenters searched out individual gay or lesbian twins and then obtained information from them about the sexual orientation of their co-twins or other siblings. The results were startling. Among women, 48 percent of MZ twins were both lesbians, compared with 16 percent of DZ twins (Bailey et al., 1993). Among men, 52 percent of MZ twins were both gay, compared with 22 percent of DZ twins (Bailey & Pillard, 1991). Although MZ twins may also be reared in more similar environments than DZ twins—they may be treated more similarly by their parents—this pattern strongly suggests that sexuality may, in part, be genetically determined. With this knowledge in hand, researchers have started

to search for the gene sequences that might control the emergence of homosexuality or heterosexuality (Bailey et al., 1999; Hamer et al., 1993; Rice et al., 1999). So, does biology determine your sexual destiny? Further research may strengthen or weaken the case, but it seems clear that some aspects of homosexuality and heterosexuality emerge in response to purely biological forces (Gladue, 1994; LeVay, 1996).

Social psychologist **Daryl Bem** (1996, 2000) has suggested that biology does not effect sexual preference directly, but rather has an indirect impact by influencing the temperaments and activities of young children. Recall from Chapter 10 that researchers have suggested that boys and girls engage in different activities—boys' play, for example, tends to be more rough-and-tumble. According to Bem's theory, depending on whether they engage in sex-typical or sex-atypical play, children come to feel dissimilar to either their same-sex or opposite-sex peers. In Bem's theory, "exotic becomes erotic": Feelings of dissimilarity lead to emotional arousal; over time this arousal is transformed into erotic attraction. For example, if a young girl feels dissimilar from other girls because she does not wish to engage in girl-typical activities, over time her emotional arousal will be transformed into homosexual feelings. Note that Bem's theory supports the assertion that homosexuality and heterosexuality arise from the same causal forces: In both cases, the gender the child perceives as dissimilar becomes, over time, eroticized. Although Bem provides a range of evidence in favor of his theory, it is still relatively new. We will see in the next several years how it fares when researchers assess its various implications.

SOCIETY AND HOMOSEXUALITY

Suppose Bem is correct to argue that childhood experiences matter enormously. Does everyone act on the urgings set down in childhood? What, perhaps, most sets homosexuality apart from heterosexuality is the continuing hostility toward homosexual behaviors in many corners of society (Herek, 1998, 2002). In a survey of 363 adults, 68 percent agreed "strongly" or "somewhat" with the statement "Sex between two men is just plain wrong"; 64 percent agreed "strongly" or "somewhat" with the statement "Sex between two women is just plain wrong" (Herek, 1994). Researchers have labeled highly negative attitudes toward gay people *homophobia*.

Most homosexuals come to the realization that they are motivated toward same-sex relationships in the hostile context of societal homophobia. Even so, research suggests that many individuals begin to recognize those feelings at quite young ages. For example, researchers asked students from the southeastern United States attending a conference for gay, lesbian, bisexual, and transgendered youth to indicate the age at which they became aware of their sexual orientation (Maguen et al., 2002). Among the gay men, the mean age was 9.6 years; among the lesbians the mean age was 10.9 years. The men reported having same-sex sexual contact at 14.9 years and the women reported same-sex contact at 16.7 years. These data suggest that many people become aware of their homosexual orientation at a time when they must still function in school environments that are often quite hostile to homosexuality (D'Augelli et al., 2002). In addition, homosexual youths must often make the difficult decision of whether to disclose their sexual orientation to their parents. Most adolescents rely on their parents for both emotional and financial support; to disclose their homosexuality puts them at risk to lose both types of sustenance. In fact, parental rejection is related to increases in suicide attempts (D'Augelli et al., 2001).

These findings for adolescents reinforce the point that most gay and lesbian individuals find homophobia more psychologically burdensome than homosexuality itself. In 1973, the American Psychiatric Association voted to remove homosexuality from the list of psychological disorders; the American Psychological Association followed in 1975 (Morin & Rothblum, 1991). Spurring this action were research reports suggesting that, in fact, most gay men and lesbians are happy, productive human beings who would not change their sexual orientation even if a "magic pill" enabled them to do so (Bell & Weinberg, 1978; Siegelman, 1972). These data suggest that much of the stress associated with homosexuality arises not from the sexual motivation itself—gay people are happy with their orientations— but from the way in which people respond to the revelation of that sexual motivation. Much of lesbians' and gay men's anxiety about homosexuality arises not from being homosexual, but from an ongoing need either to reveal ("come out") to or conceal ("stay in the closet") their sexual identity from family, friends, and coworkers (D'Augelli, 1993). As you might expect, gay men and lesbians also spend time worrying about establishing and maintaining loving relationships, just as heterosexuals do.

The willingness of lesbians and gay men to "come out" may serve as a first step toward decreasing societal hostility. Research has shown that people's attitudes toward gay men and lesbians are much less negative when they actually *know* individuals in these groups; in fact, on average the more gay men and lesbians a person knows, the more favorable is his or her attitude (Herek & Capitanio, 1996). (When we turn to the topic of prejudice in Chapter 17, we will see there again how experiences with members of minority groups can lead to more positive attitudes.) Do you know any gay, lesbian, or bisexual individuals? How have your attitudes been influenced by interactions with gay people? Are you yourself gay, lesbian, or bisexual? How have or could have the attitudes of people around you been affected by knowing that you are gay?

This brief review of homosexuality allows us to reinforce our main conclusions about human sexual motivation. Some of the impetus for sexual behaviors is internal—genetic endowment and species evolution provide internal models for both heterosexual and homosexual behaviors. But the external environment also gives rise to sexual motivation. You learn to find some stimuli particularly alluring and some behaviors culturally acceptable. In the case of homosexuality, external societal norms may work against the internal dictates of nature.

Let's move now to our third example of important motivation: the forces that set an individual's course for relative success or failure.

PUT YOURSELF TO THE TEST

- What roles do hormones play in the sexual response of non-human animals?
- What did Masters and Johnson discover about the phases of sexual response in humans?
- How do evolutionary psychologists explain differences in the sexual behaviors of men and women?
- How do sexual scripts affect the sexual behaviors of men and women?
- What evidence suggests that sexual orientation has biological roots?
- How does culture constrain the lives of homosexual individuals?

Motivation for Personal Achievement

Why do some people succeed while other people, relatively speaking, fail? Why, for example, are some people able to swim the English Channel, while other people just wave woefully from the shore? You are likely to attribute some of the difference to genetic factors like body type, and you're correct to do so. But you also know that some people are simply much more interested in swimming the English Channel than are others. So

<www.ablongman.com/gerrig17e>

we are back at one of our core reasons for studying motivation. We want, in this case, to understand the motivational forces that lead different people to seek different levels of personal achievement. Let's begin with a construct that's actually called the *need for achievement*.

◆ NEED FOR ACHIEVEMENT

As early as 1938, **Henry Murray** had postulated a need to achieve that varied in strength in different people and influenced their tendency to approach success and evaluate their own performances. **David McClelland** and his colleagues (1953) devised a way to measure the strength of this need and then looked for relationships between strength of achievement motivation in different societies, conditions that had fostered the motivation, and its results in the work world. To gauge the strength of the need for achievement, McClelland used his participants' fantasies. On what is called the **Thematic Apperception Test (TAT),** participants were asked to generate stories in response to a series of ambiguous drawings. Participants shown TAT pictures were asked to make up stories about them—to say what was happening in the picture and describe probable outcomes. Presumably, they projected into the scene reflections of their own values, interests, and motives. According to McClelland: "If you want to find out what's on a person's mind, don't ask him, because he can't always tell you accurately. Study his fantasies and dreams. If you do this over a period of time, you will discover the themes to which his mind returns again and again. And these themes can be used to explain his actions" (McClelland, 1971, p. 5).

From participant responses to a series of TAT pictures, McClelland worked out measures of several human needs, including needs for power, affiliation, and achievement. The **need for achievement** was designated as *n Ach*. It reflected individual differences in the importance of planning and working toward attaining one's goals. **Figure 11.6** shows an example of how a high *n Ach* individual and a low *n Ach* individual might interpret a TAT picture. Studies in both laboratory and real-life settings have validated the usefulness of this measure.

For example, high-scoring *n Ach* people were found to be more upwardly mobile than those with low scores; sons who had high *n Ach* scores were more likely than sons with low *n Ach* measures to advance above their fathers' occupational status (McClelland et al., 1976). Men and women who measured high on *n Ach* at age 31 tended to have higher salaries than their low *n Ach* peers by age 41 (McClelland & Franz, 1992). Do these findings indicate that high *n Ach* individuals are always willing to work harder? Not really. In the face of a task that they are led to believe will be difficult, high *n Ach* individuals quit early on (Feather, 1961). What, in fact, seems to typify high *n Ach* individuals is a need for *efficiency*—a need to get the same result for less effort. If they outearn their peers, it might be because they also value concrete feedback on how well they are doing. As a measure of progress, salary is very concrete (McClelland, 1961; McClelland & Franz, 1992).

How does a high need for achievement arise? Researchers have considered whether parenting practices can bring about a high or low need for achievement. Data come from a longitudinal analysis of a group of Boston-area children.

These men are participating in the International Games for the Disabled. How can motivation explain variability among individuals—the fact, for example, that some people do better in competition than others?

Parenting Practices and Need for Achievement

David McClelland and Carol Franz (1992) compared measures of parenting practice, collected in 1951 when the children were about 5 years old, with measures of *n Ach* and earnings, collected in 1987–1988, when the children were 41. In 1951, the parents were asked to indicate their practices with respect to feeding and toilet training the child. McClelland and Franz considered children to have experienced a high degree of *achievement pressure* when their parents had fed and toilet trained them by strict rules. Overall, there was a positive correlation between early parental achievement pressure and subsequent adult *n Ach*. Furthermore, children who had experienced a high degree of achievement pressure were earning about $10,000 more annually than their peers who had experienced little such pressure.

FIGURE 11.6

Alternative Interpretations of a TAT Picture

Story Showing High n Ach

This boy has just finished his violin lesson. He's happy at the progress he is making and is beginning to believe that all his progress is making the sacrifices worthwhile. To become a concert violinist, he will have to give up much of his social life to practice for many hours each day. Although he knows he could make more money by going into his father's business, he is more interested in being a great violinist and giving people joy with his music. He renews his personal commitment to whatever it takes to make it.

Story Showing Low n Ach

This boy is holding his brother's violin and wishes he could play it. But he knows it is not worth the time, energy, and money for lessons. He feels sorry for his brother; he has given up all the enjoyable things in life to practice, practice, practice. It would be great to wake up one day and be a top-notch musician, but it doesn't work that way. The reality is boring practice, no fun, and the strong possibility of becoming just another guy playing a musical instrument in a small-town band.

These data suggest that the degree to which you experience a need to achieve may have been established in the first few years of your life.

◆ ATTRIBUTIONS FOR SUCCESS AND FAILURE

Need for achievement is not the only variable that affects motivation toward personal success. To see why, let's begin with a hypothetical example. Suppose you have two friends who are taking the same class. On the first midterm, each gets a C. Do you think they would be equally motivated to study hard for the second midterm? Part of the answer will depend on the way in which they each explained the C to themselves.

Consider, for example, the importance of locus of control (Rotter, 1954). A *locus of control orientation* is a belief about whether the outcomes of your actions are contingent on what you do *(internal control orientation)* or on environmental factors *(external control orientation)*. In the case of the C's, your friends might *attribute* their performance to either an external cause (construction noise during the exam) or an internal cause (poor memory). **Attributions** are judgments about the causes of outcomes. (We will develop attribution theory at length in Chapter 16.) In this case, the attributions can have an impact on motivation. If your friends believe they can attribute their performance to construction noise, they are likely to study hard for the next midterm. If they think the fault lies in their poor memory, they're more likely to slack off.

Locus of control is not the only dimension along which attributions can vary (Peterson & Seligman, 1984). We can also ask: "To what extent is a causal factor likely to be stable and consistent over time, or unstable and varying?" The answer gives us the dimension of *stability* versus *instability*. Or we can ask: "To what extent is a causal factor highly specific, limited to a particular task or situation, or global, applying widely across a variety of settings?" This gives us the dimension of *global* versus *specific*.

An example of how locus of control and stability can interact is given in **Figure 11.7.** Let's stay with the example of attributions about exam grades. Your friends can interpret their grades as the result of internal factors, such as ability (a stable personality characteristic) or effort (a varying personal quality). Or they may view the grades as caused primarily by external factors such as the difficulty of the task, the actions of others (a stable situational problem), or luck (an unstable external feature). Depending on the nature of the attribution they make for this success

When success comes your way, do you give yourself full credit for the achievement? What type of attributional style would this practice reflect?

<www.ablongman.com/gerrig17e>

or failure, they are likely to experience one of the emotional responses depicted in **Table 11.3.** What is important here is that the type of interpretation will influence both their emotions and subsequent motivation—to study harder or blow off work—regardless of the true reason for the success or failure.

So far we have been considering the possibility that both of your friends will explain their C's in the same way, but it's very likely that they might arrive at different explanations. One may believe something external ("The professor gave an unfair exam"); the other may believe something internal ("I'm not smart enough for this class"). Researchers have shown that the way people explain events in their lives—from winning at cards to being turned down for a date—can become lifelong, habitual *attributional styles* (Haines et al., 1999). The way you account for your successes and failures can influence your motivation, mood, and even ability to perform appropriately. For several years, researcher **Martin Seligman** has studied the ways in which people's *explanatory style*—their degree of optimism or pessimism—affects activity and passivity, whether they persist or give up easily, take risks, or play it safe (Seligman, 1991).

In Chapter 14, we will see that an internal–global–stable explanatory style ("I never do anything right") puts individuals at risk for depression (and one of the symp-

TABLE 11.3
Attribution-Dependent Emotional Responses

Your feelings in response to success and failure depend on the kinds of attributions you make regarding the cause of those outcomes. For example, you take pride in success when you attribute it to your ability, but are depressed when you perceive lack of ability to cause failure. Or you feel gratitude when you attribute your success to the actions of others but anger when they are seen as contributing to your failure.

EMOTIONAL RESPONSES

Attribution	Success	Failure
Ability	Competence Confidence Pride	Incompetence Resignation Depression
Effort	Relief Contentment Relaxation	Guilt Shame Fear
Action of others	Gratitude Thankfulness	Anger Fury
Luck	Surprise Guilt	Surprise Astonishment

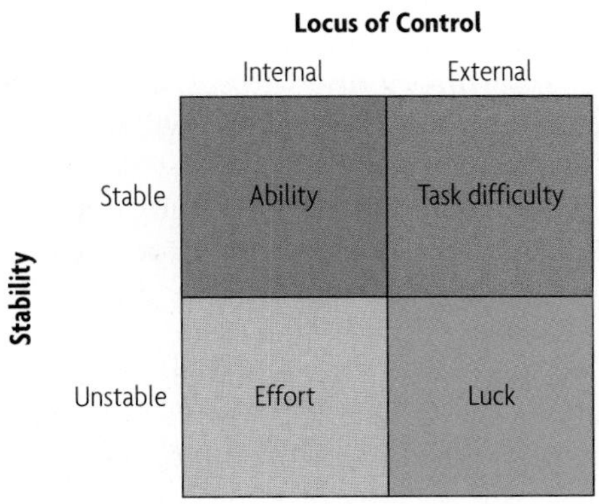

Locus of Control

FIGURE 11.7

Attributions Regarding Causes for Behavioral Outcomes

Four possible outcomes are generated with just two sources of attributions about behavior: the locus of control and the situation in which the behavior occurs. Ability attributions are made for the internal–stable combination, effort for the internal but unstable combination, a difficult task (test) when external–stable forces are assumed to be operating, and luck for the unstable–external combination.

toms of depression is impaired motivation). For now, however, let's focus on the way in which explanatory style might lead one of your friends to have an A and the other an F by the end of the semester. Seligman's research team has worked on the problem of explaining one person's ability and another's inability to resist failure. The secret ingredient has turned out to be familiar and seemingly simple: *optimism* versus *pessimism*. These two divergent ways of looking at the world influence motivation, mood, and behavior.

The *pessimistic attributional style* focuses on the causes of failure as internally generated. Furthermore, the bad situation and the individual's role in causing it are seen as stable and global—"It won't ever change and it will affect everything." The *optimistic attributional style* sees failure as the result of external causes—"The test was unfair"—and of events that are unstable or modifiable and specific—"If I put in more effort next time, I'll do better, and this one setback won't affect how I perform any other task that is important to me."

These causal explanations are reversed when it comes to the question of success. Optimists take full, personal internal–stable–global credit for success. However, pessimists attribute their success to external–unstable–global or specific factors. Because they believe themselves to be doomed to fail, pessimists perform worse than others would expect, given objective measures of their talent. A body of research supports these generalizations about optimists and pessimists. For example, one study measured the explanatory styles of 130 male salespeople in a leading United Kingdom insurance company (Corr & Gray, 1996). In the study, salesmen with more positive attributional styles were also likely to have higher sales. In everyday life, interpretations of events affect both optimists' and pessimists' levels of motivation for future performance.

To close this section, let's look at a research example of the powerful impact of causal attributions in an academic setting.

PUTTING IDEAS TO THE TEST

Attributional Retraining for Career Beliefs

When you finish college, you're going to want to get the best job possible. But how do you think that's going to happen? Are you going to get a good job because of your own skills and initiative (an internal attribution)? Or because of random circumstances and good luck (an external attribution)? Research suggests that students who believe they have control over career outcomes are more likely to meet their career aspirations. In that context, what can be done to encourage students to change their attributions from external to internal?

A team of researchers developed an intervention that they called *attributional retraining*. Groups of students who indicated that they believed they have little control over their careers viewed a videotaped conversation between a male and female graduate of their university. For the experimental group, part of the graduates' discussion focused on how they made career decisions: "I realized as I was growing up that anything worthwhile in terms of my career was going to take effort and hard work" (Luzzo et al., 1996, p. 417). The control group did not hear this type of information. After this brief intervention, members of the experimental group now indicated a more internal locus of control for career choices and also, as time passed, engaged in more behaviors related to career exploration. The control group did not show these changes (Luzzo et al., 1996).

Because of the way in which attributions affected motivation, a small amount of information about career choices had a profound effect on students' ideas about their futures.

We believe that there is much value to you in this line of psychological research. You can work at developing an optimistic explanatory style for your successes and failures. You can avoid making negative, stable,

dispositional attributions for your failures by examining possible causal forces in the situation. Finally, don't let your motivation be undermined by momentary setbacks. You can apply this research-based advice to better your life—a recurring theme of *Psychology and Life.*

◆ WORK AND ORGANIZATIONAL PSYCHOLOGY

Now suppose your positive philosophy has helped you to get a job in a big corporation. Can we predict exactly how motivated you'll be just by knowing about you, as an individual—your *n Ach* score or your explanatory style? Your individual level of motivation will depend, in part, on the overall context of people and rules in which you work. Recognizing that work settings are complex social systems, **organizational psychologists** study various aspects of human relations, such as communication among employees, socialization or enculturation of workers, leadership, attitudes and commitment toward a job and/or an organization, job satisfaction, stress and burnout, and overall quality of life at work. As consultants to businesses, organizational psychologists may assist in recruitment, selection, and training of employees. They also make recommendations about job redesign—tailoring a job to fit the person. Organizational psychologists apply theories of management, decision making, and development to improve work settings.

Let's look at a pair of theories organizational psychologists have developed to understand motivation in the workplace. *Equity theory* and *expectancy theory* attempt to explain and predict how people will respond under different working conditions. These theories assume that workers engage in certain cognitive activities, such as assessing fairness through processes of social comparison with other workers or estimating expected rewards associated with their performance.

Equity theory proposes that workers are motivated to maintain fair or equitable relationships with other relevant persons (Adams, 1965). Workers take note of their inputs (investments or contributions they make to their jobs) and their outcomes (what they receive from their jobs), and then they compare these with the inputs and outcomes of other workers. When the ratio of outcomes to inputs for Worker A is equal to the ratio for Worker B (outcome A ÷ input A = outcome B ÷ input B), then Worker A will feel satisfied. Dissatisfaction will result when these ratios are not equal. Because feeling this inequity is aversive, workers will be motivated to restore equity by changing the relevant inputs and outcomes. These changes could be behavioral (for example, reducing input by working less, increasing outcome by asking for a raise). Or they could be psychological (for example, reinterpreting the value of the inputs—"My work isn't really that good"—or the value of

<www.ablongman.com/gerrig17e>

I f you've ever had a job you didn't like, you probably know a lot about what it means to suffer from a lack of motivation: You can hardly stand the idea of reporting to work; every minute seems like an hour. An important part of having a successful career is finding a work setting that provides the types of challenges and rewards that fit your motivational needs. It probably will not surprise you that researchers have studied the match between vocations and people's individual personalities, values, and needs.

To remain motivated for career success, you would like to have a job that suits your interests and serves goals that you consider worthwhile. A widely used test for measuring vocational interests is the *Strong Interest Inventory*, which was originated in 1927 by psychologist **Edward Strong.** To construct the test, Strong first asked groups of men in different occupations to answer items about activities they liked or disliked. Then the answers given by those who were successful in particular occupations were compared with the responses of men in general to create a scale. Subsequent versions of the test, including a 1994 update, have added scales relevant to women and to newer occupations (Harmon et al., 1994). The *Strong Interest Inventory* is quite successful at relating people's likes and dislikes to appropriate occupations (Donnay & Borgen, 1996). If you take this test, a vocational counselor could tell you what types of jobs are typically held by people with interests such as yours, because these

Can Psychology Help Find Me a Career?
Megan Smallidge
Northeastern University

are the jobs that are likely to appeal to you.

Suppose you have gotten this sort of advice about what career to pursue. How do you select a particular company to join—and how does that company select you? Recently, researchers in *personnel psychology* have focused a good deal of attention on the concept of *person–organization fit*—the goal is to maximize the compatibility between people and the organizations that employ them (Dineen et al., 2002; Van Vianen, 2000). One research project has focused on the match between people's personalities and the "culture" of organizations. Consider the personality factor called Agreeableness, which encodes a continuum from "sympathetic and kind" to "cold and quarrelsome" (see Chapter 13). Consider, also, a continuum of organizational cultures from those

that are supportive and team-oriented to those that are aggressive and outcome-oriented. Do you see how these dimensions line up? Research suggests that job seekers who score high on Agreeableness will prefer organizations that are culturally supportive and team-oriented (Judge & Cable, 1997). Research of this type suggests why it is not just your own motivational states that matter for career success: The extent to which your preferences for achieving goals match the organization's preferences matters as well.

While you are thinking about the jobs that might keep you motivated to achieve your goals, here's a final factor to consider: As with so many other aspects of life, vocational interests appear to have a genetic component. In one study, researchers asked identical and fraternal twins who had been reared in different homes to complete two vocational interest surveys, like the *Strong Interest Inventory* (Moloney et al., 1991). For the two surveys, the average correlations for the identical twins were .38 and .47; the average correlations for the fraternal twins were only .05 and .06. Remember, these twins were not reared in the same homes! If you have decided to follow in your mother's or father's career path, it might very well not just be the effects of environmental indoctrination.

So, what career path will keep you motivated for success? As with so many of life's dilemmas, psychologists have carried out research that can help you make this important decision.

the outcome—"I'm lucky to have a weekly paycheck I can count on").

Have you noticed the consequences of equity or inequity in your own work situations? Consider a situation in which a coworker leaves for a better job. How does that make you feel? Equity theory suggests that you may feel like you have been unfairly left behind in an undesirable job. In fact, when coworkers leave in circumstances in which they have expressed dissatisfaction, the people remaining tend to become less productive in their jobs—they decrease productivity to restore their sense of equity (Sheehan, 1993). If you end up in a management position, you should try to prevent this pattern by addressing the psychological needs of your employees with respect to equity. For example, keep in mind the benefit of "adequate explanations."

Expectancy theory proposes that workers are motivated when they expect that their effort and performance on the job will result in desired outcomes (Harder, 1991; Porter & Lawler, 1968; Vroom, 1964). In other words, people will engage in work they find attractive (leading to favorable consequences) and achievable. Expectancy theory emphasizes three components: expectancy, instrumentality, and valence. *Expectancy* refers to the perceived likelihood that a worker's efforts will result in a certain level of performance. *Instrumentality* refers to the perception that performance will lead to certain outcomes, such as rewards. *Valence* refers to the perceived attractiveness of particular outcomes. With respect to a particular work situation, you can imagine different probabilities for these three components. You might, for example, have a job in which there is a high likelihood of reward if performance is successful (high instrumentality) but a low likelihood that performance will be successful (low expectancy) or a low likelihood that the reward will be worthwhile (low valence). According to expectancy theory, workers assess the probabilities of these three components and combine them by multiplying their individual values. Highest levels of motivation, therefore, result when all three components have high probabilities, whereas lowest levels result when any single component is zero.

Can you see how an expectancy theory analysis might help you if you were in a management position? You should be able to think more clearly about expectancy, instrumentality, and valence. You should be able to determine if one piece of the picture is out of kilter. Suppose, for example, your employees came to believe that there wasn't enough of a relationship between their efforts and how much they are rewarded. What could you do to change the workplace to restore high values for instrumentality?

As a conclusion to this section, we offer a cautionary note on achievement and motivation in work set-

How does expectancy theory explain some players' choice to favor hitting home runs over achieving a higher batting average?

tings. When you make a personal choice about how hard you can work at a career, keep a careful watch on other aspects of your life. As we shall see in the next chapter, aggressive striving for success may, in some respects, work counter to the goal of having a long and healthy life.

PUT YOURSELF TO THE TEST

➤ What have researchers discovered about differences in need for achievement?

➤ Along what dimensions do people make attributions?

➤ What impact do optimistic versus pessimistic attributional styles have on people's lives?

➤ How do equity theory and expectancy theory explain motivation in the workplace?

A Hierarchy of Needs

In the last three sections, we have focused on specific types of motivations and specific types of behaviors. To close the chapter, we return to a more global account of motivation. Our intent is to give you a general sense of the forces that could guide your life.

Humanist psychologist **Abraham Maslow** (1970) formulated the theory that basic motives form a **hierarchy of needs,** as illustrated in **Figure 11.8.** In Maslow's view, the needs at each level of the hierarchy must be satisfied—the needs are arranged in a sequence from primitive to advanced—before the next level can be achieved. At the bottom of this hierarchy are the basic *biological needs,* such as hunger and thirst. They must be met before any other needs can begin to operate. When biological needs are pressing, other needs are put on hold and are unlikely to influence your actions. When they are reasonably well satisfied, the needs at the next level—*safety needs*—motivate you. When you are no longer concerned about danger, you become motivated by *attachment needs*—needs to belong, to affiliate with others, to love, and to be loved.

Where does the need to belong, to form attachments and experience love, fit in Maslow's hierarchy?

FIGURE 11.8

Maslow's Hierarchy of Needs

According to Maslow, needs at the lower level of the hierarchy dominate an individual's motivation as long as they are unsatisfied. Once these needs are adequately met, the higher needs occupy the individual's attention.

If you are well fed and safe and if you feel a sense of social belonging, you move up to *esteem needs*—to like oneself, to see oneself as competent and effective, and to do what is necessary to earn the esteem of others.

At the top of the hierarchy are people who are nourished, safe, loved and loving, secure, thinking, and creating. These people have moved beyond basic human needs in the quest for the fullest development of their potentials, or *self-actualization.* A self-actualizing person is self-aware, self-accepting, socially responsive, creative, spontaneous, and open to novelty and challenge, among other positive attributes.

Maslow's theory is a particularly upbeat view of human motivation. At the core of the theory is the need for each individual to grow and actualize his or her highest potential. However, you know from your own experience that Maslow's strict hierarchy breaks down. You may, for example, have skipped a meal so that you could help out a friend. You may have endured the danger of a wilderness trek to boost your self-esteem. Even so, we hope Maslow's scheme will enable you to bring some order to different aspects of your motivational experiences.

We have come a long way since we asked you to consider why you got out of bed this morning. We have described the biology and psychology of hunger and eating, and the evolutionary and social dimensions of human sexuality. We have explored individual differences in people's need to achieve and explain personal success. Throughout this discussion, you have seen the intricate interplay of nature and nurture, at the level of both the species and the individual. So, with all this information in hand, why *did* you get out of bed this morning?

◆ Recapping Main Points

UNDERSTANDING MOTIVATION

- Motivation is a dynamic concept used to describe the processes directing behavior.
- Motivational analysis helps explain how biological and behavioral processes are related and why people pursue goals despite obstacles and adversity.
- Drive theory conceptualizes motivation as tension reduction.
- People are also motivated by incentives, external stimuli that are not related to physiological needs.
- Reversal theory posits opposing pairs of meta-motivational states.
- Instinct theory suggests that motivation often relies on innate stereotypical responses.
- Social and cognitive psychologists emphasize the individual's perception of, interpretation of, and reaction to a situation.

EATING

- The body has a number of mechanisms to regulate the initiation and cessation of eating.
- If individuals become restrained eaters, their diets may result in weight gain rather than weight loss.
- Eating disorders are life-threatening illnesses that may arise from cultural pressure and misperceptions of body image.

SEXUAL BEHAVIORS

- From an evolutionary perspective, sex is the mechanism for producing offspring.
- In animals, the sex drive is largely controlled by hormones.

- The work of Masters and Johnson provided the first hard data on the sexual response cycles of men and women.
- Evolutionary psychologists suggest that much of human sexual behavior reflects different mating strategies for men and women.
- Discrepancies in sexual scripts can lead to serious misunderstandings and even date rape.
- Homosexuality and heterosexuality are determined both by genetics and personal and social environments.

MOTIVATION FOR PERSONAL ACHIEVEMENT

- People have varying needs for achievement. Motivation for achievement is influenced by how people interpret success and failure.
- Two attributional styles, optimism and pessimism, lead to different attitudes toward achievement and influence motivation.
- Organizational psychologists study human motivation in work settings.

A HIERARCHY OF NEEDS

- Abraham Maslow suggested that human needs can be organized hierarchically.
- Although real human motivation is more complex, Maslow's theory provides a useful framework for summarizing motivational forces.

KEY TERMS

anorexia nervosa (p. 371)

attributions (p. 384)

bulimia nervosa (p. 371)

date rape (p. 380)

drives (p. 363)

equity theory (p. 386)

expectancy theory (p. 388)

hierarchy of needs (p. 389)

homeostasis (p. 363)

incentives (p. 364)

instincts (p. 365)

motivation (p. 362)

need for achievement (p. 383)

organizational psychologists (p. 386)

parental investment (p. 377)

reversal theory (p. 364)

sexual arousal (p. 376)

sexual scripts (p. 378)

social-learning theory (p. 366)

Thematic Apperception Test (TAT)
(p. 383)

CHAPTER 12

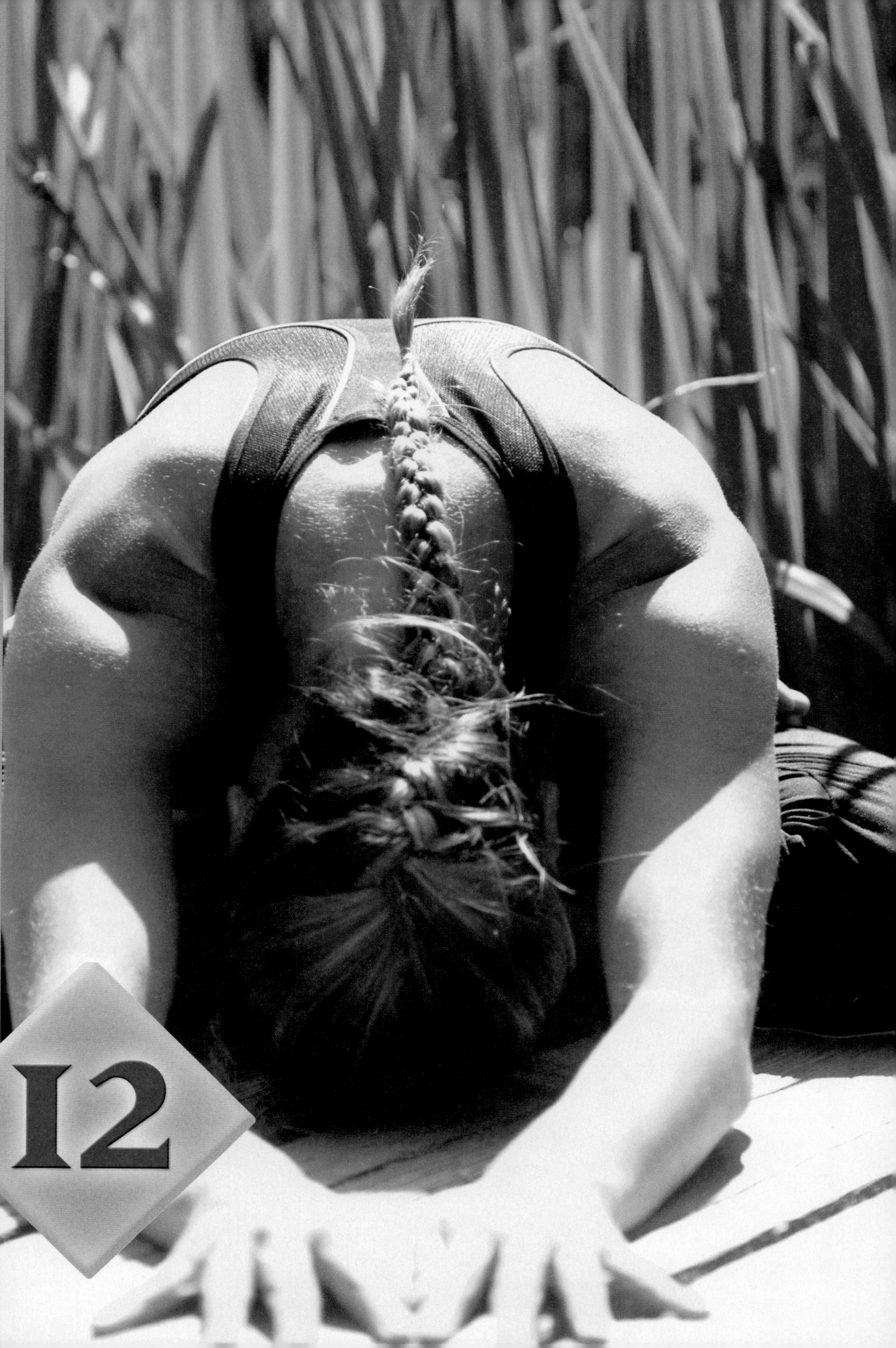

Emotion, Stress, and Health

Suppose we asked you right now, "How are you feeling?" How would you answer that question? There are at least three different types of information you might provide. First, you might reveal to us the mood you are in—the *emotions* you are feeling. Are you happy because you know you can finish reading this chapter in time to go to a party? Are you angry because your boss just yelled at you over the telephone? Second, you might tell us something more general about the amount of *stress* you are experiencing. Do you feel as if you can cope with all the tasks you have to get done? Or are you feeling a bit overwhelmed? Third, you might report on your psychological or physical *health*. Do you feel some illness coming on? Or do you feel an overall sense of wellness?

This chapter will explore interactions among these three ways in which you might answer the question "How are you feeling?"—in relation to your emotions, stress, and health. *Emotions* are the touchstones of human experience. They give richness to your interactions with people and nature and significance to your memories. In this chapter, we will discuss the experience and functions of emotions. But what happens if the emotional demands on your biological and psychological functioning are too great? You may become overwhelmed and unable to deal with the stressors of your life. This chapter will also examine how *stress* affects you and how you can combat it. Finally, we will broaden our focus to consider psychology's contributions to the study of health and illness. *Health psychologists* investigate the ways in which environmental, social, and psychological processes contribute to the development of disease. Health psychologists also use psychological processes and principles to help treat and prevent illness, while also developing strategies to enhance personal wellness.

We begin now by looking at the content and meaning of emotions.

Emotions

Just imagine what your life would be like if you could think and act but not feel. Would you be willing to give up the capacity to experience fear if you would also lose the passion of a lover's kiss? Would you give up sadness at the expense of joy? Surely these would be bad bargains, promptly regretted. We will soon see that emotions serve a number of important functions. Let us begin, however, by offering a definition of emotion and by describing the roots of your emotional experiences.

Although you might be tempted to think of emotion as only a feeling—"I feel happy" or "I feel angry"—we need a more inclusive definition of this important concept that involves both the body and the mind. Contemporary psychologists define **emotion** as a complex pattern of bodily and mental changes that includes physiological arousal, feelings, cognitive processes, visible expressions (including face and posture), and specific behavioral reactions made in response to a situation perceived as personally significant. To see why all of these components are necessary, imagine a situation in which you would feel a surge of happiness. Your physiological arousal might include a gently beating heart. Your feeling would be positive. The associated cognitive processes include interpretations, memories, and expectations that allow you to label the situation as happy. Your overt behavioral reactions might be expressive (smiling) and/or action-oriented (embracing a loved one).

Before we provide an account that unites arousal, feelings, thoughts, and actions, we need to make a distinction between emotions and moods. We have defined emotions as specific responses to specific events—in that sense, emotions are typically relatively short lived and relatively intense. By contrast, *moods* are often less intense and may last several days. There's often a weaker connection between moods and triggering events. You might be in a good or bad mood without knowing exactly why. You should keep this distinction between emotions and moods in mind as we describe the theories that explain them.

◆ BASIC EMOTIONS AND CULTURE

Suppose you could gather together in one room representatives from a great diversity of human cultures. What would be common in their experiences of emo-

Charles Darwin was one of the first to use photographs in the study of emotion. These plates are from The Expression of Emotions in Man and Animals *(1872/1965). Why did Darwin believe that emotions were the product of evolution?*

tion? For an initial answer, you might look to Charles Darwin's book *The Expression of Emotions in Man and Animals* (1872/1965). Darwin believed that emotions evolved alongside other important aspects of human and nonhuman structures and functions. He was interested in the *adaptive* functions of emotions, which he thought of not as vague, unpredictable, personal states, but as highly specific, coordinated modes of operation of the human brain. Darwin viewed emotions as inherited, specialized mental states designed to deal with a certain class of *recurring situations* in the world. Over the history of our species, humans have been attacked by predators, fallen in love, given birth to children, fought each other, confronted their mates' sexual infidelity, and witnessed the death of loved ones—innumerable times. We might expect, therefore, that certain types of emotional responses would emerge in all members of the human species. Researchers have tested this claim of the *universality of emotions* by looking at the emotional responses of newborn children as well as the consistency of facial expressions across cultures.

ARE SOME EMOTIONAL RESPONSES INNATE?

If the evolutionary perspective is correct, we would expect to find much the same patterns of emotional responses in children all over the world (Izard, 1994). **Silvan Tomkins** (1962, 1981) was one of the first psychologists to emphasize the pervasive role of immediate, unlearned affective (emotional) reactions. He pointed out that, without prior learning, infants respond to loud sounds with fear or with difficulties in breathing. They seem "prewired" to respond to certain stimuli with an emotional response general enough to fit a wide range of circumstances.

Cross-cultural research has confirmed the expectation that some emotional responses are quite similar in children from very different cultures.

PUTTING IDEAS TO THE TEST

Cross-Cultural Emotional Responses in Infants

Five- and 12-month-old children in the United States and Japan were visited in their homes. The experimenters subjected each child to a procedure in which the infant's wrists were grasped and folded across the infant's stomach. The experimenters videotaped each infant's response. Infants from both cultures moved their facial muscles in the same patterns—resulting in highly similar expressions of distress. Japanese and American infants also showed similar rates of negative vocalization and physical struggling (Camras et al., 1992).

Although this study demonstrates important cross-cultural consistency, more recent research has exposed some differences. In one study, 11-month-old children from China were consistently less emotionally expressive than their age-mates from Japan and the United States (Camras et al., 1998). These results suggest that culture acts very early in life to have an impact on innate emotional responses.

Note that infants also seem to have an innate ability to interpret the facial expressions of others. In one experiment, 4- to 6-month-old infants habituated—they showed decreasing interest—to repeated presentations of adult faces showing a single emotion drawn from the set of surprise, fear, and anger (see Chapter 10 for examples of habituation procedures with children). When the infants were subsequently shown a photograph with a different emotion, they responded with renewed interest—suggesting that surprise, fear, and anger expressions "looked different" to them, even at these very young ages (Serrano et al., 1992). Infants also produce more positive behaviors (for example, approaching movements and smiles) toward happy expressions and more negative behaviors (for example, avoidance movements and frowns) toward angry expressions. This suggests that they not only recognize but also have a very early understanding of the "meaning" of these expressions (Serrano et al., 1995).

ARE EMOTIONAL EXPRESSIONS UNIVERSAL?

We have seen that infants produce and perceive standard emotional expressions. If that is so, we might also expect to find adult members of even vastly different cultures showing reasonable agreement in the way they believe emotion is communicated by facial expressions.

According to **Paul Ekman,** the leading researcher on the nature of facial expressions, all people share an overlap in "facial language" (Ekman, 1984, 1994). Ekman and his associates have demonstrated what Darwin first proposed—that a set of emotional expressions is universal to the human species, presumably because they are innate components of our evolutionary heritage. Before you read on, take a look at **Figure 12.1** to see how well you can identify these seven universally recognized expressions of emotion (Ekman & Friesen, 1986).

There is considerable evidence that these seven expressions are recognized and produced worldwide in response to the emotions of happiness, surprise, anger, disgust, fear, sadness, and contempt. Cross-cultural researchers have asked people from a variety of cultures to identify the emotions associated with expressions in standardized photographs. Individuals are generally able to identify the expressions associated with the seven emotions.

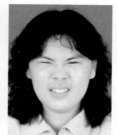

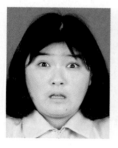

FIGURE 12.1

Judgments of Emotional Expressions

Match these seven emotion terms with the faces shown at left: fear, disgust, happiness, surprise, contempt, anger, and sadness. The answers are given at the end of the chapter.

Cross-Cultural Recognition of Facial Expressions

In one study, members of a preliterate culture in New Guinea (the Fore culture), who had had almost no exposure to Westerners or to Western culture prior to this experiment, accurately identified the emotions expressed in the Caucasian faces shown in Figure 12.1. They did so by referring to situations in which they had experienced the same emotion. For example, photo 5 (fear) suggested being chased by a wild boar when you didn't have your spear, and photo 6 (sadness) suggested your child had died. Their only confusion came in distinguishing surprise, photo 2, from fear, perhaps because these people are most fearful when taken by surprise.

Next, researchers asked other members of the culture (who had not participated in the first study) to model the expressions that they used to communicate six of the emotions (excluding contempt). When U.S. college students viewed videotapes of the facial expressions of the Fore people, they were able to identify their emotions accurately—with one exception. Not surprisingly, the Americans had difficulty distinguishing between the Fore poses of fear and surprise, the same emotions that the Fore had confused in the Western poses (Ekman & Friesen, 1971).

More recent research has compared judgments of facial expressions across individuals in Hungary, Japan, Poland, Sumatra, the United States, and Vietnam—high

agreement was found across these diverse populations (Biehl et al., 1997). The general conclusion is that people all over the world, regardless of cultural differences, race, sex, or education, express basic emotions in much the same way and are able to identify the emotions others are experiencing by reading their facial expressions.

Note that the claim of universality is focused on the basic set of seven emotions. Ekman and his colleagues make no claim that all facial expressions are universal or that cultures express all emotions in the same way (Ekman, 1994). In fact, Ekman (1972) called his position on universality the *neuro-cultural* theory, to reflect the joint contributions of the brain (the product of evolution) and culture in emotional expression. The brain specifies which facial muscles move, to produce a particular expression, when a particular emotion is aroused. Different cultures, however, impose their own constraints beyond universal biology. We reported some cultural effects in the description of the research comparing responses of members of the Fore culture and U.S. college students. The six-country comparison we cited earlier also produced some differences among the countries, against the general background of agreement (Biehl et al., 1997). For example, Japanese adults were worse at identifying anger than were U.S., Hungarian, Polish, and Vietnamese adults. Vietnamese adults were worse at identifying disgust than the participants from all the other countries.

Why might these differences arise? Let's now look directly at cultural influences on emotionality.

In what ways do cultures constrain emotional expressions in situations like funerals?

HOW DOES CULTURE CONSTRAIN EMOTIONAL EXPRESSION?

We've just seen that some aspects of emotional expression are universal. Even so, different cultures have different standards for how emotion should be managed. Some forms of emotional response, even facial expressions, are unique to each culture. Cultures establish social rules for when people may show certain emotions and for the social appropriateness of certain types of emotional displays by given types of people in particular settings (Mesquita & Frijda, 1992; Ratner, 2000). Let's look at three examples of cultures that express emotions in manners different from the Western norm. We begin with an African culture.

The Wolof people of Senegal live in a society where status and power differences among people are rigidly defined. High-caste members of this culture are expected to show great restraint in their expressions of emotionality; low-caste individuals are expected to be more volatile, particularly a caste called the *griots*. The griots, in fact, are often called upon to express the "undignified" emotions of the nobility.

> One afternoon, a group of women (some
> five nobles and two griots) were gathered near
> a well on the edge of town when another woman
> strode over to the well and threw herself down it.
> All the women were shocked at the apparent sui-
> cide attempt, but the noblewomen were shocked
> in silence. Only the griot women screamed, on
> behalf of all. (Irvine, 1990, p. 146)

Can you imagine how you would respond in this situation? It might be easier to put yourself in the place of the griots rather than in the place of the noblewomen: How could you help but scream? The answer, of course, is that the noblewomen have acquired cultural norms for emotional expression that require them not to show any overt response.

A second example of cultural variation in emotional expression arose in the life of one of your authors. At the funeral of an American friend of Syrian descent, he was surprised to see and hear a group of women shrieking and wailing when a visitor entered the funeral parlor. They then stopped just as suddenly until the next visitor arrived, when once again they started their group wailing. What is the explanation for this behavior? Because it is difficult for the family members of the deceased to sustain a high emotional pitch over the three days and nights of such wakes, they hire these professional criers to display, on their behalf, appropriately strong emotions to each newcomer. This is an expected practice among a number of Mediterranean and Near Eastern cultures.

For our third example, we need to introduce a distinction between *individualistic* and *collectivist* cultures: Individualistic cultures emphasize individuals' needs, whereas collectivist cultures emphasize the needs of the group (Triandis, 1994, 1995). Whereas individualists look for immediate personal rewards, freedom, equality, personal enjoyment, and a varied, exciting life, collectivists put high value on self-discipline and on accepting one's position in life, honoring parents and other elders, preserving one's image, and working toward long-term goals that benefit the group as a whole. Researchers have suggested that these cultural orientations will affect the expression of emotion.

Emotional Expression in Individualistic and Collectivist Cultures

What happens when someone expresses a negative emotion toward another person or group of people? Often, the situation will become socially quite awkward. That might be okay if you are a member of an individualistic culture—and are content to use expressions of negative emotions to assert your own independence. If, however, you are a member of a collectivist culture, you may shy away from displays of negative emotions to avoid causing discord in a group. To test this reasoning, a team of researchers recruited psychology students from universities in the United States (an individualistic culture) and Costa Rica (a collectivist culture) and asked them how comfortable they would feel expressing a range of positive and negative emotions toward another individual, if the individual had "caused them to experience these emotions." **Figure 12.2** displays the results. As you can see, there were no cultural differences for positive emotions. However, as predicted, students in the United States rated themselves considerably more comfortable with expressing negative emotions (Stephan et al., 1996).

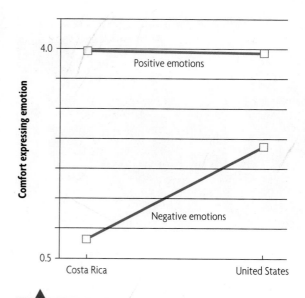

FIGURE 12.2

Emotional Expression Across Cultures

Students from the United States (an individualistic culture) and Costa Rica (a collectivist culture) were asked to indicate how comfortable they would feel expressing positive and negative emotions toward the person who had brought about the emotion. The students made their responses on a scale ranging from 0 (extremely uncomfortable) to 5 (extremely comfortable). Although there were no differences for positive emotions, students from the individualistic culture indicated more comfort with expressing negative emotions.

Next time you express a negative emotion—for example, anger toward a friend—you should consider how your comfort with that incident reflects cultural values.

When you think about the types of emotional patterns that may have evolved over the course of human experience, you should always bear in mind that culture may have the last word. Western notions of what is necessary or inevitable in emotional expression are as bound to U.S. culture as those of any other societies. Can you see how different standards for emotional expression could cause misunderstandings between people of different cultural origins?

We have seen so far that some physiological responses to emotional situations—such as smiles and grimaces—may be innate. Let's turn now to theories that consider the link between other physiological responses and their psychological interpretations.

◆ THEORIES OF EMOTION

Theories of emotion generally attempt to explain the relationship between physiological and psychological aspects of the experience of emotion. We will begin this section by discussing the responses your body gives in emotionally relevant situations. We will then review theories that explore the way these physiological responses contribute to your psychological experience of emotion.

PHYSIOLOGY OF EMOTION

What happens when you experience a strong emotion? Your heart races, respiration goes up, your mouth dries, your muscles tense, and maybe you even shake. In addition to these noticeable changes, many others occur beneath the surface. All these responses are designed to mobilize your body for action to deal with the source of the emotion. Let's look at their origins.

The *autonomic nervous system* (ANS) prepares the body for emotional responses through the action of both its sympathetic and parasympathetic divisions (see Chapter 3). The balance between the divisions depends on the quality and intensity of the arousing stimulation. With mild, *unpleasant* stimulation, the *sympathetic* division is more active; with mild, *pleasant* stimulation, the *parasympathetic* division is more active. With more intense stimulation of either kind, both divisions are increasingly involved. Physiologically, strong emotions such as fear or anger activate the body's *emergency reaction system,* which swiftly and silently prepares the body for potential danger. The sympathetic nervous system takes charge by directing the release of hormones (epi-

<www.ablongman.com/gerrig17e>

nephrine and norepinephrine) from the adrenal glands, which in turn leads the internal organs to release blood sugar, raise blood pressure, and increase sweating and salivation. To calm you after the emergency has passed, the parasympathetic nervous system inhibits the release of the activating hormones. You may remain aroused for a while after an experience of strong emotional activation, because some of the hormones continue to circulate in your bloodstream.

As we shall see when we describe specific theories of emotion, researchers have debated the question "Do particular emotional experiences give rise to distinct patterns of activity in the autonomic nervous system?" Cross-cultural research suggests that the answer to the question is yes.

PUTTING IDEAS TO THE TEST

Do Different Emotions Show Different Patterns of Autonomic Activity?

Suppose you are feeling surprised, fearful, or disgusted—but you won't tell us which. Could we measure the response of your autonomic nervous system and accurately infer what you are feeling? Paul Ekman and his colleagues (1983) set out to answer this question with a sample of professional actors in the United States. The researchers measured autonomic responses such as heart rate and skin temperature while the actors created emotions and emotional expressions. These measures revealed distinct patterns for different emotions. For example, sadness was marked by high heart rates, whereas happiness was marked by low rates; although both anger and fear produced high heart rates, anger was associated with high skin temperature, whereas fear was associated with low skin temperature.

Do these findings generalize across cultures? The same team of researchers performed another study that compared men and women from the United States to Minangkabau men from West Sumatra. Members of this culture are socialized not to display negative emotions. Would they, even so, show the same underlying autonomic patterns for negative emotions—even when they had little experience displaying the emotions? The data revealed a high level of similarity across the two cultures, leading the researchers to suggest that patterns of autonomic activity are "an important part of our common evolved biological heritage" (Levenson et al., 1992, p. 986).

These experiments suggest that members of different cultures learn to produce different overt responses—when you are angry, do you yell or do you suffer in silence?—for the same underlying bodily experiences.

Let's move now from the autonomic nervous system to the central nervous system. Integration of both the hormonal and the neural aspects of arousal is controlled by the *hypothalamus* and the *limbic system,* control systems for emotions and for patterns of attack, defense, and flight. Neuroanatomy research has particularly focused on the **amygdala** as a part of the limbic system that acts as a gateway for emotion and as a filter for memory. The amygdala does this by attaching significance to the information it receives from the senses. It plays an especially strong role in attaching meaning to negative experiences. For example, when people view pictures of fearful facial expressions, the left amygdala (each side of your brain has a separate amygdala) shows increasing activity as the intensity of the expression increases; by contrast, happy facial expressions produce less activity in the same structure the more intensely happy the face becomes (Morris et al., 1996).

Researchers have also begun to study individual differences in the amygdala's responses to emotional stimuli. One study focused on variations in a gene that affects the use of the neurotransmitter serotonin (Hariri et al., 2002). Some people are born with a short version of the gene; others are born with a long version. In the study, participants underwent fMRI scans while they viewed faces with either angry or frightened expressions. Their task was to choose a second face that showed the same emotion as the original one. The fMRI scans showed much greater activity in the right amygdalas of those participants with the short versions of the genes. This result suggests that, depending on your genetic endowment, your brain may automatically respond more so that some stimuli have a greater emotional impact.

The *cortex* is involved in emotional experiences through its internal neural networks and its connections with other parts of the body. The cortex provides the associations, memories, and meanings that integrate psychological experience and biological responses. Research using brain scanning techniques has begun to map particular responses for different emotions. For example, positive and negative emotions are not just opposite responses in the same portions of the cortex. Rather, opposite emotions lead to greatest activity in quite different parts of the brain. Consider a study in which participants underwent fMRI scans while viewing positive pictures (e.g., puppies, brownies, and sunsets) and negative pictures (angry people, spiders, and guns). The scans showed greater activity in the brain's left hemisphere for positive pictures and in the right hemisphere for negative pictures (Canli et al., 1998). In fact, researchers have suggested that there are two distinct systems in the brain that handle *approach-related* and *withdrawal-related* emotional responses (Davidson

How does the brain respond differently to experiences of puppies and spiders?

et al., 2000). Consider puppies and spiders. It is likely that most people would want to approach the puppies but withdraw from the spiders. Research suggests that different brain circuits—apportioned to the different hemispheres of the brain—underlie those responses.

We have seen so far that your body provides many responses to situations in which emotions are relevant. But how do you know which feeling goes with which

physiological response? We now review three theories that attempt an answer to this question.

JAMES–LANGE THEORY OF BODY REACTION

You might think, at first, that everyone would agree that emotions precede responses: for example, you yell at someone (response) because you feel angry (emotion). However, over 100 years ago, **William James** argued, as Aristotle had much earlier, that the sequence was reversed—you feel *after* your body reacts. As James put it, "We feel sorry because we cry, angry because we strike, afraid because we tremble" (James, 1890/1950, p. 450). This view that emotion stems from *bodily feedback* became known as the **James–Lange theory of emotion** (Carl Lange was a Danish scientist who presented similar ideas the same year as James). According to this theory, perceiving a stimulus causes autonomic arousal and other bodily actions that lead to the experience of a specific emotion (see **Figure 12.3**). The James–Lange theory is considered a *peripheralist* theory because it assigns the most prominent role in the emotion chain to visceral reactions, the actions of the autonomic nervous system that are peripheral to the central nervous system.

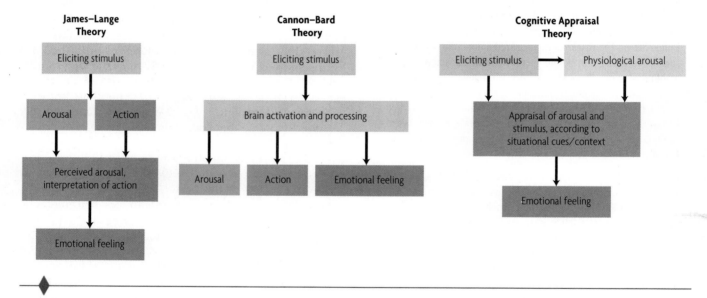

FIGURE 12.3

Comparing Three Theories of Emotion

These classic theories of emotion propose different components of emotion. They also propose different process sequences by which a stimulus event results in the experience of emotion. In the James–Lange theory, events trigger both autonomic arousal and behavioral action, which are perceived and then result in a specific emotional experience. In the Cannon–Bard theory, events are first processed at various centers in the brain, which then direct the simultaneous reactions of arousal, behavioral action, and emotional experience. In the cognitive appraisal theory, both stimulus events and physiological arousal are cognitively appraised at the same time according to situational cues and context factors, with the emotional experience resulting from the interaction of the level of arousal and the nature of appraisal.

Adapted from *Psychology*, 3e by Spencer A. Rathus. Copyright © 1987. Reprinted with permission of Wadsworth, a division of Thomson Learning.

CANNON–BARD THEORY OF CENTRAL NEURAL PROCESSES

Physiologist **Walter Cannon** (1927, 1929) rejected the peripheralist theory in favor of a *centralist* focus on the action of the central nervous system. Cannon (and other critics) raised a number of objections to the James–Lange theory (Leventhal, 1980). They noted, for example, that visceral activity is irrelevant for emotional experience—experimental animals continue to respond emotionally even after their viscera are separated surgically from the CNS. They also argued that ANS responses are typically too slow to be the source of split-second elicited emotions. According to Cannon, emotion requires that the brain intercede between the input stimulation and the output response. Signals from the thalamus get routed to one area of the cortex to produce emotional feeling and to another for emotional expressiveness.

Another physiologist, Philip Bard, also concluded that visceral reactions were not primary in the emotion sequence. Instead, an emotion-arousing stimulus has two simultaneous effects, causing both bodily arousal via the sympathetic nervous system and the subjective experience of emotion via the cortex. The views of these physiologists were combined in the **Cannon–Bard theory of emotion.** This theory states that an emotion stimulus produces two concurrent reactions, arousal and experience of emotion, that do not cause each other (see Figure 12.3). If something makes you angry, your heartbeat increases at the same time as you think "I'm ticked off!"—but neither your body nor your mind dictates the way the other responds.

The Cannon–Bard theory predicts independence between bodily and psychological responses. We will see next that contemporary theories of emotion reject the claim that these responses are necessarily independent.

COGNITIVE APPRAISAL THEORIES OF EMOTION

Because arousal symptoms and internal states are similar for many different emotions, it is possible to confuse them at times when they are experienced in ambiguous or novel situations. According to **Stanley Schachter** (1971b), the experience of emotion is the joint effect of physiological arousal and **cognitive appraisal,** with both parts necessary for an emotion to occur. All arousal is assumed to be general and undifferentiated, and arousal is the first step in the emotion sequence. You appraise your physiological arousal in an effort to discover what you are feeling, what emotional label best fits, and what your reaction means in the particular setting in which it is being experienced. **Richard Lazarus** (1991, 1995; Lazarus & Lazarus, 1994), another leading proponent of the cognitive appraisal view, maintains that "emotional experience cannot be under-

stood solely in terms of what happens in the person or in the brain, but grows out of ongoing transactions with the environment that are evaluated" (Lazarus, 1984a, p. 124). Lazarus also emphasizes that appraisal often occurs without conscious thought. When you have past experiences that link emotions to situations—here comes that bully I've clashed with before!—you need not explicitly search the environment for an interpretation of your arousal. This position has become known as the **cognitive appraisal theory of emotion** (see Figure 12.3).

To test this theory, experimenters have sometimes created situations in which environmental cues were available to provide a label for an individual's arousal.

CLASSIC
PUTTING IDEAS TO THE TEST

Arousal and Emotional Misinterpretation

A female researcher interviewed male participants who had just crossed one of two bridges in Vancouver, Canada. One bridge was a safe, sturdy bridge; the other was a wobbly, precarious bridge. The researcher pretended to be interested in the effects of scenery on creativity and asked the men to write brief stories about an ambiguous picture that included a woman. She also invited them to call her if they wanted more information about the research. Those men who had just crossed the dangerous bridge wrote stories with more sexual imagery, and four times as many of those men called the female researcher than did those who had crossed the safe bridge. To show that arousal was the independent variable influencing the emotional misinterpretation, the research team also arranged for another group of men to be interviewed 10 minutes or more after crossing the dangerous bridge, enough time for their physical arousal symptoms to be reduced. These nonaroused men did not show the signs of sexual response that the aroused men did (Dutton & Aron, 1974).

In this situation, the male participants came to an emotional judgment ("I am interested in this woman") based on a *misattribution* of the source of arousal (the woman rather than the danger of the bridge). In a similar experiment, students who performed two minutes of aerobic exercise reported less extreme emotions just after the exercise—when they could easily attribute their arousal to the exercise rather than to an emotional state—by comparison to the emotions they reported after a brief delay that made the exercise seem less relevant to continuing arousal (Sinclair et al., 1994).

What emotions would you be likely to feel if people all around you were wildly cheering your favorite team?

Some of the specific aspects of the cognitive appraisal theory have been challenged. For example, you learned earlier that arousal states—the activity of the autonomic nervous system—accompanying different emotions are not identical (Levenson et al., 1992). Therefore, interpretations of at least some emotional experiences may not require appraisal. Furthermore, experiencing strong arousal without any obvious cause does not lead to a neutral, undifferentiated state, as the theory assumes. Stop for a moment and imagine that, right now, your heart suddenly starts beating quickly, your breathing becomes fast and shallow, your chest muscles tighten, and your palms become drenched with sweat. What interpretation would you put on these symptoms? Are you surprised to learn that people generally interpret *unexplained* physical arousal as *negative,* a sign that something is wrong? In addition, people's search for an explanation tends to be biased toward finding stimuli that will explain or justify this negative interpretation (Marshall & Zimbardo, 1979; Maslach, 1979).

Another critique of the cognitive appraisal theory of emotion comes from researcher **Robert Zajonc** (pronounced Zy-Onts). Zajonc demonstrated conditions under which people have preferences—emotional responses to stimuli—without knowing why (Zajonc, 2000, 2001). In an extensive series of experiments on the *mere exposure effect,* participants were presented with a variety of stimuli, such as foreign words, Chinese characters, sets of numbers, and strange faces. These stimuli were flashed so briefly that participants could not consciously recognize the items. Later on, participants were asked how much they liked particular stimuli, some of which were old (i.e., those stimuli had been flashed below the threshold of consciousness)

whereas some were new. The participants tended to give higher ratings to the old items. Because participants experienced these positive emotions without conscious awareness of their origins, the emotional response could not emerge from an appraisal process.

It is probably safest to conclude that cognitive appraisal is an important process of emotional experience, but not the only one (Izard, 1993). Under some circumstances, you will, in fact, look to the environment (at least unconsciously) to try to interpret why you feel the way you do. Under other circumstances, however, your emotional experiences may be under the control of the innate links provided by evolution. The physiological response will not require any interpretation. These different routes to emotional experiences suggest that emotions serve a range of functions. We turn now to those functions.

◆ FUNCTIONS OF EMOTION

Why do you have emotions? What functions do emotions serve for you? To think about these questions, it might help to review your day and imagine how different it would have been if you couldn't experience or understand emotions. Let's examine some of the roles researchers have suggested that emotion plays in your life.

MOTIVATION AND ATTENTION

The very first time you wear your new sweatshirt, the shoulder seam rips. Why are you likely to storm back to the store and demand a refund? From Chapter 11, you should recognize this as a question about motivation. If you want to answer, "Because I'd be angry" or "Because I'd be disappointed," you can see that emotions often provide the impetus for action. Emotions serve a motivational function by *arousing* you to take action with regard to some experienced or imagined event. Emotions then direct and *sustain* your behaviors toward specific goals. For the love of another person, you may do all you can to attract, be near, and protect him or her. For the love of principle or of country, you may sacrifice your life.

Let's consider specific circumstances in which emotional responses have an impact on how you focus your attention. Recall from Chapter 4 that, at any given time, you can attend to only a very small subset of the objects and events available in the environment. Research suggests that your left amygdala plays an important role in giving you heightened awareness of objects that have emotional significance.

The Amygdala and Perception of Emotional Events

Under ordinary circumstances, your perception of the world is governed by a phenomenon known as the *attentional-blink effect*. This means that when your attention has become focused on one stimulus, you'll have less awareness of another one that comes shortly after. Consider an experiment in which participants had words flashed at them on a computer screen—with each word lasting about a tenth of a second and each subsequent word also coming about a tenth of a second later (Anderson & Phelps, 2001). Participants were asked to report two words presented in green type among a larger group of words presented in black type. Because of the attentional-blink effect, participants typically had some trouble on the second of the two green words: They were able to name the word correctly 61.5 percent of the time. However, when the second word evoked negative emotions (e.g., *rape* or *bastard*), performance rose dramatically to 79.8 percent. That's solid evidence that emotional stimuli command extra attention. How do we know that the amygdala plays a role in this process? The researchers replicated the experiment with patients whose left or right amygdalas had been removed to help control the seizures associated with epilepsy. Those patients whose left amygdalas had been removed showed no advantage for the emotional words over the neutral words.

This research demonstrates one way in which your brain doesn't allow events of emotional importance to escape your attention. The fact that it's the left amygdala is another piece of evidence toward the researchers' goal of providing a full account of how emotions are experienced in the brain.

Has a strong emotion, like anger, ever driven you to engage in irrational or destructive behavior?

SOCIAL FUNCTIONS OF EMOTION

On a social level, emotions serve the broad function of regulating social interactions. As a positive social glue, they bind you to some people; as a negative social repellent, they distance you from others. You back off when someone is bristling with anger, and you approach when another person signals receptivity with a smile, dilated pupils, and a "come hither" glance. You might suppress strong negative emotions out of respect for another person's status or power. Consider D. R., a woman who lost the function of her amygdala—and with it the ability to perceive anger and fear (Scott et al., 1997). Imagine what life would be like if you couldn't understand when people were trying to communicate negative emotions. For example, what would it be like not to be able to learn from others that a situation was dangerous? Or that your actions had given rise to an angry response? When D. R. lost function in her amygdala, she also lost her ability to function fully in her social world.

The emotions you experience have a strong impact on how you function in social settings. Consider the consequences of people's positive or negative moods on the ways in which they made requests.

Mood Effects on Language Use

Participants in an experiment watched short films that put them in happy, neutral, or sad moods. Once the mood was established, the experimenter asked each participant to perform a favor: Would he or she retrieve a stimulus file from a research assistant in the next room? The words the participants used to make the request were recorded. Raters (who did not know which participant had been in which mood) provided ratings of the politeness of each request. As shown in **Figure 12.4,** mood had a large impact on politeness: Sad participants were the most polite. People in sad moods appeared to be cautious about making direct—potentially impolite—demands on other people (Forgas, 1999).

Think about your own life: Are you more risk-taking in social situations when you are in a happy mood? Are you more cautious when you are in a sad mood?

Research also points to the impact of emotion on stimulating prosocial behavior (Hoffman, 1986; Isen, 1984; Schroeder et al., 1995). When individuals are made to feel good, they are more likely to engage in a variety of helping behaviors (Carlson et al., 1988). When research participants were made to feel guilty about a misdeed, they were more likely to volunteer aid

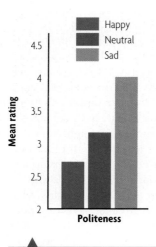

FIGURE 12.4

The Effects of Mood on Request Politeness

Participants in happy, neutral, or negative moods made requests of a stranger. Raters assessed the politeness of each request on a scale ranging from 1 (impolite) to 7 (polite). Participants in sad moods produced requests that were relatively more polite (e.g., "Would you mind getting me the stimulus file?" vs. "I need the stimulus file").

in a future situation, presumably to reduce their guilt (Carlsmith & Gross, 1969). Similarly, how people feel depends on how prosocial they have been. For example, when individuals recalled instances in which they had refused to help another person, their moods became more negative (Williamson et al., 1996). This was particularly true when the person they had refused to help was a good friend, family member, or romantic partner. How you feel is greatly affected by how well you are able to carry out your social obligations.

EMOTIONAL EFFECTS ON COGNITIVE FUNCTIONING

Emotions serve cognitive functions by influencing what you attend to, the way you perceive yourself and others, and the way you interpret and remember various features of life situations. Researchers have demonstrated that emotional states can affect learning, memory, social judgments, and creativity (Bradley, 1994; Forgas, 1995, 2000). Your emotional responses play an important role in organizing and categorizing your life experiences.

Research on the role of emotion in information processing was pioneered by **Gordon Bower** (1981, 1991) and his students. Bower's model proposes that, when a person experiences a given emotion in a particular situation, that emotion is stored in memory along with the ongoing events, as part of the same context. This pattern of memory representation gives rise to mood-congruent processing and mood-dependent memory.

Mood-congruent processing occurs when people are selectively sensitized to process and retrieve information that agrees with their current mood state. Material that is congruent with one's prevailing mood is more likely to be noticed, attended to, and processed more deeply and with greater elaborative associations (Gilligan & Bower, 1984). *Mood-dependent memory* refers to circumstances in which people find it easier to recall information when their mood at retrieval matches their mood when they first committed the information to memory (Eich, 1995; Eich & Macaulay, 2000). Here's an example of mood congruency you might have noticed: People who are in pleasant moods tend to recall more positive events from their lives than do people who are in unpleasant moods (Eich et al., 1994).

Researchers have also been interested in understanding the circumstances in which emotions have an impact on judgments and reasoning (Adolphs & Damasio, 2001). Consider the two reasoning problems given in **Table 12.1.** How would you answer the question at the end of each problem? If you analyze the situations carefully—trying to stick only to the outcomes—you'll see that in each case one person dies so that five others might live. However, most people respond differently to the scenarios: They believe it is appropriate to

TABLE 12.1

Moral Reasoning Problems

1. A runaway trolley is heading down the tracks toward five workmen who will be killed if the trolley proceeds on its present course. You are on a footbridge over the tracks, in between the approaching trolley and the five workmen. Next to you on this footbridge is a stranger who happens to be very large.

   The only way to save the lives of the five workmen is to push this stranger off the bridge and onto the tracks below where his large body will stop the trolley. The stranger will die if you do this, but the five workmen will be saved.

   Is it appropriate for you to push the stranger onto the tracks in order to save the five workmen?

2. You are at the wheel of a runaway trolley quickly approaching a fork in the tracks. On the tracks extending to the left is a group of five railway workmen. On the tracks extending to the right is a single railway workman.

   If you do nothing the trolley will proceed to the left, causing the deaths of the five workmen. The only way to avoid the deaths of these workmen is to hit a switch on your dashboard that will cause the trolley to proceed to the right, causing the death of the single workman.

   Is it appropriate for you to hit the switch in order to avoid the deaths of the five workmen?

<www.ablongman.com/gerrig17e>

You might think this question has an easy answer: Aren't some people happier than others because better things happen to them? That's true in part, but you might be surprised to learn that genetics has a large impact on how happy people are as they make their way through life.

Consider a study that used the classic methodology of behavior genetics: The researchers examined the extent to which monozygotic (MZ) twins (who are genetically identical) and dizygotic (DZ) twins (who, like other siblings, share only half their genes) showed similar reports of well-being (Lykken & Tellegen, 1996). The twins' happiness levels were measured by questionnaires that asked them to respond to statements such as "Taking the good with the bad, how happy and contented are you on the average now, compared with other people?" The researchers examined two sets of responses from MZ and DZ twins, obtained when they were roughly 20 and 30 years old. As shown in the figure, they performed a "cross-twin, cross-time" analysis: They calculated the extent to which one twin's happiness as a 30-year-old was correlated with his or her brother's or sister's happiness at age 20. The researchers found that there was virtually no relationship for the DZ twins. However, for the MZ twins, 80 percent of the relationship in the ratings from ages 20 to 30 could be explained by this cross-twin analysis.

The researchers suggested that this pattern within the pairs of MZ twins is best explained if baseline happiness—the average amount of happiness each person will experience across the life span—has a strong genetic component. This doesn't mean, of course, that there is a gene (or genes) specifically for *happiness*.

Why Are Some People Happier Than Others?
Lori Ziccardi
University of Delaware

Remember from Chapter 2 that "correlation is not causation." It could be the case that some other aspects of an individual's behaviors or experiences mediate the genetic influence on happiness. For example, there might be genes that separately affect people's experiences of positive and negative emotions—with a joint impact on average well-being (Hamer, 1996).

Are you surprised by the claim that genetics affects average happiness? As we noted at the outset, you might have thought that your happiness would be more strongly affected by the environment: Are you in a romantic relationship? How hard are your courses? What are the obstacles in your life? The researchers propose that such environmental events cause variation around an average level of happiness that was "set" at birth. As an analogy, think of the way the thermostat in your home works. Suppose you set it to 68°F—environmental events will cause variation around this temperature, but on average the temperature should be 68°F. The research on happiness suggests that each

of us has a set happiness level—analogous, for example, to 48°F, 68°F, or 88°F—which remains our average in the face of life's ups and downs. Of course, just as thermostats may function less well under extremes, some life events (e.g., marriages and the deaths of spouses) will cause people to experience levels of happiness that depart from their set point (Lucas et al., 2003).

Beyond your individual circumstances, your experience of happiness is also influenced by the context in which we now function as a species. **David Buss** (2000) has suggested that some limits are placed on human happiness by the "discrepancies between modern and ancestral environments" (p. 15). For example, although humans evolved in the context of small groups, many people now live in large urban environments in which they are mostly surrounded by large numbers of total strangers. We no longer have close bonds to the group of individuals that share our space— the types of bonds that could help us weather crises to experience happy lives. What can be done? Although you cannot turn back the tide of cultural evolution that has brought these changes about, you can try to counteract these changes by increasing your closeness to your family members and to your friends (Buss, 2000).

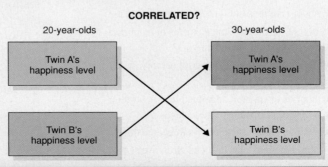

CORRELATED?

flip the switch, but they find it difficult to agree that they would actually push a stranger onto trolley tracks. One hypothesis for this difference is that the first type of problem engages emotional processing. It's hard to be unemotional about the idea of actually *pushing* someone onto the tracks. Evidence in favor of this hypothesis comes directly from the brain. In one study, researchers asked participants to consider moral reasoning problems while undergoing fMRI scans (Greene et al., 2001). As in example 1, some of the problems were *personal*—they asked participants to consider actions that required direct personal involvement. The contrasting problems, as in example 2, were relatively *impersonal*. The two types of problems led to quite different responses in the brain. In particular, for the personal problems the fMRI scans showed considerably more activity in those brain regions that had been associated, in prior research, with emotional processing. This study provides strong evidence that the content of the problems you face in life determines the way in which cognition and emotion interact to yield solutions.

One final note about the relationship between mood and cognition: Researchers have consistently demonstrated that positive affect—pleasant moods—produces more efficient and more creative thinking and problem solving (Isen et al., 1987). Consider a study in which physicians were asked to solve problems that required a certain level of creativity. Those who had been placed in a mildly pleasant mood (the experimenters gave the doctors a small gift of candy) performed reliably better on the creativity test than did those doctors in the control group (who got no prior gift) (Estrada et al., 1994). You can see an immediate application of these types of findings: You are likely to carry out your schoolwork more efficiently and creatively if you can maintain a happy mood. You might be thinking, "How am I supposed to stay happy with all the work I have to do?" As we turn now to the topic of stress, and how to cope with it, you will learn how to take cognitive control over how you are "feeling."

PUT YOURSELF TO THE TEST

- What idea about emotions did Charles Darwin originate?
- What evidence suggests that some elements of emotional responses are innate while others are not?
- What roles do the autonomic and central nervous systems play in the experience of emotions?
- How have theories of emotion attempted to explain the relationship between physiology and feelings?
- In what ways do emotions serve motivational functions?
- What roles may emotions play in social circumstances?
- What impact may emotions have on cognitive functioning?

Stress of Living

Suppose we asked you to keep track of how you are "feeling" over the course of a day. You might report that for brief periods, you felt happiness, sadness, anger, astonishment, and so on. There is one feeling, however, that people often report as a kind of background noise for much of their day-to-day experience, and that is stress (Sapolsky, 1994). Modern industrialized society sets a rapid, hectic pace for living. People often have too many demands placed on their time, are worried about uncertain futures, and have little time for family and fun. But would you be better off without stress? A stress-free life would offer no challenge—no difficulties to surmount, no new fields to conquer, and no reasons to sharpen your wits or improve your abilities. Every organism faces challenges from its external environment and from its personal needs. The organism must solve these problems to survive and thrive.

Stress is the pattern of responses an organism makes to stimulus events that disturb its equilibrium and tax or exceed its ability to cope. The stimulus events include a large variety of external and internal conditions that collectively are called stressors. A **stressor** is a stimulus event that places a demand on an organism for some kind of adaptive response: a bicyclist swerves in front of your car, your professor moves up the due date of your term paper, you're asked to run for class president. An individual's response to the need for change is made up of a diverse combination of reactions taking place on several levels, including physiological, behavioral, emotional, and cognitive. What responses might you make to each of the stressors we listed just earlier?

Figure 12.5 diagrams the elements of the stress process. Our goal for this section is to give you a clear understanding of all the features represented in this figure. We will begin by considering general physiological responses to stressors. We then describe the particular effects of different categories of stressors. Finally, we explore different methods you can use to cope with the stress in your life.

◆ PHYSIOLOGICAL STRESS REACTIONS

How would you respond if you arrived at a class and discovered that you were about to have a pop quiz? You would probably agree that this would cause you some stress, but what does that mean for your body's reactions? Many of the physiological responses we described for emotional situations are also relevant to

Whether at work or play, individuals in contemporary society are likely to encounter a stressful environment. What situations in your life do you find most stressful?

day-to-day instances of stress. Such transient states of arousal, with typically clear onset and offset patterns, are examples of **acute stress. Chronic stress,** on the other hand, is a state of enduring arousal, continuing over time, in which demands are perceived as greater than the inner and outer resources available for dealing with them. An example of chronic stress might be a continuous frustration with your inability to find time to do all the things you want to do. Let's see how your body responds to these different types of stresses.

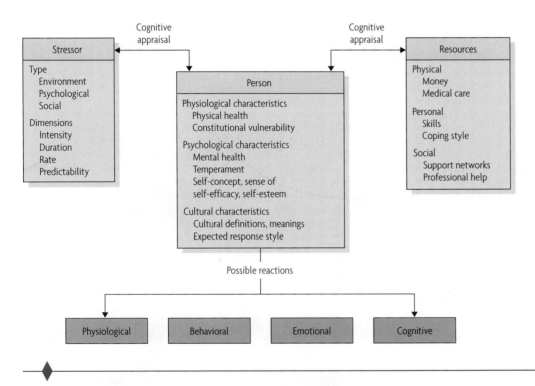

FIGURE 12.5

A Model of Stress

Cognitive appraisal of the stress situation interacts with the stressor and the physical, social, and personal resources available for dealing with the stressor. Individuals respond to threats on various levels: physiological, behavioral, emotional, and cognitive. Some responses are adaptive, and others are maladaptive or even lethal.

In the 1920s, Walter Cannon outlined the first scientific description of the way animals and humans respond to danger. He found that a sequence of activity is triggered in the nerves and glands to prepare the body either to defend itself and struggle or to run away to safety. Cannon called this dual stress response the **fight-or-flight response.** At the center of this stress response is the *hypothalamus,* which is involved in a variety of emotional responses. The hypothalamus has sometimes been referred to as the stress center because of its twin functions in emergencies: (1) It controls the autonomic nervous system (ANS) and (2) it activates the pituitary gland.

The ANS regulates the activities of the body's organs. In stressful conditions, breathing becomes faster and deeper, heart rate increases, blood vessels constrict, and blood pressure rises. In addition to these internal changes, muscles open the passages of the throat and nose to allow more air into the lungs while also producing facial expressions of strong emotion. Messages go to smooth muscles to stop certain bodily functions, such as digestion, that are irrelevant to preparing for the emergency at hand.

Another function of the autonomic nervous system during stress is to get adrenaline flowing. It signals the inner part of the adrenal glands, the *adrenal medulla,* to release two hormones, *epinephrine* and *norepinephrine,* which, in turn, signal a number of other organs to perform their specialized functions. The spleen releases more red blood corpuscles (to aid in clotting if there is an injury), and the bone marrow is stimulated to make more white corpuscles (to combat possible infection). The liver is stimulated to produce more sugar, building up body energy.

The *pituitary gland* responds to signals from the hypothalamus by secreting two hormones vital to the stress reaction. The *thyrotropic hormone* (TTH) stimulates the *thyroid gland,* which makes more energy available to the body. The *adrenocorticotropic hormone* (ACTH), known as the "stress hormone," stimulates the outer part of the adrenal glands, the *adrenal cortex,* resulting in the release of hormones that control metabolic processes and the release of sugar from the liver into the blood. ACTH also signals various organs to release about 30 other hormones, each of which plays a role in the body's adjustment to this call to arms. A summary of this physiological stress response is shown in **Figure 12.6.**

An analysis by health psychologist **Shelley Taylor** and her colleagues (2000) suggests that these physiological responses to stress may have different consequences for females than for males. Taylor et al. suggest that females do not experience *fight-or-flight.* Rather, these researchers argue that stressors lead females to experience a **tend-and-befriend response:** In times of stress, females ensure the safety of their offspring by tending to their needs; females befriend other members of their social group with the same goal of reducing the vulnerability of their offspring. You can see how this analysis of sex differences in stress responses fits with our earlier discussions of evolutionary perspectives on human behavior. For example, when we discussed human sexual behaviors in Chapter 11, we noted that men and women's *mating strategies* differ, in part, because of the relative roles men and women have played—over the course of evolution—in child rearing. The idea here is very much the same: Because of men and women's different evolutionary niches with respect to nurturing offspring, the same initial physiological responses to stress ultimately produce quite different behaviors.

Unfortunately, neither the fight-or-flight nor the tend-and-befriend response is entirely useful for contemporary lives. Many of the stressors both men and women experience on a day-to-day basis make the physiological stress responses fairly maladaptive. Suppose, for example, you are taking a difficult exam and the clock is swiftly ticking away. Although you might value the heightened attentiveness brought about by your stress response, the rest of the physiological changes do you no good: There's no one to fight or to tend, and so on. The responses that developed in the species as adaptive preparations for dealing with external dangers are counterproductive for dealing with many contemporary types of psychological stressors. This is particularly true because, as we shall see next, many people live their lives under circumstances of chronic stress.

What are the physiological consequences of chronic stress?

     <www.ablongman.com/gerrig17e>

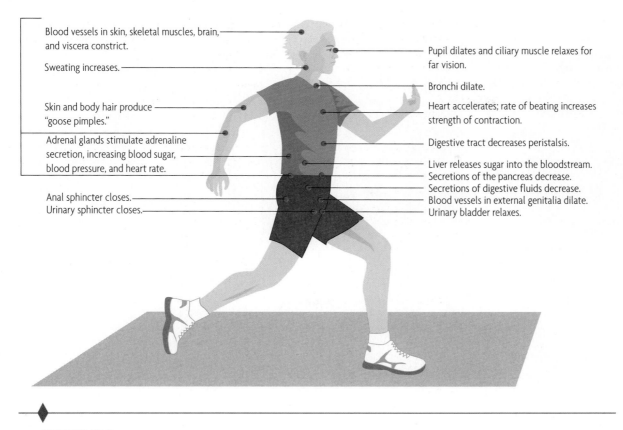

Blood vessels in skin, skeletal muscles, brain, and viscera constrict.

Sweating increases.

Skin and body hair produce "goose pimples."

Adrenal glands stimulate adrenaline secretion, increasing blood sugar, blood pressure, and heart rate.

Anal sphincter closes.
Urinary sphincter closes.

Pupil dilates and ciliary muscle relaxes for far vision.

Bronchi dilate.

Heart accelerates; rate of beating increases strength of contraction.

Digestive tract decreases peristalsis.

Liver releases sugar into the bloodstream.
Secretions of the pancreas decrease.
Secretions of digestive fluids decrease.
Blood vessels in external genitalia dilate.
Urinary bladder relaxes.

FIGURE 12.6

The Body's Reaction to Stress

Stress produces a wide range of physiological changes in your body.

THE GENERAL ADAPTATION SYNDROME (GAS) AND CHRONIC STRESS

The first modern researcher to investigate the effects of continued severe stress on the body was **Hans Selye,** a Canadian endocrinologist. Beginning in the late 1930s, Selye reported on the complex response of laboratory animals to damaging agents such as bacterial infections, toxins, trauma, forced restraint, heat, cold, and so on. According to Selye's theory of stress, many kinds of stressors can trigger the same reaction or general bodily response. All stressors call for *adaptation:* An organism must maintain or regain its integrity and well-being by restoring equilibrium, or homeostasis. The response to stressors was described by Selye as the **general adaptation syndrome (GAS).** It includes three stages: an alarm reaction, a stage of resistance, and a stage of exhaustion (Selye, 1976a, 1976b). *Alarm reactions* are brief periods of bodily arousal that prepare the body for vigorous activity. If a stressor is prolonged, the body enters a stage of *resistance*—a state of moderate arousal. During the stage of resistance, the organism can endure and *resist* further debilitating effects of prolonged stressors. However, if the stressor is sufficiently

long-lasting or intense, the body's resources become depleted and the organism enters the stage of *exhaustion*. The three stages are diagrammed and explained in **Figure 12.7.**

Selye identified some of the dangers associated with the stage of exhaustion. Recall, for example, that ACTH plays a role in the short-term response to stress. In the long term, however, its action reduces the ability of natural killer cells to destroy cancer cells and other life-threatening infections. When the body is stressed chronically, the increased production of "stress hormones" compromises the integrity of the immune system. This application of the general adaptation syndrome has proven valuable to explain **psychosomatic disorders**—illnesses that could not be wholly explained by physical causes—that had baffled physicians who had never considered stress as a cause for illness and disease. What serves the body well in adapting to acute stress impairs the body's response to chronic stress.

Selye's research makes disease seem an inevitable response to stress. We will see, however, that your psychological interpretation of what is stressful and what is not stressful—the way in which you appraise potentially stressful events—has an impact on your body's

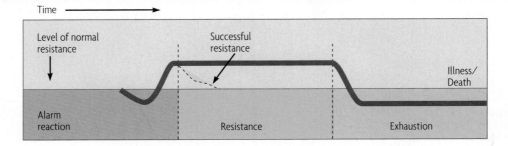

Stage I: Alarm reaction (continuously repeated throughout life)	Stage II: Resistance (continuously repeated throughout life)	Stage III: Exhaustion
• Enlargement of adrenal cortex • Enlargement of lymphatic system • Increase in hormone levels • Response to specific stressor • Epinephrine release associated with high levels of physiological arousal and negative affect • Greater susceptibility to increased intensity of stressor • Heightened susceptibility to illness (If prolonged, the slower components of the GAS are set into motion, beginning with Stage II.)	• Shrinkage of adrenal cortex • Return of lymph nodes to normal size • Sustaining of hormone levels • High physiological arousal • Counteraction of parasympathetic branch of ANS • Enduring of stressor; resistance to further debilitating effects • Heightened sensitivity to stress (If stress continues at intense levels, hormonal reserves are depleted, fatigue sets in, and individual enters Stage III.)	• Enlargement/dysfunction of lymphatic structures • Increase in hormone levels • Depletion of adaptive hormones • Decreased ability to resist either original or extraneous stressors • Affective experience—often depression • Illness • Death

Time ⟶

Level of normal resistance

Successful resistance

Illness/ Death

Alarm reaction

Resistance

Exhaustion

FIGURE 12.7

The General Adaptation Syndrome (GAS)

Following exposure to a stressor, the body's resistance is diminished until the physiological changes of the corresponding alarm reaction bring it back up to the normal level. If the stressor continues, the bodily signs characteristic of the alarm reaction virtually disappear; resistance to the particular stressor rises above normal but drops for other stressors. This adaptive resistance returns the body to its normal level of functioning. Following prolonged exposure to the stressor, adaptation breaks down; signs of alarm reaction reappear, the stressor effects are irreversible, and the individual becomes ill and may die.

physiological response. To give a full account of the effect of stress on your body, we will have to combine Selye's foundational physiological theory with later research on psychological factors.

◆ PSYCHOLOGICAL STRESS REACTIONS

Your physiological stress reactions are automatic, predictable, built-in responses over which you normally have no conscious control. However, many psychological reactions are learned. They depend on perceptions and interpretations of the world. In this section, we discuss psychological responses to different categories of stressors, such as major life changes and traumatic events.

MAJOR LIFE EVENTS

Major *changes* in life situations are at the root of stress for many people. Even events that you welcome, such as winning the lottery or getting promoted, may require major changes in your routines and adaptation to new

requirements. Recall, for example, the pattern of marital well-being we described in Chapter 10. Although the birth of a child is one of the most sought-after changes in a married couple's life, it is also a source of major stress, contributing to reduced marital satisfaction (Cowan & Cowan, 1988; Levenson et al., 1993). Thus, when you try to relate stress to changes in your life, you should consider both positive and negative changes.

The influence of life events on subsequent mental and physical health has been a target of considerable research. It started in the 1960s with the development of the Social Readjustment Rating Scale (SRRS), a simple measure for rating the degree of adjustment required by the various life changes, both pleasant and unpleasant, that many people experience. The scale was developed from the responses of adults, from all walks of life, who were asked to identify from a list those life changes that applied to them. These adults rated the amount of readjustment required for each change by comparing each to marriage, which was arbitrarily assigned a value of 50 life-change units. Researchers then calculated the total number of **life-change units (LCUs)** an individual had undergone, using the units as a measure of the amount of stress the individual had experienced (Holmes & Rahe, 1967). The SRRS was updated in the 1990s. The researchers used the same procedure of asking participants to rate the stress of life events as compared to marriage (Miller & Rahe, 1997). In this update, the LCU estimates went up 45 percent over the original values—that is, participants in the 1990s reported that they were experiencing overall much higher levels of stress than their peers had in the 1960s. Women in the 1990s also reported experiencing more stress in their lives than did men.

Table 12.2 provides a modification of this scale for college students. Before reading on, take a moment to test your level of stress on the student stress scale. What is your LCU rating? We have provided room for you to carry out this exercise three times, so that you can chart your level of stress across the semester.

Researchers have found a variety of ways to examine the relationship between life events and health outcomes. In one study, participants volunteered to be exposed to viruses that cause the common cold. Those participants who reported a rate of negative life events above the group's average were about 10 percent more likely to actually come down with a cold (Cohen et al., 1993). Consider another study that should have immediate relevance to the choices you make about how to organize your schoolwork.

PUTTING IDEAS TO THE TEST

The Health Costs of Procrastination

When a professor gives you an assignment—a stressful life event in every student's life—do you try to take care of it as soon as possible or do you put it off to the very last minute? Psychologists have developed a measurement device called the *General Procrastination Scale* (Lay, 1986) to differentiate those individuals who habitually put things off—*procrastinators*—from those who don't—*nonprocrastinators*. A pair of researchers administered this scale to students in a health psychology course who had a paper due late in the semester. The students were also asked to report, early and late in the semester, how many symptoms of physical illness they had experienced. Not surprisingly, procrastinators, on average, turned their papers in later than did nonprocrastinators; procrastinators also, on average, obtained lower grades on those papers. **Figure 12.8** displays the effect of procrastination on physical health. As you can see, early in the semester, procrastinators reported fewer symptoms, but by late in the semester, they were reporting more symptoms than their nonprocrastinating peers (Tice & Baumeister, 1997).

TABLE 12.2
Student Stress Scale

The Student Stress Scale represents an adaptation of Holmes and Rahe's Social Readjustment Rating Scale. Each event is given a score that represents the amount of readjustment a person has to make in life as a result of the change. People with scores of 300 and higher have a high health risk. People scoring between 150 and 300 points have about a 50–50 chance of serious health change within two years. People scoring below 150 have a 1 in 3 chance of serious health change. Calculate your total life-change units (LCUs) three times during the semester and then correlate those scores with any changes in your health status.

Event	Life-Change Units
Death of a close family member	100
Death of a close friend	73
Divorce between parents	65
Jail term	63
Major personal injury or illness	63
Marriage	58
Being fired from job	50
Failing an important course	47
Change in health of family member	45
Pregnancy	45
Sex problems	44
Serious argument with close friend	40
Change in financial status	39
Change of major	39
Trouble with parents	39
New girl- or boyfriend	38
Increased workload at school	37
Outstanding personal achievement	36
First quarter/semester in college	35
Change in living conditions	31
Serious argument with instructor	30
Lower grades than expected	29
Change in sleeping habits	29
Change in social activities	29
Change in eating habits	28
Chronic car trouble	26
Change in number of family get-togethers	26
Too many missed classes	25
Change of college	24
Dropping of more than one class	23
Minor traffic violations	20

My 1st total [＿＿＿] (date: ＿＿＿＿＿＿)

My 2nd total [＿＿＿] (date: ＿＿＿＿＿＿)

My 3rd total [＿＿＿] (date: ＿＿＿＿＿＿)

You see in this study why not all life events have the same impact on all people. The nonprocrastinators got to work right away and so experienced stress and symptoms early in the semester. However, the consequences for the procrastinators of avoiding the early semester stress was a great increase in physical illness toward the end of the semester. Therefore, they were likely to be feeling ill just at the point in the semester when they needed to be in good health to complete all the work they had put off! You should think about these results as you develop your own plan for navigating each semester. If you believe that you habitually procrastinate, you should consider consulting with a psychologist or school counselor to modify your behavior. Your grades and health are at stake!

TRAUMATIC EVENTS

An event that is negative but also uncontrollable, unpredictable, or ambiguous is particularly stressful. These conditions hold especially true in the case of *traumatic events*. Some traumatic events, such as rape and automobile crashes, affect individuals. Others, such as earthquakes and tornadoes, have a broader impact. In recent years, no traumatic event has had as widespread consequences as the events of September 11, 2001. On that day, attacks on the World Trade Center and the Pentagon with commercial aircraft led to the deaths of almost 3,000 people. With the goal of providing appropriate mental health care, researchers moved swiftly to assess the psychological aftermath of the attacks.

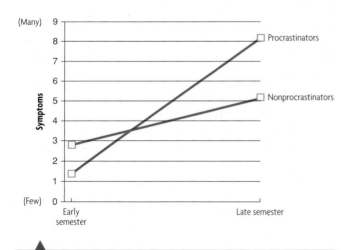

FIGURE 12.8

The Health Costs of Procrastination

Researchers identified students who were, generally, procrastinators and nonprocrastinators. The students were asked to report, early and late in the semester, how many symptoms of physical illness they had experienced. By late in the semester all students showed increases in symptoms. However—as all their work came due—procrastinators were reporting even more symptoms than their nonprocrastinating peers.

Why might TV viewing have an impact on people's experiences of PTSD?

One particular focus was on the prevalence of **posttraumatic stress disorder (PTSD).** PTSD is a stress reaction in which individuals suffer from persistent reexperiences of the traumatic event in the form, for example, of flashbacks or nightmares (*DSM-IV,* 1994). Sufferers experience an emotional numbing in relation to everyday events and feelings of alienation from other people. Finally, the emotional pain of this reaction can result in an increase in various symptoms, such as sleep problems, guilt about surviving, difficulty in concentrating, and an exaggerated startle response.

In October and November of 2001, a team of researchers conducted a Web-based survey of 2,273 adults across the United States (Schlenger et al., 2002). The survey assessed both the participants' exposure to the incidents and their mental health symptoms. As seen in **Table 12.3,** greater exposure made it more likely that people would experience PTSD. The group most affected were those who lived in the New York City metropolitan area. Those individuals were most likely to have been personally involved in the tragedy. As seen in Table 12.3, the events didn't have extra impact on people in the Washington, DC, area. The researchers suggested that the difference between New York and DC might reflect the difference between attacks on a civilian target (the World Trade Center) and a military target (the Pentagon). Table 12.3 also shows that individuals who watched the most television coverage of the events also reported higher levels of symptoms of PTSD. Researchers will continue to assess the mental health consequences of September 11: They attempt to form generalizations from people's responses to catastrophes so that they can alleviate the worst consequences when new circumstances present themselves.

As we noted earlier, people also suffer from individual traumatic events with a negative impact on their psychological health. For example, rape victims often show many of the signs of posttraumatic stress (Acierno et al., 1999). In assessments two weeks after being assaulted, 94 percent of rape victims were diagnosed with PTSD; 12 weeks after the assault, 51 percent of the victims still met diagnostic criteria (Foa & Riggs, 1995). The following excerpt of a discussion between two college students about the aftershock of being raped reveals the powerful and enduring emotions.

Alice: I was in shock for a pretty long time. I could talk about the fact that I was a rape victim, but the emotions didn't start surfacing until a month later.

Beth: During the first two weeks there were people I had chosen to tell who were very, very supportive; but after two weeks, it was like, "Okay, she's over it, we can go on now." But the farther along you get, the more support you need, because, as time passes, you become aware of your emotions and the need to deal with them.

Alice: There is a point where you deny it happened. You just completely bury it.

Beth: It's so unreal that you don't want to believe that it actually happened or that it can happen. Then you go through a long period of fear and anger.

Alice: I'm terrified of going jogging. [Alice had been jogging when she was raped.] I completely stopped any kind of physical activity after I was raped. I started it again this quarter, but every time I go jogging I have a perpetual fear. My pulse doubles. Of course I don't go jogging alone any more, but still the fear is there constantly.

Beth: There's also a feeling of having all your friends betray you. I had a dream in which I was being assaulted outside my dorm. In the dream, everyone was looking out their windows—the faces were so clear—every one of my friends lined up against the windows watching, and there were even people two feet away from me. They all saw what was happening and none of them did anything. I woke up and had a feeling of extreme loneliness. (Stanford Daily, 1982)

The emotional responses of posttraumatic stress can occur in an acute form immediately following a disaster

TABLE 12.3

The Psychological Impact of Exposure to the Events of September 11, 2001

	Probable PTSD
PROXIMITY TO CRASH SITES	
New York City metropolitan area	11.2
District of Columbia metropolitan area	2.7
Other major metropolitan area	3.6
Remainder of the United States	4.0
TELEVISION VIEWING PER DAY (in hours)	
Less than 4	0.8
4 to 7	3.9
8 to 11	4.2
12 or more	10.1

and can subside over a period of several months. We will return to the topic of PTSD when we discuss anxiety disorders in Chapter 14.

CHRONIC STRESSORS

In our discussion of physiological responses to stress, we made a distinction between stressors that are acute, with clear onsets and offsets, versus those that are chronic—that is, endure over time. With psychological stressors, it's not always easy to draw a sharp distinction. Suppose, for example, your bicycle is stolen. Originally, this is an acute source of stress. However, if you begin to worry constantly that your new bike will also be stolen, the stress associated with this event can become chronic. Researchers have found this pattern in people who suffer from serious illnesses like cancer (Andersen et al., 1994). The chronic stress of coping with the anxiety of a cancer diagnosis and treatment may impair health more rapidly than the disease alone would.

For many people, chronic stress arises from conditions in society and the environment. What cumulative effects do overpopulation, crime, economic conditions, pollution, AIDS, and the threat of terrorism have on you? How do these and other environmental stressors affect your mental well-being? Some groups of people suffer chronic stress by virtue of their socioeconomic status or racial identity, with stark consequences for overall well-being (Gallo & Matthews, 2003; Stone, 2000). Consider a study that measured economic hardships for more than a thousand participants over three decades (Lynch et al., 1997). Economic hardship was defined as household income of less than 200 percent of the federal poverty level. As assessed in 1994, the more periods of economic hardship adults experienced between 1965

These Detroit residents clamoring for post office job applications are likely to have experienced chronic stress due to unemployment or underemployment. What are some likely consequences for their physical and mental health?

and 1983, the more difficulties they had with physical functioning related to basic activities of daily living, such as cooking, shopping, and bathing. Similar effects were found for psychological and cognitive functioning. Compared to those with no period of economic hardship, people with three episodes of poverty were three times more likely to have experienced symptoms of clinical depression, they were more than five times more likely to be assessed as cynically hostile and lacking optimism, and they were more than four times more likely to report difficulties with cognitive functioning. To confirm that these results were caused by economic hardship and not by initial poor health, the researchers demonstrated comparable patterns of disability among those participants whose health at the initial measurement in 1965 had been good or excellent.

Given these research findings, you will not be surprised to learn that chronic stress can also influence children's intellectual development. Consider a study that assessed the level of stress in a group of 6- to 16-year-old children and also measured their intelligence with an IQ test (see Chapter 9). The data revealed a negative correlation between stress and the Verbal/Comprehension measure on the IQ test: On average, the higher the level of stress in the children's lives, the less well they performed on this measure (Plante & Sykora, 1994). Apparently, high levels of chronic stress play a disruptive role in children's cognitive performance. These data echo the findings we reported in Chapter 9 (see page 303) on the impact of environments on intelligence. Researchers understand that the social programs intended to improve children's lives must acknowledge the whole range of chronic stressors associated with poverty.

DAILY HASSLES

You may agree that the end of a relationship, an earthquake, or prejudice might cause stress, but what about the smaller stressors you experience on a day-to-day basis? What happened to you yesterday? You probably didn't get a divorce or survive a plane crash. You're more likely to have lost your notes or textbook. Perhaps you were late for an important appointment, or you got a parking ticket, or a noisy neighbor ruined your sleep. These are the types of recurring day-to-day stressors that confront most people, most of the time.

In a diary study, a group of white middle-class middle-aged men and women kept track of their daily hassles over a one-year period (along with a record of major life changes and physical symptoms). A clear relationship emerged between hassles and health problems: The more frequent and intense the hassles people reported, the poorer was their health, both physical and mental (Lazarus, 1981; 1984b). As daily hassles go down, well-being goes up (Chamberlain & Zika, 1990). Researchers have demonstrated that daily hassles can start to have ill effects quite early in life.

PEANUTS reprinted by permission of United Feature Syndicate, Inc.

Daily Hassles Among Kindergartners

Researchers asked 74 kindergartners to report on their daily hassles. To obtain this information, the researchers asked the children whether events such as "losing something" or "being teased" had happened in the last month. After determining whether each event had occurred, they asked the children whether the events had made them feel bad—so that the measure of daily hassles reflected how stressed the child had felt by each event. To determine the effects daily hassles had on the children, the researchers asked the kindergartners' parents and teachers to indicate the extent to which the children engaged in negative behaviors. The results showed positive correlations between daily hassles and behavior problems: On average, the children whose lives were more filled with hassles were likely to be more aggressive and disruptive in their behaviors (Creasey et al., 1995).

We often think of childhood as a time of innocence. This research suggests, however, that some children already experience a level of stress that is associated with negative outcomes.

We have been focusing largely on day-to-day hassles. It is worth noting, however, that for many people daily hassles may be balanced out by daily positive experiences (Lazarus & Lazarus, 1994). The relative balance of positive and negative experiences may have health consequences. For example, one study asked 96 men to give daily reports of positive and negative events. The men were also tested daily for the strength of their immune response. Results showed that desirable life events were associated with a stronger immune response, undesirable events with a weaker response (Stone et al., 1994). Therefore, if we want to predict your life course based on daily hassles, we also need to know something about the daily pleasures your life provides.

We have just reviewed many sources of stress in people's lives. Psychologists have recognized for quite a long time that the impact of these different types of stressors depends in large part on how effectively people can cope with them. Let's now consider how people cope successfully and unsuccessfully with stress.

◆ COPING WITH STRESS

If living is inevitably stressful, and if chronic stress can disrupt your life and even kill you, you need to learn how to manage stress. **Coping** refers to the process of dealing with internal or external demands that are perceived as straining or exceeding an individual's resources (Lazarus & Folkman, 1984). Coping may consist of behavioral, emotional, or motivational responses and thoughts. We begin this section by describing how cognitive appraisal affects what you experience as stressful. We then consider types of coping responses; we describe both general principles of coping and specific interventions. Finally, we consider some individual differences in individuals' ability to cope with stress.

APPRAISAL OF STRESS

When you cope with stressful situations, your first step is to define in what ways they are, in fact, stressful. *Cognitive appraisal* (see page 401) is the cognitive interpretation and evaluation of a stressor. Cognitive appraisal plays a central role in defining the situation— what the demand is, how big a threat it is, and what resources you have for meeting it (Lazarus, 1993; Lazarus & Lazarus, 1994). Some stressors, such as undergoing bodily injury or finding one's house on fire, are experienced as threats by almost everyone. However, many other stressors can be defined in various ways, depending on your personal life situation, the relation of a particular demand to your central goals, your competence in dealing with the demand, and your self-assessment of that competence. The situation that causes acute distress for another person may be all in a day's work for you. Try to notice, and understand, the life events that are different for you and your friends and family: Some situations cause you stress but not your friends and family; other events cause them stress but not you. Why?

Richard Lazarus, whose general theory of appraisal we addressed in our discussion of emotions, has distinguished two stages in the cognitive appraisal of demands. *Primary appraisal* describes the initial evaluation of the seriousness of a demand. This evaluation starts with the questions "What's happening?" and "Is this thing good for me, stressful, or irrelevant?" If the answer to the second question is "stressful," you appraise the potential impact of the stressor by determining whether harm has occurred or is likely to and whether action is required (see **Table 12.4**). Once you decide something must be done, *secondary appraisal* begins. You evaluate the personal and social resources that are available to deal with the stressful circumstance and consider the action options that are needed. Appraisal continues as coping responses are tried; if the first ones don't work and the stress persists, new responses are initiated, and their effectiveness is evaluated.

Cognitive appraisal is an example of a stress moderator variable. **Stress moderator variables** are those variables that change the impact of a stressor on a given type of stress reaction. Moderator variables filter or modify the

TABLE 12.4

Stages in Stable Decision Making/Cognitive Appraisal

Stage	Key Questions
1. Appraising the challenge	Are the risks serious if I don't change?
2. Surveying alternatives	Is this alternative an acceptable means for dealing with the challenge?
	Have I sufficiently surveyed the available alternatives?
3. Weighing alternatives	Which alternative is best?
	Could the best alternative meet the essential requirements?
4. Deliberating about commitment	Shall I implement the best alternative and allow others to know?
5. Adhering despite negative feedback	Are the risks serious if I *don't* change?
	Are the risks serious if I *do* change?

usual effects of stressors on the individual's reactions. For example, your level of fatigue and general health status are moderator variables influencing your reaction to a given psychological or physical stressor. When you're in good shape, you can deal with a stressor better than when you aren't. You can see how cognitive appraisal also fits the definition of a moderator variable. The way in which you appraise a stressor will determine the types of coping responses you need to bring to it. Let's now consider general types of coping responses.

TYPES OF COPING RESPONSES

Suppose you have a big exam coming up. You've thought about it—you've appraised the situation—and you're quite sure that this is a stressful situation. What can you do? It's important to note that coping can precede a potentially stressful event in the form of **anticipatory coping** (Folkman, 1984). How do you deal with the stress of the upcoming exam? How do you tell your parents that you are dropping out of school or your lover that you are no longer in love? Anticipating a stressful situation leads to many thoughts and feelings that themselves may be stress inducing, as in the cases of interviews, speeches, or blind dates. You need to know how to cope.

The two main ways of coping are defined by whether the goal is to confront the problem directly—*problem-directed coping*—or to lessen the discomfort associated with the stress—*emotion-focused coping* (Billings & Moos, 1982; Lazarus & Folkman, 1984). Several subcategories of these two basic approaches are shown in **Table 12.5.**

Let's begin with problem-directed coping. "Taking the bull by the horns" is how we usually characterize the strategy of facing up to a problem situation. This approach includes all strategies designed to deal *directly* with the stressor, whether through overt action or through realistic problem-solving activities. You face up to a bully or run away; you try to win him or her over with bribes or other incentives. Your focus is on the problem to be dealt with and on the agent that has induced the stress. You acknowledge the call to action, you appraise the situation and your resources for dealing with it, and you undertake a response that is appropriate for removing or lessening the threat. Such problem-solving efforts are useful for managing *controllable stressors*—those stressors that you can change or eliminate through your actions, such as overbearing bosses or underwhelming grades.

The emotion-focused approach is useful for managing the impact of more *uncontrollable stressors.* Suppose you are responsible for the care of a parent with Alzheimer's. In that situation, there is no "bully" whom you can eliminate from the environment; you cannot make the disease go way. Even in this situation, some forms of problem-directed coping would be useful. For example, you could modify your work sched-

Why are multiple coping strategies beneficial for individuals such as Alzheimer's caregivers?

<www.ablongman.com/gerrig17e>

TABLE 12.5

Taxonomy of Coping Strategies

Type of Coping Strategy	Example
PROBLEM-DIRECTED COPING	
Change stressor or one's relationship to it through direct actions and/or problem-solving activities	Fight (destroy, remove, or weaken the threat)
	Flight (distance oneself from the threat)
	Seek options to fight or flight (negotiating, bargaining, compromising)
	Prevent future stress (act to increase one's resistance or decrease strength of anticipated stress)
EMOTION-FOCUSED COPING	
Change self through activities that make one feel better but do not change the stressor	Somatically focused activities (use of antianxiety medication, relaxation, biofeedback)
	Cognitively focused activities (planned distractions, fantasies, thoughts about oneself)
	Therapy to adjust conscious or unconscious processes that lead to additional anxiety

ule to make it easier to provide care. However, because you cannot eliminate the source of stress, you also can try to change your feelings and thoughts about the disease. For example, you might take part in a support group for Alzheimer's caregivers or learn relaxation techniques. These approaches still constitute a coping strategy because you are acknowledging that there is a threat to your well-being and you are taking steps to modify that threat.

You will be better off if you have multiple strategies to help you cope in stressful situations (Tennen et al., 2000). For coping to be successful, your resources need to match the perceived demand. Thus, the availability of multiple coping strategies is adaptive because you are more likely to achieve a match and manage the stressful event. Consider a study that examined the ways in which Israeli citizens cope with the chronic threat of terrorism (Bleich et al., 2003). A sample of 742 adults revealed that, on average, they used 6.4 coping strategies. Those coping strategies included checking on the whereabouts of family members, talking to others about what could be done, maintaining faith in God, and avoiding television and radio broadcasts. For many stressful situations, knowing that you possess a variety of coping strategies can help increase your actual ability to meet demands. Self-confidence can insulate you from experiencing the full impact of many stressors; believing you have coping resources readily available short-circuits the stressful, chaotic response "What am I going to do?"

Researchers who study coping have discovered that some individuals meet stressors with a particular degree of resilience—they are able to achieve positive outcomes despite serious threats to their well-being (Masten, 2001). Research has focused on the types of coping skills that resilient individuals have acquired and how they have acquired them. An important part of the answer is that children who become resilient have been raised by sup-

portive parents with good parenting skills (see Chapter 10). In addition, resilient children appear to have developed coping skills that relate to their ability to regulate their own behavior (Buckner et al., 2003). They can stay focused on tasks (which allows for problem-directed coping) and control their emotional responses (which allows for emotion-focused coping) in ways that better their life outcomes.

Up to now, we have been discussing general approaches to coping with stressors. Now we review specific cognitive and social approaches to successful coping.

MODIFYING COGNITIVE STRATEGIES

A powerful way to adapt to stress is to change your evaluations of stressors and your self-defeating cognitions about the way you are dealing with them. You need to find a different way to think about a given situation, your role in it, and the causal attributions you make to explain the undesirable outcome. Two ways of mentally coping with stress are *reappraising* the nature of the stressors themselves and *restructuring* your cognitions about your stress reactions.

We have already described the idea that people control the experience of stress in their lives in part by the way they appraise life events (Lazarus & Lazarus, 1994). Learning to think differently about certain stressors, to relabel them, or to imagine them in a less-threatening (perhaps even funny) context is a form of cognitive reappraisal that can reduce stress. Worried about giving a speech to a large, forbidding audience? One stressor reappraisal technique is to imagine your potential critics sitting there in the nude—this surely takes away a great deal of their fearsome power. Anxious about being shy at a party you must attend? Think about finding someone who is shier than you and reducing his or her social anxiety by initiating a conversation.

You can also manage stress by changing what you tell yourself about it and by changing your handling of it. Cognitive-behavior therapist **Donald Meichenbaum** (1977, 1985, 1993) has proposed a three-phase process that allows for such *stress inoculation*. In Phase 1, people work to develop a greater awareness of their actual behavior, what instigates it, and what its results are. One of the best ways of doing this is to keep daily logs. By helping people redefine their problems in terms of their causes and results, these records can increase their feelings of control. You may discover, for example, that your grades are low (a stressor) because you always leave too little time to do a good job on your class assignments. In Phase 2, people begin to identify new behaviors that negate the maladaptive, self-defeating behaviors. Perhaps you might create a fixed "study time" or limit your phone calls to ten minutes each night. In Phase 3, after adaptive behaviors are being emitted, individuals appraise the consequences of their new behaviors, avoiding the former internal dialogue of put-downs. Instead of telling themselves, "I was lucky the professor called on me when I happened to have read the text," they say, "I'm glad I was prepared for the professor's question. It feels great to be able to respond intelligently in that class."

This three-phase approach means initiating responses and self-statements that are incompatible with previous defeatist cognitions. Once started on this path, people realize that they are changing—and can take full credit for the change, which promotes further successes. **Table 12.6** gives examples of the new kinds of self-statements that help in dealing with stressful situations. *Stress inoculation training* has been used successfully in a wide variety of domains.

Stress Inoculation Training for Pain Management

This study enrolled 60 male athletes who had undergone knee surgery to repair athletic injuries. Half of the athletes were assigned to a treatment group that received stress inoculation training in addition to their regular program of rehabilitation. The training focused on the types of anxiety and pain the men would experience during their period of recovery, and encouraged them to use cognitive restructuring techniques of the type we described earlier. The other 30 men just underwent the standard course of rehabilitation. All 60 participants were asked to give ratings of their subjective experience of pain before treatment began and then at the beginning of each of ten physical therapy sessions. Although the treatment and control groups did not differ before treatment or at the first test session, over the remaining nine therapy sessions men in the inoculation group reported considerably less pain than did men in the control group (Ross & Berger, 1996).

You might recall that in Chapter 4 we discussed the way in which experiences of pain are determined by both physiological and psychological factors. This experiment with recovering athletes demonstrates how coping techniques can be used to take control of some aspects of the psychological contributions to pain.

Another main component of successful coping is for you to establish **perceived control** over the stressor, a belief that you can make a difference in the course or the consequences of some event or experience (Endler et al., 2000; Roussi, 2002). If you believe that you can affect the course of an illness or the daily symptoms of a disease, you are probably adjusting well to the disorder. However, if you believe that the source of the stress is another person whose behavior you cannot influence or a situation that you cannot change, chances increase for a poor psychological adjustment to your chronic condition. Those individuals who are able to maintain perceived control even in the face of fatal diseases like AIDS reap mental and physical health benefits (Thompson et al., 1994).

While you file away these control strategies for future use, we will turn to a final aspect of coping with stress—the social dimension.

TABLE 12.6
Examples of Coping Self-Statements

Preparation

I can develop a plan to deal with it.

Just think about what I can do about it. That's better than getting anxious.

No negative self-statements, just think rationally.

Confrontation

One step at a time; I can handle this situation.

This anxiety is what the doctor said I would feel; it's a reminder to use my coping exercises.

Relax; I'm in control. Take a slow, deep breath.

Coping

When fear comes, just pause.

Keep focused on the present; what is it I have to do?

Don't try to eliminate fear totally; just keep it manageable.

It's not the worst thing that can happen.

Just think about something else.

Self-Reinforcement

It worked; I was able to do it.

It wasn't as bad as I expected.

I'm really pleased with the progress I'm making.

SOCIAL SUPPORT AS A COPING RESOURCE

Social support refers to the resources others provide, giving the message that one is loved, cared for, esteemed, and connected to other people in a network of communication and mutual obligation. In addition to these forms of *socioemotional support,* other people may provide *tangible support* (money, transportation, housing) and *informational support* (advice, personal feedback, information). Anyone with whom you have a significant social relationship—such as family members, friends, coworkers, and neighbors—can be part of your social support network in time of need.

Much research points to the power of social support in moderating the vulnerability to stress (Holahan et al., 1997). When people have other people to whom they can turn, they are better able to handle job stressors, unemployment, marital disruption, and serious illness, as well as their everyday problems of living. Consider individuals who serve as peacekeepers in the world's many troubled regions. The traumas associated with life in battle zones often leads to posttraumatic stress disorder. However, a study of Dutch peacekeepers who served in Lebanon demonstrated that those individuals who experienced higher levels of positive social interactions had fewer symptoms of PTSD (Dirkzwager et al., 2003).

Researchers are trying to identify which types of social supports are most helpful for specific life events (Helgeson & Cohen, 1996; Kuijer et al., 2000). For example, **Shelley Taylor** and her colleagues have studied the effectiveness of the different types of social supports given to cancer patients (Dakof & Taylor, 1990; Taylor, 1986). Patients varied in their assessments of the helpfulness of kinds of support. They thought it was helpful to them for spouses, but not for physicians or nurses, to "just be there." On the other hand, it was important to the patients to receive information or advice from other cancer patients or from physicians, but not from family and friends. Regardless of the source—whether doctors or family or friends—patients did not find helpful forced cheerfulness or attempts to minimize the impact of their disease. **Figure 12.9** provides a comparison of the types of social supports that were rated as most helpful for cancer patients versus patients with noncatastrophic illness, such as chronic headaches and irritable bowel syndrome (Martin et al., 1994). The data suggest, once again, that the optimal type of social support differs for different sources of stress. Can you think of some reasons why emotional support might be more helpful to cancer patients than to patients with noncatastrophic illnesses?

Researchers are also trying to determine when sources of support actually increase anxiety (Holahan et al., 1997). For example, if someone insisted on accompanying you to a doctor's appointment or to a college interview when you preferred to go alone, you might experience additional anxiety about the situation. Similarly, patients with serious diseases may find themselves unable to meet the expectations of those individuals in their social circle.

PUTTING IDEAS TO THE TEST

Expectations and Adjustment to Chronic Illness

A group of researchers examined the ways in which patients' perceptions of the expectations of the individuals around them affected their adjustment to their illness. The patients were in the final phases of renal disease; all required dialysis. The researchers asked the patients to respond to statements such as "I sometimes feel that my family and friends expect me to cope much better with my illness than I actually can" and "I sometimes think that my family and friends expect me to take more responsibility for my treatment than I can manage" on a scale ranging from *strongly disagree* to *strongly agree.* The researchers also obtained measures of how well the patients were coping with their illness. The results revealed consistent positive correlations between expectations and measures of distress. For example, patients who perceived their family and friends' expectations to be excessive were more likely to report depression and low quality of life (Hatchett et al., 1997).

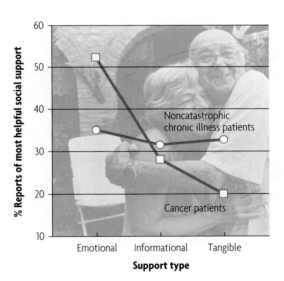

FIGURE 12.9

The Value of Social Support

Perceived social support as a function of diagnosis.

(From Martin et al., 1994; the data for cancer patients are taken from Dakof & Taylor, 1990.)

It seems quite likely that these patients' friends and family were doing their best to provide support. Even so, their expectations for the patients increased the patients' distress.

Being part of an effective social support network means that you believe others will be there for you if you need them—even if you don't actually ask for their help when you experience stress. One of the most important take-home messages from *Psychology and Life* is that you should always work at being part of a social support network and never let yourself become socially isolated.

At many points in this discussion of stress, we have noted the effect of stress on physical or psychological well-being. We will now turn directly to the ways in which psychologists apply their research knowledge to issues of illness and health.

◆ PUT YOURSELF TO THE TEST

- ❖ What are some of the major physiological responses to acute stressors?
- ❖ Why might chronic stress have a negative impact on the body and the mind?
- ❖ What is the relationship between life events and health?
- ❖ What circumstances might lead to posttraumatic stress disorder?
- ❖ What are some of the effects of daily hassles?
- ❖ What role does cognitive appraisal play in the process of coping?
- ❖ What types of strategies can people use to cope with stress?
- ❖ Why is appropriate social support an important resource for coping?

◆ Health Psychology

How much do your psychological processes contribute to your experiences of illness and wellness? We have already given you reason to believe that the right answer may be "quite a bit." This acknowledgment of the importance of psychological and social factors in health has spurred the growth of a new field, health psychology. **Health psychology** is the branch of psychology that is devoted to understanding the way people stay healthy, the reasons they become ill, and the way they respond when they do get ill. **Health** refers to the general condition of the body and mind in terms of soundness and vigor. It is not simply the absence of illness or injury, but is more a matter of how well all the body's component parts are working together. We will begin our discussion of health psychology by describing how the field's underlying philosophy departs from a traditional Western medical model of illness. We then consider the contributions of health psychology to the prevention and treatment of illness and dysfunction.

◆ THE BIOPSYCHOSOCIAL MODEL OF HEALTH

Health psychology is guided by a *biopsychosocial model* of health. We can find the roots of this perspective in many non-Western cultures. To arrive at a definition of the biopsychosocial model, we will start with a description of some of these non-Western traditions.

TRADITIONAL HEALTH PRACTICES

Psychological principles have been applied in the treatment of illness and the pursuit of health for all of recorded time. Many cultures understand the importance of communal health and relaxation rituals in the enhancement of the quality of life. Among the Navajo, for example, disease, illness, and well-being have been attributed to social harmony and mind–body interactions. The Navajo concept of **hozho** (pronounced whoa-zo) means harmony, peace of mind, goodness, ideal family relationships, beauty in arts and crafts, and health of body and spirit. Illness is seen as the outcome of any *disharmony,* caused by evil introduced through violation of taboos, witchcraft, overindulgence, or bad dreams. Traditional healing ceremonies seek to banish illness and restore health, not only through the medicine of the shaman but also through the combined efforts of all family members, who work together with the ill person to reachieve a state of hozho. The illness of any member of a tribe is seen not as his or her individual responsibility (and fault) but rather as a sign of broader disharmony that must be repaired by communal healing ceremonies. This cultural orientation guarantees that a powerful social support network will automatically come to the aid of the sufferer.

TOWARD A BIOPSYCHOSOCIAL MODEL

We have just seen that healing practices in non-Western cultures often assumed a link between the body and the mind. By contrast, modern Western scientific thinking has relied almost exclusively on a *biomedical model* that has a dualistic conception of body and mind. According

The Navajo, like people in many other cultures around the world, place a high value on aesthetics, family harmony, and physical health. What do the Navajo people consider to be the origins of illness?

to this model, medicine treats the physical body as separate from the psyche; the mind is important only for emotions and beliefs and has little to do with the reality of the body. Over time, however, researchers have begun to document types of interactions that make the strict biomedical model unworkable. You have already seen some of the evidence: Good and bad life events can affect immune function; people are more or less resilient with respect to the negative consequences of stress; adequate social support can decrease the probability of death. These realizations yield the three components of the **biopsychosocial model.** The *bio* acknowledges the reality of biological illness. The *psycho* and the *social* acknowledge the psychological and social components of health.

The biopsychosocial model links your physical health to your state of mind and the world around you. Health psychologists view health as a dynamic, multidimensional experience. Optimal health, or **wellness,** incorporates physical, intellectual, emotional, spiritual, social, and environmental aspects of your life. When you undertake an activity for the purpose of preventing disease or detecting it in the asymptomatic stage, you are exhibiting health behavior. The general goal of health psychology is to use psychological knowledge to promote wellness and positive health behaviors. Let's now consider theory and research relevant to this goal.

◆ HEALTH PROMOTION

Health promotion means developing general strategies and specific tactics to eliminate or reduce the risk that people will get sick. The prevention of illness in the 21st century poses a much different challenge than it did at the beginning of the 20th century. In 1900, the primary cause of death was infectious disease. Health practitioners at that time launched the first revolution in American public health. Over time, through the use of research, public education, the development of vac-

cines, and changes in public health standards (such as waste control and sewage), they were able to reduce substantially the deaths associated with such diseases as influenza, tuberculosis, polio, measles, and smallpox.

If researchers wish to contribute to the trend toward improved quality of life, they must attempt to decrease those deaths associated with lifestyle factors (see **Table 12.7**). Smoking, being overweight, eating foods high in fat and cholesterol, drinking too much alcohol, driving without seat belts, and leading stressful lives all play a role in heart disease, cancer, strokes, accidents, and suicide. Changing the behaviors associated with these diseases of civilization will prevent much illness and premature death.

Based on this knowledge, it's easy to make some recommendations. You are more likely to stay well if you practice good health habits, such as those listed in **Table 12.8.** Many of these suggestions probably are familiar to you already. However, health psychologists would like to use psychological principles to increase the probability that you will actually do the things you know are good for you. To show you how that works, we now consider a pair of concrete domains: smoking and AIDS.

SMOKING

It would be impossible to imagine that anyone reading this book wouldn't know that smoking is extremely dangerous. Roughly 440,000 people die each year from smoking-related illnesses (Fellows et al., 2002). Even so, 66.5 million people in the United States still smoke (Substance Abuse and Mental Health Services Administration, 2003). Seventy percent of smokers say they want to quit but are unable to do so (Centers for Disease Control and Prevention, 1997). Health psychologists would like to understand both why people begin to smoke—so that the psychologists can help prevent it—and how to assist people in quitting—so they can reap the substantial benefits of becoming ex-smokers.

TABLE 12.7

Leading Causes of Death, United States

Rank	Percent of Deaths	Cause of Death	Contributors to Cause of Death*
1	28.9	Heart disease	D, S
2	22.9	Cancer	D, S
3	6.8	Stroke	D, S
4	5.1	Respiratory diseases	S
5	4.0	All accidents	A/DA
	1.7	Motor vehicle accidents alone	A/DA
6	2.9	Diabetes	D
7	2.6	Influenza and pneumonia	S
8	2.2	Alzheimer's disease	
9	1.6	Kidney diseases	D
10	1.3	Septicemia (bacteria in the blood)	A/DA

*D = diet; S = smoking; A/DA = alcohol/drug abuse
Source: Arias & Smith, 2003

Analyses of why some people start smoking have focused on interactions of nature and nurture. For example, one study compared monozygotic and dizygotic twins for the similarity of their tobacco use (Kendler et al., 2000). (Recall that monzygotic twins share identical genetic material whereas dizygotic twins are no more genetically alike than other siblings.) The data, obtained from the Swedish Twin Registry, included twins born in several different decades. As shown in **Table 12.9,** birth cohort had a large impact on the estimates of heritability for women but not for men. For men, the genetic impact on smoking was large—the closer the estimate is to 1.0, the more genetic factors predict the behavior—and steady across groups. However, for the women the estimate increased dramatically over time. Why would this be? The researchers suggested that the "reduction in social restrictions on smoking in Sweden as the 20th century progressed permitted genetic factors . . . to increasingly express themselves" (p. 891). That is, as social restrictions on women lifted, those women who were genetically inclined to smoke were able to do so.

To understand the link between genes and smoking, researchers have often focused on personality differences that predict which people will start smoking. One personality type that has been associated with the initiation of smoking is called *sensation seeking* (Zuckerman, 1988). Individuals characterized as sensation seeking are more likely to engage in risky activities. One study compared personality assessments of men and women in the mid-1960s (1964–1967) with their smoking or nonsmoking

behavior in the late 1980s (1987–1991). Both men and women who had revealed themselves to be sensation seeking in the 1960s were more likely to be smoking 20 to 25 years later (Lipkus et al., 1994). Health psychologists understand that successful interventions to prevent the initiation of smoking must address the aspects of individuals' personalities that make smoking attractive to them.

TABLE 12.8

Ten Steps to Personal Wellness

1. Exercise regularly.
2. Eat nutritious, balanced meals (high in vegetables, fruits, and grains; low in fat and cholesterol).
3. Maintain proper weight.
4. Sleep 7 to 8 hours nightly; rest/relax daily.
5. Wear seat belts and bike helmets.
6. Do not smoke or use drugs.
7. Use alcohol in moderation, if at all.
8. Engage only in protected, safe sex.
9. Get regular medical/dental checkups; adhere to medical regimens.
10. Develop an optimistic perspective and friendships.

<www.ablongman.com/gerrig17e>

TABLE 12.9

The Impact of Social Restrictions on Estimates of Heritability for Regular Tobacco Use

Birth Years	Men	Women
1910–1924	0.53	0.00
1925–1939	0.58	0.21
1940–1958	0.51	0.64

The best approach to smoking is never to start at all. But for those of you who have begun to smoke, what has research revealed about quitting? Although many people who try to quit have relapses, an estimated 35 million Americans have quit. Ninety percent have done so on their own, without professional treatment programs. Researchers have identified stages people pass through that represent increasing readiness to quit (Norman et al., 1998, 2000):

- *Precontemplation.* The smoker is not yet thinking about quitting.
- *Contemplation.* The smoker is thinking about quitting but has not yet undertaken any behavioral changes.
- *Preparation.* The smoker is getting ready to quit.
- *Action.* The smoker takes action toward quitting by setting behavioral goals.
- *Maintenance.* The smoker is now a nonsmoker and is trying to stay that way.

This analysis suggests that not all smokers are psychologically equivalent in terms of readiness to quit. Interventions can be designed that nudge smokers up the scale of readiness, until, finally, they are psychologically prepared to take healthy action.

Successful smoking-cessation treatment requires that both smokers' physiological and psychological needs be met (Tsoh et al., 1997; U.S. Department of Health and Human Services, 2000). On the physiological side, smokers are best off learning an effective form of *nicotine replacement therapy,* such as nicotine patches or nicotine gum. On the psychological side, smokers must understand that there are huge numbers of ex-smokers and realize that it is possible to quit. Furthermore, smokers must learn strategies to cope with the strong temptations that accompany efforts to quit. Treatments often incorporate the types of cognitive coping techniques we described earlier, which allow people to alleviate the effects of a wide range of stressors. For smoking, people are encouraged to find ways to avoid or escape from situations that may bring on a renewed urge to smoke.

AIDS

AIDS is an acronym for *acquired immune deficiency syndrome.* Although hundreds of thousands are dying from this virulent disease, many more are now living with HIV infection. **HIV** *(human immunodeficiency virus)* is a virus that attacks the white blood cells (T lymphocytes) in human blood, thus damaging the immune system and weakening the body's ability to fight other diseases. The individual then becomes vulnerable to infection by a host of other viruses and bacteria that can cause such life-threatening illnesses as cancer, meningitis, and pneumonia. The period of time from initial infection with the virus until symptoms occur (incubation period) can be five years or longer. Although most of the estimated millions of those infected with the HIV virus do not have AIDS (a medical diagnosis), they must live with the continual stress that this life-threatening disease might suddenly emerge. At the present time, there are treatments that delay the onset of full-blown AIDS, but there is neither a cure for AIDS nor a vaccine to prevent its spread.

The HIV virus is not airborne; it requires direct access to the bloodstream to produce an infection. The HIV virus is generally passed from one person to another in one of two ways: (1) the exchange of semen or blood during sexual contact and (2) the sharing of intravenous needles and syringes used for injecting drugs. The virus has also been passed through blood transfusions and medical procedures in which infected blood or organs are unwittingly given to healthy people. Many people suffering from hemophilia have gotten AIDS in this way. However, everyone is at risk for AIDS.

The only way to protect oneself from being infected with the AIDS virus is to change those lifestyle habits that put one at risk. This means making permanent changes in patterns of sexual behavior and use of drug paraphernalia. Health psychologist **Thomas Coates** is part of a multidisciplinary research team that is using an array of psychological principles in a concerted effort to prevent the further spread of AIDS (Catania et al., 1994; Kegeles et al., 1996, 1999). The team is involved in many aspects of applied psychology, such as assessing psychosocial risk factors, developing behavioral interventions, training community leaders to be effective in educating people toward healthier patterns of sexual and drug behavior, assisting with the design of media advertisements and community information campaigns, and systematically evaluating changes in relevant attitudes, values, and behaviors. Successful AIDS interventions require three components (Fisher et al., 1994, 1996; Yzer et al., 1998):

Why is regular exercise an important component of a lifelong plan to reduce stress and preserve health?

- *Information.* People must be provided with knowledge about how AIDS is transmitted and how its transmission may be prevented; they should be counseled to practice safer sex (for example, use condoms during sexual contact) and use sterile needles.
- *Motivation.* People must be motivated to practice AIDS prevention.
- *Behavioral skills.* People must be taught how to put the knowledge to use.

Why are all three of these components necessary? People might be highly motivated but uninformed, or vice versa. They may have both sufficient knowledge and sufficient motivation but lack requisite skills. They may not, for example, know exactly how to overcome the social barrier of asking a partner to use a condom (Leary et al., 1994). Psychological interventions can provide role-playing experience, or other behavioral skills, to make that barrier seem less significant.

◆ TREATMENT

Treatment focuses on helping people adjust to their illnesses and recover from them. We will look at three aspects of treatment. First, we consider the role of psychologists in encouraging patients to adhere to the regimens prescribed by health-care practitioners. Next, we look at techniques that allow people to explicitly use psychological techniques to take control over the body's responses. Finally, we examine instances in which the mind can contribute to the body's cure.

PATIENT ADHERENCE

Patients are often given a *treatment regimen*. This might include medications, dietary changes, prescribed periods of bed rest and exercise, and follow-up procedures such as return checkups, rehabilitation training, and chemotherapy. Failing to adhere to treatment regimens is one of the most serious problems in health care (Clark & Becker, 1998). The rate of patient nonadherence is estimated to be as high as 50 percent for some treatment regimens. Recent research has focused on the types of individual differences that lead some individuals to comply whereas others do not.

PUTTING IDEAS TO THE TEST

Compliance for Patients on Hemodialysis

A team of researchers examined the relevance of *monitoring attentional style* to patient compliance. When they are ill, some individuals pay close attention to all aspects of the illness—they are called *high monitors*. By contrast, *low monitors* are less likely to focus their attention on their illness. It might not sound dangerous, at first, to be a high monitor. However, because of the tight attentional focus, high monitors tend to overestimate the severity of their illness. As a consequence, high monitors have lower perceived control over their illness—which, the researchers suggested, could undermine their adherence to a treatment regimen. In the current study, the researchers assessed a group of patients for their monitoring attentional style as well as their perceived control and adherence to the regimen. The results fit the pattern the researchers laid out. By comparison to low monitors, high monitors perceived less control over their illness and were also less likely to comply with the regimen specified by their doctors (Christensen et al., 1997).

Prior to reading about this study, you might have thought that people who are very focused on their illness would be more likely to take good care of themselves. Instead, the data suggest that too tight a focus on an illness can make it seem even worse than it really is—and, therefore, beyond hope of a remedy in a way that discourages patients from taking necessary actions.

Research has shown that health-care professionals can take steps to improve patient adherence. Patients are more satisfied with their health care when they trust that the efficacy of the treatment outweighs its costs. They are also more likely to comply with a regimen when practitioners communicate clearly, make sure that their patients understand what has been said, act courteously, and convey a sense of caring and supportive-

<www.ablongman.com/gerrig17e>

Healthy People 2010

If you live in the United States, your government has plans for you for the next few years: The U.S. Department of Health and Human Services has outlined a program called *Healthy People 2010* that makes concrete recommendations for the behaviors necessary for personal and societal health. The program has two broad goals: (1) to reduce the disparities in health status among different populations, such as the poor, minorities, and children, and (2) to increase the span of healthy life. Psychologists will contribute to both of these goals. With respect to the first goal, *mental health* is included in the category of "health status." For several years now, psychologists have devoted substantial energy in research and practice to improve mental health care for diverse communities. The second goal relates directly to the expertise healthy psychologists bring to the topic of health promotion. The *Healthy People 2010* program wishes people to change their health-relevant behaviors. As we have seen, that's an important topic of health psychology research.

To expand on that claim, let's look at a pair of specific goals from *Healthy People 2010*:

- To reduce the proportion of adults who engage in no leisure-time physical activity from 40 percent to 20 percent.

- To increase the proportion of adults who engage regularly in moderate physical activity (30 minutes, most days) from 15 percent to 30 percent.

You probably know why *Healthy People 2010* wishes you to get regular exercise: Major improvements in health are achieved from such aerobic exercises as bicycling, swimming, running, or even fast walking. These activities lead to increased fitness of the heart and respiratory systems, improvement of muscle tone and strength, and many other health benefits.

So, how can your knowledge of health psychology help people reap these benefits? Researchers are exploring the questions of who exercises regularly and why and are trying to determine what programs or strategies are most effective in getting people to start and continue exercising (Dishman & Buckworth, 1997). In fact, much the same model that we outlined for people's readiness to *quit* smoking applies to people's readiness to begin exercising (Marshall & Biddle, 2001; Myers & Roth, 1997). In the *precontemplation* stage, an individual is still more focused on the

barriers to exercise (for example, too little time, no exercise partners) rather than the benefits (for example, helps relaxation, improves appearance). As the individual moves through the *contemplation* and *preparation* stages toward the training stages, the emphasis shifts from barriers to benefits.

If you do not exercise regularly now, how can you get beyond precontemplation? Research suggests that individuals can learn strategies that allow them to overcome obstacles to exercise (Simkin & Gross, 1994). You can treat exercise like any other situation in which you use cognitive appraisal to cope with stress. Try to structure your life so that exercise is a healthy pleasure. You should also be aware that many college students have "rebounds" in both their eating and exercising: When periods of academic stress have passed, they return from poor eating and minimal exercising to healthy behavior (Griffin et al., 1993). How might you structure your thoughts to avoid this pattern? Try to help *Healthy People 2010* meet its goals!

ness. In addition, health professionals must recognize the role of cultural and social norms in the treatment process and involve family and friends where necessary. Some physicians critical of their profession's outdated reliance on the biomedical model argue that doctors must be taught to care in order to cure (Siegel, 1988). Compliance-gaining strategies developed from psychological research are also being used to help overcome the lack of cooperation between patients and practitioners (Putnam et al., 1994; Zimbardo & Leippe, 1991).

HARNESSING THE MIND TO HEAL THE BODY

More and more often, the treatments to which patients must adhere involve a psychological component. Many investigators now believe that psychological strategies can improve well-being. For example, many people react to stress with tension, resulting in tight muscles and high blood pressure. Fortunately, many tension responses can be controlled by psychological techniques, such as *relaxation* and *biofeedback.*

Relaxation through meditation has ancient roots in many parts of the world. In Eastern cultures, ways to calm the mind and still the body's tensions have been practiced for centuries. Today, Zen discipline and yoga exercises from Japan and India are part of daily life for many people both there and, increasingly, in the West. Growing evidence suggests that complete relaxation is a potent antistress response (Deckro et al., 2002). The **relaxation response** is a condition in which muscle tension, cortical activity, heart rate, and blood pressure all decrease and breathing slows (Benson & Stuart, 1992; Friedman et al., 1996). There is reduced electrical activity in the brain, and input to the central nervous system from the outside environment is lowered. In this low level of arousal, recuperation from stress can take place. Four conditions are regarded as necessary to produce the relaxation response: (1) a quiet environment, (2) closed eyes, (3) a comfortable position, and (4) a repetitive mental device such as the chanting of a brief phrase over and over again. The first three conditions lower input to the nervous system, while the fourth lowers its internal stimulation.

Biofeedback is a self-regulatory technique used for a variety of special applications, such as control of blood pressure, relaxation of forehead muscles (involved in tension headaches), and even diminishment of extreme blushing. As pioneered by psychologist **Neal Miller** (1978), biofeedback is a procedure that makes an individual aware of ordinarily weak or internal responses by providing clear external signals. The patient is allowed to "see" his or her own bodily reactions, which are monitored and amplified by equipment that transforms them into lights and sound cues of varying intensity. The patient's task is then to control the level of these external cues.

Let's consider one application of biofeedback. Participants who suffered from either high or low blood pressure were brought into a laboratory (Rau et al., 2003). Feedback from equipment measuring an index of the participants' blood pressure on each heart cycle was delivered to a computer screen so that growing green bars indicated changes in the right direction and growing red bars indicated changes in the wrong direction. In addition, the researchers provided verbal reinforcement: "You did it the right way!" After three training sessions, the participants were able to raise or lower their blood pressure, as desired. If you ever become concerned about your blood pressure or other physical disorders, results of this sort might encourage you to seek a course of biofeedback to complement a drug regimen.

Why does relaxation through meditation have health benefits?

PSYCHONEUROIMMUNOLOGY

In the early 1980s, researchers made a series of discoveries that confirmed another way in which the mind affects the body: Psychological states can have an impact on immune function. Historically, scientists had assumed that immunological reactions—rapid production of antibodies to counterattack substances that invade and damage the organism—were automatic biological processes that occurred without any involvement of the central nervous system. However, conditioning experiments of the type we described in Chapter 6 proved that assumption to be incorrect.

PUTTING IDEAS TO THE TEST

Conditioning and Immune Function

Groundbreaking researchers **Robert Ader** and **Nicholas Cohen** (1981) taught one group of rats to associate sweet-tasting saccharin with cyclophosphamide (CY), a drug that weakens immune response. A control group received only the saccharin. Later, when both groups of rats were given only saccharin, the animals that had been conditioned to associate saccharin with CY produced significantly fewer antibodies to foreign cells than those rats in the control group. Thus, the learned association alone was sufficient to elicit suppression of the immune system, making the experimental rats vulnerable to a range of diseases. The learning effect was so powerful that, later in the study, some of the rats died after drinking only the saccharin solution.

Results like this strongly suggested that immune function can be modified by psychological states. A new field of study, **psychoneuroimmunology,** has emerged to explore these types of results that involve psychology, the nervous system, and the immune system (Ader & Cohen, 1993; Coe, 1999).

Research over the past 25 years has confirmed that stressors—and how people cope with them—have a consistent impact on the ability of the immune system to function effectively (Kiecolt-Glaser et al., 2002). Consider one of the immune system's basic functions, to heal small wounds in your skin. In one study, a research team led by **Janet Kiecolt-Glaser** gave 13 caretakers for relatives with Alzheimer's disease (see Chapter 7) and 13 control participants standardized small wounds to their skin. On average, the Alzheimer's caretakers, who experience chronic stress, took 9 days longer for their wounds to heal (Kiecolt-Glaser et al., 1995)! Subsequent research examined the physiological mechanisms underlying this effect. For example, as seen in **Figure 12.10,** participants who reported higher levels of perceived stress in their lives had lower levels of the critical substances that regulate healing at the wound site (Glaser et al., 1999). You can see from these data how small differences in stress level may affect the speed with which a person's body can heal even the smallest scratch or scrape. From that basic insight, you can understand why research suggests that stress responses play an even more profound role with respect to the progression of serious medical conditions such as infectious diseases and cancer. Researchers wish to understand how the mind affects immune function so they can harness that power to slow these serious illnesses.

PSYCHOLOGICAL IMPACT ON HEALTH OUTCOMES

The discussion of psychoneuroimmunology allows you to understand the potential for psychological factors to have an impact on physical health. In fact, researchers have designed stress-management programs they hope will provide patients with the coping resources to help change the consequences of disease. Recall our earlier discussion of social support as a coping resource. Some researchers have found that patients who participate in support groups have longer survival times for serious illnesses. For example, in one sample of women suffering from metastatic breast cancer, those patients who participated in group therapy survived for an average of 36.6 months, compared with 18.9 months for the control group (Spiegel et al., 1989). Although not all studies have confirmed that social support leads to increased survival times, participants in stress-management programs consistently have better psychological functioning and better quality of life over the course of their diseases (Claar & Blumenthal, 2003).

One last note on treatment. Have you ever had a secret too shameful to tell anyone? If so, talking about the secret could very well improve your health. That is the conclusion from a large body of research by health psychologist **James Pennebaker** (1990, 1997; Petrie et al., 1998), who has shown that suppressing thoughts and feelings associated with personal traumas, failures, and guilty or shameful experiences takes a devastating toll on mental and physical health. Such inhibition is psychologically hard work and, over time, it undermines the body's defenses against illness. The experience of letting go often is followed by improved physical and psychological health weeks and months later. Consider the effects of emotional disclosure on the functioning of adults with rheumatoid arthritis.

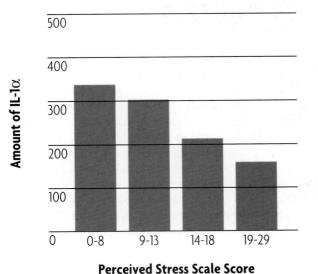

FIGURE 12.10

Perceived Stress and Immune Function

Researchers created standardized wounds on participants' forearms. Twenty-four hours later, participants reported on the stress of their daily life (high scores indicate more perceived stress). The researchers also took samples from the wound sites to assess the levels of the substance IL-1α, which regulates immune function. The data indicated that participants with the highest perceived stress had the lowest levels of IL-1α.

Health Benefits of Emotional Disclosure

Seventy-two adults with rheumatoid arthritis participated in this study. This disease leads to chronic inflammation of the peripheral joints, with accompanying pain and disability. The researchers hypothesized that sessions of emotional disclosure might help alleviate some of the stress associated with the disease and also, therefore, alleviate some of the problems in day-to-day functioning. Half of the patients were assigned to the *disclosure* group and spent 15 minutes on four consecutive days talking to a tape recorder about their deepest feelings surrounding highly stressful life events. The *control* group spent the same amount of time in a neutral task, giving descriptions of color landscapes. In the short run, disclosure patients were a bit worse off—the task stirred up a lot of negative emotions. However, three months after the treatment, the disclosure group was experiencing consistently less physical dysfunction—fewer problems, for example, with walking and bending—than were the members of the control group (Kelley et al., 1997).

If you disclose your pesonal thoughts and feelings to a friend, why might that have a positive impact on your health?

For patients in the disclosure group, the relatively simple act of revealing feelings, in private, to a tape recorder brought about measurable improvements in functioning.

◆ PERSONALITY AND HEALTH

Do you know a person like this: Someone who is driven to succeed, no matter what obstacles; someone whose high school class voted him or her "Most likely to have a heart attack before age 20"? Are you that person? As you've observed the way in which some people charge through life while others take a more relaxed pace, you may have wondered whether these different personalities affect health. Research in health psychology strongly suggests that the answer is yes.

In the 1950s, Meyer Friedman and Ray Rosenman reported what had been suspected since ancient times: There was a relationship between a constellation of personality traits and the probability of illness, specifically coronary heart disease (Friedman & Rosenman, 1974). These researchers identified two behavior patterns that they labeled Type A and Type B. The **Type A behavior pattern** is a complex pattern of behavior and emotions that includes being excessively competitive, aggressive, impatient, time urgent, and hostile. Type A people are often dissatisfied with some central aspect of their lives, are highly competitive and ambitious, and often are loners. The **Type B behavior pattern** is everything Type A is not—individuals are less competitive, less hostile, and so on. Importantly, these behavior patterns have an impact on health. In their original discussion, Friedman

and Rosenman reported that people who showed Type A behavior patterns were stricken with coronary heart disease considerably more often than individuals in the general population.

Because the Type A behavior pattern has many components, researchers have focused their attention on identifying the specific Type A elements that most often put people at risk. The personality trait that has emerged most forcefully as "toxic" is hostility.

Hostility and Coronary Heart Disease

A longitudinal study began in 1986, with 774 men in the sample who were free of any evidence of cardiovascular disease (Niaura et al., 2002). In 1986, each participant's level of hostility was measured (using a set of questions from the Minnesota Multiphasic Personality Inventory, a device we will describe in Chapter 13). Hostility is defined as the consistency with which individuals look at the world and other people in a cynical and negative manner. To display the relationship between hostility and coronary heart disease, the researchers divided the hostility scores into percentile groups. As shown in **Figure 12.11,** those individuals whose hostility scores were in the upper 20 percent had a dramatically larger number of episodes of incident coronary heart disease in the subsequent years. In this sample of men, hostility was a better predictor of future illness than several behavioral risk factors such as smoking and drinking.

<www.ablongman.com/gerrig17e>

Hostility may affect health for both physiological reasons—by leading to chronic overarousal of the body's stress responses—and psychological reasons—by leading hostile people to practice poor health habits and avoid social support (Smith & Ruiz, 2002).

The good news is that researchers have begun to implement behavioral treatments to reduce hostility and other aspects of the Type A behavior pattern (Smith & Ruiz, 2002; Thoresen & Powell, 1992). For example, one intervention was directed toward high-hostile men who had been diagnosed with coronary heart disease (Gidron et al., 1999). As part of the intervention, the men were taught how to use problem-focused coping to reduce anger; they were taught how to use cognitive restructuring to reduce cynicism. After eight weeks, men in the intervention group reported consistently lower levels of hostility than their peers in the control (non-intervention) group. In addition, the men in the intervention group had lower average blood pressure than their control peers. Do you recognize yourself in the definition of hostility? If you do, you should protect your health by seeking out this type of intervention.

To round out this section on personality and health we want to remind you of the concept of *optimism* we introduced in Chapter 12. We saw there that optimistic individuals attribute failures to external causes and to events that were unstable or modifiable (Seligman, 1991). This style of coping has a strong impact on the optimist's well-being. Researchers have demonstrated that optimism has an impact on the function of the immune system (Segerstrom et al., 1998). Optimistic people have fewer physical symptoms of illness, are faster at recovering from certain illnesses, are generally healthier, and live longer (Hegelson, 2003; Peterson et al., 1988). A positive outlook may both reduce your body's experience of chronic stress and make it more likely that you'll engage in healthy behaviors.

◆ JOB BURNOUT AND THE HEALTH-CARE SYSTEM

One final focus of health psychology is to make recommendations about the design of the health-care system. Researchers, for example, have examined the stress associated with being a health-care provider. Even the most enthusiastic health-care providers run up against the emotional stresses of working intensely with large numbers of people suffering from a variety of personal, physical, and social problems.

The special type of emotional stress experienced by these professional health and welfare practitioners has been termed *burnout* by **Christina Maslach,** a leading researcher on this widespread problem. **Job burnout** is a syndrome of emotional exhaustion, depersonalization, and reduced personal accomplishment that is often experienced by workers in professions that demand high-intensity interpersonal contact with patients, clients, or the public. Health practitioners begin to lose their caring and concern for patients and may come to treat them in detached and even dehumanized ways. They feel bad about themselves and worry that they are failures. Burnout is correlated with greater absenteeism and turnover, impaired job performance, poor relations with coworkers, family problems, and poor personal health (Maslach et al., 2001; Schaufeli et al., 1993).

Job burnout in today's workforce is reaching ever higher levels due to the effects of organizational downsizing, job restructuring, and greater concerns for profits than for employee morale and loyalty. Burnout then is not merely a concern of workers and health caregivers, but it also reveals organizational dysfunction that needs to be corrected by reexamining goals, values, workloads, and reward structures (Leiter & Maslach, 2000; Maslach & Leiter, 1997).

What recommendations can be made? Several social and situational factors affect the occurrence and level of burnout and, by implication, suggest ways of preventing or minimizing it (Leiter & Maslach, 2000; Prosser et al., 1997). For example, the quality of the patient–practitioner interaction is greatly influenced by the number of patients for whom a practitioner is providing care—the greater the number, the greater the cognitive, sensory, and emotional overload. Another factor in the quality of that interaction is the amount of direct contact with

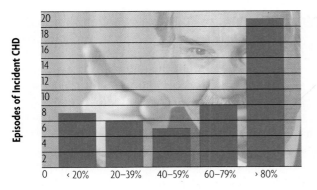

FIGURE 12.11

Hostility Predicts Coronary Heart Disease

Study participants were divided into percentile groups based on their self-reports of hostility. Men whose scores placed them in the top 20 percent on the measure (i.e., the group greater than 80 percent) had the highest levels of coronary heart disease.

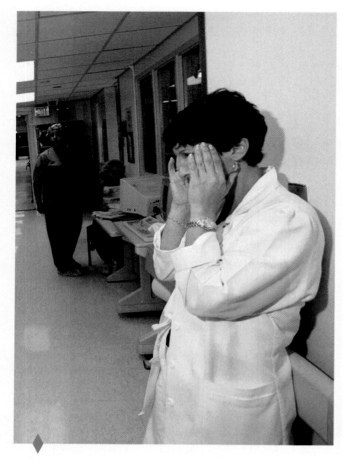

Why are health-care providers particularly prone to job burnout?

patients. Longer work hours in continuous direct contact with patients are correlated with greater burnout. This is especially true when the nature of the contact is difficult and upsetting, such as contact with patients who are dying (Catalan et al., 1996). The emotional strain of such prolonged contact can be eased by a number of means. For example, practitioners can modify their work schedules in order to withdraw temporarily from such high-stress situations. They can use teams rather than only individual contact. They can arrange opportunities to get positive feedback for their efforts.

◆ A TOAST TO YOUR HEALTH

It's time for some final advice. Instead of waiting for stress or illness to come and then reacting to it, you should set goals and structure your life in ways that are most likely to forge a healthy foundation. The following nine steps to greater happiness and better mental health are presented as guidelines to encourage you to take a more active role in your own life and to create a more positive psychological environment for yourself and others. Think of the steps as *year-round resolutions.*

1. Never say bad things about yourself. Look for sources of your unhappiness in elements that can be modified by future actions. Give yourself and others only *constructive criticism*—what can be done differently next time to get what you want?

2. Compare your reactions, thoughts, and feelings with those of friends, coworkers, family members, and others so that you can gauge the appropriateness and relevance of your responses against a suitable social norm.

3. Have several close friends with whom you can share feelings, joys, and worries. Work at developing, maintaining, and expanding your social support networks.

4. Develop a sense of *balanced time perspective* in which you can flexibly focus on the demands of the task, the situation, and your needs; be future oriented when there is work to be done, present oriented when the goal is achieved and pleasure is at hand, and past oriented to keep you in touch with your roots.

5. Always take full credit for your successes and happiness (and share your positive feelings with other people). Keep an inventory of all the qualities that make you special and unique—those qualities you can offer others. For example, a shy person can provide a talkative person with the gift of attentive listening. Know your sources of personal strength and available coping resources.

6. When you feel you are losing control over your emotions, distance yourself from the situation by physically leaving it, role playing the position of another person in the situation or conflict, projecting your imagination into the future to gain perspective on what seems an overwhelming problem now, or talking to a sympathetic listener. Allow yourself to feel and express your emotions.

7. Remember that failure and disappointment are sometimes blessings in disguise. They may tell you that your goals are not right for you or may save you from bigger letdowns later on. Learn from every failure. Acknowledge setbacks by saying, "I made a mistake," and move on. Every accident, misfortune, or violation of your expectations is potentially a wonderful opportunity in disguise.

8. If you discover you cannot help yourself or another person in distress, seek the counsel of a trained specialist in your student health department or community. In some cases, a problem

<www.ablongman.com/gerrig17e>

that appears to be psychological may really be physical, and vice versa. Check out your student mental health services before you need them, and use them without concern about being stigmatized.

9. Cultivate healthy pleasures. Take time out to relax, to meditate, to get a massage, to fly a kite, and to enjoy hobbies and activities you can do alone and by means of which you can get in touch with and better appreciate yourself.

So how are you feeling? If the stressors in your life have the potential to put you in a bad mood, we hope you'll be able to use cognitive reappraisal to minimize their impact. If you are feeling ill, we hope you'll be able to use your mind's healing capacity to speed your way back toward health. Never underestimate the power of these different types of "feelings" to exercise control over your life. Harness that power!

PUT YOURSELF TO THE TEST

- How does the biopsychosocial model of health reflect the influence of non-Western cultures?
- Why might genetic and environmental factors make it difficult for people to quit smoking?
- What are the necessary components for a successful AIDS intervention?
- What factors affect the likelihood that patients will adhere to treatment regimens?
- In what ways have researchers demonstrated that the mind has an impact on the body?
- What are the relationships between personality types and physical health?
- What are the consequences of job burnout for health-care practitioners?

◆Recapping Main Points

EMOTIONS

- Emotions are complex patterns of changes made up of physiological arousal, cognitive appraisal, and behavioral and expressive reactions.
- As a product of evolution, all humans may share a basic set of emotional responses.
- Cultures, however, vary in their rules of appropriateness for displaying emotions.
- Classic theories emphasize different parts of emotional response, such as peripheral bodily reactions or central neural processes.
- More contemporary theories emphasize the appraisal of arousal.
- Emotions serve motivational, social, and cognitive functions.

STRESS OF LIVING

- Stress can arise from negative or positive events. At the root of most stress are change and the need to adapt to environmental, biological, physical, and social demands.
- Physiological stress reactions are regulated by the hypothalamus and a complex interaction of the hormonal and nervous systems.
- Depending on the type of stressor and its effect over time, stress can be a mild disruption or lead to health-threatening reactions.
- Cognitive appraisal is a primary moderator variable of stress.

- Coping strategies either focus on problems (taking direct actions) or attempt to regulate emotions (indirect or avoidant).
- Cognitive reappraisal and restructuring can be used to cope with stress.
- Social support is also a significant stress moderator, as long as it is appropriate to the circumstances.

HEALTH PSYCHOLOGY

- Health psychology is devoted to treatment and prevention of illness.
- The biopsychosocial model of health and illness looks at the connections among physical, emotional, and environmental factors in illness.
- Illness prevention in the 21st century focuses on lifestyle factors such as smoking and AIDS-risk behaviors.
- Psychological factors influence immune function.
- Psychosocial treatment of illness adds another dimension to patient treatment.
- Individuals who are characterized by Type A (especially hostile), Type B, and optimistic behavior patterns will experience different likelihoods of illness.
- Health-care providers are at risk for burnout, which can be minimized by appropriate situational changes in their helping environment.

KEY TERMS

acute stress (p. 407)

AIDS (p. 423)

amygdala (p. 399)

anticipatory coping (p. 416)

biofeedback (p. 426)

biopsychosocial model (p. 421)

Cannon–Bard theory of emotion (p. 401)

chronic stress (p. 407)

cognitive appraisal (p. 401)

cognitive appraisal theory of emotion (p. 401)

coping (p. 415)

emotion (p. 394)

fight-or-flight response (p. 408)

general adaptation syndrome (GAS) (p. 409)

health (p. 420)

health promotion (p. 421)

health psychology (p. 420)

HIV (p. 423)

hozho (p. 420)

James–Lange theory of emotion (p. 400)

job burnout (p. 429)

life-change units (LCUs) (p. 411)

perceived control (p. 418)

posttraumatic stress disorder (PTSD) (p. 412)

psychoneuroimmunology (p. 427)

psychosomatic disorders (p. 409)

relaxation response (p. 426)

social support (p. 419)

stress (p. 406)

stress moderator variables (p. 415)

stressor (p. 406)

tend-and-befriend response (p. 408)

Type A behavior pattern (p. 428)

Type B behavior pattern (p. 428)

wellness (p. 421)

Answers for Figure 12.1 (p. 396)

First row: happiness, surprise, anger, disgust

Second row: fear, sadness, contempt

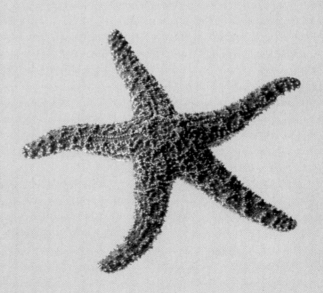

13

Understanding Human Personality

S uppose we asked you to compare and contrast your two closest friends. In what ways are they similar? In what ways are they different? It seems likely that your analysis would very quickly come to focus on your friends' *personalities*. You might, for example, assert that one is friendlier than the other or one has more self-confidence than the other. Assertions of this sort would suggest that you've brought your own personality theory to bear on your relationships—you have your own system for appraising personality. You use your beliefs to determine who in a new class would be friend or foe; you worked out techniques for dealing with your parents or teachers based on the way you read their personalities.

Psychologists define personality in many different ways, but common to all of the ways are two basic concepts: *uniqueness* and *characteristic patterns of behavior*. We will define **personality** as the complex set of psychological qualities that influence an individual's characteristic patterns of behavior across different situations and over time.

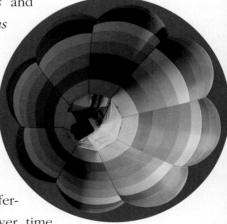

What unexpected consequences may follow from individual differences in personality?

(© The New Yorker Collection 1946 Charles Addams from cartoonbank.com. All Rights Reserved.)

Theories of personality are hypothetical statements about the structure and functioning of individual personalities. They help to achieve two of the major goals of psychology: (1) understanding the structure, origins, and correlates of personality; and (2) predicting behavior and life events based on what we know about personality. Different theories make different predictions about the way people will respond and adapt to certain conditions.

Before we examine some of the major theoretical approaches, we should ask why there are so many different (often competing) theories. Theorists differ in their approaches to personality by varying their starting points and sources of data and by trying to explain different types of phenomena. Some are interested in the structure of individual personality and others in how that personality developed and will continue to grow. Some are interested in what people do, either in terms of specific behaviors or important life events, while others study how people feel about their lives. Finally, some theories try to explain the personalities of people with psychological problems, while others focus on healthy individuals. Thus, each theory can teach something about personality, and together they can teach much about human nature.

Our goal for this chapter will be to provide you with a framework for understanding your everyday experience of personality. However, before we begin, consider this series of questions: If psychologists studied *you,* what portrait of your personality would they draw? What early experiences might they identify as

contributing to the way you now act and think? What conditions in your current life exert strong influences on your thoughts and behaviors? What makes you different from other individuals who are functioning in many of the same situations as you? This chapter should help you formulate specific answers to these questions.

In the next several sections, we consider a series of theoretical approaches to understanding personality: type and trait, psychodynamic, humanistic, social-learning, cognitive, and analyses of the self. We conclude the chapter by describing some of the assessment techniques psychologists use to understand and describe personality.

Type and Trait Personality Theories

Two of the oldest approaches to describing personality involve classifying people into a limited number of *distinct types* and scaling the degree to which they can be described by *different traits.* There seems to be a natural tendency for people to place their own and others' behavior into different categories. Let's examine the formal theories psychologists have developed to capture these differences in types and traits.

◆ CATEGORIZING BY TYPES

We are always categorizing people according to distinguishing features. These include college class, academic major, sex, and race. Some personality theorists also group people into distinct, nonoverlapping categories that are called **personality types.** Personality types are all-or-none phenomena, not matters of degree: If a person is assigned to one type, he or she could not belong to any other type within that system. Many people like to use personality types in everyday life because they help simplify the complex process of understanding other people.

One of the earliest type theories was originated in the fifth century B.C. by **Hippocrates,** the Greek physician who gave medicine the Hippocratic oath. He theorized that the body contained four basic fluids, or *humors,* each associated with a particular *temperament,* a pattern of emotions and behaviors. In the second century A.D., a later Greek physician, **Galen,** suggested that an individual's personality depended on which humor was predominant in his or her body. Galen paired

<www.ablongman.com/gerrig17e>

Hippocrates theorized that the body contained four essential fluids, or humors, each associated with a particular temperament. Clockwise: a melancholy patient suffers from an excess of black bile; blood impassions a sanguine lutenist to play; a maiden, dominated by phlegm, is slow to respond to her lover; choler, too much yellow bile, makes an angry master. Do you believe Hippocrates's personality types apply to the people you know?

Hippocrates's body humors with personality temperaments according to the following scheme:

- *Blood.* Sanguine temperament: cheerful and active
- *Phlegm.* Phlegmatic temperament: apathetic and sluggish
- *Black bile.* Melancholy temperament: sad and brooding
- *Yellow bile.* Choleric temperament: irritable and excitable

The theory proposed by Galen was believed for centuries, up through the Middle Ages, although it has not held up to modern scrutiny. (We will, however, see a modern echo of these temperaments in Hans Eysenck's trait theory, which we present on p. 439.)

In modern times, **William Sheldon** (1942) originated a type theory that related physique to temperament. He assigned people to three categories based on their body builds: *endomorphic* (fat, soft, round), *mesomorphic* (muscular, rectangular, strong), or *ectomorphic* (thin, long, fragile). Sheldon believed that endomorphs are relaxed, fond of eating, and sociable. Mesomorphs are physical people, filled with energy, courage, and assertive tendencies. Ectomorphs are brainy, artistic, and introverted; they would think about life, rather than consuming it or acting on it. For a period of time, Sheldon's theory was sufficiently influential that nude "posture" photographs were taken of thousands of students at U.S. colleges like Yale and Wellesley to allow researchers to study the relationships between body type and life factors. However, like Hippocrates's much earlier theory, Sheldon's notion of body types has proven to be of very little value in predicting an individual's behavior (Tyler, 1965).

More recently, **Frank Sulloway** (1996) has proposed a contemporary type theory based on *birth order.* Are you the *firstborn* child (or *only* child) in your family, or are you a *laterborn* child? Because you can take on only one of these birth positions, Sulloway's theory fits the criteria for being a type theory. (For people with unusual family constellations—for example, a very large age gap between two children—Sulloway still provides ways of categorizing individuals.) Sulloway makes birth-order predictions based on Darwin's idea that organisms diversify to find niches in which they will survive. According to Sulloway, firstborns have a ready-made niche: They immediately command their parents' love and attention; they seek to maintain that initial attachment by identifying and complying with their parents. By contrast, laterborn children need to find a different niche—one in which they don't so clearly follow their parents' example. As a consequence, Sulloway characterizes laterborns as "born to rebel": "they seek to excel in those domains where older siblings have not already established superiority. Laterborns typically cultivate openness to experience—a useful strategy for anyone who wishes to find a novel and successful niche in life" (Sulloway, 1996, p. 353). To test the prediction that laterborns embrace innovation whereas firstborns prefer the status quo, Sulloway examined scientific, historical, and cultural revolutions and determined the birth position of large numbers of historical and contemporary figures who had supported or opposed those revolutions. **Figure 13.1** presents data on the extent to which firstborn and laterborn scientists supported 23 innovative theories in science. As you can see, for all of the family sizes, laterborns were more likely to support the innovative theory than were firstborns. Do you have brothers or sisters? Can you find this pattern in your own family?

Do you know people whom you would label as particular "types"? Does the "type" include all there is to know about the person? Type theories often don't seem to capture more subtle aspects of people's personalities. Let's turn now to theories that allow more flexibility by differentiating individuals according to traits rather than types.

◆ DESCRIBING WITH TRAITS

Type theories presume that there are separate, discontinuous categories into which people fit, such as firstborn or laterborn. By contrast, trait theories propose *continuous dimensions,* such as intelligence or friendliness. **Traits** are enduring qualities or attributes that predispose individuals to behave consistently across situations. For

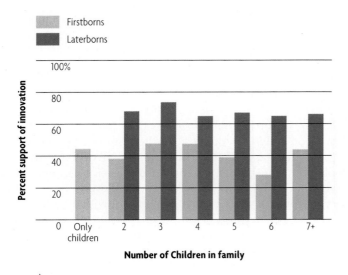

■ Firstborns
■ Laterborns

FIGURE 13.1

Birth Position and Support for Scientific Innovation

Frank Sulloway examined 23 innovative scientific theories and determined the birth positions of 1,218 scientists who had adopted or rejected those theories. For every family size, laterborns were more likely to adopt the innovative theory than were firstborns.

example, you may demonstrate honesty on one day by returning a lost wallet and on another day by not cheating on a test. Some trait theorists think of traits as *predispositions* that cause behavior, but more conservative theorists use traits only as *descriptive dimensions* that simply summarize patterns of observed behavior. Let's examine prominent trait theories.

ALLPORT'S TRAIT APPROACH

Gordon Allport (1937, 1961, 1966) viewed traits as the building blocks of personality and the source of individuality. According to Allport, traits produce coherence in behavior because they connect and unify a person's reactions to a variety of stimuli. Traits may act as *intervening variables,* relating sets of stimuli and responses that might seem, at first glance, to have little to do with each other (see **Figure 13.2**).

Allport identified three kinds of traits: cardinal traits, central traits, and secondary traits. *Cardinal traits* are traits around which a person organizes his or her life. For Mother Teresa, a cardinal trait might have been self-sacrifice for the good of others. However, not all people develop such overarching cardinal traits. Instead, *central traits* are traits that represent major characteristics of a person, such as honesty or optimism. *Secondary traits* are specific, personal features that help predict an individual's behavior but are less useful for understanding an individual's personality. Food or dress preferences are examples of secondary traits. Allport was interested in discovering the unique combination of these three types of traits that make each person a singular entity and championed the use of case studies to examine these unique traits.

Allport saw *personality structures,* rather than *environmental conditions,* as the critical determiners of individual behavior. "The same fire that melts the butter hardens the egg" was a phrase he used to show that the same stimuli can have different effects on different individuals. Many contemporary trait theories have followed in Allport's tradition.

IDENTIFYING UNIVERSAL TRAIT DIMENSIONS

In 1936, a dictionary search by Gordon Allport and his colleague H. S. Odbert found over 18,000 adjectives in

In the absence of personality test results, traits can be inferred from observed behavior. For example, Martin Luther King Jr. (left) would be thought to have the cardinal trait of peacefully resisting injustice; honesty would be one of Abraham Lincoln's central traits; and Madonna's predilection for changeable styles would be a secondary trait. What do you think may be your cardinal, central, and secondary traits?

     <www.ablongman.com/gerrig17e>

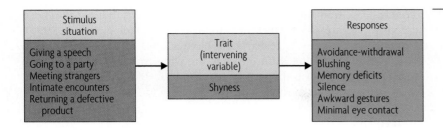

Stimulus situation		Trait (intervening variable)		Responses
Giving a speech Going to a party Meeting strangers Intimate encounters Returning a defective product	→	Shyness	→	Avoidance-withdrawal Blushing Memory deficits Silence Awkward gestures Minimal eye contact

FIGURE 13.2

Shyness as a Trait

Traits may act as intervening variables, relating sets of stimuli and responses that might seem, at first glance, to have little to do with each other.

the English language to describe individual differences. Researchers since that time have attempted to identify the fundamental dimensions that underlie that enormous trait vocabulary. They have tried to determine how many dimensions exist and which ones will allow psychologists to give a useful, universal characterization of all individuals.

Raymond Cattell (1979) used Allport and Odbert's list of adjectives as a starting point in his quest to uncover the appropriate small set of basic trait dimensions. His research led him to propose that 16 factors underlie human personality. Cattell called these 16 factors *source traits* because he believed that they provide the underlying source for the surface behaviors that we think of as personality. Cattell's 16 factors included important behavioral oppositions such as *reserved* versus *outgoing, trusting* versus *suspicious,* and *relaxed* versus *tense.* Even so, contemporary trait theorists argue that even fewer dimensions than 16 capture the most important distinctions among people's personalities.

Hans Eysenck (1973, 1990) derived just three broad dimensions from personality test data: *extraversion* (internally versus externally oriented), *neuroticism* (emotionally stable versus emotionally unstable), and *psychoticism* (kind and considerate versus aggressive and antisocial). As shown in **Figure 13.3,** Eysenck combined the two dimensions of extraversion and neuroticism to form a circular display. He suggested that each quadrant of the display represents one of the four personality types associated by Galen with Hippocrates's humors. Eysenck's trait theory, however, allows for individual variation within these categories. Individuals can fall anywhere around the circle, ranging from very introverted to very extraverted and from very unstable (neurotic) to very stable. The traits listed around the circle describe people with combinations of these two dimensions. For example, a person who is very extraverted and somewhat unstable is likely to be impulsive.

FIVE-FACTOR MODEL

Research evidence supports many aspects of Eysenck's theory. However, in recent years, a consensus has emerged that *five factors,* which overlap imperfectly with Eysenck's three dimensions, best characterize personality structure (Wiggins & Pincus, 1992). Although these five factors are not accepted by all personality

researchers (Block, 1995; Eysenck, 1992; Pervin, 1994), they now serve as a touchstone for most discussions of trait structures.

The movement toward the *five-factor model* represented attempts to find structure among the large list of traits that Allport and Odbert (1936) had extracted from the dictionary. The traits were boiled down into about 200 synonym clusters that were used to form *bipolar* trait dimensions: dimensions that have a high pole and a low pole, such as *responsible* versus *irresponsible.* Next, people were asked to rate themselves and others on the bipolar dimensions, and the ratings were subjected to statistical procedures to determine how the synonym clusters were interrelated. Using this method, several

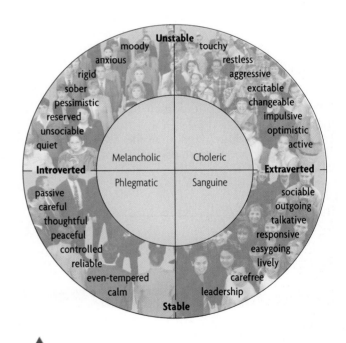

FIGURE 13.3

The Four Quadrants of Eysenck's Personality Circle

The two dimensions of extraversion and neuroticism yield a circular display. Eysenck related each quadrant of the display to one of the four personality types defined by Galen. Eysenck's trait theory, however, allows for individual variation within these categories.

independent research teams came to the same conclusion: that there are only *five basic dimensions* underlying the traits people use to describe themselves and others (Norman, 1963, 1967; Tupes & Christal, 1961).

The five dimensions are very broad, because each brings into one large category many traits that have unique connotations but a common theme. These five dimensions of personality are now called the **five-factor model,** or, more informally, the *Big Five* (McCrae & Costa, 1999). The five factors are summarized in **Table 13.1.** You'll notice again that each dimension is bipolar—terms that are similar in meaning to the name of the dimension describe the high pole, and terms that are opposite in meaning describe the low pole.

The dimensions in the five-factor model were derived from ratings collected in the 1960s, using several different sets of adjectives and many different participant samples and rating tasks. Since then, very similar dimensions have also been found in personality questionnaires, interviewer checklists, and other data (Costa & McCrae, 1992a; Digman, 1990; Wiggins & Pincus, 1992). To demonstrate the universality of the five-factor model, researchers have broadened their studies beyond the English language: The five-factor structure has been replicated in a number of languages including German, Portuguese, Hebrew, Chinese, Korean, and Japanese (McCrae & Costa, 1997). The five factors are not meant to replace the many specific trait terms that carry their own nuances and shades of meaning. Rather, they outline a taxonomy—a classification system—that allows you to give a description of all the people you know in ways that capture the important dimensions on which they differ.

We have emphasized that the five-factor model originally emerged from statistical analyses of clusters of trait terms, rather than from a theory that said, "These are the factors that must exist" (Ozer & Reise, 1994). However, researchers have started to demonstrate that there are differences in the ways that individuals' brains function that correspond to trait differences in the five-factor model.

Extraversion and the Amygdala

Recall from Chapter 12 that a brain structure called the amygdala plays an important role in the processing of emotional stimuli. However, researchers had begun to suspect that not all amygdalas—and, therefore, not all people—responded to stimuli in the same way. To test this idea, a team of researchers recruited 15 participants who differed in their level of extraversion (Canli et al., 2002). The researchers predicted that extraversion would have an impact on emotional processing because that trait captures important aspects of people's emotional lives. To look for individual differences, the researchers had the participants view fearful, happy, and neutral faces while they underwent fMRI scans. **Figure 13.4** displays the correlation between participants' self-reports of extraversion and activity in the left and right amygdalas: The areas in red are those areas for which high levels of extraversion were associated with high levels of brain activity. As you can see, extraversion was not correlated with the brains' responses to fearful faces (i.e., there are no areas in red). In fact, fearful faces activated both the left and right amygdalas, but more or less equally across all levels of extraversion. By contrast, for happy faces the highly extraverted individuals showed abundant activity in their left amygdala.

You might recall from Chapter 12 that researchers have characterized emotions as either *approach-related* or *withdrawal-related*. This study suggests that people who are most content to approach other people—that's what makes them extraverted—have more activation in brain regions that support approach-related emotions.

Supporters of the five-factor model have also tried to explain why exactly these five dimensions emerge by looking to evolution: They try to relate the five dimensions to consistent types of interactions that people had with each other and with the external world over the course of human evolution (Costa & McCrae, 1992a; McCrae et al., 2000). An evolutionary basis would help explain the universality of the five factors across diverse cultures. If this explanation is correct, we might also expect that, like other aspects of human experience that have been shaped by evolution, traits can be passed from one generation to the next. We turn now to that claim.

TABLE 13.1
The Five-Factor Model

Factor	Bipolar Definitions
Extraversion	Talkative, energetic, and assertive versus quiet, reserved, and shy
Agreeableness	Sympathetic, kind, and affectionate versus cold, quarrelsome, and cruel
Conscientiousness	Organized, responsible, and cautious versus careless, frivolous, and irresponsible
Neuroticism	Stable, calm, and contented versus anxious, unstable, and temperamental
Openness to experience	Creative, intellectual, and open-minded versus simple, shallow, and unintelligent

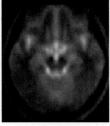

Fearful

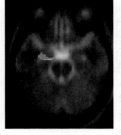

Happy

FIGURE 13.4

Extraversion Affects the Function of the Left Amygdala

Participants viewed fearful and happy faces. The figure displays in red those areas of the brain for which there was a positive correlation between extraversion and amygdala activity. For the fearful faces, there was no correlation. However, for happy faces, the most extraverted participants also showed the highest levels of activity in their left amygdalas.

◆ TRAITS AND HERITABILITY

You've probably heard people say things such as "Jim's artistic, like his mother" or "Mary's as stubborn as her grandfather." Or maybe you've felt frustrated because the characteristics that you find irritating in your siblings are those you would like to change in yourself. Let's look at the evidence that supports the heritability of personality traits.

Recall that *behavioral genetics* is the study of the degree to which personality traits and behavior patterns are inherited. To determine the effect of genetics on personality, researchers study the personality traits of family members who share different proportions of genes and who have grown up in the same or different households. For example, if a personality characteristic such as *sociability* is passed on genetically, then sociability should correlate more highly between identical, *monozygotic* twins (who share 100 percent of their genes) than between fraternal, *dizygotic* twins or other siblings (who share, on average, 50 percent of their genes).

Heritability studies show that almost all personality traits are influenced by genetic factors (Loehlin et al., 1998). The findings are the same with many different measurement techniques, whether they measure broad traits, such as extraversion and neuroticism, or specific traits, such as self-control or sociability. Let's consider one sample study.

Research with identical twins demonstrates the heritability of personality traits. Are there personality traits you believe run in your family?

The Heritability of the Five Factors

We just introduced you to the five-factor model of personality. Researchers have turned their attention to the question of whether there is a genetic basis for the factors specified by this model. In one study, a team of researchers from Germany and Poland obtained personality measures for 660 monozygotic twin pairs and 304 dizygotic twin pairs. Data were provided both by self-report (that is, the twins filled out personality inventories of the type we cover later in the chapter) and by peer report (that is, friends and family members made ratings on one or the other twin). Past research has generally only used self-report data. Critics of heritability research have worried that monozygotic and dizygotic twins may have biases in the way they compare themselves to their twins versus other individuals. The inclusion of peer report eliminates the possibility that high heritability estimates are merely consequences of twins' biases in reporting on themselves. In fact, in all cases, the personalities of monozygotic twins were rated as more similar than those of dizygotic twins. The self-ratings, for example, revealed intertwin correlations of .52 (monozygotic) versus .23 (dizygotic). Using both the self and peer data, these researchers demonstrated substantial heritability estimates for each of the factors defined by the five-factor model (Riemann et al., 1997).

Look back to Table 13.1. Which poles of the five factors seem to apply best to you? Can you find similarities between you and your parents?

Researchers continue to try to improve on the design of heritability studies. For example, because twins and other siblings are usually raised together, they share a family environment—which might cause their personalities to be correlated. Thus, researchers also use *adoption studies* to examine the inheritance of traits. In adoption studies, researchers typically try to obtain data from both biological parents (which provides an indication of genetics) and adoptive parents (which provides an indication of environment). To assess heritability, researchers assess the degree to which children's traits correlate with their biological parents' traits, as compared to correlations with their adoptive parents' traits. Adoption studies also reveal sizable genetic contributions to personality traits (Bouchard, 1994).

◆ DO TRAITS PREDICT BEHAVIORS?

Suppose we ask you to choose some trait terms that you believe apply particularly well to yourself. You might tell us, for example, that you are *very friendly*. What do we now know? If personality theories allow us to make predictions about behaviors, what can we predict from knowing that you rate yourself as being very friendly? How can we determine the validity of your belief? Let's explore this question.

One idea you might have is that knowing that a person can be characterized by a particular trait would enable you to predict his or her behavior across different *situations*. Thus, we would expect you to produce friendly behaviors in all situations. However, in the 1920s, several researchers who set out to observe trait-related behaviors in different situations were surprised to find little evidence that behavior was consistent across situations. For example, two behaviors presumably related to the trait of honesty—lying and cheating on a test—were only weakly correlated among schoolchildren (Hartshorne & May, 1928). Similar results were found by other researchers who examined the *cross-situational consistency* for other traits such as introversion or punctuality (Dudycha, 1936; Newcomb, 1929).

If trait-related behaviors are not cross-situationally consistent—that is, if people's behavior changes in different situations—why do you perceive your own and others' personalities to be relatively stable? Even more puzzling, the personality ratings of observers who know an individual from one situation correlate with the ratings of observers who know the individual from another situation. The observation that personality ratings across time and among different observers *are consistent,* while behavior ratings of a person across situations *are not consistent,* came to be called the **consistency paradox** (Mischel, 1968).

The identification of the consistency paradox led to a great deal of research (for a review, see Cervone & Shoda, 1999). Over time, the consensus emerged that the appearance of behavioral inconsistency arose, in large part, because situations had been categorized in the wrong way: The paradox fades away once theorists can provide an appropriate account of the *psychological features* of situations (Mischel & Shoda, 1995, 1999). Suppose, for example, you want to try to assess behavioral consistency by determining if a friend acts in much the same way at every party she attends. You're likely to discover that her behavior varies widely if your level of analysis is just "parties." What you need to determine is what psychologically relevant features separate parties into different categories. Perhaps your friend feels uncomfortable in situations in which she is expected to disclose personal information to strangers. As a consequence, she might seem very unfriendly at some parties (where she is expected to disclose personal information) but quite friendly at others (where she is not). Meanwhile, other situations that require her to be disclosing—such as job interviews—might also bring out negative behaviors. Thus, we find consistency in the way that features of situations elicit people's distinctive responses.

Assuming you could afford either one, which of these vacations would you prefer? What might that tell us about the ways in which personality traits interact with features of situations?

Let's consider a study that examined the psychological features of a variety of situations. The study considered activities children encounter in summer camp.

PUTTING IDEAS TO THE TEST

Consistency in Verbal Aggression

This study was carried out on a group of 6- to 12-year-old children who were referred to a summer camp for children with social adjustment problems. The researchers wished to see how accurately they could predict the situations in which individual children would produce aggressive behavior. To make these predictions, the researchers gathered data on the significant features of different camp situations with respect to the types of demands they put on the child: *cognitive* ("requires the ability to think logically"), *social* ("requires the ability to speak in front of others"), *self-regulatory* ("requires the ability to tolerate frustration"), *physical strength* ("requires physical strength, stamina"), and *motor coordination* ("requires the ability to coordinate arm and body movements"). Swimming, for example, demands physical strength and coordination but relatively little self-regulation. Fishing, by contrast, requires a high level of self-regulation alongside motor coordination.

The children were observed across the full range of camp activities and their incidents of verbal aggression—for example, threatening and teasing—were recorded for each situation. If behavioral consistency depends on the similarities in features of situations, then the higher the level of similarity between two situations, the more likely it should be that children will show the same extent of verbal aggression. This prediction was confirmed (Shoda et al., 1993a).

Note the lengths to which the researchers went to derive the relevant features of the situations. This taxonomy allows them to make claims such as "Sonja has trouble coping with situations that make high cognitive demands—and that's why she's going to be verbally aggressive in such situations." We find consistency when we have the right description of the person ("she can't cope with cognitive demands") and the situation ("this situation creates a cognitive demand").

You can apply this perspective to the traits with which you label yourself. For example, if you describe yourself as a *very friendly* person, that doesn't mean that we should expect you to perform "friendly" behaviors every moment of your life. Instead, we would expect your friendliness to differ across situations according to the psychological features of those situations. You may, for example, be very warm with close acquaintances but more formal toward your professors.

◆ EVALUATION OF TYPE AND TRAIT THEORIES

We have seen that type and trait theories allow researchers to give concise descriptions of different people's personalities. These theories have been criticized, however, because they do not generally explain how behavior is generated or how personality develops; they only identify and describe characteristics that are correlated with behavior. Although contemporary trait theorists have begun to address these concerns, trait theories typically portray a *static,* or at least stabilized, view of *personality structure* as it currently exists.

Surveys reveal that more than 50 percent of college students consider themselves to be "currently shy" individuals (Carducci & Zimbardo, 1995). Most of them say that shyness is an undesirable condition that has more negative personal and social consequences than positive effects. Another group of students say that they are "situationally shy," and not "dispositionally shy" like that majority of students. They feel "as if" they were shy in certain situations that are novel, awkward, or socially pressured, such as blind dates, singles bars, being put on the spot to perform in public without preparation. Researchers investigating shyness in adults were surprised to discover that it is the "not shy" person who is the rare, unusual breed in the United States and in every other country surveyed (Zimbardo, 1991).

Shyness may be defined as discomfort and/or inhibition in interpersonal situations that interferes with pursuing one's interpersonal or professional goals.

Why Are Some People Shy?

Eden Kram

Hobart and William Smith Colleges

Shyness may be chronic and dispositional, serving as a personality trait that is central in one's self-definition. It can be the mild reticence and social awkwardness many of us feel in new situations, but it can escalate into the extreme of a totally inhibiting fear of people (we will discuss

this *social phobia* in Chapter 14). Many shy people are also *introverted;* they have a personal preference for solitary, nonsocial activities and settings. Others are "shy extraverts," publicly outgoing yet privately shy, preferring to engage in social activities, having the social skills to do so effectively, yet doubting that others will really like or respect them (Pilkonis & Zimbardo, 1979).

So why are some people shy, while others are not? One explanation may be *nature.* Research evidence suggests that about 10 percent of infants are "born shy" (Kagan, 1994). From birth, these children are unusually cautious and reserved when they interact with unfamiliar people or situations. A complementary explanation focuses on *nurture.* As children, some individuals are ridiculed, laughed at, or singled out for public shame for some mistake; others grow up in families that make "being loved" contingent on competitive success in appearance and performance. A third explanation focuses on culture.

By contrast, psychodynamic theories of personality, to which we next turn, emphasize conflicting forces within the individual that lead to change and development.

PUT YOURSELF TO THE TEST

➤ Why are personality types defined as categories that don't overlap?

➤ What were the origins of the five-factor model of personality traits?

➤ How have researchers assessed the heritability of traits?

➤ How do traits and situations interact to affect predictions of behaviors?

Psychodynamic Theories

Common to all **psychodynamic personality theories** is the assumption that powerful inner forces shape personality and motivate behavior. **Sigmund Freud,** the originator of psychodynamic theories, was characterized by his biographer Ernest Jones as "the Darwin of the mind" (1953). Freud's theory of personality boldly attempts to explain the origins and course of personality development, the nature of mind, aspects of abnormal personality, and the way personality can be changed by therapy. Here

Shyness is highest in some Asian countries, notably Japan and Taiwan, and lowest in Israel, among nine countries studied (Zimbardo, 1991). This difference is attributed in part to cultural emphases on shame for social failure and obedience to authority in these Asian countries versus encouragement for taking risks and externalizing blame in Israel (Pines & Zimbardo, 1978). A fourth explanation accounts, in part, for a recent rise in reported prevalence of shyness in the United States: Young people are intensively involved with electronic technology. Spending long hours, typically alone, watching TV, playing video games, surfing the Web, and doing e-mail is socially isolating and reduces daily face-to-face contact. Heavy use of the Internet has the potential to make people feel lonely, isolated, and shier (Kraut et al., 1998; Nie & Erbring, 2000).

As shyness gets more extreme, it intrudes on ever more aspects of one's life to minimize social pleasures and maximize social discomfort and isolation.

There are some simple concepts and tactics we suggest for shy students to think about and try out (see Zimbardo, 1991):

- Realize that you are not alone in your shyness; every other person you see is more like you than different from you in his or her shyness.

- Shyness can be modified, even when there is a genetic component, but it takes dedication and a resolve to change, as with any long-standing habit you want to break.

- Practice smiling and making eye contact with most people you meet.

- Talk up; speak in a loud, clear voice, especially when giving your name or asking for information.

- Be the first to ask a question or make a comment in a new social situation. Be prepared with something interesting to say, and say it first; everyone appreciates an "ice breaker," and then no one will think you are shy.

- Never put yourself down. Instead, think about what you can do next time to gain the outcome you want.

- Focus on making others feel comfortable, especially searching out those other shy people. Doing so lowers your self-consciousness.

- Practice meditation, relaxation, and mental visualization of the ideal scenario before going into a situation that usually triggers your shyness.

If you are shy, we hope you will adopt these suggestions. Other students who have followed them have been released from the prison of shyness into a life filled with newfound liberties. This is one sure benefit of putting some simple psychology to work in your life. If you are not shy, then you can help friends and family who are shy by encouraging them to change their lifestyles in these ways (Henderson & Zimbardo, 1998).

we will focus only on normal personality; Freud's views on psychopathology and treatment will be treated in Chapters 14 and 15. After we explore Freud, we will describe some criticisms and reworkings of his theories.

◆ FREUDIAN PSYCHOANALYSIS

According to psychoanalytic theory, at the core of personality are events within a person's mind (*intrapsychic events*) that motivate behavior. Often, people are aware of these motivations; however, some motivation also operates at an unconscious level. The *psychodynamic* nature of this approach comes from its emphasis on these inner wellsprings of behavior, as well as the clashes among these internal forces. For Freud, *all behavior was motivated*. No chance or accidental happenings cause behavior; all acts are determined by motives. Every human action has a cause and a purpose that can be discovered through analysis of thought associations, dreams, errors, and other behavioral clues to inner passions. The primary data for Freud's hypotheses about personality came from clinical observations and in-depth case studies of individual patients in therapy. He developed a theory of normal personality from his intense study of those with mental disorders. Let's look at some of the most important aspects of Freud's theory.

DRIVES AND PSYCHOSEXUAL DEVELOPMENT

Freud's medical training as a neurologist led him to postulate a common biological basis for the behavioral patterns he observed in his patients. He ascribed the

Why did Freud believe that eating is motivated not only by the self-preservation drive to satisfy hunger but also by the "erotic" drive to seek oral gratification?

source of motivation for human actions to *psychic energy* found within each individual. Each person was assumed to have inborn instincts or drives that were *tension systems* created by the organs of the body. These energy sources, when activated, could be expressed in many different ways.

Freud originally postulated two basic drives. One he saw as involved with *self-preservation* (meeting such needs as hunger and thirst). The other he called *Eros,* the driving force related to sexual urges and preservation of the species. Freud greatly expanded the notion of human sexual desires to include not only the urge for sexual union but all other attempts to seek pleasure or to make physical contact with others. He used the term **libido** to identify the source of energy for sexual urges—a psychic energy that drives us toward sensual pleasures of all types. Sexual urges demand immediate satisfaction,

whether through direct actions or through indirect means such as fantasies and dreams.

Clinical observation of patients who had suffered traumatic experiences during World War I led Freud to add the concept of *Thanatos,* or the death instinct, to his collection of drives and instincts. Thanatos was a negative force that drove people toward aggressive and destructive behaviors. These patients continued to relive their wartime traumas in nightmares and hallucinations, phenomena that Freud could not work into his self-preservation or sexual drive theory. He suggested that this primitive urge was part of the tendency for all living things to seek to return to an inorganic state. However, this death instinct took a back seat in Freud's theoretical vehicle, which was largely driven by Eros.

According to Freud, Eros, as a broadly defined sexual drive, does not suddenly appear at puberty but operates from birth. Eros is evident, he argued, in the pleasure infants derive from physical stimulation of the genitals and other sensitive areas, or *erogenous zones.* Freud's five stages of *psychosexual development* are shown in **Table 13.2.** Freud believed that the physical source of sexual pleasure changed in this orderly progression. One of the major obstacles of psychosexual development, at least for boys, occurs in the phallic stage. Here, the 4- or 5-year-old child must overcome the *Oedipus complex.* Freud named this complex after the mythical figure Oedipus, who unwittingly killed his father and married his mother. Freud believed that every young boy has an innate impulse to view his father as a sexual rival for his mother's attentions. Because the young boy cannot displace his father, the Oedipus complex is generally resolved when the boy comes to *identify* with his father's power. (Freud was inconsistent with respect to his theoretical account of the experiences of young girls.)

TABLE 13.2

Freud's Stages of Psychosexual Development

Stage	Age	Erogenous Zones	Major Developmental Task (Potential Source of Conflict)	Some Adult Characteristics of Children Who Have Been Fixated at This Stage
Oral	0–1	Mouth, lips, tongue	Weaning	Oral behavior, such as smoking, overeating; passivity and gullibility
Anal	2–3	Anus	Toilet training	Orderliness, parsimoniousness, obstinacy, or the opposite
Phallic	4–5	Genitals	Oedipus complex	Vanity, recklessness, or the opposite
Latency	6–12	No specific area	Development of defense mechanisms	None: fixation does not normally occur at this stage
Genital	13–18	Genitals	Mature sexual intimacy	Adults who have successfully integrated earlier stages should emerge with a sincere interest in others and a mature sexuality

According to Freud, either too much gratification or too much frustration at one of the early stages of psychosexual development leads to **fixation,** an inability to progress normally to the next stage of development. As shown in Table 13.2, fixation at different stages can produce a variety of adult characteristics. The concept of fixation explains why Freud put such emphasis on early experiences in the continuity of personality. He believed that experiences in the early stages of psychosexual development had a profound impact on personality formation and adult behavior patterns.

PSYCHIC DETERMINISM

The concept of fixation gives us a first look at Freud's belief that early conflicts help *determine* later behaviors. **Psychic determinism** is the assumption that all mental and behavioral reactions (symptoms) are determined by earlier experiences. Freud believed that symptoms were not arbitrary. Rather, symptoms were related in a meaningful way to significant life events.

Freud's belief in psychic determinism led him to emphasize the **unconscious**—the repository of information that is unavailable to conscious awareness. Other writers had discussed this construct, but Freud put the concept of the unconscious determinants of human thought, feeling, and action at center stage in the human drama. According to Freud, behavior can be motivated by drives of which a person is not aware. You may act without knowing why or without direct access to the true cause of your actions. There is a *manifest* content to your behavior—what you say, do, and perceive—of which you are fully aware, but there is also a concealed, *latent* content. The meaning of neurotic (anxiety-based) symptoms, dreams, and slips of the pen and tongue is found at the unconscious level of thinking and information processing. Many psychologists today consider this concept of the unconscious to be Freud's most important contribution to the science of psychology. Much modern literature and drama, as well, explores the implications of unconscious processes for human behavior.

According to Freud, impulses within you that you find unacceptable still strive for expression. A *Freudian slip* occurs when an unconscious desire is betrayed by your speech or behavior. For example, one of your authors felt obligated to write a thank-you note although he hadn't much enjoyed the weekend he'd spent at a friend's home. He intended to write, "I'm glad we got to spend a chunk of time together." However, in a somewhat testy phone call, the friend informed him that he'd actually written "I'm glad we got to spend a *junk* of time together." Do you see how the substitution of *junk* for *chunk* could be the expression of an unconscious desire? The concept of unconscious motivation

adds a new dimension to personality by allowing for greater complexity of mental functioning.

We've now reviewed some basic aspects of Freud's theory. Let's see how they contribute to the structure of personality.

THE STRUCTURE OF PERSONALITY

In Freud's theory, personality differences arise from the different ways in which people deal with their fundamental drives. To explain these differences, Freud pictured a continuing battle between two antagonistic parts of the personality—the *id* and the *superego*—moderated by a third aspect of the self, the *ego*. Although we will refer to these three aspects almost as if they are separate creatures, keep in mind that Freud believed them all to be just different mental *processes*. He did not, for example, identify specific brain locations for the id, ego, and superego.

The **id** is the storehouse of the fundamental drives. It operates irrationally, acting on impulse and pushing for expression and immediate gratification without considering whether what is desired is realistically possible, socially desirable, or morally acceptable. The id is governed by the *pleasure principle,* the unregulated search for gratification—especially sexual, physical, and emotional pleasures—to be experienced here and now without concern for consequences.

The **superego** is the storehouse of an individual's values, including moral attitudes learned from society. The superego corresponds roughly to the common notion of *conscience*. It develops as a child comes to accept as his or her own values the prohibitions of parents and other adults against socially undesirable actions. It is the inner voice of *oughts* and *should nots*. The superego also includes the *ego ideal,* an individual's view of the kind of person he or she should strive to become. Thus, the superego is often in conflict with the id. The id wants to do what feels good, while the superego insists on doing what is right.

The **ego** is the reality-based aspect of the self that arbitrates the conflict between id impulses and superego demands. The ego represents an individual's personal view of physical and social reality—his or her conscious beliefs about the causes and consequences of behavior. Part of the ego's job is to choose actions that will gratify id impulses without undesirable consequences. The ego is governed by the *reality principle,* which puts reasonable choices before pleasurable demands. Thus, the ego would block an impulse to cheat on an exam, because of concerns about the consequences of getting caught, and it would substitute the resolution to study harder the next time or solicit the teacher's sympathy. When the id and the superego are in conflict, the ego arranges a compromise that at least partially satisfies both. However, as

TABLE 13.3
Major Ego Defense Mechanisms

Denial of reality	Protecting self from unpleasant reality by refusing to perceive it
Displacement	Discharging pent-up feelings, usually of hostility, on objects less dangerous than those that initially aroused the emotion
Fantasy	Gratifying frustrated desires in imaginary achievements ("daydreaming" is a common form)
Identification	Increasing feelings of worth by identifying self with another person or institution, often of illustrious standing
Isolation	Cutting off emotional charge from hurtful situations or separating incompatible attitudes into logic-tight compartments (holding conflicting attitudes that are never thought of simultaneously or in relation to each other); also called *compartmentalization*
Projection	Placing blame for one's difficulties on others or attributing one's own "forbidden" desires to others
Rationalization	Attempting to prove that one's behavior is "rational" and justifiable and thus worthy of the approval of self and others
Reaction formation	Preventing dangerous desires from being expressed by endorsing opposing attitudes and types of behavior and using them as "barriers"
Regression	Retreating to earlier developmental levels involving more childish responses and usually a lower level of aspiration
Repression	Pushing painful or dangerous thoughts out of consciousness, keeping them unconscious; this is considered to be *the most basic of the defense mechanisms*
Sublimation	Gratifying or working off frustrated sexual desires in substitutive nonsexual activities socially accepted by one's culture

id and superego pressures intensify, it becomes more difficult for the ego to work out optimal compromises.

REPRESSION AND EGO DEFENSE

Sometimes this compromise between id and superego involves "putting a lid on the id." Extreme desires are pushed out of conscious awareness into the privacy of the unconscious. **Repression** is the psychological process that protects an individual from experiencing extreme anxiety or guilt about impulses, ideas, or memories that are unacceptable and/or dangerous to express. The ego remains unaware of both the mental content that is censored and the process by which repression keeps information out of consciousness. Repression is considered to be the most basic of the various ways in which the ego defends against being overwhelmed by threatening impulses and ideas.

Ego defense mechanisms are mental strategies the ego uses to defend itself in the daily conflict between id impulses that seek expression and the superego's demand to deny them (see **Table 13.3**). In psychoanalytic theory, these mechanisms are considered vital to an individual's psychological coping with powerful inner conflicts. By using them, a person is able to maintain a favorable self-image and to sustain an acceptable social image. For example, if a child has strong feelings of hatred toward his father—which, if acted out, would be dangerous—repression may take over. The hostile impulse is then no longer consciously pressing for satisfaction or even recognized as existing.

However, although the impulse is not seen or heard, it is not gone; these feelings continue to play a role in personality functioning. For example, by developing a strong *identification* with his father, the child may increase his sense of self-worth and reduce his unconscious fear of being discovered as a hostile agent.

In Freudian theory, **anxiety** is an intense emotional response triggered when a repressed conflict is about to emerge into consciousness. Anxiety is a danger signal: Repression is not working! Red alert! More defenses needed! This is the time for a second line of defense, one or more additional ego defense mechanisms that will relieve the anxiety and send the distressing impulses back down into the unconscious. For example, a mother who does not like her son and does not want to care for him might use *reaction formation,* which transforms her unacceptable impulse into its opposite: "I don't hate my child" becomes "I love my child. See how I smother the dear little thing with love?" Such defenses serve the critical coping function of alleviating anxiety.

If defense mechanisms defend you against anxiety, why might they still have negative consequences for you? Useful as they are, ego mechanisms of defense are ultimately self-deceptive. When overused, they create more problems than they solve. It is psychologically unhealthy to spend a great deal of time and psychic energy deflecting, disguising, and rechanneling unacceptable urges in order to reduce anxiety. Doing so leaves little energy for productive living or satisfying human relationships. Some forms of mental illness result from excessive reliance on defense mechanisms

    <www.ablongman.com/gerrig17e>

to cope with anxiety, as we shall see in a later chapter on mental disorders.

◆ EVALUATION OF FREUDIAN THEORY

We have devoted a great deal of space to outlining the essentials of psychoanalytic theory, because Freud's ideas have had an enormous impact on the way many psychologists think about normal and abnormal aspects of personality. However, there probably are more psychologists who criticize Freudian concepts than who support them. What is the basis of some of their criticisms?

First, psychoanalytic concepts are vague and not operationally defined; thus, much of the theory is difficult to evaluate scientifically. Because some of its central hypotheses cannot be disproved, even in principle, Freud's theory remains questionable. How can the concepts of libido, the structure of personality, and repression of infantile sexual impulses be studied in any direct fashion?

A second, related criticism is that Freudian theory is good history but bad science. It does not reliably *predict* what will occur; it is applied *retrospectively*—after events have occurred. Using psychoanalytic theory to understand personality typically involves historical reconstruction, not scientific construction of probable actions and predictable outcomes. In addition, by overemphasizing historical origins of current behavior, the theory directs attention away from the current stimuli that may be inducing and maintaining the behavior.

There are three other major criticisms of Freudian theory. First, it is a developmental theory, but it never included observations or studies of children. Second, it minimizes traumatic experiences (such as child abuse) by reinterpreting memories of them as fantasies (based on a child's desire for sexual contact with a parent). Third, it has an *androcentric* (male-centered) bias because it uses a male model as the norm without trying to determine how females might be different.

Some aspects of Freud's theory, however, continue to gain acceptance as they are modified and improved through empirical scrutiny. For example, in Chapter 5, we saw that the concept of the unconscious is being systematically explored by contemporary researchers (Baars & McGovern, 1996; Westen, 1998). This research reveals that much of your day-to-day experience is shaped by processes outside of your awareness. These results support Freud's general concept but weaken the link between unconscious processes and psychopathology: Little of your unconscious knowledge will cause you anxiety or distress. Similarly, researchers have found evidence for some of the habits of mind Freud characterized as defense mechanisms (Hentschel et al., 1993; Singer, 1990).

PUTTING IDEAS TO THE TEST

Individual Differences in the Use of Defense Mechanisms

We suggested earlier that individuals are most likely to use defense mechanisms when they are experiencing anxiety. Researchers have tested this hypothesis in a variety of ways. In one study, a researcher examined the extent to which a group of young adults (23-year-olds) had achieved a stable adult identity. (Recall from Chapter 10 that, according to Erik Erikson, forming an identity is a "crisis" individuals are meant to have resolved by the end of adolescence.) Some of the individuals in this group had achieved an identity, whereas others were still in a state of crisis. If this crisis breeds anxiety, we would expect the crisis group to show evidence for more frequent use of defense mechanisms. To test this hypothesis, the researcher asked the young adults to tell stories based on cards from the *Thematic Apperception Test* (see p. 384). The stories were analyzed for evidence of defense mechanisms such as *denial* and *projection* (see Table 13.3). These analyses supported the hypothesis: Those individuals who had not yet achieved an identity were more likely to show evidence of the use of defense mechanisms (Cramer, 1997).

Some of the styles for coping with stress we described in Chapter 12 fall within the general category of defense mechanisms. You might recall, for example, that inhibiting the thoughts and feelings associated with personal traumas or guilty or shameful experiences can take a devastating toll on mental and physical health (Pennebaker, 1990; Petrie et al., 1998). These findings echo Freud's beliefs that repressed psychic material can lead to psychological distress.

Freud's theory is the most complex, comprehensive, and compelling view of normal and abnormal personality functioning—even when its predictions prove wrong. However, like any other theory, Freud's theory is best treated as one that must be confirmed or disconfirmed element by element. Freud retains his influence on contemporary psychology because some of his ideas have been widely accepted. Others have been abandoned. Some of the earliest revisions of Freud's theory arose from within his own original circle of students. Let's see how they sought to amend Freud's views.

◆ EXTENDING PSYCHODYNAMIC THEORIES

Some of those who came after Freud retained his basic representation of personality as a battleground on which unconscious primal urges conflict with social values.

Jung recognized creativity as a means to release images from both the personal and collective unconscious. Why did Jung believe in the two types of unconscious?

However, many of Freud's intellectual descendants made major adjustments in the psychoanalytic view of personality. In general, these post-Freudians have made the following changes:

- They put greater emphasis on ego functions, including ego defenses, development of the self, conscious thought processes, and personal mastery.

- They view social variables (culture, family, and peers) as playing a greater role in shaping personality.

- They put less emphasis on the importance of general sexual urges, or libidinal energy.

- They have extended personality development beyond childhood to include the entire life span.

We will now review key features of the theories of Alfred Adler, Karen Horney, and Carl Jung.

Alfred Adler (1929) rejected the significance of Eros and the pleasure principle. Adler believed that as helpless, dependent, small children, people all experience feelings of *inferiority*. He argued that all lives are dominated by the search for ways to overcome those feelings. People compensate to achieve feelings of adequacy or, more often, overcompensate in an attempt to become *superior*. Personality is structured around this underlying striving; people develop lifestyles based on particular ways of overcoming their basic, pervasive feelings of inferiority. Personality conflict arises from incompatibility between external environmental pressures and internal strivings for adequacy, rather than from competing urges within the person.

Karen Horney was trained in the psychoanalytic school but broke from orthodox Freudian theory in several ways. She challenged Freud's phallocentric emphasis on the importance of the penis, hypothesizing that male envy of pregnancy, motherhood, breasts, and suckling is a dynamic force in the unconscious of boys and men. This "womb envy" leads men to devalue women and to overcompensate by unconscious impulses toward creative work. Horney also placed greater emphasis than did Freud on cultural factors and focused on present character structure rather than on infantile sexuality (Horney, 1937, 1939). Because Horney also had influence on the development of humanistic theories, we will return to her ideas in the next section.

Carl Jung (1959) greatly expanded the conception of the unconscious. For him, the unconscious was not limited to an individual's unique life experiences but was filled with fundamental psychological truths shared by the whole human race, a **collective unconscious.** The collective unconscious explains your intuitive understanding of primitive myths, art forms, and symbols, which are the universal archetypes of existence. An **archetype** is a primitive symbolic representation of a particular experience or object. Each archetype is associated with an instinctive tendency to feel and think about it or experience it in a special way. Jung postulated many archetypes that give rise to myths and symbols: the sun god, the hero, the earth mother. *Animus* was the male archetype, while *anima* was the female archetype, and all men and women experienced both archetypes in varying degrees. The archetype of the self is the *mandala,* or magic circle; it symbolizes striving for unity and wholeness (Jung, 1973).

Jung saw the healthy, integrated personality as balancing opposing forces, such as masculine aggressiveness and feminine sensitivity. This view of personality as a constellation of compensating internal forces in dynamic balance was called **analytic psychology.** In addition, Jung rejected the primary importance of libido, so central to Freud's own theory. Jung added two equally powerful unconscious instincts: the need to create and the need to become a coherent, whole individual. In the next section on humanist theories, we will see this second need paralleled in the concept of *self-actualization.*

<www.ablongman.com/gerrig17e>

- In Freud's theory, how does the expression of the sexual drive change over the course of development?

- What is the importance of the unconscious?

- How do the id, ego, and superego interact to determine behavior?

- How do repression and defense mechanisms function?

- What aspects of Freud's theories have been accepted and rejected by later researchers?

- How have figures like Adler, Horney, and Jung critiqued and extended Freud's theories?

Humanistic Theories

Humanistic approaches to understanding personality are characterized by a concern for the integrity of an individual's personal and conscious experience and growth potential. The key feature of all humanistic theories is an emphasis on the drive toward self-actualization. **Self-actualization** is a constant striving to realize one's inherent potential—to fully develop one's capacities and talents. In this section, you will see how humanist theorists have developed this concept of self-actualization. You will learn, in addition, what additional features set humanistic theories apart from other types of personality theories.

◆ FEATURES OF HUMANISTIC THEORIES

Humanistic personality theorists, such as Carl Rogers, Abraham Maslow, and Karen Horney, believed that the motivation for behavior comes from a person's unique tendencies, both innate and learned, to develop and change in positive directions toward the goal of self-actualization. Recall from Chapter 11 that Maslow placed self-actualization at the pinnacle of his hierarchy of needs. The striving toward self-fulfillment is a constructive, guiding force that moves each person toward generally positive behaviors and enhancement of the self.

The drive for self-actualization at times comes into conflict with the need for approval from the self and others, especially when the person feels that certain obligations or conditions must be met in order to gain approval. For example, **Carl Rogers** (1947, 1951, 1977) stressed the importance of **unconditional positive regard** in raising children. By this, he meant that children should feel they will always be loved and approved of, in spite of their mistakes and misbehavior—that they do not have to earn their parents' love. He recommended that, when a child misbehaves, parents should emphasize that it is the behavior they disapprove of, not the child. Unconditional positive regard is important in adulthood, too, because worrying about seeking approval interferes with self-actualization. As an adult, you need to give and receive unconditional positive regard from those to whom you are close. Most important, you need to feel unconditional positive *self-regard,* or acceptance of yourself, in spite of the weaknesses you might be trying to change.

Although not often given due credit, Karen Horney was another major theorist whose ideas created the foundation of humanistic psychology (Frager & Fadiman, 1998). Horney came to believe that people have a "real self" that requires favorable environmental circumstances to be actualized, such as an atmosphere of warmth, the goodwill of others, and parental love of the child as a "particular individual" (Horney, 1945, 1950). In the absence of those favorable nurturing conditions, the child develops a basic anxiety that stifles spontaneity of expression of real feelings and prevents effective relations with others. To cope with their basic anxiety, individuals resort to interpersonal or intrapsychic defenses. Interpersonal defenses produce movement toward others (through excessive compliance and self-effacing actions), against others (by aggressive, arrogant, or narcissistic solutions), and away from others (through detachment). Intrapsychic defenses operate to develop for some people an unrealistic idealized self-image that generates a "search for glory" to justify it and a pride system that operates on rigid rules of conduct to live up to a grandiose self-concept. Such people often live by the "tyranny of shoulds," self-imposed obligations, such as "I should be perfect, generous, attractive, brave," and so forth. Horney believed that the goal of a humanistic therapy was to help the individual achieve the joy of self-realization and promote the inherent constructive forces in human nature that support a striving for self-fulfillment.

An important aspect of each of the theories of Maslow, Rogers, and Horney is the emphasis on self-actualization or progress toward the real self. In addition, humanistic theories have been described as being holistic, dispositional, and phenomenological. Let's see why.

Humanistic theories are *holistic* because they explain people's separate acts in terms of their entire personalities; people are not seen as the sum of discrete traits that each influence behavior in different ways. Maslow believed that people are intrinsically motivated toward the upper levels of the hierarchy of needs (discussed in Chapter 11), unless deficiencies at the lower levels weigh them down.

Humanistic theories are *dispositional* because they focus on the innate qualities within a person that exert a major influence over the direction behavior will take. Situational factors are seen as constraints and barriers (like the strings that tie down balloons). Once freed from negative situational conditions, the actualizing tendency should actively guide people to choose life-enhancing situations. However, humanistic theories are not dispositional in the same sense as trait theories or psychodynamic theories. In those views, personal dispositions are recurrent themes played out in behavior again and again. Humanistic dispositions are oriented specifically toward creativity and growth. Each time a humanistic disposition is exercised, the person changes a little, so that the disposition is never expressed in the same way twice. Over time, humanistic dispositions guide the individual toward self-actualization, the purest expression of these motives.

Humanistic theories are *phenomenological* because they emphasize an individual's frame of reference and subjective view of reality—not the objective perspective of an observer or of a therapist. Thus, a humanistic psychologist always strives to see each person's unique point of view. This view is also a present-oriented view; past influences are important only to the extent that they have brought the person to the present situation, and the future represents goals to achieve. Thus, unlike psychodynamic theories, humanistic theories do not see people's present behaviors as unconsciously guided by past experiences.

The upbeat humanist view of personality was a welcome treat for many psychologists who had been brought up on a diet of bitter-tasting Freudian medicine. Humanistic approaches focus directly on improvement—on making life more palatable—rather than dredging up painful memories that are sometimes better left repressed. The humanist perspective emphasizes each person's ability to realize his or her fullest potential.

◆ EVALUATION OF HUMANISTIC THEORIES

Freud's theory was often criticized for providing the too-pessimistic view that human nature develops out of conflicts, traumas, and anxieties. Humanistic theories arose to celebrate the healthy personality that strives for happiness and self-actualization. It is difficult to criticize theories that encourage and appreciate people, even for

their faults. Even so, critics have complained that humanistic concepts are fuzzy and difficult to explore in research. They ask, "What exactly is self-actualization?" "Is it an inborn tendency, or is it created by the cultural context?" Humanistic theories also do not traditionally focus on the particular characteristics of individuals. They are more theories about human nature and about qualities all people share than about the individual personality or the basis of differences among people. Other psychologists note that, by emphasizing the role of the self as a source of experience and action, humanistic psychologists neglect the important environmental variables that also influence behavior.

Despite these limitations, a type of contemporary research can be traced in part to the humanist tradition that focuses directly on individual *narratives* or *life stories* (McAdams, 2001). The tradition of using psychological theory to understand the details of an individual's life—to produce a *psychobiography*—can be traced back to Freud's analysis of Leonardo da Vinci (Freud, 1910/1957; see Elms, 1988, for a critique of Freud's work). **Psychobiography** is defined as "the systematic use of psychological (especially personality) theory to transform a life into a coherent and illuminating story" (McAdams, 1988, p. 2). Consider the great artist Pablo Picasso. Picasso suffered a series of traumas as a young child, including a serious earthquake and the death of a young sister. A psychobiography might attempt to explain some of Picasso's vast artistic creativity as the lifelong residue of his responses to these early traumas (Gardner, 1993).

When a well-known or historical figure is the subject of a psychobiography, a researcher may turn to published work, diaries, and letters as sources of relevant data. For more ordinary individuals, researchers may directly elicit narratives of life experiences. The request might be, for example, that the participant talk about a recent peak experience: "What were you thinking and feeling? What might this episode say about who you are, who you were, who you might be, or how you have developed over time?" (McAdams & de St. Aubin, 1992, p. 1010). The characteristic themes that emerge over series of narrative accounts support the holistic and phenomenological version of personality that was put forth by the early humanists: People construct their identities by weaving life stories out of the strands of narrative. Personal accounts provide a window on people's views of themselves and interpersonal relationships.

Humanistic theorists emphasized each individual's drive toward self-actualization. This group recognized, however, that people's progress toward this goal is determined, in part, by realities of their environments. We turn now to theories that directly examine how individuals' behaviors are shaped by their environments.

<www.ablongman.com/gerrig17e>

- Why is self-actualization central to humanistic theories?
- Why did Carl Rogers emphasize unconditional positive regard?
- What contributions did Karen Horney make to humanistic theories?
- In what ways are humanistic theories holistic, dispositional, and phenomenological?
- How do humanistic theories give rise to a focus on life stories and psychobiography?

Social-Learning and Cognitive Theories

Common to all the theories we have reviewed so far is an emphasis on hypothesized inner mechanisms—traits, instincts, impulses, tendencies toward self-actualization—that propel behavior and form the basis of a functioning personality. What most of these theories lacked, however, was a solid link between personality and particular behaviors. Psychodynamic and humanistic theories, for example, provide accounts of the total personality but do not predict specific actions. Another tradition of personality theory emerged from a more direct focus on individual differences in behavior. Recall from Chapter 6 that much of a person's behavior can be predicted from contingencies in the environment. Psychologists with a *learning theory* orientation look to the environmental circumstances that control behavior. Personality is seen as the sum of the overt and covert responses that are reliably elicited by an individual's *reinforcement history*. Learning theory approaches suggest that people are different because they have had different histories of reinforcement.

Consider a behaviorist conception of personality developed by a team of Yale University psychologists headed by John Dollard and Neal Miller (1950). Dollard and Miller introduced concepts such as learned drives, inhibition of responses, and learned habit patterns. Similar to Freud, they emphasized the roles of the motivating force of tension and the reinforcing (pleasurable) consequences of *tension reduction*. Organisms act to reduce tension produced by unsatisfied drives. Behavior that successfully reduces such tensions is repeated, even-

tually becoming a learned habit that is reinforced by repeated tension reduction. Dollard and Miller also showed that one could learn by *social imitation*—by observing the behavior of others without having to actually perform the response. Suppose a youngster sees his older sister given candy when she races to meet their father as he arrives home; the younger brother may begin to carry out the same behavior. The idea of imitation broadened the ways psychologists understood that effective or destructive habits are learned. Personality emerges as the sum of these learned habits.

Contemporary social-learning and cognitive theories often share Dollard and Miller's belief that behavior is influenced by environmental contingencies. These theories, however, go one step further to emphasize the importance of cognitive processes as well as behavioral ones, returning a thinking mind to the acting body. Those who have proposed cognitive theories of personality point out that there are important individual differences in the way people think about and define any external situation. Cognitive theories stress the mental processes through which people turn their sensations and perceptions into organized impressions of reality. Like humanistic theories, cognitive theories emphasize that you participate in creating your own personality. For example, you actively *choose* your own environments to a great extent; you do not just react passively. You weigh alternatives and select the settings in which you act and are acted upon—you choose to enter situations that you expect to be reinforcing and to avoid those that are unsatisfying and uncertain. For example, you often choose to return to restaurants where you've had good meals before, rather than always trying someplace new.

If your parents complimented you every time you got a new haircut, how might that affect your confidence about your appearance and grooming as an adult? Suppose they were regularly critical. What effect could that have?

Let's look now at more concrete embodiments of these ideas. We examine the theories of Walter Mischel, Albert Bandura, and Nancy Cantor.

◆ MISCHEL'S COGNITIVE–AFFECTIVE PERSONALITY THEORY

Walter Mischel developed an influential theory of the cognitive basis of personality. Mischel emphasizes that people actively participate in the cognitive organization of their interactions with the environment. His approach emphasizes the importance of understanding how behavior arises as a function of interactions between persons and situations (Mischel & Shoda, 1995, 1999). Consider this example:

> *John's unique personality may be seen most clearly in that he is always very friendly when meeting someone for the first time, but that he also predictably becomes rather abrupt and unfriendly as he begins to spend more time with that person. Jim, on the other hand, is unique in that he is typically shy and quiet with people who he does not know well but becomes very gregarious once he begins to know someone well.*
> *(Shoda et al., 1993a, p. 1023)*

If we were to average John's and Jim's overall friendliness, we would probably get about the same value on this trait—but that would fail to capture important differences in their behavior. According to Mischel (1973; Mischel & Shoda, 1995), how you respond to a specific environmental input depends on the variables defined in **Table 13.4.** Do you see how each variable listed would affect the way in which a person would behave in par-

ticular situations? We have given you examples for each variable. Try to invent a situation in which you would produce behavior different from the characters listed in the table, because you contrast on the particular variable. You may wonder what determines the nature of these variables for a specific individual. Mischel believes that they result from his or her history of observations and interactions with other people and with inanimate aspects of the physical environment (Mischel, 1973).

Mischel and his colleagues have demonstrated the importance of patterns of behavior in their field studies of children's experiences in summer camp.

PUTTING IDEAS TO THE TEST

Patterns of Behavior

We described one study from this project earlier, when we discussed behavioral consistency. Another study focused on children's reactions to different psychological situations, such as having another child initiate positive social contact or being warned by an adult to cease some activity. Children's reactions were coded into categories such as "talked prosocially" or "complied or gave in." In addition, at the end of the summer, camp counselors were asked to label individual children as "aggressive," "withdrawn," or "friendly." What information did they use to make these judgments? Consider the behavior of complying or giving in. Children who were ultimately rated as *friendly* had complied in situations in which they had been given warnings by an adult. Children who were ultimately rated as *withdrawn* had complied in situations in which peers had tested them (Shoda et al., 1993b).

TABLE 13.4
Person Variables in Mischel's Cognitive–Affective Personality Theory

Variable	Definition	Example
Encodings	The way you categorize information about yourself, other people, events, and situations.	As soon as Bob meets someone, he tries to figure out how wealthy he or she is.
Expectancies and beliefs	Your beliefs about the social world and likely outcomes for given actions in particular situations. Your beliefs about your ability to bring outcomes about.	Greg invites friends to the movies, but he never expects them to say "yes."
Affects	Your feelings and emotions, including physiological responses.	Cindy blushes very easily.
Goals and values	The outcomes and affective states you do and do not value; your goals and life projects.	Peter wants to be president of his college class.
Competencies and self-regulatory plans	The behaviors you can accomplish and plans for generating cognitive and behavioral outcomes.	Jan can speak English, French, Russian, and Japanese and expects to work for the U.N.

Would you feel comfortable making personality judgments about these boys from this one snapshot? Why might you want to know their patterns of behavior across different types of situations?

These results suggest that knowing the average rates at which children complied wouldn't tell you very much about their personalities. You would have to know in what situation the compliance took place to understand why one child was labeled as friendly and another as withdrawn. Mischel emphasizes that your beliefs about other people's personalities come not from taking averages but from tracking the way different situations bring out different behaviors (Mischel et al., 2002; Shoda & Mischel, 1993).

◆ BANDURA'S COGNITIVE SOCIAL-LEARNING THEORY

Through his theoretical writing and extensive research with children and adults, **Albert Bandura** (1986, 1999) has been an eloquent champion of a social-learning approach to understanding personality (recall from Chapter 6 his studies of aggressive behavior in children). This approach combines principles of learning with an emphasis on human interactions in social settings. From a social-learning perspective, human beings are not driven by inner forces, nor are they helpless pawns of environmental influence. The social-learning approach stresses the cognitive processes that are involved in acquiring and maintaining patterns of behavior and, thus, personality.

Bandura's theory points to a complex interaction of individual factors, behavior, and environmental stimuli. Each can influence or change the others, and the direction of change is rarely one way—it is *reciprocal*. Your behavior can be influenced by your attitudes, beliefs, or

prior history of reinforcement as well as by stimuli available in the environment. What you do can have an effect on the environment, and important aspects of your personality can be affected by the environment or by feedback from your behavior. This important concept, **reciprocal determinism,** implies that you must examine all components if you want to completely understand human behavior, personality, and social ecology (Bandura, 1999; see **Figure 13.5**). So, for example, if you don't generally think of yourself as an athlete, you may not choose to be active in track-and-field events, but if you live near a pool, you may nonetheless spend time swimming. If you are outgoing, you'll talk to others sitting around the pool and thereby create a more sociable atmosphere, which, in turn, makes it a more enjoyable environment. This is one instance of reciprocal determinism among person, place, and behavior.

You may recall from Chapter 6 that Bandura's social-learning theory emphasizes observational learning as the process by which a person changes his or her behavior based on observations of another person's behavior. Through observational learning, children and adults acquire an enormous range of information about their social environment. Through observation, you learn what is appropriate and gets rewarded and what

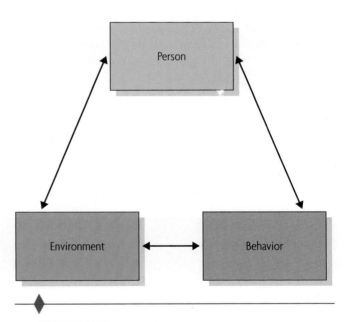

FIGURE 13.5

Reciprocal Determinism

In reciprocal determinism, the individual, the individual's behavior, and the environment all interact to influence and modify the other components.

gets punished or ignored. Because you can use memory and think about external events, you can foresee the possible consequences of your actions without having to actually experience them. You may acquire skills, attitudes, and beliefs simply by watching what others do and the consequences that follow.

As his theory developed, Bandura (1997) elaborated self-efficacy as a central construct. **Self-efficacy** is the belief that one can perform adequately in a particular situation. Your sense of self-efficacy influences your perceptions, motivation, and performance in many ways. You don't even try to do things or take chances when you expect to be ineffectual. You avoid situations when you don't feel adequate. Even when you do, in fact, have the ability—and the desire—you may not take the required action or persist to complete the task successfully, if you think you lack what it takes.

Beyond actual accomplishments, there are three other sources of information for *self-efficacy judgments:*

- vicarious experience—your observations of the performance of others
- persuasion—others may convince you that you can do something, or you may convince yourself
- monitoring of your emotional arousal as you think about or approach a task—for example, anxiety suggests low expectations of efficacy; excitement suggests expectations of success

Self-efficacy judgments influence how much effort you expend and how long you persist when faced with difficulty in a wide range of life situations (Bandura, 1997; Cervone, 2000). For example, how vigorously and persistently you study this chapter may depend more on your sense of self-efficacy than on actual ability (Zimmerman et al., 1992).

One important type of self-efficacy beliefs reflects people's judgments about their ability to regulate their own behavior. Let's look at an example of the impact of *self-regulatory efficacy* on adolescents' likelihood to engage in violent conduct.

Self-Regulatory Efficacy and Adolescent Behavior

Bandura and his colleagues (Caprara et al., 2002) predicted that those adolescents who had the *highest* levels of perceived self-regulatory efficacy would be the *least* likely to engage in violent conduct. To test this hypothesis, the researchers recruited 350 adolescents (170 boys and 180 girls) from high schools located near Rome, Italy. The students provided initial data when they were 16 years old. At that time, they provided perceptions of their perceived self-regulatory efficacy by responding to such items as "How well can you resist peer pressure to use drugs?" The students also indicated their level of violent conduct by responding to such items as "Have you ever participated in violent actions of 'gangs'?" When the students were 18, they were asked a second time about their violent conduct. The researchers examined the patterns of data to see how well perceived self-efficacy predicted violence at both ages 16 and 18. Those students who believed they were most able to control their behavior were, in fact, least likely to engage in violent activities across time. Although the girls had lower levels of violence as both 16- and 18-year-olds, both boys and girls showed the same impact of self-regulatory efficacy on violent conduct.

You can see from this study the strong correlation between what people believe they can accomplish (or prevent) and what they are actually able to do.

Bandura's theory of self-efficacy also acknowledges the importance of the environment. Expectations of failure or success—and corresponding decisions to stop trying or to persevere—may be based on perceptions of the supportiveness or unsupportiveness of the environment, in addition to perceptions of one's own adequacy or inadequacy. Such expectations are called *outcome-based expectancies.* **Figure 13.6** displays how the parts of Bandura's theory fit together. Behavioral outcomes

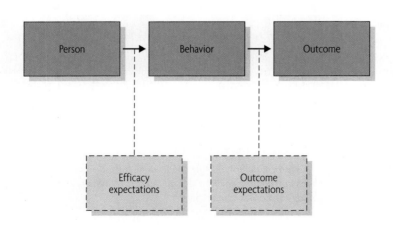

FIGURE 13.6

Bandura's Self-Efficacy Model

This model positions efficacy expectations between the person and his or her behavior; outcome expectations are positioned between behavior and its anticipated outcomes.

depend both on people's perceptions of their own abilities and their perceptions of the environment.

◆ CANTOR'S SOCIAL INTELLIGENCE THEORY

Building on these earlier cognitive and social theories, **Nancy Cantor** and her colleagues have outlined a *social intelligence* theory of personality (Cantor & Kihlstrom, 1987; Kilstrom & Cantor, 2000). **Social intelligence** refers to the expertise people bring to their experience of life tasks. The theory defines three types of individual differences:

- *Choice of life goals.* People differ as to which life goals or life tasks are most important to them. People's goals may also change over time.
- *Knowledge relevant to social interactions.* People differ with respect to the expertise they bring to tasks of social and personal problem solving.
- *Strategies for implementing goals.* People have different characteristic problem-solving strategies.

Can you see how these three dimensions interact to give rise to the different patterns of behavior you would recognize as personality? You might, for example, have two friends—one of whom is more concerned about "getting and keeping friends" whereas the other one gives more weight to "getting good grades." Or suppose two other friends both value getting good grades. Depending on what they know and how they are able to put that knowledge to use, the moment-by-moment decisions they make about how to behave could be very different. One may have been taught explicit strategies for studying, and the other muddles through without special help. The theory of social intelligence gives a new perspective on how personality predicts consistency: For a given period of time, consistency is found in people's goals, knowledge, and strategies.

Let's examine concrete circumstances in which people's disparate goals yield different outcomes: Researchers have demonstrated that *intimacy goals* have an impact on relationship satisfaction.

PUTTING IDEAS TO THE TEST

Intimacy Goals in Dating Relationships

When some people enter into relationships, their foremost goal is to create intimacy: They wish to experience circumstances in which they can foster interdependence and engage in self-disclosure. Other people are equally interested in having relationships, but for them relationships are more a pathway to desired activities (e.g., parties, sexual relations) rather than intimacy. To assess these differences in the strength of intimacy

goals, researchers asked 60 students to respond to such items as "In my dating relationships, I try to share my most intimate thoughts and feelings" (Sanderson & Cantor, 1997). The students also reported such factors as, for example, the time they actually spent with their partners in various situations as well as their relationship satisfaction. The data showed a clear pattern: The relationship satisfaction of people with *stronger* intimacy goals was less affected by the amount of time they were able to spend with their partners; their reports of relationship satisfaction were relatively high whether they spent a little or a lot of time. By comparison, the relationship satisfaction of those individuals with weaker intimacy goals was considerably lower when they spent little time with their partners.

Do you see how this pattern could follow from the individuals' goals? People with stronger intimacy goals are highly motivated to make the most of whatever time they can spend with their partners. By comparison, those with weaker intimacy goals may not be able to bring sufficient focus to maintain a satisfying relationship without abundant interactions. In this case, you recognize personality in the consistent way in which people behave in close relationships.

◆ EVALUATION OF SOCIAL-LEARNING AND COGNITIVE THEORIES

One set of criticisms leveled against social-learning and cognitive theories is that they often overlook emotion as an important component of personality. In psychodynamic theories, emotions like anxiety play a central role. In social-learning and cognitive theories emotions are perceived merely as by-products of thoughts and behavior or are just included with other types of thoughts rather than being assigned independent importance. For those who feel that emotions are central to the functioning of human personality, this is a serious flaw. Cognitive theories are also attacked for not fully recognizing the impact of unconscious motivation on behavior and affect.

A second set of criticisms focuses on the vagueness of explanations about the way personal constructs and competencies are created. Cognitive theorists have often had little to say about the developmental origins of adult personality; their focus on the individual's perception of the current behavior setting obscures the individual's history.

Despite these criticisms, cognitive personality theories have made major contributions to current thinking. Mischel's awareness of situation has brought about a better understanding of the interaction between what a person brings to a behavior setting and what that setting brings out of the person. Bandura's ideas have led to improvements in the way teachers educate children and help them achieve as well as new treatments in the areas of health, business, and sports performance. Finally, Cantor's theory shifts the search for personality consistency to the level of life goals and social strategies.

Do these cognitive personality theories provide you with insights about your own personality and behaviors? You can start to see how you define yourself in part through interactions with the environment. We turn now to theories that can add even further to your definition of self.

PUT YOURSELF TO THE TEST

◆ What is a common feature of personality accounts that emerges from learning theory?

◆ In what ways does Mischel's theory explain the interactions of persons and situations?

◆ What role does reciprocal determinism play in Bandura's theory?

◆ What are some causes and consequences of perceptions of self-efficacy?

◆ Why does Cantor's theory emphasize goals and the strategies people bring to implement them?

Self Theories

We have arrived now at theories of personality that are most immediately personal: They deal directly with how each individual manages his or her sense of *self*. What is your conception of your *self*? Do you think of your *self* reacting consistently to the world? Do you try to present a consistent *self* to your friends and family? What impact do positive and negative experiences have on the way you think about your *self*? We will begin our consideration of these questions with a brief historical review.

The concern for analysis of the self found its strongest early advocate in **William James** (1890). James identified three components of self-experience: the *material me* (the bodily self, along with surrounding physical objects), the *social me* (your awareness of how others view you), and the *spiritual me* (the self that monitors private thoughts and feelings). James believed that everything that you associate with your identity becomes, in some sense, a part of the self. This

explains why people may react defensively when their friends or family members—a part of the self—have been attacked. The concept of self was also central to psychodynamic theories. Self-insight was an important part of the psychoanalytic cure in Freud's theory, and Jung stressed that to fully develop the self, one must integrate and accept all aspects of one's conscious and unconscious life.

How has the self been treated in contemporary theory? We will first describe cognitive aspects of the self: self-concepts and possible selves. We then examine the way that people present their selves to the world. Finally, we look at the important topic of how views of the self differ across cultures.

◆ DYNAMIC ASPECTS OF SELF-CONCEPTS

The **self-concept** is a dynamic mental structure that motivates, interprets, organizes, mediates, and regulates intrapersonal and interpersonal behaviors and processes. The self-concept includes many components. Among them are your memories about yourself; beliefs about your traits, motives, values, and abilities; the ideal self that you would most like to become; the possible selves that you contemplate enacting; positive or negative evaluations of yourself (self-esteem); and beliefs about what others think of you (Brown, 1998; McGuire & McGuire, 1988). In Chapter 7, we discussed *schemas* as "knowledge packages" that embody complex generalizations about the structure of the environment. Your self-concept contains schemas about the self—*self-schemas*—that allow you to organize information about yourself, just as other schemas allow you to manage other aspects of your experience. However, self-schemas influence more than just the way you process information about yourself. Research indicates that these schemas, which you frequently use to interpret your own behavior, influence the way you process information about other people as well (Krueger & Stanke, 2001; Mussweiler & Bodenhausen, 2002). Thus, you interpret other people's actions in terms of what you know and believe about yourself.

Another important component of your cognitive sense of self may be the other *possible selves* to which you compare your current self-concept. **Hazel Markus** and her colleagues have defined **possible selves** as "the ideal selves that we would very much like to become. They are also the selves we could become, and the selves we are afraid of becoming" (Markus & Nurius, 1986, p. 954). Possible selves play a role in motivating behavior—they spur action by allowing you to consider what directions your "self" could take, for better or for worse.

Consider a study that explored individuals' ideas about whether they are prepared to become parents.

Possible Self as Parent

A team of researchers developed an assessment device intended to measure the extent to which young adults could imagine themselves becoming parents (Bloom et al., 1999). The 683 college students who participated in the study responded on a scale of *not at all like me* to *very much like me* to statements such as "In the future I see myself as the kind of person who would get married but choose not to have children." To discourage students from guessing the study's purpose, the items relevant to parenting were dispersed into a longer questionnaire. After completing the questionnaire, each student was assigned a *parent possible-self score* (PPS). On average, men and women did not differ on these scores. However, the researchers defined subsets of both men and women who were particularly high and low on the scale. The individuals in those subsets rated their perceptions of videotaped infants whose behavior ranged from happy to fussy. The high-PPS students gave consistently more favorable ratings to the infants than the low-PPS students did.

Can you think of reasons why a person's ability to envision him- or herself as a parent might have an impact on that person's interpretations of an infant's behavior?

◆ SELF-ESTEEM AND SELF-PRESENTATION

We have already acknowledged that some people have a negative self-concept, which we could also characterize as low self-esteem. A person's **self-esteem** is a *generalized* evaluation of the self. Self-esteem can strongly influence thoughts, moods, and behavior (Baumeister et al., 2003). Low self-esteem may be characterized, in part, by less certainty about the self. When high- and low-self-esteem individuals were asked to rate themselves along a number of trait dimensions (such as logical, intellectual, and likable), low-self-esteem participants, as you might expect, gave themselves overall lower ratings (Baumgardner, 1990). However, when they were also asked to provide upper and lower limits for their estimates, the low-self-esteem participants indicated larger ranges: They had a less precise sense of self than their high-self-esteem peers. Thus, part of the phenomenon of low self-esteem may be feeling that you just don't know much about yourself. Lack of self-knowledge makes it difficult to predict that one will make a success of life's endeavors.

Evidence suggests that most people go out of their way to maintain self-esteem and to sustain the integrity of their self-concept (Steele, 1988). People engage in a variety of forms of self-enhancement (Banaji & Prentice, 1994). For example, when you doubt your ability to perform a task, you may engage in **self-handicapping**

behavior. You deliberately sabotage your performance! The purpose of this strategy is to have a ready-made excuse for failure that does not imply *lack of ability* (McCrea & Hirt, 2001). Thus, if you are afraid to find out whether you have what it takes to be pre-med, you might party with friends instead of studying for an important exam. That way, if you don't succeed, you can blame your failure on low effort, without finding out whether you really had the ability to make it.

Self-Handicapping Among College Students

A pair of researchers asked college students to indicate their agreement with statements that measured self-handicapping: "I would do a lot better if I tried harder"; "I suppose I feel 'under the weather' more often than most"; "I tend to put things off to the last moment." Before their first exam, the students were asked what grade would make them happy. After the exam, they were given false feedback that their score was one-third grade below that "happy" grade (for example, if they had desired a B, they were told they got a B–). At that point, the researchers assessed the students' self-esteem. If self-handicapping protects self-esteem, we would expect high self-handicappers to suffer the least injury to self-esteem when they obtained the dissatisfying grade. That's exactly the pattern that the men in the study showed: High self-handicapping was associated with higher self-esteem. The women students, however, did not show any correlation between self-handicapping and self-esteem. The researchers speculated that men may have a stronger tendency to protect against threats to the self (Rhodewalt & Hill, 1995).

You should think about this study with respect to your own behaviors. Do you indulge in self-handicapping? Even if it protects your self-esteem (particularly if you are male), your grades are still likely to suffer! (By the way, after the study was completed, the researchers thoroughly debriefed the participants—which included explaining the purpose of the deception and giving them their real grades.)

The phenomenon of self-handicapping suggests, as well, that important aspects of self-esteem are related to *self-presentation*. Self-handicapping is more likely when people know that outcomes will be made public (Self, 1990). After all, how can someone think less well of you when your handicap is so obvious? Similar issues of self-presentation help explain behavioral differences between individuals with high and low self-esteem (Baumeister et al., 1989). People with high self-esteem present themselves to the world as ambitious, aggressive risk takers. People with low self-esteem present themselves as cautious and prudent.

In this section, we've emphasized that people engage in behaviors such as self-handicapping to maintain a high

Imagine for a moment your different "possible selves." What effect might consideration of possible selves have on your behavior?

sense of self-esteem. For that reason, you might not be surprised to learn that high self-esteem is not a good predictor of performance in many settings (Baumeister et al., 2003). In fact, it's safer to assume that high self-esteem is a consequence of success. Thus, making students feel better about themselves doesn't lead to better school performance. Rather, high self-esteem flows, in part, from success in school.

◆ THE CULTURAL CONSTRUCTION OF SELF

Our discussion so far has focused on constructs relevant to the self, such as self-esteem and possible selves, that apply quite widely across individuals. However, researchers on the self have also begun to study the way in which self-concepts and self-development are affected by differing cultural constraints. If you have grown up in a Western culture, you are likely to be pretty comfortable with the research we have reviewed so far: The theories and constructs match the ways that Western cultures conceptualize the *self*. However, the type of culture from which the Western self emerges—an *individualistic* culture—is in the minority with respect to the world's population, which includes about 70 percent *collectivist* cultures. Individualistic cultures emphasize individuals' needs, whereas collectivist cultures emphasize the needs of the group (Triandis, 1994, 1995). This overarching emphasis has important implications for how each member of these cultures conceptualizes his or her *self*: **Hazel Markus** and **Shinobu Kitayama** (1991; Kitayama et al., 1995; Markus et al., 1997) have argued that each culture gives rise to different interpretations of the meaning of self—or different *construals* of self:

- Individualistic cultures encourage **independent construals of self**—"Achieving the cultural goal of independence requires construing oneself as an individual whose behavior is organized and made meaningful primarily by reference to one's own internal repertoire of thoughts, feelings, and action, rather than by reference to the thoughts, feelings, and actions of others" (Markus & Kitayama, 1991, p. 226).

- Collectivist cultures encourage **interdependent construals of self**—"Experiencing interdependence entails seeing oneself as part of an encompassing social relationship and recognizing that one's behavior is determined, contingent on, and, to a large extent organized by what the actor perceives to be the thoughts, feelings, and actions of *others* in the relationship" (Markus & Kitayama, 1991, p. 227).

Researchers have documented the reality and implications of these distinctions in a number of ways.

One type of cross-cultural research on the self has used a measurement device called the *Twenty Statements Test* (TST) (Kuhn & McPartland, 1954). When they take this test, participants are asked to give 20 different answers to the question "Who am I?" As shown in **Table 13.5,** responses to this question typically fall into six different categories. The table also presents the results of a study in which roughly 300 students from the United States and India were asked to go through the TST procedure (Dhawan et al., 1995). The greatest difference in the table is the rate at which people gave *self-evaluations*. American students were far more likely

Self-handicapping behavior in action: Instead of studying for tomorrow's exam, you fall asleep in the library, thereby enabling yourself to say, "Well, I didn't really study" if you don't ace the test. Are there situations in which you resort to self-handicapping?

TABLE 13.5
Cross-Cultural Comparison of *Twenty Statements Test* Responses—Percent Response in Each Category

Category	Examples	INDIAN		AMERICAN	
		Male	Female	Male	Female
Social identity	I'm a student. I am a daughter.	34	28	26	26
Ideological beliefs	I believe that all human beings are good. I believe in God.	2	2	2	1
Interests	I like playing the piano. I enjoy visiting new places.	7	16	6	5
Ambitions	I want to become a doctor. I want to learn more psychology.	11	15	2	2
Self-evaluations	I am honest and hardworking. I am a tall person. I worry about the future.	35	33	64	65
Other	I have noisy friends. I own a dog.	11	6	1	0

to do so—in keeping with their independent sense of self. Indian students gave far fewer self-evaluations and, in keeping with their interdependent sense of self, somewhat more statements about social identity. Note that differences between men and women overall were rather small—culture mattered more. You might wonder how the export of Western culture affects the self-concepts of members of collectivist cultures. One study compared the TST responses of Kenyans who had virtually no exposure to Western culture—members of pastoral Samburu and Maasai tribes—to those who had moved to the Westernized capital city of Nairobi. Roughly 82 percent of the tribe members' responses on the TST were social responses; workers in Nairobi gave only 58 percent social responses, and students at the University of Nairobi gave only 17 percent social responses (Ma & Schoeneman, 1997). This pattern suggests that when a nation imports Western products, they may also import a Western sense of self.

These studies illustrate that the cultures to which people belong have a strong impact on the way they construe their selves. You have already read about the consequences of these construals in earlier chapters. For example, in Chapter 10, you learned that culture affects moral judgments (Miller & Bersoff, 1992); and in Chapter 12, you learned that culture affects emotional expression (Stephan et al., 1996). You will encounter this distinction again later in the book when, for example, we consider the question of whether ideas about *love* are influenced by construals of the self (see Chapter 16). For now, consider a study that has particular relevance to theories about the self.

PUTTING IDEAS TO THE TEST

Cross-Cultural Patterns of Self-Enhancement

Earlier we reviewed evidence that people are concerned with *self-enhancement*—bringing about positive changes in self-esteem. However, people in different cultures have different interpretations of the *self* in self-enhancement. For that reason, a team of researchers predicted that students from the United States would be more likely to choose individualistic behaviors for self-enhancement whereas students from Japan would choose collectivist behaviors (Sedikides et al., 2003). To test that idea, the researchers asked each student from the United States and Japan to spend ten minutes imagining that he or she was part of a task force responsible for solving business problems. The students were asked to consider a range of issues and write down their ideas on those issues. After performing this exercise, the students made predictions about how likely it was that they would outperform the other (imaginary) task force members on a range of behaviors. Some of those behaviors were individualistic: Would they "disagree with [their] group when [they] believe the group is wrong?" Some of those behaviors were collectivist: Would they "avoid open confrontation with [their] group?" For each behavior, the students gave responses ranging from −5 ("much less likely than the typical group member") to +5 ("much more likely than the typical group member"). As shown in **Table 13.6,** the students predicted that they would outperform their peers—the more positive numbers indicate more self-enhancement—with respect to those behaviors that were matched with their construals of self.

In what ways is an individual's sense of self different when he or she is a member of a culture with an interdependent construal of self rather than an independent construal of self?

Over the next few days, you might try to experience both construals of self by trying to attend to how the events that happen around you have an impact both on your self as an individual and your self as a member of a larger social structure.

◆ EVALUATION OF SELF THEORIES

Self theories succeed at capturing people's own concepts of their personalities and the way they wish to be perceived by others. Furthermore, examinations of cross-cultural construals of the self have had great influence on the way psychologists assess the universality of their theories. However, critics of self theory approaches to personality argue against its limitless boundaries. Because so many things are relevant to the self and to the self-concept, it is not always clear which factors are most important for predicting behavior. In addition, the emphasis on the self as a social construct is not entirely consistent with evidence that some facets of personality may be inherited. As with the other theories we have described, self theories capture some but not all of what you think of as personality.

◆

TABLE 13.6
Self-Enhancement Across Cultures

| Culture | BEHAVIORS | |
	Individualist	Collectivist
American	1.28	−0.45
Japanese	0.06	0.63

- How do self-concepts affect the ways in which people process information about themselves and others?
- What is the function of possible selves?
- What are the origins and consequences of self-esteem?
- What is the relationship between self-handicapping and self-esteem?
- Why do construals of the self have an impact across cultures?

Comparing Personality Theories

There is no unified theory of personality that a majority of psychologists can endorse. Several differences in basic assumptions have come up repeatedly in our survey of the various theories. It may be helpful to recap five of the most important differences in assumptions about personality and the approaches that advance each assumption.

1. *Heredity versus environment.* As you have learned throughout *Psychology and Life,* this difference is also referred to as *nature versus nurture.* What is more important to personality development: genetic and biological factors or environmental influences? Trait theories have been split on this issue; Freudian theory depends heavily on heredity; humanistic, social-learning, cognitive, and self theories all emphasize either environment as a determinant of behavior or interaction with the environment as a source of personality development and differences.

2. *Learning processes versus innate laws of behavior.* Should emphasis be placed on the view that personalities are modified through learning or on the view that personality development follows an internal timetable? Again, trait theories have been divided. Freudian theory has favored the inner determinant view, whereas humanists postulate an optimistic view that experience changes people. Social-learning, cognitive, and self theories clearly support the idea that behavior and personality change as a result of learned experiences.

3. *Emphasis on past, present, or future.* Trait theories emphasize past causes, whether innate or learned;

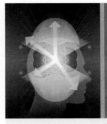
The Self on the Internet

The most pressing question many people ask themselves when they sit down for an Internet session is: Who should I be today? One of the best documented aspects of life on the Internet is that people create new identities for themselves (McKenna & Bargh, 2000; Reid, 1998). When a person enters a chat room, she might decide to be a man rather than a woman, black rather than white, 40 rather than 18, and a successful executive rather than a college sophomore. The Internet brings the concept of *possible selves* very vividly into many people's everyday lives. Let's focus on some positive consequences of these Internet selves.

Something that many people find burdensome in "real" life is that they start to feel as though they are defined rather narrowly: Repeated interactions with family, friends, bosses, and coworkers require them to remain consistent in a way that may be at odds with the person they wish to be; it is relatively difficult for people to expand into new realms of experience, given the constraints of their day-to-day social context. The Internet loosens up that social context (Bargh et al., 2003; McKenna &

Bargh, 2000). People can use the anonymity of the Internet to express new interests or explore new ideas without fear of real-world consequences. Without making radical changes (e.g., claiming to be a woman rather than a man), a person can rehearse possible selves that may be closer to his or her ideal self.

Furthermore, the anonymity of the Internet allows people to reveal more of their selves than they might otherwise be willing to disclose. Recall from Chapter 12 that people obtain positive health benefits when they make emotional disclosures (Pennebaker, 1990). The Internet offers people a broad range of opportunities to engage in such disclosure. People can find specialized chat rooms or newsgroups that explicitly provide forums for such disclosure and social support for the content of the disclosures.

Researchers have demonstrated, in fact, that people's ability to make disclosures about hidden aspects of their self can lead to greater self-acceptance. One study obtained information from people who made postings to newsgroups intended for people with marginalized

sexual identities such as homosexuality. The researchers were able to obtain anonymous data from people who were active participants in those groups (McKenna & Bargh, 1998). The data suggested that newsgroup participation led to greater self-acceptance. In fact, 37 percent of the respondents who provided data had revealed to others the secret of their marginalized identity as a consequence of newsgroup participation.

We have been focusing on the positive aspects of the Internet: People's ability to expand their sense of self and their ability to engage in self-disclosure with consequences for health and self-acceptance. There are, of course, some dangers. Anonymity can lead people to fragment their lives in ways that might lead to maladaptive behaviors (Reid, 1998). We also noted earlier that some researchers attribute a rise in the prevalence of shyness to the availability of the Internet. Still, we hope that most people will benefit from the opportunities the Internet provides to engage, very literally, in self-exploration.

Freudian theory stresses past events in early childhood; social-learning theories focus on past reinforcements and present contingencies; humanistic theories emphasize present reality or future goals; and cognitive and self theories emphasize past and present (and the future if goal setting is involved).

4. *Consciousness versus unconsciousness.* Freudian theory emphasizes unconscious processes; humanistic, social-learning, and cognitive theories emphasize conscious processes. Trait theories pay little attention to this distinction; self theories are unclear on this score.

5. *Inner disposition versus outer situation.* Social-learning theories emphasize situational factors; traits play up dispositional factors; and the others allow for an interaction between person-based and situation-based variables.

Each type of theory makes different contributions to the understanding of human personality. Trait theories provide a catalog that describes parts and structures. Psychodynamic theories add a powerful engine and the fuel to get the vehicle moving. Humanistic theories put a person in the driver's seat. Social-learning theories supply the steering wheel, directional signals, and other regulation equipment. Cognitive theories add reminders that the way the trip is planned, organized, and remembered will be affected by the mental map the driver chooses for the journey. Finally, self theories remind the driver to consider the image his or her driving ability is projecting to backseat drivers and pedestrians.

To complete our discussion of personality, we now consider personality assessment. We will describe some of the ways in which psychologists obtain information about the range of personality attributes that make each individual unique.

PUT YOURSELF TO THE TEST

- How do personality theories differ along the dimension of heredity versus environment?

- How do personality theories differ along the dimension of learning processes versus innate laws of behavior?

- How do personality theories differ with respect to their emphasis on past, present, or future?

- How do personality theories differ with respect to their emphasis on conscious versus unconscious processes?

- How do personality theories differ with respect to the dispositional versus situational causes of behavior?

Assessing Personality

Think of all the ways in which you differ from your best friend. Psychologists wonder about the diverse attributes that characterize an individual, set one person apart from others, or distinguish people in one group from those in another (for example, shy people from outgoing or depressed individuals from happy). Two assumptions are basic to these attempts to understand and describe human personality: first, that there are personal characteristics of individuals that give coherence to their behavior and, second, that those characteristics can be assessed or measured. Personality tests must also meet the standards of reliability and validity (see Chapter 9). Personality tests that pursue these goals can be classified as being either *objective* or *projective*.

◆ OBJECTIVE TESTS

Objective tests of personality are those in which scoring and administration are relatively simple and follow well-defined rules. Some objective tests are scored, and even interpreted, by computer programs. The final score is usually a single number, scaled along a single dimension (such as *adjustment* versus *maladjustment*), or a set of scores on different traits (such as impulsiveness, dependency, or extraversion) reported in comparison with the scores of a normative sample.

A *self-report inventory* is an objective test in which individuals answer a series of questions about their thoughts, feelings, and actions. One of the first self-report inventories, the *Woodworth Personal Data Sheet* (written in 1917) asked questions such as "Are you often frightened in the middle of the night?" (see DuBois, 1970). Today, a person taking a **personality inventory** reads a series of statements and indicates whether each one is true or typical for himself or herself.

The most frequently used personality inventory is the *Minnesota Multiphasic Personality Inventory,* or MMPI (Dahlstrom et al., 1975). It is used in many clinical settings to aid in the diagnosis of patients and to guide their treatment. After reviewing its features and applications, we will briefly discuss the *NEO Personality Inventory* (NEO-PI), which is used widely with nonpatient populations.

THE MMPI

The MMPI was developed at the University of Minnesota during the 1930s by psychologist Starke Hathaway and psychiatrist J. R. McKinley (Hathaway & McKinley, 1940, 1943). Its basic purpose is to diagnose individuals according to a set of psychiatric labels. The first test consisted of 550 items, which individuals determined to be either true or false for themselves or to which they responded, "Cannot say." From that item pool, scales were developed that were relevant to the kinds of problems patients showed in psychiatric settings.

The MMPI scales were unlike other existing personality tests because they were developed using an *empirical* strategy rather than the intuitive, theoretical approach that dominated at the time. Items were included on a scale only if they clearly distinguished between two groups—for example, schizophrenic patients and a normal comparison group. Each item had to demonstrate its validity by being answered similarly by members within each group but differently between the two groups. Thus, the items were not selected on a theoretical basis (what the content seemed to mean to experts) but on an empirical basis (did they distinguish between the two groups?).

The MMPI has 10 *clinical scales,* each constructed to differentiate a special clinical group (such as individuals with schizophrenia) from a normal comparison group. The test also includes *validity scales* that detect suspicious response patterns, such as blatant dishonesty, carelessness, defensiveness, or evasiveness. When an MMPI is interpreted, the tester first checks the validity scales to be sure the test is valid and then looks at the rest of the scores. The pattern of the scores—which are highest, how they differ—forms the "MMPI profile." Individual profiles are compared with those common for particular groups, such as felons and gamblers.

In the mid-1980s, the MMPI underwent a major revision, and it is now called the *MMPI-2* (Butcher et al., 1989; Butcher & Williams, 1992; Greene, 1991). The MMPI-2 has updated language and content to better reflect contemporary concerns, and new populations provided data for norms. The MMPI-2 also adds 15 new *content scales* that were derived using, in part, a theoretical method. For each of 15 clinically relevant topics (such as anxiety or family problems), items were selected on two bases: if they seemed theoretically related to the topic area and if they statistically formed a *homogeneous scale,* meaning that each scale measures a single, unified concept. The clinical and content scales of the MMPI-2 are given in **Table 13.7** and **Table 13.8.** You'll notice that most of the clinical scales measure several related concepts and that the names of the content scales are simple and self-explanatory.

The benefits of the MMPI-2 include its ease and economy of administration and its usefulness for the diagnosis of psychopathology (Butcher & Rouse, 1996). In addition, the item pool can be used for many purposes. For example, you could build a creativity scale by finding creative and noncreative groups of individuals and determining the MMPI items that they answered differently. Over the years, psychologists have developed and validated hundreds of special-purpose scales in this way. For researchers, one of the most attractive characteristics of the MMPI is the enormous archives of MMPI profiles collected over 50 years. Because all of these people have been tested on the same items in a standardized way, they can be compared either on the traditional clinical scales or on special-purpose scales (like our new "creativity" scale). These MMPI archives allow researchers to test hypotheses on MMPIs taken by people many years earlier, perhaps long before the construct being measured was even conceived.

However, the MMPI-2 is not without its critics. Its clinical scales have been criticized, for example, because they are heterogeneous—they measure several patterns at once rather than focusing on a specific clinical group. Researchers have also suggested that the changes from the original MMPI to the revised MMPI-2 were insufficient to recognize advances in personality theory; the test remains close to its empirical origins (Helmes & Reddon, 1993). Clinicians have also been concerned whether the MMPI-2 is equally valid for all racial and ethnic groups (Arbisi et al., 2002). As with any assessment device, researchers must carefully evaluate the reliability and validity of each particular use of the MMPI and MMPI-2 (Greene et al., 1997).

The MMPI was designed to assess individuals with clinical problems. In the next section, we'll describe devices more suited to assess personality in the general, nonpatient population.

◆

TABLE 13.7
MMPI-2 Clinical Scales

Hypochondriasis (Hs): Abnormal concern with bodily functions

Depression (D): Pessimism; hopelessness; slowing of action and thought

Conversion hysteria (Hy): Unconscious use of mental problems to avoid conflicts or responsibility

Psychopathic deviate (Pd): Disregard for social custom; shallow emotions; inability to profit from experience

Masculinity–femininity (Mf): Differences between men and women

Paranoia (Pa): Suspiciousness; delusions of grandeur or persecution

Psychasthenia (Pt): Obsessions; compulsions; fears; guilt; indecisiveness

Schizophrenia (Sc): Bizarre, unusual thoughts or behavior; withdrawal; hallucinations; delusions

Hypomania (Ma): Emotional excitement; flight of ideas; overactivity

Social introversion (Si): Shyness; disinterest in others; insecurity

THE NEO-PI

The NEO Personality Inventory (NEO-PI) was designed to assess personality characteristics in nonclinical adult populations. It measures the five-factor model of personality we discussed earlier. If you took the NEO-PI, you would receive a profile sheet that showed your standardized scores relative to a large normative sample on each of the five major dimensions: Neuroticism, Extraversion, Openness, Agreeableness, and Conscientiousness (Costa & McCrae, 1985). A revised version of the NEO-PI assesses 30 separate traits organized within the five major factors (Costa & McCrae, 1992b). For example, the Neuroticism dimension is broken down into six facet scales: Anxiety, Angry hostility, Depression, Self-consciousness, Impulsiveness, and Vulnerability. Much research has demonstrated that the NEO-PI dimensions are homogeneous, highly reliable, and show good criterion and construct validity (Costa &

◆

TABLE 13.8
MMPI-2 Content Scales

Anxiety	Antisocial practices
Fears	Type A (workaholic)
Obsessiveness	Low self-esteem
Depression	Social discomfort
Health concerns	Family problems
Bizarre mentation (thoughts)	Work interference
Anger and cynicism	Negative treatment indicators (negative attitudes about doctors and treatment)

McCrae, 1992a; Furnham et al., 1997). The NEO-PI is being used to study personality stability and change across the life span as well as the relationship of personality characteristics to physical health and various life events, such as career success or early retirement.

A new inventory based on the five-factor model, the *Big Five Questionnaire (BFQ),* was designed to have validity across different cultures. The scale was developed in Italy, but it shows similar psychometric characteristics for U.S. and Spanish populations, and appropriate norms are being established for French, German, Czech, Hungarian, and Polish translations (Barbaranelli et al., 1997; Caprara et al., 1993). Although the BFQ correlates highly with the NEO-PI, it differs in important ways. Factor 1 is labeled Energy or Activity rather than Extraversion (to reduce overlap with the social aspects of Agreeableness). The BFQ includes a scale to see if test takers' responses are biased toward socially desirable responses. It is simpler than the NEO-PI in having only two facets for each of the five factors. For example, Energy is composed of the facets of Dynamism and Dominance. The first is intrapersonal; the second is interpersonal. As psychology becomes more global in its concerns, such assessment instruments that work equally well across language and national boundaries are essential for conducting meaningful cross-cultural research in personality and social psychology.

◆ PROJECTIVE TESTS

Have you ever looked at a cloud and seen a face or the shape of an animal? If you asked your friends to look, too, they may have seen a reclining nude or a dragon. Psychologists rely on a similar phenomenon in their use of projective tests for personality assessment.

As we just saw, objective tests take one of two forms: Either they provide test takers with a series of statements and ask them to give a simple response (such as "true," "false," or "cannot say") or they ask test takers to rate themselves with respect to some dimension (such as "anxious" versus "nonanxious"). Thus, the respondent is constrained to choose one of the predetermined responses. *Projective tests,* by contrast, have no predetermined range of responses. In a **projective test,** a person is given a series of stimuli that are purposely ambiguous, such as abstract patterns, incomplete pictures, or drawings that can be interpreted in many ways. The person may be asked to describe the patterns, finish the pictures, or tell stories about the drawings. Projective tests were first used by psychoanalysts, who hoped that such tests would reveal their patients' unconscious personality dynamics. Because the stimuli are ambiguous, responses to them are determined partly by what the person brings to the situation—namely, inner feelings, personal motives, and conflicts from prior life experiences. These personal, idiosyncratic

aspects, which are *projected* onto the stimuli, permit the personality assessor to make various interpretations.

Projective tests are among the assessment devices most commonly used by psychological practitioners (Butcher & Rouse, 1996; Lubin et al., 1984; Piotrowski et al., 1985). They have also been used more often outside the United States, such as in the Netherlands, Hong Kong, and Japan, than objective tests like the MMPI (Piotrowski et al., 1993). Objective tests often fail to be adequately translated or adequately standardized for non-U.S. populations. Projective tests are less sensitive to language variation. However, because projective tests are so widespread, critics have often worried that they are used in ways that are not valid. As we examine two of the most common projective tests, the Rorschach test and the Thematic Apperception Test, we will discuss those issues of validity.

THE RORSCHACH

In the Rorschach test, developed by Swiss psychiatrist **Hermann Rorschach** in 1921, the ambiguous stimuli are symmetrical inkblots (Rorschach, 1942). Some are black and white and some are colored (see **Figure 13.7**). During the test, a respondent is shown an inkblot and asked, "What might this be?" Respondents are assured that there are no right or wrong answers (Exner, 1974). Testers record verbatim what people say, how much time they take to respond, the total time they take per inkblot, and the way they handle the inkblot card. Then, in a second phase called an *inquiry,* the respondent is reminded of the previous responses and asked to elaborate on them.

The responses are scored on three major features: (1) the *location,* or part of the card mentioned in the response—whether the respondent refers to the whole stimulus or to part of it and the size of the details mentioned; (2) the *content* of the response—the nature of the object and activities seen; and (3) the *determinants*—

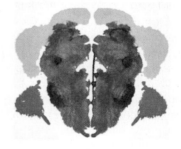

◆

FIGURE 13.7

An Inkblot Similar to Those Used in the Rorschach Test

What do you see? Does your interpretation of this inkblot reveal anything about your personality?

<www.ablongman.com/gerrig17e>

which aspects of the card (such as its color or shading) prompted the response. Scorers may also note whether responses are original and unique or popular and conforming.

You might think that ambiguous inkblots would give rise to an uninterpretable diversity of responses. In fact, researchers have devised a comprehensive scoring system for Rorschach responses that allows for meaningful comparisons among different test takers (Exner, 2003; Exner & Weiner, 1994). This scoring system specifies, for example, common categories of content response like *whole human* (the response mentions or implies a whole human form) and *blood* (the response mentions blood, either human or animal). Patterns of responses have been successfully related to normal personality characteristics as well as to psychopathology. Even so, some controversy remains about the validity of the scoring system and the Rorschach test (Exner, 2003; Garb et al., 2001).

THE TAT

In the Thematic Apperception Test (TAT), developed by **Henry Murray** in 1938, respondents are shown pictures of ambiguous scenes and asked to generate stories about them, describing what the people in the scenes are doing and thinking, what led up to each event, and how each situation will end (see **Figure 13.8**). The person administering the TAT evaluates the structure and content of the stories as well as the behavior of the individual telling them, in an attempt to discover some of the respondent's major concerns, motivations, and personality characteristics. For example, an examiner might evaluate a person as conscientious if his or her stories concerned people who lived up to their obligations and if the stories were told in a serious, orderly way. Recall from Chapter 11 that the TAT has often been used to reveal individual differences in dominant needs, such as needs for power, affiliation, and achievement (McClelland, 1961). Over several decades of research, the TAT has proven to be a valid measure of the need for achievement (Spangler, 1992).

Let us offer some concluding remarks on the subject of personality assessment. Did you see the relationship between these personality assessment devices and the theories of personality we reviewed earlier? The conclusion we reached was that each of the types of theories illuminated best different aspects of human experience. We can reach much the same conclusions for personality tests: Each has the potential to provide unique insights into an individual's personality. Clinicians most often use a combination of tests when they carry out a personality assessment. Under many circumstances, the profiles that arise from objective, even computer-based analyses may allow accurate predictions to be made for specific outcomes. Under other circumstances, clinical expertise and skilled intuition must supplement objec-

tive norms. In practice, the best predictions are made when the strengths of each approach are combined.

To close the chapter, we want you to consider a series of questions in light of what you have just learned: If psychologists studied you, what portrait of your personality would they draw? What early experiences might they identify as contributing to how you now act and think? What conditions in your current life exert strong influences on your thoughts and behaviors? What makes you different from other individuals who are functioning in many of the same situations as you? You now can see that each type of personality theory provides a framework against which you can begin to form your answers to these questions. Suppose the time has really come to paint your psychological portrait. Where would you begin?

PUT YOURSELF TO THE TEST

- What are the defining features of objective personality tests?
- How were the MMPI and the MMPI-2 developed and for what purposes?
- What are the functions of the NEO-PI and the BFQ?
- What theoretical ideas gave rise to projective personality tests?
- What are the functions of the Rorschach and the TAT?

◆Recapping Main Points

TYPE AND TRAIT PERSONALITY THEORIES

- Some theorists categorize people by all-or-none types, assumed to be related to particular characteristic behaviors.

- Other theorists view traits—attributes along continuous dimensions—as the building blocks of personality.

- The five-factor model is a personality system that maps out the relationships among common trait words, theoretical concepts, and personality scales.

- Twin and adoption studies reveal that personality traits are partially inherited.

- People display behavioral consistency when situations are defined with respect to relevant psychological features.

PSYCHODYNAMIC THEORIES

- Freud's psychodynamic theory emphasizes instinctive biological energies as sources of human motivation.

- Basic concepts of Freudian theory include psychic energy as powering and directing behavior, early experiences as key determinants of lifelong personality, psychic determinism, and powerful unconscious processes.

- Personality structure consists of the id, the superego, and the reconciling ego.

- Unacceptable impulses are repressed and ego defense mechanisms are developed to lessen anxiety and bolster self-esteem.

- Post-Freudians like Adler, Horney, and Jung put greater emphasis on ego functioning and social variables and less on sexual urges. They saw personality development as a lifelong process.

HUMANISTIC THEORIES

- Humanistic theories focus on self-actualization—the growth potential of the individual.

- These theories are holistic, dispositional, and phenomenological.

- Contemporary theories in the humanist tradition focus on individuals' life stories.

SOCIAL-LEARNING AND COGNITIVE THEORIES

- Social-learning theorists focus on understanding individual differences in behavior and personality as a consequence of different histories of reinforcement.

- Cognitive theorists emphasize individual differences in perception and subjective interpretation of the environment.

- Walter Mischel explored the origins of behaviors as interactions of persons and situations.

- Albert Bandura described the reciprocal determinism among people, environments, and behaviors.

- Nancy Cantor's theory emphasized the impact of goals, knowledge, and strategies on people's behavior.

SELF THEORIES

- Self theories focus on the importance of the self-concept for a full understanding of human personality.

- The self-concept is a dynamic mental structure that motivates, interprets, organizes, mediates, and regulates personal and interpersonal behaviors and processes.

- People engage in behaviors such as self-handicapping to maintain self-esteem.

- Cross-cultural research suggests that individualistic cultures give rise to independent construals of self, whereas collectivist cultures give rise to interdependent construals of self.

COMPARING PERSONALITY THEORIES

- Personality theories can be contrasted with respect to the emphasis they put on heredity versus environment; learning processes versus innate laws of behavior; the past, present, or future; consciousness versus unconsciousness; and inner dispositions versus outer situations.

- Each theory makes different contributions to the understanding of human personality.

ASSESSING PERSONALITY

- Personality characteristics are assessed by both objective and projective tests.
- The most common objective test, the MMPI-2, is used to diagnose clinical problems.
- The NEO-PI and BFQ are newer objective personality tests that measure five major dimensions of personality.
- Projective tests of personality ask people to respond to ambiguous stimuli.
- Two important projective tests are the Rorschach test and the TAT.

KEY TERMS

analytic psychology (p. 450)

anxiety (p. 448)

archetype (p. 450)

collective unconscious (p. 450)

consistency paradox (p. 442)

ego (p. 447)

ego defense mechanisms (p. 448)

five-factor model (p. 440)

fixation (p. 447)

id (p. 447)

independent construals of self (p. 460)

libido (p. 446)

personality (p. 435)

personality inventory (p. 464)

personality types (p. 436)

possible selves (p. 458)

projective test (p. 466)

psychic determinism (p. 447)

psychobiography (p. 452)

psychodynamic personality theories (p. 444)

reciprocal determinism (p. 455)

repression (p. 448)

self-actualization (p. 451)

self-concept (p. 458)

self-efficacy (p. 456)

self-esteem (p. 459)

self-handicapping (p. 459)

shyness (p. 444)

social intelligence (p. 457)

superego (p. 447)

traits (p. 437)

unconditional positive regard (p. 451)

unconscious (p. 447)

Psychological Disorders

Consider these words, written by a 30-year-old woman who was receiving treatment for schizophrenia: "I want to let you know what it is like to be a functional [schizophrenic] in these days and times and what someone with my mental illness faces. . . . I live pretty normal and no one can tell [I'm] mentally ill unless I tell them. . . . The delusions before I got my medicine picked any storyline it chose, and changed it at will. As time went by before help, I felt it was taking over my whole brain, and I'd cry wanting my mind and life back." What are your reactions as you read this young woman's words, an excerpt from a letter to your authors?

If your reactions are similar to ours, you feel a mixture of sadness at her plight, of delight in her willingness to do all she can to cope with the many problems her mental illness creates, of anger toward those who stigmatize her because she may act differently at times, and of hope that, with medication and therapy, her condition may improve. These are but a few of the emotions that clinical and research psychologists and psychiatrists feel as they try to understand and treat mental disorders.

This chapter focuses on the nature and causes of psychological disorders: what they are, why they develop, and how we can explain their causes. The next chapter builds on this knowledge to describe the strategies used to treat, and to prevent, mental illness. Research indicates that nearly 50 percent of young and middle-aged adults in the United States have suffered from a psychological disorder at some point in their lives (Kessler et al., 1994). Thus, many of you who read this text are likely to benefit directly from knowledge about psychopathology. Facts alone, however, will not convey the serious impact psychological disorders have on the everyday lives of individuals and families. Throughout this chapter, as we discuss categories of psychological disorders, try to envision the real people who live with such a disorder every day. We will share with you their words and lives, as we did at the start of the chapter. Let's begin now with a discussion of the concept of abnormality.

The Nature of Psychological Disorders

Have you ever worried excessively? Felt depressed or anxious without really knowing why? Been fearful of something you rationally knew could not harm you? Had thoughts about suicide? Used alcohol or drugs to escape a problem? Almost everyone will answer yes to at least one of these questions, which means that almost everyone has experienced the symptoms of a psychological disorder. This chapter looks at the range of psychological functioning that is considered unhealthy or abnormal, often referred to as *psychopathology* or *psychological disorder*. **Psychopathological functioning** involves disruptions in emotional, behavioral, or thought processes that lead to personal distress or that block one's ability to achieve important goals. The field of **abnormal psychology** is the area of psychological investigation most directly concerned with understanding the nature of individual pathologies of mind, mood, and behavior.

We begin this section by exploring a more precise definition of abnormality and then look at problems of objectivity. We then examine how this definition evolved over hundreds of years of human history.

What do you imagine the lives of people with mental illnesses are like?

◆ DECIDING WHAT IS ABNORMAL

What does it mean to say someone is *abnormal* or *suffering from a psychological disorder?* How do psychologists and other clinical practitioners decide what is abnormal? Is it always clear when behavior moves from the normal to the abnormal category? The judgment that someone has a mental disorder is typically based on the evaluation of the individual's *behavioral* functioning by people with some special authority or power. The terms used to describe these phenomena—*mental disorder, mental illness,* or *abnormality*—depend on the particular perspective, training, and cultural background of the evaluator, the situation, and the status of the person being judged.

Let's consider seven criteria you might use to label behavior as "abnormal" (*DSM-IV-TR,* 2000; Rosenhan & Seligman, 1989):

1. *Distress or disability.* An individual experiences personal distress or disabled functioning, which produces a risk of physical or psychological deterioration or loss of freedom of action. For example, a man who cannot leave his home without weeping would be unable to pursue ordinary life goals.

2. *Maladaptiveness.* An individual acts in ways that hinder goals, do not contribute to personal well-being, or interfere strongly with the goals of others and the needs of society. Someone who is drinking so heavily that she cannot hold down a job or who is endangering others through her intoxication is displaying maladaptive behavior.

3. *Irrationality.* An individual acts or talks in ways that are irrational or incomprehensible to others. A man who responds to voices that do not exist in objective reality is behaving irrationally.

4. *Unpredictability.* An individual behaves unpredictably or erratically from situation to situation, as if experiencing a loss of control. A child who smashes his fist through a window for no apparent reason displays unpredictability.

5. *Unconventionality and statistical rarity.* An individual behaves in ways that are statistically rare and that violate social standards of what is acceptable or desirable. Just being statistically unusual, however, does not lead to a psychological judgment of abnormality. For example, possessing genius-level intelligence is extremely rare, but it is also considered desirable. On the other hand, having extremely low intelligence is also rare but is considered undesirable; thus, it has often been labeled abnormal.

6. *Observer discomfort.* An individual creates discomfort in others by making them feel threatened or distressed in some way. A woman walking down the middle of the sidewalk, having a loud conversation with herself, creates observer discomfort in other pedestrians trying to avoid her.

7. *Violation of moral and ideal standards.* An individual violates expectations for how one ought to behave with respect to societal norms. By this criterion, people might be considered abnormal by some if they did not wish to work or they did not believe in God. This criterion for abnormality also becomes relevant in legal situations, a topic we address in the Psychology in Your Life box on page 480.

Can you see why most of these indicators of abnormality may not be immediately apparent to all observers? Consider just the last criterion. Are you mentally ill if you don't wish to work, even if that is abnormal with respect to the norms of society? Or consider a more serious symptom. It is "bad" to have hallucinations in our culture because they are taken as signs of mental disturbance, but it is "good" in cultures in which hallucinations are interpreted as mystical visions from spirit forces. Whose judgment is correct? At the end of this chapter, we will consider some negative consequences and dangers associated with such socially regulated judgments and the decisions based on them.

We are more confident in labeling behavior as "abnormal" when more than just one of the indicators is present and valid. The more extreme and prevalent the indicators are, the more confident we can be that they point to an abnormal condition. None of these criteria is a *necessary* condition shared by all cases of abnormality. For example, during his murder trial, a Stanford University graduate student who had killed his math professor with a hammer, and then taped to his office door a note that read "No office hours today,"

reported feeling neither guilt nor remorse. Despite the absence of personal suffering, we would not hesitate to label his overall behavior as abnormal. It is also true that no single criterion, by itself, is a *sufficient* condition that distinguishes all cases of abnormal behavior from normal variations in behavior. The distinction between normal and abnormal is not so much a difference between two independent types of behaviors as it is a matter of the degree to which a person's actions resemble a set of agreed-upon criteria of abnormality. Mental disorder is best thought of as a *continuum* that varies between *mental health* and *mental illness,* as shown in **Figure 14.1.**

How comfortable do you feel with these ideas about abnormality? Although the criteria seem fairly clear-cut, psychologists still worry about the problem of objectivity.

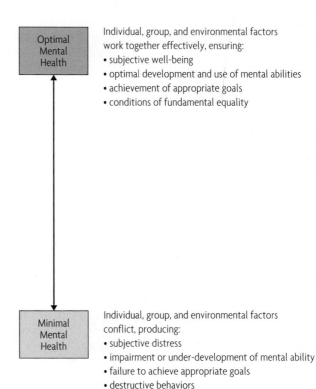

FIGURE 14.1

Mental Health Continuum

Because the distinction between normal *and* abnormal *is relative, rather than absolute, it is useful to think of mental health as a continuum. At one end are behaviors that define optimal mental health; at the other end are behaviors that define minimal mental health. In between lie gradual increases in maladaptive behaviors.*

◆ THE PROBLEM OF OBJECTIVITY

The decision to declare someone psychologically disordered or abnormal is always a *judgment* about behavior: The goal for many researchers is to make these judgments *objectively,* without any type of bias. For some psychological disorders, like depression or schizophrenia, diagnosis often easily meets the standards of objectivity. Other cases are more problematic. As we have seen throughout our study of psychology, the meaning of behavior is jointly determined by its *content* and by its *context.* The same act in different settings conveys very different meanings. A man kisses another man; it may signify a gay relationship in the United States, a ritual greeting in France, or a Mafia "kiss of death" in Sicily. The meaning of a behavior always depends on context.

Let's see why objectivity is such an important issue. History is full of examples of situations in which judgments of abnormality were made by individuals to preserve their moral or political power. Consider an 1851 report, entitled "The Diseases and Physical Peculiarities of the Negro Race," published in a medical journal. Its author, Dr. Samuel Cartwright, had been appointed by the Louisiana Medical Association to chair a committee to investigate the "strange" practices of African American slaves. "Incontrovertible scientific evidence" was amassed to justify the practice of slavery. Several "diseases" previously unknown to the white race were discovered. One finding was that blacks allegedly suffered from a sensory disease that made them insensitive "to pain when being punished" (thus, no need to spare the whip). The committee also invented the disease *drapetomania,* a mania to seek freedom—a mental disorder that caused certain slaves to run away from their masters. Runaway slaves needed to be caught so that their illness could be properly treated (Chorover, 1981)!

Once an individual has obtained an "abnormal" label, people are inclined to interpret later behavior to confirm that judgment. **David Rosenhan** (1973, 1975) and his colleagues demonstrated that it may be impossible to be judged "sane" in an "insane place."

CLASSIC
PUTTING IDEAS TO THE TEST

Being Sane in an "Insane" Place

Rosenhan and seven other sane people gained admission to different psychiatric hospitals by pretending to have a single symptom: hallucinations. All eight of these *pseudopatients* were diagnosed on admission as either paranoid schizophrenic or manic-depressive. Once admitted, they behaved normally in every way. Rosenhan observed, however, that when a sane person is in an insane place, he or she is likely to be judged insane, and any behavior is likely to be reinterpreted to fit the context. If the pseudopatients discussed their situation in a rational way with the staff, they were reported to be using "intellectualization" defenses, while their taking notes of their observations were evidence of "writing behavior." The pseudopatients remained on the wards for almost three weeks, on the average, and not one was identified by the staff as sane. When they were finally released—only with the help of spouses or colleagues—their discharge diagnosis was still "schizophrenia" but "in remission." That is, their symptoms were no longer active.

Rosenhan's research demonstrates how judgments of abnormality rely on factors beyond behavior itself.

In the view of psychiatrist **Thomas Szasz,** mental illness does not even exist—it is a "myth" (1961, 1977, 1995). Szasz argues that the symptoms used as evidence of mental illness are merely medical labels that sanction professional intervention into what are social problems—deviant people violating social norms. Once labeled, these people can be treated either benignly or harshly for their problem "of being different," with no threat of disturbing the existing status quo.

Few clinicians would go this far, in large part because the focus of much research and treatment is on understanding and alleviating personal distress. For most of the disorders we will describe in this chapter, individuals experience their own behavior as abnormal, or poorly adapted to the environment. Even so, this discussion suggests that there can be no altogether objective assessments of abnormality. As we describe each type of psychological disorder, you should try to understand why clinicians believe the cluster of symptoms represents behavior patterns that are more serious for the individual than mere violations of social norms.

To help round out your perspective on the context of psychological disorders, we will now fill in some of the history of the concept of abnormality and the treatment of abnormal behavior. We will then turn to the general causal factors researchers look to as the forces that give rise to abnormality.

◆ HISTORICAL PERSPECTIVES

Throughout history, humans have feared psychological disorders, often associating them with evil. Because of this fear, people have reacted aggressively and decisively to any behaviors they perceived as bizarre or abnormal. People who have exhibited such behaviors have been imprisoned and made subject to radical med-

<www.ablongman.com/gerrig17e>

ical treatments. Attitudes about the link between mental illness and evil may be as old as human history. Archaeologists have found prehistoric skulls with holes drilled in them. These discoveries might indicate that our ancestors believed such holes would allow the demons that had possessed a loved one to escape.

The following 10th-century invocation was intended to alleviate *hysteria,* an affliction characterized by a cluster of symptoms that included paralysis or pains, dizziness, lameness, and blindness. Hysteria was originally thought to affect only women, and it was believed to be caused by a wandering uterus under the devil's control (Veith, 1965). Notice how the invocation illustrates the role demonic forces were believed to play in psychological disorders.

> *O womb, womb, womb, cylindrical womb, red womb, white womb, fleshy womb, bleeding womb, large womb, neufredic womb, bloated womb, O demoniacal one! . . . I conjure thee, O womb, in the name of the Holy Trinity to come back to the place from which thou shouldst neither move nor turn away . . . and to return, without anger, to the place where the Lord has put thee originally. (Zilboorg & Henry, 1941, quoted in Nietzel et al., 1991, p. 19)*

In 1692, in the Massachusetts colony of Salem, numerous young women began experiencing convulsions, nausea, and weakness. They reported sensations of being pinched, pricked, or bitten. Many became temporarily blind or deaf; others reported visions and sensations of flying through the air. Such strange symptoms sparked a frantic search for an explanation. Many people theorized that the symptoms were the work of the devil, who, through the efforts of earthbound witches, had taken over the minds and bodies of the young women. These theories led to a witchcraft panic and to the execution of over 20 women believed to be witches.

Until the end of the 18th century, the mentally ill in Western societies were perceived as mindless beasts who could be controlled only with chains and physical discipline. They were not cared for in hospitals but were incarcerated with criminals. Let's see how that perspective began to change.

EMERGENCE OF THE MEDICAL MODEL

In the latter part of the 18th century, a new perspective about the origins of abnormal behavior emerged—people began to perceive those with psychological problems as *sick,* suffering from illness, rather than as *possessed* or *immoral.* As a result, a number of reforms were gradually implemented in the facilities for the

The Salem witchcraft trials were an outgrowth of a desperate attempt to affix blame for frighteningly bizarre behavior among the Puritan colonists. What general attitudes were common toward the mentally ill in those times?

insane. **Philippe Pinel** (1745–1826) was one of the first clinicians to use these ideas to attempt to develop a classification system for psychological difficulties based on the idea that disorders of thought, mood, and behavior are similar in many ways to the physical, organic illnesses. According to such a system, each disorder has a group of characteristic symptoms that distinguishes it from other disorders and from healthy functioning. Disorders are classified according to the patterns of observed symptoms, the circumstances surrounding the onset of the disturbance, the natural course of the disorder, and its response to treatment. Such classification systems are modeled after the biological classification systems naturalists use and are intended to help clinicians identify common disorders more easily.

In 1896, **Emil Kraepelin** (1855–1926), a German psychiatrist, was responsible for creating the first truly comprehensive *classification system* of psychological disorders. Strongly motivated by a belief that there was a physical basis to psychological problems, he gave the process of psychological diagnosis and classification the flavor of medical diagnosis, a flavor that remains today (Rosenhan & Seligman, 1989). His perspective is most readily seen in the terminology used by psychiatrists. They speak of *mental illness,* and *treat* mental *patients* in the hope of *curing* their *diseased* brains.

EMERGENCE OF PSYCHOLOGICAL MODELS

An alternative perspective to the medical approach focuses on the psychological causes and treatment of abnormal behavior. This perspective emerged most

In this engraving, circa 1780, Franz Mesmer entrances a salon full of fashionable ladies and gentlemen. In what form did "mesmerism" eventually become a useful technique in the treatment of some psychological disorders?

◆ THE ETIOLOGY OF PSYCHOPATHOLOGY

Etiology refers to the factors that cause or contribute to the development of psychological and medical problems. Knowing why the disorder occurs, what its origins are, and how it affects thought and emotional and behavioral processes may lead to new ways of treating and, ideally, preventing it. An analysis of causality will be an important part of our discussion of each individual disorder. Here we introduce two general categories of causal factors: biological and psychological.

BIOLOGICAL APPROACHES

Building on the heritage of the medical model, modern biological approaches assume that psychological disturbances are directly attributable to underlying biological factors. Biological researchers and clinicians most often investigate structural abnormalities in the brain, biochemical processes, and genetic influences.

The brain is a complex organ whose interrelated elements are held in delicate balance. Subtle alterations in its chemical messengers—the neurotransmitters—or in its tissue can have significant effects. Genetic factors, brain injury, and infection are a few of the causes of these alterations. We have seen in earlier chapters that technological advances in brain imaging techniques allow mental health professionals to view the structure of the brain and specific biochemical processes in living individuals without surgery. Using these techniques, biologically oriented researchers are discovering new links between psychological disorders and specific abnormalities in the brain. In addition, continuing advances in the field of behavioral genetics have improved researchers' abilities to identify the links between specific genes and the presence of psychological disorders. We will look to these different types of biological explanations throughout the chapter as we try to understand the nature of various forms of abnormality.

PSYCHOLOGICAL APPROACHES

Psychological approaches focus on the causal role of psychological or social factors in the development of psychopathology. These approaches perceive personal experiences, traumas, conflicts, and environmental factors as the roots of psychological disorders. We will outline four dominant psychological models of abnormality: the psychodynamic, the behavioral, the cognitive, and the sociocultural.

Psychodynamic. Like the biological approach, the psychodynamic model holds that the causes of psychopathology are located inside the person. However,

clearly at the end of the 18th century. It was helped along by the dramatic work of **Franz Mesmer** (1734–1815). Mesmer believed that many disorders, including hysteria, were caused by disruptions in the flow of a mysterious force that he called *animal magnetism*. He unveiled several new techniques to study animal magnetism, including one that eventually became known as *hypnotism* but was originally referred to as *mesmerism* in his honor (Darnton, 1968; Pattie, 1994).

Although Mesmer's general theory of animal magnetism was discredited, his hypnotic techniques were adopted by many researchers, including a prominent French neurologist, **Jean Charcot** (1825–1893). Charcot found that some of the symptoms of hysteria, such as paralysis of a limb, could be eliminated when a patient was under hypnosis. Hypnosis even had the power to *induce*—bring out—the symptoms of hysteria in healthy individuals, dramatically illustrating the potential of *psychological factors* to cause problems that were believed to have an exclusively physical basis.

One of Charcot's students, Sigmund Freud, continued to experiment with hypnosis. Freud used his experiments to elaborate his psychodynamic theories of personality and abnormality, which continue to influence current theories of the nature and causes of psychopathology. (He later abandoned hypnotherapy for psychoanalysis as the treatment for psychological disorders.)

Modern perspectives on abnormality most often combine aspects of both medical and psychological models of mental illness. We next consider those general types of explanations for the origins or causes of abnormality.

according to **Sigmund Freud,** who developed this model, the internal causal factors are psychological rather than biological. As we noted in earlier chapters, Freud believed that many psychological disorders were simply an extension of "normal" processes of psychic conflict and ego defense that all people experience. In the psychodynamic model, early childhood experiences shape both normal and abnormal behavior.

In psychodynamic theory, behavior is motivated by drives and wishes of which people are often unaware. Symptoms of psychopathology have their roots in *unconscious conflict* and thoughts. If the unconscious is conflicted and tension-filled, a person will be plagued by anxiety and other disorders. Much of this psychic conflict arises from struggles between the irrational, pleasure-seeking impulses of the *id* and the internalized social constraints imposed by the *superego.* The *ego* is normally the arbiter of this struggle; however, its ability to perform its function can be weakened by abnormal development in childhood. Individuals attempt to avoid the pain caused by conflicting motives and anxiety with *defense mechanisms,* such as repression or denial. Defenses can become overused, distorting reality or leading to self-defeating behaviors. The individual may then expend so much psychic energy in defenses against anxiety and conflict that there is little energy left to provide a productive and satisfying life.

Behavioral. Because of their emphasis on observable responses, behavioral theorists have little use for hypothetical psychodynamic processes. These theorists argue that abnormal behaviors are acquired in the same fashion as healthy behaviors—through learning and reinforcement. They do not focus on internal psychological phenomena or early childhood experiences. Instead, they focus on the *current* behavior and the *current* conditions or reinforcements that sustain the behavior. The symptoms of psychological disorders arise because an individual has learned self-defeating or ineffective ways of behaving. By discovering the environmental contingencies that maintain any undesirable, abnormal behavior, an investigator or clinician can then recommend treatment to change those contingencies and extinguish the unwanted behavior. Behaviorists rely on both classical and operant conditioning models (recall Chapter 6) to understand the processes that can result in maladaptive behavior.

Cognitive. Cognitive perspectives on psychopathology are often used to supplement behavioral views. The cognitive perspective suggests that the origins of psychological disorders cannot always be found in the objective reality of stimulus environments, reinforcers, and overt responses. What matters as well is the way people perceive or think about themselves and about their relations with other people and the environment.

Among the cognitive variables that can guide—or misguide—adaptive responses are a person's perceived degree of control over important reinforcers, a person's beliefs in his or her ability to cope with threatening events, and interpretations of events in terms of situational or personal factors. The cognitive approach suggests that psychological problems are the result of distortions in perceptions of the reality of a situation, faulty reasoning, or poor problem solving.

Sociocultural. The sociocultural perspective on psychopathology emphasizes the role culture plays in both the diagnosis and etiology of abnormal behavior. We already gave you a taste of the impact of culture on diagnosis when we described the problem of objectivity. We suggested that behaviors are interpreted in different ways in different cultures: the threshold at which a certain type of behavior will cause an individual problems in adjustment will depend, in part, on how that behavior is viewed in its cultural context. With respect to etiology, the particular cultural circumstances in which people live may define an environment that helps bring about distinctive types or subtypes of psychopathology. We will give you examples of such *culture-bound syndromes* in the next section on classification.

We have now given you a general sense of the types of explanations researchers give for the emergence of mental illness. It is worth noting that contemporary researchers increasingly take an *interactionist* perspective on psychopathology, seeing it as the product of a complex interaction between a number of biological and psychological factors. For example, genetic predispositions may make a person vulnerable to a psychological disorder by affecting neurotransmitter levels or hormone levels, but psychological or social stresses or certain learned behaviors may be required for the disorder to develop fully.

In the next section, we describe the efforts that have been made to classify and describe different categories of disorder.

PUT YOURSELF TO THE TEST

➤ What criteria have been used to define abnormality?
➤ Why is it not always possible to be "objective" about diagnoses of mental illness?
➤ What are some historical origins of contemporary models of mental illness?
➤ What types of biological and psychological factors contribute to the etiology of psychopathology?

Classifying Psychological Disorders

Why is it helpful to have a classification system for psychological disorders? What advantages are gained by moving beyond a global assessment that abnormality exists to distinguish among different types of abnormalities? A **psychological diagnosis** is the label given to an abnormality by classifying and categorizing the observed behavior pattern into an approved diagnostic system. Such a diagnosis is in many ways more difficult to make than a medical diagnosis. In the medical context, a doctor can rely on physical evidence, such as X rays, blood tests, and biopsies, to inform a diagnostic decision. In the case of psychological disorders, the evidence for diagnosis comes from interpretations of a person's actions. In order to create greater consistency among clinicians and coherence in their diagnostic evaluations, psychologists have helped to develop a system of diagnosis and classification that provides precise descriptions of symptoms, as well as other criteria to help practitioners decide whether a person's behavior is evidence of a particular disorder.

◆ GOALS OF CLASSIFICATION

To be most useful, a diagnostic system should provide the following three benefits:

- *Common shorthand language.* To facilitate a quick and clear understanding among clinicians or researchers working in the field of psychopathology, practitioners seek a common set of terms with agreed-upon meanings. A diagnostic category, such as *depression,* summarizes a large and complex collection of information, including characteristic symptoms and the typical course of the disorder. In clinical settings, such as clinics and hospitals, a diagnostic system allows mental health professionals to communicate more effectively about the people they are helping. Researchers studying different aspects of psychopathology or evaluating treatment programs must agree on the disorder they are observing.

- *Understanding of etiology.* Ideally, a diagnosis of a specific disorder should make clear the causes of the symptoms. Unfortunately, because there is substantial disagreement or lack of knowledge about the etiology of many psychological disorders, this goal is difficult to meet.

- *Treatment plan.* A diagnosis should also suggest what types of treatments to consider for particular disorders. Researchers and clinicians have found that certain treatments or therapies work most effectively for specific kinds of psychological disorders. For example, drugs that are quite effective in treating schizophrenia do not help and may even hurt people with depression. Further advances in knowledge about the effectiveness and specificity of treatments will make fast and reliable diagnosis even more important.

◆ DSM-IV-TR

In the United States, the most widely accepted classification scheme is one developed by the American Psychiatric Association. It is called the *Diagnostic and Statistical Manual of Mental Disorders.* The most recent version, published in 2000 as a revision of the fourth edition, is known by clinicians and researchers as **DSM-IV-TR.** It classifies, defines, and describes over 200 mental disorders.

To reduce the diagnostic difficulties caused by variability in approaches to psychological disorders, *DSM-IV-TR* emphasizes the *description* of patterns of symptoms and courses of disorders rather than etiological theories or treatment strategies. The purely descriptive terms allow clinicians and researchers to use a common language to describe problems, while leaving room for disagreement and continued research about which theoretical models best *explain* the problems.

The first version of *DSM,* which appeared in 1952 *(DSM-I),* listed several dozen mental illnesses. *DSM-II,* introduced in 1968, revised the diagnostic system to make it more compatible with another popular system, the World Health Organization's *International Classification of Diseases (ICD).* The fourth edition of the *DSM (DSM-IV,* 1994) emerged after several years of intense work by committees of scholars. To make their changes (from the *DSM-III-Revised,* which appeared in 1987), these committees carefully scrutinized large bodies of research on psychopathology and also tested proposed changes for workability in actual clinical settings. *DSM-IV* is also fully compatible with the tenth edition of the *ICD. DSM-IV-TR* (2000) incorporated a review of the research literature that had accumulated since *DSM-IV.* Because the changes largely affected the supporting text, rather than the system of classification, the revision was termed a "text revision" which yielded the name *DSM-IV-TR.*

To encourage clinicians to consider the psychological, social, and physical factors that may be associated with a psychological disorder, *DSM-IV-TR* uses dimensions, or *axes,* that portray information about all these factors (see **Table 14.1**). Most of the principal clinical

TABLE 14.1

The Five Axes of *DSM-IV-TR*

Axis	Classes of Information	Description
Axis I	Clinical disorders	These mental disorders present symptoms or patterns of behavioral or psychological problems that typically are painful or impair an area of functioning. Included are disorders that emerge in infancy, childhood, or adolescence.
Axis II	(a) Personality disorders (b) Mental retardation	These are dysfunctional patterns of perceiving and responding to the world.
Axis III	General medical conditions	This axis codes physical problems relevant to understanding or treating an individual's psychological disorders on Axes I and II.
Axis IV	Psychosocial and environmental problems	This axis codes psychosocial and environmental stressors that may affect the diagnosis and treatment of an individual's disorder and the likelihood of recovery.
Axis V	Global assessment of functioning	This axis codes the individual's overall level of current functioning in the psychological, social, and occupational domains.

disorders are contained on Axis I. Included here are all disorders that emerge in childhood, except for mental retardation. Axis II lists mental retardation as well as personality disorders. These problems may accompany Axis I disorders. Axis III incorporates information about general medical conditions, such as diabetes, that may be relevant to understanding or treating an Axis I or II disorder. Axes IV and V provide supplemental information that can be useful when planning an individual's treatment or assessing the *prognosis* (predictions of future change). Axis IV assesses psychosocial and environmental problems that may explain patients' stress responses or their resources for coping with stress. On Axis V, a clinician evaluates the global level of an individual's functioning. A full diagnosis in the *DSM-IV-TR* system would involve consideration of each of the axes.

EVOLUTION OF DIAGNOSTIC CATEGORIES

The diagnostic categories and the methods used to organize and present them have shifted with each revision of the *DSM*. These shifts reflect changes in the opinions of a majority of mental health experts about exactly what constitutes a psychological disorder and where the lines between different types of disorders should be drawn. They also reflect changing perspectives among the public about what constitutes *abnormality*.

In the revision process of each *DSM*, some diagnostic categories were dropped and others were added. For example, with the introduction of *DSM-III*, in 1980, the traditional distinction between *neurotic* and *psychotic* disorders was eliminated. **Neurotic disorders,** or *neuroses,* were originally conceived of as relatively common psychological problems in which a person did not have signs of brain abnormalities, did not display grossly irrational thinking, and did not violate basic norms; but he or she did experience subjective distress or a pattern of self-defeating or inadequate coping strategies. **Psychotic disorders,** or *psychoses,* were thought to differ in both quality and severity from neurotic problems. It was believed that psychotic behavior deviated significantly from social norms and was accompanied by a profound disturbance in rational thinking and general emotional and thought processes. The *DSM-III* advisory committees felt that the terms neurotic disorders and psychotic disorders had become too general in their meaning to have much usefulness as diagnostic categories (however, they continue to be used by many psychiatrists and psychologists to characterize the general level of disturbance in a person).

Across the editions of the *DSM,* individual diagnoses have also come and gone. One of the best examples is *homosexuality.* You may recall from Chapter 11 that it was in 1973 that the American Psychiatric Association voted to remove homosexuality from the list of psychological disorders. Until that time, homosexuality appeared in the *DSM* as a bona fide mental illness. What changed the opinions of psychiatric experts was research data demonstrating the generally positive mental health of gay men and lesbians. Homosexuality is now simply considered a variant of sexual expression. It is relevant to a diagnosis in *DSM-IV-TR* only if an individual shows "persistent and marked distress about sexual orientation" (*DSM-IV-TR,* 2000, p. 582). That diagnostic criterion could, of course, apply equally well to distressed heterosexuals.

O n March 30, 1981, the world was shocked when John Hinckley was nearly successful in his attempt to assassinate U.S. president Ronald Reagan. In June 1982, shock turned to outrage when a jury found Hinckley "not guilty by virtue of insanity." Was this outrage appropriate? What does it mean for someone to be *insane*?

Insanity is not defined in *DSM-IV-TR*; there is no accepted clinical definition of insanity. Rather, insanity is a concept that belongs to popular culture and to the legal system. The treatment of insanity in the law dates back to England in 1843, when Daniel M'Naghten was found not guilty of murder by reason of insanity. M'Naghten's intended victim was the British prime minister—M'Naghten believed that God had instructed him to commit the murder. (He accidentally killed the prime minister's secretary instead.) Because of M'Naghten's delusions, he was sent to a mental hospital rather than to prison. The anger surrounding this verdict—even Queen Victoria was infuriated—prompted the House of Lords to articulate a guideline, known as the *M'Naghten rule,* to limit claims of insanity. This rule specifies that a criminal must not "know the nature and quality of the act he was doing; or, if he did know it, that he did not know he was doing what was wrong."

Does the M'Naghten rule seem like a fair test of guilt or innocence? With advances in the understanding of mental illness, researchers became more aware of circumstances in which a criminal might know right from wrong—a criminal might understand that what he or she was doing

Is "Insanity" Really a Defense?

Sara Owen
University of Vermont

was illegal or immoral—but still might not be able to suppress the actions. (We will address this type of dissociation in the discussion of anxiety disorders on page 482.) Often, for example, people with phobias "know" that a spider can do them no harm, but they are unable to suppress panic behaviors in the presence of the spider. This perspective on mental illness was incorporated into the legal standard that was operative at Hinckley's trial. His jury agreed that Hinckley's behavior—arising from his obsession with the actress Jodie Foster—was beyond his control.

Did Hinckley go free? Not at all. He was committed to St. Elizabeth's, a psychiatric hospital in the Washington area—and, as of 2003, remains there. In fact, one of the public's main misconceptions of the insanity defense is that it allows murderers to go free (Borum & Fullero, 1999; Silver et al., 1994). Perhaps 90 percent of the individuals acquitted on

insanity pleas spend time in psychiatric care after they are found not guilty. In cases like Hinckley's, the individual is released into the community only when he or she is judged by experts no longer to be dangerous—there is often no upper limit placed on psychiatric incarceration as there would be for prison incarceration. In Hinckley's case, how certain do you think a panel of psychiatrists and psychologists would have to feel before they would agree that Hinckley could go free?

In the aftermath of Hinckley's case, many jurisdictions altered their standards for the insanity defense—the general trend was to make it more difficult to obtain a verdict of "not guilty by reason of insanity" (Appelbaum, 1994). Were these changes necessary? On practical grounds, the answer is almost certainly "no." Despite the great attention that insanity pleas receive in the media—and, thus, the public's great awareness of them—such pleas are quite rare (Kirschner & Galperin, 2001). For example, one study found that in 60,432 indictments in Baltimore, Maryland, only 190 defendants (0.31 percent) entered insanity pleas; of the 190 pleas, only 8 (4.2 percent) were successful (Janofsky et al., 1996). Thus, the likelihood that you will ever be asked to sit on a jury and judge another person as sane or insane is quite low. But suppose it did happen. Suppose, for example, you had been on the jury that considered whether Andrea Yates, a woman from Texas who systematically drowned her five young children, was sane. (The jury rejected the insanity defense.) How might the information you have acquired in this chapter have affected your judgment?

Finally, critics of earlier editions of the *DSM* had been greatly concerned that no attention was paid to cultural variation in the incidence of psychological disorders. In *DSM-IV-TR,* the description of most disorders includes information about "specific culture features." Furthermore, an appendix describes about 25 *culture-bound syndromes:* "recurrent, locality-specific patterns of aberrant behavior and troubling experience that may or may not be linked to a particular *DSM-IV* diagnostic category" (*DSM-IV-TR,* 2000, p. 898). Here are some examples:

- *Boufée delirante.* "A sudden outburst of agitated and aggressive behavior, marked confusion, and psychomotor excitement" (p. 899); reported in West Africa and Haiti.
- *Koro.* "An episode of sudden and intense anxiety that the penis (or, in females, the vulva and nipples) will recede into the body and possibly cause death" (p. 900); reported in south and east Asia.
- *Taijin kyofusho.* "An individual's intense fear that his or her body, its parts or its functions, displease, embarrass, or are offensive to other people in appearance, odor, facial expressions, or movements" (p. 903); reported in Japan.

As we describe each major form of psychological disorder, it is important to bear in mind that not all cultures treat the same behaviors as normal or abnormal.

PUT YOURSELF TO THE TEST

- What are three important goals for classifying psychological disorders?
- How has the *DSM* evolved over time to the current *DSM-IV-TR?*
- What role do the fives axes of *DSM-IV-TR* play in diagnosis?
- How does *DSM-IV-TR* address cultural variation in psychological disorders?

Major Types of Psychological Disorders

Now that we have given you a basic framework for thinking about abnormality, we get to the core information that you will want to know—the causes and consequences of major psychological disorders, such as anxiety, depression, and schizophrenia. For each category, we will begin by describing what sufferers experience and how they appear to observers. Then we will consider how each of the major biological and psychological approaches to etiology explains the development of these disorders.

There are many other categories of psychopathology that we will not have time to examine. However, what follows is a capsule summary of some of the most important we must omit:

- *Substance-use disorders* include both dependence on and abuse of alcohol and drugs. We discussed many issues of substance abuse in the broader context of states of consciousness (see Chapter 5).
- *Somatoform disorders* involve physical (soma) symptoms, such as paralysis or pains in a limb, that arise without a physical cause. This category includes the symptoms of what used to be called hysteria.
- *Sexual disorders* involve problems with sexual inhibition or dysfunction and deviant sexual practices.
- *Eating disorders,* such as anorexia and bulimia, were discussed in Chapter 11.

Throughout this chapter, we will provide estimates of the frequency with which individuals experience particular psychological disorders. These estimates arise from research projects in which mental health histories are obtained from large samples of the population, up to 20,000 people. Figures are available for the prevalence of different disorders over one-month, one-year, and lifetime periods (Kessler et al., 1994; Regier et al., 1993a, 1993b). The figures we will generally cite come from the *National Comorbidity Study (NCS),* which sampled 8,098 U.S. adults ages 15 to 54 years (Kessler et al., 1994). Although we will refer to this sample as "adults," it is important to note that the study included some teenagers and excluded older adults. It is also important to emphasize that often the same individuals have experienced more than one disorder simultaneously at some point in their life span, a phenomenon known as **comorbidity.** (*Morbidity* refers to the occurrence of disease. *Comorbidity* refers to the co-occurrence of diseases.) The NCS found that 56 percent of the people who had experienced one disorder had actually experienced two or more. Researchers have begun to study intensively the patterns of comorbidity of different psychological disorders.

As you read about the symptoms and experiences that are typical of the various psychological disturbances, you may begin to feel that some of the characteristics seem to apply to you—at least part of the time—or to someone you know. Some of the disorders that we will consider are not uncommon, so it would be surprising if they sounded completely alien. Many people have human frailties that appear on the list of criteria for a particular psychological disorder. Recognition of this familiarity can further your understanding of abnormal psychology, but you should remember that a diagnosis for any disorder depends on a number of criteria and requires the judgment of a trained mental health professional. Please resist the temptation to use this new knowledge to diagnose friends and family members as pathological. However, if the chapter leaves you uneasy about mental health issues, please note that most colleges and universities have counseling centers for students with such concerns.

We will explore anxiety and depression in depth and more briefly consider personality disorders and dissociative disorders. We then devote a section to schizophrenia.

◆ ANXIETY DISORDERS: TYPES

Everyone experiences anxiety or fear in certain life situations. For some people, however, anxiety becomes problematic enough to interfere with their ability to function effectively or enjoy everyday life. It has been estimated that almost 25 percent of the adult population has, at some time, experienced symptoms characteristic of the various **anxiety disorders** (Kessler et al., 1994). While anxiety plays a key role in each of these disorders, they differ in the extent to which anxiety is experienced, the severity of the anxiety, and the situations that trigger the anxiety. We will review five major categories: generalized anxiety disorder, panic disorder, phobic disorder, obsessive-compulsive disorder, and posttraumatic stress disorder.

GENERALIZED ANXIETY DISORDER

When a person feels anxious or worried most of the time for at least six months, when not threatened by any specific danger, clinicians diagnose **generalized anxiety disorder.** The anxiety is often focused on specific life circumstances, such as unrealistic concerns about finances or the well-being of a loved one. The way the anxiety is expressed—the specific symptoms—varies from person to person, but for a diagnosis of generalized anxiety disorder to be made, the patient must also suffer from at least three other symptoms, such as muscle tension, fatigue, restlessness, poor concentration, irritability, or sleep difficulties.

Generalized anxiety disorder leads to impaired functioning because the person's worries cannot be controlled or put aside. With the focus of attention on the sources of anxiety, the individual cannot attend sufficiently to social or job obligations. These difficulties are compounded by the physical symptoms associated with the disorder.

PANIC DISORDER

In contrast to the chronic presence of anxiety in generalized anxiety disorder, sufferers of **panic disorder** experience unexpected, severe *panic attacks* that may last only minutes. These attacks begin with a feeling of intense apprehension, fear, or terror. Accompanying these feelings are physical symptoms of anxiety, including autonomic hyperactivity (such as rapid heart rate), dizziness, faintness, or sensations of choking or smothering. The attacks are unexpected in the sense that they are not brought about by something concrete in the situation. A panic disorder is diagnosed when an individual has recurrent unexpected panic attacks and also begins to have persistent concerns about the possibility of having more attacks.

In *DSM-IV-TR,* panic disorder must be diagnosed as occurring with or without the simultaneous presence of agoraphobia. **Agoraphobia** is an extreme fear of being in public places or open spaces from which escape may be difficult or embarrassing. Individuals with agoraphobia usually fear such places as crowded rooms, malls, buses, and freeways. They are often afraid that, if they experience some kind of difficulty outside the home, such as a loss of bladder control or panic attack symptoms, help might not be available or the situation will be embarrassing to them. These fears deprive individuals of their freedom, and, in extreme cases, they become prisoners in their own homes.

Can you see why agoraphobia is related to panic disorder? For some (but not all) people who suffer from panic attacks, the dread of the next attack—the helpless feelings it engenders—can be enough to imprison them. The person suffering from agoraphobia may leave the safety of home but almost always with extreme anxiety.

Why might a situation like this one cause difficulty for a person with agoraphobia?

Fear is a rational reaction to an objectively identified external danger (such as a fire in one's home or a mugging attack) that may induce a person to flee or to attack in self-defense. In contrast, a person with a **phobia** suffers from a persistent and irrational fear of a specific object, activity, or situation that is excessive and unreasonable given the reality of the threat.

Many people feel uneasy about spiders or snakes (or even multiple-choice tests). These mild fears do not prevent people from carrying out their everyday activities. Phobias, however, interfere with adjustment, cause significant distress, and inhibit necessary action toward goals. Even a very specific, apparently limited phobia can have a great impact on one's whole life. *DSM-IV-TR* defines two categories of phobias: *social phobias* and *specific phobias* (see **Table 14.2**).

Social phobia is a persistent, irrational fear that arises in anticipation of a public situation in which an individual can be observed by others. A person with a social phobia fears that he or she will act in ways that could be embarrassing. The person recognizes that the fear is excessive and unreasonable yet feels compelled by the fear to avoid situations in which public scrutiny is possible. Social phobia often involves a self-fulfilling prophecy. A person may be so fearful of the scrutiny and rejection of others that enough anxiety is created to actually impair performance. Even when social phobics are successful in social circumstances, they do not allow that success to reflect positively on themselves (Wallace & Alden, 1997). Among U.S. adults, 13.3 percent have experienced a social phobia (Magee et al., 1996).

Specific phobias occur in response to several different types of objects or situations. As shown in Table 14.2, specific phobias are further categorized into several sub-

What turns a harmless garter snake into a threatening object of phobia?

TABLE 14.2
Common Phobias

Social phobias (fear of being observed doing something humiliating)

Specific phobias

Animal type
  Cats (ailurophobia)
  Dogs (cynophobia)
  Insects (insectophobia)
  Spiders (arachnophobia)
  Snakes (ophidiophobia)
  Rodents (rodentophobia)

Natural environment type
  Storms (brontophobia)
  Heights (acrophobia)

Blood–injection–injury type
  Blood (hemaphobia)
  Needles (belonephobia)

Situational type
  Closed spaces (claustrophobia)
  Railways (siderodromophobia)

---

types. For example, an individual suffering from an *animal-type specific phobia* might have a phobic response to spiders. In each case, the phobic response is produced either in the presence of or in anticipation of the feared specific object or situation. Research suggests that 11.3 percent of adults in the United States have experienced a specific phobia (Magee et al., 1996).

OBSESSIVE-COMPULSIVE DISORDERS

Some people with anxiety disorders get locked into specific patterns of thought and behavior.

> *Only a year or so ago, 17-year-old Jim seemed to be a normal adolescent with many talents and interests. Then, almost overnight, he was transformed into a lonely outsider, excluded from social life by his psychological disabilities. Specifically, he developed an obsession with washing. Haunted by the notion that he was dirty—in spite of what his senses told him—he began to spend more of his time cleansing himself of imaginary dirt. At first, his ritual washings were confined to weekends and evenings, but soon they began to consume all his time, forcing him to drop out of school. (Rapoport, 1989)*

Jim is suffering from a condition known as **obsessive-compulsive disorder (OCD),** which has been estimated to affect 2.5 percent of U.S. adults at some point during their lives (*DSM-IV-TR,* 2000). *Obsessions* are thoughts, images, or impulses (such as Jim's belief that he is unclean) that recur or persist despite a person's efforts to suppress them. Obsessions are experienced as an unwanted invasion of consciousness, they seem to be senseless or repugnant, and they are unacceptable to the person experiencing them. You probably have had some sort of mild obsessional experience, such as the intrusion of petty worries—"Did I really lock the door?"; or "Did I turn off the oven?" The obsessive thoughts of people with obsessive-compulsive disorder are much more compelling, cause much more distress, and may interfere with their social or occupational functioning.

Compulsions are repetitive, purposeful *acts* (such as Jim's washing) performed according to certain rules or in a ritualized manner in response to an obsession. Compulsive behavior is performed to reduce or prevent the discomfort associated with some dreaded situation, but it is either unreasonable or clearly excessive. Typical compulsions include irresistible urges to clean, to check that lights or appliances have been turned off, and to count objects or possessions.

At least initially, people with obsessive-compulsive disorder resist carrying out their compulsions. When they are calm, they view their compulsion as senseless. When anxiety rises, however, the power of the ritual compulsive behavior to relieve tension seems irresistible. Part of the pain experienced by people with this mental problem is created by their frustration at recognizing the irrationality or excessive nature of their obsessions without being able to eliminate them.

POSTTRAUMATIC STRESS DISORDER

In Chapter 12, we presented a discussion between two women who were still grappling with the aftereffects of rape. The conversation portrayed the two women's ongoing anxiety. One reported going through a "long period of fear and anger" and having dreams of being assaulted in front of her dorm, with friends watching without coming to her rescue. The other, who had been raped while jogging, was still afraid to resume running: "Every time I go jogging I have a perpetual fear. My pulse doubles. Of course I don't go jogging alone any more, but still the fear is there constantly." These women suffer from **posttraumatic stress disorder (PTSD),** an anxiety disorder that is characterized by the persistent reexperience of traumatic events through distressing recollections, dreams, hallucinations, or flashbacks. Individuals may develop PTSD in response to rape, life-threatening events or severe injury, and natural disasters. People develop PTSD both when they themselves have been the victim of the trauma and when they have witnessed others being victimized.

People who suffer from PTSD are also likely to suffer simultaneously from other psychopathologies, such as major depression, substance-abuse problems, and sexual dysfunction (Kilpatrick et al., 2003).

Research suggests that about 8 percent of adults in the United States will experience PTSD at some point during their lifetime (*DSM-IV-TR,* 2000). Overall, about three-quarters of the general population have experienced an event that could be defined as traumatic, such as a serious accident, a natural disaster, or physical abuse (Green, 1994). In one sample of college students, 84 percent reported that they had experienced at least one traumatic event; roughly one-third reported four or more separate events (Vrana & Lauterbach, 1994). Although men and women experience about the same rate of traumatic events, women are twice as likely to develop PTSD (Breslau et al., 1997). By comparison to men, childhood traumas are particularly likely to give rise to PTSD in women. Researchers are still trying to understand this gender difference.

Posttraumatic stress disorder severely disrupts sufferers' lives. How do researchers go about the complex task of exploring the origins of PTSD and other anxiety disorders? Understanding the origins gives hope to eliminating the psychological distress.

◆ ANXIETY DISORDERS: CAUSES

How do psychologists explain the development of anxiety disorders? Each of the four etiological approaches we have outlined (biological, psychodynamic, behavioral, and cognitive) emphasizes different factors. Let's analyze how each adds something unique to the understanding of anxiety disorders.

BIOLOGICAL

Various investigators have suggested that anxiety disorders have biological origins. One theory attempts to explain why certain phobias, such as those for spiders or heights, are more common than fears of other dangers, such as electricity. Because many fears are shared across cultures, it has been proposed that, at one time in the evolutionary past, certain fears enhanced our ancestors' chances of survival. Perhaps humans are born with a predisposition to fear whatever is related to sources of serious danger in the evolutionary past. This *preparedness hypothesis* suggests that we carry around an evolutionary tendency to respond quickly and "thoughtlessly" to once-feared stimuli (Öhman & Mineka, 2001; Seligman, 1971). However, this hypothesis does not explain types of phobias that develop in response to objects or situations that would not have had survival meaning over evolutionary history, like fear of needles or driving or elevators.

<www.ablongman.com/gerrig17e>

The ability of certain drugs to relieve and of others to produce symptoms of anxiety offers evidence of a biological role in anxiety disorders (Nutt & Malizia, 2001). For example, recall from Chapter 3 that when the level of the neurotransmitter GABA in the brain becomes low, people often experience feelings of anxiety. As we shall see in Chapter 15, drugs that affect GABA levels are used as successful treatments for some types of anxiety disorders.

Researchers are also using imaging techniques to examine the brain bases of these disorders. Consider a study of posttraumatic stress disorder.

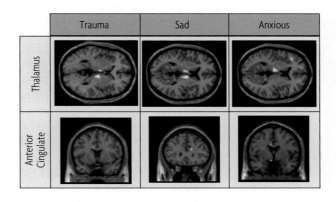

PUTTING IDEAS TO THE TEST

PTSD and Brain Activity

Some people who suffer traumatic events develop PTSD whereas others do not. A team of researchers used fMRI scans to explore differences in patterns of brain activity for individuals in those two categories (Lanius et al., 2003). The study focused on the brain activity that arose when the individuals recalled memories of sad, anxious, and traumatic events. As shown in **Figure 14.2**, those individuals who had experienced a trauma but not developed PTSD showed more activity in areas of the brain (the thalamus and the anterior cingulate) that play a role in emotional processing compared to individuals whose traumatic experiences led to PTSD. These differences in brain activity applied for all three types of memories (i.e., sad, anxious, and traumatic). The generality of the finding suggests that the traumatic experiences for the individuals who developed PTSD led to a broad disruption of the way in which their brains respond to emotional events.

This study illustrates why brain imaging techniques can help deepen the understanding of the biological bases of anxiety disorders. Similar results have emerged for other disorders. For example, PET scans have revealed a difference in the function of GABA receptors between the brains of individuals who suffer from panic disorder and those of control individuals (Malizia et al., 1998). These differences may help explain the onset of panic disorder. MRI techniques have revealed very widespread abnormalities in OCD patients' brains with respect to a much lower volume of myelinated nerve fibers than in normal brains (Jenike et al., 1996). Researchers are trying to understand the relationship between these brain abnormalities and the symptoms of OCD.

Finally, family and twin studies suggest that there is a genetic basis for the predisposition to experience anxiety disorders (Hettema et al., 2001). For example, the

FIGURE 14.2

Brain Activity and Emotional Memories

The study compared individuals who developed PTSD in response to traumatic experiences with those who did not. Members from each group recalled emotional memories while undergoing fMRI scans. The figure shows more brain activity for the group of individuals without PTSD across memories of traumatic, sad, and angry events.

probability that a pair of identical twins both suffered from a panic disorder was twice as great as the probability that both fraternal twins were sufferers (Skre et al., 1993). Still, it's important to remember that nature and nurture always interact. For example, recall from Chapter 13 that many aspects of personality are heritable. Research suggests that part of the influence of genes on PTSD arises because people with different personality traits make life choices that decrease or increase the probability that they will experience traumas (Stein et al., 2002).

PSYCHODYNAMIC

The psychodynamic model begins with the assumption that the symptoms of anxiety disorders come from underlying psychic conflicts or fears. The symptoms are attempts to protect the individual from psychological pain. Thus, panic attacks are the result of unconscious conflicts bursting into consciousness. Suppose, for example, a child represses conflicting thoughts about his or her wish to escape a difficult home environment. In later life, a phobia may be activated by an object or situation that symbolizes the conflict. A bridge, for example, might come to symbolize the path that the person must traverse from the world of home and family to the outside world. The sight of a bridge would then force the unconscious conflict into awareness, bringing with it the fear and anxiety common to phobias. Avoiding bridges would be a symbolic attempt to stay clear of anxiety about the childhood experiences at home.

In obsessive-compulsive disorders, the obsessive behavior is seen as an attempt to displace anxiety created by a related but far more feared desire or conflict. By substituting an obsession that symbolically captures the forbidden impulse, a person gains some relief. For example, the obsessive fears of dirt experienced by Jim, the adolescent we described earlier, may have their roots in the conflict between his desire to become sexually active and his fear of "dirtying" his reputation. Compulsive preoccupation with carrying out a minor ritualistic task also allows the individual to avoid the original issue that is creating unconscious conflict.

BEHAVIORAL

Behavioral explanations of anxiety focus on the way symptoms of anxiety disorders are reinforced or conditioned. Investigators do not search for underlying unconscious conflicts or early childhood experiences, because these phenomena can't be observed directly. As we saw in Chapter 6, behavioral theories are often used to explain the development of phobias, which are seen as classically conditioned fears: Recall Little Albert, in whom John Watson and Rosalie Rayner instilled a fear of a white rat (see page 179). The behavioral account suggests that a previously neutral object or situation becomes a stimulus for a phobia by being paired with a frightening experience. For example, a child whose mother yells a warning when he or she approaches a snake may develop a phobia about snakes. After this experience, even thinking about snakes may produce a wave of fear. Phobias continue to be maintained by the reduction in anxiety that occurs when a person withdraws from the feared situation.

A behavioral analysis of obsessive-compulsive disorders suggests that compulsive behaviors tend to reduce the anxiety associated with obsessive thoughts—thus reinforcing the compulsive behavior. For example, if a woman fears contamination by touching garbage, then washing her hands reduces the anxiety and is therefore reinforcing. In parallel to phobias, obsessive-compulsive disorders continue to be maintained by the reduction in anxiety that follows from the compulsive behaviors.

COGNITIVE

Cognitive perspectives on anxiety concentrate on the perceptual processes or attitudes that may distort a person's estimate of the danger that he or she is facing. A person may either overestimate the nature or reality of a threat or underestimate his or her ability to cope with the threat effectively. For example, before delivering a speech to a large group, a person with a social phobia may feed his or her anxiety:

What if I forget what I was going to say? I'll look foolish in front of all these people. Then I'll get even more nervous and start to perspire, and my voice will shake, and I'll look even sillier. Whenever people see me from now on, they'll remember me as the foolish person who tried to give a speech.

People who suffer from anxiety disorders may often interpret their own distress as a sign of impending disaster. Their reaction may set off a vicious cycle in which the person fears disaster, which leads to an increase in anxiety, which in turn worsens the anxiety sensations and confirms the person's fears (Beck & Emery, 1985).

Psychologists have tested this cognitive account by measuring *anxiety sensitivity:* individuals' beliefs that bodily symptoms—such as shortness of breath or heart palpitations—may have harmful consequences. People high in anxiety sensitivity are likely to agree with statements such as "When I notice that my heart is beating rapidly, I worry that I might have a heart attack." In one study, researchers assessed the anxiety sensitivity of a group of students who were about to undergo a stressful course of U.S. Air Force Academy basic cadet training. Approximately 20 percent of those students who measured above the 90th percentile on anxiety sensitivity experienced panic attacks during the five-week course, compared to 6 percent for the rest of the group (Schmidt et al., 1997). These data suggest that some individuals may experience panic attacks because they interpret their bodily arousal in a fearful fashion.

Research has also found that anxious patients contribute to the *maintenance* of their anxiety by employing cognitive biases that highlight the threatening stimuli. For example, one study examined people's ability to name either body-related words (e.g., *dizzy, fainting,* and *breathless*) versus control words (e.g., *delicate, slow,* and *friendly*) when they were presented on a computer screen for only 1/100th of a second. Individuals who suffered from panic disorder showed much greater ability to recognize the body-related words than did the healthy controls (Pauli et al., 1997). Similarly, patients whose symptoms of obsessive-compulsive disorder focused on issues of cleanliness watched a researcher touch a series of objects with a "clean and unused" tissue or a "dirty and already used" tissue. In a later memory test, these OCD patients showed greater ability to recall which objects were "dirty" than which were "clean" (Ceschi et al., 2003). Studies of this type confirm that people suffering from anxiety disorders focus their attention on aspects of the world that may help to sustain their anxiety.

Each of the major approaches to anxiety disorders may explain part of the etiological puzzle. Continued

<www.ablongman.com/gerrig17e>

research of each approach will clarify causes and, therefore, potential avenues for treatment. Now that you have this basic knowledge about anxiety disorders, we'd like you to consider the next of the three major categories of abnormality we are covering in some detail—*mood disorders*.

◆ MOOD DISORDERS: TYPES

There have almost certainly been times in your life when you would have described yourself as terribly depressed or incredibly happy. For some people, however, extremes in mood come to disrupt normal life experiences. A **mood disorder** is an emotional disturbance, such as severe depression or depression alternating with mania. Researchers estimate that roughly 19 percent of adults have suffered from mood disorders (Kessler et al., 1994). We will describe two major categories: major depressive disorder and bipolar disorder.

MAJOR DEPRESSIVE DISORDER

Depression has been characterized as the "common cold of psychopathology," both because it occurs so frequently and because almost everyone has experienced elements

What are some differences between the occasional feelings of unhappiness that most people feel and the symptoms of major depressive disorder?

of the full-scale disorder at some time in his or her life. Everyone has, at one time or another, experienced grief after the loss of a loved one or felt sad or upset when failing to achieve a desired goal. These sad feelings are only one symptom experienced by people suffering from a **major depressive disorder** (see **Table 14.3**). Consider one individual's description of his struggle to carry out normal daily tasks while in the depths of depression:

> *I can remember lying frozen in bed, crying because I was too frightened to take a shower and at the same time knowing that showers are not scary. I ran through the individual steps in my mind: You sit up, turn and put your feet on the floor, stand, walk to the bathroom, open the bathroom door, go to the edge of the tub. . . . Hoping that someone else could open the bathroom door, I would, with all the force in my body, sit up; turn and put my feet on the floor; stand; then feel so incapacitated and frightened that I would roll over and lie face down. (Solomon, 1998, pp. 48–49)*

Recall that we noted that disorders often occur simultaneously. Here, depression and anxiety are comorbid.

People diagnosed with depression differ in terms of the severity and duration of their symptoms. While many individuals struggle with clinical depression for only several weeks at one point in their lives, others experience depression episodically or chronically for many years. Estimates of the prevalence of mood

◆

TABLE 14.3
Characteristics of Major Depressive Disorder

Characteristics	Example
Dysphoric mood	Sad, blue, hopeless; loss of interest or pleasure in almost all usual activities.
Appetite	Poor appetite; significant weight loss
Sleep	Insomnia or hypersomnia (sleeping too much)
Motor activity	Markedly slowed down (motor retardation) or agitated
Guilt	Feelings of worthlessness; self-reproach
Concentration	Diminished ability to think or concentrate; forgetfulness
Suicide	Recurrent thoughts of death; suicidal ideas or attempts

disorders reveal that about 21 percent of females and 13 percent of males suffer a major depression at some time in their lives (Kessler et al., 1994).

Depression takes an enormous toll on those afflicted, on their families, and on society. A study undertaken on behalf of the World Health Organization estimated the loss of healthy life years that could be attributed to physical and mental illnesses (Murray & Lopez, 1996). In this analysis, major depressive disorder ranked second (behind heart disease) in terms of the burden it places on people's lives around the world. In the United States, depression accounts for the majority of all mental hospital admissions, but it is still believed to be underdiagnosed and undertreated. Fewer than half of those who suffer from major depressive disorder receive any professional help (Regier et al., 1993b).

BIPOLAR DISORDER

Bipolar disorder is characterized by periods of severe depression alternating with manic episodes. A person experiencing a **manic episode** generally acts and feels unusually elated and expansive. However, sometimes the individual's predominant mood is irritability rather than elation, especially if the person feels thwarted in some way. During a manic episode, a person often experiences an inflated sense of self-esteem or an unrealistic belief that he or she possesses special abilities or powers. The person may feel a dramatically decreased need to sleep and may engage excessively in work or in social or other pleasurable activities.

Caught up in a manic mood, the person shows unwarranted optimism, takes unnecessary risks, promises anything, and may give everything away. Consider this first-person account:

> *Manic depression is about buying a dozen bottles of Heinz ketchup and all eight bottles of Windex in stock at the Food Emporium on Broadway at 4:00 A.M., flying from Zurich to the Bahamas and back to Zurich in three days to balance the hot and cold weather, [and] carrying $20,000 in $100 bills in your shoes into the country on your way back from Tokyo. . . . It's about blips and burps of madness, moments of absolute delusion, bliss, and irrational and dangerous choices made in order to heighten pleasure and excitement and to ensure a sense of control. (Behrman, 2002)*

When the mania begins to diminish, people are left trying to deal with the damage and predicaments they created during their period of frenzy. Thus manic episodes almost always give way to periods of severe depression.

The duration and frequency of the mood disturbances in bipolar disorder vary from person to person. Some people experience long periods of normal functioning punctuated by occasional short manic or depressive episodes. A small percentage of unfortunate individuals go right from manic episodes to clinical depression and back again in continuous, unending cycles that are devastating to them, their families, their friends, and their coworkers. While manic, they may gamble away life savings or give lavish gifts to strangers, acts that later add to guilt feelings when they are in the depressed phase. Bipolar disorder is much rarer than major depressive disorder, occurring in about 1.6 percent of adults and distributed equally between males and females (Kessler et al., 1994).

◆ MOOD DISORDERS: CAUSES

What factors are involved in the development of mood disorders? We will address this question from the biological, psychodynamic, behavioral, and cognitive perspectives. Note that, because of its prevalence, major depressive disorder has been studied more extensively than bipolar disorder. Our review will reflect that distribution of research.

BIOLOGICAL

Several types of research provide clues to the contribution of biology to mood disorders. For example, the ability of different drugs to relieve manic and depressive symptoms provides evidence that different brain states underlie the two extremes of bipolar disorder. Reduced levels of two chemical messengers in the brain, serotonin and norepinephrine, have been linked to depression; increased levels of these neurotransmitters are associated with mania. However, the exact biochemical mechanisms of mood disorders have not yet been discovered (Nestler et al., 2002).

A dramatic example of a biological approach to understanding one type of psychological disorder comes from research on an unusual form of depression. Some people regularly become depressed during the winter months, especially in the long Scandinavian winters when daylight hours are short (see **Figure 14.3**). This disturbance in mood has been appropriately named *seasonal affective disorder,* or *SAD* (Rosenthal et al., 1984; Young et al., 1997). Researchers have devised a therapy that is quite effective at alleviating SAD: Patients are systematically exposed to bright white fluorescent light (Blehar & Rosenthal, 1989). Researchers have speculated that the light therapy may affect the activity of the neurotransmitter serotonin which, as we mentioned earlier, has been implicated as a causal factor in depression.

<www.ablongman.com/gerrig17e>

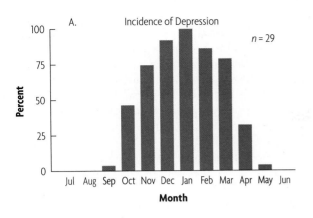

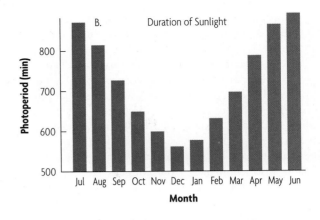

FIGURE 14.3

Seasonal Affective Disorder

People who suffer from seasonal affective disorder experience symptoms of depression during seasons with short sunlight. The figure displays a strong inverse relationship between the incidence of depression (part A) and the duration of sunlight (part B).

PUTTING IDEAS TO THE TEST

Serotonin and Seasonal Affective Disorder

Patients suffering from SAD received a course of light therapy—two hours of bright fluorescent light—each evening in their homes. Only patients for whom the light therapy brought about relief (12 out of 14 patients) participated in the second phase of the study, which tested the idea that light therapy affects brain serotonin levels. Patients in an experimental group were put on a diet that was intended to lower the level of brain serotonin; control patients consumed a diet intended to maintain serotonin levels. Patients in the experimental group experienced a relapse of SAD symptoms; control patients did not. This pattern suggests that light therapy was initially responsible for restoring serotonin to levels that allowed patients to experience relief from depression (Neumeister et al., 1997).

You might expect that people would have to take drugs to affect the actions of neurotransmitters in their brains. (We will describe some of these drugs in Chapter 15.) This study suggests, however, that light therapy can have the same effects as some psychoactive drugs. Both types of treatments—drug therapy or light therapy—support the role of a biological imbalance in the etiology of the disorder. Meanwhile, if you recognize yourself in the description of SAD, you should throw some light on the subject—you!

Researchers have also begun to use brain imaging techniques to understand the causes and consequences of mood disorders (Liotti et al., 2002; Strakowski et al., 2002). For example, researchers have used fMRI to demonstrate that the brains of people who suffer from bipolar disorder respond differently when they are in depressed versus manic states (Blumberg et al., 2003). **Figure 14.4** reports the data from 36 individuals with

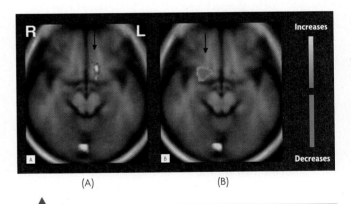

(A)   (B)

FIGURE 14.4

Brain Activity and Bipolar Disorder

Individuals with bipolar disorder underwent fMRI scans while performing a cognitive task. The brain response was different in an area known as caudal ventral prefrontal cortex (cVPFC) depending on whether the individuals were experiencing elevated, depressed, or balanced moods. As shown in A, individuals in depressed moods showed increased left cVPFC activity by comparison to those in balanced moods. As shown in B, individuals in elevated moods showed reduced right cVPFC activity by comparison to those in balanced moods.

bipolar disorder. At the time of the study, 11 were in elevated moods, 10 were in depressed moods, and 15 were in *euthymic* (or balanced) emotional states. All of the individuals performed the same cognitive task—naming the colors in which words were printed—while undergoing fMRI scans. Figure 14.4 indicates that particular regions of cortex were more active or less active depending on each individual's particular phase of bipolar disorder.

The contribution of biology to the etiology of mood disorders is also confirmed by evidence that the incidence of mood disorder is influenced by genetic factors (Johnson et al., 2002). Studies of twins show that when one identical twin is afflicted by a mood disorder, there is a 67 percent chance that the second twin will also have the disorder; the figure for fraternal twins, who do not share identical genetic material, is only 20 percent (Ciaranello & Ciaranello, 1991; Gershon et al., 1987). You will see in Psychology in the 21st Century that researchers have begun to make progress identifying the actual genes that have an impact on individuals' predispositions to experience mood disorders.

Let's see now what the three major psychological approaches can add to your understanding of the onset of mood disorders.

PSYCHODYNAMIC

In the psychodynamic approach, unconscious conflicts and hostile feelings that originate in early childhood are seen to play key roles in the development of depression. Freud was struck by the degree of self-criticism and guilt that depressed people displayed. He believed that the source of this self-reproach was anger, originally directed at someone else, that had been turned inward against the self. The anger was believed to be tied to an especially intense and dependent childhood relationship, such as a parent–child relationship, in which the person's needs or expectations were not met. Losses, real or symbolic, in adulthood reactivate hostile feelings, now directed toward the person's own ego, creating the self-reproach that is characteristic of depression.

BEHAVIORAL

Rather than searching for the roots of depression in the unconscious, the behavioral approach focuses on the effects of the amount of positive reinforcement and punishments a person receives (Lewinsohn, 1975; Lewinsohn et al., 1985). In this view, depressed feelings result when an individual receives insufficient positive reinforcements and experiences many punishments in the environment following a loss or other major life changes. Without sufficient positive reinforcement, a person begins to feel sad and withdraws. This state of sadness is initially reinforced by increased attention and sympathy from others (Biglan,

1991). Typically, however, friends who at first respond with support grow tired of the depressed person's negative moods and attitudes and begin to avoid him or her. This reaction eliminates another source of positive reinforcement, plunging the person further into depression. Research also shows that depressed people tend to underestimate positive feedback and overestimate negative feedback (Kennedy & Craighead, 1988; Nelson & Craighead, 1977).

COGNITIVE

At the center of the cognitive approach to depression are two theories. One theory suggests that negative *cognitive sets*—"set" patterns of perceiving the world—lead people to take a negative view of events in their lives for which they feel responsible. The second theory, the *explanatory style* model, proposes that depression arises from the belief that one has little or no personal control over significant life events. Each of these models explains some aspects of the experience of depression. Let's see how.

Aaron Beck (1983, 1985, 1988), a leading researcher on depression, has developed the theory of cognitive sets. Beck has argued that depressed people have three types of negative cognitions, which he calls the *cognitive triad* of depression: negative views of themselves, negative views of ongoing experiences, and negative views of the future. Depressed people tend to view themselves as inadequate or defective in some way, to interpret ongoing experiences in a negative way, and to believe that the future will continue to bring suffering and difficulties. This pattern of negative thinking clouds all experiences and produces the other characteristic signs of depression. An individual who always anticipates a negative outcome is not likely to be motivated to pursue any goal, leading to the *paralysis of will* that is prominent in depression.

In the explanatory style view, pioneered by **Martin Seligman** (see Chapter 11), individuals believe, correctly or not, that they cannot control future outcomes that are important to them. Seligman's theory evolved from research that demonstrated depressionlike symptoms in dogs (and later in other species). Seligman and Maier (1967) subjected dogs to painful, unavoidable shocks: No matter what the dogs did, there was no way to escape the shocks. The dogs developed what Seligman and Maier called **learned helplessness.** Learned helplessness is marked by three types of deficits: *motivational deficits*—the dogs were slow to initiate known actions; *emotional deficits*—they appeared rigid, listless, frightened, and distressed; and *cognitive deficits*—they demonstrated poor learning in new situations. Even when put in a situation in which they could, in fact, avoid shock, they did not learn to do so (Maier & Seligman, 1976).

<www.ablongman.com/gerrig17e>

According to cognitive theories, under what circumstances could a poor grade or an unhappy romance lead to major depression?

Seligman believed that depressed people are also in a state of learned helplessness: They have an expectancy that nothing they can do matters (Abramson et al., 1978; Peterson & Seligman, 1984; Seligman, 1975). However, the emergence of this state depends, to a large extent, on how individuals explain their life events. As we discussed in Chapter 11, there are three dimensions of explanatory style: *internal-external, global-specific,* and *stable-unstable.* Suppose that you have just received a poor grade on a psychology exam. You attribute the negative outcome on the exam to an internal factor ("I'm stupid"), which makes you feel sad, rather than to an external one ("The exam was really hard"), which would have made you angry. You could have chosen a less stable internal quality than intelligence to explain your performance ("I was tired that day"). Rather than attributing your performance to an internal, stable factor that has global or far-reaching influence (stupidity), you could even have limited your explanation to the psychology exam or course ("I'm not good at psychology courses"). Explanatory style theory suggests that individuals who attribute failure to internal, stable, and global causes are vulnerable to depression. This prediction has been confirmed repeatedly (Peterson & Vaidya, 2001; Seligman, 1991).

Cognitive theories of depression share the view that the ways in which depressed people think about themselves and the events in their lives are likely to keep them depressed. For example, people have a general tendency toward *self-verification*—they seek information that confirms their self-concept (Swann, 1990, 1997). This tendency has negative consequences for depressed individuals.

Self-Verification and Depression

Researchers differentiated three groups of individuals: One group was depressed, the second group was nondepressed but experienced low self-esteem, and the third group was nondepressed and had high self-esteem. The participants in each group completed a packet of questionnaires in preparation for an interview. During the interview, the participants were told that two graduate students had examined those questionnaires and each had written a "personality summary" in advance of a full personality assessment of the individual. In fact, all participants received the same summaries—one was positive ("this person seems well adjusted, self-confident, happy" and so on) and one was negative ("this person seems unhappy, unconfident, uncomfortable around others" and so on). Based on these summaries, participants were asked to choose which full assessment they would like to read. The results are presented in **Table 14.4.** As you can see, depressed individuals were disproportionately interested in reading the negative assessments; individuals with low self-esteem also showed a tendency to prefer negative feedback whereas those with high self-esteem clearly preferred positive feedback. Table 14.4 also provides data for each group on how accurate they believed the positive and negative summaries to be. Note that only depressed participants believed that the negative summary was more accurate (Giesler et al., 1996).

You might have expected that depressed people would try to "pull themselves out of it" by seeking positive feedback. This experiment demonstrates that, instead, they seek information that is consistent with their

TABLE 14.4
Self-Verification and Depression

	Depressed	Low Self-Esteem	High Self-Esteem
Percent choosing negative assessment	82	64	25
Perceived accuracy of summary[a]			
Positive summary	5.67	6.60	9.70
Negative summary	7.89	6.48	2.45
Difference	−2.22	0.12	7.25

[a]Accuracy ratings were made on an 11-point scale ranging from not at all (1) to very much (11) accurate.

What factors help explain why more women than men experience depression?

depression—and almost certainly functions to perpetuate that depression.

In Chapter 15, we will see that insights generated from cognitive theories of depression have given rise to successful forms of therapy. For now, there are two other important aspects of the study of depression that we will review: the large differences between the prevalence of depression in men and women and the link between depression and suicide.

◆ GENDER DIFFERENCES IN DEPRESSION

One of the central questions of research on depression is why women are afflicted twice as often as men. One factor that contributes to this difference is, unfortunately, quite straightforward: On average, women experience more negative events and life stressors than men do (Hankin & Abramson, 2001; Nolen-Hoeksema, 2002). For example, women have a greater likelihood of experiencing physical or sexual abuse, and they are more likely to live in poverty while being the primary caregiver for children and elderly parents. Thus, women's lives provide more of the types of experiences that lay the groundwork for serious depression.

Other gender differences explain why women may become more depressed once that groundwork has been laid. For example, women may be more likely to have the type of internal–global–stable explanatory style. There are also other cognitive factors at work. Research by **Susan Nolen-Hoeksema** (2002; Nolen-Hoeksema et al., 1999) points to the response styles of men and women once they begin to experience negative moods. According to this view, when women experience sadness, they tend to think about the possible causes and implications of their feelings. In contrast, men attempt actively to distract themselves from depressed feelings, either by focusing on something else or by engaging in a physical activity that will take their minds off their current mood state. This model suggests that it is the more thoughtful, *ruminative* response style of women, the tendency to focus obsessively on their problems, that increases women's vulnerability to depression. From a cognitive approach, paying attention to your negative moods can increase your thoughts of negative events, which eventually increases the quantity and/or the intensity of negative feelings. Men who ruminate are also at risk for depression. The gender difference emerges because more women ruminate (Nolen-Hoeksema et al., 1999).

There is a relationship between the gender differences in life experiences and the gender differences in cognitive styles. Researchers believe that women might, for example, explain negative events in ways different from men because they have more of them to explain (Hankin & Abramson, 2001). Suppose bad events happen to you with great frequency. Wouldn't you start to attribute those events to something about you rather than something about the world? This overall pattern suggests that the gender differences in depression will endure as long as gender differences in life experiences endure.

◆ SUICIDE

"The will to survive and succeed had been crushed and defeated. . . . There comes a time when all things cease to shine, when the rays of hope are lost" (Shneidman, 1987, p. 57). This sad statement by a suicidal young man reflects the most extreme consequence of any psychological disorder—*suicide*. While most depressed people do not commit suicide, analyses suggest that many suicides are attempted by those who are suffering from depression (Conner et al., 2001). In the general U.S. population, the number of deaths officially designated as suicide is around 30,000; because many suicides are attributed to accidents or other causes, the actual rate is probably much higher. Because depression occurs more frequently in women, it is not surprising that women *attempt* suicide about three times more often than men do; attempts by men, however, are more often successful. This difference occurs largely

<www.ablongman.com/gerrig17e>

Highly successful individuals, like rock star Kurt Cobain, are not immune to the feelings of despair that can trigger suicide. What has research revealed about the relationship between depression and suicide?

because men use guns more often, and women tend to use less lethal means, such as sleeping pills (Berman & Jobes, 1991).

One of the most alarming social problems in recent decades is the rise of *youth suicide*. Although suicide is the eleventh leading cause of death in the United States for all ages, it is third for people ages 15 to 24 (Arias et al., 2003). For every completed suicide, there may be as many as 8 to 20 suicide attempts. A survey of 694 college freshmen revealed that 26 percent had considered suicide during the past 12 months; 2 percent had actually attempted suicide in the past 12 months; and 10 percent had attempted suicide at some point in their lives (Meehan et al., 1992). Despite fewer attempts, adolescent boys are over four times more likely to succeed than are adolescent girls (Bingham et al., 1994). Note that the suicide rates for African American youths of both sexes are much lower than those for white youths, although no clear explanation has emerged for this finding (Bingham et al., 1994; Murphy, 2000). These racial differences remain in place across the life span. Elderly white men are at greatest risk for suicide and African American women least, when data are compared across race, gender, and age.

Youth suicide is not a spur-of-the-moment, impulsive act, but, typically, it occurs as the final stage of a period of inner turmoil and outer distress. The majority of young suicide victims have talked to others about their intentions or have written about them. Thus, talk

of suicide should always be taken seriously (Marttunen et al., 1998). What lifestyle patterns predispose adolescents to attempt suicide? The breakup of a close relationship is a leading traumatic incident for both sexes (Gould et al., 1996). Other significant incidents that create shame and guilt can overwhelm immature egos and lead to suicide attempts. Such incidents include being assaulted, beaten, raped, or arrested for the first time. Furthermore, gay and lesbian youths are at even higher risk for suicide than are other adolescents (D'Augelli et al., 2001; Remafedi, 1999). These higher suicide rates undoubtedly reflect the relative lack of social support for homosexual orientation. Suicide is an extreme reaction that occurs especially when adolescents feel unable to cry out to others for help. Being sensitive to signs of suicidal intentions and caring enough to intervene are essential for saving the lives of both youthful and mature people who have come to see no exit for their troubles except total self-destruction.

We have now reviewed two of the major classes of psychopathology: anxiety disorders and mood disorders. Before we turn to the topic of schizophrenia, we briefly consider personality disorders and dissociative disorders.

◆ PERSONALITY DISORDERS

A **personality disorder** is a long-standing (chronic), inflexible, maladaptive pattern of perceiving, thinking, or behaving. These patterns can seriously impair an individual's ability to function in social or work settings and can cause significant distress. They are usually recognizable by the time a person reaches adolescence or early adulthood. There are many types of personality disorders (*DSM-IV-TR* recognizes 10 types). We will discuss four examples: paranoid, histrionic, narcissistic, and antisocial personality disorders.

People with *paranoid personality disorders* show a consistent pattern of distrust and suspiciousness about the motives of the individuals with whom they interact. People who suffer from this disorder suspect that other people are trying to harm or deceive them. They may find hidden unpleasant meanings in harmless situations. They expect their friends and spouses or partners to be disloyal.

Histrionic personality disorder is characterized by patterns of excessive emotionality and attention seeking. People with this disorder always wish to be the center of attention. If they are not, they may do something inappropriate to regain that spot. Sufferers offer strong opinions with great drama but with little evidence to back up their claims. They also react to minor occasions with overblown emotional responses.

People with a *narcissistic personality disorder* have a grandiose sense of self-importance, a preoccupation with fantasies of success or power, and a need for

In a career where power and financial gain are pursued at all costs, could antisocial personality disorder be an asset?

constant admiration. These people often have problems in interpersonal relationships; they tend to feel entitled to special favors with no reciprocal obligations, to exploit others for their own purposes, and to have difficulty recognizing and experiencing how others feel.

Antisocial personality disorder is marked by a long-standing pattern of irresponsible or unlawful behavior that violates social norms. Lying, stealing, and fighting are common behaviors. People with antisocial personality disorder often do not experience shame or remorse for their hurtful actions. Violations of social norms begin early in their lives—disrupting class, getting into fights, and running away from home. Their actions are marked by indifference to the rights of others. Antisocial personality disorder is often comorbid with other pathologies. For example, in one study, about 25 percent of individuals who met criteria for opioid (for example, opium, morphine, and heroin) abuse were also diagnosed with antisocial personality disorder (Brooner et al., 1997).

Although personality disorders have been studied less than other types of disorders, evidence is beginning to accumulate that these disorders have a genetic component (Coolidge et al., 2001; Nigg & Goldsmith, 1994). If you recall the discussion in Chapter 13 about the strong heritability of personality traits, you might not be surprised that disorders of those traits are also heritable. Research has also focused on the environmental circumstances that give rise to personality disorders (Paris, 2003). Consider this study of the relationship between parenting practices and antisocial personality traits.

PUTTING IDEAS TO THE TEST

Parents' Behaviors and Antisocial Personality Traits

A team of researchers assessed 742 men and women for personality traits that met *DSM-IV* criteria for antisocial personality disorder (Reti et al., 2002). The participants reported on their parents' behaviors toward them during childhood by completing the *Parental Bonding Instrument* (PBI). The PBI posed a range of questions to which participants responded on a four-point scale. Some of the questions measured the extent to which parents showed caring for the child (e.g., "Could make me feel better when I was upset"). Other questions measured the extent to which parents restricted the child's behavior (e.g., "Let me dress in any way I pleased"). A third type of question measured the extent to which parents allowed the child psychological freedom (e.g., "Tried to control everything I did"). The researchers looked for relationships between the participants' responses on the PBI and the extent to which they showed antisocial personality traits. The researchers found that the people who reported low levels of parental care had high levels of antisocial personality traits. Also, those individuals who believed that their mothers had been particularly overprotective also had high levels of antisocial personality traits.

The researchers were quick to assert that correlation is not causation. It's possible that parenting behaviors brought about antisocial personality traits; it's also possible that children whose behavior was influenced by antisocial traits negatively affected the way their parents behaved toward them. Still, the results suggest that researchers could observe family patterns to determine what children might be at risk to develop adult forms of antisocial personality disorder.

◆ DISSOCIATIVE DISORDERS

A **dissociative disorder** is a disturbance in the integration of identity, memory, or consciousness. It is important for people to see themselves as being in control of their behavior, including emotions, thoughts, and actions. Essential to this perception of self-control is the sense of selfhood—the consistency of different aspects of the self and the continuity of identity over time and place. Psychologists believe that, in dissociated states, individuals escape from their conflicts by giving up this precious consistency and continuity—in a sense, disowning part of themselves. The forgetting of important personal experiences, a process caused by psychological factors in the absence of any organic dysfunction, called **dissociative amnesia,** is one example of disso-

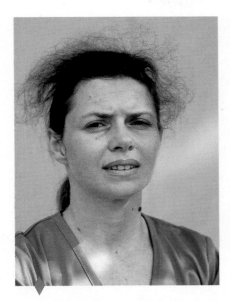

When found in a park in Florida, this woman (dubbed "Jane Doe" by authorities) was emaciated, incoherent, and near death. She was suffering from severe amnesia in which she had lost not only the memory of her name and her past but also the ability to read and write. What types of traumas may lead to dissociative amnesia?

ciation. Psychologists have begun to document the degree to which such memory dissociation may accompany instances of sexual and physical childhood abuse (Draijer & Langeland, 1999). Other types of severe traumas—such as the firestorm that struck Oakland and Berkeley, California, in 1991, resulting in a loss of 25 lives and over a billion dollars in damage—also produce dissociative symptoms (Koopman et al., 1996).

Dissociative identity disorder (DID), formerly known as *multiple personality disorder,* is a dissociative mental disorder in which two or more distinct personalities exist within the same individual. At any particular time, one of these personalities is dominant in directing the individual's behavior. Dissociative identity disorder is popularly known as *split personality,* and sometimes mistakenly called *schizophrenia,* a disorder, as we shall see in the next section, in which personality often is impaired but is not split into multiple versions. In DID, each of the emerging personalities contrasts in some significant way with the original self—it might be outgoing if the person is shy, tough if the original personality is weak, and sexually assertive if the other is fearful and sexually naive. Each personality has a unique identity, name, and behavior pattern. In some cases, dozens of different characters emerge to

help the person deal with a difficult life situation. Here is an excerpt from a first-person account of a woman who experiences DID (Mason, 1997, p. 44):

> *Just as waves turn the ocean inside out and rearrange the water, different ones of us cycle in and out in an ebb and flow that is sometimes gentle, sometimes turbulent. A child colors with Crayola markers. She moves aside to make way for the administrator, who reconciles the bank statement. A moment later, the dead baby takes over and lies paralyzed on the floor. She remains that way for a while, but no one gets upset—it's her turn. The live baby stops in her crawl, engrossed by a speck of dust. The cooker prepares meals for three days and packages each separately—we all have different likes and dislikes. A terrified one screams aloud, a wounded one moans, a grieving one wails.*

Can you put yourself in this woman's place, and imagine what it would be like to have this range of "individuals"—the child, the dead baby, the live baby, the cooker, and so on—inside your one head?

Some psychologists believe that multiple personalities develop to serve a vital survival function. DID victims may have been beaten, locked up, or abandoned by those who were supposed to love them—those on whom they were so dependent that they could not fight them, leave them, or even hate them. Instead, the psychodynamic perspective suggests that these victims have fled their terror symbolically through dissociation. They have protected their egos by creating stronger internal characters to help cope with the ongoing traumatic situation. Typically, DID victims are women who report being severely abused physically or sexually by parents, relatives, or close friends for extended periods during childhood. One study obtained questionnaire data from 448 clinicians who had treated cases of dissociative identity disorders and major depressions (used for comparative purposes). As shown in **Table 14.5,** the dominant feature of the 355 DID cases is the almost universal reports of abuse, with incidents often starting around age 3 and continuing for more than a decade. Although the 235 comparison patients with depression disorder also had a high incidence of abuse, it was significantly less than that experienced by those with DID (Schultz et al., 1989).

Although these data—and personal accounts of the type we quoted earlier—seem compelling, many psychologists remain skeptical about the diagnosis of DID (Lilienfeld & Lynn, 2003). No solid data exist about the prevalence of this disorder (*DSM-IV-TR,* 2000). Skeptics have often suggested that therapists who "believe" in DID may create DID—these therapists question their

TABLE 14.5

Responses to Inquiries Regarding Abuse: Comparing Dissociative Identity Disorder and Depression

Questionnaire Item	DID (%)	Major Depression (%)
Abuse incidence	98	54
Type(s)		
Physical	82	24
Sexual	86	25
Psychological	86	42
Neglect	54	21
All of above	47	6
Physical and sexual	74	14
	(N = 355)	(N = 235)

What psychological disorders of childhood might lead to classroom disruptions?

patients, often under hypnosis, in a way that encourages multiple personalities to "emerge." Other psychologists believe that sufficient evidence has accumulated in favor of the DID diagnosis to indicate that it is not just the product of zealous therapists (Gleaves et al., 2001). The safest conclusion may be that of the group of people diagnosed with DID, some cases are genuine whereas other cases emerge in response to therapists' demands.

◆ PSYCHOLOGICAL DISORDERS OF CHILDHOOD

Our discussion so far has largely focused on adults who suffer from psychopathology. It is important to note, however, that many individuals begin to experience symptoms of mental illness in childhood and adolescence. Researchers have recently intensified their study of the types of stressors that increase the risk of psychopathology in young lives (Grant et al., 2003). For example, the gender difference for the prevalence of depression begins to emerge around age 13 (Hankin & Abramson, 2001). Researchers seek to understand how boys' and girls' lives diverge, early on, to yield a relative disproportion of depressed girls versus depressed boys.

DSM-IV-TR also identifies a range of disorders that are "usually first diagnosed in infancy, childhood, or adolescence." We discussed one of these disorders, *mental retardation*, in Chapter 9. Here, we focus on *attention-deficit hyperactivity disorder* and *autistic disorder*.

The definition of *attention-deficit hyperactivity disorder* (ADHD) refers to two clusters of symptoms

(*DSM-IV-TR*, 2000). First, children must show a degree of *inattention* that is not consistent with their level of development. They might, for example, have difficulty paying attention in school or often lose items such as toys or school assignments. Second, children must show signs of *hyperactivity-impulsivity* that, once again, is not consistent with their developmental level. Hyperactive behaviors include squirming, fidgeting, and excessive talking; impulsive behaviors include blurting out answers and interrupting. A diagnosis of ADHD requires that children have shown these patterns of behavior for at least six months before age 7.

Researchers estimate the prevalence of ADHD to be 3 to 7 percent of school-age children in the United States (Root & Resnick, 2003). The diagnosis of ADHD is complicated by the fact that many children are prone to episodes of inattention, hyperactivity, or impulsiveness. For that reason, the diagnosis has sometimes been controversial: People have worried that children's normal disorderliness was being labeled as abnormal. However, there is now a large consensus among clinicians that some children's behavior reaches a level at which it is maladaptive—the children are unable to control their behavior or complete tasks. As with the other disorders we've described, researchers have considered both the nature and nurture of ADHD. Twin and adoption studies have provided strong evidence for the heritability of the disorder (Thapar, 2003). There are also important environmental variables that are associated with ADHD.

For example, children who come from families with economic disadvantages or families with high levels of conflict are more likely to experience the disorder (Biederman et al., 2002).

Children with *autistic disorder* present severe disruption in their ability to form social bonds. They are likely to have greatly delayed and very limited development of spoken language as well as very narrow interests in the world. Consider a report on a child who was diagnosed with this disorder:

> [Audrey] seemed frightened by nearly any changes in her customary routine, including the presence of strange people. She either shrank from contact with other children or avoided them altogether, seemingly content to engage in nonfunctional play by herself for hours at a time. When she was with other children, she seldom engaged in reciprocal play or even copied any of their motor movements. (Meyer, 2003, p. 244)

Estimates of the prevalence of autistic disorder (and related disorders) range from about 30 to 60 per 10,000 children (Fombonne, 2003; Yeargin-Allsopp et al., 2003). What has become clear, however, is that the number of cases of autistic disorder has risen sharply over the last 20 or 30 years. Researchers are exploring various theories to explain the origins of the disorder.

As with ADHD, autistic disorder has a large genetic component. In fact, researchers have begun to identify the variations in the human genome that may predispose individuals to experience the disorder (Pericak-Vance, 2003). Researchers have also discovered brain markers of the disorder. For example, individuals with autistic disorder experience more rapid brain growth than do their peers (Cody et al., 2002; Courchesne et al., 2003). The ongoing question is how such brain abnormalities bring about the symptoms of the disorder.

Researchers have suggested that individuals who suffer from autistic disorder have an inability to develop an understanding of other people's mental states (Baron-Cohen, 2000). Under ordinary circumstances, children develop what has been called a *theory of mind*. At first, they interpret the world only from their own perspective. However, with rapid progress between ages 3 and 4, children develop an understanding that other people have different knowledge, beliefs, and intentions than they do. Research suggests that individuals with autistic disorder lack the ability to develop this understanding. Without a theory of mind, it is quite difficult for people to establish social relationships. Individuals with autistic disorder find it virtually impossible to understand and predict other people's behavior, making everyday life seem mysterious and hostile.

Schizophrenic Disorders

Everyone knows what it is like to feel depressed or anxious, even though most of us never experience these feelings to the degree of severity that constitutes a disorder. Schizophrenia, however, is a disorder that represents a qualitatively different experience from normal functioning. A **schizophrenic disorder** is a severe form of psychopathology in which personality seems to disintegrate, thought and perception are distorted, and emotions are blunted. The person with a schizophrenic disorder is the one you most often conjure up when you think about madness or insanity.

For many of the people afflicted with schizophrenia, the disease is a life sentence without possibility of parole, endured in the solitary confinement of a mind that must live life apart. Although schizophrenia is relatively rare—approximately 0.7 percent of U.S. adults have suffered from schizophrenia at some point in their lives (Kessler et al., 1994)—this figure translates to around two million people affected by this most mysterious and tragic mental disorder. Half of the beds in this nation's mental institutions are occupied by schizophrenic patients, because many spend their entire adult lives hospitalized, with little hope of ever returning to a "normal" existence.

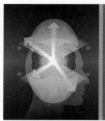

PSYCHOLOGY IN THE 21ST CENTURY

Pinpointing Interactions of Nature and Nurture

Throughout this chapter, we have asserted that major types of mental illnesses have a genetic component. The majority of those claims have been based on methods that should be quite familiar to you by this point in *Psychology and Life*. Researchers, for example, compare the rate at which monozygotic and dizygotic twins share the same psychopathology to offer estimates of the heritability of each type of disorder (Coolidge et al., 2001; Hettema et al., 2001). However, in recent years, researchers have begun to move beyond calculations of heritability to pinpoint the actual differences in genetic material that predispose some individuals to experience mental illness. Let's consider a study that establishes an important relationship between genetic variation and life experiences in the etiology of depression.

When we discussed mood disorders, we noted that disruptions in the function of the neurotransmitter serotonin play a role in depression. For that reason, researchers have focused attention on a gene that has an impact on the serotonin system (Caspi et al., 2003). The gene comes in short (s) and long (l) forms. (In Chapter 12 we described a study that assessed the impact of this gene on the amygdala's response to emotion stimuli [Hariri et al., 2002].) For 847 individuals in a longitudinal study in New Zealand, researchers determined their status for

this gene. In the sample, 17 percent had two short versions of the gene (s/s), 51 percent had one short and one long (s/l), and 31 percent had two long versions (l/l). The participants themselves provided information about the stressors they had weathered in their lives. For ages 21 to 26, they indicated whether they had experienced such events as employment or financial crises, health problems, or relationship issues. Across the genotypes (i.e., s/s, s/l, l/l), no one group experienced more life stressors than another. That's an important result: It suggests that any group differences in the prevalence of depression cannot be attributed to easier or harder lives. Instead, we learn that people's genotypes predispose them to respond differently to similar experiences.

The researchers' final step was to determine which participants in the study had

suffered from major depressive disorder. As seen in the figure, the pattern that emerged was quite dramatic. In general, people who had experienced more stressful life events were more likely to experience an episode of major depression. However, as the figure shows, genotypes had an important impact as well. For participants in possession of one or, more so, two copies of the short version of the gene, the impact of negative life events was amplified.

This study makes many of the ideas we've discussed about nature and nurture quite concrete. These researchers have demonstrated that a known genetic difference in combination with negative life events greatly increases the likelihood that people will experience depression. Breakthroughs in the understanding of the human genome allow researchers to determine exactly how nature and nurture interact.

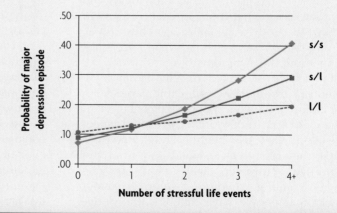

Mark Vonnegut, son of novelist Kurt Vonnegut, was in his early twenties when he began to experience symptoms of schizophrenia. In *The Eden Express* (1975), he tells the story of his break with reality and his eventual recovery. Once, while pruning some fruit trees, his reality became distorted:

I began to wonder if I was hurting the trees and found myself apologizing. Each tree began to take on personality. I began to wonder if any of them liked me. I became completely absorbed in looking at each tree and began to notice that they were ever so slightly luminescent, shining with a soft inner light that played around the branches. And from out of nowhere came an incredibly wrinkled, iridescent face. Starting as a small point infinitely distant, it rushed forward, becoming infinitely huge. I could see nothing else. My heart had stopped. The moment stretched forever. I tried to make the face go away but it mocked me. . . . I tried to look the face in the eyes and realized I had left all familiar ground. (1975, p. 96)

Vonnegut's description gives you a glimpse at the symptoms of schizophrenia.

In the world of schizophrenia, *thinking* becomes illogical; associations among ideas are remote or without apparent pattern. **Hallucinations** often occur, involving imagined sensory perception—sights, smells, or, most commonly, sounds (usually voices)—that patients assume to be real. A person may hear a voice that provides a running commentary on his or her behavior or may hear several voices in conversation. **Delusions** are also common; these are false or irrational beliefs maintained in spite of clear contrary evidence. *Language* may become incoherent—a "word salad" of unrelated or made-up words—or an individual may become mute. *Emotions* may be flat, with no visible expression, or they may be inappropriate to the situation. *Psychomotor behavior* may be disorganized (grimaces, strange mannerisms), or posture may become rigid. Even when only some of these symptoms are present, deteriorated functioning in work and interpersonal relationships is likely as the patient withdraws socially or becomes emotionally detached.

Psychologists divide the symptoms between a positive category and a negative category. During *acute* or *active phases* of schizophrenia, the positive symptoms—hallucinations, delusions, incoherence, and disorganized behavior—are prominent. At other times, the negative symptoms—social withdrawal and flattened emotions—become more apparent. Some individuals, such as Mark Vonnegut, experience only one or a couple of acute phases of schizophrenia and recover to live normal lives. Others, often described as chronic sufferers, experience either repeated acute phases with short periods of negative symptoms or occasional acute phases with extended periods of negative symptoms. Even the most seriously disturbed are not acutely delusional all the time.

◆ MAJOR TYPES OF SCHIZOPHRENIA

Because of the wide variety of symptoms that can characterize schizophrenia, investigators consider it not a single disorder but rather a constellation of separate types. The five most commonly recognized subtypes are outlined in **Table 14.6.**

◆

TABLE 14.6

Types of Schizophrenic Disorders

Types of Schizophrenia	Major Symptoms
Disorganized	Inappropriate behavior and emotions; incoherent language
Catatonic	Frozen, rigid, or excitable motor behavior
Paranoid	Delusions of persecution or grandeur
Undifferentiated	Mixed set of symptoms with thought disorders and features from other types
Residual	Free from major symptoms but evidence from minor symptoms of continuation of the disorder

DISORGANIZED TYPE

In this subtype of schizophrenia, a person displays incoherent patterns of thinking and grossly bizarre and disorganized behavior. Emotions are flattened or inappropriate to the situation. Often, a person acts in a silly or childish manner, such as giggling for no apparent reason. Language can become so incoherent, full of unusual words and incomplete sentences, that communication with others breaks down. If delusions or hallucinations occur, they are not organized around a coherent theme.

> *Mr. F. B. was a hospitalized patient in his late twenties. When asked his name, he said he was trying to forget it because it made him cry whenever he heard it. He then proceeded to cry vigorously for several minutes. Then, when asked about something serious and sad, Mr. F. B. giggled or laughed. When asked the meaning of the proverb "When the cat's away, the mice will play," Mr. F. B. replied, "Takes less place. Cat didn't know what mouse did and mouse didn't know what cat did. Cat represented more on the suspicious side than the mouse. Dumbo was a good guy. He saw what the cat did, put himself with the cat so people wouldn't look at them as comedians." (Zimbardo, personal communication, 1957)*

Mr. F. B.'s mannerisms, depersonalized, incoherent speech, and delusions are the hallmarks of the disorganized type of schizophrenia.

CATATONIC TYPE

The major feature of the catatonic type of schizophrenia is a disruption in motor activity. Sometimes people with this disorder seem frozen in a stupor. For long periods of time, the individual can remain motionless, often in a bizarre position, showing little or no reaction to anything in the environment. At other times, these patients show excessive motor activity, apparently without purpose and not influenced by external stimuli. The catatonic type is also characterized by extreme *negativism,* an apparently unmotivated resistance to all instructions.

PARANOID TYPE

Individuals suffering from this form of schizophrenia experience complex and systematized delusions focused around specific themes:

- *Delusions of persecution.* Individuals feel that they are being constantly spied on and plotted against and that they are in mortal danger.
- *Delusions of grandeur.* Individuals believe that they are important or exalted beings—millionaires, great inventors, or religious figures such as Jesus Christ. Delusions of persecution may accompany delusions of grandeur—an individual is a great person but is continually opposed by evil forces.
- *Delusional jealousy.* Individuals become convinced—without due cause—that their mates are unfaithful. They contrive data to fit the theory and "prove" the truth of the delusion.

Individuals with paranoid schizophrenia rarely display obviously disorganized behavior. Instead, their behavior is likely to be intense and quite formal.

UNDIFFERENTIATED TYPE

This is the grab-bag category of schizophrenia, describing a person who exhibits prominent delusions, hallucinations, incoherent speech, or grossly disorganized behavior that fits the criteria of more than one type or of no clear type. The hodgepodge of symptoms experienced by these individuals does not clearly differentiate among various schizophrenic reactions.

RESIDUAL TYPE

Individuals diagnosed as residual type have usually suffered from a major past episode of schizophrenia but are currently free of major positive symptoms such as hallucinations or delusions. The ongoing presence of the disorder is signaled by minor positive symptoms or negative symptoms like flat emotion. A diagnosis of residual type may indicate that the person's disease is entering *remission,* or becoming dormant.

◆ CAUSES OF SCHIZOPHRENIA

Different etiological models point to very different initial causes of schizophrenia, different pathways along which it develops, and different avenues for treatment. Let's look at the contributions several of these models

can make to an understanding of the way a person may develop a schizophrenic disorder.

GENETIC APPROACHES

It has long been known that schizophrenia tends to run in families (Bleuler, 1978; Kallmann, 1946). Three independent lines of research—family studies, twin studies, and adoption studies—point to a common conclusion: Persons related genetically to someone who has had schizophrenia are more likely to become affected than those who are not (Owen & O'Donovan, 2003). A summary of the risks of being affected with schizophrenia through various kinds of relatives is shown in **Figure 14.5.** Schizophrenia researcher **Irving Gottesman** (1991) pooled these data from about 40 reliable studies conducted in Western Europe between 1920 and 1987; he dropped the poorest data sets. As you can see, the data are arranged according to degree of genetic relatedness, which correlates highly with the degree of risk. For example, when both parents have suffered from schizophrenia, the risk for their offspring is 46 percent, as compared with 1 percent in the general population. When only one parent has had schizophrenia, the risk for the offspring drops sharply, to 13 percent. Note also that the probability that identical twins will both have schizophrenia is roughly three times greater than the probability for fraternal twins.

Researchers have also used adoption studies to demonstrate that the etiology of schizophrenia is greatly influenced by genetic factors (Kety et al., 1994). Consider a study that assessed the incidence of thought disorders in biological and adoptive relatives of schizophrenic patients.

PUTTING IDEAS TO THE TEST

Thought Disorders in Schizophrenic Patients' Biological and Adoptive Relatives

Schizophrenic participants in this study were drawn from a larger sample of individuals who had developed the disorder after having been adopted. A control sample was matched to the schizophrenic sample on variables such as sex and age; participants in the control sample had experienced no psychiatric hospitalizations. Tape recordings were made of the patients' and controls' speech, as well as the speech of their biological relatives—to assess the importance of genetics—and their adopted relatives—to assess the importance of environment. Based on these speech samples, each individual (that is, patients and relatives) was assigned a thought disorder score, using a set of categories specified by a measure called the Thought Disorder Index (TDI). Results are presented in

<www.ablongman.com/gerrig17e>

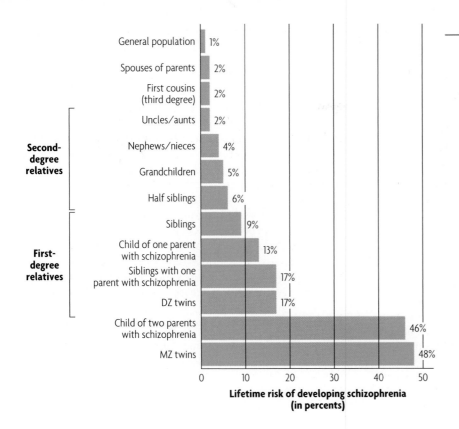

General population 1%

Spouses of parents 2%

First cousins (third degree) 2%

Second-degree relatives
Uncles/aunts 2%
Nephews/nieces 4%
Grandchildren 5%
Half siblings 6%

First-degree relatives
Siblings 9%
Child of one parent with schizophrenia 13%
Siblings with one parent with schizophrenia 17%
DZ twins 17%
Child of two parents with schizophrenia 46%
MZ twins 48%

0   10   20   30   40   50
Lifetime risk of developing schizophrenia (in percents)

FIGURE 14.5

Genetic Risk of Developing Schizophrenia

The graph shows average risks for developing schizophrenia. Data were compiled from family and twin studies conducted in European populations between 1920 and 1987; the degree of risk correlates highly with the degree of genetic relatedness.

Except when the label indicates otherwise, the data reflect the relationship between an individual and someone who has been diagnosed with schizophrenia. For example, the D2 twin of someone diagnosed with schizophrenia has a 17 percent chance of sharing the diagnosis.

Table 14.7—higher TDI scores indicate more disordered thought. The results indicate that the biological relatives of the schizophrenic adoptees had higher levels of disordered thought than did the biological relatives of control adoptees. However, the adoptive relatives of both groups did not differ in their thought disorders. This pattern of data suggests that genetics matters more than environment in predicting who will experience thought disorders (Kinney et al., 1997).

Almost all the adoptees had been separated from their biological families shortly after birth. Therefore, whatever forces were leading to very high levels of thought disorder in the schizophrenic adoptees and relatively high levels in their biological relatives cannot be attributed to environmental factors.

While there is certainly a strong relationship between genetic similarity and schizophrenia risk, even in the groups with the greatest genetic similarity, the risk factor is less than 50 percent (see Figure 14.5). This indicates that, although genes play a role, environmental conditions may also be necessary to give rise to the disorder. A widely accepted hypothesis for the cause of schizophrenia is the *diathesis-stress hypothesis*. According to the **diathesis-stress hypothesis,** genetic factors

place the individual at risk, but environmental stress factors must impinge in order for the potential risk to be manifested as a schizophrenic disorder. Once we have considered other biological aspects of schizophrenia, we will review the types of environmental stressors that may speed the emergence of this disorder.

TABLE 14.7

Thought Disorder Scores for Schizophrenic Adoptees, Control Adoptees, and Their Relatives

SCORES ON THE THOUGHT DISORDER INDEX

	Schizophrenic Adoptees	Control Adoptees	Difference
The adoptees themselves	4.82	1.15	3.67
All their biological relatives	1.37	0.99	0.38
Their biological siblings and half-siblings	1.44	0.82	0.62
Their adoptive relatives	1.11	1.31	−0.20

BRAIN FUNCTION AND BIOLOGICAL MARKERS

Another biological approach to the study of schizophrenia is to look for abnormalities in the brains of individuals suffering from the disorder. Much of this research now relies on brain imaging techniques that allow direct comparisons to be made between the structure and functioning of the brains of individuals with schizophrenia and normal control individuals. For example, the magnetic resonance procedure has been used to show that the *ventricles*—the brain structures through which cerebrospinal fluid flows—are enlarged in up to 50 percent of individuals with schizophrenia (Degreef et al., 1992). MRI studies also demonstrate that individuals with schizophrenia have measurably thinner regions in frontal and temporal lobes of cerebral cortex; the loss of neural tissue presumably relates to the disorder's behavioral abnormalities (Kuperberg et al., 2003). Imaging techniques have also revealed that individuals with schizophrenia may have patterns of brain activity different from those of normal controls. For example, one study examined identical twins in which either one or both members of each pair had schizophrenia (Berman et al., 1992). Only those individuals who actually had schizophrenia showed lower activity in the frontal lobes of the brain. This research design allows "genetics" to be held constant, to reveal this other biological aspect of the disorder.

Researchers continue to add to the list of *biological markers* for schizophrenia. A biological marker is a "measurable indicator of a disease that may or may not be causal" (Szymanski et al., 1991, p. 99). In other words, a biological marker may be correlated with a disease, although it does not bring the disease about. At present no known marker perfectly predicts schizophrenia, but markers have great potential value for diagnosis and research. For example, persons with schizophrenia are more likely than normal people to have an eye movement dysfunction when they scan the visual field. This biological marker can be quantified in individuals and is related to the presence of schizophrenia in families (Clementz & Sweeney, 1990; Lencer et al., 2000). Researchers continue to probe to find the specific elements of eye movements that most precisely set individuals with schizophrenia apart from patients with other mental disorders (Katsanis et al., 1997; Sweeney et al., 1994). Precise knowledge of biological markers may help researchers determine what groups of individuals are at risk for developing the disorder.

Given the wide range of symptoms of schizophrenia, you are probably not surprised by the comparably wide range of biological abnormalities that may be either causes or consequences of the disorder. What are the ways in which features of the environment may prompt people who are at risk to develop the disease?

FAMILY INTERACTION AS ENVIRONMENTAL STRESSOR

If it is difficult to prove that a highly specific biological factor is a *sufficient* cause of schizophrenia, it is equally hard to prove that a general psychological one is a *necessary* condition. Sociologists, family therapists, and psychologists have all studied the influence of family role relationships and communication patterns in the development of schizophrenia. The hope is to identify environmental circumstances that increase the likelihood of schizophrenia—and to protect at-risk individuals from those circumstances.

Research has provided evidence for theories that emphasize the influence of *deviations* in parental communication on the development of schizophrenia (Miklowitz & Tompson, 2003). These deviations include a family's inability to share a common focus of attention and parents' difficulties in taking the perspective of

These four genetically identical women each experience a schizophrenic disorder, which suggests that heredity plays a role in the development of schizophrenia. For each of the Genain quadruplets, the disorder differs in severity, duration, and outcome. In general, how do genetics and environment interact to produce instances of schizophrenia?

<www.ablongman.com/gerrig17e>

Are there certain destructive or self-contradictory patterns within the family that can contribute to the onset of schizophrenia?

other family members or in communicating clearly and accurately. Studies suggest that the speech patterns of families with a schizophrenic member show less responsiveness and less interpersonal sensitivity than those of normal families.

Uncertainty remains over whether deviant family patterns are a cause of schizophrenia, a reaction to an individual's developing symptoms of schizophrenia, or both. To help answer this question, researchers undertake *prospective* studies: They measure family function to see which patterns predict who will develop schizophrenia, or experience relapses, in the future. For example, one study focused on the *empathy* skills of patients' relatives with respect to their ability to perceive the patients' mood states (Giron & Gomez-Beneyto, 1998). Over a two-year period, the patients whose relatives had shown low levels of empathy were more likely to suffer relapses in their symptoms of schizophrenia. This study is consistent with other findings that family factors play an important role in influencing the functioning of an individual after the first symptoms appear.

PUTTING IDEAS TO THE TEST

Expressed Emotion and Symptom Relapse

To examine the role of family communication in schizophrenia, researchers have defined the concept of *expressed emotion.* Families are high on expressed emotion if they make a lot of critical comments about the patient, if they are emotionally overinvolved with the patient (that is, if they are overprotective and intrusive), and if they have a generally hostile attitude toward the patient. One study gathered data on the families of 69 schizophrenic patients who were living at home during a period in which they were considered stable. Each family was evaluated for the extent of its expressed emotion. When the patients' condition was assessed nine months later, 50 percent of the patients from high-expressed-emotion homes had experienced a relapse, whereas only 17 percent of patients from low-expressed-emotion homes had done so. Nonetheless, some aspects of expressed emotion were beneficial to the patients. Those patients whose families were emotionally overinvolved had better social adjustment nine months later. Perhaps the rigid family environment helped the patients make the difficult transition from hospitalization to the outside world (King & Dixon, 1996).

This study replicates the general pattern that when parents reduce their criticism, hostility, and intrusiveness toward a schizophrenic offspring, the recurrence of acute schizophrenic symptoms and the need for rehospitalization are also reduced (Wearden et al., 2000). The implication is that treatment should be for the entire family as a *system,* to change the operating style toward the disturbed child.

The number of explanations of schizophrenia that we have reviewed—and the questions that remain despite significant research—suggests how much there is to learn about this powerful psychological disorder. Complicating understanding is the likelihood that the phenomenon called schizophrenia is probably better thought of as a group of disorders, each with potentially distinct causes. Genetic predispositions, brain processes, and family interactions have all been identified as participants in at least some cases. Researchers must still determine the exact ways in which these elements may combine to bring about schizophrenia.

PUT YOURSELF TO THE TEST

- What are positive versus negative symptoms of schizophrenia?
- What are the five different types of schizophrenia?
- What evidence supports a genetic component for schizophrenia?
- What has been discovered about brain abnormalities and genetic markers?
- What patterns of family interactions may contribute to the emergence, continuation, or relapse of symptoms?

The Stigma of Mental Illness

One of our most important goals for this chapter has been to demystify mental illness—to help you understand how, in some ways, abnormal behavior is really ordinary. People with psychological disorders are often labeled as *deviant;* society exacts costly penalties from those who deviate from its norms (see **Figure 14.6**). However, the deviant label is not true to prevailing realities: When 50 percent of young and middle-aged adults in the United States report having experienced some psychiatric disorder in their lifetime (Kessler et al., 1994), psychopathology is, at least statistically, relatively normal.

Even given the frequency with which psychopathology touches "normal lives," people who are psychologically disordered are often stigmatized in ways that most physically ill people are not. A **stigma** is a mark or brand of disgrace; in the psychological context, it is a set of negative attitudes about a person that places him or her apart as unacceptable (Clausen, 1981). The woman with schizophrenia we quoted at the beginning of the chapter had this to say: "The patient and public, in my [opinion] needs to be educated about mental illness, because people ridicule and mistreat, even misunderstand us at crucial times." Another recovered patient wrote, "For me, the stigma of mental illness was as devastating as the experience of hospitalization itself." She went on to describe her personal experience in vivid terms:

> *Prior to being hospitalized for mental illness, I lived an enviable existence. Rewards, awards, and invitations filled my scrapbook. . . . The crises of mental illness appeared as a nuclear explosion in my life. All that I had known and enjoyed previously was suddenly transformed, like some strange reverse process of nature, from a butterfly's beauty into a pupa's cocoon. There was a binding, confining quality to my life, in part chosen, in part imposed. Repeated rejections, the awkwardness of others around me, and my own discomfort and self-consciousness propelled me into solitary confinement.*
>
> *My recovery from mental illness and its aftermath involved a struggle—against my own body, which seemed without energy and stamina, and against a society that seemed reluctant to embrace me. (Houghton, 1980, pp. 7–8)*

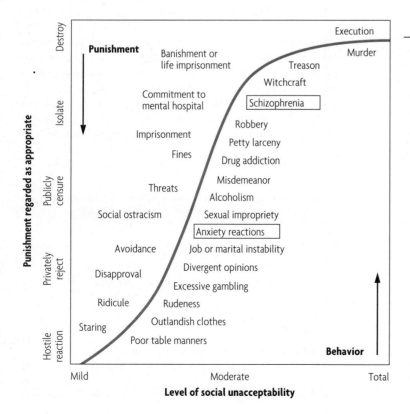

FIGURE 14.6

"Let the Punishment Fit the Crime"

This figure illustrates a continuum of behaviors that are deemed increasingly unacceptable and are responded to with increasing severity. In essence, each reaction is a punishment for deviance. Thus, behavior toward those who suffer from psychopathology can be seen to resemble behavior toward criminals or other deviants.

Negative attitudes toward the psychologically disturbed come from many sources: The mass media portray psychiatric patients as prone to violent crime; jokes about the mentally ill are acceptable; families deny the mental distress of one of their members; legal terminology stresses mental incompetence. People also stigmatize themselves by hiding current psychological distress or a history of mental health care.

Researchers have documented a number of ways in which the stigma of mental illness has a negative impact on people's lives (Farina et al., 1996; Wright et al., 2000). In one sample of 84 men who had been hospitalized for mental illness, 6 percent reported having lost a job because of their hospitalization; 10 percent reported having been denied an apartment or room; 37 percent reported being avoided by others; and 45 percent reported that others had used their history of mental illness to hurt their feelings. Only 6 percent of the men reported no incidents of rejection (Link et al., 1997). This group of men went through a year-long course of treatment that resulted in considerable improvement in their mental health. Even so, at the end of that year, there were no changes in their perception of stigma: Despite their improvements in functioning, the patients did not expect to be treated any more kindly by the world. This type of research shows the great duality of many people's experience with mental disorders: Seeking help—allowing one's problems to be labeled—generally brings both relief *and* stigma; treatment improves quality of life at the same time that stigma degrades it (Rosenfield, 1997).

An added difficulty is that people with mental illness often internalize expectations of rejections that may, in turn, bring about negative interactions (Link et al., 1997). Consider this classic experiment.

CLASSIC
PUTTING IDEAS TO THE TEST

Expectations of Rejection

Twenty-nine men who had formerly been hospitalized for mental illness volunteered to participate in this study. They believed that the research concerned the difficulties ex-psychiatric patients have with finding jobs. The participants were informed that they would interact with a personnel trainee recruited from a business establishment. Half of the participants were told that the trainee knew of their status as ex-psychiatric patients; the other half were told that the trainee had been led to believe they had been medical or surgical patients at the hospital. In fact, the "trainee" was a confederate of the experimenter who did not have any prior information about the participants' beliefs about his knowledge. That is, he did not know which partici-

pants thought that *he* knew that they were ex-patients. Therefore, any differences in the interactions during the time the participants and confederate spent together can be attributed to the participants' *expectations*. In fact, the participants who believed themselves to have been labeled as ex-psychiatric patients talked less during the session and performed less well on a cooperative task. Furthermore, the confederate rated members of this group as more "tense and anxious" without, again, knowing which group each participant was in (Farina et al., 1971).

The important conclusion here is that people who believe that others have attached the "mental illness" label to them may change their interactions in a way that brings about genuine discomfort: The expectation of rejection can create rejection; mental illness can be another of life's unfortunate self-fulfilling prophecies.

A final note on stigma: Research suggests that people who have had prior contact with individuals with mental illnesses hold attitudes that are less affected by stigma (Couture & Penn, 2003). For example, students who read a vignette about a man named Jim who had recovered from schizophrenia were more optimistic about Jim's future prospects when the students had had prior contact with someone who suffered from a mental illness (Penn et al., 1994). Similarly, students' ratings of the dangerousness of patients with schizophrenia were lower when they had had prior contact (Penn et al., 1999). We hope that one consequence of reading this chapter and the next will be to help modify your beliefs about what it means to be mentally ill and what it means to be "cured"—and to increase your tolerance and compassion for mentally ill individuals.

In making sense of psychopathology, you are forced to come to grips with basic conceptions of normality, reality, and social values. In discovering how to understand, treat, and, ideally, prevent psychological disorders, researchers not only help those who are suffering and losing out on the joys of living, they also expand the basic understanding of human nature. How do psychologists and psychiatrists intervene to right minds gone wrong and to modify behavior that doesn't work? We shall see in the next chapter on therapies.

PUT YOURSELF TO THE TEST

- ➤ In the context of mental illness, what does stigma mean?
- ➤ What are some consequences of stigma?
- ➤ What types of experiences reduce stigma?

Recapping Main Points

THE NATURE OF PSYCHOLOGICAL DISORDERS

- Abnormality is judged by the degree to which a person's actions resemble a set of indicators that include distress, maladaptiveness, irrationality, unpredictability, unconventionality, observer discomfort, and violation of standards or societal norms.

- In earlier times, mentally ill individuals were often treated as possessed by demons or less than human.

- Contemporary approaches to mental illness began with the recognition that mental disorders are illnesses that can be treated.

- There are a number of approaches to studying the etiology of psychopathology.

- The biological approach concentrates on abnormalities in the brain, biochemical processes, and genetic influences.

- Psychological approaches include psychodynamic, behavioral, cognitive, and sociocultural models.

CLASSIFYING PSYCHOLOGICAL DISORDERS

- Classification systems for psychological disorders should provide a common shorthand for communicating about general types of psychopathologies and specific cases.

- The most widely accepted diagnostic and classification system is *DSM-IV-TR*.

- *DSM-IV-TR* uses a multidimensional system of five axes that encourages mental health professionals to consider psychological, physical, and social factors that might be relevant to a specific disorder.

MAJOR TYPES OF PSYCHOLOGICAL DISORDERS

- The five major types of anxiety disorders are generalized, panic, phobic, obsessive-compulsive, and posttraumatic stress.

- Mood disorders involve disturbances of emotion. Major depressive disorder is the most common affective disorder, while bipolar disorder is much rarer.

- Suicides are most frequent among people suffering from depression.

- Biological and psychological explanations account for different aspects of the etiology of anxiety and mood disorders.

- Personality disorders are patterns of perception, thought, or behavior that are long-standing and inflexible and that impair an individual's functioning.

- Dissociative disorders involve a disruption of the integrated functioning of memory, consciousness, or personal identity.

- ADHD and autistic disorder are diagnosed in childhood.

SCHIZOPHRENIC DISORDERS

- Schizophrenia is a severe form of psychopathology that is characterized by extreme distortions in perception, thinking, emotion, behavior, and language.

- The five subtypes of schizophrenia are disorganized, catatonic, paranoid, undifferentiated, and residual.

- Evidence for the causes of schizophrenia has been found in a variety of factors including genetics, brain abnormalities, and family processes.

THE STIGMA OF MENTAL ILLNESS

- Those with psychological disorders are often stigmatized in ways that most physically ill people are not.

- Although treatment for psychological disorders brings about positive changes, the stigma associated with mental illness has a negative impact on quality of life.

KEY TERMS

abnormal psychology (p. 472)

agoraphobia (p. 482)

anxiety disorders (p. 482)

bipolar disorder (p. 488)

comorbidity (p. 481)

delusions (p. 499)

diathesis-stress hypothesis (p. 501)

dissociative amnesia (p. 494)

dissociative disorder (p. 494)

dissociative identity disorder (DID)
  (p. 495)

DSM-IV-TR (p. 478)

etiology (p. 476)

fear (p. 483)

generalized anxiety disorder (p. 482)

hallucinations (p. 499)

insanity (p. 480)

learned helplessness (p. 490)

major depressive disorder (p. 487)

manic episode (p. 488)

mood disorder (p. 487)

neurotic disorders (p. 479)

obsessive-compulsive disorder (OCD)
  (p. 483)

panic disorder (p. 482)

personality disorder (p. 4931)

phobia (p. 483)

posttraumatic stress disorder (PTSD)
  (p. 484)

psychological diagnosis (p. 478)

psychopathological functioning
  (p. 472)

psychotic disorders (p. 479)

schizophrenic disorder (p. 497)

social phobia (p. 483)

specific phobias (p. 483)

stigma (p. 504)

CHAPTER 15

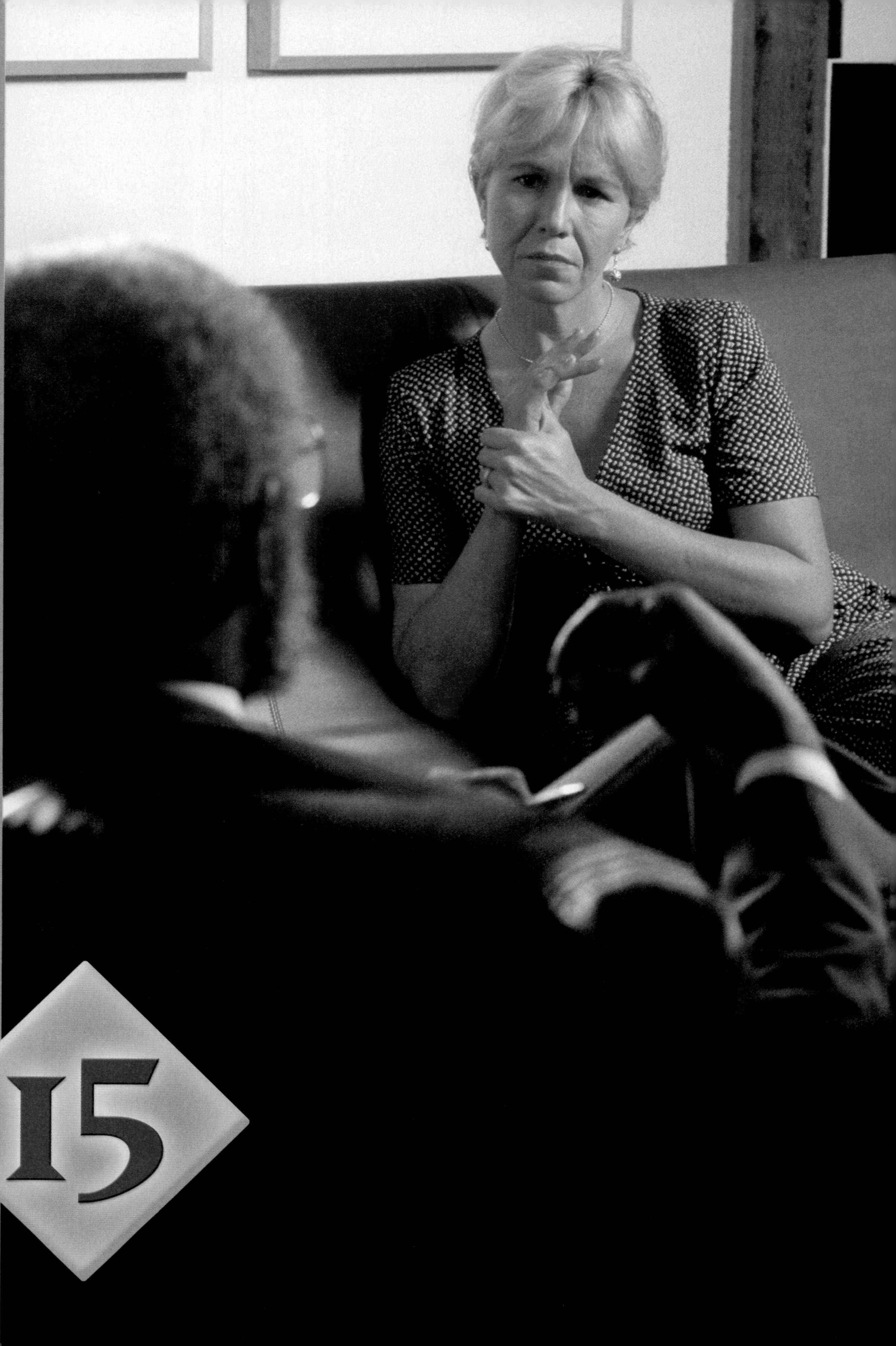

Therapies for Psychological Disorders

As you read Chapter 14, you might at some points have felt overwhelmed by all the ways in which individuals can experience mental illness. Fortunately, psychologists and other providers of mental health care have worked intently to create therapies that address the full range of psychopathology. We will see in this chapter that researchers continue to generate innovations in therapeutic techniques. The more researchers learn about the causes and consequences of psychopathology—the research we described in Chapter 14—the better they are able to fine-tune their repertory of therapies.

In this chapter, we will examine the types of therapies that can help restore personal control to individuals with a range of disorders. We address a number of formidable questions: How has the treatment of psychological disorders been influenced by historical, cultural, and social forces? How do theory, research, and practice interact as researchers develop and test treatment methods? What can be done to influence a mind ungoverned by ordinary reason, to modify uncontrolled behavior, to alter unchecked emotions, and to correct abnormalities of the brain?

This chapter surveys the major types of treatments currently used by health-care providers: psychoanalysis, behavior modification, cognitive alteration, humanistic therapies, and drug therapies. We will examine the way these treatments work. We will also evaluate the validity of claims about the success of each therapy.

The Therapeutic Context

There are different types of therapies for mental disorders, and there are many reasons some people seek help (and others who need it do not). The purposes or goals of therapy, the settings in which therapy occurs, and the kinds of therapeutic helpers also vary. Despite any differences between therapies, however, all are *interventions* into a person's life, designed to change the person's functioning in some way.

◆ GOALS AND MAJOR THERAPIES

The therapeutic process can involve four primary tasks or goals:

1. Reaching a *diagnosis* about what is wrong, possibly determining an appropriate psychiatric *(DSM-IV-TR)* label for the presenting problem, and classifying the disorder.

2. Proposing a probable *etiology* (cause of the problem)—that is, identifying the probable origins of the disorder and the functions being served by the symptoms.

3. Making a *prognosis,* or estimate, of the course the problem will take with and without any treatment.

4. Prescribing and carrying out some form of *treatment,* a therapy designed to minimize or eliminate the troublesome symptoms and, perhaps, their sources.

Biomedical therapies focus on changing the mechanisms that run the central nervous system. Practiced largely by psychiatrists and physicians, these therapies try to alter brain functioning with chemical or physical interventions, including surgery, electric shock, and drugs that act directly on the brain–body connection.

Psychological therapies, which are collectively called **psychotherapy,** focus on changing the faulty behaviors people have learned: the words, thoughts, interpretations, and feedback that direct daily strategies for living. These therapies are practiced by clinical psychologists as well as by psychiatrists. There are four major types of psychotherapies: psychodynamic, behavioral, cognitive, and existential-humanistic.

The *psychodynamic* approach views neurotic suffering as the outer symptom of inner, unresolved traumas and conflicts. Psychodynamic therapists treat mental disorder with a "talking cure," in which a therapist helps a person develop insights about the relation between the overt symptoms and the unresolved hidden conflicts that presumably caused them.

Behavior therapy treats the behaviors themselves as disturbances that must be modified. Disorders are viewed as learned behavior patterns rather than as the symptoms of mental disease. Behaviors are transformed in many ways, including changing reinforcement contingencies for desirable and undesirable responding, extinguishing conditioned responses, and providing models of effective problem solving.

Cognitive therapy tries to restructure the way a person thinks by altering the often distorted self-statements a person makes about the causes of a problem. Restructuring cognitions changes the way a person defines and explains difficulties, often enabling the person to cope with the problems.

Therapies that have emerged from the *humanistic tradition* emphasize the patients' values. They are directed toward self-actualization, psychological growth, the development of more meaningful interpersonal relationships, and the enhancement of freedom of choice. They tend to focus more on improving the functioning of essentially healthy people than on correcting the symptoms of seriously disturbed individuals.

◆ THERAPISTS AND THERAPEUTIC SETTINGS

When psychological problems arise, most people initially seek out informal counselors who operate in familiar settings. Many people turn to family members, close friends, personal physicians, lawyers, or favorite teachers for support, guidance, and counsel. Those with religious affiliations may seek help from a clergy member. Others get advice and a chance to talk by opening up to bartenders, salesclerks, cabdrivers, or other people willing to listen. In our society, these informal therapists carry the bulk of the daily burden of relieving frustration and conflict. When problems are limited in scope, informal therapists can often help.

Although more people seek out therapy now than in the past, people usually turn to trained mental health professionals only when their psychological problems become severe or persist for extended peri-

Cathy □ Cathy Guisewite

ods of time. When they do, they can turn to several types of therapists.

A **clinical social worker** is a mental health professional whose specialized training in a school of social work prepares him or her to work in collaboration with psychiatrists and clinical psychologists. Unlike many psychiatrists and psychologists, these counselors are trained to consider the social contexts of people's problems, so these practitioners may also involve other family members in the therapy or at least become acquainted with clients' homes or work settings.

A **pastoral counselor** is a member of a religious group who specializes in the treatment of psychological disorders. Often, these counselors combine spirituality with practical problem solving.

A **clinical psychologist** is required to have concentrated his or her graduate school training in the assessment and treatment of psychological problems, completed a supervised internship in a clinical setting, and earned a Ph.D. or Psy.D. These psychologists tend to have a broader background in psychology, assessment, and research than do psychiatrists.

A **counseling psychologist** also typically has obtained a Ph.D. or Psy.D. He or she usually provides guidance in areas such as vocation selection, school problems, drug abuse, and marital conflict. Often, these counselors work in community settings related to the problem areas—within a business, a school, a prison, the military service, or a neighborhood clinic—and use interviews, tests, guidance, and advising to help individuals solve specific problems and make decisions about future options.

A **psychiatrist** must have completed all medical school training for an M.D. degree and also have undergone some postdoctoral specialty training in mental and emotional disorders. Psychiatrists are trained more in the biomedical basis of psychological problems, and

they are currently the only therapists who can prescribe medical or drug-based interventions.

A **psychoanalyst** is a therapist with either an M.D. or a Ph.D. degree who has completed specialized postgraduate training in the Freudian approach to understanding and treating mental disorders.

These different types of therapists practice in many settings: hospitals, clinics, schools, and private offices. Some humanistic therapists prefer to conduct group sessions in their homes in order to work in a more natural environment. Community-based therapies, which take the treatment to the client, may operate out of local storefronts or houses of worship. Finally, therapists who practice *in vivo* therapy work with clients in the life setting that is associated with their problem. For example, they work in airplanes with clients who suffer from flying phobias or in shopping malls with people who have social phobias.

In the past few years, psychotherapists have also begun to provide mental health care using e-mail or the Internet (King & Moreggi, 1998; Taylor & Luce, 2003). In this type of computer-assisted therapy, individuals often interact with their therapists through exchanges of e-mail. Researchers have been quick to point out both potential dangers and benefits of therapy on the Internet. On the dangers side, researchers worry that patients may be misdiagnosed if they present limited or distorted information without the extra scrutiny that is possible face-to-face (King & Moreggi, 1998). Furthermore, consumers rarely are able to verify the credentials of on-line therapists; in cyberspace anyone can claim to be an expert. Despite these dangers, e-mail therapy may also provide unique opportunities for therapists and their clients. For example, some therapists believe that the relative anonymity of this form of therapy allows clients to reveal their most pressing problems and concerns more quickly and with less embarrassment;

individuals may be more honest when they don't have to worry about their therapist's overt reactions to their difficult confessions (Grohol, 1998).

People who enter therapy are usually referred to as either patients or clients. The term **patient** is used by professionals who take a biomedical approach to the treatment of psychological problems. The term **client** is used by professionals who think of psychological disorders as "problems in living" and not as mental illnesses. We will use the preferred term for each approach: *patient* for biomedical and psychoanalytic therapies and *client* for other therapies.

Whatever the form of the treatment, it's important that the individual seeking help enter into an effective therapeutic alliance. A *therapeutic alliance* is a mutual relationship that a client or patient establishes with a therapist: The individual and the therapist collaborate to bring about relief. Research suggests that the quality of the therapeutic alliance has an impact on psychotherapy's ability to bring about improved mental health (Joyce et al., 2003). When you enter into therapy, you should believe that you can establish a strong therapeutic alliance with your therapist.

Before looking at contemporary therapies and therapists in more detail, we will first consider the historical contexts in which treatment of the mentally ill was developed and then broaden the Western perspective with a look at the healing practices of other cultures.

◆ HISTORICAL AND CULTURAL CONTEXTS

What kind of treatment might you have received in past centuries if you were suffering from psychological problems? If you had lived in Europe or the United States, chances are the treatment would not have helped and could even have been harmful. In other cultures, treatment of psychological disorders has usually been seen within a broader perspective of religious and social values that yielded more humane treatment.

HISTORY OF WESTERN TREATMENT

Population increases and migration to big cities in 14th-century Western Europe created unemployment and social alienation. These conditions led to poverty, crime, and psychological problems. Special institutions were soon created to warehouse society's three emerging categories of "misfits": the poor, criminals, and the mentally disturbed.

In 1403, a London hospital—St. Mary of Bethlehem—admitted its first patient with psychological problems. For the next 300 years, mental patients of the hospital were chained, tortured, and exhibited to an admission-paying public. Over time, a mispronunciation of Bethlehem—*bedlam*—came to mean *chaos,* because of the horrible confusion reigning in the hospital and the dehumanized treatment of patients there (Foucault, 1975).

It wasn't until the late 18th century that the perception of psychological problems as *mental illness* emerged in Europe. The French physician **Philippe Pinel** wrote in 1801, "The mentally ill, far from being guilty people deserving of punishment, are sick people whose miserable state deserves all the consideration that is due to suffering humanity. One should try with the most simple methods to restore their reason" (Zilboorg & Henry, 1941, pp. 323–324).

In the United States, psychologically disturbed individuals were confined for their own protection and for the safety of the community, but they were given no treatment. However, by the mid-1800s, when psychology as a field of study was gaining some credibility and respectability, "a cult of curability" emerged throughout the country. Insanity was then thought to be related to the environmental stresses brought on by the turmoil of newly developing cities. Eventually, madness came to be viewed as a social problem to be cured through

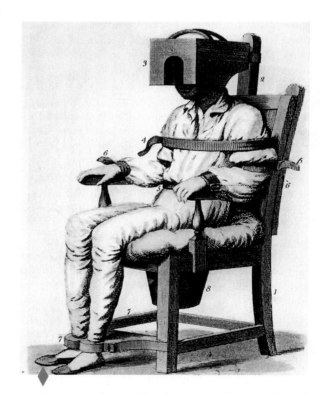

Treatment of mental disorders in the 18th century focused on banishing "ill humors" from the body. Shown here is the "tranquilizing chair" advocated by Philadelphia physician Benjamin Rush. Why did attitudes toward the treatment of the mentally ill change?

    <www.ablongman.com/gerrig17e>

"mental hygiene," just as contagious physical diseases were being treated by physical hygiene.

In the 1900s, **Clifford Beers** spurred on the mental hygiene movement. Eventually, the confinement of the mentally ill assumed a new *rehabilitative* goal. The *asylum* then became the central fixture of this social-political movement. The disturbed were confined to asylums in rural areas, far from the stress of the city, not only for protection but also for treatment (Rothman, 1971). Unfortunately, many of the asylums that were built became overcrowded. The humane goal of rehabilitation was replaced with the pragmatic goal of *containing* strange people in remote places. These large, under-staffed state mental hospitals became little more than human warehouses for disturbed individuals (Scull, 1993). Beginning in the 1960s, reformers began to agitate against these warehouses, in favor of the *deinstitution-alization* of at least those mental patients who could thrive with outpatient treatment and appropriate community supports. Unfortunately, many deinstitutionalized patients do not obtain adequate assistance in their communities. For example, researchers found that 24 percent of a sample of 438 individuals with serious mental illnesses were homeless (Kuno et al., 2000).

CULTURAL SYMBOLS AND RITUALS OF CURING

Our review of these historical trends in the treatment of psychological disorders has been limited to Western views and practices, which emphasize the uniqueness of the individual, independence, and personal responsibility for success and failure. Both demonology and the disease model are consistent with this emphasis, regarding mental disorder as something that happens *inside* a person and as an individual's failure.

This view is not shared by many other cultures (Triandis, 1995). The research of *cultural anthropologists* has provided analyses of the explanations and treatments for psychological disorders across different cultures (Bourguignon, 1979; Evans-Pritchard, 1937; Kluckhohn, 1944; Marsella, 1979). For example, in the African worldview, the emphasis is on cooperation, interdependence, tribal survival, unity with nature, and collective responsibility (Nobles, 1976). It is contrary to the thinking of many non-European cultures to treat mentally ill individuals by *removing* them from society. In many African cultures, healing takes place in a social context, involving a distressed person's beliefs, family, work, and life environment. The African use of group support in therapy has been expanded into a procedure called "network therapy," in which a patient's entire network of relatives, coworkers, and friends becomes involved in the treatment (Lambo, 1978).

In many cultures, the treatment of mental and physical disease is bound up with religion and witchcraft.

Certain human beings, called *shamans,* are given special mystical powers to help in the transformation of their distressed fellow beings. **Shamanism** is an ancient and powerful spiritual tradition that has been practiced for close to 30,000 years. In the shamanistic tradition, suffering and disease are diagnosed as powerlessness. This cultural belief system *personalizes* the vague forces of fate or chance that intervene in one's life to create problems. Such personalization permits direct action to be taken against presumed evildoers and direct help to be sought from assumed divine healers (Middleton, 1967). Often, the pathological state that is seen as a result of the spirit possession of the afflicted person is transformed by therapeutic intervention of shaman healers. Drumming, chanting, and other rituals are used to inspire awe and induce altered states of consciousness that facilitate the quest for knowledge and empowerment (Walsh, 1990).

Common to folk-healing ceremonies are the important roles of symbols, myths, and rituals (Lévi-Strauss, 1963). **Ritual healing** ceremonies infuse special emotional intensity and meaning into the healing process. They heighten patients' suggestibility and sense of importance, and, combined with the use of symbols, they connect the individual sufferer, the shaman, and the society to supernatural forces to be won over in the battle against madness (Devereux, 1961). One therapeutic practice used in a number of healing ceremonies is *dissociation of consciousness,* in which the distressed person or a faith healer enters an altered state of consciousness. In Western views, dissociation is itself a symptom of mental disorder to be prevented or corrected; in other cultures, as consciousness is altered, good spirits are communicated with and evil spirits are exorcised. The use of ceremonial alteration of consciousness can be seen among the cult of Puerto Rican *Espiritistas* in New York City, whose healing ceremonies involve communication with good spirits that are believed to exist outside the person (Garrison, 1977).

Although shamans and other healers play special roles in ritual ceremonies, the healing power most often transcends the individual healer and resides in greater spiritual forces (Katz, 1982, 1993). In describing healing practices in Fiji, psychologist **Richard Katz** writes, "Becoming connected to the spiritual dimension demands commitment to a healing power beyond the self, and entails humility about one's own contribution to healing. The Fijian healer does not claim personal ownership of *mana* [spiritual power derived from the culture's ancestors], or take personal credit for its healing effects" (pp. 327–328). Katz makes an explicit comparison to Western practice: "In contrast, the Western physician is more likely to claim control over, if not ownership of, the ability to cure or heal. Competence—knowing what to do, or at least not revealing that one doesn't know—is stressed over natural human vulnerability" (p. 328).

Some of these non-Western views have begun to work their way into Western practices (Katz, 1982, 1993). The influence of the social-interactive concept and the focus on the *family context* and *supportive community* are evident in newer therapeutic approaches that emphasize social support networks and family therapy. Other Western practitioners work with shamans in an effort to integrate Western psychotherapies that involve self-analysis with the therapies of collectivist societies that view the individual within the current communal context. These attempts at integration make therapies more culturally appropriate to a wider range of clients (Kraut, 1990).

With this brief overview of historical trends and some cultural variations in mind, it is time to investigate in some detail each of the major types of therapies being practiced today.

Psychodynamic Therapies

*P*sychodynamic therapies assume that a patient's problems have been caused by the psychological tension between unconscious impulses and the constraints of his or her life situation. These therapies locate the core of the disorder inside the disturbed person.

◆ FREUDIAN PSYCHOANALYSIS

Psychoanalysis, as developed by **Sigmund Freud,** is an intensive and prolonged technique for exploring unconscious motivations and conflicts in neurotic, anxiety-ridden individuals. As we saw in earlier chapters, Freudian theory views anxiety disorders as inabilities to resolve adequately the inner conflicts between the unconscious, irrational impulses of the *id* and the internalized social constraints imposed by the *superego.* The goal of psychoanalysis is to establish intrapsychic harmony that expands awareness of the forces of the *id,* reduces overcompliance with the demands of the *superego,* and strengthens the role of the *ego.*

Of central importance to a therapist is to understand the way a patient uses the process of *repression* to handle conflicts. Symptoms are considered to be messages from the unconscious that something is wrong. A psychoanalyst's task is to help a patient bring repressed thoughts to consciousness and to gain *insight* into the relationship between the current symptoms and the repressed conflicts. In this psychodynamic view, therapy succeeds and patients recover when they are "released from repression" established in early childhood. Because a central goal of a therapist is to guide a patient toward discovering insights into the relationships between present symptoms and past origins, psychodynamic therapy is often called **insight therapy.**

Traditional psychoanalysis is an attempt to reconstruct long-standing repressed memories and then work through painful feelings to an effective resolution. Accordingly, it is a therapy that takes a long time (several years at least, with as many as five sessions a week). It also requires introspective patients who are verbally fluent, highly motivated to remain in therapy, and willing and able to undergo considerable expense. (Newer forms of psychodynamic therapy are making therapy briefer in total duration.) Therapists in the psychodynamic tradition use several techniques to bring repressed conflicts to consciousness and to help a patient resolve them (Henry et al., 1994). These techniques include free association, analysis of resistance, dream analysis, and analysis of transference and countertransference.

FREE ASSOCIATION AND CATHARSIS

The principal procedure used in psychoanalysis to probe the unconscious and release repressed material is called **free association.** A patient, sitting comfortably in a chair or lying in a relaxed position on a couch, lets his or her mind wander freely and gives a running account of thoughts, wishes, physical sensations, and mental images. The patient is encouraged to reveal every thought or feeling, no matter how unimportant it may seem.

Freud maintained that free associations are *predetermined,* not random. The task of an analyst is to track the associations to their source and identify the significant patterns that lie beneath the surface of what are appar-

Why is psychoanalytic therapy, originally practiced in Freud's study, often called the "talking cure"?

ently just words. The patient is encouraged to express strong feelings, usually toward authority figures, that have been repressed for fear of punishment or retaliation. Any such emotional release, by this or other processes within the therapeutic context, is called **catharsis.**

RESISTANCE

A psychoanalyst attaches particular importance to subjects that a patient does *not* wish to discuss. At some time during the process of free association, a patient will show **resistance**—an inability or unwillingness to discuss certain ideas, desires, or experiences. Such resistances are conceived of as *barriers* between the unconscious and the conscious. This material is often related to an individual's sexual life (which includes all things pleasurable) or to hostile, resentful feelings toward parents. When the repressed material is finally brought into the open, a patient generally claims that it is unimportant, absurd, irrelevant, or too unpleasant to discuss. The therapist believes the opposite. Psychoanalysis aims to break down resistances and enable the patient to face these painful ideas, desires, and experiences.

DREAM ANALYSIS

Psychoanalysts believe that dreams are an important source of information about a patient's unconscious motivations. When a person is asleep, the superego is presumably less on guard against the unacceptable impulses originating in the id, so a motive that cannot be expressed in waking life may find expression in a dream. In analysis, dreams are assumed to have two kinds of content: *manifest* (openly visible) content that people remember upon awakening and *latent* (hidden) content—the actual motives that are seeking expression

but are so painful or unacceptable that they are expressed in disguised or symbolic form. Therapists attempt to uncover these hidden motives by using **dream analysis,** a therapeutic technique that examines the content of a person's dreams to discover the underlying or disguised motivations and symbolic meanings of significant life experiences and desires.

TRANSFERENCE AND COUNTERTRANSFERENCE

During the course of the intensive therapy of psychoanalysis, a patient usually develops an emotional reaction toward the therapist. Often, the therapist is identified with a person who has been at the center of an emotional conflict in the past—most often a parent or a lover. This emotional reaction is called **transference.** Transference is called *positive transference* when the feelings attached to the therapist are those of love or admiration and *negative transference* when the feelings consist of hostility or envy. Often, a patient's attitude is ambivalent, including a mixture of positive and negative feelings. An analyst's task in handling transference is a difficult one because of the patient's emotional vulnerability; however, it is a crucial part of treatment. A therapist helps a patient to interpret the present transferred feelings by understanding their original source in earlier experiences and attitudes (Henry et al., 1994).

Personal feelings are also at work in a therapist's reactions to a patient. **Countertransference** refers to what happens when a therapist comes to like or dislike a patient because the patient is perceived as similar to significant people in the therapist's life. In working through countertransference, a therapist may discover some unconscious dynamics of his or her own. The therapist becomes a "living mirror" for the patient and the patient, in turn, for the therapist. If the therapist fails to recognize the operation of countertransference, the therapy may not be as effective (Winarick, 1997). Because of the emotional intensity of this type of therapeutic relationship and the vulnerability of the patient, therapists must be on guard about crossing the boundary between professional caring and personal involvement with their patients. The therapy setting is obviously one with an enormous power imbalance that must be recognized, and honored, by the therapist.

◆ LATER PSYCHODYNAMIC THERAPIES

Freud's followers retained many of his basic ideas but modified certain of his principles and practices. In general, these therapists place more emphasis than Freud did on: (1) a patient's *current* social environment (less focus on the past); (2) the continuing influence of life

Are Lives Haunted by Repressed Memories?

Adam Whitehurst

University of North Carolina at Chapel Hill

On September 22, 1969, 8-year-old Susan Nason vanished from her northern California neighborhood. In December 1969, her body was found. For 20 years, no one knew who had murdered her. Then, in 1989, Susan's friend Eileen Franklin-Lipsker contacted county investigators. Eileen told them that, with the help of psychotherapy, she had recalled a long-repressed, horrifying memory about what had happened to Susan. In the fall of 1990, Eileen testified that, over two decades earlier, she had witnessed her father, George Franklin, sexually assault Susan and then bludgeon her to death with a rock (Marcus, 1990; Workman, 1990). Eileen reported that her father had threatened to kill her if she ever told anyone. This testimony was sufficient to have George Franklin convicted of first-degree murder.

How, in theory, had these memories remained hidden for 20 years? The answer to this mystery finds its roots in Sigmund Freud's concept of repressed memories. As we just reminded you, Freud (1923) theorized that some people's memories of life experiences become sufficiently threatening to their psychological well-being that the individuals banish the memories from consciousness—they repress them. Clinical psychologists are often able to help clients take control of their lives by interpreting disruptive life patterns as the consequences of repressed memories; an important goal of therapy is to achieve catharsis with respect to these repressed memories.

But not all experiences of repressed memories remain in the therapist's office. In recent years, there has been an explosion of mass-media claims for the dramatic recovery of repressed memories. After long

intervals of time, individuals report sudden vivid recollections of horrifying events, such as murders or childhood sexual abuse. Could all these claims be real? Our review of memory research in Chapter 7—particularly research on eyewitness memories—provided you with grounds for skepticism (Wells & Loftus, 2003). You might recall from that research that people will report as true memories information that was provided from an artificial source. They will do so even when, as witnesses, they have been specifically warned that they have been misled. Thus, being in confident possession of a memory provides no assurance of the ultimate source of that memory.

In fact, the popular media have in recent years frequently provided reports of repressed memories that can serve as an "artificial source." What an individual saw on TV could be reborn as a personal memory if information about the TV as source somehow got lost. Thus, media

descriptions of repressed memories will potentially lead some individuals to "recover" the same memories. Basically, the individual has lost access to the *source* of the memory but held on to the *content* (Johnson et al., 1993).

Clinicians also worry that therapists who believe in repressed memories may, through the mechanisms of psychotherapy, implant those beliefs in their patients (Lynn et al., 2003). For example, researchers have studied women who have ultimately retracted charges of childhood sexual abuse—these women had come to understand that their "memories" of abuse could not have been real. These studies provide evidence that therapists often instigated the patients' efforts to find these memories—and verbally rewarded them when the "memories" came to light (de Rivera, 1997). Cases of this sort have convinced clinicians that they must study the social forces that are at work in therapy to discover how the therapist's theory is translated into the patient's reality (Lynn et al., 1997).

Belief in the recovery of repressed memories may provide a measurable benefit for patients in psychotherapy. In fact, some portion of recovered memories are valid recollections of earlier traumatic experiences (Schooler & Eich, 2000; Williams, 1995). Even so, if you come to explore the question of whether repressed memories from your past can help explain present discomfort, you should ensure that you are not passively accepting someone else's version of your life. Fortunately for George Franklin, doubts about his daughter's repressed memories led his verdict to be overturned.

experiences (not just childhood conflicts); (3) the role of social motivation and interpersonal relations of love (rather than of biological instincts and selfish concerns); (4) the significance of ego functioning and development of the self-concept (less on the conflict between id and superego).

In Chapter 13, we noted two other prominent theorists, Carl Jung and Alfred Adler. To get a flavor of more contemporary psychodynamic approaches, here we will look at the work of Harry Stack Sullivan and Melanie Klein (see Ruitenbeek, 1973, for a look at other members of the Freudian circle).

Harry Stack Sullivan (1953) felt that Freudian theory and therapy did not recognize the importance of social relationships and a patient's needs for acceptance, respect, and love. Mental disorders, he insisted, involve not only traumatic intrapsychic processes but also troubled interpersonal relationships and even strong societal pressures. A young child needs to feel secure and to be treated by others with caring and tenderness. Anxiety and other mental ills arise out of insecurities in relations with parents and significant others. In Sullivan's view, a self-system is built up to hold anxiety down to a tolerable level. This self-system is derived from a child's interpersonal experiences and is organized around conceptions of the self as the *good-me* (associated with the mother's tenderness), the *bad-me* (associated with the mother's tensions), and the *not-me* (a dissociated self that is unacceptable to the rest of the self).

Therapy based on this interpersonal view involves observing a *patient's feelings* about the *therapist's attitudes*. The therapeutic interview is seen as a social setting in which each party's feelings and attitudes are influenced by the other's. The patient is gently provoked to state his or her assumptions about the therapist's attitudes. Above all, the therapeutic situation, for Sullivan, was one in which the therapist learned and taught lovingly (Wallach & Wallach, 1983).

Melanie Klein (1975) defected from Freud's emphasis on the Oedipus conflict as the major source of psychopathology. Because of Freud's focus on neurotic symptoms arising from the oedipal period (ages 4 to 5), the task he set for therapeutic intervention was to interpret and illuminate these unconscious sexual conflicts. However, some analytic therapists had difficulty treating patients whose conflicts seemed to arise from earlier times, before they had verbal memory, which often resulted in more extreme pathologies. They often suffered from feelings of unreality, emptiness, and a loss of meaning in life. Klein suggested that primitive forms of the superego appear in the first months of life. Instead of oedipal sexual conflicts as the most important organizing factors of the psyche, Klein argued that a *death instinct* preceded sexual awareness

In what ways did the theories of Melanie Klein and Sigmund Freud differ?

and led to an innate aggressive impulse that was equally important in organizing the psyche. She contended that the two fundamental organizing forces in the psyche are aggression and love, where aggression *splits* and love *unites* the psyche. Aggressive splitting of the world rejects what is hated and keeps what is desired; love creates unity and wholeness. For Klein, love was not just erotic fulfillment but a true kindness and authentic caring for others. However, this conscious love is connected to remorse over destructive hate and potential violence toward those we love. Thus, Klein explained "one of the great mysteries that all people face, that love and hate—our personal heaven and hell—cannot be separated from one another" (Frager & Fadiman, 1998, p. 135). Klein's view that the building blocks of how we experience the world emerge from our relations to loved and hated *objects*—significant people in our lives—has become central to a prominent type of psychoanalytic theory and practice called **object relations theory.** Klein also pioneered the use of forceful therapeutic interpretations of both aggressive and sexual drives in analytic patients.

We already noted that psychoanalytic therapy often requires a long period of time to achieve its goals. Often, however, people are suffering from disorders that require more speedy remedies. Behavior therapies, to which we turn next, provide the potential for swift relief from symptoms.

➤ Why is psychodynamic therapy also known as insight therapy?

➤ What techniques might Freudian therapists use to bring about catharsis?

➤ What principles guide therapy based on Harry Stack Sullivan's theories?

➤ Why is object relations theory central to Melanie Klein's views?

Behavior Therapies

While psychodynamic therapies focus on presumed inner causes, behavior therapies focus on observable outer behaviors. Behavior therapists argue that abnormal behaviors are acquired in the same way as normal behaviors—through a learning process that follows the basic principles of conditioning and learning. Behavior therapies apply the principles of conditioning and reinforcement to modify undesirable behavior patterns associated with mental disorders.

The terms **behavior therapy** and **behavior modification** are often used interchangeably. Both refer to the systematic use of principles of learning to increase the frequency of desired behaviors and/or decrease that of problem behaviors. The range of deviant behaviors and personal problems that typically are treated by behavior therapy is extensive and includes fears, compulsions, depression, addictions, aggression, and delinquent behaviors. In general, behavior therapy works best with specific rather than general types of personal problems: It is better for a phobia than for unfocused anxiety.

The therapies that have emerged from the theories of conditioning and learning are grounded in a pragmatic, empirical research tradition. The central task of all living organisms is to learn how to adapt to the demands of the current social and physical environment. When organisms do not learn how to cope effectively, their maladaptive reactions can be overcome by therapy based on principles of learning (or relearning). The target behavior is not assumed to be a symptom of any underlying process. The symptom itself is the problem. Psychodynamic therapists predicted that treating only the outer behavior without confronting the true, inner problem would result in *symptom substitution,* the appearance of a new physical or psychological problem. However, research has shown that when pathological behaviors are eliminated by behavior therapy, new symptoms are not substituted (Kazdin, 1982; Wolpe, 1986). "On the contrary, patients whose target symptoms improved often reported improvement in other, less important symptoms as well" (Sloane et al., 1975, p. 219).

Let's look at the different forms of behavior therapies that have brought relief to distressed individuals.

◆ COUNTERCONDITIONING

Why does someone become anxious when faced with a harmless stimulus, such as a spider, a nonpoisonous snake, or social contact? The behavioral explanation is that the anxiety arises due to the simple conditioning principles we reviewed in Chapters 6 and 14: Strong emotional reactions that disrupt a person's life "for no good reason" are often conditioned responses that the person does not recognize as having been learned previously. In **counterconditioning,** a new response is conditioned to replace, or "counter," a maladaptive response. The earliest recorded use of behavior therapy followed this logic. **Mary Cover Jones** (1924) showed that a fear could be *unlearned* through conditioning. (Compare with the case of Little Albert in Chapter 6.)

> Her patient was Peter, a 3-year-old boy who, for some unknown reason, was afraid of rabbits. The therapy involved feeding Peter at one end of a room while the rabbit was brought in at the other end. Over a series of sessions, the rabbit was gradually brought closer until, finally, all fear disappeared and Peter played freely with the rabbit.

Following in Cover Jones's footsteps, behavior therapists now use several counterconditioning techniques, including systematic desensitization, implosion, flooding, and aversion therapy.

EXPOSURE THERAPIES

The central component of **exposure therapy** is that individuals are made to confront the object or situation that causes anxiety. The therapeutic principle is that exposure permits counterconditioning—people learn to remain relaxed in circumstances that once would have made them highly anxious. Individual exposure therapies differ with respect to the time course and circumstances in which people are exposed to their sources of anxiety.

For example, **Joseph Wolpe** (1958, 1973) observed that the nervous system cannot be relaxed and agitated at the same time because incompatible processes cannot be activated simultaneously. This insight was central to the *theory of reciprocal inhibition* that Wolpe applied to the treatment of fears and phobias. Wolpe taught his patients to *relax* their muscles and then to *imagine* visually their feared situation. They did so in gradual steps that moved from initially remote associations to direct images. Psychologically confronting the feared stimulus while being relaxed and doing so in a *graduated* sequence is the therapeutic technique known as **systematic desensitization.**

Desensitization therapy involves three major steps. First, the client identifies the stimuli that provoke anxiety and arranges them in a hierarchy ranked from weakest to strongest. For example, a student suffering from severe test anxiety constructed the hierarchy in **Table 15.1.** Note that she rated immediate anticipation of an examination (No. 14) as more stressful than taking the exam itself (No. 13). Second, the client is trained in a system of progressive deep-muscle relaxation. Relaxation training requires several sessions in which the client learns to distinguish between sensations of tension and relaxation and to let go of tension in order to achieve a state of physical and mental relaxation. Finally, the actual process of desensitization begins: The relaxed client vividly imagines the weakest anxiety

stimulus on the list. If it can be visualized without discomfort, the client goes on to the next stronger one. After a number of sessions, the most distressing situations on the list can be imagined without anxiety.

Systematic desensitization represents a gradual course of exposure to stimuli that provoke anxiety. Therapists have explored a variety of other techniques, some of which bring about exposure with less delay. For example, in a technique known as *flooding*, clients agree to be put directly into the phobic situation. A person with claustrophobia is made to sit in a dark closet, and a child with a fear of water is put into a pool. Researchers successfully treated a 21-year-old student's phobia of balloon pops by having him experience three sessions in which he endured hundreds of balloons being popped (Houlihan et al., 1993). In the third session, the student was able to pop the last 115 balloons himself. Another form of flooding therapy begins with the use of imagination. In this procedure, the client may listen to a tape that describes the most terrifying version of the phobic fear in great detail for an hour or two. Once the terror subsides, the client is then taken to the feared situation.

When exposure techniques were first created, therapists brought about exposure through mental imagery or actual contact. In recent years, clinicians have turned to virtual reality to provide exposure therapy (Glanz et al., 2003). Consider this study that compared virtual reality therapy to standard exposure therapy for individuals with *acrophobia*—a fear of heights.

TABLE 15.1

Hierarchy of Anxiety-Producing Stimuli for a Test-Anxious College Student (in order of increasing anxiety)

1. A month before an examination.
2. Two weeks before an examination.
3. A week before an examination.
4. Five days before an examination.
5. Four days before an examination.
6. Three days before an examination.
7. Two days before an examination.
8. One day before an examination.
9. The night before an examination.
10. The examination paper face down.
11. Awaiting the distribution of examination papers.
12. Before the unopened doors of the examination room.
13. In the process of answering an examination paper.
14. On the way to the university on the day of an examination.

PUTTING IDEAS TO THE TEST

Treatments for Acrophobia

A team of researchers recruited 33 people suffering from acrophobia (Emmelkamp et al., 2002). Roughly half of the group (16 participants), received a standard form of exposure therapy. The researchers took them to actual physical locations that became successively more anxiety-provoking with respect to the fear of heights—a mall with several levels, a fire escape, and a roof garden. The participants experienced each location until their anxiety had diminished. The remainder of the participants visited the same locations—but as virtual environments. As with their peers who went out into the world, they remained in each virtual location until their anxiety had diminished. To measure the effectiveness of each intervention, the researchers assessed the participants' lingering discomfort toward heights on measures such as an *attitudes toward heights questionnaire.* Both types of therapies yielded consistent and lasting relief for the participants. There were no differences in the effectiveness of the two types of therapies.

Exposure therapies have proved to be highly effective for alleviating phobias. Virtually reality techniques hold out the promise of providing powerful exposure experiences without the time and expense of venturing out into the real world.

Exposure therapy has also been used to combat obsessive-compulsive disorders. For example, one woman who was obsessed with dirt compulsively washed her hands over and over until they cracked and bled. She even thought of killing herself because this disorder totally prevented her from leading a normal life. Under the supervision of a behavior therapist, she confronted the things she feared most—dirt and trash—and eventually even touched them. She gave up washing and bathing her hands and face for five days. Note that behavior therapy here has an added component, *response prevention*. Not only is the client exposed to what is feared (dirt and trash), but she is also prevented from performing the compulsive behavior that ordinarily reduces her anxiety (washing). The therapy teaches the woman to reduce anxiety without engaging her compulsion.

AVERSION THERAPY

The forms of exposure therapy we've described help clients deal directly with stimuli that are not really harmful. What can be done to help those who are *attracted* to stimuli that *are* harmful? Drug addiction, sexual perversions, and uncontrollable violence are human problems in which deviant behavior is elicited by tempting stimuli. **Aversion therapy** uses counter-conditioning procedures to pair these stimuli with strong noxious stimuli such as electric shocks or nausea-producing drugs. In time, the same negative reactions are elicited by the tempting stimuli, and the person develops an aversion that replaces his or her former desire. For example, aversion therapy has been used with individuals who engage in *self-injurious behaviors,* such as hitting their heads or banging their heads against other objects. When an individual performs such a behavior, he or she is given a mild electric shock. This treatment effectively eliminates self-injurious behaviors in some, but not all, patients (Duker & Seys, 1996).

In the extreme, aversion therapy resembles torture, so why would anyone submit voluntarily to it? Usually, people do so only because they realize that the long-term consequences of continuing their behavior pattern will destroy their health or ruin their careers or family lives. They may also be driven to do so by institutional pressures, as has happened in some prison treatment programs. However, use of aversion therapy in institutional rehabilitation programs has become regulated by ethical guidelines and state laws. The hope is that, under these restrictions, it will be therapeutic rather than coercive.

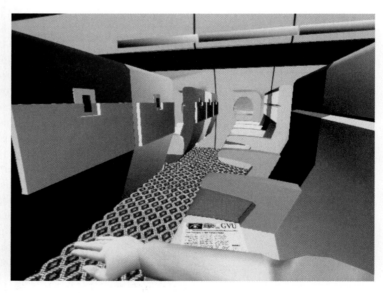

How might a behavior therapist use exposure therapy to help a client overcome a fear of flying?

◆ CONTINGENCY MANAGEMENT

Counterconditioning procedures are appropriate when one response can be replaced with another. Other behavior modification procedures rely on the principles of operant conditioning that arose in the research tradition pioneered by **B. F. Skinner. Contingency management** refers to the general treatment strategy of changing behavior by modifying its consequences. The two major techniques of contingency management in behavior therapy are *positive reinforcement strategies* and *extinction strategies.*

POSITIVE REINFORCEMENT STRATEGIES

When a response is followed immediately by a reward, the response tends to be repeated and to increase in frequency over time. This central principle of operant learning becomes a therapeutic strategy when it is used to modify the frequency of a desirable response as it replaces an undesirable one. Dramatic success has been obtained from the application of positive reinforcement procedures to behavior problems.

You might recall from Chapter 6 a technique called *shaping* in which researchers reinforce successive approximations to a desired behavior. Consider how shaping was used to improve the athletic performance of a 21-year-old university pole vaulter (Scott et al., 1997). The vaulter didn't sufficiently extend his arms (holding the pole) above his head before planting the pole to lift himself off. The research team used a photoelectric beam that beeped when the vaulter achieved the desired extension and broke the beam. In Chapter 6, we also described *token economies,* in which desired behaviors (for example, practicing personal care or taking medication) are explicitly defined, and token payoffs are given by institutional staff when the behaviors are performed. These tokens can later be exchanged for an array of rewards and privileges (Kazdin, 1994; Martin & Pear, 1999). These systems of reinforcement are especially effective in modifying patients' behaviors regarding self-care, upkeep of their environment, and frequency of their positive social interactions.

In another approach, therapists differentially reinforce behaviors that are incompatible with the maladaptive behavior. This technique has been used successfully with individuals in treatment for drug addiction.

PUTTING IDEAS TO THE TEST

Behaviorial Treatments for Drug Addiction

Researchers recruited 70 men and women who were seeking treatment for cocaine dependence. All the participants received a series of counseling sessions that imparted strategies and skills for overcoming dependence. In addition, 36 participants received vouchers each time they produced a urine specimen that was drug free. The vouchers were each worth \$0.25 and could be used to purchase retail items. The first time participants produced a negative urine specimen, they were given 10 vouchers. As long as they kept producing negative specimens, the number of vouchers on each occasion increased. For these participants, reinforcement with vouchers was *contingent* on being drug free. The remaining 34 participants were also given vouchers; however, their reinforcement was *noncontingent:* Each member of the noncontingent group was yoked to a member of the contingent group so that he or she got the same levels of reinforcement at the same times. Because of this design, we can be confident that any effect of the vouchers was a product of contingency and not reinforcement alone. In fact, contingency had an enduring impact on cocaine use: Both at the end of the study and one year later, participants in the contingent group were consistently more successful at abstaining from cocaine than their peers in the noncontingent group (Higgins et al., 2000).

You might recognize the same philosophy at work here as the one that motivated the counterconditioning procedures we described earlier: Basic principles of learning are used to increase the probability of adaptive behaviors.

EXTINCTION STRATEGIES

Why do people continue to do something that causes pain and distress when they are capable of doing otherwise? The answer is that many forms of behavior have multiple consequences—some are negative, and some are positive. Often, subtle positive reinforcements keep a behavior going despite its obvious negative consequences. For example, children who are punished for misbehaving may continue to misbehave if punishment is the only form of attention they seem to be able to earn.

Extinction strategies are useful in therapy when dysfunctional behaviors have been maintained by unrecognized reinforcing circumstances. Those reinforcers can be identified through a careful situational analysis, and then a program can be arranged to withhold them in the presence of the undesirable response. When this approach is possible, and everyone in the situation who might inadvertently reinforce the person's behavior cooperates, extinction procedures work to diminish the frequency of the behavior and eventually to eliminate the behavior completely. Consider a classroom example. Researchers discovered that attention from their peers was reinforcing the disruptive behavior of four elementary school children. By having their classmates provide attention to appropriate behaviors and ignore disruptive behaviors, the researchers were able to eliminate the children's patterns of misbehavior (Broussard & Northup, 1997).

Even symptoms of schizophrenia can be maintained and encouraged by unintentional reinforcement. Consider the following circumstances. It is standard procedure in many psychiatric hospitals for the staff to ask patients frequently, as a form of social communication, "How are you feeling?" Patients often misinterpret this question as a request for diagnostic information, and they respond by thinking and talking about their feelings, unusual symptoms, and hallucinations. Such responding is likely to be counterproductive, since it leads staff to conclude that the patients are self-absorbed and not behaving normally. In fact, the more bizarre the symptoms and verbalizations, the more attention the staff members may show to the patient, which reinforces continued expression of bizarre symptoms. In a classic study, dramatic decreases in symptoms were observed when hospital staff members were simply instructed to ignore the behavior and to give attention to the patients only when they were behaving normally (Ayllon & Michael, 1959).

◆ SOCIAL-LEARNING THERAPY

The range of behavior therapies has been expanded by social-learning theorists who point out that humans learn by observing the behavior of other people. Often, you learn and apply rules to new experiences through symbolic means, such as watching other people's experiences in life, in a movie, or on TV. **Social-learning therapy** is designed to modify problematic behavior patterns by arranging conditions in which a client will observe models being reinforced for a desirable form of responding. This vicarious learning process has been of special value in overcoming phobias and building social skills. We have noted in earlier chapters that this social-learning theory was largely developed through the pioneering research of **Albert Bandura** (1977, 1986). Here we will mention only two aspects of his approach: imitation of models and social-skills training.

IMITATION OF MODELS

Social-learning theory predicts that individuals acquire responses through observation. Thus, it should be the case that people with phobias should be able to unlearn fear reactions through imitation of models. For example, in treating a phobia of snakes, a therapist will first demonstrate fearless approach behavior at a relatively minor level, perhaps approaching a snake's cage or touching a snake. The client is aided, through demonstration and encouragement, to imitate the modeled behavior. Gradually, the approach behaviors are shaped so that the client can pick up the snake and let it crawl freely over him or her. At no time is the client forced to perform any behavior. Resistance at any level is overcome by having the client return to a previously successful, less threatening level of approach behavior.

The power of this form of **participant modeling** can be seen in research comparing this technique with symbolic modeling, desensitization, and a control condition. In *symbolic modeling therapy*, individuals who had been trained in relaxation techniques watched a film in which several models fearlessly handled snakes; they could stop the film and try to relax whenever a scene made them feel anxious. In the control condition, no therapeutic intervention was used. As you can see in **Figure 15.1,** participant modeling was clearly the most successful of these techniques. Snake phobia was eliminated in 11 of the 12 individuals in the participant modeling group (Bandura, 1970).

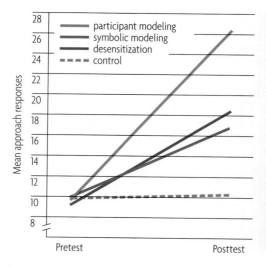

◆

FIGURE 15.1

Participant Modeling Therapy

The subject shown in the photo first watched a model make a graduated series of snake-approach responses and then repeated them herself. She eventually was able to pick up the snake and let it crawl about on her. The graph compares the number of approach responses subjects made before and after receiving participant modeling therapy (most effective) with the behavior of those exposed to two other therapeutic techniques and a control group.

SOCIAL-SKILLS TRAINING

A major therapeutic innovation encouraged by social-learning therapists involves training people with inadequate social skills to be more effective. Many difficulties arise for someone with a mental disorder, or even just an everyday problem, if he or she is socially inhibited, inept, or unassertive. *Social skills* are sets of responses that enable people to effectively achieve their social goals when approaching or interacting with others. These skills include knowing *what* (content) to say and do in given situations in order to elicit a desired response (consequences), *how* (style) to say and do it, and *when* (timing) to say and do it. One of the most common social-skills problems is lack of assertiveness—an inability to state one's own thoughts or wishes in a clear, direct, nonaggressive manner (Alberti & Emmons, 1990; Bower & Bower, 1991). To help people overcome such a problem, many social-learning therapists recommend **behavioral rehearsal**—visualizing how one should behave in a given situation and the desired positive consequences. Rehearsal can be used to establish and strengthen any basic skill, from personal hygiene to work habits to social interactions.

Adult pathology is often preceded by deficits in social skills in childhood. Therefore, considerable research and therapy are directed at building competence in withdrawn and disturbed children (Fantuzzo et al., 1996; Pfiffner & McBurnett, 1997). For example, one study provided an intervention based on guided imagery to increase the peer acceptance of social isolates.

PUTTING IDEAS TO THE TEST

An Intervention for Social Isolation

The researchers observed 6- to 8-year-old boys and girls during recess and identified a group of children who were relatively isolated from their peers (Hernández-Guzmán et al., 2002). A subset of the children received social skills training that the researchers intended to increase the likelihood that they would engage in social play. The training involved guided imagery: The children were asked to imagine themselves approaching a peer ("You softly tell [David]: 'Would you play with me?'") and anticipating their peers' reactions. At first, the children were asked to imagine rejection ("Someone else calls [David] and he leaves"); over time, they visualized success ("OK, let's play.") The researchers measured the students' percentage of socialization—the extent to which they engaged in social play with their peers—before and after the intervention. As seen in **Table 15.2,** children who received social skills training through guided imagery showed great improvement with respect to their untreated peers in the control group.

The treatment group continued to show an advantage over their peers three months after the end of the intervention, a month into the next school year.

◆ GENERALIZATION TECHNIQUES

An ongoing issue of concern for behavior therapists is whether new behavior patterns generated in a therapeutic setting will actually be used in the everyday situations faced by their clients (Kazdin, 1994). This question is important for all therapies, because any measure of treatment effectiveness must include maintenance of long-term changes that go beyond a therapist's couch, clinic, or laboratory.

When essential aspects of a client's real-life setting are absent from the therapy program, behavioral changes accomplished through therapy may be lost over time after therapy terminates. To prevent this gradual loss, it has become common practice to build generalization techniques into the therapeutic procedure itself. These techniques attempt to *increase* the similarity of target behaviors, reinforcers, models, and stimulus demands between therapy and real-life settings. For example, behaviors are taught that are likely to be reinforced naturally in a person's environment, such as showing courtesy or consideration. Rewards are given on a partial reinforcement schedule to ensure that their effect will be maintained in the real world, where rewards are not always forthcoming. Expectation of tangible extrinsic rewards is gradually *faded out,* while social approval and more naturally occurring consequences, including reinforcing self-statements, are incorporated.

Behavior therapists, for example, used a fading procedure with a 7-year-old boy who frequently stole from his classmates (Rosen & Rosen, 1983). The boy was fined or awarded "points" (which could be exchanged for reinforcers such as extra recess) when a check revealed whether he did or did not have other children's possessions. At first, these checks were made every 15 minutes.

TABLE 15.2

Children's Socialization with Peers Before and After Guided Imagery Training for Social Skills

	Pre-Test	Post-Test
Treatment	50.3	66.8
Control	57.0	48.3

Note: The figures are percentage socialization (out of 100 percent).

Over time, they were faded out to only once every 2 hours. Finally, the possession checks were eliminated. Even after the direct manipulation of reinforcers had been faded out, the boy did not return to stealing.

Before we move on to cognitive therapies, take a few minutes to review the major differences between the two psychotherapies outlined thus far—the psychoanalytic and the behavioral—as summarized in **Table 15.3.**

TABLE 15.3

Comparison of Psychoanalytic and Behavioral Approaches to Psychotherapy

Issue	Psychoanalysis	Behavior Therapy
Basic human nature	Biological instincts, primarily sexual and aggressive, press for immediate release, bringing people into conflict with social reality.	Similar to other animals, people are born only with the capacity for learning, which follows similar principles in all species.
Normal human development	Growth occurs through resolution of conflicts during successive stages. Through identification and internalization, mature ego controls and character structures emerge.	Adaptive behaviors are learned through reinforcement and imitation.
Nature of psychopathology	Pathology reflects inadequate conflict resolutions and fixations in earlier development, which leave overly strong impulses and/or weak controls. Symptoms are defensive responses to anxiety.	Problematic behavior derives from faulty learning of maladaptive behaviors. The *symptom* is the problem; there is no *underlying disease*.
Goal of therapy	Psychosexual maturity, strengthened ego functions, and reduced control by unconscious and repressed impulses are attained.	Symptomatic behavior is eliminated and replaced with adaptive behaviors.
Psychological realm emphasized	Motives, feelings, fantasies, and cognitions are experienced.	Therapy involves behavior and observable feelings and actions.
Time orientation	The orientation is discovering and interpreting past conflicts and repressed feelings in light of the present.	Concerned only about client's reinforcement history. Present behavior is examined and treated.
Role of unconscious material	This is primary in classical psychoanalysis and somewhat less emphasized by neo-Freudians.	There is no concern with unconscious processes or with subjective experience even in the conscious realm.
Role of insight	Insight is central; it emerges in "corrective emotional experiences."	Insight is irrelevant and/or unnecessary.
Role of therapist	The therapist functions as a *detective*, searching out basic root conflicts and resistances; detached and neutral, to facilitate transference reactions.	The therapist functions as a *trainer*, helping patients unlearn old behaviors and/or learn new ones. Control of reinforcement is important; interpersonal relationship is minor.

<www.ablongman.com/gerrig17e>

- Why do behavior therapies target adaptive and maladaptive behaviors?
- What features allow exposure therapies to combat anxiety disorders?
- What procedures are used for aversion therapies?
- How are positive reinforcement and extinction used for contingency management?
- What principles of social learning are used for modeling and social skills training?

Cognitive Therapies

Cognitive therapy attempts to change problem feelings and behaviors by changing the way a client thinks about significant life experiences. The underlying assumption of such therapy is that abnormal behavior patterns and emotional distress start with problems in *what* people think (cognitive content) and *how* they think (cognitive process). Cognitive therapies focus on changing different types of cognitive processes and providing different methods of cognitive restructuring. We discussed some of these approaches in Chapter 12 as ways to cope with stress and improve health. In this section, we will describe two major forms of cognitive therapy: alteration of false belief systems and cognitive behavior modification.

◆ CHANGING FALSE BELIEFS

Some cognitive behavior therapists have, as their primary targets for change, beliefs, attitudes, and habitual thought patterns. These cognitive therapists argue that many psychological problems arise because of the way people think about themselves in relation to other people and the events they face. Faulty thinking can be based on (1) unreasonable attitudes ("Being perfect is the most important trait for a student to have"), (2) false premises ("If I do everything they want me to, then I'll be popular"), and (3) rigid rules that put behavior on automatic pilot so that prior patterns are repeated even when they have not worked ("I must obey authorities"). Emotional distress is caused by cognitive misunderstandings and by failure to distinguish between current reality and one's imagination (or expectations).

A cognitive therapist helps a patient to correct faulty patterns of thinking by substituting more effective problem-solving techniques. **Aaron Beck** (1976) has successfully pioneered cognitive therapy for the problem of depression. He states the formula for treatment in simple form: "The therapist helps the patient to identify his warped thinking and to learn more realistic ways to formulate his experiences" (p. 20). For example, depressed individuals may be instructed to write down negative thoughts about themselves, figure out why these self-criticisms are unjustified, and come up with more realistic (and less destructive) self-cognitions.

Beck believes that depression is maintained because depressed patients are unaware of the negative automatic thoughts that they habitually formulate, such as "I will never be as good as my brother"; "Nobody would like me if they really knew me"; and "I'm not smart enough to make it in this competitive school." A therapist then uses four tactics to change the cognitive foundation that supports the depression (Beck & Rush, 1989; Beck et al., 1979):

- Challenging the client's basic assumptions about his or her functioning.
- Evaluating the evidence the client has for and against the accuracy of automatic thoughts.
- Reattributing blame to situational factors rather than to the patient's incompetence.
- Discussing alternative solutions to complex tasks that could lead to failure experiences.

This therapy is similar to behavior therapies in that it centers on the present state of the client.

One of the worst side effects of being depressed is having to live with all the negative feelings and lethargy associated with depression. Becoming obsessed with thoughts about one's negative mood brings up memories of all the bad times in life, which worsens the depressive feelings. By filtering all input through a darkly colored lens of depression, depressed people see criticism where there is none and hear sarcasm when they listen to praise—further "reasons" for being depressed. Cognitive therapies arrest depression's downward spiral by helping the client not to become further depressed about depression itself (Teasdale, 1985). Researchers continue to use insights into the experience of depression to refine cognitive therapies (Jacobson et al., 1996; Teasdale et al., 1995). For example, one study provided evidence that a therapy is most effective when its features match the patients' own beliefs about the reasons that they have become depressed (Addis & Jacobson, 1996). Working with these kinds of results, clinicians can tailor appropriate interventions for individual clients.

One of the earliest forms of cognitive therapy was the **rational-emotive therapy (RET)** developed by **Albert Ellis** (1962, 1995; Windy & Ellis, 1997). RET is a comprehensive system of personality change based on the transformation of irrational beliefs that cause undesirable, highly charged emotional reactions, such as severe anxiety. Clients may have core values *demanding* that they succeed and be approved, *insisting* that they be treated fairly, and *dictating* that the universe be more pleasant.

Rational-emotive therapists teach clients how to recognize the "shoulds," "oughts," and "musts" that are controlling their actions and preventing them from choosing the lives they want. They attempt to break through a client's closed-mindedness by showing that an emotional reaction that follows some event is really the effect of unrecognized beliefs about the event. For example, failure to achieve orgasm during intercourse (event) is followed by an emotional reaction of depression and self-derogation. The belief that is causing the emotional reaction is likely to be "I am sexually inadequate and may be impotent because I failed to perform as expected." In therapy, this belief (and others) is openly disputed through rational confrontation and examination of alternative reasons for the event, such as fatigue, alcohol, false notions of sexual performance, or reluctance to engage in intercourse at that time or with that particular partner. This confrontation technique is followed by other interventions that replace dogmatic, irrational thinking with rational, situationally appropriate ideas.

Rational-emotive therapy aims to increase an individual's sense of self-worth and the potential to be self-actualized by getting rid of the system of faulty beliefs that block personal growth. As such, it shares much with humanistic therapies, which we consider later in the chapter.

◆ COGNITIVE BEHAVIOR MODIFICATION

You are what you tell yourself you can be, and you are guided by what you believe you ought to do. This is a starting assumption of **cognitive behavior modification.** This therapeutic approach combines the cognitive emphasis on changing false beliefs with the behavioral focus on reinforcement contingencies in the modification of performance. Unacceptable behavior patterns are modified by *cognitive restructuring*—changing a person's negative self-statements into constructive coping statements.

A critical part of this therapeutic approach is the discovery by therapist and client of the way the client

Suppose you were learning to knit. Assuming you wanted to get better at it over time, what would be the best internal message to give yourself about the activity?

thinks about and expresses the problem for which therapy is sought. Once both therapist and client understand the kind of thinking that is leading to unproductive or dysfunctional behaviors, they develop new self-statements that are constructive and minimize the use of self-defeating ones that elicit anxiety or reduce self-esteem (Meichenbaum, 1977, 1985, 1993). For example, they might substitute the negative self-statement "I was really boring at that party; they'll never ask me back" with constructive criticism: "Next time, if I want to appear interesting, I will plan some provocative opening lines, practice telling a good joke, and be responsive to the host's stories." Instead of dwelling on negatives in past situations that are unchangeable, the client is taught to focus on positives in the future.

Cognitive behavior modification builds expectations of being effective. Therapists know that building these expectations increases the likelihood that people will behave effectively. Through setting attainable goals, developing realistic strategies for attaining them, and evaluating feedback realistically, you develop a sense of mastery and *self-efficacy* (Bandura, 1992, 1997). As we saw in Chapter 13, your sense of self-efficacy influences your perceptions, motivation, and performance in many ways. Self-efficacy judgments influence how much effort you expend and how long you persist in the face of difficult life situations (Schwarzer, 1992). The modeling procedures we described earlier allow individuals to increase feelings of *behavioral* self-efficacy: They learn that they can carry out a certain range of behaviors. In contrast, therapy for *cognitive* self-efficacy changes the way clients think about their abilities. For example, in one study, students who believed that a decision-making task would *enhance* their abilities outperformed a second group who thought that the task would only gauge the abilities they already had (Wood & Bandura, 1989). In the study, types of thoughts like "I can learn to do better" actually allowed the students to become better.

PUT YOURSELF TO THE TEST

◆ What is the general goal of cognitive therapies?

◆ How does cognitive therapy for depression correct faulty patterns of thinking?

◆ How does rational-emotive therapy attempt to change clients' closed-mindedness?

◆ In cognitive behavior modification, how are thoughts used to affect behaviors?

Humanistic Therapies

Humanistic theories have at their core the concept of a whole person in the continual process of changing and of becoming. Although environment and heredity place certain restrictions, people always remain free to choose what they will become by creating their own values and committing to them through their own decisions. Along with this *freedom to choose,* however, comes the burden of responsibility. Because you are never fully aware of all the implications of your actions, you experience anxiety and despair. You also suffer from guilt over lost opportunities to achieve your full potential. Psychotherapies that apply the principles of this general theory of human nature attempt to help clients define their own freedom, value their experiencing selves and the richness of the present moment, cultivate their individuality, and discover ways of realizing their fullest potential (self-actualization).

In some cases, humanistic therapies also absorbed the lessons of *existentialist* approaches to human experience (May, 1975). This approach emphasizes people's ability to meet or be overwhelmed by the everyday challenges of existence. Existential theorists suggest that individuals suffer from *existential crises:* problems in everyday living, a lack of meaningful human relation-

How might volunteer work help people to maximize their human potential?

ships, and an absence of significant goals. A clinical version of existential theory, which integrates its various themes and approaches, assumes that the bewildering realities of modern life give rise to two basic kinds of human maladies. Depressive and obsessive syndromes reflect a retreat from these realities; sociopathic and narcissistic syndromes reflect an exploitation of these realities (Schneider & May, 1995).

The humanistic philosophy also gave rise to the **human-potential movement,** which emerged in the United States in the late 1960s. This movement encompassed methods to enhance the potential of the average human being toward greater levels of performance and greater richness of experience. Through this movement, therapy originally intended for people with psychological disorders was extended to mentally healthy people who wanted to be more effective, more productive, and happier human beings.

Let's examine two types of therapies in the humanistic tradition: client-centered therapy and Gestalt therapy.

◆ CLIENT-CENTERED THERAPY

As developed by **Carl Rogers** (1951, 1977), *client-centered therapy* has had a significant impact on the way many different kinds of therapists define their relationships to their clients. The primary goal of **client-centered therapy** is to promote the healthy psychological growth of the individual.

The approach begins with the assumption that all people share the basic tendency to self-actualize—that is, to realize their potential. Rogers believed that "it is the inherent tendency of the organism to develop all its capacities in ways which seem to maintain or enhance the organism" (1959, p. 196). Healthy development is hindered by faulty learning patterns in which a person accepts the evaluation of others in place of those provided by his or her own mind and body. A conflict between the naturally positive self-image and negative external criticisms creates anxiety and unhappiness. This conflict, or *incongruence,* may function outside of awareness, so that a person experiences feelings of unhappiness and low self-worth without knowing why.

The task of Rogerian therapy is to create a therapeutic environment that allows a client to learn how to behave in order to achieve self-enhancement and self-actualization. Because people are assumed to be basically good, the therapist's task is mainly to help remove barriers that limit the expression of this natural positive tendency. The basic therapeutic strategy is to recognize, accept, and clarify a client's feelings. This is accomplished within an atmosphere of *unconditional positive regard*—nonjudgmental acceptance and respect for the client. The therapist allows his or her own feelings and thoughts to be transparent to the client. In addition to maintaining this genuineness, the therapist tries to experience the client's feelings. Such total empathy requires that the therapist care for the client as a worthy, competent individual—not to be judged or evaluated but to be assisted in discovering his or her individuality (Meador & Rogers, 1979).

The emotional style and attitude of the therapist are instrumental in *empowering* the client to attend once again to the true sources of personal conflict and to remove the distracting influences that suppress self-actualization. Unlike practitioners of other therapies, who interpret, give answers, or instruct, the client-centered therapist is a supportive listener who reflects and, at times, restates the client's evaluative statements and feelings. Client-centered therapy strives to be *nondirective* by having the therapist merely facilitate the client's search for self-awareness and self-acceptance.

Rogers believed that, once people are freed to relate to others openly and to accept themselves, individuals have the potential to lead themselves back to psychological health. This optimistic view and the humane relationship between therapist-as-caring-expert and client-as-person have influenced many practitioners.

◆ GESTALT THERAPY

Gestalt therapy focuses on ways to unite mind and body to make a person whole (recall the Gestalt school of perception, described in Chapter 4). Its goal of self-awareness is reached by helping clients express pent-up feelings and recognize unfinished business from past conflicts that is carried into new relationships and must be completed for growth to proceed. **Fritz Perls** (1969), the originator of Gestalt therapy, asked clients to act out fantasies concerning conflicts and strong feel-

ings and also to re-create their dreams, which he saw as repressed parts of personality. Perls said, "We have to *re-own* these projected, fragmented parts of our personality, and re-own the hidden potential that appears in the dream" (1969, p. 67).

In Gestalt therapy workshops, therapists encourage participants to regain contact with their "authentic inner voices" (Hatcher & Himelstein, 1996). Among the best known methods of Gestalt therapy is the *empty chair technique.* To carry out this technique, the therapist puts an empty chair near the client. The client is asked to imagine that a feeling, a person, an object, or a situation is occupying the chair. The client then "talks" to the chair's occupant. For example, clients would be encouraged to imagine their mother or father in the chair and reveal feelings they might otherwise be unwilling to reveal. The clients can then imagine those feelings in the chair to "talk" to the feelings about the impact they have on the clients' lives. This technique allows clients to confront and explore strong unexpressed feelings that may interfere with psychological well-being.

Group Therapies

All the treatment approaches outlined thus far are primarily designed as one-to-one relationships between a patient or client and a therapist. Many people, however, now experience therapy as part of a group. There are several reasons why group therapy has flourished and, in some cases, may even be more effective than individual therapy (Fuhriman & Burlingame, 1994). Some advantages are practical. Group therapy is less expensive to participants and allows small numbers of mental health personnel to help more clients.

What are some strengths of group therapies?

Other advantages relate to the power of the group setting. The group (1) is a less threatening situation for people who have problems dealing on their own with authority; (2) allows group processes to be used to influence individual maladaptive behavior; (3) provides people with opportunities to observe and practice interpersonal skills within the therapy session; and (4) provides an analogue of the primary family group, which enables corrective emotional experiences to take place.

Some of the basic premises of group therapies differ from those of individual therapy. The social setting of group therapies provides an opportunity to learn how one comes across to others, how the self-image that is projected differs from the one that is intended or personally experienced. In addition, the group provides confirmation that one's symptoms, problems, and "deviant" reactions are not unique but often are quite common. Because people tend to conceal from others negative information about themselves, it is possible for many people with the same problem to believe "It's only me." The shared group experience can help to dispel this pluralistic ignorance in which many share the same false belief about their unique failings. In addition, the group of peers can provide social support outside the therapy setting.

◆ MARITAL AND FAMILY THERAPY

Much group therapy consists of strangers coming together periodically to form temporary associations from which they may benefit. Marital and family therapy brings meaningful, existing units into a therapy setting. *Couples counseling* for marital problems seeks to clarify the typical communication patterns of the partners and then to improve the quality of their interaction (Napier, 2000). By seeing a couple together, and often

by videotaping and replaying their interactions, a therapist can help them appreciate the verbal and nonverbal styles they use to dominate, control, or confuse each other. Each party is taught how to reinforce desirable responding in the other and withdraw reinforcement for undesirable reactions. They are also taught nondirective listening skills to help the other person clarify and express feelings and ideas. Couples therapy has been shown to reduce marital crises and keep marriages intact (Baucom et al., 1998; Johnson, 2003).

In *family therapy,* the client is a whole nuclear family, and each family member is treated as a member of a *system* of relationships (Fishman & Fishman, 2003). A family therapist works with troubled family members to help them perceive what is creating problems for one or more of them. The focus is on altering the *psychological spaces* between people and the interpersonal dynamics of people acting as a unit, rather than on changing processes within maladjusted individuals. Consider a family therapy intervention that addressed adolescent drug use.

PUTTING IDEAS TO THE TEST

Family Therapy and Adolescent Drug Use

A team of researchers took a family therapy approach to reducing adolescent drug use: Their important assumption was that the adolescents in the study were more likely to eliminate drug use if the overall family context was changed. As a consequence, the family therapy was targeted toward improving both the adolescents' functioning and their mothers' and fathers' parenting practices. Early in the six months of therapy, observations of the families indicated that negative parenting practices (for example, expressions of negative emotion, verbal aggression) outnumbered positive ones (for example, optimism, affection)—72 to 53 percent; at the end of therapy, positive practices outnumbered negative ones—77 to 47 percent. Moreover, the children of the parents who showed overall parenting improvement were also likely to have substantially reduced their drug use (Schmidt et al., 1996).

This study illustrates the importance of the family therapy approach. By engaging the whole family, the therapeutic intervention changed environmental factors that may have originally driven the adolescents to initiate drug use and abuse.

Family therapy can reduce tensions within a family and improve the functioning of individual members by helping clients recognize the positive as well as the negative aspects in their relationships. **Virginia Satir** (1967), a developer of family therapy approaches, noted that the family therapist plays many roles, acting as an interpreter and clarifier of the interactions that are taking place in the therapy session and as influence agent, mediator, and referee. Most family therapists assume that the problems brought into therapy represent *situational* difficulties between people or problems of social interaction, rather than *dispositional* aspects of individuals. These difficulties may develop over time as members are forced into or accept unsatisfying roles. Nonproductive communication patterns may be set up in response to natural transitions in a family situation—loss of a job, a child's going to school, dating, getting married, or having a baby. The job of the family therapist is to understand the structure of the family and the many forces acting on it. Then he or she works with the family members to dissolve "dysfunctional" structural elements while creating and maintaining new, more effective structures (Fishman, 1993).

◆ COMMUNITY SUPPORT GROUPS

A dramatic development in therapy has been the surge of interest and participation in *self-help groups*. It is estimated that about 10 million U.S. adults attend such groups every year (Kessler et al., 1997). These support group sessions are typically free, especially when they are not directed by a health-care professional, and they give people a chance to meet others with the same problems who are surviving and sometimes thriving. The self-help concept applied to community group settings was pioneered by Alcoholics Anonymous (AA), which was founded in 1935. However, it was the women's consciousness-raising movement of the 1960s that helped to extend self-help beyond the arena of alcoholism. Now support groups deal with four basic categories of problems: addictive behavior, physical and mental disorders, life transition or other crises, and the traumas experienced by friends or relatives of those with serious problems. In recent years, people have begun to turn to the Internet as another venue for self-help groups (Zuckerman, 2003). In general, Internet self-help groups engage the same range of issues as their physical counterparts (Davison et al., 2000). However, the Internet provides a particularly important meeting place for people who suffer from conditions that limit mobility, such as chronic fatigue syndrome and multiple sclerosis: An inability to attend meetings physically no longer denies people the benefits of self-help.

Researchers have begun to investigate what properties of self-help groups can make them most effective. Self-help groups appear to serve a number of functions for their members: For example, they provide people with a sense of hope and control over their problems, they engage social support for people's suffering, and they provide a forum for dispensing and acquiring information about disorders and treatments (Riessman, 1997; Schiff & Bargal, 2000). If you consider joining a self-help group, it is important to note that these groups have the most positive impact on people's feelings of well-being when they are satisfied with the group (Schiff & Bargal, 2000). For example, one study found that individuals who affiliated most strongly with AA after treatment for alcoholism showed the lowest levels of continuing substance abuse. Strong affiliation with AA apparently allowed these individuals to maintain their behavioral self-efficacy with respect to the control of their alcoholism (Morgenstern et al., 1997).

A valuable development in self-help is the application of group therapy techniques to the situations of terminally ill patients. The goals of such therapy are to help patients and their families live lives as fulfilling as possible during their illnesses, to cope realistically with impending death, and to adjust to the terminal illness (Fobair, 1997; LeGrand, 1991). One general focus of such support groups for the terminally ill is to help patients learn how to live fully until they "say goodbye" (Nungesser, 1990).

The group therapies are our final examples of types of therapies that are based purely on psychological interventions. We will now analyze how biomedical therapies work to alter the brain in order to affect the mind.

PUT YOURSELF TO THE TEST

➤ What are some benefits of group therapies?

➤ Why does marital and family therapy often focus on systems of relationships?

➤ What features of self-help groups make them beneficial to mental health?

Biomedical Therapies

The ecology of the mind is held in delicate balance. When something goes wrong with the brain, we see the consequences in abnormal patterns of behavior and peculiar cognitive and emotional reactions. Similarly, environmental, social, or behavioral disturbances, such as drugs and violence, can alter brain chemistry and function. Biomedical therapies most often treat mental disorders as problems in the brain. We will describe four biomedical approaches to alleviating the symptoms of psychological disorders: psychosurgery, electroconvulsive therapy (ECT), repetitive transcranial magnetic stimulation (rTMS), and drug therapies.

◆ PSYCHOSURGERY

The headline in the *Los Angeles Times* read, "Bullet in the Brain Cures Man's Mental Problem" (2/23/1988). The article revealed that a 19-year-old man suffering from severe obsessive-compulsive disorder had shot a .22-caliber bullet through the front of his brain in a suicide attempt. Remarkably, he survived, his pathological symptoms were cured, and his intellectual capacity was not affected, although some of the underlying causes of his problems remained.

This case illustrates the potential effects of one of the most direct biomedical therapies: surgical intervention in the brain. Such intervention involves lesioning (severing) connections between parts of the brain or removing small sections of the brain. These therapies are often considered methods of last resort to treat psychopathologies that have proven intractable to other, less extreme forms of therapy. **Psychosurgery** is the general term for surgical procedures performed on brain tissue to alleviate psychological disorders. In medieval times, psychosurgery involved "cutting the stone of folly" from the brains of those suffering from madness, as shown vividly in many engravings and paintings from that era.

Modern psychosurgical procedures include severing the fibers of the corpus callosum to reduce violent seizures of epilepsy, as we saw in Chapter 3; severing pathways that mediate limbic system activity (amygdalotomy); and prefrontal lobotomy. The best known form of psychosurgery is the **prefrontal lobotomy,** an operation that severs the nerve fibers connecting the frontal lobes of the brain with the diencephalon, especially those fibers of the thalamic and hypothalamic areas. The procedure was developed by neurologist **Egas Moniz,** who, in 1949, won a Nobel Prize for this treatment, which seemed to transform the functioning of mental patients.

The original candidates for lobotomy were agitated patients with schizophrenia and patients who were compulsive and anxiety-ridden. The effects of this psychosurgery were dramatic: A new personality emerged without intense emotional arousal and, thus, without overwhelming anxiety, guilt, or anger. However, the operation permanently destroyed basic aspects of human nature. The lobotomy resulted in inability to plan ahead, indifference to the opinions of others, childlike actions, and the intellectual and emotional flat-

ness of a person without a coherent sense of self. (One of Moniz's own patients was so distressed by these unexpected consequences that she shot Moniz, partially paralyzing him.) Because the effects of psychosurgery are permanent, its negative effects severe and common, and its positive results less certain, its continued use is very limited.

◆ ECT AND rTMS

Electroconvulsive therapy (ECT) is the use of electric shock applied to the brain to treat psychiatric disorders such as schizophrenia, mania, and, most often, depression. The technique consists of applying weak electric current (75 to 100 volts) to a patient's temples for a period of time from 1/10 to a full second until a convulsion occurs. The convulsion usually runs its course in 45 to 60 seconds. Patients are prepared for this traumatic intervention by sedation with a short-acting barbiturate and muscle relaxant, which renders the patient unconscious and minimizes the violent physical reactions (Abrams, 1992).

Electroconvulsive therapy has proven extremely successful at alleviating the symptoms of serious depression (Sackheim et al., 2000). ECT is particularly important because it works quickly. Typically, the symptoms of depression are alleviated in a three- or four-day course of treatment, as compared with the one- to two-week time window for drug therapies. Even so, most therapists hold ECT as a treatment of last resort. ECT is often reserved for emergency treatment for suicidal or severely malnourished, depressed patients and for patients who do not respond to antidepressant drugs or can't tolerate their side effects.

If ECT is so effective, why has it so often been demonized? For example, in 1982, the citizens of Berkeley, California, voted to ban the use of electroconvulsive shock in any of their community mental health facilities (the action was later overturned on legal grounds). Scientific unease with ECT centers largely on the lack of understanding of how it works. The therapy was originated when clinicians observed that patients who suffered from both schizophrenia and epilepsy showed improvement in their symptoms of schizophrenia after epileptic seizures. The clinicians conjectured that the same effect could be obtained with artificially induced seizures. Although the conjecture proved correct in part—ECT is much more effective at alleviating depression than schizophrenia—researchers have yet to fit a definitive theory to this chance observation.

Critics have also worried about potential side effects of ECT (Breggin, 1979, 1991). ECT produces temporary disorientation and a variety of memory deficits. Patients often suffer amnesia for events in the

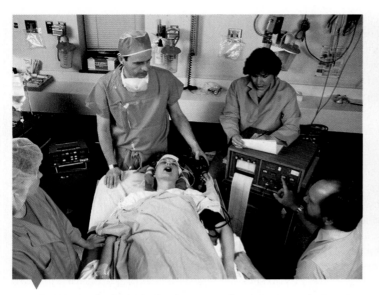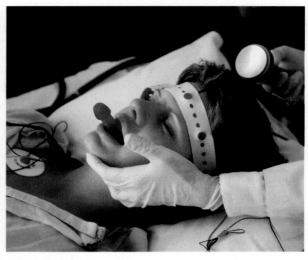

Electroconvulsive therapy has been very effective in cases of severe depression. Why does it remain controversial as a treatment?

period of time preceding the treatment; the amnesia becomes more severe the longer the course of treatment. Research has shown, however, that patients generally recover their specific memories within months of the treatment (Cohen et al., 2000). As a way of minimizing even short-term deficits, ECT is now often administered to only one side of the brain so as to reduce the possibility of speech impairment. Such unilateral ECT is an effective antidepressant.

In recent years, researchers have explored an alternative to ECT called **repetitive transcranial magnetic stimulation (rTMS).** As you might recall from Chapter 3, people who undergo rTMS receive repeated pulses of magnetic stimulation to the brain. As with ECT, researchers have not yet determined why rTMS can bring relief for major depressive disorder and other forms of psychopathology. However, evidence is mounting that rTMS can be just as effective as, for example, ECT (Grunhaus et al., 2003). Researchers are working to determine how variables such as the intensity of the magnetic stimulation affect rTMS's ability to bring relief (Padberg et al., 2002).

Let's now see why drug therapies have become the most popular form of biomedical intervention for psychopathology.

◆ DRUG THERAPY

In the history of the treatment of mental disorders, nothing has rivaled the revolution created by the discovery of drugs that can calm anxious patients, restore contact with reality in withdrawn patients, and suppress hallucinations in psychotic patients. This new therapeutic era began in 1953 with the introduction of tranquilizing drugs, notably *chlorpromazine,* into hospital

treatment programs. Emerging drug therapies gained almost instant recognition and status as an effective way to transform patient behavior. **Psychopharmacology** is the branch of psychology that investigates the effects of drugs on behavior. Researchers in psychopharmacology work to understand the effect drugs have on some biological systems and the consequent changes in responding.

The discovery of *drug therapies* had profound effects on the treatment of severely disordered patients. No longer did mental hospital staff have to act as guards, putting patients in seclusion or straitjackets; staff morale improved as rehabilitation replaced mere custodial care of the mentally ill (Swazey, 1974). Moreover, the drug therapy revolution had a great impact on the U.S. mental hospital population. Over half a million people were living in mental institutions in 1955, staying an average of several years. The introduction of chlorpromazine and other drugs reversed the steadily increasing numbers of patients. By the early 1970s, it was estimated that fewer than half the country's mental patients actually resided in mental hospitals; those who did were institutionalized for an average of only a few months.

The drugs we will describe that alleviate symptoms of various mental disorders are widely prescribed. As mental health care comes increasingly under the direction of health maintenance organizations (HMOs), cost-cutting practices are limiting the number of patients' visits to therapists for psychological therapies while substituting cheaper drug therapies. Researchers have documented great increases in prescriptions for drug therapies (Pincus et al., 1998). For that reason, it is important to understand the positive and negative features of drug therapies.

                     <www.ablongman.com/gerrig17e>

Three major categories of drugs are used today in therapy programs: *antipsychotic, antidepressant,* and *antianxiety* medications (see **Table 15.4**). As their names suggest, these drugs chemically alter specific brain functions that are responsible for psychotic symptoms, depression, and extreme anxiety.

ANTIPSYCHOTIC DRUGS

Antipsychotic drugs alter symptoms of schizophrenia such as delusions, hallucinations, social withdrawal, and occasional agitation (Dawkins et al., 1999). Antipsychotic drugs work by reducing the activity of the neurotransmitter dopamine in the brain. Drugs like *chlorpromazine* (marketed under the U.S. brand name *Thorazine*) and *haloperidol* (marketed as *Haldol*) block or reduce the sensitivity of dopamine receptors. *Clozapine* (marketed as *Clozaril*), the newest major antipsychotic drug, both directly decreases dopamine activity and increases the level of serotonin activity, which inhibits the dopamine system. Although these drugs function by decreasing the overall level of brain activity, they are not just tranquilizers. For many patients, they do much more than merely eliminate agitation. They also relieve or reduce the positive symptoms of schizophrenia, including delusions and hallucinations.

There are, unfortunately, negative side effects of antipsychotic drugs. Because dopamine plays a role in motor control, muscle disturbances frequently accompany a course of drug treatment. *Tardive dyskinesia* is a particular disturbance of motor control, especially of the facial muscles, caused by antipsychotic drugs. Patients who develop this side effect experience involuntary jaw, lip, and tongue movements. The newer drug clozapine blocks dopamine receptors more selectively, resulting in a lower probability of motor disturbance. Unfortunately, *agranulocytosis,* a rare disease in which the bone marrow stops making white blood cells, develops in 1 to 2 percent of patients treated with clozapine.

Researchers continue to examine the consequences of drug use over long periods of time as well as consequences when patients cease taking the drugs. The rate of relapse when patients go off the drugs is quite high—three-quarters have new symptoms within one year (Gitlin et al., 2001). Even patients who remain on the newer drugs such as clozapine have about a 15 to 20 percent chance of relapse (Leucht et al., 2003). Thus, antipsychotic drugs do not cure schizophrenia—they do not eliminate the underlying psychopathology. Fortunately, they are reasonably effective at controlling the disorder's most disruptive symptoms.

TABLE 15.4

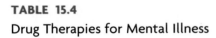

Drug Therapies for Mental Illness

Disorder	Type of Therapy	Examples
Schizophrenia	Antipsychotic drug	chlorpromazine (Thorazine) haloperidol (Haldol) clozapine (Clozaril)
Depression	Tricyclic antidepressant	imipramine (Tofranil) amitriptyline (Elavil)
	Selective serotonin reuptake inhibitor	fluoxetine (Prozac) paroxetine (Paxil) sertraline (Zoloft)
	MAO inhibitor	phenelzine (Nardil) isocarboxazid (Marplan)
Bipolar disorder	Mood stabilizer	lithium (Lithonate)
Anxiety disorders	Benzodiazepines	diazepam (Valium) alprazolam (Xanax)
	Antidepressant drug	fluoxetine (Prozac)

ANTIDEPRESSANT DRUGS

Antidepressant drugs work by increasing the activity of the neurotransmitters norepinephrine and serotonin (Holmes, 1994). Recall from Chapter 3 that nerve cells communicate by releasing neurotransmitters into synaptic clefts (the small gaps between neurons). *Tricyclics,* such as *Tofranil* and *Elavil,* reduce the reuptake (removal) of the neurotransmitters from the synaptic cleft. Drugs such as *Prozac* are known as *selective serotonin reuptake inhibitors* (SSRIs) because they specifically reduce the reuptake of serotonin. The *monoamine oxidase* (MAO) *inhibitors* limit the action of the enzyme monoamine oxidase, which is responsible for breaking down (metabolizing) norepinephrine. When MAO is inhibited, more of the neurotransmitter is left available. Thus, each type of drug leaves more neurotransmitters available to bring about neural signals.

Antidepressant drugs can be successful at relieving the symptoms of depression, although as many as 50 percent of patients will not show improvement (Hollon et al., 2002). (Those patients may be candidates for ECT or rTMS.) Because antidepressant drugs affect important neurotransmitter systems in the brain, they have the potential for serious side effects. For example, people taking SSRIs such as Prozac may experience symptoms such as nausea, insomnia, nervousness, and sexual dysfunction. Tricyclics and MAO inhibitors may cause dry mouth, difficulty sleeping, and memory impairment. Research suggests that most of the major antidepressant drugs are roughly equal, across individuals, in their ability to bring relief (Hollon et al., 2002). For that reason, it is important for each individual to find the drug that yields the fewest side effects for him or her personally.

Lithium salts have proven effective in the treatment of bipolar disorders (Schou, 2001). People who experience uncontrollable periods of hyperexcitement, when their energy seems limitless and their behavior extravagant and flamboyant, are brought down from their state of manic excess by doses of lithium. Between 60 and 80 percent of patients treated with lithium have a good chance of recovery (Walden et al., 1998). However, for those people suffering from bipolar disorders who cycle frequently between manic episodes and depression, lithium appears to be less effective than other treatments such as the drug *valproate,* which was originally developed as a drug to prevent seizures.

ANTIANXIETY DRUGS

Like antipsychotic and antidepressant drugs, antianxiety drugs generally have their effect by adjusting the levels of neurotransmitter activity in the brain. Different drugs are most effective at relieving different types of anxiety disorders (Spiegel et al., 2000). Generalized anxiety disorder is best treated with a *benzodiazepine,* such as *Valium* or *Xanax,* which increases the activity of the

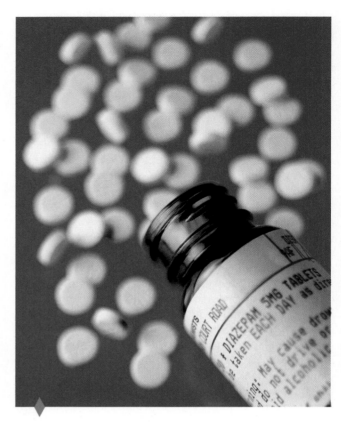

Why should people be cautious when they undertake drug therapies?

neurotransmitter GABA. Because GABA regulates inhibitory neurons, increases in GABA activity decrease brain activity in areas of the brain relevant to generalized anxiety responses. Panic disorders, as well as agoraphobia and other phobias, can be treated with antidepressant drugs, although researchers do not yet understand the biological mechanism involved. Obsessive-compulsive disorder, which may arise from low levels of serotonin, responds particularly well to drugs, like Prozac, that specifically affect serotonin function.

As with drugs that treat schizophrenia and mood disorders, benzodiazepines affect a major neurotransmitter system and therefore have a range of potential side effects (Rivas-Vazquez, 2003). People who begin a course of therapy may experience daytime drowsiness, slurred speech, and problems with coordination. The drugs may also impair cognitive processes such as attention and memory. Furthermore, people who begin treatment with benzodiazepines often experience drug tolerance—they must increase their dosage to maintain a stable effect (see Chapter 5). Discontinuation of treatment might also lead to withdrawal symptoms. Because of the potential for psychological and physical dependence, people should undertake treatment with antianxiety drugs in careful consultation with a health care provider.

- Why has psychosurgery been largely abandoned as a treatment practice?
- How effective is electroconvulsive therapy for treating depression?
- What have researchers learned about repetitive transcranial magnetic stimulation?
- What neurotransmitter systems do antipsychotic, antidepressant, and antianxiety drugs typically affect?
- Why do most drug therapies involve the risk of side effects?

Treatment Evaluation and Prevention Strategies

Suppose you have come to perceive a problem in your life that you believe could be alleviated by interaction with a trained clinician. We have mentioned a great variety of types of therapies. How can you know which one of them will work best to relieve your distress? How can you be sure that *any* of them will work? In this section, we examine the projects researchers undertake to test the effectiveness of particular therapies and make comparisons between different therapies. The general goal is to discover the most efficient way to help people overcome distress. We also consider briefly the topic of *prevention:* How can psychologists intervene in people's lives to prevent mental illness before it occurs?

◆ EVALUATING THERAPEUTIC EFFECTIVENESS

British psychologist **Hans Eysenck** (1952) created a furor some years ago by declaring that psychotherapy does not work at all! He reviewed available publications that reported the effects of various therapies and found that patients who received no therapy had just as high a recovery rate as those who received psychoanalysis or other forms of insight therapy. He claimed that roughly two-thirds of all people with neurotic problems would recover spontaneously within two years of the onset of the problem.

Researchers met Eysenck's challenge by devising more accurate methodologies to evaluate the effective-

ness of therapy. What Eysenck's criticism made clear was that researchers needed to have appropriate control groups. For a variety of reasons, *some* percentage of individuals in psychotherapy *does* improve without any professional intervention. This **spontaneous-remission effect** is one *baseline* criterion against which the effectiveness of therapies must be assessed. Simply put, doing something must be shown to lead to a greater percentage of improved cases than doing nothing.

Similarly, researchers generally try to demonstrate that their treatment does more than just take advantage of clients' own expectations of healing. You may recall our earlier discussions of *placebo* effects: In many cases, people's mental or physical health will improve because they expect that it will improve. The therapeutic situation helps bolster this belief by putting the therapist in the specific social role of *healer* (Frank & Frank, 1991). Although the placebo effects of therapy are an important part of the therapeutic intervention, researchers typically wish to demonstrate that their specific form of therapy is more effective than a **placebo therapy** (a neutral therapy that just creates expectations of healing) (Enserink, 1999).

In recent years, researchers have evaluated therapeutic effectiveness using a statistical technique called meta-analysis. **Meta-analysis** provides a formal mechanism for detecting the general conclusions to be found in data from many different experiments. In many psychological experiments, the researcher asks, "Did most of my participants show the effect I predicted?" Meta-analysis treats experiments like participants. With respect to the effectiveness of therapy, the researcher asks, "Did most of the outcome studies show positive changes?"

"OF COURSE I'VE BECOME MORE MATURE SINCE YOU STARTED TREATING ME. YOU'VE BEEN AT IT SINCE I WAS FOURTEEN YEARS OLD."

Therapies and Brain Activity

In this chapter, we've made a number of distinctions among types of therapies. However, our most basic distinction has been between psychological and biomedical approaches to treatment. It has often been the practice to use a computer analogy to motivate this distinction: If we think of the brain as a computer, we can say that mental illness may arise from either the brain's hardware or in the software that programs its actions. With respect to this analogy, biomedical treatments focus on changing the hardware whereas psychological treatments focus on changing the software. However, cutting-edge research blurs the distinction between hardware and software: There is growing evidence that biomedical and psychological therapies produce many of the same changes in the brain.

Consider a study that examined the brain changes that accompanied treatment for social phobia (Furmark et al., 2002). Each of the ten men and eight women in the study met *DSM-IV* criteria for the disorder. The researchers placed

them into one of three groups. One group of participants was given the drug citalopram (which has the prescription name *Celexa*). At the end of the nine-week treatment period, the researchers did blood assays to ensure that the participants had adhered to their drug regimen. A second group of participants received eight weekly sessions of therapy. In each three-hour session, participants engaged in simulated exposure to feared situations and cognitive restructuring. The third group of participants was the control group. (After the period of the experiment, they began the drug regimen.)

To assess the impact of the drug and cognitive-behavioral therapies, all the participants were asked to deliver brief speeches while they underwent PET scans. The situation was intended to be quite threatening for individuals with social phobia: An audience of six to eight people surrounded the scanner bed while the participants gave their $2\frac{1}{2}$-minute speeches. With respect to behavioral measures (e.g., the extent to which partic-

ipants experienced anxiety during their speeches), both treatment groups showed substantial and roughly equivalent improvement as compared to the control group. Moreover, as shown in the figure, the PET scans demonstrated decreased brain activity (again, relative to the control group) in much the same locations in the brain. Of importance, the decreased activity was in areas of the brain (e.g., the amygdala) that play a role in emotional responses.

Researchers have found similar patterns for other disorders. For example, PET scans detected the same changes in brain function for patients who underwent either behavioral or drug therapy for obsessive-compulsive disorder (Baxter et al., 1992; Schwartz et al., 1996). Similarly, patients who experienced either a form of cognitive therapy or drug therapy for major depressive disorder showed similar brain changes (Brody et al., 2002). In each of these cases, it hasn't been enough to show just that the two types of therapies affect the same areas of the brain. Researchers have also argued that changes in those areas are related to the relief that patients experience.

In light of these results, researchers can now shift their attention to *how:* How is it that psychotherapy can restore the brain's balance in the same systems affected by drugs? How, for example, can cognitive therapy have a similar impact on the brain's use of the neurotransmitter serotonin as does a drug that is specifically designated as a selective serotonin reuptake inhibitor (Brody et al., 2002)? These types of questions will help set the research agenda for the first part of the 21st century.

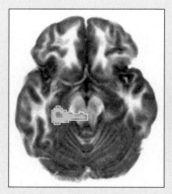

Cognitive-behavioral group therapy (compared to control)

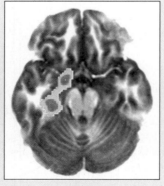

Drug therapy (compared to control)

Consider **Figure 15.2,** which presents the results of meta-analyses of the research literature on treatments for depression (Hollon et al., 2002). The figure compares results for three types of psychotherapies and medications (averaged across different types of antidepressant drugs) to placebo treatments. We described psychodynamic and cognitive behavioral therapies earlier in the chapter. Interpersonal therapy focuses on a patient's current life and interpersonal relationships. As you can see, across all the studies reviewed in the meta-analyses that contributed to this figure, interpersonal therapy, cognitive behavioral therapy, and drug therapies had a consistently larger impact than did placebos. At least for treatment of depression, classic psychodynamic therapy did not fare well.

Note that these data reflect the impact of each type of treatment alone. Researchers have assessed the effectiveness of psychotherapy alone versus psychotherapy combined with drug therapy. One study found that combination therapy was most successful (Keller et al., 2000). Of 519 participants who completed a course of treatment, 55 percent of the participants who received only drug therapy met the study's criterion for symptom relief, as did 52 percent of the participants who received only psychotherapy. For participants who received both drug therapy and psychotherapy, 85 percent showed the same level of improvement.

Because of such findings, contemporary researchers are less concerned about asking *whether* psychotherapy works and more concerned about asking why it works and whether any one treatment is most effective for any particular problem and for certain types of patients (Drozd & Goldfried, 1996; Goldfried et al., 1990). For example, much treatment evaluation has been carried out in research settings that afford reasonable control over patients (often, the studies exclude individuals who have more than one disorder) and procedures (therapists are rigorously trained to minimize differences in treatment). Researchers need to ensure that therapies that work in research settings also work out in community settings in which patients and therapists have more diversity of symptoms and experience (Hohmann & Shear, 2002). Another important issue for evaluation research is to assess the likelihood that individuals will complete a course of treatment. In almost all circumstances, some people choose to discontinue treatments (Klein et al., 2003; Wierzbicki & Pekarik, 1993). Researchers seek to understand who leaves treatment and why—with the ultimate hope of creating treatments to which most everyone can adhere.

Figure 15.3 provides a general flowchart for the way theory, clinical observation, and research all play a role in the development and evaluation of any form of treatment (for both mental and physical disorders). It shows the type of systematic research needed to help clinicians discover if their therapies are making the differences that their theories predict. On one side, you see clinical observation—clinicians' own experience with a new procedure. Often, new treatments first get tested without rigorous experimental control. On the other side of the figure, you see a theory being developed. The theory makes predictions about what should work, which may be confirmed in laboratory studies. These two types of insights—clinical and experimental—are combined to yield a new therapy.

In the final section of this chapter, we reflect on an important principle of life: Whatever the effectiveness of treatment, it is often better to prevent a disorder than to heal it once it arises.

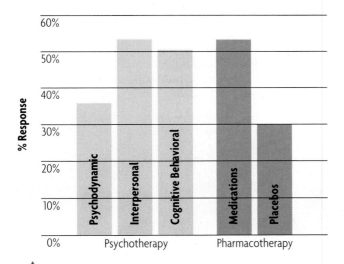

FIGURE 15.2

Treatment Evaluation for Depression

The figure displays the results from meta-analyses of treatments for depression. For each treatment, the figure presents the percentage of patients who typically respond to each category of treatment. For example, about 50 percent of patients taking antidepressant medication experience recognizable symptom relief whereas 50 percent do not.

◆ PREVENTION STRATEGIES

Two friends were walking on a riverbank. Suddenly, a child swept downstream in the current. One of the friends jumped in the river and rescued the child. Then the two friends resumed their stroll. Suddenly, another child appeared in the water. The rescuer jumped in and again pulled the victim to safety. Soon, a third drowning child swept by. The still-dry friend began to trot up the riverbank. The rescuer yelled, "Hey, where are you going?" The dry one replied, "I'm going to get the bastard that's throwing them in." (Wolman, 1975, p. 3)

The moral of this story is clear: *Preventing* a problem is the best solution. The traditional therapies we have examined here share the focus of changing a person who is already distressed or disabled. They begin to do their work after the problem behaviors show up and after the suffering starts. By the time someone elects to go into therapy or is required to, the psychological disorder has "settled in" and had its disruptive effects on the person's daily functioning, social life, job, or career.

The goal of *preventing* psychological problems can be realized at several different levels (Rabins, 1992; Reiss & Price, 1996). *Primary* prevention seeks to pre-

vent a condition before it begins. Steps might be taken, for example, to provide individuals with coping skills so they can be more resilient or to change negative aspects of an environment that might lead to anxiety or depression (Durlak & Wells, 1997; Kaplan, 2000). *Secondary* prevention attempts to limit the duration and severity of a disorder once it has begun. This goal is realized by means of programs that allow for early identification and prompt treatment. For example, based on the meta-analyses we described for depression, a mental health practitioner might recommend a combination of psychotherapy and drug therapy to optimize secondary prevention (Keller et al., 2000). *Tertiary* prevention limits the long-term impact of a psychological disorder by seeking to prevent a relapse. For example, we noted earlier that individuals with schizophrenia who discontinue drug therapy have a very high rate of relapse (Gitlin et al., 2001). To engage in tertiary prevention, mental health practitioners would recommend that their patients with schizophrenia continue their courses of antipsychotic drugs.

The implementation of these three types of prevention has signaled major shifts in the focus and in the basic paradigms of mental health care. The most important of these paradigm shifts are: (1) supplementing treatment with prevention; (2) going beyond a medical disease model to a public health model; (3) focusing on situations and ecologies that put people at risk and away from "at-risk people"; and (4) looking for precipitating factors in life settings rather than for predisposing factors in people (Ammerman & Hersen, 1997; Kendrick et al., 1996).

The medical model is concerned with treating people who are afflicted; a public health model includes

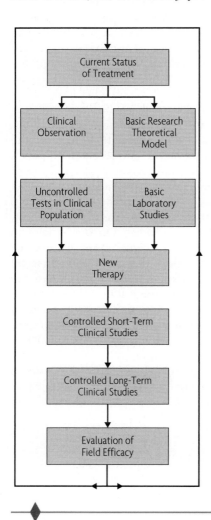

FIGURE 15.3

Building Better Therapies

Flowchart of stages in the development of treatments for mental/physical disorders.

How can prevention strategies encourage people to build "mental hygiene" habits to minimize the need for treatment?

identifying and eliminating the causes of disease and illness that exist in the environment. In this approach, an affected individual is seen as the host or carrier—the end product of an existing process of disease. When programs can change the conditions that breed illness, there will be no need to change people later with expensive, extensive treatments. The dramatic reduction of many contagious and infectious diseases, such as tuberculosis, smallpox, and malaria, came about through this approach. With psychopathology, too, many sources of environmental or organizational stress can be identified. Programs can be designed to alleviate them, thus reducing the number of people who will be exposed. The field of **clinical ecology** expands the boundaries of biomedical therapies by relating disorders, such as anxiety and depression, to environmental irritants, such as chemical solvents, noise pollution, seasonal changes, and radiation (Bell, 1982). Some therapists have broadened the definition of environment, as it contributes to psychopathology, to include all features of the external environment that interfere with normal adaptations in daily life (Ghadirian & Lehmann, 1993). These include nutritional influences, psychoactive substances, terrorism, natural disasters, and the availability of social support networks.

Preventing mental disorders is a complex and difficult task. It involves not only understanding the relevant causal factors, but overcoming individual, institutional, and governmental resistance to change. A major research effort will be needed to demonstrate the long-range utility of prevention and the public health approach to psychopathology in order to justify the expense in the face of the many other problems that demand immediate solutions. The ultimate goal of prevention programs is to safeguard the mental health of all members of our society.

PUT YOURSELF TO THE TEST

- Why are therapies compared to placebos to evaluate their effectiveness?
- What conclusions can be drawn from meta-analyses of treatments for depression?
- What challenges do researchers face to design and implement effective therapies?
- What are three types of prevention in which people can engage?
- What features define the field of clinical ecology?

Recapping Main Points

THE THERAPEUTIC CONTEXT

- Therapy requires that a diagnosis be made and a course of treatment be established.
- Therapy may be medically or psychologically oriented.
- The four major types of psychotherapies are psychodynamic, behavior, cognitive, and humanistic.
- A variety of professionals practice therapy.
- In earlier times, treatment for those with mental problems was often harsh and dehumanizing.
- A disease model of mental illness led to a more humane treatment of patients.
- Cultural anthropology shows that many cultures have ways of understanding and treating mental disorders that can generate important lessons for Western practice.

PSYCHODYNAMIC THERAPIES

- Psychodynamic therapies grew out of Sigmund Freud's psychoanalytic theory.
- Freud emphasized the role of unconscious conflicts in the etiology of psychopathology. Psychodynamic therapy seeks to reconcile these conflicts.
- Free association, attention to resistance, dream analysis, transference, and countertransference are all important components of this therapy.
- Other psychodynamic theorists place more emphasis on the patient's current social situation and interpersonal relationships.

BEHAVIOR THERAPIES

- Behavior therapies use the principles of learning and reinforcement to modify or eliminate problem behaviors.
- Counterconditioning techniques replace negative behaviors, like phobic responses, with more adaptive behaviors.
- Exposure is the common element in phobia-modification therapies.

- Contingency management uses operant conditioning to modify behavior, primarily through positive reinforcement and extinction.
- Social-learning therapy uses models and social-skills training to help individuals gain confidence about their abilities.

COGNITIVE THERAPIES

- Cognitive therapy concentrates on changing negative or irrational thought patterns about the self and social relationships.
- Cognitive therapy has been used successfully to treat depression.
- Rational-emotive therapy helps clients recognize that their irrational beliefs about themselves interfere with successful life outcomes.
- Cognitive behavior modification calls for the client to learn more constructive thought patterns in reference to a problem and to apply the new technique to other situations.

HUMANISTIC THERAPIES

- Humanistic therapies work to help individuals become more fully self-actualized.
- Therapists strive to be nondirective in helping their clients establish a positive self-image that can deal with external criticisms.
- Gestalt therapy focuses on the whole person—body, mind, and life setting.

GROUP THERAPIES

- Group therapy allows people to observe and engage in social interactions as a means to reduce psychological distress.
- Family and marital therapy concentrates on situational difficulties and interpersonal dynamics of the couple or family group as a system in need of improvement.
- Community and Internet self-help groups allow individuals to obtain information and feelings of control in circumstances of social support.

BIOMEDICAL THERAPIES

- Biomedical therapies concentrate on changing physiological aspects of mental illness.
- Psychosurgery is rarely used because of its radical, irreversible effects.
- Electroconvulsive therapy and repetitive transcranial magnetic stimulation (rTMS) can be effective with depressed patients.
- Drug therapies include antipsychotic medications for treating schizophrenia as well as antidepressants and antianxiety drugs.

TREATMENT EVALUATION AND PREVENTION STRATEGIES

- Research shows that many therapies work better than the mere passage of time or nonspecific placebo treatment.
- Evaluation projects are helping to answer the question of what makes therapy effective.
- Prevention strategies are necessary to stop psychological disorders from occurring and minimize their effects once they have occurred.

KEY TERMS

aversion therapy (p. 520)
behavioral rehearsal (p. 523)
behavior modification (p. 518)
behavior therapy (p. 518)
biomedical therapies (p. 510)
catharsis (p. 515)
client (p. 512)
client-centered therapy (p. 527)
clinical ecology (p. 539)
clinical psychologist (p. 511)
clinical social worker (p. 511)
cognitive behavior modification (p. 526)
cognitive therapy (p. 525)
contingency management (p. 521)
counseling psychologist (p. 511)
counterconditioning (p. 518)

countertransference (p. 515)
dream analysis (p. 515)
electroconvulsive therapy (ECT) (p. 531)
exposure therapy (p. 518)
free association (p. 514)
Gestalt therapy (p. 528)
human-potential movement (p. 527)
insight therapy (p. 514)
meta-analysis (p. 535)
object relations theory (p. 517)
participant modeling (p. 522)
pastoral counselor (p. 511)
patient (p. 512)
placebo therapy (p. 535)
prefrontal lobotomy (p. 531)
psychiatrist (p. 511)

psychoanalysis (p. 514)
psychoanalyst (p. 511)
psychopharmacology (p. 532)
psychosurgery (p. 531)
psychotherapy (p. 510)
rational-emotive therapy (RET) (p. 526)
repetitive transcranial magnetic stimulation (rTMS) (p. 532)
resistance (p. 515)
ritual healing (p. 513)
shamanism (p. 513)
social-learning therapy (p. 522)
spontaneous-remission effect (p. 535)
systematic desensitization (p. 519)
transference (p. 515)

Social Cognition and Relationships

I magine circumstances in which you've done everything to get to a job interview on time, but nothing has gone your way. The electricity went off during the night, so your alarm didn't wake you. The friend who was supposed to give you a ride had a flat tire. When you tried to get money for a taxi, the ATM ate your card. When you finally get to the office, you know what the manager is thinking: "Why would I give a job to someone this unreliable?" You want to protest, "It's not me, it's the circumstances!" As you have contemplated this scenario, you have begun to enter the world of *social psychology*—that area of psychology that investigates the ways in which individuals create and interpret social situations.

Social psychology is the study of the ways in which thoughts, feelings, perceptions, motives, and behavior are influenced by interactions and transactions between people. Social psychologists try to understand behavior within its social context. This social context is the vibrant canvas on which are painted the movements, strengths, and vulnerabilities of the social animal. Defined broadly, the social context includes the real, imagined, or symbolic presence of other people; the activities and interactions that take place between people; the features of the settings in which behavior occurs; and the expectations and norms that govern behavior in a given setting (Sherif, 1981).

In this chapter and the next, we explore several major themes of social psychological research. For much of this chapter we focus on **social cognition,** which is the processes by which people select, interpret, and remember social information. We examine the ways in which people construct social reality and the ways in which attitudes are formed and changed. We then consider circumstances of prejudice, in which beliefs and attitudes have distressing consequences for social interactions. Finally, we consider the relationships of liking and loving. Throughout this chapter, we illustrate how research in social psychology has immediate applications to your life. As you shall see, in Chapter 17, we extend our analysis of social psychology's relevance beyond the personal to societal concerns. In both chapters, abstract theory meets the stern test of practicality, as we attempt to answer this question: Does psychological knowledge make a difference in the everyday lives of people and society?

Constructing Social Reality

To open the chapter, we asked you to imagine everything that could go wrong in advance of a job interview. When you finally arrive at the manager's office you have very different interpretations of the same event. You know you've been a victim of circumstances. However, at least in the short run, the manager judges you only by what is readily apparent: You are late and you are disheveled. That's what we mean by *constructing social reality*. The manager considers the evidence you present and makes an interpretation of the situation. If you still wish to get the job, you'll have to get the manager to construct a new interpretation.

Let's look at one classic social psychological example in which people's beliefs led them to view the same situation from different vantage points and make contrary conclusions about what "really happened." The study concerned a football game that took place some years ago between two Ivy League teams. An undefeated Princeton team played Dartmouth in the final game of the season. The game, which Princeton won, was rough,

filled with penalties and serious injuries to both sides. After the game, the newspapers of the two schools offered very different accounts of what had happened.

CLASSIC

PUTTING IDEAS TO THE TEST

Can We Ever Say What "Really Happened"?

A team of social psychologists, intrigued by the different perceptions, surveyed students at both schools, showed them a film of the game, and recorded their judgments about the number of infractions committed by each of the teams. Nearly all Princeton students judged the game as "rough and dirty," none saw it as "clean and fair," and most believed that Dartmouth players started the dirty play. In contrast, the majority of Dartmouth students thought both sides were equally to blame for the rough game, and many thought it was "rough, clean, and fair." Moreover, when the Princeton students viewed the game film, they "saw" the Dartmouth team commit twice as many penalties as their own team. When viewing the same film, Dartmouth students "saw" both sides commit the same number of penalties (Hastorf & Cantril, 1954).

This study makes clear that a complex social occurrence, such as a football game, cannot be observed in an objective, unbiased fashion. Social situations obtain significance when observers *selectively encode* what is happening in terms of what they expect to see and want to see. In the case of the football game, people *looked* at the same activity, but they *saw* two different games.

Why are fans who watch their favorite team play likely to perceive more instances of unfair play on the part of the opposing team?

To explain how the Princeton and Dartmouth fans came to such different interpretations of the football game returns us to the realm of *perception*. Recall from Chapter 4 that you often must put prior knowledge to work to interpret ambiguous perceptual objects. The principle is the same for the football game—people bring past knowledge to bear on the interpretation of current events—but the objects for perceptual processing are people and situations. **Social perception** is the process by which people come to understand and categorize the behaviors of others. In this section, we will focus largely on two issues of social perception. First, we consider how people make judgments about the forces that influence other people's behavior, their *causal attributions*. Next, we discuss how processes of social perception can sometimes bring the world in line with expectations.

◆ THE ORIGINS OF ATTRIBUTION THEORY

One of the most important inferential tasks facing all social perceivers is to determine the causes of events. You want to know the whys of life. Why did my girlfriend break off the relationship? Why did he get the job and not I? Why did my parents divorce after so many years of marriage? All such whys lead to an analysis of possible causal determinants for some action, event, or outcome. **Attribution theory** is a general approach to describing the ways the social perceiver uses information to generate causal explanations.

Attribution theory originated in the writings of **Fritz Heider** (1958). Heider argued that people continually make causal analyses as part of their attempts at general comprehension of the social world. People, he suggested, are all *intuitive psychologists* who try to figure out what people are like and what causes their behavior, just as professional psychologists do. Heider believed that the questions that dominate most attributional analyses are whether the cause of a behavior is found in the person (internal or *dispositional* causality) or in the situation (external or *situational* causality) and who is responsible for the outcomes. How do people make those judgments?

Harold Kelley (1967) formalized Heider's line of thinking by specifying the variables that people use to make their attributions. Kelley made the important observation that people most often make causal attributions for events under conditions of *uncertainty*. You rarely, if ever, have sufficient information to know for sure what caused someone to behave in a particular way. Kelley believed that people grapple with uncertainty by accumulating information from multiple events and using the *covariation principle*. The **covariation principle** suggests that people should attribute a be-

havior to a causal factor if that factor was present whenever the behavior occurred but was absent whenever it didn't occur. Suppose, for example, you are walking down a street and you see a friend pointing at a horse and screaming. What evidence would you gather to decide whether your friend is crazy (a dispositional attribution) or danger is afoot (a situational attribution)?

Kelley suggested that people make this judgment by assessing covariation with respect to three dimensions of information relevant to the person whose acts they are trying to explain: distinctiveness, consistency, and consensus.

- *Distinctiveness* refers to whether the behavior is specific to a particular situation—does your friend scream in response to all horses?
- *Consistency* refers to whether the behavior occurs repeatedly in response to this situation—has this horse made your friend scream in the past?
- *Consensus* refers to whether other people also produce the same behavior in the same situation—is everyone pointing and screaming?

Each of these three dimensions plays a role in the conclusions you draw. Suppose, for example, that your friend was the only one screaming. Would that make you more likely to make a dispositional or a situational attribution?

Thousands of studies have been conducted to refine and extend attribution theory beyond the solid foundation provided by Heider and Kelley (Fiske & Taylor, 1991). Many of those studies have concerned themselves with conditions in which attributions depart from a systematic search of available information. We will describe four types of circumstances in which bias may creep into your attributions.

◆ THE FUNDAMENTAL ATTRIBUTION ERROR

Suppose you have made an arrangement to meet a friend at 7 o'clock. It's now 7:30, and the friend still hasn't arrived. How might you be explaining this event to yourself?

- I'm sure something really important happened that made it impossible for her to be here on time.
- What a jerk! Couldn't she try a little harder?

We've given you a choice again between a situational and a dispositional attribution. Research has shown that people are more likely, on average, to choose the second type, the dispositional explanation (Ross & Nisbett, 1991). This tendency is so strong, in fact, that social psychologist **Lee Ross** (1977) labeled it the fundamental attribution error. The **fundamental attribution error (FAE)** represents the dual tendency for people to overestimate dispositional factors (blame or credit people) and to underestimate situational factors (blame or credit the environment) when searching for the cause of some behavior or outcome.

Let's look at a laboratory example of the FAE. Ross and his colleagues (1977) created an experimental version of a "College Bowl" type of quiz game in which participants became questioners or contestants by the flip of a coin. The questioner was instructed to ask challenging questions to which he or she knew the answers. The contestant tried, often in vain, to answer the questions. At the end of the session, the questioner, the contestant, and observers (other participants who had watched the game) rated the general knowledge of both questioner and contestant. The results are shown in **Figure 16.1.** As you can see, questioners seem to believe that both they and the contestants are average. Both contestants and observers, however, rate the questioner as much more knowledgeable than the contestant—and contestants even rate themselves to be a bit below average! Is this fair? It should be clear that the situation confers a great advantage on the questioner. (Wouldn't you prefer to be the one who gets to ask the questions?) The contestants' and observers' ratings ignore the way in which the situ-

ation allowed one person to look bright and the other to look dull. That's the fundamental attribution error.

You should be on a constant lookout for instances of the FAE. However, this may not always be easy: It often takes a bit of "research" to discover the situational roots of behavior. Situational forces are often invisible. You can't, for example, *see* social norms; you can only see the behaviors they give rise to. What can you do to avoid the FAE? Particularly in circumstances in which you are making a dispositional attribution that is negative ("What a jerk!"), you should take a step back and ask yourself, Could it be something about the situation that is bringing about this behavior? You might think of such an exercise as "attributional charity." Do you see why?

This advice may be particularly important to those of us who live in Western society, because evidence suggests that the FAE is due, in part, to cultural sources (Miller, 1984). Recall the discussion in Chapter 13 of cultural differences in construals of the self. As we explained there, most Western cultures embody *independent construals of self,* whereas most Eastern cultures embody *interdependent construals of self* (Markus & Kitayama, 1991). Research demonstrates that, as a function of the culture of interdependence, members of non-Western cultures are less likely to focus on individual actors in situations. Let's see how this cultural difference affects reporting of news events.

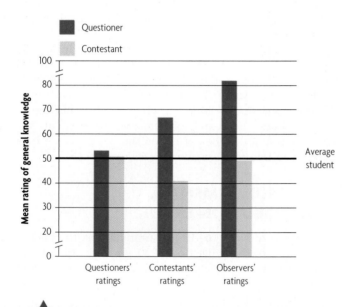

FIGURE 16.1

Ratings of Questioners' and Contestants' General Knowledge

After the quiz game, questioners, contestants, and observers rated each of the participant's general knowledge with respect to a rating of 50 for the average student. Questioners believed that both they and the contestants were average. However, both contestants and observers rated the questioner as much more knowledgeable than the contestant. Furthermore, contestants rated themselves to be a bit below average.

PUTTING IDEAS TO THE TEST

Attributions about Financial Scandals

Researchers selected articles from newspapers in the United States (*The New York Times*) and Japan (*Asahi Shimbun*) that reported on financial scandals such as the 1995 collapse of England's oldest bank, Barings. A research assistant, who was blind to the study's purpose, read each article to extract excerpts in which causal explanations were offered. For each excerpt, another pair of blind research assistants judged whether the explanation offered was dispositional—it attributed blame to an individual—or situational—it attributed blame to an organization. The patterns of attributions were strikingly different for the two sets of articles. U.S. writers tended to make stronger dispositional attributions, whereas Japanese writers made stronger situational attributions (Menon et al., 1999).

An impressive feature of this study is that it captures cultural attributional styles as they are written for newspaper articles. The study makes clear one way in which a cultural style of attribution is transmitted and maintained for all those who are exposed to the media in a particular culture.

◆ SELF-SERVING BIASES

One of the most startling findings in the College Bowl study was the contestants' negative evaluation of their own abilities. This suggests that people will make the FAE even at their own expense. (In fact, you should recall from Chapter 14 that one theory of the origins of depression suggests that depressed people make too many negative attributions to themselves rather than to situational causes.) In many circumstances, however, people do just the opposite—their attributions err in the direction of being self-serving. A **self-serving bias** leads people to take credit for their successes while denying or explaining away responsibility for their failures. In many situations, people tend to make dispositional attributions for success and situational attributions for failure (Gilovich, 1991): "I got the prize because of my ability"; "I lost the competition because it was rigged."

These patterns of attribution may be good for short-term self-esteem. However, it may often be more important to have an accurate sense of what causal forces are at work in your life outcomes. Consider how you do in your classes. If you get an A, what attributions do you make? How about if you get a C? Research has demonstrated that students tend to attribute high grades to their own efforts and low grades to factors external to themselves (McAllister, 1996). In fact, professors show the same pattern—they make attributions to themselves for students' successes but not their failures. Once again, can you see what impact this pattern of attributions might have on your GPA? If you don't think about the external causes for your successes (for example, "That first exam was easy"), you might fail to study enough the next time; if you don't think about the dispositional causes for failures (for example, "I shouldn't have stayed so long at that party"), you also might never get around to studying hard enough. We emphasized earlier that you should strive to avoid the FAE when you think about others' behavior. Similarly, you might examine attributions about your own behavior to weed out (non-self-serving) self-serving biases.

People also indulge in self-serving biases when they are members of groups: They are more likely to attribute group successes to themselves and failures to other group members. You may be pleased, however, to learn that friendship puts limits on this effect.

PUTTING IDEAS TO THE TEST

Friendship and Self-Serving Biases

Experimental participants were asked to engage in a task that measured creativity with either a friend or a stranger. After completing the task, each participant was given feedback on the success of his or her group relative to a large normative sample. Irrespective of their actual performance, half the participants were given *success* feedback (i.e., they were told their performance was in the 93rd percentile); half were given *failure* feedback (i.e., they were told their performance was in the 31st percentile). All the participants were then asked to rate who was more responsible for the test outcome on a scale that ranged from 1 (the other participant) to 10 (myself). As seen in **Figure 16.2**, participants who engaged in the task with a stranger made considerably stronger attributions to themselves for success than for failure (Campbell et al., 2000). Participants' attributions in circumstances of success and failure were more consistent when their partners had been their friends.

Next time you are engaged in a group activity, try to see how this experiment applies to the way in which you make attributions of responsibility to different members of the group.

Why does it matter so much what attributions you make? Recall the example of your tardy friend. Suppose that, because you don't seek information about the situation, you decide that she isn't actually interested in being your friend. Can that incorrect belief actually cause the person to be unfriendly toward you in the future? To address that question, we turn now to the power of beliefs and expectations in constructing social reality.

FIGURE 16.2

Patterns of Attributions to Friends and Strangers

Experimental participants were asked to rate who was responsible for their groups' success or failure on a task. With strangers, participants showed a pattern of self-serving biases: They made stronger attributions to themselves when the group had succeeded than when it had failed. Ratings were more consistent when the participants' partners were their friends.

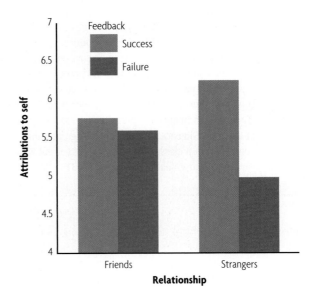

◆ EXPECTATIONS AND SELF-FULFILLING PROPHECIES

Can beliefs and expectations go beyond coloring the way you interpret experiences to actually shape social reality? Much research suggests that the very nature of some situations can be modified significantly by the beliefs and expectations people have about them. **Self-fulfilling prophecies** (Merton, 1957) are predictions made about some future behavior or event that modify behavioral interactions so as to produce what is expected. Suppose, for example, you go to a party expecting to have a great time. Suppose a friend goes expecting it to be boring. Can you imagine the different ways in which the two of you might behave, given these expectations? These alternative ways of behaving may, in turn, alter how others at the party behave toward you. In that case, which of you is actually more likely to have a good time at the party?

One of the most powerful demonstrations of self-fulfilling prophecies took its cue from a play by George Bernard Shaw. In Shaw's *Pygmalion* (popularized as the musical *My Fair Lady*), a street waif is transformed into a proper society lady under the intense training of her teacher, Professor Henry Higgins. The effect of social expectancy, or the *Pygmalion effect,* was re-created in a classic experiment by psychologist **Robert Rosenthal** in conjunction with school principal Leonore Jacobson.

How do self-fulfilling prophecies affect the likelihood that children will engage in underage drinking?

CLASSIC

PUTTING IDEAS TO THE TEST

Expectations Can Change IQ

Elementary school teachers in Boston were informed by researchers that their testing had revealed that some of their students were "academic spurters." The teachers were led to believe that these particular students were "intellectual bloomers who will show unusual gains during the academic year." In fact, there was no objective basis for that prediction; the names of these late bloomers were chosen randomly. However, by the end of that school year, 30 percent of the children arbitrarily named as spurters had gained an average of 22 IQ points! Almost all of them had gained at least 10 IQ points. Their gain in intellectual performance, as measured by a standard test of intelligence, was significantly greater than that of their control group classmates who had started out with the same average IQ (Rosenthal & Jacobson, 1968).

How did the teachers' false expectations get translated into such positive student performance? Rosenthal (1974) points to at least four processes that were activated by the teachers' expectations (see also Jussim,

1986). First, the teachers acted more warmly and more friendly toward the "late bloomers," creating a climate of social approval and acceptance. Second, they put greater demands—involving both quality and level of difficulty of material to be learned—on those for whom they had high hopes. Third, they gave more immediate and clearer feedback (both praise and criticism) about the selected students' performance. Finally, the teachers created more opportunities for the special students to respond in class, show their stuff, and be reinforced, thus giving them hard evidence that they were indeed as good as the teachers believed they were.

What is unusual, of course, about the situation in the Boston classrooms is that the teachers were purposefully given false expectations. This methodology allowed Rosenthal and Jacobson to demonstrate the full potential for self-fulfilling prophecies. In most real-world situations, however, expectations are based on fairly accurate social perceptions (Jussim, 1991). Teachers, for example, expect certain students to do well because those students arrive in the classroom with better qualifications; and those students, typically, do show the best performance. Research has suggested, in fact, that self-fulfilling prophecies have the greatest effect on the lives of low-achieving students (Madon et al., 1997). When teachers expect them to do poorly, they may do even worse; when teachers expect them to do well, that has the potential to turn their school lives around.

Much of the research on self-fulfilling prophecies has focused on school success. However, researchers have found evidence in other domains that people's mistaken beliefs and expectations can have an influence on what actually happens. For example, one study focused on mothers' expectations about the likelihood that their children would engage in underage drinking (Madon et al., 2003). Mothers know a fair amount about their children. For that reason, their expectations of how much their children might drink in the future were fairly accurate. Still, to the extent that mothers were, in fact, inaccurate, their children's drinking behavior tended to be correlated with those mistaken expectations. This was particularly true when mothers underestimated how much their children would drink: The children, in fact, planned to drink less than would have been expected based on background factors (such as peers' alcohol use and past alcohol use).

As you consider these studies on self-fulfilling prophecies, you might wonder what behaviors teachers and mothers perform that allow their mistaken expectations to be confirmed. Let's see now how a person's choice of behaviors can affect the construction of social reality.

◆ BEHAVIORS THAT CONFIRM EXPECTATIONS

Consider the Boston classrooms once again. We have already noted that the teachers performed a series of behaviors that enabled them, in the long run, to confirm their expectations. **Mark Snyder** (1984) introduced the term **behavioral confirmation** to label the process by which someone's expectations about another person actually influence the second person to behave in ways that confirm the original hypothesis. For example, imagine you were about to interview someone, and you were told that the person was shy or introverted. Which of these questions might you select to ask (Snyder & Swann, 1978)?

- What would you do if you wanted to liven things up at a party?
- In what situations do you wish you could be more outgoing?
- What factors make it hard for you to really open up to people?
- In what situations are you most talkative?

Suppose you chose the second question—as many experimental participants did when they believed they were going to talk to someone introverted. Isn't it likely that even a very extraverted person could give you reasonable answers to the question? Thus an expectation—"I'm going to talk to someone who is an introvert"—leads to a behavioral choice—"I'm going to ask the kind of question you ask an introverted person"—which leads to potential confirmation of the expectation—"If he could answer this question, I guess he really is introverted."

How powerful are the forces of behavioral confirmation? An initial answer to this question is similar to the one we developed with respect to the likelihood of self-fulfilling prophecies: It depends on the availability of accurate information from the environment.

PUTTING IDEAS TO THE TEST

Limits on Behavioral Confirmation

Researchers created circumstances in which one set of undergraduate women, the *perceivers,* were given false expectations about the extraversion or introversion of a second set of women, the *targets.* Each of the targets had, in fact, provided ratings that allowed the experimenters to identify her as an introvert or extravert. However, some of the target women had certain (strong) self-conceptions on this dimension, whereas other of the target women had uncertain (weak) self-conceptions. What happened when the perceivers interacted with the targets? When the targets had uncertain self-conceptions, behavioral confirmation reigned: The perceivers elicited behavior from the targets that confirmed the initial expectation. However, when the targets had more solid and certain self-conceptions, that self-conception shone through contrary to the perceivers' expectations (Swann & Ely, 1984).

Once again you can see that expectations have their greatest effect when the actual state of the world—the "reality" of the target—is ambiguous or uncertain. In those circumstances, you are most likely to go beyond the "data" to make inferences about the underlying reality.

The extent of behavioral confirmation also depends on the motivations the target has with respect to the interaction. In another study, male *perceivers* were led to believe—they were shown photographs—that the female *targets* at the other end of a phone conversation were either of normal weight or obese. In some cases, the women (whose actual weight was unrelated to the photographs) were asked to participate in the conversations to gain knowledge about the personality of the man to whom they were speaking; in other cases, the women's goal was to have a smooth and pleasant interaction with their male partner. In general, this latter situation produced behavioral confirmation: The *targets* were rated as producing behaviors that conformed to an obesity stereotype (for example, they were rated as less sociable and less happy). However, when the *targets* were motivated to obtain knowledge, behavioral confirmation was *not* found (Snyder & Haugen, 1995). This experiment suggests that the normal impulse to have smooth social interactions makes it *more* possible for people to remake the world in line with their own beliefs and attitudes, including stereotypes.

The research we have described in this section leads naturally to the question, How do attitudes and expectations arise? In the experiments we have reviewed, participants are typically told what to believe. But what happens in the real world, when you arrive at expectations on your own? In the next section, we consider the question of how attitudes are formed and changed—and we examine the links among beliefs, attitudes, and action.

PUT YOURSELF TO THE TEST

- What does it mean to say that people construct social reality?
- What are some of the important variables that affect people's causal attributions?
- What is meant by the fundamental attribution error?
- Why might self-serving biases have an impact on future outcomes?
- What are some limits on self-fulfilling prophecies?
- Under what circumstances might behaviors confirm expectations?

Attitudes, Attitude Change, and Action

Have you already had a chance today to express an *attitude?* Has someone asked you, "What do you think of my shirt?" or "Was the chicken any good?" An **attitude** is a positive or negative evaluation of people, objects, and ideas. You may have favorable attitudes toward day-care workers, sports cars, and tax cuts, and unfavorable attitudes toward telemarketers, contemporary art, and astrology. This definition of attitude allows for the fact that many of the attitudes you hold are not overt; you may not be consciously aware that you harbor certain attitudes. Attitudes are important

because they influence your behavior and how you construct social reality. Recall the Princeton–Dartmouth football game. Those people who favored Princeton "saw" a different game from those people who favored Dartmouth; attributions about events were made in line with their attitudes. What are the sources of your attitudes, and how do they affect your behaviors?

◆ ATTITUDES AND BEHAVIORS

We have already defined attitudes as positive or negative evaluations. We'll begin this section by giving you an opportunity to make an evaluation. To what extent do you agree with this statement? (Circle a number.)

I enjoy movies that star Ben Affleck.

1 —— 2 —— 3 —— 4 —— 5 —— 6 —— 7 —— 8 —— 9
Strongly   Neutral   Strongly
disagree   agree

Let's say that you gave a rating of 3—you disagree somewhat. What is the origin of that judgment? We can identify three types of information that give rise to your attitude:

- *Cognitive.* What thoughts do you have in response to "Ben Affleck"?
- *Affective.* What feelings does the mention of "Ben Affleck" evoke?
- *Behavioral.* How do you behave when, for example, you have the opportunity to see one of Ben Affleck's movies?

Some combination of these types of information most likely guided your hand when you circled "3" (or some other number). Your attitudes also generate responses in the same three categories. If you believe yourself to have a somewhat negative attitude toward Ben Affleck, you might say, "He isn't a serious actor" (cognitive), "He looked better when he first started out" (affective), or "After *Gigli*, I'm going to wait to read his reviews" (behavioral).

It isn't too hard to measure an attitude, but is that attitude always an accurate indication of how people will actually behave? You know from your own life experiences that the answer is "no": People will say they dislike Ben Affleck but spend good money to see him anyway. At the same time, sometimes people's behaviors *do* follow their attitudes: They say they won't pay to see Ben Affleck, and they don't. How can you determine when attitudes will or will not predict behavior? Researchers have worked hard to answer that question—to identify the circumstances in which the link is strongest between people's attitudes and how they act (Ajzen & Sexton, 1999; Fazio & Towles-Schwen, 1999).

How does your attitude toward Ben Affleck affect your willingness to watch his movies?

One property of attitudes that predicts behavior is *accessibility*—the strength of the association between an attitude object and a person's evaluation of that object (Fazio, 1995). When we asked you about Ben Affleck, did an answer rush to mind or did you have to consider the question for a while? The more quickly an answer rushed in, the more likely it is that your behavior will be consistent with that attitude. But how do attitudes become more accessible? Research suggests that attitudes are more accessible when they are based on *direct experience:* You will have a more accessible attitude about Ben Affleck movies if you've experienced several of them yourself rather than hearing or reading about them indirectly. Attitudes are also more accessible when they have been rehearsed more often: Just as you might expect, the more often you've formulated an attitude about something (consider "chocolate" versus "kiwi"), the more accessible is the attitude. Rehearsal makes attitudes more accessible even when you've been lying.

Lying and Attitude Accessibility

Suppose someone asks you how you feel about Ben Affleck and you decide to lie to be polite. What impact does lying have on your attitude and your subsequent behavior? Researchers have tested the hypothesis that because lies make your *real* attitude more accessible, they actually make your behavior more consistent with that real attitude (Johar & Sengupta, 2002). In the study, participants were asked to consider four brands of candy bars that were unfamiliar to them—the researchers imported them from Canada. After considering information associated with each candy bar, participants in one group were asked to indicate their true attitude toward each brand five times. Participants in a second group were asked to express the opposite of their true feelings—they were asked to lie five times. A third group served as a control group and did not express their opinions. At the end of the study, participants were asked to choose the candy bar they most wanted to sample. **Table 16.1** shows the correlations between the participants' true attitude ratings and the brands they selected. As you can see, for both true and false expressions of attitudes the correlation is higher than in the control condition. Thus, lying made people's behaviors more consistent with what they really thought rather than with what they said.

Each time the participants prepared a lie, they had to examine mentally their true attitudes. That process of examination made their true attitudes more accessible.

Attitudes also are better predictors of behavior when the attitudes and behaviors are measured at the same level of *specificity*. Consider the data presented in **Table 16.2.** In this study, the researchers were trying to predict the likelihood that members of an initial sample of 270 women, ages 18 to 38, would use birth control pills. You can see in Table 16.2 that the more *specific* the question the women were asked about their attitudes

TABLE 16.1

Accessibility Improves Attitude–Behavior Correlations

	Correlation between True Attitude and Behavioral Choice
True expression of attitude	0.61
False expression of attitude	0.54
Control	0.39

TABLE 16.2
Specificity Improves
Attitude–Behavior Correlations

Attitude Measured	Correlation with Behavior of Using Birth Control
Attitude toward birth control	.08
Attitude toward birth control pills	.32
Attitude toward using birth control pills	.52
Attitude toward using birth control pills during the next two years	.57

Specificity ↓

Note: Researchers were trying to predict the likelihood that women would use birth control pills in the next two years. The more specific the question the women were asked about their attitudes, the higher was the correlation with their actual behavior.

was, the higher was the correlation with their actual specific behavior (Davidson & Jaccard, 1979). (Recall that the closer a correlation is to 1 or –1, the stronger is the relationship.) The concept of specificity also applies to the specific *exemplars* you call to mind when you produce an attitude (Sia et al., 1997). Suppose, for example, we asked you to agree or disagree with the statement "I trust politicians." Your judgment would depend on which politician or politicians came to mind: Was it George Washington, Winston Churchill, Bill Clinton, or George W. Bush? If we asked you the same question in a week, your judgment—your report of your general attitude—might change if some other set of politicians came to mind.

Why might someone be able to predict your vote from the speed with which you express an attitude?

When your attitudes are based on different subsets of information, they may change radically over time: When you gave us your attitude about Ben Affleck, were you thinking about the film *Armageddon*, *Daredevil*, or *Gigli*? Only when the "evidence" for your attitude remains stable over time can we expect to find a strong relationship between your evaluation (thoughts) and what you do (actions).

◆ PROCESSES OF PERSUASION

We've just seen that, under appropriate circumstances, attitudes can predict behavior. That's good news for all the people who spend time and money to affect your attitudes. But quite often others *can't* affect your attitudes when they want to do so. You don't change brands of toothpaste each time you see a peppy new commercial with scads of pearly-toothed actors; you don't change your political affiliation each time a candidate looks into the camera and declares sincerely that he or she deserves your vote. Many people in your life indulge in **persuasion**—deliberate efforts to change your attitudes. For persuasion to take place, certain conditions must be met. Let's explore some of those conditions.

To begin, we introduce the **elaboration likelihood model,** a theory of persuasion that defines how likely it is that people will focus their cognitive processes to elaborate upon a persuasive message (Petty & Wegener, 1999; Petty et al., 2003). This model makes a critical distinction between *central* and *peripheral routes* to persuasion. The central route represents circumstances in which people think carefully about a persuasive communication so that attitude change depends on the strength of the arguments. When someone is trying to convince you that gasoline should cost $5 a gallon, you are likely to process the information in this careful fashion. The peripheral route represents circumstances in which people do not focus critically on the message but respond to superficial cues in the situation. When a sexy model is placed in front of the product someone wishes you to buy, the seller is hoping you'll avoid critical thought. The central or peripheral route that people take depends in large part on their *motivation* with respect to the message: Are they willing and able to think carefully about the persuasive content?

If you take a close look at the messages that surround you, you will quickly come to the conclusion that advertisers, for example, often count on you to take the peripheral route. Why do advertisers pay celebrities to sell their products? Do you really believe that Hollywood actors worry enormously about which long-distance phone service will produce bigger savings? Presumably, the advertisers hope that you won't evaluate the arguments too closely—instead, they hope you'll let yourself be persuaded by your general feelings of warmth toward the actor hawking the product.

Why do advertisers pay celebrities to endorse their products?

Now ask yourself this question: Under what circumstances are you likely to feel sufficiently motivated to take the central route to persuasion? The answer is important both to people who wish you would (because they think they have strong arguments) and people who wish you wouldn't (because, as we just suggested, they want to persuade you with superficial cues). One example of a characteristic of a persuasive message that prompts you to take the central route is *personal relevance:* You are more likely to evaluate arguments carefully when information is personally relevant (Eagly & Chaiken, 1993). Suppose, for example, you listened to two speeches in succession. The first

speaker argued that Hollywood should produce more 3-D movies; the second argued that college tuitions should be raised 50 percent. Which speech would be more likely to engage the central route? Let's look now at an experiment that considers the importance of personal relevance to your experience of fictional worlds.

PUTTING IDEAS TO THE TEST

Personal Relevance in Fictional Worlds

Are you persuaded by the information you encounter in fictional worlds—information from the novels you read, the movies you watch, and so on? A team of researchers suggested that the extent to which you will be persuaded depends, in part, on the personal relevance of the fictional setting. Participants in the study were students at Yale and Princeton universities. Some students from each school read a story that was set at Princeton; the remaining students read a story that was identical except that it was set at Yale. The characters in the stories discussed real-world issues, like whether sunlight is good for the skin or mental illnesses are contagious. The researchers reasoned that participants would be more likely to treat information as personally relevant when they read the story set at their *home* school: For example, a Princeton student reading a story set at Princeton would be more motivated to read the story carefully and consider the characters' arguments. As shown in **Figure 16.3,** the results confirmed this prediction. The students showed attitude change in the direction of the arguments made in the story only when it was set at the *away* school (for example, the Princeton version for Yale students). That is, when the information was not personally relevant, the students failed to carry out central processing to expose the weaknesses in the story information. Without this central processing, the students were persuaded by the story (Prentice et al., 1997).

FIGURE 16.3

Persuasion and Personal Relevance

Students read stories that were set either at their "home" school—and therefore were personally relevant—or set at an "away" school. Personal relevance should make it more likely that the students will centrally process the story information and thus be less persuaded by it. In fact, persuasion in the direction of the story only occurred when students read the "away" school versions (for example, when the Yale students read the Princeton version of the story). This finding supports the prediction that the personally relevant "home" school versions led to central processing and rejection of the story arguments, whereas the not personally relevant "away" school versions led to peripheral processing and acceptance of the story arguments.

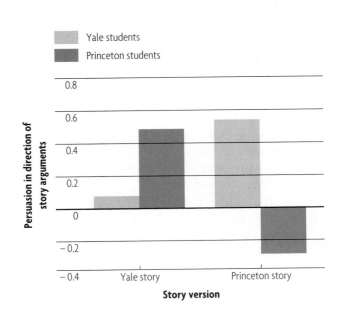

Note that the two versions of the story were identical, except for their settings. Thus, the difference in persuasion can only be attributed to the extent to which students were motivated to take the central route and evaluate the information carefully (Prentice & Gerrig, 1999). Next time you sit down to watch a TV show, you should consider what types of persuasion might go on via the peripheral route if the content is not personally relevant—by virtue of the setting, characters, and so on—to you.

Another factor that influences your choice of routes is the match between the type of attitude and the type of argument (Ajzen & Sexton, 1999). Earlier, we suggested that both cognitive and affective experiences give rise to attitudes. Research suggests that attitudes are more likely to change when advertisers match cognitive-based arguments to cognitive-based attitudes and affect-based arguments to affect-based attitudes.

PUTTING IDEAS TO THE TEST

The Match Between Advertisements and Attitudes

What is the basis of your attitudes toward brands of *coffee*? You are likely to make evaluations based on your *cognitive* responses: How do they taste? How much do they cost? Now think about *greeting cards*. For greeting cards, you're more likely to be swayed by *affective* responses: Do they make you smile? Will they capture the right quality relationship? In one experiment, participants were exposed to either cognitive-based or affective-based advertisements for products, including coffee and greeting cards. A cognitive-based ad might read, "The delicious, hearty flavor and aroma of Sterling Blend coffee come from a blend of the freshest coffee beans"; an emotion-based ad might read, "The coffee you drink says something about the type of person you are. It can reveal your rare, discriminating taste." After participants read each of a series of ads, they listed thoughts to indicate how favorably they felt toward the product. As you can see in **Figure 16.4**, there was a strong effect of the match: Participants produced more favorable thoughts when the type of message (for example, cognitive-based ads) matched the type of attitude (for example, cognitive-based attitudes) (Shavitt, 1990).

In your own efforts to change people's attitudes you should also be able to put this result to use: Does the attitude have a strong cognitive component or a strong affective component? How can you tailor your persuasive message accordingly?

◆ PERSUASION BY YOUR OWN ACTIONS

In the last section, we described factors that influence people's ability to change others' attitudes. However, there are forces at work in a number of circumstances

---

that cause people to bring about their *own* attitude change. Imagine a situation in which you've vowed not to eat any extra calories. You arrive at work, and there's a cake for your boss's birthday. You consume a piece. Did you break your vow? That is, should you have a negative attitude about your own behavior? Aren't you likely to think what you did was okay? Why? We describe two analyses of self-persuasion, *dissonance theory* and *self-perception theory*.

DISSONANCE THEORY

One of the most common assumptions in the study of attitudes is that people like to believe that their attitudes remain consistent over time (Eagly & Chaiken, 1993). This striving for consistency was explored within the field of social psychology in the theory of *cognitive dissonance*, as developed by **Leon Festinger** (1957). **Cognitive dissonance** is the state of conflict someone experiences *after* making a decision, taking an action, or being exposed to information that is contrary to prior beliefs, feelings, or values. Suppose, for example, you chose to buy a car against a friend's advice. Why might you be overly defensive about the car? It is assumed that when a person's cognitions about his or her behavior and relevant attitudes are dissonant—they do not follow one to

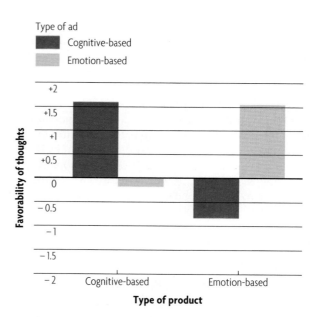

FIGURE 16.4

Emotion- and Cognitive-Based Ads and Products

When the type of advertisement (emotion- or cognitive-based) matched the dimension of evaluation underlying the object— emotions for greeting cards and cognitions for coffee—people reacted more favorably to the product. (The favorability of thoughts was measured on a scale ranging from −3 to +3.)

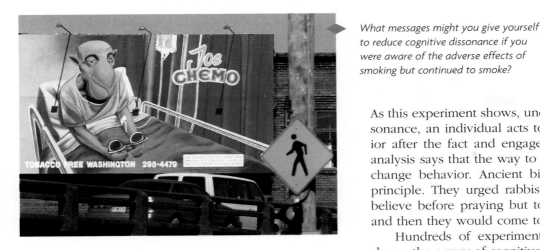

What messages might you give yourself to reduce cognitive dissonance if you were aware of the adverse effects of smoking but continued to smoke?

the next—an aversive state arises that the person is motivated to reduce. Dissonance-reducing activities modify this unpleasant state. In the case of your car, being defensive—overstating its value—makes you feel better about going against your friend's advice. (Dissonance also might lead you to think less well of your friend.)

Dissonance has motivational force—it impels you to take action to reduce the unpleasant feeling (Wood, 2000). The motivation to reduce dissonance increases with the magnitude of the dissonance created by a cognitive inconsistency. In other words, the stronger the dissonance, the greater the motivation to reduce it. In a classic dissonance experiment, college students told a lie to other students and came to believe in their lie when they got a small, rather than a large, reward for doing so.

CLASSIC
PUTTING IDEAS TO THE TEST

Dissonance Makes Lies True

Stanford students participated in a very dull task and were then asked (as a favor to the experimenter, because his assistant hadn't shown up) to lie to another participant by saying that the task had been fun and interesting. Half the participants were paid $20 to tell the lie, while the others were paid only $1. The $20 payment was sufficient external justification for lying, but the $1 payment was an inadequate justification. The people who were paid $1 were left with dissonant cognitions: "The task was dull" and "I chose to lie by telling another student it was fun and interesting without a good reason for doing so."

To reduce their dissonance, these $1 participants changed their evaluations of the task. They later expressed the belief that they found "it really was fun and interesting—I might like to do it again." In comparison, the participants who lied for $20 did not change their evaluations—the task was still a bore; they had only lied "for the money" (Festinger & Carlsmith, 1959).

As this experiment shows, under conditions of high dissonance, an individual acts to justify his or her behavior after the fact and engages in self-persuasion. This analysis says that the way to change attitudes is first to change behavior. Ancient biblical scholars knew this principle. They urged rabbis not to insist that people believe before praying but to get them to pray first—and then they would come to believe.

Hundreds of experiments and field studies have shown the power of cognitive dissonance to change attitudes and behavior (Eagly & Chaiken, 1993; Wicklund & Brehm, 1976). Recently, however, researchers have begun to question whether dissonance effects generalize to other cultures. Consider again the way the concept of *self* changes from culture to culture. As we noted earlier, North Americans typically view themselves as *independent,* distinct from others in the environment; members of Asian cultures typically view themselves as *interdependent,* fundamentally interconnected with others. Does the cultural concept of the self affect the experience of cognitive dissonance?

PUTTING IDEAS TO THE TEST

Culture and Cognitive Dissonance

Groups of Canadian and Japanese participants were asked to choose the 10 CDs out of a group of 40 available CDs that they would most like to own. Next, they rank-ordered those 10 compact disks from most to least desirable and provided ratings (on a scale that ranged from "wouldn't like this CD at all" to "would like this CD very much"). The experimenters then asked the participants to choose a CD to take home—as compensation for participating in the study. The choices were limited to CDs from the middle of the participants' lists: They typically were asked to choose between their fifth- and sixth-ranked choices. Finally, participants were asked to go through and rate their top 10 choices once again. How might those ratings change from the first to the second time? According to dissonance theory, when you make a tough choice—like the one between your fifth- and sixth-ranked alternatives—you should adjust your attitudes to feel better about the outcome of the choice: "If I chose the Janet Jackson CD [originally No. 5], I must really like it *much* better than the R.E.M. [originally No. 6]." In fact, Canadian participants gave evidence for this change in attitude—the ratings for the chosen CD moved in a positive direction from those for the unchosen CD. Japanese participants, by contrast, showed no effects of dissonance—their choice did not systematically affect their ratings (Heine & Lehman, 1997).

This research suggests that people only experience cognitive dissonance—they only seek to maintain consistency within their self-concept—when they have an *independent* concept of the self. If you are ever in circumstances in which you must make decisions jointly with members of other cultures, you will want to reflect on the culture's impact on the way you all think and act after the decision has been made.

SELF-PERCEPTION THEORY

Dissonance theory describes one way in which people, at least in Western cultures, allow their behaviors ("I chose that CD") to have an impact on their attitudes ("I must like it much better than my other option"). *Self-perception theory,* developed by **Daryl Bem** (1972), identifies other circumstances in which behaviors inform attitudes. According to **self-perception theory,** you infer what your internal states (beliefs, attitudes, motives, and feelings) are or should be by perceiving how you are acting now and recalling how you have acted in the past in a given situation. You use that self-knowledge to reason backward to the most likely causes or determinants of your behavior. For example, the self-perceiver responds to the question, "Do you like psychology?" by saying, "Sure, I'm taking the basic course and it's not required, I do all the readings, I pay attention during lectures, and I'm getting a good grade in the course." In other words, you answer a question about personal preferences by a behavioral description of relevant actions and situational factors—rather than undertaking an intense search of thoughts and feelings.

Self-perception theory lacks the motivational components of dissonance theory. Because self-perception fills in missing attitudes—you look to your behavior to learn how you feel—self-perception processes occur mainly when you are in ambiguous situations and dealing with unfamiliar events (Fazio, 1987). In these situations, you have a need to discover how you feel about some novel object of attitudinal scrutiny—if you find yourself laughing during your first Jim Carrey movie, you may infer a favorable attitude toward him. One flaw in the process of gaining self-knowledge through self-perception is that people are often insensitive about the extent to which their behavior is influenced by situational forces. You can see this if we return a final time to the College Bowl experiment. Recall that the participants who labored unsuccessfully as contestants rated their own general knowledge relatively low. Imagine what it must have been like to be in their position. Over and over you would hear yourself saying, "I don't know the answer to that question." Can you see how observation of this behavior—the process of self-perception—could give rise to a negative self-evaluation?

Let's return to the attitudes you might express toward yourself if you eat a slice of cake at your boss's birthday party. According to dissonance theory, you need to resolve the inconsistency between your vow ("I won't consume any extra calories") and your behavior (eating a piece of cake). There are many things you can do to avoid feeling bad: Perhaps you'd reason, "I can't afford to have my boss be angry at me by declining a piece of cake." Similarly, according to self-perception theory, you look at your behavior to calculate your attitude. If you think, "Because I ate cake, my boss's birthday must have been very important," you'll also escape any negative impact on your self-esteem. Self-persuasion can sometimes be useful!

◆ COMPLIANCE

In this section so far, we have discussed what attitudes are and how they might be changed. It should be clear to you, however, that most often what people want you to do is change your *behavior:* People wish to bring about **compliance**—a change in behavior consistent with their direct requests. When advertisers spend a lot of money for TV commercials, they don't just want you to feel good about their products—they want you to march into a store and buy them. Similarly, doctors want you to follow their medical advice. Social psychologists have extensively studied the way in which individuals bring about compliance with their requests (Cialdini, 2001). We will describe some of those techniques and note how wily salespeople often use them to get you to do things you might not otherwise have done.

RECIPROCITY

One of the rules that dominates human experience is that when someone does something for you, you should do something for that person as well—this is called the **reciprocity norm.** Laboratory research has shown that even very small favors can lead participants to do much larger favors in return (Regan, 1971). Salespeople use reciprocity against you by appearing to do you a favor: "I'll tell you what, I'll take $5 off the price" or "Here's a free sample just for agreeing to talk to me today." This strategy puts you in a position of psychological distress if you don't return the favor and buy the product.

Another compliance technique that arises from the reciprocity norm has often been called the *door-in-the-face technique:* When people say "no" to a large request, they will often say "yes" to a more moderate request.

The Door-in-the-Face Technique

In one experiment, students were asked to spend two hours every week for two years as counselors for juvenile delinquents. They all said "no." Next, they were asked if they would serve as chaperones for some of the delinquents on a trip to the zoo. When they had previously said "no" to the large request, 50 percent of the students agreed to this smaller request. When a different group of students was approached, who had never been asked the large request, only 17 percent of them agreed to serve as chaperones (Cialdini et al., 1975).

What can you do if you want to increase the probability that your neighbors will recycle?

How does this technique invoke the reciprocity norm? When people making requests go from the large to the moderate request, they have done something for you: Now you must do something for them—or risk violating the norm. You agree to the smaller request!

COMMITMENT

The door-in-the-face technique moves you from a large to a moderate request. Salespeople also know that if they can get you to *commit* yourself to some small concession, they can probably also get you to commit to something larger. In experiments, people who agreed to small requests (for example, signing petitions) were more likely subsequently to agree to a bigger request (for example, putting large signs on their lawn) (Freedman & Fraser, 1966). This is often called the *foot-in-the-door technique:* Once people get a foot in the door, they can use your sense of commitment to increase your later compliance. Salespeople use this technique against you by getting you to make a decision and then subtly changing the deal: "I know this is the car you want to buy, but my manager will only let me give you a $200 discount"; "I know you're the sort of person who buys quality goods, so I know you won't mind paying a little extra." This strategy makes you feel inconsistent or foolish if you don't go through with the purchase.

SCARCITY

People dislike feeling that they can't have something (or, from another perspective, people like to have things others can't). Participants, for example, give higher ratings to the taste of chocolate chip cookies that come from a jar with just two cookies than to those that come from a jar of ten (Worchel et al., 1975). How does the principle of *scarcity* apply in the marketplace? Salespeople know that they can increase the likelihood of your purchase if they make goods seem scarce: "This is the last one I have, so

I'm not sure you should wait until tomorrow"; "I have another customer who's planning to come back and get this." This strategy makes you feel as if you are missing a critical opportunity by not buying now.

In explaining these compliance techniques, we have provided a couple of examples of things you might *want* to do: You might want to volunteer your time or sign petitions for good causes. However, you can see that much of the time people use these techniques to get you to do things you probably *wouldn't* want to do. How can you defend yourself against wily salespeople and their kin? You should try to catch them using these strategies—and resist their efforts. Try to ignore meaningless favors. Try to avoid foolish consistency. Try to detect false claims of scarcity. Always take time to think and reason before acting. Your knowledge of social psychology can make you an all-round wiser consumer.

In this section we have described attitudes and behaviors and the relationships between them. However, we have not yet touched on circumstances in which attitudes in the form of *prejudice* may lead to destructive behaviors. We turn now to the topic of prejudice and document both how it comes about and procedures that may be effective to reduce or eliminate it.

- What three components define attitudes?
- What properties of attitudes increase the correlations between attitudes and behaviors?
- What are the central and peripheral routes to persuasion?
- What impact does people's consideration of their own behavior have on their attitudes?
- What forces have researchers demonstrated will raise the probability of compliance?

Prejudice

O f all human weaknesses, none is more destructive to the dignity of the individual and the social bonds of humanity than prejudice. Prejudice is the prime example of social reality gone awry—a situation created in the minds of people that can demean and destroy the lives of others. **Prejudice** is a learned attitude toward a target object, involving negative feelings (dislike or fear), negative beliefs (stereotypes) that justify the attitude, and a behavioral intention to avoid, control, dominate, or eliminate those in the target group. Nazi leaders, for example, passed laws to enforce their prejudiced beliefs that Jews were subhuman and trying to bring about the downfall of Aryan culture. A false belief qualifies as prejudice when it resists change even in the face of appropriate evidence of its falseness. People display prejudice, for example, when they assert that African Americans are all lazy despite their hardworking African American colleagues. Prejudiced attitudes serve as biasing filters that influence the way individuals are perceived and treated once they are categorized as members of a target group.

Social psychology has always put the study of prejudice high on its agenda in an effort to understand its complexity and persistence and to develop strategies to change prejudiced attitudes and discriminatory behavior (Allport, 1954; Duckitt, 1992; Jones, 1997). In fact, the Supreme Court's 1954 decision to outlaw segregated public education was, in part, based on research, presented in federal court by social psychologist **Kenneth Clark,** that showed the negative impact on black children of their separate and unequal education (Clark & Clark, 1947). In this section, we will describe the progress social psychologists have made in their efforts to understand the origins and effects of prejudice, as well as their efforts to help reverse its effects.

◆ ORIGINS OF PREJUDICE

One of the sad truths from the study of prejudice is that it is easy to get people to show negative attitudes toward people who do not belong to the same "group." **Social categorization** is the process by which people organize their social environment by categorizing themselves and others into groups. The simplest and most pervasive form of categorizing consists of an individual

How did Kenneth Clark contribute to the end of segregated schooling?

determining whether people are like him or her. This categorization develops from a "me versus not me" orientation to an "us versus them" orientation: People divide the world into **in-groups**—the groups with which they identify as members—and **out-groups**—the groups with which they do not identify. These cognitive distinctions result in an **in-group bias,** an evaluation of one's own group as better than others (Jones, 1997). People defined as part of the out-group almost instantly are candidates for hostile feelings and unfair treatment.

The most minimal of distinctive cues is sufficient to trigger the formation of bias and prejudice against those in an out-group.

PUTTING IDEAS TO THE TEST

Random Assignment Creates Group Solidarity

In a series of experiments in Holland, participants were randomly divided into two groups: a blue group and a green group. According to the participants' group membership, they were given either blue or green pens and asked to write on either blue or green paper. The experimenter addressed participants in terms of their group color. Even though these color categories had no intrinsic psychological significance and assignment to the groups was completely arbitrary, participants gave a more positive evaluation of their own group than of the other. Furthermore, this in-group bias, based solely on color identification, appeared even before the group members began to work together on an experimental task (Rabbie, 1981).

If you've spent any time watching late night (or early morning) television, you've certainly been subjected to the types of advertisements that attempt to sell you sets of knives or CDs that you really don't need. If you pay close attention to these ads, you'll often see that they are structured to take strong advantage of the quirks of human compliance (Cialdini, 2001).

Let's look at one particular method that researchers have called the *That's-Not-All* (TNA) Technique (Burger, 1986; Burger et al., 1999). Suppose you have been offered five CDs of "The Greatest Hits of the '70s" for three easy payments of only $29.95. However, before you can make your decision the announcer adds, "But that's not all: Act now and we'll also include—at no extra cost—a bonus CD with 12 more songs!" Does the addition of the extra CD make it more likely that you'll accept the offer? It probably should—you're getting more for the same money. Suppose, however, that you'd been offered the six CDs (for three easy payments of only $29.95) all at the same time, without the "that's not all." You'd be getting exactly the same amount of merchandise (six CDs) for the same money. Would you be equally likely to make the purchase?

Here's another common version of the TNA technique. They offer you the five CDs for three easy payments of $29.95 but then, before you can respond, they announce that (for a limited time only) the price has been reduced to three payments of $24.95. Again, compare this to circumstances in which they always offer you the merchandise at the lower price.

Do Late Night TV Ads Really Work?

Lara Torsky

University of Maryland at College Park

Would you be equally likely to make the purchase?

If you think about both these variations, you'll probably guess correctly that the TNA staging has a major impact on people's compliance. Consider a study that was framed as a psychology club bake sale (Burger, 1986). When community members approached the table to ask prices, they were told one of two things. In one condition (which, for the study, was the control condition), they were told that a cupcake with two cookies was 75¢. In a second condition (the TNA condition), potential customers were told that the cupcake was 75¢. However, before they could respond, they were told "wait a second" and told that the deal also included two cookies. In the control condition, 40 percent of the potential customers closed the deal. In the TNA condition, the success rate was

73 percent. Remember, everyone was getting the same overall deal—what mattered quite a bit was the way in which the deal unfolded in time.

Why does that's-not-all work? One explanation is the reciprocity norm that we have already described: The seller has done something for you (added to the deal) and now you should do something for him or her (buy the product). Another explanation points to the type of anchoring phenomenon we described in Chapter 8. The original deal serves as an anchor point against which you decide whether you are at all interested. If you have some interest, then the added bonus seals the deal. For that reason, that's-not-all doesn't work if the original deal isn't sufficiently attractive (Burger et al., 1999). For example, in one study college students were asked to make a donation of $5 to a charity. In the control condition, they were told directly that if they donated $5 they would receive a mug. In the TNA condition, they were first asked to make the donation but, before they could respond, they were told "you'll get the mug too." In the control condition, 63 percent of the students agreed to the donation; in the TNA condition, only 23 percent of the students agreed. That's-not-all fails in this case because the initial offer ("Give $5" with no mention of the mug) strikes most students as unreasonable.

In light of this research, you can watch late night advertisements with a trained eye. How often are they using the TNA technique? How well have the advertisers done in framing an initial offer that doesn't immediately make you say no?

How does prejudice arise, and why is it so difficult to eradicate?

Prejudice and Racial Category Judgments

A group of undergraduates completed a scale that measured their attitudes toward African Americans. Based on their responses, half of the group was classified as prejudiced and the other half nonprejudiced. Next, all the students were asked to view a series of faces and label them aloud as either "white" or "black." Some of the faces were easily classified, whereas other faces were ambiguous. The researchers hypothesized that prejudiced individuals care more about making "correct" racial judgments. Thus, the researchers predicted that the prejudiced students would take longer to provide answers for the ambiguous faces. In fact, prejudiced individuals took almost a second longer than the nonprejudiced individuals when making judgments of the ambiguous faces (Blascovich et al., 1997).

This experiment suggests how important it is to individuals with prejudiced attitudes to define who qualifies as "us" and who qualifies as "them." Researchers have also begun to develop an explicit measure of *nonprejudice* that captures the idea that people without prejudice are less likely to focus on the differences among individuals (Phillips & Ziller, 1997). People who fall high on the *universal orientation scale* tend to endorse statements such as "When I meet someone I tend to notice similarities between myself and the other person" and reject statements such as "I can tell a great deal about a person by knowing his or her gender." Thus, some people appear to have a fundamental ability to overcome the tendency to experience the world in terms of in-groups and out-groups.

We have seen so far that people's categorization of the world into "us" and "them" can swiftly lead to prejudice. Let's look at the way in which prejudice functions through applications of stereotypes.

◆ EFFECTS OF STEREOTYPES

We can use the power of social categorization to explain the origins of many types of prejudice. To explain how prejudice affects day-to-day interactions, we must explore the memory structures that provide important support for prejudice, stereotypes. **Stereotypes** are generalizations about a group of people in which the same characteristics are assigned to all members of a group. You are no doubt familiar with a wide range of stereotypes. What beliefs do you have about men and women? Jews, Muslims, and Christians? Asians, African Americans, Native Americans, Hispanics, and Caucasians? How do those beliefs affect your day-to-day interactions with members of those groups? Do you avoid members of some of these groups based on your beliefs?

What is at work even in this "color" experiment is the very swift action of social categorization.

Many experiments have examined the consequences of in-group versus out-group status (Hewstone et al., 2002). This research points to the conclusion that, for the most part, people show favoritism toward those people who are members of their own group rather than bias against members of the other group. For example, people typically rate members of their in-group more highly (on pleasantness, diligence, and so on) than they do members of the out-group. However, that's because they have positive feelings toward the in-group and neutral feelings toward the out-group. Thus, one can have an in-group bias without also having the negative feelings that constitute prejudice.

Unfortunately, in some circumstances people's feelings about out-groups are guided by learned prejudices. In those cases, in-group bias may become more purposeful. Prejudice easily leads to **racism**—discrimination against people based on their skin color or ethnic heritage—and **sexism**—discrimination against people based on their sex. The instant tendency toward defining "us" against "them" becomes even more powerful when the perception grows that resources are scarce and that goods can be given only to one group, at the expense of the other. In fact, people who express a high degree of prejudice are much more careful about making judgments about who belongs to which categories of humanity.

<www.ablongman.com/gerrig17e>

Why might prejudiced beliefs affect individuals' ability to categorize these racially ambiguous faces?

Because stereotypes so powerfully encode *expectations,* they frequently contribute to the types of situations we described earlier in this chapter, in which people construct their own social reality. Consider the potential role stereotypes play to generate judgments about what "exists" in the environment. People are prone to fill in "missing data" with information from their stereotypes: "I'm not going to get in a car with Hiroshi—all Asians are terrible drivers." Similarly, people may knowingly or unknowingly use stereotypical information to produce *behavioral confirmation.* If, for example, you reason that Jewish friends are likely to be cheap, you may never give them opportunities to prove otherwise. Worse than that, to maintain consistency, people are likely to discount information that is inconsistent with their stereotyped beliefs.

PUTTING IDEAS TO THE TEST

Discounting Stereotype-Inconsistent Information

What happens when you are presented with information, some of which supports your beliefs and some of which contradicts them? In one study, researchers classified students as having high or low prejudice toward homosexuals. Each student subsequently read a pair of scientific studies about homosexuality. One of those studies concluded that, consistent with the stereotype, homosexuality is associated with cross-gender behaviors. The other study came to the stereotype-inconsistent conclusion that homosexuality is not associated with cross-gender behaviors. When the high- and low-prejudice students evaluated the *quality* of each study, they gave consistently higher ratings to the study that supported their point of view. For example, high-prejudice

students found more merit in the study that supported the cross-gender stereotype. Furthermore, as a consequence of reading a pair of studies that were intended to exactly balance each other out, the students on average reported that their beliefs had shifted further in the direction of their original attitudes (Munro & Ditto, 1997).

This experiment suggests why information alone can typically not reduce prejudice: People tend to devalue information that is inconsistent with their prior stereotype. (We will see in the next section more successful methods for overcoming prejudice.)

Let us remind you about another effect of stereotypes that we introduced in the context of intelligence testing. Recall that in Chapter 9, we discussed racial differences among IQ scores. In that section, we reviewed evidence that suggests that members of stereotyped groups suffer from what **Claude Steele** and his colleagues have called *stereotype threat* (Steele, 1997; Steele & Aronson, 1995, 1998). Stereotype threat occurs when people are placed in situations to which negative aspects of stereotypes are relevant. For example, in Chapter 9, we provided evidence that African Americans' performance on aptitude tests is impaired when they believe the outcome of the test is relevant to the stereotype of black underachievement. We remind you of this result here to emphasize the forces that sustain negative stereotypes—and the way they deform the lives of people who are stereotyped.

Even if you do not believe yourself to be a prejudiced person, you still are likely aware of the stereotypes that exist in contemporary society. Knowledge of these stereotypes might prompt you to use them in some ways, below the level of conscious awareness (Crandall & Eshleman, 2003; Devine & Monteith, 1999). Even people whose explicit beliefs are not prejudiced may produce automatic acts of prejudice as a function of the messages they have unknowingly internalized from many sources in their current and earlier environments. Consider your best friends: Do they belong to the same ethnic group as you do? If so, why might this be the case?

We have come to the rather troubling conclusion that prejudice is easy to create and difficult to remove. Even so, from the earliest days of social psychology, researchers have attempted to reverse the march of prejudice. Let's now sample some of those efforts.

◆ REVERSING PREJUDICE

One of the classic studies in social psychology was also the first demonstration that arbitrary "us" versus "them" divisions could lead to great hostility. In the summer of 1954, **Muzafer Sherif** and his colleagues (1961/1988) brought two groups of boys to a summer camp at Robbers Cave State Park in Oklahoma. The two groups were dubbed the "Eagles" and the "Rattlers." Each group forged its own camp bonds—for example, the boys hiked, swam, and prepared meals together—in ignorance of the other group for about a week. The groups' introduction to each other consisted of a series of competitive activities like baseball, football, and a tug-of-war. From this beginning, the rivalry between the groups grew violent. Group flags were burned, cabins were ransacked, and a near-riotlike food fight broke out. What could be done to reduce this animosity?

CLASSIC
PUTTING IDEAS TO THE TEST

The Importance of Interdependence

The experimenters tried a propaganda approach, by complimenting each group to the other. That did not work. The experimenters tried bringing the groups together in noncompetitive circumstances. That did not work either. Hostility seethed even when the groups were just watching a movie in the same place. Finally, the experimenters hit on a solution. What they did was to introduce problems that could be solved only through *cooperative action* on *shared goals*. For example, the experimenters arranged for the camp truck to break down. Both groups of boys were needed to pull it back up a steep hill. In the face of mutual dependence, hostility faded away. In fact, the boys started to make "best friends" across group boundaries.

The Robbers Cave experiment disproved the idea that simple contact between hostile groups alone will reduce prejudice (Allport, 1954). The boys did not like each other any better just by being in each others' company. Instead, the experiment provided evidence for the **contact hypothesis**—a program combating prejudice must foster personal interaction in the pursuit of shared goals (Dovidio et al., 2003). Take a moment to consider how you might apply these lessons to situations that matter to you. Suppose, for example, that you are managing employees who cannot get along. What intervention might you design?

In the intergroup competition phase of the Robbers Cave experiment, the "Eagles" and "Rattlers" pulled apart—but in the end, they pulled together. What general conclusions about contact and prejudice can be drawn from this study?

Social psychologist **Elliot Aronson** and his colleagues (1978) developed a program anchored in the Robbers Cave philosophy to tackle prejudice in newly desegregated classrooms in Texas and California. The research team created conditions in which fifth-grade students had to depend on one another rather than compete against one another to learn required material. In a strategy known as the *jigsaw technique,* each pupil is given part of the total material to master and then share with other group members. Performance is evaluated on the basis of the overall group presentation. Thus, every member's contribution is essential and valued.

Interracial conflict has decreased in **jigsaw classrooms**—classes in which jigsawing has united formerly hostile white, Latino, and African American students in a common-fate team (Aronson, 2002; Aronson & Gonzalez, 1988). Consider the story of one young boy named Carlos. Carlos, who had been ignored because his primary language was not English, was assigned a vital part of the team assignment on Joseph Pulitzer. The other teammates had to figure out how to get him to share the information he was responsible for providing. In response to his teammates' patience and encouraging comments, Carlos felt needed, developed affection for the group members, and also discovered that learning was fun. Both his self-esteem and his grades increased. (We are happy to report that Carlos went on to Harvard Law School after graduating from a Texas college.)

Although most of our examples have looked at prejudice within the United States, virtually every society defines in-groups and out-groups. Researchers have carried out studies around the world to determine what types of contact between people lead to reduced prejudice. For example, **Thomas Pettigrew** (1997) examined data from nearly 4,000 people in France, the Netherlands, England, and the former West Germany and came to the conclusion that friendship with out-group members lowers prejudice. Let's consider a study that adds further weight to that conclusion.

PUTTING IDEAS TO THE TEST

Prejudice in East and West Germany

Although Germany was reunited in October 1990, the inhabitants of the former East and West Germany still show important differences: When social scientists assess the level of prejudice and violence toward foreigners, the data consistently show that East Germans are much more hostile. Researchers tested the hypothesis that an important force that contributes to the ongoing hostility arises from East Germany's historic isolation (Wagner et al., 2003): Fewer foreigners reside in East Germany, providing fewer opportunities for the type of contact that reduces prejudice. A study with 2,893 East and West German

participants confirmed this hypothesis. Each participant provided information about his or her level of prejudice by responding to statements such as "Foreigners living in Germany are a problem for the social system." Each participant also indicated his or her level of personal contact by responding to questions such as "Are there any foreigners among your friends?" Those individuals who had more foreign friends reported, on average, lower levels of prejudice. Because the inhabitants of East Germany had fewer opportunities to have foreign friends, their prejudice levels remained relatively high.

Why is friendship so effective? Friendships allow people to learn about out-group members: They may come to identify and empathize with out-group members. Friendships may also foster a process of *deprovincialization:* When people learn more about out-group social norms and customs, they may become less "provincial" about the correctness of their in-group processes (Pettigrew, 1997).

Social psychology has no great solution to end prejudice all at once. It does, however, provide a set of ideas to eliminate prejudice's worst effects slowly but surely, in each small locality. It is worth taking a moment to contemplate the prejudices you have enforced or endured—to see how you might begin to make adjustments in your own small locality.

We have just considered circumstances in which psychological forces drive individuals apart. In the final section of this chapter, we examine the opposite situations in which people are drawn together in relationships of liking and loving.

PUT YOURSELF TO THE TEST

- What is the relationship between in-group bias and prejudice?
- What impact do stereotypes have on people's behavior?
- What types of interactions help people to overcome prejudice?
- Why do friendships help to eliminate prejudice?

Social Relationships

How do you choose the people with whom you share your life? Why do you seek the company of your friends? Why are there some people for whom your feelings move beyond friendship to feelings of romantic love? Social psychologists have developed a variety of answers to these questions of *interpersonal attraction*. (But don't worry, no one yet has taken all the mystery out of love!)

◆ LIKING

Have you ever stopped to examine how and why you acquired each of your friends? The first part of this answer is straightforward: People tend to become attracted to others with whom they are in close *proximity*—you see and meet them because they live or work near you. This factor probably requires little explanation, but it might be worth noting that there is a general tendency for people to like objects and people just by virtue of *mere exposure:* As we explained in Chapter 12, the more you are exposed to something or someone, the more you like it (Zajonc, 1968). This mere exposure effect means that, on the whole, you will come to like more and more the people who are nearby. As we shall see in the Psychology in the 21st Century box, however, the computer age is giving a

Why does proximity—in physical space or cyberspace—affect liking?

new meaning to the idea of proximity. Many people now maintain relationships over networks of computers. Although a friend may be geographically quite distant, daily messages appearing on a computer screen can make the person seem psychologically very close. Let's look now at other factors that can lead to attraction and liking.

PHYSICAL ATTRACTIVENESS

For better or worse, *physical attractiveness* often plays a role in the kindling of friendship. There is a strong stereotype in Western culture that physically attractive people are also good in other ways. A review of more than 70 studies suggested that the physical attractiveness stereotype has its largest effect on people's judgments about social competence—people believe that the attractive are likely to be more sociable and extraverted than are the less attractive (Eagly et al., 1991). Attractiveness has a much smaller effect, however, on people's judgments of intelligence or predictions about career success. In light of the social basis of the stereotype, it might not surprise you that physical attractiveness plays a role in liking.

CLASSIC
PUTTING IDEAS TO THE TEST

Pursuing Physically Attractive Partners

In one study, researchers randomly assigned incoming University of Minnesota freshmen to couples as blind dates for a large dance. The researchers collected a variety of information about each student along dimensions of intelligence and personality. On the night of the dance and in later follow-ups the students were asked to evaluate their dates and indicate how likely they were to see the individual again. The results were clear, and very similar for both men and women. Beauty mattered more than high IQs, good social skills, or good personalities. Only those matched by chance with beautiful or handsome blind dates wanted to pursue the relationship further (Walster et al., 1966).

Physical attractiveness appears to predict liking in different cultures as well. For example, Chinese 10th- to 12th-graders accorded greater status to their classmates who were physically attractive (Dong et al., 1996). However, as we noted in Chapter 12, cultures differ with respect to their standards for physical beauty. African Americans, for example, associate fewer negative personality traits with obesity than do Anglo-Americans (Hebl & Heatherton, 1998; Jackson & McGill, 1996).

<www.ablongman.com/gerrig17e>

SIMILARITY

A famous adage on *similarity* suggests that "birds of a feather flock together." Is this correct? Research evidence suggests that, under many circumstances, the answer is yes. Similarity on dimensions such as beliefs, attitudes, and values fosters friendship. Why might that be so? People who are similar to you can provide a sense of personal validation, because a similar person makes you feel that the attitudes, for example, you hold dear are, in fact, the right ones (Byrne & Clore, 1970). Furthermore, dissimilarity often leads to strong repulsion (Rosenbaum, 1986). When you discover that someone holds opinions that are different from yours, you may evoke from memory past instances of interpersonal friction. That will motivate you to stay away—and if you stay away from dissimilar people, only the similar ones will be left in your pool of friends.

If you are living in a dormitory while you attend college, you can look around you to see similarity at work. Do you perceive successful roommates to be similar? Researchers have looked at the similarity of roommates on a variety of dimensions. For example, one study assessed the *communication traits* of pairs of roommates: How similar were they on dimensions such as their willingness to communicate? Roommates who were similar at the positive ends of the trait dimensions (for example, they were both willing to communicate) liked each other more than mismatched pairs or pairs that were both unwilling to communicate (Martin & Anderson, 1995). If you are in a dorm, you can try to confirm this pattern in the field!

RECIPROCITY

Finally, you tend to like people whom you believe like you. Do you recall our discussion of salespeople's use of *reciprocity?* The rule that you should give back what you receive applies to friendship as well. People give back "liking" to people whom they believe have given "liking" to them (Backman & Secord, 1959; Kenny & La Voie, 1982). Furthermore, because of the way your beliefs can affect your behaviors, believing that someone likes or dislikes you can help bring that relationship about (Curtis & Miller, 1986). Can you predict how you would act toward someone you believe likes you? Toward someone you believe dislikes you? Suppose you act with hostility toward someone you think doesn't like you. Do you see how your belief could become a self-fulfilling prophecy? When we look out at the social world, our judgments about which acquaintances are united by a "liking" relationship tend to be heavily guided by reciprocity. That is, if we know that Person A particularly likes Person B, we infer that Person B has the same feelings toward Person A (Kenny et al., 1996).

The evidence we have reviewed suggests that most of your friends will be people you encounter frequently, and people with whom you share the bonds of similarity and reciprocity. But what have researchers found about more intense relationships people call "loving"?

◆ LOVING

Many of the same forces that lead to liking also get people started on the road to love—in most cases, you will first like the people you end up loving. (However, some people report loving certain relatives that they don't particularly like as individuals.) What special factors have social psychologists learned about loving relationships?

THE EXPERIENCE OF LOVE

What does it mean to experience *love?* You should take a moment to think how you would define this important concept. Do you think your definition would agree with your friends' definitions? Researchers have tried to answer this question in a variety of ways, and some consistency has emerged. People's conceptualizations of love cluster into three dimensions (Aron & Westbay, 1996):

- *Passion*—sexual passion and desire
- *Intimacy*—honesty and understanding
- *Commitment*—devotion and sacrifice

Would you characterize all your loving relationships as including all three dimensions? You're probably thinking, "not *all* of them." In fact, it is important to make a distinction between "loving" someone and being "in love" with someone (Meyers & Berscheid, 1997). Most people report themselves to "love" a larger category of people than the group with whom they are "in love"—who among us hasn't been heartbroken to hear the words, "I love you, but I'm not *in* love with you"? Being "in love" implies something more intense and special—this is the type of experience that includes sexual passion.

Although it is possible to state some general features of loving relationships, your knowledge of the world has probably led you to the correct generalization that there are individual differences in the way that people experience love. Researchers have been particularly interested in understanding individual differences in people's ability to sustain loving relationships over an extended period of time. In recent years, attention has often focused on *adult attachment style* (Fraley & Shaver, 2000; Shaver & Hazan, 1994). Recall from Chapter 10 the importance of the quality of a child's attachment to his or her parents for smooth social development. Researchers began to wonder how much impact that early attachment might have later in life, as the children grew up to have committed relationships and children of their own.

What are the types of attachment styles? **Table 16.3** provides three statements about close relationships (Hazan & Shaver, 1987; Shaver & Hazan, 1994). Please take a moment to note which statement fits you best. When asked which of these statements best describes them, the majority of people (55 percent) choose the first statement; this is a *secure* attachment style. Sizable minorities select the second statement (25 percent, an *avoidant* style) and the third (20 percent, an *anxious-ambivalent* style). Attachment style has proven to be an accurate predictor of relationship quality (Mikulincer et al., 2002; Tidwell et al., 1996). Compared with individuals who chose the other two styles, securely attached individuals had the most enduring romantic relationships as adults. Attachment style also predicts the ways in which individuals experience jealousy in relationships (Sharpsteen & Kirkpatrick, 1997). For example, people with an anxious style tend to experience jealousy more frequently and more intensely than do people with a secure attachment style.

Let us make one final distinction. Many loving relationships start out with a period of great intensity and absorption, which is called *passionate* love. Over time, there is a tendency for relationships to migrate toward a state of lesser intensity but greater intimacy, called *companionate love* (Berscheid & Walster, 1978). When you find yourself in a loving relationship, you may do

Companionate feelings for someone you were once passionate about do not signal "falling out of love": On the contrary, they are a natural outgrowth of romance and a vital ingredient to most long-term partnerships.

well to anticipate that transition—so that you don't misinterpret a natural change as a process of falling "out of love." Even so, the decline of passionate love may not be as dramatic as the stereotype of long-committed couples suggests. Researchers find a reasonable level of passionate love as much as 30 years into a relationship (Aron & Aron, 1994). When you enter a loving relationship, you can have high hopes that the passion will endure in some form, even as the relationship grows to encompass other needs.

Note that experiences of love are also influenced by cultural expectations. At various moments in this chapter, we've alluded to the cultural dimension of independence versus interdependence: Cultures with independent construals of self value the person over the collective; interdependent cultures put greater value on shared cultural goals rather than on individual ones. How does this apply to your love life? If you choose a life partner based on your own feelings of love, you are showing preference for your personal goals; if you choose a partner with an eye to how that individual will mesh with your family's structure and concerns, you are being more attuned to collective goals. Cross-cultural research has led to the very strong generalization that members of independent cultures put much greater emphasis on love (Dion & Dion, 1996). Consider the question, "If a man (woman) had all the other qualities you desired, would you marry this person if you were not in love with him (her)?" Only 3.5 percent of a sample of male and female undergraduates in the United States answered yes; 49 percent of a comparable group of students in India answered yes (Levine et al., 1995). Members of independent cultures are also more

---

TABLE 16.3
Styles of Adult Attachment for Close Relationships

Statement 1:

I find it relatively easy to get close to others and am comfortable depending on them. I don't often worry about being abandoned or about someone getting too close to me.

Statement 2:

I am somewhat uncomfortable being close to others; I find it difficult to trust them completely, difficult to allow myself to depend on them. I am nervous when anyone gets too close, and often, love partners want me to be more intimate than I feel comfortable being.

Statement 3:

I find that others are reluctant to get as close as I would like. I often worry that my partner doesn't really love me or won't want to stay with me. I want to get very close to my partner, and this sometime scares people away.

---

demanding of their potential partners. Because people in these cultures have stronger ideas about personal fulfillment within relationships, they also expect more from marriage partners (Hatfield & Sprecher, 1995).

WHAT FACTORS ALLOW RELATIONSHIPS TO LAST?

It seems likely that everyone reading this book—and certainly everyone *writing* this book—has been in a relationship that didn't last. What happened? Or, to put the question in a more positive light, what can researchers say about the types of situations, and people in those situations, that are more likely to lead to long-term loving relationships?

One theory conceptualizes people in close relationships as having a feeling that the "other" is included in their "self" (Aron et al., 1991; Aron & Aron, 1994). Consider the series of diagrams given in **Figure 16.5.** Each of the diagrams represents a way you could conceptualize a close relationship. If you are in a romantic relationship, can you say which of the diagrams seems to capture most effectively the extent of interdependence between you and your partner? Research has shown that people who perceive the most overlap between self and other—those people who come to view the other as included within the self—are most likely to remain committed to their relationships over time (Aron et al., 1992; Aron & Fraley, 1999).

What other factors contribute to the likelihood that someone will remain in a relationship? *Interdependence theory* examines people's needs with respect to their social interactions (Rusbult & Van Lange, 2003). This perspective suggests that commitment is based on a series of judgments (Drigotas & Rusbult, 1992, p. 65):

- The degree to which each of several needs is important in the individual's relationship. Important needs are intimacy, sex, emotional involvement, companionship, and intellectual involvement.

- The degree to which each of those needs is satisfied in that relationship.

- For each need, whether there is anyone other than the current partner with whom the individual has an important relationship.

- The degree to which each need is satisfied by the alternative relationship.

As you might expect, this model predicts that people are more likely to stay in a relationship when the relationship satisfies important needs that cannot be satisfied by anyone else. Thus, if *companionship* is very important to you—you enjoy spending leisure time with other people—and a person with whom you share a relationship provides more companionship than anyone else you know, you're likely to feel committed to that relationship. This will be true even if your partner is not your first choice on dimensions that matter less. The dependence model also offers insight into why people will stay in relationships in which they have been physically abused (Choice & Lamke, 1999). In a sample of

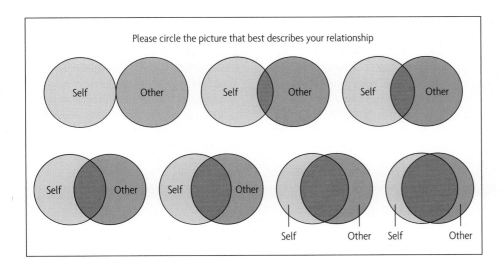

FIGURE 16.5

The Inclusion of Other in the Self (IOS) Scale

If you are in a romantic relationship, which diagram best captures the interdependence of you and your partner? Research with the IOS scale suggests that people who most perceive the other as included with the self are most likely to stay committed to their relationships.

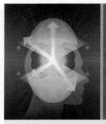

Relationships and the Internet

Does anyone doubt that the advent of the Internet has had a broad impact on how people initiate and conduct their close relationships? Consider a 13-year-old boy named Daniel from New York City whose "new girlfriend" is a 13-year-old named Rachel from South Carolina. Daniel and Rachel have not been able to exchange pictures over the Internet. When Daniel's mother suggested that they send photos through the U.S. mail, her son replied, "Mom, she's not going to give me her address" (Gardner, 2000, p. 40). Clearly, until late in the 20th century, this is not the type of relationship most boys would've had in mind for their "new girlfriend." Let's explore the impact of the Internet on relationships.

Studies have shown that social interaction is one of Internet users' most frequent activities. In one survey of roughly 4,100 people, 90 percent used the Internet to exchange e-mail and 24 percent participated in chat rooms (Nie & Erbring, 2000). Other research suggests that a good number of relationships forged in cyberspace make their way into the physical world. Consider a study that involved 568 individuals (59 percent women and 41 percent

men) who had made postings to newsgroups (McKenna et al., 2002). In that sample, 63 percent had spoken on the telephone with an acquaintance they'd made on the Internet; 54 percent had met face-to-face with an Internet acquaintance. A follow-up study two years later showed that many of the relationships formed over the Internet were still going strong. In fact, 15 percent of the sample had become engaged to someone they'd met on the Internet, and 10 percent had married an Internet partner.

We noted earlier that *proximity* is an important ingredient for liking: You need to meet people before they can become your friends or romantic partners. The studies we've just cited indicate that the Internet provides an important new mechanism to establish psychological proximity in the absence of geographic proximity. In fact, some evidence suggests that relationships get off to a better start when they begin on the Internet rather than face-to-face (Bargh et al., 2002). In one study using college students, participants interacted on two occasions with the same partner. For half of the pairs, both interactions were face-to-face. For the other half, an Internet interaction pre-

ceded the face-to-face meeting. At the end of the second interaction, the participants were asked how much they liked their partners on a scale ranging from −7 (strong dislike) to +7 (strong like). Those participants whose first interaction had taken place over the Internet reported consistently greater liking for their partners (with a mean of 4.70) than did their peers who had met only face-to-face (with a mean of 2.45). Why might that be? The researchers speculated that the initial Internet interaction allowed participants to be less affected by surface features of their partners such as physical attractiveness. Furthermore, the momentary anonymity of the Internet likely encouraged people to be more self-disclosing, which also may increase liking.

Research attention has often focused on the lives of people whose use or overuse of the Internet decreases real-life social activity (Kraut et al., 1998; Nie & Erbring, 2000). However, the studies we've cited here suggest that the Internet may also be a positive force for many or most people's social and romantic lives. Perhaps someday Daniel may even get his girlfriend's address.

100 women at a shelter for battered women, the women who saw themselves as having few alternatives—often for economic reasons—were still committed to returning to their relationships (Rusbult & Martz, 1995). Thus, people may be quite unhappy in a relationship and yet depend on the relationship.

Throughout this chapter, we've seen how individuals construct and respond to aspects of their social worlds. We've seen, for example, how your attitudes are forged in the social cauldron and how those attitudes can lead to the very different outcomes of prejudice and love. We've encouraged you to examine your behaviors, to see the way in which your interpretation of social setting helps to explain important aspects of your day-to-day experiences. In the next chapter, we will see how the same types of forces control your own behavior and the behaviors of larger groups of people.

PUT YOURSELF TO THE TEST

- ➤ Why does physical attractiveness contribute to liking?
- ➤ Why do similarity and reciprocity increase liking?
- ➤ How does the importance of the features of loving relationships change over time?
- ➤ What impact does adult attachment style have on relationships?
- ➤ What factors help determine which relationships will last?

Recapping Main Points

CONSTRUCTING SOCIAL REALITY

- Each person constructs his or her own social reality.
- Social perception is influenced by beliefs and expectations.
- Attribution theory describes the judgments people make about the causes of behaviors.
- Several biases, such as the fundamental attribution error, self-serving biases, and self-fulfilling prophecies, can creep into attributions and other judgments and behaviors.
- However, the influence of expectations is limited by accurate information you have about the world.

ATTITUDES, ATTITUDE CHANGE, AND ACTION

- Attitudes are positive or negative evaluations of objects, events, or ideas.
- Not all attitudes accurately predict behaviors; they must be highly accessible or highly specific.
- According to the elaboration likelihood model, the central route to persuasion relies on careful analyses of arguments, whereas the peripheral route relies on superficial features of persuasive situations.
- The match between the basis for an attitude and the type of argument also affects the argument's effectiveness.
- Dissonance theory and self-perception theory consider attitude formation and change that arise from behavioral acts.
- To bring about compliance, people can exploit reciprocity, commitment, and scarcity.

PREJUDICE

- Even arbitrary, minimal cues can yield prejudice when they define an in-group and an out-group.
- Stereotypes affect the way in which people evaluate behaviors and information in the world.
- Researchers have eliminated some of the effects of prejudice by creating situations in which members of different groups must cooperate to reach shared goals.
- Cross-cultural studies also suggest that friendship plays an important role in eliminating prejudice.

SOCIAL RELATIONSHIPS

- Interpersonal attraction is determined in part by proximity, physical attractiveness, similarity, and reciprocity.
- Loving relationships are defined with respect to passion, intimacy, and commitment.
- Adult attachment style affects the quality of relationships.
- A person's commitment to a loving relationship is related to the level of closeness and interdependence.

   <www.ablongman.com/gerrig17e>

KEY TERMS

attitude (p. 550)

attribution theory (p. 545)

behavioral confirmation (p. 549)

cognitive dissonance (p. 554)

compliance (p. 556)

contact hypothesis (p. 562)

covariation principle (p. 545)

elaboration likelihood model (p. 552)

fundamental attribution error (FAE)
(p. 545)

in-group bias (p. 558)

in-groups (p. 558)

jigsaw classrooms (p. 563)

out-groups (p. 558)

persuasion (p. 552)

prejudice (p. 558)

racism (p. 560)

reciprocity norm (p. 556)

self-fulfilling prophecy (p. 548)

self-perception theory (p. 556)

self-serving bias (p. 547)

sexism (p. 560)

social categorization (p. 558)

social cognition (p. 544)

social perception (p. 545)

social psychology (p. 543)

stereotypes (p. 560)

Social Processes, Society, and Culture

We have come to the moment in *Psychology and Life* when we consider the most extreme consequences of the way in which social forces act on human behavior. Some of the content of this chapter will be quite disturbing with respect to the potential it reveals for destructive and inhumane acts. We consider the power of situations, aggressive behavior, and the circumstances that can lead to acts of genocide. At the same time, we describe the innate drive of the human species to be prosocial—to perform altruistic acts of generosity with no expectation of reward. Ultimately, we hope that this chapter strikes an optimistic note by suggesting how the insights generated through social science research can help relieve some of the world's tension.

Students often find the topics discussed in this chapter both provocative and disconcerting. We hope you will have the opportunity to discuss and debate the full implications with your classmates. You should finish the chapter with an understanding of how the social psychological forces acting on each individual can, as individuals join together in groups, produce some of the most intimidating moments of world history.

The Power of the Situation

Throughout *Psychology and Life,* we have seen that psychologists who strive to understand the causes of behavior look in many different places for their answers. Some look to genetic factors and others to biochemical and brain processes, while still others focus on the causal influence of the environment. Social psychologists believe that the primary determinant of behavior is the nature of the social situation in which that behavior occurs. They argue that social situations exert significant control over individual behavior, often dominating personality and a person's past history of learning, values, and beliefs. In this section, we will review both classic research and recent experiments that together explore the effect of subtle but powerful situational variables on people's behavior.

◆ ROLES AND RULES

What *social roles* are available to you? A **social role** is a socially defined pattern of behavior that is expected of a person when functioning in a given setting or group. Different social situations make different roles available. When you are at home, you may accept the role of "child" or "sibling." When you are in the classroom, you accept the role of "student." At other times still, you are a "best friend" or "lover." Can you see how these different roles immediately make different types of behaviors more or less appropriate and also available to you?

...or not to open? How do people learn the etiquette for ...receiving gifts in different cultures?

Situations are also characterized by the operation of **rules,** behavioral guidelines for specific settings. Some rules are *explicitly* stated in signs (DON'T SMOKE, NO EATING IN CLASS) or are explicitly taught to children (Respect the elderly, Never take candy from a stranger). Other rules are *implicit*—they are learned through transactions with others in particular settings. How loud you can play your stereo, how close you can stand to another person, when you can call your teacher or boss by a first name, and what is the suitable way to react to a compliment or a gift—all of these actions depend on the situation. For example, the Japanese do not open a gift in the presence of the giver, for fear of not showing sufficient appreciation; foreigners not aware of this unwritten rule will misinterpret the behavior as rude instead of sensitive. Next time you get in an elevator, try to determine what rules you have learned about that situation. Why do people usually speak in hushed tones or not at all?

Ordinarily, you might not be particularly aware of the effects of roles and rules, but one classic social psychological experiment, the *Stanford Prison Experiment,* put these forces to work with startling results (Haney & Zimbardo, 1977; Zimbardo, 1975; replicated in Australia by Lovibond et al., 1979).

CLASSIC
PUTTING IDEAS TO THE TEST

Social Roles in a Simulated Prison

On a summer Sunday in California, a siren shattered the serenity of college student Tommy Whitlow's morning. A police car screeched to a halt in front of his home. Within minutes, Tommy was charged with a felony, informed of his constitutional rights, frisked, and handcuffed. After he was booked and fingerprinted, Tommy was blindfolded and transported to the Stanford County Prison, where he was stripped, sprayed with disinfectant, and issued a smock-type uniform with an I.D. number on the front and back. Tommy became prisoner 647. Eight other college students were also arrested and assigned numbers.

Tommy and his cellmates were all volunteers who had answered a newspaper ad and agreed to be participants in a two-week experiment on prison life. By random flips of a coin, some of the volunteers had been assigned to the role of prisoners; the rest became guards. All had been selected from a large pool of student volunteers who, on the basis of extensive psychological tests and interviews, had been judged as law-abiding, emotionally stable, physically healthy, and "normal-average." The prisoners lived in the jail around the clock; the guards worked standard eight-hour shifts.

What happened once these students had assumed their randomly assigned roles? In guard roles, college students who had

<www.ablongman.com/gerrig17e>

been pacifists and "nice guys" behaved aggressively—sometimes even sadistically. The guards insisted that prisoners obey all rules without question or hesitation. Failure to do so led to the loss of a privilege. At first, privileges included opportunities to read, write, or talk to other inmates. Later on, the slightest protest resulted in the loss of the "privileges" of eating, sleeping, and washing. Failure to obey rules also resulted in menial, mindless work such as cleaning toilets with bare hands, doing push-ups while a guard stepped on the prisoner's back, and spending hours in solitary confinement. The guards were always devising new strategies to make the prisoners feel worthless.

As prisoners, psychologically stable students soon behaved pathologically, passively resigning themselves to their unexpected fate. Less than 36 hours after the mass arrest, Prisoner 8412, one of the ringleaders of an aborted prisoner rebellion that morning, began to cry uncontrollably. He experienced fits of rage, disorganized thinking, and severe depression. On successive days, three more prisoners developed similar stress-related symptoms. A fifth prisoner developed a psychosomatic rash all over his body when the Parole Board rejected his appeal.

Because of the dramatic and unexpectedly severe emotional and behavioral effects observed, those five prisoners with extreme stress reactions were released early from this unusual prison, and the psychologists were forced to terminate their two-week study after only six days. Although Tommy Whitlow said he wouldn't want to go through it again, he valued the personal experience because he learned so much about himself and about human nature. Fortunately, he and the other students were basically healthy, and they readily bounced back from this highly charged situation. Follow-ups over many years revealed no lasting negative effects. The participants had all contributed to an important lesson: The power of the simulated prison situation had created a new *social reality*—a real prison—in the minds of the jailers and their captives.

By the conclusion of the Stanford Prison Experiment, guards' and prisoners' behavior differed from each other in virtually every observable way (see **Figure 17.1**). Yet it was only chance, in the form of random assignment, that had decided their roles—roles that had created status and power differences that were validated in the prison situation. No one taught the participants to play their roles. Without ever visiting real prisons, all the participants learned something about the interaction between the powerful and the powerless (Banuazizi & Movahedi, 1975). A guard type is someone who limits the freedom of prisoner types to manage their behavior and make them behave more predictably. This task is aided by the use of *coercive rules,* which include explicit punishment for violations.

The Stanford Priso[...]
a new "social [...]
of good behavi[...]
the dynamics of [...]
the student guards [...]
their roles so powerf[...]

Prisoners can only *react* to the social structure of a prisonlike setting created by those with power. Rebellion or compliance are the only options of the prisoners; the first choice results in punishment, while the second results in a loss of autonomy and dignity.

The student participants had already experienced such power differences in many of their previous social interactions: parent–child, teacher–student, doctor–patient, boss–worker, male–female. They merely refined and intensified their prior patterns of behavior for this particular setting. Each student could have played either role. Many students in the guard role reported being surprised at how easily they enjoyed controlling other people. Just putting on the uniform was enough to transform them from passive college students into aggressive prison guards. What sort of person do *you* become when you slip in and out of different roles? Where does your sense of personal self end and your social identity begin?

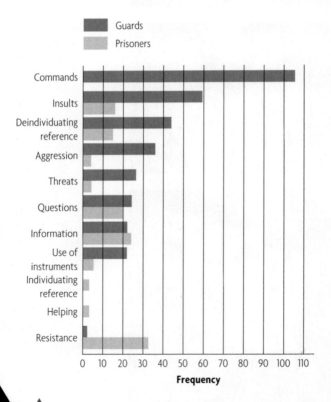

ring the Stanford Prison Experiment, the randomly assigned *of prisoners and guards drastically affected participants'* *ior. The observations recorded in the six-day interaction* *ow that across 25 observation periods, the prisoners* *more passive resistance, while the guards became* *ating, controlling, and hostile.*

◆ SOCIAL NORMS

In addition to the expectations regarding role behaviors, groups develop many expectations for the ways their members *should* act. The specific expectations for socially appropriate attitudes and behaviors that are embodied in the stated or implicit rules of a group are called **social norms.** Social norms can be broad guidelines; if you are a member of Democrats for Social Action, you may be expected to hold liberal political beliefs, while members of the Young Republicans will advocate more conservative views. Social norms can also embody specific standards of conduct. For example, if you are employed as a waiter or a waitress, you will be expected to treat your customers courteously no matter how unpleasant and demanding they are to you.

Belonging to a group typically involves discovering the set of social norms that regulates desired behavior in the group setting. This adjustment occurs in two ways: You notice the *uniformities* in certain behaviors of all or most members, and you observe the *negative consequences* when someone violates a social norm.

Norms serve several important functions. Awareness of the norms operating in a given group situation helps orient members and regulate their social interaction. Each participant can anticipate how others will enter the situation, how they will dress, and what they are likely to say and do, as well as what type of behavior will be expected of them to gain approval. You often feel awkward in new situations precisely because you may be unaware of the norms that govern the way you ought to act. Some tolerance for deviating from the standard is also part of the norm—wide in some cases, narrow in others. For example, shorts and a T-shirt might be marginally acceptable attire for a religious ceremony; a bathing suit would almost certainly deviate too far from the norm. Group members are usually able to estimate how far they can go before experiencing the coercive power of the group in the form of ridicule, reeducation, and rejection.

◆ CONFORMITY

When you adopt a social role or bend to a social norm, you are, to some extent, *conforming* to social expectations. **Conformity** is the tendency for people to adopt the behavior and opinions presented by other group members. Why do you conform? Are there circumstances under which you ignore social constraints and act independently? Social psychologists have studied two types of forces that may lead to conformity:

- **Informational influence** processes—wanting to be correct and to understand the right way to act in a given situation.

- **Normative influence** processes—wanting to be liked, accepted, and approved of by others.

We will describe classic experiments that illustrate each type of influence.

INFORMATIONAL INFLUENCE: SHERIF'S AUTOKINETIC EFFECT

Many life situations in which you must make decisions about behaviors are quite ambiguous. Suppose, for example, you are dining at an elegant restaurant with a large group of people. Each place at the table is set with a dazzling array of silverware. How do you know which fork to use when the first course arrives? Typically, you would look to other members of the party to help you make an appropriate choice. This is *informational influence*.

A classic experiment, conducted by **Muzafer Sherif** (1935), demonstrated how informational influence can lead to **norm crystallization**—norm formation and solidification.

Informational Influence Produces Norms

Participants were asked to judge the amount of movement of a spot of light, which was actually stationary but that appeared to move when viewed in total darkness with no reference points. This is a perceptual illusion known as the *autokinetic effect*. Originally, individual judgments varied widely. However, when the participants were brought together in a group consisting of strangers and stated their judgments aloud, their estimates began to converge. They began to see the light move in the same direction and in similar amounts. Even more interesting was the final part of Sherif's study—when alone in the same darkened room after the group viewing, these participants continued to follow the group norm that had emerged when they were together.

When individuals become dependent on a group—such as a religious cult—for basic feelings of self-worth, they are prone to extremes of conformity. Twenty thousand identically dressed couples were married in this service conducted by the Reverend Sun Myung Moon. More recently, in August 1995, Moon simultaneously married 360,000 "Moonie" couples who were linked by satellite in 500 worldwide locations. Why do people find comfort in such large-scale conformity?

Once norms are established in a group, they tend to perpetuate themselves. In later research, these autokinetic group norms persisted even when tested a year later and without former group members witnessing the judgments (Rohrer et al., 1954). Norms can be transmitted from one generation of group members to the next and can continue to influence people's behavior long after the original group that created the norm no longer exists (Insko et al., 1980). How do we know that norms can have transgenerational influence? In autokinetic effect studies, researchers replaced one group member with a new one after each set of autokinetic trials until all the members of the group were new to the situation. The group's autokinetic norm remained true to the one handed down to them across several successive generations (Jacobs & Campbell, 1961). Do you see how this experiment captures the processes that allow real-life norms to be passed down across generations?

NORMATIVE INFLUENCE: THE ASCH EFFECT

What is the best way to demonstrate that people will sometimes conform because of *normative influence*—their desire to be liked, accepted, and approved of by others? One of the most important early social psychologists, **Solomon Asch** (1940, 1956), created circumstances in which participants made judgments under conditions in which the physical reality was absolutely clear—but the rest of a group reported that they saw that reality differently. Male college students were led to believe they were in a study of simple visual perception. They were shown cards with three lines of differing lengths and asked to indicate which of the three lines was the same length as the standard line (see **Figure 17.2**). The lines were different enough so that mistakes were rare, and their relative sizes changed on each series of trials.

PUTTING IDEAS TO THE TEST

Yielding to Lying Lines?

The participants were seated next to last in semicircles of six to eight other students. Unknown to the participants, the others were all experimental confederates—accomplices of the experimenter—who were following a prearranged script. On the first three trials, everyone in the circle agreed on the correct comparison. However, the first confederate to respond on the fourth trial matched two lines that were obviously different. So did all members of the group up to the participant. That student had to decide if he should go along with everyone else's view of the situation and conform or remain independent, standing by what he clearly saw. That dilemma was repeated for the naive participant on 12 of the 18 trials. The participants showed signs of disbelief and obvious discomfort when faced with a majority who saw the world so differently. What did they do?

Roughly one-fourth of the participants remained completely independent—they never conformed. However, between 50 and 80 percent of the participants (in different studies in the research program) conformed with the false majority estimate at least once, while a third of the participants yielded to the majority's wrong judgments on half or more of the critical trials.

Asch describes some participants who yielded to the majority most of the time as "disoriented" and "doubt-ridden"; he states that they "experienced a powerful impulse not to appear different from the majority" (1952, p. 396). Those who yielded underestimated the influence of the social pressure and the frequency of their conformity; some even claimed that they really had seen the lines as the same length, despite their obvious discrepancy.

In other studies, Asch varied three factors: the size of the unanimous majority, the presence of a partner who dissented from the majority, and the size of the discrepancy between the correct physical stimulus comparison and the majority's position. He found that strong conformity effects were elicited with a unanimous majority of only three or four people. However, giving the naive participant a single ally who dissented from the majority opinion had the effect of sharply reducing conformity, as can be seen in Figure 17.2. With a partner, the participant was usually able to resist the pressures to conform to the majority (Asch, 1955, 1956).

How should we interpret these results? Asch himself was struck by the rate at which participants did *not* conform (Friend et al., 1990). He reported this research as studies in "independence." In fact, two-thirds of the time, participants gave the correct, nonconforming answer. However, most descriptions of Asch's experiment have emphasized the one-third conformity rate.

Accounts of this experiment also often fail to note that not all participants were alike: The number of individuals who never conformed, about 25 percent, was roughly equal to the number who always or almost always conformed. Thus, Asch's experiment teaches two complementary lessons. On the one hand, we find that people are not entirely swayed by normative influence—they assert their independence on a majority of occasions (and some people always do). On the other hand, we find that people will sometimes conform, even in the most unambiguous situations. That potential to conform is an important element of human nature.

CONFORMITY IN EVERYDAY LIFE

Although you've almost certainly never faced the exact circumstances of the Asch experiment, you can no doubt recognize conformity situations in your everyday life. Many of these situations are easy to spot. You might notice, for example, that you are wearing clothes that you find rather silly because someone has declared them to be fashionable. (Certainly that's true of *other* people.) Also, as we noted in Chapter 10, adolescents often conform with their peer groups with respect to risky behaviors such as drug use.

There are also subtler instances of conformity that may not be immediately apparent to you. Consider a study that examined how long it took people to provide either majority or minority answers to questions about both important and mundane topics.

PUTTING IDEAS TO THE TEST

The Minority Slowness Effect

When was the last occasion on which you offered an opinion that differed from the majority around you? In what ways did you find it difficult? A series of studies demonstrated that people with minority opinions took consistently more times to voice their opinions (Bassili, 2003). In an initial study, interviews called 714 students at the University of Toronto and asked them to respond to statements such as "We should be tolerant of groups that do not share basic Canadian values." For that statement, 88 percent of the students responded "agree" with an average response time of 2.71 seconds. Almost all the other students, 11 percent, said "disagree" (the rest gave other responses) with an average response time of 4.59 seconds. Thus, participants took 1.88 seconds longer to give a minority opinion. In a sample of 191 Indiana University students, the same pattern emerged for attitudes toward activities (for example, sewing and swimming) and objects (for example, snakes and chocolate chip cookies). A majority of 76 percent of the sample took on average 1.28 seconds to say that they like dentists whereas a minority 24 percent took on average 1.72 seconds to say they dislike them.

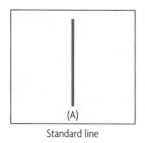

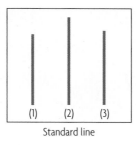

Standard line   Standard line

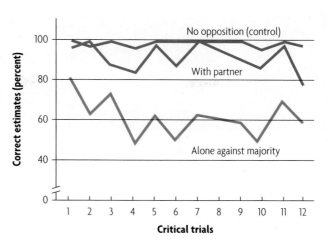

FIGURE 17.2

Conformity in the Asch Experiments

In this photo from Asch's study, it is evident that the naive participant, Number 6, is distressed by the unanimous majority's erroneous judgment. The typical stimulus array is shown at the top left. At top right, the graph illustrates conformity across 12 critical trials when solitary participants were grouped with a unanimous majority, as well as their greater independence when paired with a dissenting partner. A lower percentage of correct estimates indicates the greater degree of an individual's conformity to the group's false estimate.

You should bear in mind that participants were not offering these opinions in a particularly public fashion. In the first study, they were giving their response to a single interviewer who did not offer any sort of feedback; in the second study they were pushing "like" or "dislike" keys on a computer. Even so, when they gave opinions that failed to conform to the majority, they hesitated to do so.

MINORITY INFLUENCE AND NONCONFORMITY

Given the power of the majority to control resources and information, it is not surprising that people regularly conform to groups. As we've just seen, majority

power even extends to how long it takes people to offer their opinions in private. Yet you know that sometimes individuals persevere in their personal views. How can this happen? How do people escape group domination, and how can anything new (counternormative) ever come about? Are there any conditions under which a small minority can turn the majority around and create new norms?

While researchers in the United States have concentrated their studies on conformity, in part because conformity is intertwined with the democratic process, some European social psychologists have instead focused on the power of the few to change the majority. **Serge Moscovici** of France pioneered the study of

I f you've ever tried to make a decision as part of a group, you know that it can be quite torturous. Imagine, for example, that you have just seen a movie with a bunch of friends. Although you thought the movie was "OK," by the end of a postmovie discussion you find yourself agreeing that it was "an incredible piece of trash." Is this change after group discussion typical? Are the judgments groups make consistently different from individuals' judgments? Researchers in social psychology have documented two forces that operate when groups make decisions: *group polarization* and *groupthink.*

Your postmovie experience is an example of **group polarization:** Groups show a tendency to make decisions that are more extreme than the decisions that would be made by the members acting alone. Suppose, for example, you asked each member of the movie group to provide an attitude rating toward the movie; subsequently, as a group you agree on a single value to reflect your group attitude. If the group's rating is more extreme than the average of the individuals' ratings, that would be an instance of polarization. Depending on the initial group tendency—toward caution or risk—group polarization will tend to make a group more cautious or more risky. Researchers have suggested that two types of processes underlie group polarization: the *information-influence* model and the *social comparison* model (Liu & Latané, 1998). The information-influence model

How Do Groups Affect Decision Making?
Erin Beatty
St. Michael's College

suggests that group members contribute different information to a decision. If you and your friends each have a different reason for disliking a movie a little bit, all that information taken together would provide the evidence that you should actually dislike the movie a lot. The social comparison model suggests that group members strive to capture their peers' regard by representing a group ideal that is a bit more extreme than the group's true norm. Thus, if you come to decide that everyone was unhappy with a movie, you could try to present yourself as particularly astute by stating a more extreme opinion. If everyone in a group tries to capture the group's esteem in that same fashion, polarization will result.

Group polarization is one consequence

of a general pattern of thought called *groupthink.* **Irving Janis** (1982) coined the term **groupthink** for the tendency of a decision-making group to filter out undesirable input so that a consensus may be reached, especially if it is in line with the leader's viewpoint. Janis's theory of groupthink emerged from his historical analysis of the Bay of Pigs invasion of Cuba in 1960. This disastrous invasion was approved by President Kennedy after Cabinet meetings in which contrary information was minimized or suppressed by those advisors to the president who were eager to undertake the invasion. From his analysis of this event, Janis outlined a series of features that he believed would predispose groups to fall prey to groupthink: He suggested, for example, that groups that were highly cohesive, insulated from experts, and operated under directed leadership would make groupthink decisions. Researchers have attempted to verify Janis's ideas through both further historical analyses and laboratory experiments (Esser, 1998). This body of research suggests that groups are particularly vulnerable to groupthink when they embody a collective desire to maintain a shared positive view of a group (Turner & Pratkanis, 1998). Group members must understand that dissent often improves the quality of a group decision even if it may detract, on the surface, from the group's positive feel.

The next time you are involved in a group enterprise, see if you can detect these processes at work.

minority influence. In one study where participants were given color-naming tasks, the majority correctly identified the color patches, but two of the experimenter's confederates consistently identified a green color as blue. Their consistent minority opposition had no immediate effect on the majority, but, when later tested alone, some of the participants shifted their judgments by moving the boundary between blue and green toward the blue side of the color continuum (Moscovici, 1976; Moscovici & Faucheux, 1972). Eventually, the power of the many may be undercut by the conviction of the dedicated few (Moscovici, 1980, 1985).

You can conceptualize these effects with respect to the distinction we introduced earlier between normative influence and informational influence (Wood et al., 1994). Minority groups have relatively little normative influence: Members of the majority are typically not particularly concerned about being liked or accepted by the minority. On the other hand, minority groups do have informational influence: Minorities can encourage group members to understand issues from multiple perspectives (Peterson & Nemeth, 1996). Unfortunately, this potential for informational influence may only infrequently allow minorities to overcome majority members' normative desire to distance themselves from deviant or low-consensus views (Wood, 2000).

In society, the majority tends to be the defender of the status quo. Typically, the force for innovation and change comes from the minority members or from individuals who are either dissatisfied with the current system or able to visualize new options and create alternative ways of dealing with current problems. The conflict between the entrenched majority view and the dissident minority perspective is an essential precondition of innovations that can lead to positive social change.

If you came upon an unattended plate of dollar bills with a sign directing you to TAKE ONE, would you obey it as these Candid Camera participants did?

◆ SITUATIONAL POWER: *CANDID CAMERA* REVELATIONS

Social psychologists have attempted to demonstrate the power of social norms and social situations by devising experiments that reveal the ease with which smart, independent, rational, good people can be led into behaving in ways that are less than optimal. Although social psychologists have shown the serious consequences of situational power such as the social roles that turn ordinary students into aggressive prison guards, it is equally possible to demonstrate this principle with humor. Indeed, *Candid Camera* scenarios, created by intuitive social psychologist **Allen Funt,** have been doing so for nearly 50 years. Funt showed how human nature follows a situational script to the letter. Millions in his TV audiences laughed when a diner stopped eating a hamburger whenever a DON'T EAT counter light flashed; when pedestrians stopped and waited at a red street light above the *sidewalk* on which they were walking; when highway drivers turned back after seeing a road sign that read DELAWARE IS CLOSED; and when customers jumped from one white tile to another in response to a store sign that instructed them not to walk on black tiles. One of the best *Candid Camera* illustrations of the subtle power of implicit situational rules to control behavior is the "elevator caper." A person riding a rigged elevator first obeyed the usual silent rule to face the front, but when a group of other passengers all faced the rear, the hapless victim followed the new emerging group norm and faced the rear as well.

We see in these slice-of-life episodes the minimal situational conditions needed to elicit unusual behaviors in ordinary people. You laugh because people who appear similar to you behave foolishly in response to small modifications in their commonplace situations. You implicitly distance yourself from them by assuming you would not act that way. The lesson of much social psychological research is that, more than likely, you would behave exactly as others have if you were placed in the same situation. Poet John Donne wrote, "No man is an island, entire of itself; every man is a piece of the continent." People are all interconnected by the situations and norms and rules they share. The wise reply to someone who asks how *you* would act if you were in a situation in which people behaved in evil, foolish, or irrational ways is, "I don't know. It depends on how powerful the situation is."

We have reached the important conclusion that situations play a substantial role in determining people's behavior. However, you've almost certainly had real-life experiences in which you have come to understand that you and a friend disagree about exactly what took place—what the situation was. In the next section, we explore the idea that different people interpret the same situations in different ways.

We have reached the important conclusion that situations play a substantial role in determining people's behavior. In the next two sections we will revisit that conclusion with respect to positive and negative behaviors—altruism and aggression. We will also see how other factors, such as our genetic inheritance, play a role in determining who might help and who might do harm within particular situations.

PUT YOURSELF TO THE TEST

- What did the Stanford Prison Experiment demonstrate about social roles?
- How do social norms define acceptable attitudes and behavior?
- How do informational and normative influence affect conformity?
- How have experimenters demonstrated the impact of informational and normative influence?
- In what ways are minorities able to have an impact on majority views?

Altruism and Prosocial Behavior

You see the same images after almost every tragedy: People risk their own lives to try to save the lives of others. Recall, for example, the horror of the World Trade Center attack. People from all the over the country converged on Ground Zero with the hope of finding and aiding survivors. Such tragedies show the human species's potential for **prosocial behaviors,** behaviors that are carried out with the goal of helping other people. Beyond that, these tragedies often demonstrate **altruism**—the prosocial behaviors a person carries out without considering his or her own safety or interests. Much of what defines a *culture* or *society* is people's willingness to help each other. As members of a culture or society, people cooperate and make sacrifices for the good of other members. We begin this section by considering why it is that people are willing to perform acts of altruism.

◆ THE ROOTS OF ALTRUISM

Let's start with a concrete example of altruism, reported in a daily newspaper (Porstner, 1997):

> A Bay Shore man pulled in front of and stopped a swerving car on the Southern State Parkway in Lindenhurst Thursday, saving a

Connecticut man whom police said may have suffered a seizure.

> "I just got up real close in front of him and just slowed down so he would hit me," said [the driver, age] 25. "That was the only way I could get his moving car to a stop."

What response do you have to this report? Can you imagine risking your own life—or, at least, your own car—to save someone else's life? As this event unfolded, what do you imagine the Bay Shore driver might have been thinking to himself? Do you believe he calculated costs and benefits before he acted?

When you consider examples like this courageous driver, it seems fairly natural to conclude that there is some basic human motive to be altruistic. In fact, the existence of altruism has sometimes been controversial. To understand why, you must think back to the discussion of evolutionary forces we presented in Chapters 3 and 11. According to the evolutionary perspective, the main goal of life is to reproduce so that one can pass on one's genes. How, in that context, does altruism make sense? Why should you risk your life to aid others? There are two answers to this question, depending on whether the "others" are family members or strangers.

For family members, altruistic behaviors makes some sense because—even if you imperil your own survival—you aid the general survival of your gene pool. In fact, when asked about who they might aid in life-or-death situations, people are relatively sensitive to their genetic overlap.

◆ What social forces turn people like workers in India after the 2001 earthquake into heroes?

Altruism Toward Kin

College students from the United States and Japan were asked to consider scenarios in which they could only save one of three individuals in grave peril. For example, in one scenario the three individuals were sleeping in a rapidly burning house. In each scenario, the individuals differed with respect to their imagined *kinship* with the students. Some were close relatives, such as brothers (0.5 overlap in genes); others were more distant, such as cousins (0.125 overlap). The students were asked to indicate which individual they would be most likely to save. As you can see in **Figure 17.3,** the closer the kinship, the more likely people were to "save" that individual. The figure also shows a comparison condition in which the situation wasn't life-or-death: The students were asked how they would deal with more everyday decisions, like choosing someone for whom they would run an errand. The results still show the effects of kinship, but the relationship is not quite as strong. That is, the "life-or-death" scenarios yield more extreme evaluations of kinship than the "everyday" scenarios. The results were the same for both Japanese and U.S. students (Burnstein et al., 1994).

Students in this study didn't actually have to rescue anyone from a burning house, yet you can see how kinship affected their choices. Although it's unlikely that anyone was explicitly reasoning "I have to protect the gene pool," if people follow the pattern represented in Figure 17.3, gene pool protection would emerge.

But how about non-kin? Why, for example, was the driver willing to risk his own survival to preserve some-one else's genes? To explain altruism toward acquaintances and strangers, theorists have explored the concept of **reciprocal altruism** (Trivers, 1971). This concept suggests that people perform altruistic behaviors because they, in some sense, expect that others will perform altruistic behaviors for them: I will save you when you are drowning with the expectation that you would save me, in the future, when I am drowning. Thus, expectations of reciprocity endow altruism with survival value. You have already become acquainted with this concept in other guises. In Chapter 16, for example, we introduced the *norm of reciprocity* to explain one way in which people can bring about compliance. When someone does a favor for you, you are in a state of psychological distress until you can return the favor—this distress, apparently, has its roots in evolution because it helps increase survival. Because of these evolutionary underpinnings, altruism is not unique to the human species. In fact, anthropologists have identified patterns of reciprocal altruism among a variety of species, such as vampire bats and chimpanzees, that function in social groups (Nielsen, 1994).

Note, however, that the concept of reciprocal altruism cannot explain all facets of cooperation in social species. Researchers have produced evidence that, in many situations, both human and nonhuman animals continue to cooperate and share resources without expectations of reciprocity (Matheson & Bernstein, 2000; Wedekind & Milinski, 2000; Widdig et al., 2000). For example, the small number of successful hunters among the !Kung people, hunter-gatherers who live in northwestern Botswana and neighboring parts of Namibia, share the meat from animals they kill with the other members of their camp even though they cannot expect to obtain comparable resources in return from the less skilled

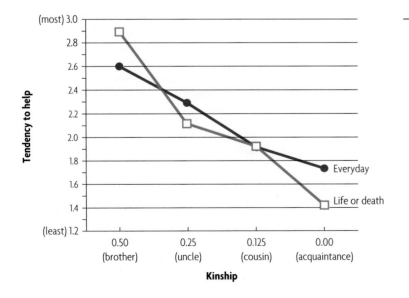

FIGURE 17.3

Tendency to Help Kin

Students were asked to indicate which relatives, of differing degrees of kinship, they were most likely to save in life-or-death and everyday circumstances. Although closeness had an effect on both types of judgments, it mattered more for life-or-death situations.

hunters (Hawkes, 1993). Based on these types of observations, researchers continue the search for a broader range of explanations for the existence of altruism.

Given that altruism appears to have an evolutionary basis, do individual differences in altruism affect a contemporary individual's ability to pass on his or her genes? Recall that in Chapter 11, we explored some of the factors evolutionary psychologists have suggested guide people's mate selections. Our discussion of altruism allows us to add another factor to this list.

Women Value Altruistic Men

Female undergraduates watched a videotaped conversation between an experimenter and a male confederate. During the conversation, the confederate revealed his attitude toward altruistic behaviors. In the *high-altruism* condition, he talked about helping others and then volunteered to do a boring task, rather than allowing someone else to do it. In the *low-altruism* condition, the confederate talked about watching out for his own interests and opted to leave the boring task to someone else. After watching the conversation, the female participants were asked to rate the confederate on a number of dimensions, including physical and sexual attractiveness and social and dating desirability. Although the very same males appeared in the low- and high-altruism conditions, the women rated them as considerably more attractive and desirable when they were committed to altruistic behaviors (Jensen-Campbell et al., 1995).

Contrary to the old saying, in this study, nice guys finished first. In evolutionary terms, the results suggest that women prefer men who will actively share their resources to help nurture offspring. In this light, we have another reason why altruism remained part of the human genome: Women believed that men who provided evidence of altruistic behaviors would make better fathers.

◆ MOTIVES FOR PROSOCIAL BEHAVIOR

In the last section, we suggested that altruism—a motive to sacrifice for others—has an innate basis. We now consider altruism in the context of other motives for prosocial behavior. Researcher **Daniel Batson** (1994) suggests that there are four forces that prompt people to act for the public good:

- *Altruism.* Acting in response to a motive to benefit others, as in the case of the driver who saved another person's life.
- *Egoism.* Performing prosocial behaviors ultimately in one's own self-interest; someone might perform

a helping behavior to receive a similar favor in return (for example, compliance with a request) or to receive a reward (for example, money or praise).

- *Collectivism.* Performing prosocial behaviors to benefit a particular group; people might perform helping behaviors to improve circumstances for their families, fraternities or sororities, political parties, and so on.
- *Principlism.* Performing prosocial behaviors to uphold moral principles; someone might act in a prosocial manner because of a religious or civic principle.

You can see how each of these motives might apply in different situations.

Although each motive may lead people to perform behaviors in the service of others, they also sometimes can act in competition (Batson & Powell, 2003). Suppose, for example, that you must decide how to allocate a scarce resource to several people. You might be thinking, "I'd give the same amount to all individuals," because the principle of *justice* suggests that each person should have equal access to resources. Suppose, however, that other motives come into play that lead you to favor one individual over the others.

Empathy Can Lead to Injustice

Participants in an experiment were asked to allocate raffle tickets either to a whole group or to individuals within the group. If the tickets were given to the whole group, each member would get the same number of tickets—a *justice* outcome. However, in one condition of the experiment, the participants read an autobiographical message from someone they were led to believe was a group member; the message revealed that that person had just been dumped by a long-time romantic partner. How does this information affect people's distributions of raffle tickets? When the participants were encouraged to try to imagine how the student would feel, they gave extra tickets to the dumped individual. *Empathy*—the participants' emotional identification with the student—won out over *justice* (Batson et al., 1999).

Daniel Batson and his colleagues have provided several demonstrations in favor of the *empathy-altruism hypothesis:* When you feel empathy toward another individual, those feelings evoke an altruistic motive to provide help. In the experiment we just described, the immediate altruistic goal proved stronger for some participants than the more abstract goal of justice. In a similar fashion, empa-

<www.ablongman.com/gerrig17e>

What prosocial motive explains why people band together to protect the environment?

thy can give rise to altruistic behaviors that favor an individual over the collective good (Batson et al., 1995).

You can see why it's important to consider each behavior in light of the full situation: What looks at first like *anti*social behavior—for example, violating principles of justice—may turn out, from a different vantage point, to be *pro*social behavior. A social psychology lesson we emphasized in the first section of this chapter was how much people's behaviors are constrained by situations. We have just had a first hint of such constraints for prosocial behavior. Next, we describe a classic program of research that demonstrated fully how much people's willingness to help—their ability to follow through on prosocial motives—depends on characteristics of the situation.

◆ THE EFFECTS OF THE SITUATION ON PROSOCIAL BEHAVIOR

This program of research began with a tragedy. From the safety of their apartment windows, 38 respectable, law-abiding citizens in Queens, New York, for more than half an hour watched a killer stalk and stab a woman in three separate attacks. Two times the sound of the bystanders' voices and the sudden glow of their bedroom lights interrupted the assailant and frightened him off. Each time, however, he returned and stabbed the victim again. Not a single person telephoned the police during the assault; only one witness called the police after the woman was dead (Rosenthal, 1964). This newspaper account of the murder of Kitty Genovese shocked a nation that could not accept the idea of such apathy or hard-heartedness on the part of its responsible citizenry.

But is it fair to pin the label of "apathy" or "hard-hearted" on these bystanders? Or can we explain their inaction in terms of situational forces? To make the case for situational forces, **Bibb Latané** and **John Darley** (1970) carried out a classic series of studies. Their goal

was to demonstrate that **bystander intervention**—people's willingness to help strangers in distress—was very sensitive to precise characteristics of the situation. They ingeniously created in the laboratory an experimental analogue of the bystander-intervention situation.

CLASSIC

PUTTING IDEAS TO THE TEST

When Will People Help?

The participants were male college students. Each student, placed in a room by himself with an intercom, was led to believe that he was communicating with one or more students in an adjacent room. During the course of a discussion about personal problems, he heard what sounded like one of the other students having an epileptic seizure and gasping for help. During the "seizure," it was impossible for the participant to talk to the other students or to find out what, if anything, they were doing about the emergency. The dependent variable was the speed with which the participant reported the emergency to the experimenter.

It turned out that the likelihood of intervention depended on the number of bystanders the participant thought were present. The more people he thought were present, the slower he was in reporting the seizure, if he did so at all. As you can see in **Figure 17.4**, everyone in a two-person situation intervened within 160 seconds, but nearly 40 percent of those who believed they were part of a larger group never bothered to inform the experimenter that another student was seriously ill (Darley & Latané, 1968).

The murder of Kitty Genovese, in a pleasant Queens neighborhood, shocked the nation. Why did so many responsible citizens fail to intervene when they heard her cries for help?

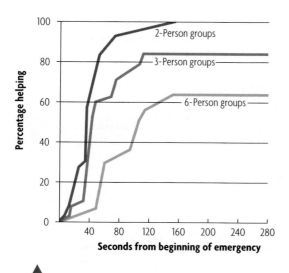

FIGURE 17.4

Bystander Intervention in an Emergency

The more people present, the less likely that any one bystander will intervene. Bystanders act most quickly in two-person groups.

This result arises from a **diffusion of responsibility.** When more than one person *could* help in an emergency situation, people often assume that someone else *will* or *should* help—so they back off and don't get involved.

Diffusion of responsibility is only one of the reasons that bystanders may fail to help. Let's explore more of the facets of many emergency situations.

BYSTANDERS MUST NOTICE THE EMERGENCY

In the seizure study, the situation was rigged so that participants had to notice what was going on. In many real-life circumstances, however, people who are pursuing their own agendas—they may, for example, be on their way to work or an appointment—may not even notice that there is a situation in which they can help. In one dramatic experiment, students at the Princeton Theological Seminary thought they were going to be evaluated on their sermons, one of which was to be about the parable of the Good Samaritan—a New Testament figure who takes time to help a man lying injured by the roadside.

CLASSIC

PUTTING IDEAS TO THE TEST

Who Notices Emergencies?

The seminarians had to deliver their lectures in a different building from the one in which they were initially briefed. Some were randomly assigned to a *late* condition, in which they had to hurry to make the next session, others to an *on-time* condi-

tion, and a third group to an *early* condition. When each seminarian walked down an alley between the two buildings, he came upon a man slumped in a doorway, coughing and groaning. On their way to deliver a sermon about the Good Samaritan, these seminary students now had the chance to practice what they were about to preach. Did they? Of those who were in a hurry because they were late, only 10 percent helped. If they were on time, 45 percent helped the stranger. Most bystander intervention came from those who were early— 63 percent of these seminarians acted as Good Samaritans (Darley & Batson, 1973).

How should we evaluate the "late" seminarians? Perhaps the seminarians were so caught up in their own concerns that they failed to even "notice" the emergency situation. Perhaps they noticed, but in their hurry, they did not pay careful enough attention to determine how serious the situation was. In either case, you see that helping behavior depends on taking the time to evaluate a situation accurately.

BYSTANDERS MUST LABEL EVENTS AS AN EMERGENCY

Many situations in life are ambiguous. You don't want to embarrass yourself by trying to give mouth-to-mouth resuscitation to someone who is merely asleep. To decide if a situation is an emergency, you typically see how other people are responding (Latané & Darley, 1970). (You should recall the earlier discussion of informational influence in Chapter 17.) Consider this first-person account from one of your authors who was attending a lecture at which the speaker appeared to be on the brink of fainting:

> *The speaker is flustered and his rapid delivery is clearly slowing down. Is it to emphasize his final points or because he is about to collapse? Maybe he needs to sit down, but how can I tell without interrupting him? What if I am reading the situation wrong, and then everyone will think I'm a fool? But suppose I am right and he passes out before finishing, and falls off the stage? He will surely get hurt smashing down into the seats. I'll know that I could have prevented his accident and did not.*

You can see here how hard it is, even for someone with a firm grasp on the psychological forces at work in such a situation, to commit himself to action when no one else seems to be labeling the situation as an emergency. Here's how the situation ended:

> *I stood up in front of the speaker and put my arms up toward him. He looked down at me in total confusion. I imagined what my students*

<www.ablongman.com/gerrig17e>

and colleagues were thinking of my seemingly bizarre behavior as I wrapped my arms around the honored guest speaker, moments before he finished his distinguished lecture. Just then, the speaker went limp, unconscious, and fell on me. We crashed back into the first row seats.

The decision to intervene, as you can see, proved to be prudent. However, from this brief account, you can see how very stressful it is to make a personal decision to define a situation as an emergency.

BYSTANDERS MUST FEEL RESPONSIBILITY

We have already seen that an important factor in non-intervention is the diffusion of responsibility. If you find yourself in a situation in which you need help, you should do everything you can to cause bystanders to focus responsibility on themselves and overcome this force. You should point directly toward someone and say, "You! I need your help." Consider two studies that involved apparent crimes. In the first study, New Yorkers watched as a thief snatched a women's suitcase in a fast-food restaurant when she left her table. In the second, beachgoers watched as a thief snatched a portable radio from a beach blanket when the owner left it for a few minutes.

CLASSIC
PUTTING IDEAS TO THE TEST

Creating a Sense of Responsibility

In each experiment, the would-be theft victim (the experimenter's accomplice) asked the soon-to-be observer of the crime either, "Do you have the time?" or "Will you please keep an eye on my bag (radio) while I'm gone?" The first interaction elicited no personal responsibility, and the bystanders simply stood by idly as the thefts unfolded. However, of those who agreed to watch the victim's property, almost every bystander intervened. They called for help, and some even tackled the runaway thief on the beach (Moriarty, 1975).

These experiments suggest that the act of requesting a favor forges a special human bond that involves other people in ways that materially change the situation. This is another instance in which it would be wrong to make an attribution of apathy when people fail to stop the theft. The social psychological power of the small commitment—"Will you watch this for me?"—turned almost every bystander into someone who cared enough to help.

In this section, we have discussed prosocial behaviors—those circumstances in which people come to each others' aid. We suggested that the motivation to help may be part of each human's genetic inheritance. However, human nature presents a mixture of prosocial and antisocial impulses. In the next section, we move to another type of behavior—*aggression*—that may also be encoded in the human genome.

PUT YOURSELF TO THE TEST

- What sets altruistic behaviors apart from other types of prosocial behaviors?
- How does an evolutionary perspective explain altruistic behavior?
- What four motives explain prosocial behavior and why might they come into conflict?
- What situational forces influence whether people will engage in prosocial behaviors?

Aggression

To introduce the concept of altruism, we quoted a newspaper article about a heroic act. Unfortunately, newspapers are much more likely to contain reports on acts of **aggression:** a person's behaviors that cause psychological or physical harm to another individual. These were some headlines from a single issue of *The New York Times,* September 29, 2003:

- Survivor Describes Stabbing on Subway
- Afghan Soldiers Killed in Ambush
- 11 Killed in Bombing in Colombian City
- In the Bronx, Little Pity for a Beaten Cabby

Just from this brief sample, you can see the many ways in which people aggress against one another. You can see why, consequently, it is so important to psychologists that they understand the causes of aggression. The ultimate goal, of course, is to try to use psychological knowledge to help reduce societal levels of aggression.

◆ EVOLUTIONARY PERSPECTIVES

In the section on prosocial behavior, we posed a puzzle of evolution: Why is it that people would risk their own lives to benefit others? The existence of aggressive behaviors, however, has posed no similar puzzle. In evolutionary terms, animals commit aggressive behaviors to ensure themselves access to desired mates and to protect the resources that allow themselves and their offspring to survive. In his classic book *On Aggression,* **Konrad Lorenz** (1966) documented a range of aggressive activity in the animal kingdom. In the course of his review, Lorenz also documented the mechanisms that keep aggression in check: "A raven can peck out the eye of another with one thrust of its beak, a wolf can rip the jugular vein of another with a single bite. There would be no more ravens and no more wolves if reliable inhibitions did not prevent such actions" (p. 240). On Lorenz's view, this is what sets the human species apart: He argued that humans do not have appropriately evolved mechanisms to *inhibit* their aggressive impulses. Lorenz believed that these inhibitory mechanisms failed to evolve because, until the invention of artificial weapons, humans could not do each other much harm. When weapons appeared, Lorenz suggested that the human species's "position was very nearly that of a dove which, by some unnatural trick of nature, has suddenly acquired the beak of a raven" (p. 241).

Research in response to Lorenz's work has contradicted his assessment of human aggression in two ways (Lore & Schultz, 1993). First, field research with a variety of animal species suggests that many other species commit the same range of aggressive acts as do humans. For example, even seemingly mild-mannered chimpanzees gang up on and kill their own kind (Goodall, 1986). Aggression in other species is not particularly good news for humans—it just seems that we're no worse—but it does suggest less of an evolutionary discontinuity. Second, research suggests that humans have more inhibitory control over their use of aggression than Lorenz suggested. In fact, humans make choices with respect to their display of aggression conditioned on their social environments. As we will see later in this section, cultures specify norms for circumstances in which aggression is acceptable or required. We will suggest there that cultures themselves play a critical role in determining the extent to which people are "able" to inhibit aggression.

Evolutionary analysis suggests that a drive for survival may have endowed many or most species with an innate predisposition toward some forms of violence. For humans, however, it is nonetheless the case that different members of the species are more or less likely to perform aggressive behaviors. We next consider those individual differences in aggression.

◆ INDIVIDUAL DIFFERENCES

Why are some individuals more aggressive than others? In the context of Lorenz's evolutionary claims, you can see why one hypothesis that researchers have pursued is that there is a genetic component to individual differences in rates of aggression. Researchers have sought an answer to the genetics of aggression using many of the methodologies we've illustrated in earlier chapters. They have, for example, compared the similarity of identical (monozygotic, MZ) and fraternal (dizygotic, DZ) twins with respect to aggressive personalities; in

Why do so many species of animals engage in aggressive behaviors? What did Konrad Lorenz believe makes human aggression unique?

other cases, they have estimated the contributions of nature and nurture by examining children raised in adoptive homes. These studies typically demonstrate a strong genetic component for aggressive behavior (DiLalla, 2002; Miles & Carey, 1997). For example, MZ twins consistently show higher correlations for aggressiveness than do DZ twins. Let's consider one study that looks at genetic contributions very early in life.

Here, students mourn the victims of the Columbine massacre. Why do people so often turn to aggression as a solution to their problems?

PUTTING IDEAS TO THE TEST

Antisocial Behavior Among Five-Year-Old Children

The study involved 1,116 families in England and Wales with MZ or DZ twins (Arseneault et al., 2003). The study focused on the range of antisocial behaviors the children were displaying at age five. These behaviors include aggressive acts ("uses force to take something from another child") as well as more general opposition behavior ("spiteful, tries to get revenge"). The study obtained four different sources of information about the children's antisocial behavior: Mothers and teachers reported on the children, the children provided self-reports, and observers interacted with the children in their homes and rated their behavior. These four sources of information allowed the researchers to determine whether genetics makes a contribution to antisocial behavior across different situations. In fact, the comparison between MZ and DZ twins established that across the four types of reports, 82 percent of the variation in antisocial behavior could be explained by genetic factors.

This study supports the conclusion that some individuals have a greater genetic predisposition toward aggression than do others.

Researchers have also focused attention on brain and hormonal differences that may mark a predisposition toward aggressive behavior. As we saw in Chapter 12, several brain structures, such as the amygdala and portions of cortex, play roles in the expression and regulation of emotion. With respect to aggression, it is critical that brain pathways function effectively so that individuals can control the expression of negative emotion. If, for example, people experience inappropriate levels of activation in the amygdala, they may not be able to inhibit the negative emotions that lead to aggressive behaviors (Davidson et al., 2000).

Attention has also focused on the neurotransmitter serotonin. Research suggests that inappropriate levels of serotonin may impair the brain's ability to regulate negative emotions and impulsive behavior (Enserink, 2000). For example, one study demonstrated that men with higher life histories of aggression showed decreased response in the serotonin system to a drug (fenfluramine) that typically has a considerable impact on that system (Manuck et al., 2002). Recall from Chapter 14 that researchers have begun to explore consequences of variations in the actual genes that underlie serotonin function. In this study as well, the researchers showed that a particular genetic variation was likely to affect serotonin function in a way that put people at risk for high levels of aggressive behavior.

Finally, studies suggest that some individual differences in aggression may reflect muted stress responses. For example, one project related levels of the stress hormone *cortisol* to the aggressive behavior of 7- to 12-year-old boys: The most aggressive boys had the most muted stress response (McBurnett et al., 2000). These results suggest that some individuals may not experience the types of physiological stress responses that inhibit most people from behaving in a dramatically aggressive fashion: Their bodies do not experience the negative consequences of negative behaviors and emotions.

Personality research on aggression has pointed to the importance of differentiating categories of aggressive behaviors: People with different personality profiles are likely to engage in different types of aggression. One important distinction separates *impulsive aggression* from *instrumental aggression* (Berkowitz, 1993; Caprara et al., 1996). **Impulsive aggression** is produced in reaction to situations and is emotion-driven: People respond with aggressive acts in the heat of the moment. If you see people get into a fistfight after a car accident, that is impulsive aggression. **Instrumental aggression** is goal-directed (the aggression serves as the *instrument* for some goal) and cognition-based: People carry out acts of aggression, with premeditated thought, to achieve specific aims. If you see someone knock an elderly woman down to steal her purse, that is instrumental aggression. Research has confirmed that those individuals with high propensities toward one or the other of these types of violence have distinct sets of personality traits (Caprara et al., 1996). For example, individuals who reported a propensity toward impulsive aggression were likely, in general, to be characterized as high on the factor of *emotional responsivity*. That is, they were likely, in general, to report highly emotional responses to a range of situations. By contrast, individuals who reported a propensity toward instrumental aggression were likely to score high on the factor of *positive evaluation of violence*. These individuals believed that many forms of violence are justified, and they also did not accept moral responsibility for aggressive behaviors. You learn from this analysis that not all types of aggression arise from the same underlying personality factors.

Most people are not at the extremes of either impulsive or instrumental aggression: They do not lose their tempers at the least infraction or purposefully commit acts of violence. Even so, in some situations, even the most mild-mannered individuals will perform aggressive acts. We look now at the types of situations that may often provide the triggering conditions for aggression.

◆ SITUATIONAL INFLUENCES

Take a moment now to think back to the last time you engaged in aggressive behavior. It may not have been physical aggression: You may just have been verbally abusive toward some other individual, with the intent of causing psychological distress. How would you explain why that particular situation gave rise to aggression? Did you have a long history of conflict with the individual or was it just a one-time interaction? Were you inclined toward an aggressive act because of something very specific or were you just feeling frustrated at that moment? These are some of the questions researchers have asked when they've examined the links between situations and aggression. When we've asked our own students to think about their aggressive acts, they've given us a variety of answers, as you will see in what follows.

FRUSTRATION-AGGRESSION HYPOTHESIS

I'd been having a really bad day. I needed to register late for a course. I couldn't find anyone to help me. When I was told for the thousandth time, "You've got to go to a different office," I got so angry I practically kicked a hole in the door.

This anecdote provides an instance of a general relationship captured by the **frustration-aggression hypothesis**

(Dollard et al., 1939). According to this hypothesis, *frustration* occurs in situations in which people are prevented or blocked from attaining their goals; a rise in frustration then leads to a greater probability of aggression. The link between frustration and aggression has obtained a high level of empirical support (Berkowitz, 1993, 1998). For example, children who are frustrated in their expectation that they will be allowed to play with highly attractive toys act aggressively toward those toys when they finally have an opportunity to play (Barker et al., 1941). Researchers have used this relationship to explain aggression at both the personal and societal levels.

Aggression and the Economy

Do you recognize this news story? A man gets fired from a job and goes back to kill the boss who fired him, as well as several coworkers. Could this count as an instance of frustration (that is, the frustrated goal of earning a living) leading to aggression? To provide a general answer to this question, a team of researchers examined the relationship between San Francisco's unemployment rate and the rate at which people in that city were committed for being "dangerous to others." This analysis allows for predictions across a whole community: What unemployment rate is likely to lead to the highest levels of violence? The researchers found that violence increased as unemployment increased, but only to a certain point. When unemployment got too high, violence began to fall again. Why might that be? The researchers speculated that people's fears that they too might lose their jobs helped inhibit frustration-driven tendencies toward violence (Catalano et al., 1997, 2002).

Why do some types of day-to-day experiences make even the calmest people contemplate aggressive acts?

This study suggests how individual and societal forces interact to produce a net level of violence. We can predict a certain level of aggression based on the frustration each individual experiences in an economy with rising unemployment. However, as people realize that expressions of aggression may imperil their own employment, violence is inhibited. You can probably recognize these forces in your day-to-day experiences: There are many situations in which you might feel sufficiently frustrated to express aggression, but you also understand that an expression of aggression will work against your long-term best interest.

Frustration doesn't always lead to aggression. When, for example, the frustration is brought about unintentionally—suppose a child spills juice on his mother's new dress—people are less likely to become aggressive than when the action is intentional (Burnstein & Worchel, 1962). At the same time, other situations that are not frustrating with respect to goals, but bring about negative emotional states, can also lead to aggression. We see such a situation in another student anecdote.

TEMPERATURE AND AGGRESSION

It was a hot summer day, and the air conditioning in my car was broken. This guy cut me off. I chased after him and tried to run him off the road.

Is there a relationship between temperature and aggression? Consider the data plotted in **Figure 17.5.** This figure is taken from a study that examined the effects of temperature on assaults for a two-year period in Minneapolis, Minnesota; the plot is based on 36,617 reported assaults (Cohn & Rotton, 1997). (A similar study of 18,687 assaults in Dallas, Texas, yielded the same general pattern [Rotton & Cohn, 2000]). As you can see, there is a strong relationship between how cold or hot it is and how likely it is that people will commit assaults. In fact, the figure doesn't tell quite the whole story: The relationship between temperature and assault is actually strongest in the late evening and early morning hours (that is, 9 P.M. to 3 A.M.).

Why might this be so? An explanation of these data relies on both societal and psychological forces. At a societal level, you probably guessed that it's more likely that people will commit assault when they are more likely to be out and about. That is, in warmer weather, people are more likely to be outdoors and, therefore, are also more likely to be "available" as assault victims. You can also provide the same analysis for time of day: In the 9 P.M. to 3 A.M. hours, people are typically less constrained by work or other responsibilities. Furthermore, by the late evening hours, people may have been drinking alcohol or using other substances that lower their inhibition for aggression (Ito et al., 1996).

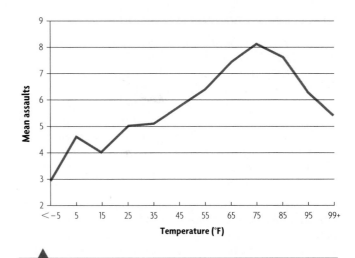

FIGURE 17.5

Temperature and Aggression

The figure presents average number of assaults (in a three-hour period) as a function of the temperature in that period. (°F = degrees Fahrenheit.) Aggression rises steadily as the temperature warms up to about 75°F.

Given all these societal explanations for increased aggression, do we also need to invoke psychology? The answer is yes. Another important component of an explanation for the data in Figure 17.5 is the way in which people cope with and interpret the discomfort associated with high temperatures. Recall the discussion of appraisal and emotions in Chapter 12. Suppose on a 75-degree day you're having a conversation with someone that makes you feel hot and uncomfortable. Do you attribute the emotion to the temperature or to your adversary? To the extent that you misattribute your emotion to another person, rather than to the situation, you're more likely to become aggressive toward that person. (You might recognize this from Chapter 16 as a dangerous consequence of the fundamental attribution error.) Why does heat matter most in the late evening and early morning? As the day goes on, it may become harder to remember "I'm feeling this way because it's hot" and not just conclude "I'm feeling this way because this bozo is making me crazy." If all of this is true, why does Figure 17.5 show a decline in assaults when temperatures become very hot, beginning around 75 degrees? Researchers have speculated that at very high temperatures, people might experience sufficient discomfort to withdraw from abrasive situations rather than stay and fight (Cohn & Rotton, 1997).

A third student anecdote illustrates how situations elicit hostility that gets amplified over time.

DIRECT PROVOCATION AND ESCALATION

I was sitting in the library trying to get some work done. These two women were having a really loud conversation that was bothering a lot of people. I asked them to quiet down, and they pretty much ignored me. I asked again about five minutes later, and they only started talking louder. Finally, I told them they were both stupid, ugly jerks and that if they didn't shut up I was going to pick them up and throw them out of the library. That worked.

It's not going to surprise you that *direct provocation* will also give rise to aggression. That is, when someone behaves in a way that makes you angry or upset—and you think that behavior was intentional—you are more likely to respond with some form of physical or verbal aggression (Johnson & Rule, 1986). The effects of direct provocation are consistent with the general idea that situations that produce negative affect will lead to aggression. The intentionality of the act matters because you are less likely to interpret an unintentional act in a negative way. (Recall that we made the similar observation that frustration is less likely to lead to aggression when it is brought about unintentionally.)

Researchers have looked at issues of provocation to assess the causes of extreme violence in schools.

PUTTING IDEAS TO THE TEST

Teasing, Rejection, and Violence

Researchers reviewed 15 instances of shootings that occurred in schools between 1995 and 2001 (Leary et al., 2003). The most publicized of these was the incident at Columbine High School in 1999 that led to the deaths of 12 students and one teacher. All told, in that six-year period students killed nearly 40 individuals including, in some cases, themselves. The researchers examined extensive reports of the 15 incidents to determine the extent to which the perpetrators had been the victims of either chronic teasing, rejection, or bullying or an acute episode of humiliation or romantic rejection. These factors were present in 12 of the 15 incidents. For example, the perpetrators at Columbine left behind videotapes in which they recounted the teasing and ostracism they believed they had endured. In several of the incidents, the perpetrator's victims were drawn from the group of peers who had mistreated them.

Note that these data in no way *excuse* the killer's actions—they only help to *explain* them. In most of these situations, there were other causal forces in play. For example, in 10 of the 15 incidents, the perpetrators had shown previous signs of psychological distress

such as depression and animal abuse. Still, it's important to keep in mind that provocation can lead to extreme acts of aggression.

A second characteristic of the anecdote with which we opened this section, beyond provocation, is *escalation:* Because less intense responses to the provocation had no effect, the student's response became more aggressive over time. Researchers have demonstrated that aggressive responses will, in fact, escalate in the face of a persistent annoyance. For example, in one study, participants were unable to get members of a group to share resources (Mikolic et al., 1997). (The group members were privately instructed by the experiments not to cooperate.) Over the course of the session, the participants' verbal remarks progressed from *demanding statements* ("We need it now"), through *angry statements* ("I'm really getting annoyed with you"), all the way to *abusive statements* (for example, "You guys are total jerks"). In fact, the strength of the responses followed a very orderly sequence of escalation. The experimenters suggested that people have learned an *escalation script.* This memory structure encodes cultural norms for the sequence with which people should ratchet up the aggressiveness of their responses to continuing provocation. Can you see how the escalation script also refers back to the relationship between frustration and aggression? The failures of the initial attempts to change the situation likely lead to feelings of frustration that also will increase the likelihood of more intense aggression.

We've now considered some of the situational forces that may lead you to produce psychological or physical aggression. It's important to note that our examples all refer to impulsive aggression rather than to instrumental aggression. As we explained earlier, instrumental aggression refers to circumstances in which people use aggression to achieve an end—for example, when muggers use physical force to commit their crimes. That type of aggression must be explained as a component of a larger theory of criminality. We have been concerned here largely with circumstances in which ordinary individuals find themselves committing impulsive aggressive acts. In the next section, we will see, even so, that cultural differences constrain levels of both individual and criminal aggression.

◆ CULTURAL CONSTRAINTS

We have seen so far that aggressive behaviors are part of your evolutionary inheritance and that certain situations are more likely to evoke aggressive behavior. Even so, several types of data suggest that the probability that an individual will display aggression is highly constrained by cultural values and norms (Segall et al., 1997). To make this point, we need go no further than comparisons between the murder rate in the United

<www.ablongman.com/gerrig17e>

Why might Gandhi's philosophy of nonviolent resistance have been particularly appropriate for the culture of India?

States and other countries: You are seven to ten times more likely to be murdered in the United States than in most European countries (Lore & Schultz, 1993). What psychological forces give rise to such a vast difference in murder rates? If you are a citizen of the United States, you should have considerable interest in answers to this question.

CONSTRUALS OF THE SELF AND AGGRESSIVE BEHAVIOR

To begin an examination of culture and aggression, we return to a distinction in cultural construals of the self that has loomed large in several places in *Psychology and Life:* As explained earlier, most Western cultures embody *independent construals of self,* whereas most Eastern cultures embody *interdependent construals of self* (Markus & Kitayama, 1991). What are the consequences for aggressive behavior? Studies have shown that if you think of yourself as fundamentally interconnected with other members of your culture, you will be less likely to respond aggressively—an act of aggression, after all, would be an act against your "self." For example, in one study Japanese and U.S. preschoolers, average age roughly $4^1/_2$ years, were asked to use dolls to act out endings to stories involving conflicts (Zahn-Waxler et al., 1996). The U.S. children scored considerably higher both on measures of aggressive verbalizations—U.S. children were more likely to say things such as "I hate you"—and aggressive behaviors—U.S. children were more likely to act out behaviors with the dolls such as pushing and hitting. This experiment

suggests that the Japanese children have already internalized the cultural norm of interdependence that weighs against bringing harm to others. The U.S. children, by contrast, show evidence for an independent self that must be protected from others' insults.

Although we have identified this major cultural divide between independence and interdependence, it is also possible to find more fine-grained cultural differences nested within this overarching perspective. For example, **Richard Nisbett** (Nisbett & Cohen, 1996) and his colleagues have extensively studied regional attitudes and behaviors within the United States with respect to uses of aggression. One consistent difference that has emerged is that southern behavior is guided by a *culture of honor,* in which "even small disputes become contests for reputation and social status" (Cohen et al., 1996, p. 945). The culture of honor doesn't sanction all forms of aggression—only those aggressive behaviors that are used to protect property or redress personal insults (Cohen & Nisbett, 1994).

PUTTING IDEAS TO THE TEST

Northern and Southern Responses to Insults

Researchers arranged for male college students—northerners and southerners—to endure a mild insult: While the participant walked down a hallway, an experimental confederate bumped each participant with his shoulder and called him an "asshole." (Students in the control group did not experience this event.) The researchers predicted that southerners would react more dramatically than their northern peers to the bump and insult. One measure the researchers used to gauge the students' reactions was based on the game of "chicken" in which two people drive toward each other until one swerves out of the way. In this case, a second confederate marched directly at each approaching participant. The researchers measured how close each participant got to the confederate before he changed path. As you can see in **Figure 17.6,** the mild insult had a dramatic effect on southern students' behavior. Without an insult, they were actually more polite than the northerners—they "gave way" sooner. However, when southerners had been bumped, they turned away considerably later (Cohen et al., 1996).

Many people in the United States share the general sense that southern culture is more polite than northern culture—you'd rather ask directions from someone in Richmond than someone in New York City. This experiment echos that belief, in the sense that southerners in the control group made way for the confederate earlier than did their northern peers. However, this general

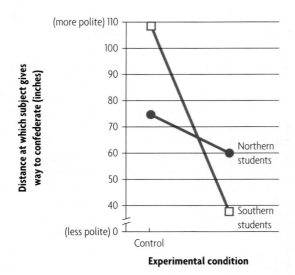

FIGURE 17.6

The Effects of Insults on Northerners and Southerners

Northern and southern students in the experimental group suffered a minor insult. Although southerners were more polite without an insult, they became considerably less likely to give way in a game of "chicken" after they had been insulted.

aura of politeness broke down quite quickly when an attack had been made on the students' sense of honor. Thus, even within the overarching independent construal of self that characterizes most U.S. citizens, southern males react more sharply when that sense of self is challenged and their "honor" is on the line (Nisbett & Cohen, 1996).

NORMS OF AGGRESSIVE BEHAVIOR

We have suggested so far that cultures that embody independent construals of self are more likely to give rise to aggressive behavior. This observation, however, doesn't explain the difference in murder rates we cited earlier: The European countries whose murder rates are vastly lower than that in the United States mostly share the same overarching independent culture. What other cultural forces are at work?

One major factor that has been identified for the United States is the availability of aggressive models in the environment. In Chapter 6, we discussed research suggesting that children very readily adapt aggressive behaviors from watching adult models. For example, children who watched adult models punching, hitting, and kicking a large plastic BoBo doll later showed a greater frequency of the same behaviors than did children in control conditions who had not observed the

aggressive models (Bandura et al., 1963). We also suggested in Chapter 6 that television in the United States beams an enormous number of aggressive models directly into children's homes—exposure to violence is highly related to adult levels of aggression (Comstock & Scharrer, 1999; Huesmann et al., 2003).

Researchers have developed the *general aggression model* to explain the relationship between exposure to violent media (television, movies, and so on) and aggressive behavior. This model suggests that people acquire a general set of aggression-related knowledge structures through their experiences of media violence: On this view, "each violent media episode is essentially one more trial to learn that the world is a dangerous place, that aggression is an appropriate way to deal with conflict and anger, and that aggression works" (Bushman & Anderson, 2002, p. 1680). Consider a study that examined the short-term impact of violent video games.

PUTTING IDEAS TO THE TEST

Violent Video Games and Hostile Expectations

Researchers asked 224 college undergraduates to play either violent video games (for example, Mortal Kombat) or nonviolent video games (for example, 3D Pinball) (Bushman & Anderson, 2002). After playing for 20 minutes, the participants were asked to complete what they believed to be an unrelated task. The participants read incomplete stories and indicated what they thought would happen next. For example, in one story, Todd was rear-ended when he braked quickly at a yellow light. Participants wrote answers to the question, "What happens next?" Those students who played the violent video games gave consistently more aggressive outcomes for the stories. For example, participants suggested that Todd would kick out a window or stab or shoot the other driver.

This study illustrates that those students who had just played violent video games versus nonviolent video games were ready to provide much more aggressive responses. In general, children and young adults who play video games have higher levels of aggressive behaviors and aggression-related thoughts and feelings (Anderson & Bushman, 2001). Exposure to these games—and other violent media—makes the world seem more dangerous. In that context, aggression becomes an appropriate response to a dangerous world.

Unfortunately, for many children the world does present real dangers. Children may be exposed to ggressive acts in their homes. We noted in Chapter 6

Why should parents worry that children who play violent video games may be prone to more real-world aggression?

that children who are physically punished often begin themselves to use aggression as a tactic for controlling others' behaviors. In addition, many children in the United States grow up in inner-city communities in which violence is daily and chronic (Osofsky, 1997; Schwartz & Proctor, 2000). Researchers have only begun to explore the consequences of exposure to violence for children's mental health and their inclination to aggressive behavior.

We end this section on cultural norms for aggressive behavior by noting that those norms can be quite local and quite stable. Consider two adjacent Zapotec villages in the state of Oaxaca, Mexico (Scott, 1992). One of the villages is violent and the other nonviolent: The violent village has a murder rate five times as great as the nonviolent village. The villages have been on the same spots since at least the 1500s; they are highly similar with respect to religion and economics. More or less, the only explanation for their differing characters is the stability of culture: One way or another each village has acquired a characteristic level of violence, and that has stayed stable over time. This is a salient real-world example of the processes of norm transmission and preservation we described in earlier in this chapter. Similarly, with its modern modes of mass communication, the United States has become a very large village that preserves norms of aggressive behavior.

In this section we have described far too many reasons why people might engage in aggressive behavior. We turn now to aggression on a broader scale. We examine the forces that bring groups of people into conflict and interventions that might help alleviate some of those conflicts.

PUT YOURSELF TO THE TEST

➤ What does an evolutionary perspective suggest about the origins of aggressive behavior?

➤ Why do researchers believe that genetic and biological factors play a role in aggression?

➤ Why do situational forces such as frustration and provocation lead to aggressive behaviors?

➤ How do construals of the self affect the expression of aggression?

➤ Why do experiences of violent media affect aggressive thoughts and behaviors?

The Psychology of Conflict and Peace

We begin this final section on a somber note: In these early years of the 21st century, the globe is still littered with instances of catastrophic violence born from religious, racial, and cultural prejudice. What can be done? In the opening chapter of *Psychology and Life*, we characterized psychologists as a "rather optimistic group" because they believe that the theories and results of psychology can be used to better people's lives. In these final sections of *Psychology and Life,* we wish to carry through on that optimistic message. Although we will begin by documenting more of the psychological forces that can lead to devastating behaviors, that discussion will generate insights that can form the basis for constructive change. Our endpoint will be a discussion of *peace psychology,* a multidisciplinary effort to use social science knowledge to further the cause of world peace. This is the note of optimism on which we wish you to end your first experience of psychology.

We begin with perhaps the most classic study in the social psychological canon—research carried out by Stanley Milgram in an effort to understand some of the vast horrors of World War II.

◆ OBEDIENCE TO AUTHORITY

What made thousands of Nazis willing to follow Hitler's orders and send millions of Jews to the gas chambers? Did character defects lead them to carry out orders blindly? Did they have no moral values? How can we explain the willingness of cult members to take their own lives and the lives of others? How about you? Are there any conditions under which you would blindly obey an order from your religious leader to poison others and then commit suicide? Could you imagine being part of the massacre of hundreds of innocent citizens of the Vietnamese village of My Lai by U.S. soldiers who were following the orders of their superiors (Hersh, 1971; Opton, 1970, 1973)? Your answer—as ours used to be— is most likely, "No! What kind of person do you think I am?" After reading this section, we hope you may be more willing to answer, "Maybe. I don't know for sure." Depending on the power of the social forces operating, you might do what other human beings have done in those situations, however horrible and alien their actions may seem—to you and to them—outside that setting.

The most convincing demonstration of situational power over individual behavior was created by Stanley Milgram, a student of Solomon Asch. Milgram's research (1965, 1974) showed that the blind obedience of Nazis during World War II was less a product of dispositional characteristics (their unusual personality or German national character) than it was the outcome of situational forces that could engulf anyone. Milgram's program of obedience research is one of the most controversial because of its significant implications for real-world phenomena and the ethical issues it raises.

THE OBEDIENCE PARADIGM

To separate the variables of personality and situation, Milgram used a series of 19 separate controlled laboratory experiments involving more than 1,000 partici-

pants. Milgram's first experiments were conducted at Yale University, with male residents of New Haven and surrounding communities who received payment for their participation. In later variations, Milgram took his obedience laboratory away from the university. He set up a storefront research unit in Bridgeport, Connecticut, recruiting through newspaper ads a broad cross section of the population, varying widely in age, occupation, and education and including members of both sexes.

Milgram's basic experimental paradigm involved individual participants delivering a series of what they thought were extremely painful electric shocks to another person. These volunteers thought they were participating in a scientific study of memory and learning. They were led to believe that the educational purpose of the study was to discover how punishment affects memory, so that learning could be improved through the proper balance of reward and punishment. In their *social roles* as *teachers,* the participants were to punish each error made by someone playing the role of *learner.* The major rule they were told to follow was to increase the level of shock each time the learner made an error until the learning was errorless. The white-coated experimenter acted as the *legitimate authority* figure—he presented the rules, arranged for the assignment of roles (by a rigged drawing of lots), and ordered the teachers to do their jobs whenever they hesitated or dissented. The dependent variable was the final level of shock—on a shock machine that went up to 450 volts in small, 15-volt steps—that a teacher gave before refusing to continue to obey the authority.

THE TEST SITUATION

The study was staged to make a participant think that, by following orders, he or she was causing pain and suffering and perhaps even killing an innocent person. Each teacher had been given a sample shock of 45 volts to feel the amount of pain it caused. The learner was a pleasant, mild-mannered man, about 50 years old, who mentioned something about a heart condition but was willing to go along with the procedure. He was strapped into an "electric chair" in the next room and communicated with the teacher via an intercom. His task was to memorize pairs of words, giving the second word in a pair when he heard the first one. The learner soon began making errors—according to a prearranged schedule— and the teacher began shocking the learner. The protests of the victim rose with the shock level. At 75 volts, he began to moan and grunt; at 150 volts, he demanded to be released from the experiment; at 180 volts, he cried out that he could not stand the pain any longer. At 300 volts, he insisted that he would no longer take part in the experiment and must be freed. He yelled out about his heart condition and screamed. If a teacher hesitated or protested delivering the next shock, the experimenter said, "The experiment requires that you continue" or "You have no other choice, you *must* go on."

As you might imagine, the situation was stressful for the participants. Most participants complained and protested, repeatedly insisting they could not continue. Women participants often were in tears as they dissented. That the experimental situation produced considerable conflict in the participants is readily apparent from their protests:

- 180 volts delivered: "He can't stand it! I'm not going to kill that man in there! You hear him hollering? He's hollering. He can't stand it. What if something happens to him? . . . I mean, who is going to take the responsibility if anything happens to that gentleman?" [The experimenter accepts responsibility.] "All right."

- 195 volts delivered: "You see he's hollering. Hear that. Gee, I don't know." [The experimenter says, "The experiment requires that you go on."] "I know it does, sir, but I mean—huh—he don't know what he's in for. He's up to 195 volts" (Milgram, 1965, p. 67).

Even when there was only silence from the learner's room, the teacher was ordered to keep shocking him more and more strongly, all the way up to the button that was marked "Danger: Severe Shock XXX (450 volts)."

TO SHOCK OR NOT TO SHOCK?

When 40 psychiatrists were asked by Milgram to predict the performance of participants in this experiment, they estimated that most would not go beyond 150 volts (based on a description of the experiment). In their professional opinions, fewer than 4 percent of the participants would still be obedient at 300 volts, and only about 0.1 percent would continue all the way to 450 volts. The psychiatrists presumed that only those few individuals who were *abnormal* in some way, sadists who enjoyed inflicting pain on others, would blindly obey orders to continue up to the maximum shock.

The psychiatrists based their evaluations on presumed *dispositional* qualities of people who would engage in such abnormal behavior; they were, however, overlooking the power of this special situation to influence the thinking and actions of most people caught up in its social context. The remarkable and disturbing conclusion is just how wrong these experts were: *The majority of participants obeyed the authority fully.* No participant quit below 300 volts. Sixty-five percent delivered the maximum 450 volts to the learner. Note that most people *dissented* verbally, but the majority did not *disobey* behaviorally. From the point of view of the victim, that's a critical difference. If you were the victim, would it matter much that the participants said they didn't want to continue hurting you (they dissented), if they then shocked you repeatedly (they obeyed)?

The results of the Milgram studies were so unexpected that researchers worked hard to rule out alternative interpretations of the results. One possibility was that the participants did not really believe the "cover story" of the experiment. They might have believed that the victim was not really getting hurt. This alternative was ruled out by a study that made the effects of being obedient vivid, immediate, and direct for the participants. College students thought they were training a puppy by shocking him each time he made a mistake. The students actually saw the puppy jump and heard him squeal each time they pressed a button to activate an electrified grid beneath his paws. How many people would continue to shock the puppy and watch him suffer? Even under these vivid circumstances, three-fourths of all students delivered the maximum shock possible (Sheridan & King, 1972).

Milgram's obedience experiment: the "teacher" (participant) with experimenter (authority figure), the shock generator, and the "learner" (the experimenter's confederate). What aspects of the situation affected the likelihood that the teachers would continue to the maximum shock level?

Another alternative explanation for participants' behavior is that the effect is limited to the *demand characteristics* of the experimental situation. **Demand characteristics** are cues in an experimental setting that influence participants' perceptions of what is expected of them and systematically influence their behavior. Suppose Milgram's participants guessed that his results would be more interesting if they kept giving shocks—so they played along. Further research showed that obedience to authority does not rely on the demands of an unusual experimental setting. It can happen in any natural setting.

CLASSIC

PUTTING IDEAS TO THE TEST

Obedience in a Real-World Setting

A team of researchers performed the following field study to test the power of obedience in the natural setting of a hospital. A nurse (the participant) received a call from a staff doctor whom she had not met. He told her to administer some medication to a patient so that it could take effect by the time he arrived. He would sign the drug order after he got to the ward. The doctor ordered a dose of 20 milligrams of a drug called *Astroten.* The label on the container of Astroten stated that 5 milligrams was the usual dose and warned that the maximum dose was 10 milligrams.

Would a nurse administer an excessive dose of a drug on the basis of a telephone call from an unfamiliar person when doing so was contrary to standard medical practice? When this dilemma was *described* to 12 nurses, 10 *said* they would disobey. However, what the nurses *did* was another, by now familiar, story. When another group of them was actually in the situation, almost every nurse obeyed. Twenty-one of 22 had started to pour the medication (actually a harmless substance) before a physician researcher stopped them (Hofling et al., 1966).

These results suggest that Milgram's findings cannot be attributed solely to participants responding to the demands of the experiment.

WHY DO PEOPLE OBEY AUTHORITY?

Milgram's research suggests that, to understand why people obey authority, you need to look closely at the psychological forces at work in the situation. We saw earlier how often situational factors constrain behaviors; in Milgram's research, we see an especially vivid instance of that general principle. Milgram and other researchers manipulated a number of aspects of the experimental circumstances to demonstrate that the obedience effect is overwhelmingly due to situational variables and not personality variables. **Figure 17.7** displays the level of obedience found in different situations. Obedience is quite high, for example, when a peer first models obedience, when a participant acts as an *intermediary bystander* assisting another person who actually delivers the shock, or when the victim (the learner) is physically remote from the teacher. Obedience is quite low when the learner demands to be shocked, when two authorities give contradictory commands, or when the authority figure is the victim. These findings all point to the idea that the *situation,* and not differences among individual participants, largely controlled behavior.

Two reasons people obey authority in these situations can be traced to the effects of *normative* and *informational* sources of influence, which we discussed earlier: People want to be liked (normative influence), and they want to be right (informational influence). They tend to do what others are doing or requesting in order to be socially acceptable and approved. In addition, when in an ambiguous, novel situation—like the experimental situation—people rely on others for cues as to what is the appropriate and correct way to behave. They are more likely to do so when experts or credible communicators tell them what to do. A third factor in the Milgram paradigm is that participants were probably confused about *how* to *disobey;* nothing they said in dissent satisfied the authority. If they had a simple, direct way out of the situation—for example, by pressing a "quit" button—it is likely more would have disobeyed (Ross, 1988). Finally, obedience to authority in this experimental situation is part of an *ingrained habit* that is learned by children in many different settings—obey authority without question (Brown, 1986). This heuristic usually serves society well when authorities are legitimate and deserving of obedience. The problem is that the rule gets overapplied. Blind obedience to authority means obeying any and all authority figures simply because of their ascribed status, regardless of whether they are unjust or just in their requests and commands.

THE MILGRAM EXPERIMENTS AND YOU

What is the personal significance to you of this obedience research? What choices will you make when faced with moral dilemmas throughout your life? Take a moment to reflect on the types of obedience to authority situations that might arise in your day-to-day experience. Suppose you were a salesclerk. Would you cheat customers if your boss encouraged such behavior? Suppose you were a member of Congress. Would you vote along party lines, rather than vote your conscience?

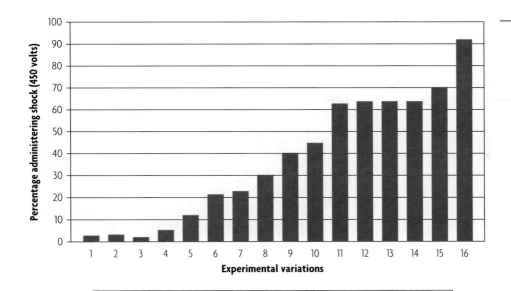

FIGURE 17.7

Obedience in Milgram's Experiments

The graph shows a profile of weak to strong obedience effects across Milgram's many experimental variations.

From *The Obedience Experiments*, A.G. Miller, "Obedience in Milgram's Experiments." Copyright © 1986 Praeger. Reproduced with permission of Greenwood Publishing Group, Inc., Westport, CT.

Percentage administering shock (450 volts)

Experimental variations

1. Learner demands to be shocked
2. Authority as victim—an ordinary man commanding
3. Two authorities—contradictory commands
4. Partcipants free to choose shock level
5. Two peers rebel
6. An ordinary man gives orders
7. Remote authority
8. Touch proximity
9. Proximity
10. Institutional context
11. Voice feedback
12. Remote victim
13. Women as participants
14. Two authorities—one as victim
15. The participant as bystander
16. A peer administers shock

Milgram's obedience research challenges the myth that evil lurks in the minds of evil people—the bad "they" who are different from the good "us" or "you," who would never do such things. Our purpose in recounting these findings is not to debase human nature, but to make clear that even normal, well-meaning individuals are subject to the potential for frailty in the face of strong situational and social forces.

Finally, we wish to add a note on heroism. Suppose the majority of people who are comparable to you yield to powerful group forces. In our view, if you are able to resist, that qualifies you as heroic. The hero is the person who can act mindfully, out of conscience, when others are all conforming, or who can take the moral high road when others are standing by silently, allowing evil deeds to go unchallenged. Perhaps your knowledge of situational forces that make possible the "banality of evil" can nudge you in the direction of heroism.

◆ THE PSYCHOLOGY OF GENOCIDE AND WAR

We have seen so far that the human species has a distinct predilection to obey authority. However, it takes more than an appreciation of this feature of human nature to explain why at some times and in some places one group undertakes the systematic destruction of another group—**genocide**—and why, far more often, one group goes to war or takes less formal aggressive action toward another group. In this section, we will analyze some of the historical and psychological forces

Would you risk your life to defy authority in defense of your beliefs, as this young Chinese student did in a student-led rebellion?

that lead populations to pursue the path of highly organized aggression.

Psychologist **Ervin Staub** (1989, 2000) has studied campaigns of genocide throughout history and has offered an account of the sets of cultural and psychological forces that make campaigns of terror possible:

- The starting point is often severely difficult life conditions for members of a society—harsh economic circumstances, political upheaval, and so on.

- Under these conditions of difficulty, people will intensify the ordinary impulse to define in-groups and out-groups that we described in Chapter 16. In this case, out-groups become *scapegoats* for the ills of society. In many instances, as in Nazi Germany, the scapegoating becomes part of the cultural or political ideology shared by the nation's leaders and citizens.

- Because the scapegoat group is blamed for society's ills, it becomes easy to justify violence against them. These incidents of violence lead to *just world thinking* (Lerner, 1980): Perpetrators and bystanders come to believe—because we live in a just world—that the victims must have done something to bring the violence upon themselves. Thus, Germans of the Nazi era came to believe that the Jews deserved their fate because of the imagined harm they had done to the German state.

- The violence also comes to justify itself—to stop the violence would mean to admit that it had been wrong to begin with. Furthermore, when regimes carry out organized violence without sanctions from other nations, the world community's passivity is taken as evidence of the justice of the regime's actions. This was the case with the "ethnic cleansing" massacres that followed the dissolution of Yugoslavia in 1991—although images of the massacres were widely transmitted, the world community took no action for several years.

Consider the case of Cambodia (Hinton, 1996). The situation began with difficult life conditions: Starting in the late 1960s, the country suffered economic hardships as well as bombings by the United States as war spread to Cambodia from its neighbor Vietnam. A new regime began to identify scapegoats, and the scapegoats became the targets of extreme violence: The Communists who captured the city of Phnom Penh in 1975 identified a number of ideological enemies who needed to be eliminated to put a new society into place. Former military and political leaders were arrested and often executed. The definition of "class enemies" swiftly became broader, however, as teachers, students, bureaucrats, and professionals were denounced as potential traitors. The killing gathered momentum because it was

A Cambodian man tends skulls from the "killing fields." What sequence of events may create a context for mass murders?

in service to such a powerful ideology and a clearly defined goal: The country must be rid of its internal enemies. Finally, as has most often been the case, the world community did not intervene.

CONCEPTS AND IMAGES OF THE "ENEMY"

We have suggested that an important way station on the path to genocide is scapegoating. We can see the same process at work, even when the endpoint is not systematic murder. Consider the attitudes of young adults in the former East Germany after the collapse of the socialist system. In national surveys, individuals aged 15 to 20 revealed themselves to hold, on average, quite negative attitudes toward groups such as Poles and Turks. The major reason for these negative attitudes appears to be the threat of economic and cultural competition (Watts, 1996). That is, the Poles and Turks are suspected of contributing to the economic hardship of the transition from communism to democracy by taking jobs and income away from Germans. This perception of economic threat fits the model we described earlier: Prejudice and willingness to discriminate do not arise spontaneously; they require societal circumstances that foster the belief that an "enemy" is consuming scarce resources. This sets the context for violence.

When regimes scapegoat the "enemy," they often also *dehumanize* them—they attempt to convince people to conceive of the group as nonhuman objects to be hated and destroyed. This process of dehumanization is also particularly critical to the conduct of war. Although most cultures oppose individual aggression as a crime, nations train millions of soldiers to kill. The challenge for leaders is to convert the act of murder into patriotism (Harle, 2000). Part of this mass social influence involves dehumanizing the soldiers of the other side

<www.ablongman.com/gerrig17e>

into "the enemy." This dehumanization is accomplished by political rhetoric and by the media, in their vivid depictions of the enemy. According to army veterans, a soldier's most important weapon in war is not a gun but this internalized view of the hated "enemy" (see **Figure 17.8**). Thus, young soldiers become psychologically programmed to be wartime killers by these distorted images of anyone their government decides to label as the enemy.

In many cases, the images will not be literal representations but rather the mental images that politicians invoke to rally populations and send troops off to war. The most vivid example of this process in recent U.S. history was the regularity with which Saddam Hussein was likened to Adolph Hitler in the context of the 1990 Gulf War (Voss et al., 1992). By establishing this mapping in the public's mind, then President George Bush and other political leaders were able to call forth Americans' vast stores of anti-Hitler sentiment. Research suggests that such references to history are effective to persuade some, but not all, people.

PUTTING IDEAS TO THE TEST

The Impact of Lessons from History

Participants in a study were asked to read an account of a conflict between two fictitious countries, Afslandia and Bagumba, about disputed territory (Beer et al., 1987; Bourne et al., 2003). Some participants also read brief texts that put the conflict in a historical context. One group read a text that described the human suffering of soldiers during World War I. A second group read a text that described the process of appeasement that enabled Hitler to gain power in World War II. The control group just read the basic text describing Afslandia and Bagumba. After reading their materials, all three groups selected what they believed to be appropriate reactions from a set that varied in their conflict level from 1 (for example, "Afslandia accepts the Bagumban head of state as its own head of state") to 15 (for example, "Afslandia firebombs 5 of Bagumba's major cities"). The researchers predicted that the historical material would have a different impact on participants' judgments depending on their personality characteristics. For that reason, participants also gave self-reports that indicated whether they were relatively high in dominance ("dominant, assertive, aggressive, stubborn, competitive, bossy") versus relatively low in dominance ("submissive, humble, mild, easily led, accommodating"). **Figure 17.9** shows that historical material had opposite effects on people who were more or less dominant. High dominant individuals tended to recommend that the nations react at higher levels of conflict whereas low dominant individuals tended to recommend lower levels of conflict.

Note that in control circumstances—without the historical contexts—the high and low dominance groups were more or less the same in their responses. It was the contemplation of the lessons of history that drove their responses apart. The historical context, apparently, helped participants develop their own inclinations toward aggression or submission.

WHY WILL PEOPLE GO TO WAR?

When countries' leaders contemplate going to war, they do so with virtually certain knowledge that there will be

This is the Enemy

FIGURE 17.8

Faces of the Enemy

How does military psychology convert killing into patriotism? Note how in each of these caricatures the designated enemy is given monstrous and dehumanized characteristics.

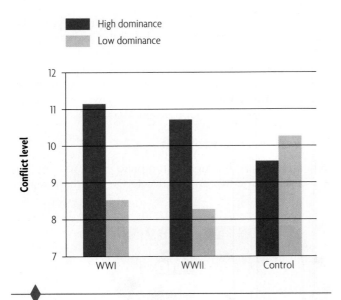

High dominance
Low dominance

FIGURE 17.9

Recommendations for Responses to Conflicts

Participants were asked to recommend how two fictitious countries should react to a dispute over territory. Depending on the participants' personalities with respect to the dimension of dominance, material that provided a historical context led participants to recommend reactions with either higher or lower levels of conflict.

negative consequences. Modern warfare no longer spares civilians—one of the great innovations of World War II was to target civilian populations to break "the will of the people." Even when a war is fought at great distance, as the Gulf War was for citizens of the United States, wars inevitably produce casualties on both sides. How does a country or other group determine that a cause is of sufficient importance that the loss of life is warranted? Most often this type of question is answered in a history class: Countries go to war, we have learned, to protect their territory, their people, or their economic interests. In this section, however, we briefly discuss some of the more psychological factors that lead individuals to choose to participate in war.

We can ask, for example, why it is that people will sacrifice their lives for their nations. That may be the ultimate act of altruism—to give up one's life in service of some cause. Recall from earlier in the chapter that the evolutionary perspective identifies the desire to protect family members (that is, to preserve one's genes) as one important root of altruism. Some researchers have suggested that people have internalized an association between "family" and "nation" (Stern, 1995): We talk about our "motherland" or "fatherland" and being "sons" or "daughters" of our country. Is this association sufficient to explain why people will die for their countries? Do

people who march off to war construct a "social reality" in which they believe that, ultimately, they are protecting the interests of their literal family? You can see why this is an important question for psychologists to address.

We can acquire additional insight into psychological aspects of war making by examining the circumstances that prompted the Serbians to undertake the aggressive acts in 1992 that led to sustained war in Bosnia (White, 1996). The Serbians, apparently, feared that they would become a persecuted minority after the disintegration of Yugoslavia in 1991. We have already seen how reasonable a fear this may be for a minority in times of strife. Here is the testimony of one Bosnian Serb policeman, recorded by a British journalist (Glenny, 1994; cited in White, 1996, p. 111):

> *He confirmed the countless observations I had made while talking with local fighters of all nationalities—he was not a man of evil. On the contrary, he explained how he found it very difficult to shoot at the other side of the village, because he knew everybody who lived there. But the war had somehow arrived and he had to defend his home. The man was confused and upset by events, but he now perceived the Green Berets [Muslims] and Ustashas [Croats] as a real threat to his family.*
>
> *"We cannot let them form an Islamic state here," he said with genuine passion. "Are you sure they want to?" I asked him. "Of course they want to. I don't understand why you people outside don't see that we are fighting for Europe against a foreign religion."*

In the context of this anticipated persecution, it was easy for Serbians to think of themselves as innocent even while they began to undertake aggressive action. From their psychological standpoint, they weren't the aggressors but the victims. As the conflict unfolded, Serbian leaders such as Slobodan Milosevic fanned the Serbian people's "persecution mania" to maintain the belief that they were right to make war. In the long run, the Serbians turned to massacres—"ethnic cleansing"—to remove all possible "persecutors" from their midst. We see how willing people are to go to war to protect themselves from enemies real, imagined, or created by their leaders.

What this analysis suggests is that, at least in modern times, countries rarely go to war with the goal of domination or conquest. Rather, countries come to believe—even when the rest of the world characterizes them as aggressors—that they are protecting interests that are important to their survival and identity. Countries, of course, are made of up of millions of individuals. Enough of those individuals must sufficiently internalize the values at stake to be willing to sacrifice their lives. Whatever the "real" causes of war revealed

<www.ablongman.com/gerrig17e>

by historical analysis, it is these individual, psychological forces that prompt people to endure war's hardships.

In this section so far, we have seen some of the ways in which psychological forces create the context that makes war—and atrocities committed in the context of wars—seem entirely reasonable. As the last topic of *Psychology and Life,* we turn to the efforts *peace psychologists* make to use psychological forces to promote peaceful coexistence.

◆ PEACE PSYCHOLOGY

It is time now to turn these analyses around, to see how we can harness social psychology to wage peace instead of war. Psychology is uniquely equipped to study the question of how to help resolve the dilemmas of national and international disharmony. The American Psychological Association includes the division of **peace psychology.** The division works to promote peace within nations, communities, and families. It encourages research, education, and training on issues concerning the causes, consequences, and prevention of violence and destructive conflict. We provide two examples of how applications of psychology can serve these goals.

ANALYZING FORMS OF LEADERSHIP AND GOVERNMENT

Some of the earliest research on what we now call *peace psychology* was inspired by world historical events culminating in World War II. Social psychologists sought to understand how leaders and forms of government emerge to exert considerable power on group behavior. What psychological constraints explain the emergence of Adolf Hitler in Germany and Benito Mussolini in Italy? These leaders forged individuals into mindless masses with unquestioning loyalty to fascist ideologies. Their authoritarian regimes threatened democracies and freedom everywhere. Modern social psychology developed out of this crucible of fear, prejudice, and war. Early social psychologists focused on understanding the nature of the *authoritarian personality* behind the fascist mentality (Adorno et al., 1950), the effects of propaganda and persuasive communications (Hovland et al., 1949), and the impact of group atmosphere and leadership styles on group members (Lewin et al., 1939).

The pioneering figure in social psychology was **Kurt Lewin,** a German refugee who escaped Nazi oppression. Lewin could not help but wonder how his nation could succumb totally to the tyranny of an autocratic, fascist dictator. He witnessed the spectacle of rallies of tens of thousands of people shouting allegiance to their *Führer.* This was a frightening testimony to the dynamic power of groups to transform the minds and actions of individuals and the power of an individual to affect the masses. Lewin investigated **group dynamics**—the ways in which leaders directly influenced their followers and the ways in which group processes changed the behavior of individuals.

In 1939, Lewin and his colleagues designed an experiment to investigate the effects of different leadership styles on group function. They wanted to find out if people are happier or more productive under autocratic or under democratic leadership. To assess the effects of different leadership styles, the researchers created three experimental groups, gave them different types of leaders, and observed the groups in action. The participants were four small groups of 10-year-old boys, who met after school. The group leaders were men trained to play each of the three leadership styles as they rotated from one to another group. When they acted as *autocratic leaders,* the men were to make all decisions and work assignments but not participate in the group activity. As *democratic leaders,* they were to encourage and assist group decision making and planning. Finally, when they acted as *laissez-faire leaders,* their job was to allow complete freedom with little leader participation.

CLASSIC
PUTTING IDEAS TO THE TEST

The Effects of Leadership Style

The results of this experiment suggested a number of generalizations. First, *autocratic* leaders produced a mixed bag of effects on their followers—some positive and some quite negative. At times, the boys worked very hard, but typically only when the leader—acting as boss—was watching them. What most characterized the boys in the autocratic groups was their high level of aggression. These boys showed up to *30 times more hostility* when under autocratic leaders than they did under the other types of leaders. They demanded more attention, were more likely to destroy their own property, and showed more scapegoating behavior—using weaker individuals as displaced targets for their frustration and anger.

As for the *laissez-faire groups,* not much good resulted. They were the most inefficient of all, doing the least amount of work and of the poorest quality. In the absence of any social structure, they simply fooled around. However, when the same groups were *democratically run,* members worked the most steadily and were most efficient. The boys showed the highest levels of interest, motivation, and originality under democratic leadership. When discontent arose, it was likely to be openly expressed. Almost all the boys preferred the democratic group to the others. Democracy promoted more group loyalty and friendliness. There were more mutual praise, more friendly remarks, more sharing, and, overall, more playfulness (Lewin et al., 1939).

Democracy proved superior psychologically to the other forms of group atmosphere, as well as more productive. Democratic leaders also generated the healthiest reactions from group members, while autocratic-leader groups generated the most destructive individual reactions.

What was true in Lewin's classroom seems also to be true in the real world. Consider the finding that authoritarian leadership leads to increased hostility. We can find a real-world correlate to that finding in analyses that relate type of government to instances of *democide*—genocide and other forms of mass murder (Rummel, 1994). If you examine **Figure 17.10,** you see that totalitarian governments—such as Communist Russia and China—have been responsible for vast numbers of deaths; authoritarian governments—such as Idi Amin's reign in Uganda—have been responsible for fewer deaths, but democratic governments, though certainly not innocent of bloodshed, have produced fewest of all. Figure 17.10 also provides a comparison to the number of deaths caused by battles in war. You should note that the great majority of deaths caused by authoritarian and totalitarian regimes were victims not of war but of other programs of mass murder. Ideological considerations aside, the world suffers least when democratic systems of government are in place to ensure that power cannot be used according to the whims of a small elite, with deadly consequences.

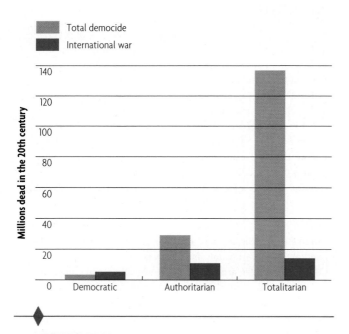

FIGURE 17.10

Types of Regimes and Democide

Totalitarian regimes are most likely to commit democide (genocide and other forms of mass murder). The comparison to war dead demonstrates that vastly more people are murdered by governments outside the context of war.

What psychological measures might allow Northern Ireland to continue its progress toward peace?

The overall conclusion we can draw from research on forms of leadership is that democracy works best. We derive that insight from research on groups quite small (groups of young boys) and quite large (whole countries). You should also apply this insight to the smallest and largest groups in your own life!

FOSTERING CONTACT TO FACILITATE CONFLICT RESOLUTION

Many of the antagonisms that give rise to conflict and violence are quite ancient. The Serbs who waged war in Bosnia, for example, traced their fear of persecution back to the Battle of Kosovo Field in 1389. What can be done in these situations? The main approach peace psychologists take is the same one we described for healing other types of prejudices: People must be brought together in cooperative settings that can foster mutual trust and shared goals.

Such an approach is now being attempted, for example, in Northern Ireland. In an attempt to begin a healing process between Catholics and Protestants, the United Kingdom began in 1989 to fund Community Relations programs intended "to develop cross-community contact and cooperation; to promote greater mutual understanding; [and] to increase respect for other cultural traditions" (Knox, 1994, p. 600). Not every political unit in Northern Ireland undertook a community relations program, giving researchers the opportunity to make comparisons to assess the programs' effects. These comparisons indicate at least limited progress: After four years, the programs had succeeded, for example, in reducing participants' estimates of prejudice against Catholics (Knox, 1994). Other attempts to heal Northern Ireland are being made among schoolchildren (Cairns et al., 1995). Most children in this troubled region attend schools that are strictly segregated by religion. However, in the past 20 years, schools have been founded that bring Protestant and Catholic students and faculty together. These changes in schooling have yet to provide definitive data on whether cross-community friendships can change political values. However, the important suggestion from both the community and school interventions is that governments can—and perhaps should—expend their resources to create situations of mutual contact in service of shared goals (Cairns & Darby, 1998).

We turn to another of the world's major trouble spots, the Middle East, to describe the program of Israeli–Palestinian workshops conducted by psychologist **Herbert Kelman** (1997, 1999) and his colleagues. Over several years, Kelman's group has invited Palestinians and Israelis to participate in meetings in which they engaged in *interactive problem solving* with respect to the ongoing conflicts in their regions, such as the fate of settlements in occupied territories. The participants in this process were promised privacy and confidentiality as well as open and analytical discussion. They were encouraged to have appropriate expectations: No pressure was created to produce agreement among all the participants. Third-party members were present to facilitate conversation but did not mediate between the parties.

Kelman's group initiated these workshops at a time when it was still nearly unheard of for Palestinians and Israelis to meet at all. The workshops presented environments in which participants could have opportunities for direct interaction that could potentially foster mutual understanding. Moreover, graduates of the workshop could bring the insights they had gained into the broader, real-world political arena—along with a first approximation of the types of relationships and dialogue that are required for progress toward peace.

The violence in both Northern Ireland and the Middle East has, unfortunately, not come to an end. There are militant groups in each region with political, economic, and religious agendas that encourage violence and segregation over peace and integration. This continuing reality reminds us that change often comes in small increments. Nations and groups modify their responses only when education toward peace takes firm hold among their people (Staub, 2003). Insights from psychological research have helped to produce some concrete programs for that education toward peace. The results are sufficiently important and encouraging to keep psychologists—that "rather optimistic group"—diligently at work.

A Personal Endnote

We have come to the end of our journey through *Psychology and Life*. As you think back, we hope you will realize just how much you have learned on the way. Yet we have barely scratched the surface of the excitement and challenges that await the student of psychology. We hope you will pursue your interest in psychology and that you may even go on to contribute to this dynamic enterprise as a scientific researcher or a clinical practitioner or by applying psychological knowledge to the solution of social and personal problems.

Playwright Tom Stoppard reminds us that "every exit is an entry somewhere else." We'd like to believe that the entry into the next phase of your life will be facilitated by what you have learned from *Psychology and Life* and from your introductory psychology course. In that next journey, may you infuse new life into the psychology of human endeavors while strengthening the connections among all the people you encounter.

Richard Gerrig

Phil Zimbardo

Recapping Main Points

THE POWER OF THE SITUATION

- Human thought and action are affected by situational influences.
- Being assigned to play a social role, even in artificial settings, can cause individuals to act contrary to their beliefs, values, and dispositions.
- Social norms shape the attitudes and behaviors of group members.
- Classic research by Sherif and Asch illustrated the informational and normative forces that lead to conformity.
- Minority influence may arise as a consequence of informational influence.

ALTRUISM AND PROSOCIAL BEHAVIOR

- Researchers have tried to explain why people engage in prosocial behaviors, particularly altruistic behaviors that do not serve their own interests.
- Evolutionary explanations focus on kinship and reciprocity.
- People also engage in prosocial behaviors to serve their self-interest, to benefit particular communities, and to uphold social principles.
- Bystander intervention studies show that situations largely determine who is likely or unlikely to help in emergencies.

AGGRESSION

- From an evolutionary perspective, aggressive behaviors arose because people needed to ensure their ability to preserve their genes.
- Individual differences in aggressive behavior are reflected both in genetic analyses and in brain and hormone function.

- Different personality profiles predict propensities toward either impulsive or instrumental aggression.
- Although there are inhibitions to aggressive behavior, situations arise that prompt people to respond aggressively.
- Frustration can lead to aggression; ongoing irritation will escalate the level of aggression.
- Different cultures provide different norms for aggressive behavior depending, in part, on cultural construals of the self.

THE PSYCHOLOGY OF CONFLICT AND PEACE

- Milgram's studies on obedience are a powerful testimony to the influence of the situational factors that can lead ordinary people to sanction and participate in organized aggression.
- Some of the same processes that foster prejudice can, in the long run, lead to mass murder and genocide.
- Leaders create images of the enemy as less than human.
- People sacrifice themselves for their country in response to fears and threats to their families and communities.
- Peace psychologists look for ways to help resolve competition and hostilities among nations.
- Democratic societies are least likely to commit mass murder.
- Programs fostering interaction between traditional "enemies" may help to prepare the way for peace.

KEY TERMS

aggression (p. 587)

altruism (p. 582)

bystander intervention (p. 585)

conformity (p. 576)

demand characteristics (p. 598)

diffusion of responsibility (p. 586)

frustration-aggression hypothesis (p. 590)

genocide (p. 599)

group dynamics (p. 603)

group polarization (p. 580)

groupthink (p. 580)

impulsive aggression (p. 589)

informational influence (p. 576)

instrumental aggression (p. 589)

norm crystallization (p. 577)

normative influence (p. 576)

peace psychology (p. 603)

prosocial behaviors (p. 582)

reciprocal altruism (p. 583)

rules (p. 574)

social norms (p. 576)

social role (p. 574)

Glossary

Abnormal psychology The area of psychological investigation concerned with understanding the nature of individual pathologies of mind, mood, and behavior.

Absolute threshold The minimum amount of physical energy needed to produce a reliable sensory experience; operationally defines as the stimulus level at which a sensory signal is detected half the time.

Accommodation 1. The process by which the ciliary muscles change the thickness of the lens of the eye to permit variable focusing on near and distant objects. 2. According to Piaget, the process of restructuring or modifying cognitive structures so that new information can fit into them more easily; this process works in tandem with assimilation.

Acquisition The stage in a classical conditioning experiment during which the conditioned response is first elicited by the conditioned stimulus.

Action potential The nerve impulse activated in a neuron that travels down the axon and causes neurotransmitters to be released into a synapse.

Acute stress A transient state of arousal with typically clear onset and offset patterns.

Addiction A condition in which the body requires a drug in order to function without physical and psychological reactions to its absence; often the outcome of tolerance and dependence.

Ageism Prejudice against older people, similar to racism and sexism in its negative stereotypes.

Aggression Behaviors that cause psychological or physical harm to another individual.

Agoraphobia An extreme fear of being in public places or open spaces from which escape may be difficult or embarrassing.

AIDS Acronym for acquired immune deficiency syndrome, a syndrome caused by a virus that damages the immune system and weakens the body's ability to fight infection.

Algorithm A step-by-step procedure that always provides the right answer for a particular type of problem.

All-or-none law The rule that the size of the action potential is unaffected by increases in the intensity of stimulation beyond the threshold level.

Altruism Prosocial behaviors a person carries out without considering his or her own safety or interests.

Alzheimer's disease A chronic organic brain syndrome characterized by gradual loss of memory, decline in intellectual ability, and deterioration of personality.

Amacrine cells Cells that integrate information across the retina; rather than sending signals toward the brain, amacrine cells link bipolar cells to other bipolar cells and ganglion cells to other ganglion cells.

Ambiguity Property of perceptual object that may have been more than one interpretation.

Amnesia A failure of memory caused by physical injury, disease, drug use, or psychological trauma.

Amygdala The part of the limbic system that control emotion, aggression, and the formation of emotional memory.

Analytic psychology A branch of psychology that views the person as a constellation of compensatory internal forces in a dynamic balance.

Anchoring heuristic An insufficient adjustment up or down from an original starting value when judging the probable value of some event or outcome.

Animal cognition The cognitive capabilities of nonhuman animals; researchers trace the development of cognitive capabilities across specifies and the continuity of capabilities from nonhuman to human animals.

Anorexia nervosa An eating disorder in which an individual weighs less than 85 percent of her or his expected weight but still expresses intense fear of becoming fat.

Anticipatory coping Efforts made in advance of a potentially stressful event to overcome, reduce, or tolerate the imbalance between perceived demands and available resources.

Anxiety An intense emotional response caused by the preconscious recognition that a repressed conflict id about to emerge into consciousness.

Anxiety disorders Mental disorders marked by psychological arousal, feeling of tension, and intense apprehension without apparent reason.

Archetype A universal, inherited, primitive, and symbolic representation of a particular experience or object.

Assimilation According to Piaget, the process whereby new cognitive elements.

Association cortex The parts of the cerebral cortex in which many high-level brain processes occur.

Attachment Emotional relationship between a child and the regular caregiver.

Attention A state of focused awareness on a subset of the available perceptual information.

Attitude The learned, relatively stable tendency to respond to people, concepts, and events in an evaluative way.

Attributions Judgments about the causes of outcomes.

Attribution theory A social-cognitive approach to describing the ways the social perceiver uses information to generate causal explanations.

Audience design The process of shaping a message depending on the audience for which it is intended.

Auditory cortex The area of the temporal lobes that receives and processes auditory information.

Auditory nerve The nerve that carries impulses form the cochlea to the cochlear nucleus of the brain.

Automatic processes Processes that do not require attention; they can often be performed along with other tasks without interference.

Autonomic nervous system (ANS) The subdivision of the peripheral nervous system that controls the body's involuntary motor responses by connecting the sensory receptors to the central nervous system (CNS) and the CNS to the smooth muscle, cardiac muscle, and glands.

Availability heurisitic A judgment based on the information readily available in memory.

Aversion therapy A type of behavioral therapy used to treat individuals attracted to harmful stimuli; an attractive stimulus is paired with a noxious stimulus in order to elicit a negative reaction to the target stimulus.

Axon The extended fiber of a neuron through which nerve impulses travel from the soma to the terminal buttons.

Basic level The level of categorization that can be retrieved from memory most quickly and used most efficiently.

Basilar membrane A membrane in the cochlea that, when set into motion, stimulates hair cells that produce the neural effects of auditory stimulation.

Behavior The actions by which an organism adjusts to its environment.

Behavior analysis The area of psychology that focuses on the environmental determinants of learning and behavior.

<www.ablongman.com/gerrig17e>

Behavior data Observational reports about the behavior of organisms and the conditions under which the behavior occurs or changes.

Behavior modification The systematic use of principles of learning to increase the frequency of desired behaviors and/or decrease the frequency of problem behaviors.

Behavior therapy See behavior modification.

Behavioral confirmation The process by which people behave in ways that elicit from others specific expected reactions and then use those reactions to confirm their beliefs.

Behavioral measures Overt actions and reactions that are observed and recorded, exclusive of self-reported behavior.

Behavioral neuroscience A multidisciplinary field that attempts to understand the brain processes that underlie behavior.

Behavioral rehearsal Procedures used to establish and strengthen basic skills; as used in social-skills training programs, requires the client to rehears a desirable behavior sequence mentally.

Behaviorism A scientific approach that limits the study of psychology to measurable or observable behavior.

Behaviorist perspective The psychological perspective primarily concerned with observable behavior that can be objectively recorded and with the relationships of observable behavior to environmental stimuli.

Belief-bias effect A situation that occurs when a person's prior knowledge, attitudes, or values distort the reasoning process by influencing the person to accept invalid arguments.

Between-subjects design A research design in which different groups of participants are randomly assigned to experimental conditions or to control conditions.

Biofeedback A self-regulatory technique by which an individual acquires voluntary control over nonconscious biological processes.

Biological constraints on learning Any limitations on an organism's capacity to learn that are caused by the inherited sensory, response, or cognitive capabilities of members of a given species.

Biological perspective The approach to identifying causes of behavior that focuses on the functioning of the genes, the brain, the nervous system, and the endocrine system.

Biomedical therapies Treatments for psychological disorders that alter brain functioning with chemical or physical interventions such as drug therapy, surgery, or electroconvulsing therapy.

Biopsychosocial model A model of health and illness that suggests that links among the nervous system, the immune system, behavioral styles, cognitive processing, and environmental domains of health.

Bipolar cells Nerve cells in the visual system that combine impulses from many receptors and transmit the results to ganglion cells.

Bipolar disorder A mood disorder characterized by alternating periods of depression and mania.

Bottom-up processing Perceptual analyses based on the sensory data available in the environment; results of analysis are passed upward toward more abstract representations.

Brain stem The brain structure that regulates the body's basic life processes.

Brightness The dimension of color space that captures the intensity of light.

Broca's area The region of the brain that translates thoughts into speech or signs.

Bulimia nervosa An eating disorder characterized by binge eating followed by measures to purge the body of excess calories.

Bystander intervention Willingness to assist a person in need of help.

Cannon–Bard theory of emotion A theory stating that an emotional stimulus produces two co-occurring reactions—arousal and experience of emotion—that do not cause each other.

Case study Intensive observation of a particular individual or small group of individuals.

Catharsis The process of expressing strongly felt but usually repressed emotions.

Central nervous system (CNS) The part of the nervous system consisting of the brain and spinal cord.

Centration A thought pattern common during the beginning of the preoperational stage of cognitive development; characterized by the child's inability to take more than one perceptual factor into account at the same time.

Cerebellum The region of the brain attached to the brain stem that controls motor coordination, posture, and balance as well as the ability to learn control of body movements.

Cerebral cortex The outer surface of the cerebrum.

Cerebral hemispheres The two halves of the cerebrum, connected by the corpus callosum.

Cerebrum The region of the brain that regulates higher cognitive and emotional functions.

Child-directed speech A special form of speech with an exaggerate and high-pitched intonation that adults use to speak to infants and young children.

Chronic stress A continuous state of arousal in which an individual perceives demands as greater than the inner and outer resources available for dealing with them.

Chronological age The number of months or years since an individual's birth.

Chunking The process of taking single items of information and recoding them on the basis of similarity or some other organizing principle.

Circadian rhythm A consistent pattern of cyclical body activities, usually lasting 24 to 25 hours and determined by an internal biological clock.

Classical conditioning A type of learning in which a behavior (conditioned response) comes to be elicited by a stimulus (conditioned stimulus) that has acquired its power through an association with a biologically significant stimulus (unconditioned stimulus).

Client The term used by clinicians who think of psychological disorder as problems in living, and not as mental illnesses, to describe those being treated.

Client-centered therapy A humanistic approach to treatment that emphasizes the healthy psychological growth of the individual based on the assumption that all people share the basic tendency of human nature toward self-actualization.

Clinical ecology A field of psychology that related disorders such as anxiety and depression to environmental irritants and sources of trauma.

Clinical psychologist An individual who has earned a doctorate in psychology and whose training is in the assessment and treatment of psychological problems.

Clinical social worker A mental health professional whose specialized training prepares him or her to consider the social context of people's problems.

Cochlea The primary organ of hearing; a fluid-filled coiled tube located in the inner ear.

Cognition Processes of knowing, including attending, remembering, and reasoning; also the content of the processes, such as concepts and memories.

Cognitive appraisal theory of emotion A theory stating that the experience of emotion is the joint effect of physiological arousal and cognitive appraisal, which serves to determine how an ambiguous inner state of arousal will be labeled.

Cognitive behavior modification A therapeutic approach that combines the cognitive emphasis on the role of thoughts and attitudes influencing motivations and response with the behavioral emphasis on changing performance through modification of reinforcement contingencies.

Cognitive development The development of processes if knowing, including imagining, perceiving, reasoning, and problem solving.

Cognitive dissonance The theory that the tension-producing effects of incongruous cognitions motivate individuals to reduce such tension.

Cognitive map A mental representation of physical space.

Cognitive neuroscience A multidisciplinary field that attempts to understand the brain processes that underlie higher cognitive functions in humans.

Cognitive perspective The perspective on psychology that stresses human thought and the processes of knowing, such as attending, thinking, remembering, expecting, solving problems, fantasizing, and consciousness.

Cognitive processes Higher mental processes, such as perception, memory, language, problem solving, and abstract thinking.

Cognitive psychology The study of higher mental processes such as attention, language use, memory, perception, problem solving, and thinking.

Cognitive science The interdisciplinary field of study of the approach systems and processes that manipulate information.

Cognitive therapy A type of psychotherapeutic treatment that attempts to change feeling and behaviors by changing the way a client thinks about or perceived significant life experiences.

Collective unconscious The part of an individual's unconscious that is inherited, evolutionarily developed, and common to all members of the species.

Comorbidity The experience of more than one disorder at the same time.

Compliance A change in behavior consistent with a communication source's direct requests.

Complementary colors Colors opposite each other on the color circle; when additively mixed, they create the sensation of white light.

Concepts Mental representations of kinds or categories of items and ideas.

Conditioned reinforcers In classical conditioning, formerly neutral stimuli that have become reinforcers.

Conditioned response (CR) In classical conditioning, a response elicited by some previously neutral stimulus that occurs as a result of pairing the neutral stimulus with an unconditioned stimulus.

Conditioned stimulus (CS) In classical conditioning, a previously neutral stimulus that comes to elicit a conditioned response.

Conditioning The ways in which events, stimuli, and behavior become associated with one another.

Cones Photoreceptors concentrated in the center of the retina that are responsible for visual experience under normal viewing conditions for all experiences of color.

Conformity The tendency for people to adopt the behaviors, attitudes, and values of other members of a reference group.

Confounding variable A stimulus other than the variable an experimenter explicitly introduces into a research setting that affects a participant's behavior.

Consciousness A state of awareness of internal events and the external environment.

Conservation According to Piaget, the understanding that physical properties do not change when nothing is added or taken away, even though appearances may change.

Consistency paradox The observation that personality ratings across time and among different observers are consistent, while behavior ratings across situations are not consistent.

Contact comfort Comfort derived from an infant's physical contact with the mother or caregiver.

Contact hypothesis The prediction that contact between groups will reduce prejudice only if the contact includes features such as cooperation toward shared goals.

Contextual distinctiveness The assumption that the serial position effect can be altered by the context and the distinctiveness of the experience being recalled.

Contingency management A general treatment strategy involving changing behavior by modifying its consequences.

Controlled processes Processes that require attention; it is often difficult to carry out more than one controlled process at a time.

Convergence The degree to which the eyes turn inward to fixate on an object.

Coping The proves of dealing with internal or external demands that are perceived to be threatening or overwhelming.

Corpus callosum The mass of nerve fibers connecting the two hemispheres of the cerebrum.

Correlational coefficient (r) A statistic that indicates the degree of relationship between two variables.

Correlational methods Research methodologies that determine to what extent two variables, traits, or attributes are related.

Counseling psychologist Psychologist who specializes in providing guidance in areas such as vocational selections, school problems, drug abuse, and marital conflict.

Counterconditioning A technique used in therapy to substitute a new response for a maladaptive one by means of conditioning procedures.

Countertransference Circumstances in which a psychoanalyst develops personal feelings about a client because of perceived similarity of the client to significant people in the therapist's life.

Covariation principle A theory that suggests that people attribute a behavior to a causal factor if that factor was present whenever the behavior occurred but was absent whenever it did occur.

Creativity The ability to generate ideas or products that are both novel and appropriate to the circumstances.

Criterion validity The degree to which test scores indicate a result on a specific measure that is consistent with some other criterion of the characteristic being assessed; also known as predictive validity.

Cross-sectional design A research method in which groups of participants of different chronological ages are observed and compared at a given time.

Crystallized intelligence The facet of intelligence involving the knowledge a person has already acquired and the ability to access that knowledge; measures by vocabulary, arithmetic, and general information tests.

Cutaneous senses The skin senses that register sensations or pressure, warmth, and cold.

Dark adaptation The gradual improvement of the eyes' sensitivity after a shift in illumination from light to near darkness.

Date rape Unwanted sexual violation by social acquaintance in the context of a consensual dating situation.

Daytime sleepiness The experience of excessive sleepiness during daytime activities; the major complaint of patients evaluated at sleep disorder centers.

Debriefing A procedure conducted at the end of an experiment in which the researcher provides the participant with as much information about the study as possible and makes sure that no participant leaves feeling confused, upset, or embarrassed.

Decision aversion The tendency to avoid decision making; the tougher the decision, the greater the likelihood of decision aversion.

Decision making The process of choosing between alternatives; selecting or rejecting available options.

Declarative memory Memory for information such as facts and events.

Deductive reasoning A form of thinking in which one draws a conclusion that is intended to follow logically from two or more statements or premises.

Delusions False or irrational beliefs maintained despite clear evidence to the contrary.

Demand characteristics Cues in an experimental setting that influence the participants' perception of what is expected of them and that systematically influence their behavior within that setting.

Dendrites The branched fibers of neurons that receive incoming signals.

Dependent variable In an experimental setting, a variable that the researcher measures to assess the impact of a variation in an independent variable.

Determinism The doctrine that all events—physical, behavioral, and mental—are determined by specific causal factors that are potentially knowable.

Developmental age The chronological age at which most children show a particular level of physical or mental development.

Developmental psychology The branch of psychology concerned with interaction between physical and psychological processes

<www.ablongman.com/gerrig17e>

and with stages of growth from conception throughout the entire life span.

Diathesis-stress hypothesis A hypothesis about the cause of certain disorders, such as schizophrenia, that suggests that genetic factors predispose an individual to a certain disorder, but that environmental stress factors must impinge in order for the potential risk to manifest itself.

Dichotic listening An experimental technique in which a different auditory stimulus is simultaneously presented to each ear.

Difference threshold The smallest physical difference between two stimuli that can still be recognized as a difference; operationally defined as the point at which the stimuli are recognized as different half of the time.

Diffusion of responsibility In emergency situations, the larger the number of bystanders, the less responsibility any one of the bystanders feels to help.

Discriminative stimuli Stimuli that act as predictors of reinforcement, signaling when particular behaviors will result in positive reinforcement.

Dissociative amnesia The inability to remember important personal experiences, caused by psychological factors in the absence of any organic dysfunction.

Dissociative disorder A personality disorder marked by a disturbance in the integration of identity, memory, or consciousness.

Dissociative identity disorder (DID) A dissociative mental disorder in which two or more distinct personalities exist within the same individual; formerly knows as multiple personality disorder.

Distal stimulus In the processes of perception, the physical object in the world, as contrasted with the proximal stimulus, the optical image on the retina.

Divergent thinking An aspect of creativity characterized by an ability to produce unusual but appropriate responses to problems.

DNA (deoxyribonucleic acid) The physical basis for the transmission of genetic information.

Double-blind control An experimental technique in which biased expectations of experimenters are eliminated by keeping both participants and experimental assistants unaware of which participants have received which treatment.

Dream analysis The psychoanalytic interpretation of dreams used to gain insight into a person's unconscious motives or conflicts.

Dream work In Freudian dream analysis, the process by which the internal censor transforms the latent content of a dream into manifest content.

Drives Internal states that arise in response to a disequilibrium in an animal's physiological needs.

DSM-IV-TR The current diagnostic and statistical manual of the American Psychological Association that classifies, defines, and describes mental disorders.

Echoic memory Sensory memory that allows auditory information to be stored for brief durations.

Ego The aspect of personality involved in self-preservation activities and in directing instinctual drives and urges into appropriate channels.

Ego defense mechanisms Mental strategies (conscious or unconscious) used by the ego to defend itself against conflicts experienced in the normal course of life.

Egocentrism In cognitive development, the inability of a young child at the preoperational stage to take the perspective of another person.

Elaborative rehearsal A technique for improving memory by enriching the encoding of information.

Electroconvulsive therapy (ECT) The use of electroconvulsive shock as an effective treatment for severe depression.

Electroencephalogram (EEG) A recording of the electrical activity of the brain.

Elaboration likelihood model A theory of persuasion that defines how likely it is that people will focus their cognitive processes to elaborate upon a message and therefore follow the central and peripheral routes to persuasion.

Emotion A complex pattern of changes, including physiological arousal, feelings, cognitive processes, and behavioral reactions, made in response to a situation perceived to be personally significant.

Emotional intelligence Type of intelligence defined as the abilities to perceive, appraise, and express emotions accurately and appropriate, to use emotions to facilitate thinking, to understand and analyze emotions, to use emotional knowledge effectively, and to regulate one's emotions to promote both emotional and intellectual growth.

Encoding The process by which a mental representation is formed in memory.

Encoding specificity The principle that subsequent retrieval of information is enhanced if cues received at the time of recall are consistent with those present at the time of encoding.

Endocrine system The network of glands that manufacture and secrete hormones into the bloodstream.

Engram The physical memory trace for information in the brain.

Episodic memories Long-term memories for autobiographical events and the contexts in which they occurred.

EQ The emotional intelligence counterpart of IQ.

Equity theory A cognitive theory of work motivation that proposes that workers are motivated to maintain fair and equitable relationships with other relevant persons; also, a model that postulates that equitable relationships are those in which the participants' outcomes are proportional to their inputs.

Estrogen The female sex hormone, produced by the ovaries, that is responsible for the release of eggs from the ovaries as well as for the development and maintenance of female reproductive structures and secondary sex characteristics.

Etiology The causes of, or factor related to, the development of a disorder.

Excitatory inputs Information entering a neuron that signals it to fire.

Expectancy effects Results that occur when a researcher or observer subtly communicates to participants the kind of behavior he or she expects to find, thereby creating that expected reaction.

Expectancy theory A cognitive theory of work motivation that proposes that workers are motivated when they expect their efforts and job performance to result in desired outcomes.

Experience-sampling method As experimental method that assists researchers in describing the typical contents of consciousness; participants are asked to record what they are feeling and thinking whenever signaled to do so.

Experimental methods Research methodologies that involve the manipulation of independent variables in order to determine their effects on the dependent variables.

Explicit uses of memory Conscious effort to encode or recover information through memory processes.

Exposure therapy A behavioral technique in which clients are exposed to the objects or situations that cause them anxiety.

Evolutionary perspective The approach to psychology that stresses the importance of behavioral and mental adaptiveness, based on the assumption that mental capabilities evolved over millions of years to serve particular adaptive purposes.

Evolutionary psychology The study of behavior and mind using the principles of evolutionary theory.

Extinction In conditioning, the weakening of a conditioned association in the absence of a reinforcer or unconditioned stimulus.

Face validity The degree to which test items appear to be directly related to the attribute the researcher wishes to measure.

Fear A rational reaction to an objectively identified external danger that may induce a person to flee or attack in self-defense.

Fight-or-flight response A sequence of internal activities triggered when an organism is faced with a threat; prepares the body for combat and struggle or for running away to safety; recent evidence suggests that the response is characteristic only of males.

Figure Object like regions of the visual field that are distinguished from background.

Five-factor model A comprehensive descriptive personality system that maps out the relationships among common traits, theoretical concepts, and personality scales; informally called the Big Five.

Fixation A state in which a person remains attached to objects or activities more appropriate for an earlier stage of psychosexual development.

Fixed-interval schedule A schedule of reinforcement in which a reinforcer is delivered for the first response made after a fixed period of time.

Fixed-ratio schedule A schedule of reinforcement in which a reinforcer is delivered for the first response made after a fixed number of responses.

Fluid intelligence The aspect of intelligence that involves the ability to see complex relationships and solve problems.

Formal assessment The systematic procedures and measurement instruments used by trained professionals to assess an individual's functioning, aptitudes, abilities, or mental states.

Foundational theories Frameworks for initial understanding formulated by children to explain their experiences of the world.

Fovea Area of the retina that contains densely packed cones and forms the point of sharpest vision.

Frame A particular description of a choice; the perspective from which a choice is described or framed affects how a decision is made and which option is ultimately exercised.

Free association The therapeutic method in which a patient gives a running account of thoughts, wishes, physical sensations, and mental images as they occur.

Frequency theory The theory that a tone produces a rate of vibration in the basilar membrane equal to its frequency, with the result that pitch can be coded by the frequency of the neural response.

Frontal lobe Region of the brain located above the lateral fissure and in front of the central sulcus; involved in motor control and cognitive activities.

Frustration-aggression hypothesis According to this hypothesis, frustration occurs in situations in which people are prevented or blocked from attaining their goals; a rise in frustration then leads to a greater probability of aggression.

Functional fixedness An inability to perceive a new use for an object previously associated with some other purpose; adversely affects problem solving and creativity.

Functionalism The perspective on mind and behavior that focuses on the examination of their functions in an organism's interactions with the environment.

Functional MRI (fMRI) A brain imaging technique that combines benefits of both MRI and PET scans by detecting magnetic changes in the flow of blood to cells in the brain.

Fundamental attribution error (FAE) The dual tendency of observers to underestimate the impact of situational factors and to overestimate the influence of dispositional factors on a person's behavior.

g According to Spearman, the factor of general intelligence underlying all intelligent performance.

Ganglion cells Cells in the visual system that integrate impulses from many bipolar cells in a single firing rate.

Gate-control theory A theory about pain modulation that proposes that certain cells in the spinal cord act as gates to interrupt and block some pain signals while sending others to the brain.

Gender A psychological phenomenon that refers to learned sex related behaviors and attitudes of males and females.

Gender identity One's sense of maleness or femaleness; usually includes awareness and acceptance of one's biological sex.

Gender roles Sets if behaviors and attitudes associated by society being male or female and expressed publicly by the individual.

General adaptation syndrome (GAS) The pattern of nonspecific adaptational physiological mechanisms that occurs in response to continuing threat by almost any serious stressor.

Generalized anxiety disorder An anxiety disorder in which an individual feels anxious and worried most of the time for at least six months when not threatened by any specific danger or object.

Generativity A commitment beyond one's self and one's partner to family, work society, and future generations; typically, a crucial state in development in one's 30s and 40s.

Genes The biological units of heredity; discrete sections of chromosomes responsible for transmission of traits.

Genetics The study of the inheritance of physical and psychological traits from ancestors.

Genocide The systematic destruction of one group of people, often an ethnic or racial group, by another.

Genome The genetic information for an organism, stored in the DNA of its chromosomes.

Genotype The genetic structure an organism inherits from its parents.

Gestalt psychology A school of psychology that maintains that psychological phenomena can be understood only when viewed as organized, structured wholes, not when broken down into primitive perceptual elements.

Gestalt theory Therapy that focuses on ways to unite mind and body to make a person whole.

Glia The cells that hold neurons together and facilitate neural transmission, remove damaged and dead neurons, and prevent poisonous substances in the blood from reaching the brain.

Goal-directed selection A determinant of why people select some parts of sensory input for further processing; it reflects the choices made as a function of one's own goals.

Ground The backdrop of background areas of the visual field, against which figures stand out.

Group dynamics The study of how group processes change individual functioning.

Group polarization The tendency for groups to make decisions that are more extreme than the decisions that would be made by the members acting alone.

Group think The tendency of a decision-making group to filter out undesirable input so that a consensus may be reached, especially if it is in line with the leader's viewpoint.

Hallucinations False perceptions that occur in the absence of objective stimulation.

Health A general condition of soundness and vigor of body and mind; not simply the absence of illness or injury.

Health promotion The development and implementation of general strategies and specific tactics to eliminate or reduce the risk that people will become ill.

Health psychology The field of psychology devoted to understanding the ways people stay healthy, the reasons they become ill, and the ways they respond when they become ill.

Heredity The biological transmission of traits from parents to offspring.

Heritability The relative influence of genetics—versus environment—in determining patterns of behavior.

Heritability estimate A statistical estimate of the degree of inheritance of a given trait or behavior, assessed by the degree of similarity between individuals who vary in their extent of genetic similarity.

Heuristics Cognitive strategies, or "rules of thumb," often used as shortcuts in solving a complex inferential task.

Hierarchy of needs Maslow's view that basic human motives form a hierarchy and that the needs at each level of the hierarchy must be satisfied before the next level can be achieved; these needs progress from basic biological needs to the need for self-actualization.

Hippocampus The part of the limbic system that is involved in the acquisition of explicit memory.

HIV Human immunodeficiency virus, a virus that attacks white blood cells (T lymphocytes) in human blood, thereby weakening the functioning of the immune system; HIV causes AIDS.

Homeostasis Constancy or equilibrium of the internal conditions of the body.

Horizontal cells The cells that integrate information across the retina; rather than sending signals towards the brain, horizontal cells connect receptors to each other.

Hormones The chemical messengers, manufactured and secreted by the endocrine glands, that regulate metabolism and influence body growth, mood, and sexual characteristics.

Hozho A Navajo concept referring to harmony, peace of mind, goodness, ideal family relationships, beauty in arts and crafts, and health of body and spirit.

Hue The dimension of color space that captures the qualitative experience of the color of light.

Human behavior genetics The area of study that evaluates the genetic component of individual differences in behaviors and traits.

Humanistic perspective A psychological model that emphasizes an individual's phenomenal world and inherent capacity for making rational choices and developing to maximum potential.

Human-potential movement The therapy movement that encompasses all those practices and methods that release the potential of the average human being for greater levels of performance and greater richness experience.

Hypnosis An altered state of awareness characterized by deep relaxation, susceptibility to suggestions, and changes in perception, memory, motivation, and self-control.

Hypnotizability The degree to which an individual is responsive to standardized hypnotic suggestion.

Hypothalamus The brain structure that regulates motivated behavior (such as eating and drinking) and homeostasis.

Iconic memory Sensory memory in the visual domain; allows large amounts of information to be stored for very brief durations.

Id The primitive, unconscious part of the personality that represents the internalization of society's values, standards, and morals.

Identification and recognition Two ways of attaching meaning to percepts.

Illusion An experience of a stimulus pattern in a manner that is demonstrably incorrect but shared by others in the same perceptual environment.

Implicit uses of memory Availability of information through memory processes without conscious effort to encode or recover information.

Impulsive aggression Cognition-based and goal-directed aggression carried out with premeditated thought, to achieve specific aims.

Imprinting A primitive form of learning in which some infant animals physically follow and form an attachment to the first moving object they see and/or hear.

Incentives External stimuli or rewards that motivate behavior although they do not relate directly to biological needs.

Independent construals of self Conceptualization of the self as individual whose behavior is organized primarily by reference to one's own thoughts, feelings, and actions, rather than by reference to the thoughts, feelings, and actions of others.

Independent variable In an experimental setting, a variable that the researcher manipulates with the expectation of having an impact on values of the dependent variable.

Inductive reasoning A form of reasoning in which a conclusion is made about the probability of some state of affairs, based on the available evidence and past experience.

Informational influence Group effects that arise from individuals' desire to be correct and right and to understand how best to act in a given situation.

In-group bias An evaluation of one's own group as better than others.

In-groups The groups with which people identify as members.

Inhibitory inputs Information entering a neuron that signals it not to fire.

Insanity The legal (not clinical) designation for the state of an individual judged to be legally irresponsible or incompetent.

Insight therapy A technique by which the therapist guides a patient toward discovering insights between present symptoms and past origins.

Instincts Preprogrammed tendencies that are essential to a species's survival

Instinctual drift The tendency for learned behavior to drift toward instinctual behavior over time.

Instrumental aggression Cognition-based and goal-directed aggression carried out with premeditated thought, to achieve specific aims.

Internalization According to Vygotsky, the process through which children absorb knowledge from the social context.

Intimacy The capacity to make a full commitment—sexual, emotional, and moral—to another person.

Insomnia The chronic inability to sleep normally; symptoms include difficulty in falling asleep, frequent waking, inability to return to sleep, and early-morning awakening.

Intelligence The global capacity to profit from experience and to go beyond given information about the environment.

Intelligence quotient (IQ) An index derived from standardized tests of intelligence; originally obtained by dividing an individual's mental age by chronological age and then multiplying by 100; now directly computed as an IQ test score.

Interdependent construals of self Conceptualization of the self as part of an encompassing social relationship; recognizing that one's behavior is determined, contingent on, and, to a large extent organized by what the actor perceived to be the thoughts, feelings, and actions of others.

Interferences Missing information filled on the basis of a sample of evidence or on the basis of prior beliefs and theories.

Internal consistency A measure of reliability; the degree to which a test yields similar scores across its different parts, such as an odd versus even items.

Interneurons Brain neurons that relay messages from sensory neurons to other interneurons or to motor neurons.

Ion channels The portions of neurons' cell membranes that selectively permit certain ions to flow in and out.

James–Lange theory of emotion A peripheral-feedback theory of emotion stating that an eliciting stimulus triggers a behavioral response that sends different sensory and motor feedback to the brain and creates the feeling of a specific emotion.

Jigsaw classrooms Classrooms that use a technique known as jigsawing, in which each pupil is given part of the total material to master and then share with other group members.

Job burnout The syndrome of emotional exhaustion, depersonalization, and reduced personal accomplishment, often experienced by workers in high-stress jobs.

Judgment The process by which people form opinions, reach conclusions, and make critical evaluations of events and people based on available material; also, the product of the mental activity.

Just noticeable difference (JND) The smallest difference between two sensations that allows them to be discriminated.

Kinesthetic sense The sense concerned with bodily position and movement of the body parts relative to one another.

Language-making capacity The innate guidelines or operating principles that children bring to task of learning a language.

Language production What people say, sign, and write, as well as the processes they go through to produce these messages.

Latent content In Freudian dream analysis, the hidden meaning of a dream.

Law of effect A basic law of learning that states that the power of a stimulus to evoke a response is strengthened when the response is followed by a reward and weakened when it is not followed by a reward.

Learned helplessness A general pattern of nonresponding in the presence of noxious stimuli that often follows after an organism has previously experienced noncontingent, inescapable aversive stimuli.

Learning A process based on experience that results in a relatively permanent change in behavior or behavioral potential.

Learning disorder A disorder defined by a large discrepancy between individuals measured IQ and their actual performance.

Learning-performance distinction The difference between what has been learned and what is expressed in overt behavior.

Lesions Injuries to or destruction of brain tissue.

Levels-of-processing theory A theory that suggests that the deeper the level at which information was processed, the more likely it is to be retained in memory.

Libido The psychic energy that drives individuals toward sensual pleasures of all types; especially sexual ones.

Life-change units (LCUs) In stress research, the measure of the stress levels of different types of change experienced during a given period.

Lightness constancy The tendency to perceive the whiteness, grayness, or blackness of objects as constant across changing the levels of illuminations.

Limbic system The region of the brain that regulates emotional behavior, basic motivational urges, and memory, as well as major physiological functions.

Long-term memory (LTM) Memory processes associated with the preservation of information for retrieval at any later time.

Longitudinal design A research design in which the same participants are observed repeatedly, sometime over many years.

Loudness A perceptual dimension of sound influenced by the amplitude of a sound wave; sound waves in large amplitudes are generally experienced as loud and those with small amplitudes as soft.

Lucid dreaming The theory that conscious awareness of dreaming is a learnable skill that enables dreamers to control the direction and content of their dreams.

Magnetic resonance imaging (MRI) A technique for brain imaging that scans the brain using magnetic fields and radio waves.

Major depressive disorder A mood disorder characterized by intense feelings of depression over and extended time, without the manic high phase of bipolar depression.

Manic episode A component of bipolar disorder characterized by periods of extreme elation, unbounded euphoria without sufficient reason, and grandiose thoughts or feelings about personal abilities.

Manifest content In Freudian dream analysis, the surface content of a dream, which is assumed to mask the dream's actual meaning.

Maturation The continuing influence of heredity throughout development, the age-related physical and behavioral changes characteristic of a species.

Meditation A form of consciousness alteration designed to enhance self-knowledge and well-being through reduced self-awareness.

Medulla The region of the brain stem that regulates breathing, waking, and heartbeat.

Memory The mental capacity to encode, store, and retrieve information.

Menarche The onset of menstruation.

Mental age In Binet's measure of intelligence, the age at which a child is performing intellectually, expressed in terms of the average age at which normal children achieve a particular score.

Mental retardation Condition in which individuals have IQ scores 70 to 75 or below and also demonstrate limitations in the ability to bring adaptive skills to bear on life tasks.

Mental set The tendency to respond to a new problem in the manner used to respond to a previous problem.

Meta-analysis A statistical technique for evaluating hypotheses by providing a formal mechanism for detecting the general conclusions found in data from many different experiments.

Metamemory Implicit of explicit knowledge about memory abilities and effective memory strategies; cognition about memory.

Mnemonics Strategies or devices that use familiar information during the encoding of new information to enhance subsequent access to the information in memory.

Mood disorder A mood disturbance such as severe depression or depression alternating with mania.

Morality A system of beliefs and values that ensures that individuals will keep their obligations to others in society and will behave in ways that do not interfere with the rights and interests of others.

Motor cortex The region of the cerebral cortex that controls the action of the body's voluntary muscles.

Motor neurons The neurons that carry messages away from the central nervous system toward the muscles and glands.

Motivation The process of starting, directing, and maintaining physical and psychological activities; includes mechanisms involved in preferences for one activity over another and the vigor and persistence of responses.

Narcolepsy A sleep disorder characterized by an irresistible compulsion to sleep during the daytime.

Natural selection Darwin's theory that favorable adaptations to features of the environment allow some members of a species to reproduce more successfully than others.

Need for achievement (n Ach) An assumed basic human need to strive for achievement of goals which motivates a wide range of behavior and thinking.

Negative punishment A behavior is followed by the removal of an appetitive stimulus, decreasing the probability of that behavior.

Negative reinforcement A behavior is followed by the removal of an aversive stimulus, increasing the probability of that behavior.

Neurogenesis The creation of new neurons.

Neuron A cell in the nervous system specialized to receive, process, and/or transmit information to other cells.

Neuromodulator Any substance that modifies or modulates the activities of the postsynaptic neuron.

Neuroscience The scientific study of the brain and of the links between brain activity and behavior.

Neurotic disorders Mental disorders in which a person does not have signs of brain abnormalities and does not have signs of brain abnormalities and does not display grossly irrational thinking or violate basic norms but does experience subjective distress; a category dropped from DSM-III.

Neurotransmitters The Chemical messengers released from neurons that cross the synapse from one neuron to another, stimulating the postsynaptic neuron.

Nonconscious Not typically available to consciousness or memory.

Non-REM (NREM) sleep The period during which a sleeper does not show rapid eye movement; characterized by less dream activity than during REM sleep.

Norm crystallization The convergence of the expectations of a group of individuals into a common perspective as they talk and carry out activities together.

Normative influence Group effects that arise from individuals' desire to be liked, accepted, and approved of by others.

Normative investigations Research efforts designed to describe what is characteristic of a specific age or developmental stage.

Norms Standards based on measurements of a large group of people; used for comparing the scores of an individual with those of others within a well-defined group.

Object permanence The recognition that objects exist independently of an individual's action or awareness; an important cognitive acquisition of infancy.

Object relations theory Psychoanalytic theory that originated Melanie Klein's view that the building blocks of how people experience the world emerge from their relations to loved and hated objects (significant people in their lives).

Observational learning The process of learning new responses by watching the behavior of another.

Observer bias The distortion of evidence because of the personal motives and expectations of the viewer..

Obsessive-compulsive disorder (OCD) A mental disorder characterized by obsessions—recurrent thoughts, images, or impulses that recur or persist despite efforts to suppress them—and compulsions—repetitive, purposeful acts performed according to certain rules or in a ritualized manner.

Occipital lobe Rearmost region of the brain; contains primary visual cortex.

Olfactory bulb The center where odor-sensitive receptors sent their signals, located just below the frontal lobes of the cortex.

Operant Behavior emitted by an organism that can be characterized in terms of the observable effects it has on the environment.

Operant conditioning Learning in which the probability of a response is changed by a change in its consequences.

Operant extinction When a behavior no longer produces predictable consequences, its return to the level of occurrence it had before operant conditioning.

Operational definition A definition of a variable or condition in terms of the specific operation or procedure used to determine its presence.

Opponent-process theory The theory that all color experiences arise from three systems, each of which includes two "opponent" elements (red versus green, blue versus yellow, and black versus white).

Optical nerve The axons of the ganglion cells that carry information from the eye toward the brain.

Organizational psychologists Psychologists who study various aspects of the human work environment, such as communication among employees, socialization or enculturation of workers, leadership, job satisfaction, stress and burnout, and overall quality of life.

Out-groups The groups with which people do not identify.

Overregularization A grammatical error, usually appearing during early language development, in which rules of the language are applied too widely, resulting in incorrect linguistic forms.

Pain The bodies response to noxious stimuli that are intense enough to cause, or threaten to cause, tissue damage.

Panic disorder An anxiety disorder in which sufferers experience unexpected, severe panic attacks that begin with a feeling of intense apprehension, fear, or terror.

Parallel forms Different versions of a test used to assess test reliability; the change of forms reduces effects of direct practice, memory, or the desire of an individual to appear consistent on the same items.

Parallel processes Two or more mental processes that are carried out simultaneously.

Parasympathetic division The subdivision of the autonomic nervous system that monitors the routine operation of the body's internal functions and conserves and restores body energy.

Parental investment The time and energy parents must spend raising their offspring.

Partial reinforcement effect The behavioral principle that states that responses acquired under intermittent reinforcement are more difficult to extinguish than those acquired with continuous reinforcement.

Parenting practices Specific parenting behaviors that arise in response to particular parental goals.

Parenting styles The manner in which parents rear their children; an authoritative parenting style, which balances demandingness and responsiveness, is seen as the most effective.

Parietal lobe Region of the brain behind the frontal lobe and above the lateral fissure; contains somatosensory cortex.

Participant modeling A therapeutic technique in which a therapist demonstrates the desired behavior and a client is aided, through supportive encouragement, to imitate the modeled behavior.

Pastoral counselor A member of a religious order who specializes in the treatment of psychological disorders, often combining spirituality with practical problem solving.

Patient The term used by those who take a biomedical approach to the treatment of psychological problems to describe the person being treated.

Peace psychology An interdisciplinary approach to the prevention of nuclear war and the maintenance of peace.

Perceived control The belief that one has the ability to make a difference in the course of the consequences of some event or experience; often helpful in dealing with stressors.

Perception The processes that organize information in the sensory image and interpret it as having been produced by properties of objects or events in the external, three-dimensional world.

Perceptual constancy The ability to retain an unchanging percept of an object despite variations in the retinal image.

Perceptual organization The processes that put sensory information together to give the perception of a coherent scene over the whole visual field.

Peripheral nervous system (PNS) The part of the nervous system composed of the spinal and cranial nerves that connect the body's sensory receptors to the CNS and the CNS to the muscles and glands.

Personality The psychological qualities of an individual that influence a variety of characteristic behavior patterns across difference situations and over time.

Personality disorder A chronic, inflexible, maladaptive pattern of perceiving, thinking, and behaving that seriously impairs an individual's ability to function in social or other settings.

Personality inventory A self-report questionnaire used for personality assessment that includes a series of items about personal thoughts, feelings, and behaviors.

Personality types Distinct patterns of personality characteristics used to assign people to categories; qualitative differences, rather than differences in degree, used to discriminate among people.

Persuasion Deliberate efforts to change attitudes.

PET scans Brain images produced by a device that obtains detailed pictures of activity in the living brain by recording the radioactivity emitted by cells during different cognitive or behavioral activities.

Phenotype The observable characteristics of an organism, resulting from the interaction between the organism's genotype and its environment.

Pheromones Chemical signals released by organisms to communicate with other members of the species often serve as long-distance sexual attractors.

Phi phenomenon The simplest form of apparent motion, the movement illusion in which one or more stationary lights going on and off in succession are perceived as a single moving light.

Phobia A persistent and irrational fear of a specific object, activity, or situation that is excessive and unreasonable, given the reality of the threat.

Phonemes Minimal units of speech in any given language that make a meaningful difference in speech and production and reception, r and l are two distinct phonemes in English but variations of one in Japanese.

Photoreceptors Receptor cells in the retina that are sensitive to light.

Physiological dependence The process by which the body becomes adjusted to an dependent on a drug.

Pitch Sound quality of highness or lowness; primarily dependent on the frequency of the sound wave.

Pituitary gland Located in the brain, the gland that secretes growth hormone and influences the secretion of hormones by other endocrine glands.

Place theory The theory that different frequency tones produce maximum activation at different locations along the basilar membrane, with the result that pitch can be coded by the place at which activation occurs.

Placebo control An experimental condition in which treatment is not administered; it is used in cases where a placebo effect might occur.

Placebo effect A change in behavior in the absence of an experimental manipulation.

Placebo therapy A therapy interdependent of any specific clinical procedures that results in client improvement.

Plasticity Changes in the performance of the brain; may involve the creation of new synapses or changes in the function of existing synapses.

Pons the region of the brain stem that connects the spinal cord with the brain and links parts of the brain to one another.

Population The entire set of individuals to which generalizations will be made based on an experimental sample.

Positive punishment A behavior is followed by the presentation of an aversive stimulus, decreasing the probability of that behavior.

Positive reinforcement A behavior is followed by the presentation of an appetitive stimulus, increasing the probability of that behavior.

Possible selves The ideal selves that a person would like to become, the selves a person could become, and the selves a person is afraid of becoming; components of the cognitive sense of self.

Posttraumatic stress disorder (PTSD) An anxiety disorder characterized by the persistent reexperience of traumatic events through distressing recollections, dreams, hallucinations, or dissociative flashbacks; develops in response to rapes, life-threatening events, severe injury, and natural disasters.

Preconscious memories Memories that are not currently conscious but that can easily be called into consciousness when necessary.

Predictive validity See criterion validity.

Prefrontal lobotomy An operation that severs the nerve fibers connecting the frontal lobes of the brain with the diencephalons, especially those fibers id the thalamic and hypothalamic areas; best known form of psychosurgery.

Prejudice A learned attitude toward a target object, involving negative affect (dislike or fear), negative beliefs (stereotypes) that justify the attitude, and a behavioral intention to avoid, control, dominate, or eliminate the target object.

Primacy effect Improved memory for items at the start of a list.

Primary effect Improved memory for items at the start of a list.

Primary reinforcers Biologically determined reinforcers such as food and water.

Priming In the assessment of implicit memory, the advantage conferred by prior exposure to a word or situation.

Proactive interference Circumstances in which past memories make it more difficult to encode and retrieve new information.

Problem solving Thinking that is directed toward solving specific problems and that moves from an initial state to a goal state by means of a set of mental operations.

Problem space The elements that make up a problem: the initial state, the incomplete information or unsatisfactory conditions the person starts with; the goal state, the set of information or state the person wishes to achieve; and the set of operations, the steps the person takes to move from the initial state to the goal state.

Procedural memory Memory for how things get done; the way perceptual, cognitive, and motor skills are acquired, retained, and used.

Projective test A method of personality assessment in which an individual is presented with a standardized set of ambiguous, abstract stimuli and asked to interpret their meanings; the individual's responses are assumed to reveal inner feelings, motives, and conflicts.

Prosocial behaviors Behaviors that are carried out with the goal of helping other people.

Prototype The most representative example of a category.

Proximal stimulus The optical image on the retina; contrasted with the distal stimulus, the physical object in the world.

Psychiatrist An individual who has obtained an M.D. degree and also has completed postdoctoral specialty training in mental and emotional disorders; a psychiatrist may prescribe medications for the treatment of psychological disorders.

Psychic determinism The assumption that mental and behavioral reactions are determined by previous experiences.

Psychoactive drugs Chemicals that affect mental processes and behavior by temporarily changing conscious awareness of reality.

Psychoanalysis The form of psychodynamic therapy developed by Freud; an intensive prolonged technique for exploring unconscious motivations and conflicts in neurotic, anxiety-ridden individuals.

Psychoanalyst An individual who has earned either a Ph.D. or an M.D. degree and has completed postgraduate training in the Freudian approach to understanding and treating mental disorders.

Psychobiography The use of psychological (especially personality) theory to describe and explain an individual's course through life.

Psychodynamic personality theories Theories of personality that share the assumption that personality is shaped by and behavior is motivated by inner forces.

Psychodynamic perspective A psychological model in which behavior is explained in terms of past experiences and motivational forces; actions are viewed as stemming from inherited instincts, biological drives, and attempts to resolve conflicts between personal needs and social requirements.

Psychological assessment The use of specified procedures to evaluate the abilities, behaviors, and personal qualities of people.

Psychological dependence The psychological need or craving for a drug.

Psychological diagnosis The label given to psychological abnormality by classifying and categorizing the observed behavior pattern into an approved diagnostic system.

Psychology The scientific study of the behavior or individuals and their mental processes.

Psychometrics The field of psychology that specializes in mental testing.

Psychometric function A graph that plots the percentage of detections of a stimulus (on the vertical axis) for each stimulus intensity (on the horizon axis).

Psychoneuroimmunology The research area that investigates interactions between psychological processes, such as responses to stress, and the functions of the immune system.

Psychopathological functioning Disruptions in emotional, behavioral, or thought processes that lead to personal distress or block one's ability to achieve important goals.

Psychopharmacology The branch of psychology that investigates the effects of drugs on behavior.

Psychophysics The study of the correspondence between physical simulation and psychological experience.

Psychosurgery A surgical procedure performed on brain tissue to alleviate psychological disorder.

Psychotherapy Any of a group of therapies, used to treat psychological disorders, that focus on changing faulty behaviors, thoughts, perceptions, and emotions that may be associated with specific disorders.

Psychotic disorders Severe mental disorders in which a person experiences impairments in reality testing manifested through thought, emotional, or perceptual difficulties; no longer used as diagnostic category after DSM-III.

Psychosomatic disorders Physical disorders aggravated by or primarily attributable to prolonged emotional stress or other psychological causes.

Psychological dependence The psychological need or craving for a drug.

Psychosocial stages Proposed by Erik Erikson, successive developmental stages that focus on an individual's orientation toward the self and others; these stages incorporate both the sexual and social aspects of a person's developmental and the social conflicts that arise from the interaction between the individual and the social environment.

Physical development The bodily changes, maturation, and growth that occur in an organism starting with conception and continuing across the life span.

Puberty The process through which sexual maturity is attained.

Punisher Any stimulus that, when made contingent upon a response, decreases the probability of that response.

Racism Discrimination against people based on their skin color or ethnic heritage.

Rapid eye movements (REM) A behavioral sign of the phase of sleep during which the sleeper is likely to be experiencing dream-like mental activity.

Rational-emotive therapy (RET) A comprehensive system of personality change based on changing irrational beliefs that cause undesirable, highly charged emotional reactions such as severe anxiety.

Reasoning The process of thinking in which conclusions are drawn from a set of facts; thinking directed toward a given goal or objective.

Recall A method of retrieval in which an individual is required to reproduce the information previously presented.

Recency effect Improved memory for items at the end of a list.

Receptive field The area of the visual field to which a neuron in the visual system responds.

Receptive field The visual are from which a given ganglion cell receives information.

Reciprocal altruism The idea that people perform altruistic behaviors because they expect that others will perform altruistic behaviors for them in turn.

Reciprocal determinism A concept of Albert Bandura's social learning theory that refers to the notion that a complex reciprocal interaction exist among the individual, his or her behavior, and environmental stimuli and that each of these components affects the others.

Reciprocity norm Expectation that favors will be returned—if someone does something for another person, that person should do something in return.

Recognition A method of retrieval in which an individual is required to identify stimuli as having been experienced before.

Reconstructive memory The process of putting information together based on general types of stored knowledge in the absence of a specific memory representation.

Reflex An unlearned response elicited by specific stimuli that have biological relevance for an organism.

Refractory period The period of rest during which a new nerve impulse cannot be activated in a segment of an axon.

Reinforcement contingency A consistent relationship between a response and the changes in the environment that it produces.

Reinforcer Any stimulus that, when made contingent upon a response, increases the probability of that response.

Relative motion parallax A source of information about depth in which the relative distances of objects from a viewer determine the amount and direction of their relative motion in the retinal image.

Relaxation response A condition in which muscle tension, cortical activity, heart rate, and blood pressure decrease and breathing slows.

Reliability The degree to which a test produces similar scores each time it is used; stability or consistency of the scores produced by an instrument.

Repetitive transcranial magnetic stimulation (rTMS) A technique for producing temporary inactivation of brain areas using repeated pulses of magnetic stimulation.

Representative sample A subset of a population that closely matches the overall characteristics of the population with respect to the distribution of males and females, racial and ethnic groups, and so on.

Representativeness heuristic A cognitive strategy that assigns an object to a category on the basis of a few characteristics regarded as representative of that category.

Repression The basic defense mechanism by which painful or guilt producing thoughts, feelings, or memories are excluded from conscious awareness.

Resistance The inability or unwillingness of a patient in psychoanalysis to discuss certain ideas, desires, or experiences.

Response bias The systematic tendency as a result of nonsensory factors for an observer to favor responding in a particular way.

Resting potential The polarization of cellular fluid within a neuron, which provides the capability to produce an action potential.

Reticular formation The region of the brain stem that alerts the cerebral cortex to incoming sensory signals and is responsible for maintaining consciousness and awakening from sleep.

Retina The layer at the back of the eye that contains photoreceptors and converts light energy to neutral responses.

Retinal disparity The displacement between the horizontal positions of corresponding images in the two eyes.

Retrieval The recovery of stored information from memory.

Retrieval cues Internally or externally generated stimuli available to help with the retrieval of a memory.

Retroactive interference Circumstances in which the formation of new memories makes it more difficult to recover older memories.

Reversal theory Theory that explains human motivation in terms of reversals from one to the other opposing metamotivational states.

Ritual healing Ceremonies that infuse special emotional intensity and meaning into the healing process.

Rods Photoreceptors concentrated in the periphery of the retina that are most active in dim illumination; rods do not produce sensation of color.

Rules Behavioral guidelines for acting in certain ways in certain situations.

Sample A subset of a population selected as participants in an experiment.

Saturation The dimension of color space that captures the purity and vividness of color sensations.

Schedules of reinforcement In operant conditioning, the patterns of delivering and withholding reinforcement.

Schemas General conceptual frameworks, or clusters of knowledge, regarding objects, people, and situations; knowledge packages that encode generalizations about the structure of the environment.

Schemes Piaget's term for cognitive structures that develop as infants and young children learn to interpret the world and adapt to their environment.

Schizophrenic disorder Severe form of psychopathology characterized by the breakdown of integrated personality functioning, withdrawal from reality, emotional distortions, and disturbed thought processes.

Scientific method The set of procedures used for gathering and interpreting objective information in a way that minimizes error and yields dependable generalizations.

Selective optimization with compensation A strategy for successful aging in which one makes the most gains while minimizing the impact of losses that accompany normal aging.

Selective social interaction theory The view that suggests that, as people age, they become more selective in choosing social partners who satisfy their emotional needs.

Self-actualization A concept in personality psychology referring to a person's constant striving to realize his or her potential and to develop inherent talents and capabilities.

Self-concept A person's mental model of his or her abilities and attributes.

Self-efficacy The set of beliefs that one can perform adequately in a particular situation.

Self-esteem A generalized evaluative attitude toward the self that influences both moods and behavior and that exerts a powerful effect on a range of personal and social behaviors.

Self-fulfilling prophecy A prediction made about some future behavior or event that modifies interactions so as to produce what is expected.

Self-handicapping The process of developing, in anticipation of failure, behavioral reactions and explanations that minimize ability deficits as possible attributions for the failure.

Self-perception theory The idea that people observe themselves in order to figure out the reasons they act as they do; people infer what their internal states are by perceiving how they are acting in a given situation.

Self-report measures The self-behaviors that are identified through a participant's own observations and reports.

Semantic memories Generic, categorical memories, such as the meanings of words and concepts.

Sensation The process by which stimulation of a sensory receptor gives rise to neutral impulses that result in an experience, or awareness, of conditions inside or outside the body.

Sensory adaptation A phenomenon in which receptor cells lose their power to respond after a period of unchanged stimulation; allows a more rapid reaction to new sources of information.

Sensory neurons The neurons that carry messages from sense receptors toward the central nervous system.

Sensory memory The initial memory processes involved in the momentary preservation of fleeting impressions of sensory stimuli.

Sensory receptors Specializes cells that convert physical signals into cellular signals that are processed by the nervous system.

Serial position effect A characteristic of memory retrieval in which the recall of beginning and end items on a list is often better than recall of items appearing in the middle.

Serial processes Two or more mental processes that are carried out in order, one after the other.

Set A temporary readiness to perceive or react to a stimulus in a particular way.

Sex chromosomes Chromosomes that contain the genes that code for the development of male or female characteristics.

Sex differences Biologically based characteristics that distinguish males from females.

Sexism Discrimination against people because of their sex.

Sexual arousal The motivational state of excitement and tension brought about by physiological and cognitive reactions to erotic stimuli.

Sexual scripts Socially learned programs of sexual responsiveness.

Shamanism A spiritual tradition that involves both healing and gaining contact with the spirit world.

Shape constancy The ability to perceive the true shape of an object despite variations in the size of the retinal image.

Shaping by successive approximations A behavioral method that reinforces responses that successively approximate and ultimately match the desired response.

Short-term memory (STM) Memory processes associated with preservation of recent experiences and with retrieval of information from long-term memory; short-term memory is of limited capacity and stores information for only a short length of time without rehearsal.

Shyness An individual's discomfort and/or inhibition in interpersonal situations that interferes with pursuing interpersonal professional goal.

Signal detection theory A systematic approach to the problem of response bias that allows an experimenter to identify and separate the roles of sensory stimuli and the individual's criterion level in producing the final response.

Size constancy The ability to perceive the true size of an object despite variations in the size of its retinal image.

Sleep apnea A sleep disorder of the upper respiratory system that causes the person to stop breathing while asleep.

Social categorization The process by which people organize the social environment by categorizing themselves and others into groups.

Social cognition The process by which people select, interpret, and remember social information.

Social development The ways in which individuals' social interactions and expectations change across the life span.

Social intelligence A theory of personality that refers to the expertise people bring to their experience of life tasks.

Social-learning therapy A form of treatment in which clients observe models' desirable behaviors being reinforced.

Social-learning theory The learning theory that stresses the role of observation and the imitation of behaviors observed in others.

Social norms The expectation a group has for its members regarding acceptable and appropriate attitudes and behaviors.

Social perception The process by which a person comes to know or perceive the personal attributes.

Social phobia A persistent, irrational fear that arises in anticipation if a public situation in which an individual can be observed by others.

Social psychology The branch of psychology that studies the effect of social variables on individual behavior, attitudes, perceptions, and motives; also studies group and intergroup phenomena.

Social role A socially defined pattern of behavior that is expected of a person who is functioning in a given setting or group.

Social support Resources, including material aid, socioemotional support, and informational aid, provided by others to help a person cope with stress.

Socialization The lifelong process whereby an individual's behavioral patterns, values, standards, skills, attitudes, and motives are shaped to conform to those regarded as desirable in a particular society.

Sociobiology A field of research that focuses on evolutionary explanations for the social behavior and social systems of humans and other animal species.

Sociocultural perspective The psychological perspective that focuses on cross-cultural differences in the causes and consequences of behavior.

Soma The cell body of a neuron, containing the nucleus and cytoplasm.

Somatic nervous system The subdivision of the peripheral nervous system that connects the central nervous system to the skeletal muscles and skin.

Somatosensory cortex The region of the parietal lobes that processes sensory input from various body areas.

Somnambulism A disorder that causes sleepers to leave their beds and wander while still remaining asleep; also known as sleepwalking.

Sound localization The auditory processes that allow the spatial origins of environmental sounds.

Specific phobias Phobias that occur in response to specific types of objects or situations.

Split-half reliability A measure of the correlation between test takers' performance on different halves (e.g., odd- and even-numbered items) of a test.

Spontaneous recovery The reappearance of an extinguished conditioned response after a rest period.

Spontaneous-remission effect The improvement of some mental patients and clients in psychotherapy without and professional interventional; a baseline criterion against which the effectiveness of therapies must be assessed.

Standardization A set of uniform procedures for treating each participant in a test, interview, or experiment, or for recording data.

Stereotypes Generalizations about a group of people in which the same characteristics are assigned to all members of a group.

Stereotype threat The threat associated with being at risk for confirming a negative stereotype of one's group.

Stigma The negative reaction of people to an individual or group because of some assumed inferiority or source of difference that is degraded.

Stimulus discrimination A conditioning process in which an organism learns to respond differently to stimuli that differ from the conditioned stimulus on some dimension.

Stimulus-driven capture A determinant of why people select some parts of sensory input for further processing; occurs when features of stimuli—objects in the environment—automatically capture attention, independent of the local goals of a perceiver.

Stimulus generalization The automatic extension of conditioned responding to similar stimuli that have never been paired with the unconditioned stimulus.

Storage The retention of encoded material over time.

Stress The pattern of specific and nonspecific responses an organism makes to stimulus events that disturb its equilibrium and tax or exceed its ability to cope.

Stress moderator variables Variables that change the impact of a stressor on a given type of stress reaction.

Stressor An internal or external event or stimulus that induces stress.

Structuralism The study of the structure of mind and behavior; the view that all human mental experience can be understood as a combination of simple elements or events.

Superego The aspect of personality that represents the internalization of society's values, standards, and morals.

Sympathetic division The subdivision of the autonomic nervous system that deals with emergency response and the mobilization of energy.

Synapse The gap between one neuron and another.

Synaptic transmission The relaying information from one neuron to another across the synaptic gap.

Systematic desensitization A behavioral therapy technique in which a client is taught to prevent the arousal of anxiety by confronting the feared stimulus while relaxed.

Taste-aversion learning A biological constraint on learning in which an organism learns in one trial to avoid a food whose ingestion is followed by illness.

Temporal lobe Region of brain found below the lateral fissure; contains auditory cortex.

Tend-and-befriend response A response to stressors that is hypothesized to be typical for females; stressors prompt females to protect their offspring and join social groups to reduce vulnerability.

Terminal buttons The bulblike structures at the branched endings of axons that contain vesicles filled with neurotransmitters.

Test–retest reliability A measure of the correlation between the scores of the same people on the same test given on two different occasions.

Testosterone The male sex hormone, secreted by the testes, that stimulates production of sperm and is also responsible for the development of male secondary sex characteristics.

Thalamus The brain structure that relays sensory impulses to the cerebral cortex.

Thematic Apperception Test (TAT) A projective test in which pictures of ambiguous scenes are presented to an individual, who is encouraged to generate stories about them.

Theory An organized set of concepts that explains a phenomenon or set of phenomena.

Think-aloud protocols Reports made by experimental participants of the mental processes and strategies they use while working on a task.

Three-term contingency The means by which organisms learn that, in the presence of some stimuli but not others, their behavior is likely to have a particular effect on the environment.

Timbre The dimension of auditory sensation that reflects the complexity of a sound wave.

Tolerance A situation that occurs with continued use of a drug in which an individual requires greater dosages to achieve the same effect.

Top-down processing Perceptual processes in which information from an individual's past experience, knowledge, expectations, motivations, and background influence the way a perceived object is interpreted and classified.

Traits Enduring personal qualities or attributes that influence behavior across situations.

Transduction Transformation of one form of energy into another; for example, light is transformed into neutral impulses.

Transfer-appropriate processing The perspective that suggests that memory is best when the type of processing carried out at encoding matches the processes carried out at retrieval.

Transference The process by which a person in psychoanalysis attaches to a therapist feelings formerly held toward some significant person who figured into past emotional conflict.

Trichromatic theory The theory that there are three types of color receptors that produce the primary color sensations of red, green, and blue.

Type A behavior pattern A complex pattern of behaviors and emotions that includes excessive emphasis on competition, aggression, impatience, and hostility; hostility increases the risk of coronary heart disease.

Type B behavior pattern As compared to Type A behavior pattern, a less competitive, less aggressive, less hostile pattern of behavior and emotion.

Unconditional positive regard Complete love and acceptance of an individual by another person, such as a parent for a child, with no conditions attached.

Unconditioned response (UCR) In classical conditioning, the response elicited by an unconditioned stimulus without prior training or learning.

Unconditioned stimulus (UCS) In classical conditioning, the stimulus that elicits an unconditioned response.

Unconscious The domain of the psyche that stores repressed urges and primitive impulses.

Validity The extent to which a test measures what it was intended to measure.

Variable In an experimental setting, a factor that varies in amount and kind.

Variable-interval schedule A schedule of reinforcement in which a reinforcer is delivered for the first response made after a variable period of time whose average is predetermined.

Variable-ratio schedule A schedule of reinforcement in which a reinforcer is delivered for the first response made after a variable number of responses whose average is predetermined.

Vestibular sense The sense that tells how one's own body is oriented in the world with respect to gravity.

Visual cortex The region of the occipital lobes in which visual information is processed.

Volley principle An extension of frequency theory, which proposes that when peaks in a sound wave come too frequently for a single neuron to fire at each peak, several neurons fire as a group at the frequency of the stimulus tone.

Weber's law An assertion that the size of a difference threshold is proportional to the intensity of the standard stimulus.

Wellness Optimal health, incorporating the ability to function fully and actively over the physical, intellectual, emotional, spiritual, social, and environmental domains of health.

Wisdom Expertise in the fundamental pragmatics of life.

Within-subjects design A research design that uses each participant as his or her own control; for example, the behavior of an experimental participant before receiving treatment might be compared to his or her behavior after receiving treatment.

Working memory A memory resource that is used to accomplish tasks such as reasoning and language comprehension; consists of the phonological loop, visuospatial sketchpad and central executive.

Zygote The single cell that results when a sperm fertilizes an egg.

References

Abelin, T., Muller, P., Buehler, A., Vesanen, K., & Imhof, P. R. (1989, January 7). Controlled trial of transdermal nicotine patch in tobacco withdrawal. *The Lancet*, pp. 7–10.

Abrams, R. (1992). *Electroconvulsive therapy*. New York: Oxford University Press.

Abramson, L. Y., Seligman, M. E. P., & Teasdale, J. D. (1978). Learned helplessness in humans: Critique and reformulation. *Journal of Abnormal Psychology, 87,* 32–48, 49–74.

Acierno, R., Resnick, H., Kilpatrick, D. G., Saunders, B., & Best, C. L. (1999). Risk factors for rape, physical assault, and post-traumatic stress disorder in women: Examination of differential multivariate relationships. *Journal of Anxiety Disorders, 13,* 541–563.

Adams, J. L. (1986). *Conceptual blockbusting* (3rd ed.). New York: Norton.

Adams, J. S. (1965). Inequity in social exchange. In L. Berkowitz (Ed.), *Advances in experimental social psychology* (Vol. 2, pp. 267–299). New York: Academic Press.

Addis, M. E., & Jacobson, N. S. (1996). Reasons for depression and the process and outcome of cognitive-behavioral psychotherapies. *Journal of Consulting and Clinical Psychology, 64,* 1417–1424.

Ader, R., & Cohen, N. (1981). Conditioned immunopharmacological responses. In R. Ader (Ed.), *Psychoneuroimmunology* (pp. 281–319). New York: Academic Press.

Ader, R., & Cohen, N. (1993). Psychoneuroimmunology: Conditioning and stress. *Annual Review of Psychology, 44,* 53–85.

Adler, A. (1929). *The practice and theory of individual psychology*. New York: Harcourt, Brace & World.

Adolphs, R., Tranel, D., Damasio, H., & Damasio, A. (1994). Impaired recognition of emotion in facial expressions following bilateral damage to the human amygdala. *Nature, 372,* 669–672.

Adolphs, R., Tranel, D., Hamann, S., Young, A. W., Calder, A. J., Phelps, E. A., Anderson, A., Lee, G. P., & Damasio, A. R. (1999). Recognition of facial emotion in nine individuals with bilateral amygdala damage. *Neuropsychologia, 37,* 1111–1117.

Adolphs, R., & Damasio, A. R. (2001). The interaction of affect and cognition: A neurobiological perspective. In J. P. Forgas (Ed.), *Handbook of affect and social cognition* (pp. 27–49). Mahwah, NJ: Erlbaum.

Adorno, T. W., Frenkel-Brunswick, E., Levinson, D. J., & Sanford, R. N. (1950). *The authoritarian personality*. New York: Harper.

Aghajanian, G. K., & Marek, G. J. (1999). Serotonin and hallucinogens. *Neuropsychopharmacology, 21* (Suppl.), 16S–23S.

Ainsworth, M. D. S., Blehar, M., Waters, E., & Wall, S. (1978). *Patterns of attachment*. Hillsdale, NJ: Erlbaum.

Ajzen, I., & Sexton, J. (1999). Depth of processing, belief congruence, and attitude-behavior correspondence. In S. Chaiken & Y. Trope (Eds.), *Dual-process theories in social psychology* (pp. 117–138). New York: Guilford.

Akmajian, A., Demers, R. A., Farmer, A. K., & Harnish, R. M. (1990). *Linguistics*. Cambridge, MA: The MIT Press.

Alberti, R. E., & Emmons, M. L. (1990). *Your perfect right—A guide to assertive living*. San Luis Obispo, CA: Impact Publishers.

Aldrich, M. S. (1992). Narcolepsy. *Neurology, 42*(Suppl. 6), 34–43.

Alexander, G. M. (2003). An evolutionary perspective of sex-typed toy preferences: Pink, blue, and the brain. *Archives of Sexual Behavior, 32,* 7–14.

Allen, J. P., & Land, D. (1999). Attachment in adolescence. In J. Cassidy & P. R. Shaver (Eds.), *Handbook of attachment: Theory, research, and clinical applications*. New York: The Guilford Press.

Allen, M., Donohue, W. A., Griffin, A., Ryan, D., & Turner, M. M. M. (2003). Comparing the influence of parents and peers on the choice to use drugs. *Criminal Justice & Behavior, 30,* 163–186.

Allison, D. B., Heshka, S., Neale, M. C., Lykken, D. T., & Heymsfield, S. B. (1994). A genetic analysis of relative weight among 4,020 twin pairs, with an emphasis on sex effects. *Health Psychology, 13,* 362–365.

Allison, T., & Cicchetti, D. (1976). Sleep in mammals: Ecological and constitutional correlates. *Science, 194,* 732–734.

Allport, G. W., & Odbert, H. S. (1936). Trait-names, a psycholexical study. *Psychological Monographs, 47*(1, Whole No. 211).

Allport, G. W. (1937). *Personality: A psychological interpretation*. New York: Holt, Rinehart & Winston.

Allport, G. W. (1954). *The nature of prejudice*. Cambridge, MA: Addison-Wesley.

Allport, G. W. (1961). *Pattern and growth in personality*. New York: Holt, Rinehart & Winston.

Allport, G. W. (1966). Traits revisited. *American Psychologist, 21,* 1–10.

Amabile, T. M. (1983). *The social psychology of creativity*. New York: Springer-Verlag.

American Psychological Association. (1992). Ethical principles of psychologists and code of conduct. *American Psychologist, 47,* 1597–1611.

American Psychological Association. (2002). Ethical principles of psychologists and code of conduct. *American Psychologist, 57,* 1060–1073.

American Psychological Association. (2003). Summary report of journal operations, 2001. *American Psychologist, 57,* 659–660.

American Psychological Association. (2003). Summary report of journal operations, 2002. *American Psychologist, 58,* 663–664.

Ammerman, R. T., & Hersen, M. (1997). *Handbook of prevention and treatment with children and adolescents: Intervention in the real world context*. New York: Wiley.

Andersen, B., Kiecolt-Glaser, J. K., & Glaser, R. (1994). A biobehavioral model of cancer stress and disease course. *American Psychologist, 49,* 389–404.

Anderson, A. D., & Phelps, E. A. (2001). Lesions of the human amygdala impair enhanced perception of emotionally salient events. *Nature, 411,* 305–309.

Anderson, A. E., & DiDomenico, L. (1992). Diet vs. shape content of popular male and female magazines: A dose-response relationship to the incidence of eating disorders? *International Journal of Eating Disorders, 11,* 283–287.

Anderson, C. (2003). The psychology of doing nothing. *Psychological Bulletin, 129,* 139–166.

<www.ablongman.com/gerrig17e>

Anderson, C. A., & Bushman, B. J. (2001). Effects of violent video games on aggressive behavior, aggressive cognition, aggressive affect, physiological arousal, and prosocial behavior: A meta-analytic review of the scientific literature. *Psychological Science, 12,* 353–359.

Anderson, J. R. (1987). Skill acquisition: Compilation of weak-method problem-solutions. *Psychological Review, 94,* 192–210.

Anderson, J. R. (1996). ACT: A simple theory of complex cognition. *American Psychologist, 51,* 355–365.

Anderson, V. L., Levinson, E. M., Barker, W., & Kiewra, K. R. (1999). The effects of meditation on teacher perceived occupational stress, state and trait anxiety, and burnout. *School Psychology Quarterly, 14,* 3–25.

Andrews, E. L. (1990, April 29). *A nicotine drug patch to end smoking. The New York Times Index* (Vol. 139, Section 1, Col. 1, p. 27, June 3, 1990).

Angier, N. (1999). *Woman: An intimate geography.* Boston, MA: Houghton Mifflin.

Anliker, J. A., Bartoshuk, L., Ferris, A. M., & Hooks, L. D. (1991). Children's food preferences and genetic sensitivity to the bitter taste of 6-*n*-propylthiouracil (PROP). *American Journal of Clinical Nutrition, 54,* 316–320.

Applebaum, P. S. (1994). *Almost a revolution: Mental health law and the limits of change.* New York: Oxford University Press.

Apter, M. J. (1989). *Reversal theory: Motivation, emotion, and personality.* London: Routledge.

Apter, M. J. (Ed.) (2001). *Motivational styles in everyday life: A guide to reversal theory.* Washington, DC: American Psychological Association.

Apter, M. J., & Batler, R. (1997). Gratuitous risk: A study of parachuting. In S. Svebak & M. J. Apter (Eds.), *Stress & health: A reversal theory perspective* (pp. 119–129). Washington, DC: Taylor & Francis.

Arbisi, P. A., Ben-Porath, Y. S., & McNulty, J. (2002). A comparison of MMPI-2 validity in African American and Caucasian psychiatric inpatients. *Psychological Assessment, 14,* 3–15.

Arendt, H. (1963). *Eichmann in Jerusalem: A report on the banality of evil.* New York: Viking Press.

Arendt, H. (1971). Organized guilt and universal responsibility. In R. W. Smith (Ed.), *Guilt: Man and society.* Garden City, NY: Doubleday Anchor Books.

Arias, E., & Smith, B. L. (2003). Deaths: Preliminary data for 2001. *National Vital Statistics Reports, 51*(5), 1–48.

Arkin, R. M. (Ed.). (1990). Centennial celebration of the principles of psychology. *Personality and Social Psychology Bulletin, 16*(4).

Aron, A., & Aron, E. N. (1994). Love. In A. L. Weber & J. H. Harvey (Eds.), *Perspectives on close relationships* (pp. 131–152). Boston: Allyn & Bacon.

Aron, A., Aron, E. N., & Smollan, D. (1992). Inclusion of other in the self scale and the structure of interpersonal closeness. *Journal of Personality and Social Psychology, 63,* 596–612.

Aron, A., Aron, E. N., Tudor, M., & Nelson, G. (1991). Close relationships as including other in the self. *Journal of Personality and Social Psychology, 60,* 241–253.

Aron, A., & Fraley, B. (1999). Relationship closeness as including other in the self: Cognitive underpinnings and measures. *Social Cognition, 17,* 140–160.

Aron, A., & Westbay, L. (1996). Dimensions of the prototype of love. *Journal of Personality and Social Psychology, 70,* 535–551.

Aronson, E. (2002). Building empathy, compassion, and achievement in the jigsaw classroom. In J. Aronson (Ed.), *Improving academic achievement: Impact of psychological factors on education* (pp. 209–225). San Diego, CA: Academic Press.

Aronson, E., Blaney, N., Stephan, C., Sikes, J., & Snapp, M. (1978). *The jigsaw classroom.* Beverly Hills, CA: Sage.

Aronson, E., & Gonzalez, A. (1988). Desegregation jigsaw, and the Mexican-American experience. In P. A. Katz & D. Taylor (Eds.), *Towards the elimination of racism: Profiles in controversy.* New York: Plenum Press.

Arseneault, L., Moffitt, T. E., Caspi, A., Taylor, A., Rijsdijk, F. V., Jaffee, S. F., Ablow, J. C., & Measelle, J. R. (2003). Strong genetic effects of cross-situational antisocial behaviour among 5-year-old children according to mothers, teachers, examiner-observers, and twins' self-reports. *Journal of Child Psychology and Psychiatry, 44,* 832–848.

Asch, S. E. (1940). Studies in the principles of judgments and attitudes: 11. Determination of judgments by group and by ego standards. *Journal of Social Psychology, 12,* 433–465.

Asch, S. E. (1952). *Social psychology.* Englewood Cliffs, NJ: Prentice Hall.

Asch, S. E. (1955). Opinions and social pressure. *Scientific American, 193*(5), 31–35.

Asch, S. E. (1956). Studies of independence and conformity: A minority of one against a unanimous majority. *Psychological Monographs, 70*(9, Whole No. 416).

Aserinsky, E., & Kleitman, N. (1953). Regularly occurring periods of eye mobility and concomitant phenomena during sleep. *Science, 118,* 273–274.

Ayllon, T., & Michael, J. (1959). The psychiatric nurse as a behavioral engineer. *Journal of the Experimental Analysis of Behavior, 2,* 323–334.

Ayres, T. J., Jonides, J., Reitman, J. S., Egan, J. C., & Howard, D. A. (1979). Differing suffix effects for the same physical stimulus. *Journal of Experimental Psychology: Human Learning and Memory, 5,* 315–321.

Baars, B. J. (1992). A dozen completing-plans techniques for inducing predictable slips in speech and action. In B. J. Baars (Ed.), *Experimental slips and human error: Exploring the architecture of volition* (pp. 129–150). New York: Plenum Press.

Baars, B. J. (1997). *In the theater of consciousness.* New York: Oxford University Press.

Baars, B. J., Cohen, J., Bower, G. H., & Berry, J. W. (1992). Some caveats on testing the Freudian slip hypothesis. In B. J. Baars (Ed.), *Experimental slips and human error: Exploring the architecture of volition* (pp. 289–313). New York: Plenum Press.

Baars, B. J., & McGovern, K. (1994). Consciousness. *Encyclopedia of Human Behavior, 1,* 687–699.

Baars, B. J., & McGovern, K. (1996). Cognitive views of consciousness: What are the facts? How can we explain them? In M. Velmans (Ed.), *The science of consciousness* (pp. 63–95). London: Routledge.

Baars, B. J., Motley, M. T., & MacKay, D. G. (1975). Output editing for lexical status in artificially elicited slips of the tongue. *Journal of Verbal Learning and Verbal Behavor, 14,* 382–391.

Backman, C. W., & Secord, P. F. (1959). The effect of perceived liking on interpersonal attraction. *Human Relations, 12,* 379–384.

Baddeley, A. D. (1986). *Working memory.* New York: Oxford University Press.

Baddeley, A. D. (1992). Working memory. *Science, 255,* 556–559.

Baddeley, A. D. (1994). The magical number seven: Still magic after all these years? *Psychological Review, 101,* 353–356.

Baddeley, A. D., & Andrade, J. (2000). Working memory and the vividness of imagery. *Journal of Experimental Psychology: General, 129,* 126–145.

Bahrick, H. P., Bahrick, P. O., & Wittlinger, R. P. (1975). Fifty years of memory for names and faces: A cross-sectional approach. *Journal of Experimental Psychology: General, 104,* 54–75.

Bailey, J. M., & Pillard, R. C. (1991). A genetic study of male sexual orientation. *Archives of General Psychiatry, 48,* 1089–1096.

Bailey, J. M., Pillard, R. C., Dawood, K., Miller, M. B., Farrer, L. A., Trivedi, S., & Murphy, R. L. (1999). A family history study of male sexual orientation using three independent samples. *Behavior Genetics, 29,* 79–86.

Bailey, J. M., Pillard, R. C., Neale, M. C., & Agyei, Y. (1993). Heritable factors influence sexual orientation in women. *Archives of General Psychiatry, 50,* 217–223.

Bailey, M. B., & Bailey, R. E. (1993). "Misbehavior": A case history. *American Psychologist, 48,* 1157–1158.

Baillargeon, R. (1986). Representing the existence and the location of hidden objects: Object permanence. I. 6- and 8-month-old infants. *Cognition, 23,* 21–41.

Baillargeon, R. (1987a). Young infants reasoning about the physical and spatial properties of a hidden object. *Cognitive Development, 2,* 179–200.

Baillargeon, R. (1987b). Object permanence in $3\frac{1}{2}$- and $4\frac{1}{2}$-month-old infants. *Developmental Pyschology, 23,* 655–664.

Baillargeon, R., & DeVos, J. (1991). Object permanence in young infants: Further evidence. *Child Development, 62,* 1227–1246.

Balch, W. R., & Lewis, B. S. (1996). Music-dependent memory: The roles of tempo change and mood mediation. *Journal of Experimental Psychology: Learning, Memory, and Cognition, 22,* 1354–1363.

Balda, R. P., Kamil, A. C., Bednekoff, P. A., & Hile, A. G. (1997). Species differences in spatial memory performance on a three-dimensional task. *Ethology, 103,* 47–55.

Baldwin, A. L., & Baldwin, C. P. (1973). Study of mother–child interaction. *American Scientist, 61,* 714–721.

Ballenger, J. C. (1999). Current treatments of the anxiety disorders in adults. *Biological Psychiatry, 46,* 1579–1594.

Becker, M. W., Pashler, H., & Anstis, S. M. (2000). The role of iconic memory in change-detection tasks. *Perception, 29,* 273–286.

Baltes, P. B. (1993). The aging mind: Potential and limits. *The Gerontologist, 33,* 580–594.

Baltes, P. B., & Kunzmann, U. (2003). Wisdom. *Psychologist, 16,* 131–133.

Baltes, P. B., & Staudinger, U. M. (1993). The search for a psychology of wisdom. *Current Directions in Psychological Science, 2,* 75–80.

Baltes, P. B., Smith, J., & Staudinger, U. M. (1992). Wisdom and successful aging. In T. B. Sonderegger (Ed.), *The Nebraska Symposium on Motivation: Vol. 39. The psychology of aging* (pp. 123–167). Lincoln: University of Nebraska Press.

Banaji, M. R., & Prentice, D. A. (1994). The self in social contexts. *Annual Review of Psychology, 45,* 297–332.

Bancroft, J. (1978). The relationship between hormones and sexual behavior in humans. In J. B. Hutchinson (Ed.), *Biological determinants of sexual behavior* (pp. 493–519). New York: Wiley.

Bandura, A. (1970). Modeling therapy. In W. S. Sahakian (Ed.), *Psychopathology today: Experimentation, theory and research.* Itasca, IL: Peacock.

Bandura, A. (1977). *Social learning theory.* Englewood Cliffs, NJ: Prentice Hall.

Bandura, A. (1986). *Social foundations of thought and action: A social cognitive theory.* Englewood Cliffs, NJ: Prentice Hall.

Bandura, A. (1992). Exercise of personal agency through the self-efficacy mechanism. In R. Schwarzer (Ed.), *Self-efficacy: Thought control of action* (pp. 3–38). Washington, DC: Hemisphere.

Bandura, A. (1997). *Self-efficacy: The exercise of control.* New York: Freeman.

Bandura, A. (1999). Social cognitive theory of personality. In L. A. Pervin & O. P. John (Eds.), *Handbook of personality: Theory and research* (2nd ed.) (pp. 154–196). New York: Guilford Press.

Bandura, A., Ross, D., & Ross, S. A. (1963). Imitation of film-mediated aggressive models. *Journal of Abnormal and Social Psychology, 66,* 3–11.

Banks, W. C. (1990). *In Discovering Psychology, Program 16* [PBS video series]. Washington, DC: Annenberg/CPB Program.

Banuazizi, A., & Movahedi, S. (1975). Interpersonal dynamics in a simulated prison: A methodological analysis. *American Psychologist, 30,* 152–160.

Banyai, E. I., & Hilgard, E. R. (1976). Comparison of active-alert hypnotic induction with traditional relaxation induction. *Journal of Abnormal Psychology, 85,* 218–224.

Barbaranelli, C., Caprara, G. V., & Maslach, C. (1997). Individuation and the Five Factor Model of personality traits. *European Journal of Psychological Assessment, 13,* 75–84.

Bar-Hillel, M., & Neter, E. (1993). How alike is it versus how likely is it: A disjunction fallacy in probability judgments. *Journal of Personality and Social Psychology, 65,* 1119–1131.

Bargh, J. A., Fitzsimons, G. M., & McKenna, K. Y. A. (2003). The self, online. In S. J. Spencer, S. Fein, M. P. Zanna, & J. M. Olson (Eds.), *Motivated social perception: The Ontario symposium* (Vol. 9, pp. 195–213). Mahwah, NJ: Erlbaum.

Bargh, J. A., McKenna, K. Y. A., & Fitzsimons, G. M. (2002). Can you see the real me? Activation and expression of the "true self" on the Internet. *Journal of Social Issues, 58,* 33–48.

Barinaga, M. (1993). Carbon monoxide: Killer to brain messenger in one step. *Science, 259,* 309.

Barton, N. (2000). The rapid origin of reproduction isolation. *Science, 290,* 462–463.

Barker, L. M., Best, M. R., & Domjan, M. (Eds.). (1978). *Learning mechanisms in food selection.* Houston: Baylor University Press.

Barker, R., Dembo, T., & Lewin, D. (1941). Frustration and aggression: An experiment with young children. *University of Iowa Studies in Child Welfare, 18*(1).

Barnett, W. S. (1998). Long-term cognitive and academic effects of early childhood education of children in poverty. *Preventive Medicine, 27,* 204–207.

Barondes, S. H. (1994). Thinking about Prozac. *Science, 263,* 1102–1103.

Baron-Cohen, S. (2000). Theory of mind and autism: A fifteen year review. In S. Baron-Cohen, H. Tager-Flusberg, & D. J. Cohen (Eds.), *Understanding other minds: Perspectives from developmental cognitive neuroscience* (pp. 3–20). Oxford: Oxford University Press.

Bartlett, F. C. (1932). *Remembering: A study in experimental and social psychology.* Cambridge, U.K.: Cambridge University Press.

Bartoshuk, L. (1990, August–September). Psychophysiological insights on taste. *Science Agenda,* 12–13.

Bartoshuk, L. M. (1993). The biological basis of food perception and acceptance. *Food Quality and Preference, 4,* 21–32.

Bartoshuk, L. M., & Beauchamp, G. K. (1994). Chemical senses. *Annual Review of Psychology, 45,* 419–449.

Bartoshuk, L. M., Duffy, V. B., & Miller, I. J. (1994). PTC/PROP tasting: Anatomy, psychophysics, and sex effects. *Physiology and Behavior, 56,* 1165–1171.

Bassili, J. N. (2003). The minority slowness effect: Subtle inhibitions in the expression of views not shared by others. *Journal of Personality and Social Psychology, 84,* 261–276.

Basso, E. B. (1987). The implications of a progressive theory of dreaming. In B. Tedlock (Ed.), *Dreaming: Anthropological and psychological interpretations* (pp. 86–104). Cambridge, U.K.: Cambridge University Press.

Batson, C. D. (1994). Why act for the public good? Four answers. *Personality and Social Psychology Bulletin, 20,* 603–610.

Batson, C. D., Ahmad, N., Yin, J., Bedell, S. J., Johnson, J. W., Templin, C. M., & Whiteside, A. (1999). Two threats to the common good: Self-interested egoism and empathy-induced altruism. *Personality and Social Psychology Bulletin, 25,* 3–16.

Batson, C. D., Klein, T. R., Highberger, L., & Shaw, L. L. (1995). Immorality from empathy-induced altruism: When compassion and justice conflict. *Journal of Personality and Social Psychology, 68,* 1042–1054.

Batson, C. D., & Powell, A. A. (2003). Altruism and prosocial behavior. In T. Millon & M. J. Lerner (Eds.), *Handbook of psychology: Personality and social psychology* (Vol. 5, pp. 463–484). New York: Wiley.

Baucom, D. H., Shoham, V., Mueser, K. T., Daiuto, A. D., & Stickle, T. R. (1998). Empirically supported couple and family interventions for marital distress and adult mental health problems. *Journal of Consulting and Clinical Psychology, 66,* 53–88.

Baudry, M., Davis, J. L., & Thompson, R.F. (Eds.) (1999). *Advances in synaptic plasticity.* Cambridge, MA: MIT Press.

Baumeister, R. F. (2000). Gender differences in erotic plasticity: The female sex drive as socially flexible and responsive. *Psychological Bulletin, 126,* 347–374.

Baumeister, R. F., Campbell, J. D., Krueger, J. I., & Vohs, K. D. (2003). Does high self-esteem cause better performance, interpersonal success, happiness, or healthy lifestyles? *Psychological Science in the Public Interest, 4,* 1–44.

Baumeister, R. F., & Twenge, J. M. (2002). Cultural suppression of female sexuality. *Review of General Psychology, 6,* 166–203.

Baumeister, R. F., Tice, D. M., & Hutton, D. G. (1989). Self-presentational motivations and personality differences in self-esteem. *Journal of Personality, 57,* 547–579.

Baumgardner, A. H. (1990). To know oneself is to like oneself: Self-certainty and self-affect. *Journal of Personality and Social Psychology, 58,* 1062–1072.

Baxter, L. R., Schwartz, J. M., Bergman, K. S., Szuba, M. P., Guze, B. H., Mazziotta, J. C., Alazraki, A., Selin, C. E., Ferng, H. K., Munford, P., & Phelps, M. E. (1992). Caudate glucose metabolic rate changes with both drug and behavior therapy for obsessive-compulsive disorder. *Archives of General Psychiatry, 49,* 681–689.

Bayley, N. (1956). Individual patterns of development. *Child Development, 27,* 45–74.

Beattie, J., Baron, J., Hershey, J. C., & Spranca, M. D. (1994). Psychological determinants of decision attitude. *Journal of Behavioral Decision Making, 7,* 129–144.

Beck, A. T. (1976). *Cognitive therapy and emotional disorders.* New York: International Universities Press.

Beck, A. T. (1983). Cognitive theory of depression: New perspectives. In P. J. Clayton & J. E. Barrett (Eds.), *Treatment of depression: Old controversies and new approaches* (pp. 265–290). New York: Raven Press.

Beck, A. T. (1985). Cognitive therapy. In H. I. Kaplan & J. Sandock (Eds.), *Comprehensive textbook of psychiatry* (4th ed.). Baltimore: Williams & Wilkins.

Beck, A. T. (1988). Cognitive approaches to panic disorders: Theory and therapy. In S. Rachman & J. D. Maser (Eds.), *Panic: Psychological perspectives.* New York: Guilford Press.

Beck, A. T., & Emery, G. (1985). *Anxiety disorders and phobias: A cognitive perspective.* New York: Basic Books.

Beck, A. T., & Rush, A. J. (1989). Cognitive therapy. In H. I. Kaplan & B. Sadock (Eds.), *Comprehensive textbook of psychiatry* (Vol. 5). Baltimore: Williams & Wilkins.

Beck, A. T., Rush, A. J., Shaw, B. F., & Emery, G. (1979). *Cognitive therapy of depression.* New York: Guilford Press.

Beer, F. A., Healy, A. F., Sinclair, G. P., & Bourne, L. E., Jr. (1987). War cues and foreign policy acts. *American Political Science Review, 81,* 701–715.

Behrman, A. (2002). *Electroboy.* New York: Random House.

Beiser, M., & Gotowiec, A. (2000). Accounting for native/non-native differences in IQ scores. *Psychology in the Schools, 37,* 237–252.

Bell, A. P., & Weinberg, M. S. (1978). *Homosexualities: A study of diversity among men and women.* New York: Simon & Schuster.

Bell, I. R. (1982). *Clinical ecology.* Bolinas, CA: Common Knowledge Press.

Bell, S. T., Kuriloff, P. J., & Lottes, I. (1994). Understanding attributions of blame in stranger rape and date rape situations: An examination of gender, race, identification, and students' social perceptions of rape victims. *Journal of Applied Social Psychology, 24,* 1719–1734.

Bem, D. (2000). The exotic-becomes-erotic theory of sexual orientation. In J. Bancroft (Ed.), *The role of theory in sex research* (pp. 67–81). Bloomington: Indiana University Press.

Bem, D. J. (1972). Self-perception theory. In L. Berkowitz (Ed.), *Advances in experimental social psychology* (Vol. 6, pp. 1–62). New York: Academic Press.

Bem, D. J. (1996). Exotic becomes erotic: A developmental theory of sexual orientation. *Psychological Review, 103,* 320–335.

Bem, S. L. (1974). The measurement of psychological androgyny. *Journal of Consulting and Clinical Psychology, 42,* 155–162.

Bem, S. L. (1981). *The Bem Sex Role Inventory: Professional manual.* Palo Alto, CA: Consulting Psychology Press.

Benedict, R. (1938). Continuities and discontinuities in cultural conditioning. *Psychiatry, 1,* 161–167.

Benedict, R. (1959). *Patterns of culture.* Boston: Houghton Mifflin.

Benenson, J. F., Apostoleris, N. H., & Parnass, J. (1997). Age and sex differences in dyadic and group interaction. *Developmental Psychology, 33,* 538–543.

Benhamou, S., & Poucet, B. (1996). A comparative analysis of spatial memory processes. *Behavioural Processes, 35,* 113–126.

Benington, J. H., & Heller, H. C. (1994). Does the function of REM sleep concern non-REM sleep or waking? *Progress in Neurobiology, 44,* 433–449.

Benington, J. H., & Heller, H. C. (1995). Restoration of brain energy metabolism as the function of sleep. *Progress in Neurobiology, 45,* 347–360.

Benson, H., & Stuart, E. M. (Eds.). (1992). *The wellness book.* New York: Simon & Schuster.

Bergman, E. T., & Roediger, H. L., III. (1999). Can Bartlett's repeated reproduction experiments be replicated? *Memory & Cognition, 27,* 937–947.

Berkowitz, L. (1993). *Aggression: Its causes, consequences, and control.* New York: McGraw-Hill.

Berkowitz, L. (1998). Affective aggression: The role of stress, pain, and negative affect. In R. G. Geen & E. Donnerstein (Eds.), *Human aggression: Theories, research, and implications for public policy* (pp. 49–72). San Diego, CA: Academic Press.

Berlin, B., & Kay, P. (1969). *Basic color terms: Their universality and evolution.* Berkeley: University of California Press.

Berlyne, D. E. (1960). *Conflict, arousal, and curiosity.* New York: McGraw-Hill.

Berman, A. L., & Jobes, D. A. (1991). *Adolescent suicide: Assessment and intervention*. Washington, DC: American Psychological Association.

Berman, K. F., Torrey, E. F., Daniel, D. G., & Weinberger, D. R. (1992). Regional cerebral blood flow in monozygotic twins discordant and concordant for schizophrenia. *Archives of General Psychiatry, 49,* 927–934.

Bernard, L. L. (1924). *Instinct*. New York: Holt, Rinehart & Winston.

Berndt, T. J. (1992). Friendship and friends' influence in adolescence. *Current Directions in Psychological Science, 1,* 156–159.

Bernstein, I. L. (1991). Aversion conditioning in response to cancer and cancer treatment. *Clinical Psychology Review, 11,* 185–191.

Berscheid, E., & Walster, E. H. (1978). *Interpersonal attraction* (2nd ed.). Reading, MA: Addison-Wesley.

Bertenthal, B. I., & Fischer, K. W. (1978). Development of self-recognition in the infant. *Developmental Psychology, 14,* 44–50.

Bickerton, D. (1990). *Language and species*. Chicago: University of Chicago Press.

Biederman, J., Faraone, S. V., & Monteaux, M. C. (2002). Differential effect of environmental adversity by gender: Rutter's index of adversity in a group of boys and girls with and without ADHD. *American Journal of Psychiatry, 159,* 1556–1562.

Biehl, M., Matsumoto, D., Ekman, P., Hearn, V., Heider, K., Kudoh, T., & Ton, V. (1997). Matsumoto and Ekman's Japanese and Caucasian facial expressions of emotion (JACFEE): Reliability data and cross-national differences. *Journal of Nonverbal Behavior, 21,* 3–21.

Biglan, A. (1991). Distressed behavior and its context. *Behavior Analyst, 14,* 157–169.

Billings, A. G., & Moos, R. H. (1982). Family environments and adaptation: A clinically applicable typology. *American Journal of Family Therapy, 20,* 26–38.

Binet, A. (1911). *Les idées modernes sur les enfants*. Paris: Flammarion.

Bingham, C. R., Bennion, L. D., Openshaw, D. K., & Adams, G. R. (1994). An analysis of age, gender and racial differences in recent national trends of youth suicide. *Journal of Adolescence, 17,* 53–71.

Blascovich, J., Wyer, N. A., Swart, L. A., & Kibler, J. L. (1997). Racism and racial categorization. *Journal of Personality and Social Psychology, 72,* 1364–1372.

Bleich, A., Gelkopf, M., & Solomon, Z. (2003). Exposure to terrorism, stress-related mental health symptoms, and coping behaviors among a nationally representative sample in Israel. *JAMA, 290,* 612–620.

Bleuler, M. (1978). The long-term course of schizophrenic psychoses. In L. C. Wynne, R. L. Cromwell, & S. Mattysse (Eds.), *The nature of schizophrenia: New approaches to research and treatment* (pp. 631–636). New York: Wiley.

Block, J. (1995). A contrarian view of the five-factor approach to personality description. *Psychological Bulletin, 117,* 187–215.

Blood, A. J., & Zatorre, R. J. (2001). Intensely pleasurable responses to music correlate with activity in brain regions implicated in reward and emotion. *Proceedings of the National Academy of Sciences. 98,* 11818–11823.

Bloom, K., Delmore-Ko, P., Masataka, N., & Carli, L. (1999). Possible self as parent in Canadian, Italian, and Japanese young adults. *Canadian Journal of Behavioural Science, 31,* 198–207.

Blos, P. (1965). *On adolescence: A psychoanalytic interpretation*. New York: The Free Press.

Blumberg, H. P., Leung, H.-C., Skudlarski, P., Lacadie, C. M., Fredericks, C. A., Harris, B. C., Charney, D. S., Gore, J. C., Krystal, J. H., & Peterson, B. S. (2003). A functional magnetic resonance imaging study of bipolar disorder. *Archives of General Psychiatry, 60,* 601–609.

Bock, K. (1990). Structure in language: Creating form in talk. *American Psychologist, 45,* 1221–1236.

Bock, K. (1996). Language production: Methods and methodologies. *Psychonomic Bulletin & Review, 3,* 395–421.

Bock, K., & Levelt, W. (1994). Language production: Grammatical encoding. In M. A. Gernsbacher (Ed.), *Handbook of psycholinguistics* (pp. 945–984). San Diego, CA: Academic Press.

Bohlin, G., Hagekull, B., & Rydell, A.-M. (2000). Attachment and social functioning: A longitudinal study from infancy to middle childhood. *Social Development, 9,* 24–39.

Boldizar, J. P., Wilson, K. L., & Deemer, D. K. (1989). Gender, life experiences, and moral judgment development: A process-oriented approach. *Journal of Personality and Social Psychology, 57,* 229–238.

Bond, C. F., Jr., Pitre, U., & van Leeuwen, M. D. (1991). Encoding operations and the next-in-line effect. *Personality and Social Psychology Bulletin, 17,* 435–441.

Bond, L. (1995). Unintended consequences of performance assessment: Issues of bias and fairness. *Educational Measurement: Issues and Practice, 14,* 21–24.

Borum, R., & Fulero, S. M. (1999). Empirical research on the insanity defense and attempted reforms: Evidence toward informed policy. *Law and Human Behavior, 23,* 117–135.

Bouchard, C., Tremblay, A., Nadeau, A., Despres, J. P., Theriault, G., Boulay, M. R., Lortie, G., Leblanc, C., & Fournier, G. (1989). Genetic effect in resting and exercise metabolic rates. *Metabolism, 38,* 364–370.

Bouchard, T. J. (1994). Genes, environment, and personality. *Science, 264,* 1700–1701.

Bourguignon, E. (1979). *Psychological anthropology: An introduction to human nature and cultural differences*. New York: Holt, Rinehart & Winston.

Bourne, L. E., Jr., Healy, A. F., & Beer, F. A. (2003). Military conflict and terrorism: General psychology informs international relations. *Review of General Psychology, 7,* 189–202.

Bowd, A. D., & Shapiro, K. J. (1993). The case against laboratory animal research in psychology. *Journal of Social Issues, 49,* 133–142.

Bowden, E. M., & Beeman, M. J. (1998). Getting the right idea: Semantic activation in the right hemisphere may help solve insight problems. *Psychological Science, 9,* 435–440.

Bower, G. H. (1981). Mood and memory. *American Psychologist, 36,* 129–148.

Bower, G. H. (1991). Mood congruity of social judgements. In J. P. Forgas (Ed.), *Emotional & social judgments* (pp. 31–54). Oxford: Pergamon Press.

Bower, S. A., & Bower, G. H. (1991). *Asserting yourself: A practical guide for positive change*. Reading, MA: Addison-Wesley. (Original work published 1976)

Bowers, J. S., & Marsolek, C. J. (Eds.) (2003). *Rethinking implicit memory*. London: Oxford University Press.

Bowlby, J. (1969). *Attachment and loss, Vol 1. Attachment*. New York: Basic Books.

Bowlby, J. (1973). *Attachment and loss, Vol 2. Separation, anxiety and anger*. London: Hogarth.

Bradley, M. M. (1994). Emotional memory: A dimensional analysis. In S. H. M. van Goozen, N. E. Van de Poll, & J. A. Sergeant (Eds.), *Emotions: Essays on emotion theory* (pp. 97–134). Hillsdale, NJ: Erlbaum.

Braginsky, B., & Braginsky, D. (1967). Schizophrenic patients in the psychiatric interview: An experimental study of their effectiveness at manipulation. *Journal of Consulting Psychology, 31,* 543–547.

Brainerd, C. J. (1996). Piaget: A centennial celebration. *Psychological Science, 7,* 191–195.

Brakke, K. E., & Savage-Rumbaugh, E. S. (1995). The development of language skills in bonobo and chimpanzee—I. Comprehension. *Language & Communication, 15,* 121–148.

Breedlove, S. M. (1994). Sexual differentiation of the human nervous system. *Annual Review of Psychology, 45,* 389–418.

Breggin, P. R. (1979). *Electroshock: Its brain disabling effects.* New York: Springer.

Breggin, P. R. (1991). *Toxic psychiatry.* New York: St. Martin's Press.

Bregman, A. S. (1981). Asking the "what for" question in auditory perception. In M. Kobovy & J. Pomerantz (Eds.), *Perceptual organization* (pp. 99–118). Hillsdale, NJ: Erlbaum.

Breland, K., & Breland, M. (1951). A field of applied animal psychology. *American Psychologist, 6,* 202–204.

Breland, K., & Breland, M. (1961). A misbehavior of organisms. *American Psychologist, 16,* 681–684.

Breslau, N., Davis, G. C., Andreski, P., Peterson, E. L., & Schultz, L. R. (1997). Sex differences in posttraumatic stress disorder. *Archives of General Psychiatry, 54,* 1044–1048.

Bretherton, I. (1996). Internal working models of attachment relationships as related to resilient coping. In G. G. Noam & K. W. Fischer (Eds.), *Development and vulnerability in close relationships* (pp. 3–27). Mahwah, NJ: Erlbaum.

Brewer, J. B., Zhao, Z., Desmond, J. E., Glover, G. H., & Gabrieli, J. D. E. (1998). Making memories: Brain activity that predicts how well visual experience will be remembered. *Science, 281,* 1185–1187.

Broadbent, D. E. (1958). *Perception and communication.* London: Pergamon Press.

Brody, A. L., Saxena, S., Stoessel, P., Gillies, L. A., Fairbanks, L. A., Alborzian, S., Phelps, M. E., Huang, S.-C., Wu, H.-M., Ho, M. L., Ho, M. K., Au, S. C., Maidment, K., & Baxter, L. R., Jr. (2002). Regional brain metabolic changes in patients with major depression treated with either paroxetine or interpersonal therapy. *Archives of General Psychiatry, 58,* 631–640.

Brody, N. (1997b). Intelligence, schooling, and society. *American Psychologist, 52,* 1046–1050.

Broman, S. H., Nichols, P. I., & Kennedy, W. A. (1975). *Preschool IQ: Prenatal and early developmental correlates.* Hillsdale, NJ: Erlbaum.

Bronfenbrenner, U. (1999). Environments in developmental perspective: Theoretical and operational models. In S. L. Friedman & T. D. Wachs (Eds.), *Measuring environment across the lifespan: Emerging methods and concepts* (pp. 3–28). Washington, DC: American Psychological Association.

Bronfenbrenner, U., & Ceci, S. J. (1994). Nature–nurture reconceptualized in developmental perspective: A bioecological model. *Psychological Review, 101,* 568–586.

Brooner, R. K., King, V. L., Kidorf, M., Schmidt, C. W., & Bigelow, G. E. (1997). Psychiatric and substance abuse comorbidity among treatment-seeking opioid abusers. *Archives of General Psychiatry, 54,* 71–80.

Broughton, W. A., & Broughton, R. J. (1994). Psychosocial impact of narcolepsy. *Sleep, 17*(Suppl. 8), S45–S49.

Broussard, C., & Northup, J. (1997). The use of functional analysis to develop peer interventions for disruptive classroom behavior. *School Psychology Quarterly, 12,* 65–76.

Brown, J. D. (1998). *The self.* New York: McGraw-Hill.

Brown, N. R., & Siegler, R. S. (1992). The role of availability in the estimation of national populations. *Memory & Cognition, 20,* 406–412.

Brown, R. (1976). Reference: In memorial tribute to Eric Lenneberg. *Cognition, 4,* 125–153.

Brown, R. (1986). *Social psychology: The second edition.* New York: The Free Press.

Brownell, K. D., & Rodin, J. (1994). The dieting maelstrom: Is it possible and advisable to lose weight? *American Psychologist, 49,* 781–791.

Buboltz, W. C., Jr., Soper, B., Brown, F., & Jenkins, S. (2002). Treatment approaches for sleep difficulties in college students. *Counselling Psychology Quarterly, 15,* 229–237.

Buchner, A., & Wippich, W. (2000). On the reliability of implicit and explicit memory measures. *Cognitive Psychology, 40,* 227–259.

Buckner, J. C., Mezzacappa, E., & Beardslee, W. R. (2003). Characteristics of resilient youths living in poverty: The role of self-regulatory processes. *Development and Psychopathology, 15,* 139–162.

Bukowski, W. M., Newcomb, A. F., & Hartup, W. W. (Eds.). (1998). *The company they keep: Friendship in childhood and adolescence.* New York: Cambridge University Press.

Buntain-Ricklefs, J. J., Kemper, K. J., Bell, M., & Babonis, T. (1994). Punishments: What predicts adult approval. *Child Abuse & Neglect, 18,* 945–955.

Burchinal, M. R., Roberts, J. E., Riggins, R., Jr., Zeisel, S. A., Neebe, E., & Bryant, D. (2000). Relating quality of center-based child care to early cognitive and language development longitudinally. *Child Development, 71,* 338–357.

Burger, J. M., Reed, M., DeCesare, K., Rauner, S., & Rozolis, J. (1999). The effects of initial request size on compliance: More about the that's-not-all technique. *Basic and Applied Social Psychology, 21,* 243–249.

Burger, J. M. (Wagner, U., van Dick, R.,). Increasing compliance by improving the deal: The that's-not-all technique. *Journal of Personality and Social Psychology, 51,* 277–283.

Burnstein, E., Crandall, C., & Kitayama, S. (1994). Some neo-Darwinian decision rules for altruism: Weighing cues for inclusive fitness as a function of the biological importance of the decision. *Journal of Personality and Social Psychology, 67,* 773–789.

Burnstein, E., & Worchel, P. (1962). Arbitrariness of frustration and its consequences for aggression in a social situation. *Journal of Personality, 30,* 528–540.

Bush, G., Luu, P., Posner, M. I. (2000). Cognitive and emotional influences in anterior cingulate cortex. *Trends in Cognitive Sciences, 4,* 215–222.

Bushman, B. J., & Anderson, C. J. (2002). Violent video games and hostile expectations: A test of the general aggression model. *Personality and Social Psychology Bulletin, 28,* 1679–1686.

Buss, D. M. (1999). *Evolutionary psychology: The new science of mind.* Boston, MA: Allyn & Bacon.

Buss, D. M. (2000). The evolution of happiness. *American Psychologist, 55,* 15–23.

Buss, D. M., & Schmitt, D. P. (1993). Sexual strategies theory: An evolutionary perspective on human mating. *Psychological Review, 100,* 204–232.

Butcher, J. N., Dahlstrom, W. G., Graham, J. R., Tellegen, A., & Kaemmer, B. (1989). *Manual for the restandardized Minnesota Multiphasic Personality Inventory: MMPI-2. An administrative and interpretive guide.* Minneapolis: University of Minnesota Press.

Butcher, J. N., & Rouse, S. V. (1996). Personality: Individual differences and clinical assessment. *Annual Review of Psychology, 47,* 87–111.

Butcher, J. N., & Williams, C. L. (1992). *Essentials of MMPI-2 and MMPI-A interpretation.* Minneapolis: University of Minnesota Press.

Bykov, K. M. (1957). *The cerebral cortex and the internal organs*. New York: Academic Press.

Byrne, D., & Clore, G. L. (1970). A reinforcement model of evaluative processes. *Personality: An International Journal, 1*, 103–128.

Cabeza, R., & Nyberg, L. (2000). Imaging cognition II: An empirical review of 275 PET and fMRI studies. *Journal of Cognitive Neuroscience, 12*, 1–47.

Cairns, E., & Darby, J. (1998). The conflict in Northern Ireland: Causes, consequences, and controls. *American Psychologist, 53*, 754–760.

Cairns, E., Wilson, R., Gallagher, T., & Trew, K. (1995). Psychology's contribution to understanding conflict in Northern Ireland. *Peace and Conflict: Journal of Peace Psychology, 1*, 131–148.

Campbell, W. K., Sedikides, C., Reeder, G. D., & Elliot, A. J. (2000). Among friends? An examination of friendship and the self-serving bias. *British Journal of Social Psychology, 39*, 229–239.

Campfield, L. A., Smith, F. J., & Burn, P. (1998). Strategies and potential molecular targets for obesity treatment. *Science, 280*, 1383–1387.

Campos, J. J., Barrett, K. C., Lamb, M. E., Goldsmith, H. H., & Stenberg, C. (1983). *Socioemotional development* (Vol. 2). New York: Wiley.

Campos, J. J., Bertenthal, B. I., & Kermoian, R. (1992). Early experience and emotional development: The emergence of wariness of heights. *Psychological Science, 3*, 61–64.

Camras, L. A., Oster, H., Campos, J., Campos, R., Ujiie, T., Miyake, K., Wang, L., & Meng, Z. (1998). Production of emotional facial expressions in European American, Japanese, and Chinese infants. *Developmental Psychology, 34*, 616–628.

Camras, L. A., Oster, H., Campos, J. J., Miyake, K., & Bradshaw, D. (1992). Japanese and American infants' responses to arm restraint. *Developmental Psychology, 28*, 578–583.

Canli, T., Desmond, J. E., Zhao, Z., Glover, G., & Gabrieli, J. D. E. (1998). Hemispheric asymmetry for emotional stimuli detected with fMRI. *NeuroReport, 9*, 3233–3239.

Canli, T., Sivers, H., Whitfield, S. L., Gotlib, I. H., & Gabrieli, J. D. E. (2002). Amygdala response to happy faces as a function of extraversion. *Science, 296*, 2191.

Cannon, W. B. (1927). The James–Lange theory of emotion: A critical examination and an alternative theory. *American Journal of Psychology, 39*, 106–124.

Cannon, W. B. (1929). *Bodily changes in pain, hunger, fear, and rage* (2nd ed.). New York: Appleton-Century-Crofts.

Cannon, W. B. (1934). Hunger and thirst. In C. Murchison (Ed.), *A handbook of general experimental psychology*. Worcester, MA: Clark University Press.

Cannon, W. B., & Washburn, A. L. (1912). An explanation of hunger. *American Journal of Physiology, 29*, 441–454.

Cantor, N., & Kihlstrom, J. R. (1987). *Personality and social intelligence*. Englewood Cliffs, NJ: Prentice Hall.

Cantor, N., & Mischel, W. (1979). Traits as prototypes: Effects on recognition memory. *Journal of Personality and Social Psychology, 35*, 38–48.

Caprara, G. V., Barbaranelli, C., Borgoni, L., & Perugini, M. (1993). The Big Five Questionnaire: A new questionnaire for the measurement of the five factor model. *Personality and Individual Differences, 15*, 281–288.

Caprara, G. V., Barbaranelli, C., & Zimbardo, P. G. (1996). Understanding the complexity of human aggression: Affective, cognitive, and social dimensions of individual differences in propensity toward aggression. *European Journal of Personality, 10*, 133–155.

Caprara, G. V., Regalia, C., & Bandura, A. (2002). Longitudinal impact of perceived self-regulatory efficacy on violent conduct. *European Psychologist, 7*, 63–69.

Carducci, B. J., & Zimbardo, P. G. (1995, November/December). Are you shy? *Psychology Today, 28*, 34–40.

Carey, S. (1978). The child as word learner. In M. Hale, J. Bresnan, & G. A. Miller (Eds.), *Linguistic theory and psychological reality* (pp. 265–293). Cambridge, MA: The MIT Press.

Carey, S. (1985). *Conceptual change in childhood*. Cambridge, MA: The MIT Press.

Carlsmith, J. M., & Gross, A. (1969). Some effects of guilt on compliance. *Journal of Personality and Social Psychology, 11*, 232–240.

Carlson, M., Charlin, V., & Miller, N. (1988). Positive mood and helping behavior: A test of six hypotheses. *Journal of Personality and Social Psychology, 55*, 211–229.

Carlson-Radvansky, L. A., & Irwin, D. E. (1995). Memory for structural information across eye movements. *Journal of Experimental Psychology: Learning, Memory, and Cognition, 21*, 1441–1458.

Carmichael, L. (1970). The onset and early development of behavior. In P. H. Mussen (Ed.), *Carmichael's manual of child psychology* (3rd ed., Vol. 1). New York: Wiley.

Carstensen, L. L. (1991). Selectivity theory: Social activity in life-span context. In K. W. Schaie (Ed.), *Annual review of geriatrics and gerontology* (Vol. 11). New York: Springer.

Carstensen, L. L. (1998). A life-span approach to social motivation. In J. Heckhausen & C. S. Dweck (Eds.), *Motivation and self-regulation across the life span* (pp. 341–364). New York: Cambridge University Press.

Carstensen, L. L., & Freund, A. M. (1994). The resilience of the aging self. *Developmental Review, 14*, 81–92.

Carstensen, L. L., & Pasupathi, M. (1993). Women of a certain age. In S. Matteo (Ed.), *American women in the nineties: Today's critical issues* (pp. 66–78). Boston: Northeastern University Press.

Carter, J. H. (1982). The effects of aging on selected visual functions: Color vision, glare sensitivity, field of vision, and accommodation. In R. Sekuler, D. Kline, & K. Dismukes (Eds.), *Aging and human visual function* (pp. 121–130). New York: Liss.

Cartwright, R. D. (1982). The shape of dreams. In *1983 yearbook of science and the future*. Chicago: Encyclopaedia Britannica.

Caspi, A., Sugden, K., Moffitt, T. E., Taylor, A., Craig, I. W., Harrington, H., McClay, J., Mill, J., Martin, J., Braithwaite, A., & Poulton, R. (2003). Influence of life stress on depression: Moderation by a polymorphism in the 5-HTT gene. *Science, 301*, 386–389.

Catalan, J., Burgess, A., Pergami, A., Hulme, N., Gazzard, B., & Phillips, R. (1996). The psychological impact on staff of caring for people with serious diseases: The case of HIV infection and oncology. *Journal of Psychosomatic Research, 42*, 425–435.

Catalano, R., Novaco, R., & McConnell, W. (1997). A model of the net effect of job loss on violence. *Journal of Personality and Social Psychology, 72*, 1440–1447.

Catalano, R., Novaco, R. W., & McConnell, W. (2002). Layoffs and violence revisited. *Aggressive Behavior, 28*, 233–247.

Catania, J. A., Coates, T. J., & Kegeles, S. (1994). A test of the AIDS risk reduction model: Psychosocial correlates of condom use in the AMEN cohort survey. *Health Psychology, 13*, 548–555.

Caterina, M. J., Leffler, A., Malmberg, A. B., Martin, W. J., Trafton, J., Petersen-Zeitz, K. R., Koltzenburg, M., Basbaum, A. I., & Julius, D. (2000). Impaired nociception and pain sensation in mice lacking the capsaicin receptor. *Science, 288*, 306–313.

Cattell, R. B. (1963). Theory of fluid and crystallized intelligence: A critical experiment. *Journal of Educational Psychology, 54*, 1–22.

Cattell, R. B. (1979). *Personality and learning theory*. New York: Springer.

Ceci, S. J. (1999). Schooling and intelligence. In S. J. Ceci & W. M. Williams (Eds.), *The nature-nurture debate: The essential readings* (pp. 168–175). Oxford, U.K.: Blackwell.

Ceci, S. J., & Liker, J. K. (1986). A day at the races: A study of IQ, expertise, and cognitive complexity. *Journal of Experimental Psychology: General, 115,* 255–266.

Centers for Disease Control and Prevention. (1997). Cigarette smoking among adults—United States, 1995. *Morbidity and Mortality Weekly Report, 46,* 1217–1220.

Cervone, D. (2000). Thinking about self-efficacy. *Behavior Modification, 24,* 30–56.

Cervone, D., & Shoda, Y. (Eds.). (1999). *The coherence of personality: Social-cognitive bases of consistency, variability, and organization*. New York: Guilford Press.

Ceschi, G., van der Linden, M., Dunker, D., Perroud, A., & Brédart, S. (2003). Further exploration memory bias in compulsive washers. *Behaviour Research and Therapy, 41,* 737–748.

Chae, Y. M. (1998). Expert systems in medicine. In J. Liebowitz (Ed.), *The handbook of applied expert systems* (pp. 32-1-32–20). Boca Raton, FL: CRC Press.

Chamberlain, K., & Zika, S. (1990). The minor events approach to stress: Support for the use of daily hassles. *British Journal of Psychology, 81,* 469–481.

Champoux, M., Boyce, W. T., & Suomi, S. J. (1995). Biobehavioral comparisons between adopted and nonadopted rhesus monkey infants. *Journal of Developmental and Behavioral Pediatrics, 16,* 6–13.

Chan, A. Y., & Wethington, E. (1998). Factors promoting marital resilience among interracial couples. In H. I. McCubbin, E. A. Thompson, A. I. Thompson, & J. E. Fromer (Eds.), *Resiliency in Native American and immigrant families* (pp. 71–87). Thousand Oaks, CA: Sage.

Chandrasekaran, B., & Mittal, S. (1999). Deep versus compiled knowledge approaches to diagnostic problem-solving. *International Journal of Human-Computer Studies, 51,* 357–368.

Chapman, P. D. (1988). *Schools as sorters: Lewis M. Terman, applied psychology, and the intelligence testing movement, 1890–1930*. New York: New York University Press.

Chase, W. G., & Ericsson, K. A. (1981). Skilled memory. In J. R. Anderson (Ed.), *Cognitive skills and their acquisition*. Hillsdale, NJ: Erlbaum.

Chaudhari, N., Landin, A. M., & Roper, S. D. (2000). A metabotropic glutamate receptor variant functions as a taste receptor. *Nature Neuroscience, 3,* 113–119.

Chaves, J. F. (1999). Applying hypnosis in pain management: Implications of alternative theoretical perspectives. In I. Kirsch, A. Capafons, E. Cardeña-Buelna, & S. Amigó (Eds.), *Clinical hypnosis and self-regulation: Cognitive-behavioral perspectives* (pp. 227–247). Washington, DC: American Psychological Association.

Chen, I. (1990, July 13). Quake may have caused baby boom in Bay Area. *The San Francisco Chronicle,* p. A3.

Cheney, D. L., & Seyfarth, R. M. (1990). *How monkeys see the world*. Chicago: University of Chicago Press.

Cheng, P. W., & Holyoak, K. J. (1985). Pragmatic reasoning schemas. *Cognitive Psychology, 17,* 391–416.

Cherry, E. C. (1953). Some experiments on the recognition of speech, with one and with two ears. *Journal of the Acoustical Society of America, 25,* 975–979.

Chess, S., & Thomas, A. (1984). *Origins and evolution of behavior disorders*. New York: Brunner/Mazel.

Choice, P., & Lamke, L. K. (1999). Stay/leave decision-making processes in abusive dating relationships. *Personal Relationships, 6,* 351–367.

Chomsky, N. (1965). *Aspects of a theory of syntax*. Cambridge, MA: The MIT Press.

Chomsky, N. (1975). *Reflections on language*. New York: Pantheon Books.

Chorover, S. (1981, June). *Organizational recruitment in "open" and "closed" social systems: A neuropsychological perspective*. Conference paper presented at the Center for the Study of New Religious Movements, Berkeley, California.

Christensen, A. J., Moran, P. J., Lawton, W. J., Stallman, D., & Voights, A. L. (1997). Monitoring attentional style and medical regimen adherence in hemodialysis patients. *Health Psychology, 16,* 256–262.

Cialdini, R. B. (2001). *Influence: Science and practice* (4th ed.), Boston, MA: Allyn & Bacon.

Cialdini, R. B., Vincent, J. E., Lewis, S. K., Catalan, J., Wheeler, D., & Darby, B. L. (1975). Reciprocal concessions procedure for inducing compliance: The door-in-the-face technique. *Journal of Personality and Social Psychology, 31,* 206–215.

Ciaranello, R. D., & Ciaranello, A. L. (1991). Genetics of major psychiatric disorders. *Annual Review of Medicine, 42,* 151–158.

Claar, R. L., & Blumenthal, J. A. (2003). The value of stress-management interventions in life-threatening medical conditions. *Current Directions in Psychological Science, 12,* 133–137.

Clark, E. V. (2003). *First language acquisition*. Cambridge: Cambridge University Press.

Clark, H. H. (1996). *Using language*. Cambridge, U.K.: Cambridge University Press.

Clark, H. H., & Clark, E., V. (1977). *Psychology and language: An introduction to psycholinguistics*. New York: Harcourt Brace Jovanovich.

Clark, H. H., & Marshall, C. R. (1981). Definite reference and mutual knowledge. In A. K. Joshi, B. Webber, & I. Sag (Eds.), *Elements of discourse understanding* (pp. 10–63). Cambridge, U.K.: Cambridge University Press.

Clark, H. H., & Van Der Wege, M. M. (2002). Psycholinguistics. In H. Pashler & D. Medin (Eds.), *Stevens' handbook of experimental psychology: Vol 3. Memory and cognitive processes* (pp. 209–259). New York: Wiley.

Clark, K., & Clark, M. (1947). Racial indentification and preference in Negro children. In T. M. Newcomb & E. L. Hartley (Eds.), *Readings in social psychology* (pp. 169–178). New York: Holt.

Clark, N. M., & Becker, M. H. (1998). Theoretical models and strategies for improving adherence and disease management. In S. A. Shumaker & E. B. Schron (Eds.), *The handbook of health behavior change* (pp. 5–32). New York: Springer.

Clarke-Stewart, K. A. (1991). A home is not a school: The effects of child care on children's development. *Journal of Social Issues, 47,* 105–123.

Clarke-Stewart, K. A. (1993). *Daycare*. Cambridge, MA: Harvard University Press.

Clausen, J. A. (1981). Stigma and mental disorder: Phenomena and mental terminology. *Psychiatry, 44,* 287–296.

Clementz, B. A., & Sweeney, J. A. (1990). Is eye movement dysfunction a biological marker for schizophrenia? A methodological review. *Psychological Bulletin, 108,* 77–92.

Clopton, N. A., & Sorell, G. T. (1993). Gender differences in moral reasoning: Stable or situational? *Psychology of Women Quarterly, 17,* 85–101.

Cody, H., Pelphrey, K., & Piven, J. (2002). Structural and functional magnetic resonance imaging of autism. *International Journal of Developmental Neuroscience, 20,* 421–438.

Coe, C. L. (1999). Psychosocial factors and psychoneuroimmunology within a lifespan perspective. In D. P. Keating & C. Hertzman (Eds.), *Developmental health and the wealth of* nations: *Social, biological, and educational dynamics* (pp. 201–219). New York: The Guilford Press.

Cogan, J. C., Bhalla, S. K., Sefa-Dedeh, A., & Rothblum, E. D. (1996). A comparison study of United States and African students on perceptions of obesity and thinness. *Journal of Cross-Cultural Psychology, 27,* 98–113.

Cohen, D., & Nisbett, R. E. (1994). Self-protection and the culture of honor: Explaining southern violence. *Personality and Social Psychology Bulletin, 20,* 551–567.

Cohen, D., Nisbett, R. E., Bowdle, B. R., & Schwarz, N. (1996). Insult, aggression, and the Southern culture of honor: An "experimental ethnography." *Journal of Personality and Social Psychology, 70,* 945–960.

Cohen, D., Taieb, O., Flament, M., Benoit, N., Chevret, S., Corcos, M., Fossati, P., Jeammet, P., Allilaire, J. F., & Basquin, M. (2000). Absence of cognitive impairment at long-term follow-up in adolescents treated with ECT for severe mood disorder. *American Journal of Psychiatry, 157,* 460–462.

Cohen, M. N. (2002). An anthropologist looks at "race" and IQ testing. In J. M. Fish (Ed.), *Race and intelligence: Separating science from myth* (pp. 201–223). Mahwah, NJ: Erlbaum.

Cohen, S., Tyrrell, D. A. J., & Smith, A. P. (1993). Negative life events, perceived stress, negative affect, and susceptibility to the common cold. *Journal of Personality and Social Psychology, 64,* 131–140.

Cohn, E. G., & Rotton, J. (1997). Assault as a function of time and temperature: A moderator-variable time-series analysis. *Journal of Personality and Social Psychology, 72,* 1322–1334.

Coleman, R. M. (1986). *Wide awake at 3:00 a.m.: By choice or by chance?* New York: Freeman.

Coles, C. (1994). Critical periods for prenatal alcohol exposure. *Alcohol Health & Research World, 18,* 22–29.

Collaer, M. L., & Hines, M. (1995). Human behavioral sex differences: A role for gonadal hormones during early development? *Psychological Bulletin, 118,* 55–107.

Collins, M. A., & Amabile, T. M. (1999). Motivation and creativity. In R. J. Sternberg (Ed.), *Handbook of creativity* (pp. 297–312). Cambridge, U.K.: Cambridge University Press.

Collins, W. A., Maccoby, E. E., Steinberg, L., Hetherington, E. M., & Bornstein, M. H. (2000). Contemporary research on parenting: The case for nature and nurture. *American Psychologist, 55,* 218–232.

Comstock, G., & Scharrer, E. (1999). *Television: What's on, who's watching, and what it means.* San Diego, CA: Academic Press.

Conner, K. R., Duberstein, P. R., Conwell, Y., Seidlitz, L., & Caine, E. D. (2001). Psychological vulnerability to completed suicide: A review of empirical studies. *Suicide and Life-Threatening Behavior, 31,* 367–385.

Cook, T. D., Churck, M. B., Ajanaku, S., Shadish, W. R., Jr., Kim, J. R., & Cohen, R. (1996). The development of occupational aspirations and expectations among inner-city boys. *Child Development, 67,* 3368–3385.

Coolidge, F. L., Thede, L. L., & Jang, K. L. (2001). Heritability of personality disorders in childhood: A preliminary investigation. *Journal of Personality Disorders, 15,* 33–40.

Coren, S., Ward, L. M., & Enns, J. T. (1999). *Sensation and perception* (5th ed.). Fort Worth, TX: Harcourt Brace.

Corina, D. P., & McBurney, S. L. (2001). The neural representation of language in users of American Sign Language. *Journal of Communication Disorders, 34,* 455–471.

Corr, P. J., & Gray, J. A. (1996). Attributional style as a personality factor in insurance sales performance in the UK. *Journal of Occupational and Organizational Psychology, 69,* 83–87.

Corso, J. F. (1977). Auditory perception and communication. In J. E. Birren & K. W. Schaie (Eds.), *Handbook of the psychology of aging* (pp. 535–553). New York: Van Nostrand Reinhold.

Costa, P. T., Jr., & McCrae, R. R. (1985). *The NEO Personality Inventory manual.* Odessa, FL: Psychological Assessment Resources.

Costa, P. T., Jr., & McCrae, R. R. (1992a). Four ways five factors are basic. *Personality and Individual Differences, 13,* 653–665.

Costa, P. T., Jr., & McCrae, R. R. (1992b). *Revised NEO Personality Inventory (NEO-PI-R) and NEO Five-Factor Inventory (NEO-FFI) professional manual.* Odessa, FL: Psychological Assessment Resources.

Courchesne, R., Carper, R., & Akshoomoff, N. (2003). Evidence of brain overgrowth in the first year of life in autism. *JAMA, 290,* 337–344.

Couture, S., & Penn, D. (2003). Interpersonal contact and the stigma of mental illness: A review of the literature. *Journal of Mental Health, 12,* 291–306.

Cowan, C. P., & Cowan, P. (2000). *When partners become parents: The big life change for couples.* Mahwah, NJ: Erlbaum.

Cowan, C. P., & Cowan, P. A. (1988). Changes in marriage during the transition to parenthood. In G. Y. Michaels & W. A. Goldberg (Eds.), *The transition to parenthood: Current theory and research.* Cambridge, U.K.: Cambridge University Press.

Cowan, C. P., Cowan, P. A., Heming, G., Garrett, E., Coysh, W. S., Curtis-Boles, H., & Boles, A. J., III. (1985). Transitions to parenthood: His, hers, and theirs. *Journal of Family Issues, 6,* 451–481.

Cowan, N. (1993). Activation, attention, and short-term memory. *Memory & Cognition, 21,* 162–167.

Cowan, P., & Cowan, C. P. (1998). New families: Modern couples as new pioneers. In M. A. Mason, A. Skolnick, & S. D. Sugarman (Eds.), *All our families: New policies for a new century.* New York: Oxford University Press.

Cowan, W. M. (1979, September). The development of the brain. *Scientific American, 241,* 106–117.

Cowles, J. T. (1937). Food tokens as incentives for learning by chimpanzees. *Comparative Psychology Monographs, 74,* 1–96.

Craik, F. I. M. (1994). Memory changes in normal aging. *Current Directions in Psychological Science, 3,* 155–158.

Craik, F. I. M. (1999). Age-related changes in human memory. In D. C. Park & N. Schwarz (Eds.), *Cognitive aging: A primer* (pp. 75–92). Philadelphia: Psychology Press.

Craik, F. I. M., & Lockhart, R. S. (1972). Levels of processing: A framework for memory research. *Journal of Verbal Learning and Verbal Behavior, 11,* 671–684.

Cramer, P. (1997). Identity, personality, and defense mechanisms: An observer-based study. *Journal of Research in Personality, 31,* 58–77.

Crandall, C. S., & Eshleman, A. (2003). A justification-suppression model of the expression and experience of prejudice. *Psychological Bulletin, 129,* 414–446.

Cranson, R. W., Orme-Johnson, D. W., Gackenbach, J., Dillbeck, M. C., Jones, C. H., & Alexander, C. N. (1991). Transcendental meditation and improved performance on intelligence-related measures: A longitudinal study. *Personality and Individual Differences, 12,* 1105–1116.

Creasey, G., Mitts, N., & Catanzaro, S. (1995). Associations among daily hassles, coping, and behavior problems in nonreferred kindergartners. *Journal of Child Clinical Psychology, 24,* 311–319.

Crockett, L. J., & Silbereisen, R. K. (Eds.). (2000). *Negotiating adolescence in times of social change.* New York: Cambridge University Press.

Crowder, R. G. (1976). *Principles of learning and memory.* Hillsdale, NJ: Erlbaum.

Crowder, R. G. (1992). Eidetic imagery. In L. R. Squire (Ed.), *Encyclopedia of learning and memory* (pp. 154–156). New York: Macmillan.

Crowder, R. G., & Morton, J. (1969). Precategorical acoustic storage (PAS). *Perception and Psychophysics, 8,* 815–820.

Cummins, D. D. (1996). Evidence of deontic reasoning in 3- and 4-year-old children. *Memory & Cognition, 24,* 823–829.

Cummins, D. D. (1999). Cheater detection is modified by social rank: The impact of dominance on the evolution of cognitive functions. *Evolution and Human Behavior, 20,* 229–248.

Curtis, R. C., & Miller, K. (1986). Believing another likes or dislikes you: Behaviors making the beliefs come true. *Journal of Personality and Social Psychology, 51,* 284–290.

Cutting, J. C., & Bock, K. (1997). That's the way the cookie bounces: Syntactic and semantic components of experimentally elicited idiom blends. *Memory & Cognition, 25,* 57–71.

Cutting, J. C., & Proffitt, D. (1982). The minimum principle and the perception of absolute, common and relative motions. *Cognitive Psychology, 14,* 211–246.

Czeisler, C. A., Duffy, J. F., Shanahan, T. L., Brown, E. N., Mitchell, J. F., Rimmer, D. W., Ronda, J. M., Silva, E. J., Allan, J. S., Emens, J. S., Dijk, D.-J., & Kronauer, R. E. (1999). Stability, precision, and near-24-hour period of the human circadian pacemaker. *Science, 284,* 2177–2181.

Dahlstrom, W. G., Welsh, H. G., & Dahlstrom, L. E. (1975). *An MMPI handbook, Vol. 1: Clinical interpretation.* Minneapolis: University of Minnesota Press.

Dakof, G. A., & Taylor, S. E. (1990). Victims' perceptions of social support: What is helpful from whom? *Journal of Personality and Social Psychology, 58,* 80–89.

Damasio, H., Grabowski, T., Frank, R., Galaburda, A. M., & Damasio, A. R. (1994). The return of Phineas Gage: Clues about the brain from the skull of a famous patient. *Science, 264,* 1102–1105.

Daneman, M., & Carpenter, P. A. (1980). Individual differences in working memory and reading. *Journal of Verbal Learning and Verbal Behavior, 19,* 450–466.

Darley, J., & Latané, B. (1968). Bystander intervention in emergencies: Diffusion of responsibility. *Journal of Personality and Social Psychology, 8,* 377–383.

Darley, J. M., & Batson, C. D. (1973). From Jerusalem to Jericho: A study of situational and dispositional variables in helping behavior. *Journal of Personality and Social Psychology, 27,* 100–108.

Darling, N., & Steinberg, L. (1993). Parenting style as context: An integrative model. *Psychological Bulletin, 113,* 487–496.

Darnton, R. (1968). *Mesmerism and the end of the Enlightenment in France.* Cambridge, MA: Harvard University Press.

Darwin, C. (1965). *The expression of emotions in man and animals.* Chicago: University of Chicago Press. (Original work published 1872)

Darwin, C. J., Turvey, M. T., & Crowder, R. G. (1972). The auditory analogue of the Sperling partial report procedure: Evidence for brief auditory stage. *Cognitive Psychology, 3,* 255–267.

D'Augelli, A. R. (1993). Preventing mental health problems among lesbian and gay college students. *The Journal of Primary Prevention, 13,* 245–261.

D'Augelli, A. R., Hershberger, S. L., & Pilkington, N. W. (2001). Suicidality patterns and sexual orientation-related factors among lesbian, gay, and bisexual youths. *Suicide and Life-Threatening Behavior, 31,* 250–264.

D'Augelli, A. R., Pilkington, N. W., & Hershberger, S. L. (2002). Incidence and mental health impact of sexual orientation victimization of lesbian, gay, and bisexual youths in high school. *Social Psychology Quarterly, 17,* 148–167.

Davidson, A. R., & Jaccard, J. J. (1979). Variables that moderate the attitude-behavior relation: Results of a longitudinal survey. *Journal of Personality and Social Psychology, 37,* 1364–1376.

Davidson, R. J., Jackson D.C., & Kalin, N. H. (2000). Emotion, plasticity, context, and regulation: Perspectives for affective neuroscience. *Psychological Bulletin, 126,* 890–909.

Davidson, R. J., Putnam, K. M., & Larson, C. L. (2000). Dysfunction in the neural circuitry of emotion regulation? A possible prelude to violence. *Science, 289,* 591–594.

Davies, I. R. L., Sowden, P. T., Jerrett, D. T., Jerret, T., & Corbett, G. G. (1998). A cross-cultural study of English and Setswana speakers on a colour triads task: A test of the Sapir-Whorf hypothesis. *British Journal of Psychology, 89,* 1–15.

Davison, K. P., Pennebaker, J. W., & Dicerson, S. S. (2000). Who talks? The social psychology of illness support groups. *American Psychologist, 55,* 202–217.

Dawkins, K., Lieberman, J. A., Lebowitz, B. D., & Hsiao, J. K. (1999). Antipsychotics: Past and future. *Schizophrenia Bulletin, 25,* 395–405.

DeCasper, A. J., & Prescott, P. A. (1984). Human newborns' perception of male voices: Preference, discrimination, and reinforcing value. *Developmental Psychology, 17,* 481–491.

Deckro, G. R., Ballinger, K. M., Hoyt, M., Wilcher, M., Dusek, J., Myers, P., Greenberg B., Rosenthal, D. S., & Benson, H. (2002). The evaluation of a mind/body intervention to reduce psychological distress and perceived stress in college students. *Journal of American College Health, 50,* 281–287.

Degreef, G., Ashari, M., Bogerts, B., Bilder, R. M., Jody, D. N., Alvir, J. M. J., & Lieberman, J. A. (1992). Volumes of ventricular system subdivisions measured from magnetic resonance images in first-episode schizophrenic patients. *Archives of General Psychiatry, 49,* 531–537.

Dehaene, S., & Akhavein, R. (1995). Attention, automaticity, and levels of representation in number processing. *Journal of Experimental Psychology: Learning, Memory, and Cognition, 21,* 314–326.

Dejin-Karlsson, E., Hsonson, B. S., Oestergren, P.-O., Sjoeberg, N.-O., & Karel, M. (1998). Does passive smoking in early pregnancy increase the risk of small-for-gestational age infants? *American Journal of Public Health, 88,* 1523–1527.

Delaney, A. J., & Sah, P. (1999). GABA receptors inhibited by benzodiazepines mediate fast inhibitory transmission in the central amygdala. *Journal of Neuroscience, 19,* 9698–9704.

Delprato, D. J., & Midgley, B. D. (1992). Some fundamentals of B. F. Skinner's behaviorism. *American Psychologist, 47,* 1507–1520.

Dement, W. C., & Vaughan, C. (1999). *The promise of sleep.* New York: Delacorte Press.

Dennett, D. C. (1987). Consciousness. In R. L. Gregory (Ed.), *The Oxford companion to the mind* (pp. 160–164). New York: Oxford University Press.

Denton, K., & Zarbatany, L. (1996). Age differences in support processes in conversations between friends. *Child Development, 67,* 1360–1373.

de Rivera, J. (1997). The construction of false memory syndrome: The experience of retractors. *Psychological Inquiry, 8,* 271–292.

De Valois, R. L., & Jacobs, G. H. (1968). Primate color vision. *Science, 162,* 533–540.

Devereux, G. (1961). Mohave ethnopsychiatry and suicide: The psychiatric knowledge and psychic disturbances of an Indian tribe. *Bureau of American Ethnology (Bulletin 175).* Washington, DC: Smithsonian Institution.

Devine, P. G., & Monteith, M. J. (1999). Automaticity and control in stereotyping. In S. Chaiken & Y. Trope (Eds.), *Dual-process theories in social psychology* (pp. 339–360). New York: Guilford.

De Witte, P. (1996). The role of neurotransmitters in alcohol dependence: Animal research. *Alcohol & Alcoholism, 31* (Suppl. 1), 13–16.

Dew, M. A., Hoch, C. C., Buysse, D. J., Monk, T. H., Begley, A. E., Houck, P. R., Hall, M., Kupfer, D. J., & Reynolds, C. F. (2003). Healthy older adults' sleep predicts all-cause mortality at 4 to 19 years of follow-up. *Psychosomatic Medicine, 65,* 63–73.

Dewsbury, D. A. (1981). Effects of novelty on copulatory behavior: The Coolidge effect and related phenomena. *Psychological Bulletin, 89,* 464–482.

Dhawan, N., Roseman, I. J., Naidu, R. K., Thapa, K., & Rettek, S. I. (1995). Self-concepts across two cultures: India and the United States. *Journal of Cross-Cultural Psychology, 26,* 606–621.

Digman, J. M. (1990). Personality structure: Emergence of the five-factor model. *Annual Review of Psychology, 41,* 417–440.

DiLalla, L. F. (2002). Behavior genetics of aggression in children: Reviews and future directions. *Developmental Review, 22,* 593–622.

Di Marzo, V., Fontana, A., Cadas, H., Schinelli, S., Cimino, G., Schwartz, J.-C., & Piomelli, D. (1994). Formation and inactivation of endogenous cannabinoid anadamide in central neurons. *Nature, 372,* 686–691.

Dineen, B. R., Ash, S. R., & Noe, R. A. (2002). A web of applicant attraction: Person-organization fit in the context of Web-based recruitment. *Journal of Applied Psychology, 87,* 723–734.

Dinges, M. M., & Oetting, E. R. (1993). Similarity in drug use patterns between adolescents and their friends. *Adolescence, 28,* 253–266.

Dion, K. K., & Dion, K. L. (1996). Cultural perspectives on romantic love. *Personal Relationships, 3,* 5–17.

Dirkzwager, A. J. E., Bramsen, I., & van der Ploeg, H. M. (2003). Social support, coping, life events, and posttraumatic stress symptoms among former peacekeepers: A prospective study. *Personality and Individual Differences, 34,* 1545–1559.

Dishman, R. K., & Buckworth, J. (1997). Adherence to physical activity. In W. P. Morgan (Ed.), *Physical activity and mental health* (pp. 63–80). Washington, DC: Taylor & Francis.

Dixon, R. A. (1999). Concepts and mechanisms of gains in cognitive aging. In D. C. Park & N. Schwarz (Eds.), *Cognitive aging: A primer* (pp. 23–41). Philadelphia: Psychology Press.

Dollard, J., Doob, L. W., Miller, N., Mower, O. H., & Sears, R. R. (1939). *Frustration and aggression.* New Haven: Yale University Press.

Dollard, J., & Miller, N. E. (1950). *Personality and psychotherapy.* New York: McGraw-Hill.

Domhoff, G. W. (1996). *Finding meanings in dreams: A quantitative approach.* New York: Plenum.

Domhoff, G. W. (1999). Drawing theoretical implications from descriptive empirical findings on dream content. *Dreaming, 9,* 201–210.

Domjan, M., & Purdy, J. E. (1995). Animal research in psychology. *American Psychologist, 50,* 496–503.

Donald, M. (1995). The neurobiology of human consciousness: An evolutionary approach. *Neuropsychology, 33,* 1087–1102.

Donchin, E., Spencer, K. M., & Wijesinghe, R. (2000). The mental prosthesis: Assessing the speed of a P300-based brain-computer interface. *IEEE Transactions on Rehabilitation Engineering, 8,* 174–179.

Dong, Q., Weisfeld, G., Boardway, R. H., & Shen, J. (1996). Correlates of social status among Chinese adolescents. *Journal of Cross-Cultural Psychology, 27,* 476–493.

Donnay, D. A. C., & Borgen, F. H. (1996). Validity, structure, and content of the 1994 Strong Interest Inventory. *Journal of Counseling Psychology, 43,* 275–291.

Dosher, B. A., & Corbett, A. T. (1982). Instrument inferences and verb schemata. *Memory & Cognition, 10,* 531–539.

Dovidio, J. F., Gaertner, S. L., & Kawakami, K. (2003). Intergroup contact: The past, present, and the future. *Group Processes & Intergroup Relations, 6,* 5–21.

Downing, P. E., Jiang, Y., Shuman, M., & Kanwisher, N. (2001). A cortical area selective for visual processing of the human body. *Science, 293,* 2470–2473.

Draijer, N., & Langeland, W. (1999). Childhood trauma and perceived parental dysfunction in the etiology of dissociative symptoms in psychiatric inpatients. *American Journal of Psychiatry, 156,* 379–385.

Drayna, D. Manichaikul, A., deLange, M., Snieder, H., & Spector, T. (2001). Genetic correlates of musical pitch recognition in humans. *Science, 291,* 1969–1972.

Drigotas, S. M., & Rusbult, C. E. (1992). Should I stay or should I go? A dependence model of breakups. *Journal of Personality and Social Psychology, 62,* 62–87.

Drozd, J. F., & Goldfried, M. R. (1996). A critical evaluation of the state-of-the-art in psychotherapy outcome research. *Psychotherapy, 33,* 171–180.

Dryfoss, J. G. (1990). *Adolescents at risk: Prevalence and prevention.* New York: Oxford University Press.

DSM-IV. (1994). *Diagnostic and statistical manual of mental disorders* (4th ed.). Washington, DC: American Psychiatric Association.

DSM-IV-TR. (2000). *Diagnostic and statistical manual of mental disorders* (4th ed., Text revision). Washington, DC: American Psychiatric Association.

DuBois, D. L., Burk-Braxton, C., Swenson, L. P., Tevendale, H. D., Lockerd, E. M., & Moran, B. L. (2002). Getting by with a little help from self and others: Self-esteem and social support as resources during early adolescence. *Developmental Psychology, 38,* 822–839.

DuBois, P. H. (1970). *A history of psychological testing.* Boston: Allyn & Bacon.

Duckitt, J. (1992). Psychology and prejudice: A historical analysis and integrative framework. *American Psychologist, 47,* 1182–1193.

Dudycha, G. J. (1936). An objective study of punctuality in relation to personality and achievement. *Archives of Psychology, 204,* 1–53.

Duker, P. C., & Seys, D. M. (1996). Long-term use of electrical aversion treatment with self-injurious behavior. *Research in Developmental Disabilities, 17,* 293–301.

Duncker, D. (1945). On problem solving. *Psychological Monographs, 58* (No. 270).

Durkin, S. J., & Paxton, S. J. (2002). Predictors of vulnerability to reduced body image satisfaction and psychological well-being in response to exposure to idealized female media images in adolescent girls. *Journal of Psychosomatic Research, 53,* 995–1005.

Durlak, J. A., & Wells, A. M. (1997). Primary prevention mental health programs for children and adolescents: A meta-analytic review. *American Journal of Community Psychology, 25,* 115–152.

Dutton, D. G., & Aron, A. P. (1974). Some evidence for heightened sexual attraction under conditions of high anxiety. *Journal of Personality and Social Psychology, 30,* 510–517.

Dweck, C. S. (1975). The role of expectations and attributions in the alleviation of learned helplessness. *Journal of Personality and Social Psychology, 31,* 674–685.

Eagly, A. H., Ashmore, R. D., Makhijani, M. G., & Longo, L. C. (1991). What is beautiful is good, but . . . : A meta-analytic review of research on the physical attractiveness stereotype. *Psychological Bulletin, 110,* 109–128.

Eagly, A. H., & Chaiken, S. (1993). *The psychology of attitudes.* Fort Worth, TX: Harcourt Brace Jovanovich.

Ebbinghaus, H. (1973). *Psychology: An elementary text-book.* New York: Arno Press. (Original work published 1908)

Eckensberger, L. H., & Zimba, R. F. (1997). The development of moral judgment. In J. W. Berry, P. R. Dasen, & T. S. Saraswathi (Eds.), *Handbook of cross-cultural psychology: Vol. 2. Basic processes and human development* (pp. 299–338). Boston: Allyn & Bacon.

Edinger, J. D., Fins, A. I., Glenn, D. M., Sullivan, R. J., Jr., Bastian, L. A., Marsh, G. R., Dailey, D., Hope, T. V., Young, M., Shaw, E., & Vasilas, D. (2000). Insomnia and the eye of the beholder: Are there clinical markers of objective sleep disturbances among adults with and without insomnia complaints? *Journal of Consulting and Clinical Psychology, 68,* 593–596.

Eich, E. (1995). Searching for mood dependent memory. *Psychological Science, 6,* 67–75.

Eich, E., & Macaulay, D. (2000). Fundamental factors in mood-dependent memory. In J. P. Forgas (Ed.), *Feeling and thinking: The role of affect in social cognition* (pp. 109–130). New York: Cambridge University Press.

Eich, E., Macaulay, D., & Ryan, L. (1994). Mood dependent memory for events of the personal past. *Journal of Experimental Psychology: General, 123,* 201–215.

Ekman, P. (1972). Universal and cultural differences in facial expressions of emotion. In J. Cole (Ed.), *Nebraska symposium on motivation.* Lincoln: University of Nebraska Press.

Ekman, P. (1984). Expression and the nature of emotion. In K. R. Scherer & P. Ekman (Eds.), *Approaches to emotion.* Hillsdale, NJ: Erlbaum.

Ekman, P. (1994). Strong evidence for universals in facial expressions: A reply to Russell's mistaken critique. *Psychological Bulletin, 115,* 268–287.

Ekman, P., & Friesen, W. V. (1971). Constants across cultures in the face and emotion. *Journal of Personality and Social Psychology, 17,* 124–129.

Ekman, P., & Friesen, W. V. (1986). A new pan-cultural facial expression of emotion. *Motivation and Emotion, 10,* 159–168.

Elbert, T., Pantev, C., Wienbruch, C., Rockstroh, B., & Taub, E. (1995). Increased cortical representation of the fingers of the left hand in string players. *Science, 270,* 305–307.

Elms, A. C. (1988). Freud as Leonardo: Why the first psychobiography went wrong. *Journal of Personality, 56,* 19–40.

Emmelkamp, P. M. G., Krijn, M., Hulsbosch, A. M., de Vries, S., Schuemie, M. J., & van der Mast, C. A. P. G. (2002). Virtual reality treatment versus exposure in vivo: A comparative evaluation in acrophobia. *Behaviour Research and Therapy, 40,* 509–516.

Endler, N. S., Macrodimitris, S. D., & Kocovski, N. L. (2000). Controllability in cognitive and interpersonal tasks: Is control good for you? *Personality & Individual Differences, 29,* 951–962.

Engle, R. W. (2002). Working memory capacity as executive attention. *Current Directions in Psychological Science, 11,* 19–23.

Enserink, M. (1999). Can the placebo be the cure? *Science, 284,* 238–240.

Enserink, M. (2000). Searching for the mark of Cain. *Science, 289,* 575–579.

Ericsson, K. A., & Chase, W. G. (1982). Exceptional memory. *American Scientist, 70,* 607–615.

Ericsson, K. A., & Simon, H. A. (1993). *Protocol analysis: Verbal reports as data* (rev. ed.). Cambridge, MA: The MIT Press.

Erikson, E. (1963). *Childhood and society.* New York: Norton.

Esler, W. P., & Wolfe, M. S. (2001). A portrait of Alzheimer secretases—new features and familiar faces. *Science, 293,* 1449–1454.

Espie, C. A. (2002). Insomnia: Conceptual issues in the development, persistence, and treatment of sleep disorder in adults. *Annual Review of Psychology, 53,* 215–243.

Esser, J. K. (1998). Alive and well after 25 years: A review of groupthink research. *Organizational Behavior and Human Decision Processes, 73,* 116–141.

Estrada, C. A., Isen, A. M., & Young, M. J. (1994). Positive affect improves creative problem solving and influences reported source of practice satisfaction in physicians. *Motivation and Emotion, 18,* 285–299.

Evans, D. A., Funkenstein, H. H., Albert, M. S., Scherr, P. A., Cook, N. R., Chown, M. J., Hebert, L. E., Hennekens, C. H., & Taylor, J. O. (1989). Prevalence of Alzheimer's disease in a community population of older persons. *Journal of the American Medical Association, 262,* 2251–2256.

Evans, J. S. B., Barston, J. L., & Pollard, P. (1983). On the conflict between logic and belief in syllogistic reasoning. *Memory and Cognition, 11,* 295–306.

Evans, J. St. B. T., Newstead, S. E., Allen, J. L., & Pollard, P. (1994). Debiasing by instruction: The case of belief bias. *European Journal of Cognitive Psychology, 6,* 263–285.

Evans-Pritchard, E. E. (1937). *Witchcraft, oracles and magic among the Azande.* Oxford: Oxford University Press.

Exner, J. E., Jr. (1974). *The Rorschach: A comprehensive system: Vol. 1.* New York: Wiley.

Exner, J. E., Jr. (2003). *The Rorschach: A comprehensive system* (4th ed.). New York: John Wiley & Sons.

Exner, J. E., Jr., & Weiner, I. B. (1994). *The Rorschach: A comprehensive system: Vol. 3. Assessment of children and adolescents* (2nd ed.). New York: Wiley.

Eysenck, H. J. (1952). The effects of psychotherapy: An evaluation. *Journal of Consulting Psychology, 16,* 319–324.

Eysenck, H. J. (1973). *The inequality of man.* London: Temple Smith.

Eysenck, H. J. (1990). Biological dimensions of personality. In L. A. Pervin (Ed.), *Handbook of personality theory and research* (pp. 244–276). New York: Guilford Press.

Eysenck, H. J. (1992). Four ways five factors are not basic. *Personality and Individual Differences, 13,* 667–673.

Fagot, B. I., & Hagan, R. (1991). Observations of parent reactions to sex-stereotyped behaviors: Age and sex effects. *Child Development, 62,* 617–628.

Fantuzzo, J., Sutton-Smith, B., Atkins, M., Meyers, R., Stevenson, H., Coolahan, K., Weiss, A., & Manz, P. (1996). Community-based resilient peer treatment of withdrawn maltreated school children. *Journal of Consulting and Clinical Psychology, 64,* 1377–1386.

Fantz, R. L. (1963). Pattern vision in newborn infants. *Science, 140,* 296–297.

Farina, A., Fischer, E. H., Boudreau, L. A., & Belt, W. E. (1996). Mode of target presentation in measuring the stigma of mental disorder. *Journal of Applied Social Psychology, 26,* 2147–2156.

Farina, A., Gliha, D., Boudreau, L. A., Allen, J. G., & Sherman, M. (1971). Mental illness and the impact of believing others know about it. *Journal of Abnormal Psychology, 77,* 1–5.

Farine, J. P., Everaerts, C., Abed, D., & Ntari, M. (1996). Pheromonal emission during the mating behavior of *Eurycotis floridana* (Walker) (Dictyoptera: Blattidea). *Journal of Insect Behavior, 9,* 197–213.

Fazio, R. H. (1987). Self-perception theory: A current perspective. In M. P. Zanna, J. M. Olson, & C. P. Herman (Eds.), *Social influence: The Ontario Symposium* (Vol. 5, pp. 129–150). Hillsdale, NJ: Erlbaum.

Fazio, R. H. (1995). Attitudes as object-evaluation associations: Determinants, consequences, and correlates of attitude accessibility. In R. E. Petty & J. A. Krosnick (Eds.), *Attitude strength: Antecedents and consequences* (pp. 247–282). Mahwah, NJ: Erlbaum.

Fazio, R. H., & Towles-Schwen, T. (1999). The MODE model of attitude-behavior processes. In S. Chaiken & Y. Trope (Eds.), *Dual-process theories in social psychology* (pp. 97–116). New York: Guilford.

Feather, N. T. (1961). The relationship of persistence at a task to expectation of success and achievement related motives. *Journal of Abnormal and Social Psychology, 63,* 552–561.

Fechner, G. T. (1966). *Elements of psychophysics* (H. E. Adler, Trans.). New York: Holt, Rinehart & Winston. (Original work published 1860)

Fellows, J. L., Trosclair, A., Adams, E. K., & Rivera, C. C. (2002, April 12). Annual smoking-attributable mortality, years of potential life lost, and economic costs—United States, 1995-1999. (2002). *Morbidity and Mortality Weekly Report, 51,* 300–303.

Fernald, A., & Morikawa, H. (1993). Common themes and cultural variations in Japanese and American mothers' speech to infants. *Child Development, 64,* 637–656.

Fernandez-Ballesteros, R. (2002). Social support and quality of life among older people in Spain. *Journal of Social Issues, 58,* 645–659.

Ferster, C. B., & Skinner, B. F. (1957). *Schedules of reinforcement.* New York: Appleton-Century-Crofts.

Festinger, L. (1957). *A theory of cognitive dissonance.* Stanford, CA: Stanford University Press.

Festinger, L., & Carlsmith, J. M. (1959). Cognitive consequences of forced compliance. *Journal of Abnormal and Social Psychology, 58,* 203–211.

Fields, H. L., & Levine, J. D. (1984). Placebo analgesia: A role for endorphins. *Trends in Neuroscience, 7,* 271–273.

Fields, R. D., & Stevens-Graham, B. (2002). New insights into neuro-glia communication. *Science, 298,* 556–562.

Fiorito, G., & Scotto, P. (1992). Observational learning in *Octopus vulgaris. Science, 256,* 545–547.

Fisher, B. S., Cullen, F. T., & Turner, M. G. (2000). *The sexual victimization of college women.* Washington, DC: National Institute of Justice.

Fisher, J. D., Fisher, W. A., Misovich, S. J., Kimble, D. L., & Malloy, T. E. (1996). Changing AIDS risk behavior: Effects of an intervention emphasizing AIDS risk reduction information, motivation and behavioral skills in a college student population. *Health Psychology, 15,* 114–123.

Fisher, J. D., Fisher, W. A., Williams, S. S., & Malloy, T. E. (1994). Empirical tests of an information-motivation-behavioral skills model of AIDS-prevention behavior with gay men and heterosexual university students. *Health Psychology, 13,* 238–250.

Fisher, S., & Greenberg, R. (1996). *Freud scientifically appraised.* New York: Wiley.

Fishman, H. C. (1993). *Intensive structural therapy: Treating families in their social context.* New York: Basic Books.

Fishman, H. C., & Fishman, T. (2003). Structural family therapy. In G. P. Sholevar & L. D. Schwoeri (Eds.), *Textbook of family and couples therapy: Clinical applications* (pp. 35–54). Washington, DC: American Psychiatric Publishing.

Fiske, S. T., & Taylor, S. E. (1991). *Social cognition.* New York: McGraw-Hill.

Flavell, J. H. (1985). *Cognitive development* (2nd ed.). Englewood Cliffs, NJ: Prentice Hall.

Flavell, J. H. (1996). Piaget's legacy. *Psychological Science, 7,* 200–203.

Fleming, I. (1959). From a view to a kill. In *For your eyes only* (pp. 1–30). New York: Charter Books.

Foa, E. B., & Riggs, D. S. (1995). Posttraumatic stress disorder following assault: Theoretical considerations and empirical findings. *Current Directions in Psychological Science, 4,* 61–65.

Fobair, P. (1997). Cancer support groups and group therapies. *Journal of Psychosocial Oncology, 15,* 43–81.

Folkman, S. (1984). Personal control and stress and coping processes: A theoretical analysis. *Journal of Personality and Social Psychology, 46,* 839–852.

Fombonne, E. (2003). The prevalence of autism. *JAMA, 289,* 87–89.

Ford, C. S., & Beach, F. A. (1951). *Patterns of sexual behavior.* New York: Harper & Row.

Forgas, J. P. (1995). Mood and judgment: The affect infusion model (AIM). *Psychological Bulletin, 117,* 39–66.

Forgas, J. P. (1999). Feeling and speaking: Mood effects on verbal communication strategies. *Personality and Social Psychology Bulletin, 25,* 850–863.

Forgas, J. P. (Ed.). (2000). *Feeling and thinking: The role of affect in social cognition.* New York: Cambridge University Press.

Foucault, M. (1975). *The birth of the clinic.* New York: Vintage Books.

Foulkes, D. (1962). Dream reports from different states of sleep. *Journal of Abnormal and Social Psychology, 65,* 14–25.

Fowler, H. (1965). *Curiosity and exploratory behavior.* New York: Macmillan.

Fowler, R. D. (1999). Report of the association. *American Psychologist, 54,* 539–558.

Frager, R., & Fadiman, J. (1998). *Personality and personal growth.* New York: Longman.

Fraley, R. C., & Shaver, P. R. (2000). Adult romantic attachment: Theoretical developments, emerging controversies, and unanswered questions. *Review of General Psychology, 4,* 132–154.

Frank, J. D., & Frank, J. B. (1991). *Persuasion and healing: A comparative study of psychotherapy* (3rd ed.). Baltimore: Johns Hopkins University Press.

Frank, M. E., & Nowlis, G. H. (1989). Learned aversions and taste qualities in hamsters. *Chemical Senses, 14,* 379–394.

Franklin, N., & Tversky, B. (1990). Searching imagined environments. *Journal of Experimental Psychology: General, 119,* 63–76.

Freedman, J. L., & Fraser, S. C. (1966). Compliance without pressure: The foot-in-the-door technique. *Journal of Personality and Social Psychology, 4,* 195–202.

Freedman, M. S., Lucas, R. J., Soni, B., von Schantz, M., Muñoz, M., David-Gray, Z., & Foster, R. (1999). Regulation of mammalian circadian behavior by non-rod, non-cone, ocular photoreceptors. *Science, 284,* 502–507.

Freud, A. (1946). *The ego and the mechanisms of defense.* New York: International Universities Press.

Freud, A. (1958). Adolescence. *Psychoanalytic Study of the Child, 13,* 255–278.

Freud, S. (1915). Instincts and their vicissitudes. In S. Freud, *The collected papers*. New York: Collier.

Freud, S. (1923). *Introductory lectures on psycho-analysis* (J. Riviera, Trans.). London: Allen & Unwin.

Freud, S. (1957). Leonardo da Vinci and a memory of his childhood. In J. Strachey (Ed. and Trans.), *The standard edition of the complete psychological works of Sigmund Freud* (Vol. 11, pp. 59–137). London: Hogarth Press. (Original work published 1910)

Freud, S. (1965). *The interpretation of dreams*. New York: Avon. (Original work published 1900)

Freund, A. M., & Baltes, P. B. (1998). Selection, optimization, and compensation as strategies of life management: Correlations with subjective indicators of successful aging. *Psychology and Aging, 13,* 531–543.

Friedman, M., & Rosenman, R. F. (1974). *Type A behavior and your heart*. New York: Knopf.

Friedman, R., Myers, P., Krass, S., & Benson, H. (1996). The relaxation response: Use with cardiac patients. In R. Allan & S. S. Scheidt (Eds.), *Heart and mind: The practice of cardiac psychology* (pp. 363–384). Washington, DC: American Psychological Association.

Friend, R., Rafferty, Y., & Bramel, D. (1990). A puzzling misinterpretation of the Asch "conformity" study. *European Journal of Social Psychology, 20,* 29–44.

Fromkin, V. A. (Ed.). (1980). *Errors in linguistic performance: Slips of the tongue, pen, and hand*. New York: Academic Press.

Fromm, E., & Shor, R. E. (Eds.). (1979). *Hypnosis: Developments in research and new perspectives* (2nd ed.). Hawthorne, NY: Aldine.

Fuhriman, A., & Burlingame, G. M. (Eds.) (1994). *Handbook of group psychotherapy: An empirical and clinical synthesis*. New York: Wiley.

Fuligni, A. J. (1997). The academic achievement of adolescents from immigrant families: The roles of family background, attitudes, and behavior. *Child Development, 68,* 351–363.

Fuller, B., Holloway, S. D., & Liang, X. (1996). Family selection of child-care centers: The influence of household support, ethnicity, and parental practices. *Child Development, 67,* 3320–3337.

Furmark, T., Tillfors, M., Marteinsdottir, I., Fischer, H., Pissiota, A., Långström, B., & Fredrikson, M. (2002). Common changes in cerebral blood flow in patients with social phobia treated with citalopram or cognitive-behavioral therapy. *Archives of General Psychiatry, 59,* 425–433.

Furnham, A., Crump, J., & Whelan, J. (1997). Validating the NEO Personality Inventory using assessor's ratings. *Personality & Individual Differences, 22,* 669–675.

Fussell, S. R., & Krauss, R. M. (1992). Coordination of knowledge in communication: Effects of speakers' assumptions about what others know. *Journal of Personality and Social Psychology, 62,* 378–391.

Gabrieli, J. D. E., Brewer, J. B., Desmond, J. E., & Glover, G. H. (1997). Separate neural bases of two fundamental memory processes in the human medial temporal lobe. *Science, 276,* 264–266.

Gabrieli, J. D. E., Desmond, J. E., Demb, J. B., Wagner, A. D., Stone, M.V., Vaidya, C. J., & Glover, G. H. (1996). Functional magnetic resonance imaging of semantic memory processes in the frontal lobes. *Psychological Science, 7,* 278–283.

Gackenbach, J., & LaBerge, S. (Eds.). (1988). *Conscious mind, sleeping brain: Perspectives on lucid dreaming*. New York: Plenum Press.

Gaines, S. O., Jr., & Agnew, C. R. (2003). Relationship maintenance in intercultural couples: An interdependence analysis. In D. Canary & M. Dainton (Eds.), *Maintaining relationships through communication: Relational, contextual, and cultural variations* (pp. 231–253). Mahwah, NJ: Erlbaum.

Galambos, N. L., Barker, E. T., & Almeida, D. M. (2003). Parents *do* matter: Trajectories of change in externalizing and internalizing problems in early adolescence. *Child Development, 74,* 578–594.

Gallo, L. C., & Matthews, K. A. (2003). Understanding the association between socioeconomic status and physical health: Do negative emotions play a role? *Psychological Bulletin, 129,* 10–51.

Galton, F. (1869). *Hereditary genius*. London: Macmillan.

Galton, F. (1907). *Inquiries into human faculty and its development*. London: Dent Publishers. (Original work published 1883)

Garb, H. N., Wood, J. M., Nezworski, M. T., Grove, W. M., & Stejskal, W. J. (2001). Toward a resolution of the Rorschach controversy. *Psychological Assessment, 13,* 433–448.

Garcia, J. (1990). Learning without memory. *Journal of Cognitive Neuroscience, 2,* 287–305.

Garcia, J. (1993). Misrepresentations of my criticisms of Skinner. *American Psychologist, 48,* 1158.

Garcia, J., & Koelling, R. A. (1966). The relation of cue to consequence in avoidance learning. *Psychonomic Science, 4,* 123–124.

Garcia, M. M., Shaw, D. S., Winslow, E. B., & Yaggi, K. E. (2000). Destructive sibling conflict and the development of conduct problems in young boys. *Developmental Psychology, 36,* 44–53.

Gardner, H. (1983). *Frames of mind*. New York: Basic Books.

Gardner, H. (1993). *Creating minds*. New York: Basic Books.

Gardner, H. (1999a). *The disciplined mind*. New York: Simon & Schuster.

Gardner, H. (1999b). *Intelligence reframed*. New York: Basic Books.

Gardner, R., Jr. (2000, June 12). Parenting: Is AOL worse than TV? *New York, 33,* 38–41.

Gardner, R. A., & Gardner, B. T. (1969). Teaching sign language to a chimpanzee. *Science, 165,* 664–672.

Garland, A. F., & Zigler, E. (1993). Adolescent suicide prevention. *American Psychologist, 48,* 169–182.

Garrison, V. (1977). The "Puerto Rican syndrome" in psychiatry and Espiritismo. In V. Crapanzano & V. Garrison (Eds.), *Case studies in spirit possession*. New York: Wiley Interscience.

Gatchel, R. J., & Oordt, M. S. (2003). Acute and chronic pain conditions. In R. J. Gatchel, & M. S. Oordt (Eds.), *Clinical health psychology and primary care: Practical advice and clinical guidance for successful collaboration* (pp. 117–134). Washington, D.C.: American Psychological Association.

Gawin, F. H. (1991). Cocaine addiction: Psychology and neurophysiology. *Science, 251,* 1580–1586.

Gazzaniga, M. (1970). *The bisected brain*. New York: Appleton-Century-Crofts.

Gazzaniga, M. S. (1985). *The social brain*. New York: Basic Books.

Gegenfurtner, K. R., & Sperling, G. (1993). Information transfer in iconic memory experiments. *Journal of Experimental Psychology: Human Perception and Performance, 19,* 845–866.

Gelman, S. A., & Wellman, H. M. (1991). Insides and essences: Early understandings of the non-obvious. *Cognition, 38,* 213–244.

Gelman, S. A. (2003). *Origins of essentialism in everyday thought*. London: Oxford University Press.

Gelman, S. A., & Lakshmi, R. (2002). Folk biology as a window into cognitive development. *Human Development, 45,* 61–68.

Gelman, S. A., & Raman, L. (2002). Folk biology as a window into cognitive development. *Human Development, 45,* 61–68.

Gergen, K. J., Gulerce, A., Lock A., & Misra, G. (1996). Psychological science in a cultural context. *American Psychologist, 51,* 496–503.

Gerra, G., Zaimovic, A., Ferri, M., Zambelli, U., Timpano, M., Neri, E., Marzocchi, G. F., Delsignore, R., & Brambilla, F. (2000). Long-lasting effects of ±(3,4-methylenedioxymethamphetamine (*Ecstasy*) on serotonin system function in humans. *Biological Psychiatry, 47,* 127–136.

Gerrig, R. J., & Banaji, M. R. (1994). Language and thought. In R. J. Sternberg (Ed.), *Handbook of perception and cognition: Vol. 2. Thinking and problem solving* (pp. 233–261). Orlando, FL: Academic Press.

Gerrig, R. J., & Egidi, G. (2003). Cognitive psychological foundations of narrative experiences. In D. Herman (Ed.), *Narrative theory and the cognitive sciences* (pp. 31–53). Stanford, CA: CSLI Publications.

Gershon, E. S., Berrettini, W., Nurnberger, J., Jr., & Goldin, L. (1987). Genetics of affective illness. In H. Y. Meltzer (Ed.), *Psychopharmacology: The third generation of progress* (pp. 481–491). New York: Raven Press.

Ghadirian, A. M., & Lehmann, H. E. (1993). *Environment and psychopathology.* New York: Springer.

Giambra, L. M., & Arenberg, D. (1993). Adult age differences in forgetting sentences. *Psychology and Aging, 8,* 451–462.

Gibbons, A. (2002). Hot spots of brain evolution. *Science, 296,* 837.

Gibson, E. J., & Walk, R. D. (1960). The "visual cliff." *Scientific American, 202,* 64–71.

Gibson, J. J. (1979). *An ecological approach to visual perception.* Boston: Houghton Mifflin.

Gidron, Y., Davidson, K., & Bata, I. (1999). The short-term effects of a hostility-reduction intervention on male coronary heart disease patients. *Health Psychology, 1999,* 416–420.

Giesler, R. B., Josephs, R. A., & Swann, W. B., Jr. (1996). Self-verification in clinical depression: The desire for negative evaluation. *Journal of Abnormal Psychology, 105,* 358–368.

Gillespie, J. M., Byrne, B., & Workman, L. J. (1995). An intensive reunification program for children in foster care. *Child & Adolescent Social Work Journal, 12,* 213–228.

Gilligan, C. (1982). *In a different voice: Psychological theory and women's development.* Cambridge, MA: Harvard University Press.

Gilligan, S., & Bower, G. H. (1984). Cognitive consequences of emotional arousal. In C. Izard, J. Kagan, & R. Zajonc (Eds.), *Emotions, cognitions, and behavior* (pp. 547–588). Cambridge, U.K.: Cambridge University Press.

Gilovich, T. (1991). *How we know what isn't so: The fallibility of human reason in everyday life.* New York: The Free Press.

Giron, M., & Gomez-Beneyto, M. (1998). Relationship between empathic family attitude and relapse in schizophrenia: A two-year follow-up prospective study. *Schizophrenia Bulletin, 24,* 619–627.

Giros, B., Jaber, M., Jones, S. R., Wightman, R. M., & Caron, M. G. (1996). Hyperlocomotion and indifference to cocaine and amphetamine in mice lacking the dopamine transporter. *Nature, 379,* 606–612.

Gitlin, M., Nuechterlein, K., Subotnik, K. L., Ventura, J., Mintz, J., Fogelson, D. L., Bartzokis, G., & Aravagiri, M. (2001). Clinical outcome following neuroleptic discontinuation in patients with remitted recent-onset schizophrenia. *American Journal of Psychiatry, 158,* 1835–1842.

Gladue, B. A. (1994). The biopsychology of sexual orientation. *Current Directions in Psychological Science, 3,* 150–154.

Glanz, K., Rizzo, A., & Graap, K. (2003). Virtual reality for psychotherapy: Current reality and future possibilities. *Psychotherapy: Theory, Research, Practice, Training, 40,* 55–67.

Glaser, R., Kiecolt-Glaser, J. K., Marucha, P. T., MacCallum, R. C., Laskowski, B. F., & Malarkey, W. B. (1999). Stress-related changes in proinflammatory cytokine production in wounds. *Archives of General Psychiatry, 56,* 450–456.

Gleaves, D. H., May, M. C., & Cardeña, E. (2001). An examination of the diagnostic validity of dissociative identity disorder. *Clinical Psychology Review, 21,* 577–608.

Glenny, M. (1994). *The fall of Yugoslavia.* New York: Penguin.

Gobet, F., & Simon, H. A. (1996). The roles of recognition processes and look-ahead search in time-constrained expert problem solving: Evidence from grand-master-level chess. *Psychological Science, 7,* 52–55.

Goddard, H. H. (1914). *The Kallikak family: A study of the heredity of feeble-mindedness.* New York: Macmillan.

Goddard, H. H. (1917). Mental tests and immigrants. *Journal of Delinquency, 2,* 243–277.

Goldfried, M. R., Greenberg, L., & Marmar, C. (1990). Individual psychotherapy: Process and outcome. *Annual Review of Psychology, 41,* 659–688.

Goldin-Meadow, S. (2003). *The resilience of language: What gesture creation in deaf children can tell us about how all children learn language.* New York: Psychology Press.

Goldin-Meadow, S., & Mylander, C. (1990). Beyond the input given: The child's role in the acquisition of language. *Language, 66,* 323–355.

Goldstein, E. B. (1999). *Sensation & perception* (5th ed.). Pacific Grove, CA: Brooks/Cole Publishing Company.

Goodall, J. (1986). *The chimpanzees of Gombe: Patterns of behavior.* Cambridge, MA: Harvard University Press.

Goodall, J. (1990). *Through a window: My thirty years with the chimpanzees of Gombe.* Boston: Houghton Mifflin.

Gooden, D. R., & Baddeley, A. D. (1975). Context-dependent memory in two natural environments: On land and under water. *British Journal of Psychology, 66,* 325–331.

Goodison, T., & Siegel, S. (1995). Learning and tolerance to the intake suppressive effect of cholecystokinin in rats. *Behavioral Neuroscience, 109,* 62–70.

Gorfein, D. S. (Ed.) (2001). *On the consequences of meaning selection: Perspectives on resolving lexical ambiguity.* Washington, DC: American Psychological Association.

Goshen-Gottstein, Y., Moscovitch, M., & Melo, B. (2000). Intact implicit memory for newly formed verbal associations in amnesic patients following single study trials. *Neuropsychology, 14,* 570–578.

Gottfredson, L. S. (1997a). Mainstream science on intelligence: An editorial with 52 signatories, history, and bibliography. *Intelligence, 24,* 13–23.

Gottfredson, L. S. (1997b). Why *g* matters: The complexity of everyday life. *Intelligence, 24,* 79–132.

Gottman, J. M. (1994). *What predicts divorce?* Hillsdale, NJ: Erlbaum.

Gottman, J. M., & Levenson, R. W. (2000). The timing of divorce: Predicting when a couple will divorce over a 14-year period. *Journal of Marriage and the Family, 62,* 737–745.

Gould, E., & Gross, C. G. (2002). Neurogenesis in adult mammals: Some progress and problems. *The Journal of Neuroscience, 22,* 619–623.

Gould, M. S., Fisher, P., Parides, M., Flory, M., & Shaffer, D. (1996). Psychosocial risk factors of child and adolescent completed suicide. *Archives of General Psychiatry, 53,* 1155–1162.

Gould, S. J. (1981). *The mismeasure of man.* New York: Norton.

Gould, S. J. (2002). *The structure of evolutionary theory.* Cambridge, MA: Belknap Press.

Graesser, A. C., Singer, M., & Trabasso, T. (1994). Constructing inferences during narrative text comprehension. *Psychological Review, 101,* 371–395.

Grant, B. R., & Grant, P. (1989). *Evolutionary dynamics of a natural population.* Princeton: Princeton University Press.

Grant, K. E., Compas, B. E., Stuhlmacher, A. F., Thurm, A. E., McMahon, S. D., & Halpert, J. A. (2003). Stressors and child and adolescent psychopathology: Moving from markers to mechanisms of risk. *Psychological Bulletin, 129,* 447–466.

Grant, L., & Evans, A. (1994). *Principles of behavior analysis.* New York: HarperCollins.

Grant, P. R., & Grant, B. R. (2002). Unpredictable evolution in a 30-year study of Darwin's finches. *Science, 296,* 707–711.

Gray, M. R., & Steinberg, L. (1999). Unpacking authoritative parenting: Reassessing a multidimensional construct. *Journal of Marriage and the Family, 61,* 574–587.

Green, B. L. (1994). Psychosocial research in traumatic stress: An update. *Journal of Traumatic Stress, 7,* 341–362.

Green, D. M., & Swets, J. A. (1966). *Signal detection theory and psychophysics.* New York: Wiley.

Greene, J. D., Sommerville, R. B., Nystrom, L. E., Darley, J. M., & Cohen, J. D. (2001). An fMRI investigation of emotional engagement in moral judgment. *Science, 293,* 2105–2108.

Greene, R. L. (1991). *The MMPI-2/MMPI: An interpretive manual.* Boston: Allyn & Bacon.

Greene, R. L., Gwin, R., & Staal, M. (1997). Current status of MMPI–2 research: A methodologic overview. *Journal of Personality Assessment, 68,* 20–36.

Greenfield, P. M. (1997). You can't take it with you: Why ability assessments don't cross cultures. *American Psychologist, 52,* 1115–1124.

Greeno, C. G., & Wing, R. R. (1994). Stress-induced eating. *Psychological Bulletin, 115,* 444–464.

Greenwald, A. G., Spangenber, E. R., Pratkanis, A. R., & Eskenazi, J. (1991). Double-blind tests of subliminal self-help audiotapes. *Psychological Science, 2,* 119–122.

Grice, H. P. (1968). Utterer's meaning, sentence-meaning, and word-meaning. *Foundations of Language, 4,* 1–18.

Grice, H. P. (1975). Logic and conversation. In P. Cole & J. L. Morgan (Eds.), *Syntax and semantics: Vol. 3. Speech acts* (pp. 41–58). New York: Academic Press.

Griffin, K., Friend, R., Eitel, P., & Lobel, M. (1993). Effects of environmental demands, stress, and mood on health practices. *Journal of Behavioral Medicine, 16,* 1–19.

Grigorenko, E. L. (2000). Heritability and intelligence. In R. J. Sternberg (Ed.), *Handbook of intelligence* (pp. 53–91). Cambridge, England: Cambridge University Press.

Grohol, J. M. (1998). Future clinical directions: Professional development, pathology, and psychotherapy on-line. In J. Gackenbach (Ed.), *Psychology and the Internet: Intrapersonal, interpersonal, and transpersonal implications* (pp. 111–140). San Diego, CA: Academic Press.

Gross, C. G. (2000). Neurogenesis in the adult brain: Death of a dogma. *Nature Reviews Neuroscience, 1,* 67–73.

Grunhaus, L., Schreiver, S., Dolberg, O. T., Polak, D., & Dannon, P. N. (2003). A randomized controlled comparison of electro-convulsive therapy and repetitive transcranial magnetic stimulation in severe and resistant nonpsychotic major depression. *Biological Psychiatry, 53,* 324–331.

Guilford, J. P. (1961). Factorial angles to psychology. *Psychological Review, 68,* 1–20.

Guilford, J. P. (1985). The Structure-of-Intellect model. In B. B. Wolman (Ed.), *Handbook of intelligence.* New York: Wiley.

Guilleminault, C., Poyares, D., Aftab, F., & Palombini, L. (2001). Sleep and wakefulness in somnambulism: A spectral analysis study. *Journal of Psychosomatic Research, 51,* 411–416.

Gumperz, J. J., & Levinson, S. C. (Eds.). (1996). *Rethinking linguistic relativity.* Cambridge, U.K.: Cambridge University Press.

Gura, T. (2000). Tracing leptin's partners in regulating body weight. *Science, 287,* 1738–1741.

Gura, T. (2003). Obesity drug pipeline not so fat. *Science, 299,* 849–852.

Haas, S. M. (2003). Relationship maintenance in same-sex couples. In D. Canary & M. Dainton (Eds.), *Maintaining relationships through communication: Relational, contextual, and cultural variations* (pp. 209–230). Mahwah, NJ: Erlbaum.

Haas, S. M., & Stafford, L. (1998). An initial examination of maintenance behaviors in gay and lesbian relationships. *Journal of Social and Personal Relationships, 15,* 846–855.

Haines, B. A., Metalsky, G. I., Cardamone, A. L., & Joiner, T. (1999). Interpersonal and cognitive pathways in to the origins of attributional style: A developmental perspective. In T. E. Joiner & J. C. Coyne (Eds.), *The interactional nature of depression; Advances in interpersonal approaches* (pp. 65–92). Washington, DC: American Psychological Association.

Hall, D., & Suboski, M. D. (1995). Visual and olfactory stimuli in learned release of alarm reactions by zebra danio fish (*Brachydanio rerio*). *Neurobiology of Learning and Memory, 63,* 229–240.

Hall, G. S. (1904). *Adolescence: Its psychology and its relations to physiology, anthropology, sociology, sex, crime, religion and education* (Vols. 1 and 2). New York: D. Appleton.

Hamer, D. H. (1996). The heritability of happiness. *Nature Genetics, 14,* 125–126.

Hamer, D. H., Hu, S., Magnuson, V. L., Hu, N., & Pattatucci, A. M. L. (1993). A linkage between DNA markers on the X chromosome and male sexual orientation. *Science, 261,* 321–327.

Hamilton, M., & Rajaram, S. (2001). The concreteness effect in implicit and explicit memory tests. *Journal of Memory and Language, 44,* 96–117.

Haney, C., & Zimbardo, P. G. (1977). The socialization into criminality: On becoming a prisoner and a guard. In J. L. Tapp & F. L. Levine (Eds.), *Law, justice and the individual in society: Psychological and legal issues* (pp. 198–223). New York: Holt, Rinehart & Winston.

Hankin, B. L., & Abramson, L. Y. (2001). Development of gender differences in depression: An elaborated cognitive vulnerability-transactional stress model. *Psychological Bulletin, 127,* 773–796.

Hargadon, R., Bowers, K. S., & Woody, E. Z. (1995). Does counter-pain imagery mediate hypnotic analgesia? *Journal of Abnormal Psychology, 104,* 508–516.

Harder, J. W. (1991). Equity theory versus expectancy theory: The case of major league baseball free agents. *Journal of Applied Psychology, 76,* 458–464.

Hardy, J., & Selkoe, D. J. (2002). The amyloid hypothesis of Alzheimer's disease: Progress and problems on the road to therapeutics. *Science, 297,* 353–356.

Hariri, A. R., Mattay, V. S., Tessitore, A., Kolachana, B., Fera, F., Goldman, D., Egan, M. F., & Weinberger, D. R. (2002). Serotonin transporter genetic variation and the response of the human amygdala. *Science, 297,* 400–403.

Harle, V. (2000). *The enemy with a thousand faces: The tradition of the other in western political thought and history.* Westport, CT: Praeger.

Harlow, H. F. (1965). Sexual behavior in the rhesus monkey. In F. Beach (Ed.), *Sex and behavior.* New York: Wiley.

Harlow, H. F., Harlow, M. K., & Meyer, D. R. (1950). Learning motivated by a manipulation drive. *Journal of Experimental Psychology, 40,* 228–234.

Harlow, H. F., & Zimmerman, R. R. (1958). The development of affectional responses in infant monkeys. *Proceedings of the American Philosophical Society, 102,* 501–509.

Harlow, J. M. (1868). Recovery from the passage of an iron bar through the head. *Publications of the Massachusetts Medical Society, 2,* 327–347.

Harmon, L. W., Hansen, J. C., Borgen, F. H., & Hammer, A. L. (1994). *Strong Interest Inventory applications and technical guide.* Palo Alto, CA: Consulting Psychologists Press.

Harris, B. (1979). Whatever happened to Little Albert? *American Psychologist, 34,* 151–160.

Harrison, L. M., Kastin, A. J., & Zadina, J. E. (1998). Opiate tolerance and dependence: Receptors, G-proteins, and antiopiates. *Peptides, 19,* 1603–1630.

Harrison, Y., & Horne, J. A. (1996). Long-term sleep extension—Are we really chronically sleep deprived? *Psychophysiology, 33,* 22–30.

Hart, J. T. (1965). Memory and the feeling-of-knowing experience. *Journal of Educational Psychology, 56,* 208–216.

Hartshorne, H., & May, M. A. (1928). *Studies in the nature of character, Vol. 1: Studies in deceit.* New York: Macmillan.

Hartup, W. H. (1996). The company they keep: Friendships and their developmental significance. *Child Development, 67,* 1–13.

Hastorf, A. H., & Cantril, H. (1954). They saw a game: A case study. *Journal of Abnormal and Social Psychology, 49,* 129–134.

Hatcher, C., & Himelstein, P. (Eds.). (1996). *The handbook of Gestalt therapy.* Northvale, NJ: Jason Aronson.

Hatchett, L., Friend, R., Symister, P., & Wadhwa, N. (1997). Interpersonal expectations, social support, and adjustment to chronic illness. *Journal of Personality and Social Psychology, 73,* 560–573.

Hatfield, E., & Sprecher, S. (1995). Men's and women's preferences in marital partners in the United States, Russia, and Japan. *Journal of Cross-Cultural Psychology, 26,* 728–750.

Hathaway, S. R., & McKinley, J. C. (1940). A multiphasic personality schedule (Minnesota): I. Construction of the schedule. *Journal of Psychology, 10,* 249–254.

Hathaway, S. R., & McKinley, J. C. (1943). *Minnesota Multiphasic Inventory manual.* New York: Psychological Corporation.

Hawkes, K. (1993). Why hunter-gatherers work. *Current Anthropology, 34,* 341–351.

Hazan, C., & Shaver, P. (1987). Romantic love conceptualized as an attachment process. *Journal of Personality and Social Psychology, 52,* 511–524.

Hazeltine, E., & Ivry, R. B. (2002). Can we teach the cerebellum new tricks? *Science, 296,* 1979–1980.

Healy, A. F., & McNamara, D. S. (1996). Verbal learning and memory: Does the modal model still work? *Annual Review of Psychology, 47,* 143–172.

Hearst, E. (1988). Fundamentals of learning and conditioning. In R. C. Atkinson, R. J. Herrnstein, G. Lindzey, & R. D. Luce (Eds.), *Stevens' handbook of experimental psychology: Vol. 2. Learning and Cognition* (2nd ed., pp. 3–109). New York: Wiley.

Hebl, M. R., & Heatherton, T. F. (1998). The stigma of obesity in women: The difference is black and white. *Personality and Social Psychology Bulletin, 24,* 417–426.

Hegelson, V. S. (2003). Cognitive adaptation, psychological adjustment, and disease progression among angioplasty patients: 4 years later. *Health Psychology, 22,* 30–38.

Heider, F. (1958). *The psychology of interpersonal relationships.* New York: Wiley.

Heine, S. J., & Lehman, D. R. (1997). Culture, dissonance, and self-affirmation. *Personality and Social Psychology Bulletin, 23,* 389–400.

Hektner, J. M., & Csikszentmihalyi, M. (2002). The experience sampling method: Measuring the context and the content of lives. In R. B. Bechtel & A. Churchman (Eds.), *Handbook of environmental psychology* (pp. 233–243). New York: John Wiley & Sons.

Helgeson, V. S., & Cohen, S. (1996). Social support and adjustment to cancer: Reconciling descriptive, correlational, and intervention research. *Health Psychology, 15,* 135–148.

Helmes, E., & Reddon, J. R. (1993). A perspective on developments in assessing psychopathology: A critical review of the MMPI and MMPI–2. *Psychological Bulletin, 113,* 453–471.

Helmuth, L. (2002a). Long-awaited technique spots Alzheimer's toxin. *Science, 297,* 752–753.

Helmuth, L. (2002b). New Alzheimer's treatments that may ease the mind. *Science, 297,* 1260–1262.

Henderson, L., & Zimbardo, P. G. (1998). Shyness. In *Encyclopedia of Mental Health.* San Diego: Academic Press.

Henry, W. P., Strupp, H. H., Schacht, T. E., & Gaston, L. (1994). Psychodynamic approaches. In A. E. Bergin & S. L. Garfield (Eds.), *Handbook of psychotherapy and behavior change* (4th ed., pp. 467–508). New York: Wiley.

Hentschel, U., Smith, G., Ehlers, W., & Draguns, J. G. (Eds.). (1993). *The concept of defense mechanisms in contemporary psychology.* New York: Springer-Verlag.

Herek, G. M. (Ed.). (1998). *Stigma and sexual orientation: Understanding prejudice against lesbians, gay men, and bisexuals.* Newbury Park, CA: Sage.

Herek, G. M., & Capitanio, J. P. (1996). "Some of my best friends": Intergroup contact, concealable stigma, and heterosexuals' attitudes toward gay men and lesbians. *Personality and Social Psychology Bulletin, 22,* 412–424.

Herek, G. M. (2002). Gender gaps in public opinion about lesbians and gay men. *Public Opinion Quarterly, 66,* 40–66.

Herman, C. P., & Polivy, J. (1996). *What does abnormal eating tell us about normal eating?* In H. Meiselman & H. MacFie (Eds.), *Food choice, acceptance, and consumption* (pp. 207–238). London: Blackie Academic & Professional.

Hernández-Guzmán, L., González, S., & López, F. (2002). Effect of guided imagery on children's social performance. *Behavioural and Cognitive Psychotherapy, 30,* 471–483.

Hernnstein, R. J., & Murray, C. (1994). *The bell curve.* New York: The Free Press.

Hersh, S. M. (1971). *My Lai 4: A report on the massacre and its aftermath.* New York: Random House.

Hertzog, C., Dixon, R. A., & Hultsch, D. F. (1990). Relationships between metamemory, memory predictions, and memory task performance in adults. *Psychology and Aging, 5,* 215–227.

Herz, R. S. (1997). The effects of cue distinctiveness on odor-based context-dependent memory. *Memory & Cognition, 25,* 375–380.

 <www.ablongman.com/gerrig17e>

Hettema, J. M., Neale, M. C., & Kendler, K. S. (2001). A review and meta-analysis of the genetic epidemiology of anxiety disorders. *American Journal of Psychiatry, 158,* 1568–1578.

Hewstone, M., Rubin, M., & Willis, H. (2002). Intergroup bias. *Annual Review of Psychology, 53,* 575–604.

Hickok, G., Love-Geffen, T., & Klima, E. S. (2002). Role of the left hemisphere in sign language comprehension. *Brain & Language, 82,* 167–178.

Higgie, M., Chenoweth, S., & Blows, M. W. (2000). Natural selection and the reinforcement of mate recognition. *Science, 290,* 519–521.

Higgins, S. T., Wong, C. J., Badger, G. J., Ogden, D. E. H., & Dantona, R. L. (2000). Contingent reinforcement increases cocaine abstinence during outpatient treatment and 1 year of follow-up. *Journal of Consulting and Clinical Psychology, 68,* 64–72.

Hilgard, E. R. (1986). *Psychology in America: A historical survey.* San Diego: Harcourt Brace Jovanovich.

Hilgetag, C.-C., O'Neill, M. A., & Young, M. P. (1996). Indeterminate organization of the visual system. *Science, 271,* 776–777.

Hinton, A. L. (1996). Agents of death: Explaining the Cambodian genocide in terms of psychosocial dissonance. *American Anthropologist, 98,* 818–831.

Hintzman, D. L. (1986). "Schema abstraction" in a multiple-trace memory model. *Psychological Review, 93,* 411–428.

Hobson, J. A. (1988). *The dreaming brain.* New York: Basic Books.

Hobson, J. A., & McCarley, R. W. (1977). The brain as a dream state generator: An activation-synthesis hypothesis of the dream process. *American Journal of Psychiatry, 134,* 1335–1348.

Hoffman, C., Lau, I., & Johnson, D. R. (1986). The linguistic relativity of person cognition: An English–Chinese comparison. *Journal of Personality and Social Psychology, 51,* 1097–1105.

Hoffman, L. W. (1989). Effects of maternal employment in the two-parent family. *American Psychologist, 44,* 283–292.

Hoffman, M. L. (1986). Affect, cognition, and motivation. In R. Sorrentino & E. Higgins (Eds.), *Handbook of motivation and cognition: Foundations of social behavior* (pp. 244–280). New York: Guilford Press.

Hofling, C. K., Brotzman, E., Dalrymple, S., Graves, N., & Pierce, C. M. (1966). An experimental study in nurse–physician relationships. *Journal of Nervous and Mental Disease, 143*(2), 171–180.

Hohmann, A. A., & Shear, M. K. (2002). Community-based intervention research: Coping with the "noise" of real life in study design. *American Journal of Psychiatry, 159,* 201–207.

Holahan, C. J., Moos, R. H., & Bonin, L. (1997). Social support, coping, and psychological adjustment: A resource model. In G. R. Pierce, B. Lakey, I. G. Sarason, & B. R. Sarason (Eds.), *Sourcebook of social support and personality* (pp. 3–18). New York: Plenum.

Holden, C. (1998). No last word on language origins. *Science, 282,* 1455–1458.

Holen, M. C., & Oaster, T. R. (1976). Serial position and isolation effects in a classroom lecture simulation. *Journal of Educational Psychology, 68,* 723–725.

Hollon, S. D., Thase, M. E., & Markowitz, J. C. (2002). Treatment and prevention of depression. *Psychological Science in the Public Interest, 3,* 39–77.

Holmbeck, G. N., & O'Donnell, D. (1991). Discrepancies between perceptions of decision making and behavioral autonomy. In R. L. Paikoff (Ed.), *Shared views in the family during adolescence* (pp. 51–69). San Francisco: Jossey-Bass.

Holmes, D. S. (1994). *Abnormal psychology.* New York: HarperCollins.

Holmes, T. H., & Rahe, R. H. (1967). The social readjustment rating scale. *Journal of Psychosomatic Research, 11*(2), 213–218.

Holtgraves, T., & Skeel, J. (1992). Cognitive biases in playing the lottery: Estimating the odds and choosing the numbers. *Journal of Applied Social Psychology, 22,* 934–952.

Holyoak, K. J., & Nisbett, R. E. (1988). Induction. In R. J. Sternberg & E. E. Smith (Eds.), *The psychology of human thought* (pp. 50–91). Cambridge, U. K.: Cambridge University Press.

Holyoak, K. J., & Spellman, B. A. (1993). Thinking. *Annual Review of Psychology, 44,* 265–315.

Holyoak, K. J., & Thagard, P. (1997). The analogical mind. *American Psychologist, 52,* 35–44.

Hopson, J. L. (1979). *Scent signals: The silent language of sex.* New York: Morrow.

Horne, J., & Ostberg, O. (1976). A self-assessment questionnaire to determine morningness-eveningness in human circadian rhythms. *International Journal of Chronobiology, 4,* 97–110.

Horney, K. (1937). *The neurotic personality of our time.* New York: Norton.

Horney, K. (1939). *New ways in psychoanalysis.* New York: Norton.

Horney, K. (1945). *Our inner conflicts: A constructive theory of neurosis.* New York: Norton.

Horney, K. (1950). *Neurosis and human growth.* New York: Norton.

Houghton, J. (1980). One personal experience: Before and after mental illness. In J. G. Rabkin, L. Gelb, & J. B. Lazar (Eds.), *Attitudes toward the mentally ill: Research perspectives* (pp. 7–14). Rockville, MD: National Institutes of Mental Health.

Houlihan, D., Schwartz, C., Miltenberger, R., & Heuton, D. (1993). The rapid treatment of a young man's balloon (noise) phobia using *in vivo* flooding. *Journal of Behavior Therapy and Experimental Psychiatry, 24,* 233–240.

Hovland, C. I., Lumsdaine, A. A., & Sheffield, F. D. (1949). *Experiments on mass communication.* Princeton, NJ: Princeton University Press.

Hudson, D. L., & Cohen, M. E. (2000). *Neural networks and artificial intelligence for biomedical engineering.* New York: IEEE Press.

Huesmann, L. R., Moise-Titus, J., Podolski, C.-L., & Eron, L. D. (2003). Longitudinal relations between children's exposure to TV violence and their aggressive and violent behavior in young adulthood: 1977–1992. *Developmental Psychology, 39,* 201–221.

Huey, R. B., Gilchrist, G. W., Carlson, M. L., Berrigan, D., & Serra, L. (2000). Rapid evolution of a geographic cline in size in an introduced fly. *Science, 287,* 308–309.

Hull, C. L. (1943). *Principles of behavior: An introduction to behavior theory.* New York: Appleton-Century-Crofts.

Hull, C. L. (1952). *A behavior system: An introduction to behavior theory concerning the individual organism.* New Haven: Yale University Press.

Hultsch, D. F., Hertzog, C., Dixon, R. A., & Small, B. J. (1998). *Memory change in the aged.* Cambridge, U.K.: Cambridge University Press.

Hultsch, D. F., Hertzog, C., Small, B. J., & Dixon, R. A. (1999). Use it or lose it: Engaged lifestyle as a buffer of cognitive decline in aging? *Psychology and Aging, 14,* 245–263.

Hume, D. (1951). In L. A. Selby-Bigge (Ed.), *An enquiry concerning human understanding.* London: Oxford University Press. (Original work published 1748)

Hummert, M. L. (1999). A social cognitive perspective on age stereotypes. In T. M. Hess & R. Blanchard-Fields (Eds.), *Social cognition and aging* (pp. 175–196). San Diego, CA: Academic Press.

Humphrey, T. (1970). The development of human fetal activity and its relation to postnatal behavior. In H. W. Reese & L. P. Lipsitt (Eds.), *Advances in child development and behavior* (Vol. 5). New York: Academic Press.

Hunt, E., & Agnoli, F. (1991). The Whorfian hypothesis: A cognitive psychology perspective. *Psychological Review, 92,* 377–389.

Hurvich, L., & Jameson, D. (1974). Opponent processes as a model of neural organization. *American Psychologist, 29,* 88–102.

Huston, A. C., McLoyd, V. C., & Coll, C. G. (Eds.). (1994). Children and poverty: Issues in contemporary research [Special issue]. *Child Development, 65*(2).

Hyde, J. S., & Durik, A. M. (2000). Gender differences in erotic plasticity—evolutionary or sociocultural forces? Comment on Baumeister (2000). *Psychological Bulletin, 126,* 375–379.

Insko, C. A., Thibaut, J. W., Moehle, D., Wilson, M., Diamond, W. D., Gilmore, R., Solomon, M. R., & Lipsitz, A. (1980). Social evolution and the emergence of leadership. *Journal of Personality and Social Psychology, 39,* 431–448.

Irvine, J. T. (1990). Registering affect: Heteroglossia in the linguistic expression of emotion. In C. A. Lutz & L. Abu-Lughod (Eds.), *Language and the politics of emotions* (pp. 126–161). Cambridge, U. K.: Cambridge University Press.

Irwin, D. E. (1991). Information integration across saccadic eye movements. *Cognitive Psychology, 23,* 420–456.

Isaacs, E. A., & Clark, H. H. (1987). References in conversations between experts and novices. *Journal of Experimental Psychology: General, 116,* 26–37.

Isen, A. M. (1984). Toward understanding the role of affect in cognition. In R. Wyer & T. Srull (Eds.), *Handbook of social cognition* (pp. 174–236). Hillsdale, NJ: Erlbaum.

Isen, A. M., Daubman, D. A., & Nowicki, G. P. (1987). Positive affect facilitates creative problem solving. *Journal of Personality and Social Psychology, 52,* 1122–1131.

Ishii-Kuntz, M. (1990). Social interaction and psychological well-being: Comparison across stages of adulthood. *International Journal of Aging and Human Development, 30,* 15–36.

Ito, T. A., Miller, N., & Pollock, V. E. (1996). Alcohol and aggression: A meta-analysis on the moderating effects of inhibitory cues, triggering events, and self-focused attention. *Psychological Bulletin, 120,* 60–82.

Izard, C. E. (1993). Four systems for emotion activation: Cognitive and noncognitive processes. *Psychological Review, 100,* 68–90.

Izard, C. E. (1994). Innate and universal facial expressions: Evidence from developmental and cross-cultural research. *Psychological Bulletin, 115,* 288–299.

Jackson, L. A., & McGill, O. D. (1996). Body type preferences and body characteristics associated with attractive and unattractive bodies by African Americans and Anglo Americans. *Sex Roles, 35,* 295–307.

Jackson, R. S., Creemers, J. W. M., Ohagi, S., Raffin-Sanson, M.-L., Sanders, L., Montague, C. T., Hutton, J. C., & O'Rahilly, S. (1997). Obesity and impaired prohormone processing associated with mutations in the human prohormone convertase 1 gene. *Nature Genetics, 16,* 303–306.

Jacobs, R. C., & Campbell, D. T. (1961). The perpetuation of an arbitrary tradition through several generations of a laboratory microculture. *Journal of Abnormal and Social Psychology, 62,* 649–658.

Jacobsen, P. B., Bovbjerg, D. H., Schwartz, M. D., Andrykowski, M. A., Futterman, A. D., Gilewski, T., Norton, L., & Redd, W. H. (1993). Formation of food aversions in cancer patients receiving repeated infusions of chemotherapy. *Behaviour Research and Therapy, 31,* 739–748.

Jacobson, N. S., Dobson, K. S., Truax, P. A., Addis, M. E., Koerner, K., Gollan, J. K., Gortner, E., & Prince, S. (1996). A component analysis of cognitive-behavioral treatment for depression. *Journal of Consulting and Clinical Psychology, 64,* 295–304.

Jaffee, S., & Hyde, J. S. (2000). Gender differences in moral orientation: A meta-analysis. *Psychological Bulletin, 126,* 703–726.

Jahnke, J. C. (1965). Primacy and recency effects in serial-position curves of immediate recall. *Journal of Experimental Psychology, 70,* 130–132.

James, S. E., & Murphy, B. C. (1998). Gay and lesbian relationships in a changing social context. In C. J. Patterson & A. R. D'Augelli (Eds.), *Lesbian, gay, and bisexual identities in families: Psychological perspectives* (pp. 99–121). New York: Oxford University Press.

James, W. (1882). Subjective effects of nitrous oxide. *Mind, 7,* 186–208.

James, W. (1892). *Psychology.* New York: Holt.

James, W. (1902). *The varieties of religious experience.* New York: Longmans, Green.

James, W. (1950). *The principles of psychology* (2 vols.). New York: Holt, Rinehart & Wilson. (Original work published 1890)

Janis, I. (1982). *Groupthink* (2nd ed.). Boston: Houghton Mifflin.

Janis, I. L., & Frick, F. (1943). The relationship between attitudes toward conclusions and errors in judging logical validity of syllogisms. *Journal of Experimental Psychology, 33,* 73–77.

Janofsky, J. S., Dunn, M. H., Roskes, E. J., Briskin, J. K., & Rudolph, M. S. L. (1996). Insanity defense pleas in Baltimore City: An analysis of outcome. *American Journal of Psychiatry, 153,* 1464–1468.

Janowitz, H. D., & Grossman, M. I. (1950). Hunger and appetite: Some definitions and concepts. *Journal of the Mount Sinai Hospital, 16,* 231–240.

Janz, N. K., & Becker, M. H. (1984). The health belief model: A decade later. *Health Education Quarterly, 11,* 1–47.

Jedrej, M. C. (1995). *Ingessana: The religious institutions of a people of the Sudan–Ethiopia borderland.* Leiden: Brill.

Jenike, M. A., Breiter, H. C., Baer, L., Kennedy, D. N., Savage, C. R., Olivares, M. J., O'Sullivan, R. L., Shera, D. M., Rauch, S. C., Keuthen, N., Rosen, B. R., Caviness, V. S., & Filipek, P. A. (1996). Cerebral structural abnormalities in obsessive-compulsive disorder. *Archives of General Psychiatry, 53,* 625–632.

Jenkins, L., Myerson, J., Hale, S., & Fry, A. F. (1999). Individual and developmental differences in working memory across the life span. *Psychonomic Bulletin & Review, 6,* 28–40.

Jensen, A. R. (1962). Spelling errors and the serial position effect. *Journal of Educational Psychology, 53,* 105–109.

Jensen-Campbell, L. A., Graziano, W. G., & West, S. G. (1995). Dominance, prosocial orientation, and female preferences: Do nice guys really finish last? *Journal of Personality and Social Psychology, 68,* 427–440.

Johar, G. V., & Sengupta, J. (2002). The effects of dissimulation on the accessibility and predictive power of weakly held attitudes. *Social Cognition, 20,* 257–293.

Johnson, J. R., & Vickers, Z. M. (1993). The effects of flavor and macronutrient composition of preloads on liking, hunger, and subsequent intake in humans. *Appetite, 21,* 15–31.

Johnson, M. K., Hashtroudi, S., & Lindsay, D. S. (1993). Source monitoring. *Psychological Bulletin, 114,* 3–28.

Johnson, S. M. (2003). The revolution in couple therapy: A practitioner-scientist perspective. *Journal of Marital and Family Therapy, 29,* 365–384.

Johnson, T. D., & Gottlieb, G. (1981). Visual preferences of imprinted ducklings are altered by the maternal call. *Journal of Comparative and Physiological Psychology, 95*(5), 665–675.

Johnson, T. E., & Rule, B. G. (1986). Mitigating circumstances, information, censure, and aggression. *Journal of Personality and Social Psychology, 50,* 537–542.

Johnson, W., McGue, M., Gaist, D., Vaupel, J. W., & Christensen, K. (2002). Frequency and heritability of depression symptomatology in the second half of life: Evidence from Danish twins over 45. *Psychological Medicine, 32,* 1175–1185.

Johnson-Laird, P. N., & Wason, P. C. (1977). A theoretical analysis of insight into a reasoning task. In P. N. Johnson-Laird & P. C. Wason (Eds.), *Thinking* (pp. 143–157). Cambridge, U.K.: Cambridge University Press.

Jones, E. (1953). *The life and works of Sigmund Freud.* New York: Basic Books.

Jones, J. M. (1997). *Prejudice and racism* (2nd ed.). New York: McGraw-Hill.

Jones, J. M., Levine, I. S., & Rosenberg, A. A. (Eds.). (1991). Homelessness [Special issue]. *American Psychologist, 46*(11).

Joyce, A. S., Ogrodniczuk, J. S., Piper, W. E., & McCallum, M. (2003). The alliance as mediator of expectancy effects in short-term individual therapy. *Journal of Consulting and Clinical Psychology, 71,* 672–679.

Joyce, L. (1990). Losing the connection. *Stanford Medicine,* pp. 19–21.

Judge, T. A., & Cable, D. M. (1997). Applicant personality, organizational culture, and organization attraction. *Personnel Psychology, 50,* 359–392.

Jung, C. G. (1959). The concept of the collective unconscious. In *The archetypes and the collective unconscious, collected works* (Vol. 9, Part 1, pp. 54–74.). Princeton, NJ: Princeton University Press. (Original work published 1936)

Jung, C. G. (1973). *Memories, dreams, reflections* (Rev. ed., A. Jaffe, Ed.). New York: Pantheon Books.

Jusczyk, P. W. (2003). Chunking language input to find patterns. In D. H. Rakison & L. M. Oakes (Eds.), *Early category and concept development.* London: Oxford University Press.

Jusczyk, P. W., & Aslin, R. N. (1995). Infants' detection of the sound patterns of words in fluent speech. *Cognitive Psychology, 29,* 1–23.

Jussim, L. (1991). Social perception and social reality: A reflection-construction model. *Psychological Review, 98,* 54–73.

Kabat-Zinn, J. (1990). *Full catastrophe living: Using the wisdom of your body and mind to face stress, pain, and illness.* New York: Dell Publishing.

Kagan, J. (1994). *Galen's prophesy: Temperament in human nature.* New York: Basic Books.

Kahneman, D. (1991). Judgment and decision making: A personal view. *Psychological Science, 2,* 142–145.

Kahneman, D. (1992). Reference points, anchors, norms, and mixed feelings. *Organizational Behavior and Human Decision Processes, 51,* 296–312.

Kahneman, D., & Tversky, A. (1973). On the psychology of prediction. *Psychological Review, 80,* 237–251.

Kallmann, F. J. (1946). The genetic theory of schizophrenia: An analysis of 691 schizophrenic index families. *American Journal of Psychiatry, 103,* 309–322.

Kamil, A. C., & Balda, R. P. (1990). Spatial memory in seed-caching corvids. In G. H. Bower (Ed.), *The psychology of learning and motivation* (Vol. 26, pp. 1–25). San Diego: Academic Press.

Kamil, A. C., Balda, R. P., Olson, D. P., & Good, S. (1993). Returns to emptied cache sites by Clark's nutcrackers, *Nucifraga columbiana*: A puzzle revisited. *Animal Behaviour, 45,* 241–252.

Kamin, L. J. (1969). Predictability, surprise, attention, and conditioning. In B. A Campbell & R. M. Church (Eds.), *Punishment and aversive behavior* (pp. 279–296). New York: Appleton-Century-Crofts.

Kantrowitz, B., & McGinn, D. (2000, June 19). When teachers are cheaters. *Newsweek, 135,* 48–49.

Kaplan, C. A., & Simon, H. A. (1990). In search of insight. *Cognitive Psychology, 22,* 374–419.

Kaplan, R. M. (2000). Two pathways to prevention. *American Psychologist, 55,* 382–396.

Karin-D'Arcy, M. R., & Povinelli, D. J. (2002). Do chimpanzees know what each other see? A closer look. *International Journal of Comparative Psychology, 15,* 21–54.

Karney, B. R., & Bradbury, T. N. (1995). The longitudinal course of marital quality and stability: A review of theory, method, and research. *Psychological Bulletin, 118,* 3–34.

Kassebaum, N. L. (1994). Head Start: Only the best for America's children. *American Psychologist, 49,* 1123–1126.

Katsanis, J., Kortenkamp, S., Iacono, W. G., & Grove, W. M. (1997). Antisaccade performance in patients with schizophrenia. *Journal of Abnormal Psychology, 106,* 468–472.

Katz, R. (1982). *Boiling energy: Community healing among the Kalahari Kung.* Cambridge, MA: Harvard University Press.

Katz, R. (1993). *The straight path: A story of healing and transformation in Fiji.* Reading, MA: Addison-Wesley.

Kay, P., & Kempton, W. (1984). What is the Sapir-Whorf hypothesis? *American Anthropologist, 86,* 65–79.

Kazdin, A. E. (1982). The token economy: A decade later. *Journal of Applied Behavior Analysis, 15,* 431–445.

Kazdin, A. E. (1994). *Behavior modification in applied settings* (5th ed.). Pacific Grove, CA: Brooks/Cole.

Kegeles, S. M., Hays, R. B., & Coates, T. J. (1996). The Mpowerment project: A community-level HIV prevention intervention for young gay men. *American Journal of Public Health, 86,* 1129–1136.

Kegeles, S. M., Hays, R. B., Pollack, L. M., & Coates, T. J. (1999). Mobilizing young gay and bisexual men for HIV prevention: A two-community study. *AIDS, 13,* 1753–1762.

Keiger, D. (1993, November). Touched with fire. *Johns Hopkins Magazine,* pp. 38, 40–44.

Keller, M. B., McCullough, J. P., Klein, D. N., Arnow, B., Dunner, D. L., Gelenberg, A. J., Markowitz, J. C., Nemeroff, C. B., Russell, J. M., Thase, M. E., Trivedi, M. H., & Zajecka, J. (2000). A comparison of nefazodone, the cognitive behavioral-analysis system of psychotherapy, and their combination for the treatment of chronic depression. *New England Journal of Medicine, 342,* 1462–1470.

Kelley, H. H. (1967). Attribution theory in social psychology. In D. Levine (Ed.), *Nebraska symposium on motivation* (Vol. 15). Lincoln: University of Nebraska Press.

Kelley, J. E., Lumley, M. A., & Leisen, J. C. C. (1997). Health effects of emotional disclosure in rheumatoid arthritis patients. *Health Psychology, 16,* 331–340.

Kelman, H. C. (1997). Group processes in the resolution of international conflicts: Experiences from the Israeli–Palestinian case. *American Psychologist, 52,* 212–220.

Kelman, H. C. (1999). Interactive problem solving as a metaphor for international conflict resolution: Lessons for the policy process. *Peace & Conflict: Journal of Peace Psychology, 5,* 201–218.

Kempermann, G. (2002). Why new neurons? Possible functions for adult hippocampal neurogenesis. *Journal of Neuroscience, 22,* 635–638.

Kendler, H. H. (1987). *Historical foundations of modern psychology.* Chicago: Dorsey Press.

Kendler, K. S., Thornton, L. M., & Pedersen, N. L. (2000). Tobacco consumption in Swedish twins reared apart and reared together. *Archives of General Psychiatry, 57,* 886–892.

Kendrick, T., Tylee, A., & Freeling (Eds.) (1996). *The prevention of mental illness in primary care.* Cambridge, U.K.: Cambridge University Press.

Kennedy, P. R., Bakay, R. A. E., Moore, M. M., Adams, K., & Goldwaithe, J. (2000). Direct control of a computer from the human central nervous system. *IEEE Transactions on Rehabilitation Engineering, 8,* 198–202.

Kennedy, R. E., & Craighead, W. E. (1988). Differential effects of depression and anxiety on recall of feedback in a learning task. *Behavior Therapy, 19,* 437–454.

Kenny, D. A., Bond, C. F., Jr., Mohr, C. D., & Horn, E. M. (1996). Do we know how much people like one another? *Journal of Personality and Social Psychology, 71,* 928–936.

Kenny, D. A., & La Voie, L. (1982). Reciprocity of interpersonal attraction: A confirmed hypothesis. *Social Psychology Quarterly, 45,* 54–58.

Kessel, N. (1989). Genius and mental disorder: A history of ideas concerning their conjunction. In P. Murray (Ed.), *Genius: The history of an idea* (pp. 196–212). London: Basil Blackwell.

Kessler, R. C., McGonagle, K. A., Zhao, S., Nelson, C. B., Hughes, M., Eshleman, S., Wittchen, H. U., & Kendler, K. S. (1994). Lifetime and 12-month prevalence of DSM-III-R psychiatric disorders in the United States. *Archives of General Psychiatry, 51,* 8–19.

Kessler, R. C., Mickelson, K. D., & Zhao, S. (1997). Patterns and correlates of self-help group membership in the United States. *Social Policy, 27,* 27–46.

Kety, S. S., Wender, P. H., Jacobsen, B., Ingraham, L. J., Jansson, L., Faber, B., & Kinney, D. K. (1994). Mental illness in the biological and adoptive relatives of schizophrenic adoptees: Replication of the Copenhagen study in the rest of Denmark. *Archives of General Psychiatry, 51,* 442–455.

Kiecolt-Glaser, J. K., Marucha, P. T., Malarkey, P. T., Mercado, A. M., & Glaser, R. (1995). Slowing of wound healing by psychological stress. *Lancet, 346,* 1194–1196.

Kiecolt-Glaser, J. K., McGuire, L., Robles, T. F., & Glaser, R. (2002). Psychoneuroimmunology: Psychological influences on immune function and health. *Journal of Consulting and Clinical Psychology, 70,* 537–547.

Kihlstrom, J. F., & Cantor, N. (2000). Social intelligence. In R. J. Sternberg (Ed.), *Handbook of intelligence* (pp. 359–369). New York: Cambridge University Press.

Killen, M., & Hart, D. (Eds.). (1999). *Morality in everyday life: Developmental perspectives.* New York: Cambridge University Press.

Kilpatrick, D. G., Ruggiero, K. J., Acierno, R., Saunders, B. E., Resnick, H. S., & Best, C. L. (2003). Violence and risk of PTSD, major depression, substance abuse/dependence, and comorbidity: Results from the National Survey of Adolescents. *Journal of Consulting and Clinical Psychology, 71,* 692–700.

Kim, M. S., & Cave, K. R. (1995). Spatial attention in visual search for features and feature conjunctions. *Psychological Science, 6,* 376–380.

Kimura, D. (1999). *Sex and cognition.* Cambridge, MA: MIT Press.

King, S., & Dixon, M. J. (1996). The influence of expressed emotion, family dynamics, and symptom type on the social adjustment of schizophrenic young adults. *Archives of General Psychiatry, 53,* 1098–1104.

King, S. A., & Moreggi, D. (1998). Internet therapy and self-help groups—The pros and cons. In J. Gackenbach (Ed.), *Psychology and the Internet: Intrapersonal, interpersonal, and transpersonal implications* (pp. 77–109). San Diego, CA: Academic Press.

Kinney, D. K., Holzman, P. S., Jacobsen, B., Jansson, L., Faber, B., Hildebrand, W., Kasell, E., & Zimbalist, M. E. (1997). Thought disorder in schizophrenic and control adoptees and their relatives. *Archives of General Psychiatry, 54,* 475–479.

Kinsey, A. C., Martin, C. E., & Pomeroy, W. B. (1948). *Sexual behavior in the human male.* Philadelphia: Saunders.

Kinsey, A. C., Pomeroy, W. B., Martin, C. E., & Gebhard, R. H. (1953). *Sexual behavior in the human female.* Philadelphia: Saunders.

Kintner, C. (2002). Neurogenesis in embryos and in adult neural stem cells. *Journal of Neuroscience, 22,* 639–643.

Kintsch, W. (1974). *The representation of meaning in memory.* Hillsdale, NJ: Erlbaum.

Kirsch, I., & Lynn, S. J. (1995). The altered state of hypnosis: Changes in the theoretical landscape. *American Psychologist, 50,* 846–858.

Kirsch, I., & Lynn, S. J. (1998). Dissociation theories of hypnosis. *Psychological Bulletin, 123,* 100–115.

Kirschner, S. M., & Galperin, G. J. (2001). Psychiatric defenses in New York County: Pleas and results. *Journal of the American Academy of Psychiatry and the Law, 29,* 194–201.

Kisilevsky, B. S., Hains, S. M. J., Lee, K., Xie, X., Huang, H., Ye, H. H., Zhang, K., & Wang, Z. (2003). Effects of experience on fetal voice recognition. *Psychological Science, 14,* 220–224.

Kitamura, C., Thanavishuth, C., Burnham, D., & Luksaneeyanawin, S. (2002). Universality and specificity in infant-directed speech: Pitch modifications as a function of infant age and sex in a tonal and non-tonal language. *Infant Behavior & Development, 24,* 372–392.

Kitayama, S., Markus, H. R., & Lieberman, C. (1995). The collective construction of self-esteem: Implications for culture, self, and emotion. In J. A. Russell, J. Fernandez-Dols, T. Manstead, & J. Wellenkamp (Eds.), *Everyday conceptions of emotion* (pp. 523–550). Dordrecht: Kluwer.

Kite, M. E., & Wagner, L. S. (2002). Attitudes toward older adults. In T. D. Nelson (Ed.) (2002). *Ageism: Stereotyping and prejudice against older persons* (pp. 130–161). Cambridge, MA: MIT Press.

Klein, E. B., Stone, W. N., Hicks, M. W., & Pritchard, I. L. (2003). Understanding dropouts. *Journal of Mental Health Counseling, 25,* 89–100.

Klein, K. E., & Wegmann, H. M. (1974). The resynchronization of human circadian rhythms after transmeridian flights as a result of flight direction and mode of activity. In L. E. Scheving, F. Halberg, & J. E. Pauly (Eds.), *Chronobiology* (pp. 564–570). Tokyo: Igaku.

Klein, M. (1975). *The writings of Melanie Klein* (Vols. 1–4). London: Hogarth Press and the Institute of Psychoanalysis.

Kluckhohn, C. (1944). Navaho witchcraft. *Papers of the Yale University Peabody Museum* (Vol. 24, No. 2). New Haven: Yale University Press.

Knee, C. R., & Boon, S. D. (2001). When the glass is half-empty: Framing effects and evaluations of a romantic partner's attributes. *Personal Relationships, 8,* 249–263.

Knoedler, A. J., Hellwig, K. A., & Neath, I. (1999). The shift from recency to primacy with increasing delay. *Journal of Exper-*

<www.ablongman.com/gerrig17e>

imental Psychology: Learning, Memory, and Cognition, 25, 474–487.

Knox, C. (1994). Conflict resolution at the microlevel: Community relations in Northern Ireland. *Journal of Conflict Resolution, 38,* 595–619.

Koffka, K. (1935). *Principles of Gestalt psychology.* New York: Harcourt Brace.

Kohlberg, L. (1964). Development of moral character and moral ideology. In M. L. Hoffman & L. W. Hoffman (Eds.), *Review of child development research* (Vol. 1). New York: Russell Sage Foundation.

Kohlberg, L. (1981). *The philosophy of moral development.* New York: Harper & Row.

Köhler, W. (1947). *Gestalt psychology.* New York: Liveright.

Kolb, B. (1989). Development, plasticity, and behavior. *American Psychologist, 44,* 1203–1212.

Koopman, C., Classen, C., & Spiegel, D. (1996). Dissociative responses in the immediate aftermath of the Oakland/Berkeley firestorm. *Journal of Traumatic Stress, 9,* 521–540.

Koren, G., Nulman, I., Rovet, J., Greenbaum, R., Loebstein, M., & Einarson, T. (1998). Long-term neurodevelopmental risks in children exposed in utero to cocaine: The Toronto adoption study. In J. A. Harvey & B. E. Kosofsky (Eds.), *Cocaine: Effects on the developing brain* (pp. 306–313). New York: New York Academy of Sciences.

Koriat, A. (1993). How do we know what we know? The accessibility model of the feeling of knowing. *Psychological Review, 100,* 609–639.

Koriat, A. (1995). Dissociating knowing and the feeling of knowing: Further evidence for the accessibility model. *Journal of Experimental Psychology: General, 124,* 311–333.

Koriat, A., & Fischoff, B. (1974). What day is today? An inquiry into the process of time orientation. *Memory & Cognition, 2,* 201–205.

Koriat, A., & Levy-Sadot, R. (1999). Processes underlying metacognitive judgments: Information-based and experience-based monitoring of one's own knowledge. In S. Chaiken & Y. Trope (Eds.), *Dual-process theories in social psychology* (pp. 483–502). New York: Guilford.

Kortegaard, L. S., Hoerder, K., Joergensen, J., Gillberg, C., & Kyvik, K. O. (2001). A preliminary population-based twin study of self-reported eating disorder. *Psychological Medicine, 31,* 361–365.

Kosslyn, S. M. (1980). *Image and mind.* Cambridge, MA: Harvard University Press.

Kosslyn, S. M., Pascual-Leone, A., Felician, O., Camposano, S., Keenan, J. P., Thompson, W. L., Ganis, G., Sukel, K. E., & Alpert, N. M. (1999). The role of area 17 in visual imagery: Convergent evidence from PET and rTMS. *Science, 284,* 167–170.

Kotovsky, K., Hayes, J. R., & Simon, H. A. (1985). Why are some problems hard? Evidence from Tower of Hanoi. *Cognitive Psychology, 17,* 248–294.

Kotovsky, K., & Simon, H. A. (1990). What makes some problems really hard: Explorations in the problem space of difficulty. *Cognitive Psychology, 22,* 143–183.

Kraepelin, E. (1921). *Manic-depressive disorder and paranoia.* London: Churchill Livingstone.

Kraut, A. M. (1990). Healers and strangers: Immigrant attitudes toward the physician in America—A relationship in historical perspective. *Journal of the American Medical Association, 263,* 1807–1811.

Kraut, R., Patterson, M., Lundmark, V., Kiesler, S., Mukopadhyay, T., & Scherlis, W. (1998). Internet paradox: A social technology that reduces social involvement and psychological well being? *American Psychologist, 53,* 1017–1031.

Krueger, J., & Stanke, D. (2001). The role of self-referent and other-referent knowledge in perceptions of group characteristics. *Personality & Social Psychology Bulletin, 27,* 878–888.

Kübler, A., Kotchoubey, B., Kaiser, J., Wolpaw, J.R., & Birbaumer, N. (2001). Brain–computer communication: Unlocking the locked in. *Psychological Bulletin, 127,* 358–375.

Kuest, J., & Karbe, H. (2002). Cortical activation studies in aphasia. *Current Neurology and Neuroscience Reports, 2,* 511–515.

Kuhn, M. H., & McPartland, T. S. (1954). An empirical investigation of self-attitudes. *American Sociological Review, 19,* 68–76.

Kuijer, R. G., Ybema, J. F., Buunk, B. P., De Jon, G. M., Thijs-Boer, F., & Sanderman, R. (2000). Active engagement, protective buffering, and overprotection: Three ways of giving support by intimate partners of patients with cancer. *Journal of Social and Clinical Psychology, 19,* 256–275.

Kujawski, J. H., & Bower, T. G. R. (1993). Same-sex preferential looking during infancy as a function of abstract representation. *British Journal of Developmental Psychology, 11,* 201–209.

Kuno, E., Rothbard, A. B., Averyt, J., & Culhane, D. (2000). Homelessness among persons with serious mental illness in an enhanced community-based mental health system. *Psychiatric Services, 51,* 1012–1016.

Kuperberg, G. R., Broome, M. R., McGuire, P. K., David, A. S., Eddy, M., Ozawa, F., Goff, D., West, W. C., Williams, S. C. R., van der Kouwe, A. J. W., Salat, D. H., Dale, A. M., & Fischl, B. (2003). Regionally localized thinning of the cerebral cortex in schizophrenia. *Archives of General Psychiatry, 60,* 878–888.

LaBerge, S., & DeGracia, D. J. (2000). Varieties of lucid dreaming experience. In R. G. Kunzendorf & B. Wallace (Eds.), *Individual differences in conscious experience* (pp. 269–307). Amsterdam: John Benjamins Publishing Company.

LaBerge, S., & Levitan, L. (1995). Validity established of DreamLight cues for eliciting lucid dreaming. *Dreaming: Journal of the Association for the Study of Dreams, 5,* 159–168.

LaBerge, S., & Rheingold, H. (1990). *Exploring the world of lucid dreaming.* New York: Ballantine Books.

Lachman, R., Lachman, J. L., & Butterfield, E. C. (1979). *Cognitive psychology and information processing.* Hillsdale, NJ: Erlbaum.

Ladd, G. W., & Cairns, E. (1996). Children: Ethnic and political violence. *Child Development, 67,* 14–18.

Lambo, T. A. (1978). Psychotherapy in Africa. *Human Nature, 1,* 32–39.

Lander, E. S., & Weinberg, R. A. Genomics: Journey to the center of biology. *Science, 287,* 1777–1782.

Lang, F. R., & Carstensen, L. L. (1994). Close emotional relationships in late life: Further support for proactive aging in the social domain. *Psychology and Aging, 9,* 315–324.

Lanius, R. A., Williamson, P. C., Hopper, J., Densmore, M., Boksman, K., Gupta, M. A., Neufeld, R. W. J., Gati, J. S., & Menon, R. S. (2003). Recall of emotional states in posttraumatic stress disorder: An fMRI investigation. *Biological Psychiatry, 53,* 204–210.

Larner, A. J., Moss, J., Rossi, M. L., & Anderson, M. (1994). Congenital insensitivity to pain: A 20-year follow up. *Journal of Neurology, Neurosurgery & Psychiatry, 57,* 973–974.

Lashley, K. S. (1929). *Brain mechanisms and intelligence.* Chicago: University of Chicago Press.

Lashley, K. S. (1950). In search of the engram. In *Physiological mechanisms in animal behavior: Symposium of the Society for Experimental Biology.* New York: Academic Press.

Latané, B., & Darley, J. M. (1970). *The unresponsive bystander: Why doesn't he help?* New York: Appleton-Century-Crofts.

Laumann, E. O., & Gagnon, J. H. (1995). A sociological perspective on sexual action. In R. G. Parker & J. H. Gagnon (Eds.), *Conceiving sexuality: Approaches to sex research in a postmodern world* (pp. 183–213). New York: Routledge.

Lay, C. H. (1986). At last my research article on procrastination. *Journal of Research in Personality, 20,* 474–495.

Lazarus, R. S. (1981, July). Little hassles can be hazardous to your health. *Psychology Today,* pp. 58–62.

Lazarus, R. S. (1984a). On the primacy of cognition. *American Psychologist, 39,* 124–129.

Lazarus, R. S. (1984b). Puzzles in the study of daily hassles. *Journal of Behavioral Medicine, 7,* 375–389.

Lazarus, R. S. (1991). Cognition and motivation in emotion. *American Psychologist, 46,* 352–367.

Lazarus, R. S. (1993). From psychological stress to the emotions: A history of changing outlooks. *Annual Review of Psychology, 44,* 1–21.

Lazarus, R. S. (1995). Vexing research problems inherent in cognitive-mediational theories of emotion—and some solutions. *Psychological Inquiry, 6,* 183–196.

Lazarus, R. S., & Folkman, S. (1984). *Stress, appraisal, and coping.* New York: Springer.

Lazarus, R. S., & Lazarus, B. N. (1994). *Passion and reason: Making sense of our emotions.* New York: Oxford University Press.

Leaper, C. (2000). The social construction and socialization of gender during development. In P. H. Miller & E. K. Scholnick (Eds.), *Toward a feminist developmental psychology* (pp. 127–152). New York: Routledge.

Leary, M. R., Kowalski, R. M., Smith, L., & Phillips, S. (2003). Teasing, rejection, and violence: Case studies of the school shootings. *Aggressive Behavior, 29,* 202–214.

Leary, M. R., Tchividjian, L. R., & Kraxberger, B. E. (1994). Self-presentation can be hazardous to your health: Impression management and health risk. *Health Psychology, 13,* 461–470.

Leathers, S. J. (2002). Parental visiting and family reunification: Could inclusive practice make a difference? *Social Welfare, 81,* 595–616.

LeCompte, D. C., & Watkins, M. J. (1995). Grouping in primary memory: The case of the compound suffix. *Journal of Experimental Psychology: Learning, Memory, and Cognition, 21,* 96–102.

Lee, M., Zimbardo, P., & Bertholf, M. (1977, November). Shy murderers. *Psychology Today,* pp. 68–70, 76, 148.

Lee-Sammons, W. H., & Whitney, P. (1991). Reading perspectives and memory for text: An individual differences analysis. *Journal of Experimental Psychology: Learning, Memory, and Cognition, 17,* 1074–1081.

Leger, D. (1992). *Biological foundations of behavior: An integrative approach.* New York: HarperCollins.

LeGrand, L. E. (1991). United we cope: Support groups for the dying and bereaved. *Death Studies, 15,* 207–230.

Leiter, M. P., & Maslach, C. (1988). The impact of interpersonal environment on burnout and organizational commitment. *Journal of Organizational Behavior, 9,* 297–308.

Lencer, R., Malchow, C. P., Trillenberg-Krecker, K., Schwinger, E., & Arolt, V. (2000). Eye-tracking dysfunction (ETD) in families with sporadic and familial schizophrenia. *Biological Psychiatry, 47,* 391–401.

Lennon, R. T. (1985). Group tests of intelligence. In B. B. Wolman (Ed.), *Handbook of intelligence* (pp. 825–847). New York: Wiley.

Lerner, M. (1980). *The belief in a just world: A fundamental delusion.* New York: Plenum Press.

Leucht, S., Barnes, T. R. E., Kissling, W., Engel, R. R., Correll, C., & Kane, J. M. (2003). Relapse prevention in schizophrenia with new-generation antipsychotics: A systematic review and exploratory meta-analysis of randomized, controlled trials. *American Journal of Psychiatry, 160,* 1209–1222.

LeVay, S. (1996). *Queer science: The use and abuse of research into homosexuality.* Cambridge, MA: The MIT Press.

Levenson, R. W., Carstensen, L. L., & Gottman, J. M. (1993). Long-term marriage: Age, gender, and satisfaction. *Psychology and Aging, 8,* 301–313.

Levenson, R. W., Ekman, P., Heider, K., & Friesen, W. V. (1992). Emotion and autonomic nervous system activity in the Minangkabau of West Sumatra. *Journal of Personality and Social Psychology, 62,* 972–988.

Leventhal, H. (1980). Toward a comprehensive theory of emotion. In L. Berkowitz (Ed.), *Advances in experimental social psychology* (Vol. 13, pp. 139–207). New York: Academic Press.

Leventhal, T., & Brooks-Gunn, J. (2000). The neighborhoods they live in: The effects of neighborhood on child and adolescent outcomes. *Psychological Bulletin, 126,* 309–337.

Levine, R., Sato, S., Hashimoto, T., & Verma, J. (1995). Love and marriage in eleven cultures. *Journal of Cross-Cultural Psychology, 26,* 544–571.

Levine, S. B. (1998). *Sexuality in mid-life.* New York: Plenum.

Levi-Strauss, C. (1963). The effectiveness of symbols. In C. Levi-Strauss (Ed.), *Structural anthropology.* New York: Basic Books.

Levy, B., & Langer, E. (1994). Aging free from negative stereotypes: Successful memory in China and among the American deaf. *Journal of Personality and Social Psychology, 66,* 989–997.

Levy, G. D., & Fivush, R. (1993). Scripts and gender: A new approach for examining gender-role development. *Developmental Review, 13,* 126–146.

Levy, J. A. (1994). Sex and sexuality in later life stages. In A. Rossi (Ed.), *Sexuality across the life course* (pp. 287–309). Chicago: University of Chicago Press.

Levy, S. R., Plaks, J. E., & Dweck, C. S. (1999). Modes of social thought: Implicit theories and social understanding. In S. Chaiken & Y. Trope (Eds.), *Dual-process theories in social psychology* (pp. 179–202). New York: Guilford.

Lewin, K. (1936). *Principles of topological psychology.* New York: McGraw-Hill.

Lewin, K., Lippitt, R., & White, R. K. (1939). Patterns of aggressive behavior in experimentally created "social climates." *Journal of Social Psychology, 10,* 271–299.

Lewinsohn, P. M. (1975). The behavioral study and treatment of depression. In M. Hersen, R. M. Eisler, & P. M. Miller (Eds.), *Progress in behavior modification* (pp. 19–64). New York: Academic Press.

Lewinsohn, P. M., Hoberman, H. M., Teri, L., & Hautzinger, M. (1985). An integrative theory of depression. In S. Reiss & R. Bootzin (Eds.), *Theoretical issues in behavior therapy* (pp. 331–359). San Diego: Academic Press.

Lewis, J. R. (1995). *The dream encyclopedia.* Detroit: Visible Ink Press.

Lewis, M. (1991). Ways of knowing: Objective self-awareness or consciousness. *Developmental Review, 11,* 231–243.

Lewis, M. (1999). Social cognition and the self. In P. Rochat (Ed.), *Early social cognition: Understanding others in the first months of life* (pp. 81–98). Mahwah, NJ: Erlbaum.

Lilienfeld, S. O., & Lynn, S. J. (2003). Dissociative identity disorder: Multiple personalities, multiple controversies. In S. O. Lilienfeld, S. J. Lynn, & J. M. Lohr (Eds.), *Science and pseudoscience in clinical psychology* (pp. 109–142). New York: Guilford Press.

<www.ablongman.com/gerrig17e>

Lindsay, D. S. (1990). Misleading suggestions can impair eyewitnesses' ability to remember event details. *Journal of Experimental Psychology: Learning, Memory, and Cognition, 16,* 1077–1083.

Lindsay, D. S. (1993). Eyewitness suggestibility. *Current Directions in Psychological Science, 2,* 86–89.

Link, B. G., Struening, E. L., Rahav, M., Phelan, J. C., & Nuttbrock, L. (1997). On stigma and its consequences: Evidence from a longitudinal study of men with dual diagnoses of mental illness and substance abuse. *Journal of Health and Social Behavior, 38,* 177–190.

Liotti, M., Mayberg, H. S., McGinnis, S., Brannan, S. L., & Jerabek, P. (2002). Unmasking disease-specific cerebral blood flow abnormalities: Mood challenge in people with remitted unipolar depression. *American Journal of Psychiatry, 159,* 1830–1840.

Lipkus, I. M., Barefoot, J. C., Williams, R. B., & Siegler, I. C. (1994). Personality measures as predictors of smoking initiation and cessation in the UNC Alumni Heart Study. *Health Psychology, 13,* 149–155.

Liu, J. H., & Latané, B. (1998). Extremitization of attitudes: Does thought- and discussion-induced polarization cumulate? *Basic and Applied Social Psychology, 20,* 103–110.

Liu, W., McGucken, E., Clements, M., DeMarco, C., Vichienchom, K., Hughes, C., Humayun, M., Weiland, J., Greenber, R., & de Juan, E. (2000). Multiple-unit artificial retina chipset system to benefit the visually impaired. *IEEE Transactions on Rehabilitation Engineering,* in press.

Liu, W., Vichienchom, K., Clements, M., DeMarco, S. C., Hughes, C., McGucken, E., Humayun, M. S., de Juan, E., Weiland, J. D., & Greenberg, R. (2000). A neuro-stimulus chip with telemetry unit for retinal prosthetic device. *IEEE Journal of Solid-State Circuits, 35,* 1487–1497.

Lloyd-Jones, T. J., & Luckhurst, L. (2002). Effects of plane rotation, task, and complexity on recognition of familiar and chimeric objects. *Memory & Cognition, 30,* 499–510.

Locke, J. (1975). *An essay concerning human understanding.* Oxford: P. H. Nidditch. (Original work published 1690)

Lockhart, R. S., & Craik, F. I. M. (1990). Levels of processing: A retrospective commentary on a framework for memory research. *Canadian Journal of Psychology, 44,* 87–122.

Loehlin, J. C. (2000). Group differences in intelligence. In R. J. Sternberg (Ed.), *Handbook of intelligence* (pp. 176–193). Cambridge, U.K.: Cambridge University Press.

Loehlin, J. C., McCrae, R. R., Costa, P. T., & John, O. P. (1998). Heritabilities of common and measure-specific components of the big five personality factors. *Journal of Research in Personality, 32,* 431–453.

Loftus, E. F. (1979). *Eyewitness testimony.* Cambridge, MA: Harvard University Press.

Loftus, E. F. (1992). When a lie becomes memory's truth: Memory distortion after exposure to misinformation. *Current Directions in Psychological Science, 1,* 121–123.

Loftus, E. F., & Palmer, J. C. (1974). Reconstruction of automobile destruction: An example of the interaction between language and memory. *Journal of Verbal Learning and Verbal Behavior, 13,* 585–589.

Logan, G. D. (1988). Toward an instance theory of automatization. *Psychological Review, 95,* 492–527.

Logan, G. D. (1992). Shapes of reaction-time distributions and shapes of learning curves: A test of the instance theory of automaticity. *Journal of Experimental Psychology: Learning, Memory, and Cognition, 18,* 883–914.

Logan, G. D. (2002). Parallel and serial processes. In H. Pashler & J. Wixted (Eds.), *Stevens' handbook of experimental psychology: Vol 4. Methodology in experimental psychology* (pp. 271–300). New York: Wiley.

Logue, A. W. (1991). *The psychology of eating & drinking: An introduction* (2nd ed.). New York: Freeman.

Loomis, A. L., Harvey, E. N., & Hobart, G. A. (1937). Cerebral states during sleep as studied by human brain potentials. *Journal of Experimental Psychology, 21,* 127–144.

Lore, R. K., & Schultz, L. A. (1993). Control of human aggression: A comparative perspective. *American Psychologist, 48,* 16–25.

Lorenz, K. (1966). *On aggression.* New York: Harcourt, Brace, & World.

Lourenço, O., & Machado, A. (1996). In defense of Piaget's theory: A reply to 10 common criticisms. *Psychological Review, 103,* 143–164.

Lovibond, S. H., Adams, M., & Adams, W. G. (1979). The effects of three experimental prison environments on the behavior of nonconflict volunteer subjects. *Australian Psychologist, 14,* 273–285.

Lubart, T. I. (1994). Creativity. In R. J. Sternberg (Ed.), *Handbook of perception and cognition: Vol. 2. Thinking and problem solving* (pp. 289–332). Orlando, FL: Academic Press.

Lubin, B., Larsen, R. M., & Matarazzo, J. D. (1984). Patterns of psychological test usage in the United States: 1935–1982. *American Psychologist, 39,* 451–455.

Lucas, R. E., Clark, A. E., Georgellis, Y., & Diener, E. (2003). Reexamining adaptation and the set point model of happiness: Reactions to changes in marital status. *Journal of Personality and Social Psychology, 84,* 527–539.

Luchins, A. S. (1942). Mechanization in problem solving. *Psychological Monographs, 54* (No. 248).

Luo, M., Fee, M. S., & Katz, L. C. (2003). Encoding pheromonal signals in the accessory olfactory bulb of behaving mice. *Science, 299,* 1196–1201.

Luzzo, D. A., James, T., & Luna, M. (1996). Effects of attributional retraining on the career beliefs and career exploration behavior of college students. *Journal of Counseling Psychology, 43,* 415–422.

Lykken, D., & Tellegen, A. (1996). Happiness is a stochastic phenomenon. *Psychological Science, 7,* 186–189.

Lynch, J. W., Kaplan, G. A., & Shema, S. J. (1997). Cumulative impact of sustained economic hardship on physical, cognitive, psychological, and social functioning. *New England Journal of Medicine, 337,* 1889–1895.

Lynn, S. J., Lock, T., Loftus, E. F., Krackow, E., & Lilienfeld, S. O. (2003). The remembrance of things past: Problematic memory recovery techniques in psychotherapy. In S. O. Lilienfeld, S. J. Lynn, & J. M. Lohr (Eds.), *Science and pseudoscience in clinical psychology* (pp. 205–239). New York: Guilford Press.

Lyons, N. (1983). Two perspectives: On self, relationships, and morality. *Harvard Educational Review, 53,* 125–146.

Lytton, H., & Romney, D. M. (1991). Parents' differential socialization of boys and girls: A meta-analysis. *Psychological Bulletin, 109,* 267–296.

Ma, V., & Schoeneman, T. J. (1997). Individualism versus collectivism: A comparison of Kenyan and American self-concepts. *Basic and Applied Social Psychology, 19,* 261–273.

Maas, J. (1998). *Power sleep: The revolutionary program that prepares your mind for peak performance.* New York: Villard.

Maccoby, E. E. (1998). *The two sexes: Growing up apart, coming together.* Cambridge, MA: Harvard University Press.

Maccoby, E. E., & Martin, J. A. (1983). Socialization in the context of the family: Parent–child interaction. In E. M. Hetherington

(Ed.), *Handbook of child psychology: Vol. 4. Socialization, personality, and social development* (pp. 1–101). New York: Wiley.

MacDonald, M. C. (1993). The interaction of lexical and syntactic ambiguity. *Journal of Memory and Language, 32,* 692–715.

MacLeod, C., & Campbell, L. (1992). Memory accessibility and probability judgments: An experimental evaluation of the availability heuristic. *Journal of Personality and Social Psychology, 63,* 890–902.

Madon, S., Guyll, M., Spoth, R. L., Cross, S. E., & Hilbert, S. J. (2003). The self-fulfilling influence of mother expectations on children's underage drinking. *Journal of Personality and Social Psychology, 84,* 1188–1205.

Madon, S., Jussim, L., & Eccles, J. (1997). In search of the powerful self-fulfilling prophecy. *Journal of Personality and Social Psychology, 72,* 791–809.

Magee, W. J., Eaton, W. W., Wittchen, H.-U., McConagle, K. A., & Kessler, R. C. (1996). Agoraphobia, simple phobia, and social phobia in the national comorbidity survey. *Archives of General Psychiatry, 53,* 159–168.

Magnusson, D. (1987). Adult delinquency in the light of conduct and physiology at an early age: A longitudinal study. In D. Magnusson & A. Ohman (Eds.), *Psychopathology* (pp. 221–234). Orlando, FL: Academic Press.

Magnusson, D., & Bergman, L. R. (1990). A pattern approach to the study of pathways from childhood to adulthood. In L. N. Robins & M. Rutter (Eds.), *Straight and devious pathways from childhood to adulthood* (pp. 101–115). Cambridge, U.K.: Cambridge University Press.

Maguen, S., Floyd, F. J., Bakeman, R., & Armistead, L. (2002). Developmental milestones and disclosure of sexual orientation among gay, lesbian, and bisexual youths. *Applied Developmental Psychology, 23,* 219–233.

Mahoney, A., Donnelly, W. O., Lewis, T., & Maynard, C. (2000). Mother and father self-reports of corporal punishment and severe physical aggression toward clinic-referred youth. *Journal of Clinical Child Psychology, 29,* 266–281.

Mahoney, J. L., Stattin, H., & Magnusson, D. (2001). Youth recreation centre participation and criminal offending: A 20-year longitudinal study of Swedish boys. *International Journal of Behavioral Development, 25,* 509–520.

Maier, N. R. F. (1931). Reasoning in humans: II. The solution of a problem and its appearance in consciousness. *Journal of Comparative Psychology, 12,* 181–194.

Maier, S. F., & Seligman, M. E. P. (1976). Learned helplessness: Theory and evidence. *Journal of Experimental Psychology, 105,* 3–46.

Main, M., & George, C. (1985). Responses of abused and disadvantaged toddler to distress in agemates: A study in the day care setting. *Developmental Psychology, 21,* 407–412.

Malinowski, B. (1927). *Sex and repression in savage society.* London: Routledge & Kegan Paul.

Malizia, A. L., Cunningham, V. J., Bell, C. J., Liddle, P. F., Jones, T., & Nutt, D. J. (1998). Decreased brain GABA-sub(A)-benzodiazepine receptor binding in panic disorder: Preliminary results from a quantitative PET study. *Archives of General Psychiatry, 55,* 715–720.

Malizia, A. L., & Nutt, D. J. (1995). Psychopharmacology of benzodiazepines: An update. *Human Psychopharmacology: Clinical and Experimental, 10*(Suppl. 1), S1–S14.

Mandel, D. R., Jusczyk, P. W., & Pisoni, D. B. (1995). Infants' recognition of the sound patterns of their own names. *Psychological Science, 5,* 314–317.

Manuck, S. B., Flory, J. D., Muldoon, M. F., & Ferrell, R. E. (2002). Central nervous system serotonergic responsivity and aggressive disposition in men. *Physiology & Behavior, 77,* 705–709.

Maquet, P. (2001). The role of sleep in learning and memory. *Science, 294,* 1048–1052.

Marcus, A. D. (1990, December 3). Mists of memory cloud some legal proceedings. *The Wall Street Journal,* p. B1.

Markovitz, H., & Nantel, G. (1989). The belief-bias effect in the production and evaluation of logical conclusions. *Memory & Cognition, 17,* 11–17.

Markowitsch, H. J. (2000). Neuroanatomy of memory. In E. Tulving & F. I. M. Craik (Eds.), *The Oxford handbook of memory* (pp. 465–484). Oxford, U.K.: Oxford University Press.

Marks, A. R., & Crowder, R. G. (1997). Temporal distinctiveness and modality. *Journal of Experimental Psychology: Learning, Memory, and Cognition, 23,* 164–180.

Markus, H., & Nurius, P. (1986). Possible selves. *American Psychologist, 41,* 954–969.

Markus, H. R., & Kitayama, S. (1991). Culture and the self: Implications for cognition, emotion, and motivation. *Psychological Review, 98,* 224–253.

Markus, H. R., Mullally, P. R., & Kitayama, S. (1997). Selfways: Diversity in modes of cultural participation. In U. Neisser & D. A. Jopling (Eds.), *The conceptual self in context* (pp. 13–61). Cambridge, U.K.: Cambridge University Press.

Marsella, A. J. (1979). Cross-cultural studies of mental disorders. In A. J. Marsella, R. G. Sharp, & T. J. Ciborowski (Eds.), *Perspectives on cross-cultural psychology* (pp. 233–262). New York: Academic Press.

Marshall, G. D., & Zimbardo, P. G. (1979). Affective consequences of inadequately explained physiological arousal. *Journal of Personality and Social Psychology, 37,* 970–988.

Marshall, S. J., & Biddle, S. J. H. (2001). The transtheoretical model of behavior change: A meta-analysis of applications to physical activity and exercise. *Annals of Behavioral Medicine, 23,* 229–246.

Martin, G., & Pear, J. (1999). *Behavior modification: What it is and how to do it* (6th ed.). Upper Saddle River, NJ: Prentice-Hall.

Martin, M. M., & Anderson, C. M. (1995). Roommate similarity: Are roommates who are similar in their communication traits more satisfied? *Communication Research Reports, 12,* 46–52.

Martin, R., Davis, G. M., Baron, R. S., Suls, J., & Blanchard, E. B. (1994). Specificity in social support: Perceptions of helpful and unhelpful provider behaviors among irritable bowel syndrome, headache, and cancer patients. *Health Psychology, 13,* 432–439.

Martin, R. J., White, B. D., & Hulsey, M. G. (1991). The regulation of body weight. *American Scientist, 79,* 528–541.

Marttunen, M. J., Henriksson, M. M., Isometsae, E. T., Heikkinen, M. E., Aro, H. M., & Loennqvist, J. K. (1998). Completed suicide among adolescents with no diagnosable psychiatric disorder. *Adolescence, 33,* 669–681.

Marx, B. P., & Gross, A. M. (1995). Date rape: An analysis of two contextual variables. *Behavior Modification, 19,* 451–463.

Marx, J. (2001). New leads on the "how" of Alzheimer's. S*cience, 293,* 2192–2194.

Marx, J. (2003). Cellular warriors in the battle of the bulge. *Science, 299,* 846–849.

Maslach, C. (1979). Negative emotional biasing of unexplained arousal. *Journal of Personality and Social Psychology, 37,* 953–969.

Maslach, C., & Leiter, M. P. (1997*). The truth about burnout: How organizations cause personal stress and what to do about it.* San Francisco: Jossey-Bass.

Maslach, C., Schaufeli, W. B., & Leiter, M. P. (2001). Job burnout. *Annual Review of Psychology, 52,* 397–422.

Maslow, A. H. (1968). *Toward a psychology of being* (2nd ed.). Princeton, NJ: Van Nostrand.

Maslow, A. H. (1970). *Motivation and personality* (Rev. ed.). New York: Harper & Row.

Mason, L. E. (1997, August 4). Divided she stands. *New York, 30,* 42–49.

Mason, M. A., Skolnick, A., & Sugarman, S. D. (Eds.). (1998). *All our families: New policies for a new century.* New York: Oxford University Press.

Masten, A. S. (2001). Ordinary magic: Resilience processes in development. *American Psychologist, 56,* 227–238.

Masters, W. H., & Johnson, V. E. (1966). *Human sexual response.* Boston: Little, Brown.

Masters, W. H., & Johnson, V. E. (1970). *Human sexual inadequacy.* Boston: Little, Brown.

Masters, W. H., & Johnson, V. E. (1979). *Homosexuality in perspective.* Boston: Little, Brown.

Matheson, M. D., & Bernstein, I. S. (2000). Grooming, social bonding, and agonistic aiding in rhesus monkeys. *American Journal of Primatology, 51,* 177–186.

Mattson, S. N., Schoenfeld, A. M., Riley, E. P. (2001). Teratogenic effects of alcohol on the brain. *Alcohol Research & Health, 25,* 185–191.

Maurer, D., Lewis, T. L., Brent, H. P., & Levin, A. V. (1999). Rapid improvement in the acuity of infants after visual input. *Science, 286,* 108–110.

May, R. (1975). *The courage to create.* New York: Norton.

Mayer, J. D., & Salovey, P. (1997). What is emotional intelligence? In P. Salovey & D. Sluyter (Eds.), *Emotional development and emotional intelligence: Educational implications* (pp. 3–31). New York: Basic Books.

Mayer, J. D., Salovey, P., & Caruso, D. (2000). Models of emotional intelligence. In R. J. Sternberg (Ed.), *Handbook of intelligence* (pp. 396–420). Cambridge, U.K.: Cambridge University Press.

Mayes, A. R. (2000). Selective memory disorders. In E. Tulving & F. I. M. Craik (Eds.), *The Oxford handbook of memory* (pp. 427–440). Oxford, U.K.: Oxford University Press.

McAdams, D. P. (1988). Biography, narrative, and lives: An introduction. *Journal of Personality, 56,* 1–18.

McAdams, D. P. (2001). The psychology of life stories. *Review of General Psychology, 5,* 100–122.

McAdams, D. P., & de St. Aubin, E. (1992). A theory of generativity and its assessment through self-report, behavioral acts, and narrative themes in autobiography. *Journal of Personality and Social Psychology, 62,* 1003–1015.

McAdams, D. P., & de St. Aubin, E. (Eds.). (1998). *Generativity and adult development: How and why we care for the next generation.* Washington, DC: American Psychological Association.

McAllister, H. A. (1996). Self-serving bias in the classroom: Who shows it? Who knows it? *Journal of Educational Psychology, 88,* 123–131.

McBurnett, K., Lahey, B. B., Rathouz, P. J., & Loeber, R. (2000). Low salivary cortisol and persistent aggression in boys referred for disruptive behavior. *Archives of General Psychiatry, 57,* 38–43.

McClelland, D. C. (1961). *The achieving society.* Princeton, NJ: Van Nostrand.

McClelland, D. C. (1971). *Motivational trends in society.* Morristown, NJ: General Learning Press.

McClelland, D. C., Atkinson, J. W., Clark, R. A., & Lowell, E. L. (1953). *The achievement motive.* New York: Appleton-Century-Crofts.

McClelland, D. C., Atkinson, J. W., Clark, R. A., & Lowell, E. L. (1976). *The achievement motive* (2nd ed.). New York: Irvington.

McClelland, D. C., & Franz, C. E. (1992). Motivational and other sources of work accomplishments in mid-life: A longitudinal study. *Journal of Personality, 60,* 679–707.

McCrae, R. R., & Costa, P. T., Jr. (1997). Personality trait structure as a human universal. *American Psychologist, 52,* 509–516.

McCrae, R. R., & Costa, P. T., Jr. (1999). A five-factor theory of personality. In L. A. Pervin & O. P. John (Eds.), *Handbook of personality: Theory and research* (2nd ed., pp. 139–153). New York: Guilford Press.

McCrae, R. R., Costa, P. T., Jr., Ostendorf, F., Angleitner, A., Hrebickova, M., Avia, M. D., Sanz, J., Sanchez-Bernardos, M. L., Kusdil, M. E., Woodfield, R., Saunders, P. R., & Smith, P. B. (2000). Nature over nurture: Temperament, personality, and life span development. *Journal of Personality and Social Psychology, 78,* 173–186.

McCrae, S. M., & Hirt, E. R. (2001). The role of ability judgments in self-handicapping. *Personality & Social Psychology Bulletin, 27,* 1378–1389.

McGuire, W. J., & McGuire, C. V. (1988). Content and process in the experience of self. In L. Berkowitz (Ed.), *Advances in experimental social psychology* (Vol. 21, pp. 97–144). New York: Academic Press.

McKenna, K. Y. A., & Bargh, J. A. (1998). Coming out in the age of the Internet: Identity "demarginalization" through virtual group participation. *Journal of Personality and Social Psychology, 75,* 681–694.

McKenna, K. Y. A., & Bargh, J. A. (2000). Plan 9 from cyberspace: The implications of the Internet for personality and social psychology. *Personality and Social Psychology Review, 4,* 57–75.

McKenna, K. Y. A., Green, A. S., & Gleason, M. (2002). Relationship formation on the Internet: What's the big attraction? *Journal of Social Issues, 58,* 9-31.

McKone, E., & Trynes, K. (1999). Acquisition of novel traces in short-term implicit memory: Priming for nonwords and new associations. *Memory & Cognition, 27,* 619–632.

McKoon, G., & Ratcliff, R. (1992). Inference during reading. *Psychological Review, 99,* 440–446.

McNeil, B. J., Pauker, S. G., Sox, H. C., Jr., & Tversky, A. (1982). On the elicitation of preferences for alternative therapies. *New England Journal of Medicine, 306,* 1259–1262.

Mcphail, E. M. (1998). *The evolution of consciousness.* Oxford, U.K.: Oxford University Press.

McPherson, K. S. (1985). On intelligence testing and immigration legislation. *American Psychologist, 40,* 242–243.

Mead, M. (1928). *Coming of age in Samoa.* New York: Morrow.

Mead, M. (1939). *From the South Seas: Studies of adolescence and sex in primitive societies.* New York: Morrow.

Meador, B. D., & Rogers, C. R. (1979). Person-centered therapy. In R. J. Corsini (Ed.), *Current psychotherapies* (2nd ed., pp. 131–184). Itasca, IL: Peacock.

Meany, M. J., Aitken, D. H., Van Berkel, C. Bhatnagar, S., & Sapolsky, R. M. (1988). Effect of neonatal handling on age-related impairments associated with the hippocampus. *Science, 239,* 766–768.

Meehan, P. J., Lamb, J. A., Saltzman, L. E., & O'Carroll, P. W. (1992). Attempted suicide among young adults: Progress toward a meaningful estimate of prevalence. *American Journal of Psychiatry, 149,* 41–44.

Meichenbaum, D. (1977). *Cognitive-behavior modification: An integrative approach*. New York: Plenum.

Meichenbaum, D. (1985). *Stress inoculation training*. New York: Pergamon Press.

Meichenbaum, D. (1993). Changing conceptions of cognitive behavior modification: Retrospect and prospect. *Journal of Consulting and Clinical Psychology, 61,* 202–204.

Meier, R. P. (1991). Language acquisition by deaf children. *American Scientist, 79,* 60–70.

Melzack, R. (1973). *The puzzle of pain*. New York: Basic Books.

Melzack, R. (1980). Psychological aspects of pain. In J. J. Bonica (Ed.), *Pain*. New York: Raven Press.

Melzack, R. (1999). Pain and stress: A new perspective. In R. J. Gatchel & D. C. Turk (Eds.), *Psychosocial factors in pain: Critical perspectives* (pp. 89–106). New York: Guilford Press.

Menaker, M. (2003). Circadian photoreception. *Science, 299,* 213–214.

Menon, T., Morris, M. W., Chiu, C., & Hong, Y. (1999). Culture and construal of agency: Attribution to individual versus group dispositions. *Journal of Personality and Social Psychology, 76,* 701–717.

Merton, R. K. (1957). *Social theory and social structures*. New York: The Free Press.

Mervis, C. B., & Rosch, E. (1981). Categorization of natural objects. *Annual Review of Psychology, 32,* 89–115.

Mesquita, B., & Frijda, N. H. (1992). Cultural variations in emotions: A review. *Psychological Bulletin, 112,* 179–204.

Metcalfe, J. (2000). Metamemory: Theory and data. In E. Tulving & F. I. M. Craik (Eds.), *The Oxford handbook of memory* (pp. 197–211). Oxford, U.K.: Oxford University Press.

Metcalfe, J., Schwartz, B. L., & Joaquim, S. G. (1993). The cue-familiarity heuristic in metacognition. *Journal of Experimental Psychology: Learning, Memory, and Cognition, 19,* 851–861.

Meyer, R. G. (2003). *Case studies in abnormal behavior* (6th ed.). Boston, MA: Allyn & Bacon.

Meyers, S. A., & Berscheid, E. (1997). The language of love: The difference a preposition makes. *Personality and Social Psychology Bulletin, 23,* 347–362.

Michael, R. T., Gagnon, J. H., Laumann, E. O., & Kolata, G. (1994). *Sex in America: A definitive survey*. Boston: Little, Brown.

Middlebrooks, J. C., & Green, D. C. (1991). Sound localization by human listeners. *Annual Review of Psychology, 42,* 135–159.

Middleton, J. (Ed.). (1967). *Magic, witchcraft, and curing*. Garden City, NY: Natural History Press.

Mignot, E. (1998). Genetic and familial aspects of narcolepsy. *Neurology, 50* (Suppl.), S16–S22.

Miklowitz, D. J., & Tompson, M. C. (2003). Family variables and interventions in schizophrenia. In G. P. Sholevar & L. D. Schwoeri (Eds.), *Textbook of family and couples therapy: Clinical applications* (pp. 585–617). Washington, DC: American Psychiatric Publishing.

Mikolic, J. M., Parker, J. C., & Pruitt, D. G. (1997). Escalation in response to persistent annoyance: Groups versus individuals and gender effects. *Journal of Personality and Social Psychology, 72,* 151–163.

Mikulincer, M., Florian, V., Cowan, P. A., & Cowan, C. P. (2002). Attachment security in couple relationships: A systematic model and its implications for family dynamics. *Family Process, 41,* 405–434.

Miles, D. R., & Carey, G. (1997). Genetic and environmental architecture of human aggression. *Journal of Personality and Social Psychology, 72,* 207–217.

Milgram, S. (1965). Some conditions of obedience and disobedience to authority. *Human Relations, 18,* 56–76.

Milgram, S. (1974). Obedience to authority. New York: Harper & Row.

Miller, G. A. (1956). The magic number seven plus or minus two: Some limits in our capacity for processing information. *Psychological Review, 63,* 81–97.

Miller, J. G., & Bersoff, D. M. (1992). Culture and moral judgment: How are conflicts between justice and interpersonal responsibilities resolved? *Journal of Personality and Social Psychology, 62,* 541–554.

Miller, J. G. (1984). Culture and the development of everyday social explanation. *Journal of Personality and Social Psychology, 46,* 961–978.

Miller, J. G., Bersoff, D. M., & Harwood, R. L. (1990). Perceptions of social responsibilities in India and in the United States: Moral imperatives or personal decisions? *Journal of Personality and Social Psychology, 58,* 33–47.

Miller, M. A., & Rahe, R. H. (1997). Life changes scaling for the 1990s. *Journal of Psychosomatic Research, 43,* 279–292.

Miller N. E. (1978). Biofeedback and visceral learning. *Annual Review of Psychology, 29,* 373–404.

Miller, N. E. (1985). The value of behavioral research on animals. *American Psychologist, 40,* 423–440.

Minckley, R. L., Buchmann, S. L., & Wcislo, W. J. (1991). Bioassay evidence for a sex attractant pheromone in the large carpenter bee *Xylocopa varipuncta* (Anthophoridea: Hymenoptera). *Journal of Zoology, 224,* 285–291.

Mindell, J. A. (1997). Children and sleep. In M. R. Pressman & W. C. Orr (Eds.), *Understanding sleep: The evaluation and treatment of sleep disorders* (pp. 427–439). Washington, DC: American Psychological Association.

Mischel, W. (1968). *Personality and assessment*. New York: Wiley.

Mischel, W. (1973). Toward a cognitive social learning reconceptualization of personality. *Psychological Review, 80,* 252–283.

Mischel, W., & Shoda, Y. (1995). A cognitive-affective system theory of personality: Reconceptualizing situations, dispositions, dynamics, and invariance in personality structure. *Psychological Review, 102,* 246–268.

Mischel, W., & Shoda, Y. (1999). Integrating dispositions and processing dynamics within a unified theory of personality: The cognitive-affective personality system. In L. A. Pervin & O. P. John (Eds.), *Handbook of personality: Theory and research* (2nd ed., pp. 197–218). New York: Guilford Press.

Mischel, W., & Shoda, Y., & Mendoza-Denton, R. (2002). Situation-behavior profiles as a locus of consistency in personality. *Current Directions in Psychological Science, 11,* 50–54.

Mitchell, K. J., & Johnson, M. K. (2000). Source monitoring: Attributing mental experiences. In E. Tulving & F. I. M. Craik (Eds.), *The Oxford handbook of memory* (pp. 179–195). London: Oxford University Press.

Mitchell, K. J., & Zaragoza, M. S. (1996). Repeated exposure to suggestion and false memory: The role of contextual variability. *Journal of Memory and Language, 35,* 246–260.

Moffitt, A., Karmer, M., & Hoffmann, R. (Eds.). (1993). *The functions of dreaming*. Albany: State University of New York Press.

Mokdad, A. H., Ford, E. S., Bowman, B. A., Dietz, W. H., Vinicor, F., Bales, V. S., & Marks, J. S. (2003). Prevalence of obesity, diabetes, and obesity-related health risk factors, 2001. *JAMA, 289,* 76–79.

Moloney, D. P., Bouchard, T. J., Jr., & Segal, N. L. (1991). A genetic and environmental analysis of the vocational interests of monozygotic and dizygotic twins reared apart. *Journal of Vocational Behavior, 39,* 76–109.

Moncrieff, R. W. (1951). *The chemical senses.* London: Leonard Hill.

Montague, C. T., Farooqi, I. S., Whitehead, J. P., Soos, M. A., Rau, H., Wareham, N. J., Sewter, C. P., Digby, J. E., Mohammed, S. N., Hurst, J. A., Cheetham, C. H., Earley, A. R., Barnett, A. H., Prins, J. B., & O'Rahilly, S. (1997). Congenital leptin deficiency is associated with severe early-onset obesity in humans. *Nature, 387,* 903–908.

Moore, P. (1990). In *Discovering Psychology,* Program 18 [PBS video series]. Washington, DC: Annenberg/CPB Program.

Moore-Ede, M. C. (1993). *The twenty-four-hour society: Understanding human limits in a world that never stops.* Reading, MA: Addison-Wesley.

Morgan, A. H., Hilgard, E. R., & Davert, E. C. (1970). The heritability of hypnotic susceptibility of twins: A preliminary report. *Behavior Genetics, 1,* 213–224.

Morgan, A. H., Johson, D. L., & Hilgard, E. R. (1974). The stability of hypnotic susceptibility: A longitudinal study. *International Journal of Clinical and Experimental Hypnosis, 22,* 249–257.

Morgenstern, J., Labouvie, E., McCrady, B. S., Kahler, C. W., & Frey, R. M. (1997). Affiliation with Alcoholics Anonymous after treatment: A study of its therapeutic effects and mechanisms of action. *Journal of Consulting and Clinical Psychology, 65,* 768–777.

Moriarty, T. (1975). Crime, commitment and the responsive bystander: Two field experiments. *Journal of Personality and Social Psychology, 31,* 370–376.

Morin, S. F., & Rothblum, E. D. (1991). Removing the stigma: Fifteen years of progress. *American Psychologist, 46,* 947–949.

Morris, J. S., Frith, C. D., Perrett, D. I., Rowland, D., Young, A. W., Calder, A. J., & Dolan, R. J. (1996). A differential neural response in the human amygdala to fearful and happy facial expressions. *Nature, 383,* 812–815.

Moscovici, S., & Faucheux, C. (1972). Social influence, conformity bias, and the study of active minorities. In L. Berkowitz (Ed.), *Advances in experimental social psychology* (Vol. 6). New York: Academic Press.

Moscovici, S. (1980). Toward a theory of conversion behavior. In L. Berkowitz (Ed.), *Advances in experimental social psychology* (Vol. 13, pp. 209–239). New York: Academic Press.

Moscovici, S. (1985). Social influence and conformity. In G. Lindzey & E. Aronson (Eds.), *The handbook of social psychology* (3rd ed., pp. 347–412). New York: Random House.

Moskowitz, B. A. (1978). The acquisition of language. *Scientific American, 239*(11), 92–108.

Motley, M. T., & Baars, B. J. (1979). Effects of cognitive set upon laboratory-induced verbal (Freudian) slips. *Journal of Speech and Hearing Research, 22,* 421–432.

Mumme, D. L., & Fernald, A. (2003). The infant as onlooker: Learning from emotional reactions observed in a television scenario. *Child Development, 74,* 221–237.

Munro, G. D., & Ditto, P. H. (1997). Biased assimilation, attitude polarization, and affect in reactions to stereotype-relevant scientific information. *Personality and Social Psychology Bulletin, 23,* 636–653.

Murata, P. J., McGlynn, E. A., Siu, A. L., & Brook, R. H. (1992). *Prenatal care.* Santa Monica, CA: The Rand Corporation.

Murphy, M. C., & Archer, J. (1996). Stressors on the college campus: A comparison of 1985–1993. *Journal of College Student Development, 37,* 20–28.

Murphy, S. L. (2000). Deaths: Final data for 1998. *National Vital Statistics Reports, 48*(11), 1–106.

Murray, C. J. L., & Lopez, A. D. (Eds.) (1996). *The global burden of disease and injury series.* Cambridge, MA: Harvard University Press.

Murray, H. A. (1938). *Explorations in personality.* New York: Oxford University Press.

Murray, J. B. (1995). Evidence for acupuncture's analgesic effectiveness and proposals for the physiological mechanisms involved. *Journal of Psychology, 129,* 443–461.

Mussweiler, T., & Bodenhausen, G. V. (2002). I know you are, but what am I? Self-evaluative consequences of judging in-group and out-group members. *Journal of Personality and Social Psychology, 82,* 19–32.

Myers, R. S., & Roth, D. L. (1997). Perceived benefits of and barriers to exercise and stage of exercise adoption in young adults. *Health Psychology, 16,* 277–283.

Napier, A. Y. (2000). Making a marriage. In W. C. Nichols, M. A. Pace-Nichols, D. S. Becvar, & A. Y. Napier (Eds.), *Handbook of family development and intervention* (pp. 145–170). New York: Wiley.

National Sleep Foundation. (2000). *2000 omnibus sleep in America poll* [On-line]. Available: www.sleepfoundation.org/publications/2000poll.html

National Sleep Foundation. (2003). *2003 sleep in America poll* [On-line]. Available:www.sleepfoundation.org/polls/2003Sleep PollExecSumm.pdf.

Natsoulas, T. (1998). Consciousness and self-awareness. In M. Ferrari & R. J. Sternberg (Eds.), *Self-awareness: Its nature and development* (pp. 12–33). New York: The Guilford Press.

Neath, I. (1993). Contextual and distinctive processes and the serial position function. *Journal of Memory and Language, 32,* 820–840.

Neath, I. (1998). *Human memory: An introduction to research, data, and theory.* Pacific Grove, CA: Brooks/Cole.

Neath, I., & Crowder, R. G. (1990). Schedules of presentation and temporal distinctiveness in human memory. *Journal of Experimental Psychology: Learning, Memory, and Cognition, 16,* 316–327.

Neath, I., & Knoedler, A. J. (1994). Distinctiveness in serial position effects in recognition and sentence processing. *Journal of Memory and Language, 33,* 776–795.

Neath, I., Surprenant, A. M., & Crowder, R. G. (1993). The context-dependent stimulus suffix effect. *Journal of Experimental Psychology: Learning, Memory, and Cognition, 19,* 698–703.

Neisser, U. (1967). *Cognitive psychology.* New York: Appleton-Century-Crofts.

Neisser, U., Boodoo, G., Bouchard, T. J., Jr., Boykin, A. W., Brody, N., Ceci, S. J., Halpern, D. F., Loehlin, J. C., Perloff, R., Sternberg, R. J., & Urbina, S. (1996). Intelligence: Knowns and unknowns. *American Psychologist, 51,* 77–101.

Nelson, R. E., & Craighead, W. E. (1977). Selective recall of positive and negative feedback, self-control behaviors and depression. *Journal of Abnormal Psychology, 86,* 379–388.

Nelson, T. D. (Ed.) (2002). *Ageism: Stereotyping and prejudice against older persons.* Cambridge, MA: MIT Press.

Nelson, T. O. (1996). Consciousness and metacognition. *American Psychologist, 51,* 102–116.

Nestler, E. J., Gould, E., Manji, H., Bucan, M., Duman, R. S., Gershenfeld, H. K., Hen, R., Koester, S., Lederhendler, I., Meaney, M. J., Robbins, T., Winsky, L., & Zalcman, S. (2002). Preclinical models: Status of basic research in depression. *Biological Psychiatry, 52,* 503–528.

Neumeister, A., Praschak-Rieder, N., Heßelmann, B., Rao, M.-L., Glück, J., & Kasper, S. (1997). Effects of tryptophan depletion on drug-free patients with seasonal affective disorder during a stable response to bright light therapy. *Archives of General Psychiatry, 54,* 133–138.

Néveus, T., Cnattingius, S., Olsson, U., & Hetta, J. (2001). Sleep habits and sleep problems among a community sample of schoolchildren. *Acta Paediatr, 90,* 1450–1455.

Newcomb, T. M. (1929). *The consistency of certain extrovert-introvert behavior traits in 50 problem boys* (Contributions to Education, No. 382). New York: Columbia University Press.

Newell, A., & Simon, H. A. (1972). *Human problem solving.* Englewood Cliffs, NJ: Prentice Hall.

Newstead, S. E., Pollard, P., Evans, J. St. B. T., & Allen, J. L. (1992). The source of belief bias effects in syllogistic reasoning. *Cognition, 45,* 257–284.

Nhat Hanh, T. (1991). *Peace is every step: The path of mindfulness in everyday life.* New York: Bantam.

Niaura, R., Todaro, J. F., Stoud, L., Sprio, A., III, Ward, K. D., & Weiss, S. (2002). Hostility, the metabolic syndrome, and incident coronary heart disease. *Health Psychology, 21,* 588–593.

Nicoll, C., Russell, S., & Katz, L. (1988, May 26). Research on animals must continue. *San Francisco Chronicle,* p. A25.

Nie, N. H., & Erbring, L. (2000). *Internet and society: A preliminary report.* Stanford, CA: Stanford Institute for the Quantitative Study of Society.

Nielsen, F. (1994). Sociobiology and sociology. *Annual Review of Sociology, 20,* 267–303.

Nietzel, M. T., Bernstein, D. A., & Milich, R. (1991). *Introduction to clinical psychology.* Englewood Cliffs, NJ: Prentice Hall.

Nigg, J. T., & Goldsmith, H. H. (1994). Genetics of personality disorders: Perspectives from personality and psychopathology research. *Psychological Bulletin, 115,* 346–380.

Nisbett, R. E. (1995). Race, IQ, and scientism. In S. Fraser (Ed.), *The Bell Curve wars: Race, intelligence, and the future of America* (pp. 36–57). New York: Basic Books.

Nisbett, R. E. (1998). Race, genetics, and IQ. In C. Jencks & M. Phillips (Eds.), *The black–white test score gap* (pp. 86–102). Washington, DC: Brookings Institution Press.

Nisbett, R. E., & Cohen, D. (1996). *Culture of honor: The psychology of violence in the South.* Boulder, CO: Westview Press.

Nobles, W. W. (1976). Black people in white insanity: An issue for black community mental health. *Journal of Afro-American Issues, 4,* 21–27.

Nolen-Hoeksema, S. (1990). *Sex differences in depression.* Stanford, CA: Stanford University Press.

Nolen-Hoeksema, S. (2002). Gender differences in depression. In I. H. Gotlib & C. L. Hammen (Eds.), *Handbook of depression* (pp. 492–509). New York: Guilford.

Nolen-Hoeksema, S., Larson, J., & Grayson, C. (1999). Explaining the gender difference in depressive symptoms. *Journal of Personality and Social Psychology, 77,* 1061–1072.

Norman, G. J., Velicer, W. F., Fava, J. L., & Prochaska, J. O. (1998). Dynamic topology clustering within the stages of change for smoking cessation. *Addictive Behaviors, 23,* 139–153.

Norman, G. J., Velicer, W. F., Fava, J. L., & Prochaska, J. O. (2000). Cluster subtypes within stage of change in a representative sample of smokers. *Addictive Behaviors, 25,* 183–204.

Norman, W. T. (1963). Toward an adequate taxonomy of personality attributes: Replicated factor structure in peer nomination personality ratings. *Journal of Abnormal and Social Psychology, 66,* 574–583.

Norman, W. T. (1967). *2,800 personality trait descriptors: Normative operating characteristics for a university population* (Research Rep. No. 08310–1-T). Ann Arbor: University of Michigan Press.

Nosofsky, R. M., Kruschke, J. K., & McKinley, S. C. (1992). Combining exemplar-based category representations and connectionist learning rules. *Journal of Experimental Psychology: Learning, Memory, and Cognition, 18,* 211–233.

Nungesser, L. G. (1990). *Axioms for survivors: How to live until you say goodbye.* Santa Monica, CA: IBS Press.

Nurmi, J. E. (1991). How do adolescents see their future? A review of the development of future orientation and planning. *Developmental Review, 11,* 1–59.

Nutt, D. J., & Malizia, A. L. (2001). New insights into the role of the GABA-sub(A)-benzodiazepine receptor in psychiatric disorder. *British Journal of Psychiatry, 179,* 390–396.

Nyberg, L., & Cabeza, R. (2000). Brain imaging of memory. In E. Tulving & F. I. M. Craik (Eds.), *The Oxford handbook of memory* (pp. 501–519). Oxford, U.K.: Oxford University Press.

Nyberg, L., Cabeza, R., & Tulving, E. (1996). PET studies of encoding and retrieval: The HERA model. *Psychonomic Bulletin & Review, 3,* 135–148.

Oaksford, M., & Chater, N. (1994). A rational analysis of the selection task as optimal data selection. *Psychological Review, 101,* 608–631.

Oaksford, M., Chater, N., Grainger, B., & Larking, J. (1997). Optimal data selection in the reduced array selection task (RAST). *Journal of Experimental Psychology: Learning, Memory, and Cognition, 23,* 441–458.

Oezgen, E., & Davies, I. R. L. (2002). Acquisition of categorical color perception: A perceptual learning approach to the linguistic relativity hypothesis. *Journal of Experimental Psychology: General, 131,* 477–493.

Offer, D., Ostrov, E., & Howard, K. I. (1981a). *The adolescent: A psychological self-portrait.* New York: Basic Books.

Offer, D., Ostrov, E., Howard, K. I., & Atkinson, R. (1988). *The teenage world: Adolescents' self-image in ten countries.* New York: Plenum Medical.

Offer, D., & Schonert-Reichl, K. A. (1992). Debunking the myths of adolescence: Findings from recent research. *Journal of the American Academy of Child and Adolescent Psychiatry, 31,* 1003–1014.

O'Guinn, T. C., & Shrum, L. J. (1997). The role of television in the construction of consumer reality. *Journal of Consumer Research, 23,* 278–294.

Ohayon, M. M., Guilleminault, C., & Priest, R. G. (1999). Night terrors, sleepwalking, and confusional arousals in the general population: Their frequency and relationship to other sleep and mental disorders. *Journal of Clinical Psychiatry, 60,* 268–276.

Öhman, A., & Mineka, S. (2001). Fears, phobias, and preparedness: Toward an evolved module of fear and fear learning. *Psychological Review, 108,* 483–522.

Oishi, S. (2003). The experiencing and remembering of well-being: A cross-cultural analysis. *Personality and Social Psychology Bulletin, 28,* 1398–1406.

Olson, D. J., Kamil, A. C., Balda, R. P., & Nims, P. J. (1995). Performance of four seed-caching corvid species in operant tests of nonspatial and spatial memory. *Journal of Comparative Psychology, 109,* 173–181.

Olton, D. S. (1992). Tolman's cognitive analyses: Predecessors of current approaches in psychology. *Journal of Experimental Psychology: General, 121,* 427–428.

Opton, E. M., Jr. (1970). Lessons of My Lai. In N. Sanford & C. Comstock (Eds.), *Sanctions for evil*. San Francisco: Jossey-Bass.

Opton, E. M., Jr. (1973). "It never happened and besides they deserved it." In W. E. Henry & N. Stanford (Eds.), *Sanctions for evil* (pp. 49–70). San Francisco: Jossey-Bass.

O'Regan, J. K. (1992). Solving the "real" mysteries of visual perception: The world as an outside memory. *Canadian Journal of Psychology, 46*, 461–488.

Ornstein, R. E. (1991). *The evolution of consciousness*. New York: Simon & Schuster.

Orr, W. C. (1997). Obstructive sleep apnea: Natural history and varieties of clinical presentation. In M. R. Pressman & W. C. Orr (Eds.), *Understanding sleep: The evaluation and treatment of sleep disorders* (pp. 267–281). Washington, DC: American Psychological Association.

Osofsky, J. D. (Ed.). (1997). *Children in a violent society*. New York: Guilford.

Owen, M. J., & O'Donovan, M. C. (2003). Schizophrenia and genetics. In R. Plomin, J. C. DeFries, I. W. Craig, & P. McGuffin (Eds.), *Behavioral genetics in the postgenomic era* (pp. 463–480). Washington, DC: American Psychological Association.

Owens, J., Bower, G. H., & Black, J. B. (1979). The "soap opera" effect in story recall. *Memory & Cognition, 7*, 185–191.

Ozer, D. J., & Reise, S. P. (1994). Personality assessment. *Annual Review of Psychology, 45, 357–388.*

Padberg, R., Zwanzger, P., Keck, M. E., Kathmann, N., Mikhaiel, P., Ella, R., Rupprecht, P., Thoma, H., Hampel, H., Toschi, N., & Möller, H.-J. (2002). Repetitive transcranial magnetic stimulation (rTMS) in major depression: Relation between efficacy and stimulation intensity. *Neuropsychopharmacology, 27,* 638–645.

Paivio, A. (1995). Imagery and memory. In M. S. Gazzaniga (Ed.), *The cognitive neurosciences* (pp. 977–986). Cambridge, MA: MIT Press.

Paris, J. (2003). *Personality disorders over time: Precursors, course, and outcome*. Washington, DC: American Psychiatric Publishing, Inc.

Park, S. M., & Gabrieli, J. D. E. (1995). Perceptual and nonperceptual components of implicit memory for pictures. *Journal of Experimental Psychology: Learning, Memory, and Cognition, 21,* 1583–1594.

Parker, S., Nichter, M., Nichter, M., Vuckovic, N., Sims, C., & Ritenbaugh, C. (1995). Body image and weight concerns among African American and White adolescent females: Differences that make a difference. *Human Organization, 54,* 103–114.

Parr, W. V., & Siegert, R. (1993). Adults' conceptions of everyday memory failures in others: Factors that mediate the effects of target age. *Psychology and Aging, 8,* 599–605.

Parsons, L. M., & Osherson, D. (2001). New evidence for distinct right and left brain systems for deductive versus probabilistic reasoning. *Cerebral Cortex, 11, 954–965.*

Pascalis, O., de Schonen, S., Morton, J., Deruelle, C., & Fabre-Grenet, M. (1995). Mother's face recognition by neonates: A replication and extension. *Infant Behavior & Development, 18,* 79–85.

Pashler, H. (1992). Attentional limitations in doing two tasks at the same time. *Current Directions in Psychological Science, 1,* 44–48.

Pashler, H. (1994). Dual-task interference in simple tasks: Data and theory. *Psychological Bulletin, 116,* 220–244.

Pasternak, T., Bisley, J. W., & Calkins, D. (2003). Visual processing in the primate brain. In M. Gallager & R. J. Nelson (Eds.), *Handbook of psychology: Biological psychology* (Vol. 3, pp. 139–185). New York: John Wiley & Sons.

Patterson, C. J. (2002). Lesbian and gay parenthood. In M. H. Bornstein (Ed.), *Handbook of parenting: Vol. 3: Being and becoming a parent* (2nd ed.) (pp. 317–338). Mahwah, NJ: Erlbaum.

Patterson, G. R. (2002). The early development of coercive family process. In J. B. Ried, G. R. Patterson, & J. J. Snyder (Eds.), *Antisocial behavior in children and adolescents: A developmental analysis and the Oregon model for intervention* (pp. 25–44). Washington, DC: American Psychological Association.

Pattie, F. A. (1994). *Mesmer and animal magnetism: A chapter in the history of medicine*. New York: Edmonston.

Pauli, P., Dengler, W., Wiedemann, G., Montoya, P., Flor, H., Birbaumer, N., & Buchkremer, G. (1997). Behavioral and neuropsychological evidence for altered processing of anxiety-related words in panic disorder. *Journal of Abnormal Psychology, 106,* 213–220.

Pavlov, I. P. (1927). *Conditioned reflexes* (G. V. Anrep, Trans.). London: Oxford University Press.

Pavlov, I. P. (1928). *Lectures on conditioned reflexes: Twenty-five years of objective study of higher nervous activity (behavior of animals)* (Vol. 1, W. H. Gantt, Trans.). New York: International Publishers.

Pederson, D. R., & Moran, G. (1996). Expressions of the attachment relationship outside of the strange situation. *Child Development, 67,* 915–927.

Penick, S., Smith, G., Wienske, K., & Hinkle, L. (1963). An experimental evaluation of the relationship between hunger and gastric motility. *American Journal of Physiology, 205,* 421–426.

Penn, D. L., Guynan, K., Daily, T., Spaulding, W. D., Garbin, C. P., & Sullivan, M. (1994). Dispelling the stigma of schizophrenia: What sort of information is best? *Schizophrenia Bulletin, 20,* 567–578.

Penn, D. L., Kommana, S., Mansfield, M., & Link, B. G. (1999). Dispelling the stigma of schizophrenia: II. The impact of information on dangerousness. *Schizophrenia Bulletin, 25,* 437–446.

Pennebaker, J. W. (1990). *Opening up: The healing power of confiding in others*. New York: Morrow.

Pennebaker, J. W. (1997). Writing about emotional experiences as a therapeutic process. *Psychological Science, 8,* 162–166.

Penton-Voak, I. S., & Perrett, D. I. (2000). Female preference for male faces changes cyclically: Further evidence. *Evolution and Human Behavior, 21,* 39–48.

Penton-Voak, I. S., Perrett, D. I., Castles, D. L., Kobayashi, T., Burt, D. M., Murray, L. K., & Minamisawa, R. (1999). Menstrual cycle alters face preference. *Nature, 399,* 741–742.

Pericak-Vance, M. A. (2003). The genetics of autistic disorder. In R. Plomin, J. C. DeFries, I. W. Craig, & P. McGuffin (Eds.), *Behavioral genetics in the postgenomic era* (pp. 267–288). Washington, DC: American Psychological Association.

Perkins, D. N. (1988). Creativity and the quest for mechanism. In R. J. Sternberg & E. E. Smith (Eds.), *The psychology of human thought* (pp. 309–336). Cambridge, U.K.: Cambridge University Press.

Perls, F. S. (1969). *Gestalt therapy verbatim*. Lafayette, CA: Real People Press.

Pervin, L. A. (1994). A critical analysis of current trait theory. *Psychological Inquiry, 5,* 103–113.

Peterson, C., & Seligman, M. E. P. (1984). Causal explanations as a risk factor for depression: Theory and evidence. *Psychological Review, 91,* 347–374.

Peterson, C., Seligman, M. E. P., & Valliant, G. E. (1988). Pessimistic explanatory style is a risk factor for physical illness: A thirty-five year longitudinal study. *Journal of Personality and Social Psychology, 55,* 23–27.

Peterson, C., & Vaidya, R. S. (2001). Explanatory style, expectations, and depressive symptoms. *Personality and Individual Differences, 31,* 1217–1223.

Peterson, D., & Goodall, J. (1993). *Visions of Caliban: On chimpanzees and people.* Boston: Houghton Mifflin.

Peterson, L. R., & Peterson, M. J. (1959). Short-term retention of individual verbal items. *Journal of Experimental Psychology, 58,* 193–198.

Peterson, R. S., & Nemeth, C. J. (1996). Focus versus flexibility: Majority and minority influence can both improve performance. *Personality and Social Psychology Bulletin, 22,* 14–23.

Petrie, K. J., Booth, R. J., & Pennebaker, J. W. (1998). The immunological effects of thought suppression. *Journal of Personality and Social Psychology, 75,* 1264–1272.

Petrinovich, L. F. (1998). *Darwinian dominion: Animal welfare and human interests.* Cambridge, MA: The MIT Press.

Pettigrew, T. F. (1997). Generalized intergroup contact effects on prejudice. *Personality and Social Psychology Bulletin, 23,* 173–185.

Petty, R. E., & Wegener, D. T. (1999). The elaboration likelihood model: Current status and controversies. In S. Chaiken & Y. Trope (Eds.), *Dual-process theories in social psychology* (pp. 41–72). New York: Guilford.

Petty, R. E., Wheeler, S. C., & Tormala, Z. L. (2003). Persuasion and attitude change. In T. Millon & M. J. Lerner (Eds.), *Handbook of psychology: Personality and social psychology* (Vol. 5, pp. 353–382). New York: Wiley.

Pfiffner, L. J., & McBurnett, K. (1997). Social skills training with parent generalization: Treatment effects for children with attention deficit disorder. *Journal of Consulting and Clinical Psychology, 65,* 749–757.

Phillips, D. P. (1993). Representation of acoustic events in primary auditory cortex. *Journal of Experimental Psychology: Human Perception and Performance, 19,* 203–216.

Phillips, S. T., & Ziller, R. C. (1997). Toward a theory and measure of the nature of nonprejudice. *Journal of Personality and Social Psychology, 72,* 420–432.

Piaget, J. (1929). *The child's conception of the world.* New York: Harcourt, Brace.

Piaget, J. (1954). *The construction of reality in the child.* New York: Basic Books.

Piaget, J. (1965). *The moral judgment of the child* (M. Gabain, Trans.). New York: Macmillan.

Piaget, J. (1977). *The development of thought: Equilibrium of cognitive structures.* New York: Viking Press.

Piccione, C., Hilgard, E. R., & Zimbardo, P. G. (1989). On the degree of stability of measured hypnotizability over a 25-year period. *Journal of Personality and Social Psychology, 56,* 289–295.

Pich, E. M., Pagliusi, S. R., Tessari, M., Talabot-Ayer, D., van Juijsduijnen, R. H., & Chaimulera, C. (1997). Common neural substrates for the addictive properties of nicotine and cocaine. *Science, 275,* 83–85.

Pilcher, J. J., & Walters, A. S. (1997). How sleep deprivation affects psychological variables related to college students' cognitive performance. *Journal of American College Health, 46,* 121–126.

Pilkonis, P. A., & Zimbardo, P. G. (1979). The personal and social dynamics of shyness. In C. E. Izard (Ed.), *Emotions in personality and psychopathology* (pp. 131–160). New York: Plenum Press.

Pincus, H. A., Tanielian, T. L., Marcus, S. C., Olfson, M., Zarin, D. A., Thompson, J., & Zito, J. M. (1998). Prescribing trends in psychotropic medications. *Journal of the American Medical Association, 279,* 526–531.

Pines, A., & Zimbardo, P. G. (1978). The personal and cultural dynamics of shyness: A comparison between Israelis, American Jews and Americans. *Journal of Psychology and Judaism, 3,* 81–101.

Pinker, S. (1994). *The language instinct: How the mind creates language.* New York: Morrow.

Piotrowski, C., Keller, J. W., & Ogawa, T. (1993). Projective techniques: An international perspective. *Psychological Reports, 72,* 179–182.

Piotrowski, C., Sherry, D., & Keller, J. W. (1985). Psychodiagnostic test usage: A survey of the Society for Personality Assessment. *Journal of Personality Assessment, 49,* 115–119.

Pitts, D. G. (1982). The effects of aging on selected visual functions: Dark adaptation, visual acuity, stereopsis, and brightness contrast. In R. Sekuler, D. Kline, & K. Dismukes (Eds.), *Aging and human visual function* (pp. 131–159). New York: Liss.

Plante, T. G., & Sykora, C. (1994). Are stress and coping associated with WISC-III performance among children? *Journal of Clinical Psychology, 50,* 759–762.

Plomin, R., DeFries, J. C., Craig, I. W., & McGuffin, P. (2003). Behavioral genetics. In R. Plomin, J. C, DeFries, I. W. Craig, & P. McGuffin (Eds.), *Behavioral genetics in the postgenomic era* (pp. 3–15). Washington, DC: American Psychological Association.

Plomin, R., & Petrill, S. A. (1997). Genetics and intelligence: What's new? *Intelligence, 24,* 53–77.

Plous, S. (1996a). Attitudes toward the use of animals in psychological research and education: Results from a national survey of psychology majors. *Psychological Science, 7,* 352–358.

Plous, S. (1996b). Attitudes toward the use of animals in psychological research and education: Results from a national survey of psychologists. *American Psychologist, 51,* 1167–1180.

Polivy, J., & Herman, C. P. (1999). Distress and eating: Why do dieters overeat? *International Journal of Eating Disorders, 26,* 153–164.

Poppen, P. J. (1995). Gender and patterns of sexual risk taking in college students. *Sex Roles, 32,* 545–555.

Porkka-Heiskanen, T., Strecker, R. E., Thakkar, M., Bjørkum, A. A., Greene, R. W., & McCarley, R. W. (1997). Adenosine: A mediator of the sleep-inducing effects of prolonged wakefulness. *Science, 276,* 1265–1268.

Porstner, D. (1997, July 26). Man stops car with own. *Newsday,* p. A32.

Porter, L. W., & Lawler, E. E. (1968). *Managerial attitudes and performance.* Homewood, IL: Irwin.

Poucet, B. (1993). Spatial cognitive maps in animals: New hypotheses on their structure and neural mechanisms. *Psychological Review, 100,* 163–182.

Poulos, C. X., & Cappell, H. (1991). Homeostatic theory of drug tolerance: A general model of physiological adaptation. *Psychological Review, 98,* 390–408.

Povinelli, D. J., Landau, K. R., & Perilloux, H. K. (1996). Self-recognition in young children using delayed versus live feedback: Evidence of a developmental asynchrony. *Child Development, 67,* 1540–1554.

Povinelli, D. J., & Prince, C. G. (1998). When self met other. In M. Ferrari & R. J. Sternberg (Eds.), *Self-awareness: Its nature and development*. New York: The Guilford Press.

Powley, T. (1977). The ventromedial hypothalamic syndrome, satiety, and a cephalic phase hypothesis. *Psychological Review, 84,* 89–126.

Pratt, M. W., Golding, G., Hunter, W., & Norris, J. (1988). From inquiry to judgment: Age and sex differences in patterns of adult moral thinking and information-seeking. *International Journal of Aging and Human Development, 27,* 109–124.

Premack, D. (1965). Reinforcement theory. In D. Levine (Ed.), *Nebraska symposium on motivation* (pp. 128–180). Lincoln: University of Nebraska Press.

Premack, D. (1971). Language in chimpanzee? *Science, 172,* 808–822.

Prentice, D. A., & Gerrig, R. J. (1999). Exploring the boundary between fiction and reality. In S. Chaiken & Y. Trope (Eds.), *Dual-process theories in social psychology* (pp. 529–546). New York: Guilford.

Prentice, D. A., Gerrig, R. J., & Bailis, D. S. (1997). What readers bring to the experience of fictional texts. *Psychonomic Bulletin & Review, 4,* 416–420.

Price, D. D. (2000). Psychological and neural mechanisms of the affective dimension of pain. *Science, 288,* 1769–1772.

Price, R. (1980). *Droodles.* Los Angeles: Price/Stern/Sloan. (Original work published 1953)

Prosser, D., Johnson, S., Kuipers, E., Szmukler, G., Bebbington, P., & Thornicroft, G. (1997). Perceived sources of work stress and satisfaction among hospital and community mental health staff, and their relation to mental health, burnout, and job satisfaction. *Journal of Psychosomatic Research, 43,* 51–59.

Putnam, D. E., Finney, J. W., Barkley, P. L., & Bonner, M. J. (1994). Enhancing commitment improves adherence to a medical regimen. *Journal of Consulting and Clinical Psychology, 62,* 191–194.

Quine, W. V. O. (1960). *Word and object.* Cambridge, MA: The MIT Press.

Rabbie, J. M. (1981). The effects of intergroup conpetition and cooperation on intra- and intergroup relationships. In J. Grzelak & V. Derlega (Eds.), *Living with other people: Theory and research on cooperation and helping.* New York: Academic Press.

Rabins, P. V. (1992). Prevention of mental disorder in the elderly: Current perspectives and future prospects. *Journal of the American Geriatric Society, 40,* 727–733.

Rachlin, H. (1990). Why do people gamble and keep gambling despite heavy losses? *Psychological Science, 1,* 294–297.

Rainnie, D. G., Grunze, H. C. R., McCarley, R. W., & Greene, R. W. (1994). Adenosine inhibition of mesopontine cholinergic neurons: Implications for EEG arousal. *Science, 263,* 689–692.

Rajaram, S., & Coslett, H. B. (2000). New conceptual associative learning in amnesia: A case study. *Journal of Memory and Language, 43,* 291–315.

Rajaram, S., & Roediger, H. L., III (1993). Direct comparison of four implicit memory tests. *Journal of Experimental Psychology: Learning, Memory, and Cognition, 19,* 765–776.

Rajaram, S., Srinivas, K., & Roediger, H. L., III. (1998). A transfer-appropriate processing account of context effects in word-fragment completion. *Journal of Experimental Psychology: Learning, Memory, and Cognition, 24,* 993–1004.

Rand, C. S., & Kuldau, J. M. (1992). Epidemiology of bulimia and symptoms in a general population: Sex, age, race, and socio-economic status. *International Journal of Eating Disorders, 11,* 37–44.

Rand, C. S. W., & Kuldau, J. M. (1990). The epidemiology of obesity and self-defined weight problem in the general population: Gender, race, age, and social class. *International Journal of Eating Disorders, 9,* 329–343.

Randall, C. L. (2001). Alcohol and pregnancy: Highlights from three decades of research. *Journal of Studies on Alcohol, 62,* 554–561.

Rao, S. C., Rainer, G., & Miller, E. K. (1997). Integration of what and where in the primate prefrontal cortex. *Science, 276,* 821–824.

Rapoport, J. L. (1989, March). The biology of obsessions and compulsions. *Scientific American,* pp. 83–89.

Rapp, B., & Goldrick, M. (2000). Discreteness and interactivity in spoken word production. *Psychological Review, 107,* 460–499.

Rasmussen, T., & Milner, B. (1977). The role of early left-brain injury in determining lateralization of cerebral speech functions. *Annals of the New York Academy of Sciences, 299,* 355–369.

Ratcliff, R. (1978). A theory of memory retrieval. *Psychological Review, 85,* 59–108.

Ratcliff, R., & McKoon, G. (1978). Priming in item recognition: Evidence for the propositional structure of sentences. *Journal of Verbal Learning and Verbal Behavior, 17,* 403–418.

Ratner, C. (2000). A cultural-psychological analysis of emotions. *Culture and Psychology, 6,* 5–39.

Rau, H., Bührer, M., & Wietkunat, R. (2003). Biofeedback of R-wave-to-pulse interval normalizes blood pressure. *Applied Psychophysiology and Biofeedback, 28,* 37–46.

Raynor, H. A., & Epstein, L. H. (2001). Dietary variety, energy regulation, and obesity. *Psychological Bulletin, 127,* 325–341.

Reder, L. M., & Ritter, F. E. (1992). What determines initial feelings of knowing? Familiarity with question terms, not with the answer. *Journal of Experimental Psychology: Learning, Memory, and Cognition, 18,* 435–452.

Redfern, P., Minors, D., & Waterhouse, J. (1994). Circadian rhythms, jet lag, and chronobiotics: An overview. *Chronobiology International, 11,* 253–265.

Reed, S. B., Kirsch, I., Wickless, C., Moffitt, K. H., & Taren, P. (1996). Reporting biases in hypnosis: Suggestion of compliance? *Journal of Abnormal Psychology, 105,* 142–145.

Regan, R. T. (1971). Effects of a favor and liking on compliance. *Journal of Experimental Social Psychology, 7,* 627–639.

Regier, D. A., Farmer, M. E., Rae, D. S., Myers, J. K., Kramer, M., Robins, L. N., George, L. K., Karno, M., & Locke, B. Z. (1993a). One-month prevalence of mental disorders in the United States and sociodemographic characteristics: The Epidemiological Catchment Area Study. *Acta Psychiatrica Scandinavica, 88,* 35–47.

Regier, D. A., Narrow, W. E., Rae, D. S., Manderscheid, R. W., Locke, B. Z., & Goodwin, F. K. (1993b). The de facto US mental and addictive disorders service system: Epidemiologic Catchment Area prospective 1-year rates of disorders and services. *Archives of General Psychiatry, 50,* 85–94.

Reid, E. (1998). The self and the Internet: Variations on the illusion of one self. In J. Gackenbach (Ed.), *Psychology and the Internet: Intrapersonal, interpersonal, and transpersonal implications* (pp. 29–42). San Diego, CA: Academic Press.

Reid, J. B., Patterson, G. R., & Snyder, J. J. (Eds.) (2002). *Antisocial behavior in children and adolescents: A developmental analysis and the Oregon model for intervention.* Washington, DC: American Psychological Association.

Reisine, T. (1995). Opiate receptors. *Neuropharmacology, 34,* 463–472.

Reiss, D., & Price, R. H. (1996). National research agenda for prevention research: The National Institute of Mental Health report. *American Psychologist, 51,* 1109–1115.

Remafedi, G. (1999). Sexual orientation and youth suicide. *Journal of the American Medical Association, 282,* 1291–1292.

Rescorla, R. A. (1966). Predictability and number of pairings in Pavlovian fear conditioning. *Psychonomic Science, 4,* 383–384.

Rescorla, R. A. (1988). Pavlovian conditioning: It's not what you think it is. *American Psychologist, 43,* 151–160.

Reti, I. M., Samuels, J. F., Eaton, W. W., Bienvenu, O. J., III, Costa, P. T., Jr., & Nestadt, G. (2002). Adult antisocial personality traits are associated with experiences of low paternal care and maternal overprotection. *Acta Psychiatrica Scandinavica, 106,* 126–133.

Rhodewalt, F., & Hill, S. K. (1995). Self-handicapping in the classroom: The effects of claimed self-handicaps on responses to academic failure. *Basic and Applied Social Psychology, 16,* 397–416.

Ricaurte, G. A., Yuan, J., Hatzidimitriou, G., Cord, B. J., McCann, U. D. (2002). Severe dopaminergic neurotoxicity in primates after a common recreational dose regimen of MDMA ("ecstasy"). *Science, 297,* 2260–2263.

Rice, G., Anderson, C., Risch, N., & Ebers, G. (1999). Male homosexuality: Absence of linkage to microsatellite markers at Xq28. *Science, 284,* 665–667.

Richards, M. H., Crowe, P. A., Larson, R., & Swarr, A. (1998). Developmental patterns and gender differences in the experience of peer companionship during adolescence. *Child Development, 69,* 154–163.

Riemann, R., Angleitner, A., & Strelau, J. (1997). Genetic and environmental influences on personality: A study of twins reared together using the self- and peer report NEO-FFI scales. *Journal of Personality, 65,* 449–475.

Riessman, F. (1997). Ten self-help principles. *Social Policy, 27,* 6–11.

Rinck, M., Hähnel, A., Bower, G. H., & Glowalla, U. (1997). The metrics of spatial situation models. *Journal of Experimental Psychology: Learning, Memory, and Cognition, 23,* 622–637.

Rips, L. J. (1990). Reasoning. *Annual Review of Psychology, 41,* 321–353.

Rivas-Vazquez, R. A. (2003). Benzodiazepines in contemporary clinical practice. *Professional Psychology: Research and Practice, 34,* 424–428.

Roberts, A. H., Kewman, D. G., Mercier, L., & Hovell, M. (1993). The power of nonspecific effects in healing: Implications for psychosocial and biological treatments. *Clinical Psychology Review, 13,* 375–391.

Rodin, J. (1981). Current status of the internal-external hypothesis for obesity: What went wrong? *American Psychologist, 26,* 361–372.

Roediger, H. L., III, Gallo, D. A., & Geraci, L. (2002). Processing approaches to cognition: The impetus from the levels-of-processing framework. *Memory, 10,* 319–332.

Rogers, C. R. (1947). Some observations on the organization of personality. *American Psychologist, 2,* 358–368.

Rogers, C. R. (1951). *Client-centered therapy: Its current practice, implications and theory.* Boston: Houghton Mifflin.

Rogers, C. R. (1977). *On personal power: Inner strength and its revolutionary impact.* New York: Delacorte.

Rogers, M., & Smith, K. (1993). Public perceptions of subliminal advertising: Why practitioners shouldn't ignore this issue. *Journal of Advertising Research, 33*(2), 10–18.

Rogers, S. (1993). How a publicity blitz created the myth of subliminal advertising. *Public Relations Quarterly, 37,* 12–17.

Rogoff, B. (1990). *Apprenticeship in thinking: Cognitive development in social context.* New York: Oxford University Press.

Rogoff, B. (2003). *The cultural nature of human development.* London: Oxford University Press.

Rogoff, B., & Chavajay, P. (1995). What's become of research on the cultural basis of cognitive development? *American Psychologist, 50,* 859–877.

Rohrer, J. H., Baron, S. H., Hoffman, E. L., & Swinder, D. V. (1954). The stability of autokinetic judgment. *Journal of Abnormal and Social Psychology, 49,* 595–597.

Roid, G. (2003). Stanford-Binet intelligence scale (5th ed.). Itasca, IL: Riverside Publishing.

Rolls, B. J., Rowe, E. A., Rolls, E. T., Kingston, B., Megson, A., & Gunary, R. (1981). Variety in a meal enhances food intake in man. *Physiology & Behavior, 26,* 215–221.

Rolls, E. T. (1994). Neural processing related to feeding in primates. In C. R. Legg & D. Booth (Eds.), *Appetite: Neural and behavioural bases* (pp. 11–53). Oxford, U.K.: Oxford University Press.

Rolls, E. T. (2000). Memory systems in the brain. *Annual Review of Psychology, 51,* 599–630.

Root, R. W., II, & Resnick, R. J. (2003). An update on the diagnosis and treatment of attention-deficit/hyperactivity disorder in children. *Professional Psychology: Research and Practice, 34,* 34–41.

Rorschach, H. (1942). *Psychodiagnostics: A diagnostic test based on perception.* New York: Grune & Stratton.

Rosch, E. H. (1973). Natural categories. *Cognitive Psychology, 4,* 328–350.

Rosch, E. H. (1978). Principles of categorization. In E. Rosch & B. B. Lloyd (Eds.), *Cognition and categorization* (pp. 27–48). Hillsdale, NJ: Erlbaum.

Rosch, E. H., Mervis, C. B., Gray, W. D., Johnson, D. M., & Boyes-Braem, P. (1976). Basic objects in natural categories. *Cognitive Psychology, 8,* 382–439.

Rosen, H. S., & Rosen, L. A. (1983). Eliminating stealing: Use of stimulus control with an elementary student. *Behavior Modification, 7,* 56–63.

Rosenbaum, M. E. (1986). The repulsion hypothesis: On the non-development of relationships. *Journal of Personality and Social Psychology, 51,* 1156–1166.

Rosenfield, S. (1997). Labeling mental illness: The effects of received services and perceived stigma on life satisfaction. *American Sociological Review, 62,* 660–672.

Rosenhan, D. L. (1973). On being sane in insane places. *Science, 179,* 250–258.

Rosenhan, D. L. (1975). The contextual nature of psychiatric diagnoses. *Journal of Abnormal Psychology, 84,* 462–474.

Rosenhan, D. L., & Seligman, M. E. P. (1989). *Abnormal psychology* (2nd ed.). New York: Norton.

Rosenkoetter, L. I. (1999). The television situation comedy and children's prosocial behavior. *Journal of Applied Social Psychology, 29,* 979–993.

Rosenthal, A. M. (1964). *Thirty-eight witnesses.* New York: McGraw-Hill.

Rosenthal, N. E., Sack, D. A., Gillin, J. C., Lewy, A. J., Goodwin, F. K., Davenport, Y., Mueller, P. S., Newsome, D. A., & Wehr, T. A. (1984). Seasonal affective disorder: A description of the syndrome and preliminary findings with light therapy. *Archives of General Psychiatry, 41,* 72–80.

Rosenthal, R. (1966). *Experimenter effects in behavioral research*. New York: Appleton-Century-Crofts.

Rosenthal, R. (1994). Science and ethics in conducting, analyzing, and reporting psychological research. *Psychological Science, 5,* 127–134.

Rosenthal, R., & Fode, K. L. (1963). The effect of experimenter bias on the performance of the albino rat. *Behavioral Science, 8,* 183–189.

Rosenzweig, M. R. (1996). Aspects of the search for neural mechanisms of memory. *Annual Review of Psychology, 47,* 1–32.

Rosenzweig, M. R. (1999a). Continuity and change in the development of psychology around the world. *American Psychologist, 54,* 252–259.

Rosenzweig, M. R. (1999b). Effects of differential experience on brain and cognition throughout the life span. In S. H. Broman & J. M. Fletcher (Eds.), *The changing nervous system: Neurobehavioral consequences of early brain disorders* (pp. 25–50). New York: Oxford University Press.

Ross, B. H., & Kennedy, P. T. (1990). Generalizing from the use of earlier examples in problem solving. *Journal of Experimental Psychology: Learning, Memory, and Cognition, 16,* 42–55.

Ross, L. (1988). Situational perspectives on the obedience experiments. [Review of the obedience experiments: A case study of controversy in social science]. *Contemporary Psychology, 33,* 101–104.

Ross, L., Amabile, T., & Steinmetz, J. (1977). Social roles, social control and biases in the social perception process. *Journal of Personality and Social Psychology, 37,* 485–494.

Ross, L., & Nisbett, R. E. (1991). *The person and the situation: Perspectives of social psychology*. New York: McGraw-Hill.

Ross, M. J., & Berger, R. S. (1996). Effects of stress inoculation training on athletes' postsurgical pain and rehabilitation after orthopedic injury. *Journal of Consulting and Clinical Psychology, 64,* 406–410.

Rossell, S. L., Bullmore, E. T., Williams, S. C. R., & David, A. S. (2001). Brain activation during automatic and controlled processing of semantic relations: A priming experiment using lexical decision. *Neuropsychologia, 39,* 1167–1176.

Roth, T., Roehrs, T., Carskadon, M. A., & Dement, W. C. (1989). Daytime sleepiness and alertness. In M. Kryser, T. Roth, & W. C. Dement (Eds.), *Principles and practices of sleep medicine* (pp. 14–23). New York: Saunders.

Rothenberg, A. (1990). *Creativity and madness*. Baltimore: The Johns Hopkins University Press.

Rothenberg, A. (2001). Bipolar illness, creativity, and treatment. *Psychiatric Quarterly, 72,* 131–147.

Rothman, D. J. (1971). *The discovery of the asylum: Social order and disorder in the new republic*. Boston: Little, Brown.

Rotter, J. B. (1954). *Social learning and clinical psychology*. Englewood Cliffs, NJ: Prentice Hall.

Rotton, J., & Cohn, E. G. (2000). Violence as a curvilinear function of temperature in Dallas: A replication. *Journal of Personality and Social Psychology, 78,* 1074–1081.

Roussi, P. (2002). Discriminative facility in perceptions of control and its relation to psychological distress. *Anxiety, Stress, & Coping: An International Journal, 15,* 179–191.

Rowe, D. C. (1997). A place at the policy table? Behavior genetics and estimates of family environmental effects on IQ. *Intelligence, 24,* 133–158.

Rozin, P., & Fallon, A. E. (1987). A perspective on disgust. *Psychological Review, 94,* 23–41.

Rozin, P., Millman, L., & Nemeroff, C. (1986). Operation of the laws of sympathetic magic in disgust and other domains. *Journal of Personality and Social Psychology, 50,* 703–712.

Rubin, D. C., & Kontis, T. C. (1983). A schema for common cents. *Memory & Cognition, 11,* 335–341.

Rubin, J. Z., Provenzano, F. J., & Luria, Z. (1974). The eye of the beholder: Parents' views on sex of newborns. *American Journal of Orthopsychiatry, 44,* 512–519.

Ruch, R. (1937). *Psychology and life*. Glenview, IL: Scott, Foresman.

Rucker, C. E., III, & Cash, T. F. (1992). Body images, body-size perceptions, and eating behaviors among African-American and White college women. *International Journal of Eating Disorders, 12,* 291–299.

Ruitenbeek, H. M. (1973). *The first Freudians*. New York: Jason Aronson.

Rummel, R. J. (1994). Power, genocide and mass murder. *Journal of Peace Research, 31,* 1–10.

Runco, M. A. (1991). *Divergent thinking*. Norwood, NJ: Ablex.

Rundle, H. D., Nagel, L., Boughman, J. W., & Schluter, D. (2000). Natural selection and parallel speciation in sympatric sticklebacks. *Science, 287,* 306–308.

Rusbult, C. E., & Martz, J. M. (1995). Remaining in an abusive relationship: An investment model analysis of nonvoluntary dependence. *Personality and Social Psychology Bulletin, 21,* 558–571.

Rusbult, C. E., & Van Lange, P. A. M. (2003). Interdependence, interaction, and relationships. *Annual Review of Psychology, 54,* 351–375.

Ryan, L., Hatfield, C., & Hofstetter, M. (2002). Caffeine reduces time-of-day effects on memory performance in older adults. *Psychological Science, 13,* 68–71.

Ryckman, R. M., Graham, S. S., Thornton, B., Gold, J. A., & Lindner, M. A. (1998). Physical size stereotyping as a mediator of attributions of responsibility in an alleged date-rape situation. *Journal of Applied Social Psychology, 28,* 1876–1888.

Ryff, C. D. (1989). In the eye of the beholder: Views of psychological well-being among middle-aged and older adults. *Psychology and Aging, 4,* 195–210.

Saarinen, T. F. (1987). *Centering of mental maps of the world: Discussion paper*. Tucson: University of Arizona, Department of Geography and Regional Development.

Saberi, K. (1996). An auditory illusion predicted from a weighted cross-correlation model of binaural interaction. *Psychological Review, 103,* 137–142.

Sackheim, H. A., Prudic, J., Devanand, D. P., Nobler, M. S., Lisanby, S. H., Peyser, S., Fitzsimons, L., Moody, B. J., & Clark, J. (2000). A prospective, randomized, double-blind comparison of bilateral and right unilateral electroconvulsive therapy at different stimulus intensities. *Archives of General Psychiatry, 57,* 425–434.

Sagi, A., Koren-Karie, N., Gini, M., Ziv, Y., & Joels, T. (2002). Shedding further light on the effects of various types and quality of early child care on infant-mother attachment relationship: The Haifa Study of Early Child Care. *Child Development, 73,* 1166–1186.

Salthouse, T. A. (1996). The processing-speed theory of adult age differences in cognition. *Psychological Review, 103,* 403–428.

Samuda, R. J. (1998). *Psychological testing of American minorities* (2nd ed.). Thousand Oaks, CA: Sage.

Samuel, A. G. (1981). Phonemic restoration: Insights from a new methodology. *Journal of Experimental Psychology: General, 110,* 474–494.

Samuel, A. G. (1991). A further examination of attentional effects in the phonemic restoration illusion. *Quarterly Journal of Experimental Psychology: Human Experimental Psychology, 43A,* 679–699.

Sanderson, C. A., & Cantor, N. (1997). Creating satisfaction in steady dating relationships: The role of personal goals and situational affordances. *Journal of Personality and Social Psychology, 73,* 1424–1433.

Sapir, E. (1964). *Culture, language, and personality.* Berkeley: University of California Press. (Original work published 1941)

Sapolsky, R. M. (1994). *Why zebras don't get ulcers: A guide to stress, stress-related disease, and coping.* New York: Freeman.

Satir, V. (1967). *Conjoint family therapy* (Rev. ed.). Palo Alto, CA: Science and Behavior Books.

Savage-Rumbaugh, S., Shanker, S. G., & Taylor, T. J. (1998). *Apes, language, and the human mind.* New York: Oxford University Press.

Scarr, S. (1998). American child care today. *American Psychologist, 53,* 95–108.

Scarr, S., & Eisenberg, M. (1993). Child care research: Issues, perspectives, and results. *Annual Review of Psychology, 44,* 613–644.

Scarr, S., Phillips, D., & McCartney, K. (1990). Facts, fantasies and the future of child care in the United States. *Psychological Science, 1,* 26–35.

Schab, F. R. (1990). Odors and the remembrance of things past. *Journal of Experimental Psychology: Learning, Memory, and Cognition, 16,* 648–655.

Schachter, S. (1971a). Some extraordinary facts about obese humans and rats. *American Psychologist, 26,* 129–144.

Schachter, S. (1971b). *Emotion, obesity and crime.* New York: Academic Press.

Schaeken, W., De Booght, G., Vandierendonck, A., & d'Ydewalle, G. (Eds.). (2000). *Deductive reasoning and strategies.* Mahwah, NJ: Erlbaum.

Schaie, K. W. (1993). Ageist language in psychological research. *American Psychologist, 48,* 49–51.

Schaie, K. W. (1994). The course of adult intellectual development. *American Psychologist, 49,* 304–313.

Schaie, K. W., & Willis, S. L. (1986). Can decline in adult intellectual functioning be reversed? *Developmental Psychology, 22,* 223–232.

Schaufeli, W. B., Maslach, C., & Marek, T. (1993). *Professional burnout: Recent developments in theory and research.* Washington, DC: Taylor & Francis.

Schiff, M., & Bargal, D. (2000). Helping characteristics of self-help and support groups: Their contribution to participants' subjective well-being. *Small Group Research, 31,* 275–304.

Schlenger, W. E., Caddell, J. M., Ebert, L., Jordan, B. K., Rourke, K. M., Wilson, D., Thalji, L., Dennis, J. M., Fairbank, J. A., & Kulka, R. A. (2002). Psychological reactions to terrorist attacks: Findings from the National Study of Americans' reactions to September 11. *JAMA, 288,* 581–588.

Schlitz, M. (1997). *Dreaming for the community: Subjective experience and collective action among the Anchuar Indians of Ecuador.* Research proposal. Marin, CA: Institute of Noetic Sciences.

Schmitt, D. P., Shackelford, T. K., Duntley, J., Tooke, W., & Buss, D. M. (2001). The desire for sexual variety as a key to understanding basic human mating strategies. *Personal Relationships, 8,* 425–455.

Schmidt, L. A. & Trainor, L. J. (2001). Frontal brain electrical activity (EEG) distinguishes *valence* and *intensity* of musical emotions. *Cognitive and Emotion, 15,* 487–500.

Schmidt, N. B., Lerew, D. R., & Jackson, R. J. (1997). The role of anxiety sensitivity in the pathogenesis of panic: Prospective evaluation of spontaneous panic attacks during acute stress. *Journal of Abnormal Psychology, 106,* 355–364.

Schmidt, S. E., Liddle, H. A., & Dakof, G. A. (1996). Changes in parenting practices and adolescent drug abuse during multidimensional family therapy. *Journal of Family Psychology, 10,* 12–27.

Schneider, K., & May, R. (1995). *The psychology of existence: An integrative, clinical perspective.* New York: McGraw-Hill.

Scholnick, E. K., Nelson, K., Gelman, S. A., & Miller, P. H. (1999). *Conceptual development: Piaget's legacy.* Mahwah, NJ: Erlbaum.

Schooler, J. W., & Eich, E. (2000). Memory for emotional events. In E. Tulving & F. I. M. Craik (Eds.), *The Oxford handbook of memory* (pp. 379–392). Oxford, U.K.: Oxford University Press.

Schou, M. (2001). Lithium treatment at 52. *Journal of Affective Disorders, 67,* 21–32.

Schreiber, T. A., & Sergent, S. D. (1998). The role of commitment in producing misinformation effects in eyewitness testimony. *Psychonomic Bulletin & Review, 5,* 443–448.

Schroeder, D. A., Penner, L. A., Dovido, J. F., & Piliavin, J. A. (1995). *The psychology of helping and altruism.* New York: McGraw-Hill.

Schultz, R., Braun, R. G., & Kluft, R. P. (1989). Multiple personality disorder: Phenomenology of selected variables in comparison to major depression. *Dissociation, 2,* 45–51.

Schwartz, B. L., & Metcalfe, J. (1992). Cue familiarity but not target retrievability enhances feeling-of-knowing judgments. *Journal of Experimental Psychology: Learning, Memory, and Cognition, 18,* 1074–1083.

Schwartz, D., & Proctor, L. J. (2000). Community violence exposure and children's social adjustment in the school peer group: The mediating roles of emotion regulation and social cognition. *Journal of Consulting and Clinical Psychology, 68,* 670–683.

Schwartz, J. M., Stoessel, P. W., Baxter, L. R., Martin, K. M., & Phelps, M. E. (1996). Systematic changes in cerebral glucose metabolic rate after successful behavior modification treatment of obsessive-compulsive disorder. *Archives of General Psychiatry, 53,* 109–113.

Schwarzer, R. (Ed.). (1992). *Self-efficacy: Thought control of action.* Washington, DC: Hemisphere.

Scott, D., Scott, L. M., & Goldwater, B. (1997). A performance improvement program for an international-level track and field athlete. *Journal of Applied Behavior Analysis, 30,* 573–575.

Scott, K. K., Young, A. W., Calder, A. J., Hellawell, D. J., Aggleton, J. P., & Johnson, M. (1997). Impaired auditory recognition of fear and anger following bilateral amygdala lesions. *Nature, 385,* 254–257.

Scull, A. (1993). *A most solitary of afflictions: Madness and society in Britain 1700–1900.* London: Yale University Press.

Searle, J. R. (1979b). Literal meaning. In J. R. Searle (Ed.), *Expression and meaning* (pp. 117–136). Cambridge, U.K.: Cambridge University Press.

Sedikides, C., Gaertner, L., & Toguchi, Y. (2003). Pancultural self-enhancement. *Journal of Personality and Social Psychology, 84,* 60–79.

Segall, M. H., Ember, C. E., & Ember, M. (1997). Aggression, crime, and warfare. In J. W. Berry, M. H. Segall, & C. Kagitçibasi (Eds.), *Handbook of cross-cultural psychology: Vol. 3. Social behaviors and applications* (pp. 213–254). Boston: Allyn & Bacon.

Segerstrom, S. C., Taylor, S. E., Kemeny, M. E., & Fahey, J. L. (1998). Optimism is associated with mood, coping and immune change in response to stress. *Journal of Personality and Social Psychology, 74,* 1646–1655.

Seidenberg, M. S., & Petitto, L. A. (1979). Signing behavior in apes: A critical review. *Cognition, 7,* 177–215.

Seidler, R. D., Purushotham, A., Kim S.-G., Ugurbil, K., Willingham, D., & Ashe, J. (2002). Cerebellum activation associated with performance change but no motor learning. *Science, 296,* 2043–2046.

Sekuler, R., & Blake, R. (2001). *Perception* (4th ed.). New York: McGraw-Hill.

Self, E. A. (1990). Situational influences on self-handicapping. In R. L. Higgins, C. R. Snyder, & S. Berglas (Eds.), *Self-handicapping: The paradox that isn't* (pp. 37–68). New York: Plenum Press.

Selfridge, O. G. (1955). Pattern recognition and modern computers. *Proceedings of the Western Joint Computer Conference.* New York: Institute of Electrical and Electronics Engineers.

Seligman, M. E. P. (1975). *Helplessness: On depression, development, and death.* San Francisco: Freeman.

Seligman, M. E. P. (1991). *Learned optimism.* New York: Norton.

Seligman, M. E. P., & Maier, S. F. (1967). Failure to escape traumatic shock. *Journal of Experimental Psychology, 74,* 1–9.

Selye, H. (1976a). *Stress in health and disease.* Reading, MA: Butterworth.

Selye, H. (1976b). *The stress of life* (2nd ed.). New York: McGraw-Hill.

Serpell, R. (2000). Intelligence and culture. In R. J. Sternberg (Ed.), *Handbook of intelligence* (pp. 549–577). Cambridge, U.K.: Cambridge University Press.

Serpell, R., & Boykin, A. W. (1994). Cultural dimensions of cognition: A multiplex, dynamic system of constraints and possibilities. In R. J. Sternberg (Ed.), *Handbook of perception and cognition: Vol. 2. Thinking and problem solving* (pp. 369–408). Orlando, FL: Academic Press.

Serrano, J. M., Iglesias, J., & Loeches, A. (1992). Visual discrimination and recognition of facial expressions of anger, fear, and surprise in 4- to 6-month-old infants. *Developmental Psychobiology, 25,* 411–425.

Serrano, J. M., Iglesias, J., & Loeches, A. (1995). Infants' responses to adult static facial expressions. *Infant Behavior and Development, 18,* 477–482.

Shafir, E. (1993). Choosing versus rejecting: Why some options are both better and worse than others. *Memory & Cognition, 21,* 546–556.

Shapiro, K. F. (1998). *Animal models of human psychology: Critique of science, ethics, and policy.* Seattle, WA: Hogrefe & Huber.

Shapiro, L. P., Nagel, H. N., & Levine, B. A. (1993). Preferences for a verb's complements and their use in sentence processing. *Journal of Memory and Language, 32,* 96–114.

Shapiro, S. L., Schwartz, G. E., & Bonner, G. (1998). Effects of mindfulness-based stress reduction on medical and premedical students. *Journal of Behavioral Medicine, 21,* 581–599.

Sharpsteen, D. J., & Kirkpatrick, L. A. (1997). Romantic jealousy and adult romantic attachment. *Journal of Personality and Social Psychology, 72,* 627–640.

Shaver, P. R., & Hazan, C. (1994). Attachment. In A. L. Weber & J. H. Harvey (Eds.), *Perspectives on close relationships* (pp. 110–130). Boston: Allyn & Bacon.

Shavitt, S. (1990). The role of attitude objects in attitude functions. *Journal of Experimental Social Psychology, 26,* 124–148.

Shaywitz, B. A., Shaywitz, S. E., Pugh, K. R., Constable, R. T., Skudlarski, P., Fulbright, K., Bronen, R. A., Fletcher, J. M., Shankweller, D. P., Katz, L., & Gore, J. C. (1995). Sex differences in the functional organization of the brain for language. *Nature, 373,* 607–609.

Shealy, C. N. (1995). From *Boys Town* to *Oliver Twist:* Separating fact from fiction in welfare reform and out-of-home placement for children and youth. *American Psychologist, 50,* 565–580.

Sheehan, E. P. (1993). The effects of turnover on the productivity of those who stay. *Journal of Social Psychology, 133,* 699–706.

Sheldon, W. (1942). *The varieties of temperament: A psychology of constitutional differences.* New York: Harper.

Shepard, R. N. (1978). Externalization of mental images and the act of creation. In B. S. Randhawa & W. E. Coffman (Eds.), *Visual learning, thinking, and communicating.* New York: Academic Press.

Shepard, R. N. (1984). Ecological constraints on internal representation: Resonant kinematics of perceiving, imagining, thinking and dreaming. *Psychological Review, 91,* 417–447.

Shepard, R. N., & Cooper, L. A. (1982). *Mental images and their transformations.* Cambridge, MA: The MIT Press.

Shepard, R. N., & Jordan, D. S. (1984). Auditory illusions demonstrating that tones are assimilated to an internalized musical scale. *Science, 226,* 1333–1334.

Sheridan, C. L., & King, R. G. (1972). Obedience to authority with an authentic victim. Proceedings from the 80th Annual Convention. *American Psychological Association, Part I, 7,* 165–166.

Sherif, C. W. (1981, August). *Social and psychological bases of social psychology.* The G. Stanley Hall Lecture on social psychology, presented at the annual convention of the American Psychological Association, Los Angeles. 1961.

Sherif, M. (1935). A study of some social factors in perception. *Archives of Psychology, 27*(187).

Sherif, M., Harvey, O. J., White, B. J., Hood, W. R., & Sherif, C. W. (1988). *The Robbers Cave experiment: Intergroup conflict and cooperation.* Middletown, CT: Wesleyan University Press. (Original work published 1961)

Sherrod, K., Vietze, P., & Friedman, S. (1978). *Infancy.* Monterey, CA: Brooks/Cole.

Shettleworth, S. J. (1993). Where is the comparison in comparative cognition? *Psychological Science, 4,* 179–184.

Shiffrar, M. (1994). When what meets where. *Current Directions in Psychological Science, 3,* 96–100.

Shiffrin, R. M. (1993). Short-term memory: A brief commentary. *Memory & Cognition, 21,* 193–197.

Shiffrin, R. M., & Schneider, W. (1977). Controlled and automatic human information processing: II. Perceptual learning, automatic attending, and a general theory. *Psychological Review, 84,* 127–190.

Shimamura, A. P., Berry, J. M., Mangels, J. A., Rusting, C. L., & Jurica, P. J. (1995). Memory and cognitive abilities in university professors: Evidence for successful aging. *Psychological Science, 6,* 271–277.

Shneidman, E. S. (1987, March). At the point of no return. *Psychology Today,* pp. 54–59.

Shoda, Y., Mischel, W., & Wright, J. C. (1993a). The role of situational demands and cognitive competencies in behavior organization and personality coherence. *Journal of Personality and Social Psychology, 65,* 1023–1035.

Shoda, Y., Mischel, W., & Wright, J. C. (1993b). Links between personality judgments and contextualized behavior patterns: Situation-behavior profiles of personality prototypes. *Social Cognition, 11,* 399–429.

Shortliffe, E. H. (1976). *Computer-based medical consultations—MYCIN.* New York: Elsevier/North Holland.

Shulman, S. (1993). Close friendships in early and middle adolescence: Typology and friendship reasoning. In B. Laursen (Ed.), *Close friendships in adolescence* (pp. 55–71). San Francisco: Jossey-Bass.

Sia, T. L., Lord, C. G., Blessum, K. A., Ratcliff, C. D., & Lepper, M. R. (1997). Is a rose always a rose? The role of social category exemplar change in attitude stability and attitude-behavior consistency. *Journal of Personality and Social Psychology, 72,* 501–514.

Siegel, B. (1988). *Love, medicine and miracles.* New York: Harper & Row.

Siegel, J. M. (2001). The REM sleep-memory consolidation hypothesis. *Science, 294,* 1058–1063.

Siegel, R. K. (1992). *Fire in the brain.* New York: Dutton.

Siegel, S. (1984). Pavlovian conditioning and heroin overdose: Reports by overdose victims. *Bulletin of the Psychonomic Society, 22,* 428–430.

Siegel, S. (1999). Drug anticipation and drug addiction: The 1998 H. David Archibald lecture. *Addiction, 94,* 1113–1124.

Siegel, S., Hinson, R. E., Krank, M. D., & McCully, J. (1982). Heroin "overdose" death: The contribution of drug-associated environmental cues. *Science, 216,* 436–437.

Siegelman, M. (1972). Adjustment of homosexual and heterosexual women. *British Journal of Psychiatry, 120,* 477–481.

Siegler, R. S., & Crowley, K. (1991). The microgenetic method: A direct means for studying cognitive development. *American Psychologist, 46,* 606–620.

Silver, E., Cirincione, C., & Steadman, H. J. (1994). Demythologizing inaccurate perceptions of the insanity defense. *Law & Human Behavior, 18,* 63–70.

Silverman, A. B., Reinherz, H. Z., & Giaconia, R. M. (1996). The long-term sequelae of child and adolescent abuse: A longitudinal community study. *Child Abuse & Neglect, 20,* 709–723.

Simkin, L. R., & Gross, A. M. (1994). Assessment of coping with high-risk situations for exercise relapse among healthy women. *Health Psychology, 13,* 274–277.

Simmons, J. A., Ferragamo, M. J., & Moss, C. F. (1998). Echo-delay resolution in sonar images of the big brown bat, *Eptesicus fuscus. Proceedings of the National Academy of Sciences of the United States, 95,* 12647–12652.

Simon, H. A. (1973). The structure of ill-structured problems. *Artificial Intelligence, 4,* 181–202.

Simon, H. A. (1979). *Models of thought* (Vol. 1). New Haven: Yale University Press.

Simon, H. A. (1989). *Models of thought* (Vol. 2). New Haven: Yale University Press.

Simons, D. J. (1996). In sight, out of mind: When object representations fail. *Psychological Science, 7,* 301–305.

Simons, D. J. (2000). Current approaches to change blindness. *Visual Cognition, 7,* 1–15.

Sinclair, R. C., Hoffman, C., Mark, M. M., Martin, L. L., & Pickering, T. L. (1994). Construct accessibility and the misattribution of arousal: Schachter and Singer revisited. *Psychological Science, 5,* 15–19.

Singer, D. G., & Singer, J. L. (1990). *The house of make-believe.* Cambridge, MA: Harvard University Press.

Singer, J. L. (Ed.). (1990). *Repression and dissociation.* Chicago: University of Chicago Press.

Singer, L. T., Arendt, R., Minnes, S., Farkas, K., Salvator, A., Kirchner, H. L., & Kliegman, R. (2002). Cognitive and motor outcomes of cocaine-exposed infants. *Journal of the American Medical Association, 287,* 1952–1960.

Singer, T., Verhaegen, P., Ghisletta, P., Lindenberger, U., & Baltes, P. B. (2003). The fate of cognition in very old age: Six-year longitudinal findings in the Berlin Aging Study (BASE). *Psychology & Aging, 18,* 318–331.

Sireteanu, R. (1999). Switching on the infant brain. *Science, 286,* 59–61.

Skinner, B. F. (1938). *The behavior of organisms.* New York: Appleton-Century-Crofts.

Skinner, B. F. (1953). *Science and human behavior.* New York: Macmillan.

Skinner, B. F. (1966). What is the experimental analysis of behavior? *Journal of the Experimental Analysis of Behavior, 9,* 213–218.

Skinner, B. F. (1972). *Beyond freedom and dignity.* Toronto: Bantam Books.

Skinner, B. F. (1990). Can psychology be a science of mind? *American Psychologist, 45,* 1206–1210.

Skre, I., Onstad, S., Torgersen, S., Kygren, S., & Kringlen, E. (1993). A twin study of DSM-III-R anxiety disorders. *Acta Psychiatrica Scandinavica, 88,* 85–92.

Slaski, M., & Cartwright, S. (2002). Health, performance and emotional intelligence: An exploratory study of retail managers. *Stress and Health, 18,* 63–68.

Sloane, R. B., Staples, F. R., Cristol, A. H., Yorkston, N. J., & Whipple, K. (1975). *Psychotherapy versus behavior therapy.* Cambridge, MA: Harvard University Press.

Slobin, D. I. (1982). Universal and particular in the acquisition of language. In E. Wanner & L. Gleitman (Eds.), *Language acquisition: The state of the art* (pp. 128–170). Cambridge, U.K.: Cambridge University Press.

Slobin, D. I. (1985). Crosslinguistic evidence for the language-making capacity. In D. Slobin (Ed.), *The crosslinguistic study of language acquisition: Vol. 2. Theoretical issues* (pp. 1157–1256). Hillsdale, NJ: Erlbaum.

Slobin, D. I., & Aksu, A. (1982). Tense, aspect, and modality in the use of the Turkish evidential. In P. J. Hopper (Ed.), *Tense-aspect: Between semantics & pragmatics* (pp. 185–200). Amsterdam: Benjamins.

Sloman, S. A., Hayman, C. A. G., Ohta, N., Law, J., & Tulving, E. (1988). Forgetting in primed fragment completion. *Journal of Experimental Psychology: Learning, Memory, and Cognition, 14,* 223–239.

Slovic, P. (1995). The construction of preference. *American Psychologist, 50,* 364–371.

Smith, J., & Baltes, P. B. (1990). Wisdom-related knowledge: Age/cohort differences in response to life-planning problems. *Developmental Psychology, 26,* 494–505.

Smith, M. V. (1996). Linguistic relativity: On hypotheses and confusions. *Communication & Cognition, 29,* 65–90.

Smith, S. L., & Donnerstein, E. (1998). Harmful effects of exposure to media violence: Learning of aggression, emotional desensitization, and fear. In R. G. Geen & E. Donnerstein (Eds.), *Human aggression: Theories, research, and implications for public policy* (pp. 167–202). San Diego, CA: Academic Press.

Smith, T. W., & Ruiz, J. M. (2002). Psychosocial influences on the development and course of coronary heart disease: Current status and implications for research and practice. *Journal of Consulting and Clinical Psychology, 70,* 548–568.

Snyder, M. (1984). When beliefs create reality. In L. Berkowitz (Ed.), *Advances in experimental social psychology* (Vol. 18, pp. 247–305). New York: Academic Press.

Snyder, M., & Haugen, J. A. (1995). Why does behavioral confirmation occur? A functional perspective on the role of the target. *Personality and Social Psychology Bulletin, 21,* 963–974.

Solomon, A. (1998, January 12). Anatomy of melancholy. *New Yorker, 73,* 46–61.

Solso, R. L., & McCarthy, J. E. (1981). Prototype formation of faces: A case study of pseudomemory. *British Journal of Psychology, 72,* 499–503.

<www.ablongman.com/gerrig17e>

Sommer, W., Heinz, A., Leuthold, H., Matt, J., & Schweinberger, S. R. (1995). Metamemory, distinctiveness, and event-related potentials in recognition memory for faces. *Memory & Cognition, 23,* 1–11.

Sonnad, S. S., Moyer, C. A., Patel, S., Helman, J. I., Garetz, S. L., & Chervin, R. D. (2003). A model to facilitate outcome assessment of obstructive sleep apnea. *International Journal of Technology Assessment in Health Care, 19,* 253–260.

Sowell, E. R., Trauner, D. A., Gamst, A., & Jernigan, T. L. (2002). Development of cortical and subcortical brain structures in childhood and adolescence: A structural MRI study. *Developmental Medicine & Child Neurology, 44,* 4–16.

Spangler, W. D. (1992). Validity of questionnaire and TAT measures of need for achievement: Two meta-analyses. *Psychological Bulletin, 112,* 140–154.

Spearman, C. (1927). *The abilities of man.* New York: Macmillan.

Spence, M. J., & DeCasper, A. J. (1987). Prenatal experience with low-frequency maternal-voice sounds influences neonatal perception of maternal voice samples. *Infant Behavior and Development, 10,* 133–142.

Spence, M. J., & Freeman, M. S. (1996). Newborn infants prefer the maternal low-pass filtered voice, but not the maternal whispered voice. *Infant Behavior and Development, 19,* 199–212.

Sperling, G. (1960). The information available in brief visual presentations. *Psychological Monographs, 74,* 1–29.

Sperling, G. (1963). A model for visual memory tasks. *Human Factors, 5,* 19–31.

Sperry, R. W. (1968). Mental unity following surgical disconnection of the cerebral hemispheres. *The Harvey Lectures,* Series 62. New York: Academic Press.

Spiegel, D., Bloom, J. R., Kraemer, H. C., & Gottheil, E. (1989, October 14). Effect of psychosocial treatment on survival of patients with metastatic breast cancer. *The Lancet,* pp. 888–891.

Spiegel, D. A., Wiegel, M., Baker, S. L., & Greene, K. A. I. (2000). Pharmacological management of anxiety disorders. In D. I. Mostofsky & D. H. Barlow (Eds.), *The management of stress and anxiety in medical disorders* (pp. 36–65). Boston, MA: Allyn & Bacon.

Spielman, A. J., & Glovinsky, P. B. (1997). The diagnostic interview and differential diagnosis for complaints of insomnia. In M. R. Pressman & W. C. Orr (Eds.), *Understanding sleep: The evaluation and treatment of sleep disorders* (pp. 125–160). Washington, DC: American Psychological Association.

Spitz, R. A., & Wolf, K. (1946). Anaclitic depression. *Psychoanalytic Study of Children, 2,* 313–342.

Squire, L. R., Amaral, D. G., Zola-Morgan, S., Kritchevsky, M., & Press, G. (1989). Description of brain injury in the amnesic patient N. A. based on magnetic resonance imaging. *Experimental Neurology, 105,* 23–35.

Stahl, S. M. (1998). Getting stoned without inhaling: Anandamide is the brain's natural marijuana. *Journal of Clinical Psychiatry, 59,* 566–567.

Stams, G.-J. J. M., Juffer, F., van Ijzendoorn, M. H. (2002). Maternal sensitivity, infant attachment, and temperament in early childhood predict adjustment in middle childhood: The case of adopted children and their biologically unrelated parents. *Developmental Psychology, 38,* 806–821.

Stanford Daily. (1982, February 2, pp. 1, 3, 5). Rape is no accident, say campus assault victims.

Staub, E. (1989). *The roots of evil: The origins of genocide and other group violence.* New York: Cambridge University Press.

Staub, E. (2000). Genocide and mass killing: Origins, prevention, healing and reconciliation. *Political Psychology, 21,* 367–382.

Staub, E. (2003). Notes on cultures of violence, cultures of caring and peace, and the fulfillment of basic human needs. *Political Psychology, 24,* 1–21.

Steele, C. M. (1988). The psychology of self-affirmation: Sustaining the integrity of the self. In L. Berkowitz (Ed.), *Advances in experimental social psychology* (Vol. 21, pp. 261–302). New York: Academic Press.

Steele, C. M. (1997). A threat in the air: How stereotypes shape intellectual identity and performance. *American Psychologist, 6,* 613–629.

Steele, C. M., & Aronson, J. (1995). Stereotype threat and the intellectual test performance of African Americans. *Journal of Personality and Social Psychology, 69,* 797–811.

Steele, C. M., & Aronson, J. (1998). Stereotype threat and the test performance of academically successful African Americans. In C. Jencks & M. Phillips (Eds.), *The black–white test score gap* (pp. 401–427). Washington, DC: Brookings Institution Press.

Stein, M. B., Jang, K. L., Taylor, S., Vernon, P. A., & Livesley, W. J. (2002). Genetic and environmental influences on trauma exposure and posttraumatic stress disorder symptoms: A twin study. *American Journal of Psychiatry, 159,* 1675–1681.

Steinberg, L., Lamborn, S. D., Dornbusch, S. M., & Darling, N. (1992). Impact of parenting practices on adolescent achievement: Authoritative parenting, school involvement, and encouragement to succeed. *Child Development, 63,* 1266–1281.

Stemberger, J. P. (1992). The reliability and replicability of naturalistic speech error data: A comparison with experimentally induced errors. In B. J. Baars (Ed.), *Experimental slips and human error: Exploring the architecture of volition* (pp. 195–215). New York: Plenum Press.

Stephan, W. G., Stephan, C. W., & de Vargas, M. C. (1996). Emotional expression in Costa Rica and the United States. *Journal of Cross-Cultural Psychology, 27,* 147–160.

Stern, M., & Karraker, K. H. (1989). Sex stereotyping of infants: A review of gender labeling studies. *Sex Roles, 20,* 501–522.

Stern, P. C. (1995). Why do people sacrifice for their nations? *Political Psychology, 16,* 217–235.

Stern, W. (1914). The psychological methods of testing intelligence. *Educational Psychology Monographs* (No. 13).

Sternberg, R. J. (1985). *Beyond IQ.* Cambridge, MA: Cambridge University Press.

Sternberg, R. J. (1986). *Intelligence applied.* San Diego: Harcourt Brace Jovanovich.

Sternberg, R. J. (1994). Intelligence. In R. J. Sternberg (Ed.), *Handbook of perception and cognition: Vol. 2. Thinking and problem solving* (pp. 263–288). Orlando, FL: Academic Press.

Sternberg, R. J. (1999). The theory of successful intelligence. *Review of General Psychology, 3,* 292–316.

Sternberg, R. J., & Lubart, T. I. (1996). Investing in creativity. *American Psychologist, 51,* 677–688.

Sternberg, R. J., & Lubart, T. I. (1999). The concept of creativity: Prospects and paradigms. In R. J. Sternberg (Ed.), *Handbook of creativity* (pp. 3–15). Cambridge, U.K.: Cambridge University Press.

Sternberg, R. J., & Grigorenko, E. L. (2000). *Teaching for successful intelligence.* Arlington Heights, IL: Skylight Training and Publishing Inc.

Sternberg, R. J., & O'Hara, L. A. (1999). Creativity and intelligence. In R. J. Sternberg (Ed.), *Handbook of creativity* (pp. 251–272). Cambridge, U.K.: Cambridge University Press.

Sternberg, S. (1966). High-speed scanning in human memory. *Science, 153,* 652–654.

Sternberg, S. (1969). Memory-scanning: Mental processes revealed by reaction time experiments. *American Scientist, 57,* 421–457.

Stevens, J. A., Fonlupt, P., Shiffrar, M., & Decety, J. (2000). New aspects of motion perception: Selective neural encoding of apparent human movements. *Neuroreport, 11,* 109–115.

Stevenson, H. W., Chen, C., & Lee, S. Y. (1993). Mathematics achievement of Chinese, Japanese, and American children: Ten years later. *Science, 259,* 53–58.

Stickgold, R., Hobson, J. A., Fosse, R., & Fosse, M. (2001). Sleep, learning, and dreams: Off-line memory reprocessing. *Science, 294,* 1052–1057.

Stone, A. A., Neale, J. M., Cox, D. S., Napoli, A., Valdimarsdottir, H., & Kennedy-Moore, E. (1994). Daily events are associated with a secretory immune response to an oral antigen in men. *Health Psychology, 13,* 440–446.

Stone, R. (2000). Stress: The invisible hand in Eastern Europe's death rates. *Science, 288,* 1732–1733.

Strakowski, S. M., DelBello, M. P., Zimmerman, M. E., Getz, G. E., Mills, N. P., Ret, J., Shear, P., & Adler, C. M. (2002). Ventricular and periventricular structural volumes in first-versus multiple-episode bipolar disorder. *American Journal of Psychiatry, 159,* 1841–1847.

Strassberg, Z., Dodge, K. A., Pettit, G. S., & Bates, J. E. (1994). Spanking in the home and children's subsequent aggression toward kindergarten peers. *Development and Psychopathology, 6,* 445–461.

Strauch, I., & Lederbogen, S. (1999). The home dreams and waking fantasies of boys and girls between ages 9 and 15: A longitudinal study. *Dreaming, 9,* 153–161.

Straus, M. A., & Kantor, G. K. (1994). Corporal punishment of adolescents by parents: A risk factor in the epidemiology of depression, suicide, alcohol abuse, child abuse, and wife beating. *Adolescence, 29,* 543–561.

Straus, M. A., & Stewart, J. H. (1999). Corporal punishment by American parents: National data on prevalence, chronicity, severity, and duration, in relation to child and family characteristics. *Clinical Child and Family Psychology Review, 2,* 55–70.

Striegel-Moore, R. H., Dohm, F. A., Kraemer, H. C., Taylor, C. B., Daniels, S., Crawford, P. B., & Schreiber, G. B. (2003). Eating disorders in white and black women. *American Journal of Psychiatry, 160,* 1326–1331.

Stunkard, A. J., Harris, J. R., Pedersen, N. L., & McClearn, G. E. (1990). The body mass index of twins who have been reared apart. *New England Journal of Medicine, 322,* 1483–1487.

Substance Abuse and Mental Health Service Administration. (2003). *The national survey on drug use and health.* Available: http://www.samhsa.gov/oas/nhsda/2k1nhsda/vol2/toc.htm.

Suchman, A. L., & Ader, R. (1989). Placebo response in humans can be shaped by prior pharmacologic experience. *Psychosomatic Medicine, 51,* 251.

Sullivan, H. S. (1953). *The interpersonal theory of psychiatry.* New York: Norton.

Sulloway, F. J. (1996). *Born to rebel: Birth order, family dynamics, and creative lives.* New York: Pantheon.

Suomi, S. J. (1999). Developmental trajectories, early experiences, and community consequences: Lessons from studies with rhesus monkeys. In D. P. Keating & C. Hertzman (Eds.), *Developmental health and the wealth of nations: Social, biological, and educational dynamics* (pp. 185–200). New York: The Guilford Press.

Suzuki, L. A., & Valencia, R. R. (1997). Race-ethnicity and measured intelligence: Educational implications. *American Psychologist, 52,* 1103–1114.

Swann, W. B., Jr. (1990). To be adored or to be known? The interplay of self-enhancement and self-verification. In R. M. Sorrentino & E. T. Higgins (Eds.), *Handbook of motivation and cognition* (Vol. 2). New York: Guilford Press.

Swann, W. B., Jr. (1997). The trouble with change: Self-verification and allegiance to the self. *Psychological Science, 8,* 177–180.

Swann, W. B., Jr., & Ely, R. J. (1984). A battle of wills: Self-verification versus behavioral confirmation. *Journal of Personality and Social Psychology, 46,* 1287–1302.

Swazey, J. P. (1974). *Chlorpromazine in psychiatry: A study of therapeutic innovation.* Cambridge, MA: The MIT Press.

Sweeney, J. A., Clementz, B. A., Haas, G. L., Escobar, M. D., Drake, K., & Frances, A. J. (1994). Eye tracking dysfunction in schizophrenia: Characterization of component eye movement abnormalities, diagnostic specificity, and the role of attention. *Journal of Abnormal Psychology, 103,* 222–230.

Szasz, T. (1995). The origin of psychiatry: The alienist as nanny for troublesome adults. *History of Psychiatry, 6,* 1–19.

Szasz, T. S. (1961). *The myth of mental illness.* New York: Harper & Row.

Szasz, T. S. (1977). *The manufacture of models.* New York: Dell.

Szymanski, S., Kane, J. M., & Leiberman, J. A. (1991). A selective review of biological markers in schizophrenia. *Schizophrenia Bulletin, 17,* 99–111.

Tacon, A. M., McComb, J., Caldera, Y., & Randolph, P. Mindfulness meditation, anxiety reduction, and heart disease: A pilot study. *Family and Community Health, 26,* 25–33.

Tanofsky-Kraff, M., Wilfley, D. E., & Spurrell, E. (2000). Impact of interpersonal and ego-related stress on restrained eaters. *International Journal of Eating Disorders, 27,* 411–418.

Taylor, C. B., & Luce, K. H. (2003). Computer- and internet-based psychotherapy interventions. *Current Directions in Psychological Science, 12,* 18–22.

Taylor, M. G. (1996). The development of children's beliefs about social and biological aspects of gender differences. *Child Development, 67,* 1555–1571.

Taylor, S. E. (1986). *Health psychology.* New York: Random House.

Taylor, S. E., Klein, L. C., Lewis, B. P., Gruenewald, T. L., Gurung, R. A. R., & Updegraff, J. A. (2000). Biobehavioral responses to stress in females: Tend-and-befriend, not fight-or-flight. *Psychological Review, 107,* 411–429.

Teasdale, J. D. (1985). Psychological treatments for depression: How do they work? *Behavior Research and Therapy, 23,* 157–165.

Teasdale, J. D., Segal, Z., & Williams, J. M. G. (1995). How does cognitive therapy prevent depressive relapse and why should attentional control (mindfulness) training help? *Behaviour Research and Therapy, 33,* 25–39.

Tedlock, B. (Ed.). (1987). *Dreaming: Anthropological and psychological interpretations.* Cambridge, U.K.: Cambridge University Press.

Templin, M. (1957). Certain language skills in children: Their development and interrelationships. *Institute of Child Welfare Monograph,* Series No. 26. Minneapolis: University of Minnesota Press.

Tennen, H., Affleck, G., Armeli, S., & Carney, M. A. (2000). A daily process approach to coping: Linking theory, research, and practice. *American Psychologist, 55,* 626–636.

Terman, L. M. (1916). *The measurement of intelligence.* Boston: Houghton Mifflin.

Terman, L. M., & Merrill, M. A. (1937). *Measuring intelligence.* Boston: Houghton Mifflin.

Terman, L. M., & Merrill, M. A. (1960). *The Stanford-Binet intelligence scale.* Boston: Houghton Mifflin.

Terman, L. M., & Merrill, M. A. (1972). *Stanford-Binet intelligence scale—manual for the third revision, Form L-M.* Boston: Houghton Mifflin.

Thapar, A. (2003). Attention deficit hyperactivity disorder: New genetic findings, new directions. In R. Plomin, J. C. DeFries, I. W. Craig, & P. McGuffin (Eds.), *Behavioral genetics in the postgenomic era* (pp. 445–462). Washington, DC: American Psychological Association.

Theeuwes, J., Kramer, A. F., Hahn, S., & Irwin, D. E. (1998). Our eyes do not always go where we want them to go: Capture of the eyes by new objects. *Psychological Science, 9,* 379–385.

Thomas, A. K., & Loftus, E. F. (2002). Creating bizarre false memories through imagination. *Memory & Cognition, 30,* 423–431.

Thomas, E., & Wingert, P. (2000, June 19). Bitter lessons. *Newsweek, 135,* 50, 51–52.

Thompson, S. C., Nanni, C., & Levine, A. (1994). Primary versus secondary and central versus consequence-related control in HIV-positive men. *Journal of Personality and Social Psychology, 67,* 540–547.

Thoresen, C. E., & Powell, L. H. (1992). Type A behavior pattern: New perspectives on theory, assessment, and intervention. *Journal of Consulting and Clinical Psychology, 60,* 595–604.

Thorndike, E. L. (1898). Animal intelligence. *Psychological Review Monograph Supplement, 2*(4, Whole No. 8).

Thorndike, R. L., Hagen, E. P., & Sattler, J. M. (1986). *Stanford-Binet intelligence scale* (4th ed.). Chicago: Riverside.

Tice, D. M., & Baumeister, R. F. (1997). Longitudinal study of procrastination, performance, stress, and health: The costs and benefits of dawdling. *Psychological Science, 8,* 454–458.

Tidwell, M.-C. O., Reis, H. T., & Shaver, P. R. (1996). Attachment, attractiveness, and social interaction: A diary study. *Journal of Personality and Social Psychology, 71,* 729–745.

Todd, J. T., & Morris, E. K. (1992). Case histories in the great power of steady misrepresentation. *American Psychologist, 47,* 1441–1453.

Todd, J. T., & Morris, E. K. (1993). Change and be ready to change again. *American Psychologist, 48,* 1158–1159.

Todrank, J., & Bartoshuk, L. M. (1991). A taste illusion: Taste sensation localized by touch. *Physiology & Behavior, 50,* 1027–1031.

Tolman, E. C. (1948). Cognitive maps in rats and men. *Psychological Review, 55,* 189–208.

Tolman, E. C., & Honzik, C. H. (1930). "Insight" in rats. *University of California Publications in Psychology, 4,* 215–232.

Tomkins, S. (1962). *Affect, imagery, consciousness* (Vol. 1). New York: Springer.

Tomkins, S. (1981). The quest for primary motives; Biography and autobiography of an idea. *Journal of Personality and Social Psychology, 41,* 306–329.

Tomoyasu, N., Bovbjerg, D. H., & Jacobsen, P. B. (1996). Conditioned reactions to cancer chemotherapy: Percent reinforcement predicts anticipatory nausea. *Physiology & Behavior, 59,* 273–276.

Torrance, E. P. (1974). *The Torrance tests of creative thinking: Technical-norms manual.* Bensenville, IL: Scholastic Testing Services.

Townsend, J. T. (1971). A note on the identifiability of parallel and serial processes. *Perception & Psychophysics, 10,* 161–163.

Townsend, J. T. (1990). Serial vs. parallel processing: Sometimes they look like Tweedledum and Tweedledee but they can (and should) be distinguished. *Psychological Science, 1,* 46–54.

Trainor, L. J., Austin, C. M., & Desjardins, R. N. (2000). Is infant-directed speech prosody a result of the vocal expression of emotion? *Psychological Science, 11,* 188–195.

Treisman, A., & Gormican, S. (1988). Feature analysis in early vision: Evidence from search asymmetries. *Psychological Review, 95,* 15–48.

Treisman, A., & Sato, S. (1990). Conjunction search revisited. *Journal of Experimental Psychology: Human Perception and Performance, 16,* 459–478.

Triandis, H. C. (1990). Cross-cultural studies of individualism and collectivism. In J. Berman (Ed.), *Nebraska Symposium on Motivation, 1989* (pp. 41–133). Lincoln: University of Nebraska Press.

Triandis, H. C. (1994). *Culture and social behavior.* New York: McGraw-Hill.

Triandis, H. C. (1995). *Individualism and collectivism.* Boulder, CO: Westview.

Trivers, R. L. (1971). The evolution of reciprocal altruism. *Quarterly Review of Biology, 46,* 35–57.

Trivers, R. L. (1972). Parental investment and sexual selection. In B. Campbell (Ed.), *Sexual selection and the descent of man* (pp. 139–179). Chicago: Aldine.

Trueswell, J. C. (1996). The role of lexical frequency in syntactic ambiguity resolution. *Journal of Memory and Language, 35,* 566–585.

Tsang, C.D., Trainor, L. J., Santesso, D. L., Tasker, S. L., & Schmidt, L.A. (2001). Frontal EEG responses as a function of affective musical features. In R. J. Zatorre & I. Peretz (Eds.), *Annals of the New York Academy of Sciences: Vol. 930. The Biological foundations of music* (pp. 439–442). New York: New York Academy of Sciences.

Tsoh, J. Y., McClure, J. B., Skaar, K. L., Wetter, D. W., Cinciripini, P. M., Prokhorov, A. V., Friedman, K., & Gritz, E. (1997). Smoking cessation 2: Components of effective intervention. *Behavioral Medicine, 23,* 15–27.

Tulving, E. (1972). Episodic and semantic memory. In E. Tulving & W. Donaldson (Eds.), *Organization of memory.* New York: Academic Press.

Tulving, E., Kapur, S., Craik, F. I. M., Moscovitch, M., & Houle, S. (1994). Hemispheric encoding/retrieval asymmetry in episodic memory: Positron emission tomography findings. *Proceedings of the National Academy of Sciences of the United States of America, 91,* 2016–2020.

Tulving, E., & Thompson, D. M. (1973). Encoding specificity and retrieval processes in episodic memory. *Psychological Review, 80,* 352–373.

Tupes, E. G., & Christal, R. C. (1961). *Recurrent personality factors based on trait ratings* (Tech. Rep. No. ASD-TR–61–97). Lackland Air Force Base, TX: U.S. Air Force.

Turk, D. C., & Okifuji, A. (2003). Psychological factors in chronic pain: Evolution and revolution. *Journal of Consulting and Clinical Psychology, 70,* 678–690.

Turner, M. E., & Pratkanis, A. R. (1998). A social identity maintenance model of groupthink. *Organizational Behavior and Human Decision Processes, 73,* 210–235.

Tversky, A., & Kahneman, D. (1973). Availability: A heuristic for judging frequency and probability. *Cognitive Psychology, 5,* 207–232.

Tversky, A., & Kahneman, D. (1981). The framing of decisions and the psychology of choice. *Science, 211,* 453–458.

Tversky, A., & Shafir, E. (1992). Choice under conflict: The dynamics of deferred decision. *Psychological Science, 3,* 358–361.

Tyler, L. E. (1965). *The psychology of human differences* (3rd ed.). New York: Appleton-Century-Crofts.

Underwood, B. J. (1948). Retroactive and proactive inhibition after five and forty-eight hours. *Journal of Experimental Psychology, 38,* 28–38.

Underwood, B. J. (1949). Proactive inhibition as a function of time and degree of prior learning. *Journal of Experimental Psychology, 39,* 24–34.

U. S. Department of Health and Human Services. (2000). *Reducing tobacco use: A report of the Surgeon General.* Atlanta, GA: U.S. Department of Health and Human Services.

Urban, J., Carlson, E., Egeland, B., & Stroufe, L. A. (1991). Patterns of individual adaptation across childhood. *Development and Psychopathology, 3,* 445–460.

Urbszat, D., Herman, C. P., & Polivy, J. (2002). Eat, drink, and be merry, for tomorrow we diet: Effects of anticipated deprivation on food intake in restrained and unrestrained eaters. *Journal of Abnormal Psychology, 111,* 396–401.

Uttal, D. H., & Perlmutter, M. (1989). Toward a broader conceptualization of development: The role of gains and losses across the life span. *Developmental Review, 9,* 101–132.

Vaillant, G. E. (1977). *Adaptation to life.* Boston: Little, Brown.

Valenstein, E. S. (Ed.). (1980). *The psychosurgery debate.* New York: Freeman.

Valenza, E., Simion, F., Cassia, V. M., & Umilta, C. (1996). Face preference at birth. *Journal of Experimental Psychology: Human Perception & Performance, 22,* 892–903.

Vandewater, K., & Vickers, Z. (1996). Higher-protein foods produce greater sensory-specific satiety. *Physiology & Behavior, 59,* 579–583.

Van IJzendoorn, M. H., & Kroonenberg, P. M. (1988). Cross-cultural patterns of attachment: A meta-analysis of the Strange Situation. *Child Development, 59,* 147–156.

Van Vianen, A. E. M. (2000). Person-organization fit: The match between newcomers' and recruiters' preferences for organizational culture. *Personnel Psychology, 53,* 113–149.

Vaughan, E., & Seifert, M. (1992). Variability in the framing of risk issues. *Journal of Social Issues, 48*(4), 119–135.

Veith, I. (1965). *Hysteria: The history of the disease.* Chicago: University of Chicago Press.

Vonnegut, M. (1975). *The Eden express.* New York: Bantam.

Voss, J. F., Kennet, J., Wiley, J., & Schooler, T. Y. E. (1992). Experts at debate: The use of metaphor in the U.S. Senate Debate on the Gulf Crisis. *Metaphor and Symbolic Activity, 7,* 197–214.

Vrana, S., & Lauterbach, D. (1994). Prevalence of traumatic events and post-traumatic psychological symptoms in a nonclinical sample of college students. *Journal of Traumatic Stress, 7,* 289–302.

Vroom, V. H. (1964). *Work and motivation.* New York: Wiley.

Vu, H., Kellas, G., Metcalf, K., & Herman, R. (2000). The influence of global discourse on lexical ambiguity resolution. *Memory & Cognition, 28,* 236–252.

Vu, H., Kellas, G., & Paul, S. T. (1998). Sources of constraint on lexical ambiguity resolution. *Memory & Cognition, 26,* 979–1001.

Wagner, A. D., Schacter, D. L., Rotte, M., Koutstaal, W., Maril, A., Dale, A. M., Rosen, B. R., & Buckner, R. L. (1998). Building memories: Remembering and forgetting of verbal experiences as predicted by brain activity. *Science, 281,* 1188–1191.

Wagner, U., van Dick, R., Pettigrew, T. F., & Christ, O. (2003). Ethnic prejudice in East and West Germany: The explanatory power of intergroup contact. *Group Processes & Intergroup Relations, 6,* 23–37.

Walden, J., Normann, C., Langosch, J., Berger, M., & Grunze, H. (1998). Differential treatment of bipolar disorder with old and new antiepileptic drugs. *Neuropsychobiology, 38,* 181–184.

Wallace, S. T., & Alden, L. E. (1997). Social phobia and positive social events: The price of success. *Journal of Abnormal Psychology, 106,* 416–424.

Wallach, M. A., & Wallach, L. (1983). *Psychology's sanction for selfishness.* San Francisco: Freeman.

Wallach, M. A., & Kogan, N. (1965). *Modes of thinking in young children.* New York: Holt, Rinehart & Winston.

Walsh, R. N. (1990). *The spirit of shamanism.* Los Angeles: J. P. Tarcher.

Walster, E., Aronson, V., Abrahams, D., & Rottman, L. (1966). Importance of physical attractiveness in dating behavior. *Journal of Personality and Social Psychology, 5,* 508–516.

Walters, C. C., & Grusec, J. E. (1977). *Punishment.* San Francisco: Freeman.

Ward, C. D., & Cooper, R. P. (1999). A lack of evidence in 4-month-old human infants for paternal voice preference. *Developmental Psychobiology, 35,* 49–59.

Warren, R. M. (1970). Perceptual restoration of missing speech sounds. *Science, 167,* 392–393.

Washburn, M. (1908). *The animal mind.* New York: Macmillan.

Wasserman, E. A. (1993). Comparative cognition: Beginning the second century of study of animal intelligence. *Psychological Bulletin, 113,* 211–228.

Wasserman, E. A. (1994). Animal learning and comparative cognition. In I. P. Levin & J. V. Hinrichs (Eds.), *Experimental psychology: Contemporary methods and applications* (pp. 117–164). Dubuque, IA: Brown & Benchmark.

Wasserman, E. A., DeVolder, C. L., & Coppage, D. J. (1992). Non-similarity-based conceptualization in pigeons via secondary or mediated generalization. *Psychological Science, 3,* 374–379.

Watkins, L. R., & Mayer, D. J. (1982). Organization of the endogenous opiate and nonopiate pain control systems. *Science, 216,* 1185–1193.

Watson, J. B. (1913). Psychology as the behaviorist views it. *Psychological Review, 20,* 158–177.

Watson, J. B. (1919). *Psychology from the standpoint of a behaviorist.* Philadelphia: Lippincott.

Watson, J. B. (1924). *Behaviorism.* New York: Norton.

Watson, J. B., & Rayner, R. (1920). Conditioned emotional reactions. *Journal of Experimental Psychology, 3,* 1–14.

Watterlond, M. (1983). The holy ghost people. Reprinted in A. L. Hammond & P. G. Zimbardo (Eds.), *Readings on human behavior: The best of* Science *'80–'86* (pp. 48–55). Glenview, IL: Scott, Foresman.

Watts, M. W. (1996). Political xenophobia in the transition from socialism: Threat, racism and ideology among East German youths. *Political Psychology, 17,* 97–126.

Wearden, A. J., Tarrier, N., Barrowclough, C., Zastowny. T. R., & Rahill, A. A. (2000). A review of expressed emotion research in health care. *Clinical Psychology Review, 20,* 633–666.

Webb, W. B. (1974). Sleep as an adaptive response. *Perceptual and Motor Skills, 38,* 1023–1027.

Wechsler, D. (1997). *Manual for the Wechsler Adult Intelligence Scale-III*. San Antonio, TX: Psychological Corporation.

Wechsler, D. (2002). *WPPSI-III manual*. San Antonio, TX: Psychological Corporation.

Wechsler, D. (2003). *WISC-IV manual*. San Antonio, TX: Psychological Corporation.

Wedekind, C., & Milinski, M. (2000). Cooperation through image scoring in humans. *Science, 288*, 850–852.

Weiner, J. (1994). *The beak of the finch*. New York: Knopf.

Weinfield, N. S., Ogawa, J. R., & Sroufe, L. A. (1997). Early attachment as a pathway to adolescent peer competence. *Journal of Research on Adolescence, 7*, 241–265.

Weingardt, K. R., Loftus, E. F., & Lindsay, D. S. (1995). Misinformation revisited: New evidence for the suggestibility of memory. *Memory & Cognition, 23*, 72–82.

Weisberg, R. W. (1986). *Creativity: Genius and other myths*. New York: Freeman.

Weisberg, R. W. (1994). Genius and madness? A quasi-experimental test of the hypothesis that manic-depression increases creativity. *Psychological Science, 5*, 361–367.

Weisberg, R. W. (1996). Causality, quality, and creativity: A reply to Repp. *Psychological Science, 7*, 123–124.

Weldon, M. S., Roediger, H. L., III, Beitel, D. A., Johnston, T. R. (1995). Perceptual and conceptual processes in implicit and explicit tests with picture fragment and word fragment cues. *Journal of Memory & Language, 34*, 268–285.

Wellman, H. M., & Inagaki, K. (1997). *The emergence of core domains of thought*. San Francisco: Jossey-Bass.

Wells, G. L., & Loftus, E. F. (2003). Eyewitness memory for people and events. In A. M. Goldstein (Ed.), *Handbook of psychology: Forensic psychology* (Vol. 11, pp. 149–160). New York: John Wiley & Sons.

Werker, J. F. (1991). The ontogeny of speech perception. In I. G. Mattingly & M. Studdert-Kennedy (Eds.), *Modularity and the motor theory of speech perception* (pp. 91–109). Hillsdale, NJ: Erlbaum.

Werker, J. F., & Lalond, F. M. (1988). Cross-language speech perception: Initial capabilities and developmental change. *Developmental Psychology, 24*, 672–683.

Werker, J. F., & Tees, R. C. (1999). Influences on infant speech processing: Toward a new synthesis. *Annual Review of Psychology, 50*, 509–535.

Wertheim, E. H., Paxton, S. J., Schutz, H. K., & Muir, S. L. (1997). Why do adolescent girls watch their weight? An interview study examining sociocultural pressures to be thin. *Journal of Psychosomatic Research, 42*, 345–355.

Wertheimer, M. (1923). Untersuchungen zur lehre von der gestalt, II. *Psychologische Forschung, 4*, 301–350.

Westen, D. (1998). The scientific legacy of Sigmund Freud: Toward a psychodynamically informed psychological science. *Psychological Bulletin, 124*, 333–371.

Wever, E. G. (1949). *Theory of hearing*. New York: Wiley.

Whitbourne, S. K., & Hulicka, I. M. (1990). Ageism in undergraduate psychology texts. *American Psychologist, 45*, 1127–1136.

White, J. L., & Mitler, M. M. (1997). The diagnostic interview and differential diagnosis for complaints of excessive daytime sleepiness. In M. R. Pressman & W. C. Orr (Eds.), *Understanding sleep: The evaluation and treatment of sleep disorders* (pp. 161–175). Washington, DC: American Psychological Association.

White, L., & Edwards, J. N. (1990). Emptying the nest and parental well-being: An analysis of national panel data. *American Sociological Review, 55*, 235–242.

White, R. K. (1996). Why the Serbs fought: Motives and misperceptions. *Peace and Conflict: Journal of Peace Psychology, 2*, 109–128.

Whorf, B. L. (1956). In J. B. Carroll (Ed.), *Language, and reality: Selected writings of Benjamin Lee Whorf*. Cambridge, MA: The MIT Press.

Wickelgren, I. (2003). Tapping the mind. *Science, 299*, 496–499.

Wicklund, R. A., & Brehm, J. W. (1976). *Perspectives on cognitive dissonance*. Hillsdale, NJ: Erlbaum.

Widdig, A., Streich, W. J., & Tembrock, G. (2000). Coalition formation among male Barbary macaques (*Macaca sylvanus*). *American Journal of Primatology, 51*, 37–51.

Wierzbicki, M., & Pekarik, G. (1993). A meta-analysis of psychotherapy dropout. *Professional Psychology: Research & Practice, 24*, 190–195.

Wiggins, J. S. (1973). *Personality and prediction: Principles of personality and prediction: Principles of personality assessment*. Reading, MA: Addison-Wesley.

Wiggins, J. S., & Pincus, A. L. (1992). Personality: Structure and assessment. *Annual Review of Psychology, 43*, 473–504.

Williams, L. M. (1995). Recovered memories of abuse in women with documented child sexual victimization histories. *Journal of Traumatic Stress, 8*, 649–673.

Williams, W. M., Blythe, T., White, N., Li, J., Gardner, H., Sternberg, R. J. (2002). Practical intelligence for school: Developing metacognitive sources of achievement in adolescence. *Developmental Review, 22*, 162–210.

Williams, W. M., & Ceci, S. J. (1997). Are Americans becoming more or less alike? Trends in race, class, and ability differences in intelligence. *American Psychologist, 52*, 1226–1235.

Williamson, G. M., Clark, M. S., Pegalis, L. J., & Behan, A. (1996). Affective consequences of refusing to help in communal and exchange relationships. *Personality and Social Psychology Bulletin, 22*, 34–47.

Wilson, R. I., & Nicoll, R. A. (2002). Endocannabinoid signaling in the brain. *Science, 296*, 678–682.

Wilson, S. I., & Edlund, T. (2001). Neural induction: Toward a unifying mechanism. *Nature Neuroscience, 4*, 1161–1168.

Wilson, T. D., Houston, C. E., Etling, K. M., & Brekke, N. (1996). A new look at anchoring effects: Basic anchoring and its antecedents. *Journal of Experimental Psychology: General, 125*, 387–402.

Winarick, K. (1997). Visions of the future: The analyst's expectations and their impact on the analytic process. *American Journal of Psychoanalysis, 57*, 95–109.

Windy, D., & Ellis, A. (1997). *The practice of rational emotive behavior therapy*. New York: Springer.

Witt, S. D. (1997). Parental influence of children's socialization to gender roles. *Adolescence, 32*, 253–259.

Witte, K., & Noltemeier, (2002). The role of information in mate-choice copying in female sailfin mollies (poecilia latipinna). *Behavioral Ecology and Sociobiology, 52*, 194–202.

Wolcott, S., & Strapp, C. M. (2002). Dream recall frequency and dream detail as mediated by personality, behavior, and attitude. *Dreaming, 12*, 27–44.

Wolf, M., Risley, T., & Mees, H. (1964). Application of operant conditioning procedures to the behavior problems of an autistic child. *Behavior Research and Therapy, 1*, 305–312.

Wolfe, J. M. (1992). The parallel guidance of visual attention. *Current Directions in Psychological Science, 1*, 124–128.

Wolfson, A. R., & Carskadon, M. A. (1998). Sleep schedules and daytime functioning in adolescents. *Child Development, 69,* 875–887.

Wolman, C. (1975). Therapy and capitalism. *Issues in Radical Therapy, 3*(1).

Wolpe, J. (1958). *Psychotherapy by reciprocal inhibition.* Stanford, CA: Stanford University Press.

Wolpe, J. (1973). *The practice of behavior therapy* (2nd ed.). New York: Pergamon Press.

Wolpe, J. (1986). Misconceptions about behaviour therapy: Their sources and consequences. *Behaviour Change, 3,* 9–15.

Wood, J. M., & Bootzin, R. R. (1990). The prevalence of nightmares and their independence from anxiety. *Journal of Abnormal Psychology, 99,* 64–68.

Wood, J. M., Bootzin, R. R., Kihlstrom, J. F., & Schacter, D. L. (1992). Implicit and explicit memory for verbal information presented during sleep. *Psychological Science, 3,* 236–239.

Wood, N., & Cowan, N. (1995a). The cocktail party phenomenon revisited: How frequent are attention shifts to one's name in an irrelevant auditory channel? *Journal of Experimental Psychology: Learning, Memory, and Cognition, 21,* 255–260.

Wood, N., & Cowan, N. (1995b). The cocktail party phenomenon revisited: Attention and memory in the classic selective listening procedure of Cherry (1953). *Journal of Experimental Psychology: General, 124,* 243–262.

Wood, R. E., & Bandura, A. (1989). Impact of conceptions of ability on self-regulatory mechanisms and complex decision making. *Journal of Personality and Social Psychology, 56,* 407–415.

Wood, W. (2000). Attitude change: Persuasion and social influence. *Annual Review of Psychology, 51,* 539–570.

Wood, W., & Eagly, A. H. (2002). A cross-cultural analysis of the behavior of women and men: Implications for the origins of sex differences. *Psychological Bulletin, 128,* 699–727.

Woods, S. C., Seeley, R. J., Porte, D., Jr., & Schwartz, M. W. (1998). Signals that regulate food intake and homeostasis. *Science, 280,* 1378–1383.

Worchel, S., Lee, J., & Adewole, A. (1975). Effects of supply and demand on ratings of object value. *Journal of Personality and Social Psychology, 32,* 906–914.

Workman, B. (1990, December 1). Father guilty of killing daughter's friend, in '69. *San Francisco Examiner-Chronicle,* pp. 1, 4.

Wright, E. R., Gronfein, W. P., & Owens, T. J. (2000). Deinstitutionalization, social rejection, and the self-esteem of former mental patients. *Journal of Health and Social Behavior, 41,* 68–90.

Wright, R. (1994). *The moral animal.* New York: Pantheon Books.

Wundt, W. (1907). *Outlines of psychology* (7th ed., C. H. Judd, Trans.). Leipzig: Englemann. (Original work published 1896)

Yantis, S. (1993). Stimulus-driven attentional capture. *Current Directions in Psychological Science, 2,* 156–161.

Yantis, S., & Jonides, J. (1996). Attentional capture by abrupt onsets: New perceptual objects or visual masking? *Journal of Experimental Psychology: Human Perception and Performance, 22,* 1505–1513.

Yau, J., & Smetana, J. G. (1996). Adolescent–parent conflict among Chinese adolescents in Hong Kong. *Child Development, 67,* 1262–1275.

Yeargin-Allsopp, M., Rice, C., Karapurkar, T., Doernberg, N., Boyle, C., & Murphy, C. (2003). Prevalence of autism in a US Metropolitan area. *JAMA, 289,* 49–55.

Yoon, C., May, C. P., & Hasher, L. (1999). Aging, circadian arousal patterns, and cognition. In D. C. Park & N. Schwarz (Eds.), *Cognitive aging: A primer* (pp. 151–172). Philadelphia: Psychology Press.

Young, M. A., Meaden, P. M., Fogg, L. F., Cherin, E. A., & Eastman, C. I. (1997). Which environmental variables are related to the onset of seasonal affective disorder? *Journal of Abnormal Psychology, 106,* 554–562.

Young, M. E., & Wasserman, E. A. (2001). Evidence for a conceptual account of same-different discrimination learning in the pigeon. *Psychonomic Bulletin & Review, 8,* 677–684.

Yzer, M. C., Fisher, J. D., Bakker, A. B., Siero, F. W., & Misovich, S. J. (1998). The effects of information about AIDS risk and self-efficacy on women's intentions to engage in AIDS preventive behavior. *Journal of Applied Social Psychology, 28,* 1837–1852.

Zahn-Waxler, C., Friedman, R. J., Cole, P. M., Mizuta, I., & Hiruma, N. (1996). Japanese and United States preschool children's responses to conflict and distress. *Child Development, 67,* 2462–2477.

Zajonc, R. B. (1968). Attitudinal effects of mere exposure. *Journal of Personality and Social Psychology. Monograph Supplement, 9*(2, Part 2), 1–27.

Zajonc, R. B. (2000). Feeling and thinking: Closing the debate over the independence of affect. In J. P. Forgas (Ed.), *Feeling and thinking: The role of affect in social cognition* (pp. 31–58). New York: Cambridge University Press.

Zajonc, R. B. (2001). Mere exposure: A gateway to the subliminal. *Current Directions in Psychological Science, 10,* 224–228.

Zaslow, M. J. (1991). Variation in child care quality and its implications for children. *Journal of Social Issues, 47,* 125–138.

Zeineh, M. M., Engel, S. A., Thompson, P. M., & Bookheimer, S. Y. (2003). Dynamics of the hippocampus during encoding and retrieval of face-name pairs. *Science, 299,* 577–580.

Zelazo, P. D., Helwig, C. C., & Lau, A. (1996). Intention, act, and outcome in behavioral prediction and moral judgment. *Child Development, 67,* 2478–2492.

Zelinski, E. M., Gilewski, M. J., & Schaie, K. W. (1993). Individual differences in cross-sectional and 3-year longitudinal memory performance across the adult life span. *Psychology and Aging, 8,* 176–186.

Zenderland, L. (1998). *Measuring minds: Henry Herbert Goddard and the origins of American intelligence testing.* Cambridge: Cambridge University Press.

Zentall, T. R., Sutton, J. E., & Sherburne, L. M. (1996). True imitative learning in pigeons. *Psychological Science, 7,* 343–346.

Zhang, Y., Proenca, R., Maffel, M., Barone, M., Leopold, L., & Friedman, J. M. (1994). Positional cloning of the mouse *obese* gene and its human homologue. *Nature, 372,* 425–432.

Zigler, E., & Muenchow, S. (1992). *Head Start: The inside story of America's most successful educational experiment.* New York: Basic Books.

Zigler, E., & Styfco, S. J. (1994). Head Start: Criticisms in a constructive context. *American Psychologist, 49,* 127–132.

Zilboorg, G., & Henry, G. W. (1941). *A history of medical psychology.* New York: Norton.

Zimbardo, P. G. (1975). On transforming experimental research into advocacy for social change. In M. Deutsch & H. Hornstein (Eds.), *Applying social psychology: Implications for research, practice and training.* Hillsdale, NJ: Erlbaum.

Zimbardo, P. G. (1991). *Shyness: What it is, what to do about it* (Rev. ed.). Reading, MA: Addison-Wesley. (Original book published 1977)

Zimbardo, P. G., & Leippe, M. (1991). *The psychology of attitude change and social influence.* New York: McGraw-Hill.

Zimbardo, P. G., & Montgomery, K. D. (1957). The relative strengths of consummatory responses in hunger, thirst, and exploratory drive. *Journal of Comparative and Physiological Psychology, 50,* 504–508.

Zimbardo, P. G., & Radl, S. L. (1999). *The shy child* (2nd ed.). Los Altos, CA: Malor Press.

Zimmerman, B. J., Bandura, A., & Martinez-Pons, M. (1992). Self-motivation for academic attainment: The role of self-efficacy beliefs and personal goal setting. *American Educational Research Journal, 29,* 663–676.

Zuckerman, E. (2003). Finding, evaluating, and incorporating Internet self-help resources into psychotherapy practice. *Journal of Clinical Psychology, 59,* 217–225.

Zuckerman, M. (1988). Sensation seeking, risk taking, and health. In M. P. Janisse (Ed.), *Individual differences, stress, and health psychology* (pp. 72–88). New York: Springer-Verlag.

Zuckerman, M. (1990). Some dubious premises in research and theory on racial differences: Scientific, social, and ethical issues. *American Psychologist, 45,* 1297–1303.

Zwaan, R. A., & Radvansky, G. A. (1998). Situation models in language comprehension and memory. *Psychological Bulletin, 123,* 162–185.

Name Index

Carlson-Radvansky, L. A., 127
Carmichael, L., 318
Carpenter, P. A., 217
Carskadon, M. A., 154
Carstensen, L. L., 337, 350, 357
Carter, J. H., 323
Cartwright, R. D., 151
Cartwright, S., 298, 474
Cash, T. F., 374
Caspi, A., 498
Catalan, J., 430
Catalano, R., 590
Catania, J. A., 423
Caterina, M. J., 123
Cattell, R., 295, 439
Cave, K. R., 147
Ceci, S. J., 297, 303, 317
Cervone, D., 442, 456
Ceschi, G., 486
Chae, Y. M., 273
Chaiken, S., 553, 554, 555
Chamberlain, K., 414
Chan, A. Y., 348
Chandrasekaran, B., 273
Chapman, P. D., 291
Charcot, J., 476
Chase, W. G., 215
Chater, N., 270
Chaudhari, N., 119
Chavajay, P., 329, 330
Chaves, J. F., 160
Chen, I., 32
Cheney, D. L., 145, 258
Cheng, P. W., 270
Cherry, E. C., 125
Chess, S., 188
Choice, P., 567
Chomsky, N., 335
Chorover, S., 474
Christal, R. C., 440
Christensen, A. J., 424
Cialdini, R. B., 556, 557, 559
Ciaranello, A. L., 490
Ciaranello, R. D., 490
Cicchetti, D., 151
Cici, S. J., 302
Claar, R. L., 427
Clark, E. V., 256, 334
Clark, H. H., 251, 253, 256
Clark, K., 558
Clark, M., 558
Clark, N. M., 424
Clarke-Stewart, K. A., 342
Clausen, J. A., 504
Clementz, B. A., 502
Clopton, N. A., 356
Clore, G. L., 565
Coates, T., 423
Cobain, K., 493
Cognan, J. C., 372
Cohen, D., 532, 593–594
Cohen, M. E., 273
Cohen, M. N., 303
Cohen, N., 426, 427
Cohen, S., 411, 419
Cohn, E. G., 591

Coleman, R. M., 149
Coles, C., 319
Collaer, M. L., 352
Collins, M. A., 308
Collins, W. A., 340
Columbus, C., 99
Comstock, G., 200, 594
Conner, K. R., 492
Cook, T. D., 346
Coolidge, F. L., 494, 498
Cooper, L. A., 261
Cooper, R. P., 320
Corbett, A. T., 257
Coren, S., 112
Corina, D. P., 76
Corr, P. J., 386
Corso, J. F., 323
Coslett, H. B., 239
Costa, P. T., Jr., 440, 465–466
Couture, S., 505
Cover Jones, M., 518
Cowan, C. P., 348, 410
Cowan, N., 125, 143, 213
Cowan, P., 348, 410
Cowan, W. M., 318
Cowles, J. T., 187
Cox, C., 372
Craighead, W. E., 490
Craik, F. I. M., 224, 331, 332
Cramer, P., 449
Crandall, C. S., 562
Cranson, R. W., 161
Creasey, G., 415
Crockett, L. J., 336
Crowder, R. G., 212, 214, 219, 221
Crowley, K., 317
Csikszentmihalyi, M., 144
Cummins, D. D., 270
Curie, C., 302
Curie, I., 302
Curie, M., 302
Curtis, R. C., 565
Cutting, J. C., 128, 254
Czeisler, C. A., 149

Dahlstrom, W. G., 464
Dakof, G. A., 419
Dalie, S., 97
Damasio, A. R., 404
Damasio, H., 71
Daneman, M., 217
Darby, J., 605
Darley, J. M., 585, 586
Darling, N., 340, 341
Darnton, R., 476
Darwin, C., 56–58, 197, 286, 394, 395
Darwin, C. J., 212
D'Augelli, A. R., 382, 493
Davidson, A. R., 86, 552
Davidson, R. J., 399–400, 589
Davies, I. R. L., 259
Da Vinci, L., 452
Davison, K. P., 530

Dawkins, K., 533
DeCasper, A. J., 319, 320
Deckro, G. R., 426
DeGracia, D. J., 157
Degreef, G., 502
Dehaene, S., 249
Dejin-Karlsson, E., 319
Delaney, A. J., 164
Delprato, D. J., 171
Dement, W. C., 154
Denton, K., 317
De Rivera, J., 516
Descartes, R., 62–63
De St. Aubin, E., 350
De Valois, R. L., 112
Devereux, G., 513
Devine, P. G., 562
DeVos, J., 328
Dew, M. A., 150
Dewey, J., 10–11
De Witte, P., 164
Dewsbury, D. A., 375
Dhawan, N., 460
DiDomenico, L., 372
Digman, J. M., 440
DiLalla, L. F., 589
Di Marzo, V., 164
Dineen, B. R., 387
Dinges, M. M., 345
Dion, K. K., 566
Dion, K. L., 566
Dirkzwager, A. J. E., 419
Dishman, R. K., 425
Ditto, P. H., 561
Dixon, M. J., 503
Dixon, R. A., 316, 330
Dollard, J., 453, 590
Domhoff, G. W., 155, 156
Domjan, M., 39
Donald, M., 145
Donchin, E., 83
Donders, F. C., 247
Donnay, D. A. C., 387
Donnerstein, E., 200
Dosher, B. A., 257
Dovidio, J. F., 562
Downing, P. E., 107
Draijer, N., 495
Drayna, D., 61
Drigotas, S. M., 567
Drozd, J. F., 537
Dryfoss, J. G., 336
Dudycha, G. J., 442
Duker, P. C., 520
Duncker, D., 268
Durik, A. M., 378
Durkin, S. J., 372
Durlak, J. A., 538
Dutton, D. G., 400
Dweck, C. S., 367

Eagly, A. H., 352, 553, 554, 555, 564
Ebbinghaus, H., 9, 206–207, 208, 223
Eckensberger, L. H., 355
Edinger, J. D., 153

Edlund, T., 88
Edwards, J. N., 349
Egidi, G., 257
Eich, E., 404, 516
Einstein, A., 261
Eisenberg, M., 337
Ekman, P., 395, 396, 399
Elbert, T., 88
Elizabeth II, England, 316
Ellis, A., 526
Elman, J. L., 135
Elms, A. C., 452
Ely, R. J., 549
Emery, G., 486
Emmelkamp, P. M. G., 519
Emmons, M. L., 523
Endler, N. S., 418
Engle, R. W., 217
Enserink, M., 535, 589
Epstine, L. H., 368
Erbring, L., 445, 568
Ericsson, K. A., 144, 215, 266–267
Erikson, E., 337–338, 345, 347, 350
Eshleman, A., 562
Esler, W. P., 237
Espie, C. A., 153
Esser, J. K., 580
Estrada, C. A., 406
Evans, A., 171, 189
Evans, D. A., 237
Evans, J. S. B., 270
Evans-Pritchard, E. E., 513
Exner, J. E., Jr., 466, 467
Eysenck, H., 437, 439, 535

Fadiman, J., 451, 517
Fagot, B. I., 353
Fallon, A. E., 179
Fantuzzo, J., 523
Faraday, M., 260–261
Farina, A., 505
Farine, J. P., 118, 375
Faucheux, C., 580
Fazio, R. H., 550, 551, 556
Feather, N. T., 383
Fechner, G., 99
Fellows, J. L., 421
Fernald, A., 30, 333
Fernandez-Ballesteros, R., 347
Ferster, C. B., 192
Festinger, L., 366, 554–555
Fields, H. L., 121
Fields, R. D., 80
Fiorito, G., 199
Fischer, K. W., 148
Fischoff, B., 219
Fisher, B. S., 380
Fisher, J. D., 423
Fisher, S., 155
Fishman, H. C., 529, 530
Fishman, T., 529
Fiske, S. T., 545
Fivush, R., 353
Flavell, J. G., 326, 328

Fleming, I., 262
Foa, E. B., 413
Fobair, P., 530
Folkman, S., 415, 416
Fombonne, E., 497
Ford, C. S., 375
Forgas, J. P., 403, 404
Foucault, M., 512
Foulkes, D., 154
Fowler, H., 364
Fowler, R. D., 19
Fox, M. J., 88
Frager, R., 451, 517
Fraley, B., 567
Fraley, R. C., 565
Frank, J. B., 535
Frank, J. D., 535
Frank, M. E., 119
Franklin, G., 516
Franklin, N., 262–263
Franklin-Lipsker, E., 516
Frantz, R., 320
Franz, C. E., 383
Fraser, S. C., 557
Freedman, J. L., 557
Freedman, M. S., 149
Freeman, M. S., 319
Freud, A., 12, 344
Freud, S., 12, 15, 43, 143–144, 155, 307, 341, 344, 347, 366, 444, 445–449, 452, 458, 476, 477, 490, 514–515, 516, 517
Freund, A. M., 331, 350, 357
Frick F., 270
Friedman, M., 428
Friedman, R., 426
Friend, R., 578
Friesen, W. V., 395, 396
Frijda, N. H., 397
Fromkin, V. A., 254
Fromm, E., 159
Fuhriman, A., 528
Fulero, S. M., 480
Fuligni, A. J., 346
Fuller, B., 342
Funt, A., 581
Furmark, T., 536
Furnham, A., 466
Fussell, S. R., 253

Gabrieli, J. D. E., 240
Gabrieli, J. D. F., 225
Gackenbach, J., 157
Gage, P., 63, 64, 71
Gagnon, J. H., 379
Gaines, S. O., Jr., 348
Galambos, N. L., 345
Galen, 436–437, 439
Gallo, L. C., 413
Galperin, G. J., 480
Galton, F., 286–287
Gandhi, M., 593
Garb, H. N., 467
Garcia, J., 177, 193, 194–195
Garcia, M. M., 32
Gardner, B. T., 258
Gardner, H., 297–298, 299, 307–308, 452

Gardner, R. A., 258
Gardner, R., Jr., 568
Garland, A. F., 345
Garrison, V., 513
Gatchel, R. J., 121
Gawin, F. H., 164
Gazzaniga, M., 74, 75
Gegenfurtner, K. R., 211
Gelman, S. A., 328, 329
Gendron, J., 86
Genovese, K., 585
George, C., 343
Gergen, K. J., 15
Gerra, G., 163
Gerrig, R. J., 257, 260, 554
Gershon, E. S., 490
Ghadirian, A. M., 539
Giambra, L. M., 332
Gibbons, A., 59
Gibson, E., 321
Gibson, J. J., 128
Gidron, Y., 429
Giesler, R. B., 491
Gillespie, J. M., 343
Gilligan, C., 355–356
Gilligan, S., 404
Gilovich, T., 547
Giron, M., 503
Giros, B., 164
Gitlin, M., 533, 538
Gladue, B. A., 381
Glanz, K., 519
Glaser, R., 427
Gleaves, D. H., 496
Glenny, M., 602
Glovinsky, P. B., 153
Gobet, F., 267
Goddard, H., 287, 300–301
Gogwiec, A., 303
Goldfried, M. R., 537
Goldin-Meadow, S., 335
Goldrick, M., 254
Goldsmith, H. H., 494
Goldstein, E. B., 134
Gomez-Beneyto, M., 503
Gonzalez, A., 563
Goodall, J., 36, 588
Gooden, D. R., 219
Goodison, T., 181
Gorfein, D. S., 256
Gormican, S., 147
Goshen-Gottstein, Y., 239
Gottesman, I., 500
Gottfredson, L. S., 290, 305
Gottlieb, G., 339
Gottman, J. M., 349
Gould, E., 89
Gould, M. S., 493
Gould, S. J., 57, 302
Graesser, A. C., 257
Graham, M., 307
Grant, K. E., 496
Grant, L., 171, 189
Grant, P., 57, 58
Grant, R., 57, 58
Gray, J. A., 386
Gray, M. R., 340

Green, B. L., 484
Green, D. C., 117
Green, D. M., 101
Greenberg, R., 155
Greene, J. D., 406
Greene, R. L., 465
Greenfield, P. M., 305
Greeno, C. G., 370
Greenwald, A. G., 33
Grice, H. P., 251, 252
Griffin, K., 425
Grigorenko, E. L., 299, 302
Grohol, M., 512
Gross, A., 404
Gross, A. M., 380, 425
Gross, C. G., 89
Grossman, M. I., 368
Grunhaus, L., 532
Grusec, J. E., 189
Guilford, J. P., 295–296
Guilleminault, C., 153
Guisewite, C., 511
Gumperz, J. J., 259
Gura, T., 370

Haas, S. M., 348
Hagan, R., 353
Haines, B. A., 385
Hall, D., 199
Hall, G. S., 9, 344
Halsey, C., 342
Hamer, D. H., 381, 405
Hamilton, M., 225
Haney, C., 574
Hankin, B. L., 492, 496
Harder, J. W., 388
Hardy, J., 237
Hargadon, R., 160
Hariri, A. R., 399, 498
Harle, V., 600
Harlow, H. F., 341, 343, 364
Harlow, J. M., 63
Harmon, L. W., 387
Harris, B., 179
Harrison, L. M., 164
Harrison, Y., 151
Hart, D., 354
Hart, J. T., 227, 229
Hartshorne, H., 442
Hartup, W. H., 345
Hastorf, A. H., 544
Hatcher, C., 528
Hatchett, L., 419
Hathaway, S., 464
Haugen, J. A., 550
Hawkes, S., 584
Hazan, C., 565, 566
Hazeltine, E., 70
Healy, A. F., 216
Hearst, E., 174
Heatherton, T. F., 374, 564
Hebl, M. R., 374, 564
Hegelson, V. S., 429
Heider, F., 367, 545
Heine, S. J., 555
Hektner, J. M., 144
Helgeson, V. S., 419
Heller, H. C., 152, 156
Helmes, E., 465
Helmholtz, H. von, 112, 116

Helmuth, L., 237
Henderson, L., 445
Henry, G. W., 475, 512
Henry, W. P., 514, 515
Hentschel, U., 449
Herek, G. M., 381, 382
Hering, E., 112
Herman, P., 369–370
Hernández-Guzmán, L., 523
Hernnstein, R. J., 302
Hersen, M., 538
Hersh, S. M., 596
Hertzog, C., 332
Herz, R. S., 219
Hess, W., 64
Hettema, J. M., 485, 498
Hewstone, M., 560
Hickok, G., 76
Higgie, M., 58
Higgins, M., 521
Hilgard, E. R., 9, 158
Hilgetag, C. C., 108
Hill, S. K., 459
Himelstein, P., 528
Hinckley, J., 480
Hines, M., 352
Hinton, A. L., 600
Hintzman, D. L., 231
Hippocrates, 436, 437, 439
Hirt, E. R., 459
Hitler, A., 287, 601
Hobson, J. A., 156
Hoffman, C., 233
Hoffman, L. W., 342
Hoffman, M. L., 403
Hofling, C. K., 598
Hohmann, A. A., 537
Holahan, C. J., 419
Holden, C., 59
Holen, M. C., 228
Hollon, S. D., 534, 537
Holmbeck, G. N., 345
Holmes, D. S., 534
Holmes, T. H., 411
Holtgraves, T., 277
Holyoak, K. J., 270, 271
Honzik, C. H., 197
Hopson, J. L., 375
Horne, J. A., 26, 151
Horney, K., 450, 451
Houghton, J., 504
Houlihan, D., 519
Hovland, C. I., 603
Howe, El, 156
Hubel, D., 107
Hudson, D. L., 273
Huesmann, L. R., 200, 594
Huey, R. B., 57
Hulicka, I. M., 351
Hull, C., 363
Hultsch, D. F., 331
Humayun, M., 109
Hume, D., 193
Hummert, M. L., 351
Humphrey, T., 318
Hunt, E., 260
Hurvich, L., 112
Hussein, S., 601
Huston, A. C., 336

Hyde, J. S., 356, 378

Inagaki, K., 328
Insko, C. A., 577
Irvine, J. T., 397
Irwin, D. E., 127
Isaacs, E. A., 253
Isen, A. M., 403, 406
Ishii-Kuntz, M., 347
Ito, T. A., 591
Ivry, R. B., 70
Izard, C. E., 395, 402

Jaccard, J. J., 552
Jackon, R. S., 370
Jackson, L. A., 564
Jacobs, G. H., 112
Jacobs, R. C., 577
Jacobsen, P. B., 195
Jacobson, L., 548
Jacobson, N. S., 525
Jaffee, S., 356
Jahnke, J. C., 219
James, H., 9
James, S. E., 348
James, W., 9, 11, 142, 145, 161, 162, 365, 400, 458
Jameson, D., 112
Janis, I. L., 270, 580
Janofsky, J. S., 480
Janowitz, H. D., 368
Jedrej, M. C., 156
Jenike, M. A., 485
Jenkins, L., 217
Jensen, A. R., 228
Jensen-Campbell, L. A., 584
Jobes, D. A., 493
Johar, G. V., 551
Johnson, J. R., 368
Johnson, M. K., 235, 236, 516
Johnson, S. M., 529
Johnson, T. D., 339
Johnson, T. E., 592
Johnson, V. E., 376–377
Johnson, W., 490
Johnson-Laird, P. N., 270
Jones, E., 444
Jones, J. M., 339, 558
Jonides, J., 124
Jordan, D. S., 98
Joyce, A. S., 512
Joyce, L., 84
Judge, T. A., 387
Jung, C., 450, 458
Jusczyk, P. W., 334
Jussim, L., 548

Kabaat-Zinn, J., 160
Kagan, J., 444
Kahneman, D., 274, 275, 276, 277, 279, 280
Kallikak, M., 300
Kallman, F. J., 500
Kamil, A. C., 197
Kamin, L. J., 178
Kantarowitz, B., 310
Kantor, G. K., 188
Kaplan, C. A., 267
Kaplan, R. M., 538
Karbe, H., 88
Karin-D'Arry, M. R., 258

Karney, B. R., 349
Karraker, K. H., 352
Kasparov, G., 267
Kassebaum, N. L., 304
Katsanis, J., 502
Katz, R., 513–514
Kay, P., 259
Kazdin, A. E., 190, 518, 521, 523
Kegeles, S. M., 423
Keiger, D., 308
Kekulé, A. F., 156, 260
Keller, M. B., 537, 538
Kelley, H., 545
Kelley, J. E., 428
Kelman, H., 605
Kempermann, G., 89
Kempton, W., 259
Kendler, H. H., 9, 11
Kendler, K. S., 422
Kendrick, T., 538
Kennedy, J. R., 580
Kennedy, P. T., 83, 271
Kennedy, R. E., 490
Kenny, D. A., 565
Kessel, N., 308
Kessler, R. C., 472, 481, 482, 488, 497, 530
Kety, S. S., 500
Kiecolt-Glaser, J., 427
Kihlstrom, J. R., 457
Killen, J., 580
Kilpatrick, D. J., 484
Kim, M. S., 147
Kimura, D., 77
King, M. L., Jr., 438
King, R. G., 597
King, S. A., 503, 511
Kinney, D. K., 501
Kinsey, A., 378, 380
Kintner, C., 88
Kintsch, W., 256
Kirkpatrick, L. A., 566
Kirsch, I., 158, 159
Kirschner, S. M., 480
Kisilevsky, B. S., 320
Kitamura, C., 333
Kitayama, S., 460, 546, 593
Kite, M. E., 351
Klein, K. E., 149
Klein, M., 517
Kleitman, N., 150
Kluckhohn, C., 513
Knee, C. R., 279
Knoedler, A. J., 219
Knox, C., 604
Koelling, R. A., 195
Koffka, K., 126
Kogan, N., 307
Kohlberg, L., 354–355
Köhler, W., 126
Kolb, B., 318
Kontis, T. C., 233
Koopman, C., 495
Koren, G., 319
Koriat, A., 219, 229
Kortegaard, L. S., 372
Kosslyn, S. M., 64, 261

Kotovsky, K., 267
Kraepelin, E., 475
Kram, E., 444–445
Krauss, R. M., 253
Kraut, R., 445, 568
Kronenberg, P. M., 339
Krueger, J., 458
Kübler, A., 83
Kuest, J., 88
Kuhn, M. H., 460
Kuijer, R. G., 419
Kujawski, J. H., 352
Kuldau, J. M., 361, 374
Kuno, E., 513
Kunzmann, U., 331
Kuperberg, G. R., 502

LaBerge, S., 157–158
Ladd, G. W., 336
Lalond, F. M., 333
Lambo, T. A., 513
Lamke, L. K., 567
Land, D., 345
Lander, E. S., 60
Landin, A. M., 119
Lang, F. R., 357
Lange, C., 400
Langeland, W., 495
Langer, E., 332
Lanius, R. A., 485
Larner, A. J., 121
Larson, G., 198
Lashley, K., 238
Latané, B., 580, 585, 586
Laumann, E. O., 379
Lauterbach, D., 484
La Voie, L., 565
Lawler, E. E., 387
Lay, C. H., 411
Lazarus, B. N., 400, 415, 417
Lazarus, R. S., 400, 414, 415, 416, 417
Leaper, C., 353
Leary, M. R., 424, 592
Leathers, S. J., 343
LeCompte, D. C., 212
Lederbogen, S., 156
Lee, M., 45
Lee-Sammons, W. H., 217
Leger, D., 193
LeGrand, L. E., 530
Lehman, D. R., 555
Lehmann, H. E., 539
Lein, E. B., 537
Leippe, M., 425
Leiter, M. P., 429
Lencer, R., 502
Lennon, R. T., 291
Lerner, M., 600
Leucht, S., 533
Levanthal, H., 400
LeVay, S., 381
Levelt, W., 254
Levenson, R. W., 349, 399, 402, 410
Leventhal, T., 336
Levine, J. D., 121
Levine, R., 566

Levine, S. B., 324
Levinson, S. C., 259
Lévi-Strauss, C., 513
Levitan, L., 157
Levy, B., 332
Levy, G. D., 353
Levy, J. A., 324
Levy, S. R., 233
Levy-Sadot, R., 229
Lewin, K., 367, 603
Lewinsohn, P. M., 490
Lewis, B. S., 219
Lewis, J. R., 155
Lewis, M., 148
Lieu, J. H., 580
Liker, J. K., 297
Lilienfeld, S. O., 495
Lincoln, A., 438
Lindsay, D. S., 236
Link, B. G., 505
Liotti, M., 489
Lipkus, I. M., 422
Liu, W, 109
Lloyd-Jones, T. J., 261
Locke, J., 144, 324–325
Lockhart, R. S., 224
Loehlin, J. C., 302, 303, 441
Loftus, E. F., 235, 236, 516
Logan, G. D., 249
Logue, A. W., 367, 368
Loomis, A. L., 150
Lopez, A. D., 488
Lore, R. K., 588, 593
Lorenz, K., 339, 588
Lourenço, O., 328, 329
Lovibond, S. H., 574
Lubart, T. I., 307, 308
Lubin, B., 466
Lucas, R. E., 405
Luce, K. H., 511
Luckhurst, L., 261
Luo, M., 118, 375
Luzzo, D. A., 386
Lykken, D., 405
Lynch, J. W., 413
Lynn, S. J., 158, 159, 495, 516
Lyons, N., 356
Lytton, H., 353

Ma, V., 461
Maas, J., 153–154
Macaulay, D., 404
Maccoby, E. E., 340, 353
MacDonald, M. C., 256
Machado, A., 328, 329
Macleod, C., 275
Madon, S., 549
Madonna, 438
Magee, W. J., 483
Magnusson, D., 344
Maguen, S., 382
Mahoney, A., 188
Mahoney, J. L., 344
Maier, N. R. F., 268
Maier, S. F., 490
Main, M., 343

Runco, M. A., 307
Rundle, H. D., 57
Rusbult, C. E., 567, 569
Rush, A. J., 525
Ryan, L., 26, 29
Ryckman, R. M., 380
Ryff, C. D., 350

Saarinen, T. F., 263
Saberi, K., 98
Sackheim, H. A., 531
Sagi, A., 342
Sah, P., 164
Salovey, P., 297
Salthouse, T. A., 331
Samuda, R. J., 305
Samuel, A. G., 135, 136
Sanderson, C. A., 457
Sapir, E., 259
Sapolsky, R. M., 406
Satis, V., 530
Sato, S., 147
Savage-Rumbaugh, E. S., 258
Scarr, S., 337, 342
Schab, F. R., 219
Schachter, S., 369, 400
Schaeken, W., 269
Schaie, K. W., 331, 351
Scharrer, E., 594
Schaufeli, W. B., 429
Scheider, W., 249
Schiff, M., 530
Schlenger, W. E., 412
Schlitz, M., 155
Schmidt, L. A., 378
Schmidt, N. B., 86, 486
Schmidt, S. E., 529
Schmitt, D. P., 378
Schneider, K., 527
Schoeneman, T. J., 461
Schonert-Reichl, K. A., 344
Schooler, J. W., 516
Schou, M., 534
Schreiber, T. A., 236
Schroeder, D. A., 403
Schultz, L. A., 588
Schultz, R., 495
Schwartz, B. L., 229
Schwartz, D., 595
Schwartz, J. M., 536
Schwarzer, R., 526
Scott, D., 192, 403, 521
Scotto, P., 199
Scull, A., 513
Searle, J. R., 260
Secord, P. F., 565
Sedikides, C., 461
Segall, M. H., 592
Segerstrom, S. C., 429
Seidenberg, M. S., 258
Seidler, R. D., 70
Seifert, M., 280

Sekuler, R., 119
Self, E. A., 459
Selfridge, O. G., 137
Seligman, M. E. P., 384, 385, 429, 472–473, 475, 490–491
Selkoe, D. J., 237
Selye, H., 409
Sengupta, J., 551
Sergent, S. D., 236
Serpell, R., 305, 330
Serrano, J. M., 395
Seurat, G., 5, 6
Sexton, J., 550, 554
Seyfarth, R. M., 145, 258
Seys, D. M., 520
Shafir, E., 278, 280
Shapiro, K. J., 39
Shapiro, L. P., 256
Shapiro, S. L., 160
Sharpsteen, D. J., 566
Sharrer, E., 200
Shaver, P. R., 565, 566
Shavitt, S., 554
Shaw, G. B., 548
Shaywitz, B. A., 77
Shealy, C. N., 343
Shear, M. K., 537
Sheehan, E. P., 388
Sheldon, W., 437
Shepard, R. N., 98, 128, 156, 260, 261
Sheridan, C. L., 597
Sherif, C. W., 544
Sherif, M., 562, 577
Sherrington, C., 172
Sherrod, K., 343
Shettleworth, S. J., 197
Shiffrar, M., 128
Shiffrin, R. M., 213, 249
Shimamura, A. P., 331
Shneidman, E. S., 492
Shoda, Y., 442, 443, 454–455
Sholnick, E. K., 328
Shor, R. E., 159
Shortliffe, E. H., 273
Shrum, L. J., 276
Shulman, S., 345
Shultz, L. A., 593
Sia, T. L., 552
Siegel, J. M., 152
Siegel, R. K., 161
Siegel, S., 180–181
Siegelman, M., 382
Siegert, R., 330
Siegler, R. S., 276, 317
Silbereisen, L. K., 336
Silver, E., 480
Silverman, A. B., 343
Simkin, L. R., 425
Simmons, J. A., 117
Simon, H. A., 144, 265, 266–267, 274

Simon, T., 290
Simons, D. J., 127
Sinclair, R. C., 400
Singer, D. G., 200
Singer, J. L., 200, 449
Singer, L. T., 319
Singer, T., 330
Sireteanu, R., 320
Skeel, J., 277
Skinner, B. F., 13, 171, 182–183, 184, 190, 192, 521
Skre, U., 485
Slaski, M., 298
Sloane, R. B., 518
Slobin, D. I., 259, 335
Sloman, S. A., 224
Slovic, P., 278
Smallidge, M., 389
Smetana, J. G., 345
Smith, J., 331
Smith, K., 33
Smith, M. V., 260
Smith, S. L., 200
Smith, T. W., 429
Snyder, M., 549, 550
Socrates, 9
Solomon, A., 487
Solso, R. L., 230
Sommer, W., 65
Sonnad, S. S., 153
Sorell, G. T., 356
Sowell, E. R., 323
Spangler, W. D., 467
Spearman, C., 295
Spellman, B. A., 270
Spence, M. J., 319
Sperling, G., 211, 212
Sperry, R., 74
Spiegel, D., 160, 534
Spielman, A. J., 153
Spitz, R. A., 343
Spooner, W. A., 253–254
Squire, L. R., 239
Stafford, L., 348
Stahl, S. M., 164
Stams, G.-J. J. M., 340
Stanke, D., 458
Staub, E., 600, 605
Staudinger, U. M., 330, 331
Stead, D., 228
Steele, C. M., 305, 459, 561
Steens, J. A., 128
Stein, M. B., 485
Steinberg, L., 340, 341
Stemberger, J. P., 254
Stephan, W. G., 398, 461
Stern, M., 352
Stern, P. C., 602
Stern, W., 291
Sternberg, R. J., 290, 296–297, 299, 307, 308

Sternberg, S., 216
Stevens-Graham, B., 80
Stevenson, H., 306
Stewart, J. H., 188
Stickgold, R., 152, 156
Stone, A. A., 415
Stong, S., 192
Stoppard, T., 605
Strakowski, S. M., 489
Strapp, C. M., 156
Strassberg, Z., 188
Strauch, I., 156
Straus, M. A., 188
Stravinsky, I., 307
Striegel-Moore, R. H., 374
Strong, E., 387
Stuart, E. M., 426
Stunkard, A. J., 370
Styfco, S. J., 304–305
Suboski, M. D., 199
Sullivan, H. S., 517
Sulloway, F., 437, 438
Suomi, S., 343
Suzuki, L. A., 302, 303
Swann, W. B., Jr., 491, 549
Swazey, J. P., 532
Sweeney, J. A., 502
Swets, J. A., 101
Sykora, C., 414
Szasz, T., 474
Szymanski, S., 502

Tacon, A. M., 161
Tanofsky-Kraff, W., 370
Taylor, C. B., 511
Taylor, M. G., 352
Taylor, S. E., 408, 419, 545
Teasdale, J. D., 525
Tedlock, B., 155
Tees, R. C., 333
Tellegen, A., 405
Templin, M., 334
Tennen, H., 417
Terman, L. M., 287, 291, 301
Teresa, Mother, 438
Terman, L. M., 287, 291, 301
Thagard, P., 271
Thapar, A., 496
Theeuwes, J., 124
Thomas, A. K., 188, 235
Thomas, E., 310
Thompson, S. C., 418
Thomson, D., 218
Thorndike, E. L., 181–182, 291
Thorsen, C. E., 429
Tice, D. M., 411
Tidwell, M.-C. O., 566
Titchener, E., 9, 10, 142
Todd, J. T., 193
Todrank, J., 98
Tolman, E. C., 197
Tomkins, S., 395
Tomoyasu, N., 196

Tompson, M. C., 502
Torrance, E. P., 307
Torsky, Lara, 559
Towles-Schwen, T., 550
Townsend, J. T., 216
Trainor, L. J., 86, 333
Trebby, J., 299
Treisman, A., 147
Triandis, H. C., 297, 397, 460, 513
Trivers, R. L., 377, 583
Trueswell, J. C., 256
Trynes, K., 213
Tsang, C. D., 86
Tsoh, J. T., 423
Tulving, E., 218, 222, 240
Tupes, E. G., 440
Turk, D. C., 121
Turner, M. E., 580
Tversky, A., 274, 275, 276, 277, 280
Tversky, B., 262–263
Twenge, J. M., 378
Tyler, L. E., 437

Underwood, B. J., 223
Urban, J., 340
Urbszat, D., 371
Uttal, D. H., 316

Vaidya, R. S., 491
Vaillant, G., 350
Va Lange, P. A. M., 567
Valencia, R. R., 302, 303
Valenza, E., 320
Van Der Wege, M. M., 251
Vandewater, K., 368
Van Gogh, V., 309
Van IJzendoorn, M. H., 339
Van Vianen, A. E. M., 387
Vaughan, C., 154
Vaughan, E., 280
Veith, I., 475
Vicary, J. M., 40
Vickers, Z. M., 368
Victoria, England, 480
Voltaire, 97
Vonnegut, K., 498
Vonnegut, M., 498–499
Voss, J. R., 601
Vrana, S., 484
Vroom, V. H., 388
Vu, H., 144, 256
Vygotsky, L., 329–330

Wagner, A. D., 240
Wagner, L. S., 351
Wagner, U., 563
Walden, J., 534

Walk, R., 321
Wallace, S. T., 483
Wallach, L., 517
Wallach, M. A., 307
Walsh, R. N., 513
Walster, E. H., 564, 566
Walters, A. S., 154
Walters, C. C., 189
Ward, C. D., 320
Warren, R. M., 135
Washburn, A. L., 367–368
Washburn, M., 10
Wason, P. C., 270
Wasserman, E. A., 197, 198–199
Watkins, L. R., 121
Watkins, M. J., 212
Watson, J., 12–13, 171, 179, 319, 486
Watterlond, M., 162
Watts, M. W., 600
Wearden, A. J., 503
Webb, W. B., 151
Weber, E., 102
Wechsler, D., 292–293
Wedekind, C., 583
Wegener, D. T., 552
Wegmann, H. M., 149
Weinberg, M. S., 382
Weinberg, R. A., 60
Weiner, I. B., 467
Weiner, J., 57
Weinfield, N. S., 340
Weingardt, K. R., 236
Weisberg, R., 308
Weldon, M. S., 225
Wellman, H. M., 328, 329
Wells, A. M., 538
Wells, G. L., 235, 516
Werker, J. F., 333
Wertheim, E. H., 372
Wertheimer, M., 10, 126
Westbay, L., 565
Westen, D., 144, 146, 449
Wethington, E., 348
Wever, E. G., 116
Whalen, H., 8
Whitbourne, S. K., 351
White, J. L., 154
White, L., 349
White, R. K., 602
Whitehurst, A., 516
Whitlow, T., 574
Whitney, P., 217
Whorf, B. L., 259
Wickelgren, I., 83
Wicklund, R. A., 555
Widdig, A., 583
Wierzbicki, M., 537
Wiesel, T., 107
Wiggins, J. S., 286, 439, 440
Williams, C. L., 465

Subject Index

Anxiety sensitivity, 486
Anxiety-to-excitement reversal, 365
Anxious-ambivalent attachment style, 566
Aphasia, Broca's, 74
Appetitive stimuli, 183
Application of theory, 17
Appreciation, 170
Approach-related emotions, 440
Aqueous humor, 104
Arbitrary anchors, 277
Archetypes, 450
Artificial intelligence (AI), 273
Asch effect, 577–578, 579
Aspirations, 346–347
Assessment. *See also* Intelligence assessment
    criterion validity, 288–289
    defined, 286
    face validity, 288
    formal assessment, 287–289
    history of, 286–287
    norms, 289–290
    of personality, 464–467
    reliability and, 287–288
    standardization and, 289–290
    validity and, 288–289
Assimilation, 234, 325
Association cortex, 72
Athletic performance, shaping and, 192
Attachment
    child abuse and, 343
    cupboard theory of, 341
    needs, 388
    social development and, 339–340
    styles, 565–566
Attention, 122
    filter theory of, 125
    focus of, 122–124
    perceptual grouping, 125–126
    unattended information, 124–215
Attentional-blink effect, 403
Attentional bottleneck, 250
Attentional processes, 122–125, 249
Attention-deficit hyperactivity disorder (ADHD), 496–497
Attitudes
    advertisements and, 554
    behaviors and, 550–552
    commitment and, 557
    compliance, 556–557
    dissonance theory, 554–556
    lying and, 551
    reciprocity norm, 556–557
    self-perception theory, 556
Attractiveness, 564
Attributional styles, 385
Attributions, 384–386
Attribution theory, 545
    fundamental attribution error (FAE), 545–546
Audience design, 251–253
Auditory cortex, 72, 115, 116
Auditory nerve, 116
Auditory system, 114–116
Australopithecus afarensis, 14
Authoritarian parents, 340–341
Authoritarian personality, 603
Authoritative parents, 340
Autistic disorder, 497
Autocratic leaders, 603–604
Autohypnosis, 160
Automatic processes, 249–250

Autonomic nervous system (ANS), 66
    diagram of, 68
    and emotions, 398
    fight-or-flight response, 408
Availability heuristic, 275–276
Aversion therapy, 520
Avoidance conditioning, 184
Avoidant attachment style, 566
Awareness, consciousness and, 142–144
Axons, 79–80
    action potential and, 83
    of ganglion cells, 105
Aztecs, 162

Backward conditioning, 174, 175
Bad-me self, 517
Balanced time perspective, 430
Bandura's cognitive social-learning theory, 455–457
Barbiturates, 164
Bar graphs, 47
Basic level, 232
Basilar membrane, 115–116
Bathers (Seurat), 5, 6
Battle of Kosovo Field, 604
Bay of Pigs invasion, 580
Bedlam, 512
Behavioral confirmation, 549–550
    stereotypes and, 561
Behavioral data, 5
Behavioral geneticists, 17
Behavioral measures, 35–37
Behavioral neuroscience, 14
Behavioral rehearsal, 523
Behavioral theories
    of anxiety disorders, 486
    of mental illness, 477
    of mood disorders, 490
Behavior analysis, 17, 171–172
Behaviorism, 13, 171
    radical behaviorism, 171
Behaviorism (Watson), 171
Behaviorist perspective, 12–13
    aggression, analysis of, 16
Behavior modification, 518
    cognitive behavior modification, 526–527
Behaviors
    attitudes and, 550–552
    conceptual behavior, 198–199
    continuum of unacceptable behaviors, 504
    defined, 4
    dissonance and, 555
    environmental consequences and, 182
    experimental analysis of, 182–183
    genetics and, 61–62
    heredity and, 56–62
    learning and, 170
    motivation and, 362
    personality traits predicting, 442–443
    self-perception theory, 556
    units of, 5–6
Behavior therapies, 510, 518–525
    comparison of, 524
Beliefs
    belief-bias effect, 269–270
    placebo effect and, 28
Bell-shaped curve, 50–52
    and intelligence, 286–287
    for intelligence scores, 293
Bem Sex-Role Inventory (BSRI), 45

Benzodiazepine, 87, 534
Between-subjects designs, 29
Beyond Freedom and Dignity (Skinner), 171
Biases. *See also* Prejudice
    in Freudian psychoanalysis, 449
    response bias, 101
    self-serving biases, 547
Binge eating, 371–372
Binocular cues, 129–130
Biofeedback, 426
Biological markers for schizophrenia, 502
Biological needs, 388
Biological perspective, 13–14
    aggression, analysis of, 16
Biological preparedness, 195
Biological sciences, 4
Biology. *See also* Brain
    anxiety disorders, causes of, 484–485
    and behavior, 62–79
    learning and, 192–196
    and mental illness, 476
    mood disorders and, 488–490
    motivation and, 362
    sexual preference and, 381
Biomedical model of health, 420–421
Biomedical therapies, 510, 530–535
Biopsychosocial model of health, 420–421
Bipedalism, 59
Bipolar cells, 105
Bipolar disorder, 488
    brain activity and, 489
    drug therapies for, 533
    lithium salts, 534
    personality traits, 439–440
Birds, cognitive maps and, 197
Birth order, 437, 438
Blindness
    change blindness, 127
    color blindness, 112
    restoration of sight, 109
Blind spots, 105–106
Blood-brain barrier, 80
Bodily kinesthetic intelligence, 298
Body image, 371–374
Body size
    culture and, 372–373
    judgments of, 373
Bonobos, language and, 258
Bosnian war, 602
Bottom-up processing, 135–136
Botulism, 87
Boufée delirante, 481
Bounded rationality, 274
Brain, 55–56. *See also* Nervous system
    aggression and, 589
    amyotrophic lateral sclerosis (ALS), 83
    bipolar disorder and, 489
    blood-brain barrier, 80
    Broca's area, 63
    coordination of areas of, 71
    deductive reasoning and, 271–272
    development of, 319
    dreams and, 156
    eating and, 367
    electroconvulsive therapy (ECT), 531–532
    electroencephalogram (EEG), 65

emotions and, 399–400
encephalization, 59
gender and, 77
hand-eye coordination, 76
hemispheric lateralization of, 74–77
imaging activity of, 64–66
inductive reasoning and, 271–272
interventions in, 63–66
language and, 63, 72–74
memory and, 238, 240–241
MRI (magnetic resonance imaging) of, 65
neurogenesis, 89
PET scans, 65
plasticity of, 88–89
posttraumatic stress disorder (PTSD) and, 485
psychosurgery, 531
recording activity of, 64–66
repetitive transcranial magnetic stimulation (rTMS), 63–64
schizophrenia and, 502
split-brain patients, 74–75
stem cells and injuries, 88
structures of, 68–74
therapies and, 536
visual imagery, localizing, 64
visual system, processes of, 106–108
Brain-computer interface, 83
Brain stem, 68, 70
Brightness of color, 110, 112
Broca's aphasia, 74
Broca's area, 63, 73
Bulimia nervosa, 371–372
Burnout, 429–430
Business sense, 297
Bystander intervention, 585–587

Caffeine, 164–165
Cambodia, killing fields of, 600
Cancer, taste aversions and, 195
Candid Camera, 581
Cannabionoids, 164
Cannabis, 163
Cannon-Bard theory of central neural processes, 401
Cantor's social intelligence theory, 457
Capsaicin, 123
Carbon monoxide, 87
Cardinal traits, 438
Case studies, 37
Cataplexy, 153
Catatonic type of schizophrenia, 499–500
Categorization
    as memory structure, 230
    prototypes and, 231
    Strange Situation Test and, 340
Catharsis, 514–515
Caudal ventral prefrontal cortex (cVPFC), 489
Causal attributions, 545
Causal predictions, 7
Causation, correlation and, 31
Celera Genomics Corporation, 61
Censorship and dreams, 155
Central executive, 216
Central nervous system (CNS), 66–67
Central sulcus, 71
Central tendency, measure of, 48–49
Central traits, 438
Centration, 326

intelligence assessment and, 305–306
language and, 257–260
love and, 566–567
moral development and, 355–357
reality, cultural constructions of, 146
self-construction of, 460–462
and self-enhancement, 461
sexual norms and, 378
treatment and, 513–514
well-being and, 144, 145
Culture-bound syndromes, 477, 481
Culture of honor, 593
Cupboard theory of attachment, 341
Curare, 87
Current performance estimates, 291
Cutaneous senses, 119–120

Dani people, Papula New Guinea, 259
Dark adaptation, 105
Data, 5. *See also* Statistics
processing, data-driven, 135
Date rape, 380
Day care, 342
Daytime sleepiness, 153–154
Deafness, 116
Death
leading causes of, 422
lifestyle factors and, 421
self-help groups and, 530
of spouse, 349
suicide, 492–493
Death instincts, 366, 517
Debriefing research participants, 38–39
Decibels, 114
Decision aversion, 280–281
Decision making, 274, 278–281
decision aversion, 280–281
framing of decisions, 279–280
heuristics and, 266
signal detection theory (SDT) and, 101
tough decisions, avoiding, 281
Declarative memory, 208–209
Deductive reasoning, 268–272
brain bases of, 271
Deep judgments, 224, 225
Defense mechanisms, 449
mental illness and, 477
Dehumanizing the enemy, 600–601
Deinstitutionalization, 513
Delay conditioning, 174–175
Delirium tremens, 161
Delusions
antipsychotic drugs and, 533
in paranoid type of schizophrenia, 500
in schizophrenia, 499
Demand characteristics, 598
Demandingness, 340
Demanding statements, 592
Democide, 604
Democratic leaders, 603–604
Demonology, 513
Dendrites, 79
Denial, mental illness and, 477
Dentate gyrus (DG), 241
Dependent variables, 26
Depolarized cells, 82
Depressants, 164

Depression
antidepressant drugs, 534
cognitive therapy for, 525
cognitive triad of, 490
drug therapies for, 533
electroconvulsive therapy (ECT) and, 531–532
gender differences in, 492
major depressive disorder, 487–488
psychodynamic therapy and, 537
self-verification and, 491
treatment evaluation for, 537
Deprovincialization, 563
Depth cues, 128
Depth perception, 128–132
binocular information, 129–130
pictorial cues, 130–132
Descriptions in psychology, 5–6
Descriptive statistics, 46–50
Desensitization
television violence and, 200
therapy, 519
Despair conflict, 338
Destructive sibling conflict, 32
Determinism, 24
Developmental age, 317
Developmental psychologists, 17
Developmental psychology, 315–316
Diagnosis, 510
Diathesis-stress hypothesis, 501
Dichotic listening, 125
Dieting, 369–371
Difference thresholds, 102–103
Differential reinforcement, 192
Diffusion of responsibility, 586
Direct observations, 36
Direct provocation and aggression, 592
Disclosure and health, 428
Discrimination. *See* Prejudice
Disease. *See also* Mental illness
chronic illness and stress, 419
stress and, 409–410
treatment of, 424–428
"The Diseases and Physical Peculiarities of the Negro Race" (Cartwright), 474
Disharmony, 420
Disinhibited eating, 370
Disorganized type of schizophrenia, 499
Displacement, 449
Dispositional attributions, 547
Dispositional causality, 545
Dispositional forces, 367
Dissociation of consciousness, 513
Dissociative amnesia, 494–495
Dissociative disorders, 494–496
Dissociative identity disorder (DID), 495
Dissonance
culture and, 555
theory, 554–556
Distal stimuli, 94–96
Distinctiveness, 545
Distracter object, 30
Divergent thinking, 307
Diversity of inquiry, 17
Divorce, 349
Dizygotic (DZ) twins. *See* Twin studies
DNA (deoxyribonucleic acid), 60
genomes and, 61

Door-in-the-face technique, 556–557
Dopamine, 87
alcohol and, 164
Double-blind control, 29
Dream logs, 156
Dreams, 154–157
culture and interpretation of, 155–156
Freudian analysis, 155
lucid dreaming, 157–158
nightmares, 157
physiological theories of, 156
psychoanalysis and, 515
Dream work, 155
Drives, 363–364
Droodles, 135
Drug addiction, 163
behavioral treatment for, 521
family therapy and, 529
Drugs
AIDS risk and, 423
altered states of consciousness and, 162–165
conditioning and, 180–181
hallucinations and, 161
psychoactive drugs, 163–165
varieties of, 163–164
Drug therapies, 532–534
antipsychotic drugs, 533
Drunk driving, 164
DSM editions, evolution of, 478–481
DSM-IV-TR (Diagnostic and Statistical Manual of Mental Disorders), 478–479
Dyads, 353

Ears. *See* Hearing
Eating, 367–374
and body image, 371–374
central responses, 368–369
obesity, 369–371
physiology of, 367–369
psychology of, 369–371
Eating disorders, 481
race and, 374
Ebbinghaus illusion, 98
Echoic memory, 212–213
Echolocation, 117
Economy
and aggression, 590
stress and, 413–414
Ecstasy (MDMA), 163
Ectomorphs, 437
Education
practical intelligence for school (PIFS), 299
tracking of students, 305
Educational psychologists, 17
Ego, 447–448, 514
defense mechanisms, 448
Egocentrism, 326
Ego ideal, 447
Ego-integrity conflict, 338
Egoism, 584
Eidetic imagery, 212
Elaboration likelihood model, 552–553
Elaborative rehearsal, 226, 228
Elavil, 534
Electroconvulsive therapy (ECT), 531–532
Electroencephalograms (EEGs), 65
locked-in syndrome and, 83
sleep and, 149–150
Electromagnetic spectrum, 110

E-mail, mental health care and, 511–512
Emergencies
bystander intervention and, 585–587
threats, reactions to, 408
Emotional deficits, 490
Emotional intelligence, 297–298
Emotion-focused coping, 416–417
Emotions, 86, 393–394
advertisements and, 554
arousal and, 401–402
attribution-dependent emotional responses, 385
brain functions and, 399–400
Cannon-Bard theory of, 401
classical conditioning and, 179–180
comparison theories of, 400
culture and, 394–398
expressed emotion concept, 503
expression and culture, 397–398
functional MRI (fMRI) scans, 240, 399, 406–407
functions of, 402–406
of infants, 395
as innate, 395
instincts and, 366
James-Lange theory of, 400
moral reasoning and, 404
pain and, 121–122
physiology of, 398–399
in schizophrenia, 499
social functions of, 403
theories of, 398–402
universality of, 395–396
Empathy, justice and, 584
Empiricism, 324–325
Employment
aspirations and expectations, 346
equity theory and, 386–388
expectancy theory and, 388
motivation for, 387
organizational psychology and, 386–388
Empty chair technique, 528
Empty nest, 349
Encephalization, 59
Encoding. *See* Memory
Endocrine glands, 77
Endocrine system, 77–79
major glands and functions, 78
Endogenous morphines, 87–88, 121
Endomorphs, 437
Endorphins, 87–88
drugs and, 164
pain and, 121
Enemy, establishing, 600–601
Engram, 238–239
Enlightenment, 161
Environment
attention-deficit hyperactivity disorder (ADHD) and, 496–497
behavior and, 182
brain plasticity and, 88
and cognitive-affective personality theory, 454
human deprivation, 343–344
infants and, 320–321
intelligence, 303–305
personality and, 462
self-efficacy and, 456–457
Environmental conditions, 438

Environmental stimuli, 103
Epilepsy, 74
Epinephrine
  and emotions, 398–399
  and fight-or-flight response, 408
Episodic memories, 222
Equity theory, 386–388
Erogenous zones, 120, 446
Eros, 446
Erotic plasticity, 378
Erotic stimuli, 376
Errors, judgment and, 274–275
Escalation of aggression, 592
Escalation script, 592
Escape conditioning, 184
Espiritistas, 513
Esteem needs, 388
Estrogens, 78, 375
Ethics
  animal research, 39
  of intelligence assessment, 309–310
  research, ethical issues in, 38–39
Ethnicity. See also Prejudice
  eating disorders and, 374
Etiology, 510
  of mental illness, 476–477
Eugenics movement, 287
Euthymic emotional state, 490
Evolution, 56–60
  and aggression, 588
  cultural evolution, 59
  human evolution, 59–60
Evolutionary perspective, 14
  aggression, analysis of, 16
  learning and, 170
Evolutionary psychology, 62
Excitatory inputs, 81–82
Excitement phase, 376
Exemplars, 231, 552
Exhaustion stage, 409
Existentialist approaches, 527
Expectancy effects, 28
Expectancy theory, 388
Expectations, 346–347
  behaviors confirming, 549–550
  IQ and, 548
  mental illness and, 505
  motivation and, 366–367
  perception and, 136–137
  self-fulfilling prophecies and, 548–549
  stereotypes and, 561
  video games and, 594
Experience
  attitudes and, 551
  biological perspective and, 14
  brain plasticity and, 88
  learning and, 171
  reasoning ability and, 270
  self-efficacy judgments and, 456
  self-experience, components of, 458
Experience-sampling method, 144–145
Experimental methods, 27
Experimental psychologists, 17
Experiments. See Research
Expert systems, 273
Explanations in psychology, 6
Explanatory style, 491
Explicit memory, 207–208
  amnesia and, 239
Exposure therapies, 518–520, 519–520

The Expression of Emotions in Man and Animals (Darwin), 394, 395
External ear, 115
Extinction, 175–176
  operant extinction, 184
  strategies, 521–522
Extraversion, 439
  amygdala and, 440. 441
Eyes. See Visual system
Eyewitness memory, 235–236

Face validity, 288
Factor analysis, 295
Fading procedures, 523
Failure, attributions for, 384–386
False beliefs, changing, 525–526
Family, 348–349. See also Parents
  altruism in, 582–583
  healing and, 514
  schizophrenia and, 502–503
Family therapy, 529–530
Fantasy, 449
Fears. See also Phobias
  conditioning, 179–180
  flooding therapy, 519
  infants and, 321
Feelings-of-knowing, 227, 229
Fenfluramine, 589
Fetus, 318
Fight-or-flight response, 408
Figures, 125–126
Fiji, healing in, 513
Filter, observer bias as, 25
Filter theory of attention, 125
Five-factor model, 439–440
Fixations, 127, 446, 447
Fixed alternatives to questions, 35
Fixed-interval (FI) schedules, 191–192
Fixed-ratio (FR) schedules, 191
Flooding therapy, 519
Fluency, 307
Fluid intelligence, 295, 330–331
Foot-in-the-door technique, 557
Forensic psychologists, 17
Formal assessment, 287–289
Formal operations stage, 328
Foundational theories, 328–329
Fovea, 105
Framing of decisions, 279–280
Free association, 514–515
Freedom to choose, 527
Free recall, 219
Frequencies, 47
  distributions, 46–47
Frequency (sound), 113
  pitch and, 116
  of pure tones, 114
Freudian psychoanalysis, 445–449
  evaluation of, 449
Freudian slip, 447
Friends
  in adolescence, 345
  gender roles and, 353
  liking and, 564–565
  and self-serving biases, 547
Frontal lobes, 71
  in adolescence, 323
Frustration-aggression hypothesis, 590–591
Functional fixedness, 268
Functionalism, 10–11
Functional MRI (fMRI), 65
  emotions and, 240, 399, 406–407

Fundamental attribution error (FAE), 545–546

GABA (gamma-aminobutyric acid), 87
  alcohol and, 164
  antianxiety drugs and, 534
Galápagos Islands, 57
Gambling, representativeness and, 277
Ganglion cells, 105
  receptive fields of, 107
Gases as neurotransmitters, 88
Gate-control theory, 121–122
Gays. See Homosexuality
Gender. See also Homosexuality
  altruism and, 584
  brain functions and, 77
  color blindness and, 112
  defined, 352
  and depression, 492
  development, 351–354
  eating disorders and, 371
  identity, 352
  moral reasoning and, 355–357
  sexual behaviors and, 378
  smoking and, 422
  suicide and, 493
  taste and, 123
  tend-and-befriend response, 408
Gender roles, 352
  acquisition of, 353–354
General adaptation syndrome (GAS), 409–410
General aggression model, 594
General intelligence factor, 295
Generalizations, 271
Generalization techniques, 523–524
Generalized anxiety disorder, 482
  drug therapies, 534
General knowledge test, 224–225
General Procrastination Scale, 411
Generativity, 350–351
Genes, 60–61
Genetic material, 60
Genetics, 60–61
  aggression and, 588–589
  attention-deficit hyperactivity disorder (ADHD) and, 496–497
  autistic disorder and, 497
  behavior and, 56–62
  color blindness, 112
  emotions and, 399
  genius and, 287
  and happiness, 405
  intelligence and, 300–303
  narcolepsy and, 153
  obesity and, 370
  personality and, 441–442, 462
  schizophrenia and, 500–501
  sleep needs and, 150
  taste and, 123
Genius and heredity, 287
Genocide, 599–603
Genomes, 61
Genotypes, 58–59
  for cultural evolution, 59
  variations in, 60–62
German measles, 318
Germany, prejudice in, 563
Gestalt psychology, 9
  perceptual grouping principles, 126

Gestalts, 10
  perceptual arrays and, 126
GHB, 164
Glia, 80
Goals
  selection, goal-directed, 122, 124
  and social intelligence theory, 457
  state of problem, 265
Gombe chimpanzee study, 36
Gonads, 375
Good continuation, law of, 126
Good-me self, 517
Good Samaritans, 585–587
Government, forms of, 603–604
Grammar, 333
  acquisition of, 334–336
Grandeur, delusions of, 500
Graphs, 47–48
Grounds, 126
Groups
  dynamics, 603
  norms, 289
  polarization, 580
  self-serving biases in, 547
Group therapies, 528–530
Groupthink, 580
Guided imagery, 523
Gulf War, 601, 602

Habitats, 57
Habitual criminal murderers, 45
Habituation, 328
Haldol, 533
Hallucinations, 161
  antipsychotic drugs and, 533
  perception and, 98
  in schizophrenia, 499
Hallucinogens, 163
Haloperidol, 533
Hammer of ear, 115
Hand-eye coordination, 76
Happiness, 405
  evolutionary perspective on, 62
  steps for, 430–431
Hashish, 163
Head Start program, 304–305
Health, 4–5. See also Mental illness
  biomedical model of, 420–421
  biopsychosocial model of, 420–421
  continuum of, 473
  defined, 420
  emotional disclosure and, 428
  expert systems and, 273
  job burnout, 429–430
  mind and, 425–427
  personality and, 428–429
  promotion of, 421–424
  psychological factors and, 427–428
  psychoneuroimmunology, 426–427
  and smoking, 421–423
  steps for, 430–431
  treatment of illnesses, 424–428
Health and Human Services Department
  research, ethical standards for, 38
Health psychologists, 17, 394, 420–431
Healthy People 2010, 425

Hearing, 113–117. *See also* Sound
  aging and, 323–324
  auditory system, 114–116
  impairments, 116
  physiology of, 114–117
  range of, 114
  sound localization, 117
  structure of ear, 115
Heart disease, personality and, 428–429
Hemodialysis, 424
Hemophilia, 423
Hereditary Genius (Galton), 286
Heredity. *See* Genetics
Heritability, 61
  estimate, 302
  five factors, 442
  personality traits and, 441–442
Heroin, conditioning and, 181
Hertz (Hz), 113
Heterosexual couples, 348
Heuristics, 266
  anchoring heuristic, 277–278
  availability heuristic, 275–276
  and judgment, 274–278
  representativeness heuristic, 276–277
Hierarchies of concepts, 232
Hierarchy of needs, 388–389
High-altruism condition, 584
Hippocampus, 70–71
  cannabinoids and, 164
  encoding in, 241
  and memory, 238
  retrieval in, 241
Histograms, 47, 48
History of psychology, 9–11
Histrionic personality disorder, 493
HIV/AIDS, 423–424
HMOs (health maintenance organizations), 532
Holistic approach, 13
Holy Ghost people, 161–162
Homelessness, 513
Homeostasis, 70, 363–364
Homophobia, 381
Homosexuality, 380–382
  couples, 348
  DSM editions and, 479
  society and, 381–382
  stereotypes and, 561
Horizontal cells, 105
Hormones, 77–79, 375
  and emotions, 398–399
Hostility and health, 428–429
Hozho, 420
Hues, *seeing*, 110–112
Human body, visual processing of, 107–108
Human deprivation, 343–344
Human development
  in adolescence, 322–323
  in adulthood, 323–324
  cross-sectional design research, 317
  developmental psychology, 315–316
  in life span, 318–324
  longitudinal design research, 317
  normative investigations, 317
  prenatal development, 318–319
  study of, 316–317
Human factors psychologists, 17
Human Genome Project, 61
  obesity and, 370
Humanistic theories, 13, 451–453

aggression, analysis of, 16
  as dispositional, 452
  as holistic, 451–452
  as phenomenological, 452
Humanistic therapies, 510, 527–528
Human-potential movement, 527
Humors, 436–437
Hunger sensations, 367–368
Hyperactivity-impulsivity, 496
Hypercomplex cells, 107
Hypnosis, 158–160
  effects of, 159–160
  hypnotic induction, 158–159
  pain, minimizing, 160
  stimulating, 159
Hypnotherapy, 476
Hypnotic induction, 158–159
Hypnotizability, 158–159
Hypothalamus, 69, 70
  eating and, 368–369
  emotions and, 399
  endocrine system and, 77, 78–79
  fight-or-flight response, 408
Hypotheses
  contact hypothesis, 562–563
  defined, 24
  diathesis-stress hypothesis, 501
  frustration-aggression hypothesis, 590–591
  perceptual processes and, 96
  preparedness hypothesis, 484
  on subliminal messages, 34
  testing of, 27–28
Hysteria, 475
  somatoform disorders, 481

Iconic memory, 210–212
Id, 447, 514
  mental illness and, 477
Identification, 94, 449
  processes, 134–137
Identity changes, 127
Ill-defined problems, 265
Illusions
  Ames room illusion, 132–133
  in daily life, 98–99
  perception and, 98–99
  Ponzo illusion, 131
Imagination, 235
Imitation of models, 522
Immigration and intelligence, 300
Immigration Restriction Act, 300
Immune function, 426
  stress and, 427
Implicit memory
  amnesia and, 239
  encoding and, 224
  priming and, 224–225
Imprinting, 339
Impulsive aggression, 589
Incentives, 364
Incongruence, 528
Independent construals of self, 546
Independent variables, 26
Indian Yogic traditions, 9
Individualistic cultures, 397–398, 460
Inductive reasoning, 271–272
  brain bases of, 271–272
Industrial-organizational psychologists, 17
Infancy. *See also* Cognitive development
  development in, 319–321
  emotions in, 395

Inferences, 257
Inferential statistics, 46, 50–52
Inferiority feelings, 450
Informational influence, 576, 577
Informational support, 419
Information explosion, 41
Informative stimulus, 178
Informed consent requirement, 38
Ingrained habits, 598
In-groups, 558, 560
Inhibitory inputs, 81–82
Initial state of problem, 265
Innate intelligence measures, 291
Inner ear, 115
Insanity. *See* Mental illness
Insanity defense, 480
Insight therapy, 514
Insomnia, 152–153
Instincts, 365–366
Instinctual drift, 193–194
Instrumental aggression, 589–590
Instrumentality, 388
Insults experiment, 593–594
Intelligence, 285–286. *See also* Intelligence assessment
  in adulthood, 330–331
  creativity and, 307
  culture and, 305–306
  defined, 290
  environment and, 303–305
  expectations and, 548
  heredity and, 300–303
  history of comparisons, 300–301
  multiple intelligences, 297–298
  psychometrics, 295–296
  race and, 301, 302–303
  social intelligence theory, 457
  theories of, 295–299
  triarchic theory of, 296–297
  twin studies on, 301–302
Intelligence assessment, 290–294
  culture and, 305–306
  history of comparisons, 300–301
  on Internet, 294
  interpreting IQ scores, 293–294
  labels and, 310
  society and, 309–311
  Stanford-Binet Intelligence Scale, 291
  stress and, 414
  Wechsler Intelligence Scales, 292–293
Intelligence quotient (IQ), 291
Intentional deception in research, 38
Interactive problem solving, 605
Interdependence theory, 567
Interdependent construals of self, 460, 546
Interference, 222–223
Intermediary bystanders, 598
Internal consistency and reliability, 288
Internalization, 330
Internal working model, 340
International Classification of Diseases (ICD), 478
International Union of Psychological Science, 19
Internet
  IQ tests on, 294
  mental health care on, 511
  personal relationships and, 568
  psychology topics, sites with, 41
  self and, 463
  self-help groups, 530

sleep and, 154
Interneurons, 80
Interpersonal intelligence, 298
Interpersonal therapy, 537
Interposition, 130–131
The Interpretation of Dreams (Freud), 155
Intervals, 47
Interventions, 7–8
Interviews, 35
Intestines, 78
Intimacy
  in adulthood, 347–350
  companionate love and, 566
  goals, 457
  isolation and, 338
  of late-in-life relationships, 349–350
Intrapersonal intelligence, 298
Invariant properties, 132
In vivo therapy, 511
Ion channels, 82
Ions, 82
Iris, 104
Irresponsible traits, 439
Isolation
  in Freudian theory, 449
  intimacy and, 338

James-Lange theory of emotion, 400
Jealousy, delusional, 500
Jet lag, 149
Jigsaw classrooms, 563
Job burnout, 429–430
Jobs. *See* Employment
Johns Hopkins University, 9
Judgment, 274
  anchoring heuristic, 277–278
  availability heuristic, 275–276
  creativity and, 308
  heuristics and, 266, 274–278
  representativeness heuristic, 276–277
  stored memories and, 276
Justice
  interpersonal responsibility and, 356
  principle, 584
  standards of, 355–356
Just noticeable difference (JND), 102–103
Just world thinking, 600

Kinesthetic sense, 120–121
Kinship and altruism, 582–583
Knowledge
  compilation, 209
  deductive reasoning and, 269
  organized knowledge, 229
Koro, 481

Labels
  intelligence assessment and, 310
  mental illness and, 474
Laissez-faire leaders, 603
Language, 251–260. *See also* Speech errors
  acquisition of, 332–336
  ambiguity in, 255–256
  animals learning, 258
  audience design and, 251–253
  brain and, 63, 72–74
  capacity to create, 335
  color judgments and, 259
  common grounds, 253
  community membership and, 253

consciousness and, 145
and culture, 257–260
electroconvulsive therapy
  (ECT) and, 532
evolution and, 59
Grice's maxims in production,
  252
and lateralized brain functions,
  75
perceiving speech and words,
  332–334
products of understanding,
  256–257
propositions and, 256–257
psychosocial stages and, 338
in schizophrenia, 499
semantic memories, 222
stereotypes and, 233
thought and, 257–260
unconscious processes and,
  144
understanding, 254–257
word meanings, learning, 334
Latent content, 447
of dreams, 155, 515
Lateral fissure, 71
Lateral hypothalamus (LH), 368
Lateralized brain functions, 74
Lawful patterns of relationships,
  24
Law of effect, 182
Leadership, forms of, 603–604
Learned helplessness, 490–491
Learning, 170. *See also* Memory
behavior and, 170
biology and, 193–196
cognitive influences on,
  196–201
consistent change and,
  170–171
defined, 170–172
experience and, 171
instinctual drift, 193–194
observational learning,
  199–201
personality and, 462
social-learning theories,
  453–458
taste-aversion learning,
  194–196
word meanings, 334
Learning disorders, 294
Learning-performance distinction,
  170
Left hemisphere of brain, 75
Left visual field, 77
Lens of eye, 104
Lesbians. *See* Homosexuality
Lesions in brain, 63
Leveling, 234
Levels of analysis, 5
Levels-of-processing theory, 224
Lexical ambiguity, 255–256
Lexical meaning, 333
Libido, 446
Lieben und Arbeten, 347
Life changes and stress, 410–412
Life-change units (LCU), 411
Life instincts, 366
Life span development, 316
Life stories, 452
Lifestyles
AIDS risk and, 423
suicide and, 493
Light. *See also* Colors
constancy, lightness, 134
Liking, 564–565
of foods, 368

proximity and, 568
Limbic system, 67, 70
emotions and, 399
Linear perspective, 131
Linguistic copresence, 253
Linguistic intelligence, 298
Linguistic relativity, 259
Listeners, 251
Lithium salts, 534
Little Albert, fear conditioning of,
  179
Lobotomy, 531
Locked-in syndrome, 83
Locomotion. *See* Walking
Locus of control, 384–385
Logical-mathematical intelligence,
  298
Longitudinal design research, 317
Long-term mating, 378
Long-term memory (LTM),
  218–229
categorization and, 230
concepts and, 230
context and, 218–221
elaborative rehearsal, 226, 228
encoding, 218–221
  processes of, 223–225
episodic memories, 222
eyewitness memory, 235–236
hierarchies of concepts, 232
interference, 222–223
levels-of-processing theory, 224
metamemory, 227, 229
mnemonics, 226–227, 228
perception, memory structures
  and, 233
priming, 224–225
prototypes, 230–232
reconstructive memory, 234–236
retrieval
  cues, 221–223
  processes of, 223–225
schemas, 232–233
semantic memories, 222
serial position effect, 219–221
structures in, 229–236
transfer-appropriate processing,
  224
unstructured information and,
  225–227
Loudness, 114
Loving relationships, 565–569
culture and, 566–567
duration of, 567–569
Low-altruism condition, 584
LSD (lysergic acid diethylamide),
  87, 163
hallucinations and, 161
Lucid dreaming, 157–158
Lying, 551
dissonance and, 555

Maintenance rehearsal, 214–215
Maintenance stage, 423, 425
Major life events, 410–412
Mandala, 450
Manic episodes, 488
Manifest content of dreams, 155,
  515
Marijuana, 163–164
Marital therapy, 529–530
Marriage, 348
in late adulthood, 349
Material me, 458
Mating strategies, 408
Maturation, 321–322
Mayans and dreams, 155
Maze learning, 197

MDMA, 163
Mean, 48–49
Measure of central tendency,
  48–49
Measures of variability, 49
Median, 48
Meditation, 160–161
and health, 426
Medulla, 67–68
Meissner corpuscles, 119
Memory, 205–206. *See also* Brain;
  Implicit memory; Long-
  term memory (LTM);
  Moods; Short-term
  memory (STM)
acetylcholine and, 87
aging and, 331–332
amnesia, 239–240
antianxiety drugs and, 534
biology and, 236–241
brain and, 238, 240–241
categorization and, 230
concepts and, 230
declarative memory, 208–209
defined, 206
dreams and, 156
Ebbinghaus on, 206–207
echoic memory, 212–213
elaborative rehearsal, 226, 228
electroconvulsive therapy
  (ECT) and, 531–532
encoding, 209–210
  in hippocampus, 241
  implicit memory, 224
  and long-term memory
    (LTM), 218–221, 223–225
  specificity of, 228
engram, 238–239
explicit memory, 207–208
eyewitness memory, 235–236
hierarchies of concepts, 232
iconic memory, 210–212
metamemory, 227, 229
mnemonics, 226–227, 228
postevent information, 235–236
preconscious memories, 142,
  143
priming, 224–225
procedural memory, 208–209
propositions and, 257
prototypes, 230–232
reconstructive memory, 234–236
retrieval, 209–210
  cue familiarity hypothesis,
    229
  in hippocampus, 241
  long-term memory (LTM),
    cues for, 221–223, 223–225
  from short-term memory
    (STM), 216
schemas, 232–233
selective storage, 146
sensory memory, 210–213
serial position effect, 228
short-term memory (STM),
  213–218
sources of, 235
span, 213–214
  working memory, test for,
    217
storage, 209–210
  judgment and, 276
subliminal influence and, 33
types of memories, 207–209
working memory, 213, 216–218
Menarche, 323
Menopause, 324
Menstruation, 323

menopause, 324
Mental age, 291
Mental asylums, 513
Mental hospitals, 532
Mental illness. *See also*
  Treatments
anxiety disorders, 482–484
behavioral theories of, 477
biological approaches to, 476
classification of disorders,
  478–481
cognitive theories of, 477
continuum of, 473
creativity and, 307–308
criteria for, 472–473
culture and treatment of,
  513–514
as defense, 480
dissociative disorders, 494–496
etiology of, 476–477
goals for therapies, 510
historical perspectives, 474–476
major types of, 481–497
medical model of, 475
mood disorders, 487–492
nature of, 472–477
objectivity and, 474
personality disorders, 493–494
prevention strategies, 537–539
prognosis of, 479
psychodynamic model of,
  476–477
psychological models of,
  475–476
sociocultural theories of, 477
stigma of, 504–505
suicide, 492–493
treatment plan for, 478
Mental operations, 326
Mental processes, 4
Mental resources, 247–250
Mental retardation, 293–294, 496
Mental rotation, 261
Mental sets, 137
inductive reasoning and, 271
Mere exposure effect, 402
Merkel disks, 119
Mesmerism, 476
Mesomorphs, 437
Meta-analysis, 535, 537
Metamemory, 227, 228, 229
Metamotivational states, 364–365
Methamphetamines, 164
Method of loci, 226–227
Middle East conflict, 605
Milgram experiments, 596–599
Mindfulness meditation, 160
Minnesota Multiphasic
  Personality Inventory
  (MMPI), 45, 464–465
Minority groups. *See also* Race
conformity and, 579–581
Misattribution of arousal source,
  401
Mischel's cognitive-affective
  personality theory, 454–458
MMPI-2, 465
M'Naghten rule, 480
Mnemonics, 226–227, 228
Mode, 48
Monitoring attentional style, 424
Monoamine oxidase (MAO)
  inhibitors, 534
Monozygotic (MZ) twins. *See*
  Twin studies
Mood-congruent processing, 404
Mood disorders. *See also*
  Depression

<www.ablongman.com/gerrig17e>

causes of, 488–492
Moods, 394
  cognition and, 406
  memory, 275
    mood-dependent memory, 404
  request politeness and, 404
Moral behavior, 354
Moral development, 354–358
  culture and, 355–357
  gender and, 355–357
  Kohlberg's stages of, 354–355
Moral reasoning, 354
  emotions and, 404
  stages of, 354–355
Morbidity, 481
Morphemes, 333, 3353
Morphine, 87–88, 121, 164
Mortality frame, 279
Motion
  cues, 129–130
  depth information and, 130
  perception, 128
Motion sickness, 120
Motivation, 361–362
  defined, 362
  dissonance and, 555
  drives, 363–364
  for employment, 387
  expectations and, 366–367
  hierarchy of needs and, 388–389
  and instincts, 365–366
  organizational psychology and, 386–388
  for personal achievement, 382–388
  reversal theory, 364–365
  sources of, 363–367
Motivational deficits, 490
Motor cortex, 71, 73
Motor neurons, 79
Motor sets, 137
Müller-Lyer illusion, 98
Multiple intelligences, 297–298
Multiple interpretations, 96
Multiple personality disorder, 495
Multiple sclerosis (MS), 84
Multiple unit artificial retina chipset (MARC), 109
Muscles, 72
Music
  and emotions, 86
  intelligence, musica;, 298
MYCIN system, 273
Myelin sheath, 81
  and multiple sclerosis (MS), 84

Naloxone, 87
Names, attention to, 125
Nanometers, 110
Narcissistic personality disorder, 493–494
Narcolepsy, 153
Narratives, 452
National Comorbidity Study (NCS), 481
Nativisim, 325
Naturalistic observations, 36
Naturalist intelligence, 298
Natural selection, 57–58
  evolutionary psychology, 62
  genotypes, 58–59
  phenotypes, 58–59
  sociobiology and, 61–62
Nature *versus* nurture, 56
  and homosexuality, 380–381
  interactions of, 498

personality and, 462
Navajo people, 420, 421
Nay-sayers, 102
Nazis, obedience to, 596
Near point of focus, 104
Necker cube, 97
Needs
  achievement, need for, 383–384
  hierarchy of needs, 388–389
  sleep needs, 150
Negative afterimage, 111
Negative punishment, 184, 187
Negative reinforcement, 183–184
Negative transference, 515
Negativism, 500
Neglecting parents, 341
Neo-Freudian theory, 12
NEO Personality Inventory (NEO-PI), 464, 465–466
Nerve deafness, 116
Nerve fibers, 121
Nervous system, 66–68, 79–89
  and emotions, 398
  hierarchical organization of, 67
Neuro-cultural theory, 396
Neurogenesis, 89
Neuromatrix theory of pain, 122
Neuromodulators, 87
Neurons, 79–80
  action potentials, 81–84
  excitatory inputs, 81–82
  glial cells, 81
  inhibitory inputs, 81–82
  refractory period, 84
  resting potential, 81
  sound localization and, 117
  structures of, 80
Neuroscience, 14, 63. *See also* Brain
Neurotic disorders, 439, 479
Neurotransmitters, 84–87
  functions of, 85–87
  gases as, 87
Neutral stimulus, 173
Next-in-line effect, 226
Nicotine, 164–165
  replacement therapy, 423
Nightmares, 157
  posttraumatic stress disorder (PTSD), 412–413
Nitric oxide, 87
Nitrous oxide, 162
Nodes of Ranvier, 84
Noise, 114
  phonemic restoration and, 135–136
  sustained exposure to, 116
Nonconformity, 579–581
Nonconscious processes, 142, 143
Non-REM (NREM) sleep, 150
Nontasters, 123
Norepinephrine, 87
  antidepressant drugs and, 534
  and emotions, 399
  and fight-or-flight response, 408
Normal distribution. *See* Bell-shaped curve
Normative influence, 576, 577–578
Normative investigations, 317
Normative population, 289
Norm of reciprocity, 583
Norms
  assessment and, 289–290
  social norms, 576
Northern Ireland conflict, 604

Nose dot test, 148
Not-me self, 517
NREM sleep, 154
Number processing, 249–250

Obedience, 596–599
  in real-world setting, 598
  reasons for, 598
Obesity, 369–371
  genetics and, 370
Objective self-awareness, 148
Objective tests of personality, 464–466
Objectivity, 5, 6
Object permanence, 326
Object relations theory, 517
Observable behavior, 171
Observation, 35–37
Observational learning, 199–201
Observer bias, 25–27
Obsessive-compulsive disorders, 483–484
  exposure therapy for, 520
Occipital lobes, 71
  visual cortex in, 72
Occlusion, depth and, 130–131
Odors. *See* Smell
Oedipus conflict, 446, 517
Olfactory bulb, 118
Olfactory cilia, 118
On Aggression (Lorenz), 588
Open-ended questions, 35
Operant chamber, 183
Operant conditioning, 181–193, 182–183
  operant extinction, 184
  personal chart for, 185
  punishment, 184
Operant extinction, 184
Operants, 182
Operational definitions, 25–27
Operationalization, 26
Opiates, 164
Opponent-process theory of color, 112
Optic chiasma, 106
Optic nerve, 105, 106
Optic tracts, 106
Optimism, 385–386
Optimistic attributional style, 385–386
Organizational psychology, 386–388
Organized knowledge, 229
Orgasm, 377–378
Orienting response, 173
The Origin of Species (Darwin), 57
Outcome-based expectancies, 456–457
Out-groups, 558, 560
Ovaries, 78
Overextending words, 334
Overregularization, 336

Pain
  gate-control theory, 121–122
  hypnotic analgesia, 160
  sense of, 121–122
  stress inoculation training and, 418
  withdrawal reflex, 80–81
Pancreas, 78
Panic disorder, 482
Papillae, 119
Paradoxical sleep, 150
Parallel forms and reliability, 287–288

Parallel processes, 247–248
Paralysis of will, 490
Paranoid delusions, 164
Paranoid personality disorders, 493
Paranoid type of schizophrenia, 500
Parasympathetic nervous system, 66–68
  and emotions, 398–399
Paratelic motivational states, 364
Parathyroid gland, 78
Parental Bonding Instrument (PBI), 494
Parent possible-self score (PPS), 459
Parents
  adolescents and, 345
  and antisocial personality traits, 494
  gender roles and, 353
  investment, parental, 377–378
  need for achievement and, 383
  possible self as, 459
  practices of, 341
  schizophrenia and, 502–503
  styles and, 340–341
  transition to parenting, 348–349
Parietal lobe, 71
Parkinson's disease, 87
Partial reinforcement schedules, 190
Partial-report method, 212
Participant modeling therapy, 522
Passionate love, 566
Pastoral counselors, 511
Patient adherence, 424–425
Pattern recognition, 106
Pavlovian conditioning, 173
PCP, 163
Peace psychology, 603–605
  conflict resolution and, 604–605
Peers. *See* Friends
Peg-word method, 227
Perceived control and stress, 418
Perceivers in behavioral confirmation, 549–550
Perception, 93. *See also* Depth perception
  and ambiguity, 96–97
  attentional processes, 122–125
  bottom-up processing, 135–136
  constancies, perceptual, 132–134
  contexts, influence of, 136–137
  defined, 94
  of distal stimulus, 95–96
  expectations, influence of, 136–137
  identification processes, 134–137
  illusions and, 98–99
  laws of, 126
  memory structures and, 233
  motion perception, 128
  organizational processes in, 122–134
  pitch perception theories, 116–117
  of proximal stimulus, 96
  recognition processes, 134–137
  sets, 137
  social perception, 545
  spatial integration, 127–128
  temporal integration, 127–128
  top-down processing, 135–136

Perceptual constancy, 132–134
Perceptual grouping, 125–126
Perceptual instability, 97
Perceptual organization, 94
Perceptual sets, 137
Perceptual similarity, 199
Performance, learning and, 170
Peripheral nervous system (PNS), 66–68
Permission situations, 270
Persecution delusions, 500
Perseverance and motivation, 363
Personal achievement, 382–388
  attributions for, 384–386
  need for, 383–384
  organizational psychology and, 386–388
Personal construction of reality, 146
Personality, 435–436
  aggression and, 589–590
  Allport's trait approach, 438
  assessment of, 464–467
  birth order an, 437
  body types and, 437
  and cognitive-affective personality theory, 454
  consistency paradox, 442–443
  cross-situational consistency, 442
  disorders, 493–494
  evaluation of theories, 443–444
  five-factor model, 439–440
  Freudian psychoanalysis, 445–449
  and health, 428–429
  humanistic theories, 451–453
  inventory, 464
  Minnesota Multiphasic Personality Inventory (MMPI), 464–465
  NEO Personality Inventory (NEO-PI), 464, 465–466
  objective tests of, 464–466
  projective tests of, 466–467
  psychodynamic theories of, 444–451
  psychosexual development, 445–447
  Rorschach test, 466–467
  structure of, 447–448
  structures, 438
  Thematic Apperception Test (TAT), 467
  theories, 462–464
  traits, 437–440
    behavior predictions and, 442–443
    and heritability, 441–442
    types of, 436–437
Personality psychologists, 17
Personality structure, 443–444
Personal relationships
  Internet and, 568
  loving relationships, 565–569
Personal relevance, 553–554
Personnel psychology, 387
Person-organization fit, 387
Perspectives in psychology, 11–16
  comparison of, 15–16
Persuasion
  elaboration likelihood model of, 552–553
  personal relevance and, 553–554
  process of, 552–554
  self-efficacy judgments and, 456

Pessimism, 385–386
Pessimistic attributional style, 385–386
PET scans, 65
  amyloid B-peptide (AB) and, 237
  memory information, 240
  reasoning tasks and, 271
  therapies and, 536
Phenotypes, 58–59
Pheromones, 118, 375
Phi phenomenon, 128
Phobias, 195, 483. See also Social phobias
  behavior therapies and, 518
  exposure therapies, 519–520
  flooding therapy, 519
  symbolic modeling therapy, 522
Phonemes, 333
Phonemic restoration, 135–136
Phonetics, 333
Phonological loop, 216
Phonology, 333
Photographic memory, 211–213
Photographs, emotions and, 394
Photoreceptors, 104–105
Physical attractiveness, 564
Physical copresence, 253
Physical development, 318
Physical growth, 321–322
Physical rotation, 261
Physiological dependence on drugs, 163
Pictorial cues to depth, 130–132
Pinna, 115
Pitch, 113
  heritability of perception, 61
  theories of, 116–117
Pituitary gland, 78–79
  and fight-or-flight response, 408
Pixels, 109
Placebo effects, 28–29
  hypnosis and, 158
  psychotherapy and, 535
  in subliminal influence research, 33
Placebos, 29, 88, 121
Placebo therapy, 535
Place recognition, 106
Place theory, 116
Planning function of consciousness, 146
Plasticity, 88–89
Plateau phase, 376
Pleasure principle, 47
Pleistocene era, 14
Poggendorf illusion, 98
Polarized cells, 82
Pons, 70
Ponzo illusion, 131
Population research sample, 30
Positive evaluation of violence, 590
Positive punishment, 184
Positive reinforcement strategies, 183–184, 521
Positive transference, 515
Possible selves, 458
Postevent information, 235–236
Postsynaptic membrane, 84
Posttraumatic stress disorder (PTSD), 412–413, 484
  brain activity and, 485
Potassium (K+) ions, 81
Practical intelligence, 297, 299

Practical intelligence for school (PIFS), 299
Pragmatic reasoning schema, 270
Pragmatics, 333
Preconscious memories, 142, 143
Precontemplation stage, 423, 425
Preconventional morality stage, 355
Predictions in psychology, 7
Predictive validity, 288–289
Predispositions, 438
Prefrontal cortex, 86
Prefrontal lobotomy, 531
Pregnancy, 318–319
  sexual risk taking, 379
Prejudice, 558–563. See also Stereotypes
  origins of, 558, 560
  reversing, 562–563
Premack principle, 190
Prenatal development, 318–319
Prenatal stokes, 319
Preoperational stage, 326
Preparation stage, 423, 425
Preparedness hypothesis, 484
Presynaptic membrane, 84
Prevention strategies, 537–539
Primacy effect, 219
Primary appraisal of stress, 415
Primary prevention, 538
Primary reinforcers, 187
Priming, 224–225
Principalism, 584
Principled morality stage, 355
Principles of contrast, 334
The Principles of Psychology (James), 9
Principles of Psychology (Kendler), 9
Proactive interference, 223
Problem-directed coping, 416–417
Problem solving, 265–268
  analogical problem solving, 271
  functional fixedness, 268
  heuristics, 266
  improving on, 267–268
  inductive reasoning and, 271
  think-aloud protocols, 266–267
Problem spaces, 265–266
Procedural memory, 208–209
  amnesia and, 239
Procrastination, costs of, 411
Prognosis
  of mental illness, 479
  treatment, 510
Progressive education, 11
Projection, 449
Projective tests of personality, 466–467
Proofs, 268
Propositions, 256–257
Prosocial behavior, 584–587
Prototypes, 230–232
Proximal stimuli, 94–96
Proximity, law of, 126
Proximity-promoting signals, 339
Prozac, 534
Psilocybe mushrooms, 162
Psychedelics, 163
Psychiatrists, 511
Psychic determinism, 447
Psychic energy, 366, 446
Psychoactive disorders, 163–165
Psychoanalysis, 445–449, 511, 514–515
  comparison of approaches, 524

Psychobiographies, 452
Psychodynamic perspective, 12, 476–477
  aggression, analysis of, 16
  of anxiety disorders, 485–486
  of mood disorders, 490
  personality theories, 444–451
  therapies, 510, 514–518
Psychological assessment, 286
Psychological dependence, 163
Psychological disorders. See Mental illness
Psychological measurement, 34–37
  behavioral measures, 35–37
  case studies, 37
  observation, 35–37
  reliability, creating, 34–35
  self-reports, 35
  validity and, 34–35
Psychological spaces, 529
Psychologists
  clinical psychologists, 511
  counseling psychologists, 511
  types of, 16–18
  work settings for, 18
Psychology
  defined, 4
  goals of, 5–8
  reasons for studying, 8
Psychology from the Standpoint of a Behaviorist (Watson), 171
Psychology (James), 142
Psychometrics, 100, 295–296
Psychomotor behavior, 499
Psychoneuroimmunology, 426–427
Psychopharmacologists, 17
Psychopathology, 472
Psychopharmacology, 532
Psychophysics, 99–103
  absolute thresholds, 99–100
  difference thresholds, 102–103
  response bias, 101–102
  signal detection theory (SDT), 101–102
  transduction, 103
Psychosexual development, 445–447
Psychosocial stages, 337–338
Psychosomatic disorders, 409
Psychosurgery, 69, 531
Psychotherapy, 510
Psychotic disorders, 479
Psychoticism, 439
Puberty, 323
Pubescent growth spurt, 322–323
Public verifiability of research, 24
Punishers, 184
Punishment, 184, 187
  aggression and, 188–189
Pupil of eye, 104
Pure tones, 114
Purposive instincts, 365
Pygmalion effect, 548
Pygmalion (Shaw), 548

Quality of life, 421
Quantifying intelligence, 286, 290–291
Questionnaires, self-reports on, 35

Race. See also Prejudice
  and eating disorders, 374
  intelligence and, 301, 302–303
  jigsaw classrooms and, 563
  suicide and, 493

Racism, 560
Radical behaviorism, 171
Random assignment, 558
  coercive rules and, 575
Random assignment of
  participants, 29–30
Range of data, 49
Rank order, 47
Rape, 380
  date rape, 380
  posttraumatic stress disorder
    (PTSD) and, 413
Rational-emotive therapy (RET),
  526
Rationalization, 449
Ratio schedules, 191–192
Raw data, 46
Reaction formation, 449
Reaction time, 247
Reality
  cultural constructions of, 146
  denial of, 449
  personal construction of, 146
  principle, 447
Real-world knowledge, 270
Reappraising stressors, 417–418
Reasoning, 265
  belief-bias effect, 269–270
  brain bases of, 271–272
  deductive reasoning, 268–272
  expert systems, 273
  inductive reasoning, 271–272
Recall, 221
  encoding and, 218
Recency effect, 219–220
Receptive fields, 107
Receptor molecules, 84
Reciprocal altruism, 583
Reciprocal determinism, 455
Reciprocal inhibition theory, 519
Reciprocity
  altruism and, 583
  friends and, 565
  norm, 556–557
Recognition, 94, 221
  encoding and, 218
  processes, 134–137
Reconstructive memory, 234–236
  eyewitness memory, 235–236
Reference points, 279
Refractory period, 84
Regression, 449
Rehearsal
  elaborative rehearsal, 226, 228
  and memory, 214–215
Reinforcement contingencies,
  183–187
  discriminative stimuli, 184–185
  history, 453
  punishment, 184–185
  schedules of reinforcement,
    190–192
  shaping, 192–193
  token economies, 190
  using, 185–187
Reinforcers, 183
  children and, 186
  conditioned reinforcers, 187,
    190
  Premack principle, 190
  properties of, 187–190
Rejection and aggression, 592
Relative motion parallax, 130
Relative refractory period, 84
Relative size and depth, 131
Relaxation
  and health, 426
  hypnotic induction and, 158

response, 426
Reliability, 34–35
  assessment and, 287–288
  parallel forms and, 287–288
  validity and, 289
Religion
  conflict and, 604–605
  ecstacy, religious, 161–162
  hallucinations and, 161
  pastoral counselors, 511
*Remembering: A Study in
  Experimental and Social
  Psychology* (Bartlett), 234
REM sleep, 150
  lucid dreaming and, 157
Repeated pairings, 173
Repetitive transcranial magnetic
  stimulation (rTMS), 63–64,
  532
Representations and speech,
  254
Representativeness heuristic,
  276–277
Representative sample, 30
Repression, 448, 514
  ideas, repressed, 143–144
  of memories, 516
  mental illness and, 477
Reproduction
  aging and, 324
  sexual strategies and, 377–378
Request politeness, 404
Research, 17
  animal research, ethical issues
    in, 39
  between-subjects designs, 29
  on cognitive development, 328
  control procedures, 29–30
  correlational methods, 30–33
  critical thinking and, 40–41
  debriefing participants, 38–39
  elements of experiment, 27
  ethical issues, 38–39
  on heritability, 61
  human development studies,
    317
  informed consent requirement,
    38
  intentional deception in, 38
  methods of, 27–30
  observer bias, 25–27
  operational definitions, 25–27
  process of, 24–34
  psychological measurement,
    34–37
  random assignment of
    participants, 29–30
  reliability, 34–35
  risk/gain assessment, 38
  self-reports, 35
  standardization, 25–27
  on subliminal influence, 33–34
  and 21st century psychology, 18
  validity of, 34–35
  within-subjects design, 30
Residual type of schizophrenia,
  500
Resistance, 409, 515
Resolution phase, 377
Response bias, 101–102
Response prevention, 520
Response selection, 247
Responsibility
  creating sense of, 586–587
  motivation and, 363
Responsible traits, 439
Responsiveness, 340
Resting potential, 82

Resting state of cell, 82
Restoration, NREM sleep and,
  151–152
Restrained eating, 369–370
Restrictive function of
  consciousness, 146
Restructuring stress reactions,
  417–418
Retention interval, 221
Reticular formation, 68
Retina, 104–106
  disparity, retinal, 129–130
  images, 95
  pathways, retinal, 105
  restoration of site and, 109
Retirement, 316
Retrieval. *See* Memory
Retroactive interference, 223
Retrograde amnesia, 239
Reversal theory, 364–365
  anxiety-to-excitement reversal,
    365
Reversibility, 328
Right hemisphere of brain,
  74–76
Right visual field, 75
Risk/gain assessment, 38
Ritual healing ceremonies, 513
Robbers Cave experiment,
  562–563
Rods and cones, 104–105
  restoration of site and, 109
  types of, 112
Rohypnol, 164
Roofies, 164
Rooting reflex, 320
Rorschach test, 466–467
Rote learning, 206
Rubella, 318
Rules, 574–576

Saccule, 120
Safety needs, 388
Sailfin mollies, 375–376
Sample
  IQ scores, distribution of, 293
  research sample, 30
Satiety cues, 368
Saturation of color, 110
Scapegoats, 600
  aversions, 196
Scarcity, 557
Schedules of reinforcement,
  190–192
Schemas, 232–233
  pragmatic reasoning schema,
    270
  self-schemas, 458
Schemes, 325
Schizophrenia, 471, 497–503
  assessment, manipulation of,
    288
  biological markers for, 502
  brain function and, 502
  catatonic type of, 499–500
  causes of, 500–503
  disorganized type of, 499
  dopamine and, 87
  drug therapies for, 533
  expressed emotion and, 503
  family interaction and, 502–503
  genetics and, 500–501
  lobotomy and, 531
  paranoid type of, 500
  residual type of, 500
  shock treatment, 531–532
  split personality and, 495
  types of, 499–500

undifferentiated type, 500
unintentional reinforcement
  and, 522
School psychologists, 17
Scientific method, 4, 24
Scientific predictions, 7
Seasonal affective disorder
  (SAD), 488–489
Secondary appraisal of stress,
  415
Secondary gains, 187
Secondary prevention, 538
Secondary traits, 438
Secrets and health, 427
Secure attachment style, 566
Selective advantage, 58
Selective encoding, 544–545
Selective optimization with
  compensation, 331, 357
Selective social interaction
  theory, 349–350
Selective storage, 146
Self
  culture and, 460–462
  dissonance and, 555
  Internet and, 463
  self-system, 517
Self-actualization, 13, 388, 450,
  451–453, 453
Self-awareness, 142
  objective self-awareness, 148
Self-concept, 458–459
  and mood disorders, 491
Self-condemnation, avoiding, 355
Self-confidence, 417
Self construals, 460
  and aggressive behavior,
    593–594
  independent construals of self,
    546
  interdependent construals of
    self, 546
Self-efficacy, 456
  cognitive behavior
    modification and, 526
Self-enhancement, 461
Self-esteem, 459–460
  subliminal influence and, 33
Self-evaluations
  culture and, 460–461
  self-perception theory, 556
Self-fulfilling prophecies, 548–549
Self-handicapping behavior, 459
Self-help groups, 530
Self-hypnosis, 160
Self-injurious behaviors, 520
Self-insight, 458
Self-perception theory, 556
Self-presentation, 459–460
Self-preservaton drive, 446
Self-regulatory efficacy, 456
Self-reports, 35
  inventory, 464
Self-schemas, 232, 458
Self-serving biases, 547
Self theories, 458–462
  evaluation of, 462
Self-verification, 491
Semantic memories, 222
Semantics, 333
Sensation, 93. *See also*
  Psychophysics
  absolute thresholds, 99–100
  defined, 94
Sensation seeking, 422
Sense of self, 142
  consciousness and, 146
Sensitivity of skin, 119–120

Sensorimotor stage, 325–326
Sensory adaptation, 100–101
Sensory cortex, 71
Sensory memory, 210–213
Sensory neurons, 80
Sensory process, 101
Sensory receptors, 94, 103
Sensory-specific satiety, 368
Sensuality, 93–94
Sentences
    meaning, 251
    structures, 255
September 11th attacks, 412–413
Serial position effect, 219–221, 228
Serial processes, 247–248
Serotonin, 87
    aggression and, 589
    antidepressant drugs and, 534
    antipsychotic drugs and, 533
    and seasonal affective disorder (SAD), 489
Set of operations for problem, 265
Sets, 137
Sex chromosomes, 60–61
Sex differences, 352–353
Sexism, 560
Sexual arousal
    emotional misinterpretation and, 401–402
    in humans, 376–377
Sexual behavior, 374–382. See also Homosexuality
    aging and, 324
    AIDS risk and, 423
    evolution of, 377–378
    frequency of sexual activity, 379
    nonhuman sexual behaviors, 374–376
    number of partners, 379
    phases of, 376–377
    pheromones and, 118
    risk taking, 379–380
    of sailfin mollies, 375–376
    strategies for, 377
Sexual disorders, 481
Sexual norms, 378–380
Sexual scripts, 378–380
Shadowing, 125
Shallow judgments, 224, 225
Shamanism, 155, 513
Shape constancy, 133
Shaping technique, 521
Sharpening, 234
Shock treatment, 531–532
Short-term mating, 378
Short-term memory (STM), 213–218
    accommodating to capacity of, 214–216
    capacity limits on, 213–214
    chunking and, 215–216
    retrieval from, 216
    working memory and, 216–217
Shyness, 6, 45, 444–445
    tactics for, 445
Sibling conflict, 32
Sight. See Visual system
Signal detection theory (SDT), 101–102
Significant difference, 52
Similarity
    and friendships, 565
    law of, 126
Simple cells, 107
Simultaneous conditioning, 174, 175

Sine waves, 113
Situational causality, 545
Situational forces, 367
Situational power, 574–582
    and aggression, 590–592
    Candid Camera revelations, 581–582
    prosocial behavior and, 585–587
Size constancy, 132–133
Size/distance relation, 131
Skin senses, 119–120
Slave Market with the Disappearing Bust (Dali), 97
Sleep, 149–154. *See also* Dreams
    circadian rhythms, 149
    cycle, 149–151
    disorders, 152–154
    Internet and, 154
    reasons for, 151–152
    stages of, 151
Sleep Alert, 153–154
Sleep apnea, 153
Sleep spindles, 150
Sleep walking, 153
SLIP (Spoonerisms of Laboratory-Induced Predisposition), 146–147, 254
Smell, 118
    long-term memory (LTM) and, 219
    sexual arousal and, 375
    taste and, 119
Smoking, 421–423
    stages for quitting, 423
Soap opera effect, 234
Social categorization, 558, 560
Social cognition, 544
Social desirability, 35
Social development, 336–351
    in adolescence, 343–347
    in adulthood, 347–351
    average life course, 336–337
    day care and, 342
    Erikson's psychosocial stages, 337–338
    parenting and, 340–341
Social imitation, 453
Social intelligence theory, 457
Social-interactive concept, 514
Socialization, 338–344
    contact comfort, 341, 343
    gender-role socialization, 353–354
    goals, 341
    human deprivation and, 343–344
Social-learning theories, 366–367, 453–458
    Bandura's cognitive social-learning theory, 455–457
    evaluation of, 457–458
    therapies, 522–523
Social me, 458
Social norms, 576
Social phobias, 483
    brain changes and treatment, 536
Social psychologists, 16–17, 543–544
Social Readjustment Rating Scale (SRRS), 410–411
Social reality, 544–550, 575
Social relationships, 563–569
Social roles, 574–576
    obedience and, 596
Social rules, 574–576

Social sciences, 4
Social-skills training, 523
Social support
    job burnout and, 429
    and stress, 419–420
    Type A behavior and, 429
Social workers, clinical, 511
Society
    emotions and, 403
    and homosexuality, 381–382
    intelligence assessment and, 309–311
Sociobiology, 61–62
Sociocultural perspective, 15
    aggression, analysis of, 16
    of mental illness, 477
Socioeconomic status, 303–305
Socioemotional support, 419
Sodium (Na+) ions, 81–82
Soma, 79
Somatic nervous system, 66–68
Somatoform disorders, 481
Somatosensory cortex, 72, 73
Somnambulism, 153
Sound. *See also* Hearing; Language
    echoic memory, 212–213
    localization, 117
    loudness, 114
    physics of, 113
    pitch of, 113
    pressure, 114
    psychological dimensions of, 113–114
    timbre of, 114
Sound shadow, 117
Source traits, 439
Spanking, 188–189
Spatial integration, 127–128
Spatial intelligence, 298
Spatial memory, 197
Spatial mental models, 262–263
Speakers, 251
    meaning of, 251
Species-specific instincts, 366
Specific phobias, 483
Speech. *See* Language; Speech errors
Speech errors, 254
    speech errors and, 147
    unconscious and, 147
Speed of recognition, 216
Sperm production, 324
Spicy foods, 123
Spinal cord, 66, 68
Spiritual me, 458
Split-brain patients, 74–77
    hand-eye coordination, 76
Split-half reliability, 287, 288
Split personality, 495
Spontaneous recovery, 175–176
Spontaneous-remission effect, 535
Spoonerisms, 146–147, 253–254
Sports psychologists, 17
SSRIS (selective serotonin reuptake inhibitors), 534
St. Mary of Bethlehem, 512
Stability, attributions and, 384–385
Standard deviation (SD), 49
Standard exposure therapy, 519
Standardization, 25–26
    assessment and, 289–290
Stanford-Binet Intelligence Scale, 291
Stanford Prison Experiment, 574–576

Stanford Shyness Survey, 45
Statistics
    correlation coefficients, 50
    descriptive statistics, 46–50
    frequency distributions, 46–47
    graphs, 47–48
    inferential statistics, 46, 50–52
    measure of central tendency, 48–49
    misuse of, 52–53
    relationships, statistical, 295
    significance, statistical, 51–52
    significant difference, 52
    statistical significance, 51–52
    variability, measures of, 49
Stem cells, 89
Stereotypes
    creativity and insanity, 308
    discounting information, 561
    effects of, 560–562
    intelligence assessment and, 305–306
    language and, 233
    sexual behavior, stereotyped, 375
    vulnerability, 305–306
Stereotype threat, 305–306, 561
Sternberg's triarchic theory of intelligence, 296–297
Stigma of mental illness, 504–505
Stimulants, 164–165
Stimuli
    distal stimuli, 94–96
    jus noticeable difference (JND), 102–103
    perceptual similarity, 199
    proximal stimuli, 94–96
    psychometric function and, 100
Stimulus categorization, 247
Stimulus discrimination, 177
Stimulus-driven capture, 122, 124
Stimulus generalization, 176–177
Stimulus-response (S-R) connection, 181–182
Stirrup of ear, 115
Storage. *See* Memory
Straight-line rule, 128
Strange Situation Test, 339–340
Street smarts, 297
Stress, 406–420
    aggression and, 589
    anticipatory coping, 416
    body's reaction to, 409
    chronic illness and, 419
    chronic stressors, 413–414
    cognitive appraisal of, 415–416
    coping with, 415–420
    daily life and, 414–415
    emergency reactions to threats, 408
    fight-or-flight response, 408
    general adaptation syndrome (GAS), 409–410
    and immune function, 427
    job burnout, 429–430
    model of, 407
    modifying cognitive strategies and, 417–418
    perceived control and, 418
    physiological reactions to, 406–410
    posttraumatic stress disorder (PTSD), 412–413, 484
    psychological reactions to, 410–415
    social support and, 419–420
    tend-and-befriend response, 408

<www.ablongman.com/gerrig17e>

Credits

2, © Anton Vengo/SuperStock; 5, TL, © Myrleen Ferguson Cate/PhotoEdit; 5, TR, © Tony Savino/the Image Works; 5, BL; © David Young-Wolff/PhotoEdit; 5, BR, © Michael Schwarz/The Image Works; 6, George S. Seurat, *Bathers at Asnieres*. National Gallery, London. Copyright Erich Lessing/Art Resource, NY; 7, © Jeff Greenberg/PhotoEdit; 9 and 10, Archives of the History of American Psychology/University of Akron; 11, © Michael Newman/PhotoEdit; 12, The Granger Collection; 14, Courtesy American Museum of Natural History Library; 17, © Michael Grecco/Stock Boston; 22, © Mehau Kulyk/Photo Researchers, Inc.; 25, John Bazemore/AP/Wide World Photos; 28, Edouard Berne/Stone/GettyImages, Inc.; 32, © Kwama Zikomo/SuperStock; 35, © Jeff Greenberg/PhotoEdit; 36, Michael K. Nichols/National Geographic Image Collection; 39, Richard T. Nowitz/PhotoTake; 40, © *Jacksonville Journal Courier*/The Image Works; 54, © Alfred Pasieka/Photo Researchers, Inc.; 56, VLC/Antonio Mo/Taxi/GettyImages, Inc.; 60, Dan McCoy/Rainbow; 64T, Reprinted with permission from Damasio H, Grabowski T, Frank R, Galaburda, AM, Damasio AR: The return of Phineas Gage: Clues about the brain from a famous patient. *Science*, 264:1102–1105, © 1994, American Association for the Advancement of Science. Photo courtesy of H. Damasio, Human Neuroanatomy and Neuroimaging Laboratory, Department of Neurology, University of Iowa; 64B, © Jiang Jin/SuperStock; 66, Stone/UHB Trust/GettyImages, Inc.; 65, Courtesy of Marcus E. Raichle, M.D., Washington University School of Medicine; 78, Roadell Hickman/*The Plain Dealer*/AP/Wide World Photos; 80, © D. W. Fawcett/Komuro/Photo Researchers, Inc.; 88, Joe Marquette/AP/Wide World Photos; 89, Tim Maylon and Paul Biddle/SPL/Photo Researchers, Inc.; 92, Michael Cogliantry/The Image Bank/GettyImages, Inc.; 92, David Lissy/Index Stock; 97, *Slave Market with the Disappearing Bust of Voltaire* (1940). Oil on canvas. $18\frac{1}{2}$ x $25\frac{3}{8}$ inches. Collection of The Salvador Dali Museum, St. Petersburg, Florida. © 2004 Gala-Salvador Dali Foundation, Figueres (Artist Rights Society [ARS] New York. © 2004 Salvador Dali Museum, Inc.; 100, © David Kelly Crow/PhotoEdit; 101, Stefan May/Stone Allstock/GettyImages, Inc.; 104, W. E. Harvey/Photo Researchers, Inc.; 108, Reprinted with permission from PE Downing et al., SCIENCE 293:2473 (2001). © 2004 AAAS; 110, © Alan Levanson/Stock Boston; 114, Jerry S. Mendoza/AP/Wide World Photos; 116, © Bob Daemmrich/Stock Boston; 117, Stephen Kraseman/Stone/GettyImages, Inc.; 119, © Norbert Schwerin/The Image Works; 121T, David Ball/Index Stock; 121B, © Pic Tommy Hindley/Professional Sport/Topham/The Image Works; 122, © Fuji Photos/The Image Works; 123, Scott Foresman; 129, Dennis O'Clair/Stone/GettyImages, Inc.; 131L, Andy Levin/Photo Researchers, Inc.; 131R, Michael Dwyer/Stock Boston; 132, William J. Herbert/Stone Allstock/GettyImages, Inc.; 133, © David Wells/The Image Works; 134, Bob Rowan/Corbis; 136, Scott Forsman; 140, Thomas Hoeffgen/Taxi/GettyImages, Inc.; 142, © David Young-Wolff/PhotoEdit; 143L, © Bonnie Kamin/PhotoEdit; 143TR, N. Durrell/McKenna/Photo Researchers, Inc.; 143BR, © Ulrike Welsch/PhotoEdit; 149L, Jim Sugar/Corbis; 149R, Chuck Solomon/Sports Illustrated © Time, Inc.; 152, © Spencer Grant/PhotoEdit; 158, Courtesy of Dr. Phillip G. Zimbardo; 160, © Peter Hvizdak/The Image Works; 162, Mike Maple/Woodfin Camp & Assoc.; 165, Chuck Savage/The Stock Market; 168, © Philip & Karen Smith/SuperStock; 170, © PAL/Topham/The Image Works; 171, Ken Heyman/Woodfin Camp & Assoc.; 172, © Bettmann/Corbis; 176, © Innervisions 1994; 179T, Archives of the History of American Psychology; 179B, PhotoFest; 180T, © David Young-Wolff/PhotoEdit; 180B, Hulton Archive Photos; 182, SuperStock; 187, © Cindy Charles/PhotoEdit; 190, Yerkes Regional Primate Research Center, Emory University; 192, Stephen Ferry/Liaison Agency, Inc.; 194T, Gerald Davis/Woodfin Camp & Assoc.; 194B, John Warden/Stone/GettyImages, Inc.; 196, Courtesy Dr. Stuart R. Ellins/California State University, San Bernadino; 200, Courtesy Dr. Albert Bandura, Stanford University; 201, © David Young-Wolff/PhotoEdit; 204, The Image Bank/GettyImages, Inc./Yellow Dog Productions; 206, AP/Wide World Photos; 208, © SuperStock; 214, © Bill Aron/PhotoEdit; 215, Kevin Horan/Stone/GettyImages, Inc.; 217, © Joseph Nettis/Stock Boston; 219, Spencer Grant/Photo Researchers, Inc.; 222, © Jeff Greenberg/PhotoEdit; 226, © Lon C. Diehl/PhotoEdit; 230, © Tom McCarthy/PhotoEdit; 234, © 1995 Comstock, Inc.; 236, © John Neubauer/PhotoEdit; 241, Reprinted with permission from MM Zeineh et al., SCIENCE 299:577–580 (2003). © Copyright 2004 AAAS; 244, Joe McBride/Stone/GettyImages, Inc.; 249, © David Young-Wolff/PhotoEdit; 250, Reprinted from NEUROPSYCHOLOGIA, Vol. 39, 2001, pp. 1167–1176, Rossell et al.: "Brain activation during automatic and controlled processing of semantic relations: a priming experiment using lexical-decision". © Copyright 2004, with permission from Elsevier; 251, Stuart Cohen/© 1995/Comstock, Inc.; 253, Fred Bavendam/Peter Arnold; 256, AP/Wide World Photos; 258, Steve Winter/Language Research Center/GSU; 259, Karl Muller/Woodfin Camp & Assoc.; 267, Will & Demi McIntyre/Photo Researchers, Inc.; 272, Reprinted from CEREBRAL CORTEX, Vol. 11, p. 959, 2001. Parsons and Osherson, "New evidence for distinct right and left brain systems for deductive versus probabilistic reasoning" © Copyright Oxford University Press 2004; 275, © 1995 Comstock, Inc.; 280, © David Frazier/The Image Works; 284, Tobi Corney/Stone/GettyImages, Inc.; 286, Science Library/Photo Researchers, Inc.; 289, © Laura Dwight/PhotoEdit; 292, © Mary Kate Denny/PhotoEdit; 297, © J. Griffin/The Image Works; 300, Brown Brothers; 302, © Bettmann/Corbis; 303, AP/Wide World Photos; 304L, Ed Clark/TimePix; 304R, Gary Buss/Taxi/GettyImages, Inc.; 308L, Kaz Mori/The Image Bank/GettyImages, Inc.; 308R, © SuperStock; 309, The Granger Collection; 310, © Tony Freeman/PhotoEdit; 314, Denis Felix/Taxi/GettyImages, Inc.; 316L, Popperfoto/Hulton Archive, 316M, Hulton Archive, 316R, Topham/The Image Works; 317L, Brown Brothers; 317R, Nathan Bilow/Allsport Photography/GettyImages, Inc.; 318, Lennart Nelson/*A Child Is Born*/Bonniers; 320T, © Elizabeth Crews/The Image Works; 320B, © Alan Carey/The Image Works; 321, Birnbach/Monkmeyer; 322, © Mike Greenlar/The Image Works, 323, © Robert W. Ginn/PhotoEdit; 324, Donna Day/Stone/GettyImages, Inc.; 326, Lew Merrim/Monkmeyer; 327, Marcia Weinstein; 330T, © McLaughlin/The Image Works, 330B, AP/Wide World Photos; 335, © DPA/The Image Works; 338, Sarah Putnam/Index Stock; 339, © Nina Leen/Timepix; 340, © Bob Daemmrich/The Image Works; 343, Martin Rogers/Stone/GettyImages, Inc.; 346, © Jeff Greenberg/The Image Works; 349, Eyewire Collection/PhotoDisc/GettyImages, Inc.; 352, J. P. Williams/Stone/GettyImages, Inc.; 353, © Tony Freeman/PhotoEdit; 360, © SuperStock; 362, Jo McBride/Stone/GettyImages, Inc.; 363, AP/Wide World Photos; 365, John Shaw/Bruce Coleman, Inc.; 368, © James Shaffer/PhotoEdit; 372T, Jon Kopaloff/© 2003 GettyImages, Inc.; 372B, AP/Wide World Photos; 375, SuperStock; 377, © B. Bachman/The Image Works; 380, © Esbin/Anderson/The Image Works; 381, © SuperStock; 383, © Bob Daemmrich/Stock Boston; 384T, © M. Antman/The Image Works; 384B, © *Syracuse Newspapers*/The Image Works; 387, Reuters/Jeff Topping/Archive Photos; 388, © Rach Epstein/The Image Works; 392, © SuperStock; 394, Photography Collection Miriam and Ira D. Wallach Division of Art, Prints and Photographs. The New York Public Library, Astor, Lenox and Tilden Foundation; 396, Dr. Paul Ekman/Human Interaction Library/University of California/San Francisco; 397L, © Burbank/The Image Works; 397R, Kathy Willens/AP/Wide World Photos; 400L, © Topham/The Image Works; 400R, © Michael J. Doolittle/The Image Works; 402, © Bonnie Kamin/PhotoEdit; 403, © Robert Brenner/PhotoEdit; 407L, © Phil Martin/PhotoEdit; 407R, © Robert Brenner/PhotoEdit; 408, © Esbin-Anderson/The Image Works; 412, Phil Coale/AP/Wide World Photos; 414, Jim West/Impact Visuals; 416, © Bill Aron/PhotoEdit; 421, © Terry Eiler/Stock Boston; 424, Ginnette P. Adams/AP/Wide World Photos; 426, © Jeff Greenberg/The Image Works; 428, © Richard Lord/The Image Works; 430, © Tony Savino/The Image Works; 434, Ron Chapple/Taxi/GettyImages, Inc.; 437, Courtesy of Zentralbibliothek, Zurich; 438L, The Granger Collection; 438M, Bettmann/Corbis; 438R, Reuters/Jonathan Evans/Archive Photos; 441T, Reprinted with permission from T Canli et al., SCIENCE 296:2191 (2002). Copyright © 2004 AAAS; 441B, © SuperStock; 443L, Doug Arman/Stone/GettyImages, Inc.; 443R, Gary Braasch/Woodfin Camp & Assoc.; 446, Jake Rais/Stone/GettyImages, Inc.; 450, Art © Jim Berris/Photo, Rafael Marcia/Photo Researchers, Inc.; 453, 454, © Richard Hutchings/PhotoEdit; 460T, © Steve Rubin/The Image Works; 460B, © Esbin-Anderson/The Image Works; 462, © Steve Maines/Stock Boston; 467, Reprinted by permission of the publishers from Henry A. Murray, THEMATIC APPERCEPTION TEST, Plate 12F, Cambridge, Mass.: Harvard University Press, Copyright © 1943 by the President & Fellows of Harvard College. © 1971 by Henry A. Murray; 470, Denis Felix/Taxi/GettyImages, Inc.; 472, Jack Rezmicki/The Stock Market; 475, *The Trial of George Jacobs*, August 5, 1692, oil on canvas by T. H. Mattenson, 1855. Photograph courtesy Peabody Essex Museum; 476, The Granger Collection; 482, © David Grossman/the Image Works; 483, William Hubbell/Woodfin Camp & Assoc.; 485, Reprinted from BIOLOGICAL PSYCHIATRY, 53, 204–210, RA Lanius et al.,"Recall of emotional states in posttraumatic stress disorder: An fMRI investigation". © Copyright 2004 with permission from Society of Biological Psychiatry; 487, *Melancholia*, 1988, Amy Wicherski/SuperStock; 489, Reprinted with permission from ARCHIVES OF GENERAL PSYCHIATRY, 60, 601–609, HP Blumberg, et al., "A functional magnetic resonance imaging study of bipolar disorder." © Copyright 2003 American Medical Association; 491, © Esbin-Anderson/The Image Works; 492, Britt Erianson/The Image Bank/GettyImages, Inc.; 493, AP/Wide World Photos; 494, Photomondo/FPG International; 495, © Susan Greenwood/Liaison Agency; 496, © David Young-Wolff/PhotoEdit; 502, Lab of Psychology and Psychopathy, National Institute of Mental Health; reproduced by permission of Edna Morlock; 503, © Robert Brenner/PhotoEdit; 508, Zigy Kaluzny/Stone/GettyImages, Inc.; 512, The Granger Collection; 515, AP/Wide World Photos; 517, Wellcome Library, London; 520, © Bob Mahoney/The Image Works; 522, Courtesy of Dr. Philip G. Zimbardo; 526, © Stephen Frisch/Stock Boston; 527, © Michelle Bridwell/PhotoEdit; 529, © Bob Daemmrich/The Image Works; 532L, James Wilson/Woodfin Camp & Assoc.; 532R, Will McIntyre/Photo Researchers, Inc.; 534, Digital Vision Ltd.; 536, Reprinted with permission from ARCHIVES OF GENERAL PSYCHIATRY, 59, 425–433, T. Furmark, et al., "Common changes in cerebral blood flow in patients with social phobia treated with citalopram or cognitive-behavioral therapy. © Copyright 2004 American Medical Association; 538, Stewart Cohen/Stone/GettyImages, Inc.; 542, Peter Adams/The Image Bank/GettyImages, Inc.; 544, AP/Wide World Photos; 548, © David Young-Wolff/Stone/GettyImages, Inc.; 551, Kevin Winter © 2003 GettyImages, Inc.; 552, Francis Specker/AP/Wide World Photos; 553, Tony Hawk © 1998 Courtesy of National Fluid Milk Processor Promotion Board; 555, AP/Wide World Photos; 557, © Susan Van Etten-Lawson/PhotoEdit; 558, AP/World Wide Photos; 560, © Bob Daemmrich/The Image Works; 561L, © Bill Aron/PhotoEdit; 561R, © W. Hill, Jr./The Image Works; 562, Dr. O. J. Harvey, University of Colorado; 564, © Rhoda Sidney/PhotoEdit; 566, Bruce Ayers/Stone/GettyImages, Inc.; 572, Elliott Minor/AP/Wide World Photos; 574, Michael S. Yamashita/Woodfin Camp & Assoc.; 575, Courtesy of Dr. Philip G. Zimbardo; 577, Kaku Kurita/Liaison Agency; 579, Courtesy of William Vandivert; 581, Everett Collection; 582, AP/Wide World Photos; 585T, © David Young-Wolff/PhotoEdit; 585B, AP/Wide World Photos; 588L, © M. Reardon/Photo Researchers, Inc.; 588R, © Catherine Ursillo/Photo Researchers, Inc.; 589, AP/Wide World Photos; 590, © Bob Daemmrich/The Image Works; p. 593, Hulton/Archive Photos; 595, Raynald Mackechnie/Stone Allstock/GettyImages, Inc.; 597, From the film *Obedience* © by Stanley Milgram, by permission of Alexandra Milgram; 599, AP/Wide World Photos; 600, AP/Wide World Photos; 601, S. Keen (1986) Faces of the Enemy: Reflections of the hostile imagination. © 1986 by Sam Keen. All rights reserved. Reprinted by permission of HarperCollins Publishers, Inc.; 604, AP/Wide World Photos.

PRACTICE TESTS

Prepared by Richard J. Gerrig and Philip G. Zimbardo

CHAPTER 1 Psychology and Life

What Makes Psychology Unique

1. The conclusions about behavior that are made by psychologists are based on
   a. information that is collected objectively.
   b. the casual observations psychologists make in their daily lives.
   c. their personal beliefs and value systems.
   d. intuition and common sense.

2. In her introductory course on research methods, the professor is giving a short classroom presentation on the "scientific method." She is most likely to mention the
   a. reliance of researchers on intuition in their theories.
   b. steps used by researchers to analyze and solve problems.
   c. general inability of psychologists to draw conclusions from their data.
   d. importance of authority and personal beliefs in the determination of truth.

3. Which of the following is the best example of an objective observation?
   a. She saw him running to first base as fast as he could.
   b. She saw him look away when he felt others were watching him.
   c. He closed all of his open files and turned off the computer.
   d. The dog lowered its head knowing it had behaved badly.

4. The young violinist practices many hours each day, striving to improve her skills. When her teacher speaks of her as being strongly motivated and perfectionistic, he is emphasizing _____ variables.
   a. environmental
   b. situational
   c. descriptive
   d. internal

5. Two workers are complaining about the fact that their supervisor still does not know their names, despite the fact that they have been working for the company for nearly a year. One suggests that this may be due to a poor memory, while the other thinks that it is more likely a result of their supervisor not liking them. In order to resolve this difference of opinion, psychologists would most likely
   a. see how well each hypothesis predicts behavior in a related situation.
   b. carefully measure the confidence each worker has in his hypothesis.
   c. favor dispositional variables as an explanation.
   d. show a strong bias toward situational variables.

6. The coach of a soccer team feels that his athletes would perform better if he made the practices more challenging. In a psychological context, the coach's belief is most similar to
   a. a dispositional variable.
   b. the goal of explanation.
   c. the goal of description.
   d. a causal prediction.

7. A psychologist works in a public school in an economically-depressed neighborhood. She has developed a teaching program that enhances each child's self-esteem. This program most clearly satisfies psychology's goal of
   a. description.
   b. control.
   c. explanation.
   d. prediction.

The Evolution of Modern Psychology

8. In compiling a list of historical facts, a psychology student has gotten only one of his "facts" correct. Which is it?
   a. G. Stanley Hall wrote a two-volume work entitled *Principles of Psychology*.
   b. Wilhelm Wundt founded the American Psychological Association.
   c. Edward Titchener was one of the first psychologists in the United States.
   d. William James established the world's first experimental psychology laboratory.

9. Structuralism was based on the assumption that
   a. mental experience can be understood as the combination of basic components.
   b. introspective analyses of consciousness are too reductionistic.
   c. consciousness is a property of mind in continual interaction with the environment.
   d. the way to explain behavior is by specifying antecedent environmental conditions.

10. The way in which the mind understands many experiences as organized wholes, rather than the sum of simple parts, was studied by
    a. Sigmund Freud.
    b. Max Wertheimer.
    c. John Dewey.
    d. William James.

11. If you were a proponent of functionalism, you would be most concerned with trying to determine
    a. the feelings that are associated with specific thoughts and emotions.
    b. where human motivation is represented in the brain.
    c. the purposes served by behavioral acts.
    d. the exact nature of the mind.

12. One way in which Neo-Freudian theorists have broadened traditional psychodynamic theory is by proposing that
    a. unconscious processes are important.
    b. human behavior is completely rational.
    c. personality develops over an individual's entire lifetime.
    d. systematic scientific research into the nature of personality is unnecessary.

13. Most research psychologists would agree that the _____ perspective is most favored today.
    a. behavioral
    b. cognitive
    c. sociocultural
    d. evolutionary

14. While browsing through the "pop psych" section of the local bookstore, you come across a paperback that looks interesting. In the preface, you read that the emphasis is on the whole person, and it includes literary, historical, and artistic references. The book seems to be taking a _____ perspective.
    a. humanistic
    b. behavioristic
    c. cognitive
    d. evolutionary

What Psychologists Do

15. A teenager has decided that he wants to be a psychologist some day. He is most interested in the topics of peer pressure and conformity. If you were to advise him, you should suggest that he look into the field of _____ psychology.
    a. clinical
    b. human factors
    c. school
    d. social

16. Which of these questions is most likely to be addressed by a developmental psychologist?
    a. Why are some concepts easier to remember than others?
    b. How can you teach a dog to roll over and play dead?
    c. Which part of the brain is associated with dreaming?
    d. Do newborn babies recognize their mother's voice?

17. A psychologist works with business executives in a training program to develop leadership skills. She probably has expertise in the field of _____ psychology.
    a. school
    b. educational
    c. industrial–organizational
    d. community

18. A woman is concerned because her best friend is experiencing personal problems. If the woman were to make a recommendation, she should suggest that her friend might benefit from seeing a(n) _____ psychologist.
    a. counseling
    b. educational
    c. developmental
    d. social

19. A forensic psychologist is most likely to
    a. work in the human resources department of a large business.
    b. conduct research on the physiological bases of memory.
    c. give a workshop to teachers of special needs children.
    d. help select a jury for a defense attorney.

20. According to a survey of American Psychological Association members who hold doctoral degrees in psychology, about one in _____ has an independent practice.
    a. two
    b. three
    c. four
    d. five

21. Surveys show that the number of psychologists in the world is
    a. fewer than 100,000.
    b. well over 500,000.
    c. between three and four million.
    d. approximately ten million.

CHAPTER 2 Research Methods in Psychology

The Process of Research

1. Psychology is considered a science because it
   a. publishes findings in journals.
   b. relies on critical thinking.
   c. proposes hypotheses and theories that appear reasonable.
   d. follows the rules of the scientific method.

2. A psychologist is studying the effect that relaxation techniques have on stress reduction. Thirty participants are taught one relaxation technique and thirty others use a different technique. Each participant's level of stress is then measured with a paper-and-pencil questionnaire. The independent variable is the _____ and the dependent variable is the _____
   a. type of relaxation technique; level of stress
   b. level of stress; number of participants in each group
   c. one relaxation technique; other relaxation technique
   d. type of relaxation technique; number of participants in each group

3. In testing the effect of a new ointment on a skin rash, a drug company enlists four groups of participants. One group gets an older drug, a second group gets an experimental drug, a third group gets a placebo, and a fourth group receives no treatment. Researchers measure the number of days it takes for the rash to disappear. The dependent variable is the
   a. older drug.
   b. experimental drug.
   c. placebo.
   d. number of days it takes for the rash to disappear.

4. In which of the following research designs does each participant serve as his or her own control?
   a. between-subjects
   b. placebo control
   c. within-subjects
   d. double-blind control

5. Imagine that you are collecting data for a food manufacturer. You have been asked to determine which of two snack crackers people prefer. One of the crackers is fat-free and the other is not, but the samples you are using are numbered so that neither you nor the participants know which is which. You are using a
   a. double-blind control procedure.
   b. correlational method.
   c. naturalistic observation procedure.
   d. placebo control procedure.

6. All you know about a study is that a researcher has used the correlational method. Which of the following is most likely to be a conclusion?
   a. The more education one has, the more he or she is likely to earn in a lifetime.
   b. People sleep better in a room that is completely dark.
   c. Cats escape from puzzle boxes fastest when they receive food as a reward.
   d. Practice improves performance on a motor task.

7. Suppose you read an editorial in a newspaper that says that states that have instituted a death penalty have shown a decrease in violent crimes. Assuming that the data are accurate, you can conclude that
   a. the death penalty is a deterrent to violent crime.
   b. an unknown variable is causing the relationship.
   c. there are fewer violent crimes in states that have a death penalty.
   d. violent criminals have probably moved to states that do not have a death penalty.

Psychological Measurement

8. A teacher constructs tests in algebra and calculus. By mistake, she gives her algebra students the calculus test. Her students can correctly argue that the test results are
   a. not reliable or valid.
   b. not reliable.
   c. not valid.
   d. valid, but not reliable.

9. Which of the following is a self-report measure?
   a. the speed with which a rat runs a maze
   b. how quickly a person can say whether a word is a noun
   c. a person's written responses to an attitude questionnaire
   d. whether children act aggressively after watching cartoons

10. Which of the following is an open-ended question?
   a. Did you vote in the last election?
   b. What are the pros and cons of living in a big city?
   c. Should the President's policy on health care be supported?
   d. Are you in favor of abolishing the electoral college?

11. A teacher wants to measure the amount of time her students are "on-task" and "off-task." It would be best if she uses a
    a. face-to-face interview.
    b. questionnaire.
    c. self-report measure.
    d. behavioral measure.

12. A student in a research methods class has been asked to come up with an idea for a naturalistic observation. The only acceptable idea is to
    a. stand near a yield sign to see whether more male or female drivers yield.
    b. question park rangers about their experiences in nature.
    c. record his own emotions while watching either a horror film or a comedy.
    d. see if his friend gets a higher score on a videogame if he is offered a prize.

Ethical Issues in Human and Animal Research

13. Must psychological researchers respect the basic rights of participants in their studies? If the answer is yes, how is this ensured?
    a. No — scientists have the freedom to conduct research as they see fit.
    b. Yes — judicial hearings are held in administrative courts prior to all research.
    c. Yes — special committees oversee every research proposal.
    d. Yes — researchers are "honor bound" to respect the basic rights of participants.

14. Which of the following is NOT an ethical issue in human and animal research?
    a. representative sampling
    b. informed consent
    c. debriefing
    d. intentional deception

15. A researcher has just completed a study. During the study, participants were partly deceived, and some were made to feel embarrassment. After collecting the data, the researcher met briefly with the participants, thanked them, and paid them for their time. Should the researcher have done anything else?
    a. No, since the participants were paid, the researcher did not need to do anything else.
    b. Yes, the participants should have gone through a formal debriefing process.
    c. Yes, the researcher should have told them not to be embarrassed.
    d. Yes, the participants should have been asked to give informed consent after the study was over.

16. In a recent survey of the attitudes of students and members of the American Psychological Association toward the use of animals in research, it was found that
    a. students and their professors strongly supported studies involving physical pain or death.
    b. fewer than 50 percent believed that observational studies in naturalistic settings were appropriate.
    c. the percentages who supported studies involving caging or confinement depended in part on the type of animal.
    d. students and their professors strongly disapproved of the use of animals in undergraduate psychology courses.

Becoming a Wiser Research Consumer

17. Someone who wants to be a "critical thinker" should do all of the following EXCEPT
    a. be willing to go beyond information as it is presented.
    b. maintain the goal of understanding the substance of arguments.
    c. avoid being seduced by style and image.
    d. be quick to criticize the motives of psychologists who carry out research.

18. In order to become a wiser consumer of research knowledge, one should
    a. keep in mind that correlation is the same as causation.
    b. first consider how to disprove something before seeking confirming evidence.
    c. remember not to be concerned with operational definitions of concepts.
    d. accept the most obvious explanation that is given rather than seeking alternatives.

19. One problem with psychological information that is available on the World Wide Web is that
    a. most Websites maintain exceptionally high standards for submitted information.
    b. there are no on-line versions of psychological journals or researcher Web pages.
    c. it is often difficult to determine if a source is legitimate.
    d. only a few experts are consulted prior to the posting of information on the Web.

Statistical Supplement

Analyzing the Data

20. All of the following are examples of descriptive statistics EXCEPT the
    a. range.
    b. standard deviation.
    c. significance test.
    d. correlation coefficient.

21. A seventh-grader has been asked to compile some statistics on the ages of her family members. She is 12 years old, and has younger twin brothers, who are 10 years old. Her parents are both 34. She should determine that, in her family, the
   a. median is greater than the mean.
   b. mean is greater than the median.
   c. mode is greater than the median.
   d. mode is greater than the mean.

22. Which statistical measure of variability indicates the average difference between the scores in a distribution and their mean?
   a. range
   b. deviation score
   c. correlation coefficient
   d. standard deviation

23. Which of the following correlation coefficients is the weakest?
   a. +0.20
   b. −0.01
   c. −0..50
   d. −0.99

24. When describing the data collected in an experiment, a researcher comments that the distribution of scores was "skewed." This means that
   a. there was a normal curve.
   b. there was a normal distribution.
   c. the median, mode, and mean values were all the same.
   d. the scores clustered toward one end.

Becoming a Wise Consumer of Statistics

25. A researcher has collected data from a small group of participants. Most of the scores cluster around a midpoint, but one or two scores are extremely high. Under these conditions, it probably would be best for the researcher to
   a. throw out the one or two extremely high scores before presenting the data.
   b. counterbalance the extremely high scores by weighing more heavily any low scores.
   c. compute a mean to represent the data.
   d. consider using the median or mode to represent the data.

26. In order for consumers to avoid being deceived when it comes to interpreting statistical claims, the authors of the textbook make the point that
   a. small samples are less likely to be misleading than large samples.
   b. large samples are less likely to be misleading than small samples.
   c. people should avoid being distracted by comparisons of various measures of central tendency.
   d. one can have more confidence when measures of central tendency vary widely.

27. Which of the following statements best characterizes the viewpoint of the authors with respect to the use of statistics?
   a. Though statistics can be applied correctly and ethically, they also can be used poorly or deceptively.
   b. It is best to accept statistics for what they are: facts that are bolstered by authority.
   c. Regardless of the source or the methods used to acquire statistics, it is best for consumers to disbelieve them.
   d. Though politicians and businesses misuse statistics, consumers can believe statistics that are presented by psychologists.

CHAPTER 3 The Biological and Evolutionary Bases of Behavior

Heredity and Behavior

1. The 13 species of finches studied by Darwin helped illustrate the principle of natural selection because
   a. they sought out environments in which it was easy for them to obtain food.
   b. they were more likely than other species to live in family clusters.
   c. the shapes of their beaks suggested adaptation to different environments.
   d. they chose nesting sites that made it easy to camouflage their eggs.

2. According to evolutionary theory, an organism's success is measured by the
   a. level of intelligence it acquires.
   b. number of offspring it produces.
   c. amount of territory it controls.
   d. size it achieves.

3. The casting director for a film is searching through photographs in an attempt to find someone who looks like a wizard. Of most interest would be the actor's
   a. phenotype.
   b. genotype.
   c. genome.
   d. genes.

4. According to evolutionary theory, an organism that has a selective advantage is
   a. more likely to have a phenotype.
   b. more likely to pass on its genotype.
   c. less likely to survive in its environment.
   d. more likely to move to a new environment.

5. Which sequence of steps correctly summarizes the process of natural selection?
   a. selection of fittest genotype, competition for resources, environmental pressure, reproductive success, frequency of genotype increases
   b. competition for resources, reproductive success, frequency of genotype increases, selection of fittest genotype, environmental pressure
   c. environmental pressure, competition for resources, selection of fittest genotype, reproductive success, frequency of genotype increases
   d. reproductive success, competition for resources, frequency of genotype increases, environmental pressure, selection of fittest genotype

6. Which of the following is the most basic genetic material?
   a. genome
   b. gene
   c. DNA
   d. chromosome

7. If you inherit a Y chromosome from your father, you are born with
   a. female characteristics.
   b. male characteristics.
   c. 47 chromosomes.
   d. extra genes.

Biology and Behavior

8. A surgeon wants to be able to see both anatomical details and the function of a patient's brain. It will be best if he uses _____ to accomplish both goals
   a. repetitive transcranial magnetic stimulation
   b. EEG tracings
   c. a PET scan
   d. functional MRI

9. A test question asks you to draw the hierarchical organization of the human nervous system. In your sketch, you should be sure to show that
   a. the peripheral nervous system can be divided into the central and somatic divisions.
   b. sympathetic and parasympathetic are divisions of the autonomic nervous system.
   c. the autonomic nervous system is composed of the peripheral and central nervous system.
   d. the two divisions of the central nervous system are the somatic and autonomic nervous systems.

10. Your professor is having difficulty learning the names of his students. If you were to search for a biological basis for this difficulty, one logical place to start would be the brain structure known as the
    a. pons.
    b. thalamus.
    c. hypothalamus.
    d. hippocampus.

11. The brain stem includes all of the following structures EXCEPT the
    a. reticular formation.
    b. medulla.
    c. hypothalamus.
    d. pons.

12. You are watching a bad science fiction movie. An evil scientist is cloning humans, but things are going wrong. In one case, a clone apparently has a malfunctioning endocrine system. This is most likely because of problems with the
    a. hippocampus.
    b. thalamus.
    c. hypothalamus.
    d. cerebellum.

13. A friend of yours creates drawings of the brain for a publisher. When you visit her she is working on a representation that shows the amount of area in the motor cortex that is devoted to different parts of the body. The drawing should show the largest area to be the one that controls the
    a. fingers, thumb, and muscles involved in speech.
    b. eyes and ears.
    c. back muscles.
    d. bottoms of both parts of the legs and feet.

14. A patient has no difficulty understanding what is said to him, but is not able to produce words to convey his understanding. It is possible that he has damage to
    a. the motor cortex.
    b. Wernicke's area.
    c. the visual cortex.
    d. the angular gyrus.

The Nervous System in Action

15. In the pairings below, which part of the cell is matched correctly with its description?
    a. axon — bulblike structure through which stimulation of nearby glands, muscles, or other neurons is made possible.
    b. dendrite — extends outward from the cell body and receives incoming signals.
    c. soma — conducts information along its length, at the end of which can be found terminal buttons.
    d. terminal button — contains the nucleus and cytoplasm that sustains its life.

16. Glial cells have many functions. However, they do NOT
    a. make up a blood–brain barrier around blood vessels in the brain.
    b. help guide newborn neurons to appropriate locations in the brain.
    c. take up excess neurotransmitters and other substances at the gaps between neurons.
    d. prevent an insulating cover from forming around some types of axons.

17. When excitatory inputs to a nerve cell are sufficiently strong with respect to inhibitory inputs, the neuron becomes _____ and a(n) _____ occurs.
    a. polarized; action potential
    b. polarized; refractory period
    c. depolarized; refractory period
    d. depolarized; action potential

18. The all-or-none law states that
    a. the size of the action potential is unaffected by increases in the intensity of the stimulation beyond the threshold level.
    b. once excitatory inputs sum to reach the threshold level, the nerve stops firing.
    c. the size of the action potential diminishes along the length of the axon.
    d. once started, the action potential needs outside stimulation to keep itself moving.

19. Multiple sclerosis is a devastating disorder that is caused by
    a. insufficient supplies of GABA.
    b. deterioration of the myelin sheath.
    c. the presence of nodes of Ranvier.
    d. a prolonged refractory period.

20. A neurotransmitter has crossed a synapse and successfully bound itself to a receptor molecule on a second neuron. This process will
    a. have no effect on the second neuron.
    b. increase the probability that the second neuron will fire.
    c. decrease the probability that the second neuron will fire.
    d. either increase or decrease the probability that the second neuron will fire.

21. Research on mood disorders points to the role of the neurotransmitter _____ as a biological factor underlying some forms of depression.
    a. norepinephrine
    b. acetylcholine
    c. epinephrine
    d. dopamine

CHAPTER 4 Sensation and Perception

Sensing, Organizing, Identifying, and Recognizing

1. In the context of perception, synthesis involves the integration and combination of simple sensory features. It occurs in the _____ stage of perceptual processing.
   a. perceptual organization
   b. identification
   c. sensation
   d. recognition

2. Suppose you are watching a television show with the sound turned off. The television sits on a table in front of a wall and you are sitting on a couch about ten feet from the television. In this example, the proximal stimulus is
   a. not present.
   b. the television set.
   c. the wall.
   d. the optical image on the retina.

3. Illusions differ from hallucinations in that illusions
   a. involve distortions.
   b. are due to unusual physical or mental states.
   c. are shared by others.
   d. exist only in the visual sense.

Sensory Knowledge of the World

4. A child who has had multiple ear infections is being tested for hearing loss. She is presented with sounds of various intensities and is asked to indicate when she hears the sound. This procedure is most similar to that used by psychophysicists who are studying
   a. the just noticeable difference.
   b. absolute thresholds.
   c. difference thresholds.
   d. response biases.

5. On a signal detection task, a nay-sayer is likely to be relatively _____ on misses and very _____ on false alarms.
   a. low; high
   b. low; low
   c. high; high
   d. high; low

6. A difference threshold is operationally defined as the
   a. point at which stimuli are recognized as different half of the time.
   b. point at which stimuli are recognized as different all of the time.
   c. point at which stimuli are occasionally recognized as different.
   d. smallest physical energy that can be detected.

The Visual System

7. If all the cones in your eyes stopped functioning, then you would
   a. be totally blind.
   b. no longer have color vision.
   c. only have sight at the center of the visual field.
   d. have poorest vision when illumination was near darkness.

8. A friend bought an intensely red shirt at a flea market. After he washed it, however, the red color faded quite a bit. The dimension of color that has changed is called
   a. hue.
   b. brightness.
   c. intensity.
   d. saturation.

9. Suppose you are staring at a dark blue circle on a computer screen. Suddenly, the screen changes to a light grey background. Based on opponent-process theory, what color circle will you see?
   a. blue
   b. red
   c. green
   d. yellow

Hearing

10. A trained musician can listen to a complex piece of music and distinguish the various instruments. This is due to the dimension of sound known as
    a. amplitude.
    b. timbre.
    c. pitch.
    d. loudness.

11. Which of the following structures is located between the eardrum and the cochlea?
    a. basilar membrane
    b. tympanic membrane
    c. pinna
    d. hammer

12. Which structure in the ear provides a function that is comparable to that of the rods and cones in the eye?
    a. the hair cells on the basilar membrane
    b. the tympanic membrane
    c. the round window
    d. the cochlea

13. Which of the following does not belong with the others?
    a. place theory
    b. the volley principle
    c. frequency theory
    d. opponent-process theory

Your Other Senses

14. The hair cells on the basilar membrane perform the same function for hearing as the _____ perform for the sense of smell.
    a. olfactory bulbs
    b. papillae
    c. olfactory cilia
    d. saccules

15. Which of the following correctly lists the basic taste qualities?
    a. sweet, sour, bitter, saline, unami
    b. aromatic, bland, rotten, spicy

c. texture, temperature, consistency
d. simple, compound, complex, combination

16. Motion sickness can occur when the signals from the _____ sense conflict with those from the _____ sense.
a. kinesthetic; auditory
b. kinesthetic; vestibular
c. visual; vestibular
d. visual; auditory

17. Which sense allows you to touch your finger to your nose when your eyes are closed?
a. olfactory
b. vestibular
c. kinesthetic
d. auditory

18. Which of the following statements is most consistent with Melzack's gate-control theory of pain?
a. As there are no physical causes for pain, the experience must originate entirely in the brain.
b. Pain is like a gate, its intensity swinging from extreme to slight and back again.
c. Cells in the spinal cord block some pain signals and let others get through to the brain.
d. All pain signals reach the brain; selective attention is then given to some signals, but not to others.

Organizational Processes in Perception

19. A young music student wants to be a cellist. As she listens to her teacher play, she focuses her attention on the way her teacher is holding the bow and the angle between the bow and the strings. The student's attentional focus best exemplifies the attentional process known as
a. stimulus-driven capture.
b. goal-directed selection.
c. dichotic listening.
d. bottom-up processing.

20. Opponents of the early filter theory of attention cited the fact that some listeners in dichotic listening tasks were
a. recalling things that should have been ignored.
b. completely filtering out all ignored material.
c. remembering information that should have been ignored.
d. unable to shadow information such as their names.

21. In a test of basic shape recognition, the second-grade teacher quickly draws various shapes and asks her students to identify them. The fact that the students recognize the shapes as complete even though they are incomplete is an example of the perceptual process known as
a. figure and ground.
b. retinal disparity.

c. interposition.
d. closure.

22. When two stationary spots of light in different positions in the visual field are turned on and off alternately at a rate of about four or five times per second, a viewer is likely to experience
a. the phi phenomenon.
b. relative motion parallax.
c. retinal disparity.
d. interposition.

23. In order to benefit from the depth cues of retinal disparity and convergence, an individual must
a. be able to see with both eyes.
b. keep one eye closed.
c. be viewing objects from a considerable distance.
d. slowly move his or her head back and forth.

24. The Ponzo illusion is a result of the way the visual system interprets
a. texture gradients.
b. converging lines.
c. shape constancy.
d. relative motion parallax.

25. Lightness constancy works because the _____ of light reflected off an object remains about the same even as the _____ of light changes.
a. percentage; saturation
b. percentage; absolute amount
c. absolute amount; percentage
d. absolute amount; saturation

Identification and Recognition Processes

26. Sensory data is the starting point for _____ processing.
a. top-down
b. bottom-up
c. conceptually driven
d. contextual

27. The veteran pharmacist has few problems reading doctors' handwritten prescriptions even though they appear illegible to others because his years of experience allow him to anticipate what certain doctors are likely to write. This example illustrates the importance of
a. top-down processing.
b. bottom-up processing.
c. phonemic restoration.
d. data-driven processing.

28. A friend who is proofreading your paper notices several typographical errors you missed. Your inability to catch these errors is most likely the result of
a. the law of proximity.
b. bottom-up processing.
c. perceptual set.
d. data-driven processing.

CHAPTER 5 Mind, Consciousness, and Alternate States

The Contents of Consciousness

1. When defining consciousness, the authors of the textbook say that it
   a. can only refer to a general state of mind.
   b. can refer to a general state of mind or to its specific contents.
   c. should not be defined, as it is too ambiguous a term.
   d. is the same as "sense of self."

2. On the very first page of his classic 1892 text, William James endorsed a definition of psychology as the description and explanation of
   a. psychopathology.
   b. behavior.
   c. animal and human intelligence.
   d. states of consciousness.

3. Your knowledge that the professional baseball season in the United States ends with the World Series and that politicians refer to Red states and Blue states are bits of information that function silently in the background until consciously needed. They best exemplify
   a. the unconscious.
   b. nonconscious processes.
   c. preconscious memories.
   d. unattended information.

4. From the time of the English philosopher John Locke until the time of Sigmund Freud, most thinkers firmly believed that
   a. rational beings had access to all the activities of their own minds.
   b. traumatic events and taboo desires were kept from consciousness through repression.
   c. unconscious processes affected all human behavior.
   d. human consciousness was identical to animal consciousness.

5. Participants in a research study are asked to report what they are thinking about when they receive alerts on their cellphones throughout the day. The researcher is using the _____ method.
   a. "text message"
   b. think-aloud
   c. experience-sampling
   d. lucid dreaming

The Functions of Consciousness

6. Which of the following is the best example of the restrictive function of consciousness?
   a. A basketball player ignores the fans waving in the background as he takes a shot.
   b. A man plans a surprise birthday party for his wife.
   c. You stroll through the park on a beautiful summer day.
   d. A group of students chat's before their history class.

7. After watching a political debate on television, two people come to different conclusions about who won the debate. Their differing perspectives can be attributed to the fact that each of them has a different
   a. planning function of consciousness.
   b. cultural construction of reality.
   c. personal construction of reality.
   d. subjective self-awareness.

8. If you were a research participant in an experiment that used the SLIP technique, the psychologist would most likely be studying
   a. shadowing.
   b. speech errors.
   c. balance.
   d. dreams.

9. In a cross-cultural study that is described in the textbook, European American and Asian students were asked to complete surveys that measured their sense of emotional well-being throughout the day. A week later, they provided retrospective ratings of the extent to which they had experienced positive moods. The results revealed that
   a. there were no differences in either the daily surveys or the retrospective reports for either European Americans or Asians.
   b. the retrospective reports of Asian students were more accurate that the retrospective reports of European American students.
   c. the European Americans reported more positive moods throughout the day, but fewer positive moods when looking back retrospectively.
   d. the Asians reported more positive moods throughout the day, but fewer positive moods when looking back retrospectively.

Sleep and Dreams

10. The "fine tuning" that is necessary to help people synchronize their internal clocks with a 24-hour cycle is mediated by
    a. exposure to sunlight.
    b. diet and exercise.
    c. variations in the daily temperature.
    d. the circulatory system.

11. With respect to jet lag, flying _____ creates greater problems because your biological clock can be more readily _____.
    a. eastbound; lengthened
    b. eastbound; shortened
    c. westbound; lengthened
    d. westbound; shortened

12. If you are like most people and experience about eight hours of sleep each night, on a typical night you will go through the sleep cycle about _____ times, and the length of your REM sleep will _____ with each sleep cycle.
    a. four to six; decrease
    b. four to six; increase
    c. eight to ten; decrease
    d. eight to ten; increase

13. In which sleep disorder does a person stop breathing a number of times throughout the night?
   a. sleep apnea
   b. somnambulism
   c. insomnia
   d. narcolepsy

14. People who have narcolepsy
   a. experience total loss of muscle control brought about by emotional excitement.
   b. are addicted to narcotics.
   c. have a periodic compulsion to sleep during the daytime.
   d. stop breathing in their sleep.

15. Researchers have found cultural differences with respect to dreams. For example, in certain Mayan subgroups
   a. dreamers are careful not to awaken at night, so dream memories will not be disrupted.
   b. only the shamans are allowed to recount and discuss dreams.
   c. people rarely dream.
   d. mothers ask their children each morning to talk about their dreams.

16. People who are lucid dreamers are capable of
   a. keeping their eyes still during their dreams.
   b. having daydreams that are as lucid as night dreams.
   c. having vivid dreams during non-REM sleep.
   d. controlling the content of their dreams.

Altered States of Consciousness

17. Research on hypnosis has found that
   a. hypnotizability is a relatively stable attribute over time.
   b. hypnotizability is correlated with gullibility and conformity.
   c. most people score very high on the Stanford Hypnotic Susceptibility Scale.
   d. older adults are more hypnotizable than are teenagers.

18. A person who practices mindfulness meditation learns to
   a. generate peaceful mental images.
   b. let thoughts and memories pass freely through the mind.
   c. regulate breathing through focused concentration.
   d. minimize all forms of external stimulation.

19. A man is telling his friends about his hallucinations. How are they most likely to react?
   a. His friends will probably assume that the man is mentally ill.
   b. Their reaction will depend on the culture in which the man lives.
   c. They are most likely to react as though he has taken a drug.
   d. They will probably assume that the hallucinations are religious revelations.

20. Some religious groups, such as the Holy Ghost people of Appalachia, engage in practices such as snake handling to prove faith and achieve changes in consciousness. To prepare for these experiences they
   a. drink poison.
   b. take psychoactive drugs.
   c. quietly meditate in small groups.
   d. listen to long sermons, sing, and dance wildly.

21. Each time an addict takes his heroin, he needs a slightly bigger dose to get the same effect. This is a phenomenon known as
   a. psychological dependence.
   b. craving.
   c. tolerance.
   d. addiction.

22. Drugs classified as depressants achieve their effects, in part, by facilitating neural communication at synapses that use the neurotransmitter
   a. dopamine.
   b. GABA.
   c. acetylcholine.
   d. serotonin.

23. With respect to their overall effects, _____ increase arousal and _____ decrease arousal.
   a. barbiturates; amphetamines
   b. opiates; barbiturates
   c. amphetamines; barbiturates
   d. benzodiazepines; opiates

The Study of Learning

1. A student spends weeks studying for his psychology test and dazzles his friends with his knowledge of the material. When the test is handed out in class, however, the student's mind goes blank. A learning psychologist would say that this disaster is most likely a problem with
   a. learning.
   b. heredity.
   c. performance.
   d. motivation.

2. At the beginning of a lecture on the topic of learning, the professor asks for examples from the students. Which of the following is the best example of learning?
   a. A dog naps when it is tired.
   b. A baby squirms when it is tickled.
   c. A child whines to get attention.
   d. Your finger hurts if you cut it.

3. B.F. Skinner wrote the book entitled _____ and is most closely associated with the approach known as _____.
   a. *Psychology from the Standpoint of a Behaviorist;* radical behaviorism
   b. *Beyond Freedom and Dignity;* radical behaviorism
   c. *Psychology from the Standpoint of a Behaviorist;* behaviorism
   d. *Beyond Freedom and Dignity;* behaviorism

4. A student goes to a lecture by a famous behavior analyst. She is most likely to hear him say that
   a. he is most interested in the subjective experiences that people report.
   b. each species responds to a different set of laws when it comes to learning.
   c. the secret to understanding motivation can be found within the limbic system.
   d. his goal is to discover the environmental determinants of learning and behavior.

Classical Conditioning: Learning Predictable Signals

5. A child becomes terrified by the loud noises when he goes through the Haunted Mansion at the amusement park. The next time his parents take him to the amusement park, he becomes afraid when he sees the Haunted Mansion. Viewed from the point of view of classical conditioning, the Haunted Mansion is a _____ and the child's fear when he sees it is a _____.
   a. CS; CR
   b. CS; UCR
   c. UCS; UCR
   d. UCS; CR

6. Using a puff of air as the UCS, a girl classically conditions her dog to blink whenever she says "blink." The girl's parrot overhears the procedure and says "blink" all day long while the girl is at school. When the girl returns, she says "blink" to her dog but gets no response. It appears as though
   a. spontaneous recovery has occurred.
   b. extinction has taken place.
   c. the dog's behavior has generalized.
   d. the girl used a backward conditioning procedure.

7. Imagine that you are conducting a study using classical conditioning. You present a CS, but then turn it off before presenting a UCS a second later. The procedure you are following is called _____ conditioning.
   a. trace
   b. delay
   c. simultaneous
   d. backward

8. You read about a classical conditioning study done by Pavlov in which he presented a 1,500-Hz tone to a dog, followed by a mild electric shock. On some trials, however, he presented 1,000-Hz or 2,000-Hz tones without the shock. You can correctly conclude that Pavlov was studying
   a. backward conditioning.
   b. blocking.
   c. stimulus generalization.
   d. stimulus discrimination.

9. Robert Rescorla's research in the mid-1960s challenged the belief that classical conditioning results from the
   a. informativeness of the CS.
   b. mere pairing of the CS and UCS.
   c. contingent relationship between the CS and UCS.
   d. law of effect.

10. MTV reports that the leader of a band has died of a heroin overdose. Other members of his band reveal that he had a daily habit. On the basis of research conducted by Shepard Siegel, you should find it most relevant that
    a. he had been using heroin for many years.
    b. when he used heroin, he typically did so in the presence of other band members.
    c. he also had an alcohol problem.
    d. his overdose occurred while he was alone in an unfamiliar hotel.

Operant Conditioning: Learning About Consequences

11. When comparing the types of punishment, it is important to remember that
   a. both positive punishment and negative punishment involve the presentation of a stimulus.
   b. both positive punishment and negative punishment involve the removal of a stimulus.
   c. positive punishment involves the presentation of a stimulus whereas negative punishment involves the removal of a stimulus.
   d. negative punishment involves the presentation of a stimulus whereas positive punishment involves the removal of a stimulus.

12. A child's tantrum has gotten to her parents, so they tell her that if she doesn't stop, she will not be allowed to go to her ballet lesson, which she loves. This is an example of the reinforcement contingency known as
   a. positive reinforcement.
   b. negative reinforcement.
   c. positive punishment.
   d. negative punishment.

13. A girl intends to change her brother's behavior by using the Premack Principle. The first thing she should do is decide
   a. what she can use as a positive punisher.
   b. which behaviors are high- and low-probability.
   c. what she can use as a primary reinforcer.
   d. how often she should use negative reinforcers.

14. When the young B.F. Skinner was running out of rat pellets when conducting research, he economized by giving the rats food only after a certain interval of time, no matter how many times the rats pressed in between. Under this partial reinforcement, Skinner found that the rats
   a. stopped responding immediately.
   b. learned less quickly.
   c. responded longer during extinction training.
   d. responded less vigorously during extinction training.

15. A pigeon pecks at a disk for a short period of time to gain access to food, then stops pecking for about 30 seconds. It then returns to pecking and repeats the cycle. The pigeon is most likely on a _____ schedule of reinforcement.
   a. FI-30
   b. FR-30
   c. VI-30
   d. VR-30

16. Salesperson A is paid weekly for the sales that he makes. Salesperson B's pay is based on every 10 sales he makes. Salesperson A is working under a _____ schedule of reinforcement, and Salesperson B is working under a _____ schedule of reinforcement.
   a. fixed-interval; fixed-ratio
   b. fixed-interval; variable-ratio
   c. fixed-ratio; fixed-interval
   d. variable-ratio; variable-interval

17. A dog's owner is trying to teach him to fetch the newspaper. At first, he gives the dog a treat every time he sniffs around the newspaper. Next, the dog will only receive a treat if he picks up the newspaper. Eventually, the dog will only receive a treat if he carries the newspaper inside the house. This example best illustrates
   a. partial reinforcement.
   b. shaping by successive approximations.
   c. the Premack principle.
   d. conditioned reinforcement.

Biology and Learning

18. When Keller and Marion Breland attempted to train animals by using operant conditioning techniques, they found several instances of animal "misbehavior." The Breland's attributed this misbehavior to the
   a. use of partial reinforcement.
   b. use of shaping by successive approximations.
   c. tendency of punishment to have a suppressive effect on behavior.
   d. tendency of learned behavior to drift toward instinctual behavior.

19. Compared to other examples of classical conditioning, the learning of taste aversions in animals
   a. is easier to extinguish.
   b. requires a greater number of US-UCS pairings.
   c. can be learned with a long delay between CS and illness.
   d. does not seem to involve a CS-UCS association.

20. The research on taste-aversion learning by John Garcia and his colleague Robert Koelling demonstrated that
   a. it was possible to shape complex behavior by using successive approximations.
   b. organisms are biologically prepared to learn certain associations.
   c. all conditioning is based entirely on the relationship between stimuli and behavior.
   d. Pavlov was correct in his contention that learning results from contiguity.

21. In a study that is described in the textbook, some women who were being treated with chemotherapy for breast cancer developed taste aversions that quickly disappeared. This finding suggests the possibility that
   a. humans can reason about what causes aversions and undergo extinction.
   b. humans are less likely than animals to be classically conditioned.
   c. taste aversions are, for the most part, short-lived.
   d. the women had not really learned taste aversions, but something similar.

Cognitive Influences on Learning

22. One important finding that resulted from Edward Tolman's research on cognitive maps was that rats could
  a. solve mazes by using paths that had never been reinforced.
  b. solve mazes after watching monkeys perform correctly.
  c. find their way to hidden food after long delays.
  d. press a bar in the right pattern to gain access to a maze.

23. Why have researchers working in Tolman's tradition chosen to study the species of bird known as Clark's nutcracker?
  a. The bird appears to have superior reasoning ability.
  b. These birds do not seem to have the ability to form cognitive maps.
  c. Operant conditioning techniques do not seem to be effective when dealing with this species.
  d. The spatial memory of the bird is noteworthy.

24. A child notices that a parent praises and hugs a playmate for sharing. The child then begins sharing also. The child is demonstrating learning through
  a. the operation of the Premack principle.
  b. vicarious punishment.
  c. vicarious reinforcement.
  d. an internal cognitive map.

25. In a study of the relationship between childhood TV viewing and adult aggression that is described in the textbook, researchers measured two years of viewing starting in either first or third grade, then interviewed those same children fifteen years later. The researchers concluded that
  a. there was no relationship between the extent to which children watched violent TV shows and their subsequent behavior as adults.
  b. there was a strong relationship between childhood aggression and the individuals' viewing of TV violence as adults.
  c. the adults who had watched the most violent TV as children were the least likely to display aggression.
  d. the findings were consistent with the view that early viewing of violent TV shows causes later aggression.

CHAPTER 7 Memory

What is Memory?

1. As a classroom assignment, you are to design a study of memory that is based on the work of the great German psychologist Hermann Ebbinghaus. If you want to do a similar experiment, you should use a task in which participants are required to learn
   a. lists of foreign words.
   b. the lyrics to the national anthem.
   c. the rules of baseball.
   d. how to draw from memory.

2. Your knowledge of how the Statue of Liberty was obtained and where it is located is an example of _____ memory; your knowledge of how to ride your bike in the Tour de France is an example of _____ memory.
   a. declarative; procedural
   b. declarative; declarative
   c. procedural; declarative
   d. procedural; procedural

3. After seeing how much money professional golfers make, you decide to go to a friend, who is an excellent golfer, for some pointers on your golf swing. The fact that your friend has difficulty expressing verbally what needs to be done may best be explained by the idea that
   a. knowledge of the golf swing is a declarative memory.
   b. your friend doesn't have conscious access to the content of his procedural memory.
   c. the knowledge compilation process has not yet taken place with respect to your friend's golf swing.
   d. because he is so experienced, your friend no longer has a procedural memory for playing golf.

4. Being able to use knowledge at some later time requires the operation of three mental processes. Which of the following is NOT one of these processes?
   a. retrieval
   b. storage
   c. recoding
   d. encoding

Sensory Memory

5. The teacher in your art history class is showing slides of Renaissance art. The images that you see initially occupy your _____ memory.
   a. short-term
   b. procedural
   c. echoic
   d. iconic

6. George Sperling's research on iconic memory, in which he compared performance using the whole-report and partial-report procedures, led to the conclusion that iconic memory
   a. lasts for about 18 seconds.
   b. has a large capacity.
   c. contains about seven items of information.
   d. is the same as short-term memory.

7. A college classmate claims that the reason he does so well on tests is that he has a "photographic memory." You should tell him that research has shown that
   a. this type of memory is quite rare in adults.
   b. he is not alone, as most people have photographic memory.
   c. photographic memory is more common in adults than in children.
   d. it is more likely that he has eidetic imagery.

8. In a study of echoic memory that is described in the textbook, participants listened to lists of letters that were followed by a suffix that sounded like a sheep's baa. When researchers looked at whether the sound disrupted echoic memory, they found that it displaced information in echoic memory only when the
   a. sound was presented to the left ear.
   b. sound was made by a sheep.
   c. participants believed the sound was made by a human.
   d. participants believed the sound was made by a sheep.

Short-Term Memory and Working Memory

9. George Miller suggested that the "magic number" for performance on random lists of meaningful, familiar items was _____ items; current researchers have estimated the pure contribution of STM to memory span is _____ items.
   a. two to four; seven to nine
   b. five to nine; two to four
   c. nine to eleven; two to four
   d. two to four; nine to eleven

10. The textbook describes a famous participant, S.F., who was able to memorize 84 digits though his memory for letters was still only about seven items. This study made the point that
    a. there are large individual differences in short-term memory capacity among adults.
    b. the capacity of short-term memory has been underestimated.
    c. memory can be improved through maintenance rehearsal.
    d. chunking is a valuable memory strategy.

11. In the context of Alan Baddeley's research, which of the following terms does NOT belong with the others?
    a. central executive
    b. iconic memory
    d. phonological loop
    d. visuospatial sketchpad

12. In a study of working memory span that is described in the textbook, low-, middle-, and high-span people were asked to read a story about a home from either the perspective of a potential homebuyer or a potential burglar. Subsequently, they were asked to recall the story twice, once from their original perspective, and then a second time from the switched perspective. The researchers found that
    a. the advantage of high-span participants was shown only on the original perspective.
    b. only middle-span participants did equally well on both perspectives.
    c. low-span participants did better than the other readers on the switched perspective.
    d. high-span participants did better than the other readers on the switched perspective.

Long-Term Memory: Encoding and Retrieval

13. While at a crowded party, a woman waves to you from across the room. You know she looks familiar, but you can't quite figure out who she is. Finally, it dawns on you: she is your dentist's assistant. Your memory difficulty can best be explained by
    a. levels of processing.
    b. retroactive interference.
    c. proactive interference.
    d. encoding specificity.

14. Two students are in a class in which ten students must make a presentation. Student A hopes that the professor will remember her presentation well. Student B prefers that his presentation be forgotten. On the basis of the serial position effect, it will be best for both of them if Student A presents _____ and Student B presents _____.

    a. last; first
    b. last; in the middle
    c. in the middle; last
    d. in the middle; first

15. Which question could best clarify whether a person's recollection of a specific item is episodic or semantic in nature?
    a. Do you remember the context in which you acquired the memory?
    b. How easy is it for you to remember the information?
    c. Can you remember the information without retrieval cues?
    d. Do you need short-term memory to recall the information?

16. When required to change the password to his e-mail account, a computer user found it difficult to remember his new password. Now, three password changes later, he can't remember the old one when he tries to. The difficulties this computer user has had remembering his passwords can most accurately be attributed to
    a. retroactive interference.
    b. proactive interference.
    c. first retroactive interference and now proactive interference.
    d. first proactive interference and now retroactive interference.

17. A researcher who is interested in studying priming effects in memory would be most likely to investigate the effect that
    a. new experiences have on the memory of older experiences.
    b. hints have on the ability to remember.
    c. monetary reward has on a participant's memory.
    d. prior experience with a word has on a later experience.

18. At the grocery store you notice a woman looking at various parts of her body and then picking up certain grocery items. Curious about her behavior, you ask her what she is doing. She says that she prefers not to use shopping lists, but rather "stores" the items she needs by imagining they are located in different parts of her body. This woman is using the mnemonic device known as
    a. the method of loci.
    b. acronyms.
    c. peg-word method.
    d. metamemory.

19. After completing a standardized test, a student feels confident about some of the answers he has given and less confident about others. Research on these "feelings-of-knowing" has shown that such feelings
    a. are more likely to be accurate in women than in men.
    b. are no more accurate than would be expected by chance.
    c. can be quite accurate.
    d. are usually inaccurate.

Structures in Long-Term Memory

20. When asked to rate examples of vehicles, a participant says that a bicycle is a good example of a vehicle and that a wheelbarrow is a bad example. Psychologists who study concepts are most likely to say that the participant has come to this conclusion because
    a. he often rides bicycles, but seldom rides in wheelbarrows.
    b. bicycles share more features with the prototypical member of the category.
    c. others have told him that bicycles are better examples of the category.
    d. he can identify bicycles more quickly when shown pictures.

CHAPTER 8 Cognitive Processes

Studying Cognition

1. A classmate tells you that she is trying to study stimulus categorization using Donders's logic. You would expect her to try to create two experimental tasks
   a. that both require stimulus generalization.
   b. in which stimulus generalization precedes response selection.
   c. that involve only parallel processes.
   d. that differ by only one mental process.

2. As a research assistant, your task is to record how long it takes a research participant to press a button when a bell rings. The measurement you are using is called
   a. reaction time.
   b. the subtraction method.
   c. mental speed.
   d. parallel processing time.

3. Which of the following is most likely to be a controlled attentional process?
   a. A child follows instructions on how to dribble a basketball.
   b. A teenager hops on his skateboard and zips down the sidewalk.
   c. You listen to a friend tell you of her troubles while you are jogging.
   d. You sign your name for yet another autograph seeker.

4. Researchers who study mental processes generally assume that
   a. reaction time decreases as the number of mental tasks increases.
   b. people have limited resources that must be allocated to different mental tasks.
   c. the absolute time mental processing takes is unrelated to the nature of the task.
   d. serial processing is identical to parallel processing.

5. In an example of mental processing that is presented in the textbook, you are asked to determine whether pairs of numbers (rendered as Arabic numerals or written out) are physically different. People usually find it harder to make these judgments when the numbers are conceptually _____ because of _____ processes that interfere.
   a. close together; serial
   b. far apart; automatic
   c. close together; automatic
   d. far apart; controlled

Language Use

6. Having studied language production, the words "quantity, quality, relation and manner" should make most sense to you in the context of
   a. Grice's maxims.
   b. spoonerisms.
   c. heuristics.
   d. think-aloud protocols.

7. Imagine that you are lost on the streets of San Francisco. When you stop someone to ask for directions, she asks you whether you are familiar with the city. She is probably trying to figure out whether you share
   a. Grice's maxims.
   b. linguistic copresence.
   c. physical copresence.
   d. community membership.

8. Which of the following is an example of a spoonerism?
   a. By the light of the silvery moon I want to spoon.
   b. A stitch in time saves nine.
   c. You have tasted the whole worm.
   d. Red sky at night, sailor's delight; red sky at morning, sailor take warning.

9. Read the following sentence: "The stadium that the band played in sat on a hill." Based on the research with propositional representation in memory, will the words stadium and hill be represented together in memory?
   a. Yes, because these words belong to the same proposition.
   b. Yes, because these words are closely linked in meaning.
   c. No, because the words are very apart in the actual structure of the sentence.
   d. Maybe, but research can not yet determine whether this happens.

10. Researchers who have studied language understanding have found that the types of inferences people make are LEAST likely to be
    a. based on information taken from memory.
    b. logical.
    c. especially far-reaching.
    d. designed to help people figure out what the speaker meant.

11. Suppose you were around to hear a lecture from Edward Sapir. Which of the following statements are you most likely to have heard him say?
    a. "Language and thought are not related."
    b. "Differences in language create differences in thought."
    c. "Language processes are primarily learned, while thought processes, which are indicative of intelligence, are primarily inborn."
    d. "Linguistic communities are so complex that one speaker of a language will think very differently from another speaker of that same language."

Visual Cognition

12. In a study that is described in the textbook, researchers presented students with examples of the letter R and its mirror image that had been rotated various amounts. As the letter appeared, the student had to identify it as either the normal R or its mirror image. An analysis of participant reaction times revealed that
   a. the farther the letter was from normal, the faster it was mentally rotated.
   b. reaction times were proportional to the degree to which each letter had to be mentally rotated.
   c. there was no relationship between the degree to which each letter had to be mentally rotated and reaction times.
   d. most participants were unable to perform the task, as they had difficulty mentally rotating the letters.

13. Imagine that you participate in a study in which you are asked to memorize a detailed image of a tall tower with a ticket booth at the bottom and a flagpole on the top. Then, you are asked to recall the image and focus mentally on the ticket booth. With respect to your visual scanning abilities, it is most likely that
   a. it will take you longer to say whether there is a flagpole on the top than whether there is a customer at the ticket booth.
   b. it will take you longer to say whether there is a customer at the ticket booth than whether there is a flagpole on the top.
   c. it will take about the same amount of time to say there is a customer at the ticket booth as it will take to say that there is a flagpole on the top.
   d. your performance will be more influenced by whether the image is presented in color or black-and-white than the relative position of the objects in the image.

14. In a study that is described in the textbook, thousands of students from 49 different countries were asked to draw a world map. The study found that the majority of maps
   a. had a Eurocentric worldview.
   b. placed the student's home country in the middle of the map.
   c. showed all of the continents to be of equal size, with Africa in the middle.
   d. only included the home country of the student, leaving other areas of the world blank.

Problem Solving and Reasoning

15. Cognitive psychologists who study problem solving have found that people often use strategies or rules-of-thumb that are called
   a. algorithms.
   b. think-aloud protocols.
   c. heuristics.
   d. problem spaces.

16. Researchers who study problem solving are most likely to use think-aloud protocols to learn about
   a. mental operations.
   b. well-defined problems.
   c. initial states.
   d. goal states.

17. When you pull out a kitchen drawer you notice that a screw is loose in the handle. You don't have a screwdriver handy, so you reach into the drawer and pull out a knife. Unlike many people, you were able to overcome
   a. the availability heuristic.
   b. functional fixedness.
   c. parallel processing.
   d. the belief-bias effect.

18. Your teacher has presented you with the following syllogism: All poisonous things taste bitter. Arsenic does not taste bitter. Therefore, arsenic is not poisonous. The fact that you are likely to reject the conclusion, without thinking much about the logic of the syllogism, is due to
   a. decision aversion.
   b. functional fixedness.
   c. the availability heuristic.
   d. the belief-bias effect.

19. The "Monk" puzzle, which is presented in the textbook, becomes relatively easy to solve if one uses a _____ representation.
   a. hierarchical
   b. verbal
   c. mathematical
   d. visual

20. As a parent, you would like to help your children improve their problem solving skills. When you attempt to teach them the useful technique of analogical problem solving, however, you are likely to find that they
   a. try to use analogical problem-solving techniques for all problems.
   b. do not always see the relevance of past problems.
   c. prefer to use deductive reasoning techniques.
   d. do not do well with concrete analogies.

Judgment and Decision Making

21. According to cognitive psychologist Herbert Simon, the "bounded rationality" of human thought processes is the result of the
   a. tendency of people to be too affected by their past experiences.
   b. tendency to use deductive reasoning rather than inductive reasoning when solving problems.
   c. way that language has evolved in humans.
   d. application of limited resources to situations that demand immediate responses.

22. Cognitive psychologists distinguish between _____ which is the process by which you form opinions, reach conclusions, and make critical evaluations of events and people, and _____ which is the process of choosing between alternatives, selecting and rejecting available options.
    a. framing; problem solving
    b. problem solving; framing
    c. judgment; decision making
    d. decision making; judgment

23. Research has shown that mood affects memory; when people are in happy moods, they tend to have happy memories, and when people are in sad moods, they tend to have memories of sad events. This finding is consistent with the _____ heuristic.
    a. availability
    b. representativeness
    c. anchoring
    d. belief-bias

24. You have just started work as a car salesman and are getting some training. The topic for today is the anchoring bias. Which of the following questions are you learning to ask?
    a. "What color and model of car are you interested in?"
    b. "Why not take this car for a test drive? I'll get the keys from the manager."
    c. "What's the most you think someone would pay for a car this well-designed?"
    d. "Don't you want a car that your friends will envy?"

25. Imagine that you are listening to a debate between a developer and an environmentalist about whether a new shopping mall should be built. The developer emphasizes how many new jobs will be created. The environmentalist emphasizes the loss of green space and the pollution created by increased traffic. Each debater is trying to influence audience members by encouraging them to
    a. resist overcoming mental sets.
    b. use the representativeness heuristic.
    c. carry out deductive reasoning.
    d. adopt a particular decision frame.

26. Researchers who have studied decision aversion have found that people
    a. cannot imagine how unhappy they will feel if the decision they make leads to a bad outcome.
    b. don't like to be accountable for decisions that lead to bad outcomes.
    c. like making decisions for others.
    d. like making decisions that will cause some people to have more and some people to have less of some desired good.

CHAPTER 9 Intelligence and Intelligence Assessment

What is Assessment?

1. The book *Heredity Genius* was written by
   a. Sir Francis Galton.
   b. Alfred Binet.
   c. J.P. Guilford.
   d. Howard Gardner.

2. A friend tells you that she was given an aptitude test by the school counselor and received a score of 120. In order to provide a context for interpreting the score, she also needs to provide you with information about the test's
   a. norms.
   b. validity.
   c. reliability.
   d. standardization.

3. A child thinks that people with bigger heads are smarter and suggests that you can measure how smart someone is by simply measuring the size of their head. If such a measure were developed for use with adults, it would probably be
   a. valid but not reliable.
   b. reliable but not valid.
   c. both valid and reliable.
   d. neither valid nor reliable.

4. Which of the following is NOT a type of validity?
   a. face
   b. test-retest
   c. construct
   d. criterion

Intelligence Assessment

5. When Alfred Binet developed the first workable intelligence test, he
   a. was careful to exclude girls from the sample.
   b. chose questions for the test that could only be scored subjectively.
   c. demonstrated that important aspects of intelligence are inherited.
   d. used scores to identify children who needed special help.

6. Which of the following is the correct formula for determining IQ?
   a. IQ = (CA+MA) x 100
   b. IQ = (MA-CA) x 100
   c. IQ = (MA/CA) x 100
   d. IQ = MA(CA x 100)

7. Which of the following is a performance subtest on the WAIS-III?
   a. digit symbol-coding
   b. digit span
   c. comprehension
   d. arithmetic

8. In order to be classified as mentally retarded, individuals must
   a. be above the age of 18.
   b. obtain IQ scores of 70–75 or below.
   c. obtain IQ scores of 70–75 or below and have limitations in adaptive skills.
   d. obtain IQ scores of 70–75 or below, have limitations in adaptive skills, and be diagnosed with a learning disorder.

9. Imagine that you are visiting a museum exhibit on theories of intelligence. In one case there is a large red sphere marked with the letter g surrounded by many small yellow spheres marked with the letter s. It's most likely that this display is on the theory of
   a. J.P. Guilford.
   b. Alfred Binet.
   c. Raymond Cattell.
   d. Charles Spearman.

Theories of Intelligence

10. You have decided to develop your own items for a test of fluid intelligence. To be consistent with other tests, you should probably include items that test
    a. arithmetic skills.
    b. general information.
    c. abstract problem solving.
    d. knowledge of vocabulary.

11. In his "structure of intellect" model, J.P. Guilford specifies three features of intellectual tasks. They are
    a. content, product, and operation.
    b. units, classes, and relations.
    c. memory, cognition, and divergent production.
    d. visual, auditory, and symbolic.

12. In Robert Sternberg's triarchic theory of intelligence, the task of selecting strategies and monitoring progress toward success is handled by
    a. knowledge acquisition components.
    b. performance components.
    c. metacognitive components.
    d. creative intelligence.

13. On the basis of Howard Gardner's approach to intelligence, you might expect a world-class sculptor to excel in the area of _____ intelligence, and a salesperson to be strong with respect to _____ intelligence.
    a. naturalist; linguistic
    b. logical-mathematical; intrapersonal
    c. bodily kinesthetic; linguistic
    d. spatial; interpersonal

The Politics of Assessment

14. Researchers who have reviewed the studies on heritability of IQ conclude that about _____ percent of the variance in IQ scores is due to genetic makeup.
a. 10
b. 25
c. 50
d. 75

15. In a classroom discussion of IQ, a student says that because IQ has been found to be highly heritable, the IQ differences found among different racial groups must be genetic. Is the student's logic correct?
a. Yes, because the members of the different racial groups are all members of the same society, so heritability estimates that apply to one group apply to all groups.
b. Yes, because whatever is heritable is by definition based on genetic transmission.
c. No, because heritability studies use correlations whereas group differences use IQ tests scores.
d. No, because heritability that is based on an estimate within one group cannot be used to interpret differences between groups.

16. Research that has been conducted on the Head Start program suggests that preschool interventions
a. permanently change the IQs of children who participate.
b. have little effect on IQs, even in the short run.
c. cannot overcome many of the negative effects of poverty.
d. are unable to help children prepare for school.

17. Before a girl begins her math test, her teacher warns her that she should try extra hard because this is the kind of test on which girls often do poorly. With respect to the concept of stereotype threat, what effect is the teacher's warning likely to have?
a. It should help the girl to overcome the impact of stereotype threat.
b. It should increase the likelihood that the girl will perform poorly.
c. It will have little effect, because stereotype threat is unrelated to gender.
d. The impact will depend on whether the teacher is a male or a female.

18. When researcher Harold Stevenson tracked the mathematics achievement of Chinese, Japanese, and U.S. children and also asked students, teachers, and parents to contrast the importance of studying hard versus innate intelligence, he found that Japanese children have much _____ levels of achievement than U.S. children and that people in the U.S. believe that innate intelligence is _____ important than studying hard.
a. higher; more
b. higher; less
c. lower; more
d. lower; less

Creativity

19. A musician is considered by his peers to be creative. According to the definition of creativity used by psychologists, the musician's behavior would be best characterized as
a. unique and artistic.
b. original.
c. exceptionally talented.
d. novel and appropriate.

20. When researchers have investigated the relationship between creativity and IQ, they have found that
a. there is no correlation between the two measures.
b. there is an inverse relationship; the higher a person's IQ, the lower a person's creativity.
c. there is a direct relationship; the higher a person's IQ, the higher their level of creativity.
d. there is a weak or moderate correlation up to an IQ of about 120, but with increasing IQs the correlation decreases.

21. While taking a test as part of an application for a job designing toys, you are asked questions such as "How many uses can you think of for a paper clip?" and "Name as many different means of transportation as you can in five minutes." Questions such as these focus most directly on _____ thinking.
a. convergent
b. divergent
c. algorithmic
d. crystallized

22. When creativity researcher Robert Weisberg examined the artistic output of the composer Robert Schumann, who was diagnosed with bipolar disorder, he found that the composer produced _____ compositions when he was in a manic state than when he was in a depressive state; further, the manic compositions were of _____ the depressive compositions.
a. more; lower quality than
b. more; the same quality as
c. fewer; higher quality than
d. fewer; the same quality as

Assessment and Society

23. According to the authors of the textbook, the primary goal of psychological assessment is to
a. make accurate assessments of people that are as free as possible of errors of assessors' judgments.
b. replace the objective judgments of evaluators with more subjective measures that are open to critical evaluation.
c. show people their strengths and weaknesses so that they will become more fully functioning members of society.
d. determine which of the various theories of intelligence best explains the development of intelligence.

24. Assessment is a controversial area within psychology. The authors of the textbook cite all of the following as major ethical concerns EXCEPT the
    a. fairness of test-based decisions.
    b. utility of tests for evaluating education.
    c. implications of using test scores as labels to categorize individuals.
    d. training of psychometricians who are qualified to administer assessments.

25. With respect to the concern that test outcomes can take on the status of unchangeable labels, the authors of the textbook suggest that labels often lead to
    a. blaming society for failure rather than the individuals who have failed.
    b. blaming the victim for failure and thereby taking society off the hook.
    c. focusing attention inappropriately on educational systems that need to accommodate learners.
    d. the mislabeling of people as "normal" when they are really "abnormal."

26. The point made by Phil Zimbardo in relating a personal anecdote about the relationship between test scores and his career as a professional psychologist is that people
    a. should use their test scores to help in the process of career development.
    b. need to remember that tests have been developed to be both reliable and valid.
    c. can overcome negative predictions based on their test scores.
    d. should not be forced to take tests, for any reason.

CHAPTER 10 Human Development Across the Life Span

Studying Development

1. Which of the following is most likely to be a finding from a normative investigation?
   a. It is easier to teach a child subtraction after he has learned addition.
   b. The average child sits without support at 5.5 months.
   c. Aggression is a personality trait that remains fairly stable over time.
   d. Children who grow up in bilingual homes seem to have few language problems.

2. When a developmental psychologist uses a longitudinal design, he or she tests participants of _____ at _____.
   a. the same age; the same time
   b. different ages; the same time
   c. the same age; different times
   d. different ages; different times

3. Compared to longitudinal studies, a disadvantage of cross-sectional designs is that
   a. they are typically more costly.
   b. it is more difficult to keep track of participants.
   c. they generally take longer to complete.
   d. the results cannot be generalized widely, to various cohorts.

Physical Development Across the Life Span

4. When fertilization occurs, the single cell that results is called the
   a. fetus.
   b. embryo.
   c. zygote.
   d. sperm.

5. Pregnant women who use cocaine expose the fetus to physical impairment. The brain systems most damaged by cocaine are those responsible for controlling
   a. sight.
   b. hearing.
   c. attention.
   d. movement.

6. When you touch a newborn's cheek, her head turns, seeking something to suck. This prewired response is known as the _____ reflex.
   a. rooting
   b. sucking
   c. startle
   d. survival

7. Developmental psychologists use an apparatus called the visual cliff to test an infant's
   a. crawling ability.
   b. attachment to its mother.
   c. depth perception.
   d. visual preferences.

8. A baby is tightly bound by his mother in a cradle-board, common to his culture. With respect to his ability to walk later, research suggests that this experience will
   a. delay walking and the sequence of locomotion that he goes through.
   b. delay walking, but not the sequence of locomotion that he goes through.
   c. change the sequence of locomotion that he goes through.
   d. have no impact on the physical process of walking, but will affect his emotional response to exploring his environment.

Cognitive Development Across the Life Span

9. While flipping through the channels on late-night television, you hear a character in a film say that "the evolutionary legacy that each child brings into the world is the mold that shapes development." You should conclude that the character is most likely
   a. John Locke.
   b. Margaret Mead.
   c. Eleanor Maccoby.
   d. Jean-Jacques Rousseau.

10. Research into the cognitive abilities of children who are in the sensorimotor stage has determined that they
    a. believe that solid objects can pass through other solid objects.
    b. are incapable of determining object boundaries by perceiving relative motion.
    c. are less perceptually and cognitively sophisticated than Piaget claimed.
    d. already rely on certain processes to help them organize their perceptual world.

11. The 4-year-old child who talks baby talk to her 2-year-old sister, but not to her 7-year-old brother, challenges Piaget's claim that 4-year-old children are
    a. decentered.
    b. preoperational.
    c. animistic.
    d. egocentric.

Acquiring Language

12. When Janet Werker measured the ability of infants learning English or Hindi, as well as adults who spoke English or Hindi, to hear the differences between certain Hindi phonemes, she found that
    a. only the infants learning Hindi could hear the differences .
    b. only the infants learning English could hear the differences.
    c. only the adults could hear the differences.
    d. of the participants older than 8 months, only the Hindi speakers or speakers-to-be could hear the differences.

13. Linguist Noam Chomsky has attempted to explain the acquisition of grammar by suggesting that
    a. children are born with mental structures that facilitate comprehension and production.
    b. parents help to accelerate the acquisition process by correcting children's grammatical inaccuracies.
    c. children eventually learn that the key to the acquisition of grammatical rules is overregularization.
    d. the role of child-directed speech has been severely underestimated.

14. A two-year-old's speech is described as telegraphic because it is
    a. used to convey emotional content.
    b. made up of single words, linked together with no grammatical structure.
    c. filled with short, simple sequences, using mostly nouns and verbs.
    d. intense and surprising, as are most telegrams.

Social Development Across the Life Span

15. A child is ending her preschool years. According to the theory of Erik Erikson, she is probably in the _____ stage of psychosocial development.
    a. autonomy vs. self-doubt
    b. initiative vs. guilt
    c. trust vs. mistrust
    d. generativity vs. stagnation

16. In the Strange Situation Test, a securely attached child will _____ when the parent leaves the room and _____ when the parent returns.
    a. show some distress; seek proximity, comfort, and contact
    b. act pleased; act dazed and confused
    c. become quite upset and anxious; show anger
    d. seem aloof; actively avoid and ignore the parent

17. A child's parents demand that he conform to appropriate rules of behavior, but at the same time they attempt to keep channels of communication open to foster their child's ability to regulate himself. Psychologists would characterize this parenting style as
    a. neglecting.
    b. authoritarian.
    c. authoritative.
    d. indulgent.

18. When Harry Harlow raised infant monkeys with terry cloth and wire "mothers," he found that the monkeys
    a. were more likely to become attached to the artificial mother who provided food.
    b. did not know how to be mothers themselves.
    c. were able to have normal sexual relationships.
    d. showed no adjustment problems once they were allowed to interact with other monkeys.

19. In a study that is described in the textbook, researchers examined the occupational aspirations and expectations for second- to eighth-grade boys in either poor minority neighborhoods or affluent white neighborhoods. When looking at the low-income boys, they found that, compared to boys from affluent neighborhoods, their
    a. aspirations and expectations were lower.
    b. aspirations were higher but their expectations were lower.
    c. expectations were higher, but their aspirations were lower.
    d. expectations were lower, but their aspirations were higher.

20. Researchers on marriage and parenthood have found that
    a. children's births tend to push husbands and wives in directions opposite traditional gender roles.
    b. both men and women typically become depressed when they are left with an "empty nest."
    c. marital satisfaction generally improves as a child or children pass through their adolescent years.
    d. marital satisfaction typically decreases after the birth of a first child.

Gender Development

21. When psychologists talk about an individual's sense of maleness or femaleness, including awareness and acceptance of one's sex, they are referring to a person's
    a. biological sex.
    b. gender.
    c. gender roles.
    d. gender identity.

22. In a study that is described in the textbook, researchers examined the extent to which 4- and 6-year-old children in same-sex groups played with one other child or engaged in activities involving larger group of children. The results revealed that
    a. boys had fewer different partners during the play period.
    b. girls were more likely to play with each partner for a longer period of time.
    c. girls were more likely to play in pairs.
    d. only the 6-year-old girls were more likely to engage in activities that involved the whole group.

23. Compared to her brother, a girl's play group is likely to be
    a. mixed-sex in nature.
    b. more concerned with consensus.
    c. more concerned with power.
    d. more concerned with dominance.

Moral Development

24. According the Lawrence Kohlberg's stage approach to morality, a person at the highest level of moral reasoning would engage in moral behavior in order to
a. be true to universal principles.
b. avoid pain or not to get caught.
c. gain acceptance and avoid disapproval.
d. follow rules and avoid censure by authorities.

25. In contrast to the view of Lawrence Kohlberg, Carol Gilligan has proposed that men's moral reasoning is based on _____, whereas women are more concerned with _____.
a. justice; caring for others
b. reason; emotion
c. doing; feeling
d. dominance; submission

26. In a cross-cultural study of responses to moral dilemmas that is presented in the textbook, schoolchildren and adults in India and the United states were asked to choose which courses of action they thought characters should take. The researchers concluded that
a. the participants from India were much more likely to favor interpersonal responsibility options over justice options.
b. the participants from the United States were much more likely to favor interpersonal responsibility options over justice options.
c. there were no differences between the groups of participants in terms of their favoring of justice or interpersonal responsibility options.
d. women from both cultures tended to favor interpersonal responsibility whereas men from both cultures favored justice options.

Learning to Age Successfully

27. In their prescription for successful aging, the authors of the textbook suggest that
a. many of the changes that are stereotypically associated with aging are functions of decay.
b. the "use it or lose it" rule applies only to physical domains.
c. the "use it or lose it" rule applies only to cognitive domains.
d. the trick to prospering is to solidify one's gains and minimize one's losses.

28. A friend tells you that his grandmother has decided she wants to make a living playing high-stakes poker. A pretty good card player, she gives up all games except poker and sharpens her skills by reading all that she can about poker. She enters low-stakes tournaments to get used to competition. Does this plan for successful aging omit any important strategies?
a. Yes, it omits optimization.
b. Yes, it omits selection.
c. Yes, it omits compensation.
d. No, it includes all of the strategies for successful aging.

29. In their suggestions for how learning how to make choices across the lifespan, the authors of the textbook suggest all of the following EXCEPT
a. selecting goals that are most important to you.
b. coming to realize that things happen for a reason.
c. compensating when your progress is blocked.
d. optimizing your performance.

CHAPTER 11 Motivation

Understanding Motivation

1. Which of the following results argues against the idea that all behavior is motivated by tension reduction?
   a. Water-deprived rats explore a new environment before they drink.
   b. People prefer exposure to moderate temperatures.
   c. A cat will eat when it is hungry.
   d. A tired organism will rest.

2. The teacher has presented a slide that is entitled "Metamotivational States." You can safely assume that the topic of the lecture is _____ theory.
   a. drive
   b. instinct
   c. incentive
   d. reversal

3. Research by cultural anthropologists such as Ruth Benedict and Margaret Mead undermined instinct theories by showing that
   a. instincts were different from culture to culture.
   b. Freud's ideas applied only to collectivist cultures.
   c. there were large behavior differences between cultures.
   d. individualist cultures valued instincts more than collectivist cultures.

4. The fact that you work harder at your workplace than other employees would be explained by a behaviorist in terms of
   a. telic and paratelic states.
   b. willpower.
   c. internal drives or instincts.
   d. differences in reinforcement histories.

5. Your high-school guidance counselor was a strong proponent of the idea that motivation is shaped by expectations and personal values, and that discrepancies between expectations and reality can be motivating. It sounds like she had been reading work by
   a. Clark Hull.
   b. Julian Rotter.
   c. Janet Polivy.
   d. David McClelland.

Eating

6. Halfway through a big holiday dinner that your mother has prepared for you, you feel full. Physiologically, the peripheral information that signaled fullness is the fact that your
   a. VMH is being stimulated.
   b. LH is being stimulated.
   c. stomach is contracting.
   d. stomach is distended.

7. In early laboratory studies of the mechanisms underlying eating behavior, animals consumed less food if
   a. the lateral hypothalamus was stimulated.
   b. the ventromedial hypothalamus was lesioned.
   c. either the lateral hypothalamus was lesioned or the ventromedial hypothalamus was stimulated.
   d. either the lateral hypothalamus was stimulated or the ventromedial hypothalamus was lesioned.

8. Imagine that you are at a restaurant with a group of friends. You have eaten a lot and feel full, but when a friend orders a dessert, you offer to share it with him. Your desire to eat the dessert exemplifies what is known as
   a. restrained eating.
   b. unrestrained eating.
   c. satiety.
   d. sensory-specific satiety.

9. In a study of the effects of anticipated diets on restrained and unrestrained eaters that is described in the textbook, some female college students were led to believe that they would be placed on diets. When given the opportunity to "taste test" cookies, the greatest number of cookies was eaten by the
   a. restrained eaters who were told they would be on a diet.
   b. unrestrained eaters who were told they would be on a diet.
   c. restrained eaters who were not told they would be on a diet.
   d. unrestrained eaters who were not told they would be on a diet.

10. Women in high school and college tend to suffer from eating disorders more than nonstudents do. It has been suggested that this is the result of the
    a. desire to look attractive yet participate in social eating and drinking with friends.
    b. higher levels of stress experienced in high school and college women compared to nonstudents.
    c. relationship found between higher levels of education and susceptibility to eating disorders.
    d. greater acceptance of the ideal body types portrayed in popular women's magazines.

Sexual Behaviors

11. The research of William Masters and Virginia Johnson described several phases in the human sexual response cycle. The plateau phase occurs
    a. before the excitement phase.
    b. after the orgasm phase.
    c. during the orgasm phase.
    d. between the excitement and orgasm phases.

12. A current debate among evolutionary psychologists concerns whether _____ have evolved a _____ mating strategy.
   a. men; long-term
   b. men; short-term
   c. women; short-term
   d. women; long-term

13. Sexual scripts explain why
   a. animal sexual behavior is more influenced by hormones.
   b. humans and animals may have different mating strategies.
   c. different cultures may have different sexual practices.
   d. men and women have similar sexual response cycles.

14. According to Daryl Bem, sexual preference
   a. is based on "exotic becoming non-erotic" activities.
   b. may be caused by emotional arousal associated with engaging in sex-atypical behavior.
   c. is associated with biological factors for heterosexual behavior but emotional arousal factors for homosexual behavior.
   d. is directly caused by biological forces.

15. When it comes to sources of anxiety, gay men and lesbians report that they are LEAST concerned with
   a. the fact that they are gay or lesbian.
   b. people's responses to their sexual orientations.
   c. the difficulty of establishing and maintaining loving relationships.
   d. having to decide whether to reveal or conceal their homosexuality.

Motivation for Personal Achievement

16. Which personality test was used by David McClelland to assess the need for achievement?
   a. Rorschach test
   b. Thematic Apperception Test (TAT)
   c. Minnesota Multiphasic Personality Inventory (MMPI-2)
   d. NEO Personality Inventory (NEO-PI)

17. A person has received a high n Ach score on a test. You can expect that this person will
   a. tend to persist when working on tasks they believe to be difficult.
   b. show a need for efficiency, trying to get the same result for less effort.
   c. earn considerably less than his or her peers.
   d. not be concerned with concrete feedback on how they are doing.

18. A man who has an external locus of control is most likely to
   a. feel that his life will be changed by a lottery ticket.
   b. believe that his own abilities will affect life outcomes.
   c. reject the idea that his life has been predetermined.
   d. feel that he will do better if he works harder.

19. Friends refer to you as an "eternal optimist." If this is true, you are likely to attribute your successes to _____ causes.
   a. internal, stable, and global
   b. internal, unstable, and global
   c. external, stable, and specific
   d. external, unstable, and specific

20. Using the language of expectancy theory, which of the following business plans has low instrumentality and high valence?
   a. Every worker is guaranteed a $10,000 bonus at the end of the year.
   b. Every worker is guaranteed a $100 bonus at the end of the year.
   c. A few workers will receive a $10,000 bonus at the end of the year.
   d. A few workers will receive a $100 bonus at the end of the year.

A Hierarchy of Needs

21. According to Abraham Maslow, a person will not be motivated to seek security, comfort, tranquility, and freedom from fear until they have satisfied their _____ needs.
   a. esteem
   b. attachment
   c. self-actualization
   d. biological

22. Of the needs that are listed, which of the following follows Maslow's hierarchy of needs in order from lowest to highest?
   a. biological, esteem, attachment
   b. safety, esteem, self-actualization
   c. attachment, safety, esteem
   d. self-actualization, esthetic, safety

23. Which of the following statements most accurately represents the view of the authors of the textbook with respect to Maslow's theory of motivation?
   a. The only part of the theory that has received experimental support is the idea of a strict hierarchy of needs.
   b. Although Maslow's theory is a particularly upbeat view of human motivation, the strict hierarchy breaks down at times.
   c. The theory does not seem to be useful in helping people to understand different aspects of their own motivational experiences.
   d. Maslow's approach presents a particularly negative view of human nature that is similar to Freud's.

CHAPTER 12 Emotion, Stress, and Health

Emotions

1. Charles Darwin believed that emotions were
   a. uniquely individualistic expressions of feelings and affect.
   b. specific situational behaviors that change over time.
   c. culturally specific behaviors that are unique to the individual.
   d. inherited mental states designed to deal with recurring situations.

2. In the context of Paul Ekman's research on the basic set of emotions, which of the following is out of place?
   a. hate
   b. fear
   c. surprise
   d. anger

3. There's a new student in school and you are trying to figure out whether she is from an individualistic or collectivist culture. As you observe her behavior, it would be most useful to see if she
   a. expresses negative emotions toward another individual.
   b. expresses positive emotions toward another individual.
   c. produces a fight-or-flight response.
   d. produces a tend-and-befriend response.

4. With respect to the physiology of emotion, the amygdala plays an especially strong role in
   a. the interpretation of signals coming from the cortex.
   b. regulating the activities of the parasympathetic nervous system.
   c. attaching meaning to negative experiences.
   d. the interpretation of emotional tones of voice.

5. The best way to test the cognitive appraisal theory of emotion would be to
   a. surgically separate the internal organs from the central nervous system.
   b. see whether environmental cues are used to help label a person's arousal.
   c. see whether people experience emotions in familiar situations.
   d. measure how long it takes for autonomic nervous system responses to appear.

6. In an extensive series of experiments on the "mere exposure effect," psychologist Robert Zajonc demonstrated that
   a. people can identify emotions by their unique pattern of physiological changes.
   b. the speed with which emotional reactions can occur rules out cognitive interpretation.
   c. it is possible to have feelings without knowing why.
   d. emotional reactions must be innate, since newborns experience them.

7. A person who is depressed sees numerous examples of depressing events filling the magazine he is reading and doesn't seem to notice the uplifting and humorous items that appear equally frequently. This sounds like an example of what Gordon Bower referred to as
   a. mood-congruent processing.
   b. mood-dependent memory.
   c. cognitive appraisal.
   d. Type A behavior.

Stress of Living

8. Health psychologist Shelley Taylor and her colleagues have suggested that females experience a _____ response to stressors, which helps to ensure the safety of their offspring and reduce future vulnerability.
   a. fight-or-flight
   b. emotion-focused coping
   c. alarm
   d. tend-and-befriend

9. Which of the following is known as the "stress hormone?"
   a. thyrotropic hormone (TTH)
   b. adrenocorticotropic hormone (ACTH)
   c. epinephrine
   d. norepinephrine

10. In the context of Hans Selye's general adaptation syndrome, which of the following is out of place?
   a. arousal stage
   b. alarm reaction
   c. resistance stage
   d. exhaustion stage

11. Research on the psychological aftereffects of traumatic events has shown that
   a. people rarely seek social contact after a tragedy.
   b. a residual stress pattern may persist after the tragedy.
   c. few people pass through recognizable stages.
   d. people readily ignore the emotional impact of the tragedy.

12. If a friend is under stress and you want to give him advice that shows an emotion-focus, you should say
   a. "Can you do anything to get out of the situation?"
   b. "You have to find ways to fight the threat."
   c. "Is there some kind of compromise you can find?"
   d. "You have to plan ways to distract yourself from the situation."

13. Your teacher has a handout that lists the following three questions: What are your personal resources? What are your social resources? What action options are available? Today's lecture topic is most likely to be
    a. primary appraisal.
    b. secondary appraisal.
    c. stress inoculation.
    d. perceived control.

14. In the context of social support, cancer patients report receiving the most benefit from
    a. informational support.
    b. emotional support.
    c. tangible support.
    d. the absence of support.

Health Psychology

15. The biomedical model and the biopsychosocial model of health differ in that the
    a. biopsychosocial model acknowledges the link between the mind and the body.
    b. biopsychosocial model minimizes the importance of physical illness.
    c. biomedical model is largely concerned with psychosomatic illnesses.
    d. biomedical model draws on traditional health practices.

16. A friend has been smoking for several years. She hasn't made any behavioral changes yet, but she has started to think seriously about quitting. She is most likely at the _____ stage.
    a. precontemplation
    b. preparation
    c. contemplation
    d. maintenance

17. In a study of compliance for patients on hemodialysis that is described in the textbook, researchers assessed a group of patients for their monitoring attentional style, perceived control over their illness, and adherence to a treatment regimen. As predicted, researchers found that
    a. high monitors were more likely to comply with the specified regimen.
    b. high monitors perceived more control over their illness.
    c. low monitors were more likely to comply with the specified regimen.
    d. there were no differences between high and low monitors with respect to perceived control over their illness.

18. In this procedure, an individual is made aware of weak or internal bodily reactions, which are monitored and amplified by equipment that transforms the reactions into clear external signals. By controlling the level of these external cues, the individual can learn to control the bodily reactions. This is a description of
    a. the relaxation response.
    b. patient adherence.
    c. biofeedback.
    d. stress inoculation training.

19. Which characteristic of Type A people seems most to put them at risk?
    a. impatience with others
    b. hostility
    c. time urgency
    d. excessive competitiveness

20. Research by Christina Maslach on burnout in the health-care system has led to the suggestion that it might be possible to decrease the likelihood of job burnout by
    a. avoiding the use of teams in health care settings.
    b. increasing the number of patients each worker sees.
    c. ensuring that workers are in direct contact with patients for long periods of time.
    d. arranging workers' schedules so they get temporary breaks from patient care.

21. The authors of the textbook suggest nine steps to greater happiness and better mental health. These guidelines include all of the following EXCEPT to
    a. remember that failure and disappointment are sometimes blessings in disguise; they may tell you that your goals are not right for you.
    b. never say bad things about yourself, giving only constructive criticism.
    c. always take full credit for your successes and happiness and share your positive feelings with other people.
    d. concentrate only on the "here and now," for no one can truly control the future and the past is past.

Type and Trait Personality Theories

1. Your friends describe you as cheerful and active. According to the personality theory of Hippocrates, you must have an excess of which bodily humor?
   a. phlegm
   b. blood
   c. black bile
   d. yellow bile

2. In the context of William Sheldon's type theory of personality, which of the following does not belong with the others?
   a. hypermorphic
   b. mesomorphic
   c. ectomorphic
   d. endomorphic

3. According to the approach of Frank Sulloway, _____ children are likely to identify and comply with their parents and _____ children are "born to rebel."
   a. only; firstborn
   b. firstborn; only
   c. firstborn; laterborn
   d. laterborn; only

4. A woman believes that she possesses several major personality characteristics, but that there is no single trait that organizes her life. Using the terminology associated with Gordon Allport, she believes herself to be better described by _____ traits than by a _____ trait.
   a. cardinal; central
   b. cardinal; secondary
   c. central; cardinal
   d. secondary; central

5. According to the five-factor model, personality can be classified along the dimensions of
   a. energy, creativeness, emotional stability, hostility and persistence.
   b. egocentrism, introversion, punctuality, openness to experience, and sociability.
   c. introversion, extroversion, neuroticism, shyness, and hostility.
   d. neuroticism, conscientiousness, openness to experience, extraversion, and agreeableness.

6. Although he is usually quiet and unassuming, in the courtroom he is a bold and self-confident prosecutor. This illustrates what is known as
   a. the consistency paradox.
   b. self-handicapping.
   c. an ego defense mechanism.
   d. reciprocal determinism.

Psychodynamic Theories

7. According to Freud's theory of personality, boys must overcome the Oedipus complex during the _____ stage of psychosexual development.
   a. anal
   b. oral
   c. genital
   d. phallic

8. Instead of studying for your psychology test, you are watching an awful movie on late-night television. When one of the characters says, "I can't wait. I want that gold and I want it now. I don't care what happens!" which of Freud's personality structures should it remind you of?
   a. id
   b. ego
   c. superego
   d. either the id or superego

9. A teenager was yelled at by his teacher. When he gets home, his little brother's bicycle is blocking his way, so he throws it into the garage. Inside his house, he yells at the dog to stop barking. This behavior best exemplifies the defense mechanism of
   a. reaction formation.
   b. sublimation.
   c. projection.
   d. displacement.

10. This personality theorist believes that, as small children, people all experience feelings of inferiority and that all lives are dominated by the search for ways to overcome those feelings. Who is it?
    a. Alfred Adler
    b. Karen Horney
    c. Carl Jung
    d. Carl Rogers

Humanistic Theories

11. Someone you know tells you that he wants to be a humanistic personality theorist. This does not surprise you because he is
    a. motivated primarily by sex and aggression.
    b. generally negative in his view of the world.
    c. always encouraging you to reach your full potential.
    d. a strong advocate of learning principles such as positive reinforcement.

12. Which humanistic personality theorist believed that the absence of favorable nurturing conditions causes a child to develop a basic anxiety that stifles spontaneity of expression of real feelings and prevents effective relations with others, in turn leading to interpersonal or intrapsychic defenses?
   a. Sigmund Freud
   b. Karen Horney
   c. Carl Rogers
   d. Abraham Maslow

13. The idea that we do not really know what another person's subjective view of life is like until we "walk in their shoes," is similar to the characteristic of humanistic theories described as
   a. holistic.
   b. dispositional.
   c. phenomenological.
   d. unconditional.

Social-Learning and Cognitive Theories

14. The gathering was pretty quiet until "the life of the party" arrived. His outgoing nature got others energized and soon everyone was laughing and talking. This is an example of what Albert Bandura referred to as
   a. self-efficacy.
   b. self-esteem.
   c. reciprocal determinism.
   d. vicarious experience.

15. All you know about a college student is that she is low in self-efficacy and that she has signed up for an advanced mathematics course. From this information, you can predict that this student may not
   a. understand the material that is presented in the course.
   b. have the ability that is necessary to take the course.
   c. be sufficiently motivated to take the course.
   d. believe that she will do well in the course.

16. Suppose you want to use Nancy Cantor's social intelligence theory to make comparisons between two of your friends. You might ask them to describe to you what
   a. situations make them feel most inadequate.
   b. life goals or life tasks matter most to them.
   c. important behaviors they have learned by watching other people.
   d. aspects of their possible selves they consider to be most important.

Self Theories

17. The _____ is a dynamic mental structure that motivates, interprets, organizes, mediates, and regulates intrapersonal and interpersonal behaviors and processes.
   a. self-concept
   b. self-schema
   c. id
   d. collective unconscious

18. In a study that is described in the textbook, researchers gave participants an assessment device that measured the extent to which young adults could imagine themselves becoming parents, and assigned participants "parent-possible-self (PPS)" scores. High- and low-PPS participants then rated their perceptions of videotaped infants whose behavior ranged from happy to fussy. It was found that
   a. women received higher PPS scores than men.
   b. men received higher PPS scores than women.
   c. high-PPS participants gave consistently more favorable ratings to the infants.
   d. low-PPS participants gave consistently more favorable ratings to the infants.

19. A skater is about to take the ice to perform her routine for the judges in an important competition. Which statement is she likely to make if she is self-handicapping?
   a. "I practiced really hard, but I'm still not sure I will do well."
   b. "I'm sure I will have a great performance."
   c. "The judges are likely to emphasize the technical aspects of my performance."
   d. "It's too bad I didn't get enough sleep last night with all the noise."

Comparing Personality Theories

20. Which theory of personality places the greatest emphasis on the heredity side of the nature versus nurture issue?
   a. humanistic
   b. social-learning
   c. cognitive
   d. Freudian

21. For the most part, social-learning theories emphasize _____ and trait theories play up _____ in their explanations of personality.
   a. future goals; past reinforcements
   b. situational factors; dispositional factors
   c. heredity; the environment
   d. the present; the past

22. When discussing the various contributions to the understanding of human personality made by each type of theory, the authors of the textbook come to the conclusion that
   a. each theory makes different contributions.
   b. cognitive theories contribute the most in the area of motivation.
   c. humanistic theories are most important in the understanding of planning, organization, and memory.
   d. psychodynamic theory emphasize the importance of the self-image.

Assessing Personality

23. A major difference between the NEO-PI and the MMPI-2 is that the NEO-PI
   a. was first used as a projective test of intelligence.
   b. was designed to be used with nonclinical adult populations.
   c. has a greater number of clinical scales than the MMPI-2.
   d. has yet been found to be reliable.

24. At the end of a job interview, the applicant is given the MMPI. He wants to make a good impression, so when he sees questions such as "I don't always tell the truth," and "I sometimes say things that are best left unsaid," he answers that these statements are not true. It is likely that the person scoring the test will
   a. not notice anything unusual about the responses.
   b. be impressed with the applicant's moral character.
   c. detect the questionable validity of the test.
   d. give the applicant a high score on the neuroticism scale.

25. When a person takes the Thematic Apperception Test, they are asked to
   a. fill out a questionnaire that contains 550 items.
   b. generate stories about ambiguous scenes.
   c. respond to questions about symmetrical inkblots.
   d. answer a series of questions about thoughts, feelings, and actions.

CHAPTER 14 Psychological Disorders

The Nature of Psychological Disorders

1. A man cannot hold down a job because of a serious drinking problem. Which criterion of abnormality does this meet?
   a. violation of moral and ideal standards
   b. irrationality
   c. maladaptiveness
   d. unpredictability

2. The first truly comprehensive classification system of psychological disorders was developed by
   a. Emil Kraepelin.
   b. Philippe Pinel.
   c. Thomas Szasz.
   d. Jean Charcot.

3. Hypnotism had its origins in a technique developed by
   a. David Rosenhan.
   b. Franz Mesmer.
   c. Sigmund Freud.
   d. Martin Seligman.

4. In their discussion of the etiology of psychopathology, the authors of the textbook make the point that contemporary researchers increasingly take a(n) _____ perspective.
   a. sociocultural
   b. cognitive
   c. biological
   d. interactionist

Classifying Psychological Disorders

5. Which of the following is LEAST likely to be stated as a goal of the classification of psychological disorders?
   a. describing the causes of disorders
   b. providing a common shorthand language
   c. suggesting appropriate treatments
   d. explaining the stigma of mental illness

6. Compared to making medical diagnoses, it is more difficult to make a psychological diagnosis because psychological diagnoses
   a. rely on interpretations of a person's actions.
   b. rely on physical evidence.
   c. require more training than psychologists usually have.
   d. must be made without any diagnostic manual.

7. Clinical psychologists who work with people who have psychological disorders rely on a reference manual known by the acronym
   a. MMPI.
   b. NEO-PI.
   c. DSM-IV-TR.
   d. TAT.

8. Personality disorders and mental retardation are classes of information found on Axis _____ of the DSM-IV-TR.
   a. I
   b. II
   c. III
   d. V

Major Types of Psychological Disorders

9. One of the findings of the National Comorbidity Study was that
   a. people who have experienced one disorder often experience others in their lifetimes.
   b. the system of classification of psychological disorders needs to be revised annually.
   c. the number of people suffering from psychological disorders is steadily declining.
   d. there is no available information on the prevalence of different disorders.

10. A boy refuses to play outside because he is deathly afraid that he will be stung by a bee. He is still willing to take the school bus and play with friends in their homes. This child most likely suffers from
    a. a social phobia.
    b. agoraphobia.
    c. a specific phobia.
    d. obsessive-compulsive disorder.

11. Which theoretical approach contends that obsessive-compulsive disorders are maintained by the reduction in anxiety that follows from compulsive behaviors.
    a. behavioral
    b. psychodynamic
    c. cognitive
    d. biological

12. A search of your family history reveals a distant relative who had a psychological disorder. Unfortunately, the records do not indicate the specific type of disorder. Your best guess should be
    a. schizophrenia.
    b. obsessive-compulsive disorder.
    c. antisocial personality disorder.
    d. mood disorder.

13. An award-winning documentary on suicide is most likely to mention that
    a. suicide rates for African American youths of both sexes are much lower than those for white youths.
    b. the suicide rate has gone down steadily since the mid-1970s.
    c. few adolescents reveal their suicidal feelings before they take their own lives.
    d. men are more likely to attempt suicide than are women.

14. If a woman feels that she is not the center of attention, she does something inappropriate to regain that spotlight. She often offers strong opinions, but rarely offers factual support for her ideas, and she reacts to minor occasions with overblown emotional responses. It sounds as though she may have _____ personality disorder.
   a. narcissistic
   b. histrionic
   c. antisocial
   d. paranoid

15. If you were to write a paper on dissociative identity disorder (DID), you would probably want to mention that it
   a. is the same as schizophrenia.
   b. is now known as multiple personality disorder.
   c. is often associated with reports of childhood abuse.
   d. does not appear to have any adaptive purpose.

Schizophrenic Disorders

16. A common symptom of schizophrenia is
   a. seasonal affective disorder.
   b. multiple personalities.
   c. posttraumatic stress.
   d. auditory hallucinations.

17. A person who has schizophrenia may suffer from delusions. A delusion is a(n)
   a. imagined sensory perception.
   b. false or irrational belief.
   c. inappropriate emotion.
   d. strange mannerism.

18. In which type of schizophrenia is an individual currently free of symptoms such as hallucinations or delusions, but still has minor positive symptoms or negative symptoms such as flat emotion, and is considered to be entering remission?
   a. residual
   b. undifferentiated c.disorganized
   d. catatonic

19. Research on the biological aspects of schizophrenia has shown that
   a. schizophrenia is associated with inadequate amounts of the neurotransmitter dopamine.
   b. the brain's ventricles are smaller in many individuals who have schizophrenia.
   c. there are biological markers for schizophrenia.
   d. there are apparently no differences in brain functioning that distinguish people who have schizophrenia.

20. A widely accepted view of the cause of schizophrenia says that genetic factors place an individual at risk, but environmental stress factors must be present in order for the potential risk to be manifested as a disorder. This description sounds most like
   a. a stigma.
   b. the diathesis-stress hypothesis.
   c. a biological marker.
   d. comorbidity.

21. A youngster has begun to show developing signs of possible schizophrenia. According to researchers who have undertaken prospective studies, parents should
   a. try to "nip the problem in the bud" by pointing out the problem behaviors to the youngster.
   b. ignore the problem behaviors as they will probably go away on their own.
   c. reduce their criticism, hostility, and intrusiveness toward the child.
   d. remember that the problem is the child's and that nothing the family members do can make a difference.

The Stigma of Mental Illness

22. To say that there is a "stigma" associated with mental illness means that
   a. there are negative attitudes about the person that makes him or her feel unacceptable.
   b. there are many subtleties in the form that mental illness can take.
   c. it is difficult for practicing clinicians to know which form of treatment is most likely to be successful.
   d. it has dual causes; biological and environmental.

23. In a study that is described in the textbook, ex-psychiatric patients interacted in pairs with a confederate of the experimenter who was posing as a personnel trainee recruited from a business establishment. Participants were led to believe that the trainee had been told they were either medical or psychiatric patients. The results demonstrated the importance of
   a. understanding the etiology of mental illness.
   b. the DSM-IV-TR in the diagnosis of mental disorders.
   c. lack of experience on the process of stigmatization.
   d. self-fulfilling prophecies on expectations of rejection.

24. Research suggests that people who have had contact with individuals with mental illness
   a. better realize how dangerous the mentally ill can be.
   b. are less likely to stigmatize such individuals.
   c. are more likely to stigmatize such individuals.
   d. better realize that there is no reason to be optimistic about treatment outcomes.

CHAPTER 15 Therapies for Psychological Disorders

The Therapeutic Context

1. By choosing a clinical psychologist over a psychiatrist, one is more likely to be treated by someone who
   a. can prescribe drugs.
   b. has completed medical school.
   c. has a broader background in psychology, assessment, and research.
   d. has received more training in the biomedical bases of psychological problems.

2. Cultural anthropologists who have looked at differences between Western and non-Western treatment of individuals with psychological disorders have found that non-Western cultures typically
   a. do not remove mentally ill individuals from society.
   b. believe in the use of asylums.
   c. only use Western-trained clinicians to treat psychopathology.
   d. have abandoned religion and witchcraft as treatment methods.

3. Which statement best reflects the role of the mental asylum during the mental hygiene movement of the 1900s?
   a. It was developed to contain the poor, criminals, and the mentally disturbed.
   b. Its purpose has always been to offer treatment to those who could not help themselves.
   c. Initially, it was looked upon as a money-making instrument of the state.
   d. It evolved from having the goal of rehabilitation to the more practical goal of containment.

Psychodynamic Therapies

4. A _____ is a member of a religious group who specializes in the treatment of psychological disorders, often combining spirituality with practical problem solving.
   a. clinical social worker
   b. pastoral counselor
   c. counseling psychologist
   d. psychoanalyst

5. During a therapy session, the therapist realizes that he really dislikes the patient, who reminds him of his own mother. It sounds like the therapist might be experiencing
   a. catharsis.
   b. resistance.
   c. transference.
   d. countertransference.

6. Freud's followers retain many of his basic ideas but tended to disagree with his emphasis on
   a. childhood conflicts.
   b. the current social environment.
   c. the significance of the self-concept.
   d. interpersonal relations of love.

Behavior Therapies

7. A man wants to stop drinking alcohol. He has begun a treatment in which he is given a drug that will make him violently ill if he takes a drink. This treatment is known as
   a. aversion therapy.
   b. rational-emotive therapy.
   c. cognitive restructuring.
   d. humanistic therapy.

8. A woman has a terrible fear of snakes. It has gotten to the point where she is afraid to walk on the grass because a snake might bite her. Which therapeutic technique is most likely to put her in contact with a real snake earliest in the course of treatment?
   a. aversion therapy
   b. systematic desensitization
   c. behavioral rehearsal
   d. flooding

9. In a treatment program for cocaine-dependent participants that is described in the textbook, researchers evaluated the use of monetary vouchers for cocaine abstinence. It was found that
   a. the absolute level of reinforcement had to be kept quite high.
   b. maintaining a level amount of reinforcement was essential to the treatment process.
   c. reinforcement had to be contingent on the participants' behavior for it to be effective.
   d. noncontingent reinforcement was as effective as contingent reinforcement.

Cognitive Therapies

10. Cognitive therapists have become well known for the treatment of
    a. schizophrenia.
    b. depression.
    c. bipolar disorder.
    d. phobias.

11. Imagine that you are a therapist who uses cognitive behavior modification techniques. Which of the following statements by a client would you be most eager to pursue?
    a. "When I see a spider my heart starts racing."
    b. "I never really got along with my father."
    c. "Other people just don't like me."
    d. "I seem to be working all of the time."

12. Rational-emotive therapy (RET) is similar to humanistic therapy in that its goal is to help clients to
    a. increase an individual's sense of self-worth and potential to be self-actualized.
    b. develop an elaborate social support network.
    c. learn how to use problem-focused coping strategies more effectively.
    d. use the principles of learning and reinforcement to modify or eliminate problem behaviors.

Humanistic Therapies

13. A _____ therapist strives to be nondirective, merely facilitating the client's search for self-awareness and self-acceptance.
   a. client-centered
   b. rational-emotive
   c. existential
   d. insight

14. In a classroom exercise, you are asked to play the role of a client-centered therapist. When your "client" sobs, "My life is so hopeless, what should I do?" you should respond,
   a. "The reason you feel hopeless is because you are hopeless."
   b. "Why do you feel guilty? What have you done wrong?"
   c. "Don't you think it's about time to get over this feeling of hopelessness and move on?"
   d. "You sound unhappy and confused."

15. Those who practice _____ therapy encourage an atmosphere of unconditional positive regard, maintaining genuineness with the client, and total empathy.
   a. Rogerian
   b. cognitive behavior modification
   c. participant modeling
   d. insight

16. Which type of therapist is most likely to use the "empty chair" technique during treatment?
   a. psychodynamic
   b. biomedical
   c. Gestalt
   d. behavioral

Group Therapies

17. Compared to individual therapy, group therapy is
   a. more expensive.
   b. somewhat more threatening for people who have problems dealing on their own with authority.
   c. more likely to provide people with opportunities to observe and practice interpersonal skills.
   d. less likely to allow people to see that many other people share the same problem.

18. A family therapist is most likely to
   a. view family problems as being biologically caused.
   b. view each member as a part of the whole family system.
   c. focus attention on the behaviors of the most maladjusted family members.
   d. focus attention on the cognitions of the most maladjusted family members.

19. A woman regularly attends meetings of Alcoholics Anonymous (AA), works closely with the leadership of the organization to help plan meetings and reach out to the community, and feels a strong bond to the group. Research suggests that, compared to people who do not have as strong an attachment to AA, this woman will
   a. be more likely to abuse alcohol.
   b. have more of a sense that she can control her alcoholism.
   c. probably relapse in the course of the next several months.
   d. be more likely to become addicted to other substances.

Biomedical Therapies

20. A patient who has schizophrenia and who is compulsive and anxiety-ridden undergoes an operation known as a prefrontal lobotomy. Following recovery from surgery, this patient is likely to
   a. suffer prolonged and severe bouts of amnesia.
   b. be unable to plan ahead and be indifferent to the opinions of others.
   c. suffer few noticeable side effects, feel energized and focused on the future.
   d. continue to feel anxiety and compulsiveness, but to a lesser degree.

21. One of the main advantages of electroconvulsive therapy over drug therapies for depression is that
   a. it works more quickly.
   b. treatment only lasts for one day.
   c. the reasons for its effectiveness are well understood.
   d. it never produces any memory deficits.

22. Antipsychotic drugs seem to work by reducing the activity of the neurotransmitter _____ in the brain.
   a. norepinephrine
   b. serotonin
   c. dopamine
   d. GABA

23. Tardive dyskinesia and agranulocytosis are side effects of
   a. electroconvulsive therapy.
   b. antipsychotic drugs.
   c. repetitive transcranial magnetic stimulation (rTMS).
   d. prefrontal lobotomy.

24. Benzodiazepines, such as Valium and Xanax, _____ the activity of the neurotransmitter GABA, and are useful in the treatment of _____.
   a. maintain constant levels of; schizophrenia
   b. increase; depression
   c. decrease; mood disorders
   d. increase; generalized anxiety disorder

Treatment Evaluation and Prevention Strategies

25. Part of the recovery that patients experience when they go into therapy arises from their own expectations of healing. This is known as
    a. spontaneous remission.
    b. ritual healing.
    c. transference.
    d. the placebo effect.

26. In a meta-analysis of treatment effectiveness for depression that is presented in the textbook, it was found that
    a. classic psychodynamic therapy was the most effective treatment.
    b. no form of therapy had greater success than placebo treatment.
    c. about half the patients taking antidepressant medication experienced symptom relief.
    d. patients treated with cognitive behavioral therapy showed the poorest level of improvement.

27. Imagine that you are setting up a mental health program in a rural community. Your goals are to identify people who are suffering from psychological disorders and to try to limit the duration and severity of the disorder. Your program provides _____ prevention services.
    a. primary
    b. secondary
    c. tertiary
    d. pre-primary

CHAPTER 16 Social Cognition and Relationships

Constructing Social Reality

1. When Fritz Heider argued that all people are "intuitive psychologists," he was expressing his belief that people
   a. prefer inductive reasoning over deductive reasoning.
   b. respond primarily on the basis of emotions rather than reason.
   c. try to figure out what people are like and what causes their behavior.
   d. prefer situational explanations of behavior.

2. In the context of the covariation principle, which of the following does not belong with the others?
   a. compliance
   b. distinctiveness
   c. consistency
   d. consensus

3. A classmate agrees to pick you up on the way to school the day of an important test. On the way to your place, however, he encounters a terrible traffic jam caused by an accident and so he arrives over an hour late. Your tendency to think of him as unreliable is an example of
   a. the fundamental attribution error.
   b. cognitive dissonance.
   c. a self-fulfilling prophecy.
   d. compliance.

4. In general, people tend to take credit for their successes and deny responsibility for their failures. Psychologists refer to this tendency as the
   a. self-fulfilling prophecy.
   b. fundamental attribution error.
   c. self-serving bias.
   d. elaboration likelihood model.

5. In an experiment that is described in the textbook, elementary school teachers were informed by researchers that some of their students were "academic spurters" who could be expected to show unusual gains during the academic year. This study demonstrated the importance of
   a. self-fulfilling prophecies.
   b. cognitive dissonance.
   c. the contact hypothesis.
   d. jigsaw classrooms.

6. A friend has invited you and a few other friends who you do not know to dinner. Without your knowledge, she has told the others that you are very introverted. On the basis of research on behavioral confirmation, will the other guests still believe you to be introverted at the end of the meal?
   a. Yes, if you have a strong self-conception on this dimension.
   b. Yes, if you have a weak self-conception on this dimension.
   c. No, because behavioral confirmation is unaffected by self-conception.
   d. No, because self-conceptions always outweigh perceivers' expectations.

Attitudes, Attitude Change, and Action

7. Theorists have suggested that three types of information give rise to attitudes. Which of the following is NOT one of those types of information?
   a. cognitive
   b. behavioral
   c. personal
   d. behavioral

8. After vetoing your choices for a research paper, your teacher has talked you into writing a paper on attitude change. It would probably be most helpful if you type the word(s) _____ into your Internet search engine.
   a. persuasion
   b. attribution
   c. social cognition
   d. social perception

9. The elaboration likelihood model is a theory of persuasion that makes a critical distinction between _____ routes to persuasion.
   a. environmental and situational
   b. primary and secondary
   c. central and peripheral
   d. strong and weak

10. When advertisers pay celebrities to sell their products, they are counting on
    a. the principle of reciprocity.
    b. the importance of personal relevance.
    c. customers taking a central route to persuasion.
    d. customers taking a peripheral route to persuasion.

11. A father is who is filling out his income tax return suddenly remembers that he gave a lecture to his daughter on the importance of honesty earlier in the day. According to Leon Festinger, the fact that the parent has just bent the rules on charitable deductions will lead him to experience
    a. informational influence.
    b. self-serving bias.
    c. cognitive dissonance.
    d. groupthink.

12. In a study that was described in the textbook, students participated in a very dull task and were then asked to lie to another participant by saying that the task had been fun and interesting. The results of the study showed that the students who were paid
    a. $1 refused to lie.
    b. $1 later expressed the belief that the task was really fun and interesting.
    c. $20 refused to lie.
    d. $20 later expressed the belief that the task was really fun and interesting.

13. A charity seeking donations has sent you free address labels. This is an example of the marketing technique known as
    a. scarcity.
    b. the foot-in-the-door.
    c. reciprocity.
    d. the door-in-the-face.

Prejudice

14. The defining characteristic of prejudice is that it
    a. involves negative feelings such as fear or dislike.
    b. is a learned attitude.
    c. is intended to create feelings of group solidarity.
    d. resists change in the face of evidence of its falseness.

15. A boy tells his little sister that she can't be a member of his club, so she forms her own club, which she says is better than his. The girl's belief is an example of the social categorization process known as
    a. in-group bias.
    b. out-group bias.
    c. sexism.
    d. behavioral confirmation.

16. In an experiment that is described in the textbook, undergraduate students who had been classified by an earlier test as either prejudiced or nonprejudiced were asked to view a series of faces and label them aloud as either "white" or "black." Some of the faces were easily classified, whereas others were ambiguous. Consistent with the researchers predictions, the
    a. nonprejudiced participants took longer when judging the ambiguous faces.
    b. prejudiced participants took longer when judging the ambiguous faces.
    c. prejudiced participants labeled more of the faces "black."
    d. nonprejudiced participants labeled all of the faces "white."

17. In a study that is described in the textbook, students who were classified as having high or low prejudice toward homosexuals read a pair of scientific studies about homosexuality that were either stereotype-consistent or stereotype-inconsistent. In part, the results showed that
    a. the students gave higher ratings to the study that opposed their point of view.
    b. only the high-prejudice students changed their attitudes because of the studies.
    c. only the low-prejudice students changed their attitudes because of the studies.
    d. after reading the studies, attitudes shifter further in the direction of original attitudes.

18. In the classic "Robbers Cave" study of prejudice by Muzafer Sherif, the prejudicial attitudes of groups of boys were changed by
    a. putting the group leaders on the paid staff of the camp.
    b. fostering personal interactions in the cooperative pursuit of shared goals.
    c. encouraging competition between the groups.
    d. planting negative rumors about the leaders of each of the groups.

19. In a program aimed at reversing prejudice, social psychologist Elliot Aronson developed the _____ technique, which requires students to depend on one another rather than compete.
    a. contact
    b. jigsaw
    c. in-groups
    d. reciprocity

Social Relationships

20. In a study that is described in the textbook, incoming college students were randomly assigned to couples as blind dates for a large dance. When asked to evaluate their dates and indicate how likely they were to see the individual again, the most important factor was
    a. different for men and women.
    b. intelligence.
    c. physical attractiveness.
    d. personality.

21. In part, research on physical attractiveness has shown that people who are believed to be attractive are also most likely believed to be
    a. rich.
    b. unintelligent.
    c. intelligent.
    d. extraverted.

22. In the context of love, which of the following does not belong with the others?
    a. passion
    b. commitment
    c. intimacy
    d. reciprocity

23. In the context of adult attachment style, if you are like the majority of people, you are most likely to agree with which of the following statements?
    a. I find it relatively easy to get close to others and am comfortable depending on them.
    b. I want to get very close to my partner, and this sometimes scares people away.
    c. I often worry that my partner doesn't really love me or won't want to stay with me.
    d. I am somewhat uncomfortable being close to others.

24. In the context of the research on love, is the feeling that the "other" is included in one's "self" important?
   a. Yes, because couples with the least overlap between "other" and "self" are most likely to remain committed.
   b. Yes, because couples with the most overlap between "other" and "self" are most likely to remain committed.
   c. No, because how a person feels about the "self" is more important than how one feels about the "other."
   d. It appears to be important for females, but not for males.

25. Research on women at a shelter for battered women found that, consistent with the dependence model of commitment, the women often stayed with their abusers and were still committed to returning to their relationships because they
   a. feared the threats made by the abusers.
   b. suffered from clinical depression.
   c. felt that the commitments they made were for a lifetime.
   d. saw themselves as having few alternatives economically.

CHAPTER 17 Social Processes, Society, and Culture

The Power of the Situation

1. The women on the college softball team are having a hard time with their coach. They disagree with many of her decisions, and feel that she plays favorites. However, they are hesitant to challenge or stand up to her, even though they have never been told not to do so. Their behavior follows what a social psychologist would call
   a. an implicit rule.
   b. an explicit rule.
   c. social reality.
   d. reciprocal altruism.

2. A graduate student is running a computer simulation of the Stanford Prison Experiment. He wants to duplicate the methodology of the original experiment. He should be sure to program the computer to
   a. choose passive individuals for the role of guard.
   b. choose aggressive individuals for the role of guard.
   c. assign the guard and prisoner roles randomly.
   d. choose passive individuals for the role of prisoner.

3. In order to be an accepted member of a particular "biker" club, you have to wear the right clothes, share the group's attitudes and opinions, and be able to use and understand the "language" of the group. These implicit rules exemplify what social psychologists refer to as
   a. norm crystallization.
   b. social norms.
   c. demand characteristics.
   d. groupthink.

4. You overhear a conversation among a group of teenagers. One of them says something that leads you to believe that he is particularly sensitive to the normative influence of his peer group. He is most likely to have said,
   a. "I'm not going to the party because I'm sure I won't have a good time."
   b. "I'm not sure what would be the best way to act in this situation."
   c. "It's really important to me to be liked and accepted by my friends."
   d. "I didn't help because I wasn't sure it was an emergency."

5. The classic research by Muzafer Sherif on informational influence using the autokinetic effect demonstrated that
   a. group norms can persist across generations of participants.
   b. each group has one participant who takes over the leadership role.
   c. norms break down when participants are tested individually.
   d. participants directly criticize group members who do not conform to group norms.

6. Solomon Asch's experiment on conformity is an important demonstration of
   a. norm crystallization.
   b. normative influence.
   c. the minority slowness effect.
   d. reciprocal altruism.

7. In a meeting with other executives, a vice-president is focusing attention on the motion that has just been presented. While others simply accept what is said, she consistently brings up important, relevant ideas that contradict the majority view. This is an example of the potential for group members in the minority to
   a. create a norm of reciprocity.
   b. find allies who also refuse to conform.
   c. have informational influence.
   d. have normative influence.

Altruism and Prosocial Behavior

8. While driving to the store, you pass a car that has pulled over to the side of the road. Apparently, the driver does not know how to fix a flat tire, so you stop to help. A social psychologist would say that your behavior exemplifies
   a. conformity.
   b. diffusion of responsibility.
   c. altruism.
   d. norm crystallization.

9. You have just started reading a social psychology experiment on the topic of altruism. You can anticipate that the dependent variable in the research is going involve some aspect of
   a. aggression.
   b. prosocial behavior.
   c. obedience.
   d. conformity.

10. When theorists use the concept of reciprocal altruism to understand behavior, they are most likely attempting to explain altruistic behavior directed toward
    a. older relatives.
    b. brothers and sisters.
    c. children by their parents.
    d. non-family members.

11. You decide to help a friend move, knowing that some day you will be moving and your friend may help you out in return. Daniel Batson would categorize your helping behavior as an example of
    a. altruism.
    b. principlism.
    c. collectivism.
    d. egoism.

12. When Bibb Latané and John Darley carried out a classic series of studies of prosocial behavior, they found that bystander "apathy" could be explained by
    a. personality characteristics.
    b. situational forces.
    c. one's prior experience with authority figures.
    d. childhood experiences.

13. In a study that is described in the textbook, seminary students who were going to deliver a sermon about the Good Samaritan were made to come across a man in obvious need of assistance. The man was most likely to receive help from seminarians who
    a. had ample time to help.
    b. were in a big hurry.
    c. noticed others were available to help.
    d. saw others were watching to see if they would help.

14. Imagine that you are reading a book on a crowded beach. You have to leave some personal items for a few minutes and are concerned that they might be taken. On the basis of studies of bystanders that are mentioned in the textbook, you should
    a. ask someone to keep an eye on your items.
    b. announce in a loud voice that you will be back shortly.
    c. put a note on your blanket saying that you are watching the items from a distance.
    d. never leave the items.

Aggression

15. In his book, *On Aggression,* Konrad Lorenz states the view that
    a. humans can not do each other much harm.
    b. there are sociocultural explanations of aggression in humans that make it unnecessary to postulate evolutionary explanations.
    c. species will act aggressively only against members of other species.
    d. humans do not have appropriately evolved mechanisms to inhibit aggressive impulses.

16. Researchers who are looking for biological factors that may mark a predisposition toward aggressive behavior have focused on the neurotransmitter
    a. acetylcholine.
    b. serotonin.
    c. dopamine.
    d. epinephrine.

17. Which of the following is the best example of instrumental aggression?
    a. A girl gets angry with her brother so she pushes him off his bike.
    b. A parent yells at his children when he gets home because he is frustrated with what is happening at work.
    c. Some teenagers make fun of a classmate who is punished by the teacher.
    d. A football player tries to injure an opponent because the opponent is the best player on the team.

18. Suppose some children are frustrated in their expectation that they will be allowed to play with highly attractive toys. Consistent with the frustration-aggression hypothesis, when they finally have an opportunity to play with those toys, they are most likely to
    a. act aggressively toward other children, but not to the toys.
    b. be happy to finally have the opportunity to play with the toys and play nicely.
    c. act aggressively toward the toys.
    d. reject the opportunity to play with the l toys.

19. Some theorists have suggested that, in response to continuing provocation, people apply memory structures that have encoded cultural norms for "ratcheting up" aggressiveness. This is known as
    a. altruism.
    b. an escalation script.
    c. the culture of honor.
    d. the general aggression model.

20. In a study of regional differences in responses to insults that is described in the textbook, researchers arranged for northern and southern male college students to endure a mild bump and insult. Subsequently, the students were observed in a situation in which they had to get out of the way of another person. Generalizing from the results of this study to all northerners and southerners, you should predict that
    a. southerners typically will be more polite, but react more dramatically to an insult.
    b. northerners typically will be more polite, but react more dramatically to an insult.
    c. southerners typically will be less polite, and react more dramatically to an insult.
    d. northerners typically will be less polite, and react more dramatically to an insult.

21. In a study of aggression that is described in the textbook, college undergraduates were recruited to play either violent or nonviolent video games, then were asked to read incomplete stories and indicate what they thought would happen next. The results showed that
    a. those who played the violent video games predicted fewer aggressive outcomes for the stories.
    b. those who played the violent video games predicted more aggressive outcomes for the stories.
    c. there were no differences in the predictions made by either group of undergraduates.
    d. there were no differences in predictions, but those who played the violent video games expressed markedly hostile attitudes toward the experimenters.

The Psychology of Conflict and Peace

22. Suppose you were a participant in Stanley Milgram's research on obedience. If you had protested when delivering shocks to the learner, Milgram would have
    a. ended the study immediately.
    b. presented a small shock to you.
    c. verbally ordered you to continue.
    d. physically forced you to continue.

23. In his research on group dynamics, Kurt Lewin found that _____ leadership produced groups that were the most inefficient and did work that was of poor quality and quantity.
    a. laissez-faire
    b. democratic
    c. autocratic
    d. authoritarian

24. A new elementary-school teacher has an autocratic style in the classroom. On the basis of research by Kurt Lewin, the teacher can expect her students to be
    a. attentive and undemanding.
    b. inventive and independent, but also aggressive at times.
    c. shy and withdrawn.
    d. hard working, but only when the teacher is watching them.

25. People of different political persuasions are debating various forms of government. The person who suggests that democratic governments are the best can find support for his conclusion from psychologists who have done research
    a. only on whole countries.
    b. only with groups of young boys.
    c. only in laboratories.
    d. on both small groups and whole countries.

26. In his early workshops with Palestinians and Israelis, the psychologist Herbert Kelman attempted to resolve conflict by
    a. engaging participants in interactive problem solving.
    b. creating pressure to produce agreement among all participants.
    c. engaging third-party members who mediated between the parties.
    d. publicly identifying participants.

ANSWER KEY

Answers for the tests read DOWN the page.

Answers for CHAPTER 1

1. a	7. b	12. c	17. c
2. b	8. c	13. b	18. a
3. c	9. a	14. a	19. d
4. d	10. b	15. d	20. b
5. a	11. c	16. d	21. b
6. d			

Answers for CHAPTER 2

1. d	8. c	15. b	22. d
2. a	9. c	16. c	23. b
3. d	10. b	17. d	24. b
4. c	11. d	18. b	25. d
5. a	12. a	19. c	26. d
6. a	13. c	20. c	27. b
7. c	14. a	21. b	

Answers for CHAPTER 3

1. c	7. b	12. c	17. d
2. b	8. d	13. a	18. a
3. a	9. b	14. a	19. b
4. b	10. d	15. b	20. d
5. c	11. c	16. d	21. a
6. c			

Answers for CHAPTER 4

1. a	8. d	15. a	22. a
2. d	9. d	16. c	23. a
3. c	10. b	17. c	24. b
4. b	11. d	18. c	25. b
5. d	12. a	19. b	26. b
6. a	13. d	20. a	27. a
7. b	14. c	21. d	28. c

Answers for CHAPTER 5

1. b	7. c	13. a	19. b
2. d	8. b	14. c	20. d
3. c	9. d	15. d	21. c
4. a	10. a	16. d	22. b
5. c	11. a	17. a	23. c
6. a	12. b	18. b	

Answers for CHAPTER 6

1. c	8. d	14. c	20. b
2. c	9. b	15. a	21. a
3. b	10. d	16. a	22. a
4. d	11. c	17. b	23. d
5. a	12. b	18. d	24. c
6. b	13. d	19. c	25. d
7. a			

Answers for CHAPTER 7

1. a	8. c	15. a	21. c
2. a	9. b	16. d	22. b
3. b	10. d	17. d	23. a
4. c	11. b	18. a	24. c
5. d	12. d	19. c	25. c
6. b	13. d	20. b	26. d
7. a	14. b		

Answers for CHAPTER 8

1. d	8. c	15. c	21. d
2. a	9. a	16. a	22. c
3. a	10. c	17. b	23. a
4. b	11. b	18. d	24. c
5. c	12. b	19. d	25. d
6. a	13. a	20. b	26. b
7. d	14. b		

Answers for CHAPTER 9

1. a	8. c	15. d	21. b
2. a	9. d	16. c	22. b
3. b	10. c	17. b	23. a
4. b	11. a	18. a	24. d
5. d	12. c	19. d	25. b
6. c	13. d	20. d	26. c
7. a	14. c		

Answers for CHAPTER 10

1. b	9. d	16. a	23. b
2. c	10. d	17. c	24. a
3. d	11. d	18. b	25. a
4. c	12. d	19. a	26. a
5. c	13. a	20. d	27. d
6. a	14. c	21. d	28. c
7. c	15. b	22. b	29. b
8. b			

Answers for CHAPTER 11

1. a	7. c	13. c	19. a
2. d	8. d	14. b	20. c
3. c	9. a	15. a	21. d
4. d	10. a	16. b	22. b
5. b	11. d	17. b	23. b
6. d	12. c	18. a	

Answers for CHAPTER 12

1. d	7. a	12. d	17. c
2. a	8. d	13. b	18. c
3. a	9. b	14. b	19. b
4. c	10. a	15. a	20. d
5. b	11. b	16. c	21. d
6. c			

Answers for CHAPTER 13

1. b	8. a	14. c	20. d
2. a	9. d	15. d	21. b
3. c	10. a	16. b	22. a
4. c	11. c	17. a	23. b
5. d	12. b	18. c	24. c
6. a	13. c	19. d	25. b
7. d			

Answers for CHAPTER 14

1. c	7. c	13. a	19. c
2. a	8. b	14. b	20. b
3. b	9. a	15. c	21. c
4. d	10. c	16. d	22. a
5. d	11. a	17. b	23. d
6. b	12. d	18. a	24. b

Answers for CHAPTER 15

1. c	8. d	15. a	22. c
2. a	9. c	16. c	23. b
3. d	10. b	17. c	24. d
4. b	11. c	18. b	25. d
5. d	12. a	19. b	26. c
6. a	13. a	20. b	27. b
7. a	14. d	21. a	

Answers for CHAPTER 16

1. c	8. a	14. d	20. c
2. a	9. c	15. a	21. d
3. a	10. d	16. b	22. d
4. c	11. c	17. d	23. a
5. a	12. b	18. b	24. b
6. b	13. c	19. b	25. d
7. c			

Answers for CHAPTER 17

1. a	8. c	15. d	21. b
2. c	9. b	16. b	22. c
3. b	10. d	17. d	23. a
4. c	11. d	18. c	24. d
5. a	12. b	19. b	25. d
6. b	13. a	20. a	26. a
7. c	14. a		